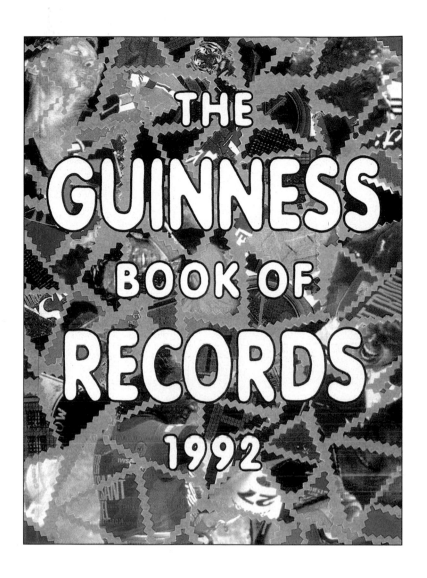

THE
GUINNESS
BOOK OF
RECORDS
1992

EDITOR

Donald McFarlan

FOUNDING EDITOR

Norris D. McWhirter

GUINNESS PUBLISHING

ACKNOWLEDGEMENTS

The Editor of *The Guinness Book of Records* wishes to thank:

DEPUTY EDITORS
Sheila Goldsmith
Nicholas Heath-Brown
Maria Morgan
Stewart Newport

SPORTS EDITOR
Peter J Matthews

CORRESPONDENCE EDITOR
Martin Day

ASSOCIATE AMERICAN EDITORS
Michelle D McCarthy
Mark Young

DESIGN MANAGER
David L Roberts

DESIGN AND LAYOUT
Amanda Ward

CONSULTANT PICTURE EDITOR
Alex P Goldberg

PICTURE ADMINISTRATOR
Muriel Ling

INFORMATION SYSTEMS MANAGER
Alex E Reid

ADMINISTRATION ASSISTANT
Ann Collins

PRODUCTION DIRECTOR
Chris Lingard

SECRETARIAL SUPPORT
Debbie Bigmore
Sallie Collins
Felicity Goodman

PRESS AND PUBLIC RELATIONS OFFICER
Cathy Brooks

CONTRIBUTORS: Andrew Adams; Robin Adams; John Arblaster; Howard Bass; Michael Benton; Dennis Bird; Richard Boehmer; David Boyd; Robert Brooke; Ian Buchanan; Bob Burton; Henry Button; A Carder; Clive Carpenter; Chris Cavey; David Cheslin; Michael Chrimes/The Institution of Civil Engineers; Nobby Clarke; Graham Dyer; Colin Dyson; Keith Escott; Clive Everton; Paulette Foyle; Andrew Frankel; Bill Frindall; Tim Furniss; Steven Goldberg; Ian Goold; Stan Greenberg; Liz Hawley; Albert Herbert; Ron Hildebrant; Rick Hogben; Sir Peter Johnson; Gene Jones; Ove Karlsson; John Lawson; Douglas Liddell; Peter Lunn; Tessa McWhirter; John Marshall; Timothy Mickelburgh; Andy Milroy; Alan Mitchell; David Mondey; John Moody; Patrick Moore; Ian Morrison; Susann Palmer; Colin Pelton; John Randall; Chris Rhys; Patrick Robertson; Dan Roddick; Jack Rollin; Adrian Room; Peter Rowan; Irvin Saxton; Robert Shopland; Colin Smith; Ian Smith; Graham Snowdon; Juhani Virola; Tony Waltham; Ray Waterman; David Wells; Rick Wilson; Tony Wood.

Grateful acknowledgement is also made to the governing bodies and organizations who have helped in our researches.

COVER DESIGN
Joanne Bloomer

ARTWORK, MAPS AND DIAGRAMS: Ad Vantage Studios; Kathy Aldridge; Rob and Rhoda Burns/Drawing Attention; Pat Gibbon; Peter Harper; Matthew Hillier; Jon Preston/Maltings Partnership; Neil Randon; Mandy Sedge. Special thanks are extended to Marie Helene Cambos, Anne Jones, Robert McMahon and James Matthew Clift for their help in selecting illustrations for this edition.

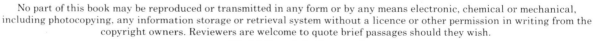

British Library Cataloguing in Publication Data
Guinness book of records.-38th edition
1. Records of achievement-Collections-Serials
031'.02

ISBN 0-85112-378-3. Australian edition 0-85112-379-1

'Guinness' is a registered trade mark of Guinness Publishing Ltd.

Printed and bound in Spain by Printer Industria Gráfica S.A., Barcelona

Introduction
By The Editor, Donald McFarlan

When *The Guinness Book of Records* was first published in 1955 it simply contained researched information regarding the highest, largest, smallest, fastest and slowest. Over the years the book has become more of an institution, with people actively setting out to be included in it by breaking the published records. And why not? If you know you are the best at some particular area of endeavour it may well be that *The Guinness Book of Records* is the only place where this fact will be recognized.

If you wish to claim a record you should make contact in writing with this office. We will advise you regarding any rules and guidelines. Because of the large volume of mail which we receive, we would be grateful if you could make contact at least a month before the record attempt. In addition, a last-minute check should also be made in case the published record has recently been broken.

Please bear in mind that we are much more likely to publish a record which betters an existing category. Occasionally, we do introduce new categories if they relate to an activity which has become the subject of widespread interest, but pressure of space usually means that if we do this an existing category has to be dropped.

This year we have made several major changes to the order and design of the book. We hope you like the new book and would always welcome your comments.

EDITOR:
DONALD McFARLAN
OCTOBER 1991

GUINNESS PUBLISHING LTD, 33 LONDON ROAD, MIDDLESEX, EN2 6DJ, ENGLAND

The story of the Guinness Book

On Saturday 10 November 1951, Sir Hugh Beaver (1890–1967) was out shooting on The North Slob, by the river Slaney in County Wexford in the south-east of Ireland. Some golden plover were missed by the party. That evening at Castlebridge House it was realized that it was not possible to confirm in reference books whether or not the golden plover was Europe's fastest game bird.

In August 1954 argument arose as to whether grouse were even faster. Sir Hugh, managing director of Guinness thought that there must be numerous other questions debated nightly in the 81 400 pubs in Britain and in Ireland, but there was no book with which to settle arguments about records.

On 12 September 1954, Sir Hugh invited Norris and Ross McWhirter to see if their fact and figure agency in London could help. An office was set up at 107 Fleet Street and intense work began on the first slim 198 page edition. The printers bound the first copy on 27 August 1955. Well before Christmas the Guinness Book was No. 1 on the bestsellers list. It has occupied this position every year since, except 1957 and 1959 when it was not published.

The first US edition appeared in New York in 1956 followed by editions in French (1962) and German (1963). In 1967 there were first editions in Japanese, Spanish, Danish and Norwegian, while the following year editions were published in Swedish, Finnish and Italian. In the 'seventies there followed Dutch (1971); Portuguese (1974); Czech (1976); Hebrew, Serbo-Croat and Icelandic (all in 1977) and Slovene (1978). In the 1980s translations into Greek, Indonesian, Turkish, Hindi, Malay, Arabic, Thai and Hungarian followed. Since 1990 editions have been published in Russian, Polish, Bulgarian, Romanian, Korean and Macedonian.

In November 1974 the *Guinness Book* earned its own place in the *Guinness Book*. It had become the top selling copyright book in publishing history with sales of 23·9 million. By the end of 1990 the global sales surpassed 65 million, which is equivalent to 168 stacks each as high as Mount Everest.

THE RT HON EARL OF IVEAGH
PRESIDENT GUINNESS PLC
OCTOBER 1991

CONTENTS

The Earth and Space

■ **Previous page**
Sandstone canyon, Arizona, USA. (Photo: Zefa)

■ **Stars farthest - Milky Way**
These two all-sky images were constructed from data obtained on NASA's Cosmic Background Explorer (COBE). The top panel combines data at the far infrared wavelengths of 25, 60 and 100 microns as seen in blue, green and red. The image is presented in galactic co-ordinates, with the plane of the Milky Way Galaxy horizontal across the middle and the galactic centre at the centre. The bottom panel also has data at the near-infrared wavelengths of 1·2, 2·2 and 3·4 represented by the same colours. The dominant source of light at these wavelengths are stars within our Galaxy. (Photo: NASA)

The Universe

MAGNITUDE – a measure of stellar brightness such that the light of a star of any magnitude bears a ratio of 2·511886 to that of a star of the next magnitude. Thus a fifth-magnitude star is 2·511 886 brighter than a sixth magnitude star whilst a first magnitude star is 100 (or $2·511\,886^5$) times brighter. Magnitude is expressed as a negative quantity for exceptionally bright bodies such as the Sun (apparent magnitude − 26·78).

ASTRONOMICAL UNIT – the distance from the centre of the Earth to the centre of the Sun as defined in 1938, equivalent to 49 597 870 km *92 955 807 miles*.

LIGHT-YEAR – the distance travelled by light (speed 299 792·458 km/s *186 282·397 miles/sec*) in one tropical year (365·24219878 mean solar days at January 0·12 hours Ephemeris time in AD 1900) and is equivalent to 9 460 528 405 000 km *5 878 499 814 000 miles* The unit was first used in March 1888.

PARSEC – the true measure of stellar distance being the reciprocal of half of the angle in seconds of arc subtended when the position of a star is measured on both sides of the Earth's orbit (parallactic displacement against a background of 'fixed' stars). This is equivalent to 206 264·806 astronomical units 3·261633 light years or 30 856 776 000 000 km *19 173 511 000 000 miles*.

Large structures in the Universe

Our own Milky Way galaxy is only one of 10 billion galaxies. It is part of the so-called Local Group of galaxies moving at a speed of 600 km/s *370 miles/sec* with respect to the cosmological frame in the general direction of a dense concentration of galaxy clusters known as the 'Great Attractor' (a term coined by Alan Dressler (USA)). In November 1989 Margaret Geller and John Huchra (USA) announced the discovery of a 'Great Wall' in space, a concentration of galaxies in the form of a 'crumpled membrane' with a minimum extent of 280×800 million light-years ($2·6 \times 10^{21}$ km $\times$ $7·5 \times 10^{21}$ km $1·6 \times 10^{21}$ miles $\times$ $4·7 \times 10^{21}$ miles) and a depth of up to 20 million light-years ($1·5 \times 10^{20}$ km *$9·6 \times 10^{19}$ miles*). In July 1990 Juan M. Uson, Stephen P. Boughn and Jeffrey R. Kuhn (USA) announced the discovery of the largest galaxy - the central galaxy of the Abell 2029 galaxy cluster, 1070 million light-years distance in Virgo. This galaxy has a major diameter of 5 500 000 million light-years ($7·4 \times 10^{19}$ km *$4·6 \times 10^{19}$ miles)*, which is eight times the diameter of our own Galaxy (see below), and has a light output equivalent to 2 trillion (2×10^{12}) Suns.

Age of the Universe For the age of the Universe a consensus value of 14 ± 3 aeons or gigayears (an aeon or gigayear being 1000 million years) is obtained from various cosmological techniques. The equivalent value of the Hubble constant based on a Friedman model of the Universe without cosmological constant is 70 ± 15 km/s/Mpc. In 1973 an *ex nihilo* creation was postulated by Edward P. Tryon (USA). Modified versions of the Inflationary Model, originally introduced by Alan Guth (USA) in 1981, now complement the Big Bang theory of creation.

Remotest object Both the interpretation of the very large red shifts exhibited by quasars and the estimation of equivalent distances remain controversial. The record red shift of $z = 4·73$ for quasar PC 1158 + 4635 was announced by Donald Schneider, Maarten Schmidt and James Gunn in August 1989 from spectroscopic and photometric observations made between February 1988 and March 1989 using the Hale Telescope at Palomar Observatory, California, USA. If it is assumed that there is an 'observable horizon', where the speed of recession is equal to the speed of light, i.e. at 14 billion light-years or $1·32 \times 10^{23}$ km *$8·23 \times 10^{22}$ miles*, then this quasar would be at a distance of 13·2 billion light-years distant.

Farthest visible object The remotest heavenly body visible with the naked eye is the Great Galaxy in *Andromeda* (mag. 3·47), known as Messier 31. It was first noted from Germany by Simon Marius (1570–1624). It is a rotating nebula in spiral form at a distance from the Earth of about 2 309 000 light-years, or $2·18 \times 10^{19}$ km *$1·36 x 10^{19}$ miles*, and is moving towards us. It is just possible, that under ideal conditions for observations, Messier 33, the Spiral in Triangulum (mag. 5·79), can be glimpsed by the naked eye of keen-sighted people at a distance of 2 509 000 light-years.

Quasars An occultation of 3C−273, observed from Australia on 5 Aug 1962, enabled the existence of quasi-stellar radio sources ('quasars' or QSOs) to be announced by Maarten Schmidt (Netherlands b. 1929). The red shift proved to be $z = 0·158$.

Quasars have immensely high luminosity for bodies so distant and of such small diameter. It was announced in May 1983 that the quasar S5 0014 + 81 had a visual luminosity $1·1 \times 10^{15}$ times greater than that of the Sun.

The first double quasar (0957 + 56) among 1500 known quasars was announced in May 1980.

The most violent outburst observed in a quasar was recorded on 13 Nov 1989 by a joint US-Japanese team who noted that the energy output of the quasar PKS 0558-504 (which is about 2000 million light-years distant) increased by two thirds in three minutes, equivalent to the total energy released by the Sun in 340 000 years.

STARS

Nearest Excepting the special case of our own Sun, the nearest star is the very faint *Proxima Centauri*, discovered in 1915, which is 4·225 light-years ($4·00 \times 10^{13}$ km *$2·48 \times 10^{13}$ miles*) away.

The nearest 'star' visible to the naked eye is the southern hemisphere binary *Alpha Centauri*, or *Rigel Kentaurus* (4·35 light-years distant), with an apparent magnitude of − 0·29. It was discovered by Nicolas L. de Lacaille (1713–62) in *c.* 1752. In AD 29700 this binary will reach a minimum distance from the Earth of 2·84 light-years and should then be the second brightest 'star', with an apparent magnitude of −1·20.

Farthest The Solar System, with its Sun's nine principal planets, 61 satellites, asteroids and comets, is located in the outer regions of our Milky Way galaxy, orbiting at a mean distance of 29 700 light-years and with an orbital eccentricity of 0·07. The present distance from the centre is 27 700 light-years and it will reach the minimum distance of 27 600 light-years (perigalacticon) in about 15 million years' time, from the present.

The Milky Way galaxy has a diameter of about 70 000 light-years so the most distant star will be at 66 700 light-years when the Solar System is farthest from the centre (apogalacticon). At present the most distant stars are at 62 700 light-years.

The present orbital velocity of the Sun and a large number of nearby stars have been averaged to 792 000 km/h *492 000 mph* (the 'Local Standard of Rest'), which would lead to an orbital period of 237 million years.

However, the Sun's actual velocity is 97 200 km/h *60 400 mph* faster than this average.

Largest, heaviest and most luminous The largest star is the M-class supergiant *Betelgeux* (Alpha Orionis - the top left star of Orion) which is 310 light-years distant. It has a diameter of 700 million km *400 million miles* which is about 500 times greater than that of the Sun. In 1978 it was found to be surrounded not only by a dust 'shell' but also by an outer tenuous gas halo up to $8·5 \times 10^{11}$ km *$5·3 \times 10^{11}$ miles* in diameter or over 1100 times the diameter of the star.

The heaviest star is the variable *Eta Carinae*, 9100 light- years distant in the Carinae Nebula in our own galaxy, with a mass 200 times greater than our own Sun. If all the stars could be viewed at the same distance it would also be the most luminous star with a total luminosity 6 500 000 times that of the Sun. However the visually brightest star is the hypergiant Cygnus OB2 No.12 which is 5900 light years distant. It has an absolute visual magnitude of − 9·9 and is therefore visually 810 000 times brighter than the Sun. This brightness may be matched by the supergiant IV b 59 in the nearby galaxy Messier 101. During 1843 the absolute luminosity and absolute visual brightness of *Eta Carinae* temporarily increased to values 60 and 70 million times the corresponding values for the Sun.

Smallest, lightest and dimmest A mass of 0·014 that of the Sun is estimated for RG 0058.8-2807, which was discovered by I. Neill Reid and Gerard Gilmore using the UK Schmidt telescope (announced in April 1983). It is also the faintest star detected with a total luminosity only 0·0021 that of the Sun and an absolute visual magnitude of 20·2 so the visual brightness is less than one millionth of the Sun. The smallest star appears to be the white dwarf L362-81 with an estimated diameter of 5600 km *3500 miles* or only 0·0040 that of the Sun.

Brightest (As seen from earth)
Sirius A (*Alpha Canis Majoris*), also known as the Dog Star, is the brightest star of the 5776 stars visibile to the naked eye. It has an apparent magnitude of −1·46 but because of the relative motions of this star and the Sun then this should rise to a maximum value of −1·67 by c. AD 61000. Sirius is 8·64 light-years distant and has a luminosity 26 times greater than that of the Sun. It has a diameter of 2·33 million km *1·45 million miles* and a mass 2·14 times that of the Sun. The faint white dwarf companion *Sirius B* has a diameter of only 10 000 km *6000 miles*, which is less than that of the Earth, but it's mass is slightly greater than that of the Sun. *Sirius* is in the constellation *Canis Major* and is visible in the winter months of the northern hemisphere, being due south at midnight on the last day of the year.

Pulsars The earliest observation of a pulsating radio source or 'pulsar', CP 1919 (now PSR 1919 + 21), by Dr Jocelyn Burnell (*née* Bell, b. 1943) was announced from the Mullard Radio Astronomy Observatory, Cambridgeshire on 24 Feb 1968. It had been detected on 28 Nov 1967.

For pulsars whose spin rates have been accurately measured, the fastest-spinning is PSR 1937 + 214, which was discovered by a group led by Donald C. Backer in November 1982. It is in the minor constellation Vulpecula (the Little Fox), 16 000 light-years distant, and has a pulse period of 1·557806449 millisec, which is equivalent to a spin rate of 641·9282708 revolutions per sec.

The pulsar which has the slowest spin down rate and is therefore the most accurate stellar clock is PSR 1855 + 09 at only $2·1 \times 10^{-20}$ sec per sec.

Brightest and latest supernova
The brightest ever seen by historic man is believed to be SN 1006, noted in April 1006 near *Beta Lupi*, which flared for two years and attained a magnitude of −9 to −10. The remnant is believed to be the radio source G.327·6 + 14·5, nearly 3000 light-years distant.

Others have occurred in 1054, 1604, 1885, and most recently on 23 Feb 1987, when Ian Shelton sighted that designated −69 202 in the Large Magellanic Cloud 170 000 light-years distant. This supernova was visible to the naked eye when at its brightest in May 1987. A claim to have detected a fast-spinning pulsar at the centre of the supernova debris was withdrawn in February 1990.

Black Holes The concept of superdense bodies was first adumbrated by the Marquis de LaPlace (1749–1827). This term for a star that has undergone complete gravitational collapse was first used by Prof John Archibald Wheeler at an Institute for Space Studies meeting in New York City, USA on 29 Dec 1967.

The first tentative identification of a black hole was announced in December 1972 in the binary-star X-ray source Cygnus X–1.

The best candidate is LMC X–3 of 10 solar masses at 180 000 light-years distant reported in January 1983. The critical size has been estimated to be as low as a diameter of 5·9 km *3·7 miles*. One at the centre of the Seyfert galaxy, NGC 4151 in *Canes Venatici*, was estimated by Michael Preston (GB) in October 1983 to be of between 50–100 million solar masses, or up to 2×10^{35} tonnes .

Stellar planets All claims to have discovered planetary systems around other stars must be treated with suspicion. There appears to be a confusion with small dim stellar companions known as 'brown dwarfs' which are failed stars since they are too cool to trigger the fusion of hydrogen.

Of the nine possible candidates announced by Bruce Campbell, Gordon Walker and Stephenson Yang of the University of Victoria, British Columbia, Canada in August 1988, the most promising appears to be the inferred existence of a planet one and a half times the mass of Jupiter orbiting the bright star 36 Ursae Majoris A with an orbital period of three years.

Constellations The largest of the 89 constellations is *Hydra* (the Sea Serpent), which covers 1302·844 02 or 6·3 per cent of the hemisphere and contains at least 68 stars visible to the naked eye (to 5·5 mag).

The constellation *Centaurus* (Centaur), ranking ninth in area, however, embraces at least 94 such stars.

The smallest constellation is *Crux Australis* (Southern Cross) with an area of only 0·16 per cent of the whole sky, viz. 68·477 deg², compared with the 41 252·96 deg² of the whole sky.

Longest name *Torcularis Septentrionalis* is the name applied to the star omicron Piscium in the constellation Pisces.

THE SUN

Distance extremes The true distance of the Earth from the Sun is 1·000 001 02 astronomical units or 149 598 020 km *92 955 900 miles*. The orbit is elliptical and the distance of the Sun varies between a minimum (perihelion) of 147 097 800 km *91 402 300 miles* and a maximum (aphelion) of 152 098 200 km *94 509 400 miles*. Based on an orbital circumference of 939 886 400 km *584 018 400 miles* and an orbital period (sidereal year) of 365·256 366 days, the average orbital velocity is 107 210 km/h *66 620 mph*, but this varies between a minimum of 105 450 km/h *65 500 mph* at aphelion and a maximum of 109 030 km/h *67 750 mph* at perihelion.

Temperature and dimensions
The Sun has a stellar classification of a *yellow dwarf* type G2, although its mass at $1·9889 \times 10^{27}$ tonnes *$1·9575 \times 10^{27}$ tons* is 332 946·04 times that of the Earth and represents over 99 per cent of the total mass of the Solar System. The solar diameter at 1 392 140 km *865 040 miles* leads to a density of 1·408 times that of water.

The Sun has a central temperature of about 15 400 000 K and a core pressure of 25·4 PPa *1 650 million tons/in²*. It uses up about 4 million tonnes of hydrogen per sec, equal to an energy output of $3·85 \times 10^{26}$ watts, although it will take 10 000 million years to exhaust its energy supply (about 5 000 million years from the present).

The luminous intensity of the Sun is $2·7 \times 10^{27}$ candela, which is equal to a luminance of $4·5 \times 10^8$ candela/m² *290 000 candela/in²*.

Sunspots To be visible to the *protected* naked eye, a sunspot must cover about one

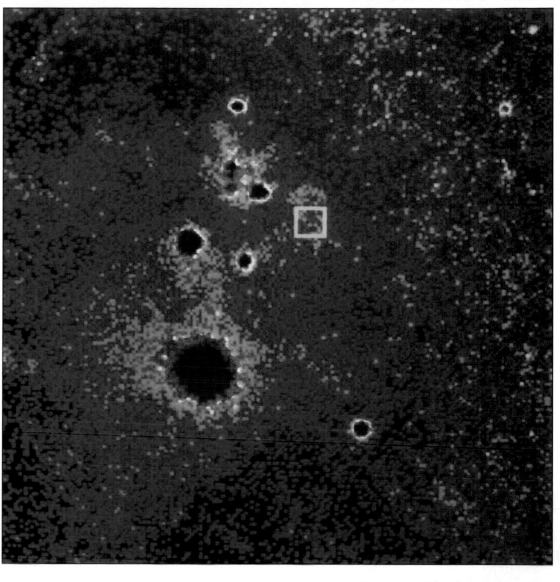

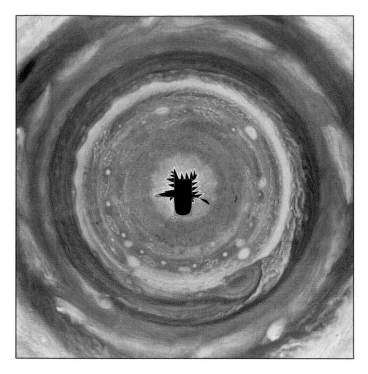

■ Largest planet - Jupiter
Jupiter is the largest of the nine major planets (including the Earth). This view shows the southern hemisphere from above the pole. It is a composite of pictures taken from Voyager I. (Photo: NASA)

two-thousandth part of the Sun's disc and thus have an area of about 1300 million km² *500 million miles²*. The largest sunspot ever noted was in the Sun's southern hemisphere on 8 Apr 1947. Its area was about 18 000 million km² *7000 million miles²*, with an extreme longitude of 300 000 km *187 000 miles* and an extreme latitude of 145 000 km *90 000 miles*. Sunspots appear darker because they are more than 1500° C *2 732° F* cooler than the rest of the Sun's surface temperature of 5507° C *9 945° F*.

In October 1957 a smoothed sunspot count showed 263, the highest recorded index since records started in 1755 (cf. the previous record of 239 in May 1778). In 1943 one sunspot lasted for 200 days, from June to December.

PLANETS

Largest The nine major planets (including the Earth) are bodies within the Solar System and revolve round the Sun in definite orbits.

Jupiter, with an equatorial diameter of 142 984 km *88 846 miles* and a polar diameter of 133 708 km *83 082 miles* is the largest of the nine major planets, with a mass 317·828 times, and a volume 1323·3 times, that of the Earth. It also has the shortest period of rotation, resulting in a Jovian day of only 9 hr 50 min 30·003 sec in the equatorial zone.

Smallest, coldest and outermost Pluto was first recorded by Clyde William Tombaugh (b. 4 Feb 1906) at Lowell Observatory, Flagstaff, Arizona, USA on 18 Feb 1930 from photographs he took on 23 and 29 January. His find was announced on 13 March.

The discovery of Pluto's companion Charon was announced on 22 Jun 1978 from the US Naval Observatory, Flagstaff, Arizona. Pluto, with a mass of about 1/500th of that of the Earth, has a diameter of 2302 km *1430 miles*, while Charon has a diameter of 1186 km *737 miles*. Their mean distance from the Sun is 5 913 514 000 km *3 674 488 000 miles*, with a period of revolution of 248·54 years. Because of their orbital eccentricity they will be temporarily closer to the Sun than Neptune in the period from 23 Jan 1979 to 15 Mar 1999. The lowest observed surface temperature of any

natural body in the Solar System is −235° C *−391° F* in the case of Neptune' large moon *Triton*, although the true surface temperature of Pluto and Charon remain to be measured.

Fastest Mercury, which orbits the Sun at an average distance of 57 909 200 km *35 983 100 miles*, has a period of revolution of 87·9686 days, so giving the highest average speed in orbit of 172 248 km/h *107 030 mph*.

Hottest For Venus a surface temperature of 462° C *864° F* has been estimated from measurements made from the USSR *Venera* and US *Pioneer* surface probes.

Nearest The fellow planet closest to the Earth is Venus, which is, at times, only 41 360 000 km *25 700 000 miles*, inside the Earth's orbit, compared with Mars' closest approach of 55 680 000 km *34 600 000 miles*, outside the Earth's orbit.

Mars, known since 1965 to be cratered, has temperatures ranging from 29·4° C *85° F* to −123° C *−190° F*.

Surface features By far the highest and most spectacular is Olympus Mons (formerly Nix Olympica) in the Tharsis region of Mars, with a diameter of 500–600 km *310–370 miles* and a height of 26 ± 3 km *75 450–95 150 ft* above the surrounding plain.

Venus has a canyon some 1600 km *1000 miles* south of the Venusian equator 6400 m *21 000 ft* deep and 400 km *250 miles* long.

The ice cliff on the Uranian moon Miranda is 5·20 km *3·23 miles* high.

Brightest and faintest Viewed from the Earth, by far the brightest of the five planets visible to the naked eye is Venus, with a maximum magnitude of −4·4.

Uranus, the first to be discovered by telescope when it was sighted by Sir William Herschel from his garden at 19 New King St, Bath on 13 Mar 1781, is only marginally visible, with a magnitude 5·5.

The faintest planet is Pluto, with a magnitude of 15·0.

Densest and least dense Earth is the densest planet, with an average figure of 5·515 times that of water, while Saturn has an average density only about one-eighth of this value or 0·685 times that of water.

Conjunctions The most dramatic recorded conjunction (coming together) of the other seven principal members of the Solar System (Sun, Moon, Mercury, Venus, Mars, Jupiter and Saturn) occurred on 5 Feb 1962, when 16° covered all seven during an eclipse in the Pacific area. It is possible that the seven-fold conjunction of September 1186 spanned only 12°.

The next notable conjunction will take place on 5 May 2000.

Largest scale model The largest scale model of the Solar System was inaugurated by the Futures' Museum, Falun, Sweden on 29 Nov 1986. A model of the Earth with a diameter of 13 mm *½ in* was placed in the museum. The Sun (diameter 1·5 m *5 ft*), and the planets (with diameters ranging from 3·5 mm *0·13 in*, to 140 mm *5½ in*) were positioned in the nearby city of Borlange some 16·2 km *10 miles* away. *Proxima Centauri* was sited in the Museum of Victoria, Melbourne, Australia.

SATELLITES

Most and least The Solar System has a total of 61 satellites with Saturn having the

most at 18, whilst Earth and Pluto only have one satellite each and Mercury and Venus none. The most recently discovered, announced on 16 Jul 1990 by Mark R. Showalter (USA), is the Saturnian satellite temporarily designated 1981 S13 which was found on eleven Voyager 2 photographs taken during the close approach in August 1981. It has a diameter of only about 20 km *12 miles* and orbits within the 322 km *200 mile* Encke gap in the A ring. E.A. Marouf and G.L. Tyler have predicted the existence of two further Saturnian satellites in the Cassini Division between the A and B rings.

Distance extremes The distance of satellites from their parent planets varies from the 9377 km *5827 miles* of Phobos from the centre of Mars to the 23 700 000 km *14 700 000 miles* of Jupiter's outer satellite *Sinope* (Jupiter IX).

Largest and smallest The largest and heaviest satellite is *Ganymede* (Jupiter III), which is 2·017 times heavier than the Earth's Moon and has a diameter of 5268 km *3273 miles*. Of satellites whose diameters have been measured the smallest is Deimos, the outermost moon of Mars. Although irregularly shaped it has an average diameter of 12·5 km *7·8 miles*. The diameter of *Leda* (Jupiter XIII) is estimated to be less than 15 km *9 miles*.

ASTEROIDS

Number and distance extremes There are estimated to be about 45 000 asteroids but only the orbits of just over 5 000 have been accurately computed. Whilst most orbit between Mars and Jupiter, average distances from the Sun vary between 116 300 000 km *72 200 000 miles* (just outside of Venus' orbit) for the Aten asteroid 1954XA (discovered 5 Dec 1954 but currently lost) and 2042 million km *1269 million miles* for the remote 2060 *Chiron* (discovered 18 Oct 1977) which orbits between Saturn and Uranus, although there is increasing evidence that this body has a cometary rather than asteroidal nature. Because of it's large orbital eccentricity the closest approach to the Sun is by the Apollo asteroid 3200 *Phaethon* (discovered on 11 Oct 1983) to within 20 890 000 km *12 980 000 miles* at perihelion, whilst the known closest approach to the Earth by an asteroid is 170 000 km *105 600 miles* on 18 Jan 1991 by 1991BA (the day after its discovery).

Largest and smallest The largest asteroid is 1 Ceres (the first discovered, by G. Piazzi at Palermo, Sicily on 1 Jan 1801) with a diameter of 936 km *582 miles*. Most asteroids are only expected to be metric/yards in diameter, the smallest reported value being 9 m *30 ft* for the closest Earth approaching asteroid 1991BA. The only asteroid visible to the naked eye is 4 Vesta (discovered 29 Mar 1807) which is 520 km *323 miles* in diameter and has a maximum apparent magnitude as viewed from the Earth of 5·0.

THE MOON

The Earth's closest neighbour in space and its only natural satellite is the Moon, which has an average diameter of 3475·1 km *2159·3 miles* and a mass of 7·348 × 10¹⁹ tonnes , or 0·0123 Earth masses, so the density is 3·344 times that of water.

The Moon orbits at a mean distance of 384 399·1 km *238 854·5 miles* centre-to-centre, although the centre of mass is displaced from the centre of figure by 1·8 km *1·1 miles* towards the Earth so that

THE MOST DISTANT MEASURED HEAVENLY BODIES

The possible existence of galaxies external to our own Milky Way system was mooted in 1789 by Sir William Herschel (1738–1822). These extra-galactic nebulae were first termed 'island universes'. Sir John Herschel (1792–1871) opined as early as 1835 that some might be more than 250 000 000 000 million miles distant. The first direct measurement of any body outside our Solar System was in 1838. Distances in the table below assume that the edge of the observable Universe is at a distance of 14 000 million light-years.

Estimated Distance in Light-years[1]	Object	Method	Astronomers	Observatory	Date
about 6 (now 11·08)	61 Cygni	Parallax	F. Bessel	Königsberg, Germany	1838
>20 (now 26)	Vega	Parallax	F. G. W. Struve	Dorpat (now Tartu), Estonia	1840
c. 200	Limit	Parallax			by 1900
900 000 (now 2·31 million)[2]	Galaxy M31	Cepheid variable	E. P. Hubble (1889–1953)	Mt. Wilson, California, USA	1924

Millions of Light-years	Recession Speed % of c	Object	Red Shift[3]	Astronomers	Observatory	Date
c.200	1·4	NGC 7619		M. L. Humason	Mt. Wilson, California, USA	early 1928
>2100	>15·0	Ursa Major No. 2		M .L. Humason & E. P. Hubble	Mt. Wilson, California, USA	by 1936[4]
4600	32·6	Cluster 1448	0·403		Palomar, California, USA	1956
5100	36·2	3C 295 in Boötes	0·461	R. Minkowski	Palomar, California, USA	June 1960
5700	41·0	QSO 3C 147	0·545	M. Schmidt & T. A. Matthews	Palomar, California, USA	February 1964[5]
11 200	80·1	QSO 3C 9	2·01	M. Schmidt	Palomar, California, USA	April 1965
11 400	81·3	QSO 0106 +01	2·11	E. M. Burbridge et al.	Palomar, California, USA	December 1965
11 400	81·4	QSO 1116 +12	2·12	C. R. Lynds & A. N. Stockton	Steward, Arizona, USA	March 1966
				M. Schmidt	Palomar, California, USA	March 1966
11 500	82·4	QSO Pks 0237 −23	2·22	H. C. Arp et al.	Palomar, California, USA	December 1966
11 700	83·7	QSO 4C 25.05	2·36	E. T. Olsen & M. Schmidt	Palomar, California, USA	December 1967[6]
12 300	87·5	QSO 4C 05.34	2·88	R. Lynds & D. Wills	Kitt Peak, Arizona, USA	March 1970
12 600	90·2	QSO OH 471	3·40	R. F. Carswell & P. A. Strittmatter	Steward, Arizona, USA	March 1973
12 700	90·7	QSO OQ 172	3·53	E. J. Wampler et al.	Lick, California, USA	May 1973
12 800	91·6	QSO Pks 2000 −330	3·78	B. A. Peterson et al.	Siding Spring, NSW, Australia	April 1982[7]
12 800	91·7	QSO Pks 1208 +1011	3·80	C. Hazard et al.	Siding Spring, NSW, Australia	February 1986[8]
12 900	92·3	QSO 0046 −293	4·01	S. J. Warren et al.	Siding Spring, NSW, Australia	September 1986[8]
12 900	92·4	QSO PC0910 +5625	4·04	M. Schmidt et al.	Palomar, California, USA	June 1987
13 000	92·6	QSO 0000 −2620	4·11	C. Hazard et al.	Siding Spring, NSW, Australia	August 1987[8]
13 100	93·4	QSO 0051 −279	4·43	S. J. Warren et al.	Siding Spring, NSW, Australia	November 1987[8]
13 200	94·1	QSO PC 1158 +4635	4·73	D. P. Schneider et al.	Palomar, California, USA	August 1989

Note: c is the notation for the speed of light. (see p. 6). [1] Term first utilized in March 1888. [2] Re-estimate by M. Rowan-Robinson in March 1988. [3] Discovered by Vesto Slipher (1875–1969) from Flagstaff, Arizona, USA in 1920. Red shift, denoted by z, is the measure of the speed of recession indicated by the ratio resulting from the subtraction of the rest wavelength of an emission line from the observed wavelength divided by the rest wavelength. [4] In 1934 Hubble opined that the observable horizon would be 3000 m light-years. [5] In December 1963 Dr I. S. Shklovsky's (USSR) suggestion that QSO 3C2 was more distant was subsequently confirmed with a value of 0·612c. [6] In October 1968 Dr Margaret Burbidge (GB) published a tentative red shift of 2·38 for QSO 5C 2.56. [7] Anglo-Australian telescope. [8] UK Schmidt telescope.

---

the distance surface-to-surface is 376 285 km *233 813 miles*. In the present century the closest approach (smallest perigee) was 356 375 km *221 441 miles* centre-to-centre on 4 Jan 1912 and the farthest distance (largest apogee) was 406 711 km *252 718 miles* on 2 Mar 1984.

The orbital period (sidereal month) is 27·321661 days, giving an average orbital velocity of 3683 km/h *2289 mph*.

The currently accepted 'giant impact' theory of the lunar origin suggests that the Moon was formed just outside of the Earth's Roche Limit (about 18 500 km *11 500 miles* from the Earth's centre) from the debris resulting from a glancing collision between the Earth and a Mars-size planetesimal. That this event must have occurred in the early history of the Solar System is indicated by the fact that the oldest lunar rocks and soils brought back to Earth by the Apollo programme crews are of a similar age to the oldest known meteorites (about 4500 million years).

The first direct hit on the Moon was achieved at 2 min 24 sec after midnight (Moscow time) on 14 Sep 1959, by the Soviet space probe *Lunar II* near the *Mare Serenitatis*.

The first photographic images of the hidden side of the Moon were collected by the USSR *Lunar III* from 6:30 a.m. on the 7 Oct 1959 from a range of up to 70 400 km *43 750 miles*, and transmitted to the Earth from a distance of 470 000 km *292 000 miles*.

Crater Only 59 per cent of the Moon's surface is directly visible from the Earth because it is in 'captured rotation', i.e. the period of rotation is equal to the period of

orbit. The largest wholly visible crater is the walled plain Bailly, towards the Moon's South Pole, which is 295 km *183 miles* across, with walls rising to 4250 m *14 000 ft*. The Orientale Basin, partly on the averted side, measures more than 965 km *600 miles* in diameter.

The deepest crater is the Newton Crater, with a floor estimated to be between 7000 and 8850 m *23 000–29 000 ft* below its rim and 2250 m *14 000 ft* below the level of the plain outside. The brightest directly visible spot on the Moon is *Aristarchus*.

Highest mountains In the absence of a sea level, lunar altitudes are measured relative to an adopted reference sphere of radius 1 738 km *1079·943 miles*. Thus the greatest elevation attained on this basis by any of the 12 US astronauts has been 7830 m *25 688 ft* on the Descartes Highlands by Capt. John Watts Young,(USN) and Major Charles M. Duke, Jr on 27 Apr 1972.

Temperature extremes When the Sun is overhead the temperature on the lunar equator reaches 117·2° C *243° F* (17·2° C *31° F* above the boiling point of water). By sunset the temperature is 14·4° C *58° F*, but after nightfall it sinks to −162·7° C *−261° F*.

ECLIPSES

Earliest recorded For the Middle East, lunar eclipses have been extrapolated to 3450 BC and solar ones to 4200 BC.

The oldest record of a total solar eclipse is on a clay tablet found in 1948 among the ruins of the ancient city of Ugarit (now in Syria).

A reassessment in 1989 suggests that this

records the eclipse of the 5 Mar 1223 BC. No centre of the path of totality for a solar eclipse crossed London for 575 years from 20 Mar 1140 to 3 May 1715.

On 14 Jun 2151 at 18:25 GMT the eclipse will be 99 per cent total in central London but total in Sheffield and Norfolk.

The most recent occasion when a line of totality of a solar eclipse crossed Great Britain was on 29 Jun 1927, for 24·5 sec at 6:23 a.m. at West Hartlepool, Cleveland. The next instance will clip the coast at St Just, Cornwall at 10:10 a.m. on Wednesday 11 Aug 1999.

On 30 Jun 1954 a total eclipse was witnessed from Unst, Shetland Islands but the centre of the path of totality was to its north.

Longest duration The maximum *possible* duration of an eclipse of the Sun is 7 min 31 sec.

The longest actually *measured* was on 20 Jun 1955 (7 min 8 sec), seen from the Philippines. An eclipse of 7 min 29 sec should occur in the mid-Atlantic Ocean on 16 Jul 2186, which will then be the longest for 1469 years.

The longest possible eclipse in the British Isles is 5 min 30 sec. That of 15 Jun 1885 lasted nearly 5 min, as will that of 20 Jul 2381 in the Borders area.

Durations can be 'extended' when observers are airborne, as on 30 Jun 1973 when an eclipse was 'extended' to 72 min aboard Concorde.

An annular eclipse may last for 12 min 24 sec.

The longest totality of any lunar eclipse is 104 minutes and has occurred many times.

Most and least frequent The highest number of eclipses possible in a year is seven, as in 1935, when there were five solar and two lunar eclipses. In 1982 there were four solar and three lunar eclipses.

The lowest possible number in a year is two, both of which must be solar, as in 1944 and 1969.

AURORAE

Most frequent Polar lights, known since 1560 as Aurora Borealis or Northern Lights in the northern hemisphere, and since 1773 as Aurora Australis in the southern, are caused by electrical solar discharges in the upper atmosphere and occur most frequently in high latitudes. Aurorae are visible at some time on *every* clear dark night in the polar areas within 20 degrees of the magnetic poles.

The extreme height of aurorae has been measured at 1000 km *620 miles*, while the lowest may descend to 72·5 km *45 miles*.

Reliable figures exist only from 1952, since when the record high and low number of nights of auroral displays in Shetland (geomagnetic Lat. 63°) has been 203 (1957) and 58 (1965).

The most recent great display in north-west Europe was that of 4–5 Sep 1958.

Lowest latitudes Extreme cases of displays in very low latitudes were recorded at Cuzco, Peru (2 Aug 1744) Honolulu, Hawaii (1 Sep 1859), and questionably, Singapore (25 Sep 1909).

Noctilucent clouds These remain sunlit long after sunset owing to their great altitude, and are thought to consist of ice crystals or meteoric dust. Regular observations (at heights of *c.* 85 km *52 miles*) in Western Europe date only from 1964; since that year the record high and low number of nights on which these phenomena have been observed have been 43 (1979) and 15 (1970).

COMETS

Earliest recorded Records date from the 7th century BC. The speeds of the estimated 2 million comets vary from 1125 km/h *700 mph* in outer space to 2 000 000 km/h *1 250 000 mph* when near the Sun. The successive appearances of Halley's Comet have been traced back to 467 BC. It was first depicted in the Nuremberg Chronicle of AD 684.

The first prediction of its return by Edmund Halley (1656–1742) proved true on Christmas Day 1758, 16 years after his death. On 13–14 Mar 1986, the European satellite *Giotto* (launched 2 Jul 1985) penetrated to within 540 km *335 miles* of the nucleus of Halley's Comet. It was established that this was 15 km *9·3 miles* in length and velvet black in colour.

Closest approach On 1 Jul 1770, Lexell's Comet, travelling at a speed of 38·5 km/sec *23·9 miles/sec* (relative to the Sun), came to within 1 200 000 km *745 000 miles* of the Earth. However, the Earth is believed to have passed through the tail of Halley's Comet, most recently on 19 May 1910.

Largest The tail of the brightest of all comets, the Great Comet of 1843, trailed for 330 000 000 km *205 000 000 miles*

The bow shock of Holmes Comet of 1892 once measured 2 400 000 km *1 500 000 miles* in diameter.

Shortest period Of all the recorded periodic comets (which are members of the Solar System), the one which most frequently returns is Encke's Comet, first identified in 1786. Its period of 1206 days (3·3 years) is the shortest established. Only one of its 53 returns has been missed by astronomers; this was in 1944. Now increasingly faint, it is expected to 'die' by February 1994.

The most frequently observed comets are Schwassmann-Wachmann I, Kopff and Oterma, which can be observed every year between Mars and Jupiter.

Longest period At the other extreme is Delavan's Comet of 1914, whose path was not accurately determined. It is not expected to return for perhaps 24 million years.

METEOROIDS

Meteoroids are of cometary or asteroidal origin. A meteor is the light phenomenon caused by the entry of a meteoroid into the Earth's atmosphere.

Meteor 'shower' The greatest shower on record occurred on the night of 16–17 Nov 1966, when the Leonid meteors (which recur every 33¼ years) were visible between western North America and eastern USSR. It was calculated that meteors passed over Arizona, USA at a rate of 2300 per min for a period of 20 min from 5 a.m. on 17 Nov 1966.

METEORITES

Meteorites When a *meteoroid* (consisting of broken fragments of cometary or asteroidal origin and ranging in size from fine dust to bodies several kilometres in diameter) penetrates to the Earth's surface, the remnant, which could be either aerolite (stony) or siderite (metallic), is described as a *meteorite*. Such events occur about 150 times per year over the whole land surface of the Earth.

In historic times, the only recorded person injured by a meteorite was Mrs Ann Hodges of Sylacauga, Alabama, USA. On 30 Nov 1954 a 4 kg *9 lb* stone, some 18 cm *7 in* in length, crashed through the roof of her home, hitting Mrs Hodges on the arm and bruising her hip. The physician who examined her, Dr Moody D. Jacobs, declared her fit but she was subsequently hospitalized as a result of the attendant publicity. The most anxious time of day for meteorophobes should be 3 p.m.

Oldest A revision by T. Kirsten in 1981 of the age estimates of meteorites which have remained essentially undisturbed after their formation suggests that the oldest which has been accurately dated is the Křahenberg meteorite at 4600 ± 20 million years, which predates the Solar System by about 70 million years.

It was reported in August 1978 that dust grains in the Murchison meteorite which fell in Australia in September 1969 may also be older than the Solar System.

Largest There was a mysterious explosion of 12½ megatons in Lat. 60° 55′ N, Long. 101° 57′ E, in the basin of the Podkamennaya Tunguska River, 40 miles north of Vanavar, in Siberia, USSR, at 00 hrs 17 min 11 sec UT on 30 Jun 1908. The cause was variously attributed to a meteorite (1927), a comet (1930), a nuclear explosion (1961) and anti-matter (1965). This devastated an area of about 3885 km² *1500 miles²* and the shock was felt as far as 1000 km (more than *600 miles*) away. The theory is now favoured that this was the terminal flare of stony debris from a comet, possibly Encke's comet, at an altitude of only 6 km or less than *20 000 ft*.

A similar event may have occurred over the Isle of Axholm, Humberside, England a few thousand years before. A stony meteorite with a diameter of 10 km *6·2 miles* striking the Earth at 55 925 mph *25 km/sec* would generate an explosive energy equivalent to 100 million megatons. Such events should not be expected to recur more than once in 75 million years.

The largest known meteorite was found in 1920 at Hoba West, near Grootfontein in Namibia and is a block 2·75 m *9 ft* long by 2·43 m *8 ft* broad, estimated to weigh 59 tonnes .

The largest meteorite exhibited by any museum is the 'Tent' meteorite, weighing 30 883 kg *68 085 lb* (30·39 tons) found in 1897 near Cape York, on the west coast of Greenland, by the expedition of Commander (later Rear-Admiral) Robert Edwin

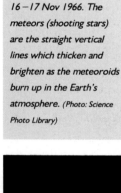

■ **Meteor shower**
The Leonid shower which was the greatest on record occurred on 16–17 Nov 1966. The meteors (shooting stars) are the straight vertical lines which thicken and brighten as the meteoroids burn up in the Earth's atmosphere. (Photo: Science Photo Library)

Peary (1856–1920). It was known to the Inuits as the Abnighito and is now exhibited in the Hayden Planetarium in New York City, USA.

The largest piece of stony meteorite recovered is a piece weighing 1770 kg *3902 lb*, part of a 4 tonne shower which struck Jilin (formerly Kirin), China on 8 Mar 1976.

The heaviest of the 22 meteorites known to have fallen on the British Isles since 1623 was one weighing at least 46·25 kg *102 lb* (the largest known fragment being 7·88 kg *17 lb 6 oz*), which fell at 4:12 p.m. on 24 Dec 1965 at Barwell, Leics.

Scotland's largest recorded meteorite fell in Strathmore, Tayside on 3 Dec 1917. It weighed 10·09 kg *22¼ lb* and was the largest of four totalling 13·324 kg *29 lb 6 oz*.

The largest recorded meteorite to fall in Ireland was the Limerick Stone of 29·5 kg *65 lb*, part of a shower weighing more than 48 kg *106 lb* which fell near Adare, Co. Limerick on 10 Sep 1813. Debris from the Bovedy Fall in Northern Ireland in 1969 spread over 80 km *50 miles*.

The larger of the two recorded meteorites to land in Wales weighed 794 g *28 oz* of which a piece weighing 723 g *25½ oz* went through the roof of the Prince Llewellyn Hotel in Beddgelert, Gwynedd shortly before 3:15 a.m. on 21 Sep 1949.

Craters It has been estimated that some 2000 asteroid Earth collisions have occurred in the last 600 million years. One hundred and two collision sites or astroblemes have been identified.

A crater 241 km *150 miles* in diameter and 805 m *½ mile* deep was attributed to a meteorite in 1962 in Wilkes Land, Antarctica. Such a crater could have been caused by a meteorite weighing 13 billion tonnes striking at 70 811 km/h *44 000 mph*. Soviet scientists reported in December 1970 an astrobleme with a diameter of 95 km *60 mile* and a maximum depth of 400 m *1300 ft* in the basin of the River Popigai.

There is a crater-like formation or astrobleme 442·5 km *275 miles* in diameter on the eastern shore of the Hudson Bay, Canada, where the Nastapoka Islands are just off the coast.

One of the largest and best-preserved craters is the Coon Butte or Barringer Crater, discovered in 1891 near Canyon Diablo, Winslow, Arizona, USA. It is 1265 m *4150 ft* in diameter and now about 175 m *575 ft* deep, with a parapet rising 40–48 m *130–155 ft* above the surrounding plain.

It has been estimated that an iron-nickel mass of some 2 million tonnes and a diameter of 61–79 m *200–260 ft* gouged this crater in *c.* 25 000 BC.

Evidence was published in 1963 discounting a meteoric origin for the crypto-volcanic Vredefort Ring (diameter 41·8 km *26 miles*), to the south-west of Johannesburg, South Africa, but this has now been reasserted.

The New Quebec (formerly the Chubb) 'Crater', first sighted on 20 Jun 1943 in northern Ungava, Canada, is 404 m *1325 ft* deep and measures 10·9 km *6·8 miles* around its rim.

Tektites The largest tektite of which details have been published weighed 3·2 kg *7·04 lb* and was found in 1932 at Muong Nong, Saravane Province, Laos. It is now in the Louvre Museum, Paris. Eight SNC meteorites (named after their find sites at

Shergotty in India, Nakla in Egypt and Chassigny in France), are believed to have emanated from Mars.

Fireball The brightest ever photographically recorded was by Dr Zdenek Ceplecha over Sumava, Czechoslovakia on 4 Dec 1974 with a momentary magnitude of −22 or 10 000 times brighter than a full Moon.

The Earth

The Earth is not a true sphere, but flattened at the poles and hence an oblate spheroid. The polar diameter of the Earth, which is 12 713·505 km *7899·806 miles*, is 42·769 km *26·575 miles* less than the equatorial diameter (12 756·274 km *7926·381 miles*). The Earth has a pear-shaped asymmetry with the north polar radius being 45 m *148 ft* longer than the south polar radius. There is also a slight ellipticity of the equator since its long axis (about longitude 37° W) is 159 m *522 ft* greater than the short axis. The greatest departures from the reference ellipsoid are a protuberance of 73 m *240 ft* in the area of Papua New Guinea and a depression of 105 m *344 ft* south of Sri Lanka, in the Indian Ocean.

The greatest circumference of the Earth, at the equator, is 40 075·02 km *24 901·46 miles*, compared with 40 007·86 km *24 859·73 miles* at the meridian. The area of the surface is estimated to be 510 065 600 km² *196 937 400 miles²*. The period of axial rotation, i.e. the true sidereal day, is 23 hr 56 min 4·0996 sec, mean time.

The mass of the Earth was first assessed by Dr Nevil Maskelyne (1732–1811) in Perthshire in 1774. The modern value is $5·974 \times 10^{21}$ tonnes and its density is 5·515 times that of water. The volume is an estimated 1 083 207 000 000 km³ *259 875 300 000 miles³*. The Earth picks up cosmic dust but estimates vary widely, with 30 000 tonnes a year being the upper limit. Modern theory is that the Earth has an outer shell or lithosphere 80 km *50 miles* thick, then an outer and inner rock layer or mantle extending 2809 km *1745 miles* deep, beneath which there is an iron-rich core of radius 3482 km *2164 miles*. If the iron-rich core theory is correct, iron would be the most abundant element in the Earth. At the centre of the core, the estimated density is 13·09 g/cm³, the temperature 4500° C and the pressure 364 GPa or 23 600 tons f/in².

Structure and Dimensions

OCEANS

The area of the Earth covered by water (the hydrosphere) is estimated to be 362 033 000 km² *139 781 000 miles²* or 70·98 per cent of the total surface. The mean depth of the hydrosphere was once estimated to be 3795 m *12 450 ft*, but recent surveys suggest a lower estimate of 3554 m *11 660 ft*. The total weight of the water is estimated to be $1·32 \times 10^{18}$ tonnes, or 0·022 per cent of the Earth's total weight. The volume of the oceans is estimated to be 1 349 900 000 km³ *323 900 000 miles³*, compared to 35 000 000 km³ *8 400 000 miles³* of fresh water.

Largest The largest ocean in the world is the Pacific. Excluding adjacent seas, it represents 45·9 per cent of the world's oceans and covers 166 241 000 km² *64 185 600 miles²* in area. The average depth is 4188 m *13 740 ft*. The shortest navigable trans-Pacific distance between Guayaquil, Ecuador and Bangkok, Thailand is 17 550 km *10 905 miles*.

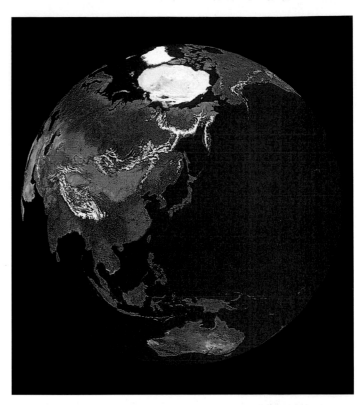

Deepest The deepest part of the ocean was first pinpointed in 1951 by HM Survey Ship *Challenger* in the Marianas Trench in the Pacific Ocean. The depth was measured by wide-band sounding at 10 863 m *35 639 ft*. Subsequent visits have resulted in slightly deeper measurements. A survey by the Soviet research ship *Vityaz* in 1957 produced a depth which was later refined to 11 034 m *36 200 ft*, and on 23 Jan 1960 the US Navy bathyscaphe *Trieste* descended to the bottom at 10 916 m *35 813 ft*. A more recent visit produced a figure of 10 924 m ± 10 m *35 839 ft ± 33 ft*, from data obtained by the survey vessel *Takuyo* of the Hydrographic Department, Japan Maritime Safety Agency in 1984, using a narrow multi-beam echo sounder.

A metal object, for example a kilogram ball of steel, dropped into water above this trench would take nearly 64 min to fall to the sea bed, where hydrostatic pressure is over 1250 bars *18 000 lb/in²*.

The deepest point in the territorial waters of the UK is an area 6 cables (*1100 m*) off the island of Raasay, near Skye, in the Inner Sound, at Lat. 57° 30′ 33″ N, Long. 5° 57′ 27″ W, which is 316 m *1037 ft* deep.

Largest sea The largest of the world's seas is the South China Sea, with an area of 2 974 600 km² *1 148 500 miles²*.

Largest gulf The largest gulf in the world is the Gulf of Mexico, with an area of 1 500 000 km² *580 000 miles²* and a shoreline of 4990 km *3100 miles* from Cape Sable, Florida, USA, to Cabo Catoche, Mexico.

Largest bay The largest bay in the world measured by shoreline length is Hudson Bay, northern Canada, with a shoreline of 12 268 km *7623 miles* and with an area of 822 300 km² *317 500 miles²*. The area of the Bay of Bengal, in the Indian Ocean, is larger, at 2 172 000 km² *839 000 miles²*.

Great Britain Great Britain's largest bay is Cardigan Bay, which has a shoreline 225 km *140 miles* long and measures 116 km *72 miles* across from the Lleyn Peninsula, Gwynedd to St David's Head, Dyfed.

Longest fjord The world's longest fjord is the Nordvest Fjord arm of the Scoresby

Sund in eastern Greenland, which extends inland 313 km *195 miles* from the sea. The longest Norwegian fjord is the Sognefjord, which extends 204 km *126·8 miles* inland from the island of Sogneoksen to the head of the Lusterfjord arm at Skjolden. Its width ranges from 2·35 km *1½ miles* at its narrowest to 5·1 km *3¼ miles* at its widest. It has a deepest point of 1296 m *4252 ft*. The longest Danish fjord is Limfjorden (160 km *100 miles*).

Longest sea loch Loch Fyne, Scotland, extends 60·5 km *37·6 miles* inland into Strathclyde.

Highest seamount The highest known submarine mountain, or seamount, is one discovered in 1953 near the Tonga Trench, between Samoa and New Zealand. It rises 8690 m *28 500 ft* from the sea bed, with its summit 365 m *1200 ft* below the surface.

Remotest spot from land The world's most distant point from land is a spot in the South Pacific, approximately 48° 30′ S, 125° 30′ W, which is about 2670 km *1660 miles* from the nearest points of land, namely Pitcairn Island, Ducie Island and Cape Dart, Antarctica. Centred on this spot is a circle of water with an area of approximately 22 421 500 km² *8 657 000 miles²* — about 18 000 km² *7000 miles²* larger than the USSR, the world's largest country.

Most southerly The most southerly part of the oceans is 85° 34′ S, 154° W, at the snout of the Robert Scott Glacier, 490 km *305 miles* from the South Pole.

Temperature The temperature of the water at the surface of the sea varies from −2° C *28·5° F* in the White Sea to 35·6° C *96° F* in the shallow areas of the Persian Gulf in summer. Ice-focused solar rays have been known to heat lake water to nearly 26·8° C *80° F*. The normal Red Sea temperature is 22°C *71·6° F*. The highest temperature recorded in the ocean is 404° C *759° F*, for a spring measured by an American research submarine some 480 km *300 miles* off the American west coast, in an expedition under the direction of Prof. Jack Diamond of Oregon State University, USA in 1985. Remote probes measured the temperature of the spring, which was kept from vaporising by the weight of water above it.

Clearest The Weddell Sea, 71° S, 15° W off Antarctica, has the clearest water of any sea. A 'Secchi' disc was visible to a depth of 80 m *262 ft* on 13 Oct 1986, as measured by Dutch researchers at the German Alfred-Wegener Institute. Such clarity corresponds to what scientists consider attainable in distilled water.

STRAITS

Longest The longest straits in the world

are the Tatarskiy Proliv or Tartar Straits between Sakhalin Island and the USSR mainland, running from the Sea of Japan to Sakhalinsky Zaliv — 800 km *497 miles*, thus marginally longer than the Malacca Straits, between Malaysia and Sumatra.

Broadest The broadest named straits in the world are the Davis Straits between Greenland and Baffin Island, Canada, with a minimum width of 338 km *210 miles*. The Drake Passage between the Diego Ramirez Islands, Chile and the South Shetland Islands is 1140 km *710 miles* across.

Narrowest The narrowest navigable straits are those between the Aegean island of Euboea and the mainland of Greece. The gap is only 40 m *45 yd* wide at Khalkis. The Seil Sound, Inner Hebrides, Scotland narrows to a point only 6 m *20 ft* wide where the Clachan bridge joins the island of Seil to the mainland, and is thus said to be a bridge across the Atlantic.

WAVES

Highest The highest officially recorded sea wave was calculated at 34 m *112 ft* from trough to crest; it was measured by Lt Frederic Margraff, USN from the USS *Ramapo* proceeding from Manila, Philippines to San Diego, California, USA on the night of 6–7 Feb 1933, during a 68 knot (*126 km/h*) hurricane. The highest instrumentally measured wave was one 26·2 m *86 ft* high, recorded by the British ship *Weather Reporter*, in the North Atlantic on 30 Dec 1972 in Lat. 59° N, Long. 19° W. It has been calculated on the statistics of the Stationary Random Theory that one wave in more than 300 000 may exceed the average by a factor of four. On 9 Jul 1958 a landslip caused a 160 km/h *100 mph* wave to wash 524 m *1720 ft* high along the fjord-like Lituya Bay in Alaska, USA.

Highest seismic The highest estimated height of a *tsunami* (often wrongly called a tidal wave) was one of 85 m *278 ft*, which appeared off Ishigaki Island, Ryukyu Chain on 24 Apr 1771. It tossed a 750-tonne block of coral more than 2·5 km *1·3 miles*. *Tsunami* (a Japanese word: *nami*, a wave; *tsu*, overflowing) have been observed to travel at 790 km/h *490 mph*. Evidence for a 300 m *1000 ft* ocean wave having occurred about 100 000 years ago was reported on 4 Dec 1984. This is believed to have broken on the southern shore of Lanai, Hawaiian Islands and was due to a meteorite, a volcanic eruption or a submarine landslide.

CURRENTS

Greatest The greatest current in the oceans is the Antarctic Circumpolar Current or West Wind Drift Current. On the basis of four measurements taken in 1982 in the Drake Passage, between South America and Antarctica, it was found to be flowing at a rate of 130 000 000 m³ *4·3 billion ft³* per sec. Results from computer modelling in 1990 estimate a higher figure of 195 000 000 m³ *6·9 billion ft³* per sec. Its width ranges from 300–2000 km *185–1240 miles* and it has a proven surface flow rate of ⁴⁄₁₀ of a knot *0·75 km/h*.

Strongest The world's strongest currents are the Nakwakto Rapids, Slingsby Channel, British Columbia, Canada (Lat. 51° 05′ N, Long. 127° 30′ W), where the flow rate may reach 16 knots *29·6 km/h*.

Great Britain The fastest current in British territorial waters is 10·7 knots *19·8 km/h* in the Pentland Firth between the Orkney Islands and Highland.

TIDES

Extreme tides are due to lunar and solar

gravitational forces affected by their perigee, perihelion and syzygies. Barometric and wind effects can superimpose an added 'surge' element. Coastal and sea-floor configurations can accentuate these forces. The normal interval between tides is 12 hr 25 min.

Greatest The greatest tides occur in the Bay of Fundy, which divides the peninsula of Nova Scotia, Canada from the United States' north-easternmost state of Maine and the Canadian province of New Brunswick. Burncoat Head in the Minas Basin, Nova Scotia, has the greatest mean spring range, with 14·5 m *47 ft 6 in*. A range of 16·6 m *54 ft 6 in* was recorded at springs in Leaf Basin, in Ungava Bay, Quebec, Canada in 1953. Tahiti experiences virtually no tide.

Great Britain The place with the greatest mean spring range in Great Britain is Beachley, on the Severn, with a range of 12·40 m *40 ft 8½ in*, compared with the British Isles' average of 4·57 m *15 ft*. Prior to 1933, tides as high as 8·80 m *28 ft 11 in* above and 6·80 m *22 ft 3½ in* below datum (total range 15·60 m *51 ft 2½ in*) were recorded at Avonmouth, though an extreme range of 15·90 m *52 ft 2½ in* for Beachley was officially accepted. In 1883 a freak tide of greater range was reported from Chepstow, Gwent.

ICEBERGS

Largest and tallest The largest iceberg on record was an antarctic tabular iceberg of over 31 000 km² *12 000 miles²*, 335 km *208 miles* long and 97 km *60 miles* wide (and thus larger than Belgium), sighted 240 km *150 miles* west of Scott Island, in the South Pacific Ocean, by the USS *Glacier* on 12 Nov 1956. The 61 m *200 ft* thick arctic ice island T.1 (360 km² *140 miles²*), discovered in 1946, was tracked for 17 years. The tallest iceberg measured was one of 167 m *550 ft* reported off western Greenland by the US icebreaker *East Wind* in 1958.

Most southerly arctic The most southerly arctic iceberg was sighted in the Atlantic by a USN weather patrol in Lat. 28° 44′ N, Long. 48° 42′ W, in April 1935. The southernmost iceberg reported in British home waters was sighted 96 km *60 miles* from Smith's Knoll, on the Dogger Bank, in the North Sea.

Most northerly antarctic The most northerly antarctic iceberg was a remnant sighted in the Atlantic by the ship *Dochra* in Lat. 26° 30′ S, Long. 25° 40′ W, on 30 Apr 1894.

LAND

There is satisfactory evidence that at one time the Earth's land surface comprised a single primeval continent of 2×10^8 km² *80 million miles²*, now termed Pangaea, and that this split about 190 million years ago, during the Jurassic period, into two supercontinents, which are termed Laurasia (Eurasia, Greenland and North America) and Gondwanaland (Africa, Arabia, India, South America, Oceania and Antarctica), named after Gondwana, India, which itself split 120 million years ago. The South Pole was apparently in the area of the Sahara as recently as the Ordovician period of *c.* 450 million years ago.

ROCKS

The age of the Earth is generally considered to be within the range of 4500 ± 70 million years, based on the lead isotope systematics. However, no rocks of this great age have yet been found on the Earth since geological processes have presumably destroyed them.

Oldest The greatest reported age for any scientifically dated rock is 3962 million years in the case of Acasta Gneisses found in May 1984. The rocks were discovered approximately 320 km *200 miles* north of Yellowknife, Northwest Territories, Canada by Dr Samuel Bowring as part of an ongoing Canadian geology survey mapping project. When the samples were analysed in June 1989, Dr Bowring and scientists from the Australian National University in Canberra established their age, using a machine called SHRIMP (Sensitive High-mass Resolution Ion MicroProbe).

Older minerals have been identified which are not rocks. Some zircon crystals discovered by Bob Pidgeon and Simon Wilde in the Jack Hills, 700 km *435 miles* north of Perth, Western Australia in August 1984 were found to be 4276 million years old, again using SHRIMP. These are the oldest fragments of the Earth's crust discovered so far.

Great Britain The oldest rocks in Great Britain are the original volcanic products from which were formed the gneiss and granulite rocks of the Scourian complex in the north-west Highlands and the Western Isles which were crystallized 2800 million years ago.

Largest The largest monolith in the world is Ayers Rock, which rises 348 m *1143 ft* above the surrounding desert plain in Northern Territory, Australia. It is 2·5 km *1·5 miles* long and 1·6 km *1 mile* wide. The nearest major town is Alice Springs, which is 400 km *250 miles* to the north-east. It was estimated in 1940 that La Gran Piedra, a volcanic plug located in the Sierra Maestra, Cuba, weighs 61 355 tonnes.

CONTINENTS

Largest Of the Earth's surface 41·25 per cent, or 210 400 000 km² *81 200 000 miles²*, is covered by continental masses of which only about two-thirds or 29·02 per cent of the Earth's surface (148 021 000 km² *57 151 000 miles²*) is land above water, with a mean height of 756 m *2480 ft* above sea level. The Eurasian land mass is the largest, with an area (including islands) of 53 698 000 km² *20 733 000 miles²*. The Afro-Eurasian land mass, separated artificially only by the Suez Canal, covers an area of 84 702 000 km² *32 704 000 miles²* or 57·2 per cent of the Earth's land mass.

Smallest The smallest continent is the Australian mainland, with an area of 7 618 493 km² *2 941 526 miles²*, which, together with Tasmania, New Zealand, Papua New Guinea and the Pacific Islands, is sometimes described as Oceania.

Land remotest from the sea The point of land remotest from the sea is at Lat. 46° 16·8′ N, Long. 86° 40·2′ E in the Dzungarian Basin, which is in the Sinkiang Uighur Autonomous Region (Xinjiang Uygur Zu zhi ju), China's most north-westerly province. It was visited by Nicholas Crane and Dr Richard Crane (GB) on 27 Jun 1986 and is at a straight-line distance of 2648 km *1645 miles* from the nearest open sea — Baydaratskaya Guba to the north (Arctic Ocean), Feni Point to the south (Indian Ocean) and Bo Hai Wun to the east (Yellow Sea).

Great Britain The point furthest from the sea in Great Britain is a point near Meriden, W Mids, which is 117 km *72½ miles* equidistant from the Severn Bridge, the Dee and Mersey estuaries and the Welland estuary in the Wash. The equivalent point in Scotland is in the Forest of Atholl, north-west Tayside, 65 km *40½ miles* equidistant from the head of Loch Leven, Inverness Firth and the Firth of Tay.

Peninsula The world's largest peninsula is Arabia, with an area of about 3 250 000 km² *1 250 000 miles²*.

ISLANDS

Largest Discounting Australia, which is usually regarded as a continental land mass, the largest island in the world is Greenland (now officially known as Kalaallit Nunaat), with an area of about 2 175 000 km² *840 000 miles²*. There is evidence that Greenland is in fact several islands overlaid by an ice cap without which it would have an area of 1 680 000 km² *650 000 miles²*. The largest sand island in the world is Fraser Island, Queensland, Australia with a sand dune 120 km *75 miles* long.

Great Britain The mainland of Great Britain is the eighth largest island in the world, with an area of 218 024 km² *84 186 miles²*. It stretches 971 km *603½ miles* from Dunnet Head in the north to Lizard Point in the south and 463 km *287½ miles* across from Porthaflod, Dyfed to Lowestoft, Suffolk. The island of Ireland (84 418 km² *32 594 miles²*) is the twentieth largest in the world.

Freshwater The largest island surrounded by fresh water (48 000 km² *18 500 miles²*) is the Ilha de Marajó in the mouth of the River Amazon, Brazil. The world's largest inland island (i.e. land surrounded by rivers) is Ilha do Bananal, Brazil (18 130 km² *7000 miles²*). The largest island in a lake is Manitoulin Island (2766 km² *1068 miles²*) in the Canadian section of Lake Huron.

Great Britain The largest lake island in Great Britain is Inchmurrin, in Loch Lomond, Strathclyde/Central with an area of 115 ha *284 acres*.

Remotest The remotest island in the world is Bouvet Island (Bouvetøya), discovered in the South Atlantic by J.B.C. Bouvet de Lozier on 1 Jan 1739, and first landed on by Capt. George Norris on 16 Dec 1825. Its position is 54° 26′ S, 3° 24′ E. This uninhabited Norwegian dependency is about 1700 km *1050 miles* from the nearest land — the uninhabited Queen Maud Land coast of eastern Antarctica.

The remotest inhabited island in the world is Tristan da Cunha, discovered in the South Atlantic by Tristão da Cunha, a Portuguese admiral, in March 1506. It has an area of 98 km² *38 miles²* and a habitable area of 31 km² *12 miles²*. The first permanent inhabitant was Thomas Currie, who landed in 1810. The island was annexed by the UK on 14 Aug 1816. After evacuation in 1961 (due to volcanic activity), 198 islanders returned in November 1963. The nearest inhabited land to the group is the island of St Helena, 2120 km *1320 miles* to the north-east. The nearest continent, Africa, is 2735 km *1700 miles* away.

The remotest of the British islets is Rockall. It is officially given as being 307 km *191 miles* west of St Kilda, Western Isles, although in June 1986 it was found by an RAF Nimrod to be 1509 m *4950 ft* to the south-east of its official location. This rock, measuring 21 m *70 ft* high and 25 m *83 ft* across, was not formally annexed until 18 Sep 1955. The remotest British island which has ever been inhabited is North Rona, which is 70·8 km *44 miles* from the next nearest land at Cape Wrath and the Butt of Lewis. It was evacuated *c.* 1844. Muckle Flugga, off Unst, in the Shetlands, is the northernmost inhabited island. It had a population of three in 1971 and is in a latitude north of southern Greenland. Just to the north of it is the rock of Out Stack in Lat. 60° 51′ 35·7″ N.

Greatest archipelago The world's greatest archipelago is the crescent of more than 13 000 islands, 5600 km *3500 miles* long, which forms Indonesia.

Highest rock pinnacle The world's highest rock pinnacle is Ball's Pyramid near Lord Howe Island in the Pacific, which is 561 m *1843 ft* high, but has a base axis of only 200 m *220 yd*. It was first scaled in 1965.

Northernmost land On 26 Jul 1978 Uffe Petersen of the Danish Geodetic

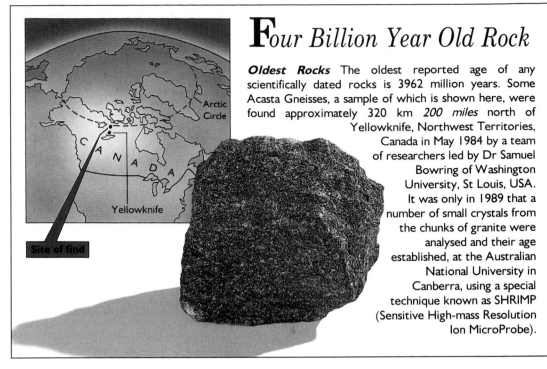

Four Billion Year Old Rock

Oldest Rocks The oldest reported age of any scientifically dated rocks is 3962 million years. Some Acasta Gneisses, a sample of which is shown here, were found approximately 320 km *200 miles* north of Yellowknife, Northwest Territories, Canada in May 1984 by a team of researchers led by Dr Samuel Bowring of Washington University, St Louis, USA. It was only in 1989 that a number of small crystals from the chunks of granite were analysed and their age established, at the Australian National University in Canberra, using a special technique known as SHRIMP (Sensitive High-mass Resolution Ion MicroProbe).

Most remote islet

The remotest of the British islets is Rockall, made famous through shipping forecasts. It is officially given as being 307 km *191 miles* west of St Kilda, Western Isles, although in June 1986 it was found to be 1509 m *4950 ft* to the south-east of its official location. In 1985 it was 'occupied' by Tom McClean for 38 days 22 hr 52 min from 25 May to 4 July.

DEEPEST CAVES BY COUNTRIES

Depth			
m	ft		
1602	5256	Réseau Jean Bernard	France
1508	4947	Shakta Pantjukhina	USSR
1441	4728	Sistema del Trave	Spain
1353	4439	Sistema Huautla	Mexico
1219	3999	Schwersystem	Austria
1210	3970	Abisso Olivifer	Italy
1198	3930	Veliko Fbrego	Yugoslavia
1159	3802	Anou Ifflis	Algeria
1020	3346	Siebenhengste System	Switzerland
308	1010	Ogof Ffynnon Ddu	Wales
214	702	Giant's Hole System	England
179	587	Reyfad Pot	Northern Ireland
142	467	Carrowmore Cavern	Republic of Ireland
76	249	Cnoc nan Uamh	Scotland

Institute observed the islet of Oodaq Ø, 30 m *100 ft* across, 1·36 km *1478 yd* north of Kaffeklubben Ø off Pearyland, Greenland in Lat. 83° 40′ 32·5″ N, Long. 30° 40′ 10·1″ W. It is 706·4 km *438·9 miles* from the North Pole.

Southernmost land The South Pole, unlike the North Pole, is on land. The Amundsen–Scott South Polar station was built there at an altitude of 2855 m *9370 ft* in 1957. It is drifting bodily with the ice cap 8–9 m *27–30 ft* per annum in the direction 43° W and was replaced by a new structure in 1975.

Newest The world's newest island is the lava islet of Fukuto Kuokanoba, near Iwo Jima in the Pacific, reported in January 1986. It measures 650 × 450 m *2132 × 1476 ft* and is 12 m *40 ft* above sea level.

Largest atoll The largest atoll in the world is Kwajalein in the Marshall Islands, in the central Pacific Ocean. Its slender coral reef 283 km *176 miles* long encloses a lagoon of 2850 km² *1100 miles²*. The atoll with the largest land area is Christmas Atoll, in the Line Islands in the central Pacific Ocean. It has an area of 642 km² *248 miles²*, of which 323 km² *125 miles²* is land. Its principal settlement, London, is only 4 km *2½ miles* distant from another settlement, Paris.

Longest reef The Great Barrier Reef off Queensland, north-eastern Australia is 2027 km *1260 statute miles* in length. Between 1959 and 1971 a large section between Cooktown and Townsville was destroyed by the Crown of Thorns starfish (*Acanthaster planci*).

DEPRESSIONS

Deepest The deepest depression so far discovered is the bedrock in the Bentley sub-glacial trench, Antarctica at 2538 m *8326 ft* below sea level. The greatest submarine depression is an area of the north-west Pacific floor which has an average depth of 4570 m *15 000 ft*. The deepest exposed depression on land is the shore surrounding the Dead Sea, now 400 m *1312 ft* below sea level. The deepest point on the bed of this saltiest of all lakes is 728 m *2388 ft* below sea level. The rate of fall in the lake surface since 1948 has been 350 mm *13·78 in* per annum. The deepest part of the bed of Lake Baikal in Siberia, USSR is 1485 m *4872 ft* below sea level.

Great Britain The lowest-lying area in Great Britain is in the Holme Fen area of the Great Ouse, in Cambridgeshire, at 2·75 m *9 ft* below sea level. The deepest depression in England is the bed of part of Lake Windermere, 28·65 m *94 ft* below sea level, and in Scotland the bed of Loch Morar, Inverness, 300·8 m *987 ft* below sea level.

Largest The largest exposed depression in the world is the Caspian Sea basin in the Azerbaijan, Russian, Kazakh and Turkmen Republics of the USSR and northern Iran. It is more than 518 000 km² *200 000 miles²*, of which 371 800 km² *143 550 miles²* is lake area. The preponderant land area of the depression is the Prikaspiyskaya Nizmennost, lying around the northern third of the lake and stretching inland for a distance of up to 450 km *280 miles*.

CAVES

Longest The most extensive cave system in the world is that under the Mammoth Cave National Park, Kentucky, USA, first entered in 1799. Explorations by many groups of cavers have revealed the interconnected cave passages beneath the Flint, Mammoth Cave and Toohey Ridges to make a system with a total mapped length which is now 560 km *348 miles*.

Great Britain The longest cave system in Great Britain is the Ease Gill system, W Yorks which now has 66 km *41 miles* of explored passage.

Largest The world's largest cave chamber is the Sarawak Chamber, Lubang Nasib Bagus, in the Gunung Mulu National Park, Sarawak, discovered and surveyed by the 1980 British–Malaysian Mulu Expedition. Its length is 700 m *2300 ft*, its average width is 300 m *980 ft* and it is nowhere less than 70 m *230 ft* high. It would be large enough to garage 7500 buses.

Underwater cave The longest explored underwater cave is the Nohoch Na Chich cave system in Quintana Roo, Mexico, with 13 290 m *43 600 ft* of mapped passages. Exploration of the system, which began in November 1987, has been carried out by the CEDAM Cave Diving Team under the leadership of Mike Madden.

Greatest descent The world depth record was set by the Groupe Vulcain in the Gouffre Jean Bernard, France at 1602 m *5256 ft* in 1989. However, this cave, explored via multiple entrances, has never been entirely descended, so the 'sporting' record for the greatest descent into a cave is recognized as 1508 m *4947 ft* in the Shakta Pantjukhina in the Russian Caucasus Mountains by a team of Ukrainian cavers in 1988.

Tallest stalagmite The tallest known stalagmite in the world is one in the Krásnohorska cave in Czechoslovakia, which is generally accepted as being about 32 m *105 ft* tall. The tallest cave column is considered to be the Flying Dragon Pillar, 39 m *128 ft* high, in Nine Dragons Cave (Daji Dong), Guizhou, China.

MOUNTAINS

Highest An eastern Himalayan peak of 8848 m *29 028 ft* above sea level on the Tibet–Nepal border (in an area first designated Chu-mu-lang-ma on a map of 1717) was discovered to be the world's highest mountain in 1852 by the Survey Department of the Government of India, from theodolite readings taken in 1849 and 1850. In 1860 its height was computed to be 8840 m *29 002 ft*. On 25 Jul 1973 the Chinese announced a height of 8848·2 m *29 029 ft 3 in*. It was named Mt Everest after Col. Sir George Everest (1790–1866), formerly Surveyor-General of India.

Everest's status as the world's highest mountain, maintained for 135 years (1852 –1987), was most recently challenged by K2 (formerly Godwin Austen), also known as Chogori, in the disputed Kashmiri Northern Areas of Pakistan, in an announcement on 6 Mar 1987 by the US K2 Expedition. Their satellite transit surveyor yielded altitudes of between 8858 and 8908 m *29 064 and 29 228 ft* as against the hitherto official 19th-century figure of 8611 m *28 250 ft*, and the 20th-century proposed height of 8760 m *28 740 ft*. However, on 13 Aug 1987 China reaffirmed their heights of 8848·2 m *29 029 ft 3 in* for Everest and 8611 m *28 250 ft* for K2. The Research Council in Rome, Italy announced on 23 Oct 1987 that new satellite measurements restored Everest to primacy at 8863 m *29 078 ft*, and put K2 down to 8607 m *28 238 ft*. It was on 31 Jul 1954 that K2 was first climbed, by A. Compagnoni and L. Lacedelli of Italy, 14 months after the summit of Everest had been reached. (For details of Everest ascents, see Mountaineering, Chapter 11.)

The mountain whose summit is farthest from the Earth's centre is the Andean peak of Chimborazo (6267 m *20 561 ft*), 158 km *98 miles* south of the equator in Ecuador, South America. Its summit is 2150 m *7057 ft* further from the Earth's centre than the summit of Mt Everest. The highest mountain on the equator is Volcán Cayambe (5878 m *19 285 ft*), Ecuador, in Long. 77° 58′ W. A mountaineer on the summit would be moving at 1671 km/h *1038 mph* relative to the Earth's centre, due to the Earth's rotation.

The highest insular mountain in the world is Puncak Jaya (formerly Puncak Sukarno, formerly Carstensz Pyramide) in Irian Jaya, Indonesia. A survey by the Australian Universities' Expedition in 1973 yielded a height of 4884 m *16 023 ft*. Ngga Pulu (also in Irian Jaya), which is now 4861 m *15 950 ft*, was in 1936 possibly *c.* 4910 m *16 110 ft* before the melting of its snow cap.

The highest mountain in the UK is Ben Nevis (1343 m *4406 ft* excluding the 3·65 m *12 ft* cairn), 6·85 km *4¼ miles* south-east of Fort William, Argyll. It was climbed before 1720, but though acclaimed the highest in 1790, was not officially recognized to be higher than Ben Macdhui (1310 m *4300 ft*) until 1870. In 1834 Ben Macdhui and Ben Nevis (Gaelic, *Beinn Nibheis*) (first reference, 1778) were respectively quoted as 1393 m *4570 ft* and 1332 m *4370 ft*. The highest mountain in England is Scafell Pike (978 m *3210 ft*) in Cumbria; in Wales the highest is Snowdon (*Yr Wyddfa*) (1085 m *3560 ft*) in Gwynedd; and in Ireland it is Carrantuohill (1041 m *3414 ft*) in Co. Kerry.

There is some evidence that, before being ground down by the ice cap, mountains in the Loch Bà area of the Isle of Mull, Strathclyde were 4575 m *15 000 ft* above sea level. There are 577 peaks and tops over 915 m *3000 ft* in the whole British Isles and 165 peaks and 136 tops in Scotland higher than England's highest point, Scafell Pike. The highest mountain off the mainland is Sgùrr Alasdair (1008 m *3309 ft*) on Skye, named after Alexander (Gaelic, *Alasdair*) Nicolson, who made the first ascent in 1873.

Unclimbed The highest unclimbed summit is Lhotse Middle Peak (8414 m *27 605 ft*) in the Khumbu district of the Nepal Himalaya. It is the tenth highest individually recognized summit in the world, Lhotse being the fourth highest mountain.

The highest unclimbed mountain is Namcha Barwa (7782 m *25 531 ft*), in the Great Bend of the Tsangpo (Brahmaputra), China.

Tallest The world's tallest mountain measured from its submarine base (6000 m *3280 fathoms*) in the Hawaiian Trough to its peak is Mauna Kea (Mountain White) on the island of Hawaii, with a combined height of 10 203 m *33 476 ft*, of which 4205 m *13 796 ft* are above sea level. Another mountain whose dimensions, but not height, exceed those of Mt Everest is the volcanic Hawaiian peak of Mauna Loa (Mountain Long) at 4170 m *13 680 ft*. The axes of its elliptical base, 4975 m *16 322 ft* below sea level, have been estimated at 119 km *74 miles* and 85 km *53 miles*. It should be noted that Cerro Aconcagua (6960 m *22 834 ft*) is more than 11 826 m *38 800 ft* above the Pacific abyssal plain (4875 m *16 000 ft* deep) or 13 055 m *42 834 ft* above the Peru–Chile Trench, which is 290 km *180 miles* distant in the South Pacific.

Greatest ranges The greatest of all mountain ranges is the submarine Mid-Ocean Ridge, extending 65 000 km *40 000 miles* from the Arctic Ocean to the Atlantic Ocean, round Africa, Asia and Australia, and under the Pacific Ocean to the west coast of North America. It has a greatest height of 4200 m *13 800 ft* above the base ocean depth.

The world's greatest land mountain range is the Himalaya-Karakoram, which contains 96 of the world's 109 peaks of over 7315 m *24 000 ft*. Himalaya derives from the Sanskrit *him*, snow; *alaya*, home.

Longest lines of sight Vatnajökull (2118 m *6952 ft*), Iceland has been seen by refracted light from the Faeroe Islands, 550 km *340 miles* distant. In Alaska, Mt McKinley (6193 m *20 320 ft*) has been sighted from Mt Sanford (4949 m *16 237 ft*) — a distance of 370 km *230 miles*. McKinley, so named in 1896, was called Denali (Great One) in the Athabascan language of North American Indians and is the highest mountain in the United States.

Greatest plateau The most extensive high plateau in the world is the Tibetan Plateau in Central Asia. The average altitude is 4875 m *16 000 ft* and the area is 200 000 km² *77 000 miles²*.

Sheerest wall Mt Rakaposhi (7772 m *25 498 ft*) rises 5·99 vertical kilometres *3·72 miles* from the Hunza Valley, Pakistan in 10 horizontal kilometres *6·21 miles* with an overall gradient of 31°.

The 975 m *3200 ft* wide north-west face of Half Dome, Yosemite, California, USA is 670 m *2200 ft* high but nowhere departs more than 7° from the vertical. It was first climbed (Class VI) in 1957 by Royal Robbins, Jerry Gallwas and Mike Sherrick.

Highest halites Along the northern shores of the Gulf of Mexico for 1160 km *725 miles* there exist 330 subterranean 'mountains' of salt, some of which rise more than 18 300 m *60 000 ft* from bedrock and appear as the low salt domes first discovered in 1862.

WATERFALLS

Highest The highest waterfall (as opposed to vaporized 'Bridal Veil') in the world is the Salto Angel in Venezuela, on a branch of the River Carrao, an upper tributary of the Caroni, with a total drop of 979 m *3212 ft* — the longest single drop is 807 m *2648 ft*. The 'Angel Falls' were named after the American pilot Jimmy Angel (died 8 Dec 1956), who recorded them in his log book on 14 Nov 1933. The falls, known by the Indians as Cherun-Meru, were first reported by Ernesto Sanchez La Cruz in 1910.

The highest waterfall in the UK is Eas a'Chùal Aluinn, from Glas Bheinn (774 m *2541 ft*), Sutherland, with a drop of 200 m *658 ft*. The greatest single drop is one of 67 m *220 ft* in the case of the Falls of Glomach, near Dornie, Highland. In England there is no clear-cut tallest waterfall. Cautley Spout, in Howgill Falls, Cumbria, with very broken cascades down a deep gully, has a total drop of 180 m *591 ft*. Scale Force, near Buttermere, Cumbria, has the longest unbroken drop, of 45 m *148 ft*. The underground cascade in the Gaping Gill Cave, Ingleborough, N Yorks descends an unbroken 111 m *365 ft*. The highest Welsh waterfall is the Pistyll-y-Llyn on the Powys–Dyfed border, which exceeds 90 m *300 ft* in descent. The highest falls in Ireland are the Powerscourt Falls (106 m *350 ft*), on the River Dargle, Co. Wicklow.

Greatest On the basis of the average annual flow, the greatest waterfalls in the world are the Boyoma (formerly Stanley) Falls in Zaïre with 17 000 m³/sec *600 000 cusec*. The flow of the Guaíra (Salto das Sete Quedas) on the Alto Paraná river between Brazil and Paraguay has at times attained a peak rate of 50 000 m³/sec *1 750 000 cusec*. It has been calculated that a waterfall 26 times greater than the Guaíra and perhaps 800 m *2625 ft* high was formed, when some 5·5 million years ago the Mediterranean basins began to be filled from the Atlantic through the Straits of Gibraltar.

Widest The widest waterfalls in the world are the Khône Falls (15–21 m *50–70 ft* high) in Laos, with a width of 10·8 km *6·7 miles* and a flood flow of 42 500 m³/sec *1 500 000 cusec*.

RIVERS

Longest The two longest rivers in the world are the Nile (*Bahr el-Nil*), flowing into the Mediterranean, and the Amazon (*Amazonas*), flowing into the South Atlantic. Which is the longer is more a matter of definition than simple measurement.

The length of the Nile watercourse, as surveyed by M. Devroey (Belgium) before the loss of a few miles of meanders due to the formation of Lake Nasser, behind the Aswan High Dam, was 6670 km *4145 miles*. This course is unitary from a hydrological standpoint and runs from the source in Burundi of the Luvironza branch of the Kagera feeder of the Victoria Nyanza via the White Nile (*Bahr el-Jebel*) to the delta in the Mediterranean.

The true source of the Amazon was discovered in 1953 to be a stream named Huaraco, deriving from the Misuie Glacier (5400 m *17 715 ft*) in the Arequipa Andes of Peru. This stream progressively becomes the Toro, then the Santiago, then the Apurimac, which in turn is known as the Ene and then the Tambo before its confluence with the Amazon prime tributary, the Ucayali. The length of the Amazon from this source to the South Atlantic via the Canal do Norte was measured in 1969 and found to be 6448 km *4007 miles* (usually quoted to the rounded-off figure of 6437 km *4000 miles*). If, however, a vessel navigating down the river follows the 'arm' (carrying 10 per cent of the river's water) to the south of Ilha de Marajó through the Furo Tajapuru and Furo dos Macacos into the Pará, the total length of the watercourse becomes 6750 km *4195 miles*. The Rio Pará is *not*, however, a tributary of the Amazon, being hydrologically part of the basin of the Tocantins, which itself flows into the Bahía de Marajó and out into the South Atlantic.

The longest river in Great Britain is the Severn, which empties into the Bristol Channel and is 354 km *220 miles* long. Its basin extends over 11 419 km² *4409 miles²*. It rises in north-western Powys, Wales, and flows through Shropshire, Hereford & Worcester, Gloucestershire and Avon and has a record 17 tributaries.

The longest river wholly in England is the Thames, which is 346 km *215 miles* long to The Nore. Its remotest source is at Seven

■ **Highest mountain**
The highest mountain in the world is Mt Everest, in the Himalayas. In recent years its status has been challenged by K2, but the Research Council in Rome, Italy announced on 23 Oct 1987 that new satellite measurements restored Everest to primacy at 8863 m 29 078 ft. (Photo: Allsport/Vandystadt)

Springs, Glos, whence the River Churn joins the other head-waters. The source of the Thames proper is Trewsbury Mead, Coates, near Cirencester, Glos. The basin measures 9948 km² *3841 miles²*. The Yorkshire Ouse's 11 tributaries aggregate 1012 km *629 miles*.

The longest river wholly in Wales is the Usk, with a length of 104·5 km *65 miles*. It rises on the border of Dyfed and Powys and flows out via Gwent into the Severn Estuary.

The longest river in Scotland is the Tay, with Dundee, Tayside on the shore of the estuary. It is 188 km *117 miles* long from the source of its remotest head-stream, the River Tummel, Tayside and has the greatest volume of any river in Great Britain, with a flow of up to 1387 m³/sec *49 000 cusec*. Of Scottish rivers the Tweed and the Clyde have most tributaries, with 11 each.

The longest river in Ireland is the Shannon, which is longer than any river in Great Britain. It rises 78·6 m *258 ft* above sea level, in Co. Cavan, and flows through a series of loughs to Limerick. It is 386 km *240 miles* long, including the 90 km *56 mile* long estuary to Loop Head. The basin area is 15 695 km² *6060 miles²*.

Shortest As with the longest river, two rivers could also be considered to be the shortest river with a name. The Roe River, near Great Falls, Montana, USA, has two forks fed by a large fresh water spring. These relatively constant forks measure 61 m *201 ft* (East Fork Roe River) and 17·7 m *58 ft* (North Fork Roe River) respectively. The Roe River flows into the

larger Missouri River. The D River, located at Lincoln City, Oregon, USA, connects Devil's Lake to the Pacific Ocean. Its length is officially quoted as 37 ± 1·5 m *120 ± 5 ft*.

Largest basin The largest river basin in the world is that drained by the Amazon (6448 km *4007 miles*), which covers about 7 045 000 km² *2 720 000 miles²*. It has some 15 000 tributaries and sub-tributaries, of which four are more than 1609 km *1000 miles* long. These include the Madeira, the longest of all tributaries, with a length of 3380 km *2100 miles*, which is surpassed by only 14 rivers in the world.

Longest sub-tributary The world's longest sub-tributary is the Pilcomayo (1609 km *1000 miles*) in South America. It is a tributary of the Paraguay (2415 km *1500 miles* long), which itself is a tributary of the Paraná (4025 km *2500 miles*).

Longest estuary The world's longest estuary is that of the often frozen Ob', in the northern USSR, at 885 km *550 miles*. It is up to 80 km *50 miles* wide.

Largest delta The world's largest delta is that created by the Ganges (Ganga) and Brahmaputra in Bangladesh and West Bengal, India. It covers an area of 75 000 km² *30 000 miles²*.

Greatest flow The greatest flow of any river in the world is that of the Amazon, which discharges an average of 120 000 m³/sec *4 200 000 cusec* into the Atlantic Ocean, increasing to more than 200 000 m³/sec *7 000 000 cusec* in full flood. The lowest 1450 km *900 miles* of the Amazon average 90 m *300 ft* in depth.

Submarine In 1952 a submarine river 400 km *250 miles* wide, known as the Cromwell current, was discovered flowing eastward 90 m *300 ft* below the surface of the Pacific for 5625 km *3500 miles* along the equator. Its volume is 1000 times that of the Mississippi.

Subterranean In August 1958 a crypto-river, tracked by radio isotopes, was discovered flowing under the Nile with six times its mean annual flow or 500 000 million m³ *20 trillion ft³*.

Largest swamp The world's largest tract of swamp is in the basin of the Pripet or Pripyat River — a tributary of the Dnieper in the USSR. These swamps cover an estimated area of 46 950 km² *18 125 miles²*.

RIVER BORES

The bore on the Qiantong Jiang (Hangzhou He) in eastern China is the most remarkable of the 60 in the world. At spring tides the wave attains a height of up to 7·5 m *25 ft* and a speed of 13–15 knots *24–27 km/h*. It is heard advancing at a range of 22 km *14 miles*. The annual downstream flood wave on the Mekong, in south-east Asia, sometimes reaches a height of 14 m *46 ft*. The greatest volume of any tidal bore is that of the Canal do Norte (16 km *10 miles* wide) in the mouth of the Amazon.

The most notable of the eight river bores in the UK is that on the Severn, which attained a measured height of 2·8 m *9 ft 3 in* on 15 Oct 1966 downstream of Stonebench, and a speed of 20 km/h *13 mph*. It travels from Framilode towards Gloucester.

LAKES AND INLAND SEAS

Largest The largest inland sea or lake in the world is the Kaspiyskoye More (Caspian Sea) in the southern USSR and Iran. It is 1225 km *760 miles* long and

its total area is 371 800 km² *143 550 miles²*. Of the total area, some 143 200 km² *55 280 miles²* (38·5 per cent) are in Iran, where it is named the Darya-ye-Khazar. Its maximum depth is 1025 m *3360 ft* and the surface is 28·5 m *93 ft* below sea level. Its estimated volume is 89 600 km³ *21 500 miles³* of saline water. Its surface has varied between 32 m *105 ft* (11th century) and 22 m *72 ft* (early 19th century) below sea level.

Deepest The deepest lake in the world is Lake Baikal in central Siberia, USSR. It is 620 km *385 miles* long and between 32–74 km *20–46 miles* wide. In 1957 the lake's Olkhon Crevice was measured and found to be 1940 m *6365 ft* deep and hence 1485 m *4872 ft* below sea level.

The deepest lake in Great Britain is the 16·57 km *10·30 mile* long Loch Morar, in Inverness. Its surface is 9 m *30 ft* above sea level and its extreme depth 310 m *1017 ft*. England's deepest lake is Wast Water (78 m *258 ft*), in Cumbria. The lake with the greatest mean depth is Loch Ness, with 130 m *427 ft*.

Highest The highest navigable lake in the world is Lake Titicaca (maximum depth 370 m *1214 ft*, with an area of about 8285 km² *3200 miles²*) in South America (4790 km² *1850 miles²* in Peru and 3495 km² *1350 miles²* in Bolivia). It is 209 km *130 miles* long and is 3811 m *12 506 ft* above sea level. There are higher lakes in the Himalayas, but most are glacial and of a temporary nature only. A survey of the area carried out in 1984 showed a lake at a height of 5414 m *17 762 ft*, named Panch Pokhri, which was 1·6 km *1 mile* long.

The highest lake in the UK is the 0·76 ha *1·9 acre* Lochan Buidhe at 1097 m *3600 ft* above sea level in the Cairngorms, Scotland. England's highest is Broad Crag Tarn (837 m *2746 ft* above sea level) on Scafell Pike, Cumbria and the highest named freshwater lake in Wales is The Frogs Pool, a tarn near the summit of Carnedd Llywelyn, Gwynedd, at 830 m *2723 ft*.

Freshwater The freshwater lake with the greatest surface area is Lake Superior, one of the Great Lakes of North America. The total area is 82 350 km² *31 800 miles²*, of which 53 600 km² *20 700 miles²* are in Minnesota, Wisconsin and Michigan, USA and 27 750 km² *11 100 miles²* in Ontario, Canada. It is 182 m *600 ft* above sea level. The freshwater lake with the greatest volume is Lake Baikal in Siberia, USSR, with an estimated volume of 23 000 km³ *5520 miles³*.

The largest lake in the UK is Lough Neagh (14·6 m *48 ft* above sea level) in Northern Ireland. It is 28·9 km *18 miles* long and 17·7 km *11 miles* wide, and has an area of 381·73 km² *147·39 miles²*. Its extreme depth is 31 m *102 ft*.

Freshwater loch The largest lake in Great Britain, and the largest inland loch in Scotland, is Loch Lomond, which is situated in the Strathclyde and Central regions at a height of 7 m *23 ft* above sea level. It is 36·44 km *22·64 miles* long and has a surface area of 70·04 km² *27·45 miles²*. Its greatest depth is 190 m *623 ft*. The lake or loch with the greatest volume is, however, Loch Ness, with 7 443 000 000 m³ *262 845 000 000 ft³*. The longest lake or loch is Loch Ness, which measures 38·99 km *24·23 miles*, although the three arms of the Y-shaped Loch Awe, Strathclyde aggregate 40·99 km *25·47 miles*. The largest lake in England is Windermere, in Cumbria. It is 17 km *10½ miles* long and has a surface area of 14·74 km² *5·69 miles²*. Its greatest depth is 66·75 m *219 ft* in the northern half. The largest *natural* lake in Wales is Llyn Tegid, with an area of 4·38 km² *1·69 miles²*, although the largest lake in Wales is that formed by the reservoir at Lake Vyrnwy, where the total surface area is 453·25 ha *1120 acres*.

Freshwater loughs The largest lough in the Republic of Ireland is Lough Corrib in Mayo and Galway. It measures 43·5 km *27 miles* in length and is 11·25 km *7 miles* across at its widest point, with a total surface area of 168 km² *65 miles²*.

Lake in a lake The largest lake in a lake is Manitou Lake (106·42 km² *41·09 miles²*) on the world's largest lake island, Manitoulin Island (2766 km² *1068 miles²*), in the Canadian part of Lake Huron. The lake itself contains a number of islands.

Underground The world's largest underground lake is believed to be that in the Drachenhauchloch cave in Namibia, discovered in 1986. Its surface has an area of 2·13 ha *5¼ acres*, and lies 60 m *200 ft* underground, over water 90 m *300 ft* deep.

Largest lagoon Lagoa dos Patos in southernmost Brazil is 254 km *158 miles* long and extends over 10 645 km² *4110 miles²*.

OTHER FEATURES

Desert Nearly an eighth of the world's land surface is arid, with a rainfall of less than 25 cm *9·8 in* per annum. The Sahara in North Africa is the largest in the world. At its greatest length it is 5150 km *3200 miles* from east to west. From north to south it is between 1275 and 2250 km *800 and 1400 miles*. The area covered by the desert is about 8 400 000 km² *3 250 000 miles²*. The land level varies from 132 m *436 ft* below sea level in the Qattâra Depression, Egypt to the mountain Emi Koussi (3415 m *11 204 ft*) in Chad. The daytime temperature range in the western Sahara may be more than 45° C or *80° F*.

Sand dunes The world's highest measured sand dunes are those in the Saharan sand sea of Isaouane-N-Tifernine of east central Algeria in Lat. 26° 42′ N, Long. 6° 43′ E. They have a wavelength of 5 km *3·1 miles* and attain a height of 430 m *1410 ft*.

Largest mirage The largest mirage on record was that sighted in the Arctic at 83° N, 103° W by Donald B. MacMillan in 1913. This type of mirage, known as the Fata Morgana, appeared as the same 'hills, valleys, snow-capped peaks extending through at least 120 degrees of the horizon' that Peary had misidentified as Crocker Land six years earlier. On 17 Jul 1939 a mirage of Snaefells Jokull (1437 m *4715 ft*) on Iceland was seen from the sea at a distance of 539–563 km *335–350 miles*.

Largest gorge The largest land gorge in the world is the Grand Canyon on the Colorado River in north-central Arizona, USA. It extends from Marble Gorge to the Grand Wash Cliffs, over a distance of 349 km *217 miles*. It varies in width from 6–20 km *4–13 miles* and is some 1615 m *5300 ft* deep. The submarine Labrador Basin canyon is 3440 km *c. 2150 miles* long.

Deepest canyon The deepest canyon is El Cañón de Colca, Peru, reported in 1929, which is 3223 m *10 574 ft* deep. It was first traversed by the Polish Expedition CANOANDES' 79 kayak team from 12 May– 14 Jun 1981. A stretch of the Kali River in central Nepal flows 5485 m *18 000 ft* below its flanking summits of the Dhaulagiri and Annapurna mountain groups. The deepest submarine canyon yet discovered is one 40 km *25 miles* south of Esperance, Western Australia, which is 1800 m *6000 ft* deep and 32 km *20 miles* wide.

Cliffs The highest sea cliffs yet pinpointed anywhere in the world are those on the north coast of east Moloka'i, Hawaii near Umilehi Point, which descend 1005 m *3300 ft* to the sea at an average gradient of more than 55°.

The highest cliffs in north-west Europe are those on the north coast of Achill Island, in Co. Mayo, Republic of Ireland, which rise 668 m *2192 ft* sheer above the sea at Croaghan. The highest cliffs in the UK are the 396 m *1300 ft* Conachair cliffs on St Kilda, Western Isles (425 m *1397 ft*). The highest sheer sea cliffs on the mainland of Great Britain are at Clo Mor, 4·8 km *3 miles* south-east of Cape Wrath, Sutherland which drop 280·7 m *921 ft*. England's highest cliff (gradient more than 45°) is Great Hangman Hill, near Combe Martin, in north Devon, which descends from 318 m *1043 ft* to the sea in 300 m *984 ft*, the last 213 m *700 ft* of which is sheer.

Natural arches The longest natural arch in the world is the Landscape Arch in the Arches National Park, 40 km *25 miles* north of Moab in Utah, USA. This natural sandstone arch spans 88 m *291 ft* and is set about 30 m *100 ft* above the canyon floor. In one place erosion has narrowed its section to 1·82 m *6 ft*. Larger, however, is the Rainbow Bridge, Utah, USA, discovered on 14 Aug 1909, which although only 84·7 m *278 ft* long, is more than 6·7 m *22 ft* wide.

Longest glaciers It is estimated that 15 600 000 km² *6 020 000 miles²*, or 10·5 per cent of the Earth's land surface, is permanently glaciated. The world's longest glacier is the Lambert Glacier, discovered by an Australian aircraft crew in Australian Antarctic Territory in 1956–57. It is up to 64 km *40 miles* wide and, with its upper section, known as the Mellor Glacier, it measures at least 402 km *250 miles* in length. With the Fisher Glacier limb, the Lambert forms a continuous ice passage about 514 km *320 miles* long. The longest Himalayan glacier is the Siachen (75·6 km *47 miles*) in the Karakoram range, though the Hispar and Biafo combine to form an ice passage 122 km *76 miles* long. The fastest-moving major glacier is the Quarayaq in Greenland, flowing 20–24 m *65–80 ft* per day.

Thickest ice The greatest recorded thickness of ice is 4·78 km *2·97 miles* measured by radio echo soundings from a US Antarctic research aircraft at 69° 9′ 38″ S, 135° 20′ 25″ E 400 km *250 miles* from the coast in Wilkes Land on 4 Jan 1975.

Deepest permafrost The deepest recorded permafrost is more than 1370 m *4500 ft*, reported from the upper reaches of the Viluy River, Siberia, USSR in February 1982.

Natural Phenomena

EARTHQUAKES

(Seismologists record all dates with the year *first*, based not on local time but on Universal Time/Greenwich Mean Time).

Greatest It is estimated that each year there are some 500 000 detectable seismic or micro-seismic disturbances, of which 100 000 can be felt and 1000 cause damage.

The deepest recorded hypocentres are of 720 km *447 miles* in Indonesia in 1933, 1934 and 1943.

The scale most commonly used to measure the size of earthquakes is Richter's magnitude scale (1954). It is named after Dr Charles Richter (1900–85) and the most commonly used form is M_s, based on amplitudes of surface waves, usually at a period of 20 sec. The largest reported magnitudes on this scale are about 8·9, but the scale does not properly represent the size of the very largest earthquakes, above M_s about 8, for which it is better to use the concept of seismic moment, M_o, devised by K. Aki in 1966. Moment can be used to derive a 'moment magnitude', M_w, first used by Hiroo Kanamori in 1977. The largest recorded earthquake on the M_w scale is the Chilean shock of 1960 May 22, which had $M_w = 9·5$, but only 8·3 on the M_s scale. For the largest events, such as the Chilean shock of 1960, the energy released is more than 10^{19} joules.

Worst death toll The greatest chronicled loss of life occurred in the earthquake which rocked every city of the Near East and eastern Mediterranean *c.* July 1201. Contemporary accounts estimate the loss of life at 1 100 000. Less uncertain is the figure of 830 000 fatalities in a prolonged earthquake (*ti chen*) in the Shensi, Shansi and Honan provinces of China, of 1556 Feb 2 (new style) (Jan 23 old style). The highest death toll in modern times has been in the Tangshan earthquake (Mag. M_s = 7·9) in eastern China on 1976 Jul 27 (local time was 3 a.m. July 28). The first figure published on 4 Jan 1977 revealed 655 237 killed, later adjusted to 750 000. On 22

■ **Largest gorge**
The largest land gorge in the world is the Grand Canyon, in Arizona, USA. It extends over a distance of 349 km 217 miles, varying in width from 6–20 km 4–13 miles. It is some 1615 m 5300 ft deep. (Photo: Spectrum)

WORLD'S STRONGEST EARTHQUAKES
Progressive list of instrumentally recorded earthquakes

Kanamori Scale Magnitudes M_W	Richter Scale Magnitude M_S	Location	Date
8·8	8·6	Ecuador	1906 31 Jan
9·0	8¼	Kamchatka, USSR	1952 4 Nov
9·1	7¾	Andreanof Islands, Aleutian Islands, USA	1957 9 Mar
9·5	8·3	Chile	1960 22 May

$\log E = 1.5M + 4.8$ (joules)

Nov 1979 the New China News Agency inexplicably reduced the death toll to 242 000.

Material damage The greatest physical devastation was in the earthquake on the Kanto plain, Japan, of 1923 Sep 1 (Mag. $M_s = 8.2$, epicentre in Lat. 35° 15′ N, Long. 139° 30′ E); in Sagami Bay the sea bottom in one area sank 400 m *1310 ft*. The official total of persons killed and missing in this *Shinsai* or great 'quake and the resultant fires was 142 807. In Tokyo and Yokohama 575 000 dwellings were destroyed. The cost of the damage was estimated at £1 billion (now £17 billion).

Great Britain and Ireland The total of the undisputed death toll for Great Britain is two — an apprentice, Thomas Grey, struck by falling masonry from Christ's Hospital Church, near Newgate, London at 6 p.m. on 6 Apr 1580, and another young person, Mabel Everet, who died of injuries four days later.

The East Anglian or Colchester earthquake of 1884 Apr 22 (9:18 a.m.) (epicentre Lat. 51° 49′ N, Long. 0° 54′ E) caused damage estimated at more than £12 000 to 1250 buildings. Langenhoe Church was wrecked. Windows and doors were rattled over an area of 137 250 km² *53 000 miles²* and the shock was felt in Exeter, Devon and Ostend, Belgium. It has been estimated to have been of Mag. 5·2 on the Richter scale.

The highest instrumentally measured Magnitude is 6·0 for the Dogger Bank event of 1931 Jun 7. The strongest Scottish tremor occurred at Inverness at 10:45 p.m. on 1816 Aug 13, and was felt over an area of 130 000 km² *50 000 miles²*.

The strongest Welsh tremor occurred in Swansea at 9:45 a.m. on 1906 Jun 27 (epicentre Lat. 51° 38′ N, Long. 4° W). It was felt over an area of 97 900 km² *37 800 miles²*.

No earthquake with its epicentre in Ireland has ever been instrumentally measured, though the effects of the North Wales shock of 1984 Jul 19 (Mag. 5 to 5·5) dislocated traffic lights in Dublin. However, there was a shock in August 1734 which damaged 100 dwellings and 5 churches.

VOLCANOES

The total number of known active volcanoes in the world is 1343, of which many are submarine. The greatest active concentration is in Indonesia, with some 200 volcanoes. The name volcano derives from the now dormant Vulcano Island (from the god of fire Vulcanus) in the Mediterranean.

Greatest explosion The greatest explosion in historic times (possibly since Santoriní in the Aegean Sea, 96 km *60 miles* north of Crete, in 1628 BC) occurred at c. 10 a.m. (local time), or 3:00 a.m. GMT, on 27 Aug 1883, with an eruption of Krakatoa, an island (then 47 km² *18 miles²*) in the Sunda

Strait, between Sumatra and Java, in Indonesia. One hundred and sixty-three villages were wiped out, and 36 380 people killed by the wave it caused. Pumice was thrown 55 km *34 miles* high and dust fell 5330 km *3313 miles* away 10 days later. The explosion was recorded four hours later on the island of Rodrigues, 4776 km *2968 miles* away, as 'the roar of heavy guns', and was heard over one thirteenth of the surface of the globe. This explosion, estimated to have had about 26 times the power of the greatest H-bomb test (by the USSR), was still only a fifth of the power of the Santoriní cataclysm.

Greatest eruption The total volume of matter discharged in the eruption of Tambora, a volcano on the island of Sumbawa, in Indonesia, 5–7 Apr 1815, was 150–180 km³ *36–43 miles³*. The energy of this 2245 km/h *1395 mph* eruption, which lowered the height of the island by 1250 m *4100 ft* from 4100 m *13 450 ft* to 2850 m *9350 ft*, was 8.4×10^{19} joules. A crater 11 km *7 miles* in diameter was formed. More than 90 000 were killed or died as a result of the subsequent famine. This compares with a probable 60–65 km³ *14–16 miles³* ejected by Santoriní (see above) and 20 km³ *5 miles³* ejected by Krakatoa (see above). The internal pressure at Tambora has been estimated at 3270 kg/cm² or *20·76 tons/in²*.

The ejecta in the Taupo eruption in New Zealand c. AD 130 has been estimated at 30 000 million tonnes of pumice moving at one time at 700 km/h *400 mph*. It flattened 16 000 km² *6180 miles²* (over 26 times the devastated area of Mount St Helens, which erupted in Washington State, USA on 18 May 1980). Less than 20 per cent of the 14×10^9 tonnes of pumice ejected in this most violent of all documented volcanic events fell within 200 km *125 miles* of the vent.

Longest lava flow The longest lava flow in historic times is a mixture of *pahoehoe* ropey lava (twisted cord-like solidifications) and *aa* blocky lava, resulting from the eruption of Laki in 1783 in southeast Iceland, which flowed 65–70 km *40½–43½ miles*. The largest known prehistoric flow is the Roza basalt flow in North America c. 15 million years ago, which had an unsurpassed length (300 km *185 miles*), area (40 000 km² *15 400 miles²*) and volume (1250 km³ *300 miles³*).

Largest active Mauna Loa in Hawaii has a dome 120 km *75 miles* long and 50 km *31 miles* wide (above sea level), with lava flows which occupy more than 5125 km² *1980 miles²* of the island. Its pit crater, Mokuaweoweo, measures 10·4 km² *4 miles²* and is 150–180 m *500–600 ft* deep. It rises 4168 m *13 677 ft* and has averaged one eruption every 3½ years since 1832, although none since 1984.

Highest active The highest volcano regarded as active is Ojos del Salado (which has fumaroles), at a height of

6887 m *22 595 ft*, on the frontier between Chile and Argentina.

Highest potentially active The highest potentially active volcano is Volcán Llullaillaco (6723 m *22 057 ft*), also on the frontier between Chile and Argentina.

Northernmost and southernmost The northernmost volcano is Beeren Berg (2276 m *7470 ft*) on the island of Jan Mayen (71° 05′ N) in the Greenland Sea. It erupted on 20 Sep 1970 and the island's 39 inhabitants (all male) had to be evacuated. It was possibly discovered by Henry Hudson the English navigator and explorer (died 1611) in 1607 or 1608, but was definitely visited by Jan Jacobsz Mayen (Netherlands) in 1614. It was annexed by Norway on 8 May 1929. The Ostenso seamount (1775 m *5825 ft*), 556 km *346 miles* from the North Pole in Lat. 85° 10′ N, Long. 133° W, was volcanic. The most southerly known active volcano is Mt Erebus (3795 m *12 450 ft*), on Ross Island (77° 35′ S) in Antarctica. It was discovered on 28 Jan 1841 by the expedition of Capt. (later Rear-Admiral Sir) James Clark Ross, RN (1800–62), and first climbed at 10 a.m. on 10 Mar 1908 by a British party of five, led by Prof. (later Lt-Col. Sir) Tannatt William Edgeworth David (1858–1934).

Largest crater The world's largest *caldera* or volcano crater is that of Toba, north-central Sumatra, Indonesia, covering 1775 km² *685 miles²*.

AVALANCHES

Greatest The greatest natural avalanches, though rarely observed, occur in the Himalayas but no estimates of their volume have been published. It was estimated that 3 500 000 m³ *120 000 000 ft³* of snow fell in an avalanche in the Italian Alps in 1885. The 400 km/h *250 mph* avalanche triggered by the Mount St Helens eruption in Washington State, USA on 18 May 1980 was estimated to measure 2800 million m³ *96 000 million ft³* (see Accidents and Disasters, Chapter 4).

GEYSERS

Tallest The Waimangu (Maori 'black water') geyser, in New Zealand, erupted to a height in excess of 457 m *1500 ft* in 1904, but has not been active since it erupted violently at 6:20 a.m. on 1 Apr 1917 and killed four people. Currently the world's tallest active geyser is the US National Parks' Service Steamboat Geyser, in Yellowstone National Park, Wyoming. During the 1980s it erupted at intervals ranging from 19 days to more than four years, although there were occasions in the 1960s when it erupted as frequently as every 4–10 days. The maximum height ranges from 60–115 m *195–380 ft*. The greatest measured water discharge was an estimated 28 000–38 000 hl *616 000–836 000 gal* by the Giant Geyser, also in Yellowstone National Park. However, this estimate, made in the 1950s, was only a rough calculation. The *Geysir* ('gusher') near Mt Hekla in south-central Iceland, from which all others have been named, spurts on occasions to 55 m *180 ft*, while the adjacent Strokkur, reactivated by drilling in 1963, spurts at 10–15 min intervals.

Weather

The meteorological records given below necessarily relate largely to the last 140–160 years, since data before that time are both sparse and often unreliable. Reliable registering thermometers were introduced as recently as c. 1820. The longest continuous observations have been maintained at the Radcliffe Observatory, Oxford since 1815, though discontinuous records have enabled the Chinese to assert that 903 BC was a very bad winter.

Palaeo-entomological evidence is that there was a southern European climate in England c. 90 000 BC, while in c. 6000 BC the mean summer temperature reached 19·4° C 67° F, or 3·3° C 6° F higher than the present. It is believed that 1·2 million years ago the world's air temperature averaged 35° C 95° F. The earliest authentic recording of British weather relates to the period 26 Aug–17 Sep 55 BC. The earliest reliably known hot summer was in AD 664 during our driest-ever century and the earliest known severe winter was that of AD 763–4. In 1683–4 there was frost in London from November to April. Frosts were recorded during August in the period 1668–89.

Most equable temperature
The location with the most equable recorded temperature over a short period is Garapan, on Saipan in the Mariana Islands, Pacific Ocean. During the nine years from 1927–35, inclusive, the lowest temperature recorded was 19·6° C 67·3° F on 30 Jan 1934 and the highest was 31·4° C 88·5° F on 9 Sep 1931, giving an extreme range of 11·8° C 21·2° F. Between 1911 and 1966 the Brazilian off-shore island of Fernando de Noronha had a minimum temperature of 18·6° C 65·5° F on 17 Nov 1913 and a maximum of 32·0° C 89·6° F on 2 Mar 1965, an extreme range of 13·4° C 24·1° F.

Greatest temperature ranges
The greatest recorded temperature ranges in the world are around the Siberian 'cold pole' in the eastern USSR. Temperatures in Verkhoyansk (67° 33′ N, 133° 23′ E) have ranged 104·4° C 188° F from −67·7° C −90° F to 36·7° C 98° F. The greatest temperature variation recorded in a day is 55·5° C 100° F (a fall from 6·7° C 44° F to −48·8° C −56° F) at Browning, Montana, USA on 23–24 Jan 1916. The most freakish rise was 27·2° C 49° F in 2 min at Spearfish, South Dakota, USA, from −20° C −4° F at 7:30 a.m. to 7·2° C 45° F at 7:32 a.m. on 22 Jan 1943. The British record is 29° C 52·2° F (−7° C 19·4° F to 22° C 71·6° F) at Tummel Bridge, Tayside on 9 May 1978.

Longest freeze
The longest recorded unremitting freeze in the British Isles was one of 40 days at the Great Dun Fell radio station, Appleby, Cumbria, from 23 Jan to 3 Mar 1986. Less rigorous early data include a frost from 5 Dec 1607 to 14 Feb 1608 and a 91-day frost on Dartmoor, Devon in 1854–5. No temperature lower than 1° C 34° F has ever been recorded on Bishop Rock, Isles of Scilly.

Upper atmosphere
The lowest temperature ever recorded in the atmosphere is −143° C −225·4° F at an altitude of about 80·5–96·5 km 50–60 miles, during noctilucent cloud research above Kronogård, Sweden from 27 Jul to 7 Aug 1963. A jet stream moving at 656 km/h 408 mph at 47 000 m 154 200 ft (46 km 29·2 miles) was recorded by Skua rocket above South Uist, Outer Hebrides on 13 Dec 1967.

Most recent white Christmas and Frost Fair
London has experienced eight 'white' or snowing Christmas Days since 1900. These have been 1906, 1917 (slight), 1923 (slight), 1927, 1938, 1956 (slight), 1970 and 1981. These were more frequent in the 19th century and even more so before the change of the calendar which by removing 3–13 September brought forward all dates subsequent to 2 Sep 1752 by 11 days. The last of the nine recorded Frost Fairs held on the Thames since 1564/5 was from December 1813 to 26 Jan 1814.

Most intense rainfall
Difficulties attend rainfall readings for very short periods, but the figure of 38·1 mm 1½ in in one min at Barst, Guadeloupe on 26 Nov 1970 is regarded as the most intense recorded in modern times. The cloudburst of 'near 609 mm 2 ft in less than a quarter of half an hour' at Oxford on the afternoon of 31 May (old style) 1682 is regarded as unacademically recorded. The most intense rainfall in Britain recorded to modern standards has been 51 mm 2 in in 12 min at Wisbech, Cambs on 27 Jun 1970.

Falsest St Swithin's Days
The legend that the weather on St Swithin's Day, celebrated on 15 July (old and new style) since AD 912, determines the rainfall for the next 40 days is one which has long persisted. There was a brilliant 13½ hr of sunshine in London on 15 Jul 1924, but 30 of the next 40 days were wet. On 15 Jul 1913 there was a downpour lasting 15 hr, yet it rained on only nine of the subsequent 40 days in London.

Best and worst British summers
According to Prof. Gordon Manley's survey over the period 1728–1978 the best (i.e. driest and hottest) British summer was that of 1976 and the worst (i.e. wettest and coldest) that of 1879. Temperatures of more than 32° C 89·8° F were recorded on 13 consecutive days (25 Jun–7 Jul 1976) within Great Britain, including 35·9° C 96·6° F at Cheltenham on 3 July. In 1983 there were 40 days with temperatures above 26·6° C 80° F in Britain between 3 July and 31 August, including 17 consecutively (3–19 July); London experienced its hottest month (July) since records began in 1840.

Humidity and discomfort
Human comfort or discomfort depends not merely on temperature but on the combination of temperature, humidity, radiation and windspeed. The United States Weather Bureau uses a Temperature-Humidity Index, which equals two-fifths of the sum of the dry and wet bulb thermometer readings plus 15. A THI of 98·2 has been twice recorded in Death Valley, California — on 27 Jul 1966 (119° F and 31 per cent) and on 12 Aug 1970 (117° F and 37 per cent). A person driving at 72 km/h 45 mph in a car without a windscreen in a temperature of −42·7° C −45° F would, by the chill factor, experience the equivalent of −87·2° C −125° F, i.e. within 2·0° C 3·6° F of the world record.

Longest-lasting rainbow
A rainbow lasting over three hours was reported from the coastal border of Gwynedd and Clwyd, north Wales on 14 Aug 1979.

Lightning
The visible length of lightning strokes varies greatly. In mountainous regions, when clouds are very low, the flash may be less than 91 m 300 ft long. In flat country with very high clouds, a cloud-to-earth flash may measure 6 km 4 miles, though in the most extreme cases such flashes have been measured at 32 km 20 miles. The intensely bright central core of the lightning channel is extremely narrow. Some authorities suggest that its diameter is as little as 1·27 cm ½ in. This core is surrounded by a 'corona envelope' (glow discharge), which may measure 3–6 m 10–20 ft in diameter.

The speed of a discharge varies from 160–1600 km/sec 100–1000 miles/sec for the downward leader track, and reaches up to 140 000 km/sec 87 000 miles/sec (nearly half

EXTREME TEMPERATURES
(Progressive recordings)

HIGH

53·0° C	127·4° F	Ouargla, Algeria	27 Aug	1884
54·4° C	130° F	Amos, California, USA	17 Aug	1885
54·4° C	130° F	Mammoth Tank, California, USA	17 Aug	1885
56·7° C	134° F	Death Valley, California, USA	10 Jul	1913
58·0° C	136·4° F	Al'Azīzīyah (el-Azizia), Libya*	3 Sep	1922

* Obtained by the US National Geographical Society but not officially recognized by the Libyan Ministry of Communications.

A reading of 60° C 140° F at Delta, Mexico in August 1953 is not now accepted because of over-exposure to roof radiation. The official Mexican record of 58·0° C 136·4° F at San Luis, Sonora on 11 Aug 1933 is not internationally accepted.

The report of a freak heat flash in Coimbra, Portugal in September 1933, said to have caused the temperature to rise to 70°C 158° F for 120 sec, is questionable.

LOW

−58·3° C	−73° F	Floeberg Bay, Ellesmere I., Canada	[1]	1852
−68° C	−90·4° F	Verkhoyansk, Siberia, USSR	3 Jan	1885
−68° C	−90·4° F	Verkhoyansk, Siberia, USSR	5 & 7 Feb	1892
−68° C	−90·4° F	Oymyakon, Siberia, USSR [2]	6 Feb	1933
−73·5° C	−100·4° F	South Pole, Antarctica	11 May	1957
−74·5° C	−102·1° F	South Pole, Antarctica	17 Sep	1957
−78·3° C	−109·1° F	Sovietskaya, Antarctica	2 May	1958
−80·7° C	−113·3° F	Vostok, Antarctica	15 Jun	1958
−81·2° C	−114·1° F	Sovietskaya, Antarctica	19 Jun	1958
−83·0° C	−117·4° F	Sovietskaya, Antarctica	25 Jun	1958
−85·7° C	−122·4° F	Vostok, Antarctica	7–8 Aug	1958
−86·7° C	−124·1° F	Sovietskaya, Antarctica	9 Aug	1958
−87·4° C	−125·3° F	Vostok, Antarctica	25 Aug	1958
−88·3° C	−126·9° F	Vostok, Antarctica	24 Aug	1960
−89·2° C	−128·6° F	Vostok, Antarctica	21 Jul	1983

[1] The earliest recorded occasion that mercury froze (at −40° C −40° F) was by M. V. Lomonosov, near Moscow, c. 1750.

[2] Population in 1986 reported to be 4000 — the world's coldest inhabited place.

the speed of light) for the powerful return stroke. Every few million strokes there is a giant discharge, in which the cloud-to-earth and return strokes flash from and to the top of the thunder clouds. In these 'positive giants' energy of up to 3 billion joules (3×10^{16} ergs) has been recorded. The temperature reaches about 30 000° C, which is more than that of the surface of the Sun.

In Britain there is an average of 3·7 strikes per km² per annum (6 strikes per mile²), and an average of 4200 per annum over London alone.

Highest waterspout The highest waterspout of which there is a reliable record was one observed on 16 May 1898 off Eden, New South Wales, Australia. A theodolite reading from the shore gave its height as 1528 m *5014 ft*. It was about 3 m *10 ft* in diameter. The Spithead waterspout off Ryde, Isle of Wight on 21 Aug 1878 was measured by sextant to be 1600 m or *'about a mile'* in height. A more realistic estimate of a waterspout was one which developed off Yarmouth, Isle of Wight on 6 Aug 1987. It was some 762 m *2500 ft* in height.

Cloud extremes The highest standard cloud form is cirrus, averaging 8250 m *27 000 ft* and above, but the rare nacreous or mother-of-pearl formation sometimes reaches nearly 24 000 m *80 000 ft* (see also Noctilucent clouds, p. 10). Cirrus cloud is composed almost entirely of ice crystals at temperatures of −40° C *−40° F* or below. The lowest is stratus, below 1066 m *3500 ft*. The cloud form with the greatest vertical range is cumulonimbus, which has been observed to reach a height of nearly 20 000 m *68 000 ft* in the tropics.

Tornadoes (see also Accidents and Disasters, Chapter 4) Britain's strongest tornado was at Southsea, Portsmouth, Hants on 14 Dec 1810 (Force 8 on the Meaden-TORRO scale). The Newmarket tornado (Force 6) of 3 Jan 1978 caused property damage estimated at up to £1 000 000. On 23 Nov 1981, 58 tornadoes were reported in one day from Anglesey to eastern England.

Highest shade temperature The highest ever recorded shade temperature is 58° C *136·4° F* at Al'Azīzīyah, Libya (alt. 111 m *367 ft*) on 13 Sep 1922. The highest in Britain is 37·1° C *98·8° F* at Cheltenham, Glos on 3 Aug 1990. The 38·6° C *100·5° F* which was once reported from Tonbridge, Kent was a non-standard exposure and is estimated to be equivalent to 36–36·7° C *97–98° F*.

Lowest screen temperature A record low of −89·2° C *−128·6° F* was registered at Vostok, Antarctica (alt. 3419 m *11 220 ft*) on 21 Jul 1983. The coldest permanently inhabited place is the Siberian village of Oymyakon (pop. 4000), 63° 16′ N, 143° 15′ E (700 m *2300 ft*), in the USSR where the temperature reached −67·8° C *−90·0° F* in 1933. Britain's lowest was −27·2° C *−17° F* on 11 Feb 1895 and again on 10 Jan 1982, both times at Braemar, Grampian. The −30·5° C *−23° F* at Blackadder, Borders, on 4 Dec 1879, and the −28·9° C *−20° F* at Grantown-on-Spey, Highland on 24 Feb 1955, were not standard exposures. The lowest official temperature in England is −26·1° C *−15° F* at Newport, Shrops on 10 Jan 1982. The lowest maximum temperature for a day was −19·1° C *−2·3° F* at Braemar, again on 10 Jan 1982.

Greatest rainfall A record 1870 mm *73·62 in* of rain fell in 24 hours in Cilaos (alt. 1200 m *3937 ft*), La Réunion, Indian Ocean on 15 and 16 Mar 1952. This is equal to 7554 tonnes of rain per acre. For a calendar month, the record is 9300 mm *366·14 in*, at Cherrapunji, Meghalaya, India in July 1861, and the 12-month record was also at Cherrapunji, with 26 461 mm *1041·78 in* between 1 Aug 1860 and 31 Jul 1861.

In Great Britain, the 24-hour record is 279 mm *11 in* at Martinstown, Dorset on 18 and 19 Jul 1955. 1436 mm *56·54 in* fell in October 1909 at Llyn Llydau, Snowdon, Gwynedd, and over a 12-month period, 6527 mm *257 in* fell at Sprinkling Tarn, Cumbria, in 1954.

Wettest place By average annual rain-

fall, the wettest place in the world is Tutunendo, in Colombia, with 11 770 mm *463·4 in* per annum. Styhead Tarn (487 m *1600 ft*), in Cumbria, with 4391 mm *172·9 in*, is Britain's wettest place.

Most rainy days Mt Wai-'ale-'ale (1569 m *5148 ft*), Kauai, Hawaii has up to 350 rainy days per annum. The place in the British Isles which has had the most rainy days in a calendar year is Ballynahinch, in Co. Galway, Republic of Ireland, with 309 in 1923.

Greatest snowfall 31 102 mm *1224½ in* of snow fell over a 12-month period from 19 Feb 1971 to 18 Feb 1972 at Paradise, Mt Rainier, in Washington State, USA. The record for a single snowstorm is 4800 mm *189 in* at Mt Shasta Ski Bowl, California, USA from 13–19 Feb 1959 and for a 24–hr period it is 1930 mm *76 in* at Silver Lake, Colorado, USA on 14–15 Apr 1921. The greatest depth of snow on the ground was 1146 cm *37 ft 7 in* at Tamarack, California, USA in March 1911. Britain's 12-month record is the 1524 mm *60 in* which fell in Upper Teesdale and also in the Denbighshire Hills, Clwyd, in 1947. London's earliest recorded snow was on 25 Sep 1885, and the latest on 2 Jun 1975. Less reliable reports suggest snow on 12 Sep 1658 (old style) and on 12 Jun 1791.

Maximum sunshine The annual average at Yuma, Arizona, USA is 90 per cent (over 4000 hr). St Petersburg, Florida, USA recorded 768 consecutive sunny days from 9 Feb 1967 to 17 Mar 1969. The best in Britain was 78·3 per cent of the maximum possible in one month (382 hours out of 488) at Pendennis Castle, Cornwall in June 1925.

Minimum sunshine At the South Pole there is nil sunshine for 182 days every year and at the North Pole the figure is nil for 176 days. From 18 November to 8 February each winter the south-eastern end of the village of Lochranza, Isle of Arran, Strathclyde is in shadow of mountains, and for the whole of December 1890, a figure of nil was registered at Westminster, London.

Barometric pressure The highest barometric pressure ever recorded was 1083·8 mb *32 in* at Agata, Siberia, USSR (alt. 262 m *862 ft*) on 31 Dec 1968. The highest in Britain was 1054·7 mb *31·15 in*, in Aberdeen on 31 Jan 1902.

The lowest sea-level pressure was 870 mb *25·69 in* in Typhoon Tip, 482 km *300 miles* west of Guam, Pacific Ocean, in Lat. 16° 44′ N, Long. 137° 46′ E, on 12 Oct 1979. Britain's lowest is 925·5 mb *27·33 in*, at Ochtertyre, near Crieff, Tayside on 26 Jan 1884.

Highest surface wind-speed A surface wind-speed of 371 km/h *231 mph* was recorded at Mt Washington (1916 m *6288 ft*), New Hampshire, USA on 12 Apr 1934. The highest speed at low level was registered on 8 Mar 1972 at the USAF base at Thule, Greenland (44 m *145 ft*), when a peak speed of 333 km/h *207 mph* was recorded. The highest speed measured to date in a tornado is 450 km/h *280 mph* at Wichita Falls, Texas, USA on 2 Apr 1958.

The record high surface wind-speed for Britain is 278 km/h *172 mph* (150 knots), on Cairn Gorm Summit (1245 m *4084 ft*), on 20 Mar 1986. A figure of 285·2 km/h *177·2 mph*, at RAF Saxa Vord, Unst, in the Shetlands on 16 Feb 1962, was not recorded with standard equipment. British tornadoes may reach 290 km/h *180 mph*. There were gales of great severity on 15 Jan 1362, 26 Nov 1703 and 16 Oct 1987.

Thunder-days At Tororo, Uganda an average of 251 days of thunder per annum was recorded for the 10-year period 1967–76. Between Lat. 35° N and 35° S there are some 3200 thunderstorms each 12 night-time hours, some of which can be heard at a range of 29 km *18 miles*. The record number of thunder-days recorded in a specific place in a calendar year in Britain is 38, twice. The first time was in 1912, at Stonyhurst, in Lancashire, and the second was in 1967, at Huddersfield, in W Yorks.

Hottest place On an annual mean basis, with readings taken over a six-year period from 1960 to 1966, the temperature at Dallol, in Ethiopia, was 34·4° C *94° F*. In Death Valley, California, USA, maximum temperatures of over 48·9° C *120° F* were recorded on 43 consecutive days, between 6 Jul and 17 Aug 1917. At Marble Bar, Western Australia (maximum 49·4° C *121° F*), 162 consecutive days with maximum temperatures of over 37·8° C *100° F* were recorded between 30 Oct 1923 and 8 Apr 1924. At Wyndham, also in Western Australia, the temperature reached 32·2° C *90° F* or more on 333 days in 1946. In Britain, annual mean temperatures of 11·5° C *52·7° F* were recorded both at Penzance, in Cornwall, and the Isles of Scilly in the period 1931 to 1960.

Coldest place Polus Nedostupnosti (Pole of Cold), Antarctica at 78° S, 96° E, is the coldest place in the world, with an extrapolated annual mean of −57·8° C −72° F. The coldest measured mean is −56·6° C −70° F, at Plateau Station, Antarctica. For Britain, the coldest mean temperature is 6·34° C 43·41° F, at Braemar, Grampian, based on readings taken between 1952 and 1981.

Driest place The annual rainfall in the Desierto de Atacama, near Calama, Chile is effectively nil. In Britain, the lowest annual mean rainfall on record is at Lee Wick Farm, St Osyth, Essex, with 513 mm *20·2 in*, based on the period 1964 to 1982. The lowest rainfall recorded in a single year was 236 mm *9·29 in* at one station in Margate, Kent in 1921.

Longest drought Desierto de Atacama, in Chile, experienced a drought for some 400 years up to 1971. Britain's longest drought lasted 73 days, from 4 Mar to 15 May 1893, at Mile End, Greater London.

Heaviest hailstones The heaviest hailstones on record, weighing 1·02 kg *2¼ lb*, are reported to have killed 92 people in the Gopalganj district of Bangladesh on

■ **Minimum sunshine**

14 Apr 1986. The heaviest hailstones in Britain fell on 5 Sep 1958 at Horsham, W Sussex, and weighed 141 g *5 oz*. Much heavier ones are sometimes reported, but usually these are coalesced rather than single stones. An ice block of 1–2 kg *35–70 oz* was reputed to have fallen at Withington, Manchester on 2 Apr 1973.

Longest sea-level fogs Sea-level fogs — with visibility less than 914·4 m *1000 yd* — persist for weeks on the Grand Banks, Newfoundland, Canada, with the average being more than 120 days per year. The duration record for Britain is 4 days 18 hours, twice, in both cases in London. The first time was from 26 Nov to 1 Dec 1948 and the second from 5 to 9 Dec 1952. Lower visibilities occur at higher altitudes. Ben Nevis is reputedly in cloud 300 days per year.

Windiest place The Commonwealth Bay, George V Coast, Antarctica, where gales reach 320 km/h *200 mph*, is the world's windiest place. In Britain, an average reading of 33·1 km/h *20·6 mph* was registered at Fair Isle in the period 1974–78.

Gems, Jewels and Precious Stones

DIAMOND

Largest. 3106 carats. This was found on 25 Jan 1905 in the Premier Mine, Pretoria, South Africa and named *The Cullinan* after the mine's discoverer Sir Thomas Cullinan. It was presented to King Edward VII in 1907. Currently the largest uncut stone is of 599 carats, found near Pretoria, South Africa in July 1986, although its existence was only announced by De Beers on 11 Mar 1988. It is expected to yield a 350-carat cut stone.

Largest cut. 530·2 carats. A 74-facet pear-shaped gem named *The Star of Africa*, it was cleaved from *The Cullinan* by Jak Asscher and polished by Henri Koe in Amsterdam in 1908. It is now in the Royal Sceptre.

Largest natural intense fancy blue. 136·25 carats. The *Queen of Holland* cushion-shaped brilliant-cut diamond was found in 1904. It was cut by Freedman & Co. in Amsterdam, and was exhibited at the Paris Exhibition in 1925. It was then sold to an Indian Maharaja, but its current owners are unknown.

Largest natural intense fancy green. 41 carats. This is housed in the Green Vaults in Dresden, Germany.

Smallest. 0·0001022 carat. D. Drukker & Zn NV of Amsterdam, Netherlands have produced a 57-facet brilliant with a diameter of 0·22 mm *0·009 in*.

Rarest colour. Blood red. The largest is a 5·05 carat flawless stone found in Tichtenburg, South Africa in 1927 and now in a private collection in the USA.

Highest priced. $12 760 000. A superb 11-sided pear-shaped mixed cut diamond of 101·84 carats was sold to Robert Mouawad at Sotheby's, Geneva, Switzerland on 14 Nov 1990. The record per carat is $975 068 for a 0·95-carat purplish-red stone sold at Christie's, New York in April 1988. A record price of £5·8 million ($10 million) was paid for a rough *uncut* diamond by Chow Tai Fook of Hong Kong on 4 Mar 1989.

■ **Minimum sunshine**
At the South Pole there is nil sunshine for 182 days every year. Work continues, however, frequently with the aid of floodlights, as is the case here at the Halley Station on Antarctica. (Photo: Science Photo Library)

■ **Longest drought**
Desierto de Atacama, near Calama, Chile experienced a drought for some 400 years up to 1971. With its annual rainfall being effectively nil, water is piped 100 km 60 miles from a water collection and storage site in the mountains to this town in the desert. (Photo: Science Photo Library)

■ **Longest drought**

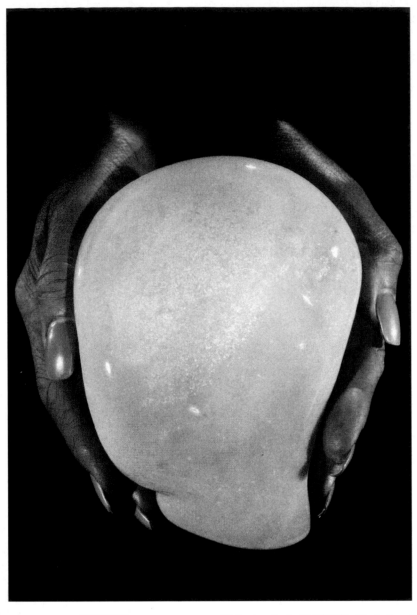

OPAL

Largest. 26 350 carats. The largest single piece of gem quality white opal was found in July 1989 at the Jupiter Field at Coober Pedy in South Australia. It has been named *Jupiter-Five* and is in private ownership.

Largest polished opal. 3749 carats. The largest free-form cabochon cut precious opal has been named 'Galaxy', and measures 139·7 × 101·6 × 41·1 mm *5½ × 4 × 1⅝ in*. It was excavated in Brazil in 1976 and was displayed by Steven Sodokoff at the Tucson Gem Show at Tucson, Arizona, USA in February 1991.

Largest black opal. 1520 carats. A stone found on 4 Feb 1972 at Lightning Ridge in Australia produced this finished gem, called the *Empress of Glengarry*. It measures 121 × 80 × 15 mm *4¾ × 3⅛ × ⅝ in*, and is owned by Peter Gray.

Largest rough black opal. 2020 carats. The largest gem quality uncut black opal was also found at Lightning Ridge, on 3 Nov 1986. After cleaning, it weighs 2020 carats and measures 100 × 66 × 63 mm *4 × 2⅝ × 2½ in*. It has been named *Halley's Comet* and is owned by a team of opal miners known as The Lunatic Hill Syndicate.

PEARL

Largest. 6·37 kg *14 lb 1 oz*. The *Pearl of Lao-tze* (also known as the *Pearl of Allah*) was found at Palawan, Philippines on 7 May 1934 in the shell of a giant clam. The property of Wilburn Dowell Cobb until his death, this molluscan concretion, 24 cm *9½ in* long by 14 cm *5½ in* diameter, was bought at auction on 15 May 1980 in San Francisco, California, USA by Peter Hoffman and Victor Barbish for $200 000. An appraisal by the San Francisco Gem Laboratory in May 1984 suggested a value of $40–42 million.

Largest cultured pearl. 138·25 carats. A 40 mm *1½ in* round cultured pearl weighing 27·65 g *1 oz* was found near Samui Island, off Thailand, in January 1988. The stone is owned by the Mikimoto Pearl Island Company, Japan.

Highest priced. $864 280. *La Régente*, an egg-shaped pearl weighing 15·13 g *302·68 grains* and formerly part of the French Crown Jewels, was sold at Christie's, Geneva, Switzerland on 12 May 1988.

TOPAZ

Largest. 22 892·5 carats. The rectangular, cushion-cut *American Golden Topaz* with 172 facets and 149·2 mm *5⅞ in* in overall width has been on display at the Smithsonian Institution, Washington, DC, USA since 4 May 1988.

JADE

Largest. 264 tonnes. A single boulder of nephrite jade was found in north-east China in March 1990. It measured 7 × 6·1 × 4·9 m *23 × 20 × 16 ft*.

AMBER

Largest. 15·25 kg *33 lb 10 oz*. The 'Burma Amber' is located in the Natural History Museum, London. Amber is a fossil resin derived from extinct coniferous trees, and often contains trapped insects.

GOLD

Largest nugget. 214·32 kg *7560 oz*. The *Holtermann Nugget* found on 19 Oct 1872 in the Beyers & Holtermann Star of Hope mine, Hill End, New South Wales, Australia contained some 99·8 kg *220 lb* of gold in a 285·7 kg *630 lb* slab of slate.

Largest pure nugget. The *Welcome Stranger* found at Moliagul, Victoria, Australia in 1869 yielded 69·92 kg *2248 troy oz* of pure gold from 70·92 kg *2280¼ oz*.

RUBY

Largest star. 2475 carats. The *Rajarathna* ruby from India, owned by G. Vidyaraj, Bangalore, India, displays an animated star of six lines and is cut as a cabochon.

Largest double star. 1370 carats. A cabochon cut gem, *Neelanjali*, also owned by G. Vidyaraj, displays 12 star lines and measures 7·62 cm *3 in* in height and 5·08 cm *2 in* in diameter.

Largest. 8500 carats. In July 1985 jeweller James Kazanjian of Beverly Hills, California, USA displayed a 14 cm *5½ in* tall red corundum (Al₂O₃) carved in the form of the Liberty Bell.

Highest priced. $4 620 000. This ruby and diamond ring made by Chaumet in Paris, France weighs 32·08 carats and was sold at Sotheby's, New York, USA on 26 Oct 1989. The record per carat is $227 300 for a ruby ring with a stone weighing 15·97 carats, which was sold at Sotheby's, New York, USA on 18 Oct 1988.

EMERALD

Largest cut. 86 136 carats. This natural beryl was found in Carnaiba, Brazil in August 1974. It was carved by Richard Chan in Hong Kong and valued at £718 000 in 1982.

Largest single crystal. 7025 carats. The largest single emerald crystal of gem quality was found in 1969 at the Cruces Mine, near Gachala, Colombia, and is owned by a private mining concern. Larger Brazilian and Russian stones do exist, but they are of low quality.

Highest priced. $3 080 000. (Single lot of emeralds.) This emerald and diamond necklace made by Cartier, London in 1937 (a total of 12 stones weighing 108·74 carats) was sold at Sotheby's, New York, USA on 26 Oct 1989. The highest price for a single emerald is $2 126 646, for a 19·77 carat emerald and diamond ring made by Cartier in 1958, which was sold at Sotheby's, Geneva, Switzerland on 2 Apr 1987. This also represented the record price per carat for an emerald, at $107 569.

SAPPHIRE

Largest carved. 2302 carats. Found at Anakie, Queensland, Australia in *c.* 1935, this corundum (Al₂O₃) was carved into a 1318-carat head of Abraham Lincoln and is now in the custody of the Kazanjian Foundation of Los Angeles, California, USA.

Largest star sapphire. 9719·50 carats. This stone, cut in London in November 1989, has been named *The Lone Star* and is owned by Harold Roper.

Highest priced. $2 791 723. A step-cut stone of 62·02 carats was sold as a sapphire and diamond ring at Sotheby's, St Moritz, Switzerland on 20 Feb 1988.

CRYSTAL BALL

Largest. 48·62 kg *106·75 lb*. The world's largest flawless rock crystal ball is 33 cm *13 in* in diameter, and was cut in China from Burmese rough material. It is now in the Smithsonian Institution in Washington, DC, USA.

The Living World

Animal Kingdom

GENERAL RECORDS

Noisiest The noisiest land animals in the world are the howling monkeys (*Alouatta*) of Central and South America. The males have an enlarged bony structure at the top of the windpipe which enables the sound to reverberate, and their fearsome screams have been described as a cross between the bark of a dog and the bray of an ass increased a thousandfold. Once they are in full voice they can be clearly heard for distances up to 16 km *10 miles*.

Most fertile It has been calculated that an individual cabbage aphid (*Brevicoryne brassica*) can give rise in a year to a mass of descendants weighing 822 million tonnes, which is more than three times the total weight of the world's human population. Fortunately the mortality rate is tremendous!

Strongest In proportion to their size, the strongest animals are the larger beetles of the family Scarabaeidae, which are found mainly in the tropics. In tests carried out on a rhinoceros beetle (sub-family Dynastinae) it was found that it could support 850 times its own weight on its back (cf. 25 per cent of its bodyweight for an adult elephant). A dor beetle (*Geotrupes stercorosus*) shifted a load weighing 80 g *2·82 oz* or 400 times its own bodyweight from one point to another and also managed to lift 100 g *3½ oz*.

Strongest bite Experiments carried out with a Snodgrass gnathodynamometer (shark-bite meter) at the Lerner Marine Laboratory in Bimini, Bahamas revealed that a 2 m *6 ft 6¾ in* long dusky shark (*Carcharhinus obscurus*) could exert a force of 60 kg *132 lb* between its jaws. This is equivalent to a pressure of 3 tonnes/cm², or 20 tonnes at the tips of the teeth.

Suspended animation In 1846 two specimens of the desert snail *Eremina desertorum* were presented to the British Museum (Natural History) as dead exhibits. They were glued to a small tablet and placed on display. Four years later, in March 1850, the Museum staff, suspecting that one of the snails was still alive, removed it from the tablet and placed it in tepid water. The snail moved and later began to feed. This hardy little creature lived for a further two years before it fell into a torpor and died.

Regeneration The sponge (Porifera) has the most remarkable powers of regeneration of lost parts of any animal, as it can regrow its entire body from a tiny fragment of itself. If a sponge is squeezed through a fine-meshed silk gauze, each piece of separated tissue will live as an individual.

Most dangerous The world's most dangerous animals (excluding Man) are the malarial parasites of the genus *Plasmodium* carried by mosquitoes of the genus *Anopheles*, which, if we exclude wars and accidents, have probably been responsible directly or indirectly for 50 per cent of all human deaths since the Stone Age. Even today, despite major campaigns to eradicate malaria, at least 200 million people are afflicted by the disease each year, and more than one million babies and children die annually from it in Africa alone.

Largest colonies The largest colonies are built by the black-tailed prairie dog (*Cynomys ludovicianus*), a rodent of the family Sciuridae found in the western USA and northern Mexico. One single 'town' discovered in 1901 contained about 400 million individuals and was estimated to cover 61 440 km² *24000 miles²*.

Greatest concentration The greatest concentration of animals ever recorded was an unbelievably huge swarm of Rocky Mountain locusts (*Melanoplus spretus*) which passed over Nebraska, USA on 15–25 Aug 1875. According to one local scientist who watched their movements for five days, these locusts covered an area of 514 374 km² *198 600 miles²* as they flew over the state. If he overestimated the size of the swarm by 50 per cent (most locusts do not fly at night), it still covered 257 187 km² *99 300 miles²*, which is approximately the area of Colorado or Oregon. It has been calculated that this swarm of locusts contained at least 12·5 trillion (10^{12}) insects, weighing 25 million tonnes. For reasons unexplained this pest mysteriously disappeared in 1902 and has not been seen since.

Most prodigious eater The larva of the Polyphemus moth (*Antheraea polyphemus*) of North America consumes an amount equal to 86 000 times its own birthweight in the first 56 days of its life. In human terms, this would be equivalent to a 3·17 kg *7 lb* baby taking in 273 tonnes of nourishment!

Champion slimmer During the 7-month lactation period, a 120-tonne female blue whale (*Balaenoptera musculus*) can lose up to 25 per cent of her bodyweight nursing her calf.

Most valuable The most valuable animals in cash terms are thoroughbred racehorses. The most paid for a yearling is $13·1 million on 23 Jul 1985 at Keeneland, Kentucky, USA by Robert Sangster and partners for *Seattle Dancer*. (see Horseracing.)

Size difference Although many differences exist in the animal world between the male and female of any species, the most striking difference in size can be seen in the marine worm *Bonellia viridis*. The females of this species are 10–100 cm *3·9–39 in* long compared with just 1–3 mm *0·039–0·12 in* for the male, making the females millions of times heavier than the males.

Slowest growth The slowest growth in the animal kingdom is that of the deep-sea clam *Tindaria callistisormis* of the North Atlantic, which takes c. 100 years to reach a length of 8 mm *0·31 in*.

Mammals Mammalia

Largest and heaviest The longest and heaviest mammal in the world, and also the largest animal ever recorded, is the blue or sulphur-bottom whale (*Balaenoptera musculus*), also called Sibbald's rorqual. The longest specimen ever recorded was a female landed in 1909 at Grytviken, South Georgia in the South Atlantic, which measured 33·58 m *110 ft 2½ in*. Another female, measuring 27·6 m *90½ ft* and caught in the Southern Ocean by the Soviet Slava whaling fleet on 20 Mar 1947, weighed 190 tonnes. Newborn calves measure 6·5–8·6 m *21 ft 3½ in–28½ ft* in length and weigh up to 3 tonnes.

The barely visible ovum of the blue-whale calf weighing a fraction of a milligram grows to a weight of c. 26 tonnes in 22¾ months, made up of 10¾ months' gestation and the first 12 months of life. This is equivalent to an increase of 3×10^{10}.

British Isles A 26·8 m *88 ft* blue whale was killed near the Bunaveneader station in Harris, Western Isles in 1904. In December 1851 the carcass of a blue whale measuring 28·87 m *94 ft 9 in* in length (girth 13·7 m *42 ft*) was brought into Bantry harbour, Co. Cork, Republic of Ireland after it had been found floating dead in the sea. A specimen stranded on the west coast of Lewis, Western Isles c. 1870 was credited with a length of 32 m *105 ft*, but the carcass was cut up by the local people before this measurement could be verified. The length was probably exaggerated or taken along the curve of the body instead of in a straight line from the tip of the snout to the notch in the flukes (the lobes of the tail).

Blue whales inhabit the colder seas and migrate to warmer waters in the winter for breeding. Observations made in the Antarctic in 1947–48 showed that a blue whale can maintain a speed of 37 km/h *23 mph* for 10 minutes when frightened. It has been calculated that a 27 m *90 ft* blue whale travelling at this speed would develop 520 hp.

The low-frequency pulses made by blue whales when communicating with each other have been measured up to 188 decibels, making them the loudest sounds emitted by any living source. They have been detected 850 km *530 miles* away.

It has been estimated that, as a result of over-hunting, there are only about 10–12 000 blue whales roaming the world's oceans today, compared with a peak estimate of c. 220 000 at the turn of the century. The species has been protected by law since 1967, although non-member countries of the International Whaling Commission, e.g. Panama, Taiwan, South Korea and the Philippines, are not bound by this agreement. An indefinite world-wide ban on commercial whaling came into force at the start of the 1985/86 season, but Japan,

Norway and Iceland are still slaughtering minke, fin and sei whales (*Balaenoptera acutorostrata*, *B. physalus* and *B. borealis*) under the guise of 'research whaling'. In 1988 Iceland caught 68 fin whales and 10 sei whales, and 300 minke whales were captured by Japanese whalers in the Southern Ocean. The ban on commercial whaling was reassessed in July 1990.

Deepest dive On 14 Oct 1955 a 14·32 m *47 ft* bull sperm whale (*Physeter catodon = macrocephalus*) was found at a depth of 1134 m *3720 ft*, its jaw entangled with a submarine cable running between Santa Elena, Ecuador and Chorillos, Peru. At this depth the whale withstood a pressure of 11 583 kPa *1680 lb/in²*. In 1970 American scientists, by triangulating the location clicks of sperm whales, calculated that the maximum depth reached by this species was 2500 m *8202 ft*. However, on 25 Aug 1969 another bull sperm whale was killed 160 km *100 miles* south of Durban, South Africa after it had surfaced from a dive lasting 1 hr 52 min, and inside its stomach were found two small sharks which had been swallowed about an hour earlier. These were later identified as *Scymnodon* sp., a type of dogfish found only on the sea floor. At this point from land the depth of water exceeds 3193 m *9876 ft* for a radius of 48–64 km *30–40 miles*, which suggests that the sperm whale sometimes descends to a depth of over 3000 m *9840 ft* when seeking food and is limited by pressure of time rather than by pressure itself.

Largest on land The largest living land animal is the African bush elephant (*Loxodonta africana*). The average adult bull stands 3·2 m *10 ft 6 in* at the shoulder and weighs 5·7 tonnes. The largest specimen ever recorded was a bull shot in Mucusso, Angola on 7 Nov 1974. Lying on its side this elephant measured 4·16 m *13 ft 8 in* in a projected line from the highest point of the shoulder to the base of the forefoot, indicating a standing height of about 3·96 m *13 ft*. Other measurements included an overall length of 10·67 m *35 ft* (tip of extended trunk to tip of extended tail) and a forefoot circumference of 1·8 m *5 ft 11 in*. The weight was computed to be 12·24 tonnes.

The endangered desert elephant of Damaraland, Namibia (reduced to 84 individuals in August 1981) is the tallest species in the world because it has proportionately longer legs than other elephants. The tallest elephant ever recorded was a bull shot near Sesfontein, Damaraland on 4 Apr 1978 after it had allegedly killed 11 people and caused widespread crop damage. Lying on its side, this mountain of flesh measured 4·42 m *14½ ft* in a projected line from the shoulder to the base of the forefoot, indicating a standing height of about 4·21 m *13 ft 10 in*. Other measurements included an overall length of 10·38 m *34 ft 1 in* and a forefoot circumference of 1·57 m *5 ft 2 in*. This particular animal weighed an estimated 8 tonnes.

UK An adult red deer (*Cervus elaphus*) stag stands 1·11 m *3 ft 8 in* at the shoulder and weighs 104–113 kg *230–250 lb*. The heaviest ever recorded was a stag killed at Glenfiddich, Grampian in 1831, which weighed 238 kg *525 lb*. The heaviest park red deer on record was a stag weighing 215 kg *476 lb* (1·37 m *4 ft 6 in* tall at the shoulder), killed at Woburn, Beds in 1836. The so-called wild pony (*Equus caballus*) may weigh up to 320 kg *700 lb* but there are no truly feral populations living today.

Largest marine The largest toothed mammal ever recorded is the sperm whale (*Physeter catodon*), also called the cachalot. In 1950 a record-sized bull measuring 20·7 m *67 ft 11 in* was captured off the Kurile Islands in the Pacific by a Soviet whaling fleet, but much larger bulls were reported in the early days of whaling. The 5 m *16 ft 4¾ in* long lower jaw of a sperm whale exhibited in the British Museum (Natural History) belonged to a bull measuring nearly 25·6 m *84 ft*, and similar lengths have been reported for other outsized individuals killed.

British Isles Thirteen cachalots have been stranded on British coasts since 1913. The largest, a bull measuring 19 m *61 ft 5 in*, was washed ashore at Birchington, Kent on 18 Oct 1914. Another bull stranded at Derryloughan, Co. Galway, Republic of Ireland on 2 Jan 1952 reportedly measured 19·8 m *65 ft*, but the carcass was so badly decomposed that there must have been some length extension.

Tallest on land The giraffe (*Giraffa camelopardalis*), which is now found only in the dry savannah and semi-desert areas of Africa south of the Sahara, is the tallest living animal. The tallest ever recorded was a Masai bull (*G. camelopardalis tippelskirchi*) named 'George', received at Chester Zoo on 8 Jan 1959 from Kenya. His 'horns' *almost* grazed the roof of the 6·09 m *20 ft* high Giraffe House when he was nine years old. 'George' died on 22 Jul 1969. Less credible heights of up to 7 m *23 ft* (measured between pegs) have been claimed for bulls shot in the field.

Smallest on land Kitti's hog-nosed bat (*Craseonycteristhonglongyai*), also called the bumblebee bat, is confined to about 21 limestone caves (population more than 2000) on the Kwae Noi River, Kanchanaburi, Thailand. Mature specimens of both sexes have a wing span of c. 160 mm *6·29 in* and weigh 1·75–2 g *0·062–0·071 oz*.

Mature specimens of Savi's white-toothed pygmy shrew (*Suncus etruscus*), also called the Etruscan shrew, which is found along the coast of the Mediterranean and southwards to Cape Province, South Africa, have a head and body length of 36–52 mm *1·32–2·04 in*, a tail length of 24–29 mm *0·94–1·14 in* and weigh 1·5–2·5 g *0·052–0·09 oz*. (See Insectivores.)

UK Mature specimens of the European pygmy shrew (*Sorex minutus*) have a head and body length of 43–64 mm *1·69–2·5 in*, a tail length of 31–46 mm *1·22–1·81 in* and weigh 2·4–6·1 g *0·084–0·213 oz*.

Smallest marine In terms of weight, the smallest totally marine mammal is probably Commerson's dolphin (*Cephalorhynchus commersonii*), also known as Le Jacobite, which is found off the tip of South America. The weights of a group of six adult specimens ranged from 23 kg *50·7 lb* to 35 kg *77·1 lb*. The sea otter (*Enhydra lutris*) of the north Pacific is of comparable size (25–38·5 kg *55–81·4 lb*), but this species sometimes comes ashore during storms.

Rarest land A number of mammals are known only from a single or type specimen. One of these is the small-toothed fruit bat (*Neopteryx frosti*), collected from Tamalanti, Sulawesi (Celebes), Indonesia in 1938.

The thylacine or Tasmanian wolf or tiger (*Thylacinus cynocephalus*), feared extinct since the last captive specimen died in Beaumaris Zoo, Hobart, Tasmania on 7 Sep 1936, was possibly identified in July 1982 when a wildlife ranger claimed he saw one of these predatory marsupials in the spot-light of his parked car. Since then, however, there have been no more positive sightings.

The red wolf (*Canis rufus*) of the south-east United States became extinct in the wild in the early 1970s, but in June 1988 it was announced that two pairs released in North Carolina from the captive breeding programme organised by the US Fish and Wildlife Service had produced cubs. By 1990 there were nine breeding wolves in the refuge and 10 in the captive breeding programme, the success of which has led to a rise in the population to 125, although not all of them are genetically pure.

The black-footed ferret (*Mustela nigripes*) of the northern United States is also extinct in the wild, but in 1988 the captive population of 25, housed in a special centre in Cheyenne, Wyoming, USA, more than doubled when the second breeding season produced 38 pups. There are now at least 300 individuals in captivity and the ferret will be reintroduced into Wyoming in the early 1990s.

Rarest marine Longman's beaked whale (*Indopacetus pacificus*) is known only from two skulls. The first specimen was discovered on a beach near MacKay, Queensland, Australia in 1922, and the second near Muqdisho, Somalia in 1955.

The vaquita or Gulf porpoise (*Phocoena sinus*) has not been sighted since 1980, and may now be extinct. Many hundreds of thousands have been accidentally killed by gillnet fishing in the last 45 years.

Fastest land Over a short distance (i.e. up to 550 m *600 yd*) the cheetah or hunting leopard (*Acinonyx jubatus*) of the open plains of east Africa, Iran, Turkmenia and Afghanistan has a probable maximum speed of 96–101 km/h *60–63 mph* on level ground. Speeds of 114, 135 and even 145 km/h *71, 84 and 90 mph* have been claimed for this animal, but these figures must be considered exaggerated. Tests in London in 1937 showed that, on an oval greyhound track over 316 m *345 yd*, a female cheetah's average speed over three runs was 69·8 km/h *43·4 mph*, compared with 72·27 km/h *44·91 mph* for the fastest racehorse (see Horseracing), but this specimen was not running flat out and had great difficulty negotiating the bends.

The fastest land animal over a sustained distance (i.e. 914 m *1000 yd* or more) is the pronghorn antelope (*Antilocapra americana*) of the western United States. Specimens have been observed to travel at 56 km/h *35 mph* for 6 km *4 miles*, at 67 km/h *42 mph* for 1·6 km *1 mile* and 88·5 km/h *55 mph* for 0·8 km *½ mile*.

UK Over a sustained distance the roe deer (*Capreolus capreolus*) can cruise at

■ **Sleepiest mammal**
In common with with some opossums and sloths, armadillos spend up to 80 per cent of their lives sleeping or dozing. Emerging here is a nine-banded armadillo (Dasypus novemcinctus), the only species of this tropical animal to range into the United States. (Photo: Bruce Coleman)

40–48 km/h *25–30 mph* for more than 32 km *20 miles*, with occasional bursts of up to 64 km/h *40 mph*. On 19 Oct 1970 a frightened runaway red deer registered a speed of 67·5 km/h *42 mph* on a police radar trap as it charged through a street in Stalybridge, Greater Manchester.

Fastest marine On 12 Oct 1958 a bull killer whale (*Orcinus orca*) measuring an estimated 6·1–7·62 m *20–25 ft* in length was timed at 55·5 km/h *34·5 mph* in the east Pacific. Similar speeds have also been reported for Dall's porpoise (*Phocoenoides dalli*) in short bursts.

Slowest The ai or three-toed sloth (*Bradypus tridactylus*) of tropical South America has an average ground speed of 1·83–2·44 m *6–8 ft* per minute (0·109 –0·158 km/h *0·068–0·098 mph*), but in the trees it can 'accelerate' to 4·57 m *15 ft* per minute (0·272 km/h *0·17 mph*). (Compare these figures with the 0·05 km/h *0·03 mph* of the common garden snail and the 0·27 km/h *0·17 mph* of the giant tortoise.)

Sleepiest Some armadillos (Dasypodidae), opossums (Didelphidae) and sloths (Bradypodidae) spend up to 80 per cent of their lives sleeping or dozing, while it is claimed that Dall's porpoise (*Phocoenoides dalli*) never sleeps at all.

Longest hibernation The barrow ground squirrel (*Spermophilus parryi barrowensis*) of Point Barrow, Alaska, USA hibernates for nine months of the year. During the remaining three months it feeds, breeds and collects food for storage in its burrow.

Oldest No other mammal can match the extreme proven 120 years attained by Man (*Homo sapiens*) (see Chapter 3). It is probable that the closest approach is made by the Asiatic elephant (*Elephas maximus*). The greatest age that has been verified with absolute certainty is 78 years in the case of a cow named 'Modoc', who died at Santa Clara, California, USA on 17 Jul 1975. She was imported into the United States from Germany in 1898 at the age of two.

Nepal's royal elephant 'Prem Prasad' was reportedly 81 when he died at Kasra, Chitwan on 27 Feb 1985, but his actual age was believed to have been 65–70 years. Sri Lanka's famous bull elephant 'Rajah', who had led the annual Perahera procession through Kandi carrying the Sacred Tooth of the Buddha since 1931, died on 16 Jul 1988 allegedly aged 81 years.

Highest living The yak (*Bos grunniens*) of Tibet and the Sichuanese Alps, China occasionally climbs to an altitude of 6100 m *20 000 ft* when foraging.

Largest herds The largest herds on record were those of the springbok (*Antidorcas marsupialis*) during migration across the plains of the western parts of southern Africa in the 19th century. In 1849 John (later Sir John) Fraser observed a *trekbokken* that took three days to pass through the settlement of Beaufort West, Cape Province. Another herd seen moving near Nels Poortje, Cape Province in 1888 was estimated to contain 100 million head, although 10 million is probably a more realistic figure. A herd estimated to be 24 km *15 miles* wide and more than 160 km *100 miles* long was reported from Karree Kloof, Orange River, South Africa in July 1896.

Longest gestation period The Asiatic elephant (*Elephas maximus*) has an average gestation period of 609 days (over 20 months) and a maximum of 760 days — more than two and a half times that of a human. By 1981 only about 35 000 survived.

Shortest gestation period The gestation periods of the American opossum (*Didelphis marsupialis*), also called the Virginian opossum, the rare water opossum or yapok (*Chironectes minimus*) of central and northern South America and the eastern native cat (*Dasyurus viverrinus*) of Australia are all normally 12–13 days, but can be as short as eight days.

Largest litter The greatest number of young born to a *wild* mammal at a single birth is 31 (30 of which survived) in the case of the tail-less tenrec (*Tenrec ecaudatus*) found in Madagascar and the Comoro Islands. The normal litter size is 12–15, although females can suckle up to 24.

Youngest breeder The streaked tenrec (*Hemicentetes semispinosus*) of Madagascar is weaned after only five days, and females can breed 3–4 weeks after their birth.

CARNIVORES

Largest on land The average adult male Kodiak bear (*Ursus arctos middendorffi*), native to Kodiak Island and the adjacent Afognak and Shuyak islands in the Gulf of Alaska, USA, has a nose-to-tail length of 2·4 m *8 ft*, with the tail measuring about 10 cm *4 in*). It stands 1·32 m *52 in* at the shoulder and weighs 476–533 kg *1050 –1175 lb*. In 1894 a weight of 751 kg *1656 lb* was recorded for a male shot at English Bay, Kodiak Island, whose *stretched* skin measured 4·11 m *13½ ft* from nose to tail. This weight was exceeded by a 'cage-fat' male in the Cheyenne Mountain Zoological Park, Colorado Springs, Colorado, USA, which scaled 757 kg *1670 lb* at the time of its death on 22 Sep 1955.

In 1981 an unconfirmed weight of over 907 kg *2000 lb* was reported for a giant bear (*Ursus a. gyas*) from Alaska on exhibition at the Space Farms Zoological Park at Beemerville, New Jersey, USA.

Weights exceeding 907 kg *2000 lb* have also been reported for the polar bear (*Ursus maritimus*), but the average adult male weighs 386–408 kg *850–900 lb* and measures 2·4 m *7 ft 9 in* from nose to tail. In 1960 a polar bear allegedly weighing 1002 kg *2210 lb* was shot at the polar entrance to Kotzebue Sound, Alaska, USA. In April 1962 the 3·38 m *11 ft 1¼ in* tall mounted specimen was put on display at the Seattle World Fair.

UK The largest land carnivore found in Britain is the badger (*Meles meles*). The average adult boar (sows are slightly smaller) measures 90 cm *3 ft* in length

(including a 10 cm *4 in* tail) and weighs 12·3 kg *27 lb* in the early spring and 14·5 kg *32 lb* at the end of the summer when it is in 'grease'. In December 1952 a boar weighing 27·2 kg *60 lb* was killed near Rotherham, S Yorks.

Smallest The smallest living member of the order Carnivora is the least weasel (*Mustela rixosa*), also called the dwarf weasel, which is circumpolar in distribution. Four races are recognized, the smallest of which is *Mustela r. pygmaea* of Siberia. Mature specimens have an overall length of 177–207 mm *6·96–8·14 in* and weigh 35–70 g *1¼–2½ oz*.

Largest feline The largest member of the cat family (Felidae) is the protected long-furred Siberian tiger (*Panthera tigris altaica*), also called the Amur or Manchurian tiger. Adult males average 3·15 m *10 ft 4 in* in length from the nose to the tip of the extended tail, stand 99–107 cm *39–42 in* at the shoulder and weigh about 265 kg *585 lb*. In 1950 a male weighing 384 kg *846·5 lb* was shot in the Sikhote Alin Mountains, Maritime Territory, USSR.

An outsized Indian tiger (*Panthera tigris tigris*) shot in northern Uttar Pradesh in November 1967 measured 3·22 m *10 ft 7 in* between pegs (3·37 m *11 ft 1 in* over the curves) and weighed 389 kg *857 lb* (cf. 2·82 m *9 ft 3 in* and 190 kg *420 lb* for an average adult male). It is now on display in the US Museum of Natural History at the Smithsonian Institution, Washington, DC, USA.

The largest tiger ever held in captivity, and the heaviest 'big cat' on record, is a nine-year-old Siberian male named 'Jaipur', owned by animal trainer Joan Byron-Marasek of Clarksburg, New Jersey, USA. This specimen measured 3·32 m *10 ft 11 in* in total length and weighed 423 kg *932 lb* in October 1986.

The average adult African lion (*Panthera leo*) measures 2·7 m *9 ft* overall, stands 91–97 cm *36–38 in* at the shoulder and weighs 181–185 kg *400–410 lb*. The heaviest wild specimen on record weighed 313 kg *690 lb* and was shot near Hectorspruit, Transvaal, South Africa in 1936.

In July 1970 a weight of 375 kg *826 lb* was reported for a black-maned lion named 'Simba' (b. Dublin Zoo, 1959) at Colchester Zoo, Essex. He died on 16 Jan 1973 at the now defunct Knaresborough Zoo, N Yorks, and his stuffed body was put on display there.

An adult male litigon (a hybrid of an Indian lion and a tigon — itself the offspring of a tiger and a lioness) named 'Cubanacan' at Alipore Zoological Gardens, Calcutta, India is also believed to weigh at least 363 kg *800 lb*. This animal stands 1·32 m *52 in* at the shoulder (cf. 1·11 m *44 in* for the lion 'Simba') and measures a record 3·5 m *11½ ft* in total length. This animal, the first and only one of its kind, was reported to have died on 12 Apr 1991.

Smallest feline The smallest member of the cat family is the rusty-spotted cat (*Felis rubiginosa*) of southern India and Sri Lanka. The average adult male has an overall length of 64–71 cm *25–28 in* (the tail measures 23–25 cm *9–10 in*) and weighs about 1·35 kg *3 lb*.

PRIMATES

Largest living The average adult male eastern lowland gorilla (*Gorilla g. graueri*) of the lowland forests of eastern Zaïre and south-western Uganda stands 175 cm *5 ft 9 in* tall and weighs 165 kg *360 lb*.

The mountain gorilla (*Gorilla g. beringei*) of the volcanic mountain ranges of western Rwanda, south-western Uganda and eastern Zaïre is of comparable size, i.e. 172·5 cm *5 ft 8 in* tall and 155 kg *343 lb* in weight, and most of the exceptionally large gorillas taken in the field have been of this race.

The greatest height (top of crest to heel) recorded for a gorilla in the wild is 1·88 m *6 ft 2 in* for a bull of the mountain race shot in the eastern Congo (Zaïre) *c.* 1920. The tallest gorilla ever kept in captivity is reportedly an eastern lowland male named 'Colossus' (b. 1966), who is currently on display at a zoo in Gulf Breeze, Florida, USA. He allegedly stands 1·88 m *6 ft 2 in* tall and weighs 260·8 kg *575 lb*, but these figures have not yet been confirmed.

A western lowland gorilla called 'Baltimore Jack', who was received at Baltimore Zoo, Maryland, USA in 1956 and later sold to Phoenix Zoo, Arizona, had exceptionally long legs for a gorilla. He reportedly stood 1·91 m *6 ft 3 in* tall, but his actual height was somewhere between 1·7 m *5 ft 7 in* and 1·75 m *5 ft 9 in* (weight 126 kg *300 lb*). He died in 1972.

The heaviest gorilla ever kept in captivity was a male of the mountain race named 'N'gagi', who died in San Diego Zoo, California, USA on 12 Jan 1944 at the age of 18. He weighed 310 kg *683 lb* at his heaviest in 1943, and 288 kg *635 lb* at the time of his death. He was 1·72 m *5 ft 7¾ in* tall and boasted a record chest measurement of 198 cm *78 in*.

UK Britain's largest captive gorilla is probably 'Djoum' (b. 1969) of Howletts Zoo, Kent, whose weight is stable at 213 kg *470 lb*. Another male example of the western lowland gorilla (*Gorilla g. gorilla*) named 'Bukhama' (b. 1960) at Dudley Zoo, W Mids was reportedly 227 kg *500 lb* in 1969, but this primate has not been weighed since.

Smallest Adult specimens of the pen-tailed shrew (*Ptilocercus lowii*) of Malaysia have a total length of 230–330 mm *9–13 in* (head and body 100–140 mm *3·93–5·51 in*, tail 130–190 mm *5·1–7·5 in*) and weigh 35–50 g *1·23–1·76 oz*.

The pygmy marmoset (*Cebuella pygmaea*) of the Upper Amazon Basin and the lesser mouse-lemur (*Microcebus murinus*) found in Madagascar are of comparable length to the shrew but heavier, with adults weighing about 50–75 g *1·76–2·64 oz* and 45–80 g *1·58–2·82 oz* respectively.

Rarest The greater bamboo broad-nosed gentle lemur (*Hapalemur simus*) of Madagascar reportedly became extinct in the early 1970s, but in 1986 a group consisting of 60–80 individuals was discovered living in a remote rainforest near Ranomafana in the south-eastern part of the island by an expedition from Duke University, Durham, North Carolina, USA.

The golden-rumped tamarin (*Leontopithecus chrysopygus*), which is now restricted to two areas of forest in the state of São Paulo, Brazil, is also on the verge of extinction, with only 75–100 surviving in 1986.

Oldest The greatest irrefutable age reported for a non-human primate is about 59 years for a male orang-utan (*Pongo pygmaeus*) named 'Guas', who died in Philadelphia Zoological Garden, Pennsylvania, USA on 9 Feb 1977. He was at least 13 years old on his arrival at the zoo on 1 May 1931.

The famous western lowland gorilla 'Massa' (b. July 1931) died on 30 Dec 1984

aged 53 years 5 months. The oldest female gorilla on record was 'Carolyn' (b. 1939) of New York Zoological Park (Bronx Zoo), USA, who died on 27 Sep 1986 at the age of 47.

The oldest chimpanzee (*Pan troglodytes*) on record was a male named 'Jimmy' at Seneca Zoo, Rochester, NY, USA, who died on 17 Sep 1985 at the age of 55 years 6 months.

Strongest In 1924 'Boma', a 74·8 kg *165 lb* male chimpanzee at Bronx Zoo, New York, USA recorded a right-handed pull (feet braced) of 384 kg *847 lb* on a dyna-

mometer (cf. 95 kg *210 lb* for a man of the same weight).

On another occasion an adult female chimpanzee named 'Suzette' (estimated weight 61 kg *135 lb*) at the same zoo registered a right-handed pull of 572 kg *1260 lb* while in a rage. A record from the USA of a 45 kg *100 lb* chimpanzee achieving a two-handed dead lift of 272 kg *600 lb* with ease suggests that, with training, a male gorilla could lift 907 kg *2000 lb*.

MONKEYS

Largest The only species of monkey reliably credited with weights of more than 45 kg *100 lb* is the mandrill (*Mandrillus sphinx*) of equatorial west Africa. The greatest reliable weight recorded is 54 kg *119 lb* for a captive male, but an unconfirmed weight of 59 kg *130 lb* has been reported. Adult females are about half the size of males.

Smallest The smallest known monkey is the pygmy marmoset (*Cebuella pygmaea*) of the Upper Amazon Basin. (See Smallest primates.)

Oldest The world's oldest monkey, a male white-throated capuchin (*Cebus capucinus*) called 'Bobo', died on 10 Jul 1988 aged 53 years following complications related to a stroke. He was originally imported from South America and donated to the Mesker Park Zoo in Evansville, Indiana, USA on 1 Jan 1935. When the zoo disbanded its monkey colony he was given to Dr Raymond T. Bartus, founder of the Geriatric Research Programme at Lederle Laboratories, American Cyanamid Co., Pearl River, NY, USA, and lived in the geriatric monkey colony from 31 Oct 1981 until his death.

PINNIPEDS

Seals, Sea-lions, Walruses

Largest The largest of the 34 known species of pinniped is the southern elephant seal (*Mirounga leonina*) of the sub-Antarctic islands. Adult bulls average 5 m *16½ ft* in length from the tip of the inflated snout to the tips of the outstretched tail flippers, have a maximum girth of 3·7 m *12 ft* and weigh about 2268 kg *5000 lb*, compared with 3 m *10 ft* and about 680 kg *1500 lb* for average adult cows. The largest accurately measured specimen was a bull killed in the south Atlantic at Possession Bay, South Georgia on 28 Feb 1913 which probably weighed at least 4 tonnes and measured 6·5 m *21 ft 4 in* after flensing (stripping of the blubber or skin). Its original length was about 6·85 m *22½ ft*. The largest recorded live specimen is a bull nicknamed 'Stalin' from South Georgia. It

was tranquilised by members of the British Antarctic Survey on 14 Oct 1989 when it weighed 2662 kg *5869 lb* and measured 5·10 m *16 ½ ft.*

UK The largest British pinniped is the grey seal (*Halichoerus grypus*), also called the Atlantic seal. The heaviest example taken from a sample group during the breeding season at the Farne Islands, Northumberland was a male weighing 310 kg *683½ lb* and measuring 2·45 m *8 ft* from the nose to the tip of the flippers.

Smallest The smallest pinnipeds are the ringed seal (*Phoca hispida*) of the Arctic and the closely related Baikal seal (*P. sibirica*) of Lake Baikal and the Caspian seal (*P. caspica*) of the Caspian Sea, USSR. Adult males measure up to 1·67 m *5½ ft* in length and can weigh up to 127 kg *280 lb*. Females are about two-thirds this size.

UK The average adult male common seal (*Phoca vitulina*) measures 1·5–1·98 m *4 ft 11 in–6½ ft* in length and weighs up to 149·6 kg *330 lb*. Females are four-fifths this size. Between July and September 1988, 2000 seals died as a result of an unidentified virus, and up to 80 per cent of the population (30 000) of the common seal may have succumbed.

Most abundant The total population of the crabeater seal (*Lobodon carcinophagus*) of Antarctica was estimated in 1977 to be nearly 15 million.

Rarest The last reliable sighting of the Caribbean or West Indian monk seal (*Monachus tropicalis*) was on Serranilla Bank off the coast of Mexico's Yucatan peninsula in 1952. In 1974 two seals were seen near Cay Verde and Cay Burro, Bahamas, but a search in 1979 found nothing. It has been suggested that these sightings (and others) may have been of Californian sea-lions (*Zalophus californianus*) which had escaped from captivity and have been recorded in the Gulf of Mexico on several occasions.

Fastest The highest swimming speed recorded for a pinniped is a short spurt of

40 km/h *25 mph* by a Californian sea-lion. The fastest-moving pinniped on land is the crabeater seal, which has been timed at speeds up to 19 km/h *11·8 mph*.

Deepest dive In about May 1988 a team of scientists from the University of California at Santa Cruz, USA tested the diving abilities of the northern elephant seal (*Mirounga anguistirostris*) off Ano Nuevo Point, California. One female reached a record depth of 1257 m *4135 ft*, and another remained submerged for 48 minutes. Similar experiments carried out by Australian scientists on southern elephant seals (*M. leonina*) in the Southern Ocean recorded a dive of 1134 m *3720 ft*, with other dives lasting nearly two hours also observed. It was discovered that the seals regularly swam down to about 820 m *2500 ft* and when they re-surfaced apparently had no 'oxygen debt'.

Oldest A female grey seal (*Halichoerus grypus*) shot at Shunni Wick, Shetland on 23 Apr 1969 was believed to be 'at least 46 years old' based on a count of dentine rings. The captive record is an estimated 41 years (1901–42) for a bull grey seal named 'Jacob' held in Skansen Zoo, Stockholm, Sweden.

BATS

Largest The only flying mammals are bats (order Chiroptera), of which there are about 950 living species. That with the greatest wing span is the Bismarck flying fox (*Pteropus neohibernicus*) of the Bismarck Archipelago and New Guinea. One specimen preserved in the American Museum of Natural History has a wing spread of 165 cm *5 ft 5 in*, but some unmeasured bats probably reach 183 cm *6 ft*.

UK Mature specimens of the very rare, large mouse-eared bat (*Myotis myotis*) have a wing span of 355–450 mm *13·97–17·71 in* and weigh up to 45 g *1·58 oz* in the case of females.

Smallest The smallest bat in the world is Kitti's hog-nosed bat. (See Smallest mammal.)

■ **Most abundant pinniped**
The population of the crabeater seal (Lobodon carcinophagus) of Antarctica was estimated at almost 15 million in 1977. (Photo: Bruce Coleman)

UK The smallest native British bat is the Pipistrelle (*Pipistrellus pipistrellus*). Mature specimens have a wing span of 190–250 mm *7·48–9·84 in* and weigh 3–8 g *0·1–0·28 oz.*

Rarest At least three species of bat are known only from the type specimen. They are: the small-toothed fruit bat (*Neopteryx frosti*) from Tamalanti, Sulawesi (Celebes) in (1938–39); *Paracoelops megalotis* from Vinh, Vietnam (1945); and *Latidens salimalii* from the High Wavy Mountains, India (1948).

UK On 23 Mar 1991 the death was reported of Britain's last surviving mouse-eared bat (*Myotis myotis*), a 19-year-old male which had lived in Sussex for 15 years forlornly waiting for a mate. The last known surviving female was killed by the felling of a tree in Sussex in 1977.

In 1987 a vagrant northern bat (*Eptesicus nilssoni*) was found hibernating in Surrey by two journalists. A native of Europe and Russia, it was the first recorded example of this species in Britain.

Fastest Because of the great practical difficulties, few data on bat speeds have been published. The greatest velocity attributed to a bat is 51 km/h *32 mph* in the case of a Mexican free-tailed bat (*Tadarida brasiliensis*), but this may have been wind-assisted. In one US experiment using an artificial mine tunnel and 17 different kinds of bat, only four of them managed to exceed 20·8 km/h *13 mph* in level flight.

Oldest The greatest age reliably reported for a bat is 32 years for a banded female little brown bat (*Myotis lucifugus*) in the United States in 1987.

Highest detectable pitch Because of their ultrasonic echolocation, bats have the most acute hearing of any terrestrial animal. Vampire bats (family Desmodontidae) and fruit bats (Pteropodidae) can hear frequencies as high as 120–210 kHz, compared with 20 kHz for the adult human limit and 280 kHz for the common dolphin (*Delphinus delphis*).

Largest colonies The largest concentration of bats found living anywhere in the world today is that of the Mexican free-tailed bat (*Tadarida brasiliensis*) in Bracken Cave, San Antonio, Texas, USA, where up to 20 million animals assemble after migration.

UK A bat colony in Greywell Canal Tunnel, Hants contains about 2000 individuals made up of six different species.

Deepest The little brown bat (*Myotis lucifugus*) has been recorded at a depth of 1160 m *3805 ft* in a zinc mine in New York, USA. The mine serves as winter quarters for 1000 members of this species, which normally roosts at a depth of 200 m *656 ft*.

RODENTS

Largest The capybara (*Hydrochoerus hydrochaeris*), also called the carpincho or water hog, of tropical South America, has a head and body length of 0·99–1·4 m *3¼–4½ ft* and can weigh up to 113 kg *250 lb* (cage-fat specimen).

UK Britain's largest rodent is the coypu (*Myocastor coypus*), adult males of which measure 76–91 cm *30–36 in* in length (including short tail) and weigh up to 13 kg *28 lb* in the wild state (18 kg *40 lb* in captivity). Also known as the nutria, it was introduced from Argentina by East Anglian fur-breeders in 1929. Three years later the first escapes were recorded and by 1960 at least 200 000 coypus were living in

East Anglia. About 80 per cent were killed by the severe winter of 1963–64, and since then the Ministry of Agriculture has carried out a campaign of extermination against this species. During the period 1981–87 trappers shot 34 000 coypus and the last known colony at St Neot's on the Great Ouse, Cambs was eliminated in 1987. Since then only two isolated coypus have been found, plus the corpse of an old male killed on a road at Barton Bendish, Norfolk on 18 Jul 1988. The trapping campaign continued until the end of 1989 and the virtual eradication of the animal was reported in April 1990.

Smallest The northern pygmy mouse (*Baiomys taylori*) of central Mexico and southern Arizona and Texas, USA measures up to 109 mm *4·3 in* in total length and weighs 7–8 g *0·24–0·28 oz.*

UK The smallest British rodent is the Old World harvest mouse (*Micromys minutus*), measures up to 135 mm *5·3 in* in total length and weighs 7–10 g *0·24–0·35 oz.*

Rarest The rarest rodents in the world are Garrido's hutia (*Capromys garridoi*) of the Canarreos Archipelago, Cuba and the little earth hutia (*C. sanfelipensis*) of Juan Garcia Cay, an islet off southern Cuba. The latter species has not been recorded since its discovery in 1970.

Oldest The greatest reliable age reported for a rodent is 27 years 3 months for a Sumatran crested porcupine (*Hystrix brachyura*), which died in the National Zoological Park, Washington, DC, USA on 12 Jan 1965.

Fastest breeder The female meadow vole (*Microtus agrestis*), found in Britain, can reproduce from the age of 25 days and can have up to 17 litters of 6–8 young in a year.

INSECTIVORES

Largest The moon rat (*Echinosorex gymnurus*), also known as Raffles' gymnure, which is found in Myanmar (formerly Burma), Thailand, Malaysia, Sumatra and Borneo, has a head and body length of 265–445 mm *10·43–17·52 in*, a tail measuring 200–210 mm *7·87–8·26 in* and weighs up to 1400 g *3·08 lb.*

The European hedgehog (*Erinaceus europaeus*) is much shorter in overall length (196–298 mm *7·71–11·73 in*), but well-fed examples have been known to weigh as much as 1900 g *4·19 lb.*

Although the much larger anteaters (families Tachyglossidae and Myrmecophagidae) feed on termites and other soft-bodied insects, they are not insectivores, but belong to the orders Monotremata and Edentata ('without teeth').

Smallest The smallest insectivore is Savi's white-toothed pygmy shrew (*Suncus etruscus*). (See Smallest mammals.)

Oldest The greatest reliable age recorded for an insectivore is over 16 years for a lesser hedgehog-tenrec (*Echinops telfairi*), which was born in Amsterdam Zoo, Netherlands in 1966 and was later sent to Jersey Zoo, Channel Islands. It died on 27 Nov 1982.

ANTELOPES

Largest The rare giant eland (*Taurotragus derbianus*) of western and central Africa may surpass 907 kg *2000 lb*. The common eland (*Taurotragus oryx*) of eastern and southern Africa has the same shoulder height of up to 1·78 m *5 ft 10 in* but is not quite so massive, although there is

one record of a 1·65 m *5 ft 5 in* bull shot in Malawi *c.* 1937 which weighed 943 kg *2078 lb*.

Smallest Mature specimens of the royal antelope (*Neotragus pygmaeus*) of western Africa measure 25–31 cm *10–12 in* at the shoulder and weigh only 3–3·6 kg *7–8 lb*, which is the size of a large brown hare (*Lepus europaeus*).

Salt's dik-dik (*Madoqua saltina*) of northeastern Ethiopia and Somalia weighs only 2·2–2·7 kg *5–6 lb* when adult, but this species stands about 35·5 cm *14 in* at the withers.

Rarest Until recently, the Arabian oryx (*Oryx leucoryx*) had not been reported in the wild since 1972 when three were killed and four others captured on the Jiddat-al-Harasis plateau, south Oman. Between March 1980 and August 1983 a total of 17 antelopes from the World Herd at San Diego Zoo, California, USA were released into the desert in south Oman under the protection of a nomadic tribe. Since then there have been at least 43 live births, and at the beginning of 1989 the wild herd totalled 60. The Arabian oryx has also been successfully reintroduced into the Shaumari Reserve in Jordan, where there are now 90 of these animals.

Oldest The greatest reliable age recorded for an antelope is 25 years 4 months for an addax (*Addax nasomaculatus*) which died

■ **Rarest antelope**
Saved from the brink of extinction by a captive breeding programme at San Diego Zoo, California, USA and strict protective measures in the wild, the Arabian oryx (Oryx leucoryx) has been successfully reintroduced into the deserts of Oman and Jordan, where its population has now reached at least 150.
(Photo: Bruce Coleman)

in Brookfield Zoo, Chicago, Illinois, USA on 15 Oct 1960.

DEER

Largest The largest deer is the Alaskan moose (*Alces alces gigas*). Adult bulls average 1·83 m *6 ft* at the shoulder and weigh *c.* 500 kg *1100 lb*. A bull standing 2·34 m *7 ft 8 in* between pegs and weighing an estimated 816 kg *1800 lb* was shot on the Yukon River in the Yukon Territory, Canada in September 1897. Unconfirmed measurements of up to 2·59 m *8 ft 6 in* at the shoulder and estimated weights of up to 1180 kg *2600 lb* have been claimed.

The record antler spread or 'rack' is 199 cm *78½ in* (skull and antlers 41 kg *91 lb*) for a set taken from a moose killed near the head-waters of the Stewart River in the Yukon, Canada in October 1897. The antlers are now on display in the Field Museum, Chicago, Illinois, USA.

UK The largest British deer is the red deer (See Largest land mammal.)

Smallest The smallest true deer (family Cervidae) is the northern pudu (*Pudu mephistopheles*) of Ecuador and Colombia. Mature specimens measure 33–35 cm *13–14 in* at the shoulder and weigh 7·2–8·1 kg *16–18 lb*.

The smallest ruminant is the lesser Malay chevrotain (*Tragulus javanicus*) of south-east Asia, Sumatra and Borneo. Adults measure 20–25 cm *8–10 in* at the shoulder and weigh 2·7–3·2 kg *6–7 lb*.

Rarest Until recently, Fea's muntjac (*Muntiacus feae*) was known only from two specimens collected on the borders of southern Myanmar (formerly Burma) and western Thailand. In December 1977 a female was received at Dusit Zoo, Bangkok, followed by two females in 1981 and three males and three females from Xizang, Tibet between February 1982 and April 1983.

Oldest The world's oldest recorded deer is a red deer (*Cervus elaphus scoticus*) named 'Bambi' (b. 8 Jun 1963), owned by the Fraser family of Kiltarlity, Beauly, Highland.

MARSUPIALS

Largest The adult male red kangaroo (*Megaleia rufa* or *Macropus rufus*) of central, southern and eastern Australia stands up to 213 cm *7 ft* tall, measures up to 245 cm *8 ft ½ in* in total length and weighs up to 85 kg *187 lb*.

Smallest The smallest known marsupial is the rare long-tailed planigale (*Planigale ingrami*), a flat-skulled mouse of north-eastern and north-western Australia. Adult males have a head and body length of 55–63 mm *2·16–2·48 in*, a tail length of 57–60 mm *2·24–2·36 in* and weigh 3·9–4·5 g *0·13–0·19 oz*.

Oldest The greatest reliable age recorded for a marsupial is 26 years 22 days for a common wombat (*Vombatus ursinus*) which died in London Zoo on 20 Apr 1906.

Fastest speed The highest speed recorded for a marsupial is 64 km/h *40 mph* for a mature female eastern grey kangaroo (*Macropus giganteus* or *M. canguru*). One large male red kangaroo died from his exertions after being paced at 1·6 km *1 mile* at 56 km/h *35 mph*.

Longest jump During the course of a chase in New South Wales, Australia in January 1951, a female red kangaroo made a series of bounds which included one of 12·80 m *42 ft*. There is also an unconfirmed report of an eastern grey kangaroo jumping nearly 13·5 m *44 ft 8½ in* on the flat.

TUSKS

Longest The longest recorded elephant tusks (excluding prehistoric examples) are a pair from Zaïre preserved in the National Collection of Heads and Horns kept by the New York Zoological Society in Bronx Park, New York City, USA. The right tusk measures 3·49 m *11 ft 5½ in* along the outside curve and the left 3·35 m *11 ft*. Their combined weight is 133 kg *293 lb*. A single tusk of 3·5 m *11 ft 6 in* has been reported. Ivory rose from $2·30 to $34/lb in the period 1970–80.

Heaviest A pair of tusks in the British Museum (Natural History) collected from an aged bull shot at the foot of Mt Kilimanjaro, Kenya in 1897 originally weighed 109 kg *240 lb* (length 3·11 m *10 ft 2½ in*) and 102 kg *225 lb* (length 3·18 m *10 ft 5½ in*) respectively, giving a total weight of 211 kg *465 lb*, but their combined weight today is 200 kg *440½ lb*. A single elephant tusk collected in Benin, Africa and exhibited at the Paris Exposition in 1900 weighed 117 kg *258 lb*.

HORNS

Longest The longest horns grown by any living animal are those of the water buffalo (*Bubalus arnee* = *B. bubalis*) of India. One huge bull shot in 1955 had horns measuring 4·24 m *13 ft 11 in* from tip to tip along the outside curve across the forehead. The longest single horn on record measured 206 cm *81¼ in* along the outside curve and was found on a specimen of domestic ankole cattle (*Bos taurus*) near Lake Ngami, Botswana. The largest spread recorded for a Texas longhorn steer is 3·2 m *10 ft 6 in*. They are currently on exhibition at the Heritage Museum, Big Springs, Texas, USA.

HORSES AND PONIES

The world's equine population is estimated to be 75 million. For record horse prices see Agriculture.

Earliest domestication The first domestication of the horse reportedly occurred in what is now the Ukraine, USSR *c.* 6500 years ago when paleolithic hunters tamed some for their flesh and milk.

Largest A 19·2-hand (1·98 m *6½ ft*) pure-bred red roan Belgian (Brabant) stallion named 'Brooklyn Supreme' (1928–48) owned by C.G. Good of Ogden, Iowa, USA weighed 1451 kg *3200 lb* at its heaviest in 1938 and had a chest girth of 259 cm *102 in*. Each of his 3·4 kg *7½ lb* shoes measured 35·5 cm *14 in* across and required 76·2 cm *30 in* of iron (cf. 55·8 cm *22 in* for 'Wandle Goliath' — see right).

In April 1973 a weight of 1459 kg *3218 lb* was reported for an 18·2-hand (1·88 m *6 ft 2 in*) Belgian (Brabant) mare named 'Wilma du Bos' (foaled 15 Jul 1966) shortly before her journey from Antwerp to her new owner, Virgie Arden of Reno, Nevada, USA. However, she was heavily in foal at the time (maximum girth 3·65 m *12 ft*). On arrival in New York she weighed 1399 kg *3086 lb*, but returned to her normal weight of 1088–1134 kg *2400–2500 lb* after foaling.

UK The 17·2-hand (1·78 m *5 ft 10 in* shire stallion 'Honest Tom 5123' (foaled 1884), owned by James Forshaw of Littleport, Cambs, weighed 1325 kg *2912 lb* in 1891. The heaviest living horse in Britain today is the 19·1½-hand (1·97 m *6 ft 5½ in*) shire gelding 'Extra Stout' (foaled 1980), owned by Samuel Smith's Old Brewery, Tadcaster, N Yorks. He weighed 1180 kg *2602 lb* on 9 Mar 1989. The 17·2-hand (1·78 m *5 ft 10 in*) champion percheron stallion 'Pinchbeck

Union Crest' (1964-88), owned by George Sneath of Pinchbeck, Spalding, Lincs, fluctuated between 1143 kg *2520 lb* and 1194 kg *2632 lb*. His famous father 'Saltmarsh Silver Crest' (1955-78) weighed 1257 kg *2772 lb* at his heaviest.

Tallest The tallest documented horse was the shire gelding 'Sampson' (later renamed 'Mammoth'), bred by Thomas Cleaver of Toddington Mills, Beds. This horse (foaled 1846) measured 21·2½ hands (2·19 m *7 ft 2½ in*) in 1850 and was later said to have weighed 1524 kg *3360 lb*.

'Boringdon Black King' (foaled 1984), a shire gelding born and bred at the National Shire Horse Centre in Plymouth, Devon, stands 19·2 hands (1·98 m *6½ ft*), making him the world's tallest living horse.

The shire geldings 'Wandle Goliath' (foaled 1977), owned by Young & Co. Brewery, Wandsworth, London, and 'Extra Stout' (see left), both measure 19·1½ hands (1·97 m *6 ft 5½ in*).

The tallest recorded non-draught horse was a Canadian thoroughbred gelding named 'Tritonis', owned by Christopher Ewing of Southfield, Michigan, USA. This show jumper, which died in September 1990 at the age of seven, stood 19·2 hands (1·98 m *6½ ft*) and weighed 952·54 kg *2100 lb*.

Smallest The Falabella of Argentina was developed over a period of 70 years by inbreeding and crossing a small group of undersized horses originally discovered in the southern part of the country. Most adult specimens stand less than 76 cm *30 in* and average 36–45 kg *80–100 lb* in weight. The smallest mature horse bred by Julio Falabella of Recco de Roca before he died in 1981 was a mare which stood 38 cm *15 in* and weighed 11·9 kg *26¼ lb*.

The stallion 'Little Pumpkin' (foaled 15 Apr 1973), owned by J.C. Williams Jr of Della Terra Mini Horse Farm, Inman, South Carolina, USA, stood 35·5 cm *14 in* and weighed 9·07 kg *20 lb* on 30 Nov 1975.

Oldest The greatest age reliably recorded for a horse is 62 years in the case of 'Old Billy' (foaled 1760), believed to be a cross between a Cleveland and eastern blood, bred by Edward Robinson of Wild Grave Farm, Woolston, Lancs. In 1762 or 1763 the horse was sold to the Mersey and Irwell Navigation Company and remained with them in a working capacity (i.e. marshalling and towing barges) until 1819 when he was retired to a farm at Latchford, near Warrington, where he died on 27 Nov 1822. The skull of this horse is preserved in the Manchester Museum, and his stuffed head (fitted with false teeth) is now on display in Bedford Museum.

The greatest age recorded for a thoroughbred racehorse is 42 years in the case of the chestnut gelding *Tango Duke* (foaled 1935), owned by Mrs Carmen J. Koper of Barongarook, Victoria, Australia. The horse died on 25 Jan 1978.

The greatest reliable age recorded for a pony is 54 years for a stallion owned by a farmer in central France (*fl.* 1919). A roan pony named 'Bonnie Lass', owned by twin sisters Sylvia Moore and Marion Atkinson of Old Harlow, Essex, died on 2 May 1987 aged 42 years. Exactly a year to the day later a moorland pony called 'Joey', belonging to June and Rosie Osborne of the Glebe Equestrian Centre, Wickham Bishop, Essex, died at the age of 44.

Strongest The greatest load ever hauled by a pair of draught-horses allegedly weighed 130·9 tonnes, which two shires with a combined weight of 1587 kg *3500 lb* pulled on a sledge litter for a distance of 402 m *1319 ft* along a frozen road at the Nester Estate near Ewen, Michigan, USA on 26 Feb 1893, but this tonnage was exaggerated. The load, which comprised 50 logs of white pine measuring 36 055 board feet, actually weighed about 42·3 tonnes.

On 23 Apr 1924 a shire gelding named 'Vulcan', owned by Liverpool Corporation, registered a pull equal to a starting load of 29·47 tonnes on a dynamometer at the British Empire Exhibition at Wembley, and a pair of shires *easily* pulled a starting load of 51 tonnes, the maximum registered on the dynamometer.

Largest mules 'Apollo' (foaled 1977) and 'Anak' (foaled 1976), owned by Herbert L. Mueller of Chicago, Illinois, USA, are the largest mules on record. 'Apollo' measures 19·1 hands (1·96 m *6 ft 5 in*) and weighs 998 kg *2200 lb*, with 'Anak' at 18·3 hands (1·905 m *6 ft 3 in*) and 952·2 kg *2100 lb*, giving a combined weight of 1950·2 kg *4300 lb*. Both are the hybrid offspring of Belgian mares and mammoth jacks.

DOGS

The United Kingdom's canine population is 6·6 million (1989 estimate), compared with 52 million for the United States and 400 million for the world.

Heaviest The heaviest breeds of domestic dog (*Canis familiaris*) are the Old English mastiff and the St Bernard, with adult males of both species regularly weighing 77–91 kg *170–200 lb*. The heaviest (and longest) dog ever recorded is 'Aicama Zorba of La-Susa' (whelped 26 Sep 1981), an Old English mastiff owned by Chris Eraclides of London. 'Zorba' stands 94 cm *37 in* at the shoulder and weighed 155·58 kg *343 lb* in November 1989. Other statistics include a chest girth of 149 cm *58¾ in*, a length of 2·53 m *8 ft 3½ in* and a neck measurement of 95·25 cm *37½ in*.

The heaviest St Bernard on record is 'Benedictine Jr Schwarzwald Hof' (whelped 1982), owned by breeders Thomas and Anne Irwin of Grand Rapids, Michigan, USA. His last recorded weight was 140·6 kg *310 lb*, with a shoulder height of 99 cm *39 in*.

Tallest The Great Dane and the Irish wolfhound can exceed 99 cm *39 in* at the shoulder. In the case of the Great Dane the extreme recorded example was 'Shamgret Danzas' (whelped 1975), owned by Mr and Mrs Comley of Milton Keynes, Bucks. He stood 105·4 cm *41½ in*, or 106·6 cm *42 in* when his hackles were raised, and weighed up to 108 kg *238 lb*. He died on 16 Oct 1984.

The Irish wolfhound 'Broadbridge Michael' (1920–29), owned by Mary Beynon of Sutton-at-Hone, Kent, stood 100·3 cm *39½ in* at the age of two.

Smallest *Miniature* versions of the Yorkshire terrier, the Chihuahua and the toy poodle have been known to weigh less than 453 g *16 oz* when mature.

The smallest mature dog on record was a matchbox-sized Yorkshire terrier owned by Arthur Marples of Blackburn, Lancs, a former editor of *Our Dogs*. This tiny atom, which died in 1945 aged nearly two, stood 6·3 cm *2½ in* at the shoulder and measured 9·5 cm *3¾ in* from the tip of its nose to the root of its tail. It weighed an incredible 113 g *4 oz*.

The smallest living adult dog is a miniature Chihuahua named 'Peanuts' (whelped 23 Sep 1986), owned by Grace Parker of Wilson's Mills, North Carolina, USA. The dog

measures 25 cm *9·84 in* from head to tail, 14 cm *5·5 in* at the shoulder and weighed 630 g *18 oz* on 25 Oct 1988.

Oldest Most dogs live between 8 and 15 years, and authentic records of dogs living over 20 years are rare. They are generally the smaller breeds. The greatest reliable age recorded for a dog is 29 years 5 months for an Australian cattle-dog named 'Bluey', owned by Les Hall of Rochester, Victoria, Australia. The dog was obtained as a puppy in 1910 and worked among cattle and sheep for nearly 20 years. He was put to sleep on 14 Nov 1939.

UK A Welsh collie named 'Taffy', owned by Evelyn Brown of Forge Farm, West Bromwich, W Mids, lived for 27 years and 313 days. He was whelped on 2 Apr 1952 and died on 9 Feb 1980.

Longest trail The 1688 km *1049 mile* Iditarod Trail from Anchorage to Nome, Alaska, USA has existed since 1910 and has been the course of an annual race since 1967. The fastest time was set by Susan Butcher (winner in 1986–87–88–89–90) in 1990 with 11 days 1 hr 53 min 23 sec. Rick Swenson has won the race a record five times (1977–79, 1981–82 and 1991).

On 8 Feb 1988 Rev. Donald Ewen McEwen, owner-musher of Nekanesu Kennels, Eldorado, Ontario, Canada, drove a 76-dog sled for 3·2 km *2 miles* single-handedly on the ice and along the shore of Lingham Lake. The team, consisting of 25 Siberian huskies and 51 Alaskan huskies, was assembled for the filming of an British TV commercial.

Rarest At the last count (March 1988), there were only 70 living examples of the American hairless terrier, 68 of them owned by Willie and Edwin Scott of Trout, Louisiana, USA.

Largest litter 'Lena', an American foxhound bitch owned by Commander W. N. Ely of Ambler, Pennsylvania, USA produced a litter of 23 on 19 Jun 1944. All the puppies survived.

On 6–7 Feb 1975 'Careless Ann', a St Bernard owned by Robert and Alice Rodden of Lebanon, Missouri, USA, also produced a litter of 23, 14 of which survived. The same number (16 survived) was produced by 'Shalimar Bootsie', a Great Dane owned by Marjorie Harris of Little Hall, near Colchester, Essex in June 1987.

Most prolific The greatest ever sire was the champion greyhound 'Low Pressure', nicknamed 'Timmy' (whelped September 1957), owned by Bruna Amhurst of Regent's Park, London. From December 1961 until his death on 27 Nov 1969 he

fathered 2414 registered puppies, with at least 600 others unregistered.

Most valuable In 1907 Clarice Ashton Cross of Ascot, Berks turned down an offer of £32 000 from the American financier and industrialist J. Pierpont Morgan for her famous Pekingese *Ch. Ch'êrh of Alderbourne* (1904–14). Mr Morgan then offered a blank cheque, but was again turned down. The largest legacy devoted to a dog was by Ella Wendel of New York, USA, who bequeathed her standard poodle 'Toby' £15 million in 1931.

Highest jump The canine high jump record for a leap and a scramble over a smooth wooden wall (without ribs or other aids) is held by a German shepherd dog named 'Volse', who scaled 3·58 m *11 ft 9 in* at a demonstration in Avignon, France in November 1989. The dog is owned by Philippe Clément of Aix-en-Provence.

'Duke', a three-year-old German shepherd dog handled by Corporal Graham Urry of RAF Newton, Notts, scaled a ribbed wall with regulation shallow slats to a height of 3·58 m *11 ft 9 in* on the BBC *Record Breakers* programme on 11 Nov 1986.

Longest jump A greyhound named 'Bang' jumped 9·14 m *30 ft* while coursing a hare at Brecon Lodge, Glos in 1849. He cleared a 1·4 m *4 ft 6 in* gate and landed on a hard road, but despite a damaged pastern bone he still managed to kill the hare.

Tracking In 1925 a Dobermann pinscher named 'Sauer', trained by Detective-Sergeant Herbert Kruger, tracked a stock-thief 160 km *100 miles* across the Great Karroo, South Africa by scent alone.

In 1923 a collie dog named 'Bobbie', lost by his owners while they were on holiday in Wolcott, Indiana, USA, turned up at the family home in Silverton, Oregon, USA six months later, after covering a distance of some 3200 km *2000 miles*. The dog, later identified by householders who had looked after him along the route, had apparently travelled back through the states of Illinois, Iowa, Nebraska and Colorado before crossing the Rocky Mountains in the depths of winter.

Top show dogs The greatest number of Challenge Certificates won by a dog is 78, compiled by the famous chow chow *Ch. U'Kwong King Solomon* (whelped 21 Jun 1968). Owned and bred by Joan Egerton of Bramhall, Cheshire, 'Solly' won his first CC at the Cheshire Agricultural Society Championship Show on 4 Jun 1969, and his 78th CC was awarded at the City of Birmingham Championship Show on 4 Sep 1976. He died on 3 Apr 1978.

LARGEST PET LITTERS

Animal/Breed	No.	Owner	Date
CAT *Burmese/Siamese*	19[1]	V. Gane, Church Westcote, Kingham, Oxon	7 Aug 1970
DOG *American foxhound*	23	W. Ely, Ambler, Pennsylvania, USA	19 Jun 1944
DOG *St Bernard*	23[2]	R. and A. Rodden, Lebanon, Missouri, USA	6–7 Feb 1975
DOG *Great Dane*	23[3]	M. Harris, Little Hall, Essex	June 1987
FERRET *Domestic*	15	J. Cliff, Denstone, Uttoxeter, Staffs	1981
GERBIL *Mongolian*	14[4]	S. Kirkman, Bulwell, Notts	May 1983
GUINEA PIG (CAVY)	12	Laboratory specimen	1972
HAMSTER *Golden*	26[5]	L. and S. Miller, Baton Rouge, Louisiana, USA	28 Feb 1974
MOUSE *House*	34[6]	M. Ogilvie, Blackpool, Lancs	12 Feb 1982
RABBIT *New Zealand white*	24	J. Filek, Cape Breton, Nova Scotia, Canada	1978

[1] 4 stillborn. [2] 14 survived. [3] 16 survived. [4] 18 killed by mother. [5] 33 survived. [6] Litter of 15 recorded in 1960s by George Meares, geneticist-owner of gerbil-breeding farm in St Petersburg, Florida, USA using special food formula.

Mousing champion
A female tortoiseshell cat named 'Towser' (b. 21 Apr 1963), owned by Glenturret Distillery Ltd near Crieff, Tayside, notched up an estimated lifetime score of 28 899. She averaged three mice per day until her death on 20 Mar 1987.

The greatest number of 'Best-in-Show' awards won by any dog in all-breed shows is 203, compiled by the Scottish terrier bitch *Ch. Braeburn's Close Encounter* (whelped 22 Oct 1978) by 10 Mar 1985. She is owned by Sonnie Novick of Plantation Acres, Florida, USA. *Ch. Clayfield's Mon Ami*, a German shepherd bitch whelped in 1973, won a unique ten dog show championships on four continents from 1975 to 1987. She is owned by Neal, Sharon, Buffy and Holly Leas of West Des Moines, Iowa, USA.

Largest show The centenary of the annual Crufts show, held outside London for the first time at the National Exhibition Centre, Birmingham, W Mids on 9–12 Jan 1991, attracted a record 22 993 entries.

Drug sniffing The greatest sniffer-dogs on record are a pair of malinoises called 'Rocky' and 'Barco'. These Belgian sheep-dogs (whelped 1984) are members of an American stop-and-search team which patrols the Rio Grande Valley ('Cocaine Alley') along the southern Texas border. In 1988 alone they were involved in 969 seizures of drugs worth $182 million, and they are so proficient at their job that Mexican drug smugglers have put a $30 000 price on their heads. 'Rocky' and 'Barco' were awarded honorary titles of Sergeant Major and always wear their stripes when on duty.

The only sniffer-dog with a 100 per cent arrest record was a German shepherd of the US Army called 'General'. From April 1974 to March 1976 this canine detective and his handler, SP4 Michael R. Harris of the 591st Military Police Company in Fort Bliss, Texas, USA, carried out 220 searches for narcotics, arrested 220 people for possession and uncovered 330 caches of drugs.

The German shepherd 'Blue' of the Los Angeles Police Department was reported in January 1986 to have assisted in apprehending 253 suspected felons.

In October 1988 another German shepherd owned by the Essex Police sniffed out 2 tonnes of cannabis worth £6 million when sent into a remote cottage on the outskirts of Harlow, Essex.

CATS

The United Kingdom's feline population is 6·5 million (1988 estimate), compared with 54·6 million for the United States.

Largest The largest of the 330 breeds of cat is the ragdoll, with males weighing 6·8–9·07 kg *15–20 lb*. In the majority of examples of domestic cat (*Felis catus*) the average weight of the adult male (tom) is 3·9 kg *8·6 lb*, compared with 3·2 kg *7·2 lb* for female or queen. Neuters and spays are generally heavier.

The heaviest domestic cat on record was a neutered male tabby named 'Himmy', owned by Thomas Vyse of Redlynch, Cairns, Queensland, Australia. At the time of his death from respiratory failure on 12 Mar 1986 at the age of 10 years 4 months he weighed 21·3 kg *46 lb 15¼ oz* (neck 38·1 cm *15 in*, waist 83·8 cm *33 in* and length 96·5 cm *38 in*).

In Feb 1988 an unconfirmed weight of 21·7 kg *48 lb* was reported for a cat named 'Edward Bear', owned by Jackie Fleming of Sydney, New South Wales, Australia.

UK An 11-year-old male tabby called 'Poppa', owned by Gwladys Cooper of Newport, Gwent, weighed 20·19 kg *44½ lb* in November 1984 and died on 25 Jun 1985.

Smallest The smallest breed of domestic cat is the Singapura or drain cat of Singapore. Adult males average 2·72 kg *6 lb* in weight and adult females 1·81 kg *4 lb*.

A male Siamese cross named 'Ebony-Eb-Honey Cat', owned by Angelina Johnston of Boise, Idaho, USA, weighed only 0·79 kg *1 lb 12 oz* in February 1984 when aged 23 months.

Oldest Cats are generally longer-lived than dogs. The average life expectancy of un-doctored, well-fed males raised under household conditions and receiving good medical attention is 13–15 years (15–17 years for intact females), but neutered males and females live on average one to two years longer.

The oldest cat ever recorded was probably the tabby 'Puss', owned by Mrs T. Holway of Clayhidon, Devon, who celebrated his 36th birthday on 28 Nov 1939 and died the next day.

A more recent and better-documented case was that of the female tabby 'Ma', owned by Alice St George Moore of Drewsteignton, Devon. This cat was put to sleep on 5 Nov 1957 at the age of 34.

The oldest cat living in Britain today is believed to be a female Siamese named 'Sukoo', owned by Joan Whithy of Kingsbridge, Devon. She celebrated her 33rd birthday on 17 Apr 1991.

Oldest twins The oldest twin cats on record were 'Beau' and 'Bubbles' (b. 17 Oct 1963), owned by Diane Phelps of Dearborn, Michigan, USA. 'Bubbles' died on 29 Apr 1985 aged 21 years 6 months and 'Beau' was put to sleep on 28 Dec 1985 aged 22 years 2 months. They were longhair and part Persian.

Largest litter A litter of 19 kittens (four stillborn) was delivered by caesarean section to 'Tarawood Antigone', a four-year-old brown Burmese, on 7 Aug 1970. Her owner, Valerie Gane of Church Westcote, Kingham, Oxon, said it was the result of a mis-mating with a half-Siamese. Of the 15 survivors, 14 were males and one female.

The largest live litter (all of which survived) was one of 14 born in December 1974 to a Persian cat named 'Bluebell', owned by Elenore Dawson of Wellington, Cape Province, South Africa.

Most prolific A tabby named 'Dusty' (b. 1935) of Bonham, Texas, USA produced 420 kittens during her breeding life. She gave birth to her last litter (a single kitten) on 12 Jun 1952.

In May 1987 'Kitty', owned by George Johnstone of Croxton, Staffs, produced two kittens at the age of 30 years, making her the oldest feline mother on record. She died in June 1989, just short of her 32nd birthday, having given birth to a known total of 218 kittens.

Most valuable In 1988 Carl Mayes, a breeder in Atlanta, Georgia, USA, turned down an offer of $10 000 for his male Singapura 'Bull', the best-known example of its breed in the United States.

Best climber On 6 Sep 1950 a four-month-old kitten, owned by Josephine Aufdenblatten of Geneva, Switzerland, followed a group of climbers to the top of the 4478 m *14 691 ft* Matterhorn in the Alps.

RABBITS AND HARES

Largest The largest breed of domestic rabbit (*Oryctolagus cuniculus*) is the Flemish giant. Adults weigh 7–8·5 kg *15·4–18·7 lb* (average toe-to-toe length when fully stretched 91 cm *36 in*), but weights up to 11·3 kg *25 lb* have been reliably reported for this breed.

In April 1980 a five-month-old French lop doe weighing 12 kg *26·45 lb* was exhibited at the Reus Fair in north-east Spain.

The heaviest recorded wild rabbit (average weight 1·58 kg *3½ lb*) was one of 3·74 kg *8 lb 4 oz*, killed on 20 Nov 1982.

Smallest The Netherland dwarf and the Polish both have a weight range of 0·9–1·13 kg *2–2½ lb* when fully grown. In 1975 Jacques Bouloc of Coulommière, France announced a new cross of the above breeds which weighed 396 g *14 oz*.

Most prolific The most prolific domestic breeds are the New Zealand white and the Californian. Does produce 5–6 litters a year, each containing 8–12 kittens during their breeding life (cf. five litters and 3–7 young for the wild rabbit).

Longest ears The longest ears are found in the lop family (four strains), and in particular the English lop. The ears of a typical example measure about 61 cm *24 in* from tip to tip (taken across the skull), and 14 cm *5·51 in* in width. In 1901 Capt. Youden exhibited a specimen in England which had ears measuring 77·4 cm *30·5 in*; it is not known, however, if this was a natural attainment or if weights had been used to stretch the ears, as the veins inside were badly varicosed.

Largest hare In November 1956 a brown hare (*Lepus europaeus*) weighing 6·83 kg *15 lb 1 oz* was shot near Welford, Northants. The average adult weight is 3·62 kg *8 lb*.

Birds Aves

Largest ratite The largest living bird is the North African ostrich (*Struthio c. camelus*), which is found in reduced numbers south of the Atlas Mountains from Upper Senegal and Niger across to the Sudan and central Ethiopia. Male examples (adult hens are smaller) of this flightless (ratite) sub-species have been recorded up to 2·74 m *9 ft* in height and

CAGED PET LONGEVITY

Animal/Species	Name (Owner), etc.	Yr	Months
RABBIT	*Flopsy* caught 6 Aug 1964, d. 29 Jun 1983 (L.B. Walker) Longford, Tasmania, Australia	18	10 ¾
GUINEA PIG	*Snowball* d. 14 Feb 1979 (M. A. Wall) Bingham, Notts	14	10 ½
GERBIL *Mongolian*	*Sahara* May 1973–4 Oct 1981 (Aaron Milstone) Lathrup Village, Michigan, USA	8	4 ½
MOUSE *House*	*Fritzy* 11 Sep 1977–24 April 1985 (Bridget Beard) West House School, Edgbaston, Birmingham, W Mids	7	7
RAT *Common*	*Rodney* January 1983–25 May 1990 (Rodney Mitchell) Tulsa, Oklahoma, USA	7	4

BIRDS

156·5 kg *345 lb* in weight. The heaviest sub-species is *S. c. australis* which can weigh 150 kg *330 lb*, although there is an unsubstantiated record of 160 kg *353 lb*.

Largest carinate The world's heaviest flying birds are the Kori bustard or paauw (*Ardeotis kori*) of north-east and southern Africa and the great bustard (*Otis tarda*) of Europe and Asia. Weights of 19 kg *42 lb* have been reported for the former, and there is an unconfirmed record of 21 kg *46·3 lb* for a male great bustard shot in Manchuria which was too heavy to fly. The heaviest reliably recorded great bustard weighed 18 kg *39·7 lb*.

The mute swan (*Cygnus olor*), which is resident in Britain, can reach 18·14 kg *40 lb* on very rare occasions, and there is a record from Poland of a cob weighing 22·5 kg *49·6 lb* which had temporarily lost the power of flight.

Bird of prey The heaviest bird of prey is the Andean condor (*Vultur gryphus*), with adult males averaging 9·09–11·3 kg *20–25 lb*. A weight of 14·1 kg *31 lb* has been claimed for an outsized male California condor (*Gymnogyps californianus*) now preserved in the California Academy of Sciences at Los Angeles, USA. This species is appreciably smaller than the Andean condor and rarely exceeds 10·4 kg *23 lb*.

Largest wing span The wandering albatross (*Diomedea exulans*) of the southern oceans has the largest wing span of any living bird, adult males averaging 3·15 m *10 ft 4 in* with wings at full stretch. The largest recorded specimen was a very old male with a wing span of 3·63 m *11 ft 11 in*, caught by members of the Antarctic research ship USNS *Eltanin* in the Tasman Sea on 18 Sep 1965. Unconfirmed measurements up to 4·22 m *13 ft 10 in* have been claimed for this species.

The only other bird reliably credited with a wing span exceeding 3·35 m *11 ft* is the vulture-like marabou stork (*Leptoptilus crumeniferus*) of tropical Africa. In 1934 an extreme measurement of 4·06 m *13 ft 4 in* was reported for a male shot in central Africa, but this can be discredited.

Smallest The smallest bird in the world is the bee hummingbird (*Mellisuga hele-*

nae) of Cuba and the Isle of Pines. Adult males (females are slightly larger) measure 57 mm *2·24 in* in total length, half of which is taken up by the bill and tail. It weighs 1·6 g *0·056 oz*, which means it is lighter than a privet hawk-moth (*Sphinx ligustri*: 2·4 g *0·084 oz*). (See Smallest nest.)

The smallest bird of prey is the 35 g *1·23 oz* white-fronted falconet (*Microhierax latifrons*) of north-western Borneo, which is sparrow-sized.

The smallest seabird is the least storm petrel (*Halocyptena microsoma*), which breeds on many of the small islands in the Gulf of California, north-western Mexico. Adult specimens average 140 mm *5½ in* in total length and weigh *c.* 28 g *1 oz*.

The smallest regularly breeding British bird is the goldcrest (*Regulus regulus*), also known as the golden crested wren. Adult specimens measure 90 mm *3·5 in* in length and weigh between 3·8 and 4·5 g *0·108* and *0·127 oz*, which means the bird is half the weight of the common wren (*Troglodytes troglodytes*).

The world's smallest species of duck is the Indian cotton teal, or Indian pygmy goose (*Nettapus coromandelianus*), found in freshwater habitats of tropical Asia and north-eastern Australia. The adult bird is 30–37 cm *12–14 in* long and the drake weighs on average 403 g *13·4 oz*. In September 1989 the first ever captive breeding of this duck was achieved at the Pensthorpe Waterfowl Trust in Fakenham, Norfolk when two eggs, removed to the safety of an incubator after being laid in the same tree-hole as the eggs of the related African pygmy goose, were successfully hatched.

Most abundant *Wild bird* The red-billed quelea (*Quelea quelea*), a seed-eating weaver of the drier parts of Africa south of the Sahara, has an estimated adult breeding population of 1·5 billion and at least 1 billion of these 'feathered locusts' are slaughtered annually without having any impact on the population. One huge roost in the Sudan contained 32 million birds.

Seabird The most abundant is probably the very small Wilson's storm petrel

(*Oceanites oceanicus*), which breeds on the Antarctic continent and adjacent sub-Antarctic islands. No population estimates have been published, but the numbers must run into hundreds of millions.

Domesticated bird The most abundant species is the chicken, the tame version of the wild red jungle fowl (*Gallus gallus*) of south-east Asia. According to the FAO (Food and Agriculture Organization of the United Nations), the world's chicken population stood at 8 295 760 000 in 1985, which means there are 1·6 chickens for every member of the human race.

Nesting bird Of the estimated 126–150 species of wild bird found in Britain, the commonest is now the blackbird (*Turdus merula*), with a breeding population of 5 million pairs. It is followed by the robin (*Erithicius rubecula*) and the blue tit (*Parus caeruleus*) with 4 million pairs each, the house sparrow (*Passer domesticus*) with 3 million pairs and the song thrush (*Turdus philamelos*) with 2·5 million pairs. Between 1964–74 the population of the wren (*Troglodytes troglodytes*) increased tenfold after a series of mild winters, and at the end of this period there were an estimated 10 million pairs. This species, however, is severely affected by cold weather, and the harsh winter of 1978–79 alone reduced the wren population by 40 per cent.

Rarest The number of threatened bird species world-wide has risen in the past 10 years from 290 to 1029 as a result of human activity, according to a survey published in October 1988. Because of the practical difficulties in assessing bird populations in the wild, it is virtually impossible to establish the identity of the world's rarest living bird.

The strongest contender until very recently was the dusky seaside sparrow (*Ammospiza nigrescens*), formerly of Titusville Marshes, Florida, USA, but the last known example (a male) died at Discovery Island, Disney World, Orlando, Florida on 16 May 1987. Some of its tissue has been frozen in the hope that future technology might allow a pure strain of dusky seaside sparrow to be resurrected through genetic cloning.

■ **Largest wing span**
The marabou stork (Leptoptilus crumeniferus) of tropical Africa is the only bird, after the wandering albatross (Diomedea exulans), reliably credited with a wing span exceeding 3·35 m 11 ft. (Photo: Bruce Coleman)

33

BIRDS

The Guam flycatcher (*Myiagra freycineti*) and the rufous fantail (*Rhipidura rufifrons*), also of Guam, were last seen in 1984 and may now also be extinct.

The Guam rail (*Rallus owstons*) has only been sighted three times since 1985.

The oa (*Moho braccatus*) of Kauai in the Hawaiian Islands, reportedly extinct, was rediscovered in 1960 in the mountain rain forests of the Alahari swamp. Its nest was found in 1979 and it was seen again in 1981. It is now protected and there may be one or two pairs left.

The crested shellduck (*Tadorna cristata*) is known from only three specimens. The last sighting was in 1971, but it may still survive in the remoter Japanese coastal regions or in adjacent waters.

The imperial woodpecker (*Campephilus imperiali*) of Mexico has not been sighted since 1958 on the Sonora–Chihuahua border, but there were unconfirmed reports from south-west Chihuahua in 1977.

The Socorro dove (*Zenaida graysoni*) of Socorro Island off the west coast of Mexico is now extinct in the wild and survives only in captivity.

The Itombwe owl is known only from the type specimen collected in 1951 while sleeping in long grass high in the Itombwe Mountains, eastern Zaïre, and the Kibale groundthrush (*Turdus kibalensis*) of western Uganda is known only from two males collected in 1966.

The sea-cliff swallow (*Hirunda perdita*) is known only from a dead specimen found on an islet off Port Sudan in 1984 and has not been recorded since.

In 1979 the Chatham Island black robin (*Petroica traversi*) was another bird on the verge of extinction, with only five surviving. By a pioneering method of cross-fostering the chicks of this wild songbird with local tom tits, however, members of the New Zealand Wildlife Service managed to increase the population to 38 by 1984. There are now over 100 of these robins spread throughout several islands. Another remarkable fact is that every living example of this species is descended from the female known as 'Old Blue'. She lived for *c*. 14 years (over twice the normal lifespan) and remained fertile right to the end. The death of this amazing little bird was officially announced in the New Zealand Parliament and her body has been preserved in a museum.

Spix's macaw (*Cyanopsitta spixii*) of Brazil, the world's most endangered parrot, has been reduced to a single specimen in the wild at July 1990. There are only 15 left in captivity around the world.

The last wild California condor (*Gymnogyps californianus*) was captured on 19 Apr 1987 in Kern County, California, USA to join 26 others held for captive breeding in San Diego Wildlife Park and Los Angeles Zoo. On 29 Apr 1988 the first California condor ever born in captivity was successfully hatched at San Diego Wildlife Park and the chick was fed successfully for six months by keepers using condor hand puppets to simulate the parent bird.

The Aldabra brush warbler (*Nesillas aldabrabus*) was not discovered until 1967, and five individuals (three males and two females) were ringed between July 1974 and February 1977. One of the males was re-sighted in 1978 and again in September 1983, but this was the last confirmed record. This species is restricted to a coastal strip 2 km *1·24 miles* long and 50 m *162 ft* wide on the northern tip of Aldabra Atoll in the Indian Ocean.

British Isles According to the British Ornithologists' Union, there are over 50 species of birds which have been recorded only once in the British Isles — most of them since the end of the Second World War.

The bird which has not been sighted for the longest period is the black-capped petrel (*Pterodroma hasitata*) of the West Indies. A specimen was caught alive on a heath at Southacre, near Swaffham, Norfolk in March or April 1850.

On 28–29 May 1979 an Aleutian tern (*Sterna aleutica*) was sighted on the Farne Islands, Northumberland. This bird breeds on the coasts of Alaska and eastern Siberia, and until then had never been recorded outside the North Pacific.

On 3 Aug 1988 a Tristram's storm petrel (*Oceanodroma tristrami*) was sighted off Sennen, near Land's End, Cornwall, more than 12 874 km *8000 miles* from its natural haunts in Japanese waters. It had never been recorded in the Atlantic before.

The most tenuously established British bird is the snowy owl (*Nyctea scandiaca*). During the period 1967–75 one pair bred regularly on Fetlar, Shetland Isles and reared a total of 21 young, but soon afterwards the old male took off for an unknown destination, having driven off all the young males and left the females without a mate. Between 19 and 22 Apr 1979 an adult male was sighted on Fair Isle, some 129 km *80 miles* further south, but it did not find its way to Fetlar. In 1984 four females were seen on Fetlar, but once again no males were in evidence. A total of 91 females have now been observed during the period 1958–86.

In 1916 an English vicar stole the eggs of the last white-tailed sea eagle (*Haliaeetus albicilla*) on Skye in the Inner Hebrides. During the period 1975–77 an attempt was made to reintroduce this bird on the island of Rhum, and 13 eaglets from Norway were released. In the summer of 1985 the first chick raised in the wild in Britain for more than 70 years took to the air. The parents of the chick successfully raised two more the following year and another two in 1987 and 1988. In November 1988 a white-tailed sea eagle was spotted near a bird reserve at Elmley, Isle of Sheppey, Kent.

Britain's rarest breeding bird is the red-backed shrike (*Lanius collurio*) of southern

and eastern England. In 1952 there were over 300 breeding pairs, but only 1–3 pairs in 1988.

The shore lark (*Eremophila alpestris*) of the east coast and the ruff (*Philomachus pugnax*) of East Anglia are both now down to three breeding pairs.

Britain's rarest breeding seabird is the Mediterranean black-headed gull (*Larus melanocephalus*), which first bred at Needs Oar Point Nature Reserve, Hants in 1968. Its range has been slowly extending in recent years.

Fastest flying The fastest living creature is the peregrine falcon (*Falco peregrinus*) when stooping from great heights during territorial displays. In one series of German experiments, a velocity of 270 km/h *168 mph* was recorded at a 30° angle of stoop, rising to a maximum of 350 km/h *217 mph* at an angle of 45°.

The white-throated spinetail swift (*Hirundapus caudacutus*) of Asia and the Alpine swift (*Apus melba*) are also extremely fast during courtship display flights, with the former timed at speeds up to 170 km/h *105·6 mph* in tests carried out in the USSR.

The fastest fliers in level flight are found among the ducks and geese (Anatidae), and some powerful species such as the red-breasted merganser (*Mergus serrator*), the eider (*Somateria mollissima*), the canvasback (*Aythya valisineria*) and the spur-winged goose (*Plectropterus gambiensis*) can probably exceed an airspeed of 104 km/h *65 mph*.

Britain's fastest game bird is the red grouse (*Lagopus l. scoticus*) which, in still air, has recorded speeds of up to 92·8–100·8 km/h *58–63 mph* over very short distances. Airspeeds up to 112 km/h *70 mph* have been claimed for the golden plover (*Pluvialis apricaria*) when flushed, but it is very doubtful whether this rapid-flying bird can exceed 80–88 km/h *50–55 mph* — even in an emergency.

Slowest flying Probably at least 50 per cent of the world's flying birds cannot exceed an air speed of 64 km/h *40 mph* in level flight. The slowest-flying bird is the American woodcock (*Scolopax minor*) which, during courtship flights, has been timed at 8 km/h *5 mph* without stalling.

Fastest wing-beat The wing-beat of the horned sungem (*Heliactin cornuta*) of tropical South America is 90 beats/sec.

Longest-lived The greatest irrefutable age reported for any bird is over 80 years for a male sulphur-crested cockatoo (*Cacatua galerita*) named 'Cocky', who died at London Zoo in 1982. He was presented to the zoo in 1925, and had been with his previous owner since 1902 when he was already fully mature.

In 1987 an unconfirmed age of *c*. 82 years was reported for a male Siberian white crane (*Crus leucogeranus*) named 'Wolfe' at the International Crane Foundation, Baraboo, Wisconsin, USA. The bird was said to have hatched out in a zoo in Switzerland *c*. 1905. He died in late 1988 after breaking his bill while repelling a visitor near his pen.

In 1964 the death was reported of a male Andean condor called 'Kuzya' at Moscow Zoo, USSR at the age of over 72 years. As this bird was already fully grown when it was received in 1892, it must have been at least 77.

The oldest ringed seabird on record is a female royal albatross (*Diomedea epomophora*) named 'Grandma' ('Blue White'), who laid an egg at Taiaroa Head, near Dunedin, South Island, New Zealand in November 1988, when she was 60 years old. She was banded for the first time in 1937 when she was a breeding adult, and such birds do not start breeding until they are 9 years old. Since then she has raised 10 chicks of her own and fostered 3 others. Her mate, 'Green White Green', is 47.

Longest flights

The greatest distance covered by a ringed bird is 22 530 km *14 000 miles* by an Arctic tern (*Sterna paradisea*), which was banded as a nestling on 5 Jul 1955 in the Kandalaksha Sanctuary on the White Sea coast and was captured alive by a fisherman 13 km *8 miles* south of Fremantle, Western Australia on 16 May 1956. The bird had flown south via the Atlantic Ocean and then circled Africa before crossing the Indian Ocean. It did not survive to make the return journey. There is also a report of an Arctic tern flying from Greenland to Australasia, but further details are lacking.

In 1990 six foraging wandering albatrosses (*Diomedea exulans*) were tracked across the Indian Ocean by satellite via radio transmitters fitted by Pierre Jouventin and Henri Weimerskirch of the National Centre for Scientific Research at Beauvoir, France. Results showed that the birds covered between 3600 and 15 000 km *2237 –9321 miles* in a single feeding trip and that they easily maintained a speed of 56 km/h *35 mph* over a distance of more than 800 km *498 miles*, with the males going to sea for up to 33 days while their partners remained ashore to incubate the eggs.

Highest flying

Most migrating birds fly at relatively low altitudes (i.e. below 91 m *300 ft*) and only a few dozen species fly higher than 914 m *3000 ft*.

The highest acceptable altitude recorded for a bird is 11 277 m *37 000 ft* for a Ruppell's vulture (*Gyps rueppellii*), which collided with a commercial aircraft over Abidjan, Côte d'Ivoire on 29 Nov 1973. The impact damaged one of the aircraft's engines, causing it to shut down, but the plane landed safely without further incident. Sufficient feather remains of the bird were recovered to allow the US Museum of Natural History to make a positive identification of this high-flier, which is rarely seen above 6096 m *20 000 ft*.

British Isles On 9 Dec 1967 about 30 whooper swans (*Cygnus cygnus*) were recorded at an altitude of just over 8230 m *27 000 ft* flying in from Iceland to winter at Loch Foyle. They were spotted by an airline pilot over the Outer Hebrides, and the height was also confirmed on radar by air traffic control.

Most airborne

The most aerial of all birds is the sooty tern (*Sterna fuscata*), which, after leaving the nesting grounds, remains continuously aloft from 3–10 years as a sub-adult before returning to land to breed.

The most aerial land bird is the common swift (*Apus apus*), which remains airborne for 2–3 years, during which time it sleeps, drinks, eats and even mates on the wing.

Fastest swimmer

The gentoo penguin (*Pygoscelis papua*) has a maximum burst of speed of *c.* 27·4 km/h *17 mph*.

Deepest dive

In 1969 a depth of 265 m *870 ft* was recorded for a small group of 10 emperor penguins (*Aptenodytes forsteri*) at Cape Crozier, Antarctica by a team of US scientists. One bird remained submerged for 18 minutes.

Vision

Birds of prey (Falconiformes) have the keenest eyesight in the avian world, and large species with eyes similar in size to those of Man have visual acuity at least twice that of human vision. It has also been calculated that a large eagle can detect a target object at a distance 3–8 times greater than that achieved by Man. Thus the golden eagle (*Aquila chrysaetos*) can detect an 46 cm *18 in* long hare at a range of 3·2 km *2 miles* in good light and against a contrasting background, and a peregrine falcon (*Falco peregrinus*) can spot a pigeon at a range of over 8 km *5 miles*.

In experiments carried out on the tawny owl (*Strix aluco*) at the University of Birmingham, W Mids in 1977, it was revealed that the bird's eye on average was only 2½ times more sensitive than the human eye. It was also discovered that the tawny owl sees perfectly adequately in daylight and that its visual acuity is only slightly inferior to that of the human.

g force

American experiments have revealed that the beak of the red-headed woodpecker (*Melanerpes erythrocephalus*) hits the bark of a tree with an impact velocity of 20·9 km/h *13 mph*. This means that when the head snaps back the brain is subject to a deceleration of about 10 g.

Longest feathers

The longest feathers grown by any bird are those of the Phoenix fowl or onagadori (a strain of red junglefowl *Gallus gallus*), which has been bred in south-western Japan since the mid-17th century. In 1972 a tail covert measuring 10·6 m *34 ft 9½ in* was reported for a rooster owned by Masasha Kubota of Kochi, Shikoku, Japan.

Among flying birds the tail feathers of the male crested pheasant (*Rheinhartia ocellata*) of south-east Asia regularly reach 173 cm *5 ft 8 in* in length and 13 cm *5 in* in width, and the central tail feathers of the Reeves' pheasant (*Syrmaticus reevesi*) of central and northern China have reached 2·43 m *8 ft* in exceptional cases.

Most and least feathers

In a series of feather counts on various species of bird a whistling swan (*Cygnus columbianus*) was found to have 25 216 feathers, 20 177 of which were on the head and neck. The ruby-throated hummingbird (*Archilochus colubris*) has only 940.

Largest egg

The average ostrich (*Struthio camelus*) egg measures 15–20 cm *6–8 in* in length, 10–15 cm *4–6 in* in diameter and weighs 1·65–1·78 kg *3·63–3·88 lb* (around two dozen hens' eggs in volume). The egg would require about 40 min for boiling, and the shell, although only 1·5 mm *0·059 in* thick, can support the weight of a 127 kg *20 st* man. On 28 Jun 1988 a 2-year-old cross between a northern and a southern ostrich (*Struthio c. camelus* and *Struthio c. australis*) laid an egg weighing a record 2·3 kg *5·07 lb* at the Kibbutz Ha'on collective farm, Israel.

UK The largest egg laid by any bird on the British list is that of the mute swan (*Cygnus olor*), which measures 109–124 mm *4·3–4·9 in* in length, 71–78·5 mm *2·8–3·1 in* in diameter and weighs 340–368 g *12–13 oz*.

Smallest egg

Eggs emitted from the oviduct before maturity, known as 'sports', are not considered to be of significance. The smallest egg laid by any bird is that of the vervain hummingbird (*Mellisuga minima*) of Jamaica. Two specimens measuring less than 10 mm *0·39 in* in length weighed 0·365 g *0·0128 oz* and 0·375 g *0·0132 oz*.

UK The smallest egg laid by a bird on the British list is that of the goldcrest (*Regulus regulus*), which is 12·2–14·5 mm *0·48–0·57 in* long, 9·4–9·9 mm *0·37–0·39 in* in diameter and weighs 0·6 g *0·021 oz*.

Longest incubation

The longest normal incubation period is that of the wandering albatross (*Diomedea exulans*), with a normal range of 75–82 days.

There is an isolated case of an egg of the mallee fowl (*Leipoa ocellata*) of Australia taking 90 days to hatch, against its normal incubation period of 62 days.

Shortest incubation

The shortest incubation period is 10 days in the case of the great spotted woodpecker (*Dendrocopus major*) and the black-billed cuckoo (*Coccyzus erythropthalmus*).

The idlest of cock birds include hummingbirds (family Trochilidae), the eider duck (*Somateria mollissima*) and golden pheasant (*Chrysolophus pictus*), among which the hen bird does 100 per cent of the incubation, whereas the female common kiwi (*Apteryx australis*) leaves this to the male for 75–80 days.

Longest bills

The bill of the Australian pelican (*Pelicanus conspicillatus*) is 34–47 cm *13·3–18·5 in* long. The longest bill in relation to overall body length is that of the sword-billed hummingbird (*Ensifera ensifera*) of the Andes from Venezuela to Bolivia. It measures 10·2 cm *4 in* in length and is longer than the bird's actual body if the tail is excluded.

■ Smallest nest

The smallest nests in the avian world are built, not surprisingly, by hummingbirds (family Trochilidae). Sizes range from the equivalent of about half a walnut to the deeper thimble-type residence. Pictured here is the broadbill hummingbird (Cynanthus latirostris)

(Photo: Bruce Coleman)

Shortest bills The shortest bills in relation to body length are found among the smaller swifts (Apodidae) and in particular that of the glossy swiftlet (*Collocalia esculenta*), which is almost non-existent.

Cuckoos It is unlikely that the cuckoo (*Culculus canorus*) has ever been *heard and seen* in Britain earlier than 2 March, on which date one was observed under acceptable conditions by William Haynes of Trinder Road, Wantage, Oxon in 1972. Because of unseasonably mild temperatures, a great spotted cuckoo, which should have been in Africa, was reported on Lundy Island, off Devon on the weekend of 24–25 Feb 1990. The two latest dates are 16 Dec 1912 at Anstey's Cove, Torquay, Devon and 26 Dec 1897 or 1898 in Cheshire.

Bird-spotters The world's leading bird-spotter or 'twitcher' is Harvey Gilston (b. 12 Oct 1922) of Lausanne, Switzerland, who had logged 6891 of the 9016 known species by April 1991.

The British life list record is 485 by Ron Johns (b. 1941) of Slough, Bucks, who started spotting in 1952. The British year list record is 359 by Lee Evans (b. 1960) of Luton, Beds, established in 1990 after travelling over 123 916 km *77 000 miles*. In an average year he travels 96 000 km *60 000 miles*.

The greatest number of species spotted in a 24-hour period is 342 by Kenyans Terry Stevenson, John Fanshawe and Andy Roberts on day two of the Birdwatch Kenya '86 event held on 29–30 November. The 48-hour record is held by Don Turner and David Pearson of Kenya, who spotted 494 species at the same event.

Peter Kaestner of Washington, DC, USA was the first person to see at least one species of each of the world's 159 bird families. He saw his final family on 1 Oct 1986. Since then Dr Ira Abramson of Miami, Florida, USA, Dr Martin Edwards and Harvey Gilston (last family seen in December 1988) have also succeeded in this achievement.

Largest nest A nest measuring 2·9 m *9½ ft* wide and 6 m *20 ft* deep was built by a pair of bald eagles (*Haliaeetus leucocephalus*), and possibly their successors, near St Petersburg, Florida, USA. It was examined in 1963 and was estimated to weigh more than 2 tonnes. The golden eagle (*Aquila chrysaetos*) also constructs huge nests, and one 4·57 m *15 ft* deep was reported from Scotland in 1954. It had been used for 45 years. The incubation mounds built by the mallee fowl (*Leipoa ocellata*) of Australia are much larger, measuring up to 4·57 m *15 ft* in height and 10·6 m *35 ft* across, and it has been calculated that the nest site may involve the mounding of 289 m³ *900 ft³* of material weighing 300 tonnes.

Smallest nest The smallest nests are built by hummingbirds (Trochilidae). That of the vervain hummingbird (*Mellisuga minima*) is about half the size of a walnut, while the deeper one of the bee hummingbird (*M. helenea*) is thimble-sized.

The smallest British nest is that of the goldcrest (*Regulus regulus*), which measures about 8–9 cm *3·14–3·54 in* in diameter.

DOMESTICATED BIRDS

Earliest The earliest domesticated bird was the greylag goose (*Anser*) of the Neolithic period (20 000 years ago) of southeastern Europe and Asia Minor.

Oldest The longest-lived domesticated bird (excluding the ostrich, which has lived up to 68 years) is the domestic goose (*Anser a. domesticus*), which normally lives about 25 years. On 16 Dec 1976 a gander named 'George', owned by Florence Hull of Thornton, Lancs, died aged 49 years 8 months. He was hatched out in April 1927.

The longest-lived small cagebird is the Canary (*Serinus canaria*). The oldest example on record is a 34-year-old cock bird named 'Joey', owned by K. Ross of Hull. The bird was purchased in Calabar, Nigeria in 1941 and died on 8 Apr 1975. The oldest budgerigar (*Melopsittacus undulatus*) was a hen bird named 'Charlie', owned by J. Dinsey of Stonebridge, London, which died on 20 Jun 1977 aged 29 years 2 months.

Reptiles Reptilia

CROCODILIANS

Largest The largest reptile in the world is the estuarine or saltwater crocodile (*Crocodylus porosus*) of south-east Asia, the Malay Archipelago, Indonesia, northern Australia, Papua New Guinea, Vietnam and the Philippines. Adult males average 4·2–4·8 m *14–16 ft* in length and weigh about 408–520 kg *900–1150 lb*. There are four protected estuarine crocodiles at the Bhitarkanika Wildlife Sanctuary, Orissa State, eastern India which measure more than 6 m *19 ft 8 in* in length. The largest individual is over 7 m *23 ft* long.

Captive The largest crocodile ever held in captivity is an estuarine/Siamese hybrid named 'Yai' (b. 10 Jun 1972) at the Samutprakarn Crocodile Farm and Zoo, Thailand. He measures 6 m *19 ft 8 in* in length and weighs 1114·27 kg *2465 lb*.

Smallest Osborn's dwarf crocodile (*Osteolaemus osborni*), found in the upper region of the Congo River, west Africa, rarely exceeds 1·2 m *3 ft 11 in* in length.

Oldest The greatest authenticated age for a crocodilian is 66 years for a female American alligator (*Alligator mississipiensis*) which arrived at Adelaide Zoo, South Australia on 5 Jun 1914 as a 2-year-old, and died there on 26 Sep 1978.

Another female of this species, named 'Smiley', at the Maritime Museum Aquarium, Gothenburg, Sweden, died on 10 Feb 1987 aged 65 years after the electricity heating its pool was accidentally turned down.

Rarest The total wild population of the protected Chinese alligator (*Alligator sinensis*) of the lower Yangtze River in the Anhui, Zhejiang and Jiangsu provinces of China is currently estimated at no more than a few hundred.

LIZARDS

Largest The largest of all lizards is the Komodo monitor or ora (*Varanus komodoensis*), a dragonlike reptile found on the Indonesian islands of Komodo, Rintja, Padar and Flores. Adult males average 225 cm *7 ft 5 in* in length and weigh about 59 kg *130 lb*. Lengths up to 9·14 m *30 ft* have been claimed for this species, but the largest specimen to be accurately measured was a male presented to an American zoologist in 1928 by the Sultan of Bima which was 3·05 m *10 ft 0·8 in* long. In 1937 this animal was put on display in St Louis Zoological Gardens, Missouri, USA for a short period. It then measured 3·10 m *10 ft 2 in* in length and weighed 166 kg *365 lb*.

The longest lizard in the world is the slender Salvadori monitor (*Varanus salva-*

dori) of Papua New Guinea, which has been reliably measured up to 4·75 m *15 ft 7 in*. Nearly 70 per cent of the total length, however, is taken up by the tail.

Smallest *Sphaerodactylus parthenopion*, a tiny gecko indigenous to the island of Virgin Gorda, one of the British Virgin Islands, is believed to be the world's smallest lizard. It is known only from 15 specimens, including some pregnant females found between 10 and 16 Aug 1964. The three largest females measured 18 mm *0·67 in* from snout to vent, with a tail of approximately the same length.

It is possible that another gecko, *Sphaerodactylus elasmorhynchus*, may be even smaller. The only known specimen was an apparently mature female with a snout-to-vent measurement of 17 mm *0·67 in* and a tail of the same length. This specimen was found on 15 Mar 1966 among the roots of a tree in the western part of the Massif de la Hotte in Haiti.

Oldest The greatest age recorded for a lizard is over 54 years for a male slow worm (*Anguis fragilis*) kept in the Zoological Museum in Copenhagen, Denmark from 1892 until 1946.

Fastest The highest speed measured for any reptile on land is 29 km/h *18 mph* for a six-lined race runner (*Cnemidophorus sexlineatus*) near McCormick, South Carolina, USA in 1941.

CHELONIANS

Largest The largest living chelonian is the leatherback turtle (*Dermochelys coriacea*), which is circumglobal in distribution. The average adult measures 1·83–2·13 m *6–7 ft* from the tip of the beak to the end of the tail (carapace 1·52–1·67 m *5–5½ ft*), about 2·13 m *7 ft* across the front flippers and weighs up to 453 kg *1000 lb*.

The largest leatherback turtle ever recorded was a male found dead on the beach at Harlech, Gwynedd on 23 Sep 1988. It measured 2·91 m *9 ft 5½ in* in total length over the carapace (nose to tail), 2·77 m *9 ft* across the front flippers and weighed an astonishing 961·1 kg *2120 lb*. It is now in the possession of the National Museum of Wales, Cardiff, S Glam and was put on public display on 16 Feb 1990. Most museums refuse to exhibit large turtles because they can drip oil for up to 50 years.

A weight of 865 kg *1908 lb* was reliably recorded for a male captured off Monterey, California, USA on 29 Aug 1961, which measured 2·54 m *8 ft 4 in* overall.

Tortoise The largest living tortoise is the Aldabra giant tortoise (*Geochelone gigantea*) of the Indian Ocean islands of Aldabra, Mauritius and the Seychelles (introduced 1874). A male tortoise named 'Esmerelda', a long-time resident on Bird Island in the Seychelles, recorded a weight of 298 kg *657 lb* on 26 Feb 1989.

Smallest The smallest of the seven species of marine turtle is the Atlantic ridley (*Lepidochelys kempi*), which has a shell length of 50–70 cm *19·7–27·6 in* and does not exceed 36 kg *80 lb*. It is also the rarest and most endangered sea turtle, with the total population in 1989 estimated at no more than 900 adult females and an unknown number of males and sub-adults.

Longest-lived The greatest authentic age recorded for a tortoise is over 152 years for a male Marion's tortoise (*Testudo sumeirii*), brought from the Seychelles to Mauritius in 1766 by the Chevalier de Fresne, who presented it to the Port Louis army garrison. This specimen, which went blind

in 1908, was accidentally killed in 1918. The greatest proven age of a continuously observed tortoise is more than 116 years for a Mediterranean spur-thighed tortoise (*Testudo graeca*).

The oldest turtle on record was an alligator snapping turtle (*Macrochelys temminckii*) at Philadelphia Zoo, Pennsylvania, USA. When it was accidentally killed on 7 Feb 1949 it was 58 years 9 months 1 day.

Fastest The highest speed claimed for any reptile is water is 35 km/h *22 mph* by a frightened Pacific leatherback turtle.

The National Tortoise Championship record is 5·48 m *18 ft* up a 1:12 gradient in 43·7 sec (0·45 km/h *0·28 mph*) by 'Charlie' at Tickhill, S Yorks on 2 Jul 1977.

Slowest In a 'speed' test carried out in the Seychelles a male giant tortoise (*Geochelone gigantea*) could cover only 4·57 m *15 ft* in 43·5 sec (0·37 km/h *0·23 mph*) despite the enticement of a female.

Deepest dive In May 1987 it was reported by Dr Scott Eckert that a leatherback turtle (*Dermochelys coriacea*) fitted with a pressure-sensitive recording device had dived to a depth of 1200 m *3973 ft* off the Virgin Islands in the West Indies.

Rarest The world's rarest chelonian is the protected short-necked swamp tortoise (*Pseudemydura umbrina*), which is confined to Ellen Brook and Twin reserves near Perth, Western Australia. The total wild population is now only 20–25, with another 22 held at Perth Zoo.

SNAKES

Longest The reticulated python (*Python reticulatus*) of south-east Asia, Indonesia and the Philippines regularly exceeds 6·24 m *20 ft 6 in.* In 1912 a specimen measuring 10 m *32 ft 9½ in* was shot near a mining camp on the north coast of Celebes in the Malay Archipelago.

Captive The longest (and heaviest) snake ever held in captivity was a female reticulated python named 'Colossus' who died in Highland Park Zoo, Pennsylvania, USA on 15 Apr 1963. She measured 8·68 m *28 ft 6 in* in length, and weighed 145 kg *320 lb* at her heaviest.

UK The longest snake found in Britian is the grass snake (*Natrix natrix*), which is found throughout southern England, parts of Wales and in Dumfries and Galloway, Scotland. The longest accurately measured specimen was probably a female killed in South Wales in 1887 which measured 1·775 m *5 ft 10 in.* In September 1816 a 2·13 m *7 ft* female was allegedly killed by a labourer at Trebun, Anglesey, Gwynedd and 'left for public curiosity at Llangefni', but further details are lacking.

Shortest The shortest snake in the world is the very rare thread snake (*Leptotyphlops bilineata*), which is known only from the islands of Martinique, Barbados and St Lucia in the West Indies. In one series of eight specimens the two longest both measured 108 mm *4·25 in.*

Heaviest The anaconda (*Eunectes murinus*) of tropical South America and Trinidad is nearly twice as heavy as a reticulated python (*Python reticulatus*) of the same length. A female shot in Brazil c. 1960 was not weighed, but as it measured 8·45 m *27 ft 9 in* in length with a girth of 111 cm *44 in* it must have scaled nearly 227 kg *500 lb*. The average adult length is 5·48–6·09 m *18–20 ft*.

The heaviest venomous snake is probably the eastern diamondback rattlesnake (*Crotalus adamanteus*) of the south-eastern United States. One specimen measuring 2·36 m *7 ft 9 in* in length weighed 15 kg *34 lb*. Adult examples average 1·52–1·83 m *5–6 ft* in length and weigh 5·5–6·8 kg *12–15 lb*.

The West African gaboon viper (*Bitis gabonica*) of the tropical rain forests is probably bulkier than this rattlesnake, but its average length is only 1·22–1·52 m *4–5 ft*. A female 1·83 m *6 ft* long was found to weigh 11·34 kg *25 lb*, and another female measuring 1·74 m *5 ft 8½ in* weighed 8·2 kg *18 lb* with an empty stomach.

In February 1973 a posthumous weight of 12·75 kg *28 lb* was reported for a 4·39 m *14 ft 5 in* long king cobra (*Ophiophagus hannah*) at New York Zoological Park (Bronx Zoo), USA. It had been ill for some time.

Oldest The greatest reliable age recorded for a snake is 40 years 3 months 14 days for a male common boa (*Boa constrictor constrictor*) named 'Popeye', who died at Philadelphia Zoo, Pennsylvania, USA on 15 Apr 1977.

Fastest The fastest-moving land snake is probably the slender black mamba (*Dendroaspis polylepis*) of the eastern part of tropical Africa. It is thought that speeds of 16–19 km/h *10–12 mph* may be possible in short bursts over level ground.

The British grass snake (*Natrix natrix*) has a maximum speed of 6·8 km/h *4·2 mph*.

Most venomous All sea snakes are venomous, but the species *Hydrophis belcheri* has a myotoxic venom a hundred times as toxic as that of the Australian taipan (*Oxyuranus scutellatus*). The snake abounds round Ashmore Reef in the Timor Sea, off the coast of north-west Australia.

The most venomous land snake is the 2 m *6 ft 6¾ in* long smooth-scaled snake (*Parademansia microlepidotus*) of the Diamantina River and Cooper's Creek drainage basins in Channel County, Queensland and western New South Wales, Australia, which has a venom nine times as toxic as that of the tiger snake (*Notechis scutatus*) of South Australia and Tasmania. One specimen yielded 110 mg *0·00385 oz* of venom after milking, enough to kill 125 000 mice, but so far no human fatalities have been reported.

More people die of snakebites in Sri Lanka than any comparable area in the world. An average of 800 people are killed annually on the island by snakes, and more than 95 per cent of the fatalities are caused by the common krait (*Bungarus caeruleus*), the Sri Lankan cobra (*Naja n. naja*) and Russell's viper (*Vipera russelli pulchella*).

The saw-scaled or carpet viper (*Echis carinatus*) bites and kills more people in the world than any other species. Its geographical range extends from West Africa to India.

UK The only venomous snake in Britain is the adder (*Vipera berus*). Since 1890 ten people have died after being bitten by this snake, including six children. The most recent recorded death was on 1 Jul 1975 when a 5-year-old was bitten at Callander, Perthshire and died 44 hours later. The longest recorded specimen was a female measuring 110·5 cm *43½ in* which was killed at Paradise Farm, Pontrilas, Hereford & Worcester in August 1977.

Longest venomous The longest venomous snake in the world is the king cobra (*Ophiophagus hannah*), also called the hamadryad, of south-east Asia and the Philippines, which has an average adult length of 3·65–4·57 m *12–15 ft*. A 5·54 m *18 ft 2 in* specimen, captured alive near Fort Dickson in the state of Negri Sembilan, Malaya in April 1937, later grew to 5·71 m *18 ft 9 in* in London Zoo. It was destroyed at the outbreak of war in 1939.

Shortest venomous The namaqua dwarf adder (*Bitis schneider*) of Namibia, has an average adult length of 200 mm *7.87 in*.

Longest fangs The longest fangs of any snake are those of the highly venomous gaboon viper (*Bitis gabonica*) of tropical Africa. The fangs of a 1·83 m *6 ft* long specimen measured 50 mm *1·96 in*. On 12 Feb 1963 a gaboon viper under severe stress sank its fangs into its own back at Philadelphia Zoo, Pennsylvania, USA and died from traumatic injury to a vital organ. It did not, as had been widely reported, succumb to its own venom.

Rarest The world's rarest snake is the St Lucia racer or couresse (*Liophis ornatus*), which inhabits only Maria Island, off St Lucia, West Indies. Estimates by Dr David Corke of the Polytechnic of East London put its population at under 100 in 1989, with no specimens held in captivity. The Round Island boa (*Bolyeria multicarinata*) of Mauritius is only known from two specimens collected in the past 40 years and probably became extinct in 1980.

UK The rarest snake of Britain's three indigenous species is the smooth snake (*Coronella austriaca*) of southern England, with a total wild population of c. 2000.

■ **Most venomous snake**
Although all sea snakes are venomous, Hydrophis belcheri, found among the coral reefs off north-west Australia, has a myotoxin which is 100 times more powerful than that of the Australian taipan (Oxyuranus scutellatus), whose bite can kill a man within minutes. (Photo: Bruce Coleman)

Amphibians Amphibia

Largest The largest species of amphibian is the Chinese giant salamander (*Andrias davidianus*), which lives in north-eastern, central and southern China. The average adult measures 114 cm *3 ft 9 in* in length and weighs 25–30 kg *55–66 lb*. One specimen collected in Hunan province measured 1·8 m *5 ft 11 in* in length and weighed 65 kg *143 lb*.

UK The largest British amphibian is the common toad (*Bufo bufo*), which is found throughout England, Scotland and Wales. A huge female collected from Marlpit Pond, Boxley, Kent measured 99 mm *3·89 in* from snout to vent and weighed 118 g *4·16 oz*.

Smallest The smallest known amphibian is the tiny Cuban frog *Sminthillus limbatus*, which is less than 12 mm *½ in* long.

UK The smallest found in Britain is the palmate newt (*Triturus helveticus*). Adult specimens measure 75–92 mm *2·95–3·62 in* in length and weigh up to 2·39 g *0·083 oz*.

The natterjack or running toad (*Bufo calamita*) has a maximum snout-to-vent length of only 80 mm *3·14 in* (female), but it is a bulkier animal.

Oldest The greatest age reliably recorded for an amphibian is 55 years for a Japanese giant salamander which died in Amsterdam Zoo, Netherlands in 1881.

Longest gestation The viviparous Alpine black salamander (*Salamandra atra*) has a gestation period of up to 38 months at altitudes above 1400 m *4600 ft* in the Swiss Alps, but this drops to 24–26 months at lower altitudes.

Rarest Only five specimens of the painted frog (*Discoglossus nigriventer*) of Lake Huleh, Israel have been reported since 1940.

UK Although cases exist where 'pet' amphibia are released into gardens and establish breeding colonies, it is illegal to introduce non-native animals into the country. Britain's rarest native amphibian is the natterjack toad (*Bufo calamita*), which is restricted to sand-dunes and heathlands with temporary pools where it breeds. Its numbers are further threatened by the disappearance of most of the inland colonies.

Highest and lowest The greatest altitude at which an amphibian has been found is 8000 m *26 246 ft* for a common toad (*Bufo bufo*) collected in the Himalayas. This species has also been found at a depth of 340 m *1115 ft* in a coal mine.

Most poisonous The most active known poison is the batrachotoxin derived from the skin secretions of the golden poison-dart frog (*Phyllobates terribilis*) of western Colombia, a species not discovered until 1973. Its skin secretions are at least 20 times more toxic than those of any other known poison-dart frog (human handlers have to wear thick gloves), and an average adult specimen contains enough poison (1900 micrograms) to kill nearly 1500 people. Rather surprisingly, this species is preyed upon by the frog-eating snake (*Leimadophis epinephelus*), which is thought to be immune to its poison.

Largest frog The largest known frog is the rare African giant or goliath frog (*Conrana goliath*) of Cameroon and Equatorial Guinea. A specimen captured in April 1989 on the Sanaga River, Cameroon by Andy Koffman of Seattle, Washington, USA had a snout-to-vent length of 36·83 cm *14½ in* (87·63 cm *34½ in* overall with legs extended) and weighed 3·66 kg *8 lb 1 oz* on 30 Oct 1989.

UK The largest frog found in Britain is the *introduced* marsh frog (*Rana r. ridibunda*). Adult males have been measured up to 96 mm *3¾ in* from snout to vent, and adult females up to 133 mm *5¼ in*, with weights of 60–95 g *1·7–3 oz*.

The largest captive frog living in Britain today is a male African bull frog *Pyxicephalus adspersus* named 'Colossus' (b. 1978), owned by Steve Crabtree of Southsea, Hants. It has a snout-to-vent length of 22·2 cm *8¾ in*, a girth of 45·7 cm *18 in* and weighs 1·89 kg *4 lb 3 oz*.

Smallest frog The smallest frog in the world is *Sminthillus limbatus* of Cuba. (See Smallest amphibian.)

Longest jump (*Competition frog jumps are invariably the aggregate of three consecutive leaps.*)

The greatest distance covered by a frog in a triple jump is 10·3 m *33 ft 5½ in* by a South African sharp-nosed frog (*Ptychadena oxyrhynchus*) named 'Santjie' at a frog Derby held at Lurula Natal Spa, Paulpietersburg, Natal, South Africa on 21 May 1977. At the annual Calaveras Jumping Jubilee held at Angels Camp, California, USA on 18 May 1986 an American bull frog (*Rana catesbeiana*) called 'Rosie the Ribeter', owned and trained by Lee Giudicci of Santa Clara, California, USA, leapt 6·55 m *21 ft 5¾ in*. 'Santjie' would have been ineligible for this contest because entrants must measure at least 10·16 cm *4 in* 'stem to stern'.

Largest toad The largest known toad is the marine toad (*Bufo marinus*) of tropical South America and Queensland, Australia (introduced). An average adult specimen weighs 453 g *1 lb*. The largest ever recorded was a female nicknamed 'Totally Awesome' (Toad Λ), owned by Blank Park Zoo, Des Moines, Iowa, USA. She was purchased in Miami, Florida on 11 May 1983, when she weighed 0·9 kg *2 lb*, and attained a peak of 2·31 kg *5 lb 1½ oz* (snout-to-vent length 24·13 cm *9½ in*) on 19 Nov 1987. She died on 8 Apr 1988, most probably from old age.

UK The largest toad and heaviest amphibian found in Britain is the common toad (*Bufo bufo*). (See Largest amphibian.)

Smallest toad The smallest toad in the world is the sub-species *Bufo taitanus beiranus*, originally of Mozambique, the largest specimen of which was 24 mm *0·95 in* long.

Fishes Gnathostomata, Agnatha

Largest marine The largest fish in the world is the plankton-feeding whale shark (*Rhincodon typus*), which is found in the warmer areas of the Atlantic, Pacific and Indian Oceans. The longest scientifically measured example on record was a 12·65 m *41½ ft* specimen captured off Baba Island, near Karachi, Pakistan on 11 Nov 1949. It measured 7 m *23 ft* round the thickest part of the body and weighed an estimated 15 tonnes.

UK An 11·12 m *36 ft 6 in* basking shark (*Cetorhinus maximus*) was washed ashore at Brighton, E Sussex in 1806. It weighed an estimated 8 tonnes.

Carnivorous The largest carnivorous fish (excluding plankton-eaters) is the comparatively rare great white shark (*Carcharodon carcharias*), also called the 'man-eater'. Adult specimens (females are larger than males) average 4·3–4·6 m *14–15 ft* in length and generally weigh between 522–771 kg *1150–1700 lb*, but larger individuals have been recorded. The length and weight record is held by a 6·4 m *21 ft* female caught off Castillo de Cojimar, Cuba in May 1945. It weighed 3312 kg *7302 lb* and yielded a 455·8 kg *1005 lb* liver.

On 17 Apr 1987 a female great white shark with a 'linear' measurement of 7·13 m *23 ft 5 in* and an estimated weight of 3000 kg *6613 lb* was caught off Malta by Alfred Cutajar. Unfortunately the preserved jaws do not confirm this extreme measurement. A formula based on the size of the shark's teeth and the perimeter measurement of its upper jaw indicate a more acceptable measurement of 5·33–5·48 m *17½–18 ft*.

Bony The longest of the bony or 'true' fishes (Pisces) is the oarfish (*Regalecus glesne*), also called the 'King of the Herrings', which has a world-wide distribution. In *c.* 1885 a specimen 7·6 m *25 ft* long, weighing 272 kg *600 lb*, was caught by fishermen off Pemaquid Point, Maine, USA. Another oarfish, seen swimming off Asbury Park, New Jersey, USA by a team of scientists from the Sandy Hook Marine Laboratory on 18 Jul 1963, was estimated to measure 15·2 m *50 ft* in length. The heaviest bony fish in the world is the ocean sunfish (*Mola mola*), which is found in all tropical, sub-tropical and temperate waters. On 18 Sep 1908 a specimen was accidentally struck by the SS *Fiona* off Bird Island about 65 km *40 miles* from Sydney, New South Wales, Australia and towed to Port Jackson. It measured 4·26 m *14 ft* between the anal and dorsal fins and weighed 2235 kg *4927 lb*.

UK The largest bony fish found in British waters is the ocean sunfish. A specimen weighing 363 kg *800 lb* stranded near Montrose, Tayside on 14 Dec 1960 was sent to the Marine Research Institute in Aberdeen, Grampian.

Largest freshwater The largest fish which spends its whole life in fresh or brackish water is the rare pla beuk (*Pangasianodon gigas*). It is confined to the Mekong River and its major tributaries in China, Laos, Cambodia and Thailand. The largest specimen, captured in the River Ban Mee Noi, Thailand, was reportedly 3 m *9 ft 10¼ in* long and weighed 242 kg *533·5 lb*. This was exceeded by the European catfish or wels (*Silurus glanis*) in earlier times (in the 19th century lengths

FISHES

■ **Largest fish**
The harmless, plankton-feeding whale shark (Rhincodon typus), found in the warmer waters of the Atlantic, Pacific and Indian Oceans, often reaches 9 m 29 ½ ft in length. (Photo: Bruce Coleman)

up to 4·57 m *15 ft* and weights up to 336·3 kg *720 lb* were reported for Russian specimens), but today anything over 1·83 m *6 ft* and 91 kg *200 lb* is considered large.

The arapaima (*Arapaima glanis*), also called the pirarucu, found in the Amazon and other South American rivers and often claimed to be the largest freshwater fish, averages 2 m *6½ ft* and 68 kg *150 lb*. The largest authentically recorded measured 2·48 m *8 ft 1½ in* in length and weighed 147 kg *325 lb*. It was caught in the Rio Negro, Brazil in 1836.

In September 1978, a Nile perch (*Lates niloticus*) weighing 188·6 kg *416 lb* was netted in the eastern part of Lake Victoria, Kenya.

UK The largest fish ever caught in a British river was a common sturgeon (*Acipenser sturio*) weighing 230 kg *507½ lb* and measuring 2·74 m *9 ft*, which was accidentally netted in the Severn at Lydney, Glos on 1 Jun 1937. Larger specimens have been taken at sea — notably one weighing 317 kg *700 lb* and 3·18 m *10 ft 5 in* in length netted by the trawler *Ben Urie* off Orkney and landed on 18 Oct 1956.

Smallest marine The shortest recorded marine fish — and the shortest known vertebrate — is the dwarf goby *Trimmatom nanus* of the Chagos Archipelago, central Indian Ocean. In one series of 92 specimens collected by the 1978–79 Joint Services Chagos Research Expedition of the British Armed Forces the adult males averaged 8·6 mm *0·338 in* in length and the adult females 8·9 mm *0·35 in*.

The lightest of all vertebrates and the smallest catch possible for any fisherman is the dwarf goby *Schindleria praematurus* from Samoa, which measures 12–19 mm *0·47–0·74 in*. Mature specimens have been

known to weigh only 2 mg, which is equivalent to 14·175 to the ounce.

British Isles Guillet's goby (*Lebutus guilleti*) does not exceed 24 mm *0·94 in*. It has been recorded from the English Channel, the west coast of Ireland and the Irish Sea.

Shark The spined pygmy shark (*Squaliolus laticaudus*) of the western Pacific matures at 150 mm *5·9 in* in length.

Smallest freshwater The shortest and lightest freshwater fish is the dwarf pygmy goby *Pandaka pygmaea*, a colourless and nearly transparent species found in the streams and lakes of Luzon in the Philippines. Adult males measure only 7·5–9·9 mm *0·28–0·38 in* in length and weigh 4–5 mg *0·00014–0·00018 oz.*

The world's smallest commercial fish is the now endangered sinarapan (*Mistichthys luzonensis*), a goby found only in Lake Buhi, Luzon, Philippines. Adult males measure 10–13 mm *0·39–0·51 in* in length, and a dried 454 g *1 lb* fish cake contains about 70 000 of them!

Fastest The maximum swimming speed of a fish is dependent on the shape of its body and tail and its internal temperature. The cosmopolitan sailfish (*Istiophorus platypterus*) is considered to be the fastest species of fish over short distances, although the practical difficulties of measuring make data extremely difficult to secure. In a series of speed trials carried out at the Long Key Fishing Camp, Florida, USA, one sailfish took out 91 m *100 yd* of line in 3 sec, which is equivalent to a velocity of 109 km/h *68 mph* (cf. 96 km/h *60 mph* for the cheetah).

Some American fishermen believe that the bluefin tuna (*Thunnus thynnus*) is the

fastest fish in the sea, and bursts of speed up to 56 knots *104 km/h* have been claimed for this species, but the highest speed recorded so far is 70 km/h *43·4 mph* in a 20 sec dash. The yellowfin tuna (*Thunnus albacares*) and the wahoo (*Acanthocybium solandri*) are also extremely fast, having been timed at 74·59 km/h *46·35 mph* and 77·05 km/h *47·88 mph* respectively during 10–20 sec sprints.

Oldest Aquaria are of too recent origin to be able to establish with certainty which species of fish can be regarded as being the longest-lived. Early indications are, however, that it may be the lake sturgeon (*Acipenser fulvescens*) of North America. In one study of the growth rings (annuli) of 966 specimens caught in the Lake Winnebago region, Wisconsin, USA between 1951 and 1954 the oldest sturgeon was found to be a male (length 2·01 m *6 ft 7 in*), which gave a reading of 82 years and was still growing.

The perch-like marine fish *Notothenia neglecta* of the Antarctic Ocean, whose blood contains a natural anti-freeze, is reported to live up to 150 years, but this claim has not yet been verified.

In July 1974 a growth-ring count of 228 years was reported for a female koi fish (a form of fancy carp), named 'Hanako', living in a pond in Higashi Shirakawa, Gifu Prefecture, Japan, but the greatest authoritatively accepted age for this species is 'more than 50 years'.

In 1948 the death was reported of an 88-year-old female European eel (*Anguilla anguilla*) named 'Putte' in the aquarium at Hälsingborg Museum, southern Sweden. She was allegedly born in the Sargasso Sea, in the North Atlantic, in 1860, and was caught in a river as a 3-year-old elver.

Oldest goldfish Goldfish (*Carassius auratus*) have been reported to live for over 50 years in China.

UK A goldfish named 'Fred', owned by A.R. Wilson of Worthing, W Sussex, died on 1 Aug 1980 aged 41 years.

Shortest-lived The shortest-lived fishes are probably certain species of the sub-order Cyprinodontei (Killifish), found in Africa and South America, which normally live for about eight months.

Most abundant The most abundant species is probably the 76 mm *3 in* long deep-sea bristlemouth *Cyclothone elongata*, which has a world-wide distribution. It would take about 500 of them to weigh 0·45 kg *1 lb*.

Deepest The greatest depth from which a fish has been recovered is 8300 m *27 230 ft* in the Puerto Rico Trench (8366 m *27 488 ft*) in the Atlantic by Dr Gilbert L. Voss of the US research vessel *John Elliott*, who took a 16·5 cm *6½ in* long *Bassogigas profundissimus* in April 1970. It was only the fifth such brotulid ever caught.

Dr Jacques Piccard and Lt Don Walsh of the US Navy reported seeing a sole-like fish about 33 cm *1 ft* long (tentatively identified as *Chascanopsetta lugubris*) from the bathyscaphe *Trieste* at a depth of 35 820 ft *10 917 m* in the Challenger Deep (Marianas Trench) in the western Pacific on 24 Jan 1960. This sighting, however, has been questioned by some authorities, who still regard the brotulids of the genus *Bassogigas* as the deepest-living vertebrates.

Most eggs The ocean sunfish (*Mola mola*) produces up to 30 million eggs, each of them measuring about 1·3 mm *0·05 in* in diameter, at a single spawning.

Fewest eggs The mouth-brooding cichlid *Tropheus moorii*, found in Lake Tanganyika, east Africa, produces seven eggs or less during normal reproduction.

Most valuable The world's most valuable fish is the Russian sturgeon (*Huso huso*). One 1227 kg *2706 lb* female caught in the Tikhaya Sosna River in 1924 yielded 245 kg *541 lb* of best-quality caviar, which would be worth £189 350 on today's market.

The 76 cm *30 in* long ginrin showa koi, which won supreme championship in nationwide Japanese koi shows in 1976, 1977, 1979 and 1980, was sold two years later for 17 million yen. In March 1986 this ornamental carp was acquired by Derry Evans, owner of the Kent Koi Centre near Sevenoaks, Kent for an undisclosed sum, but the 15-year-old fish died five months later. It has since been stuffed and mounted to preserve its beauty.

Most venomous The most venomous fish in the world are the stonefish (Synanceidae) of the tropical waters of the Indo-Pacific, and in particular *Synanceja horrida*, which has the largest venom glands of any known fish. Direct contact with the spines of its fins, which contain a strong neurotoxic poison, often proves fatal.

Most ferocious The razor-toothed piranhas of the genera *Serrasalmus*, *Pygocentrus* and *Pygopristis* are the most ferocious freshwater fish in the world. They live in the sluggish waters of the large rivers of South America, and will attack any creature, regardless of size, if it is injured or making a commotion in the water. On 19 Sep 1981 more than 300 people were reportedly killed and eaten when an overloaded passenger-cargo boat capsized and sank as it was docking at the Brazilian port of Obidos. According to one official, only 178 of the estimated number of people aboard the boat survived.

Most electric The most powerful electric fish is the electric eel (*Electrophorus electricus*), found in the rivers of Brazil, Colombia, Venezuela and Peru. An average-sized specimen can discharge 400 v at 1 amp, but measurements up to 650 v have been recorded.

Starfishes Asteroidea

Largest The largest of the 1600 known species of starfish in terms of total arm span is the very fragile brisingid *Midgardia xandaros*. A specimen collected by the Texas A & M University research vessel *Alaminos* in the southern part of the Gulf of Mexico in the late summer of 1968 measured 1380 mm *54·33 in* tip to tip, but the diameter of its disc was only 26 mm *1·02 in*. Its dry weight was 70 g *2·46 oz*.

The heaviest species of starfish is the five-armed *Thromidia catalai* of the western Pacific. One specimen collected off Ilot Amédée, New Caledonia on 14 Sep 1969 and later deposited in Nouméa Aquarium weighed an estimated 6 kg *13·2 lb* (total arm span 630 mm *24·8 in*).

British Isles The largest starfish found in British waters is the spiny starfish (*Marthasterias glacialis*). In January 1979 Jonathon MacNeil from the Isle of Barra, Western Isles found a specimen on the beach which originally spanned 76·2 cm *30 in*.

Smallest The smallest known starfish is the asterinid sea star *Patiriella parvivipara* discovered by Wolfgang Zeidler on the west coast of the Eyre peninsula, South Australia in 1975. It has a maximum radius of only 4·7 mm *0·18 in* and a diameter of less than 9 mm *0·35 in*.

Most destructive The crown of thorns (*Acanthaster planci*) of the Indo-Pacific region and the Red Sea has 12–19 arms and can measure up to 60 cm *24 in* in diameter. It feeds on coral polyps and can destroy 300–400 cm² *46½–62 in²* of coral in one day.

Deepest The greatest depth from which a starfish has been recovered is 7584 m *24 881 ft* for a specimen of *Porcellanaster ivanovi* collected by the USSR research ship *Vityaz* in the Marianas Trench in the west Pacific *c.* 1962.

Crustaceans Crustacea

(*Crabs, lobsters, shrimps, prawns, crayfish, barnacles, water fleas, fish lice, woodlice, sandhoppers, krill, etc.*)

Largest marine The largest of all crustaceans (although not the heaviest) is the taka-ashi-gani or giant spider crab (*Macrocheira kaempferi*), also called the stilt crab, which is found in deep waters off the south-eastern coast of Japan. Mature specimens usually have a body measuring 254 × 305 mm *10 × 12 in* and a claw span of 2·43–2·74 m *8–9 ft*, but unconfirmed measurements up to 5·79 m *19 ft* have been reported. A specimen with a claw span of 3·69 m *12 ft 1½ in* weighed 18·6 kg *41 lb*.

The largest species of lobster, and the heaviest of all crustaceans, is the American or North Atlantic lobster (*Homarus americanus*). On 11 Feb 1977 a specimen weighing 20·14 kg *44 lb 6 oz* and measuring 1·06 m *3 ft 6 in* from the end of the tail-fan to the tip of the largest claw was caught off Nova Scotia, Canada and later sold to a New York restaurant owner.

Europe The largest crustacean found in British waters is the common or European lobster (*Homarus vulgaris*), which averages 900–1360 g *2–3 lb*. In June 1931 an outsized specimen weighing 5·80 kg *20½ lb* and measuring 1·26 m *4 ft 1½ in* in total length was caught in a caisson during the construction of No. 3 jetty at Fowey, Cornwall. Its crushing claw weighed 1188 g *2 lb 10 oz* after the meat had been removed. Another European lobster weighing a record 10 kg *22 lb* was caught off the west coast of Floroe, Norway by an amateur fisherman in March 1988, but died before it reached Bergen in October 1988.

The largest crab found in British waters is the edible or great crab (*Cancer pagurus*). In 1895 a specimen of this crab measuring 279 mm *11 in* across the shell and weighing 6·35 kg *14 lb* was caught off the coast of Cornwall.

Largest freshwater The largest freshwater crustacean is the crayfish, or crawfish, *Astacopsis gouldi*, found in the streams of Tasmania, Australia. It has been measured up to 61 cm *2 ft* in length and may weigh as much as 4·08 kg *9 lb*. In 1934 an unconfirmed weight of 6·35 kg *14 lb* (total length 73·6 cm *29 in*) was reported for an outsized specimen caught at Bridport.

Smallest Water fleas of the genus *Alonella* may measure less than 0·25 mm *0·0098 in* in length. They are found in British waters.

The smallest known lobster is the Cape lobster (*Homarus capensis*) of South Africa, which measures 10–12 cm *3·9–4·7 in* in total length.

The smallest crabs in the world are the aptly named pea crabs (family Pinnotheridae). Some species have a shell diameter of only 6·3 mm *0·25 in*, including *Pinnotheres pisum*, which is found in British waters.

Oldest Very large specimens of the American lobster (*Homarus americanus*) may be as much as 50 years old.

Deepest The greatest depth from which a crustacean has been recovered is 10 500 m *34 450 ft* for *live* amphipods from the Challenger Deep (Marianas Trench), western Pacific by the US research vessel *Thomas Washington* in November 1980. Amphipods and isopods have also been collected in the Ecuadorean Andes at a height of 4053 m *13 300 ft*.

Largest concentration The largest single concentration of crustaceans ever recorded was an enormous swarm of krill (*Euphausia superba*) estimated to weigh 10 million tonnes and tracked by US scientists off Antarctica in March 1981.

Arachnids Arachnida

SPIDERS (Araneae)

Largest The world's largest known spider is the goliath bird-eating spider (*Theraphosa leblondi*) of the coastal rain-forests of Surinam, Guyana (formerly British Guyana) and French Guiana; isolated specimens have also been reported from Venezuela and Brazil. In February 1985 Charles J. Seiderman of New York City, USA captured a huge female just north of Paramarido, Surinam. This spider had a maximum leg span of 266·7 mm

SPIX'S MACAW (*Cyanopsitta spixii*). Also known as the little blue macaw, the wild population of this 60 cm *2 ft* long parrot has declined to a solitary male driven to mate with an equally endangered blue-winged macaw (*Ara maracana*). Between 1977 and 1987 at least 23 birds were handled illegally by two traders, all taken from the last known population. Only 15 birds are held in legitimate zoological collections and, unless the main contributors to its plight can be persuaded to release their private collections to breeding programmes, this species is heading for certain extinction in the wild.

Brazil

Species on the Brink

A small selection of the world's rarest and most endangered flora and fauna compiled from information supplied by the World Conservation Monitoring Centre, Cambridge. Artwork by Matthew Hillier for Guinness Publishing.

BAIJI (or YANGTZE RIVER) DOLPHIN (*Lipotes vexillifer*). The Baiji, which can reach lengths of 2·5 m *8 ft*, is probably the most endangered of the cetaceans (whales, dolphins and porpoises). Its population is estimated at about 300 and falling due to competition for fish supplies with China's human population (dolphins are often caught up in fishing gear) and the reduction of overall food supplies because of environmental degradation. Its survival is a high priority of the Chinese government, which has implemented an information programme especially aimed at local fishermen, and a captive breeding project is also envisaged.

IRIOMOTE CAT (*Felis iriomotensis*). Confined to the small (292 km² *113 miles²*) Japanese-owned island from which it takes its name, this average domestic cat-sized feline is not only protected by law, it has also been declared a Japanese national monument. A nocturnal and strictly territorial animal, the Iriomote was only discovered in 1967, since when its population has fallen to about 80 because of agricultural development, tourism and indigenous hostility towards conservation, which is considered prejudicial to the island's economic development.

Iriomote, east of Taiwan

Lower Yangtze river, China

CHINESE ALLIGATOR (*Alligator sinesis*). This 1·5 m *5 ft* long reptile is protected by Chinese law and was thought to be close to extinction in the early 1980s, although a few hundred probably exist in the wild. The population has been severely affected by hunters, traders and the pollution of its diet of fish, snails and crustaceans as a result of the heavy use of pesticides. Although captive breeding programmes are proving successful, the alligators cannot be reintroduced into the wild because of the lack of suitable remaining habitat, and their extinction outside captivity is expected before the end of the century, if not sooner.

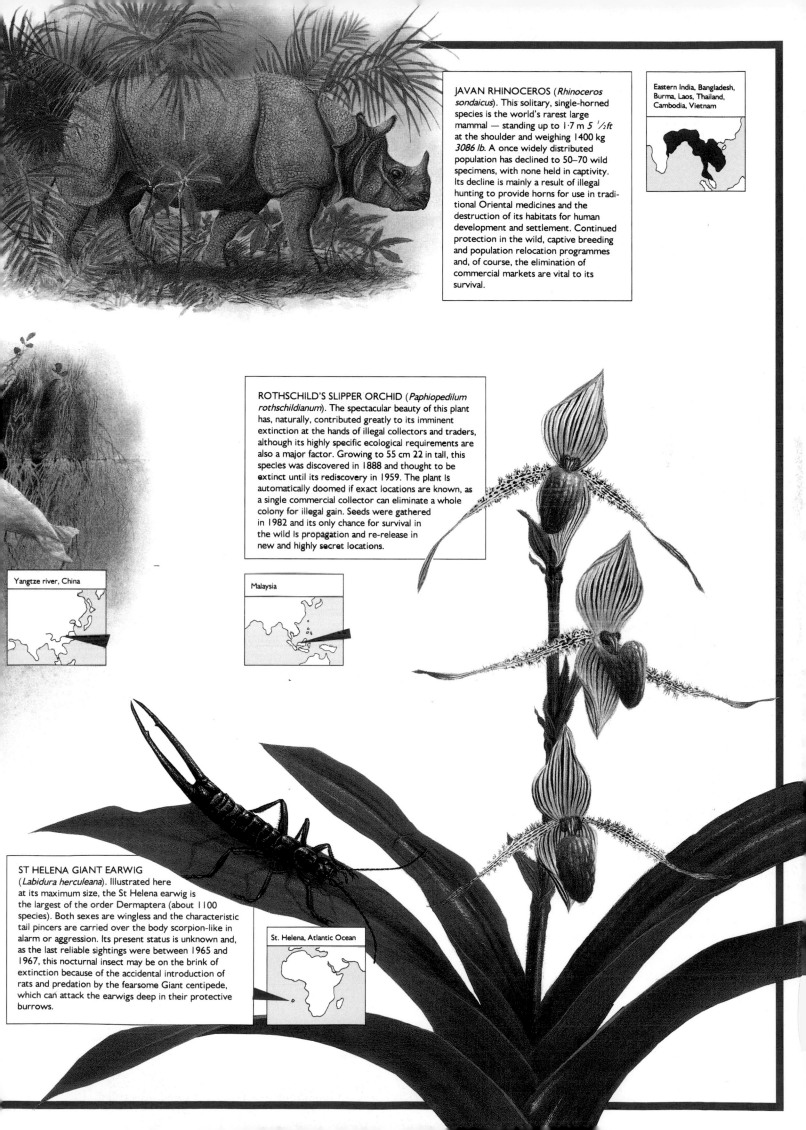

JAVAN RHINOCEROS (*Rhinoceros sondaicus*). This solitary, single-horned species is the world's rarest large mammal — standing up to 1·7 m *5 ½ft* at the shoulder and weighing 1400 kg *3086 lb*. A once widely distributed population has declined to 50–70 wild specimens, with none held in captivity. Its decline is mainly a result of illegal hunting to provide horns for use in traditional Oriental medicines and the destruction of its habitats for human development and settlement. Continued protection in the wild, captive breeding and population relocation programmes and, of course, the elimination of commercial markets are vital to its survival.

Eastern India, Bangladesh, Burma, Laos, Thailand, Cambodia, Vietnam

ROTHSCHILD'S SLIPPER ORCHID (*Paphiopedilum rothschildianum*). The spectacular beauty of this plant has, naturally, contributed greatly to its imminent extinction at the hands of illegal collectors and traders, although its highly specific ecological requirements are also a major factor. Growing to 55 cm 22 in tall, this species was discovered in 1888 and thought to be extinct until its rediscovery in 1959. The plant is automatically doomed if exact locations are known, as a single commercial collector can eliminate a whole colony for illegal gain. Seeds were gathered in 1982 and its only chance for survival in the wild is propagation and re-release in new and highly secret locations.

Yangtze river, China

Malaysia

ST HELENA GIANT EARWIG (*Labidura herculeana*). Illustrated here at its maximum size, the St Helena earwig is the largest of the order Dermaptera (about 1100 species). Both sexes are wingless and the characteristic tail pincers are carried over the body scorpion-like in alarm or aggression. Its present status is unknown and, as the last reliable sightings were between 1965 and 1967, this nocturnal insect may be on the brink of extinction because of the accidental introduction of rats and predation by the fearsome Giant centipede, which can attack the earwigs deep in their protective burrows.

St. Helena, Atlantic Ocean

■ **Strongest insect**
Rhinoceros beetles of the Dynastes and Oryctes genera of the Scarabaeidae family are the strongest animals in proportion to their size, with one specimen able to support 850 times its own bodyweight.

(Photo: Bruce Coleman)

10½ in (total body length 102 mm *4 in*) and fangs 25 mm *1 in* long. It weighed a peak 122·2 g *4·3 oz* before its death from moulting problems in January 1986.

An outsized male example collected by members of the Pablo San Martin Expedition at Rio Cavro, Venezuela in April 1965 had a leg span of 280 mm *11·02 in*; the female is built on much heavier lines.

UK Of the 617 known species of British spider covering an estimated population of over 500 billion, the cardinal spider (*Tegenaria gigantea*) of southern England has the greatest leg span. In October 1985 Lyndsay Jarrett of Marston Meysey, Wilts collected an outsized female in her home with a leg span of 139 mm *5½ in*.

The well-known 'Daddy Longlegs' spider (*Pholcus phalangioides*) rarely exceeds 114 mm *4½ in* in leg span, but one outsized specimen collected in England measured 15·2 cm *6 in* across.

The heaviest spider found in Britain is the orb weaver (*Araneus quadratus*). On 10 Sep 1979 a female weighing 2·25 g *0·079 oz* was collected at Lavington, W Sussex by J.R. Parker.

Smallest The smallest known spider is *Patu marplesi* (family Symphytognathidae) of Western Samoa in the Pacific. The type specimen (male) found in moss at *c.* 600 m *2000 ft* in Madolelei, Upolu, Western Samoa in Jan 1965 measured 0·43 mm *0·017 in* overall, which means that it was about the size of a full-stop on this page.

UK The extremely rare money spider *Glyphesis cottonae* is found only in a swamp near Beaulieu Road Station, Hants and on Thursley Common, Surrey. Adult specimens of both sexes have a body length of 1 mm *0·039 in*.

Most common The crab spiders (family Thomisidae) have a world-wide distribution.

British Isles The orb weaver *Araneus diadematus* has been recorded from all but four counties in Great Britain and the Republic of Ireland.

Rarest The most elusive of all spiders are the rare trapdoor spiders of the genus *Liphistius*, which are found in south-east Asia.

UK The most elusive spiders in Britain are the four species which are known only from the type specimen. These are the jumping spiders *Salticus mutabilis* (one male at Bloxworth, Dorset in 1860) and *Heliophanus melinus* (one female at Blox-

worth, 1870); the crab spider *Philodromus buxi* (one female at Bloxworth, pre-1879); and the cobweb spider *Robertus insignis* (one male at Norwich, Norfolk, 1906).

Oldest The longest-lived of all spiders are the primitive *Mygalomorphae* (tarantulas and allied species). One female therasophid collected in Mexico in 1935 lived for an estimated 26–28 years.

The longest-lived British spider is probably the Purse web spider (*Atypus affinis*). One specimen was kept in a greenhouse for nine years.

Fastest The fastest-moving arachnids are the long-legged sun spiders of the genus *Solpuga*, which live in the arid semi-desert regions of Africa and the Middle East. They feed on geckos and other lizards and can reach speeds of over 16 km/h *10 mph*.

Largest webs Aerial webs spun by the tropical orb weavers of the genus *Nephila* have been measured up to 573 cm *18 ft 9¾ in* in circumference.

Smallest webs The smallest webs are spun by spiders such as *Glyphesis cottonae* and cover about 48 cm² *0·75 in²*. (See Smallest spider.)

Most venomous The world's most venomous spiders are the Brazilian wandering spiders of the genus *Phoneutria*, and particularly *P. fera*, which has the most active neurotoxic venom of any living spider. These large and highly aggressive creatures frequently enter human dwellings and hide in clothing or shoes. When disturbed they bite furiously several times, and hundreds of accidents involving these species are reported annually. Fortunately an effective antivenin is available, and when deaths do occur they are usually of children under the age of seven.

SCORPIONS (Scorpiones) ━━━━━

Largest The largest of the 800 or so species of scorpion is the tropical emperor (*Pandinus imperator*) of Guinea, adult males of which can attain a body length of 18 cm *7 in* or more. Its black colouring is indicative of species found in moist or higher mountain habitats.

Smallest The smallest scorpion in the world is *Microbothus pusillus* from the Red Sea coast, which measures about 13 mm *0·5 in* in total length.

Most venomous The most venomous scorpion in the world is the Palestine yellow scorpion (*Leiurus quinquestriatus*), which ranges from the eastern part of North Africa through the Middle East to the shores of the Red Sea. Fortunately, the amount of venom it delivers is very small (0·255 mg *0·000009 oz*) and adult lives are seldom endangered, but it has been responsible for a number of fatalities among children under the age of five.

Insects Insecta

Earliest The most primitive known insect is an unidentified species of springtail (order Collembola), which dates from at least 300 million years ago. Widely distributed throughout the world, this wingless insect measures 1–10 mm *0·04–0·4 in* in length.

Heaviest The heaviest living insects are the Goliath beetles (family Scarabaeidae) of Equatorial Africa. The largest members of the group are *Goliathus regius*, *G. goliathus* (= *G. giganteus*) and *G. druryi*,

and in one series of fully-grown males (females are smaller) the lengths from the tips of the small frontal horns to the end of the abdomen measured up to 110 mm *4·33 in* and the weights ranged from 70 to 100 g *2·5–3·5 oz*. A single rhinoceros beetle of this family can support 850 times its own weight on its back. (See General records.)

The elephant beetles (*Megasoma*) of Central America and the West Indies attain the greatest dimensions in terms of volume, but they lack the massive build-up of heavy chiton forming the thorax and anterior sternum of the goliaths, and this gives them a distinct weight advantage.

UK The heaviest insect found in Britain is the stag beetle (*Lucanus cervus*), which is widely distributed over southern England. The largest specimen on record was a male collected at Sheerness, Kent in 1871 and now preserved in the British Museum (Natural History), which measures 87·4 mm *3·04 in* in length (body plus mandibles) and probably weighed over 6 g *0·21 oz* when alive.

Largest cockroach The world's largest cockroach is *Megaloblatta longipennis* of Colombia. A preserved female in the collection of Akira Yokokura of Yamagata, Japan measures 97 mm *3·81 in* in length and 45 mm *1·77 in* across.

Longest The longest insect in the world is the giant stick-insect (*Pharnacia serratipes*) of Indonesia, females of which have been measured up to 330 mm *13 in*.

The longest known beetle (excluding antennae) is the Hercules beetle (*Dynastes hercules*) of Central and South America, with lengths up to 190 mm *7·48 in*. More than half the length, however, is taken up by the prothoracic horn.

Smallest The smallest insects recorded to date are the 'feather-winged' beetles of the family Ptiliidae (= Trichopterygidae) and the battledore-wing fairy flies (parasitic wasps) of the family Mymaridae, which are smaller than some species of protozoa (single-celled animals).

The male bloodsucking banded louse (*Enderleinellus zonatus*) and the parasitic wasp *Caraphractus cinctus* may each weigh as little as 0·005 mg, or *5 670 000 to an oz*. Eggs of the latter each weigh 0·0002 mg, or *141 750 000 to an oz*.

Rarest It is estimated that there may be as many as 30 million species of insect — more than all other phyla and classes put together — but thousands are known only from a single or type specimen.

Fastest flying Experiments have proved that the widely publicized claim by an American scientist in 1926 that the deer bot-fly (*Cephenemyia pratti*) could attain a speed of 1316 km/h *818 mph* at an altitude of 3657 m *12 000 ft* was wildly exaggerated. If true, the fly would have had to develop the equivalent of 1·1 kW *1·5 hp* and consume 1½ times its own weight in food per second to acquire the energy that would be needed and, even if this were possible, it would still be crushed by the air pressure and incinerated by the friction. Acceptable modern experiments have now established that the highest maintainable airspeed of any insect, including the deer bot-fly, hawk moths (Sphingidae), horse flies (*Tabanus bovinus*) and some tropical butterflies (Hesperiidae) is 39 km/h *24 mph*, rising to a maximum of 58 km/h *36 mph* for the Australian dragonfly *Austrophlebia costalis* for short bursts.

Fastest moving The world's fastest insects are large tropical cockroaches of the family Dictyoptera. Specimens measuring about 30 mm *1·18 in* in length have been timed at 120–130 cm/sec *47–51 in/sec* (4·28–4·64 km/h *2·68–2·90 mph*), or 40–43 body lengths per second.

Highest g force The click beetle (*Athous haemorrhoidalis*) averages 400 *g* when 'jack-knifing' into the air to escape predators. One example measuring 12 mm *0·47 in* in length and weighing 40 mg *0·00014 oz* which jumped to a height of 30 cm *11¾ in* was calculated to have 'endured' a peak brain deceleration of 2300 *g* by the end of the movement.

Oldest The longest-lived insects are the splendour beetles (Buprestidae). On 27 May 1983 a *Buprestis aurulenta* appeared from the staircase timber in the home of W. Euston of Prittlewell, Southend-on-Sea, Essex after 47 years as a larva.

Loudest The loudest of all insects is the male cicada (family Cicadidae). At 7400 pulses/min its tymbal organs produce a noise (officially described by the US Department of Agriculture as 'Tsh-ee-EEEE-e-ou') detectable more than 400 m ¼ *mile* away. The only British species is the very rare mountain cicada (*Cicadetta montana*), which is confined to the New Forest area in Hampshire.

Fastest wing-beat The fastest wing-beat of any insect under natural conditions is 62 760/min by a tiny midge of the genus *Forcipomyia*. In experiments with truncated wings at a temperature of 37° C *98·6° F* the rate increased to 133 080/min. The muscular contraction–expansion cycle in 0·00045 or 1/2218th of a second also represents the fastest muscle movement ever measured.

Slowest wing-beat The slowest wing-beat of any insect is 300/min by the swallowtail butterfly (*Papilio machaon*). The average rate is 460–636 beats/min.

Largest termite mound In 1968 W. Page photographed a specimen south of Horgesia, Somalia estimated to be 8·7 m *28·5 ft* tall.

DRAGONFLIES (Odonata)

Largest *Megaloprepus caeruleata* of Central and South America has been measured up to 120 mm *4·72 in* across the wings and 191 mm *7·52 in* in body length.

UK The British species *Anax imperator* has a wing span of up to 106 mm *4·17 in*.

Smallest The smallest dragonfly in the world is *Agriocnemis naia* of Myanmar (formerly Burma). A specimen in the British Museum (Natural History) had a wing span of 17·6 mm *0·69 in* and a body length of 18 mm *0·71 in*.

UK The smallest British dragonfly is *Lestes dryas*, which has a body length of 20–25 mm *0·78–0·98 in*.

FLEAS (Siphonaptera)

Largest Siphonapterologists recognize 1830 varieties, of which the largest known is *Hystrichopsylla schefferi*, which was described from a single specimen taken from the nest of a mountain beaver (*Aplodontia rufa*) at Puyallup, Washington, USA in 1913. Females measure up to 8 mm *0·31 in* in length, which is the diameter of a pencil.

UK The largest of the 61 species found in Britain is the mole and vole flea (*Hystrichopsylla talpae*). Females have been measured up to 6 mm *0·23 in*.

Longest jump The champion jumper among fleas is the common flea (*Pulex irritans*). In one American experiment

carried out in 1910 a specimen allowed to leap at will performed a long jump of 330 mm *13 in* and a high jump of 197 mm *7¾ in*. In jumping 130 times its own height a flea subjects itself to a force of 200 *g*.

BUTTERFLIES AND MOTHS (Lepidoptera)

Largest The largest known butterfly is the protected Queen Alexandra's birdwing (*Ornithoptera alexandrae*) which is restricted to the Popondetta Plain in Papua New Guinea. Females may have a wing span exceeding 280 mm *11·02 in* and weigh over 25 g *0·88 oz*.

The largest moth in the world (although not the heaviest) is the Hercules moth (*Cosdinoscera hercules*) of tropical Australia and Papua New Guinea. A wing area of up to 263·2 cm² *40·8 in²* and a wing span of 280 mm *11 in* have been recorded. In 1948 an unconfirmed measurement of 360 mm *14·17 in* was reported for a female captured at Innisfail, Queensland, Australia and now in the Oberthur collection.

The rare owlet moth (*Thysania agrippina*) of Brazil has been measured up to 308 mm *12·16 in* wing span in the case of a female taken in 1934 and now in the collection of John G. Powers in Ontario, Canada.

UK The largest (but not the heaviest) of the 21 000 species of insect found in Britain is the very rare death's head hawkmoth (*Acherontia atropos*). One female found dead in a garden at Tiverton, Devon in 1931 had a wing span of 145 mm *5¾ in* and weighed nearly 3 g *0·10 oz*.

On 9 Jun 1988 a giant moth with a wing span of 15·2 cm *6 in* was found by workmen at a plant hire firm in Wolleston, Northants. It was later identified as a great peacock silk moth (*Saturnia pyri*) which had probably escaped from a butterfly house.

The largest butterfly found in Britain is the monarch butterfly (*Danaus plexippus*), also called the milkweed or black-veined brown butterfly, a rare vagrant which breeds in the southern United States and Central America. It has a wing span of up to 127 mm *5 in* and weighs about 1 g *0·04 oz*.

Britain's largest native butterfly is the swallowtail (*Papilio machaon britannicus*), females of which have a wing span up to 100 mm *3·93 in*. This species is now confined to the Norfolk Broads.

Smallest The smallest of the 140 000 known species of Lepidoptera is *Stigmella ridiculosa*, which has a wing span of 2 mm *0·079 in* with a similar body length and is found in the Canary Islands.

UK The moth *Johansonnia acetosae* has a wing span of 3 mm *0·19 in* and a corresponding body length.

Rarest The world's rarest butterfly is considered to be Queen Alexandra's birdwing (*Ornithoptera alexandrae*), which is found with its only source of nutrition, the vine *Aristolochia dielsiana*, in Papua New Guinea. Its population is extremely difficult to estimate as it flies very high and is seldom seen. The caterpillars are also somewhat elusive 40 m *131 ft* above the ground in the vine leaves. However, only three individuals were sighted in 1990 during surveys of an area covering 90–130 ha *222·4–321·2 acres*. (See also Largest butterfly.) Although another birdwing *Ornithoptera* (= *Troides*) *allottei* of Bougainville, Solomon Islands is known from less than a dozen specimens, this is not a true species, but a natural hybrid of

Ornithoptera victoriae and *O. urvillianus*. A male from the collection of C. Rousseau Decelle was auctioned for £750 in Paris on 24 Oct 1966.

UK Britain's rarest resident butterfly (59 species) is the large copper (*Lycaena dispar*) which became extinct in 1851 but was re-introduced in 1927 at Wood Walton Fen, Cambs, where it still survives. Already rarer than the large blue, its population is steadily declining due to drying out of the fen and it is in danger of becoming extinct again in the near future.

Although the chequered skipper (*Carterocephalus palaemon*) became extinct from England in 1975, it is relatively common in parts of Scotland.

The large blue (*Maculinea arion*) was officially declared extinct in 1979, but eggs were brought over from the island of Oland, Sweden in 1984 and hatched successfully on a site in the West Country. In 1986 another 220 eggs were obtained from Sweden, and the caterpillars distributed. At least 75 butterflies emerged and flew the following summer, and it is estimated that 4500 eggs were laid by the butterflies in 1987. The next summer 150 adult blues were recorded. They have now been introduced to half a dozen other suitable sites.

Most acute sense of smell The most acute sense of smell exhibited in nature is that of the male emperor moth (*Eudia pavonia*), which, according to German experiments in 1961, can detect the sex attractant of the virgin female at the almost unbelievable range of 11 km *6·8 miles* upwind. This scent has been identified as one of the higher alcohols ($C_{16}H_{29}OH$), of which the female carries less than 0·0001 mg.

Largest butterfly farm The Stratford-upon-Avon Butterfly Farm, Warks can accommodate 2000 exotic butterflies in authentic rain forest conditions. The total capacity of all flight areas at the farm, which opened on 15 Jul 1985, is over 4000 m³ *141 259 ft³*. The complex also comprises insect and plant houses and educational facilities.

Centipedes Chilopoda

Longest The longest known species of centipede is a large variant of the widely distributed *Scolopendra morsitans*, found on the Andaman Islands in the Bay of Bengal. Specimens up to 330 mm *13 in* in length and 38 mm *1·5 in* in width have been measured.

UK Specimens of the native British species *Henia vesuviana* exceed 70 mm *2¾ in* in length and individuals found in north-east London in 1989 by Dr Steve Hopkin of the University of Reading, Berks measured 80 mm *3[af2]3-5[af] in*.

Shortest The shortest recorded centipede is an unidentified species which measures only 5 mm *0·19 in*.

UK The British species *Lithobius dubosequi* measures up to 9·5 mm *0·374 in* in length.

Most legs *Himantarum gabrielis*, found in southern Europe, has 171–177 pairs of legs when adult.

Fastest The fastest centipede is probably *Scrutigera coleoptrata* of southern Europe, which can travel at 1·8 km/h *1·1 mph*.

Millipedes Diplopoda

Longest Both *Graphidostreptus gigas* of Africa and *Scaphistostreptus seychellarum* of the Seychelles in the Indian Ocean have been measured up to 280 mm *11·02 in* in length and 20 mm *0·78 in* in diameter.

UK The British species *Cylindroiulus londinensis* measures up to 50 mm *1·96 in.*

Shortest The shortest millipede in the world is the British species *Polyxenus lagurus*, which measures 2·1–4·0 mm *0·082–0·15 in.*

Most legs The greatest number of legs reported for a millipede is 375 pairs (750 legs) for *Illacme plenipes* of California, USA.

Segmented Worms

Annelida

Longest The longest known species of earthworm is *Microchaetus rappi* (= *M. microchaetus*) of South Africa. In *c.* 1937 a giant specimen measuring 6·7 m *22 ft* in length when naturally extended and 20 mm *0·78 in* in diameter was collected in the Transvaal.

UK The longest segmented worm found in Britain is the king rag worm (*Nereis virens*). On 19 Oct 1975 a specimen measuring 111·7 cm *44 in* when fully extended was collected by James Sawyer in Hauxley Bay, Northumberland.

The longest earthworm found in Britain is *Lumbricus terrestris*. The normal range is 90–300 mm *3·54–11·81 in*, but this species has been reliably measured up to 350 mm *13·78 in* when naturally extended. Measurements up to 508 mm *20 in* have been claimed, but in each case the body was probably macerated first. On 2 Feb 1988 an 'earthworm' reported to measure 1·83 m *6 ft* in length was found on an allotment in Stratton St Margaret, Swindon, Wilts. The specimen was later sent to the British Museum (Natural History) for identification, where it was found to be the intestine of a hedgehog. In May 1988 a man living in Herne Bay, Kent found a *live* 1·98 m *6 ft 6 in* long earthworm in his garden after a heavy rainstorm and took it to Bramble Wildlife Park near Canterbury for examination. Unfortunately, the earthworm fragmented soon afterwards and the parts were discarded before experts could make a positive identification.

Shortest The species *Chaetogaster annandalei* measures less than 0·5 mm *0·019 in* in length.

Molluscs Mollusca

(*Squids, octopuses, shellfish, snails, etc.*)

Largest invertebrate The Atlantic giant squid (*Architeuthis dux*) is the world's largest known invertebrate. The heaviest ever recorded was a 2 tonne monster which ran aground in Thimble Tickle Bay, Newfoundland, Canada on 2 Nov 1878. There are numerous types of squid, ranging in size from 1·5 cm *0·75 in* to the longest ever recorded — a 17·37 m *57 ft* giant *Architeuthis longimanus* which was washed up on Lyall Bay, Cook Strait, New Zealand in

October 1887. Its two long slender tentacles each measured 15·01 m *49 ft 3 in.*

British Isles The largest squid ever recorded in British waters was an *Architeuthis monachus* found at the head of Whalefirth Voe, Shetland on 2 Oct 1959 which measured 7·31 m *24 ft* in total length.

Largest octopus The largest known octopus is the Pacific giant (*Octopus dofleini*), which ranges from California to Alaska, USA and off eastern Asia south to Japan. It is not known exactly how large these creatures can grow but the average mature male weighs about 23 kg *51 lb* and has an arm span of about 2·5 m *8 ft.* The largest recorded specimen, found off western Canada in 1957, had an estimated arm span of 9·6 m *31½ ft* and weighed about 272 kg *600 lb.*

One huge specimen of *Octopus apollyon* caught single-handedly by skin-diver Donald E. Hagen in Lower Hoods Canal, Puget Sound, Washington, USA on 18 Feb 1973 had a relaxed radial spread of 7·01 m *23 ft* and weighed 53·8 kg *118 lb 10 oz.*

British Isles The largest octopus found in British waters is the common octopus (*Octopus vulgaris*), which can span 2·13 m *7 ft* and weigh more than 4·5 kg *10 lb.*

Largest eye The Atlantic giant squid has the largest eye of any animal, living or extinct. It has been estimated that the one recorded at Thimble Tickle Bay had eyes 400 mm *15¾ in* in diameter — almost the width of this open book!

Oldest mollusc The longest-lived mollusc is the ocean quahog (*Arctica islandica*), a thick-shelled clam found in the mid-Atlantic. A specimen with 220 annual growth rings was collected in 1982.

SHELLS

Largest The largest of all existing bivalve shells is that of the marine giant clam *Tridacna gigas*, found on the Indo-Pacific coral reefs. An outsized specimen measuring 115 cm *45·2 in* in length and weighing 333 kg *734 lb* was collected off Ishigaki Island, Okinawa, Japan in 1956, but was not scientifically examined until August 1984. It probably weighed just over 340 kg *750 lb* when alive (the soft parts weigh up to 9·1 kg *20 lb*). Another giant clam collected at Tapanoeli (Tapanula) on the north-west coast of Sumatra before 1817 and now preserved at Arno's Vale measures 137 cm *54 in* in length and weighs 230 kg *507 lb.*

British Isles The largest bivalve shell found in British waters is the fan mussel (*Pinna fragilis*). One specimen found at Tor Bay, Devon measured 37 cm *14·56 in* in length and 20 cm *7·87 in* in breadth at the hind end.

Smallest The smallest known shell-bearing species is the gastropod *Ammonicera rota*, which is found in British waters. It measures 0·5 mm *0·02 in* in diameter.

The smallest bivalve shell is the coinshell *Neolepton sykesi*, which is known only from a few examples collected off Guernsey, Channel Islands and western Ireland. It has an average diameter of 1·2 mm *0·047 in.*

Most venomous There are *c.* 400–500 species of cone shell (*Conus*), all of which can deliver a poisonous neurotoxin. The geographer (*Conus geographus*) and the court cone (*C. aulicus*), marine molluscs found from Polynesia to East Africa, are considered to be the most deadly. The venom is injected by a unique, fleshy harpoon-like proboscis and symptoms

include impaired vision, dizziness, nausea, paralysis and death. Of the twenty five people known to have been stung by these creatures, five have died, giving a mortality rate exceeding that for common cobras and rattlesnakes.

Most expensive The value of a sea-shell does not necessarily depend on its rarity or its prevalence. Some rare shells are inexpensive because there is no demand for them, while certain common shells fetch high prices because they are not readily accessible. In theory the most valuable shells in the world should be some of the unique examples collected in deep-sea trawls, but these shells are always dull and unattractive and hold very little interest for the collector. The most sought-after shell at present is probably *Cypraea fultoni*. In 1987 two live specimens were taken by a Russian trawler off Mozambique in the Indian Ocean. The larger of the two was later sold in New York to collector Dr Massilia Raybaudi of Italy for $24 000. The other was put up for sale at $17 000. A third specimen went for $6600 in June 1987 to a collector in Carmel, California, USA, who also purchased a *C. teramachii* for $6500. Another *C. fultoni* in the American Museum of Natural History, New York City, USA has been valued at $14 000.

GASTROPODS

Fastest The fastest-moving species of land snail is probably the common garden snail (*Helix aspersa*). It is probable, however, that the carnivorous (and cannibalistic) snail *Euglandina rosea* could out-pace other snails in its hunt for prey. The snail-racing equivalent of a 4-minute mile is 61 cm *24 in* in 3 min, or a 5½ day mile.

On 20 Feb 1990 a garden snail named 'Verne' completed a 31 cm *12·2 in* course at West Middle School in Plymouth, Michigan, USA in a record 2 min 13 sec at 0·233 cm/sec. The British record was set on 17 Jul 1988 when a garden snail named 'Tracker' completed a 33 cm *13 in* course at Cougham, Norfolk in 2 min 31 sec (0·219 cm/sec). The snail won a silver tankard stuffed with lettuce leaves. On 9 Jul 1988 another garden snail called 'Hercules' dragged a 241 g *8·5 oz* stone for 47 cm *18½ in* across a table in 10 min in the Basque town of Val de Trapagua, Spain.

Largest The largest known gastropod is the trumpet or baler conch (*Syrinx aruanus*) of Australia. One outsized specimen collected off Western Australia in 1979 and now owned by Don Pisor (who bought it from a fisherman in Kaohsiung, Taiwan in November 1979) of San Diego, California measures 77·2 cm *30·39 in* in length and has a maximum girth of 101 cm *39·76 in.* It weighed nearly 18·14 kg *40 lb* when alive.

The largest known land gastropod is the African giant snail (*Achatina* sp.). A specimen named 'Gee Geronimo' owned by Christopher Hudson (1955–79) of Hove, E Sussex, measured 39·3 cm *15½ in* from snout to tail when fully extended (shell length 27·3 cm *10¾ in*) in December 1978 and weighed exactly 900 g *2 lb.* The snail was collected in Sierra Leone in June 1976.

UK The largest land snail found in Britain is the Roman or edible snail (*Helix pomatia*), which measures up to 10 cm *4 in* in overall length and weighs up to 85 g *3 oz.*

Ribbon Worms
Nemertina

Longest The longest of the 550 recorded

species of ribbon worm, also called nemertines (or nemerteans), is the boot-lace worm (*Lineus longissimus*), which is found in the shallow waters of the North Sea. A specimen washed ashore at St Andrews, Fife in 1864 after a severe storm measured more than 55 m *180 ft* in length.

Immolation Some ribbon worms absorb themselves when food is scarce. One specimen under observation digested 95 per cent of its own body in a few months without apparently suffering any ill-effects. As soon as food became available the lost tissue was restored.

Jellyfishes and Corals
Cnidaria

Largest jellyfish The largest jellyfish is the Arctic giant (*Cyanea capillata arctica*) of the north-western Atlantic. One washed up in Massachusetts Bay, USA had a bell diameter of 2·28 m *7 ft 6 in* and tentacles stretching 36·5 m *120 ft*.

British Isles The largest cnidarian found in British waters is the rare lion's mane jellyfish (*Cyanea capillata*), also known as the common sea blubber. One specimen measured at St Andrew's Marine Laboratory, Fife had a bell diameter of 91 cm *35·8 in* and tentacles stretching over 13·7 m *45 ft*.

Most venomous The beautiful but deadly Australian sea wasp (*Chironex fleckeri*) is the most venomous cnidarian in the world. Its cardiotoxic venom has caused the deaths of 66 people off the coast of Queensland, Australia since 1880, with victims dying within 1–3 min if medical aid is not available. One effective defence is women's hosiery, outsize versions of which are now worn by Queensland lifesavers at surfing tournaments.

Coral The world's greatest stony coral structure is the Great Barrier Reef off Queensland, north-east Australia. It stretches for 2027 km *1260 miles* and covers an area of 207 000 km² *80 000 miles²*.

The world's largest known example of discrete coral is a stony colony of *Galaxea fascicularis* found in Sakiyama Bay off Iriomote Island, Japan on 7 Aug 1982 by Dr Shohei Shirai of the Institute for Development of Pacific Natural Resources. It has a long-axis measurement of 7·8 m *23 ft 9 in*, a height of 4 m *13 ft 1½ in* and a maximum circumference of 19·5 m *59 ft 5 in*.

Sponges Porifera

Largest The largest known sponge is the barrel-shaped loggerhead sponge (*Spheciospongia vesparium*) of the West Indies and the waters off Florida, USA. Individuals measure up to 105 cm *3 ft 6 in* in height and 91 cm *3 ft* in diameter. Neptune's cup or goblet (*Poterion patera*) of Indonesia grows to 120 cm *4 ft* in height, but it is a less bulky creature.

In 1909 a wool sponge *Hippospongia canaliculatta* measuring 183 cm *6 ft* in circumference was collected off the Bahamas. When first taken from the water it weighed 36–41 kg *80–90 lb* but this fell to 5·44 kg *12 lb* after it had been dried and relieved of all excrescences. It is now preserved in the US National Museum, Washington, DC, USA.

Smallest The widely distributed *Leucosolenia blanca* measures 3 mm *0·11 in* in height when fully grown.

Deepest Sponges have been recovered from depths of up to 5637 m *18 500 ft*.

Extinct Animals

The first dinosaur to be scientifically described was *Megalosaurus bucklandi* ('great fossil lizard') in 1824. The remains

of this bipedal flesh-eater were found by workmen before 1818 in a slate quarry near Woodstock, Oxfordshire and later placed in the University Museum, Oxford. The first fossil bone of *Megalosaurus* was actually illustrated in 1677, but its true nature was not realized until much later. It was not until 1841 that the name Dinosauria ('terrible lizards') was given to these newly-discovered giants.

Disappearance No wholly satisfactory theory has been offered for the dinosaurs' sudden extinction 65 million years ago. Evidence from the Hell Creek Formation of Montana, USA suggests that dinosaurs

■ Largest sponge
The barrel-shaped loggerhead sponge (Spheciospongia vesparia) of the Caribbean can reach 1·05 m 3 ½ft in height and 91 cm 3 ft in diameter.
(Photo: Bruce Coleman)

Most brainless
Stegosaurus ('plated lizard'), which roamed across Colorado, Oklahoma, Utah and Wyoming, USA about 150 million years ago, measured up to 9 m *30 ft* in total length but had a walnut-sized brain weighing only 70 g *2½ oz*. This represented 0·004 of 1 per cent of its computed bodyweight of 1·75 tonnes (cf. 0·074 of 1 per cent for an elephant and 1·88 per cent for a human).

dwindled in importance over a period of 5–10 million years and were replaced progressively by mammals. The gradual decline is linked to long-term changes in climates, which became cooler and more seasonal, and in the plants, which changed from lush tropical forms to temperate-zone conifers. The other view which has attracted a great deal of attention is that the dinosaurs, together with many other land and sea groups, were eliminated suddenly and catastrophically by the impact of a giant asteroid, or possibly a shower of comets, on the Earth. The impact(s) supposedly produced a vast cloud of dust which encircled the Earth, blocking out the Sun. This caused icy conditions in the northern hemisphere at least, and a cessation of photosynthesis. Plants, and consequently the animals that fed on them, died off. The evidence for this impact theory now seems very strong — the element iridium, a good indicator of extraterrestrial impact, has been found at over 100 locations world-wide at significant levels. However, a clear link between the physical results of a major impact and the selective extinctions which took place 65 million years ago has not yet been established.

Earliest known The earliest dinosaur is believed to be the *Herrerasaurus*, which is now known from an almost complete skeleton discovered in 1989 in the foothills of the Andes in Argentina by an expedition led by Paul Sereno of the University of Chicago, Illinois, USA. This specimen is thought to date from 230 million years ago and is named after Victorino Herrera, a fossil hunter who discovered fragments of bone years earlier. *Herrerasaurus* was a carnivore which stood about 2–2·5 m *6 ½–8 ft*, and weighed over 100 kg *220 lb*, and its importance in the evolutionary process is suggested by its dual-hinged jaw, a feature which did not appear in other dinosaurs for another 50 million years. Other dinosaurs of a similar age from the Late Triassic are known from incomplete remains found in Brazil, Argentina, Morocco, India and Scotland.

Largest The largest ever land animals were the sauropod dinosaurs, a group of long-necked, long-tailed, four-legged plant-eaters that lumbered around most of the world during the Jurassic and Cretaceous periods 208–65 million years ago. However, it is difficult to determine precisely which of these sauropod dinosaurs was the largest (longest, tallest or heaviest). This is because many of the supposed giants are based only on incomplete fossil remains, and also because many discoverers have tended to exaggerate the sizes of their dinosaur finds. Estimating dinosaur lengths and heights is relatively straightforward when there is a complete skeleton. However, weights are an entirely different matter, and several investigators have simply made estimates by scaling up large modern animals, such as elephants, to dinosaur size.

A more scientific approach has been to make detailed scale models of particular species of dinosaur from clay or plastic. Their volume is estimated by precise measurements of the amount of water they displace from a jar of fixed capacity. The weight can then be calculated by multiplying the volume by the assumed density of a dinosaur. Although the method is simple, results obtained by different scientists studying the same species of dinosaur can vary dramatically. For example, estimates of the bodyweight of *Brachiosaurus* range from 31·5 to 78·3 tonnes. Errors arise firstly because of

differences in the assumed corpulence of the animals in the models, and because of differences in the estimates of dinosaur density. Some scientists regard dinosaurs as having been bulky, slow-moving animals, while others see them as slender and fleet-footed. This can lead to a great range of constructions. Estimates of density used by different investigators range from 800 to 1000 kg/m³ (i.e. specific gravities of 0·8–1·0), and these also greatly affect the final weight estimates. Palaeontologists now tend to accept the lower estimates of weight.

The sauropods are divided into five main groups: cetiosaurids; brachiosaurids; diplodocids; camarasaurids; and titanosaurids. The world's biggest dinosaur has been identified at different times as a brachiosaurid, a diplodocid or a titanosaurid.

Brachiosaurids The largest (and tallest) dinosaur species for which the whole skeleton is known was *Brachiosaurus brancai* ('arm lizard') from the famous Tendaguru site in Tanzania, dated as Late Jurassic (150 million years ago). The site was excavated by German expeditions during the period 1909–11, and the bones shipped to the Humboldt Museum für Naturkunde in Berlin, Germany for preparation and assembly. A complete skeleton was constructed from the remains of several individuals and was put on display in 1937. It is the world's largest, and tallest, mounted dinosaur skeleton, measuring 22·2 m *72 ft 9½ in* in overall length (height at shoulder 6 m *19 ft 8 in*) and has a raised head height of 14 m *46 ft*. The dinosaur weighed 15–78 tonnes, depending on which estimates one chooses to believe. A weight of 30–40 tonnes seems most likely, but this could have increased by up to 33 per cent when the animal had laid down maximum amounts of body fat.

The isolated fibula of another *Brachiosaurus* in the same museum is 13 per cent larger than its equivalent in the mounted skeleton and it has been calculated that the bone must have come from a sauropod measuring 25 m *82 ft* in total length (shoulder height 6·79 m *22 ft 3½ in*), which had an estimated height of 16 m *52½ ft* to the top of its raised head and weighed 45 tonnes.

Brachiosaurus altithorax from the Late Jurassic of western Colorado, USA was similar in size to its African cousin, and weight estimates based on different specimens range from 35 to 55 tonnes.

An even larger brachiosaurid was announced from the Uncompahgre Plateau of western Colorado, USA and named *Ultrasaurus macintoshi* ('extreme lizard') in 1986. Estimates of its body length ranged up to 35 m *115 ft*, and of its weight up to 190 tonnes. However, more detailed study of the incomplete skeleton shows that *Ultrasaurus* is just a large specimen of *Brachiosaurus altithorax*, measuring about 25 m *82 ft* long and weighing 45–55 tonnes.

Fossilized footprints made by sauropod dinosaurs can also give estimates of size for animals that are not known from skeletons. Footprints called *Breviparopus taghbaloutensis* from Morocco are over 1 m *3 ft 3 in* long and may have been made by an animal weighing 50 tonnes. A similar bodyweight is estimated for trackways made by the brachiosaurid *Pleurocoelus* in Texas, USA.

Diplodocids The longest dinosaur known from a complete skeleton is *Diplodocus carnegii* ('double beam'). The remains were found in Wyoming, USA in 1899 and pieced together at the Carnegie

Museum, Pittsburgh, Pennsylvania. The skeleton was so spectacular that casts were requested by other museums, and copies may be seen in London, La Plata, Washington, Frankfurt and Paris. *Diplodocus* was 26·6 m *87½ ft* long and weighed 5·8–18·5 tonnes, the higher estimates being the most likely. Hence, *Diplodocus* was relatively light for its body length, but much of that length was made up by an extremely long whip-like tail.

An even longer diplodocid has been named *Supersaurus vivianae* ('super lizard') in 1986. It was found in the same area of Colorado as *Ultrasaurus*. The length has been estimated as up to 42 m *138 ft* and the weight as about 50 tonnes, but the skeleton is very incomplete.

In 1985 the remains of another huge diplodocid were excavated from a site near Albuquerque, New Mexico, USA. According to Dr David Gillette at the Division of State History, Utah, this giant sauropod, informally named *Seismosaurus* ('earthquake lizard'), measured an estimated 39–47 m *128–154 ft* in total length and weighed at least 50 tonnes. These estimates were given by Gillette in 1989, based on the assumption that *Seismosaurus* was 50–80 per cent longer than *Diplodocus*, based on comparisons of individual bones.

Titanosaurids Several titanosaurids ('giant lizards') have also been described as super-sized, and *Antarctosaurus giganteus* ('Antarctic lizard') from Argentina and India probably rivalled the brachiosaurids in terms of weight. Estimates range from 40–80 tonnes, with the lower figures being most likely. The skeletons of titanosaurs are generally very incomplete, but there are several thigh bones from Argentina that measure 2·3–2·4 m *7½–7¾ ft* in length.

Size limits The largest known sauropods appear to have weighed around 50–100 tonnes, but this does not necessarily represent the ultimate weight limit for a land vertebrate. Theoretical calculations suggest that some dinosaurs approached the maximum body weight possible for a terrestrial animal, namely 120 tonnes. At weights greater than this, the legs would have to be so massive to support the bulk that the dinosaur could not have moved!

UK Britain's largest known dinosaur was the diplodocid *Cetiosaurus oxoniensis* ('whale lizard'), from the upper beds of the Great Oolite at Enslow Bridge, near Oxford. Until recently this sauropod, which roamed across southern England about 170 million years ago, was credited with lengths up to 21 m *69 ft* overall and a maximum weight of 27 tonnes but in the summer of 1981 the proximal end of a *Cetiosaurus* femur over one-third larger than any others previously found was dug up by workmen in the village of Clifton Regnes, Olney, Bucks. The bone is now in the possession of the Hansford family of Ballater, Grampian and, judging by its size, this sauropod must have measured an estimated 25·6 m *84 ft* in length and weighed c. 45 tonnes.

This mass may have been nearly matched by the brachiosaur *Pelorosaurus* ('monstrous lizard') which, on the evidence of a haemal arch (the bone running beneath the vertebrae of the tail) found on the Isle of Wight, may have reached 24 m *80 ft*.

Longest Until very recently the longest dinosaurs on record were believed to be certain attenuated diplodocids. A complete reconstruction of a *Diplodocus carnegii* in the Carnegie Museum of Natural History,

Pittsburgh, Pennsylvania, USA measures 26·6 m *87 ft 6 in* in total length — head and body 6·7 m *22 ft*, body 4·5 m *15 ft*, tail 15·4 m *50 ft 6 in* — and has a mounted height of 3·58 m *11 ft 9 in* at the pelvis, the highest point of the body. But, relatively speaking, this giant was a lightweight, weighing an estimated 5·8–18·5 tonnes.

By comparison, *Supersaurus vivianae* (see Diplodocids) measured an estimated 42 m *138 ft* in total length, while *Breviparopus* (see Brachiosaurids) attained the astonishing length of 48 m *157 ft* — making it the longest vertebrate on record. Note, however, that this estimate is based on footprints only.

UK Britain's longest known dinosaurs were *Cetiosaurus oxoniensis* and *Pelorosaurus* (see Titanosaurids).

Largest land predator

The largest flesh-eating dinosaur recorded so far is *Tyrannosaurus rex* ('king tyrant lizard'). Seventy million years ago it reigned over what are now the states of Montana, Wyoming and Texas, USA and the provinces of Alberta and Saskatchewan, Canada. A composite skeleton of this nightmarish beast in the American Museum of Natural History, New York, USA has a bipedal height of 5·6 m *18 ft 6 in* (total length 10·6 m *34 ft 9 in*), and this animal is estaimated to have weighed 5·7 tonnes, or close to 7 tonnes with large fat reserves. This individual may not, however, have been fully mature, as suggested by the upper jaw-bone (maxilla) of another *Tyrannosaurus* in the Museum of Paleontology at the University of California, Berkeley which is 29 per cent longer (90 cm *35·4 in*) than the example in the American Museum of Natural History and indicates a 14 m *44 ft* theropod weighing up to 12 tonnes.

Its Mongolian relative *Tarbosaurus bataar* ('alarming lizard'), known from 13 skeletons, had a longer skull than *Tyrannosaurus* but was less heavily built. It measured 10–14 m *33–46 ft* in total length. *Dynamosaurus imperiosus* ('dynamic lizard') of Shandung province, China was also similar in size, measuring up to 14 m *46 ft* overall (bipedal length 6·1 m *20 ft*), but these tyrannosaurids were not as heavily built as their North American relative.

Allosaurs Some of the allosaurs ('other lizards') of North America, Africa, Australia and China also reached exceptional sizes, and one individual excavated near Kenton, Oklahoma, USA in 1934 measured 12·8 m *42 ft* in total length and had a bipedal height of 4·9 m *16 ft*. This specimen was more massively built than the tyrannosaurids and was named *Saurophagus maximus* ('lizard eater'). Later, however, the bones were re-examined and found to be those of another large allosaur, *Acrocanthosaurus* ('very spiky reptile'), which measured about 12 m *39 ft* overall. Seven skeletons of this terrifying carnivore have been found in Oklahoma, USA since 1950.

Recent collections of the allosaur *Epanterias amplexus* from Masonville, Colorado, USA have suggested to Dr Robert Bakker of the University of Colorado that this theropod reached a length of 15 m *50 ft* and a weight of 4 tonnes, but remains are incomplete.

Another allosaur from China, *Yangchuanosaurus magnus*, has been described as the largest non-tyrannosaurid carnosaur so far recorded. Its skull was more massive than that of *T. rex* and this species is thought to have measured over 10·36 m *34 ft* in length overall.

Spinosaurus aegyptiacus ('thorn lizard') of Niger and Egypt was even longer than the largest known tyrannosaurid, with a total length of c. 15 m *49 ft*, and it combined its tremendous length with 1·6 m *5 ft 3 in* long blade-like spines running down its back, but it was a much more lightly built theropod than the tyrannosaurids and probably did not exceed 4 tonnes.

Ornithomimosaurs Most of the ornithomimosaurs ('ostrich mimic lizards') were of modest size, but one giant from Mongolia, *Deinocheirus mirificus* ('terrible hand'), is represented by a pair of arms each 2·6 m *8 ft* long. These suggest a total body size of 7·8 m *24 ft* or more.

The megalosaurids ('great lizards') also produced some enormous examples, including *Megalosaurus ingens* from the Tendaguru site in Tanzania, and *Bahariasaurus* from Egypt and Algeria, both of which were nearly as large as *Tyrannosaurus rex*.

Smallest

The chicken-sized *Compsognathus* ('pretty jaw') of southern Germany and south-east France, and an undescribed plant-eating fabrosaurid from Colorado, USA measured 75 cm *29·5 in* from the snout to the tip of the tail and weighed about 6·8 kg *15 lb*.

Juvenile dinosaurs are even smaller: a *Psittacosaurus* from the Late Cretaceous of Mongolia was smaller than a pigeon (23–25 cm *9–10 in* long); a *Mussaurus* from the Late Triassic of Argentina was the size of a kitten (20 cm *8 in* long); and an embryo of *Orodromeus*, reported in 1988 from the Late Cretaceous of Montana, USA, still in its egg, was only 10 cm *4 in* long.

Longest neck

The sauropod *Mamenchisaurus* ('mamenchi lizard') of the Late Jurassic of Sichuan, China had the longest neck of any animal that has ever lived. It measured 11 m *36 ft* — half the total length of the dinosaur.

Longest trackway

In 1983 a series of four *Apatosaurus* (= *Brontosaurus*) trackways which ran parallel for a distance of over 215 m *705 ft* were recorded from 145-million-year-old Morrison strata in southeast Colorado, USA.

Fastest

Trackways can be used to estimate dinosaur speeds, and one from the Late Morrison of Texas, USA discovered in 1981 indicated that a carnivorous dinosaur had been moving at 40 km/h *25 mph*. Some ornithomimids (see above) were even faster, and the large-brained, 100 kg *220 lb* *Dromiceiomimus* ('emu mimic lizard') of the Late Cretaceous of Alberta, Canada could probably outsprint an ostrich, which has a top speed of 65 km/h *40 mph*.

Largest footprints

In 1932 the gigantic footprints of a large bipedal hadrosaurid ('duckbill') measuring 1·36 m *53½ in* in length and 81 cm *31·8 in* wide were discovered in Salt Lake City, Utah, USA, and other reports from Colorado and Utah refer to footprints 95–100 cm *37·4–39·4 in* wide. Footprints attributed to the largest brachiosaurids also range up to 100 cm *39·3 in* wide for the hind feet.

Largest eggs

The largest known dinosaur eggs are those of *Hypselosaurus priscus* ('high ridge lizard'), a 12·19 m *40 ft* long titanosaurid which lived about 80 million years ago. Examples found in the Durance valley near Aix-en-Provence, France in October 1961 would have had, uncrushed, a length of 300 mm *12 in* and a diameter of 255 mm *10 in* (capacity 3·3 litres *5·8 pt*).

Largest claws

The therizinosaurids ('scythe lizards') from the Late Cretaceous of the Nemegt Basin, Mongolia had the largest claws of any known animal. In the case of *Therizinosaurus cheloniformis* they measured up to 91·4 cm *36 in* along the outer curve (cf. 20·3 cm *8 in* for *Tyrannosaurus rex*). It has been suggested that these talons were designed for grasping and tearing apart large victims, but this creature had a feeble skull partially or entirely lacking teeth and probably lived on termites.

In January 1983 amateur fossil collector William Walker found a 30 cm *11·8 in* long claw-bone in a clay pit near Dorking, Surrey. Further excavations by a team from the British Museum (Natural History) revealed that the owner of this claw (believed to be a spinosaur) measured more than 9 m *29 ft 6 in* overall (estimated weight 2 tonnes) and had a bipedal height of 3–4 m *9–13 ft*. It was also distinguished from other theropods by having 128 teeth instead of the usual 64. This enigma, said to be the most important dinosaur fossil found in Europe this century, was subsequently named *Baryonyx walkeri* ('heavy claw').

Largest skull

The skulls of the long-frilled ceratopsids were the largest of all known land animals and culminated in the long-frilled *Torosaurus sp.* ('piercing lizard'). This herbivore, which measured about 7·6 m *25 ft* in total length and weighed up to 8 tonnes, had a skull measuring up to 3 m *9 ft 10 in* in length (including fringe) and weighing up to 2 tonnes. It ranged from Montana to Texas, USA.

Earliest bird

The earliest known fossil bird was the toothed, reptile-like *Archeopteryx lithographica*, which appeared c. 175 million years ago. Remains have been found in Upper Jurassic deposits in Bavaria, Germany. Despite its bird-like skull, this crow-sized animal shared many anatomical features with some of the smaller bipedal dinosaurs. Its skeletal structure suggests that it glided rather than flew, but the presence of feathers also indicates that, like modern birds, *Archeopteryx* may have been warm-blooded.

■ **Earliest bird**
Archeopteryx lithographica *dates from the Jurassic period about 175 million years ago. Although its feathers suggest that this creature was warm-blooded like modern birds, Its skeletal structure was similar to that of some smaller dinosaurs (i.e. reptilian) and, unlike modern birds,* Archeopteryx *had well-developed teeth.*
(Photo: Museum of Natural History, London)

Largest bird The largest prehistoric bird was the flightless *Dromornis stirtoni*, a huge emu-like creature which lived in central Australia 11 million years ago. Fossil leg bones found near Alice Springs in 1974 indicate that the bird must have stood c. 3 m *10 ft* tall and weighed about 500 kg *1100 lb*.

The giant moa *Dinornis maximus* of New Zealand was even taller, attaining a maximum height of 3·6 m *12 ft*, but it weighed only about 227 kg *500 lb*.

Flying bird The largest known flying bird was the giant teratorn (*Argentavis magnificens*), which lived in Argentina about 6 million years ago. Fossil remains discovered at a site 160 km *100 miles* west of Buenos Aires, Argentina in 1979 indicate that this gigantic vulture had a wing span of 7·0–7·6 m *23–25 ft* and weighed about 120 kg *265 lb*.

Seabird In 1987 an expedition from the Charleston Museum of South Carolina, USA discovered the fossil remains of a 30-million-year-old giant seabird, *Pseudodontornis sp.*, a relative of pelicans and cormorants. It had a wing span of about 5·8 m *19 ft* and weighed c. 41 kg *90 lb*.

Largest flying creature The largest ever flying creature was the pterosaur *Quetzalcoatlus northropi* ('feathered serpent'). About 70 million years ago it soared over what is now Texas, Wyoming and New Jersey, USA, Alberta, Canada and Senegal and Jordan. Partial remains discovered in Big Bend National Park, Texas, USA in 1971 indicate that this reptile must have had a wing span of 11–12 m *36–39 ft* and weighed about *113 kg* 250 lb.

UK *Ornithodesmus latidens*, from the Wealden Shales of Atherfield, Isle of Wight about 120 million years ago, had a wing span of c. 5 m *16 ft 4¼ in*.

Largest marine reptile *Kronosaurus queenslandicus*, a short-necked pliosaur from the Early Cretaceous (135 million years ago) of Australia, measured up to 15·2 m *50 ft* in length and had a 3·04 m *10 ft* long skull containing 80 massive teeth.

UK Britain's largest marine reptile was *Stretosaurus macromerus*, a short-necked pliosaur from the Kimmeridge Clay of Stretham, Cambs and Oxfordshire. A mandible found at Cumnor, Oxon and now in the University Museum, Oxford has a restored length of over 3 m *9 ft 10 in* and must have belonged to a reptile measuring at least 14 m *46 ft* in total length.

Largest crocodile The largest known crocodile was the euschian *Deinosuchus riograndensis* ('terrible crocodile'), which lived in the lakes and swamps of what is now Texas, USA about 75 million years ago. Fragmentary remains discovered in Big Bend National Park, Texas indicate a hypothetical length of 16 m *52 ft 6 in*, compared with the 15·2 m *50 ft* of the huge gharial *Rhamphosuchus* of northern India (2 million years ago) and the 14 m *46 ft* of *Sarcosuchus imperator* of Niger.

Largest chelonians The largest prehistoric chelonian was *Stupendemys geographicus*, a pelomedusid turtle which lived about 5 million years ago. Fossil remains discovered by Harvard University palaeontologists in northern Venezuela in 1972 indicate that this turtle had a carapace (shell) measuring 218–230 cm *7 ft 2 in–7 ft 6½ in* in mid-line length, measured 3 m *9 ft 10 in* in overall length and had a computed weight of 2041 kg *4500 lb* when alive.

Largest tortoise The largest prehistoric tortoise was probably *Geochelone* (= *Colossochelys*) *atlas*, which lived in what is now northern India, Myanmar (formerly Burma), Java, the Celebes and Timor, about 2 million years ago. In 1923 the fossil remains of a specimen with a carapace 180 cm *5 ft 11 in* long (223 cm *7 ft 4 in* over the curve) and 89 cm *2 ft 11 in* high were discovered near Chandigarh in the Siwalik Hills, India. This animal had a total length of 2·44 m *8 ft* and is computed to have weighed 852 kg *2100 lb* when it was alive.

Longest snake The longest prehistoric snake was the python-like *Gigantophis garstini*, which inhabited what is now Egypt about 38 million years ago. Parts of a spinal column and a small piece of jaw discovered at Fayum in the Western Desert indicate a length of about 11 m *37 ft*. Another huge fossil snake from the Middle Eocene in Mali was originally credited with a length of 23 m *75 ft 6 in*, but this measurement was over-estimated. It was actually 9 m *30 ft*.

Largest amphibian The largest amphibian ever recorded was the gharial-like *Prionosuchus plummeri*, which lived 270 million years ago. Fragmented remains were discovered in northern Brazil in 1972. These were reported in 1991 and the total body length was estimated at 9 m *30 ft* based on a 1·6 m *5 ft 3 in* long skull.

Largest fish No prehistoric fish larger than living species has yet been discovered. The claim, based on ratios from fossil teeth, that the great shark *Carcharodon megalodon* which abounded in Miocene seas some 15 million years ago measured 24 m *80 ft* in length, has now been shown to be in error. Modern estimates suggest that this shark did not exceed 13·1 m *43 ft*.

Largest insect The largest prehistoric insect was the dragonfly *Meganeura monyi*, which lived about 300 million years ago. Fossil remains (impressions of wings) discovered at Commentry, France indicate a wing extending up to 70 cm *27½ in*.

UK Britain's largest dragonfly was *Pupus diluculum* (family Meganeuridae), which is known only from a wing-impression found on a lump of coal in Bolsover colliery, Derbys in July 1978. It had an estimated wing span of 50–60 cm *19·68–23·62 in* and lived about 300 million years ago, making it the oldest flying creature so far recorded.

Largest land mammal The largest land mammal ever recorded was *Paraceratherium* (= *Baluchitherium*), a long-necked, hornless rhinocerotid which roamed across western Asia and Europe (Yugoslavia) about 35 million years ago. A restoration in the American Museum of Natural History, New York City, USA measures 5·41 m *17 ft 9 in* to the top of the shoulder hump and 11·27 m *37 ft* in total length, and this particular specimen must have weighed about 20 tonnes. The bones of this gigantic browser were first discovered in the Bugti Hills of Baluchistan, Pakistan in 1907–8.

Largest marine mammal The serpentine *Basilosaurus* (*Zeuglodon*) *cetoides*, which swam in the seas which covered modern-day Arkansas and Alabama, USA 50 million years ago, measured up to 21·3 m *70 ft* in length.

Largest mammoth The largest prehistoric elephant was the Steppe mammoth (*Mammuthus* (*Parelephas*) *trogontherii*), which, one million years ago, roamed what is now central Europe. A fragmentary skeleton found in Mosbach, Germany indicates a shoulder height of 4·5 m *14 ft 9 in*.

Largest primate The largest known primate was *Gigantopithecus* of the Middle Pleistocene of what is now northern Vietnam and southern China. Males would have stood an estimated 2·74 m *9 ft* tall and weighed about 272 kg *600 lb*. It is risky, however, to correlate tooth size and jaw depth of primates with their height and bodyweight, and *Gigantopithecus* may have had a disproportionately large head, jaws and teeth in relation to body size. The only remains discovered so far are three partial lower jaws and more than 1000 teeth.

Antlers The prehistoric giant deer (*Megaloceros giganteus*), which lived in northern Europe and northern Asia as recently as 8000 BC, had the longest horns of any known animal. One specimen recovered from an Irish bog had greatly palmated antlers measuring 4·3 m *14 ft* across, which corresponds to a shoulder height of 1·83 m *6 ft* and a weight of 499 kg *1100 lb*.

Tusks The longest tusks of any prehistoric animal were those of the straight-tusked elephant (*Palaeoloxodom antiquus germanicus*), which lived in northern Germany c. 300 000 years ago. The average length for tusks of adult bulls was 5 m *16 ft 5 in*.

A single tusk of a woolly mammoth (*Mammuthus primigenius*) preserved in the Franzens Museum at Brno, Czechoslovakia measures 5·02 m *16 ft 5½ in* along the outside curve.

In about August 1933 a single tusk of an imperial mammoth (*Mammuthus imperator*) measuring at least 4·87 m *16 ft* (anterior end missing) was unearthed near Post, Texas, USA. In 1934 this tusk was presented to the American Museum of Natural History, New York City.

The heaviest single fossil tusk on record weighed 150 kg *330 lb* with a maximum circumference of 89 cm *35 in* and is now preserved in the Museo Civico di Storia Naturale, Milan, Italy. The specimen, which is in two pieces, measures 3·58 m *11 ft 9 in* in length.

The heaviest recorded fossil tusks are a pair belonging to a 4·06 m *13 ft 4 in* tall Columbian mammoth (*Mammuthus columbi*) in the State Museum, Lincoln, Nebraska, USA. The specimens, which have a combined weight of 226 kg *498 lb* and measure 4·21 m *13 ft 9 in* and 4·14 m *13 ft 7 in* respectively, were found near Campbell, Nebraska in April 1915.

Plant Kingdom Plantea

GENERAL RECORDS

Oldest 'King Clone', the oldest known clone of the creosote plant (*Larrea tridentata*), found in south-west California, USA, was estimated in February 1980 by Prof. Frank C. Vasek to be 11 700 years old. It is possible that crustose lichens in excess of 500 mm *19·6 in* in diameter may be as old. In 1981 it was estimated that Antarctic lichens of more than 100 mm *3·9 in* in diameter are at least 10 000 years old.

Rarest Plants thought to be extinct are rediscovered each year and there are thus many plants of which specimens are known only in a single locality. The last surviving specimen (a female) of the cycad *Encephalartos woodii*, a palm-like tropical plant of a group known to have existed for 65–225 million years, is held at the Royal Botanic

Gardens, Kew, Surrey. It is possible that this plant is a hybrid of the specimen *Encephalartos altensteinii*, also at Kew. (See Oldest pot plant.)

Pennantia baylisiana, a tree found in 1945 on Three Kings Island, off New Zealand, also only exists as a female and cannot fruit.

In May 1983 it was reported that there was a sole surviving specimen of the lady's slipper orchid (*Cypripedium calceolus*) in Britain.

Northernmost The yellow poppy (*Papaver radicatum*) and the Arctic willow (*Salix arctica*) survive, the latter in an extremely stunted form, on the northernmost land at Lat. 83° N.

Southernmost Lichens resembling *Rhinodina frigida* have been found in Moraine Canyon at Lat. 86°09′S, Long. 157°30′W in 1971 and in the Horlick Mountain area, Antarctica at 86°09′S, 131°14′W in 1965.

The southernmost recorded flowering plant is the Antarctic hair grass (*Deschampsia antarctica*), which was found in Lat. 68° 21′S on Refuge Island, Antarctica on 11 Mar 1981.

Highest The greatest certain altitude at which any flowering plants have been found is 6400 m *21 000 ft* on Kamet (7756 m *25 447 ft*) by N. D. Jayal in 1955. They were *Ermania himalayensis* and *Ranunculus lobatus*.

Roots The greatest reported depth to which roots have penetrated is a calculated 120 m *400 ft* for a wild fig tree at Echo Caves, near Ohrigstad, Transvaal, South Africa. An elm tree root of at least 110 m *360 ft* was reported from Auchencraig, Largs, Ayrshire *c.* 1950. A single winter rye plant (*Secale cereale*) has been shown to produce 622·8 km *387 miles* of roots in 0·051 m³ *1·83 ft³* of earth.

Worst weeds The most intransigent weed is the mat-forming water weed *Salvinia auriculata*, found in Africa. It was detected when Lake Kariba, which straddles the border of Zimbabwe and Zambia, was filled in May 1959 and within 11 months it had choked an area of 199 km² *77 miles²*, rising to 1002 km² *387 miles²* by 1963.

The world's worst land weeds are regarded as purple nut sedge, Bermuda grass, barnyard grass, jungle rice, goose grass, Johnson grass, Guinea grass, Cogon grass and Lantana.

UK The most damaging and widespread cereal weeds in Britain are the wild oats *Avena fatua* and *A. ludoviciana*. Their seeds can withstand temperatures of 115·6° C *240° F* for 15 min and remain viable.

The largest weed in Britain is the giant hogweed (*Heracleum mantegazzianum*), which established itself from seeds brought from the Caucasus before 1862. It reaches 3·65 m *12 ft*.

Most spreading The greatest area covered by a single clonal growth is that of the wild box huckleberry (*Gaylussacia brachyera*), a mat-forming evergreen shrub first reported in 1796. A colony covering about 40 ha *100 acres* was found on 18 Jul 1920 near the Juniata River, Pennsylvania, USA. It has been estimated that this colony began 13 000 years ago.

Smallest flowering and fruiting The floating, flowering aquatic duckweed (*Wolffia angusta*) of Australia, described in 1980, is only 0·6 mm *0·0236 in* long and

0·33 mm *0·0129 in* wide. It weighs about 0·00015 g *1/100 000 oz* and its fruit, which resembles a minuscule fig, weighs 0·00007 g *400 000 to the oz*.

UK The smallest land plant regularly flowering in Britain is the chaffweed (*Cetunculus minimus*), a single seed of which weighs 0·00003 g.

Fastest growing The case of a *Hesperoyucca whipplei* of the family Liliaceae growing 3·65 m *12 ft* in 14 days was reported from Tresco Abbey, Isles of Scilly in July 1978.

Slowest flowering The slowest flowering of all plants is the rare *Puya raimondii*, the largest of all herbs, discovered at 3960 m *13 000 ft* in Bolivia in 1870. The panicle emerges after about 80–150 years of the plant's life. It then dies. One planted near sea level at the University of California's Botanical Garden, Berkeley, USA in 1958 grew to 7·6 m *25 ft* and bloomed as early as August 1986 after only 28 years. (See also Largest flowers.)

Oldest pot plant The world's oldest, and probably rarest, pot plant is the single cycad *Encephalartos altensteinii* brought from South Africa in 1775 and now housed at the Royal Botanic Gardens, Kew, Surrey. (See Rarest plant.)

Biggest collection By October 1988 Dr Julian A. Steyermark (died 15 Oct 1988) of the Missouri Botanical Garden, St Louis, Missouri, USA had made an unrivalled total of 138 000 collections, 132 500 of which belonged to his individual continuous numbered series, as opposed to specimens collected jointly with other botanists.

Biggest aspidistra The aspidistra (*Aspidistra elatior*) was introduced to Britain as a parlour palm from Japan and China in 1822. The biggest aspidistra in the world measures 142 cm *56 in* and belongs to Cliff Evans of Kiora, Moruya, New South Wales, Australia.

UK The biggest aspidistra known in Britain reached 127 cm *50 in* tall in 1979. It had more than 500 leaves spanning 1·52 m *5 ft* and was grown by Gertie James of Staveley, Chesterfield, Derbys, whose family potted it in 1873.

Earliest flower A flower believed to be 120 million years old was identified in 1989 by Dr Leo Hickey and Dr David Taylor of Yale University, Connecticut, USA from a fossil discovered near Melbourne, Victoria, Australia. The flowering angiosperm, which resembles a modern black pepper plant, had two leaves and one flower and is known as the Koonwarra plant.

Largest cactus The largest of all cacti is the saguaro (*Cereus giganteus* or *Carnegiea gigantea*), found in Arizona, southeastern California, USA and Sonora, Mexico. The green fluted column is surmounted by candelabra-like branches rising to a height of 17·67 m *57 ft 11 ¾ in* in the case of a specimen discovered in the Maricopa Mountains, 17·7 km *11 miles* east of Gila Bend, Arizona on 17 Jan 1988 by J.D. and R.M. Fairfield and R.N. and D.J. Wells. The plants have waxy white blooms which are followed by edible crimson fruit.

An armless cactus 24 m *78 ft* in height was measured in April 1978 by Hube Yates in Cave Creek, Arizona, USA. It was toppled in a windstorm in July 1986 at an estimated age of 150 years.

Mosses The tallest variety of moss is the Australian species *Dawsonia superba*, which can reach a height of 30 cm *12 in*.

The smallest is the microscopic pygmy moss (*Ephemerum*) and the longest is the brook moss (*Fontinalis*), which forms streamers up to 91 cm *3 ft* long in flowing water.

SEAWEED

Longest The longest species of seaweed is the Pacific giant kelp (*Macrocystis pyrifera*), which, although it does not exceed 65 m *215 ft* in length, can grow 45 cm *18 in* in a day.

UK The longest of the 700 species of British seaweed is the brown seaweed (*Chorda filum*), which grows to a length of 6·10 m *20 ft*. The Japanese species *Sargassum muticum*, introduced into Britain *c.* 1970, can reach 9·0 m *30 ft*.

Deepest The greatest depth at which plant life has been found is 269 m *884 ft* by Mark and Diane Littler off San Salvadore Island, Bahamas in October 1984. These maroon-coloured algae survived although 99·9995 per cent of sunlight was filtered out.

VINES AND VINEYARDS

Largest vine This was planted in 1842 at Carpinteria, California, USA. By 1900 it was yielding more than 9 tonnes of grapes in some years, and averaged 7 tonnes per year until it died in 1920. A single bunch of grapes (Red Thomson seedless) of 9·4 kg *20 lb 11½ oz* was weighed in Santiago, Chile in May 1984.

UK Britain's largest vine (1898–1964) was at Kippen, Stirling and had a girth measuring 1·52 m *5 ft* in 1956. England's largest vine is the Great Vine, planted in 1768 at Hampton Court, London. Its girth is 215·9 cm *85 in* with branches up to 34·7 m *114 ft* long and it has an average yield of

Most valuable
flower
In 1954 the Burpee
Co. $10 000 prize
offered for the
first all-white
marigold was won
on 12 Aug 1975 by
Alice Vonk of
Sully, Iowa, USA.

Longest daisy
chain
The longest daisy chain
measured 2·12 km *6980 ft
7 in* and was made in 7 hr
by villagers of Good
Easter, Chelmsford,
Essex on 27 May 1985.
The team is limited to 16.

318·8 kg *703 lb.* In 1990 Leslie Stringer of
Dartford, Kent obtained a yield of over
2300·16 kg *5071 lb* from the Dartford Won-
dervine, planted in 1979. The plant was
grown from a cutting taken from a vine
planted in Banstead, Surrey in 1962.

Largest vineyard The world's largest
vineyard extends over the Mediterranean
slopes between the Pyrenees and the Rhône
in the *départements* Gard, Hérault, Aude
and Pyrénées-Orientales. It covers an area
of 840 000 ha *2 075 685 acres,* 52·3 per cent of
which is *monoculture viticole.*

Most northerly vineyard There is a
vineyard at Sabile, Latvia, USSR is just
north of Lat. 57° N.

UK The most northerly commercial vineyard in Britain is at Renishaw Hall, near
Chesterfield, Derbys at Lat. 53° 18′ N,
comprising 2600 vines.

Most southerly vineyard The most
southerly commercial vineyards are to be
found in central Otago, South Island, New
Zealand, south of Lat. 45° S. Renton
Burgess Vineyard, south of Alexandra,
South Island, is at Lat. 44° 36′ S.

BLOOMS AND FLOWERS

Largest The largest of all blooms are
those of the parasitic stinking corpse lily
(*Rafflesia arnoldii*), which measure up to
91 cm *3 ft* across and 1·9 cm *¾ in* thick, and
attain a weight of 7 kg *15 lb.* The plants
attach themselves to the cissus vines in the
jungle of south-east Asia. True to name, the
plant has an extremely offensive scent.

UK The largest bloom of any indigenous
British flowering plant is that of the wild
white water lily (*Nymphaea alba*), which
measures 15 cm *6 in* across.

Inflorescence The largest known
inflorescence (as distinct from the largest
of all blooms) is that of *Puya raimondii,* a
rare Bolivian monocarpic member of the
Bromeliaceae family. Its erect panicle (diameter 2·4 m *8 ft*) emerges to a height of
10·7 m *35 ft* and each of these bears up to
8000 white blooms. (See also Slowest
flowering plant.) The flower-spike of an
agave measured in Berkeley, California,
USA in 1974 was found to be 15·8 m *52 ft*
long.

Blossoming plant The giant Chinese
wisteria (*Wisteria sinensis*) at Sierra
Madre, California, USA was planted in
1892 and now has branches 152 m *500 ft*
long. It covers nearly 0·4 ha *1 acre,* weighs
228 tonnes and has an estimated 1·5 million
blossoms during its blossoming period of

■ **Longest seaweed**

five weeks, when up to 30 000 people pay
admission to visit it.

Largest arrangement The largest
arrangement of a single variety of flower
was made by Johan Weisz, floral designer of
Amsterdam, and 15 assistants at the City
Hall, Aalsmeer, Netherlands from 23–25
Sep 1986. It consisted of 35 000 'Zurella'
roses and measured 21·8 m *71 ft 6 in* in
length, 7·68 m *25 ft 2 in* in width and 7·59 m
24 ft 11 in high.

Largest bouquet Thirty-six people
took 335 hr to make a bouquet 11·23 m *36 ft
10 in* high, consisting of 9299 flowers at
Annecy, France on 19 Sep 1986.

Largest wreath A wreath made by the
Clemsonville Christmas Tree Farm of
Union Bridge, Maryland, USA in
December 1989 measured 35·4 m *116 ft* in
diameter and weighed 3703·6 kg *8165 lb.*

Largest rhododendron Examples of
the scarlet *Rhododendron arboreum* reach
a height of 19·8 m *65 ft* on Mt Japfu,
Nagaland, India. The cross-section of the
trunk of a *Rhododendron giganteum,*
reputedly 27·43 m *90 ft* high from Yunnan,
China, is preserved at Inverewe Gardens,
Highland.

UK The largest rhododendron in Britain
is a specimen 7·60 m *25 ft* tall and 82·9 m
272 ft in circumference at Government
House, Hillsborough, Co. Down. A specimen 10·65 m *35 ft* high and 99 cm *3 ft 3 in* in
circumference has been measured at Tre-
gothan, Truro, Cornwall.

Largest rose tree A 'Lady Banks' rose
tree at Tombstone, Arizona, USA has a
trunk 101 cm *40 in* thick, stands 2·74 m *9 ft*
high and covers an area of 499 m² *5380 ft².* It
is supported by 68 posts and several thousand feet of piping, which enables 150
people to be seated under the arbour. The
cutting came from Scotland in 1884.

ORCHIDS

Tallest The largest of all orchids is *Grammatophyllum speciosum,* a native of Malaysia. Specimens have been recorded up to
7·62 m *25 ft* in height.

Largest flower The largest orchid
flower is that of *Phragmipedium caudatum,*
found in tropical areas of America. Its
petals grow up to 46 cm *18 in* long, giving it
a maximum diameter of 91 cm *3 ft.* The
flower is, however, much less bulky than
that of the stinking corpse lily. (See
Largest bloom.)

A height of 15 m *49 ft* has been recorded for

Galeola foliata, a saprophyte of the vanilla
family. It grows in the decaying rain forests
of Queensland, Australia, but is not free-
standing.

UK The first flowering in Britain of
Grammatophyllum wallisii from Mindanao,
Philippines at Burnham Nurseries,
Kingsteignton, Devon in 1982 produced 557
flowers.

Smallest The smallest orchid is *Pla-
tystele jungermannoides,* found in Central
America. Its flowers are just 1 mm *0·04 in* in
diameter.

Most expensive The highest price ever
paid for an orchid is 1150 guineas
(£1207.50), paid by Baron Schröder to
Sanders of St Albans for an *Odontoglossum
crispum* (var. *pittianum*) at an auction by
Protheroe & Morris of Bow Lane, London
on 22 Mar 1906. A cymbidium orchid called
'Rosanna Pinkie' was sold in the United
States for $4500 in 1952.

FRUITS AND VEGETABLES

Most nutritive An analysis of the 38
commonly eaten raw (as opposed to dried)
fruits shows that the one with the highest
calorific value is the avocado (*Persea americana*), with 163 calories per edible 100 g
741 cal/lb; it also contains vitamins A, C
and E, 2·2 per cent protein and as much as
25 per cent unsaturated oil in some varieties. Avocados probably originated in
Central and South America.

Least nutritive That with the lowest
calorific value is the cucumber (*Cucumis
sativus*), with 16 cal/100 g *73 cal/lb.*

HERBS

Herbs are not botanically defined but consist of plants whose leaves or roots are of
culinary or medicinal value.

Most heavily consumed The most
heavily consumed is coriander (*Corian-
drum sativum*), which is used in curry
powder, confectionery, bread and gin.

FERNS

Largest The largest of the more than 6000
species of fern is the tree fern (*Alsophila
excelsa*) of Norfolk Island in the South
Pacific, which attains a height of up to
18·28 m *60 ft.*

UK The tallest fern in Britain is a
bracken *Pteridium aquilinum,* measuring
over 4·8 m *16 ft* in Ruislip, Middx in 1970.

Smallest The world's smallest ferns are
Hecistopteris pumila, found in Central

■ **Largest chrysanthemum**

FRUIT, VEGETABLES, FLOWERS
WORLD RECORDS

In the interests of fairness and to minimize the risk of mistakes being made, all plants should, where possible, be entered in official international, national or local garden contests. Only produce grown primarily for human consumption will be considered for publication. The assistance of *Garden News* and the World Pumpkin Confederation is gratefully acknowledged.

TYPE	SIZE		GROWER	LOCATION	YEAR
APPLE	1·36 kg	*3 lb 1 oz*	V. Loveridge	Ross-on-Wye, Hereford & Worcester	1965
BROAD BEAN	59·3 cm	*23 ³/₈in*	T. Currie	Jedburgh, Borders	1963
	59·3 cm	*23 ³/₈in*	M. Adrian	Irvine, Strathclyde	1982
CABBAGE	56·24 kg	*124 lb*	B. Lavery	Llanharry, Mid Glam	1989
CABBAGE, RED[1]	19·05 kg	*42 lb*	R. Straw	Staveley, Derbys	1925
CARROT[2]	7 kg	*15 lb 7 oz*	I. Scott	Nelson, New Zealand	1978
CELERY	20·89 kg	*46 lb 1 oz*	B. Lavery	Llanharry, Mid Glam	1990
CHRYSANTHEMUM	2·5 m	*8 ft 2 ¹/₂in*	F. Santini	Indre-et-Loire, France	1988
COURGETTE	29·25 kg	*64 lb 8 oz*	B. Lavery	Llanharry, Mid Glam	1990
CUCUMBER[3]	8·09 kg	*17 lb 13 ¹/₂oz*	P. Vowles	Llanharry, Mid Glam	1990
DAHLIA	7·8 m	*25 ft 7 in*	R. Blythe	Nannup, Western Australia	1990
GARLIC	1·19 kg	*2 lb 10 oz*	R. Kirkpatrick	Eureka, California, USA	1985
GRAPEFRUIT	2·97 kg	*6 lb 8 ¹/₂oz*	J. and A. Sosnow	Tucson, Arizona, USA	1984
LEEK (pot)	5·5 kg	*12 lb 2 oz*	P. Harrigan	Linton, Northumberland	1987
LEMON	3·88 kg	*8 lb 8 oz*	C. and D. Knutzen	Whittier, California, USA	1983
MARROW	49·04 kg	*108 lb 2 oz*	B. Lavery	Llanharry, Mid Glam	1990
MELON	25·2 kg	*59 lb 8 oz*	B. Rogerson	Robersonville, North Carolina, USA	1990
ONION	4·93 kg	*10 lb 14 oz*	V. Throup	Silsden, W Yorks	1990
PARSNIP	4·36 m	*171 ³/₄in*	B. Lavery	Llanharry, Mid Glam	1990
PETUNIA	4·16 m	*13 ft 8 in*	B. Lawrence	Windham, New York, USA	1985
PHILODENDRON	339·55 m	*1114 ft*	F. Francis	University of Massachusetts, USA	1984
PINEAPPLE[4]	7·96 kg	*17 lb 8 oz*	Dole Philippines Inc.	South Cotabato, Philippines	1984
POTATO[5]	3·2 kg	*7 lb 1 oz*	J. East	Spalding, Lincs	1963
	3·2 kg	*7 lb 1 oz*	J. Busby	Atherstone, Warks	1982
PUMPKIN	370·36 kg	*816 lb 8 oz*	E. and R. Gancarz	Wrightstown, New Jersey, USA	1990
RADISH	12·73 kg	*28 lb 1 oz*	B. Lavery	Llanharry, Mid Glam	1990
RHUBARB	2·67 kg	*5 lb 14 oz*	E. Stone	East Woodyates, Wilts	1985
RUNNER BEAN	100·3 cm	*39 ¹/₂in*	J. Taylor	Shifnal, Shrops	1986
SQUASH	250·24 kg	*821 lb*	L. Stellpflug	Rush, New York, USA	1990
STRAWBERRY	231 g	*8·17 oz*	G. Anderson	Folkestone, Kent	1983
SUNFLOWER[6]	7·76 m tall	*25 ft 5 ¹/₂in*	M. Heijms	Oirschot, Netherlands	1986
SWEDE	22·11 kg	*48 lb 12 oz*	A. Foster	Alnwick, Northumberland	1980
TOMATO	3·51 kg	*7 lb 12 oz*	G. Graham	Edmond, Oklahoma, USA	1986
TOMATO PLANT[7]	16·3 m	*53 ft 6 in*	G. Graham	Edmond, Oklahoma, USA	1985
WATERMELON[9]	118·84 kg	*262 lb*	B. Carson	Arrington, Tennessee, USA	1990

UK NATIONAL RECORDS

BEETROOT	13·49 kg	*29 lb 12 oz*	E. Stone	East Woodyates, Wilts	1988
CARROT[2]	4·65 kg	*10 lb 4 oz*	E. Stone	East Woodyates, Wilts	1984
DAHLIA	3·3 m	*10 ft 10 in*	R. Lond	Diss, Norfolk	1989
GLADIOLUS	2·55 m	*8 ft 4 ¹/₂in*	A. Breed	Melrose, Borders	1981
GOOSEBERRY	58·5 g	*2·06 oz*	A. Dingle	Macclesfield, Cheshire	1978
GRAPEFRUIT	1·67 kg	*3 lb 11 oz*	Willington G.C.	Willington, Beds	1986
LEMON	2·13 kg	*4 lb 11 oz*	Pershore College	Pershore, Hereford & Worcester	1986
LUPIN	1·9 m	*6 ft 3 in*	K. Barnes	Guildford, Surrey	1988
MELON	6·42 kg	*14 lb 2 ³/₄oz*	R. Sainsbury	Paull, Hull, Humberside	1985
PEACH	411 g	*14 ¹/₂oz*	J. Bird	London	1984
PETUNIA	2·53 m	*8 ft 4 in*	G. Warner	Dunfermline, Fife	1978
PUMPKIN	322 kg	*710 lb*	B. Lavery	Llanharry, Mid Glam	1989
SQUASH	212·05 kg	*467 lb 12 oz*	B. Lavery	Llanharry, Mid Glam	1990
SUNFLOWER[6]	7·17 m	*23 ft 6 ¹/₂in*	F. Kelland	Exeter, Devon	1976
TOMATO	2·54 kg	*5 lb 9 ¹/₂oz*	R. Burrows	Huddersfield, W Yorks	1985
TOMATO PLANT[7]	13·96 m	*45 ft 9 ¹/₂in*	Chosen Hill School	Gloucester	1981
TURNIP[8]	16·78 kg	*37 lb*	G. Farquhar	Tillyfourie, Grampian	1987
WATERMELON[9]	16·33 kg	*36 lb*	B. Lavery	Llanharry, Mid Glam	1990

[1] The Swalwell, County Durham red cabbage of 1865, grown by William Collingwood (died 8 Oct 1867), reputedly weighed 55·7 kg *123 lb* and had a circumference of 6·57 m *259 in*.

[2] A 4·9 m *193 ¹/₄ in* long carrot was grown by Bernard Lavery of Llanharry, Mid Glam in 1990.

[3] A Vietnamese variety 1·83 m *6 ft* long was reported by L. Szabo of Debrecen, Hungary in September 1976. A.C. Rayment of Chelmsford, Essex grew one measuring 1·10 m *43 ¹/₂ in* in 1984–86. The giant cucumbers grown by Eileen Chappel, which featured for several years, have subsequently been identified as gourds.

[4] Pineapples weighing up to 13 kg *28 lb 11 oz* were reported from Tarauaca, Brazil in 1978.

[5] One weighing 8·275 kg *18 lb 4 oz* reported dug up by Thomas Siddal in his garden in Chester on 17 Feb 1795. A yield of 233·5 kg *515 lb* was achieved from a 1·1 kg *2 ¹/₂ lb* parent seed by Bowcock planted in April 1977. Six tubers weighing 24·72 kg *54 ¹/₂ lb* and belonging to Alan Nunn of Rhodes, Middleton, Lancs were reported on 18 Sep 1949.

[6] A sunflower with a head measuring 82 cm *32 ¹/₄ in* in diameter was grown by Emily Martin of Maple Ridge, British Columbia, Canada in Sep 1983. A fully mature sunflower measuring just 56 mm *2 ¹/₅ in* was grown by Michael Lenke of Lake Oswego, Oregon, USA in 1985 using a patented bonsai technique.

[7] It was reported at the Tsukuba Science Expo Centre, Japan on 28 Feb 1988 that a single plant produced 16 897 tomatoes.

[8] A 33·1 kg *73 lb* turnip was reported in December 1768 and one weighing 23·1 kg *51 lb* was reported from Alaska in 1981, but this has not been substantiated.

[9] Bill Rogerson of Robersonville, North Carolina, USA grew a watermelon which weighed 126·5 kg *279 lb* on 3 Oct 1988, but this was not measured under competition conditions.

Apple peeling
The longest single unbroken apple peel on record is one of 52·51 m *172 ft 4 in*, peeled by Kathy Wafler of Wolcott, New York, USA in 11 hr 30 min at Long Ridge Mall, Rochester, New York on 16 Oct 1976. The apple weighed 567 g *20 oz*.

Apple picking
The greatest recorded performance is 7180·33 kg *15 830 lb* picked in 8 hr by George Adrian of Indianapolis, Indiana, USA on 23 Sep 1980.

Cucumber slicing
Norman Johnson of Blackpool College, Lancs set a record of 13·4 sec for slicing a 30·48 cm *12 in* cucumber, 3·81 cm *1½ in* in diameter, at 22 slices to the inch (total 264 slices) at West Deutscher Rundfunk in Cologne, Germany on 3 Apr 1983.

Potato peeling
The greatest quantity of potatoes peeled by five people to an institutional cookery standard with standard kitchen knives in 45 min is 376·8 kg *830 lb 11 oz* (net) by Lia Sombroek, Marlene Guiamo, Ria Grol, Yvonne Renting and Nguyet Nguyen at Emmeloord, Netherlands on 15 Sep 1990.

■ Largest watermelon
Bill Carson of Arrington, Tennessee, USA proudly displays his 118·84 kg 262 lb watermelon, grown in 1990.

Most conquering conker

The most victorious untreated conker — the fruit of the common horse-chestnut (*Aesculus hippocastanum*) — was a 'five thousander plus', which won the BBC Conker Conquest in 1954. However, a professor of botany believes that this heroic specimen might well have been a 'ringer', probably an ivory or tagua nut (*Phytelephas macrocarpa*). The Guinness Book of Records *will not publish any category for the largest collection of conkers for fear that trees might suffer wholesale damage.*

Hedge laying

John Williams of Sennybridge and David James of Llanwern, Brecon, hedged by the 'stake and pleach' method a total of 241·4 m *264 yd* in 11 hr 24 min on 28 Apr 1986.

America, and *Azolla caroliniana*, which is native to the United States and has fronds down to 12 mm *½ in*.

GRASSES

Commonest The world's commonest grass is Bermuda grass (*Cynodon dactylon*). The 'Callie' hybrid, selected in 1966, grows as much as 15·2 cm *6 in* a day and stolons reach 5·5 m *18 ft* in length.

Fastest growing Some species of the 45 genera of bamboo have been found to grow up to 91 cm *36 in* per day (0·00003 km/h *0·00002 mph*).

Tallest A thorny bamboo culm (*Bambusa arundinacea*) felled at Pattazhi, Travancore, India in November 1904 measured 37 m *121½ ft*.

UK The tallest of the 160 grasses found in Great Britain is the common reed (*Phragmites communis*), which reaches a height of 2·97 m *9 ft 9 in*.

Shortest The shortest grass native to Great Britain is the very rare sand bent (*Mibora minima*) from Anglesey, which reaches a maximum height of less than 15 cm *6 in*.

LEAVES

Largest The largest leaves of any plant belong to the raffia palm (*Raphia raffia*) of the Mascarene Islands in the Indian Ocean, and the Amazonian bamboo palm (*R. toedigera*) of South America, whose leaf blades may measure up to 19·81 m *65 ft* in length with petioles up to 3·96 m *13 ft*.

The largest undivided leaf is that of *Alocasia macrorrhiza*, found in Sabah, Malaysia. A specimen found in 1966 was 3·02 m *9 ft 11 in* long and 1·92 m *6 ft 3½ in* wide, with a surface area of 3·17 m² *34·12 ft²*. A specimen of the water lily *Victoria amazonica* (Longwood hybrid) in the grounds of the Stratford-upon-Avon Butterfly Farm, Warks measured 2·4 m *8 ft* in diameter on 2 Oct 1989.

UK The largest leaves found on outdoor plants in Great Britain are those of *Gunnera manicata* from Brazil, with leaves 1·82–3·04 m *6–10 ft* across on prickly stems 1·52–2·43 m *5–8 ft* long.

Fourteen-leafed clover A fourteen-leafed white clover (*Trifolium repens*) was found by Randy Farland near Sioux Falls, South Dakota, USA on 16 Jun 1975. A fourteen-leafed red clover (*Trifolium pratense*) was reported by 12-year-old Paul Haizlip at Bellevue, Washington, USA on 22 Jun 1987.

SEEDS

Largest The largest seed in the world is that of the double coconut or coco de mer (*Lodoicea seychellarum*), the single-seeded fruit of which may weigh 18 kg *40 lb*. This grows only in the Seychelles in the Indian Ocean.

Smallest The smallest seeds are those of epiphytic (non-parasitic plants growing on others) orchids, at 992·25 million seeds/g *35 million/oz* (cf. grass pollens at up to 170·1 billion grains/g *6 billion grains/oz*). A single plant of the American ragweed can generate 8 billion pollen grains in five hours.

Most viable The most conclusive claim for the viability of seeds is that made for the Arctic lupin (*Lupinus arcticus*) found in frozen silt at Miller Creek in the Yukon, Canada in July 1954 by Harold Schmidt. The seeds were germinated in 1966 and were radiocarbon dated to at least 8000 BC, and more probably to 13 000 BC.

HEDGES

Tallest The Meikleour beech hedge in Perthshire was planted in 1746 by Jean Mercer and her husband Robert Murray Nairne. Its tapered height when trimmed now varies from 24·4 m *80 ft* to 36·6 m *120 ft* along its length of 550 m *1804 ft*. Trimming takes place every 10 years or so and was last completed in six weeks in 1988.

Yew A yew hedge in Earl Bathurst's Park, Cirencester, Glos, planted in 1720, runs for 155·5 m *510 ft*, reaches 11 m *36 ft* in height and is 4·5 m *15 ft* thick at its base. The hedge takes 20 days to trim.

Box The tallest box hedge is 12 m *40 ft* in height. It can be found at Birr Castle, Co. Offaly, Republic of Ireland and dates from the 18th century.

TREES AND WOOD

Earliest The earliest surviving species of tree is the maidenhair tree (*Ginkgo biloba*) of Zhexiang, China, which first appeared about 160 milion years ago during the Jurassic era. It was 'rediscovered' by Kaempfer (Netherlands) in 1690 and reached England *c.* 1754. It has been grown in Japan since *c*1100, where it was known as *ginkyō* ('silver apricot') and is now known as *icho*.

Oldest The oldest recorded tree was a bristlecone pine (*Pinus longaeva*) designated WPN-114, which grew at 3275 m *10 750 ft* above sea level on the north-east face of Mt Wheeler, Nevada, USA. It was found to be 5100 years old.

The oldest known *living* tree is the bristlecone pine named 'Methuselah', growing at 3050 m *10 000 ft* on the California side of the White Mountains, confirmed as 4700 years old. In March 1974 it was reported that this tree had produced 48 live seedlings. Dendrochronologists estimate the *potential* life-span of a bristlecone pine at nearly 5500 years, and that of a giant sequoia (*Sequoiadendron giganteum*) at perhaps 6000 years. No single cell lives more than 30 years.

UK Of all British trees, that with the longest life is the yew (*Taxus baccata*), for which a maximum age well in excess of 1000 years is usually conceded. The oldest known is the Fortingall yew near Aberfeldy, Tayside, part of which still grows. In 1777 this tree was over 15·24 m *50 ft* in girth and it cannot be much less than 3500 years old.

Most massive The most massive living thing on Earth is the biggest known giant sequoia (*Sequoiadendron giganteum*) named the 'General Sherman', standing 83·8 m *275 ft* tall, in the Sequoia National Park, California, USA. In 1989 it had a girth of 25·1 m *82·3 ft*, measured 1·4 m *4·5 ft* above the ground. The 'General Sherman' has been estimated to contain the equivalent of 600 120 board feet of timber, sufficient to make 5 billion matches. The foliage is blue-green, and the red-brown bark may be up to 61 cm *24 in* thick in parts. Estimates place its weight, including its root system, at 2500 tonnes, but the timber is light (288·3 kg/m³ *18 lb/ft³*).

The seed of a 'big tree' weighs only 4·7 mg *1/6000th of an oz*. Its growth at maturity may therefore represent an increase in weight of 13×10^{11}.

The tree canopy covering the greatest area is that of the great banyan (*Ficus benghalensis*) in the Indian Botanical Garden, Calcutta, with 1775 prop or supporting roots and a circumference of 412 m *1350 ft*. It covers some 1·2 ha *3 acres* and dates from before 1787. However, it is reported that a 550-year-old banyan tree known as 'Thimmamma Marrimanu' in Gutibayalu village near Kadiri Taluk, Andhra Pradesh, India spreads over 2·1 ha *5·2 acres*.

Greatest girth 'El Arbol del Tule' in the state of Oaxaca, Mexico is a 41 m *135 ft* tall Montezuma cypress (*Taxodium mucronatum*) with a girth in 1982 of 35·8 m *117·6 ft*, measured 1·52 m *5 ft* above the ground.

A circumference of 57·9 m *190 ft* was recorded for the pollarded (trimmed to encourage a more bushy growth) European chestnut (*Castanea sativa*) known as the 'Tree of the Hundred Horses' (*Castagno di Cento Cavalli*) on Mt Etna, Sicily, Italy in 1770 and 1780. It is now in three parts, widely separated. Measurements up to 54·5 m *180 ft* in circumference have been attributed to baobab trees (*Adansonia digitata*).

UK A sweet ('Spanish') chestnut (*Castanea sativa*) in the grounds of Canford School, near Poole, Dorset has a trunk measuring 13·33 m *43 ft 9 in* in circumference.

The largest living oak in Britain is at Bowthorpe Farm near Bourne, Lincs. Its girth measured 12 m *39 ft 6 in* in September 1980. The largest 'maiden' (i.e. not pollarded) oak is the 'Majesty Oak' at Fredville Park, near Nonington, Kent, with a girth of 11·60 m *38 ft 1 in* in 1973.

The largest yew with a clear trunk at 1·52 m *5 ft* above ground level measures 10·79 m *35 ft 5 in* in circumference and is at Ulcombe Church, Kent.

Fastest growing Discounting bamboo, which is not botanically classified as a tree but as a woody grass, the fastest rate of growth recorded is 10·74 m *35 ft 3 in* in 13 months by an *Albizzia falcata* planted on 17 Jun 1974 in Sabah, Malaysia. The youngest recorded age for a tree to reach 30·48 m *100 ft* is 64 months for another of the species *A. falcata* planted on 24 Feb 1975, also in Sabah.

The world's most productive forest is a plantation of eucalypts (*Eucalyptus grandis*) at Aracruz, Brazil, where the average growth rate is 70 m³ per ha per year (*2472 ft³ per 2·5 acres*).

Slowest growing The speed of growth of trees depends largely upon conditions, although some species, such as box and yew, are always slow-growing. The extreme is represented by the *Dioon edule* (Cycadaceae) measured in Mexico between 1981 and 1986 by Dr Charles M. Peters, who found the average annual growth rate to be 0·76 mm *0·03 in*; a specimen 120 years old measured 9·9 cm *3·9 in* in height.

The growing of miniature trees or *bonsai* is an oriental cult mentioned as early as *c.* 1320.

Tallest According to the researches of Dr A.C. Carder, the tallest tree ever measured was an Australian eucalyptus (*Eucalyptus regnans*) at Watts River, Victoria, Australia, reported in 1872 by forester William Ferguson. It was 132·58 m *435 ft* tall and almost certainly measured over 152·4 m *500 ft* originally. Another *Eucalyptus regnans* at Mt Baw Baw, Victoria, Australia is believed to have measured 143 m *470 ft* in 1885. The closest measured rivals to these champions have been:

m	ft	
126·5	*415*	Douglas fir (*Pseudotsuga menziesii*), Lynn Valley, British Columbia, Canada, 1902.
119·8	*393*	'Mineral' Douglas fir (*Pseudotsuga menziesii*), Washington State, USA, 1905.
115·8	*380*	'Nisqually' Douglas fir (*Pseudotsuga menziesii*), Nisqually River, Washington State, USA, 1899
114·3	*375*	'Cornthwaite' Mountain ash or giant gum (*Eucalyptus regnans*), Thorpdale, Victoria, Australia, 1880

112	*367·6*	Coast redwood (*Sequoia sempervirens*), Guerneville, California, USA, 1873. This tree was felled for timber in 1875.

The tallest tree currently standing is the 'National Geographic Society' coast redwood (*Sequoia sempervirens*) in the Redwood National Park, Humboldt County, California, USA. It stood at 113·7 m *373 ft* in October 1990, according to Ron Hildebrant of California. The 111·25 m *365 ft* 'Dyerville' giant redwood in the same park was reported felled in a storm on 27 Mar 1991.

The tallest standing broadleaf tree is an Australian mountain ash, or giant gum, (*Eucalyptus regnans*) in the Styx Valley, Tasmania, at 95 m *312 ft*.

UK The best claimant for Britain's tallest tree is a grand fir (*Abies grandis*) at Strone, Strathclyde which, has a good annual growth rate and stood at 63 m *206 ft* in 1989. The grand fir at Cairndow, Strathclyde and the Douglas firs at The Hermitage, Perth, Tayside and in Moniac Glen, Inverness, Highland were all 61–62 m *200–203 ft* tall in June 1985. Of these only the Strone grand fir can be measured from both sides.

The tallest in England is a Douglas fir (*Pseudotsuga menziesii*) measuring 57 m *187 ft* in 1990, at Broadwood, Dunster, Somerset. The tallest in Northern Ireland is a giant sequoia (*Sequoiadendron giganteum*), measuring 50 m *164 ft* in 1983, at Caledon Castle, Co. Tyrone. The tallest in Wales is a grand fir (*Abies grandis*) at Leighton Park, Powys, measuring 62 m *203 ft* in 1989. It was planted in 1886. The tallest tree in the Republic of Ireland is a sitka spruce (*Picea sitchensis*) at Curragh-

■ **Largest leaves**
Specimens of the Amazon, or royal, water lily (Victoria amazonica). The largest recorded example of this species reached a diameter of 2·4 m 8 ft at the Stratford-upon-Avon Butterfly Farm, Warks in 1989.

(Photo: Gamma)

TALLEST TREES IN THE BRITISH ISLES
(By species)

Species	Location	m	ft
ALDER (Italian)	Westonbirt, Glos	34	111
ALDER (Common)	Ashburnham Park, E Sussex	32	105
ASH	Old Roar Ghyll, St. Leonards, E Sussex	41	135
BEECH	Hallyburton House, Tayside	46	150
BEECH (Copper)	Dalguise House, Tayside	38	125
BIRCH (Silver)	Ballogie, Grampian	30	98
CEDAR (Blue Atlas)	Brockhampton Pk, Hereford & Worcs	38	125
CEDAR (of Lebanon)	Leaton Knolls, Shrops	42	140
CHESTNUT (Horse)	Ashford Chase, Petersfield, Hants	39	130
CHESTNUT (Sweet)	Tyninghame, Lothian	36	118
CYPRESS (Lawson)	Strone House, Strathclyde	40	133
CYPRESS (Leyland)	Bicton, Sidmouth, Devon	36	118
CYPRESS (Monterey)	Johnstown Castle, Co. Wexford	40	131
DOUGLAS FIR	The Hermitage, Perth, Tayside	+61	200
ELM² (Huntingdon)	Howlett's Park Zoo, Canterbury, Kent	40	132
ELM² (Wych)	Castle Howard, N Yorks	41	134
EUCALYPTUS (Blue Gum)	Glencormack, Co. Wicklow	44	144
GRAND FIR	Strone, Cairndow, Strathclyde	63	206
GINKGO	Sezincote, Glos	30	98
HEMLOCK (Western)	Murthly Castle, Dunkeld, Tayside	52	170
HOLLY	Ashburnham Park, Battle, E Sussex	24	80
HORNBEAM	Wrest Park, Shefford, Beds	32	105
LARCH (European)	Glenlee, Dumfries & Galloway	46	150
LARCH (Japanese)	Blair Castle, Fife	40	131
LIME	Duncombe Park, Helmsley, N Yorks	45	150
METASEQUOIA	Leonardslee, W Sussex	31	102
MONKEY PUZZLE	Lochnaw, Dumfries & Galloway	29	95
OAK (Common)	Leeds Castle, Maidstone, Kent	41	135
OAK (Sessile)	Whitfield House, Hereford & Worcs	42	140
OAK (Red)	Cowdray Park, Midhurst, W Sussex	35	115
OAK (Turkey)	Knightshayes, Tiverton, Devon	44	144
PEAR	Tickard's Manor, Guildford, Surrey	21	69
PINE (Corsican)	Adhurst, St. Mary, Petersfield, Hants	46	150
PLANE	Bryanston School, Blandford, Dorset	48	156
POPLAR (Black Italian)	Bowood, Wilts	46	150
POPLAR (Black, native)	Longnor Hall, Shrewsbury, Shrops	37	121
POPLAR (Lombardy)	Henrietta Park, Bath, Avon	37	121
REDWOOD (Coast)	Bodnant, Conway, Gwynedd	45	148
SILVER FIR	Armadale Castle, Skye, Highland	50	164
SPRUCE (Sitka)	Strath Earn, Tayside	61	200
SYCAMORE	Lennoxlove, Haddington, Lothian	40	132
TULIP-TREE	Taplow House, Bucks	36	120
WALNUT	Boxted Hall, Suffolk	32	105
WALNUT (Black)	Much Hadham Rectory, Herts	36	118
WELLINGTONIA	Castle Leod, Strathpeffer, Highland	53	173
WILD SERVICE	Gatton Manor, Surrey	26	87
WILLOW (Weeping)	Ashford Chase, Petersfield, Hants	24	79
WINGNUT (Caucasian)	Abbotsbury, Weymouth, Dorset	35	115
YEW	Belvoir Castle, Leics	29	95

On the night of 16–17 Oct 1987 an estimated 15 million trees were destroyed by high winds, at an estimated cost of £15 million. [1] *It was estimated in 1980 that more than 17 million of the 23 million elms in southern England had been killed since 1968 by the fungus* Ceratocystis ulmi *that causes Dutch elm disease.*

more, Co. Waterford, which measured 50·59 m *166 ft* in March 1974.

Christmas The world's tallest cut Christmas tree was a 67·36 m *221 ft* Douglas fir (*Pseudotsuga menziesii*) erected at Northgate Shopping Center, Seattle, Washington, USA in December 1950.

UK A 26·3 m *86 ft 5in* tall Norway spruce (*Picea abies*) was grown on Viscount Weymouth's Longleat estate in Wiltshire and given to the King's College, Cambridge Choir School Development Appeal for Christmas 1989.

Most leaves Little work has been done on the laborious task of establishing which species has most leaves. A large oak has perhaps 250 000 but a cypress may have some 45–50 million leaf scales.

Remotest The tree believed to be the remotest from any other is a sole Norwegian spruce (*Picea abies*) on Campbell Island, Antarctica. Its nearest companion would be over 145 km *120 miles* away on the Auckland Islands.

Most expensive The highest price ever paid for a tree is $51 000 for a single starkspur 'Golden Delicious' apple tree from near Yakima, Washington, USA, bought by a nursery in Missouri in 1959.

Largest forest The largest afforested areas in the world are the vast coniferous forests of the northern USSR, lying between Lat. 55° N and the Arctic Circle. The total wooded area amounts to 1·1 billion ha *2·7 billion acres* (25 per cent of the world's forests), of which 38 per cent is Siberian larch. The USSR is 34 per cent afforested.

The largest area of forest in the tropics remains the Amazon Basin, amounting to some 330 million ha *815 million acres*.

UK The largest forest in England is the Kielder Forest District in Northumberland, covering 39 380 ha *97 309 acres*. The largest in Wales is *Coed Morgannwg* (Forest of Glamorgan), at 17 845 ha *44 095 acres*. Scotland's most extensive forest is the Newton Stewart Forest District in Dumfries & Galloway, covering 35 275 ha *87 165 acres*.

Longest avenue The world's longest avenue comprises three parts converging on Imaichi City in the Tochigi Prefecture of Japan. Known as the Nikko Cryptomeria Avenue, its total length is 35·41 km *22 miles*, made up of the Nikko Kaido (16·52 km *10·27 miles*), the Reiheishi Kaido (13·17 km *8·18 miles*) and the Aizu-nishi Kaido (5·72 km *3·55 miles*). The avenue was planted in the period 1628–48 and over 13 500 of its original 200 000 Japanese cedar (*Cryptomeria japonica*) trees survive, at an average height of 27 m *88½ ft*.

The longest avenue of trees in the Britain is the privately-owned stretch of 1750 beeches in Savernake Forest, near Marlborough, Wilts. It measures 5·79 km *3·6 miles*.

Heaviest wood Black ironwood (*Olea laurifolia*), also called South African ironwood, has a specific gravity of up to 1·49 and weighs up to 1490 kg/m³ *93 lb/ft³*.

UK The heaviest British wood is boxwood (*Buxus sempervirens*), which weighs up to 1025 kg/m³ *64 lb/ft³*.

Lightest wood The lightest wood is *Aeschynomene hispida*, which is found in Cuba and has a specific gravity of 0·044 and a weight of only 44 kg/m³ *2¾ lb/ft³*. The wood of the balsa tree (*Ochroma pyramidale*) varies considerably in density, at 40–384 kg/m³ *2½–24 lb/ft³*. The density of cork is 240 kg/m³ *15 lb/ft³*.

Wood cutting The first recorded lumberjack sports competition was held in 1572 in the Basque region of Spain. The records set at the Lumberjack World Championships at Hayward, Wisconsin, USA (founded 1960) are:

Power Saw		8·71 sec
Ron Johnson (US)		1986
One-Man Bucking		18·96 sec
Rolin Eslinger (US)		1987
Standing Block Chop		22·05 sec
Melvin Lentz (US)		1988
Underhand Block Chop		17·84 sec
Laurence O'Toole (Australia)		1985
Two-Man Bucking		7·27 sec
Jim Colbert (US), Mike Sullivan (US)		1988
Springboard Chopping		1 min 18·45 sec
Bill Youd (Australia)		1985

Kingdom Protista

Protista were first discovered in 1676 by Antonie van Leeuwenhoek of Delft (1632–1723), a Dutch microscopist. Among Protista are characteristics common to both plants and animals. The more plant-like are termed Protophyta (protophytes), including unicellular algae, and the more animal-like are placed in the phylum Protozoa (protozoans), including amoeba and flagellates.

Largest The largest protozoans in terms of volume which are known to have existed were calcareous foraminifera, or forams, of the order Foraminiferida belonging to the genus *Nummulites*, a species of which, in the Middle Eocene rocks of Turkey, attained 22 cm *8·6 in* in diameter.

The largest existing protozoan, a species of the fan-shaped *Stannophyllum* of the order Xenophyophorida, can exceed this in length (25 cm *9·8 in* has been recorded) but not in volume.

Smallest protophytes The marine microflagellate alga *Micromonas pusilla* has a diameter of less than 2 µm (2×10^{-6} m) *0·00008 in*.

Fastest The protozoan *Monas stigmatica* has been found to move a distance equivalent to 40 times its own length in a second. No human can cover even seven times his own length in a second.

Fastest reproduction The protozoan *Glaucoma*, which reproduces by binary fission, divides as frequently as every three hours. Thus, in the course of a day it could become a great-great-great-great-great-great grandparent and the progenitor of 510 descendants.

Kingdom Fungi

Largest Marcia Wallgren of Yellow Springs, Ohio, USA found a puffball (*Calvatia gigantea*) 195·58 cm *77 in* in circumference in 1988. An example of the edible mushroom *Polyporus frondosus* weighing 32·6 kg *72 lb* was reported by Joseph Opple near Solon, Ohio, USA in September 1976.

UK The largest recorded tree fungus is a specimen of the bracket fungus *Rigidoporus ulmarius* growing from dead elm wood in the grounds of the CAB International Mycological Institute at Kew, Surrey. This perennial species measured 147 × 121 cm *57·9 × 47·7 in* with a circumference of 409 cm *161 in* on 28 Dec 1989 and is still growing. An Ash fungus (*Fomes fraxineus*) measuring 127 × 38 cm *50 × 15 in* wide was found by the forester A.D.C. LeSueur on a tree at Waddesdon, Bucks in 1954.

Most poisonous The yellowish-olive death cap (*Amanita phalloides*), which can be found in England, is regarded as the world's most poisonous fungus. From 6–15 hours after eating, the effects are vomiting, delirium, collapse and death. Among its victims was Cardinal Giulio di' Medici, Pope Clement VII (b. 1478) on 25 Sep 1534.

UK In the United Kingdom there were 39 fatalities from fungus poisoning between 1920 and 1950. As the poisonous types are mostly *Amanita* varieties, it is reasonable to assume that the deaths were predominantly due to *Amanita phalloides*. The most recent fatality was probably in 1960.

Aeroflora Fungi were once classified in the subkingdom Protophyta of the kingdom Protista. The highest total fungal spore count was 161 037/m³ *5 686 860·6/ft³* near Cardiff, S Glam on 21 Jul 1971. A plane tree pollen count of 2160/m³ *76 278·24/ft³* was recorded near London on 9 May 1971. A grass pollen count of 2824/m³ was recorded at Aberystwyth, Dyfed on 29 Jun 1961. The lowest counts of airborne allergens are nil.

Kingdom Procaryota

Earliest The earliest life-form reported from Britain is *Kakabekia barghoorniana*, a micro-organism similar in form to an orange slice, found near Harlech, Gwynedd in 1964 and dated to 4000 million years old in July 1986.

BACTERIA

Antonie van Leeuwenhoek (1632–1723)

was the first to observe bacteria, in 1675. The largest of the bacteria is the sulphur bacterium *Beggiatoa mirabilis*, which is 16–45 µm in width and which may form filaments several millimetres long.

The bacteria *Thermoactinomyces vulgaris* have been found alive in cores of mud taken from the bottom of Windermere, Cumbria and have been dated to 1500 years ago.

Smallest free-living entity The smallest of all free-living organisms are pleuro-pneumonia-like organisms (PPLO) of the *Mycoplasma*. One of these, *Mycoplasma laidlawii*, first discovered in sewage in 1936, has a diameter during its early existence of only 10^{-7} m. Examples of the strain known as H.39 have a maximum diameter of 3×10^{-7} m and weigh an estimated 10^{-16} g. Thus a 190-tonne blue whale would weigh $1·9 \times 10^{24}$ times as much.

Highest In April 1967 the US National Aeronautics and Space Administration (NASA) reported that bacteria had been discovered at an altitude of 41·13 km *25·56 miles*.

Oldest The oldest deposits from which living bacteria are claimed to have been extracted are salt layers near Irkutsk, USSR, dating from about 600 million years ago, but the discovery was not accepted internationally. The US Dry Valley Drilling Project in Antarctica claimed to have found resuscitated rod-shaped bacteria from caves up to a million years old.

Fastest The rod-shaped bacillus *Bdellovibrio bacteriovorus*, by means of a polar flagellum rotating 100 times/sec, can move 50 times its own length of 2 µm per sec. This would be the equivalent of a human sprinter reaching 320 km/h *200 mph* or a swimmer crossing the English Channel in 6 min.

Toughest The bacterium *Micrococcus radiodurans* can withstand atomic radiation of 6·5 million röntgens, or 10 000 times that fatal to the average human. In March 1983 John Barras of the University

of Oregon, USA reported bacteria from sulphurous sea-bed vents thriving at 306°C *583°F* in the East Pacific Rise at Lat. 21° N.

VIRUSES

Largest Dmitriy Ivanovsky (1864–1920) first reported filterable objects in 1892 but Martinus Willem Beijerink (1851–1931)

first confirmed the nature of viruses in 1898. These are now defined as aggregates of two or more types of chemical (including either DNA or RNA) which are infectious and potentially pathogenic. The longest known is the rod-shaped *Citrus tristeza* virus, with particles measuring 2×10^{-5} m.

Smallest The smallest known viruses are the nucleoprotein plant viruses such as the satellite of tobacco *Necrosis* virus, with spherical particles measuring 17 nm (10^{-9}) in diameter.

A putative new infectious submicroscopic organism, without nucleic acid, named a 'prion', was announced from the University of California in February 1982.

Viroids (RNA cores without a protein coating) are much smaller than viruses. They were discovered by Theodor O. Diener (US) in February 1972. Dr Rohwer of Bethesda, Maryland, USA stated in September 1984 that scrapie-specific protein was smaller than the concept of a 'yet to be identified prion'.

Parks, Zoos, Oceanaria, Aquaria

PARKS

Largest The Wood Buffalo National Park in Alberta, Canada (established 1922), covers an area of 45 211 197 ha *11 172 000 acres* (45 480 km² *17 560 miles²*).

UK The largest national park in the United Kingdom is the Lake District National Park, which has an area of 2240 km² *866 miles²*. The largest private

park in the United Kingdom is Woburn Park (1200 ha *3000 acres*), near Woburn Abbey, Beds, the seat of the Dukes of Bedford.

ZOOS

It has been estimated that throughout the world there are some 757 zoos, with an estimated annual attendance of 350 million.

Largest game reserve The world's largest zoological reserve is the Etosha National Park, Namibia. Established in 1907, its area has grown to 99 525 km² *38 427 miles²*.

Oldest zoo The earliest known collection of animals was that set up by Shulgi, a 3rd-dynasty ruler of Ur from 2097–2094 BC, at Puzurish in south-east Iraq.

The oldest known zoo is that at Schönbrunn, Vienna, Austria, built in 1752 by the Holy Roman Emperor Franz I for his wife Maria Theresa.

The oldest existing public zoological collection in the world is that of the Zoological Society of London, founded in 1826. Its collection, housed partly in Regent's Park, London (14·5 ha *36 acres*) and partly at Whipsnade Park, Beds (219 ha *541 acres*, opened on 23 May 1931), is the most comprehensive in the United Kingdom. The stocktaking on 1 Jan 1989 accounted for a total of 11 108 specimens. These comprised 2628 mammals, 1916 birds, 489 reptiles, 175 amphibians, an estimated total of 2300 fish and an estimated total of 3600 invertebrates, excluding some common species. The record annual attendances are 3 031 571 in 1950 for

Regent's Park and 756 758 in 1961 for Whipsnade.

Earliest without bars The earliest zoo without bars was that at Stellingen, near Hamburg, Germany. It was founded in 1907 by Carl Hagenbeck (1844–1913), who made use of deep pits and large pens instead of cages to separate the exhibits from visitors.

OCEANARIA

Earliest The world's first oceanarium is Marineland of Florida, opened in 1938 at a site 29 km *18 miles* south of St Augustine, Florida, USA. Up to 26·3 million litres *5 800 000 gal* of sea-water are pumped daily through two major tanks, one rectangular (30·48 m *100 ft* long by 12·19 m *40 ft* wide by 5·48 m *18 ft* deep) containing 1·7 million litres *375 000 gal*, and one circular (71 m *233 ft* in circumference and 3·65 m *12 ft* deep) containing 1·5 million litres *330 000 gal*. The tanks are seascaped, including coral reefs and even a shipwreck.

AQUARIA

Largest In terms of the volume of water held, the Living Seas Aquarium opened in 1986 at the EPCOT Center, Florida, USA is the world's largest, with a total capacity of 23·66 million litres *6·25 million gal*. It contains over 3000 fish representing 90 species.

The largest in terms of marine-life is the Monterey Bay Aquarium opened on 20 Oct 1984 in California, USA, which houses 6500 specimens (525 species) of flora and fauna in its 95 tanks. The volume of water held is 3 375 000 litres *750 000 gal*.

The Human Being

■ **Previous page**
*Child under water (Photo:
Zefa Picture Library (UK) Ltd)*

■ **Earliest footprints**
*This trail of hominid foot-
prints was found fossilized
in volcanic ash in 1978 at
Laetoli, Tanzania. It is
dated to 3·5 million years.*
(Photo: Science Photo Library)

■ **Earliest skeletal
remains**
*The most complete of the
earliest hominid skeletons
is that of 'Lucy' (40 per
cent complete) found by
Dr Donald C. Johanson
and T. Gray by the Awash
River, Hadar, Ethiopia in
November 1974. (Photo:
Science Photo Library)*

Origins
EARLIEST MAN

SCALE OF TIME *If the age of the Earth-Moon
system (latest estimate 4500 ± 70 million years) is
likened to a single year, Hominids appeared on the
scene at about 4:15 p.m. on 31 December.
Britain's earliest known inhabitants arrived at
about 11:10 p.m., the Christian era began about
14 seconds before midnight and the life span of a
120-year-old person would be about three-
quarters of a second. Present calculations indicate
that the Sun's increased heat, as it becomes a 'red
giant', will make life on Earth insupportable in
about 5500 million years. Meanwhile there may
well be colder epicycles. The period of 1000 million years is sometimes referred to as an aeon.*

*Man (Homo sapiens) is a species in the sub-family
Homininae of the family Hominidae of the super-
family Hominoidea of thee sub-order Simiae (or
Anthropoidea) of the order Primates of the
infra-class Eutheria of the sub-class Theria of the
class Mammalia of the sub-phylum Vertebrata
(Craniata) of the phylum Chordata of the subkingdom Metazoa of the animal kingdom.*

Earliest Primates These appeared in
the late Cretaceous epoch about 69 million
years ago. The earliest members of the
sub-order Anthropoidea are known from
both Africa and South America in the early
Oligocene, 34–30 million years ago, when
the two infra-orders, Platyrrhini and
Catarrhini, from the New and Old Worlds
respectively, were already distinct. New
finds from Fayum, in Egypt, are being
studied and may represent primates from
the early Oligocene period, 37 million
years.

Earliest Hominoid Hominoid remains
from Salonika in Greece are claimed by

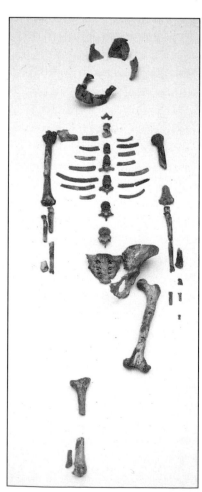

■ **Earliest skeletal remains**

field workers to be about 10 million years
old and thought to provide a link between
man and his ape ancestors. These finds,
however, require more intensive research.

Earliest hominid Characteristics
typical of the Hominidae such as the large
brain and bipedal locomotion   do not
appear until much later. The earliest
hominid relic found is an Australopithe-
cine jaw-bone with two molars 5 cm *2 in*
long found by Kiptalam Chepboi near Lake
Baringo, Kenya in February 1984 and dated
to 4 million years ago by associated fossils
and to 5·6–5·4 million years ago through
rock   correlation   by   potassium-argón
dating.

The most complete of the earliest hominid
skeletons is that of 'Lucy' (40 per cent
complete) found by Dr Donald C. Johanson
and T. Gray at Locality 162 by the Awash
River, Hadar, in the Afar region of Ethiopia
on 30 Nov 1974. She was estimated to be
c. 40 years old when she died 3 million years
ago, and she was 106 cm *3 ft 6 in* tall.

Parallel tracks of hominid footprints
extending over 24 m *80 ft* were first
discovered by Paul Abell and Dr Mary
Leakey at Laetoli, Tanzania in 1978, in
volcanic ash dating to 3·6 million years
ago. The height of the smallest what were
believed to be three individuals was estimated to be 120 cm *3 ft 11 in.*

Earliest genus—Homo The earliest
species of this genus is *Homo habilis,* or
'Handy Man', from Olduvai Gorge, Kenya,
named by Louis Leakey, Philip Tobias and
John Napier in 1964 after a suggestion from
Prof. Raymond Arthur Dart (1893–1988).

The greatest age attributed to fossils of this
genus is 1·9 million years for the skull
KNM-ER (Kenya National Museum-East
Rudolf) 1470 discovered in 1972 by Bernard
Ngeneo at Koobi Fora by Lake Turkana,
northern Kenya. It was reconstructed by
Dr Meave Leakey (*née* Epps).

The earliest stone tools are abraded core-
choppers dating from *c.* 2·5 million years
ago. They were found at Hadar, Ethiopia in
November–December 1976 by Hélène
Roche (France). Finger-(as opposed to
fist-) held quartz slicers found by Roche
and Dr John Wall (NZ) close to the Hadar
site by the Gona River are also dated to
c. 2·5 million years ago.

Earliest Homo erectus This species
(upright man), the direct ancestor of *Homo
sapiens,* was discovered by Kamoya Kimeu
on the surface at the site of Nariokotome III
to the west of Lake Turkana, Kenya in
August 1985. This skeleton of a 12-year-old-
boy 1·64 m *5 ft 5 in* in length is the most
complete of this species yet found; only a
few small pieces are missing. It is dated to
1·6 million years ago.

Europe A *Homo erectus* skull from a site
at Bilzingsleben, Germany, has been dated
by uranium dating techniques and
electron-spin resonance (ESR) to not less
than 350 000 and possible more than
400 000 years.

UK A Lower Palaeolithic hand-axe
factory and occupation site at Boxgrove,
W Sussex is thought to be more than
400 000 years old.

The oldest actual human remains ever
found in Britain are pieces of a brain case
from a specimen of *Homo sapiens,* recovered
in June 1935 and March 1936 by Dr Alvan T.
Marston from the Boyn Hill terrace in the
Barnfield Pit, near Swanscombe, Kent. The
remains were associated with a Middle
Acheulian tool culture and probably date

■ **Earliest footprints**

to the Holsteinian interglacial period (*c.*
230 000 BC).

Three hominid teeth, mandible fragments
and vertebra were found in Pontnewydd
Cave, Lower Elwy Valley, north Wales
from October 1980. They were dated by the
thorium/uranium disequilibrium method
to a little over 200 000 years.

In 1988 a jaw-bone of *homo sapiens sapiens*
(i.e. completely modern man) from a cave
near Torquay, Devon was found to be 31 000
years old by radiocarbon dating; this is
13 000 years older than a previously dated
skeleton of this species.

Oldest mummy Mummification (from
the Persian word *mūm,* wax) dates from
2600 BC or the 4th dynasty of the Egyptian
pharaohs. The oldest known mummy is that
of a high-ranking young woman who was
buried *c.* 2600 BC on a plateau near the
Great Pyramid of Cheops at Giza, or Al-
Gizeh, Egypt. Her remains, which appear
to represent the first attempts at mummification, were discovered in a 1·83 m *6 ft*
deep excavation on 17 Mar 1989, but only
her skull was intact. She is believed to have
lived in the lost kingdom of Ankh Ptah.

The oldest most complete mummy is of
Wati, a court musician of *c.* 2400 BC from
the tomb of Nefer in Saqqâra, Egypt, found
in 1944.

Dimensions
GIANTS

Growth of the body is determined by growth
hormone. This is produced by the pituitary
gland set deep in the brain. Over production in childhood produces abnormal
growth and true gigantism is the result.
The true height of human giants is frequently obscured by exaggeration and commercial dishonesty. The only admissible
evidence on the actual height of giants is

GIANTS

The only men for whom heights of 245 cm 8 ft or more have been reliably reported are the nine listed below. In seven cases, gigantism was followed by acromegaly, a disorder which causes an enlargement of the nose, lips, tongue, lower jaw, hands and feet, due to renewed activity and increase in growth hormone by an already swollen pituitary gland, which is located at the base of the brain.

John William Rogan (1871–1905) of Gallatin, Tennessee, USA [1] 264 cm *8 ft 8 in.*

John F. Carroll (1932–69) of Buffalo, New York State, USA [2] 263·5 cm *8 ft 7 3/4 in.*

Väinö Myllyrinne (1909–63) of Helsinki, Finland [3] 251·4 cm *8 ft 3 in.*

Don Koehler (1925–81) of Denton, Montana, USA [4] 248·9 cm *8 ft 2 in* ; latterly lived in Chicago.

Bernard Coyne (1897–1921) of Anthon, Iowa, USA [5] 248·9 cm *8 ft 2 in.*

Patrick Cotter (O'Brien) (1760–1806) of Kinsale, Co. Cork, Republic of Ireland [6] 246 cm *8 ft 1 in.*

'Constantine' (1872–1902) of Reutlingen, Germany [7] 245·8 cm *8 ft 0·8 in.*

Gabriel Estavao Monjane (1944–90) of Monjacaze, Mozambique [8] c. 245·7 cm *8 ft 3/4 in.*

Sulaimān 'Ali Nashnush (1943–91) of Tripoli, Libya [9] 247·6 cm *8 ft 4 in.*

[1] *Measured in a sitting position. Unable to stand owing to ankylosis (stiffening of the joints through the formation of adhesions) of the knees and hips. Weighed only 79 kg 175 lb.*

[2] *Severe kyphoscoliosis (two-dimensional spinal curvature). The figure represents his height with assumed normal spinal curvature, calculated from a standing height of 245 cm 8 ft measured on 14 Oct 1959. His standing height was 234 cm 7 ft 8 1/4 in shortly before his death.*

[3] *Stood 222 cm 7 ft 3 1/2 in at the age of 21 years. Experienced a second phase of growth in his late thirties and measured 246·8 cm 8 ft 1·2 in at the time of his death. In 1931 he reportedly weighed 196·8 kg 31 st.*

[4] *Abnormal growth started at the age of 10. He had a twin sister who is 175 cm 5 ft 9 in tall. His father was 187 cm 6 ft 2 in and his mother 177 cm 5 ft 10 in.*

[5] *Eunuchoidal giant (Daddy long-legs syndrome). Rejected by the army in 1918 when 236 cm 7 ft 9 in tall. Still growing at time of his death.*

[6] *Revised height based on skeletal remeasurement after bones exhumed on 19 Dec 1972.*

[7] *Eunuchoidal. Height estimated, as both legs were amputated after they turned gangrenous. He claimed a height of 259 cm 8 ft 6 in.*

[8] *Died January 1990 after a fall at his home .*

[9] *Operation to correct abnormal growth was successfully carried out in Rome in 1960. Died on 25 Feb 1991 of heart attack.*

that collected since 1870 under impartial medical supervision. Unfortunately even medical authors themselves are not always blameless and can include fanciful, as opposed to measured, heights.

The assertion that Goliath of Gath

EXAGGERATED HEIGHTS

The following lists a number of well-known giants whose heights have been exaggerated.

NAME	DATES	COUNTRY	HEIGHT CLAIMED			HEIGHT ACTUAL		
			cm	ft	in	cm	ft	in
Edouard Beaupre	1881–1904	Canada	251·4	8	3	236·2	7	9
Mohammad Alam Channa[1]	1956–fl. 1991	Pakistan	250·8	8	2 3/4	233·6	7	8
Fernard (Atlas) Bacheland	1923–76	Belgium	279·4	9	2	234·3	7	8 1/4
Joachim Eleizegue	1822–fl. 1845	Spain	238·7	7	10	233·6	7	8
Chang Wu-Gow	1846–93	China	279·4	9	2	233·6	7	8
Johann Petrussen	1914–fl. 1986	Iceland	264·1	8	8	231·1	7	7
Max Palmer	1928–fl. 1986	USA	245·1	8	0 1/2	231·1	7	7
Rigardus Rijnhout	1922–fl. 1955	Netherlands	278·1	9	1 1/2	229·8	7	6 1/2
Baptiste Hugo	1879–1916	France	269·2	8	10	229·8	7	6 1/2
Bernardo Gigli	1736–62	Italy	243·8	8	0	229·8	7	6 1/2
James Toller	1795–1819	England	259·0	8	6	228·6	7	6
Eddie Carmel[2]	1938–72	Israel	275·5	9	0 1/2	228·6	7	6
Daniel Cajanus	1724–49	Finland	283·2	9	3 1/2	222·2	7	3 1/2
Patrick Murphy	1834–62	Ireland	269·2	8	10	222·2	7	3 1/2
Jakop Loll (The Pomeranian Giant)	1783–1839	USSR	255·2	8	4 1/2	220·9	7	3
Paul Henoch	1852–76	Germany	251·4	8	3	218·4	7	2

[1] *Channa was medically assessed in New York on 21 Aug 1987 and found to measure 233·6 cm 7 ft 8 in (238·7 cm 7 ft 10 in in his shoes).*

[2] *The height of Eddie Carmel was estimated from photographs*

and that of Cajanus from evidence by bones. Each of the other actual heights was obtained from independent medical authority. The embalmed body of Beaupre in the anatomical museum of the University of Montreal measures 217 cm 7 ft 1 3/8 in in length.

(*c.* 1060 BC) stood 6 cubits with an arm span of 290 cm *9 ft 6 1/2 in* is open to doubt.

The Jewish historian Flavius Josephus AD 37–38, *c.*AD 100 and some of the manuscripts of the Septuagint (the earliest Greek translation of the Old Testament) attribute to Goliath the wholly credible height of 4 Greek cubits and an arm span of 208 cm *6 ft 10 in.*

Giants exhibited in circuses and exhibitions are routinely under contract not to be measured and are, almost traditionally, billed by their promoters at heights up to 45 cm *18 in* in excess of their true heights. The most recent example is Haji Mohammad Alam Channa (b. 1956) of Sehwan Sharif, Pakistan, who allegedly measured 250·8 cm *8 ft 2 3/4 in.* On 21 Aug 1987 he was measured in New York City, USA and found to be 233·6 cm *7 ft 8 in.*

TALLEST MEN

The tallest man in medical history of whom there is irrefutable evidence was Robert Pershing Wadlow, born at 6:30 a.m. on 22 Feb 1918 in Alton, Illinois, USA. On 27 Jun 1940 Dr C.M. Charles, Associate Prof. of Anatomy at Washington University's School of Medicine in St Louis, Missouri, and Dr Cyril MacBryde measured Wadlow at 272 cm *8 ft 11·1 in* (arm-span 288 cm *9 ft 5 3/4 in*). Wadlow died 18 days later at 1:30 a.m. on 15 Jul 1940 weighing 199 kg *31 st 5 lb* in an hotel in Manistee, Michigan, as a result of a septic blister on his right ankle, caused by a poorly fitting brace. Wadlow was still growing during his terminal illness and would probably have ultimately reached or just exceeded 274 cm *9 ft* in height if he had survived for another year. His greatest recorded weight was 222·7 kg (*35 st 1 lb*) on his 21st birthday. His shoes were size 37AA (47 cm *18½ in*) and his hands measured 32·4 cm *12 ¾ in* from the wrist to the tip of the middle finger.

England William Bradley (1787–1820), born in Market Weighton, East Riding, now Humberside, stood 236 cm *7 ft 9 in.*

John Middleton (1578–1623), the famous Childe of Hale, from near Liverpool, was credited with a height of 282 cm *9 ft 3 in* but a life-size impression of his right hand (length 29·2 cm *11 ½ in*, cf. Wadlow's 32·4 cm *12 ¾ in*) painted on a panel in Brasenose College, Oxford indicates his true stature was nearer 236 cm *7 ft 9 in.*

Albert Brough (1871–1919), a Nottingham publican, reached a height of 232 cm *7 ft 7 ½ in.*

Frederick Kempster (1889–1918) of Avebury, Wilts, was reported to have measured 255 cm *8 ft 4 ½ in* at the time of his death, but photographic evidence suggests that his height was 235 cm *7 ft 8 ½ in.* He measured 234 cm *7 ft 8·1 in* in 1913.

Henry Daglish, who stood 231 cm *7 ft 7 in* died in Upper Stratton, Wilts, on 15 Mar 1951, aged 25. He started growing at an abnormal rate at the age of 17 years.

The much-publicised Edward (Ted) Evans (1924–58) of Englefield Green, Surrey was reputed to have been 282 cm *9 ft 3 in*, but actually stood 235 cm *7 ft 8 ½ in.*

Scotland The tallest recorded 'true' (non-pathological) giant was Angus Macaskill (1823–63), born on the island of Berneray in the Sound of Harris, Western Isles. He stood 236 cm *7 ft 9 in* and died in St Ann's, Cape Breton Island, Nova Scotia, Canada.

Wales William Evans (1599–1634) of Monmouthshire, now Gwent, who was

ROBERT WADLOW

Weighing 3·85 kg *8 ½ lb* at birth, the abnormal growth of Robert Wadlow started at the age of 2 following a double hernia operation. His height progressed as follows:

AGE	HEIGHT cm	ft in	WEIGHT kg	lb
5	163	5 4	48	105
8	183	6 0	77	169
9	189	6 2 1/4	82	180
10	196	6 5	95	210
11	200	6 7	–	–
12	210	6 10 1/2	–	–
13	218	7 1 3/4	116	255
14	226	7 5	137	301
15	234	7 8	161	355
16	240	7 10 1/4	170	374
17	245	8 0 1/2	143[1]	315
18	253	8 3 1/2	–	–
19	258	8 5 1/2	218	480
20	261	8 6 3/4	–	–
21	265	8 8 1/4	223	491
22·4[2]	272	8 11 1/10	199	439

[1] *Following severe influenza and infection of the foot.*

[2] *Still growing during his terminal illness.*

porter to King James I, stood 228·6 cm *7 ft 6 in.*

Republic of Ireland Patrick Cotter (O'Brien) (1760–1806), born in Kinsale, Co. Cork, was 246 cm *8 ft 1 in* tall. He died at Hotwells, Bristol (see table p. 61).

Isle of Man The tallest Manxman on record was Arthur Caley of Sulby. He was variously credited with heights of 249 cm *8 ft 2 in* and 254 cm *8 ft 4 in*, but actually stood 228·6 cm *7 ft 6 in.* He died at Clyde, New Jersey, USA on 12 Feb 1889 aged 60.

Living The tallest person in the world is eunochoidal giant Chandra Barman (b. 1962) of Dacca, Bangladesh who stands 251 cm *8 ft 3 in* and is still growing after starting to grow abnormally at the age of 11.

UK The tallest man now living in the UK is Christopher Paul Greener (b. New Brighton, Merseyside, 21 Nov 1943) of Hayes, Kent, who measures 229 cm *7 ft 6 ¼ in* (weight 165 kg *26 st*).

Scotland The tallest Scotsman now living is George Gracie (b. 1938) of Forth, Lanarks, now in Strathclyde. He stands 221 cm *7 ft 3 in* and weighs 203 kg *32 st*. His brother Hugh (b. 1941) is 215 cm *7 ft 0 ½ in.*

TALLEST WOMEN

The tallest woman in medical history was the giantess Zeng Jinlian (b. 26 Jun 1964) of Yujiang village in the Bright Moon Commune, Hunan Province, central China, who was 247 cm *8 ft 1 ¾ in* when she died on 13 Feb 1982. This figure, however, represented her height with assumed normal spinal curvature because she suffered from severe scoliosis (curvature of the spine)

■ **Smallest living man**
Gul Mohammed (in right of picture) of India who is 57·5 cm 22·5 in high standing alongside Mr V.K. Sharma. (Photo: Harish Vats)

and could not stand up straight. She began to grow abnormally from the age of four months and stood 156 cm *5 ft 1 ½ in* before her fourth birthday and 217 cm *7 ft 1 ½ in* when she was 13. Her hands measured 25·5 cm *10 in* and her feet 35·5 cm *14 in* in length. Both her parents and her brother were of normal size.

The giantess Ella Ewing (1875–1913) of Gorin, Missouri, USA was billed at 249 cm *8 ft 2 in*, but this height was exaggerated. She measured 224 cm *7 ft 4 ½ in* at the age of 23, and may have attained 228·6 cm *7 ft 6 in* at the time of her death.

UK The tallest woman in British medical history was Jane ('Ginny') Bunford, (b. 26 Jul 1895) at Bartley Green, Northfield, Birmingham. Her skeleton, now preserved in the Anatomical Museum in the Medical School at Birmingham University, has a height of 223·3 cm *7 ft 4 in.* Her abnormal growth started at the age of 11 following a head injury, and on her 13th birthday she measured 198 cm *6 ft 6 in.* Shortly before her death on 1 Apr 1922 she stood 231 cm *7 ft 7 in* tall, but she had severe kyphoscoliosis and would have measured at least 241 cm *7 ft 11 in* if she had been able to stand fully erect.

Living The world's tallest woman is Sandy Allen (b. 18 Jun 1955) in Chicago, Illinois, USA and now working as a secretary in Indianapolis, Indiana. A 2·95 kg *6 ½ lb* baby, her abnormal growth began soon after birth. At 10 years of age she stood 190·5 cm *6 ft 3 in* and measured 216 cm *7 ft 1 in* when she was 16. On 14 Jul 1977 this giantess underwent a pituitary gland operation, which inhibited further growth at 231·7 cm *7 ft 7 ¼ in.* She now weighs 209·5 kg *33 st* and takes a size 16 EEE American shoe (14 ½ UK or 50 PP C).

Married couple Anna Hanen Swan (1846–88) of Nova Scotia, Canada was said to be 246 cm *8 ft 1 in* but actually measured 227 cm *7 ft 5 ½ in.* At the church of St Martin-in-the-Fields, London on 17 Jun 1871 she married Martin van Buren Bates (1845–1919) of Whitesburg, Letcher County, Kentucky, USA, who stood 219 cm *7 ft 2 ½ in*, making them the tallest married couple on record.

TALLEST TWINS

World The world's tallest identical twins are Michael and James Lanier (b. 27 Nov 1969) from Troy, Michigán, USA. They measured 216 cm *7 ft 1 in* at the age of 14 years and both now stand 223·3 cm *7 ft 4 in.* Their sister Jennifer is 157·4 cm *5 ft 2 in* tall.

The world's tallest female identical twins are Heather and Hedi Burge (b. 11 Nov 1971) from Palos Verdes, California, USA they are both 195 cm *6 ft 4 ¾ in* tall.

UK The tallest identical male twins recorded in Britain were the Knipe brothers (b. 1761) of Magherafelt, near Londonderry, who both measured 218·4 cm *7 ft 2 in.*

The tallest living male twins are Andrew and Timothy Hull (b. 23 and 24 Oct 1968 respectively) of Redditch, Worcs, who are 206·5 cm *6 ft 9·3 in* and 209 cm *6 ft 10·3 in* respectively.

The tallest identical female twins are Daphne Turner and Evelyn Staniford (née Gould) (b. 28 Apr 1931) who both measure 186 cm *6 ft 1 ½ in.* Each has a son who is over 195 cm *6 ft 5 in.*

DWARFS

The strictures that apply to giants apply

equally to dwarfs, except that exaggeration gives way to understatement. In the same way as 274 cm *9 ft* may be regarded as the limit towards which the tallest giants tend, so 58 cm *23 in* must be regarded as the limit towards which the shortest adult dwarfs or midgets tend (cf. the average length of new-born babies is 46–50 cm *18–20 in*). In the case of child dwarfs, their *ages* are often exaggerated by their agents or managers.

There are many causes of short stature in humans. They include genetic abnormalities, lack of appropriate hormones (e.g. growth hormones) and starvation. In the past dwarfism of whatever cause tended to be smaller due to lower nutritional standards. There are an estimated 3000 people of severely restricted growth (i.e. under 142 cm *4 ft 8 in* living in Britain today.

Shortest person The shortest mature human of whom there is independent evidence was Pauline Musters ('Princess Pauline'), a Dutch dwarf. She was born at Ossendrecht on 26 Feb 1876 and measured 30 cm *11·8 in* at birth. At nine years of age she was 55 cm *21·65 in* tall and weighed only 1·5 kg *3 lb 5 oz*. She died on 1 Mar 1895 in New York City, USA at the age of 19. A post mortem examination showed her to be exactly 61 cm *24 in* (there was some elongation after death). Her mature weight varied from 3·4–4 kg *7½–9 lb* and her 'vital statistics' were 47–48–43 cm *18½–19–17 in*, which suggest she was overweight.

British Isles The shortest mature human ever recorded in Britain was Joyce Carpenter (b. 21 Dec 1929), of Charford, now Hereford & Worcester, who stood 74 cm *29 in* tall and weighed 13·6 kg *30 lb*. She suffered from Morquio's disease which causes deformities of the spine and shortening of the neck and trunk. She died on 7 Aug 1973 aged 43.

In 1979 a height of 50 cm *19·68 in* and a weight of 1·98 kg *4 lb 6 oz* were reported for a nine-year-old Greek girl named Stamatoula (b. September 1969; length 15 cm *5·9 in*). When she died on 22 Aug 1985 at the Lyrion Convent, Athens, Greece she measured 67 cm *26·4 in* and weighed 5 kg *11 lb*. The child, believed to be the survivor of twins, suffered from Seckel's syndrome, also known as 'bird-headed dwarfism'.

Shortest male The shortest recorded adult male dwarf was Calvin Phillips, (b. 14 Jan 1791 in Bridgewater, Massachusetts, USA). He weighed 907 g *2 lb* at birth and stopped growing at the age of five. When he was 19 he measured 67 cm *26 ½ in* and weighed 5·4 kg *12 lb* with his clothes on. He died two years later, in April 1812, from progeria, a rare disorder characterized by dwarfism and premature senility.

William E. Jackson, alias 'Major Mite' (b. 2 Oct 1864 in Dunedin, New Zealand), measured 23 cm *9 in* long and weighed 340 g *12 oz* at birth. In November 1880 he stood 53 cm *21 in* in height and weighed 4 kg *9 lb*. He died in New York City, USA on 9 Dec 1900, when he measured 69 cm *27 in.*

The most famous midget in history was Charles Sherwood Stratton, alias 'General Tom Thumb' (b. 4 Jan 1838). When he joined up with Phineas T. Barnum the famous American showman, his birth date was changed to 4 Jan 1832 so that when billed at 77 cm *30 ½ in* at the age of 18 he was in fact 12. Tom died of apoplexy on 15 Jul 1885 at his birthplace, Bridgeport, Connecticut aged 45 and was 102 cm *3 ft 4 in* and weighed (31·7 kg *70 lb*).

Hopkins Hopkins (1737–54) of Llantrisant, Mid-Glamorgan, who suffered from progeria, was 79 cm *31 in* tall. He weighed

8·62 kg *19 lb* at the age of 7 and 6 kg *13 lb* at the time of his death.

Shortest living The world's shortest known mobile living adult is Gul Mohammed (b. 15 Feb 1957) of Delhi, India. On 19 Jul 1990 he was examined at Ram Manohar Hospital, New Delhi, and found to measure 57·15 cm *22·5 in* in height (weight 17 kg *37·47 lb*). The other members of his immediate family are of normal height.

Madge Bester (b. 26 Apr 1963) of Johannesburg, South Africa, is only 65 cm *25·5 in* tall, but she suffers from Osteogenesis imperfecta and is confined to a wheelchair. In this disease there is an inherited abnormality of collagen, which, with calcium salts, provides the rigid structure of bones. It is characterized by brittle bones and other deformities of the skeleton. Her mother Winnie is not much taller, measuring 70 cm *27·5 in*, and she too is confined to a wheelchair.

UK The shortest adult living is Michael Henbury-Ballan (b. 26 Nov 1958) of Bassett, Southampton, Hants who is 94 cm *37 in* tall and weighs 35 kg *5 ½ st*. A 2·66 kg *5 lb 14 oz* baby, he stopped growing at the age of 13. His fraternal twin brother Malcolm is 175 cm *5 ft 9 in* tall and weighs 73 kg *11 st 7 lb*.

Patrick Scanlan (b. 1966) of Maida Vale, London stands 91·4 cm *36 in* tall and weighs only 19 kg *42 lb*, but he suffers from MPs, an enzyme disease that causes severe bone abnormalities, including curvature of the spine, and cannot stand erect. He stopped growing at the age of 4 years.

Twins The shortest twins ever recorded were the primordial dwarfs Matjus and Bela Matina (b. 1903–*fl.*1935) of Budapest, Hungary, who later became naturalized American citizens. They both measured 76 cm *30 in*.

Living The world's shortest living identical twins are John and Greg Rice (b. 3 Dec 1951) of West Palm Beach, Florida, USA, who both measure 86·3 cm *34 in*.

The shortest identical twin sisters are Dorene Williams of Oakdale and Darlene McGregor of Almeda, California, USA (b. 1949), who each stand 124·4 cm *4 ft 1 in*.

Oldest There are only two centenarian dwarfs on record. The oldest was Hungarian-born Susanna Bokoyni ('Princess Susanna') of Newton, New Jersey, USA, who died aged 105 years on 24 Aug 1984. She was 101 cm *3 ft 4 in* tall and weighed 16·78 kg *37 lb*.

The other was Miss Anne Clowes of Matlock, Derbys, who died on 5 Aug 1784 aged 103 years. She was 114 cm *3 ft 9 in* tall and weighed 21·7 kg *48 lb*.

Most variable stature Adam Rainer, born in Graz, Austria in 1899, measured 118 cm *3 ft 10·45 in* at the aged of 21. He then suddenly started growing at a rapid rate, and by 1931 he had reached 218 cm *7 ft 1 ¾ in*. He became so weak as a result that he was bedridden for the rest of his life. At the time of his death on 4 Mar 1950, aged 51, he measured 234 cm *7 ft 8 in* and was the only person in medical history to have been both a dwarf and a giant.

Most dissimilar couple Nigel Wilks (200·6 cm *6 ft 6 in*) (b. 1963) of Kingston-upon-Hull, Humberside married on 30 Jun 1984 Beverley Russell (119·3 cm *4 ft*) (b. 1963) who suffers from a skeletal disorder.

TRIBES

Tallest The tallest major tribes in the world are the slender Tutsi, (also known as the Watusi) of Rwanda and Burundi, Central Africa, and the Dinka of the Sudan. In the case of the Tutsi, average adult males and females stand 195·5 cm *6 ft 5 in* and 177·8 cm *5 ft 10 in* respectively.

Shortest The smallest pygmies are the Mbuti of the Ituri forest, Zaïre, Central Africa, with an average height of 137 cm *4 ft 6 in* for men and 135 cm *4 ft 5 in* for women.

WEIGHT

Heaviest male The heaviest human in medical history was Jon Brower Minnoch (1941–1983) of Bainbridge Island, Washington State, USA, who had suffered from obesity since childhood. The 185 cm *6 ft 1 in* tall former taxi-driver was 181 kg *28 st* in 1963, 317 kg *50 st* in 1966 and 442 kg *69 st 9 lb* in September 1976.

In March 1978, Minnoch was rushed to University Hospital, Seattle, saturated with fluid and suffering from heart and respiratory failure. It took a dozen firemen and an improvized stretcher to move him from his home to a ferry-boat. When he arrived at the hospital he was put in two beds lashed together. It took 13 people just to roll him over. By extrapolating his intake and elimination rates, consultant endocrinologist Dr Robert Schwartz calculated that Minnoch must have weighed more than 635 kg *100 st*, when he was admitted, a great deal of which was water accumulation due to his congestive heart failure. After nearly two years on a 1200-calories-a-day diet the choking fluid had gone, and he was discharged at 216 kg *34 st*. In October 1981 he had to be readmitted, after putting on 91 kg over *14 st*. When he died on 10 Sep 1983 he weighed more than 363 kg *57 st*.

UK Peter Yarnall of East Ham, London weighed 374 kg *58 st* and was 177·8 cm *5 ft 10 in* tall. The former docker began putting on weight at a rapid rate in 1978 and for the last two years of his life he was bedridden. He died on 30 Mar 1984 aged 34 years and it took 10 firemen 5 hours to demolish the wall of his bedroom and winch his body down to street level. His coffin measured 288 cm *7 ft 4 in* in length, 122 cm *4 ft* across and had a depth of 83·8 cm *2 ft 9 in*.

Only three other British men had a recorded weight of more than 317·5 kg *49 st*. The most celebrated was Daniel Lambert (1770–1809) of Leicester, Leics. He stood 180 cm *5 ft 11 in* tall and weighed 335 kg *52 st* shortly before his death, and had a girth of more than 233 cm *92 in*.

Another was William Campbell (b. 1856 in Glasgow) who died on 16 Jun 1878 who was 190 cm *6 ft 3 in* tall and weighed 340 kg *53 st 8 lb*, with a 216 cm *85 in* waist and a 244 cm *96 in* chest. He was a publican at High Bridge, Newcastle upon Tyne, Tyne & Wear.

The third was the Welshman Melvin (or Melvyn) Jones (b. 1934) who died in Liverpool on 25 Jul 1988 and was buried in Bangor, Gwynedd. He stood 170 cm *5 ft 7 in* tall and weighed 330 kg *52 st*.

Republic of Ireland The heaviest is reputed to have been Roger Byrne, who was buried in Rosenallis, Co. Laoighis (Leix), on 14 Mar 1804. He died in his 54th year, and his coffin and its contents weighed 330 kg *52 st*.

Living The heaviest living man is T. J. Albert Jackson (b. 1941 as Kent Nicholson), also known as 'Fat Albert', of Canton, Mississippi, USA. He has weighed 404 kg *63 st 9 lb*. He has a 305 cm *120 in* chest, a 294 cm *116 in* waist, 178 cm *70 in* thighs and a 75 cm *29 ½ in* neck.

UK The professional wrestler Martin Ruane, alias Luke McMasters ('Giant Haystacks'), who was born in Camberwell, London in 1946 is 210·8 cm *6 ft 11 in*. He once claimed to be 317 kg *50 st*. His weight fluctuates between 286 kg *45 st* and 292 kg *46 st*.

Arthur Armitage (b. 28 Jun 1929) of Knottingley, W Yorks, weighed 305 kg *48 st* (height 175 cm *5 ft 9 in*) in October 1986. By March 1989 had stabilized at 190 kg *30 st*.

Norman Smith (b. 10 May 1957) of Slough, Berks reached a peak weight of 303 kg *47 st 11 lb* (height 184 cm *6 ft 0 ½ in*) on 10 Mar 1988, and in 1989 was reported down to 265 kg *41 st 10 lb*.

Heaviest female The heaviest woman ever recorded was probably Rosie Carnemolla (b. 1944) of Poughkeepsie, New York, USA, who registered a peak weight of 385·5 kg *60 st 10 lb* on 13 Mar 1988. A week later she was put on a carefully controlled diet which reduced her weight by 113 kg *17 st 12 lb* in six months, and then underwent an operation to reduce the size of her stomach. By September 1988 the former food addict was down to 158·7 kg *25 st*, during which time her waistline had declined from 249 cm *98 in* to 117 cm *46 in* and her US dress size from 70 to 46. Her target weight is 68 kg *10 st 10 lb*.

When Mrs Percy Pearl Washington, who suffered from polydipsia (excessive thirst), died in a Milwaukee hospital, USA on 9 Oct 1972 the scales registered only 362·8 kg *57 st 2 lb*, but earlier she was credited with a weight of 399·1 kg *62 st 12 lb*. She was 183 cm *6 ft* tall and wore a US size 62 dress.

■ **Shortest living female**
Madge Bester (b. 26 Apr 1963) of Johannesburg, South Africa, is 65 cm 25.5 in tall. (Photo: Gamma Presse)

Slimming

Ron Allen (b. 1947) sweated off 9·7 kg *21 ½ lb* of his weight of 113·4 kg *17 st 1 lb* in Nashville, Tennessee, USA in 24 hours in August 1984.

SUPER HEAVYWEIGHTS

Jon Brower Minnoch (1941–83) USA 185 cm *6 ft 1 in* **635 kg** *100 st*

Walter Hudson (b. 1944) USA 178 cm *5 ft 10 in* **544 kg** *85 st 7 lb*

Michael Walker *né* Francis Lang (b. 1934) USA 188 cm *6 ft 2 in*[1] **538 kg** *84 st 11 lb*

Robert Earl Hughes (1926–58) USA 184 cm *6 ft ½ in* **485 kg** *76 st 5 lb*

Mike Parteleno (b. 1958) USA 183 cm *6 ft* **463 kg** *73 st*

Mills Darden (1798–1857) USA 229 cm *7 ft 6 in* **462 kg** *72 st 12 lb*

Michael Edelman (b. 1964) USA **457 kg** *72 st*

John Finnerty (b. 1952) USA **453 kg** *71 st 6 lb*

'Big Tex' (1902–*fl.* 1956) USA 186 cm *6 ft 1 ½ in* **419 kg** *66 st*

Mickey Mounds (b. 1953) USA **413 kg** *65 st*[2]

John Hanson Craig (1856–94) USA 195 cm *6 ft 5 in*[3] **411 kg** *64 st 11 lb*

Michael Hebranko (b. 1954) USA 183 cm *6 ft* **410·5 kg** *64 st 9 lb*[4]

Arthur Knorr (1914–60) USA 185 cm *6 ft 1 in*[5] **408 kg** *64 st 4 lb*

T.J. Albert Jackson (b. 1941) Canton, Mississippi, USA 193 cm *6 ft 4 in* **404 kg** *63 st 9 lb*

---

[1] *Peak weight attained in 1971 as a result of drug-induced bulimia. Reduced to 167 kg 26 st 1 lb by February 1980.*

[2] *Reduced to 165 kg 26 st by February 1989.*

[3] *Won $1000 in a 'Bonny Baby' contest in New York City in 1858.*

[4] *Reduced to 98·4 kg 15 ½ st 7 lb by June 1989*

[5] *Gained 136 kg 21 st 1 lb in the last 6 months of his life.*

UK The heaviest woman ever recorded was Mrs Muriel Hopkins (b. 1931) of Tipton, W Mids, who weighed 278 kg *43 st 11 lb* (height 180 cm *5 ft 11 in*) in 1978. Shortly before her death on 22 Apr 1979 she reportedly weighed 330 kg *52 st*, but this was only an estimate, and her actual weight was found to be 301 kg *47 st 7 lb*. Her coffin measured 190 cm *6 ft 3 in* in length, 137 cm *4 ft 5 in* in width and was 114 cm *3 ft 9 in* deep.

Heaviest twins Billy Leon (1946–79) and Benny Loyd (b. 7 Dec 1946) McCrary, alias McGuire, of Hendersonville, North Carolina, USA were normal in size until the age of six when they both contracted German measles. In November 1978 they weighed 337 kg *53 st 1 lb* (Billy) and 328 kg *51 st 9 lb* (Benny) and had 213 cm *84 in* waists. As professional tag wrestling performers they were billed at weights up to 349 kg *55 st*. Billy died at Niagara Falls, Ontario, Canada on 13 Jul 1979.

Weight Loss The greatest recorded slimming feat was that of Jon Brower Minnoch (see Heaviest male) who had reduced to 216 kg *34 st* by July 1979, thus indicating a weight loss of at least 419 kg *66 st* in two years.

Michael Hebranko (b. 14 May 1953) of Brooklyn, New York, USA weighed 410·5 kg *64 st 9 lb* in July 1979. Within 15 months he lost over 226·8 kg *35 st 10 lb*, and by June 1989 he weighed 98·4 kg *15 st 7 lb*, having shed a total of 312 kg *49 st 2 lb* within a period of less than 24 months. His waist measurement was 292·1 cm *115 in* but is now 91–96 cm *36–38 in*, a reduction of about 200·6 cm *79 in*.

Paul M. Kimelman (b. 1943) of Pittsburgh, Pennsylvania, USA reduced his weight from 216 kg *34 st 11 lb* to 59 kg *9 st 4 lb* between 1 Jan 1967 and 3 Aug 1967, a loss of 162 kg *25 st* in 215 days.

Roly McIntyre (see Heaviest male) reduced his weight from 262 kg *41 st 4 lb* to 84·8 kg *13 st 5 lb* during the 22-month period April 1983–February 1985.

On 14 Mar 1982 surgeons at a hospital in New York, USA removed 67 kg *10 st* of adipose tissue from the abdominal wall of a 362 kg *57 st* man. They had to use a hoist to lift the layers of fat as they were removed.

Female The US circus fat lady Mrs Celesta Geyer (b. 1901), alias Dolly Dimples, went from 251 kg *39 st* to 69 kg *10 st 1 lb* in 1950–51, a loss of 182 kg *28 st* in 14 months. Her 'vital statistics' diminished from 200–213–213 cm *79–84–84 in* to a svelte 86–71–91 cm *34–28–36 in*. Her book *How I Lost 28 stone* was not a best-seller, perhaps because of the difficulty of would-be readers identifying with the dressmaking and other problems of losing more than 178 kg *28 st* particularly when only 150 cm *4 ft 11 in* tall. In December 1967 she was reportedly down to 50 kg *7 st 12 lb*.

The female champion in Britain is Mrs Dolly Wager (b. 1933) of Charlton, London, who, between September 1971 and 22 May 1973 reduced her weight from 200 kg *31 st 7 lb* to 69·8 kg *11 st*, so losing 130 kg *20 st 7 lb* with Weight Watchers.

Weight gaining The reported record for weight gain is held by Jon Brower Minnoch (see Heaviest male) at 91 kg *14 st* in 7 days in October 1981 after readmittance to University of Washington Hospital, Seattle, USA.

Arthur Knorr (1916–60) USA, gained 136 kg *21 st* in the last six months of his life.

Miss Doris James of San Francisco, California, USA is alleged to have gained 147 kg *23 st 3 lb* in the 12 months before her death in August 1965, aged 38, at a weight of 306 kg *48 st 3 lb*. She was only 157 cm *5 ft 2 in* tall.

Greatest differential The greatest weight difference recorded for a married couple is *c.* 589 kg *92 st 12 lb* in the case of Jon Brower Minnoch (See Heaviest male) and his 50 kg *7 st 12 lb* wife Jeannette in March 1978.

The UK record is held by the wrestler Martin Ruane, alias Luke McMasters (Giant Haystacks) and his 47·6 kg *7 ½ st* wife Rita, where their weight differential at one time may have been 270 kg *42 ½ st*.

Lightest The lightest adult on record was Lucia Zarate (1863–89 San Carlos, Mexico), an emaciated ateliotic dwarf of 67 cm *26 ½ in*, who weighed 2·13 kg *4·7 lb* at the age of 17. She 'fattened up' to 5·9 kg *13 lb* by her 20th birthday. At birth she weighed 1·1 kg *2 ½ lb*.

The thinnest recorded adults of normal height are those suffering from anorexia nervosa. Losses of up to 65 per cent of the original body-weight have been recorded in females, with a 'low' of 20 kg *3 st 3 lb* in the case of Emma Shaller (1868–90) of St Louis, Missouri, USA, who was 157 cm *5 ft 2 in* tall.

Edward C. Hagner (1892–1962), alias Eddie Masher, USA is alleged to have weighed only 22 kg *3 st 6 lb* at a height of 170 cm *5 ft 7 in*. He was also known as 'Skeleton Dude'.

In August 1825 the biceps measurement of Claude-Ambroise Seurat (1797–1826) of Troyes, France was 10 cm *4 in* and the distance between his back and his chest was less than 7·6 cm *3 in*. According to one report he stood 171 cm *5 ft 7 ½ in* and weighed 35 kg *5 st 8 lb*, but in another account he was described as being 163 cm *5 ft 4 in* and only 16 kg *2 st 8 lb*.

British Isles The lightest adult was Hopkins Hopkins (Dwarfs, see p. 62).

Robert Thorn (b. 1842) of March, Cambs weighed 22 kg *49 lb* at the age of 32. He was 137 cm *4 ft 6 in* tall and had a 68 cm *27 in* chest (expanded) 11·4 cm *4 ½ in* biceps, and a 7·6 cm *3 in* wrist. A doctor who examined him said he had practically no muscular development, 'although he could run along the road'.

Reproductivity

MOTHERHOOD

Most children The greatest officially recorded number of children born to one mother is 69, by the first of the two wives of Feodor Vassilyev (b. 1707–*fl.*1782), a peasant from Shuya, 241 km *150 miles* east of Moscow, USSR. In 27 confinements she gave birth to 16 pairs of twins, seven sets of triplets and four sets of quadruplets. The case was reported to Moscow by the Monastery of Nikolskiy on 27 Feb 1782. At least 67 who were born in the period *c.* 1725–65, survived infancy.

It was reported on 31 Jan 1989 that Mrs Maria Olivera (b. 1939) of San Juan, Argentina gave birth to her 32nd child. They are all believed to be still alive.

UK Elizabeth, wife of John Mott whom she married in 1676, of Monks Kirby, Warks, produced 42 live-born children. She died in 1720, 44 years after her marriage.

According to an inscription on a gravestone in Conway Church cemetery, Gwynedd, North Wales, Nicholas Hookes (died 27 Mar 1637) was the 41st child of his mother Alice Hookes, but further details are lacking. It has not been possible to corroborate or refute this report.

Mrs Elizabeth Greenhille (died 1681) of Abbots Langley, Herts is alleged to have produced 39 children (32 daughters, seven sons) in a record 38 confinements. Her son Thomas was the author of the *Art of Embalming* (1705).

Mrs Rebecca Town (1805–51) of Keighley, W Yorks, had 30 children, but only one survived dying at the age of three.

Mrs Ada Watson (b. 23 Jun 1886) of Cambridge gave birth to 25 children in 22 confinements, including three sets of twins, all of whom attained their majority, during the period 1904–31. She died in Roehampton, London on 5 Feb 1974.

Today's champion mothers are believed to be Mrs Margaret McNaught (b. 1923), of Balsall Heath, Birmingham (12 boys and 10 girls, all single births–two boys died in infancy).

Mrs Mabel Constable (b. 1920), of Long Itchington, Warwicks also has had 22 children, including a set of triplets and two sets of twins.

Mrs Jessie Campbell (b. 1946) of Struan, Isle of Skye, Scotland, gave birth to her 20th child on 22 Jan 1990.

Republic of Ireland In December 1949 it was reported that Mrs Mabel Murphy (b. 1898) of Lisnaskea, Co. Fermanagh had produced 28 children (12 stillborn) in a 32 year marriage, but this claim has not been fully substantiated.

Mrs Kathleen Scott (b. 4 Jul 1914) of Dublin gave birth to her 24th child on 9 Aug 1958. Twenty of her children are still alive.

Oldest mother Medical literature contains extreme but unauthenticated cases of septuagenarian mothers, such as Mrs Ellen Ellis, aged 72, of Four Crosses, Clwyd, who allegedly produced a stillborn 13th child on 15 May 1776 in her 46th year of marriage. Many very late maternities may be cover-ups for illegitimate grandchildren.

The oldest recorded mother for whom the evidence satisfied medical verification was Mrs Ruth Alice Kistler (*née* Taylor), formerly Mrs Shepard (1899–1982), of Portland, Oregon, USA. A birth certificate indicated that she gave birth to a daughter, Suzan, at Glendale, near Los Angeles, California, USA on 18 Oct 1956, when her age was 57 years 129 days.

In the *Gazette Médicale de Liége* (1 Oct 1891) Dr E. Derasse reported the case of one of his patients who gave birth to a healthy baby at the age of 59 years 5 months. The woman already had a married daughter aged 40 years.

UK Mrs Kathleen Campbell (b. 23 Apr 1932) of Ilkeston, Derbys, gave birth to a 2·92 kg *6 lb 7 oz* baby boy at Nottingham City Hospital on 9 Sep 1987 at the age of 55 years 141 days. She already had six children aged 16 to 22 years.

According to a report in the *Lancet* (1867) a woman reputedly aged 62 gave birth to triplets. She had previously borne 10 children.

Mrs Mary Higgins of Cork, Co. Cork (b. 7 Jan 1876) gave birth to a daughter, Patricia, on 17 Mar 1931 when aged 55 years 69 days.

Longest and shortest pregnancy Claims of up to 413 days have been widely reported, but accurate data are bedevilled by the increasing use of oral contraceptive pills, which is a cause of amenorrhoea (absence of menstruation). *The US Medical Investigator* of 27 Dec 1884 reported a case of 15 months 20 days and the *Histoire de l'Académie* of 1751 the most extreme case of 36 months.

In the pre-pill era English law has accepted pregnancies with extremes of 174 days (*Clark* v. *Clark*, 1939) and 349 days (*Hadlum* v. *Hadlum*, 1949).

BABIES

Heaviest Big babies (i.e. over 4·5 kg *10 lb*) are usually born to mothers who are large, overweight or have some medical problem such as diabetes. The heaviest babies of a healthy mother were two boys of a combined weight of 10·2 kg *22 lb 8 oz* born to Sig Carmelina Fedele of Aversa, Italy in September 1955 and by Caesarean section to Mrs Christina Samane at Sipetu Hospital, Transkei, South Africa on 24 May 1982. The latter boy, named Sithandawe, who suffers from Weaver's syndrome (excessive

growth in children because of abnormalities in the parents' genes), weighed 70 kg *11 st* and was 165 cm *5 ft 5 in* tall on his 6th birthday.

Mrs Anna Bates *née* Swan (1846–88), the 227 cm *7 ft 5 ½ in* Canadian giantess, gave birth to a boy weighing 10·77 kg *23 lb 12 oz* (length 76 cm *30 in*) at her home in Seville, Ohio, USA on 19 Jan 1879, but the baby died 11 hours later.

UK It was reported in a letter to the *British Medical Journal* (1 Feb 1879) from a doctor in Torpoint, Cornwall that a child born on Christmas Day 1852 weighed 9·53 kg *21 lb.*

The only other reported birthweight in excess of 9·07 kg *20 lb* is 9·13 kg *20 lb 2 oz* for a boy with a 36·8 cm *14 ½ in* chest born to a 33-year-old schoolmistress in Crewe, Cheshire on 12 Nov 1884.

On 15 Oct 1785 the 'Irish Fairy', Mrs Catherine Kelly, who was 86·3 cm *34 in* tall and weighed 9·97 kg *22 lb*, died in Norwich, Norfolk, after giving birth to a 3·17 kg *7 lb* baby which lived only 2 hours.

Lightest single births The lowest birthweight recorded for a surviving infant, of which there is definite evidence, is 283 g *10 oz* in the case of Mrs Marian Taggart (*née* Chapman) (1938–83). This baby was born six weeks premature in South Shields, Tyne & Wear. She was born unattended (length 31 cm *12 in*) and was nursed by Dr D.A. Shearer, who fed her hourly for the first 30 hours with brandy, glucose and water through a fountain-pen filler. At three weeks she weighed 821 g *1 lb 13 oz* and by her first birthday 6·29 kg *13 lb 14 oz*. Her weight on her 21st birthday was 48·08 kg *7 st 8 lb.*

Lightest twins Mary, 453 g *16 oz*, and Margaret, 538 g *19 oz*, were born on 16 Aug 1931 to Mrs Florence Stimson, Old Fletton, Peterborough, Cambs.

Longest interval between twins Mrs Danny Berg (b. 1953) of Rome, Italy, who had been on hormone treatment after suffering two miscarriages, gave birth normally to a baby girl, Diana, on 23 Dec 1987, but she was not delivered of the other twin, Monica, by Caesarean section, until 30 Jan 1988.

Test-tube babies There are various methods by which babies can be conceived outside of the mother's body. These children are usually known as 'test-tube' babies and the technique as I.V.F. (In vitro fertilization).

First Test-tube baby Lesley Brown 31, gave birth by Caesarean section to Louise (2·6 kg *5 lb 12 oz*) in Oldham General Hospital, Lancs, at 11:47 p.m. on 25 Jul 1978. Louise was externally conceived on 10 Nov 1977.

First test-tube quintuplets Alan, Brett, Connor, Douglas and Edward were born to Linda and Bruce Jacobssen at University College Hospital, London on 26 Apr 1985.

Oldest mother to have delivered following IVF A woman aged 49 years 54 days (b. Cyprus) gave birth by Caesarean section to a baby girl 2850 g *101 oz* in October 1990. The fertilized egg had been implanted in the patient's womb under the supervision of Dr Krinos Trokoudes, Director of the Pedieos I.V.F. Center in Nicosia, Cyprus.

Longest interval between 'test-tube twins' Mrs Mary Wright 38, gave birth to Amy and Elizabeth 18 months

apart from eggs fertilized by her husband in March 1984. Elizabeth was born at Stoke-on-Trent, Staffs, on 22 Apr 1987 from an egg which had been in frozen storage for 29 months.

Most premature babies James Elgin Gill was born to Brenda and James Gill, on 20 May 1987 in Ottawa, Ontario, Canada 128 days premature and weighing 0·624 kg *1 lb 6 oz.*

Twins Joanne and Mark Holding (non-identical twins) were born on 28 Feb 1988 in Portsmouth, Hants 105 days premature. Joanne weighed 0·880 kg *1 lb 15 oz* and Mark 0·825 kg *1 lb 8 oz.*

Quadruplets Tina Piper of St Leonards-on-Sea, E Sussex, was delivered of quadruplets on 10 Apr 1988, at exactly 26 weeks' term. Oliver; 1·6 kg *2 lb 9 oz*, (died February 1989), Francesca 0·96 kg *2 lb 2 oz*, Charlotte 1·03 kg *2 lb 4 ½ oz* and Georgina 1·05 kg *2 lb 5 oz* were all born at the Royal Sussex County Hospital, Brighton, Sussex.

MULTIPLE BIRTHS

'Siamese' twins Conjoined twins derive the name 'Siamese' from the celebrated Chang and Eng Bunker ('Left' and 'Right' in Thai) born at Meklong on 11 May 1811 of Chinese parents. They were joined by a cartilaginous band at the chest. They married (in April 1843) the Misses Sarah and Adelaide Yates of Wilkes County, North Carolina, USA, and fathered 10 and 12 children respectively. They died within three hours of each other on 17 Jan 1874, aged 62.

Britain's only known pair were the 'Scottish brothers', who were born near Glasgow in 1490. They were brought to the Court of King James IV of Scotland in 1491, and lived under the king's patronage for the rest of his reign. They died in 1518 aged 28 years, one brother succumbing five days before the other, who 'moaned piteously as he crept about the castle gardens, carrying with him the dead body of the brother from whom only death could separate him and to whom death would again join him'.

The British example to reach maturity were the pygopagus (joined at the buttocks back to back) twins Daisy and Violet Hilton born in Brighton, E Sussex, on 5 Feb 1908. They died in Charlotte, North Carolina, USA on 5 Jan 1969, aged 60, from Hong Kong flu.

Rarest The rarest form of conjoined twins is dicephales tetrabrachius dipus (two heads, four arms and two legs). The only known examples are Masha and Dasha Krivoshlyapovy, born in the USSR on 4 Jan 1950.

Earliest successful separation The earliest successful separation of Siamese twins was performed on xiphopagus (joined at the sternum) girls at Mount Sinai Hospital, Cleveland, Ohio, USA by Dr Jac S. Geller on 14 Dec 1952.

Oldest surviving The oldest surviving unseparated twins are the craniopagus (heads are fused at the crown) pair, Yvonne and Yvette McCarther (b. 1949) of Los Angeles, California, USA. They have rejected an operation to separate them.

Most twins In Chungchon, South Korea it was reported in September 1981 that there were unaccountably 38 pairs in only 275 families–the highest ever recorded ratio.

The highest ratio of twins in Britain is to be found on the island of North Uist in the Outer Hebrides, Scotland. In June 1985

Coincident birthdates

It should be mentioned that births are not completely random. There are some days of the year on which more births are recorded than others. It is also true that within families there are tendencies for births to occur at approximately the same (general) time, if not specific day.

The only verified example of a family producing five single children with coincident birthdays is that of Catherine (1952), Carol (1953), Charles (1956), Claudia (1961) and Cecilia (1966), born to Carolyn and Ralph Cummins of Clintwood, Virginia, USA, all on 20 February. The random odds against five single siblings sharing a birthdate would be one in 17 797 577 730 — more than 3 ½ times the world's population.

The three children of the Henriksen family of Andenes, Norway, Heidi (b. 1960), Olav (b. 1964) and Lief-Martin (b. 1968), all celebrate their birthdays infrequently, because these all fall on Leap Day – 29 February.

MULTIPLE BIRTHS

HIGHEST NUMBER REPORTED AT SINGLE BIRTH WORLD
10 (DECAPLETS)
(2 male, 8 female) Bacacay, Brazil, 22 Apr 1946 (also report from Spain, 1924 and China, 12 May 1936)

HIGHEST NUMBER MEDICALLY RECORDED[1]
WORLD
9 (NONUPLETS)
(5 male, 4 female) to Mrs Geraldine Brodrick at Royal Hospital, Sydney, Australia on 13 June 1971. 2 males stillborn. Richard (340 g *12 oz*) survived 6 days.
(all died) to patient at University of Pennsylvania, Philadelphia, USA on 29 May 1972.
(all died) reported from Bagerhat, Bangladesh, *c.* 11 May 1977 to 30-year-old mother.

UNITED KINGDOM
7 (SEPTUPLETS)
(4 boys and 3 girls) to Mrs Susan Halton (b. 1960) at Liverpool Maternity Hospital on 15 Aug 1987. The last survivor, Kane 680 g *1 lb 8 oz*, died on 31 Aug 1987.

6 (SEXTUPLETS)
(all female) to Mrs Janet Walton (b. 1952) at Liverpool Maternity Hospital on 18 Nov 1983. All survive.
(4 male, 2 female) to Mrs Jane Underhill (b. 1957) at Rosie Maternity Hospital, Cambridge on 2 May 1985. After 9 months only 3 survived.
(3 male, 3 female) to Mrs Susan Coleman at Homerton, East London on 12 Nov 1986. All survive.
(2 male, 4 female) to Mrs Sheila Ann Thorns (*née* Manning) at New Birmingham Maternity Hospital on 2 Oct 1968. Three survive. (1 male, 5 female) to Mrs Rosemary Letts (*née* Egerton) at University College Hospital, London, on 15 Dec 1969. One boy and 4 girls survive.

HIGHEST NUMBER SURVIVING[2] WORLD
6 out of 6 (3 males, 3 females) to Mrs Susan Jane Rosenkowitz (*née* Scoones) (b. Colombo, Sri Lanka, 28 Oct 1947) at Mowbray, Cape Town, South Africa on 11 Jan 1974. In order of birth they were: David, Nicolette, Jason, Emma, Grant and Elizabeth. They totalled 10·915 kg *24 lb 1 oz*
6 out of 6 (4 males, 2 females) to Mrs Rosanna Giannini (b. 1952) at Careggi Hospital, Florence, Italy on 11 Jan 1980. They are Francesco, Fabrizio, Giorgio Roberto, Letizia and Linda

UNITED KINGDOM
6 out of 6 (see above): Mrs Janet Walton and Mrs Susan Coleman

QUINTUPLETS WORLD HEAVIEST
11·35 kg *25 lb* to Mrs Lui Saulien, Chekiang, China on 7 Jun 1953.
11·35 kg *25 lb* to Mrs Kamalammal, Pondicherry, India on 30 Dec 1956.

WORLD MOST SETS
There is no recorded case of more than a single set.

QUADRUPLETS WORLD HEAVIEST
10·35 kg *22 lb 13 oz* to Mrs Ayako Takeda, Tsuchihashi Maternity Hospital, Kagoshima, Japan on 4 Oct 1978 (4 girls).

WORLD MOST SETS
4 Mde Feodor Vassilyev, Shuya, Russia (d. *ante* 1770)

TRIPLETS[3] WORLD HEAVIEST
11·96 kg *26 lb 6 oz* (unconfirmed) Iranian case (2 male, 1 female) on 18 Mar 1968

UK HEAVIEST
10·886 kg *24 lb* to Mrs Mary McDermott, of Bearpark, Co. Durham on 18 Nov 1914.

WORLD MOST SETS
15 Maddalena Granata, Italy (b. 1839–*fl.* 1886)

TWINS WORLD HEAVIEST
12·590 kg *27 lb 12 oz* (surviving) to Mrs J.P. Haskin, Fort Smith, Arkansas, USA on 20 Feb 1924.

UK HEAVIEST
The 16·1 kg *35 lb 8 oz* reported in the *Lancet* from Derbys, on 6 Dec 1884 the Warren case (2 males born live) is believed to have been a misprint for 11·6 kg *25 lb 8 oz.*

WORLD MOST SETS
16 Mde Vassilyev (see above). Note also that Mrs Barbara Zulu of Barbeton, South Africa bore 3 sets of girls and 3 mixed sets in 7 years (1967–73).

UK MOST SETS
15 Mrs Mary Jonas of Chester (died 4 Dec 1899) –all sets were mixed.

[1] Mrs Edith Bonham (died 1469) of Wishford Magna, Wilts reportedly had septuplets.
[2] The South African press were unable to verify the birth of 5 babies to Mrs Charmaine Craig (*née* Peterson) in Cape Town on 16 Oct 1980 and a sixth on 8 Nov. The reported names were Frank, Salome, John, Andrew, William and, belatedly, Deborah.
[3] Mrs Anna Steynvaait of Johannesburg, South Africa produced 2 sets within 10 months in 1960.

---

there were 36 sets aged from 82 to 2 years, a ratio of 1 to 40 (cf. the national average of 1 to 100).

Longest separated twins Through the help of New Zealand's television programme *Missing* on 27 Apr 1989, Iris (*née* Haughie) Johns and Aro (*né* Haughie) Campbell (b. 13 Jan 1914) were reunited after 75 years' separation.

Fastest triplet birth Bradley, Christopher and Carmon were born naturally to Mrs James E. Duck of Memphis, Tennessee, USA in two minutes on 21 Mar 1977.

Quindecaplets It was announced by Dr Gennaro Montanino of Rome that he had removed by hysterotomy after four months of the pregnancy the foetuses of ten girls and five boys from the womb of a 35-year-old housewife on 22 Jul 1971. A fertility drug was responsible for this unique instance of quindecaplets.

DESCENDANTS

In polygamous countries, the number of a person's descendants can become incalculable. The last Sharifian Emperor of Morocco, Moulay Ismail (1672–1727), known as 'The Bloodthirsty', was reputed to have fathered a total of 525 sons and 342 daughters by 1703 and achieved a 700th son in 1721.

At his death in April 1984 Adam Borntrager, aged 96, of Medford, Wisconsin, USA, had 707 direct descendants of whom all but 32 were living. The total extant comprised 11 children, 115 grandchildren, 529 great-grandchildren and 20 great-great-grandchildren.

Mrs Peter L. Schwartz (1902–88) had 14 children, 13 of whom are still living, 175 grandchildren, 477 great-grandchildren and 20 great-great-grandchildren.

Mrs Sarah Crawshaw (died 25 Dec 1844) left 397 descendants according to her gravestone in Stones Church, Ripponden, Halifax, W Yorks.

Seven-generation family Augusta Bunge (*née* Pagel) (b. 13 Oct 1879) of Wisconsin, USA, learned that her great-great-great-granddaughter had become a mother by receiving news of her great-great-great-great-grandson, Christopher John Bollig (b. 21 Jan 1989).

Youngest great-great-great grandmother Harriet Holmes of Newfoundland, Canada (b. 17 Jan 1899) became the youngest living great-great-great-grandmother on 8 Mar 1987 at the age of 88 years 50 days.

Most living ascendants Megan Sue Austin (b. 16 May 1982) of Bar Harbor, Maine, USA had a full set of grandparents and great-grandparents and five great-great-grandparents, making 19 direct ascendants.

Family tree The lineage of K'ung Ch'iu or Confucius (551–479 BC) can be traced back further than that of any other family. His four greats grandfather K'ung Chia is known from the 8th century BC. This man's 85th lineal descendants Wei-yi (b. 1939) and Wei-ning (b. 1947) live today in Taiwan.

Longevity

No single subject is more obscured by vanity, deceit, falsehood and deliberate fraud than human longevity. Apart from the traces left by accidental 'markers' (e.g. the residual effects of established dated events such as the Chernobyl incident), there is no known scientific method of checking the age of any part of the living body.

Centenarians surviving beyond their 113th year are in fact extremely rare and the present absolute proven limit of human longevity does not yet admit of anyone living to celebrate their 121st birthday.

■ **Longest separated twins**
Iris Johns (née Haughie) and Aro Campbell (né Haughie) were reunited after 75 years of separation.

AUTHENTIC NATIONAL LONGEVITY RECORDS

	Years	Days		Born		Died
Japan	120	237	Shigechiyo Izumi	29 Jun	1865	21 Feb 1986
United States[1]	116	88	Carrie White (Mrs) (née Joyner)	18 Nov	1874	14 Feb 1991
France	116		Jeanne Louise Calment	21 Feb	1875	fl. April 1991
United Kingdom[2]	114	208	Anna Eliza Williams (Mrs) (née Davies)	2 Jun	1873	27 Dec 1987
Canada[3]	113	124	Pierre Joubert	15 Jul	1701	16 Nov 1814
Australia	112	330	Caroline Maud Mockridge	11 Dec	1874	6 Nov 1987
Spain[4]	112	228	Josefa Salas Mateo	14 Jul	1860	27 Feb 1973
Norway	112	61	Maren Bolette Torp	21 Dec	1876	20 Feb 1989
Morocco	112		El Hadj Mohammed el Mokri (Grand Vizier)		1844	16 Sep 1957
Poland	112		Roswlia Mielczarak (Mrs)		1868	7 Jan 1981
Ireland	111	327	The Hon. Katherine Plunket	22 Nov	1820	14 Oct 1932
Netherlands[5]	111	241	Jean Michael Reyskens	11 May	1878	7 Jan 1990
Scotland[6]	111	238	Kate Begbie (Mrs)	9 Jan	1877	5 Sep 1988
South Africa[7]	111	151	Johanna Booyson	17 Jan	1857	16 Jun 1968
Sweden[8]	111	90	Wilhelmine Sande (Mrs)	24 Oct	1874	21 Jan 1986
Czechoslovakia	111	+	Marie Bernatkova	22 Oct	1857	fl. October 1968
Germany[9]	111		Maria Corba	15 Aug	1878	fl. March 1990
Finland	111	+	Fanny Matilda Nystrom	30 Sep	1878	1989
Channel Islands (Guernsey)	110	321	Margaret Ann Neve (née Harvey)	18 May	1792	4 Apr 1903
Northern Ireland	110	234	Elizabeth Watkins (Mrs)	10 Mar	1863	31 Oct 1973
Yugoslavia	110	150+	Demitrius Philipovitch	9 Mar	1818	fl. August 1928
Greece[10]	110	+	Lambrini Tsiatoura (Mrs)		1870	19 Feb 1981
USSR[11]	110	+	Khasako Dzugayev	7 Aug	1860	fl. August 1970
Italy	110	+	Damiana Sette (Sig)		1874	25 Feb 1985
Denmark	109	265	Maria Louise Augusta Bramsen	4 May	1878	23 Jan 1988
Tasmania (State of)	109	179	Mary Ann Crow (Mrs)	2 Feb	1836	31 Jul 1945
Belgium	108	327	Mathilda Vertommen-Hellemans	12 Aug	1868	4 Jul 1977
Iceland	108	45	Halldóra Bjarndóttir	14 Oct	1873	28 Nov 1981
Portugal[12]	108	+	Maria Luisa Jorge	7 Jun	1859	fl. July 1967
Malaysia	106	+	Hassan Bin Yusoff	14 Aug	1865	fl. January 1972
Luxembourg	105	228	Nicolas Wiscourt	31 Dec	1872	17 Aug 1978

[1] Ex-slave Mrs Martha Graham died at Fayetteville, North Carolina on 25 Jun 1959 reputedly aged 117 or 118. Census researches by Eckler show that she was apparently born in Dec 1844 and hence aged 114 years 6 months. Mrs Rena Glover Brailsford died in Summerton, South Carolina, on 6 Dec 1977 reputedly aged 118 yrs. The 1900 US Federal Census for Crawfish Springs Militia District of Walker County, Georgia, records an age of 77 for a Mark Thrash. If the Mark Thrash (reputedly born in Georgia in December 1822) who died near Chattanooga, Tennessee on 17 Dec 1943 was he, and the age attributed earlier was accurate, then he would have survived for 121 years. Jackson Pollard of Georgia born on 15 Dec 1869, according to his social security payments, but no birth certificate or family Bible records are available.

[2] London-born Miss Isabella Shepheard was allegedly 115 years old when she died at St Asaph, Clwyd, North Wales, on 20 Nov 1948, but her actual age was believed to have been 109 years 90 days. Isabella Sharp of Gateshead, Newcastle upon Tyne, according to baptism and burial registers was christened when aged 33 and died in Septemeber 1812 when aged 114 years.

[3] Mrs Ellen Carroll died in North River, Newfoundland, Canada on 8 Dec 1943, reputedly aged 115 years 49 days.

[4] Senor Benita Medrana of Avila died on 28 Jan 1979 allegedly aged 114 years 335 days.

[5] Thomas Peters birth was recorded 6 Apr 1745 in Leeuwarden and he died aged 111 years 354 days on 26 Mar 1857 in Arnhem

[6] Lachlen McDonald, who died on 7 Jun 1858 in Harris, Outer Hebrides, was recorded as being '110 years' on his death certificate.

[7] Mrs Susan Johanna Deporter of Port Elizabeth, South Africa was reputedly 114 years old when she died on 4 Aug 1954. Mrs Sarah Lawrence of Cape Town, South Africa was reputedly 112 on 3 Jun 1968.

[8] Mrs W. Sande was born in present-day Norway.

[9] Germany: an unnamed female died in 1979 aged 112 years, and an unnamed male aged also 112 years, in 1969. The Austrian record is 108 years (female died 1975) and the Swiss record is also 108 years (female died 1967).

[10] The claim that Liakon Efdokia died on 17 Jan 1982 aged 118 years 13 days is not substantiated by the censuses of 1971 or 1981. Birth registration before 1920 was fragmentary.

[11] There are allegedly 21 700 centenarians in the USSR (cf. 56 000 in the USA). Of these, 21 000 are ascribed to the Georgian SSR, i.e. one in every 232.

[12] Senhora Jesuina da Conceicao of Lisbon was reputedly 113 years old when she died on 10 Jun 1965.

Note: fl. is the abbreviation for the Latin = floruit, he or she was living (at the relevant date).

From data on documented centenarians, actuaries have shown that only one 115-year life can be expected in 2·1 billion lives (cf. world population which was estimated to be c. 5·3 billion by mid-1990).

The height of credulity was reached on 5 May 1933, when a news agency filed a story from China with a Beijing source that Li Chung-yun, the 'oldest man on earth', born in 1680, had just died after 256 years (sic).

The latest census in China revealed 3800 centenarians, of whom two-thirds were women. According to a 1985 census carried out in the Chinese province of Xinjiang Urgur, there were 850 centenarians in the area, four between the ages of 125 and 103.

With an estimated world-wide population of some 40 000 centenarians, only 22 per cent are male. While husbands have a better chance than bachelors, it appears that spinsters have a better chance than wives of reaching 100 years!

Oldest authentic centenarian
The greatest authenticated age to which any human has ever lived is 120 years 237 days in the case of Shigechiyo Izumi of Asan on Tokunoshima, an island 1320 km 820 miles south-west of Tokyo, Japan. He was born at Asan on 29 Jun 1865 and recorded as a 6-year-old in Japan's first census of 1871. He died in his bungalow at 12:15 GMT on 21 Feb 1986 after developing pneumonia.

Oldest living
The oldest living person in the world whose date of birth can be reliably authenticated is Jeanne Louise Calment who was born in France on 21 Feb 1875. She now lives in a nursing home in Arles, Southern France.

UK
Miss Charlotte Hughes (née Milburn) (b. 1 Aug 1877) of Marske-by-the-Sea, Hartlepool, Cleveland is the United Kingdom's oldest woman.

Joseph Randle (b. 31 Jan 1884) of Hunsdon, Ware, Herts is Britain's oldest living man.

The only UK citizens with birth and death certificates more than 112 years apart have been Mrs Anna Williams (1873–1987) (114 years 208 days), John Evans (1877–1990) (112 years 292 days) Miss Alice Stevenson (1861–1973) (112 years 39 days) and Miss Janetta Jane Thomas (1869–1982) (112 years 35 days).

Family centenarians
The first recorded case in the UK of four siblings becoming centenarians occurred on 2 Apr 1984 when Mrs Lily Beatrice Parsons (née Andrews) reached her 100th birthday. Her three sisters were Mrs Florence Eliza White (1874–1979), Mrs Maud Annie Spencer (1876–1978), Mrs Eleanor Newton Webber (1880–1983). The family came from Teignmouth, Devon.

Brother and sister, both retired head teachers, Margaret Eleanor (b. 24 May 1888) and Joseph Wood Beard (b. 13 Sep 1889) of Mansfield, Notts, have celebrated their centenary.

Oldest twins
Eli Shadrack and John Meshak Phipps were born on 14 Feb 1803 at Affington, Virginia, USA. Eli died at Hennessey, Oklahoma on 23 Feb 1911 at the age of 108 years 9 days, on which day John was still living in Shenandoah, Iowa.

On 17 Jun 1984, identical twin sisters Mildred Widman Philippi and Mary Widman Franzini of St Louis, Missouri, USA celebrated their 104th birthday. Mildred died on 4 May 1985, 44 days short of the twins' 105th birthday. The chances of identical twins both reaching 100 are now probably about one in 50 million.

UK Identical twin spinsters, Alice Maria and Emily Edith Weller were born within 15 minutes of each other on 20 Apr 1888 in Epsom, Surrey. Alice died on 21 Feb 1991 when aged 102.

The oldest living twins sister are Florence Elizabeth Blake (née Thomas) and May Mary Matilda Thomas (b. 29 Jul 1890) who live at Middleton Home, Maldon, Essex.

Oldest triplets The longest-lived triplets recorded in Great Britain were Faith Alice, Hope Fanny and Charity Sarah Stockdale of Cracoe, near Skipton, N Yorks, born on 28–29 Dec 1857. Charity was the first to die, on 30 Jul 1944, aged 86 years 213 days.

Living The oldest living triplets in the UK are Pricilla, Phyllis and Pamela Laybourne (b. 27 Oct 1910, Newport, Gwent).

Oldest quadruplets The Ottman quads of Munich, Germany, Adolf, Anne-Marie, Emma and Elisabeth, celebrated their 79th birthday on 5 May 1991.

Most reigns The greatest number of reigns during which any English subject could have lived is ten. A person born on the day (11 April) that Henry VI was deposed in 1471 had to live to only the comparatively modest age of 87 years 7 months and 6 days to see the accession of Elizabeth I on 17 Nov 1558. Such a person could have been Thomas Carn of London, reputedly born in 1471 and died 28 Jan 1578 in his 107th year.

Long spans The last Briton with 18th-century paternity was Miss Alice J. Grigg of Belvedere, Kent (died 28 Apr 1970) whose father, William was born on 26 Oct 1799. The father of Baroness Elliot of Harwood (b. 15 Jan 1903), Sir Charles Tennant Bt, was born in Glasgow on 4 Nov 1823 in the reign of George IV.

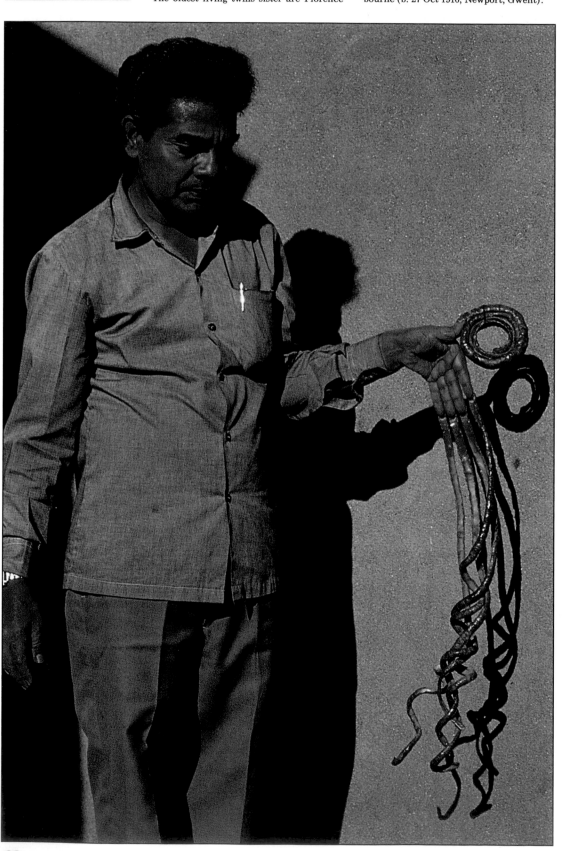

Anatomy and Physiology

Hydrogen (63 per cent) and oxygen (25·5 per cent) constitute the commonest of the 24 elements normally regarded as being in the human body. Carbon, sodium, potassium, calcium, sulphur, chlorine (as chlorides), phosphorus, iron and zinc are all present in significant quantities. Present in 'trace' quantities, but generally regarded as normal in a healthy body (even if the question of whether they are essential is a matter of controversy), are iodine, fluorine, copper, cobalt, chromium, manganese, selenium, molybdenum, vanadium (probably), nickel (probably), silicon (probably), tin (probably) and arsenic.

HANDS, FEET AND HAIR

Touch The extreme sensitivity of the fingers is such that a vibration with a movement of 0·02 of a micron can be detected.

Longest fingernails Fingernails grow about 0·05 cm *0·02 in* a week—four times faster than toenails.

The aggregate measurement of those of Shridhar Chillal (b. 1937) of Pune, India, on 19 Mar 1991 was 452·5 cm *181 in* for the five nails on his left hand (thumb 102·5 cm *41 in*, first finger 90 cm *36 in*, second and third fingers 92·5 cm *37 in*, and the fourth 92·5 cm *37 in*). He last cut his nails in 1952.

Most fingers and toes (Polydactylism) At an inquest held on a baby boy at Shoreditch in the East End of London on 16 Sep 1921 it was reported that he had 14 fingers and 15 toes.

Least toes The two-toed syndrome exhibited by some members of the Wadomo tribe of the Zambezi Valley, Zimbabwe and the Kalanga tribe of the eastern Kalahari Desert, Botswana is hereditary via a single mutated gene. These 'ostrich people', as they are known, are not handicapped by their deformity, and can walk great distances without discomfort.

Largest feet If cases of elephantiasis are excluded, then the biggest feet known are those of Haji Mohammad Alam Channa of Pakistan, (see p. 61) who wears size 22 sandals.

The owner of Britain's largest feet is John Thrupp (b. 1964) of Stratford-upon-Avon, Warks, who wears a size 21 shoe. He is 2·11 m *6 ft 11 in* tall.

Longest hair Human hair grows at the rate of about 1·27 cm *0·5 in* in a month. If left uncut it will usually grow to a maximum of 61–91 cm *2–3 ft*.

In 1780 a head of hair measuring 3·65 m *12 ft* in length and dressed in a style known as the Plica Polonica (hair closely plaited together) was sent to Dresden after adorning the head of a Polish peasant woman for 52 years. The plait of hair was 30·4 cm *11·9 in* in circumference.

In March 1989 a length of 6·4 m *21 ft* was claimed for the hair of 74-year-old Mata Jagdamba, a Yogini living in Ujjain, North India.

The hair of Diane Witt of Worcester, Massachusetts, USA measured over 3·51 m *11 ft 6 in* in May 1991. She last cut her hair 9 years ago.

Most valuable hair On 18 Feb 1988 a bookseller from Cirencester, Glos, paid £5575 for a lock of hair belonging to Lord Nelson (1758–1805) at an auction held at Crewkerne, Somerset.

Longest beard The beard of Hans N. Langseth (b. 1846 near Eidsroll, Norway) measured 5·33 m *17 ½ ft* at the time of his burial at Kensett, Iowa in 1927 after 15 years' residence in the United States. It was presented to the Smithsonian Institution, Washington, DC, in 1967.

The beard of the 'bearded lady' Janice Deveree (b. 1842 Bracken County, Kentucky, USA) was measured at 36 cm *14 in* in 1884.

Longest moustache The moustache of Birger Pellas (b. 21 Sep 1934) of Malmö, Sweden, grown since 1973, reached 306 cm *10 ft* in March 1991.

Karna Ram Bheel (1928–87) was granted permission by a New Delhi prison governor in February 1979 to keep the 238 cm *7 ft 10 in* moustache, which he had grown since

1949, during his life sentence. He used mustard, oil, butter and cream to keep it in trim.

The longest moustache in Great Britain was that of John Roy (1910–88), of Weeley, near Clacton, Essex. It attained a peak span of 189 cm *6 ft 2 ½ in* between 1939 and 2 Apr 1976. He accidentally sat on it in the bath in 1984 and lost 42 cm *16 ½ in*. He then took off the same amount from the other side to even the moustache.

The current UK champion is Ted Sedman of St Albans, Herts whose handlebar moustache measures 134·54 cm *53 in*.

DENTITION

Earliest The first deciduous or milk teeth normally appear in infants at 5–8 months, these being the upper and lower jaw first incisors. There are many records of children born with teeth, the most distinguished example being Prince Louis Dieudonné, later Louis XIV of France, who was born with two teeth on 5 Sep 1638. Molars usually appear at 24 months, but in Pindborg's case published in Denmark in 1970, a six-week premature baby was documented with eight teeth at birth, of which four were in the molar region. Shaun Keaney of Newbury, Berks was born on 10 Apr 1990 with 12 teeth but they were extracted a few days after his birth.

Most Cases of the growth in late life of a third set of teeth have been recorded several times. A reference to a case in France of a fourth dentition, known as Lison's case, was published in 1896.

Most dedicated dentist Brother Giovanni Battista Orsenigo of the Ospedale Fatebenefratelli, Rome, a monk who was also a dentist, conserved all the teeth he extracted in three enormous cases during the time he exercised his profession from 1868 to 1904. In 1903 the number was counted and found to be 2 000 744 teeth, indicating an average of 185 teeth, or nearly six total extractions a day.

Most valuable tooth In 1816 a tooth belonging to Sir Isaac Newton (1643–1727) was sold in London for £730. It was purchased by a nobleman who had it set in a ring, which he wore constantly.

Earliest false teeth From discoveries made in Etruscan tombs, partial dentures of bridge-work type were being worn in what is now Tuscany, Italy as early as 700 BC. Some were permanently attached to existing teeth and others were removable.

OPTICS

Highest visual acuity The human eye is capable of judging relative position with remarkable accuracy, reaching limits of between 3–5 sec of arc.

In April 1984 Dr Dennis M. Levi of the College of Optometry, University of Houston, Texas, USA, repeatedly identified the position of a thin white line within 0·85 sec of arc. This is equivalent to a displacement of some 6 mm *¼ in* at a distance of 1·6 km *1 mile*.

Colour sensitivity The unaided human eye, under the best possible viewing conditions, comparing large areas of colour, in good illumination, using both eyes, can distinguish 10 million different colour surfaces. The most accurate photo-electric spectrophotometers possess a precision probably only 40 per cent as good as this. About 7·5 per cent of men and 0·1 per cent of women are colour blind. The most extreme form, monochromatic vision, is very rare. The highest rate of red–green colour

blindness is in Czechoslovakia and the lowest rate among Fijians and Brazilian Indians.

BONES

Longest The thigh bone or femur is the longest. It constitutes usually 27·5 per cent of a person's stature, and may be expected to be 50 cm *19 ¾ in* long in a 183 cm *6 ft* tall man. The longest recorded bone was the femur of the German giant Constantine, who died in Mons, Belgium, on 30 Mar 1902, aged 30, it measured 76 cm *29·9 in*. The femur of Robert Wadlow, the tallest man ever recorded, measured an estimated 75 cm *29 ½ in* (see p. 61).

MUSCLES

Most active It has been estimated that the eye muscles move more than an incredible 100 000 times a day. Many of these eye movements take place during the dreaming phase of sleep. (See Longest and shortest dreams p. 74.)

Largest chest measurements The largest are among endomorphs (those with a tendency towards globularity). In the extreme case of Robert Earl Hughes (1926–58) (USA) this was 315 cm *124 in*, and T.J. Albert Jackson, currently the heaviest living man (see p. 63) has a chest measurement of 305 cm *120 in*.

Jamie Reeves (b.1962) of Sheffield, S Yorks the 'World's Strongest Man', has a chest measurement of 152·4 cm *60 in* with a height of 193 cm 6 ft 4 in. He weighs 146 kg *23 st*

The largest chest ever recorded in Britain was that of William Campbell (see p. 63) which measured 244 cm *96 in*. Among muscular subjects (mesomorphs) of normal height, *expanded* chest measurements above 142 cm *56 in* are extremely rare.

The largest muscular chest measurement recorded so far is that of American powerlifter Isaac 'Dr Size' Nesser (b. 21 Apr 1962) of Greensburg, Pennsylvania, USA, who measures 172·87 cm *68·06 in*. He is 1778·8 cm *5 ft 10 in* tall and weighs 164·2 kg *25 st 1 lb*.

Largest and smallest biceps Isaac 'Dr Size' Nesser has biceps of 66·35 cm *26 ⅛ in* cold (not pumped).

The biceps of Robert Thorn (see p. 64) measured 11·4 cm *4 ¼ in* when pumped up.

WAISTS

Largest The largest waist ever recorded was that of Walter Hudson (b. 1944) of New York, USA, which measured 302 cm *119 in* at his peak weight of 545 kg *85 st 7 lb*.

Queen Catherine de Medici (1519–89) decreed a waist measurement of 35 cm *13·77 in* for ladies of the French court, but this was at a time when females were more diminutive.

Smallest The smallest waist of normal stature was that of Mrs Ethel Granger (1905–82) of Peterborough, Cambridge, reduced from a natural 56 cm *22 in* to 33 cm *13 in* over the period 1929–39.

A measurement of 33 cm *13 in* was also claimed for the French actress Mlle Polaire (real name Emile Marie Bouchand) (1881 –1939).

NECKS

Longest The maximum measured extension of the neck by the successive fitting of copper coils, as practised by the women of the Padaung or Kareni tribe of Myanmar (formerly Burma), is 40 cm *15 ¾ in*. When

■ **Longest hair**
Mata Jagdamba, a Yogini living in Ujjain, North India has hair measuring 6·4 m 21 ft long.

Hair splitting
The greatest reported achievement in hair splitting has been that of the former champion cyclist and craftsman Alfred West (1901–85), who succeeded in splitting a human hair 17 times into 18 parts on eight occasions.

Shaving
The fastest barbers on record are Denny Rowe and Gerry Harley. Denny Rowe shaved 1994 men in 60 min with a retractor safety razor in Herne Bay, Kent on 19 Jun 1988, taking on average 1·8 sec per volunteer, and drawing blood four times. Gerry Harley, of Gillingham, Kent shaved 235 even braver volunteers with a cut-throat razor on 13 Aug 1984, averaging 15·3 sec per face. He drew blood only once.

Lifting with teeth
Walter Arfeuille of Ieper-Vlamertinge, Belgium lifted weights totalling 281·5 kg *621 lb* a distance of 17 cm *6¾ in* off the ground with his teeth in Paris, France on 31 Mar 1990.

'Hercules' John Massis (b. Wilfried Oscar Morbée, 4 Jun 1940, died 11 Jul 1988) of Oostakker, Belgium prevented a helicopter from taking off, using only a tooth bit harness, in Los Angeles, California, USA on 7 Apr 1979 for a *Guinness Spectacular* TV show.

Human Body Superlatives

THE SKULL

1 SMALLEST BONE The *stapes* or stirrup bone, one of the three auditory ossicles in the middle ear, measures from 2 –6 to 3·4 mm in length and weighs from 2·0 to 4·3 mg.

5 LONGEST NAMED MUSCLE The levator labii superioris alaeque nasi runs inwards and downwards on the face, with one branch running to the upper lip and the other to the nostril. It is the muscle which everts or curls the upper lip. Its action was particularly well demonstrated in the performances of the late Elvis Presley (1939 –77). In the late 50's he was renowned for his superlative upper lip muscle movement when singing and acting in *Love Me Tender*, one of his many early films. (See above).

6 MOST MOBILE JOINT The ball and socket joint that is the shoulder is one of the joints that is most commonly dislocated - or put out of joint. Many sportsmen and women suffer from dislocated shoulders and Bryan Robson the Manchester United and England soccer captain has been more unlucky than most in this respect. Injuries cut short his appearances in the 1986 and 1990 World Cup Final tournaments and he is pictured here leaving the field in the Mexico competition in some distress. Earlier in his career as a West Bromwich Albion player he also managed to break the same leg on 3 separate occasions in the 1976-77 season.

7 STRONGEST JOINT The strongest joint of the body is arguably the hip. The ball on the end of the femur (thigh bone), fits almost perfectly into the socket on the pelvis. It is only put out of joint by enormous force such as a high speed car crash or parachute failure.

8 LONGEST MUSCLE The longest muscle in the human body is the *sartorius* which is a narrow ribbon like muscle which runs from the pelvis and across the front of the thigh to the top of the tibia below the knee. It's action is to draw the lower limb into the cross-legged sitting position, proverbially associated with tailors. As other stronger muscles in the body can perform this action the *sartorius* could be regarded as an 'extra' of doubtful merit since it is extremely painful if torn.

2 STRONGEST MUSCLE The masseter (one each side of the mouth) is responsible for biting. In August 1986, Richard Hofmann (b. 1949) of Lake City, Florida, USA achieved a bite strength of 444 kg *975 lb* for approximately 2 secs. This figure is over six times the normal biting strength.

3 TEETH Tooth enamel is the hardest substance in the body with a Knoop number of over 300. It is also the only part of the body which remains basically unchanged through-out life. Thus a person in their 70's with a full set of teeth has enamel in their mouth that was originally formed in their mother's womb.

4 The biggest tooth is the first upper molar and one which usually has three roots.

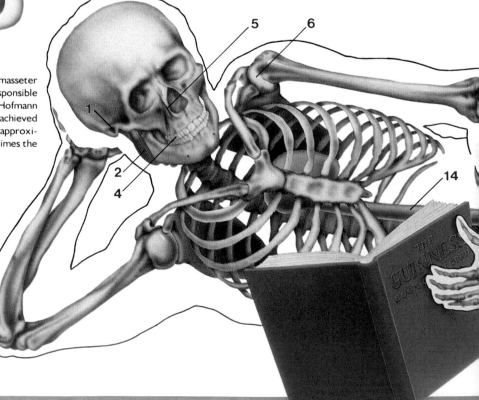

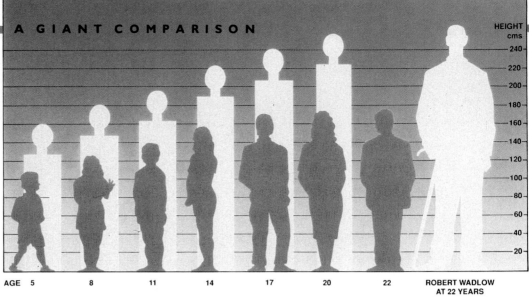

A GIANT COMPARISON

HEIGHT cms

AGE 5 8 11 14 17 20 22 ROBERT WADLOW AT 22 YEARS

9 LONGEST BONE Excluding a variable number of sesamoids (small rounded bones), there are 206 bones in the adult human body, compared with 300 for children (as they grow some bones fuse together). The thigh-bone or *femur* is the longest. It constitutes usually 27 ½ per cent of a persons stature and may extend to 50 cm *19 ¾in* in a 183 cm *6 ft* tall man. The femur of Robert Pershing Wadlow (pictured left), the tallest man ever recorded, measured an estimated 75 cm *29 ½in.*

10 MOST BROKEN BONES Barry Sheene (pictured left) who must hold the record for the most broken legs. On one occasion when he broke both legs in several places after 160 mph motorcycle crash, 26 screws and plates were used to mend his shattered bones.

11 LARGEST SESAMOID BONE The largest sesamoid bone in the body is the patella or knee cap. Most other sesamoids are only a few millimetres in diameter and are ovoid like the seeds of the sesame plant, from which they get their name. They are usually embedded tendons close to joints or where the tendons angle sharply round bone. Their function is to take compression when a tendon is going around a joint, as when kneeling on the knee.

GIGANTISM (see above)
We first grow at a rapid rate in our mothers' womb. The next time is in our teens, between the age of 11–16 for girls and 11–18 for boys.

Growth hormone controls the growth of the human body. It is produced by the pituitary gland in the brain. Excess production is usually caused by a tumour of this small gland. In childhood this results in gigantism, with disproportionately long arms and legs. Excess growth hormone in adult life produces a condition called acromegaly. It does not cause gigantism because by this stage of life the long bones of the arms and legs have stopped growing and are unable to restart. Robert Wadlow was a true giant because his height developed in childhood. We are very unlikely to see anyone like him again because modern medical techniques can stop the pituitary gland from misbehaving.

12 LARGEST NERVE
The largest nerve is the siatic nerve. This broad flat nerve is about 2 cm *0·78 in* wide and runs underneath the buttock muscle (*gluteus maximus*) and is a collection of nerve fibres from the spinal cord to the leg.

13 Within it are fibres from the region of the **largest vertebra** the 5th Lumbar.

14 LARGEST VEIN The largest is the *inferior vena cava*, which returns the blood from the lower half of the body to the heart.

15 LARGEST MUSCLE Muscle normally accounts for 40 per cent of body weight. The bulkiest of the 639 named muscles in the human body is usually the *gluteus maximus* or the buttock muscle, which extends the thigh. However, in pregnant women the uterus or womb can increase its weight from about 30 g *1 oz* to over 1 kg *2·2 lb*, larger than even the most successful body builder's buttock.

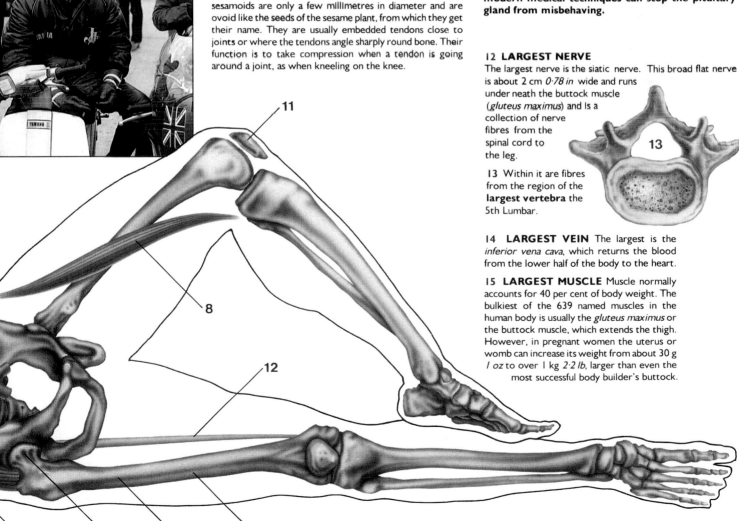

Artwork: Pat Gibbon. Photos: All-Sport, Alton Telegraph and RCA Records.

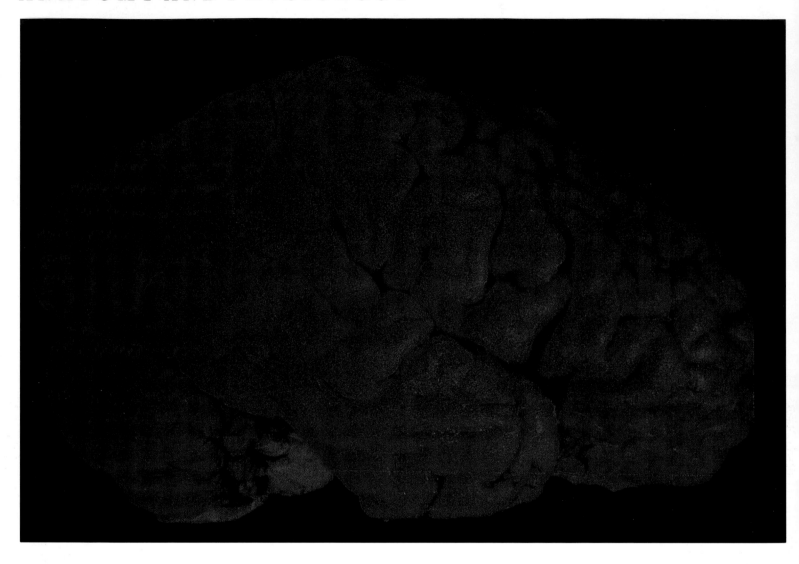

■ **Human brain**
A lateral view of the brain with the hindbrain at the left showing the cerebral cortex (grey matter). The cerebral cortex is involved in consciousness, memory, mental ability and intellect; and it is also responsible for initiating voluntary activity. (Photo: Science Photo Library)

Feminine beauty
Female pulchritude, being qualitative rather than quantitative, does not lend itself to records. It has been suggested that, if the face of Helen of Troy (*c.* 1200 BC) was capable of launching 1000 ships, a unit of beauty sufficient to launch one ship should be a millihelen.

the rings are removed, the muscles developed to support the head and neck shrink to their normal length.

BRAINS

Heaviest In normal brains there is no correlation between intelligence and size.

The heaviest brain ever recorded was that of a 50-year-old male, which weighed 2049 g *4 lb 8·29 oz* and was reported by Dr Thomas F. Hegert, chief medical examiner for District 9, State of Florida, USA, on 23 Oct 1975.

In January 1891 the *Edinburgh Medical Journal* reported the case of a 75-year-old man in the Royal Edinburgh Asylum whose brain weighed 1829 g *4 lb 0·5 oz.*

The largest female brain on record weighed 1565 g *3 lb 7·3 oz.* It belonged to a murderess.

Lightest The lightest 'normal' or non-atrophied brain on record was one weighing 1096 g *2 lb 6·7 oz* reported by Dr P. Davis and Prof. E. Wright of King's College Hospital, London in 1977. It belonged to a 31-year-old woman.

Most expensive skull The skull of Emanuel Swedenborg (1688–1772), the Swedish philosopher and theologian, was bought in London by the Royal Swedish Academy of Sciences for £5500 on 6 Mar 1977.

Human computer The fastest extraction of a 13th root from a 100-digit number, was achieved by Jaime Garcia Serrano of Bogotá, Colombia in a time of 0.15 sec on 24 May 1989 at the Hilton Hotel, Colombia.

Mrs Shakuntala Devi who comes from India demonstrated the multiplication of two 13-digit numbers 7 686 369 774 870 × 2 465 099 745 779 which were randomly selected by the Computer Department of Imperial College, London on 18 Jun 1980, in 28 sec. The correct answer which she gave was 18 947 668 177 995 426 462 773 730. Some experts on prodigies in calculation refuse to give credence to Mrs Devi on the grounds that her achievements are so vastly superior to the calculating feats of any other invigilated prodigy that the invigilation must have been defective.

Memory Bhandanta Vicitsara recited 16 000 pages of Buddhist canonical texts in Yangon, Myanmar (formerly Rangoon, Burma) in May 1974.

Gon Yang-ling, 26, has memorized more than 15 000 telephone numbers in Harbin, China according to the Xinhua News Agency. Rare instances of eidetic memory-the ability to re-project and hence 'visually' recall material-are known to science.

Dominic O'Brien of Guildford, Surrey memorized a random sequence of 35 separate packs of cards (1820) in all which had been shuffled together on a single sighting, with two corrections at the Star Inn, Furneux Pelham, Herts on 22 Jul 1990.

The greatest number of places of π Hideaki Tomoyori (b. 30 Sep 1932) of Yokohama, Japan recited 'pi' from memory to 40 000 places in 17 hr 21 min, including breaks of 4 hr 15 min breaks on 9–10 Mar 1987 at the Tsukuba University Club House.

The British record is 20 013 by Creighton

Herbert James Carvello (b. 19 Nov 1944) on 27 Jun 1980 in 9 hr 10 min at Saltscar Comprehensive School, Redcar, Cleveland.

Note: It is only the *approximation* of π at $^{22}/_7$ which recurs after its sixth decimal place and can, of course, be recited *ad nauseam*. The true value is a string of random numbers which are fiendishly difficult to memorize. The average ability for memorizing random numbers is barely more than 8, as proved by the common inability to memorise 9 or 10 digit telephone numbers.

VOICE

Greatest range The normal intelligible outdoor range of the male human voice in still air is 180 m *200 yd.* The *silbo*, the whistled language of the Spanish-speaking Canary Island of La Gomera, is intelligible across the valleys, under ideal conditions, at 8 km *5 miles.* There is a recorded case, under freak acoustic conditions, of the human voice being detectable at a distance of 17 km *10 ½ miles* across still water at night.

Screaming The highest scientifically measured emission has been one of 128 dbA by the screaming of Simon Robinson of McLaren Vale, South Australia at 'The Guinness Challenge' at Adelaide, Australia on 11 Nov 1988.

Whistling Roy Lomas achieved 122·5 decibels at 2½ m *8·20 ft* in the Deadroom at the BBC studios in Manchester on 19 Dec 1983.

Shouting Donald H. Burns of St George's, Bermuda achieved 119 dbA in shouting when he appeared on the Fuji TV film of *Narvhodo the World* at Liberty State Park, New Jersey, USA on 18 Jan 1989.

Yodelling Yodelling has been defined as 'repeated rapid changes from the chest-voice to falsetto and back again'. The most rapid recorded is ten tones (six falsetto) in 0·88 sec, by Jim Whitman of Washington, Tyne & Wear at Bethesda, Gwynedd on 16 Nov 1990.

Town crier The greatest number of wins in the national Town Criers' Contest is 11 (between 1939–73) by Ben Johnson of Fowey, Cornwall.

Lowest detectable sound The intensity of noise or sound is measured in terms of pressure. The pressure of the quietest sound that can be detected by a person of normal hearing at the most sensitive frequency of c. 2750 Hz is 2×10^{-5} Pa. One-tenth of the logarithm to this standard provides a unit termed a decibel (dbA). A noise of 30 dbA is negligible.

Highest noise levels Prolonged noise above 150 dbA will cause permanent deafness, while above 192 dbA a lethal over-pressure shock-wave can be formed. Equivalent continuous sound levels (LEQ) above 90 dbA are impermissible in factories in many countries, but this compares with 125 emitted by racing cars and 130 by amplified music.

Highest detectable pitch The upper limit is reckoned to be 20 000 Hz (cycles per sec), although it has been alleged that children with asthma can detect sounds of 30 000 Hz. Bats emit pulses at up to 90 000 Hz. It was announced in February 1964 that experiments in the USSR had conclusively proved that oscillations as high as 200 000 Hz can be detected if the oscillator is pressed against the skull.

Fastest talker Few people are able to speak *articulately* at a sustained speed above 300 words per min. The fastest broadcaster has been regarded as Gerry Wilmot (b. 6 Oct 1914 Victoria, British Columbia), the ice hockey commentator in the late forties.

Raymond Glendenning (1907–74), the BBC commentator, once spoke 176 words in 30 sec while commentating on a greyhound race.

In public life the highest speed recorded was a burst in excess of 300 words per min in a speech made in December 1961 by President John Fitzgerald Kennedy (1917–63).

John Helm of Yorkshire Television can recite the 92 Football League clubs in 26 seconds.

In vigorously controlled conditions at the Guinness World of Records Exhibition in New York on 8 Aug 1990, three record breaking contestants, Fran Capo, John Moschitta and Stephen Woodmore took part in a 'sudden-death' playoff using an unrehearsed passage chosen for its difficulty. Stephen Woodmore was the winner with a time of 448 words per minute after adjustments for intelligibility were made.

Stephen Woodmore of Orpington, Kent spoke 595 words in a time of 56·01 sec or 637·38 words per minute on ITV Programme *Motor Mouth* on 22 Sep 1990.

Hamlet's soliloquy Sean Shannon a Canadian residing in Oxford, Oxon recited Hamlet's soliloquy 'To be or not to be' (259 words) in a time of 24 sec 647·5 words per min on BBC Radio Oxford on 26 Oct 1990.

Backwards talking Steve Briers of Kilgetty, Dyfed recited the entire lyrics of Queen's album *A Night at the Opera* at BBC North-West Radio 4's 'Cat's Whiskers' on 6 Feb 1990 in a time of 9 min 58·44 sec.

BLOOD

Groups The preponderance of one blood group varies greatly from one locality to another. On a world basis Group O is the most common (46 per cent), but in some areas, for example Norway, Group A predominates.

The full description of the commonest subgroup in Britain is O MsNs, P+, Rr, Lu(a−), K−, Le(a−b+), Fy(a+b+), Jk(a+b+), which occurs in one in every 270 people.

The rarest blood group of the ABO system, one of 14 systems, is AB, which occurs in less than 3 per cent of persons in the British Isles.

The rarest type in the world is a type of Bombay blood (sub-type h-h) found so far only in a Czechoslovak nurse in 1961, and in a brother (Rh positive) and sister (Rh negative) named Jalbert in Massachusetts, USA, reported in February 1968.

Donor and recipient A 50-year-old haemophiliac, Warren C. Jyrich, required 2400 donor units of blood equivalent to 1080 litres, blood when undergoing open-heart surgery at the Michael Reese Hospital, Chicago, Illinois, USA in December 1970.

Largest artery The largest is the *aorta*, which is 3 cm *1·18 in* in diameter where it leaves the heart. By the time it ends at the level of the fourth lumbar vertebra it is about 1·75 cm *0·68 in* in diameter.

Most alcoholic subject California University Medical School, Los Angeles, USA reported in December 1982 the case of a confused but conscious 24-year-old female, who was shown to have a blood alcohol level of 1510 mg per 100 ml *1·8 grains per 0·18 pt* – nearly 19 times the UK driving limit (80 mg of alcohol per 100 ml of blood) and triple the normally lethal limit. After two days she discharged herself.

Tommy Johns of Brisbane, Queensland, Australia died in April 1988 from a brain tumour at the age of 66 years, after having been arrested nearly 3000 times for being drunk and disorderly in a public place.

The late Samuel Riley (b. 1922) of Sefton Park, Merseyside was found by a disbelieving pathologist to have a level of 1220 mg on 28 Mar 1979.

William Pitt the Younger (1759–1806), the British Prime Minister, once allegedly drank 574 bottles of claret, 854 bottles of Madeira and 2410 bottles of port in a single year!

CELLS

Biggest The biggest cell body is the ovum (egg cell) which comes from the female ovary. It is about the size of the full stop at the end of this paragraph.

Smallest Some of the smallest cells are brain cells in the cerebellum and measure about 0·005 mm.

Longest The longest cells are neurons of the nervous system. Motor neurons 1·3 m *4·26 ft* long have cell bodies (grey matter) in the lower spinal cord with axons (white matter) which carry nerve impulses this 1·3 m *4·26 ft* from the spinal cord down to the big toe. Even longer are the cell systems which carry certain sensations (vibration and positional sense) back from the big toe to the brain. Their uninterrupted length, from the toe, and up the posterior part of the spinal cord to the medulla of the brain, is about equal to the height of the body.

Fastest turnover of body cells The fastest turnover of body cells i.e. the shortest life, is in the lining of the alimentary tract (guts) where the cells are shed every 3 days.

Longest life Those with the longest life are brain cells which last for life. They may be three times as old as bone cells which may live to the grand old age of 25–30 years.

Longest memory The lymphocyte has probably the longest memory of any cell. As successive generations of lymphocytes are produced during life the cells never forget an enemy. So, for example, once a measles virus has introduced itself to the lymphocytes in the first years of life, these stalwarts of the immune system will still be ready to recognise and destroy the measles virus 70 years later. In other words you cannot get measles twice.

Largest blood cell The largest blood cells is the megakaryocyte. It spends its life in the bone marrow rarely venturing out in the main stream of the blood itself. In the marrow it produces perhaps the 'stickiest' particles in the body - the platelets. There are about 250 000 platelets in each pin prick (cu.mm) of blood. They have an important role in stopping bleeding. Once a hole is formed in a blood vessel the platelets quickly gather at the site and stick to it thus sealing the breach.

BODY TEMPERATURE

Highest Willie Jones, 52, was admitted to Grady Memorial Hospital, Atlanta, Georgia, USA on 10 Jul 1980 with heatstroke on a day when the temperature reached 32·2° C *90° F* with 44 per cent humidity. His temperature was found to be 46·5° C *115·7° F*. After 24 days he was discharged 'at prior baseline status'.

Lowest People may die of hypothermia with body temperatures of 35° C *95° F*.

■ **Loudest screamer**
The scream of Simon Robinson of McLaren Vale, South Australia was measured at 128 dBA on 11 Nov 1988.

Cardiopulmonary resuscitation

Three teams of two, consisting of David Bailey and Les Williams, Angie Drinkard and Rich Martel, and Michelle Tyler and Sherri Johnson, all completed CPR marathons (cardiopulmonary resuscitation — 15 compressions alternating with two breaths) of 120 hr 6 min from 1–6 Sep 1988 at Melbourne, Florida, USA.

Standing

The longest period on record that anyone has stood continuously is more than 17 years in the case of Swami Maujgiri Maharaj when performing the *Tapasya* or penance from 1955–November 1973 in Shahjahanpur, Uttar Pradesh, India. When sleeping he would lean against a plank. He died in September 1980 at the age of 85.

Balancing on one foot

The longest recorded duration for balancing on one foot is 34 hr by N. Ravichandran in Sathyamangalam City, Tamil Nadu, India on 17–18 Apr 1982. The disengaged foot may not be rested on the standing foot nor may any object be used for support or balance.

There are three recorded cases of individuals surviving body temperatures as low as 16° C *60·8° F*: Dorothy Mae Stevens (1929–74), who was found in an alley in Chicago, Illinois, USA on 1 Feb 1951 and whose pulse dropped to 12 beats per min. Vickie Mary Davis, at the age of 2 years 1 month, discovered in an unheated house in Marshalltown, Iowa, USA on 21 Jan 1956; and 2-year old Michael Troke, found in the snow near his home in Milwaukee, Wisconsin, USA on 19 Jan 1985.

ILLNESS AND DISEASE

Commonest The commonest noncontagious disease is periodontal disease, such as gingivitis (inflammation of the gums). In their lifetime few people completely escape the effects of tooth decay.

The commonest contagious disease in the world is coryza (acute nasopharyngitis), or the common cold.

The most resistant recorded case to being infected at the Medical Research Council Common Cold Unit, Salisbury, Wilts is that of J. Brophy, who has had one mild reaction in 24 visits.

Infestation with pinworm (*Enterobius vermicularis*) approaches 100 per cent in some tropical areas of the world.

Rarest Medical literature periodically records hitherto undescribed diseases. A disease as yet undiagnosed but predicted by a Norwegian doctor is podocytoma of the kidney. This is a potential of the cells lining that part of the kidney (glomerulus) which acts as a sieve or filter for the blood.

The last case of endemic smallpox was recorded in Ali Maow Maalin in Merka, Somalia on 26 Oct 1977. This disease is now extinct.

Kuru (literally, 'the shakes') is now believed to be extinct and was only ever found among the Fore tribe of Papua New Guinea. It is believed that the virus was transmitted during ritual mourning, when the brain of the deceased was eaten by women and children.

Most infectious and most often fatal The pneumonic form of plague, as evidenced by the Black Death of 1347–51, killed everyone who caught it – a quarter of the population of Europe and some 75 million worldwide.

Highest mortality Rabies in humans has been regarded as uniformly fatal when associated with the hydrophobia symptom (a pathological fear of drinking fluids because of painful spasms while swallowing). A 25-year-old woman, Candida de Sousa Barbosa of Rio de Janeiro, Brazil, following surgery by Dr Max Karpin, was believed to be the first ever survivor of the disease in November 1968.

Some sources prefer the case of an unnamed seven-year-old boy living near Tampa, Florida, USA who, on 23 Jun 1953, was bitten on the chest by a rabid common vampire bat (*Desmodus rotundus*). The boy was put on a course of prophylactic immunization and eventually made a full recovery.

While the *disease* rabies is regarded as being almost universally fatal, this is not to be confused with being bitten by a rabid animal. With immediate treatment the virus can be prevented from invading the nervous system and chances of survival can be as high as 95 per cent.

AIDS (Acquired Immune Deficiency Syndrome) is caused by the Human Immunodeficiency Virus (HIV). It attacks the body's immune defence system, leaving the body wide open to attack from infections, which, to a healthy person, would be fought off without any problem. Many people who are carriers of the virus (HIV) may have none of the signs or symptoms associated with the disease AIDS. It may develop later. There have been no reported recoveries from 'full blown' AIDS.

In the UK 4 354 people had been diagnosed with AIDS, with 2 493 deaths from the disease by March 1991.

Leading cause of death In industrialized countries arteriosclerosis (thickening of the arterial wall) underlies much coronary (heart attacks and strokes) and cerebrovascular disease. Deaths from these diseases of the circulatory system total 267 924 in England and Wales.

Most notorious carrier The most publicised of all typhoid carriers was Mary Mallon (real name Maria Anna Caduff), known as Typhoid Mary, who was born in Graubunden, Switzerland in 1855 and arrived as an immigrant in New York City, USA, on 11 Jan 1868. In her job as a cook she was the source of 53 outbreaks, including the 1903 epidemic of 1400 cases in Ithaca, and three deaths. She was placed under permanent detention at Riverside Hospital on North Brother Island, East River from 1915 until her death from broncho-pneumonia on 11 Nov 1938.

MEDICAL EXTREMES

Post mortem birth The longest gestation interval in a post mortem birth was one of 84 days in the case of a baby girl born on 5 Jul 1983 to a brain-dead woman in Roanoke, Virginia, USA who had been kept on a life support machine since April.

Heart arrest The longest is four hours in the case of a Norwegian fisherman, Jan Egil Refsdahl (b. 1936), who fell overboard in the icy waters off Bergen on 7 Dec 1987. He was rushed to nearby Haukeland Hospital after his body temperature fell to 24° C *77° F* and his heart stopped beating, but he made a full recovery after he was connected to a heart–lung machine normally used for heart surgery.

Pulse rates A normal adult rate is 70–78 beats per min at rest for males and 75–85 for females. (The abnormal heart may beat as fast as 300 times per min or be so slow as to be virtually undetectable). The heart rate may increase to 200 or more during violent exercise in the unfit. Super fit athletes do not have to increase their heart rates nearly as much as this. The reason is that with training the fit heart can put out a great deal more blood with each contraction. Thus it is able to produce the necessary increase of blood during exercise by only raising its rate to perhaps 140 beats per minute.

Longest coma Elaine Esposito (b. 3 Dec 1934) of Tarpon Springs, Florida, USA, never stirred after an appendectomy on 6 Aug 1941, when aged 6. She died on 25 Nov 1978 aged 43 years 357 days, having been in a coma for 37 years 111 days.

Longest and shortest dreams Dreaming sleep is characterized by rapid eye movements known as REM, first described in 1953 by William Dement of the University of Chicago, USA. The longest recorded period of REM is one of 2 hr 23 min on 15 Feb 1967 at the Department of Psychology, University of Illinois, Chicago on Bill Carskadon, who had had his previous sleep interrupted. In July 1984 the Sleep Research Centre, Haifa, Israel recorded nil REM in a 33-year-old male who had a shrapnel brain injury. (See Most active muscle.)

Largest gallstone The largest gallstone reported in medical literature was one of 6·29 kg *13 lb 14 oz* removed from an 80-year-old woman by Dr Humphrey Arthure at Charing Cross Hospital, London, on 29 Dec 1952.

In August 1987 it was reported that 23 530 gallstones had been removed from an 85-year old woman by Mr K. Whittle Martin at Worthing Hospital, W Sussex, after she complained of severe abdominal pain.

Longest in 'iron lung' Mrs Laurel Nisbet (1912–85) of La Crescenta, California, USA was in an 'iron lung' for 37 years 58 days continuously until her death.

John Prestwich (b. 24 Nov 1938) of King Langley, Herts has been dependent on a negative pressure respirator since 24 Nov 1955.

Longest patient on haemodialysis Raymond Jones (b. 14 Apr 1929) of Slough, Berks, suffered from kidney failure from the age of 34, and received continuous haemodialysis from 13 Oct 1963 until his death on 22 Mar 1991. He averaged three visits per week to the Royal Free Hospital, Hampstead, London.

Fastest nerve impulses The results of experiments published in 1966 have shown that the fastest messages transmitted by the human nervous system can travel at 288 km/h *180 mph*. With advancing age, impulses are carried 15 per cent more slowly.

Heaviest organ The skin is medically considered to be an organ. It weighs around 2·7 kg *5·9 lb* in an average adult. The heaviest internal organ is the liver at 1·5 kg *3·3 lb*. This is four times heavier than the heart.

Hiccoughing The longest recorded attack of hiccoughing is that afflicting Charles Osborne (b. 1894) of Anthon, Iowa, USA for the past 69 years from 1922. He contracted it when slaughtering a hog and has been unable to find a cure, but leads a reasonably normal life in which he has had two wives and fathered eight children. He has admitted, however, that he cannot keep in his false teeth. In July 1986 he was reported to be hiccoughing at 20–25 per min from his earlier high of 40.

Sneezing The longest lasting fit ever recorded is that of Donna Griffiths (b. 1969) of Pershore, Hereford & Worcester. She started sneezing on 13 Jan 1981 and surpassed the previous duration record of 194 days on 27 Jul 1981. She sneezed an estimated million times in the first 365 days. She achieved her first sneeze-free day on 16 Sep 1983–the 978th day.

The highest speed at which expelled particles have ever been measured to travel is 167 km/h *103·6 mph*.

Snoring The highest sound level recorded by any chronic snorer is peaks of 90 dbA measured at the Department of Medicine, University of British Columbia, Vancouver, Canada during the evening of 3 Nov 1987. The meter was placed 60 cm *2 ft* above the head of Mark Thompson Hebbard (b. 28 Feb 1947) of Richmond, British Columbia, who maintained an overall level of 85 dbA. As the Vancouver city traffic bylaw for acceptable noise is set at 80 dbA, he wonders if he is legally entitled to sleep there.

Sleeplessness Research indicates that

on the Circadian (Latin: *circa* = around; *dies* = a day) cycle for the majority peak efficiency is attained between 8 and 9 p.m. and the low point comes at 4 a.m. Victims of the very rare condition chronic colestites (total insomnia) have been known to go without definable sleep for many years.

Motionlessness Antonio Gomes dos Santos of Zare, Portugal continuously stood motionless for 15 hr 2 min 55 sec on 30 Jul 1988 at the Amoreiras Shopping Centre, Lisbon.

Fire breathers Reg Morris blew a flame from his mouth to a distance of 9·4 m *31 ft* at the Miner's Rest, Chasetown, Staffs on 29 Oct 1986.

Fire extinguishers Inge Widar Svingen, alias 'Benifax' of Norway on 10 Aug 1990 extinguished 25 270 torches of flame in his mouth in 2 hrs at Kolvereid in Nord-Trøndelag, Norway.

On 26 Jul 1986 at Port Lonsdale, Victoria, Australia, Sipra Ellen Lloyd set a female record by extinguishing 8357 torches. *Fire-eating is potentially a highly dangerous activity.*

Human salamanders The highest dry-air temperature endured by naked men in US Air Force experiments in 1960 was 204·4°C *400°F*, and for heavily clothed men 260°C *500°F*. Steaks require only 162·8°C *325°F* to cook. Temperatures of 140°C *284°F* have been found quite bearable in saunas.

Swallowing The worst reported case of compulsive swallowing involved an insane female, Mrs H. aged 42, who complained of a 'slight abdominal pain'. She proved to have 2533 objects, including 947 bent pins, in her stomach. These were removed by Drs

Chalk and Foucar in June 1927 at the Ontario Hospital, Canada. In a more recent case, 212 objects were removed from the stomach of a man admitted to Groote Schuur Hospital, Cape Town, South Africa in May 1985. They included 53 toothbrushes, two telescopic aerials, two razors and 150 handles of disposable razors.

Another compulsive swallower was a 24-year-old psychoneurotic woman, from the United States who gulped down a 12·7 cm *5 in* long iron hinge bolt from a hospital door which amazingly passed through the curve of the duodenum and the intestinal tract and broke the bed-pan when the patient successfully passed the object.

The heaviest object extracted from a human stomach has been a 2·53 kg *5 lb 3 oz* ball of hair from a 20-year-old female compulsive swallower in the South Devon and East Cornwall Hospital on 30 Mar 1895.

Hunger strike Doctors estimate that a well-nourished individual can survive without medical consequences on a diet of sugar and water for 30 days or more. The longest period for which anyone has gone without solid food is 382 days in the case of Angus Barbieri (b. 1940) of Tayport, Fife, who lived on tea, coffee, water, soda water and vitamins in Maryfield Hospital, Dundee, Angus, from June 1965 to July 1966. His weight declined from 214·1 kg *33 st 10 lb* to 80·74 kg *12 st 10 lb*. *Records claimed without continuous medical surveillance, are inadmissible.*

The longest recorded hunger strike was 385 days from 28 Jun 1972 to 18 Jul 1973 by Denis Galer Goodwin in Wakefield Prison, W Yorks, protesting his innocence of a rape charge. He was fed by tube orally.

The longest recorded case of survival without food *and* water is 18 days by Andreas Mihavecz, then 18, of Bregenz, Austria, who was put into a holding cell on 1 Apr 1979 in a local government building in Höchst, but was totally forgotten by the police. On 18 Apr 1979 he was discovered close to death having had neither food nor water. He had been a passenger in a crashed car.

Underwater In 1986 two-year-old Michelle Funk of Salt Lake City, Utah, USA, made a full recovery after spending 66 minutes underwater. The toddler fell into a swollen creek near her home while playing. When she was eventually discovered, rescue workers found she had no pulse or heartbeat. Her life was saved by the first successful bypass machine which warmed her blood, which had dropped to 66°F. Doctors at the hospital described the time she had spent under water as the 'longest documented submergence with an intact neurological outcome'.

g forces Racing driver David Purley (1945–85) survived a deceleration from 173 km/h *108 mph* to zero in 66 cm *26 in* in a crash at Silverstone, Northants on 13 Jul 1977 which involved a force of 179·8 g. He suffered 29 fractures, three dislocations and six heart stoppages. The highest g value endured on a water-braked rocket sled is 82·6 g *2·9 oz* for 0·04 sec by Eli L. Beeding, Jr at Holloman Air Force Base, New Mexico, USA on 16 May 1958. He was subsequently hospitalized for three days.

A land diver of Pentecost Island, Vanuatu (formerly the New Hebrides) dived from a platform 24·76 m *81 ft 3 in* high with liana vines attached to his ankles on 15 May 1982. His body speed was 15·24 m *50 ft* per

■ **Lung power**
The inflation of a standard 1000 g 35 oz meteorological balloon to a diameter of 2·43 m 8 ft against time was achieved by Nicholas Berkeley Mason in 45 min 8 sec at the BBC TV Centre, London on 25 Sep 1989, later shown on the Record Breakers programme.

ANATOMY AND PHYSIOLOGY

Eating

Michel Lotito (b. 15 Jun 1950) of Grenoble, France, known as Monsieur Mangetout, has been eating metal and glass since 1959. Gastroenterologists have X-rayed his stomach and have described his ability to consume 900 g *2 lb* of metal per day as unique. His diet since 1966 has included 10 bicycles, a supermarket trolley in 4½ days, 7 TV sets, 6 chandeliers and a low-calorie Cessna light aircraft, which he ate in Caracas, Venezuela. He is said to have provided the only example in history of a coffin (handles and all) ending up inside a man.

Stretcher bearing

The greatest recorded distance a stretcher case with a 63·5 kg *10 st* 'body' has been carried is 229 km *142·3 miles* in 38 hr 39 min, from 5–7 Apr 1989 by two four-man teams from 1 Field Ambulance, Canadian Forces Base, Calgary, Canada.

The record limited to Youth Organisations (under 20 years of age) and eight hours of carrying is held by eight members of the Henry Meoles School, Moreton, Wirral, Cheshire, who covered 67·62 km *42·02 miles* on 13 Jul 1980.

sec, 54 km/h *34 mph*. The jerk transmitted a momentary g force in excess of 110.

Longest stay in a hospital Miss Martha Nelson was admitted to the Columbus State Institute for the Feeble-Minded in Ohio, USA in 1875. She died in January 1975 at the age of 103 years 6 months in the Orient State Institution, Ohio after spending more than 99 years in hospitals.

Pill-taking The highest recorded total of pills swallowed by a patient is 565 939 between 9 Jun 1967 and 19 Jun 1988 by C.H.A. Kilner (1926–88) of Bindura, Zimbabwe.

Most injections A diabetic, Mrs Evelyn Ruth Winder (b. 1921) of Invercargill, New Zealand gave an estimated 62 948 insulin injections to herself over 60 years to March 1991.

Most tattoos The ultimate in being tattooed is represented by Tom Leppard of Isle of Syke. He has gone for a leopard skin design, with all the skin between the dark spots tattooed saffron yellow. The area of his body covered is approximately 3002 in², 99·2 per cent of totality.

Bernard Moeller of Pennsylvania, USA claimed to have 8960 individual tattoos at 4 Dec 1989 and Walter Stiglitz of New Jersey, USA claims 5488 separate tattoos by six different artists.

The world's most decorated woman is strip artiste 'Krystyne Kolorful' (b. 5 Dec 1952, Alberta, Canada). Her 95 per cent body suit took 10 years to complete.

Britain's most decorated woman is Rusty Field (b. 1944) of Norfolk, who after 12 years under the needle of Bill Skuse has reached 85 per cent of totality.

Both the 1980 and 1981 World's Most Beautiful Tattooed Lady Contest in the USA were won by Britain's Susan James (b. 1959).

OPERATIONS

Longest The most protracted reported operation has been one of 96 hr performed from 4–8 Feb 1951 in Chicago, Illinois, USA on Mrs Gertrude Levandowski for the removal of an ovarian cyst. During the operation her weight fell 280 kg *44 st* to 140 kg *22 st*. The patient suffered from a weak heart and surgeons had to exercise the utmost caution during the operation.

Most Padmabhushan Dr M.C. Modi, a pioneer of mass eye surgery in India since 1943, together with assistants, has performed as many as 833 cataract operations in one day, visited 45 416 villages and 10 094 632 patients, making a total of 595 019 operations to February 1990.

Dr Robert B. McClure (b. 1901) of Toronto, Canada performed a career total of 20 423 major operations from 1924 to 1978.

Joseph Ascough (1935–87) of Nottingham underwent his 341st operation (for the removal of papillomas from his windpipe) in September 1987. These wart-like growths which impede breathing first formed when he was 18 months old.

On 2 Mar 1977 Mr Jens Kjaer Jension (b. 1914) of Hoven, Denmark was discharged from a local hospital after having had 32 131 thorns removed from his body during 248 visits over a period of six years. In 1967 he had tripped and fallen into a pile of spiky berberry cuttings in his garden and was rushed unconscious to the hospital. Even today he is still troubled by thorns working their way out through the skin of his legs.

Oldest patient The greatest recorded age at which anyone has undergone an

operation is 111 years 105 days in the case of James Henry Brett, Jr (1849–1961) of Houston, Texas, USA. He underwent a hip operation on 7 Nov 1960.

The greatest age in Britain for an operation was in the case of Miss Mary Wright (b. 28 Feb 1862) who died during a thigh operation at Boston, Lincs on 22 Apr 1971 aged 109 years 53 days.

Earliest appendectomy The earliest recorded successful appendix operation was performed in 1736 by Claudius Amyand (1680–1740). He was Serjeant Surgeon to King George II (reigned 1727–60).

Earliest general anaesthesia The earliest recorded operation under general anaesthesia was for the removal of a cyst from the neck of James Venable by Dr Crawford Williamson Long (1815–78), using diethyl ether ($C_2H_5)_2O$, in Jefferson, Georgia, USA on 30 Mar 1842.

Tracheostomy Mrs Winifred Campbell (b. 6 Jul 1902) of Wanstead, London has spoken through a silver tube in her throat for 83 years.

Munchausen's syndrome The most extreme recorded case of the rare and incurable condition known as 'Munchausen's syndrome' (a continual desire to have medical treatment) was William McIlroy (b. 1906), who cost the National Health Service an estimated £2·5 million during his 50-year career as a hospital patient. During that time he had 400 major and minor operations, and stayed at 100 different hospitals using 22 aliases. The longest period he was ever out of hospital was six months. In 1979 he hung up his bedpan for the last time, saying he was sick of hospitals, and retired to an old people's home in Birmingham, W Mids where he died in 1983.

Fastest amputation The shortest time recorded for a leg amputation in the pre-anaesthetic era was 13–15 sec by Napoleon's chief surgeon, Dominique Larrey. There could have been no ligation of blood vessels.

Largest tumour The largest tumour ever recorded was Spohn's case of an ovarian cyst weighing 148·7 kg *23 st 6 lb* taken from a woman in Texas, USA in 1905. She made a full recovery.

Largest gall bladder On 15 Mar 1989 at the National Naval Medical Center in Bethesda, Maryland, USA, Prof. Bimal C. Ghosh removed a gall bladder which weighed 10·43 kglb *23 lb* from a 69 year old woman. The patient had been complaining of increasing swelling around the abdomen, and after taking away this enlarged gall bladder which weighed more than three times the average new born baby, the patient felt perfectly well and left hospital 10 days after the operation.

Surgical instruments The largest instruments are robot retractors used in abdominal surgery, introduced by Abbey Surgical Instruments of Chingford, Essex in 1968 and weighing 5 kg *11 lb*. Some bronchoscopic forceps measure 60 cm *23 ½ in* in length.

The smallest is Microcystotome a super microknife for cutting of lens capsule in eye microsurgery. The length of the working part is 0·1 mm *0·011 in* and 0·08 mm *2·03 in* wide, licenced by the Research and Technology Complex of the Russian Ministry of Health, Moscow.

TRANSPLANTS

Heart The first operation was performed on Louis Washkansky, aged 55, at the Groote Schuur Hospital, Cape Town, South

Africa between 1 a.m. and 6 a.m., on 3 Dec 1967, by a team of 30 headed by Prof. Christiaan Neethling Barnard (b. 8 Oct 1922 Beaufort West, South Africa). The donor was Miss Denise Ann Darvall, aged 25, Washkansky lived for 18 days.

Britain's first heart transplant operation took place at the National Heart Hospital, London on 3 May 1968. The patient, Frederick West, survived for 46 days.

Longest surviving William George van Buuren of California, USA (b. 24 May 1929), who received an unnamed person's heart at the Stanford Medical Center, Palo Alto, California, USA on 3 Jan 1970, is still alive today. The surgeon who performed the operation was Dr Edward Stinson.

Britain's longest-surviving heart transplant patient is Derrick H. Morris (b. 24 Mar 1930) who underwent surgery at Harefield Hospital, Greater London on 23 Feb 1980.

Youngest Paul Holt of Vancouver, British Columbia, Canada underwent a heart transplant at Loma Linda Hospital in California, USA on 16 Oct 1987 at the age of 2 hr 34 min. He was born six-weeks premature at 2·9 kg *6 lb 6 oz*.

The youngest in the UK was Hollie Roffey, who received a new heart when aged only 10 days at the National Heart Hospital in London on 29 Jul 1984. She survived for only 10 days.

First transplantee to give birth Betsy Sneith, 23, gave birth to a baby girl, Sierra (3·45 kg *7 lb 10 oz*), at Stanford University Hospital, California, USA on 17 Sep 1984. She had received a donor heart in February 1980.

Five-organ Tabatha Foster (1984–88) of Madisonville, Kentucky, USA, at the age of 3 years 143 days, received a transplanted liver, pancreas, small intestine, portions of stomach and large intestine in a 15-hour operation at the Children's Hospital, Pittsburgh, on 31 Oct 1987. Before the operation, she had never eaten solid food.

Heart–lung–liver The first triple transplant took place on 17 Dec 1986 at Papworth Hospital, Cambridge, when Mrs Davina Thompson (b. 28 Feb 1951) of Rawmarsh, S Yorks, underwent surgery for seven hours by a team of 15 headed by chest surgeon Mr John Wallwork and Prof. Sir Roy Calne.

Artificial heart On 1–2 Dec 1982 at the Utah Medical Center, Salt Lake City, Utah, USA Dr Barney B. Clark, 61, of Des Moines, Washington, was the first recipient of an artificial heart. The surgeon was Dr William C. DeVries. The heart was a Jarvik 7 designed by Dr Robert K. Jarvik (b. 11 May 1946 Midland, Michigan). Dr Clark died on 23 Mar 1983, 112 days later. William J. Schroeder survived for 620 days in Louisville, Kentucky from 25 Nov 1984 to 7 Aug 1986.

Britain's first artificial heart patient was Raymond Cook of Hucknall, Notts who temporarily received a Jarvik 7 on 2 Nov 1986 at Papworth Hospital, Cambridge, Cambs.

Kidney R. H Lawler (b. 1895) (USA) performed the first transplant of the kidney in a human at Little Company of May Hospital, Chicago, Illinois, USA on 17 Jun 1950.

The longest surviving kidney transplant patient is Kathleen Severson (b. 25 Jul 1943) of Minnesota, USA, whose operation was performed with her brother as donor on 8 Jul 1964 at the University of Minnesota Hospital.

The Human World

Political and Social

Largest political division The Commonwealth, a free association of 50 independent states and their dependencies, covers an area of 29 369 202 km² *11 339 513 miles²* with a population estimated in 1988 to be 1 384 631 000. The British Empire began to expand when Henry VII patented trade monopolies to John Cabot in March 1496 and when the East India Co. was incorporated on 31 Dec 1600.

COUNTRIES

The world comprises 171 sovereign countries and 60 separately administered non-sovereign or other territories, making a total of 231.

The United Nations still lists the *de jure* territories of East Timor (now incorporated into Indonesia),

Western Sahara (now in Morocco), the former mandated territory of Palestine and the uninhabited Canton and Enderbury Islands (now disputed between the USA and Kiribati) but does not list the three Baltic states of Estonia, Latvia and Lithuania, though their forcible incorporation into the USSR in 1940 has never been internationally recognized. Neither does it list the *de facto* territories of Taiwan, Mayotte or Spanish North Africa, the territories claimed by various countries in Antarctica, or the Australian Territory of Coral Sea Islands and Heard and McDonald Islands.

Largest The country with the greatest area is the Union of Soviet Socialist Republics (the Soviet Union), comprising 15 Union (constituent) Republics with a total area of 22 402 200 km² *8 649 500 miles²*, or 15 per cent of the world's total land area, and a total coastline (including islands) of 106 360 km *66 090 miles*. The country measures 8980 km *5580 miles* from east to west and 4490 km *2790 miles* from north to south and is 91·8 times the size of the UK. Its population in mid-1990 was an estimated 291 million.

The UK covers 244 100 km² *94 247 miles²* (including 3218 km² *1242 miles²* of inland water), or 0·16 per cent of the total land area of the world. Great Britain is the world's eighth largest island, with an area of 229 979 km² *88 795 miles²* and a coastline 7930 km *4928 miles* long, of which Scotland accounts for 4141 km *2573 miles*, Wales 685 km *426 miles* and England 3104 km *1929 miles*.

Smallest The smallest independent country in the world is the State of the Vatican City or Holy See (Stato della Città del Vaticano), which was made an enclave within the city of Rome, Italy on 11 Feb 1929. The enclave has an area of 44 ha *108·7 acres*. The maritime sovereign country with the shortest coastline is Monaco, with 5·61 km *3·49 miles*, excluding piers and breakwaters. The world's smallest republic is Nauru, less than 1 degree south of the equator in the western Pacific, which became independent on 31 Jan 1968. It has an area of 2129 ha *5263 acres* and a population of 9000 (latest estimate 1989).

The smallest colony in the world is Gibraltar (since 1969, the City of Gibraltar), with an area of 5·8 km² *2½ miles²*. However, Pitcairn Island, the only inhabited island (49 people in March 1990) of a group of four (total area 48 km² *18½ miles²*), has an area of 388 ha *960 acres/1½ miles²*. It was named after Midshipman Robert Pitcairn of HMS *Swallow* in July 1767.

The official residence, since 1834, of the Grand Master of the Order of the Knights of Malta, totalling 1·2 ha *3 acres* and comprising the Villa del Priorato di Malta on the lowest of Rome's seven hills, the 46 m *151 ft* Aventine, retains certain diplomatic privileges, as does 68 via Condotti, also in Rome. The Order has accredited representatives to foreign governments and is hence sometimes cited as the world's smallest 'state'.

Flattest and most elevated The country with the lowest 'high point' is Maldives; it attains 2·4 m *8 ft*. The country with the highest 'low point' is Lesotho. The egress of the Senqu (Orange) river-bed is 1381 m *4530 ft* above sea level.

Longest and shortest frontier The longest *continuous* frontier in the world is that between Canada and the United States, which (including the Great Lakes boundaries) extends for 6416 km *3987 miles* (excluding the frontier of 2547 km *1538 miles* with Alaska).

The frontier which is crossed most frequently is that between the United States and Mexico. It extends for 3110 km *1933 miles* and there are more than 120 000 000 crossings every year. The Sino-Soviet frontier, broken by the Sino-Mongolian border, extends for 7240 km *4500 miles*, with no reported figure for crossings. The 'frontier' of the Holy See in Rome measures 4·07 km *2·53 miles*. The land frontier between Gibraltar and Spain at La Linea, closed between June 1969 and February 1985, measures 1·53 km *1672 yd*. Zambia, Zimbabwe, Botswana and Namibia, in Africa, almost meet at a single point.

The UK's frontier with the Republic of Ireland measures 358 km *223 miles*.

Most frontiers China has the most land frontiers, with 13 — Mongolia, USSR, North Korea, Hong Kong, Macau, Vietnam, Laos, Myanmar (formerly Burma), India, Bhutan, Nepal, Pakistan and Afghanistan. These extend for 24 000 km *14 900 miles*. France, if all her *départements d'outre-mer* are included, may, on extended territorial waters, have 20.

POPULATIONS

WORLD POPULATION			
Date	**Millions**	**Date**	**Millions**
8000 BC	*c.* 6	**1970**	3698
AD 1	*c.* 255	**1975**	4080
1000	*c.* 254	**1980**	4450
1250	416	**1981**	4528
1500	460	**1982**	4607
1600	579	**1983**	4684
1700	679	**1984**	4760
1750	770	**1985**	4854
1800	954	**1986**	4917
1900	1633	**1987**	*4998
1920	1862	**1988**	5096
1930	2070	**1989**	5194
1940	2295	**1990**	5292
1950	2515	**1991**	5390
1960	3019	**2000†**	6251
		2025†	8467

* *The Population Institute of Washington, DC, USA declared that the landmark of 5 billion was reached on 7 Jul 1987 whereas the United Nations nominated 11 Jul 1987 'Baby Five Billion Day'.*

† *These projections are from the latest UN publication 'World Population Prospects 1988'. This gives no projection beyond 2025. An earlier publication in 1984 forecast that the world population will not stabilize until 2095, at about 10 500 million, but revised estimates in May 1988 said that it might be as high as 14 000 million in 2050.*

Note: *The all-time peak annual increase of 2·06 per cent in the period 1965–70 had declined to 1·73 per cent by 1985–90. By 2025 this should decline to 0·98 per cent. In spite of the reduced percentage increase, world population is currently growing by 98 million people every year.*

Using estimates made by the French demographer J. N. Biraben and others, A. R. Thatcher, a former Director of the Office of Population Censuses and Surveys, has calculated that the number of people who died between 40 000 BC and AD 1990 was nearly 60 000 million. This estimate implies that the current world population is about one eleventh of those who have ever lived.

World The average daily increase in the world's population is about 270 000 or an average of just under 200 per minute. There are, however, seasonal variations in the numbers of births and deaths throughout the year. For past, present and future estimates, see table.

Matej Gaspar, born 11 Jul 1987 in Yugoslavia, was symbolically named the world's 5 billionth inhabitant by the United Nations Secretary-General.

Most populous country The most populated country is China, which in *pinyin* is written Zhongguo (meaning 'central land'). The census of July 1990 revealed a population of 1 133 682 501, and involved 7 million census-takers. The rate of natural increase in the People's Republic of China is now estimated to be 35 068 a day or 12·8 million per year. India is set to overtake China in size of population by AD 2050, with 1591 million against 1555 million for China.

Least populous The independent state with the smallest population is the Vatican City or the Holy See (see Smallest country, above), with 750 inhabitants in 1989 and a nil return for births.

Most densely populated The most densely populated territory in the world is the Portuguese province of Macau, on the southern coast of China. It has an estimated population of 479 000 (1988) in an area of 16·9 km² *6·5 miles²*, giving a density of 28 343/km² *73 692/mile²*.

The principality of Monaco, on the south coast of France, has a population of 29 000 (1989) in an area of just 191·4 ha *473 acres,* a density equal to 15 152/km² *39 242/mile²*.

Of territories with an area of more than 1000 km² *386 miles²*, Hong Kong (1037 km² *400·5 miles²*) contains an estimated 5 800 000 (1990), giving the territory a density of 5593/km² *14 482/mile²*. Hong Kong is now the most populous of all colonies. The transcription of the name is from a local pronunciation of the Beijing dialect version of Xiang gang (meaning 'a port for incense'). The 1976 by-census showed that the West Area of the urban district of Mong Kok on the Kowloon Peninsula had a density of 252 090/km² *652 910/mile²*. In 1959, at the peak of the housing crisis, it was reported that in one house designed for 12 people the number of occupants was 459, including 104 in one room and four living on the roof.

Of countries over 2589 km² *1000 miles²* the most densely populated is Bangladesh, with a population of 114 800 000 (1990) living in 143 999 km² *55 598 miles²* at a density of 797/km² *2065/mile²*. The Indonesian island of Java (with an area of 126 295 km² *48 763 miles²*) had a population of 100 300 000 (1987), giving a density of 793/km² *2056/mile²*.

The UK (244 100 km² *94 247 miles²*) had an estimated population of 57 561 000 in mid-1991, giving a density of 236/km² *611/mile²*. The 1990 population density for the Borough of Islington, London was 11 383/km² *29 482/mile²*.

Most sparsely populated Antarctica became permanently occupied by relays of scientists from 1943. The population varies seasonally and reaches 2000 at times.

The least populated territory, apart from Antarctica, is Kalaallit Nunaat (formerly Greenland), with a population of 55 400 (1989) in an area of 2 175 000 km² *840 000 miles²*, giving a density of one person to every 39·26 km² *15·16 miles²*. Some 84·3 per cent of the island comprises an ice-cap.

The lowest population density in the UK is in Highland, Scotland with 8·0/km² *20·7/mile²*. The most sparsely populated county in England is Northumberland, with a density of 59·9/km² *155·1/mile²*.

Emigration More people emigrate from Mexico than from any other country. An estimated 800 000 illegally entered the USA in 1980 alone. The Soviet invasion of Afghanistan in December 1979 caused an influx of 2 900 000 refugees into Pakistan and a further 2 200 000 into Iran. By 1989 the number of Afghan refugees in Pakistan had increased to 3 622 000.

A total of 122 000 British citizens emigrated from the UK in 1989. Her largest number of emigrants in any one year was 360 000 in 1852, mainly from Ireland.

Immigration The country which regularly receives the most legal immigrants is the United States. It has been estimated that between 1820 and 1989 the USA received 54 978 717 *official* immigrants. One in 24 of the US population is, however, an *illegal* immigrant. In the fiscal year to September 1986, 1 615 854 people were arrested by US patrols on the Mexican border.

The peak year for immigration into the UK was the 12 months from 1 Jul 1961 to 30 Jun 1962, when about 430 000 Commonwealth citizens arrived. The number of immigrants in the year 1989 was 145 000.

Biggest demonstration A figure of

WORST DISASTERS IN THE WORLD

DISASTER	NUMBER KILLED	LOCATION	DATE
Pandemic	75 000 000	Eurasia: The Black Death (bubonic, pneumonic and septicaemic plague)	1347–51
Genocide	c. 35 000 000	Mongol extermination of Chinese peasantry	1311–40
Famine	c. 30 000 000[1]	Northern China	1959–61
Influenza	21 640 000	World-wide	1918–19
Earthquake	1 100 000	Near East and E. Mediterranean (see p. 17)	c. July 1201
Circular Storm[2]	1 000 000	Ganges Delta Islands, Bangladesh	12–13 Nov 1970
Flood	900 000	Huang Ho River, China	Oct 1887
Landslides (Triggered off by single earthquake)	180 000	Kansu Province, China	16 Dec 1920
Atomic Bomb	155 200	Hiroshima, Japan (including radiation deaths within a year)	6 Aug 1945
Conventional Bombing[3]	c. 140 000	Tokyo, Japan	10 Mar 1945
Volcanic Eruption	92 000	Tambora, Sumbawa, Indonesia	5–7 Apr 1815
Avalanches	c. 18 000[4]	Yungay, Huascarán, Peru	31 May 1970
Marine (Single ship)	c. 7700	*Wilhelm Gustloff* (25 484 tons) German liner torpedoed off Danzig by USSR submarine S-13 (only 903 survivors)	30 Jan 1945
Dam Burst	c. 5000[5]	Machhu River Dam, Morvi, Gujarat, India	11 Aug 1979
Panic	c. 4000	Chungking (Zhong qing) China, air raid shelter	6 Jun 1941
Industrial (Chemical)	3350	Union Carbide methylisocyanate plant, Bhopal, India	2–3 Dec 1984
Smog	2850	London fog, England (excess deaths)	5–13 Dec 1952
Tunnelling (Silicosis)	c. 2500	Hawk's Nest hydroelectric tunnel, W. Virginia, USA	1931–35
Fire[6] (Single building)	1670	The Theatre, Canton, China	May 1845
Explosion	1635[7]	Halifax, Nova Scotia, Canada	6 Dec 1917
Mining[8]	1572	Honkeiko Colliery, China (coal dust explosion)	26 Apr 1942
Tornado	c. 1300	Shaturia, Bangladesh	26 Apr 1989
Riot	c. 1200	New York anti-conscription riots	13–16 Jul 1863
Mass Suicide[9]	960	Jewish Zealots, Masada, Israel	73
Railway	>800	Bagmati River, Bihar, India	6 Jun 1981
Fireworks	>800	Dauphin's wedding, Seine, Paris, France	16 May 1770
Aircraft (Civil)[10]	583	KLM-Pan Am Boeing 747 ground crash, Tenerife	27 Mar 1977
Man-eating Animal	436	Champawat district, India, tigress shot by Col. Jim Corbet (died 1955)	1907
Terrorism	329	Bomb aboard Air-India Boeing 747, crashed into Atlantic south-west of Ireland, Sikh extremists suspected	23 Jun 1985
Hail	246	Moradabad, Uttar Pradesh, India	20 Apr 1888
Road[11]	176	Petrol tanker explosion inside Salang Tunnel, Afghanistan	3 Nov 1982
Offshore Oil Platform	167	Piper Alpha oil production platform, North Sea	6 Jul 1988
Submarine	130	*Le Surcouf* rammed by US merchantman *Thomas Lykes* in Caribbean	18 Feb 1942
Helicopter	54	Israel, military 'Sea Stallion', West Bank	10 May 1977
Mountaineering	43	Lenin Peak, USSR	13 Jul 1990
Ski Lift (Cable car)	42	Cavalese resort, northern Italy	9 Mar 1976
Nuclear Reactor	31[12]	Chernobyl No. 4, Ukraine, USSR	26 Apr 1986
Elevator (Lift)	23	Vaal Reefs gold mine lift fell 1·93 km *1·2 miles*	27 Mar 1980
Lightning	21	Hut in Chinamasa Kraal, near Mutari, Zimbabwe (single bolt)	23 Dec 1975
Yacht Racing	19	28th Fastnet Race—23 boats sank or abandoned in Force 11 gale	13–15 Aug 1979
Space Exploration	7	US Challenger 51L Shuttle, Cape Canaveral, Florida, USA	28 Jan 1986
Nuclear Waste Accident	high but undisclosed[13]	Venting of plutonium extraction wastes, Kyshtym, USSR	c. Dec 1957

FOOTNOTES

[1] It has been estimated that more than 5 million died in the post-World War I famine of 1920–1 in the USSR. The USSR government in July 1923 informed Mr (later President) Herbert Hoover that the ARA (American Relief Administration) had since August 1921 saved 20 million lives from famine and famine-related diseases.

[2] This figure published in 1972 for the Bangladeshi disaster was from Dr Afzal, Principal Scientific Officer of the Atomic Energy Authority Centre, Dacca. One report asserted that less than half of the population of the four islands of Bhola, Charjabbar, Hatia and Ramagati (1961 Census 1·4 million) survived. The most damaging hurricane recorded was Hurricane Hugo from 17–22 Sep 1989, which was estimated to have done $7 billion worth of damage.

[3] The number of civilians killed by the bombing of Germany has been put variously at 593 000 and 'over 635 000', including some 35 000 deaths in the raids on Dresden, Germany from 13–15 Feb 1945. Total Japanese fatalities were 600 000 (conventional) and 220 000 (nuclear).

[4] A total of 18 000 Austrian and Italian troops were reported to have been lost in the Dolomite valleys of northern Italy on 13 Dec 1916 in more than 100 snow avalanches. Some of the avalanches were triggered by gunfire.

[5] The dynamiting of a Yangtze Kiang dam at Huayuan Kow by Kuomintang (KMT) forces during the Sino-Japanese war in 1938 is reputed to have resulted in 900 000 deaths.

[6] >200 000 killed in the sack of Moscow, as a result of fires started by the invading Tatars in May 1571. Worst-ever hotel fire, 162 killed, Hotel Daeyungak, Seoul, South Korea 25 Dec 1971. Worst circus fire, 168 killed, Hartford, Connecticut, USA 6 Jul 1944.

[7] Some sources maintain that the final death toll was over 3000 on 6–7 December. Published estimates of the 11 000 killed at the BASF chemical plant explosion at Oppau, Germany on 21 Sep 1921 were exaggerated. The most reliable estimate is 561 killed.

[8] The worst gold-mining disaster in South Africa was when 182 were killed in Kinross gold mine on 16 Sep 1986.

[9] As reported by the historian Flavius Josephus (c. 37–100). In modern times, the greatest mass suicide was on 18 Nov 1978 when 913 members of the People's Temple cult died of mass cyanide poisoning near Port Kaituma, Guyana. 22 000 Japanese civilians jumped off a cliff to their deaths in June 1943 during the US Marines' assault of the island of Tarawa (now in Kiribati).

[10] The crash of JAL's Boeing 747, flight 123, near Tokyo on 12 Aug 1985, in which 520 passengers and crew perished, was the worst single plane crash in aviation history.

[11] Western estimates gave the number of deaths at c. 1100. The global aggregate death toll in road accidents was put at 25 million by September 1975.

[12] Explosion at 0123 hrs Soviet European time 26 Apr 1986. Thirty-one was the official Soviet total of immediate deaths. On 25 Apr 1991 Vladimir Shovkoshitny stated in the Ukrainian Parliament that 7000 'clean-up' workers had already died from radiation. The estimate for the eventual death toll has been put as high as 75 000 by Dr Robert Gale, a US bone transplant specialist.

[13] More than 30 small communities in a 1200 km² 460 mile² area have been eliminated from USSR maps since 1958, with 17 000 people evacuated. Possibly an ammonium nitrate-hexone explosion.

WORST DISASTERS IN THE BRITISH ISLES

DISASTER	NUMBER KILLED	LOCATION	DATE
Famine	1 500 000[1]	Ireland (famine and typhus)	1846–51
Pandemic (the Black Death)	800 000		1347–50
Influenza	225 000		Sep–Nov 1918
Circular Storm	c. 8000	'The Channel Storm'	26 Nov 1703
Smog	2850	London fog	5–13 Dec 1952
Flood	c. 2000[2]	Severn Estuary	20 Jan 1606
Bombing	1436	London	10–11 May 1941
Marine (single ship)	c. 800[3]	HMS Royal George off Spithead	29 Aug 1782
Riot	565 (min)	London anti-Catholic Gordon riots	2–13 Jun 1780
Mining	439	Universal Colliery, Senghenydd, Mid Glam	14 Oct 1913
Terrorism (aircraft)	270[4]	Bomb aboard Pan Am Boeing 747, crashed over Lockerbie, Dumfries & Galloway	21 Dec 1988
Dam Burst	250	Bradfield Reservoir, Dale Dyke, near Sheffield, S Yorks (embankment burst)	12 Mar 1864
Railway	227[5]	Triple collision, Quintinshill, Dumfries & Galloway	22 May 1915
Fire (single building)	188[6]	Theatre Royal, Exeter	5 Sep 1887
Panic	183	Victoria Hall, Sunderland, Tyne and Wear	16 Jun 1883
Offshore Oil Platform	167	Piper Alpha oil production platform, North Sea	6 Jul 1988
Landslide	144	Pantglas coal tip No. 7, Aberfan, Mid Glam	21 Oct 1966
Explosion	134[7]	Chilwell, Notts (explosives factory)	1 Jul 1918
Nuclear Reactor	see footnote[8]	Cancer deaths; Windscale (now Sellafield), Cumbria	10 Oct 1957
Submarine	99	HMS Thetis, during trials, Liverpool Bay	1 Jun 1939
Tornado	75	Tay Bridge collapsed under impact of 2 tornadic vortices	28 Dec 1879
Helicopter	45	Chinook, off Sumburgh, Shetland Islands	6 Nov 1986
Road	33[9]	Coach crash, River Dibb, near Grassington, N Yorks	27 May 1975
Lightning	31	(Annual total) Worst year on record (annual av. 12)	1914
Yacht Racing	19	28th Fastnet Race—23 boats sank or abandoned in Force 11 gale. Of 316 starters only 128 finished	13–15 Aug 1979
Avalanches	8	Lewes, E Sussex	27 Dec 1836
Mountaineering	6	On Cairn Gorm, near Aviemore (1245 m 4084 ft)	21 Nov 1971
Earthquake	2	London earthquake, Christ's Hospital (Newgate)	6 Apr 1580

FOOTNOTES

[1] Based on the net rate of natural increase between 1841 and 1851, a supportable case for a loss of population of 3 million can be made out if rates of under-enumeration of 25 per cent (1841) and 10 per cent (1851) are accepted. Potato rot (Phytophthora infestans) was first reported on 13 Sep 1845.

[2] Death tolls of 100 000 were reputed in England and Holland in the floods of 1099, 1421 and 1446.

[3] c. 4000 were lost on HM troopship Lancastria, 16 243 grt, off St Nazaire on 17 Jun 1940.

[4] The worst crash by a UK operated aircraft was that of a Dan-Air Boeing 727 from Manchester which crashed into a mountain on the Canary Islands on 25 Apr 1980, killing 146 people. There were no survivors.

[5] The 194·7 m 213 yd long troop train was telescoped to 61·2 m 67 yd. Signalmen Meakin and Tinsley were sentenced for manslaughter. Britain's worst underground train disaster was the Moorgate Tube disaster of 28 Feb 1975, when 43 persons were killed.

[6] In July 1212, 3000 were killed in the crush, burned or drowned when London Bridge caught fire at both ends. The death toll in the Great Fire of London of 1666 was only eight. History's first 'fire storm' occurred in the Quebec Yard, Surrey Docks, Southwark, London during the 300-pump fire in the Blitz on 7–8 Sep 1940. Dockland casualties were 306 killed. Britain's most destructive fire was that leading to a £165 million loss at the Army Ordnance depot, Donnington, Shrops on 24 Jun 1983.

[7] HM armed cruiser Natal blew up off Invergordon, Highland on 30 Dec 1915, killing 428.

[8] There were no deaths as a direct result of the fire, but the number of cancer deaths that might be attributed to it was estimated by the National Radiological Protection Board in 1989 to be 100.

[9] The greatest pile-up on British roads was on the M6 near Lymm Interchange, near Thelwall, Cheshire on 13 Sep 1971. Two hundred vehicles were involved, with 10 dead and 61 injured. The worst year for road deaths in Great Britain was 1941, with 9161 deaths.

2·7 million was reported from China for the demonstration against the USSR in Shanghai on 3–4 Apr 1969 following the border clashes.

Most patient 'refusenik' The USSR citizen who waited longest for an exit visa was Benyamin Bogomolny, who first applied in 1966. He arrived in Vienna on 14 Oct 1986. The person who has currently been waiting the longest is Vladimir Raiz, who first applied to emigrate in February 1973.

Tourism The most popular tourist destination is France, which in 1989 received 49 544 000 foreign tourists. The country with the greatest receipts from tourism is the United States, with $15·4 billion in 1987. The biggest spenders are Germans, who in 1987 spent $23·6 billion on foreign tourism.

The record influx of tourists into the UK was 17·3 million in 1989, which was also the record year for spending by foreign tourists, with a figure of £6945 million.

Birth rate *Highest and lowest* The crude birth rate—the number of births per 1000 population—for the whole world was estimated to be 27·1 per 1000 in 1985–90. The highest rate estimated by the United Nations for 1985–90 is 53·9 per 1000 for Kenya. Excluding the Vatican City, where the rate is negligible, the lowest recorded rate is 9·3 per 1000 (1985) for San Marino.

The crude birth rate for the UK was 13·8 in 1988 (13·8 for England and Wales, 12·9 for Scotland and 17·7 for Northern Ireland), while for the Republic of Ireland it was 16·6 registered live births per 1000 population in 1987. The annual number of births in England and Wales was highest this century in 1920 at 957 782, and lowest in 1977 at 569 259. After falling each year since 1964 when there were 875 972 births, the number started to rise again in 1978. In 1989 there were 687 725 births (on average 1884 per day or 79 per hour), of which 27 per cent were outside marriage, compared to 6 per cent in 1961.

Death rate The crude death rate—the number of deaths per 1000 population of all ages—for the whole world was an estimated 9·9 per 1000 in 1985–90. The death rate in Cambodia (formerly Kampuchea), estimated at 40·0 per 1000 for 1975–80, subsided to 16·6 in 1985–90. The estimated figure for Ethiopia from 1985–90 was 23·6. The lowest estimated rate for 1985–90 is 3·6 deaths per 1000 for the United Arab Emirates.

The crude death rate for the UK was 11·3 in 1988 (11·3 for England and Wales, 12·0 for Scotland and 10·0 for Northern Ireland). The local authority district with the high-

est SMR (Standard Mortality Ratio, where the national average is 100) was Castle Morpeth, Northumberland, where the SMR was 139 in 1988. Wealden, in E Sussex, and Oadby & Wigston, in Leics, had the lowest SMR in 1988, at 75. The 1987 rate for the Republic of Ireland was 8·8 registered deaths per 1000.

Natural increase The rate of natural increase for the whole world is estimated to be 17·2 (27·1 less 9·9) per 1000 in 1985–90 compared with a peak 22 per 1000 in 1965. The highest of the latest available recorded rates is 42·9 (53·9 less 11) from Kenya in 1985–90.

The 1988 rate for the UK was 2·5 (2·5 in England and Wales, 0·9 in Scotland and 7·7 in Northern Ireland). The rate for the first time in the first quarter of 1975 became temporarily one of natural decrease. The figure for the Republic of Ireland was 7·9 per 1000 in 1986.

The lowest rate of natural increase in any major independent country in recent times was in the former West Germany, with a negative figure of −1·3 per 1000 (10·2 births and 11·5 deaths) for 1986.

On the Isle of Man the figure is −3·8 (11·0 births and 14·8 deaths).

Marriage and divorce The marriage rate for the Northern Mariana Islands, in the Pacific Ocean, is 31·2 per 1000 population. In the UK there were 394 000 marriages in 1988—a rate of 6·9 per 1000 population. The average age at marriage in England and Wales in 1988 was 30·9 years (men) and 28·3 years (women).

The country with most divorces is the United States, with a total of 1 183 000 in 1988—a rate of 4·8 per thousand population. The all-time high rate was 5·4 per thousand population in 1979. In 1986 some 2 per cent of all *existing* marriages in the USA broke up. There were 165 700 divorces in 1988 in the UK. In England and Wales about one in ten marriages end in divorce before the fifth anniversary.

Sex ratio There were estimated to be 1012 males in the world for every 1000 females in 1988. The country with the largest recorded shortage of males is the USSR, with an estimated 1112 females to every 1000 males in 1988. The country with the largest recorded shortage of women is the United Arab Emirates, with an estimated 484 to every 1000 males, again in 1988. The ratio in the UK was 1049 females to every 1000 males at 1988, and is expected to be 1034 per 1000 by AD 2000.

Infant mortality The world infant mortality rate—the number of deaths at ages under one year per 1000 live births—in 1987 was 80·0 per 1000 live births. Based on deaths before one year of age, the lowest of the latest recorded rates is 5·0 in Japan in 1987.

In Ethiopia the infant mortality rate was unofficially estimated to be nearly 550 per 1000 live births in 1969. The highest rate recently estimated is 172·1 per 1000 in Afghanistan (1985–90).

The rate of infant mortality for the UK was 9·0 in 1988 (9·0 for England and Wales, 8·2 for Scotland and 9·0 for Northern Ireland). The corresponding rate in 1987 for the Republic of Ireland was 7·4.

Expectation of life at birth World expectation of life is rising from 47·4 years (1950–55) towards 64·5 years (1995–2000). There is evidence that life expectation in Britain in the 5th century AD was 33 years for males and 27 years for females. In the decade 1890–1900 the expectation of life among the population of India was 23·7 years.

The highest average expectation of life is in Japan, with 81·9 years for women and 75·8 years for men in 1988. The lowest expectation of life at birth recently estimated is 39·4 years for males in Ethiopia and Sierra Leone, and 42·0 years for females in Afghanistan.

The latest available figures for the UK (figures for 1986–88) are 72·2 years for males and 77·9 years for females (72·4 years for males and 78·1 years for females in England and Wales, 70·3 and 76·5 in Scotland, and 70·6 and 76·7 in Northern Ireland). For the Republic of Ireland, the figures for 1980–82 were 70·1 years for males and 75·6 for females. The British figures for 1901–10 were 48·5 years for males and 52·4 years for females.

Housing For comparison, dwelling units are defined as a structurally separated room or rooms occupied by private households of one or more people and having separate access or a common passageway to the street.

The country with the greatest number of housing units is China, with 249 270 175 in 1986.

Great Britain had an estimated stock of 22 749 000 dwellings in September 1990, of which 67·5 per cent were owner-occupied. The record number of permanent houses built in a year was 425 835 in 1968.

Physicians The country with the most physicians is the USSR, with 1 232 300, or one to every 235 persons. China had an estimated 1·4 million para-medical personnel, known as 'barefoot doctors', by 1981. There were 144 050 doctors on the General Medical Council's Principal List, and therefore entitled to practise in the UK, as at 1 Jan 1991.

Dentists The country with the most dentists is the United States, where 150 000 were registered members of the American Dental Association in 1990. The number of dentists registered in the UK as at 1 Jan 1990 was 25 918.

Psychiatrists The country with the most psychiatrists is the United States. The registered membership of the American Psychiatric Association (instituted in 1844) was 36 335 in 1990, and the membership of the American Psychological Association (instituted in 1892) was 96 000.

Largest hospital *World* The largest mental hospital in the world is the Pilgrim State Hospital, West Brentwood, Long Island, New York, USA, with 3816 beds. It formerly contained 14 200 beds. The largest psychiatric institute is at the University of California, Los Angeles, USA.

The busiest maternity hospital in the world has been the Mama Yemo Hospital, Kinshasa, Zaïre, with 42 987 deliveries in 1972. The record 'birthquake' occurred on a day in May 1976, with 175 babies born. The hospital had 599 beds.

Great Britain The largest hospital in Great Britain is the St James's University Hospital (which is also a teaching hospital), Leeds, W Yorks, with 1377 staffed beds.

The largest maternity hospital in Great Britain is the Simpson Memorial Maternity Pavilion, Edinburgh, with 193 staffed beds.

The largest children's hospital in Great Britain is the Royal Liverpool Children's Hospital (Alder Hey), Liverpool, Merseyside with 370 staffed beds.

TOWNS AND CITIES

Oldest The oldest known walled town in the world is Arihā (Jericho). The radiocarbon dating on specimens from the lowest levels reached by archaeologists indicates habitation there by perhaps 2700 people as early as 7800 BC. The settlement of Dolní Věstonice, Czechoslovakia has been dated to the Gravettian culture c. 27 000 BC. The oldest capital city in the world is Dimashq (Damascus), Syria. It has been continuously inhabited since c. 2500 BC.

Great Britain The oldest town in Great Britain is often cited as Colchester, the old British Camulodunum, headquarters of Belgic chiefs in the first century BC. However, the name of the tin trading post Salakee, St Mary's, Isles of Scilly is derived from pre-Celtic roots and hence *ante* 550 BC. The oldest borough in Britain is reputed to be Barnstaple, Devon whose charter was granted by King Athelstan (927–939) in AD 930.

The only one of the UK's 58 cities with a Saxon charter is Ripon, N Yorks which was a bishopric in 672 and had a charter dated 886.

Most populous The most populous urban agglomeration in the world is the Tokyo-Yokohama Metropolitan Area or 'Keihin Metropolitan Area' in Japan, which was listed in the United Nations *Prospects of World Urbanization, 1988* as having a population of 19 040 000 in 1985. The population of the Mexico City urban agglomeration in 1985 was given in the same publication as 16 650 000, but by 2000 it was expected to have a population of 24 440 000, against 21 320 000 for Tokyo-Yokohama.

Great Britain The most populous conurbation in Britain is London, with a population of 6 756 000 (mid-1989). The residential population of the City of London (274 ha *677·3 acres* plus 24·9 ha *61·7 acres* foreshore) is 4400 (1988 estimate) compared with 128 000 in 1801. The daytime figure is 330 000. The peak figure for London was 8 615 050 in 1939.

Largest in area The world's largest town, in area, is Mount Isa, Queensland, Australia. The area administered by the City Council is 40 978 km² *15 822 miles²*. The largest conurbation in the UK is Greater London, with an area of 1579·5 km² *609·8 miles²*.

Towns, villages and hamlets *Great Britain* The smallest place with a town council is Fordwich, in Kent (population 252 in 1991). Many towns and villages in England can claim occupation during early prehistoric times, e.g. Thatcham, Berks, but continual occupation is difficult to prove. However, from the Iron Age onwards archaeological and historical evidence is more satisfactory and there are a number of places which were undoubtedly occupied without a break. One such place is, collectively, the six villages on the Isle of Portland, which also have the distinction of having been a Royal Manor continuously from 1078 up to the present day. The most remote village on mainland Great Britain is Inverie, Highland, which is a walk of 43·5 km *27 miles* from Arnisdale, also in Highland, the nearest other village. England's largest village is Lancing, W Sussex, with an estimated population of 18 100.

Highest The highest capital in the world, before the domination of Tibet by China, was Lhasa, at an elevation of 3684 m *12 087 ft* above sea level. La Paz, administrative and *de facto* capital of Bolivia, stands at an altitude of 3631 m *11 916 ft* above sea level. Its airport, El Alto, is at 4080 m *13 385 ft*. The city was founded in 1548 by Capt. Alonso de Mendoza on the site of an Indian village named Chuquiapu. It was originally called Ciudad de Nuestra Señora de La Paz (City of Our Lady of Peace), but in 1825 was renamed La Paz de Ayacucho, its present official name. Sucre, the legal capital of Bolivia, stands at 2834 m *9301 ft* above sea level. The new town of Wenchuan, founded in 1955 on the Chinghai–Tibet road north of the Tangla range, is the highest in the world at 5100 m *16 732 ft* above sea level.

The highest village in Britain is Flash, Staffs at 462·6 m *1518 ft* above sea level. The highest in Scotland is Wanlockhead, in Dumfries & Galloway, at 420 m *1380 ft* above sea level.

Lowest The settlement of Ein Bokek, which has a synagogue, on the shores of the

PROGRESSIVE LIST OF THE WORLD'S MOST POPULOUS URBAN SETTLEMENTS

Date	Population	Name	Country
c. 27000 BC	> 100	Dolní Věstonice	Czechoslovakia
8900 BC	c. 150	Chemi Shanidar	Iraq
7800 BC	2 700	Jericho (Arihā)	Occupied Jordan
c. 6800 BC	c. 5000	Çatal Hüyük, Anatolia	Turkey
c. 3200 BC	> 5000	Hierakonopolis (Nekhen)	Egypt
3000 BC	50 000	Uruk (Erech) (now Warka)	Iraq
2200 BC	250 000	Greater Ur (now Tell Muqayyar)	Iraq
600 BC	350 000	Babylon (now al-Hillah)	Iraq
400–185 BC	500 000	Pataliputra (Patna) Bihār	India
300 BC–165 AD	600 000	Seleukia (near Baghdad)	Iraq
133 BC	1 100 000	Rome (founded c. 510 BC)	Italy
900 AD	1 500 000	Angkor	Cambodia
1279	1·0–1·5 million	Hangchow (now Hangzhou)	China
1578	707 000	Peking (Cambaluc) (now Beijing)	China
1801	1 117 290	London	United Kingdom
1939	8 615 050	London (peak)	United Kingdom
1957	8 415 400	Tokyo[1]	Japan

FOOTNOTE
[1] *For up-to-date Tokyo population figure, see Most populous.*

Dead Sea is the lowest in the world, at 393·5 m *1291 ft* below sea level.

Northernmost The northernmost village is Ny Ålesund (78° 55′ N), a coalmining settlement on King's Bay, Vest Spitsbergen, in the Norwegian territory of Svalbard, inhabited only during the winter season. The northernmost capital is Reykjavik, Iceland (64° 08′ N). Its population was estimated to be 95 800 in 1988.

Southernmost The world's southernmost village is Puerto Williams (population about 350) on the north coast of Isla Navarino, in Tierra del Fuego, Chile, 1090 km *680 miles* north of Antarctica. Wellington, North Island, New Zealand, with a 1989 population of 324 600, is the southernmost capital city (41° 17′ S). The world's southernmost administrative centre is Port Stanley, Falkland Islands (51° 43′ S), with a population of 1200.

Most remote from sea The large town most remote from the sea is Wu-lu-mu-ch'i (formerly Ürümqi) in Sinkiang, the capital of China's Sinkiang Uighur Autonomous Region, at a distance of about 2500 km *1500 miles* from the nearest coastline. Its population was estimated to be 1 060 000 in late 1987.

Royalty and Heads of State

Oldest ruling house The Emperor of Japan, Akihito (b. 23 Dec 1933), is the 125th in line from the first Emperor, Jimmu Tenno or Zinmu, whose reign was traditionally from 660 to 581 BC, but more probably from c. 40 BC to c. 10 BC.

Her Majesty Queen Elizabeth II (b. 21 Apr 1926) represents dynasties historically traceable back at least 54 generations to the 4th century AD in the case of Tegid, great grandfather of Cunedda, founder of the House of Gwynedd in Wales. If the historicity of some early Scoto-Irish and Pictish kings were acceptable, the lineage could be extended to about 70 generations.

Reigns Longest all-time The longest recorded reign of any monarch is that of Phiops II (also known as Pepi II), or Neferkare, a Sixth Dynasty pharaoh of ancient Egypt. His reign began c. 2281 BC, when he was 6 years of age, and is believed to have lasted c. 94 years. Minhti, King of Arakan (now part of Myanmar, formerly Burma), is reputed to have reigned for 95 years between 1279 and 1374. Musoma Kanijo, chief of the Nzega district of western Tanganyika (now part of Tanzania), reputedly reigned for more than 98 years from 1864, when aged 8, until his death on 2 Feb 1963. The longest reign of any European monarch was that of Afonso I Henriques of Portugal, who ascended the throne on 30 Apr 1112 and died on 6 Dec 1185 after a reign of 73 years 220 days, first as a count and then as king.

Roman occupation During the 369-year-long Roman occupation of England, Wales and parts of southern Scotland, there were 40 sole and 27 co-emperors of Rome. Of these the longest-reigning was Constantinus I (The Great) from 31 Mar 307 to 22 May 337 — 30 years 2 months.

Shortest The Crown Prince Luis Filipe of Portugal was mortally wounded at the same time that his father was killed by a bullet which severed his carotid artery, in the streets of Lisbon on 1 Feb 1908. He was thus technically King of Portugal (Dom Luis III) for about 20 minutes.

Highest post-nominal numbers The highest post-nominal number ever used to designate a member of a royal house was 75, briefly enjoyed by Count Heinrich LXXV Reuss zu Schleiz (1800–1801). All male members of this branch of the German family are called Heinrich and are successively numbered from I upwards in three sequences — the first began in 1695 (and ended with Heinrich LXXV), the second began in 1803 (and ended with Heinrich XLVII) and the third began in 1910. These are purely *personal* numbers and should not be confused with *regnal* numbers.

British regnal numbers date from the Norman Conquest. The highest is 8, used by Henry VIII (1509–47) and by Edward VIII (1936) who died as HRH the Duke of Windsor on 28 May 1972. Jacobites liked to style Henry Benedict, Cardinal York (b. 1725), the grandson of James II, as Henry IX in respect of his 'reign' from 1788 to 1807, when he died as last survivor in the male line of the House of Stuart.

Longest-lived 'royals' The longest life among the blood royal of Europe was that of the Princess Pauline Marie Madeleine of Croy (1887–1987), who celebrated her 100th birthday in her birthplace of Le Roeulx, Belgium on 11 Jan 1987.

The greatest age among European royal consorts is the 101 years 268 days of HSH Princess Leonilla Bariatinsky (b. 9 Jul 1816 in Moscow), who married HSH Prince Louis of Sayn-Wittgenstein-Sayn and died in Ouchy, Switzerland on 1 Feb 1918.

The longest-lived queen on record was Zita, Empress of Austria and Queen of Hungary, whose husband reigned as Emperor Charles I of Austria and King Charles IV of Hungary from 1916–18; she died on 14 Mar 1989 aged 96 years 309 days.

HRH Princess Alice (b. 25 Feb 1883) became the longest-lived British 'royal' ever on 15 Jul 1977 and died aged 97 years 313

BRITISH MONARCHY RECORDS

LONGEST REIGN OR TENURE

Kings
59 years 96 days[1] George III, from 1760–1820

Queens Regnant
63 years 216 days Victoria, from 1837–1901

Queens Consort
57 years 70 days Charlotte, from 1761–1818 (Consort of George III)

SHORTEST REIGN OR TENURE

Kings
77 days[2] Edward V, in 1483

Queens Regnant
13 days[3] Jane, from 6–19 Jul 1553

Queens Consort
154 days Yoleta, from 1285–6 (Second Consort of Alexander III)

LONGEST LIVED

Kings
81 years 239 days[4] George III (1738–1820)

Queens Regnant
81 years 243 days Victoria (1819–1901)

Queens Consort
90 years Lady Elizabeth Bowes Lyon, Queen Elizabeth, the Queen Mother (b. 4 Aug 1900)

MOST CHILDREN (LEGITIMATE)[5]

Kings
18 Edward I (1239–1307)

Queens Regnant
9[6] Victoria (1819–1901)

Queens Consort
15 Eleanor (c. 1244–90) and Charlotte (1744–1818)

OLDEST TO START REIGN OR CONSORTSHIP

Kings
64 years 10 months William IV (reigned 1830–7)

Queens Regnant
37 years 5 months Mary I (reigned 1553–8)

Queens Consort
56 years 53 days Alexandra (1844–1925) (Consort of Edward VII, reigned 1901–10)

YOUNGEST TO START REIGN OR CONSORTSHIP

Kings
269 days Henry VI in 1422

Queens Regnant
6 or 7 days Mary, Queen of Scots in 1542

Queens Consort
6 years 11 months Isabella (Second Consort of Richard II) in 1396

MOST MARRIED

Kings
6 times Henry VIII (1491–1547)

Queens Regnant
3 times Mary, Queen of Scots (1542–87)

Queens Consort
4 times Catherine Parr (c. 1512–1548) (Sixth Consort of Henry VIII)

MOST ALIVE SIMULTANEOUSLY

Between 30 Oct 1683 (birth of George Augustus of Hanover, later George II) and 6 Feb 1685 (death of Charles II) there were eight heads of state living simultaneously (Charles II, James II, William and Mary, Anne, George I and II, and also Richard Cromwell (died 1712), the 2nd Lord Protector and *de facto* head of state in 1658–59).

FOOTNOTES

[1] James Francis Edward, the Old Pretender, known to his supporters as James III, styled his reign from 16 Sep 1701 until his death on 1 Jan 1766 (i.e. 64 years 109 days).

[2] There is a strong probability that in pre-Conquest times Sweyn 'Forkbeard', the Danish King of England, reigned for only 40 days in 1013–14.

[3] She accepted the allegiance of the Lords of the Council (9 July) and was proclaimed on 10 July so is often referred to as the 'Nine-day Queen'.

[4] Richard Cromwell (b. 4 Oct 1626), the 2nd Lord Protector from 3 Sep 1658 until his abdication on 24 May 1659, lived under the alias John Clarke until 12 Jul 1712, aged 85 years 9 months and was thus the longest-lived head of state.

[5] Henry I (1068–1135) in addition to one (possibly two) legitimate sons and a daughter had at least 20 bastard children (9 sons, 11 daughters), and possibly 22, by six mistresses.

[6] Queen Anne (1665–1714) had 17 pregnancies, which produced only five live births.

■ **Only elected monarch**
Forty-six of the world's 171 sovereign states are not republics. The only country where the monarch is elected is Malaysia. This picture shows the coronation of the current king, Sultan Azlan Shah, in September 1989. (Photo: Gamma/ Apesteguy)

■ **Oldest Head of State**
The oldest Head of State in the world is Félix Houphouët-Boigny (b. 18 Oct 1905), president of Côte d'Ivoire (Ivory Coast). He has been his country's president since it gained independence in 1960. (Photo: Gamma/Duclos)

days on 3 Jan 1981. She fulfilled 20 000 engagements, including the funerals of five British monarchs.

Youngest king and queen Forty-six of the world's 171 sovereign states are not republics. They are headed by 1 emperor, 13 kings, 3 queens, 2 sultans, 1 grand duke, 2 princes, 3 amirs, an elected monarch, the Pope, a president chosen from and by 7 hereditary sheiks, a Head of State currently similar to a constitutional monarch, and 2 nominal non-hereditary 'princes' in one country. Queen Elizabeth II is Head of State of 16 Commonwealth countries in addition to the UK. That with the youngest king is Swaziland, where King Mswati III (see below) was crowned on 25 Apr 1986 aged 18 years 6 days. He was born Makhosetive, the 67th son of King Subhusa II. That with the youngest queen is Denmark, with Queen Margrethe II (b. 16 Apr 1940).

Heaviest monarch The world's heaviest monarch is the 1·90 m *6 ft 3 in* tall King Taufa'ahau of Tonga, who in September 1976 was weighed on the only adequate scales in the country at the airport, recording 209·5 kg *33 st*. By 1985 he was reported to have slimmed down to 139·7 kg *22 st*. His embassy car in London has the number plate '1 TON'.

Most prolific The most prolific monogamous 'royals' have been Prince Hartmann of Liechtenstein (1613–86), who had 24 children, of whom 21 were born live, by Countess Elisabeth zu Salm-Reifferscheidt (1623–88). HRH Duke Roberto I of Parma (1848–1907) also had 24 children, but by two wives. One of his daughters, Zita, Empress of Austria and Queen of Hungary (1892–1989), was exiled on 23 Mar 1919 but visited Vienna, her titles intact, on 17 Nov 1982, reminding republicans that her father succeeded to the throne of Parma in 1854.

Heads of State *Oldest and youngest* The oldest Head of State in the world is Félix Houphouët-Boigny (b. 18 Oct 1905), president of Côte d'Ivoire (b. 18 Oct 1905). The youngest is King Mswati III of Swaziland (b. 19 Apr 1968) (see above).

First female presidents Isabel Perón (b. 1931) of Argentina became the world's

first female president when she succeeded her husband on his death on 1 Jul 1974. She held office until she was deposed in a bloodless coup on 24 Mar 1976. President Vigdis Finnbogadottir (b. 1930) of Iceland became the world's first democratically elected female Head of State on 30 Jun 1980.

Meeting The largest meeting of Heads of State and Heads of Government took place on the occasion of the World Summit for Children, held on 29–30 Sep 1990. The conference at the headquarters of the United Nations in New York City, USA was attended by 71 world leaders and dealt with the plight of children world-wide.

Legislatures

PARLIAMENTS — WORLD

Earliest and oldest The earliest known legislative assembly or *ukkim* was a bicameral one in Erech, Iraq *c.* 2800 BC. The oldest legislative body is the *Althing* of Iceland, founded in AD 930. This body, which originally comprised 39 local chieftains at Thingvellir, was abolished in 1800, but restored by Denmark to a consultative status in 1843 and a legislative status in 1874. The legislative assembly with the oldest *continuous* history is the Court of Tynwald in the Isle of Man, which celebrated its millennium in 1979.

Largest The largest legislative assembly in the world is the National People's Congress of the People's Republic of China, which has 2978 members who are indirectly elected for a five-year term. The seventh congress convened in March 1988.

Smallest quorum The House of Lords has the smallest quorum, expressed as a percentage of eligible voters, of any legislative body in the world, namely less than one-third of 1 per cent. To transact business there must be three peers present, including the Lord Chancellor or his deputy. The House of Commons' quorum of 40 MPs, including the Speaker or his deputy, is 13 times as exacting.

Highest-paid legislators The most highly paid of all the world's legislators are members of the US Congress. The annual salary for members of the House of Representatives is $125 100. The basic annual salary for members of the Senate is $101 900, with an honoraria limit of $23 068. The President of the USA has a salary of $200 000 taxable, and a lifetime pension of $138 900 per annum.

Longest membership The longest span as a legislator was 83 years, by József Madarász (1814–1915). He first attended the Hungarian Parliament from 1832–86 as *oblegatus absentium* (i.e. on behalf of an absent deputy). He was a full member from 1848–50 and from 1861 until his death on 31 Jan 1915.

Longest UN speech The longest speech made in the United Nations has been one of 4 hr 29 min on 26 Sep 1960 by President Fidel Castro Ruz (b. 13 Aug 1927) of Cuba.

Filibusters The longest continuous speech in the history of the United States Senate was that of Senator Wayne Morse (1900–74) of Oregon on 24–25 Apr 1953, when he spoke on the Tidelands Oil Bill for 22 hr 26 min without resuming his seat. Interrupted only briefly by the swearing-in of a new senator, the South Carolina Senator Strom Thurmond (b. 1902) spoke against the Civil Rights Bill for 24 hr 19 min on 28–29 Aug 1957. The US national duration record on a state level is 43 hr by Texas State Senator Bill Meier against non-disclosure of industrial accidents, in May 1977.

Oldest treaty The oldest treaty still in force is the Anglo-Portuguese Treaty of Alliance, which was signed in London over 618 years ago on 16 Jun 1373. The text was confirmed 'with my usual flourish' by John de Banketre, Clerk.

Women's suffrage The earliest legislature with female voters was the Territory of Wyoming, USA in 1869, followed by the Isle of Man in 1881. The earliest country to have universal suffrage was New Zealand in 1893. The attempted exercise of the franchise by Mrs Lily Maxwell in Manchester on 26 Nov 1867 was declared illegal on 9 Nov 1868.

PARLIAMENTS — UNITED KINGDOM

Earliest The earliest known use of the term 'parliament' is in an official royal document, in the meaning of a summons to the King's (Henry III's) Council, dating from 19 Dec 1241.

■ **Oldest Head of State**

■ **Filibusters**

The Houses of Parliament of the United Kingdom in the Palace of Westminster, London had 1836 members (the House of Lords 1186, of whom *c.* 650 are active; House of Commons 650) in early 1991.

Longest The longest English Parliament was the 'Pensioners' Parliament of Charles II, which lasted from 8 May 1661 to 24 Jan 1679, a period of 17 years 8 months and 16 days. The longest United Kingdom Parliament was that of George V, Edward VIII and George VI, lasting from 26 Nov 1935 to 15 Jun 1945, a span of 9 years 6 months and 20 days.

Shortest The parliament of Edward I, summoned to Westminster for 30 May 1306, lasted only 1 day. That of Charles II at Oxford lasted 7 days, from 21–28 Mar 1681. The shortest United Kingdom Parliament was that of George III, lasting from 15 Dec 1806 to 29 Apr 1807, a period of only 4 months and 14 days.

Longest sittings The longest sitting in the House of Commons was one of 41½ hr from 4 p.m. on 31 Jan 1881 to 9:30 a.m. on 2 Feb 1881, on the question of better Protection of Person and Property in Ireland. The longest sitting of the Lords has been 19 hr 16 min from 2:30 p.m. on 29 Feb to 9:46 a.m. on 1 Mar 1968 on the Commonwealth Immigrants Bill (committee stage). The longest sitting of a standing committee was from 10:30 a.m. on 11 May to 12:08 p.m. on 13 May 1948, when Standing Committee D considered the Gas Bill through two nights for 49 hr 38 min.

Longest speeches The longest recorded continuous speech in the Chamber of the House of Commons was that of Rt Hon Henry Peter Brougham (1778–1868) on 7 Feb 1828, when he spoke for 6 hours on Law Reform. He ended at 10:40 p.m. and the report of this speech occupied 12 columns of the next day's *Times*. Brougham, created the 1st Lord Brougham and Vaux on 22 Nov 1830, then set the House of Lords record, also with 6 hours, on 7 Oct 1831, when speaking on the second reading of the Reform Bill, 'fortified by 3 tumblers of spiced wine'.

The longest back-bench speech under present, much stricter standing orders has been one of 4 hr 23 min by Ivan John Lawrence (b. 24 Dec 1936), Conservative Member for Burton, opposing the Water (Fluoridation) Bill on 6 Mar 1985. John Golding (b. 9 Mar 1931) (then Labour, Newcastle-under-Lyme) spoke for 11 hr 15 min in committee on small amendments to the British Telecommunications Bill on 8–9 Feb 1983.

The longest speech in Stormont, Northern Ireland was one of 9 hr 26 min by Thomas Gibson Henderson (1887–1970) on the Appropriations Bill from 6:32 p.m. on 26 May to 3:58 a.m. on 27 May 1936.

Greatest parliamentary petition The greatest petition has been supposed to be the Great Chartist Petition of 1848, but of the 5 706 000 'signatures' only 1 975 496 were valid.

Consequently the largest one was in support of ambulance workers in their pay dispute, when a national petition containing 4 680 727 signatures was delivered to the House of Commons on 14 Dec 1989. Since 1974, the signatures on petitions which have been presented have not been counted at the House of Commons.

Most and least time-consuming legislation The most profligate use of parliamentary time was on the Government of Ireland Bill of 1893–4, which required 82 days in the House of Commons of which 46 days were in committee. The record for a standing committee is 59 sittings for the Police and Criminal Evidence Bill, from 17 Nov 1983 to 29 Mar 1984.

The Abdication Bill (of King Edward VIII) passed all its stages in the Commons (2 hr) and the Lords (8 min) on 11–12 Dec 1936 and received the Royal Assent at 1:52 a.m. on the latter date. Several Bills have gone through the Commons without debate — most notably the Protection of Birds (Amendment) Bill 1976, which took just 67 sec in July 1976.

Private Members' Bills Balloting by private members for parliamentary time was in being at least as early as 1844. The highest recorded number of public Bills introduced by private members was 226 in 1908, but the highest number to receive Royal Assent was 27 in the Commons and 7 in the Lords in 1963–4. The least productive session was 1973–4, with nil from 42 Bills presented in the Commons and nil from 10 in the Lords.

Divisions The record number of divisions in a House of Commons day is 64 on 23–24 Mar 1971, including 57 in succession between midnight and noon. The greatest number of votes in a division was 660, with a majority of 40 (350–310) against the government of the Marquess of Salisbury on the vote of no confidence on 11 Aug 1892.

ELECTIONS — WORLD

Largest The largest elections in the world were those beginning on 22 Nov 1989 for the Indian *Lok Sabha* (Lower House), which has 543 elective seats. Out of an electorate of 498 647 786, 304 126 600 people cast their votes. 291 parties contested the elections, and there were more than 593 000 polling stations manned by 3½ million staff. As a result of the election a new government was formed under the leadership of Viswanath Pratap Singh of Janata Dal (People's Party).

■ **Smallest quorum**

Closest The ultimate in close general elections occurred in Zanzibar (now part of Tanzania) on 18 Jan 1961, when the Afro-Shirazi Party won by a single seat, after the seat of Chake-Chake on Pemba Island had been gained by a single vote.

The narrowest recorded percentage win in an election would seem to be for the office of Southern District Highway Commissioner in Mississippi, USA on 7 Aug 1979. Robert E. Joiner was declared the winner over W. H. Pyron, with 133 587 votes to 133 582. The loser thus obtained more than 49·999 per cent of the votes.

Most decisive North Korea recorded a 100 per cent turn-out of electors and a 100 per cent vote for the Workers' Party of Korea in the general election of 8 Oct 1962. The next closest approach was in Albania on 14 Nov 1982, when a single voter spoiled national unanimity for the official (and only) Communist candidates, who consequently obtained only 99·999 93 per cent of the poll in a 100 per cent turn-out of 1 627 968.

Most bent In the Liberian presidential election of 1927 President Charles D.B. King (1875–1961) was returned with a majority over his opponent, Thomas J.R. Faulkner of the People's Party, officially announced as 234 000. President King thereby claimed a 'majority' more than 15½ times greater than the entire electorate.

Highest personal majority The highest ever personal majority for any politician has been 4 726 112 in the case of Boris Yeltsin, the unofficial Moscow candidate, in the parliamentary elections held in the Soviet Union on 26 Mar 1989. Yeltsin received 5 118 745 votes out of the 5 722 937 which were cast in the Moscow constituency, his closest rival obtaining 392 633 votes. In 1956 W.R.D. Bandaranaike achieved 91·82 per cent of the poll, with 45 016 votes, in the Attanagalla constituency of Sri Lanka (then Ceylon).

Communist parties The largest national communist party outside the USSR (16 516 066 members at the end of 1990) and communist states has been the Partito Comunista Italiano, with 2 300 000 members in 1946. By 1990 its membership had dropped to 1 320 000, and on 10 Oct 1990 it was decided to change its name to Partito Democratico della Sinistra (Democratic Party of the Left). The membership in mainland China was estimated to be 48 000 000 in 1989.

The Communist Party of Great Britain, formed on 31 Jul 1920 in Cannon Street Station Hotel, London, attained its peak membership of 56 000 in December 1942. By 1990 membership had dropped to 6300, and on 27 Mar 1991 it announced that it was changing its name to the Democratic Left, bringing it into line with a number of sister parties in other countries.

Largest ballot paper On 5 Mar 1985 in the State Assembly (*Vidhan Sabha*) elections in Karnataka, India there were 301 candidates for Belgaum City.

Most coups Statisticians contend that Bolivia, since it became a sovereign country in 1825, had its 191st coup on 30 Jun 1984, when President Hernan Siles Zuazo, aged 70, was kidnapped from his official residence by more than 60 armed men.

PRIME MINISTERS AND STATESMEN

Oldest The longest-lived Prime Minister

■ **Longest-lived Prime Minister**

■ **Oldest Prime Minister**

of any country was Naruhiko Higashikuni (Japan), who was born on 3 Dec 1887 and died on 20 Jan 1990, aged 102 years 48 days. He was his country's first Prime Minister after World War II, but held office for less than two months, resigning in October 1945.

El Hadji Muhammad el Mokri, Grand Vizier of Morocco, died on 16 Sep 1957 at a reputed age of 116 Muslim (*Hijri*) years, equivalent to 112½ Gregorian years.

The oldest age at *first* appointment has been 81, by Morarji Ranchhodji Desai of India (b. 29 Feb 1896) in March 1977.

Longest term of office The longest serving current Prime Minister is HRH Prince Fatafehi Tu'ipelehake (b. 7 Jan 1922) of Tonga, who has held office since 16 Dec 1965.

Marshal Kim Il Sung (*né* Kim Sung Chu) (b. 15 Apr 1912) has been Head of Government or Head of State of the Democratic People's Republic of Korea since 25 Aug 1948.

Andrey Andreyevich Gromyko (1909–89) had been Minister of Foreign Affairs of the USSR since 15 Feb 1957 (having been Deputy Foreign Minister since 1946), when he was elected President of the USSR on 2 Jul 1985, a position he held until 30 Sep 1988. Pyotr Lomako (1904–90) served in the government of the USSR as Minister for Non-Ferrous Metallurgy from 1940–1986. He was relieved of his post after 46 years on 1 Nov 1986, aged 82, having served on the Central Committee of the CPSU since 1952.

Woman Sirimavo Bandaranaike (b. 1916) of Ceylon (now Sri Lanka) became the first woman Prime Minister when her

party, the Sri Lanka ('Blessed Ceylon') Freedom Party, won the general election in July 1960.

Youngest Currently the youngest Head of Government is HM Druk Gyalpo ('dragon king') Jigme Singye Wangchuk of Bhutan (b. 11 Nov 1955), who has been Head of Government since March 1972.

PRIME MINISTERIAL RECORDS

Though given legal warrant in the instrument of the Congress of Berlin in 1878 and awarded official recognition in a Royal Warrant of 1905, the first statutory mention of the title of Prime Minister was only in 1917. All previous acknowledged First Ministers had tenure as First Lords of the Treasury with the exception of No. 11, William Pitt, Earl of Chatham, who controlled his ministers as Secretary of State of the Southern Department or as Lord Privy Seal. The first to preside over his fellow King's ministers was Sir Robert Walpole. His ministry began in 1721, although it was not until 15 May 1730, when Viscount Townshend resigned from his position as Secretary of State, that Walpole gained absolute control of the Cabinet.

LONGEST SERVING	17 years 47 days	16th	Hon. William Pitt (1759–1806)	19 Dec 1783–3 Feb 1801
LONGEST SERVING (*20th century*)	11 years 203 days	51st	Margaret Thatcher (*née* Roberts) (b. 13 Oct 1925)	3 May 1979–22 Nov 1990
MOST MINISTRIES	5	40th	Earl Baldwin (1867–1947)	22 May 1923–28 May 1937
SHORTEST SERVICE IN OFFICE	120 days	21st	George Canning (1770–1827)	10 Apr–8 Aug 1827
YOUNGEST TO ASSUME OFFICE	24 years 205 days	16th	Hon. William Pitt (1759–1806)	19 Dec 1783 (declined when 23 years 275 days)
OLDEST FIRST TO ASSUME OFFICE	70 years 109 days	30th	Viscount Palmerston (1784–1865)	6 Feb 1855
GREATEST AGE IN OFFICE	84 years 64 days	32nd	William Gladstone (1809–98)	3 Mar 1894 (elected at 82 years 171 days)
LONGEST LIVED	92 years 322 days	46th	Earl of Stockton (1894–1986)	from 6 Apr 1984 (so surpassing No. 43)
LONGEST SURVIVAL AFTER OFFICE	41 years 45 days	12th	Duke of Grafton (1735–1811)	from 28 Jan 1770
SHORTEST LIVED	44 years	6th	Duke of Devonshire (1720–64)	died 2 Oct 1764 (exact birth date unknown)
SHORTEST MINISTRY	22 days	23rd	Duke of Wellington (1769–1852)	17 Nov–9 Dec 1834
SHORTEST POSSESSION OF SEALS	c. 48 hours	4th	Earl of Bath (1684–1764)	10–12 Feb 1746
SHORTEST PRIOR SERVICE AS MP	2 years 11 months	16th	Hon. William Pitt (1759–1806)	–19 Dec 1783
LONGEST PRIOR SERVICE AS MP	47 years	30th	Viscount Palmerston (1784–1865)	1807–6 Feb 1855
LONGEST SUBSEQUENT SERVICE AS MP	22 years 156 days	38th	Earl Lloyd George (1863–1945)	22 Oct 1922–26 Mar 1945
LONGEST SPAN AS MP (*broken*)	63 years 360 days	43rd	Sir Winston Churchill (1874–1965)	1 Oct 1900–25 Sep 1964
RICHEST	£7 ¼ million (now approx. £200 million)	28th	Earl of Derby (1799–1869)	Annual rent roll in 1869 £170 000
POOREST	£40 000 (now >£1 million) in debt	16th	Hon. William Pitt (1759–1806)	Level of personal debt by 1800
TALLEST	1·85 m *6 ft 1 in*	50th	Lord Callaghan (b. 27 Mar 1912)	
SHORTEST	1·64 m *5 ft 4¼ in*	27th	Lord John Russell (1792–1878)	Seven-month baby: max. wt. 50·7 kg *8 stone*
MOST CHILDREN (*fathered*)	15 or 16	12th	Duke of Grafton (1735–1811)	Twice married
MOST LIVING SIMULTANEOUSLY	19	8th, 11–26th, 29–30th	from birth of Peel (26th) to death of Chatham (11th)	5 Feb–11 May 1788
	19	12th, 14th–31st	from birth of Disraeli (31st) to death of Shelburne (14th)	21 Dec 1804–7 May 1805
MOST LIVING EX-PRIME MINISTERS	6	8th, 11–15th	Bute, Grafton, Chatham, North, Shelburne, Portland (Pitt) till Chatham died	19 Dec 1783–11 May 1788
MOST PRINCIPAL OFFICES	4	50th	Lord Callaghan uniquely served also as Foreign and Home Secretary and as Chancellor of the Exchequer	16 Oct 1964–4 May 1979

EUROPEAN PARLIAMENT ELECTION RECORDS

In the European Parliament elections of 15 Jun 1989 the highest majority in the 81 UK constituencies was 108 488 (L.T. Smith, Labour) in Wales South East. The lowest was 518 (Ms A.J. Pollack, Labour) in London South West. The largest and smallest electorates were 615 135 in Dorset East and Hampshire West and 317 129 in Highlands and Islands. The highest turnout was 46·8 per cent in Wales North. The lowest was 27·6 per cent in London North East. Northern Ireland voted by proportional representation. At the Hampshire Central by-election on 15 Dec 1988 there was a record low turn-out for a Euro-election in the UK, when only 14·11 per cent of the eligible electorate voted.

MAJORITIES — UNITED KINGDOM

Party The largest single-party majority was that of the Liberals in 1832, of 307 seats, with a record 66·7 per cent of the vote. In 1931 the Coalition of Conservatives, Liberals and National Labour candidates had a majority of 491 seats and 60·5 per cent of the vote. The narrowest party majority was that of the Whigs in 1847, with a single seat. The highest popular vote for a single party was 13 948 883 for Labour in 1951.

The largest majority on a division was one of 529 in favour of the government (563–34) on 21 Jan 1991, on a vote against its motion expressing full support for British forces in the Gulf during the Gulf War.

HOUSE OF LORDS

Oldest member The oldest member ever was the Rt Hon. Lord Shinwell (1884–1986), who first sat in the Lower House in November 1922 and lived to be 101 years 202 days. The oldest peer to make a maiden speech was Lord Maenan (1854–1951) at the age of 94 years 123 days (see Peerage, p. 96).

Youngest member The youngest potential member of the House of Lords is currently the Earl of Hardwicke (b. 3 Feb 1971). The youngest current member to have taken his seat is Viscount Goschen (b. 16 Nov 1965).

POLITICAL OFFICE HOLDERS

Chancellorship *Longest and shortest tenures* The Rt Hon. Sir Robert Walpole, later the 1st Earl of Orford (1676–1745), served for 22 years 5 months as Chancellor of the Exchequer, holding office continuously from 12 Oct 1715 to 12 Feb 1742, except for the period from 16 Apr 1717 to 2 Apr 1721. The briefest tenure of this office was 26 days in the case of the Baron (later the 1st Earl of) Mansfield (1705–93), from 11 Sep to 6 Oct 1767. The only man to serve four terms as Chancellor was the Rt Hon. William Ewart Gladstone (1809–98). The longest budget speech was that of the Rt Hon. David (later Earl) Lloyd George (1863–1945) on 29 Apr 1909, which lasted 4 hr 51 min but was interrupted by a 30-min laryngeal tea-break. He announced *inter alia* the introduction of car tax and petroleum duty. Mr Gladstone spoke for 4¾ hours on 18 Apr 1853.

Foreign Secretaryship *Longest tenures* The longest continuous term of office of any Foreign Secretary has been the 10 years 359 days of Sir Edward Grey (later Viscount Grey of Fallodon) from 11 Dec 1905 to 5 Dec 1916. The Rt Hon. Sir Henry John Temple, 3rd Viscount Palmerston aggregated 15 years 296 days in three spells in 1830–34, 1835–41 and 1846–51.

Speakership *Longest tenure* Arthur Onslow (1691–1768) was elected Mr Speaker on 23 Jan 1728, aged 36. He held the position for 33 years 43 days, until 18 Mar 1761, allowing for the 'lost' 11 days (3–13 Sep 1752).

MPs *Youngest* Henry Long (1420–90) was returned for an Old Sarum seat at the age of 15. His precise date of birth is unknown. Minors were debarred in law in 1695 and in fact in 1832.

The youngest ever woman MP has been Josephine Bernadette Devlin, now Mrs Michael McAliskey (b. 23 Apr 1947), elected for Mid Ulster (Independent Unity) aged 21 years 359 days on 17 Apr 1969.

Oldest Sir Francis Knollys (c. 1550–1648), 'the ancientest Parliament man in England', was re-elected for Reading in 1640 when apparently aged 90, and was probably 97 or 98 at the time of his death.

The oldest of 20th-century members has been Samuel Young (b. 14 Feb 1822), Nationalist MP for East Cavan (1892 to 1918), who died on 18 Apr 1918, aged 96 years 63 days. The oldest 'Father of the House' in parliamentary history was the Rt Hon. Charles Pelham Villiers (b. 3 Jan 1802), member for Wolverhampton South when he died on 16 Jan 1898, aged 96 years 13 days. He was a member for 63 years 6 days, having been returned at 17 elections. The oldest current member is the Rt Hon. Michael Foot, MP (Labour) for Blaenau Gwent (b. 23 Jul 1913).

Longest span Sir Francis Knollys (c. 1550–1648) was elected for Oxford in 1575 and died a sitting member for Reading 73 years later in 1648.

The longest span of service of any 20th-century MP is 63 years 11 months (1 Oct 1900 to 25 Sep 1964) by the Rt Hon. Sir Winston Leonard Spencer Churchill (1874–1965), with breaks only in 1908 and from 1922–4. The longest continuous span was that of C.P. Villiers (see above). The longest living of all parliamentarians was Theodore Cooke Taylor (1850–1952), Liberal MP for Batley from 1910–18.

Briefest span There are two 18th-century examples of posthumous elections.

Archie Hamilton, Conservative member for Epsom and Ewell, at 1·98 m *6 ft 6 in.*

Mayoralties The longest recorded mayoralty was that of Edmond Mathis (1852 –1953), *maire* of Ehuns, Haute-Saône, France for 75 years (1878–1953). The mayoralty of the City of London dates from 1192, with the 20-year term of Henry Fitz Ailwyn until 1212. Since the practice of annual elections was instituted in 1215, the longest-serving Mayor was Gregory de Rokesley, who held office for eight years (1274/75–1280/81 and 1284/85). The earliest recorded mayor of the City of York, Nigel, dates from 1142. Alderman G.T. Paine served as Mayor of Lydd, Kent for 29 consecutive years from 1931–1961. Councillor Denis Martineau was Lord Mayor of Birmingham in 1986/87, following in office his father, grandfather, great-grandfather and great-great-grandfather.

Local government service duration records The oldest local office was that of reeve, to supervise villeins. First mentioned in AD 787, it evolved to that of shire reeve, hence sheriff.

Major Sir Philip Barber (1876–1961) served as county councillor for Nottinghamshire for 63 years 41 days, from 8 Mar 1898 to 18 Apr 1961. Matthew Anderson was a member of the Borough Council of Abingdon, Oxon for 69 years 4 months, from April 1709 until August 1778. Henry Winn (1816–1914) served as parish clerk for Fulletby, near Horncastle, Lincs for 76 years. Clifford Tasker (1906–1980) of Pontefract, W Yorks was appointed as presiding officer for elections in 1921 when aged 15, and served for 59 years until March 1980.

Weight of legislation The greatest amount of legislation in a year has been 11 453 pages (83 Public General Acts and 2251 Statutory Instruments) in 1975. This compares with 46 Acts and 1130 Instruments (1998 pages) in 1928. The most Acts were 123 in 1939 and the fewest 39 in 1929 and 1942. The peak for Statutory Instruments was 2916 in 1947.

Judicial

LEGISLATION AND LITIGATION

Statutes *Oldest* The earliest surviving judicial code was that of King Ur-Hammu during the third dynasty of Ur, Iraq, *c.* 2110 BC. The oldest English statute in the Statute Book is a section of the Statute of Marlborough of 1267, retitled in 1948 'The Distress Act 1267' and most recently cited in the High Court in 1986. Some statutes enacted by Henry II (died 1189) and earlier kings are even more durable as they have been assimilated into the Common Law. An extreme example is Ine's Law concerning the administration of shires. Ine reigned over the West Saxons from AD 689–726.

Longest in the UK The weightiest piece of legislation ever written is the Income and Corporation Taxes Act 1988 of more than 1000 pages and weighing 2·5 kg *5½ lb.* Lord Houghton of Sowerby appealed to fellow peers in November 1987 'not to walk about with it' for fear of ruptures. Of old statutes, 31 George III XIV, the Land Tax Act of 1791, written on parchment, consists of 780 skins forming a roll 360 m *1170 ft* long.

Shortest The shortest statute is the Parliament (Qualification of Women) Act 1918, which runs to 27 operative words: 'A

woman shall not be disqualified by sex or marriage from being elected to or sitting or voting as a Member of the Commons House of Parliament.' Section 2 contains a further 14 words giving the short title.

Most inexplicable Certain pieces of legislation have always defied interpretation and the most inexplicable must be a matter of opinion. A judge of the Court of Session of Scotland once sent the Founding Editors his candidate, which reads: '*In the Nuts (unground), (other than ground nuts) Order, the expression nuts shall have reference to such nuts, other than ground nuts, as would but for this amending Order not qualify as nuts (unground) (other than ground nuts) by reason of their being nuts (unground).*'

Constitutions The world's oldest single-document national constitution still in force is that of the United States of America, ratified by the necessary Ninth State (New Hampshire) on 21 Jun 1788 and declared to be in effect on 4 Mar 1789.

Earliest English patent The earliest of all known English patents was that granted by Henry VI in 1449 to Flemish-born John of Utyman for making the coloured glass required for the windows of Eton College. The peak number of applications for patents filed in the UK in any one year was 63 614 in 1969. The shortest, concerning a harrow attachment, of 48 words was filed on 14 May 1956. The longest, comprising 2318 pages of text and 495 pages of drawings, was filed on 31 Mar 1965 by IBM to cover a computer.

Most protracted litigation The longest contested lawsuit ever recorded ended in Poona, India on 28 Apr 1966, when Balasaheb Patloji Thorat received a favourable judgment on a suit filed by his ancestor Maloji Thorat 761 years earlier in 1205. The points at issue were rights of presiding over public functions and precedences at religious festivals.

The dispute over the claim of the Prior and Convent (now the Dean and Chapter) of Durham Cathedral to administer the spiritualities of the diocese during a vacancy in the See grew fierce in 1283. It flared up again in 1672 and 1890; an attempt in November 1975 to settle the issue, then 692 years old, was unsuccessful. Neither side admits the legitimacy of writs of appointment issued by the other even though identical persons are named.

Fastest English hearing The law's shortest delay occurred in *Duport Steels and Others* v. *Sirs and Others*, which was heard in the High Court on 25 Jan 1980. The case was heard on appeal on 26 January, and the full hearing in the House of Lords took place on the morning of 1 February with the decision given in the afternoon.

Longest hearing The longest civil case heard before a jury is *Kemner* v. *Monsanto Co.*, which concerned an alleged toxic chemical spill in Sturgeon, Missouri, USA in 1979. The trial started on 6 Feb 1984, at St Clair County Court House, Belleville, Illinois, USA before Circuit Judge Richard P. Goldenhersh, and ended on 22 Oct 1987. The testimony lasted 657 days, following which the jury deliberated for two months. The verdict was returned on 22 October when the plaintiffs secured sums of $1 nominal compensatory damage and $16 250 000 punitive damage.

Longest British hearings The longest trial in the annals of British justice was the Tichborne personation case. The civil trial began on 11 May 1871, lasted 103 days and collapsed on 6 Mar 1872. The criminal

Capt. the Hon. Edward Legge, RN (1710–47) was returned unopposed for Portsmouth on 15 Dec 1747. News came later that he had died in the West Indies 87 days before polling. In 1780 John Kirkman, standing for the City of London, expired before polling had ended but was nonetheless duly returned. A.J. Dobbs (Lab, Smethwick), elected on 5 Jul 1945, was killed on the way to take his seat.

Women The first woman to be elected to the House of Commons was Mme Constance Georgine Markievicz (*née* Gore Booth). She was elected as member (Sinn Fein) for St Patrick's Dublin on 28 Dec 1918. The first woman to take her seat was the Viscountess Astor (1879–1964) (*née* Nancy Witcher Langhorne at Danville, Virginia, USA; formerly Mrs Robert Gould Shaw), who was elected Unionist member for the Sutton division of Plymouth, Devon on 28 Nov 1919, and took her seat 3 days later. The first woman to take her seat from the island of Ireland was Lady Fisher (*née* Patricia Smiles) as unopposed Ulster Unionist for North Down on 15 Apr 1953, as Mrs Patricia Ford. The first woman cabinet minister was the Rt Hon. Margaret Grace Bondfield (1873–1953), appointed Minister of Labour in 1929.

Heaviest and tallest The heaviest MP of all time is believed to be Sir Cyril Smith, Liberal member for Rochdale since October 1972, when in January 1976 his peak reported weight was 189·6 kg *29 st 12 lb.*

Sir Louis Gluckstein (1897–1979), Conservative member for East Nottingham (1931–45), was an unrivalled 2·02 m *6 ft 7½ in.* Currently the tallest is the Hon.

trial went on for 188 days, resulting in a sentence on 28 Feb 1874 for two counts of perjury (two 7-year consecutive terms of imprisonment with hard labour) on London-born Arthur Orton, alias Thomas Castro (1834–98), who claimed to be Roger Charles Tichborne (1829–54), the elder brother of Sir Alfred Joseph Doughty-Tichborne, 11th Bt (1839–66). The whole case thus spanned 1025 days. The jury were out for only 30 minutes.

The impeachment of Warren Hastings (1732–1818), which began in 1788, dragged on for 7 years until 23 Apr 1795, but the trial lasted only 149 days. He was appointed a member of the Privy Council in 1814. The fraud case *R.* v. *Bouzaglo and Others* ended before Judge Brian Gibbens (1912–85) on 1 May 1981 having lasted 274 days. They appealed on 10 Dec 1981. Trial costs were estimated at £2·5 million. The fluoridation case *McColl* v. *Strathclyde Regional Council* lasted 204 days ending on 27 Jul 1982 before Lord Jauncey, whose judgment in the £1 million case ran to 400 pages. The longest case in the House of Lords was *Armstrong Patents* v. *British Leyland* — seven weeks, ending on 27 Feb 1986.

Murder The longest murder trial in Britain was that at the Old Bailey, London of Reginald Dudley, 51, and Robert Maynard, 38, in the Torso Murder of Billy Moseley and Micky Cornwall which ran before Mr Justice Swanwick from 11 Nov 1976 to 17 Jun 1977 with 136 trial days. Both men were sentenced to life imprisonment (minimum 15 years). Costs were estimated to exceed £500 000 and the evidence amounted to 3 500 000 words.

Divorce The longest trial of a divorce case in Britain was *Gibbons* v. *Gibbons and Roman and Halperin*. On 19 Mar 1962, after 28 days, Mr Alfred George Boyd Gibbons was granted a decree *nisi* against his wife Dorothy for adultery with Mr John Halperin of New York City, USA.

Shortest trials The shortest recorded British murder hearings were *R.* v. *Murray* on 28 Feb 1957 and *R.* v. *Cawley* at Winchester assizes on 14 Dec 1959. Proceedings occupied only 30 seconds on each occasion.

Litigants in person Since the Union of the Parliaments in 1707 the only Scot to win an appeal in person before the House of Lords has been Mr Jack Malloch, an Aberdeen schoolmaster. In 1971 he was restored to his employment with costs under the dormant but operative Teachers Act 1882.

Dr Mark Feldman, a chiropodist, of Lauderhill, Florida, USA became the first litigant in person to secure seven figures ($1 million) before a jury in compensatory and punitive damages in September 1980. The case concerned conspiracy and fraud alleged against six other doctors.

Longest address The longest address in a British court was in *Globe and Phoenix Gold Mining Co. Ltd* v. *Amalgamated Properties of Rhodesia*. Mr William Henry Upjohn KC (1853–1941) concluded his speech on 22 Sep 1916, having addressed the court for 45 days.

Highest bail The world record for bail was set at $100 billion on Jeffrey Marsh, Juan Mercado, Yolanda Kravitz and Alvin Kravitz at the Dade County Courthouse, Miami, Florida, USA on 16 Oct 1989. The four defence attorneys in the case, concerning an armed robbery, stipulated the bail, and although a reduction was subsequently requested, this was denied. The presiding judge was David L. Tobin.

The highest bail figure in a British court is £3·5 million, which was set for Asil Nadir, the chairman of Polly Peck International, on 17 Dec 1990. He had developed the company over 20 years from a small clothing concern into an international group, but it collapsed in September 1990 and he subsequently faced 18 charges of theft and false accounting amounting to £25 million.

Longest inquiry The longest and most expensive public inquiry has been that over the projected £1200 million Sizewell B nuclear power station, Suffolk under Sir Frank Layfield QC. It began on 11 Jan 1983 and finished after 340 days of hearings on 7 Mar 1985 in the Snape Maltings, Aldeburgh. The cost to public funds was £20 million and the 3000-page eight-volume report weighed 13·6 kg *30 lb* and cost £30.

Best-attended trial The greatest attendance at any trial was at that of Major Jesús Sosa Blanco, aged 51, for an alleged 108 murders. At one point in the 12½ hr trial (5:30 p.m. to 6 a.m., 22–23 Jan 1959), 17 000 people were present in the Havana Sports Palace, Cuba. He was executed on 18 Feb 1959.

Greatest damages *Civil damages* The largest damages awarded in legal history were $11 120 million to Pennzoil Co. against Texaco Inc. concerning the latter's allegedly unethical tactics in January 1984 to break up a merger between Pennzoil and Getty Oil Co., by Judge Solomon Casseb, Jr in Houston, Texas, USA on 10 Dec 1985. An out-of-court settlement of $5 500 million was reached after a 48-hour negotiation on 19 Dec 1987.

Personal injury The greatest personal injury damages ever awarded were $78 million to the model Marla Hanson, 26, on 29 Sep 1987. Her face was slashed with razors in Manhattan, New York City, USA in June 1987. The three men convicted and now serving 5–15 years have no assets and Miss Hanson is entitled to 10 per cent of their post-prison earnings.

On 18 Jul 1986 a Bronx Supreme Court Jury awarded $65 086 000 to Mrs Agnes Mae Whitaker against the New York City Health and Hospitals Corporation for medical malpractice.

The compensation for the disaster in 1984 at the Union Carbide Corporation plant in Bhopal, India was agreed at $470 million. The Supreme Court of India passed the order for payment on 14 Feb 1989 after the settlement between the corporation and the Indian government, which represented the interests of more than 500 000 claimants.

The British record is £2·1 million, awarded in the High Court, Sheffield, S Yorks on 29 Jan 1991 to 15-year-old Garylee Grimsley, who had been left severely handicapped as a result of a car crash in 1985. Together with his mother, he brought the claim against his father, who had been driving the car in which he was a passenger, and the driver of the other car. The damages are to be paid in instalments for the rest of his life.

Breach of promise The largest sum involved in a breach of promise suit in the UK was £50 000, accepted in 1913 by Miss Daisy Markham, alias Mrs Annie Moss (died 20 Aug 1962, aged 76), in settlement against the 6th Marquess of Northampton (1885–1978).

Defamation Richard A. Sprague, a prominent lawyer from Philadelphia, Pennsylvania, USA, was awarded a record $34 million against the Philadelphia *Inquirer* on 3 May 1990 for a series of articles which the newspaper had published about him in 1973.

The $39·6 million awarded in Columbus, Ohio, USA on 1 Mar 1980 to Robert Guccione, publisher of *Penthouse*, against Larry Flynt, publisher of *Hustler*, for defamation, was reduced by Judge Craig Wright to $4 million on 17 Apr 1980.

The record damages for libel in Great Britain was the £1·5 million award to Lord Aldington, a former brigadier and former chairman of the Sun Alliance insurance company, against Count Nikolai Tolstoy, a historian, and Nigel Watts, a property developer. The award was made by a High Court jury on 30 Nov 1989 following accusations that Lord Aldington had been a war criminal.

The most expensive defamation trial in Great Britain has been the 87-day-long case of *Gee* v. *British Broadcasting Corporation*, which ran before Lord Justice Croom-Johnson from 22 Oct 1984 to 2 May 1985. The costs have been estimated at £1·5 million, excluding the BBC's internal costs, over the 681 days from the offending transmission of *That's Life* on 26 Jun 1983. Dr Gee, who was in the witness box for 27 days, received a record settlement of £100 007.

Greatest compensation for wrongful imprisonment Robert McLaughlin, 29, was awarded $1 935 000 in October 1989 for wrongful imprisonment as a result of a murder in New York City, USA in 1979 which he did not commit. He had been been sentenced to 15 years in prison and actually served six years, from 1980 to 1986, when he was released after his foster father succeeded in showing the authorities that he had nothing to do with the crime.

The greatest such compensation in Britain was £121 000, awarded to Geoffrey Davis on 12 Jun 1985. He had spent 15 years in prison for a murder that he did not commit and was freed by the Court of Appeal in July 1984.

Greatest alimony suit Belgian-born Sheika Dena Al-Fassi, 23, filed the highest-ever alimony claim of $3 billion against her former husband, Sheik Mohammed Al-Fassi, 28, of the Saudi Arabian royal family, in Los Angeles, California, USA in February 1982. Mr Marvin Mitchelson, explaining the size of the settlement claim, alluded to the Sheik's wealth, which included 14 homes in Florida alone and numerous private aircraft. On 14 Jun 1983 she was awarded $81 million and declared she would be 'very very happy' if she was able to collect.

Greatest divorce settlement The reported settlement achieved in 1982 by the lawyers of Soraya Khashóggi was £500 million plus property from her husband Adnan. Mrs Anne Bass, former wife of Sid Bass of Texas, USA, was reported to have rejected $535 million as inadequate to live in the style to which she had been made accustomed.

The highest divorce award in Great Britain was one of £1 295 000 (£1 000 000 in cash plus a £295 000 maisonette), made to Yugoslavian-born Radojka Gojkovic against her former husband in the High Court Family Division on 17 Feb 1989. The settlement was upheld by the Court of Appeal on 12 Oct 1989.

Patent case Polaroid Corporation was awarded $909·5 million in Boston, Massa-

chusetts, USA on 12 Oct 1990 in a suit involving Eastman Kodak Co. for infringing patents for instant photography cameras and films. Polaroid had filed suit in 1976, claiming that Kodak had infringed patents used in Polaroid's 1972 SX-70 system.

Largest suit The highest amount of damages ever sought to date is $675 000 000 000 000 (then equivalent to 10 times the US national wealth) in a suit by Mr I. Walton Bader brought in the US District Court, New York City, USA on 14 Apr 1971 against General Motors and others for polluting all 50 states.

Highest costs The Guinness case, involving the takeover bid by the company of Distillers in 1986, is estimated to have cost approximately £10 million. The trial at Southwark Crown Court, London, which lasted 107 days, ended on 27 Aug 1990 and resulted in jail sentences for three of the four defendants — Ernest Saunders, Gerald Ronson and Anthony Parnes. The fourth defendant, Sir (later Mr) Jack Lyons, was fined £3 000 000.

The most expensive man-hunt in police history was one costing £4 million. It terminated on 13 Jun 1981 with the arrest of Peter William Sutcliffe (the 'Yorkshire Ripper'), in Sheffield, S Yorks. His trial at the Old Bailey, London cost £250 000 and resulted in his being sentenced to life imprisonment for 13 murders (which orphaned 25 children) and seven attempted murders.

Greatest lien The greatest lien by a court is 40 000 million lire on 9 Apr 1974 upon Vittorio and Ida Riva in Milan for back taxes allegedly due on a chain of cotton mills around Turin, Italy.

Wills Shortest and longest The shortest valid will in the world is 'Vše zene', the Czech for 'All to wife', written and dated 19 Jan 1967 by Herr Karl Tausch of Langen, Germany.

The shortest will contested but subsequently admitted to probate in English law was the case of *Thorne* v. *Dickens* in 1906. It consisted of the three words 'All for mother' in which 'mother' was not his mother but his wife. The smallest will preserved by the Record Keeper is an identity disc 3·8 cm *1½ in* in diameter belonging to A.B. William Skinner, killed aboard HMS *Indefatigable* at Jutland in 1916. It had 40 words engraved on it including the signatures of two witnesses and was proved on 24 Jun 1922.

The longest will on record was that of Mrs Frederica Evelyn Stilwell Cook, proved at Somerset House, London on 2 Nov 1925. It consisted of four bound volumes containing 95 940 words.

Most durable judges The oldest recorded active judge was Judge Albert R. Alexander (1859–1966) of Plattsburg, Missouri, USA. He was the magistrate and probate judge of Clinton County until his retirement aged 105 years 8 months on 9 Jul 1965.

The greatest recorded age at which any British judge has sat on a bench was 93 years 9 months in the case of Sir William Francis Kyffin Taylor (later Lord Maenan), who was born on 9 Jul 1854 and retired as presiding judge of the Liverpool Court of Passage in April 1948, having held that position since 1903. Sir Salathiel Lovell (1619–1713) was still sitting when he died on 3 May 1713 in his 94th or 95th year. The greatest age at which a House of Lords judgment has been given is 92 in the case of the 1st Earl of Halsbury (b. 3 Sep 1823) in 1916. Lord Chief Baron of Exchequer in Ireland, the Rt Hon. Christopher Palles (1831–1920) served for 42 years, from 17 Feb 1874 until 1916.

Master of the Rolls The longest tenure of the Mastership of the Rolls since the office was inaugurated in 1286 has been 24 years 7 months by David de Wollore, from 2 Jul 1346 to 27 March 1371. The longest tenure since the Supreme Court Judicature Act of 1881 has been that of 20 years 5 months by the Rt Hon. Lord Denning (b. 23 Jan 1899), from 19 Apr 1962 to 30 Sep 1982. He had been first appointed a High Court judge in 1944. William Morland held the office for 77 days, while in 1629 Sir Humphrey May died 'soon after' his appointment on 10 April.

Youngest judge No collated records on the ages of judicial appointments exist. However, David Elmer Ward had to await the legal age of 21 before taking office after nomination in 1932 as Judge of the County Court at Fort Myers, Florida, USA.

Muhammad Ilyas passed the examination enabling him to become a Civil Judge in July 1952 at the age of 20 years 9 months, although formalities such as medicals meant that it was not until eight months later that he started work as a Civil Judge in Lahore, Pakistan.

The youngest certain age at which any English judge has been appointed is 28, in the case of Sir Ernest Wild KC (b. 1 Jan 1869) who was appointed Judge of the Norwich Guildhall Court of Record in 1897 at that age. The lowest age of appointment this century has been the 42 years 2 months of Lord Hodson in 1937.

Most judges Lord Balmerino was found guilty of treason by 137 of his peers on 28 Jul 1746. In *R.* v. *Canning* at the Old Bailey, London in 1754 Elizabeth Canning was deported to Connecticut, USA for wilful perjury by 19 judges voting 10 to 9.

Most offices The most high judicial offices held by one man were by Alexander

Wedderbarn (1733–1805), later Lord Loughborough and Earl of Rosslyn, who was Solicitor-General in 1771, Attorney-General in 1778, Chief Justice of common pleas from 1780–93, and Lord Chancellor from 27 Jan 1793 until he resigned in 1801.

Youngest English QC The earliest age at which a barrister has taken silk this century is 33 years 8 months in the case of Mr (later the Rt Hon. Sir) Francis Raymond Evershed (1899–1966) in April 1933. He was later Lord Evershed, Master of the Rolls. In the 18th century Sir Francis Buller was nepotistically given silk at the age of 31 in 1777, being a nephew of the then Lord Chancellor, Lord Bathurst.

Most successful Sir Lionel Luckhoo, senior partner of Luckhoo and Luckhoo of Georgetown, Guyana, succeeded in getting 245 successive murder charge acquittals between 1940 and 1985.

Most durable solicitors William George (1865–1967), brother of Prime Minister David Lloyd George, passed his preliminary law examination in May 1880 and was practising until December 1966 at the age of 101 years 9 months. The most durable firm is Pickering Kenyon of London, which was founded by William Umfreville in 1561.

CRIME

Mass killings China The greatest massacre ever imputed by the government of one sovereign nation against the government of another is that of 26·3 million Chinese during the regime of Mao Tse-tung (1893–1976) between 1949 and May 1965. This accusation was made by an agency of the USSR government in a radio broadcast on 7 Apr 1969. The broadcast broke down the figure into four periods: 2·8 million (1949–52); 3·5 million (1953–7); 6·7 million (1958–60); and 13·3 million (1961–May 1965).

The Walker Report published by the US Senate Committee of the Judiciary in July 1971 placed the parameters of the total death toll within China since 1949 between 32·25 and 61·7 million. An estimate of 63·7 million was published by Jean-Pierre Dujardin in *Figaro* magazine of 19–25 Nov 1978.

In Chinese history of the 13th–17th centuries there were three periods of wholesale massacre. The numbers of victims attributed to these events are assertions rather than reliable estimates. The figure put on the Mongolian invasions of northern China from 1210–19 and from 1311–40 are both of the order of 35 million, while the number of victims of the bandit leader Chang Hsien-chung (*c.* 1605–47), known as the 'Yellow Tiger', from 1643–47 in the Zechuan province has been put at 40 million.

USSR The total death toll in the Great Purge, or *Yezhovshchina*, in the USSR from 1936–38 has never been published. Evidence of its magnitude may be found in population statistics, which show a decline in population from *before* the outbreak of the 1941–45 war.

Nobel prizewinner Alexander Solzhenitsyn (b. 1918) estimated the loss of life from state repression and terrorism from October 1917 to December 1959 under Lenin, Stalin and Khrushchev at 66 700 000.

Nazi Germany The most reliable estimate of the number of Jewish victims of the Holocaust or the genocidal 'Final Solution' (*Endlösung*) ordered by Adolf Hitler (1889–1945) in April 1941 and continuing into May 1945 is 5·8 million. At the SS (*Schutzstaffel*) extermination camp (*Vernichtungslager*) known as Auschwitz-Birkenau (Oświęcim-Brzezinka), near Oświęcim (Auschwitz) in southern Poland, a minimum of 920 000 people (Soviet estimate is 4 000 000) were exterminated from 14 Jun 1940 to 18 Jan 1945. The greatest number killed in a day was 6000.

Cambodia As a percentage of a nation's total population the worst genocide appears to have been that in Cambodia (formerly Kampuchea). According to the Khmer Rouge Foreign Minister, Leng Sary, more than a third of the 8 million Khmers were killed between 17 Apr 1975 and January 1979. The highest 'class' ideals induced indifference to individual suffering to the point of serving as a warrant for massacre. Under the rule of Saloth Sar, alias Pol Pot, a founder member of the CPK (Communist Party of Kampuchea, formed in September 1960), towns, money and property were abolished and economical execution by bayonet and club introduced for such offences as falling asleep during the day, asking too many questions, playing non-communist music, being old and feeble, being the offspring of an 'undesirable' or being too well educated. Deaths at the Tuol Sleng interrogation centre reached 582 in a day.

Saving of life The greatest number of people saved from extinction by one man is an estimated 90 000 Jews in Budapest, Hungary from July 1944 to January 1945 by the Swedish diplomat Raoul Wallenberg (b. 4 Aug 1912). After escaping an assassination attempt by the Nazis, he was imprisoned without trial in the Soviet Union. On 6 Feb 1957 Mr Gromyko said prisoner Wallenberg had died in a cell in Lubyanka Jail, Moscow on 16 Jul 1947. Sighting reports within the Gulag system persisted for years after his disappearance. He was made an Honorary Citizen of the USA on 5 Oct 1981 and on 7 May 1987 a statue was unveiled to him in Budapest to replace an earlier one which had been removed.

Largest criminal organization The largest syndicate of organized crime is the Mafia or La Cosa Nostra, which has infiltrated the executive, judiciary and legislature of the United States. The name 'Mafia' is thought to be derived from the first letters of each word of the slogan 'Morte alla Francia Italia anela' — 'Death to the French is Italy's cry'. It consists of some 3000 to 5000 individuals in 25 'families' federated under 'The Commission', with an annual turnover in vice, gambling, protection rackets, tobacco, bootlegging, hijacking, narcotics, loan-sharking and prostitution which was estimated by *US News & World Report* in December 1982 at $200 billion, with a profit estimated in March 1986 by the Attorney Rudolph Giuliani at $75 billion. The biggest Mafia killing was from 11–13 Sep 1931, when 40 mafiosi were liquidated following the murder in New York of Salvatore Maranzano ('Il Capo di Tutti Capi') on 10 September. The greatest breaches of *omerta* (the vow of silence) were by Joseph Valachi who 'sang like a canary' in 1963, and by the much-bereaved Tommaso Buschetta in 1984. The latter's information led to 329 convictions and 2655 years' imprisonment, and $9·6 million in fines plus 19 life sentences, in the Sicilian Mafia or Cupola trial in Palermo from 10 Feb 1986 to 16 Dec 1987. Michele ('the Pope') and his brother Salvatore ('the Senator') Greco had been accused of slaying the Carabinieri General Dalla Chiesa in Palermo on 3 Sep 1982.

Murder rate *Highest and lowest* The country with the highest recorded murder rate is Brazil, with 104 homicides for each 100 000 of the population in 1983, or 370 per day.

The highest homicide rates recorded in New York City, USA have been 58 in a week in July 1972 and 15 in a day in June 1989.

In the Indian state of Sikkim, in the Himalayas, murder is practically unknown, while in the Hunza area of Kashmir, in the Karakoram, only one definite case by a Hunzarwal has been recorded since 1900.

In England and Wales the total number of homicides and deaths from injuries purposely inflicted by other persons in 1988 was 303.

Most prolific murderers It was established at the trial of Behram, the Indian Thug, that he had strangled at least 931 victims with his yellow and white cloth strip or *ruhmal* in the Oudh district between 1790 and 1840. It has been estimated that at least 2 000 000 Indians were strangled by Thugs (*burtotes*) during the reign of the Thugee (pronounced tugee) cult from 1550 until its final suppression by the British raj in 1853.

The greatest number of victims ascribed to a murderess has been 650, in the case of Countess Erzsebet Bathory (1560–1614) of Hungary. At her trial, which began on 2 Jan 1611, a witness testified to seeing a list of her victims in her own handwriting totalling this number. All were alleged to be young girls from near her castle at Csejthe, where she died on 21 Aug 1614. She had been walled up in her room for 3½ years after being found guilty.

20th century A total of 592 deaths was attributed to one Colombian bandit leader, Teófilo ('Sparks') Rojas, aged 27, between 1948 and his death in an ambush near Armenia, Colombia on 22 Jan 1963. Some sources attribute 3500 slayings to him during *La Violencia* of 1945–62.

In a drunken rampage lasting 8 hours on 26–27 Apr 1982, policeman Wou Bom-Kon, 27, killed 57 people and wounded 35 with 176 rounds of rifle ammunition and hand grenades in the Kyong Sang-Namdo province of South Korea. He blew himself up with a grenade.

Great Britain The biggest murder in Britain this century was committed by the unknown person or people who planted the bomb on Pan Am flight PA103, which crashed over Lockerbie, Dumfries & Galloway on 21 Dec 1988, killing a total of 270 people in the aeroplane and on the ground.

The self-confessed arsonist Bruce Lee was sent to a mental hospital by Leeds Crown Court in January 1981, but on 14 Mar 1982 he retracted his confessions to starting fires in which 26 perished. On 2 Dec 1983 the Court of Appeal quashed charges of causing 11 of the deaths.

Judith Minna Ward, 25, of Stockport, Greater Manchester was convicted on 11 separate murder charges on 4 Nov 1974 making 12 in all arising from the explosion in an army coach on the M62 near Drighlington, W Yorks on 4 Feb 1974.

Mary Ann Cotton (*née* Robson) (b. 1832 at East Rainton, Co. Durham), hanged in Durham Jail on 24 Mar 1873, is believed to have poisoned 14, possibly 20, people.

Dennis Andrew Nilsen (b. 1948), then of 23 Cranley Gardens, Muswell Hill, north London, admitted to 15 one-at-a-time murders between December 1978 and February

1983. He was sentenced to life imprisonment, with a 25-year minimum, on 4 Nov 1983 at the Old Bailey by Mr Justice Croom-Johnson for six murders and two attempted murders.

Dominic McGlinchey (b. 1955) in November 1983 admitted in a press interview to at least 30 killings in Northern Ireland. He was jailed for 10 years at Dublin's Special Criminal Court on 11 Mar 1986 for shooting with intent to resist arrest in Co. Clare, Republic of Ireland on 17 Mar 1984.

On 7 May 1981 John Thompson of Hackney, London was found guilty at the Old Bailey of the 'specimen' murder by arson of Archibald Campbell and jailed for life. There were 36 other victims at the Spanish Club, Denmark Street, London.

The worst armed rampage in Britain was at Hungerford, Berks on 19 Aug 1987, during which Michael Ryan, 27, shot dead 14 people and wounded 16 others before shooting and killing himself. Two people subsequently died from injuries sustained, bringing the total to 16.

Suicide The estimated daily rate of suicides throughout the world surpassed 1000 in 1965. The country with the highest suicide rate is Hungary, with 40 per 100 000 population in 1989. The country with the lowest recorded rate is Jordan, with just a single case in 1970 and hence a rate of 0·04 per 100 000 people. The number in China rose to 382 per day, or 16 per hour, in 1987–8.

There were 4220 suicides in 1988 in England and Wales — equivalent to 11·6 per day.

Mass poisoning On 1 May 1981 the first of more than 600 victims of the Spanish cooking oil scandal died. On 12 June it was discovered that this 8-year-old boy's cause of death was the use of 'denatured' industrial colza from rape seed. The trial of 38 defendants, including the manufacturers Ramón and Elias Ferrero, lasted from 30 Mar 1987 to 28 Jun 1988. The 586 counts on which the prosecution demanded jail sentences totalled 60 000 years.

Robbery The greatest robbery on record was that of the Reichsbank following Germany's collapse in April–May 1945. The Pentagon in Washington described the event, first published in *The Guinness Book of Records* in 1957, as 'an unverified allegation'. *Nazi Gold* by Ian Sayer and Douglas Botting, published in 1984, however, finally revealed full details and estimated that the total haul would have been equivalent to £2500 million at 1984 values.

Treasury Bills and certificates of deposit worth £292 million were stolen when a mugger attacked a money-broker's messenger in the City of London on 2 May 1990. As details of the documents stolen were quickly flashed on the City's market dealing screens and given to central banks world-wide, the chances of anyone being able to benefit from the theft were considered to be very remote.

The robbery in the Knightsbridge Safety Deposit Centre, London on 12 Jul 1987 was estimated at £30 million, the property being stolen from 113 of the 126 boxes that were broken into. The managing director Parvez Latiff, 30, was among those charged on 17 Aug 1987.

At 6:40 a.m. on 26 Nov 1983 six masked men raided the Brinks Mat Unit 7 warehouses at the Heathrow Trading Estate, Middx, removing 6800 bars of gold and platinum together with diamonds and travellers' cheques worth £26 369 778. Michael McAvoy, 32, of East Dulwich and Brian

91

Art robbery

It is arguable that the *Mona Lisa*, though never valued, is the most valuable object ever stolen. It disappeared from the Louvre, Paris on 21 Aug 1911. It was recovered in Italy in 1913, when Vincenzo Perruggia was charged with its theft.

Kidnapping

The youngest person kidnapped has been Carolyn Wharton, born at 12:46 p.m. on 19 Mar 1955 in the Baptist Hospital, Texas, USA and kidnapped, by a woman disguised as a nurse, at 1:15 p.m. aged 29 minutes.

Robinson, 41, of Lewisham were each sentenced to 25 years at the Old Bailey on 3 Dec 1984. A number of other people have been sentenced to shorter periods since then, and some are still awaiting trial.

Art On 18 Mar 1990 eleven paintings by Rembrandt, Vermeer, Degas, Manet and Flinck, plus a Chinese bronze beaker of about 1200 BC, in total worth an estimated $200 million, were stolen from the Isabella Stewart Gardner Museum in Boston, Massachusetts, USA. Although the paintings were insured against damage, none of them were insured against theft.

On 24 Dec 1985 140 'priceless' gold, jade and obsidian artifacts were stolen from the National Museum of Anthropology, Mexico City. The majority of the stolen objects were recovered in June 1989 from the Mexico City home of a man described by officials as the mastermind of the theft.

Bank During the extreme civil disorder prior to 22 Jan 1976 in Beirut, Lebanon, a guerrilla force blasted the vaults of the British Bank of the Middle East in Bab Idriss and cleared out safe deposit boxes with contents valued by former Finance Minister Lucien Dahadah at $50 million and by another source at an 'absolute minimum' of $20 million.

Train The greatest recorded train robbery occurred between 3:03 a.m. and 3:27 a.m. on 8 Aug 1963, when a General Post Office mail train from Glasgow, Strathclyde was ambushed at Sears Crossing and robbed at Bridego Bridge near Mentmore, Bucks. The gang escaped with about 120 mailbags containing £2 631 784 banknotes worth being taken to London for destruction. Only £343 448 was recovered.

Jewels The greatest recorded theft of jewels was from the bedroom of the 'well-guarded' villa of Prince Abdel Aziz bin Ahmed Al-Thani near Cannes, France on 24 Jul 1980. They were valued at $16 000 000.

The biggest theft of jewels in Britain was that from Bond Jewellers, Conduit Street, London on 20 Jun 1983, when the haul was estimated to be worth £6 million.

Greatest kidnapping ransom Historically the greatest ransom paid was that for Atahualpa by the Incas to Francisco Pizarro in 1532–3 at Cajamarca, Peru, which constituted a hall full of gold and silver, worth in modern money some $170 million.

The greatest ransom ever reported in modern times is 1500 million pesos ($60 million) for the release of the brothers Jorge Born, 40, and Juan Born, 39, of Bunge and Born, paid to the left-wing urban guerrilla group Montoneros in Buenos Aires, Argentina on 20 Jun 1975.

Greatest hijack ransom The highest amount ever paid to aircraft hijackers has been $6 million, by the Japanese government in the case of a JAL DC-8 at Dacca Airport, Bangladesh on 2 Oct 1977, with 38 hostages. Six convicted criminals were also exchanged. The Bangladesh government had refused to sanction any retaliatory action.

Largest narcotics haul The greatest drug haul ever achieved was on 28 Sep 1989, when cocaine with an estimated street value of $6–7 billion was seized in a raid on a warehouse in Los Angeles, California, USA. The haul of 20 tonnes was prompted by a tip-off from a local resident who complained about heavy lorry traffic and people leaving the warehouse 'at odd hours and in a suspicious manner'.

The bulkiest haul was 2903 tonnes of Colombian marijuana in the 14-month-long 'Operation Tiburon', carried out by the Drug Enforcement Administration. The arrest of 495 people and the seizure of 95 vessels was announced on 5 Feb 1982.

In Britain, the Home Office disclosed on 23 Dec 1977 that 13 million LSD tablets with a street value approaching £100 million had been destroyed on the conclusion of 'Operation Julie'. The largest amount of drugs seized in one operation by weight was from the *Salton Sea*, a Honduras-registered cargo ship, at Ramsgate, Kent between 4–9 Sep 1988, when 10 tonnes of cannabis were recovered.

Greatest banknote forgery The greatest forgery was the German Third Reich's forging operation, code name 'Bernhard', engineered by SS Sturmbannführer Alfred Naujocks of the Technical Dept of the German Secret Service Amt VI F in Berlin in 1940–41. It involved £150 million worth of £5 notes.

Biggest bank fraud The Banca Nazionale del Lavoro, Italy's leading bank, admitted on 6 Sep 1989 that it had been defrauded of an estimated $3 billion, with the disclosure that its branch in Atlanta, Georgia, USA had made unauthorized loan commitments to Iraq. Both the bank's chairman, Nerio Nesi, and its director general, Giacomo Pedde, resigned following the revelation.

Computer fraud Between 1964 and 1973, 64 000 fake insurance policies were created on the computer of the Equity Funding Corporation in the USA, involving $2 billion.

Stanley Mark Rifkin (b. 1946) was arrested in Carlsbad, California, USA by the FBI on 6 Nov 1978 and charged with defrauding a Los Angeles bank of $10·2 million by manipulation of a computer system. He was sentenced to 8 years' imprisonment in June 1980.

Theft It was estimated in November 1983 that the greatest theft in the world is running at $160 billion per annum. This is the value of 'bosses' time' paid for but not worked in the United States in 1983/84.

The government of the Philippines announced on 23 Apr 1986 that they had succeeded in identifying $860·8 million 'salted' by the former President Ferdinand Edralin Marcos (1917–89) and his wife Imelda. The total since November 1965 was believed to be $5–10 billion.

Maritime fraud A cargo of 180 000 tonnes of Kuwaiti crude oil on the supertanker *Salem* at Durban was sold without title to the South African government in December 1979. The ship mysteriously sank off Senegal on 17 Jan 1980 leaving the government to pay £148 million to Shell International, who owned the shipment.

CAPITAL PUNISHMENT

Capital punishment is known to date at least from the Iron Age, as evidenced by the finding of Tollund man in Denmark. The countries in which capital punishment is still prevalent include China (hundreds of shootings per annum), South Africa (about 100 hangings for rape, robbery and murder), Turkey, Iran, Saudi Arabia, Malaysia, USA (reintroduced in 38 states since January 1983 for the most heinous murders) and the USSR (23 capital offences, including profiteering, speculation and currency offences, for which 253 persons were shot in 1989). Capital punishment was first abolished *de facto* in 1798 in Liechtenstein.

Capital punishment in the British Isles was abolished in the reign of William I (1066–87) and reimposed by Henry I in the next century, reaching a peak in the reign of Edward VI (1547–53), when an average of 560 persons were executed annually at Tyburn alone. Even into the 19th century there were 223 capital crimes, although in practice people were hanged for only 25 of these. Between 1830 and 1964 the most murderers hanged in a year was 27 (24 men, 3 women) in 1903. In 1956 there were no executions. The death penalty for murder was formally abolished in Britain on 18 Dec 1969.

Largest hanging The most people hanged from one gallows were 38 Sioux Indians by William J. Duly outside Mankato, Minnesota, USA for the murder of unarmed citizens on 26 Dec 1862. The Nazi Feldkommandant simultaneously hanged 50 Greek resistance men as a reprisal measure in Athens on 22 Jul 1944.

Last hangings The last public execution in England took place outside Newgate Prison, London at 8 a.m. on 26 May 1868, when Michael Barrett was hanged for his part in the Fenian bomb outrage on 13 Dec 1867, when 12 were killed outside the Clerkenwell House of Detention, London. The last public hanging in Scotland was that of the murderer Robert Smith outside Dumfries Gaol on 12 May 1868 by the hangman Mr Askern. The last in the United States occurred at Owensboro, Kentucky in 1936. The first non-public execution was of the murderer Thomas Wells on 13 Aug 1868. The last hangings in the UK were those of Peter Anthony Allen (b. 4 Apr 1943), hanged at Walton Prison, Liverpool by Robert L. Stewart, and of John Robson Walby (b. 1 Apr 1940), alias Gwynne Owen Evans, at Strangeways Gaol, Manchester, both on 13 Aug 1964. They had been found guilty of the capital murder of John Alan West on 7 April 1964. The 15th, youngest and last woman executed this century was Mrs Ruth Ellis (*née* Neilson) for the murder of David Blakely, 25, shot outside the Magdala, Hampstead on 10 Apr 1955. She was executed on 13 July at Holloway Prison, London. The last hanging in the Republic of Ireland took place in 1954.

Last from yard-arm The last naval execution at the yard-arm was the hanging of Private John Dalliger, Royal Marines, aboard HMS *Leven* in Victoria Bay near Lu-ta, China, on 13 Jul 1860. Dalliger had been found guilty of two attempted murders.

Youngest On 26 Jun 1885 James Arcene was executed for a crime he committed when aged 10. In Britain the hanging of persons under 18 was expressly excluded in the Children's and Young Persons' Act 1933 (Section 33). No person under that age was, in fact, executed after 1887. The lowest reliably recorded age was of a boy aged eight 'who had malice, cunning and revenge' in firing two barns and who was hanged at Abingdon, Oxon in the 17th century. The youngest persons hanged since 1900 have been six 18-year-olds, the most recent of whom was Francis Robert George ('Flossie') Forsyth on 10 Nov 1960.

Oldest The oldest person hanged in the UK since 1900 was a man of 71 named Charles Frembd (*sic*) at Chelmsford Gaol on 4 Nov 1914, for the murder of his wife at Leytonstone, London. In 1822 John Smith, said to be 80, of Greenwich, south-east London, was hanged for the murder of a woman.

Last guillotinings The last person to be publicly guillotined in France was the murderer Eugene Weidmann, before a large crowd at Versailles, near Paris at 4:50 a.m. on 17 Jun 1939. The executioner was Henri Desfourneaux, who was succeeded by his nephew André Obrecht (1897–1983) in 1951, who was in turn succeeded by his niece's husband, Marcel Chevalier, in January 1978. Dr Joseph Ignace Guillotin (1738–1812) died a natural death. He had advocated the use of the machine designed by Dr Antoine Louis in 1789 in the French constituent assembly. The last use before abolition on 9 Sep 1981 was on 10 Sep 1977 at Baumettes Prison, Marseille, for torturer and murderer Hamida Djandoubi, aged 28.

Death Row The longest sojourn on Death Row was the 39 years of Sadamichi Hirasawa (1893–1987) in Sendai Jail, Japan. He was convicted in 1948 of poisoning 12 bank employees with potassium cyanide to effect a theft of £100, and died aged 94. Willie Jasper Darden, 54, survived a record six death warrants in 14 years on Death Row for the murder of a shopkeeper in 1973. His final TV interview was interrupted by a power failure caused by a test of the Florida electric chair in which he died on 15 Mar 1988. On 31 Oct 1987 Liong Wie Tong, 52, and Tan Tian Tjoen, 62, were executed for robbery and murder by firing squad in Jakarta, Indonesia after 25 years on Death Row.

Executioners The longest period of office of a public executioner was that of William Calcraft (1800–79), who was in action from 1828 to 25 May 1874 and officiated at nearly every hanging outside and later inside Newgate Prison, London. On 2 Apr 1868 he hanged the murderess Mrs Frances Kidder, 25, outside Maidstone Jail, Kent — the last public execution of a woman.

For 56 years from 1900 to the retirement of Albert Pierrepoint in February 1956, the Pierrepoint family largely monopolized the task of executing murderers and war criminals. Henry Albert (1876–1922) officiated from 1900–1911, with a record 20 executions in Britain in 1909 and the last double female execution (the baby-farmers Mrs Amelia Sachs and Mrs Annie Walters) on 3 Feb 1903. The longest-serving executioner was his eldest brother Thomas Pierrepoint from 1903–1948. Albert Pierrepoint, son of Henry Albert, officiated at the hanging of 530 men and 20 women in his career in nine countries, including a record 27 war criminals in one day in Germany. Britain's ninth and last chief prison hangman was Henry B. Allen, who was on call until the abolition of hanging for murder in 1969.

Lynching The worst year in the 20th century for lynchings in the United States has been 1901, with 130 lynchings, while the first year with no reported cases was 1952. The last lynching case recorded in Britain was that of *R.* v. *Caskie and Stevenson* on 29 Dec 1922. The accused were discharged after a verdict of not proven for murder by assault of Robert Alexander Stewart, 32, at Dalmarnock Bridge, Glasgow on 11 Sep 1922. Stewart was falsely thought by a tram conductor to be kidnapping Alistair John Sinclair, aged five, who gave evidence not under oath and standing on a seat.

Corporal punishment The last use of corporal punishment in one of HM Prisons was on 26 Jun 1962 and it was abolished in the UK by the Criminal Justice Act 1967. The treadmill which 14 prisons operated in 1878 was finally suspended on 1 Apr 1902.

PRISON SENTENCES

Longest sentences Chamoy Thipyaso, a Thai woman known as the queen of underground investing, and seven of her associates were each jailed for 141 078 years by the Bangkok Criminal Court, Thailand on 27 Jul 1989 for swindling the public through a multi-million dollar deposit-taking business. A sentence of 384 912 years was *demanded* at the prosecution of Gabriel March Grandos, 22, at Palma de Mallorca, Spain on 11 Mar 1972 for failing to deliver 42 768 letters, or 9 years per letter.

The longest sentence imposed on a mass murderer was 21 consecutive life sentences and 12 consecutive death sentences in the case of John Gacy, who killed 33 boys and young men between 1972 and 1978 in Illinois, USA. He was sentenced by a jury in Chicago, Illinois on 13 Mar 1980.

Kevin Mulgrew from the Ardoyne district of Belfast was sentenced on 5 Aug 1983 to life imprisonment for the murder of Sergeant Julian Connolley of the Ulster Defence Regiment. In addition he was given a further 963 years to be served concurrently on 84 other serious charges, including 13 conspiracies to murder and 8 attempted murders.

The longest single period served by a reprieved murderer in Great Britain this century was 40 years 11 months by John Watson Laurie, the Goat Fell or Arran murderer, who was reprieved on the grounds of insanity in November 1889. He died in Perth Penitentiary on 4 Oct 1930.

The longest prison sentence imposed by a judge under British law was one of 45 years on 24 Oct 1986 in the case of Jordanian terrorist Nezar Hindawi for his abortive bomb plot against an El Al airliner on 17 Apr 1986.

The longest single sentence passed on a woman under English law was 20 years for Mrs Lona Teresa Cohen (*née* Petra) (b. 1913) at the Old Bailey on 2 Mar 1961 for conspiring to commit a breach of the Official Secrets Act 1911. Her sentence was remitted by the Foreign Secretary on 24 Jul 1969. Judith Minna Ward (see Most prolific murderers) was sentenced to 20 years for a single offence and an aggregate 30 years on 4 Nov 1974.

Longest time served Paul Geidel (1894–1987) was convicted of second-degree murder on 5 Sep 1911 when a 17-year-old porter in a hotel in New York, USA. He was released from the Fishkill Correctional Facility, Beacon, New York aged 85 on 7 May 1980, having served 68 years, 8 months and 2 days — the longest recorded term in US history. He first refused parole in 1974.

Oldest Bill Wallace (1881–1989) was the oldest prisoner on record, spending the last 63 years of his life in Aradale Psychiatric Hospital, at Ararat, Victoria, Australia. He had shot and killed a man at a restaurant in Melbourne, Victoria in December 1925, and having been found unfit to plead, was transferred to the responsibility of the Mental Health Department in February 1926. He remained at Aradale until his death on 17 Jul 1989, shortly before his 108th birthday.

Longest in Broadmoor Special Hospital The longest period for which any person has been detained in Broadmoor Hospital, Crowthorne, Berks, which provides conditions of maximum security for patients with criminal, violent or dangerous propensities, is 76 years in the case of William Giles. He had been charged with arson but found insane, and was admitted to Broadmoor Hospital in May 1885 at the age of 10. He died there in March 1962 at the age of 87.

The longest escape from Broadmoor was one of 39 years by James Kelly, who got away on 23 Jan 1888, using a pass key made from a corset spring. After an adventurous life in Paris, France, in New York, USA and at sea he returned in April 1927 to ask for readmission. After some difficulties this was arranged. He died back in Broadmoor in September 1929.

Most arrests A record for arrests was set by Tommy Johns (1922–88) in Brisbane, Queensland, Australia on 9 Sep 1982 when he faced his 2000th conviction for drunkenness since 1957. His total at the time of his last drink on 30 Apr 1988 was 'nearly 3000'.

Greatest mass arrests The greatest mass arrest reported in a democratic country was of 15 617 demonstrators on 11 Jul 1988, rounded up by South Korean police to ensure security in advance of the 1988 Olympic Games in Seoul.

The largest in the UK occurred on 17 Sep 1961, when 1314 demonstrators supporting unilateral nuclear disarmament were arrested for obstructing highways leading to Parliament Square, London by sitting down. As a consequence of the 1926 General Strike there were 3149 prosecutions, for incitement (1760) and violence (1389).

FINES

Heaviest The largest fine ever was one of $650 million, which was imposed on the US securities house Drexel Burnham Lambert in December 1988 for insider trading. This figure represented $300 million in direct fines, with the balance to be put into an account to satisfy claims of parties that could prove they were defrauded by Drexel's actions.

The record for an individual is $200 million, which Michael Milken (see also Highest salary) agreed to pay on 24 Apr 1990. In addition, he agreed to settle civil charges filed by the Securities and Exchange Commission. The payments were in settlement of a criminal racketeering and securities fraud suit brought by the US government.

The heaviest fine ever imposed in the UK was £5 million on Gerald Ronson, the head of Heron International, announced on 28 Aug 1990 at Southwark Crown Court, London. Ronson was one of four defendants in the Guinness case concerning the company's takeover bid for Distillers.

The highest fine ever imposed on a UK company is 10 million ECUs (equivalent to £5·7 million) on ICI by the EEC for irregular trading concerning polypropylene from 1977–83, on 24 Apr 1986.

PRISONS

Largest The most capacious prison in Great Britain is Wandsworth, south London, with a certified normal accommodation of 1266. A peak occupancy of 1519 was reached on 30 Apr 1988. The highest prison walls in Great Britain are those of Lancaster Prison, measuring 11–15·85 m *36–52 ft*. The Maze Prison, near Lisburn, Northern Ireland, was opened in 1974 and covers 53·8 ha *133 acres*, with eight 100-cell blocks surrounded by a 9·1 m *30 ft* wall. The largest prison in Scotland is Barlinnie, Glasgow, with 750 single cells. Ireland's largest prison is Mountjoy Prison, Dublin, with 808 cells.

Highest population The peak average prison population, including police cell occupation, for England and Wales was 51 239 for the week beginning 17 Jul 1987. In Scotland the prison population record was 5588 in 1986 and in Northern Ireland 2934 on 16 Nov 1975.

Most secure prison After it became a maximum security federal prison in 1934, no convict was known to have lived to tell of a successful escape from the prison of Alcatraz Island in San Francisco Bay, California, USA. A total of 23 men attempted it but 12 were recaptured, five were shot dead, one drowned and five were presumed drowned. On 16 Dec 1962, just before the prison was closed on 21 Mar 1963, one man reached the mainland alive, only to be recaptured on the spot. John Chase held the record with 26 years there.

Most expensive prison Spandau Prison, in Berlin, Germany, originally built in 1887 for 600 prisoners, was used solely for the Nazi war criminal Rudolf Hess (26 Apr 1894–17 Aug 1987) for the last twenty years of his life. The cost of maintenance of the staff of 105 was estimated in 1976 to be $415 000 per annum. On 19 Aug 1987 it was announced that Hess had strangled himself with a piece of electrical flex and that he had left a note in old German script. He had remained in lone confinement at Spandau for a total of forty years. Two months after his death, the prison was demolished.

Longest escape The longest recorded escape by a recaptured prisoner was that of Leonard T. Fristoe, 77, who escaped from Nevada State Prison, USA on 15 Dec 1923 and was turned in by his son on 15 Nov 1969 at Compton, California. He had had 46 years of freedom under the name of Claude R. Willis. He had killed two sheriff's deputies in 1920.

Greatest gaol break In February 1979 a retired US Army colonel, Arthur 'Bull' Simons, led a band of 14 to break into Gasre prison, Tehran, Iran to rescue two fellow Americans. Some 11 000 other prisoners took advantage of this and the Islamic revolution in what became history's largest ever gaol break.

In July 1971, Raoul Sendic and 105 other Tupamaro guerillas escaped from a Uruguayan prison through a tunnel 91 m *298 ft* long.

The greatest gaol break in the UK was that from the Maze Prison on 25 Sep 1983, when 38 IRA prisoners escaped from Block H-7. The Provisional IRA had been first set up in Ballinamore, Co. Leitrim, Republic of Ireland in 1967.

Honours, Decorations and Awards

Oldest order The earliest honour known was the 'Gold of Honour' for extraordinary valour awarded in the 18th Dynasty *c.* 1440–1400 BC. A statuette was found at Qan-el-Kebri, Egypt. The oldest true order was the Order of St John of Jerusalem (the direct descendant of which is the Sovereign Military Order of Malta), legitimized in 1113. The prototype of the princely Orders of Chivalry is thought to be the Most Noble Order of the Garter, founded by King Edward III *c.* 1348.

Most titles The most titled person in the world is the 18th Duchess of Alba (Alba de Tormes), Doña Maria del Rosario Cayetana Fitz-James Stuart y Silva. She is 8 times a duchess, 15 times a marchioness, 21 times a countess and 19 times a Spanish grandee.

Versatility The only person to win a Victoria Cross and an Olympic Gold Medal has been Lt-Gen. Sir Philip Neame (1888–1978). He won the VC in 1914 and was an Olympic gold medallist for Britain for rifle shooting in 1924, though under the illusion at the time that he was shooting for the British Empire. The only George Cross holder who was also a Fellow of the Royal Society was Prof. Peter Victor Danckwerts (1916–85), who as a sub-lieutenant RNVR defused 16 parachute mines in under 48 hr in the London docks during the Battle of Britain in August 1940.

Victoria Cross *Double awards* The only three men ever to have been awarded a bar to the Victoria Cross (instituted 29 Jan 1856) are:

Surg.-Capt. (later Lt-Col.) Arthur Martin-Leake VC*, VD, RAMC (1874–1953) (1902 and bar 1914).
Capt. Noel Godfrey Chavasse VC*, MC, RAMC (1884–1917) (1916 and bar posthumously 1917).
Second-Lt. (later Capt.) Charles Hazlitt Upham VC*, NZMF (b. 21 Sep 1908) (1941 and bar 1942).

The most VCs awarded in a war were the 634 in World War I (1914–18). The greatest number won exclusively in a single action was 11 at Rorke's Drift in the Zulu War on 22–23 Jan 1879. The school with most recipients is Eton College, Col. H. H. Jones being the 36th (posthumously in the Falklands campaign, in 1982).

Youngest The earliest established age for a VC is 15 years 100 days for hospital apprentice Andrew (wrongly gazetted as Arthur) Fitzgibbon (b. 13 May 1845 at Peteragurh, northern India) of the Indian Medical Services for bravery at the Taku Forts in northern China on 21 Aug 1860. The youngest living VC is Capt. Rambahadur Limbu (b. 1 Nov 1939 at Chyangthapu, Nepal) of the 10th Princess Mary's Own Gurkha Rifles. The award was for his courage as a lance-corporal while fighting in the Bau district of Sarawak, east Malaysia on 21 Nov 1965. He retired on 25 Mar 1985 as a Captain.

Oldest Capt. William Raynor was the oldest person to receive the medal. It was awarded when he was 62, for the part he played in blowing up an arms store besieged by insurgents on 11 May 1857, the second day of the Indian Mutiny. The medal was retrieved on behalf of the family at a London auction in 1987, and is displayed at the RAOC Museum, Camberley, Surrey.

Longest-lived The longest-lived of all the 1351 winners of the Victoria Cross has been Lt.-Col. Harcus Strachan. He was born in Bo'ness, West Lothian on 7 Nov 1884 and died in Vancouver, British Columbia, Canada on 1 May 1982 aged 97 years 175 days.

Most highly decorated The four living persons to have been twice decorated with any of the UK's topmost decorations are Capt. C. H. Upham VC and bar; HM the Queen Mother CI, GCVO, GBE, who is a Lady of the Garter and a Lady of the Thistle; HRH the Duke of Edinburgh KG, KT, OM, GBE and HRH Prince Charles KG, KT, GCB. Britain's most highly decorated woman is the World War II British agent Mrs Odette Hallowes GC, MBE, Légion d'Honneur, Ordre St George (Belge), who survived imprisonment

and torture at the hands of the Gestapo from 1943–5. Violette Reine Elizabeth Szabo (*née* Bushnell) GC (1921–45) lost her husband in the French Legion at El Alamein in 1942. He was Etienne Szabo, Médaille Militaire, Légion d'Honneur and Croix de Guerre.

Top jet ace The greatest number of kills in jet-to-jet battles is 16, by Lt-Col. Heinz Bär (Germany) in 1945, and Capt. Joseph Christopher McConnell, Jr, of the United States Air Force, in the Korean war (1950–53). He was killed on 25 Aug 1954. It is possible that an Israeli ace may have surpassed this total in the period 1967–70, but the identity of pilots is subject to strict security.

Top woman ace The record score for any woman fighter pilot is 12, by Jnr-Lt Lydia Litvak (USSR) (b. 1921) on the Eastern Front between 1941 and 1943. She was killed in action on 1 Aug 1943.

Top-scoring air aces (World Wars I and II) The 'scores' of air aces in both wars are *still* hotly disputed. The highest figures officially attributed are:

World	United Kingdom
World War I	
80 Rittmeister Manfred Freiherr (Baron) von Richthofen (Germany)	57[1] Major James T.B. McCudden VC, DSO*, MC*, MM
World War II	
352[2] Major Erich Hartmann (Germany)	38[3] Group-Capt. (now Air Vice Marshal) James Edgar Johnson DSO**, DFC*

[1] 73 'victories' are frequently attributed to Major Edward Mannock VC, DSO**, MC*, although he actually claimed no more than 50 — the total stated in his VC citation. The figure of 73 is thought to be used so that he would appear to beat the 72 'victories' which were claimed by the Canadian pilot Lt-Col. William 'Billy' Bishop VC, although many of these are considered to be suspect.
[2] The highest total in one sortie is 13 in 17 min by Major Erich Rudorffer, on the Russian front on 6 Nov 1943.
[3] The greatest number of successes against flying bombs (V1s) was by Sqn Ldr Joseph Berry DFC** (b. Nottingham, 1920, killed 2 Oct 1944), who brought down 60 during the V1 campaign between 13 Jun and 1 Sep 1944, 57 of them at night. The most successful fighter pilot in the RAF was Sqn Ldr Marmaduke Thomas St John Pattle DFC, of South Africa, with a known total of at least 40.

Youngest award The youngest age at which an official gallantry award has ever been won is eight years in the case of Anthony Farrer, who was given the Albert Medal on 23 Sep 1916 for fighting off a cougar at Cowichan Lake, Vancouver Island, Canada to save Doreen Ashburnham. She was also awarded the AM, which, in 1971, was exchanged for the George Cross.

Most lifeboat medals Sir William Hillary (1771–1847), founder of the Royal National Lifeboat Institution in 1824, was personally and uniquely awarded four RNLI Gold Medals, in 1825, 1828 and 1830 (twice). The only triple award this century has been to Coxswain Henry Blogg GC, BEM (1876–1954) of Cromer, Norfolk, who also had four Silver Medals. The record for Silver Medals is five, by Sydney Harris of Great Yarmouth and Gorleston, Norfolk (1905 (twice), 1909, 1912 and 1916).

Most mentions in despatches The record number of 'mentions' is 23 by Field Marshal the Rt Hon. Sir Frederick Sleigh Roberts Bt, the Earl Roberts VC, VD (1832–1914).

Most post-nominal letters Lord Roberts, who was also a privy counsellor, was the only non-royal holder of eight sets of *official* post-nominal letters. Currently the record number is seven, by Marshal of the RAF the Rt Hon. Lord Elworthy KG, GCB, CBE, DSO, LVO, DFC, AFC (b. 23 Mar 1911) of New Zealand. HRH the Duke of Windsor (1894–1972) when Prince of Wales had 10 sets and was also a privy counsellor, viz. KG, PC, KT, KP, GCB, GCSI, GCMG, GCIE, GCVO, GBE, MC. He later appended the ISO but never did so in the cases of the OM, CH or DSO, of which orders he had also been sovereign.

Civilian gallantry Reginald H. Blanchford of Guernsey received the MBE for gallantry in 1950; the Queen's Commendation in 1957; the George Medal in 1958; the OBE for gallantry in 1961 for saving life from cliff-tops. He was also awarded the Life Saving Medal in Gold 1957 with golden bar 1963 and was made a Knight of Grace of the Order of St John in 1970.

USSR The USSR's highest award for valour is the Gold Star of a Hero of the Soviet Union. 12 709 Gold Stars have been awarded, 11 040 of which were World War II. The only wartime triple awards were to Marshal Georgiy Konstantinovich Zhukov (1896–1974) (subsequently awarded a fourth Gold Star), and to the leading air aces Guards Colonel (later Marshal of Aviation) Aleksandr Ivanovich Pokryshkin (1913–85) and Aviation Maj. Gen. Ivan Nikitovich Kozhedub (b. 8 Jun 1920) (Order of the Red Banner, seven times). Zhukov also uniquely had the Order of Victory (twice), the Order of Lenin (six times) and the Order of the Red Banner (thrice). The highest award of civil honour is the Gold Star of Socialist Labour, 20 424 of which have been awarded since it was established in 1938. There have been 15 awards of a third Gold Star of Socialist Labour. Leonid Ilich Brezhnev (1906–82) was four times Hero of the Soviet Union and Hero of Socialist Labour, Order of Victory (withdrawn in 1990), Order of Lenin (eight times) and Order of the Red Banner (twice).

Germany The Knight's Cross of the Iron Cross with swords, diamonds and golden oak-leaves was uniquely awarded to Col. Hans Ulrich Rudel (1916–82) for 2530 operational flying missions on the Eastern Front in the period 1941–45. He destroyed 519 Soviet armoured vehicles.

USA The highest US military decoration is the Congressional Medal of Honor. Five marines received both the Army and Navy Medals of Honor for the same deeds in 1918, and 14 officers and men received the medal on two occasions between 1864 and 1915 for two distinct acts. The Defense Department refuses to recognize any military hero as having the most awards, but various heroes have been nominated by unofficial groups. Since medals and decorations cannot be compared as to value, the title of most decorated can only be a matter of subjective evaluation. General Douglas MacArthur (1880–1964), because of his high rank and his years of military service spanning three wars, would seem to hold the best claim to 'Most Decorated American Soldier'. In addition to the Congressional Medal of Honor, he also received 58 separate awards and decorations with 16 Oak Leaf Clusters, plus 18 campaign stars.

Record price The highest price ever paid for a Victoria Cross was £126 500 for the VC awarded to Lieutenant William Rhodes-Moorhouse in 1915 for his bravery in bombing the railway junction at Courtrai, Belgium, which prevented German reinforcements from reaching the front during the second battle of Ypres. It was bought by a private collector, bidding over the telephone, at Sotheby's Battle of Britain sale at the RAF Museum, Hendon, London on 15 Sep 1990.

The record for a George Cross is £20 250 at Christie's on 14 Mar 1985, for that of Sgt Michael Willets (3rd Battalion Parachute Regiment), killed by an IRA bomb in Ulster in 1971.

Order of Merit The Order of Merit (instituted on 23 Jun 1902) is limited to 24 members. The longest-lived of the 153 holders has been the Rt Hon. Bertrand Arthur William Russell, 3rd Earl Russell, who died on 2 Feb 1970 aged 97 years 260 days. The oldest recipient was Admiral of the Fleet the Hon. Sir Henry Keppel (1809–1904), who received the Order at the age of 93 years 56 days on 9 Aug 1902. The youngest recipient has been HRH the Duke of Edinburgh, who was appointed on his 47th birthday on 10 Jun 1968.

Anti-submarine successes The highest number of U-boat kills attributed to one ship in World War II was 15, to HMS *Starling* (Capt. Frederic John Walker DSO***, RN). Captain Walker was in command at the sinking of a total of 25 U-boats between 1941 and the time of his death on 9 Jul 1944. The US Destroyer Escort *England* sank six Japanese submarines in the Pacific between 18 and 30 May 1944.

Most successful submarine captains The most successful of all World War II submarine commanders was Leutnant Otto Kretschmer, captain of the U.23 and U.99, who up to March 1941 sank one destroyer and 44 Allied merchantmen totalling 266 629 gross registered tons.

In World War I Kapitänleutnant (later Vizeadmiral) Lothar von Arnauld de la Périère, in the U.35 and U.139, sank 195 Allied ships totalling 458 856 gross registered tons. The most successful boats were the U.35, which in World War I sank 54 ships of 90 350 grt in a single voyage and 224 ships of 539 711 grt all told, and the U.48, which sank 51 ships of 310 007 grt in World War II. The largest target ever sunk by a submarine was the Japanese aircraft carrier *Shinano* (59 994 tonnes) by USS *Archerfish* (Cdr Joseph F. Enright, USN) on 29 Nov 1944.

Most valuable annual prize The value of each of the 1991 Nobel Prizes (see also p. 96) was Sw Kr 6 000 000, which at the time of printing was equivalent to approximately £570 000. The ceremonial presentations for physics, chemistry, physiology or medicine, literature and economics take place in Stockholm, Sweden, and that for peace is held in Oslo, Norway.

Most statues The world record for raising statues to oneself was set by Generalissimo Dr Rafael Leónidas Trujillo y Molina (1891–1961), former President of the Dominican Republic. In March 1960 a count showed that there were 'over 2000'. The country's highest mountain was named Pico Trujillo (later Pico Duarte). One province was called Trujillo and another Trujillo Valdez. The capital was named

Ciudad Trujillo (Trujillo City) in 1936, but reverted to its old name of Santo Domingo de Guzmán on 23 Nov 1961. Trujillo was assassinated in a car ambush on 30 May 1961, and 30 May is now celebrated as a public holiday. The man to whom most statues have been raised is Buddha. The 20th-century champion is Vladimir Ilyich Ulyanov, alias Lenin (1870–1924), busts of whom have been mass-produced, as also has been the case with Mao Tse-tung (1893–1976) and Ho Chi Minh (1890–1969).

Most honorary degrees The greatest number of honorary degrees awarded to any individual is 118, given to Rev. Father Theodore M. Hesburgh (b. 1918), president of the University of Notre Dame, Indiana, USA. These have been accumulated since 1954.

Greatest vote The largest monetary vote made by Parliament to a subject was the £400 000 given to the 1st Duke of Wellington (1769–1852) on 12 Apr 1814. He received in all £864 000. The total received by the 1st, 2nd and 3rd Dukes to January 1900 was £1 052 000.

The Royal Society The longest term as a Fellow of the Royal Society (founded 1660) has been approximately 68 years in the case of Sir Hans Sloane (1660–1753), who was elected in 1685. The longest-lived Fellow was Sir Rickard Christophers (1873–1978), who died aged 104 years 84 days. The youngest Fellow is believed to have been Sir Joseph Hodges, who was born c. 1704 and elected on 5 Apr 1716 at about 12 years of age. The oldest person to have been elected as a Fellow was Sir Rupert Edward Cecil Lee Guinness, the 2nd Earl of Iveagh (1874–1967), who was elected in 1964 at the age of 90.

■ **Victoria Cross — record price** The highest price ever paid for a Victoria Cross was £126 500 for the VC awarded to Lieutenant William Rhodes-Moorhouse in 1915. It was bought by a private collector, bidding over the telephone, at Sotheby's Battle of Britain sale at the RAF Museum, Hendon, London on 15 Sep 1990.
(Photo: Sotheby's)

NOBEL PRIZES

Earliest 1901 for Physics, Chemistry, Physiology or Medicine, Literature and Peace.

Most Prizes USA has won 206, outright or shared, including most for Physiology or Medicine (69); Physics (55); Chemistry (36), Peace (18); Economics (18). France has most for Literature (12). The United Kingdom total is 88, outright or shared, comprising Chemistry (23); Physiology or Medicine (22); Physics (20); Peace (10); Literature (8); Economics (5).

Oldest Laureate Professor Francis Peyton Rous (US) (1879–1970) in 1966 shared in Physiology or Medicine prize at the age of 87.

Youngest Laureates *At time of award:* Professor Sir Lawrence Bragg (1890–1971) 1915 Physics prize at 25. *At time of work:* Bragg, and Theodore W. Richards (US) (1868–1928), 1914 Chemistry prize for work done when 23. *Literature:* Rudyard Kipling (UK) (1865–1936) 1907 prize at 41. *Peace:* Mrs Mairead Corrigan-Maguire (Northern Ireland) (b. 27 Jan 1944) 1976 prize (shared) at 32.

Most 3 Awards: International Committee of the Red Cross, Geneva (founded 1863) Peace 1917, 1944 and 1963 (shared); 2 Awards: Dr Linus Carl Pauling (US) (b. 28 Feb 1901) Chemistry 1954 and Peace 1962; Mme Marja Sklodowska Curie (Polish-French) (1867–1934) Physics 1903 (shared) and Chemistry 1911; Professor John Bardeen (US) (1908–91) Physics 1956 (shared) and 1972 (shared); Professor Frederick Sanger (b. 13 Aug 1918) Chemistry 1958 and 1980 (shared); Office of the United Nations' High Commissioner for Refugees, Geneva (founded 1951) Peace 1954 and 1981.

Highest Prize Sw Kr 6 000 000 (for 1991), equivalent to £570 000.

Lowest Prize Sw Kr 115 000 (1923), equivalent to £6620.

Erasmus Darwin was elected on 9 Apr 1761 and was followed by his son Robert (1788 to 1848), *his* son Charles (1839 to 1882), his sons Sir George (1879 to 1912), Francis (1882 to 1925) and Horace (1903 to 1928) and Sir George's son Sir Charles (1922 to 1962), so spanning over 200 years with five generations.

Oxford and Cambridge Unions
Four brothers were Presidents of the Union in the case of the sons of the Rt Hon. Isaac Foot: Sir Dingle Foot (Balliol, 1927–8); John (Lord Foot) (Balliol, 1930–31) and the Rt Hon. Michael (Wadham, 1933–4) at Oxford, and Hugh (Lord Caradon) (St John's, 1929) at Cambridge. Lord Caradon's son, the Hon. Paul Foot, was President at Oxford (University College, 1960–61).

PEERAGE

Most ancient The oldest extant peerage is the premier Earldom of Scotland, held by the Rt Hon. Margaret of Mar, the Countess of Mar and 31st holder of this Earldom (b. 19 Sep 1940), who is the heir-at-law of Roderick or Rothri, 1st Earl (or Mormaer) of Mar, who witnessed a charter in 1114 or 1115 as 'Rothri *comes*'.

Oldest creation The greatest age at which any person has been raised to the peerage is 93 years 337 days in the case of Sir William Francis Kyffin Taylor (b. 9 Jul 1854), who was created Baron Maenan of Ellesmere, Shrops on 10 Jun 1948, and died aged 97 on 22 Sep 1951. The oldest elevation to a life peerage has been that of Emanuel Shinwell (b. 18 Oct 1884) on 2 Jun 1970 when aged 85 years 227 days. He died on 8 May 1986 aged 101 years 202 days.

Longest-lived peer The longest-lived peer ever recorded was the Rt Hon. Emanuel Shinwell (1884–1986), created a life baron in 1970. The oldest peeress recorded was the Countess Desmond, who was alleged to be 140 when she died in 1604. This claim is patently exaggerated but it is accepted that she may have been 104. Currently the oldest peer is the Rt Hon. Major the Earl of Southesk of Kinnaird Castle, Brechin, Angus (b. 23 Sep 1893).

Youngest peers Twelve Dukes of Cornwall became (in accordance with the grant by the Crown in Parliament) peers at birth as the eldest sons of a sovereign; and the 9th Earl of Chichester inherited his earldom at his birth on 14 Apr 1944, 54 days after his father's death. The youngest age at which a person has had a peerage conferred on him is 7 days old in the case of the Earldom of Chester on HRH the Prince George (later George IV) on 19 Aug 1762. The youngest to be created a life peer or peeress is Baroness Masham of Ilton, Countess of Swinton (b. 19 Apr 1935) aged 34, in 1970.

Longest and shortest peerages The longest tenure of a peerage has been 87 years 10 days in the case of Charles St Clair, Lord Sinclair, born 30 Jul 1768, succeeded 16 Dec 1775 and died aged 94 years 243 days on 30 Mar 1863.

The shortest enjoyment of a peerage was the 'split second' by which the law assumes that the Hon. Wilfrid Carlyl Stamp (b. 28 Oct 1904), the 2nd Baron Stamp, survived his father, Sir Josiah Charles Stamp, the 1st Baron Stamp, when both were killed as a result of German bombing of London on 16 Apr 1941. Apart from this legal fiction, the shortest recorded peerage was one of 30 min in the case of Sir Charles Brandon, the 3rd Duke of Suffolk, who died aged 13 or 14 just after succeeding his brother Henry, when both were suffering a fatal illness, at Buckden, Cambs on 14 Jul 1551.

Highest numbering The highest succession number borne by any peer is that of the present 35th Baron Kingsale (John de Courcy, b. 27 Jan 1941), who succeeded to the then 746-year-old barony on 7 Nov 1969. His occupations have included barman, bingo-caller and plumber.

Most creations The largest number of new hereditary peerages created in any year was 54 in 1296. The record for all peerages (including 40 life peerages) is 55 in 1964. The greatest number of extinctions in a year was 16 in 1923 and the greatest number of deaths was 44 in 1935.

Most prolific Currently the peer with the largest family is Robert Keith Rous, 6th Earl of Stradbroke (b. 25 May 1937), with seven sons and seven daughters by two different wives. The most prolific peeress ever is believed to be Mary Fitzgerald, wife of Patrick, 19th Baron Kingsale, who bore 23 children (no twins) who survived to baptism. She died in 1663.

Baronets The greatest age to which a baronet has lived is 101 years 188 days, in the case of Sir Fitzroy Donald Maclean, 10th Bt (1835–1936). He was the last survivor of the Crimean campaign of 1853–56. Capt. Sir Trevor Wheler, 13th Bt (1889–1986) was a baronet for a record 83 years 156 days. The only baronetess is Dame Maureen Dunbar of Hempriggs, who succeeded in her own right as 8th in line of a 1706 baronetcy in 1965. There are nearly 1400 baronets.

Knights *Youngest and oldest* The youngest age for the conferment of a knighthood is 29 days for HRH the Prince George (b. 12 Aug 1762) (later George IV) by virtue of his *ex officio* membership of the Order of the Garter consequent upon his creation as Prince of Wales on 17 or 19 Aug 1762. The greatest age for the conferment of a knighthood is on a 100th birthday, in the case of the Knight Bachelor Sir Robert Mayer (1879–1985), who was also made a KCVO by the Queen at the Royal Festival Hall, London on 5 Jun 1979.

Most brothers George and Elizabeth Coles of Australia had four sons knighted — Sir George (1885–1977); Sir Arthur (1892–1982); Sir Kenneth (1896–1985) and Sir Edgar (1899–1981). George re-married and had a fifth son who was also knighted — Sir Norman (1907–89).

Most freedoms Probably the greatest number of freedoms ever conferred on any man was 57 in the case of Andrew Carnegie (1835–1919), who was born in Dunfermline, Fife but emigrated to the United States in 1848. The most freedoms conferred upon any citizen of the UK is 42 for Sir Winston Churchill (1874–1965).

Military and Defence

WAR

Earliest conflict The oldest known offensive weapon is a broken wooden spear found in April 1911 at Clacton-on-Sea, Essex by S. Hazzledine Warren. This is much beyond the limit of radiocarbon dating but is estimated to have been fashioned before 200 000 BC.

Longest The longest war was the 'Hundred Years War' between England and France, which lasted from 1338 to 1453 (115 years), although it could be said that the nine Crusades from the First (1096–1104) to the Ninth (1270–91), extending over 195 years, comprised a single holy war.

Bloodiest By far the most costly war in terms of human life was World War II (1939–45), in which the total number of fatalities, including battle deaths and civilians of all countries, is estimated to have been 54·8 million, assuming 25 million USSR fatalities and 7·8 million Chinese civilians killed. The country which suffered most was Poland, with 6 028 000 or 17·2 per cent of its population of 35 100 000 killed. The total combatant death toll from World War I was 9·7 million, compared with the 15·6 million from World War II.

In the case of the UK, however, the heavier armed forces fatalities occurred in World War I (1914–18), with 765 399 killed out of 5 500 000 engaged (13·9 per cent), compared with 265 000 out of 5 896 000 engaged (4·49 per cent) in World War II.

In the Paraguayan war of 1864–70 against Brazil, Argentina and Uruguay, Paraguay's population was reduced from 1 400 000 to 220 000 survivors, of whom only 30 000 were adult males.

Dr William Brydon (1811–73) and two natives were the sole survivors of the seven-day retreat of 13 000 soldiers and camp-followers from Kabul, Afghanistan. Dr Brydon's horse died 2 days after his arrival at Jellalabad, some 115 km *70 miles* to the east on the route to the Khyber Pass, on 13 Jan 1842.

Bloodiest civil The bloodiest civil war in history was the *Taiping* ('Great Peace') rebellion, which was a revolt against the Chinese Ch'ing Dynasty between 1851 and 1864. The rebellion was led by the deranged Hung Hsiu-ch'üan (executed), who imagined himself to be a younger brother of Jesus Christ. His force was named *T'ai-p'ing T'ien-kuo* ('Heavenly Kingdom of Great Peace'). According to the best estimates the loss of life was some 20 million, including more than 100 000 killed by government forces in the sack of Nanking on 19–21 Jul 1864.

Most costly The material cost of World War II far transcended that of the rest of history's wars put together and has been estimated at $1·5 trillion. The total cost to the Soviet Union was estimated in May 1959 at 2·5 trillion roubles, while a figure of $530 billion has been estimated for the USA.

In the case of the UK the cost of £34 423 million was over five times as great as that of World War I (£6700 million) and 158·6 times that of the Boer War of 1899–1902 (£217 million).

Last battle on British soil The last pitched land battle in Britain was at Culloden Field, Drummossie Moor, near Inverness on 16 Apr 1746. The last clan battle in Scotland was between Clan Mackintosh and Clan MacDonald at Mulroy, Inverness-shire in 1689. The last battle on English soil was the Battle of Sedgemoor, Somerset on 6 Jul 1685, when the forces of James II defeated the supporters of Charles II's illegitimate son, James Scott (formerly called Fitzroy or Crofts), the Duke of Monmouth (1649–85). During the Jacobite rising of 1745–6, there was a skirmish at Clifton Moor, Cumbria on 18 Dec 1745, when forces under Prince William, Duke of Cumberland (1721–65) brushed with the rebels of Prince Charles Edward Stuart (1720–88). About 12 men were killed on the King's side and five Highlanders. This was a tactical victory for the Jacobites under Lord George Murray.

Bloodiest battle Modern The battle with the greatest recorded number of *military* casualties was the first Battle of the Somme, France, from 1 Jul–19 Nov 1916, with 1 043 896; of these 623 907 were Allied (including 419 654 British) and the rest German. The published German figure of c. 670 000 is not now accepted. Gunfire was heard on Hampstead Heath, London. The greatest death toll in a battle has been estimated at c. 2·1 million in the Battle of Stalingrad, USSR ending with the German surrender on 31 Jan 1943 by Field Marshal Friedrich von Paulus (1890–1957). The Soviet garrison commander was Gen. Vasiliy Chuikov. Additionally, only 1515 civilians from a pre-war population of more than 500 000 were found alive after the battle. The final drive on Berlin, Germany by the Soviet Army and the battle for the city which followed, from 16 Apr–2 May 1945, involved 3·5 million men, 52 000 guns and mortars, 7750 tanks and 11 000 aircraft on both sides.

Ancient Modern historians give no credence, on logistic grounds, to the casualty figures attached to ancient battles, such as the 250 000 reputedly killed at Plataea (Greeks *v.* Persians) in 479 BC or the 200 000 allegedly killed in a single day at Châlons-sur-Marne, France (Huns *v.* Romans) in AD 451.

British The bloodiest battle fought on British soil was the battle of Towton, near Tadcaster, N Yorks on 29 Mar 1461, when 36 000 Yorkists defeated 40 000 Lancastrians. The total loss has been estimated at between 28 000 and 38 000 killed. A figure of 80 000 British dead was attributed by Tacitus to the battle of AD 61 between Queen Boudicca (Boadicea) of the Iceni and the Roman Governor of Britain Suetonius Paulinus, for the reputed loss of only 400 Romans in an army of 10 000. The site of the battle is unknown but may have been near Borough Hill, Daventry, Northants, or more probably near Hampstead Heath, London. Prior to this battle the Romans had lost up to 70 000 in Colchester and London.

Greatest naval battle The greatest number of ships and aircraft ever involved in a sea–air action was 231 ships and 1996 aircraft in the Battle of Leyte Gulf, in the Philippines. It raged from 22–27 Oct 1944, with 166 Allied and 65 Japanese warships engaged, of which 26 Japanese and six US ships were sunk. In addition, 1280 US and 716 Japanese aircraft were engaged. The greatest purely naval battle of modern times was the Battle of Jutland on 31 May 1916, in which 151 Royal Navy warships were involved against 101 German warships. The Royal Navy lost 14 ships and 6097 men and the German fleet 11 ships and 2545 men. The greatest of ancient naval battles was the Battle of Salamis, Greece in September 480 BC. There were an estimated 800 vessels in the defeated Persian fleet and 380 in the victorious fleet of the Athenians and their allies, with a possible involvement of 200 000 men. The death toll at the Battle of Lepanto on 7 Oct 1571 has been estimated at 33 000.

Greatest invasion Seaborne The greatest invasion in military history was the Allied land, air and sea operation against the Normandy coasts of France on D-day, 6 Jun 1944. Thirty-eight convoys of 745 ships moved in on the first three days, supported by 4066 landing craft, carrying 185 000 men, 20 000 vehicles and 347 minesweepers. The air assault comprised 18 000 paratroopers from 1087 aircraft. The 42 available divisions had air support from 13 175 aircraft. Within a month 1 100 000 troops, 200 000 vehicles and 750 000 tons of stores were landed. The Allied invasion of Sicily from 10–12 Jul 1943 involved the landing of 181 000 men in three days.

Airborne The largest airborne invasion was the Anglo-American assault of three divisions (34 000 men), with 2800 aircraft and 1600 gliders, near Arnhem, in the Netherlands, on 17 Sep 1944.

Last on the soil of Great Britain The last invasion of Great Britain occurred on 12 Feb 1797, when the Irish-American adventurer General Tate landed at Carreg Wastad Point, Pembroke (now Dyfed) with 1400 French troops. They surrendered outside Fishguard, a few miles away, to Lord Cawdor's force of the Castlemartin Yeomanry and some local inhabitants armed with pitchforks. The UK Crown Dependency of the Falkland Islands was invaded by Argentine troops on 2 Apr 1982. British troops re-landed at San Carlos on 21 May and accepted the surrender of Brig. Gen. Mario Menéndez 24 days later, on 14 Jun 1982.

Greatest evacuation The greatest evacuation in military history was that carried out by 1200 Allied naval and civil craft from the beach-head at Dunkerque (Dunkirk), France between 27 May and 4 Jun 1940. A total of 338 226 British and French troops were taken off.

Worst sieges The worst siege in history was the 880-day siege of Leningrad, USSR by the German Army from 30 Aug 1941 until 27 Jan 1944. The best estimate is that between 1·3 and 1·5 million defenders and citizens died. This included 641 000 people who died of hunger in the city and 17 000 civilians killed by shelling. More than 150 000 shells and 100 000 bombs were dropped on the city. The longest recorded siege was that of Azotus (now Ashdod), Israel which according to Herodotus was besieged by Psamtik I of Egypt for 29 years in the period 664–610 BC.

Chemical warfare The greatest number of people killed through chemical warfare were the estimated 4000 Kurds who died at Halabja, Iraq in March 1988 when President Saddam Hussein used chemical weapons against Iraq's Kurdish minority for the support it had given to Iran in the Iran–Iraq war.

DEFENCE SPENDING

In 1989 it was estimated that the world's spending on armaments was running at an annual rate of some $1100 billion, or 5·4 per cent of the world's Gross National Product. In 1987 there were 28 123 000 full-time armed forces regulars or conscripts plus 40 289 400 reservists totalling 68 412 400. The budgeted expenditure on defence by the US government for the fiscal year 1990 was $291·4 billion. The defence expenditure of the USSR is given as 70·97 billion roubles in 1990, or $117·48 billion, but Western Intelligence Agencies still maintain that by NATO definition standards, spending is about twice as large as claimed. The UK defence budget for 1990/91 was £20·143 billion.

ARMED FORCES

Largest Numerically the largest regular armed force in the world is that of the USSR, with 3 988 000 (1990). China's People's Liberation Army's strength in 1990 was estimated to be 3 030 000 (comprising land, sea and air forces), with reductions continuing. Her reserves number around 1·2 million and her paramilitary forces of armed and unarmed militias are estimated by the International Institute for Strategic Studies at 'some 12 million'. The USA's military manpower is 2 117 900 (1990) and that of the UK 306 000 (1990).

Navies Largest The largest navy in the world in terms of manpower is the United States Navy, with a manpower of 590 500 plus 195 300 Marines in mid-1990. The active strength in 1990 included six nuclear-powered aircraft carriers, with nine others, four battleships, 34 Ballistic Missile submarines, 90 nuclear attack submarines and one diesel attack submarine, 43 cruisers, 59 destroyers, 100 frigates and 65 amphibious warfare ships. The navy of the USSR has a larger submarine fleet of 323 vessels (including 63 nuclear attack). It also has five aircraft carriers, 43 cruisers, 31 destroyers, 148 frigates and 77 amphibious warfare ships.

The strength of the Royal Navy in mid-1990 included 3 *Invincible* class carriers, 4 nuclear submarines with strategic nuclear missiles, 17 other nuclear and 11 diesel attack submarines, 13 guided weapon destroyers and 35 frigates. The uniformed strength was 63 500, including The Fleet Air Arm and Royal Marines (7600), in 1990. In 1914 the Royal Navy had 542 warships including 72 capital ships with 16 building, making it the largest navy in the world at the time.

Longest-serving admiral Admiral of the Fleet Sir Provo Wallis (1791–1892)

Shortest war

The shortest war on record was that between the UK and Zanzibar (now part of Tanzania), which lasted from 9:02 to 9:40 a.m. on 27 Aug 1896. The UK battle fleet under Rear-Admiral (later Admiral Sir) Harry Rawson (1843–1910) delivered an ultimatum to the self-appointed Sultan Sa'īd Khalid to evacuate his palace and surrender. This was not forthcoming until after 38 minutes of bombardment. Admiral Rawson received the Brilliant Star of Zanzibar (first class) from Hamud ibn Muhammad, the new Sultan. It was proposed at one time that elements of the local populace should be compelled to defray the cost of the broadsides fired.

Youngest conscripts

President Francisco Macias Nguema of Equatorial Guinea (deposed in August 1979) decreed in March 1976 compulsory military service for all boys aged between seven and 14. The edict stated that any parent refusing to hand over his or her son 'will be imprisoned or shot'.

Longest march

A team of the 29 Commando Regiment, each man carrying a 18·14 kg *40 lb* pack, including a rifle, covered the Plymouth Marathon in 4 hr 35 min 47·28 sec on 1 Nov 1987.

Army drill

On 8–9 Jul 1987 a 90-man squad of the Queen's Colour Squadron, RAF performed a total of 2 722 662 drill movements (2 001 384 rifle and 721 278 foot) at RAF Uxbridge, Middx from memory and without a word of command in 23 hr 55 min.

■ **H-Bombs**
The largest US H-bomb tested was the 18–22 megaton Bravo, *exploded at Bikini Atoll, Marshall Islands on 1 Mar 1954.*
(Photo: United Nations, New York)

first served on HMS *Cleopatra* in October 1804. Because of his service on HMS *Cleopatra* in 1805 against the French he was kept on the active list in 1870 for life. He was thus 87 years 4 months on paid active service, though he was earlier on the books as a volunteer for a further nine years from 1795–1804 — a system by which even infants could gain seniority on joining.

Armies *Oldest* The oldest army in the world is the 80–90 strong Pontifical Swiss Guard in the Vatican City, with a regular foundation dating back to 21 Jan 1506. Its origins, however, predate 1400.

Largest Numerically, the world's largest army is that of the People's Republic of China, with a total strength of some 2·3 million in mid-1990. The total size of the USSR's army in mid-1990 was estimated by the International Institute for Strategic Studies at 1 473 000 men (including 27 000–30 000 Spetsnaz), believed to be organized into 197 divisions. The strength of the British Army in early 1991 was 149 541. The basic strength maintained in Northern Ireland was 10 657. Between 1969 and April 1991, 1967 civilians and 898 armed forces and police personnel had been killed in the province.

Oldest soldiers The oldest 'old soldier' of all time was probably John B. Salling of the army of the Confederate States of America and the last accepted survivor of the US Civil War (1861–65). He died in Kingsport, Tennessee, USA on 16 Mar 1959, aged 113 years 1 day. The oldest Chelsea pensioner, based *only* on the evidence of his tombstone, was 111-year-old William Hiseland (6 Aug 1620–7 Feb 1732). The longest-serving British soldier has been Field Marshal Sir William Gomm (1784–1875), who was an ensign in 1794 and Constable of the Tower of London over 80 years later at his death aged 91.

Youngest soldiers Marshal Duke of Caxias (25 Aug 1803–7 May 1880), Brazilian military hero and statesman, entered his infantry regiment at the age of five in 1808. Probably the youngest enlistment in the 20th century was that of William Frederick Price (b. 1 Jun 1891), who was

enlisted into the army at Aldershot on 23 May 1903, aged 11 years 356 days.

Tallest soldiers The tallest soldier of all time was Väinö Myllyrinne (1909–63), who was conscripted into the Finnish Army when he was 2·21 m *7 ft 3 in* and later grew to 2·51 m *8 ft 3 in*. The British Army's tallest soldier was Benjamin Crow, who was signed on at Lichfield, Staffs in November 1947 when he was 2·15 m *7 ft 1 in* tall. Edward Evans (1924–58), who later grew to 2·35 m *7 ft 8½ in*, was in the army when he was 2·08 m *6 ft 10 in*.

British regimental records The oldest regular regiment in the British Army is the Royal Scots, raised in French service in 1633, though the Buffs (Royal East Kent Regiment) can trace their origin to independent companies in Dutch pay as early as 1572. The Coldstream Guards, raised in 1650, were, however, placed on the establishment of the British Army before the Royal Scots and the Buffs. The oldest armed body in the UK is the Queen's Bodyguard of the Yeomen of the Guard, formed in 1485. The Honourable Artillery Company, senior regiment of the Territorial Army, formed from the Fraternity of St George, Southwark, London received its charter from Henry VIII in 1537 but this lapsed until it was re-formed in 1610. The infantry regiment with most battle honours is the Royal Highland Fusiliers (Princess Margaret's Own Glasgow and Ayrshire Regiment), with 208. The most senior regiment of the Reserve Army is the Royal Monmouthshire Royal Engineers (Militia), formed on 21 Mar 1577 and never disbanded, with battle honours at Dunkirk, 1940 and Normandy, 1944.

Greatest mutiny In World War I, 56 French divisions comprising some 650 000 men and their officers, refused orders on the Western Front sector of General Robert Nivelle in April 1917 after the failure of his offensive.

Longest march The longest march in military history was the famous Long March by the Chinese Communists in 1934–35. In 368 days, of which 268 days

were days of movement, from October to October, their force of some 100 000 covered 9650 km *6000 miles* from Juichin, in Kiangsi to Yenan, in Shensi. They crossed 18 mountain ranges and 24 rivers, and eventually reached Yenan with only about 8000 surviors following continual rearguard actions against nationalist Kuomintang (KMT) forces.

On the night of 12–13 Sep 1944 a team of nine from B Company 4th Infantry Battalion of the Irish Army made a night march of 67·59 km *42 miles* in full battle order carrying 18·1 kg *40 lb* in 11 hr 49 min.

Air forces Oldest The earliest autonomous air force is the Royal Air Force, which can be traced back to 1878, when the War Office commissioned the building of a military balloon. The Royal Engineers Balloon Section and Depot was formed in 1890 and the Air Battalion of the Royal Engineers followed on 1 Apr 1911. On 13 May 1912 the Royal Flying Corps was formed, with both Military and Naval Wings, the latter being renamed the Royal Naval Air Service. The Royal Air Force was formed on 1 Apr 1918 from the RFC and the RNAS, and took its place alongside the Royal Navy and the Army as a separate service with its own Ministry. The Prussian Army used a balloon near Strasbourg, France as early as 24 Sep 1870.

Largest The greatest air force of all time was the United States Army Air Corps (now the US Air Force), which had 79 908 aircraft in July 1944 and 2 411 294 personnel in March 1944. The US Air Force, including strategic missile forces, had 571 000 and 7642 aircraft personnel in early 1990. The USSR Air Force had 420 000 men in mid-1990. It had 10 723 aircraft. In addition, the USSR's Offensive Strategic Rocket Forces had about 260 000 operational personnel in mid-1990. The strength of the Royal Air Force in 1990 was 89 600, with 65 operational squadrons.

BOMBS

Heaviest The heaviest conventional bomb ever used operationally was the Royal Air Force's *Grand Slam*, weighing 9975 kg *22 000 lb* and measuring 7·74 m *25 ft 5 in* long, dropped on Bielefeld railway viaduct, Germany on 14 Mar 1945. In 1949 the United States Air Force tested a bomb weighing 19 050 kg *42 000 lb* at Muroc Dry Lake, California, USA. The heaviest known nuclear bomb was the MK 17 carried by US B-36 bombers in the mid-1950s. It weighed 19 050 kg *42 000 lb* and was 7·37 m *24 ft 6 in* long.

Atomic The first atom bomb dropped on Hiroshima, Japan by the United States at 8:16 a.m. on 6 Aug 1945 had an explosive power equivalent to that of 12·5 kilotons of trinitrotoluene ($C_7H_5O_6N_3$), called TNT. Code-named *Little Boy*, it was 3·04 m *10 ft* long and weighed 4080 kg *9000 lb*. It burst c. 580 m *1900 ft* above the city centre. The most powerful thermonuclear device so far tested is one with a power equivalent to that of 57 megatons of TNT, detonated by the USSR in the Novaya Zemlya area at 8:33 a.m. GMT on 30 Oct 1961. The shockwave circled the world three times, taking 36 hr 27 min for the first circuit. Some estimates put the power of this device at between 62 and 90 megatons. The largest US H-bomb tested was the 18–22 megaton *Bravo*, exploded at Bikini Atoll, Marshall Islands on 1 Mar 1954. On 9 Aug 1961, Nikita Khrushchev, then the Chairman of the Council of Ministers of the USSR, declared that the Soviet Union was capable of constructing a 100-megaton bomb, and

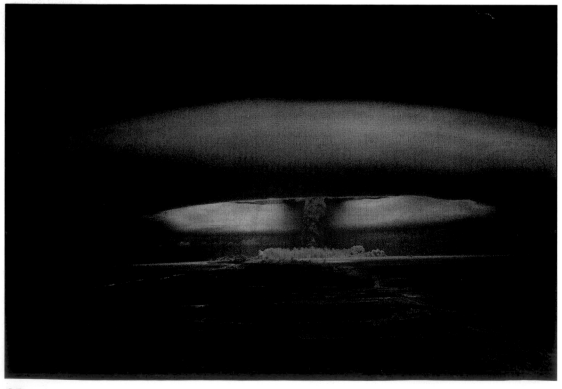

announced the possession of one during a visit to what was then East Berlin, East Germany on 16 Jan 1963. Such a device could make a crater in rock 107 m *355 ft* deep and 2·9 km *1·8 miles* wide, with a fireball 13·9 km *8·6 miles* in diameter.

Largest nuclear weapons The most powerful ICBM (inter-continental ballistic missile) is the USSR's SS-18 (Model 5), believed to be armed with 10 750-kiloton MIRVs (multiple independently targetable re-entry vehicles). Earlier models had a single 20-megaton warhead. The US Titan II carrying a W-53 warhead was rated at 5–9 megatons but has now been withdrawn, leaving the 1–2 megaton W-56 as the most powerful US weapon.

Largest 'conventional' explosion The largest use of conventional explosive was for the demolition of the fortifications and U-boat pens at Helgoland, Germany on 18 Apr 1947. A net charge of 4061 tonnes (7122 tonnes gross) was detonated by Commissioned Gunner E.C. Jellis of the naval team headed by Lt F.T. Woosnam RN aboard HMS *Lasso* lying 14·5 km *9 miles* out to sea.

TANKS

Earliest The first tank was *No. 1 Lincoln*, modified to become *Little Willie*, built by William Foster & Co. Ltd of Lincoln. It first ran on 6 Sep 1915. Tanks were first taken into action by the Heavy Section, Machine Gun Corps, which later became the Royal Tank Corps, at the Battle of Flers-Courcelette in France on 15 Sep 1916. The Mark I Male tank, armed with a pair of 6-pounder guns and four machine guns, weighed 28·4 tonnes and was driven by a motor developing 105 hp, which gave it a maximum road speed of 4·8–6·4 km/h *3–4 mph*.

Heaviest and fastest The heaviest tank ever constructed was the German Panzer Kampfwagen Maus II, which weighed 192 tonnes. By 1945 it had reached only the experimental stage and was not developed further. The heaviest operational tank used by any army was the 75·2 tonne 13-man French Char de Rupture 2C bis of 1922. It carried a 155-mm howitzer and had two 250 hp engines giving a maximum speed of 12 km/h *8 mph*. The world's most heavily armed tank since 1972 has been the Soviet T-72, with a 125 mm *4⅞ in* high velocity gun. The British AVRE *Centurion* has a 165 mm *6½ in* low-velocity demolition gun. The world's fastest tank is the British Scorpion AFV, which can touch 80 km/h *50 mph* with a 75 per cent payload.

The heaviest British armoured vehicle ever built was the 79-tonne prototype 'Tortoise'. With a crew of seven and a designed speed of 19 km/h *12 mph*, this tank had a width 5 cm *2 in* less than that of the one-time operational 66-tonne 'Conqueror'.

GUNS

Earliest Although it cannot be accepted as proven, it is believed that the earliest guns were constructed in both China and in north Africa in c. 1250. The earliest representation of an English gun is contained in an illustrated manuscript dated 1326, now at Oxford. The earliest anti-aircraft gun was an artillery piece on a high-angle mounting used in the Franco-Prussian War of 1870 by the Prussians against French balloons.

Largest The largest gun ever constructed was used by the Germans in the siege of Sevastopol, USSR in July 1942. It was of a calibre of 800 mm *31½ in* with a barrel 28·87 m *94 ft 8½ in* long. Internally it was

named *Schwerer Gustav*, and was one of three guns which were given the general name of *Dora*, although the other two were not finished and so were not used in action. It was built by Krupp, and its remains were discovered near Metzenhof, Bavaria in August 1945. The whole assembly of the gun was 42·9 m *141 ft* long and weighed 1344 tonnes, with a crew of 1500. The range for an 8·1 tonne projectile was 46·67 km *29 miles.*

During World War I the British Army used a gun of 457 mm *18 in* calibre. The barrel alone weighed 127 tonnes. In World War II the *Bochebuster*, a train-mounted howitzer with a calibre of 457 mm *18 in* firing a 1133 kg *2500 lb* shell to a maximum range of 20 850 m *22 800 yd*, was used from 1940 onwards as part of the Kent coast defences.

Greatest range The greatest range ever attained by a gun was achieved by the HARP (High Altitude Research Project) gun, consisting of two 419 mm *16½ in* calibre barrels in tandem 36·4 m *119·4 ft* long and weighing 150 tonnes, at Yuma, Arizona, USA. On 19 Nov 1966 an 84 kg *185 lb* projectile was fired to an altitude of 180 km *111·8 miles* or *590 550 ft*. The static V3 underground firing tubes built in 50° shafts near Mimoyècques, near Calais, France to bombard London were never operative.

The famous long-range gun which shelled Paris in World War I was the *Kaiser Wilhelm Geschütz*, with a calibre of 210 mm *8¼ in*, a designed range of 127·9 km *79½ miles* and an achieved range of 122 km *76 miles* from the Forest of Crépy in March 1918. The *Big Berthas* were mortars of 420 mm *16·53 in* calibre and with a range of less than 14·5 km *9 miles.*

Mortars The largest mortars ever constructed were Mallet's mortar (Woolwich Arsenal, London, 1857) and the *Little David* of World War II, made in the USA. Each had a calibre of 914 mm *36 in*, but neither was ever used in action. The heaviest mortar employed was the tracked German 600 mm *23·6 in* siege piece *Karl*, of which there were seven such mortars built. Only six of these were actually used in action, although never all at the same time, at Sevastopol, USSR in 1942, at Warsaw, Poland in 1944, and at Budapest, Hungary, also in 1944.

Largest cannon The highest-calibre cannon ever constructed is the *Tsar Pushka* (*King of Cannons*), now housed in the Kremlin, Moscow, USSR. It was built in the 16th century with a bore of 920 mm *36·2 in* and a barrel 3·18 m *10 ft 5 in* long. It weighs 39·4 tonnes or 2400 *poods (sic)*. The Turks fired up to seven shots per day from a bombard 7·92 m *26 ft* long, with an internal calibre of 1066 mm *42 in*, against the walls of Constantinople (now Istanbul) from 12 Apr–29 May 1453. It was dragged by 60 oxen and 200 men and fired a 543 kg *1200 lb* stone cannon ball.

Military engines The largest military catapults, or onagers, could throw a missile weighing 27 kg *60 lb* a distance of 457 m *500 yd.*

Conscientious objector *Most obdurate* The only conscientious objector to be six times court-martialled in World War II was Gilbert Lane of Wallington, Surrey. He served 31 months' detention and 183 days' imprisonment.

Nuclear delivery vehicles As of mid-1990 the USSR deployed 2497 nuclear delivery launchers compared to the USA's 1930 as counted under the START (Strategic Arms Reduction Talks) rules and

compared to the START proposed limit of 1600. Again under START counting rules, the USSR could deliver a maximum of 11 641 warheads and the USA 13 398, but this is a theoretical total and not necessarily the number held. The START proposed limit for nuclear warheads is 6000.

Education

Compulsory education was first introduced in 1819 in Prussia. It became compulsory in the UK in 1870.

University *Oldest* The Sumerians had scribal schools or *É-Dub-ba* soon after 3500 BC. The oldest existing educational institution in the world is the University of Karueein, founded in AD 859 in Fez, Morocco. The University of Bologna, the oldest in Europe, was founded in 1088.

The oldest university in the UK is the University of Oxford, which came into being c. 1167. The oldest of the existing colleges is probably University College (1249), though its foundation is less well documented than that of Merton in 1264. The earliest college at Cambridge University is Peterhouse, founded in 1284. The largest college at either university is Trinity College, Cambridge, founded in 1546. The oldest university in Scotland is the University of St Andrews, Fife. Established as a university in 1410, theology and medicine may have been taught there since c. AD 900.

Greatest enrolment The university with the greatest enrolment in the world is the University of Rome, Italy (founded 1303), which had 180 000 students in 1987, although the number had declined to 166 000 by 1990. Britain's largest university is the University of London, with 54 521 internal students and 24 856 external students (1988/89), totalling 79 377. The Open University at Walton Hall near Milton Keynes, Bucks was first called the University of the Air and was granted a Royal Charter on 30 May 1969. In 1990 it supported 84 196 undergraduate and associate registered students following undergraduate or diploma in education courses, 4786 postgraduate students and 15 817 student-course registrations for associate short-courses. There were 2867 full-time staff and 5705 tutorial and counselling staff, most of whom held full-time posts with other universities and colleges.

EDUCATION

Largest The largest existing university building in the world is the M.V. Lomonosov State University on the Lenin Hills, south of Moscow, USSR. It stands 240 m 787 ft 5 in tall, and has 32 storeys and 40 000 rooms. It was constructed from 1949–53.

Professor Youngest The youngest at which anybody has been elected to a chair in a university is 19 years in the case of Colin MacLaurin (1698–1746), who was elected to Marischal College, Aberdeen as Professor of Mathematics on 30 Sep 1717. In 1725 he was made Professor of Mathematics at Edinburgh University on the recommendation of Sir Isaac Newton (1642–1727), who was a professor at Cambridge at the age of 26. Henry Phillpotts (1778–1869) became a don at Magdalen College, Oxford on 25 Jul 1795 aged 17 years 80 days.

Most durable Dr Joel Hildebrand (1881–1983), Professor Emeritus of Physical Chemistry at the University of California, Berkeley, USA, first became an assistant professor in 1913 and published his 275th research paper 68 years later in 1981. The longest period for which any professorship has been held in Britain is 63 years in the case of Thomas Martyn (1735–1825), Professor of Botany at Cambridge University from 1762 until his death. The last professor-for-life was the pathologist Prof. Henry Roy Dean (1879–1961) for his last 39 years at Cambridge.

Most graduates in family Mr and Mrs Harold Erickson of Naples, Florida, USA saw all of their 14 children — 11 sons and three daughters — obtain university or college degrees between 1962 and 1978.

Youngest undergraduate and graduate The most extreme recorded case of undergraduate juvenility was that of William Thomson (1824–1907), later Lord Kelvin, who entered Glasgow University at the age of 10 years 4 months in October 1834 and matriculated on 14 November the same year. Adragon Eastwood De Mello (b. 5 Oct 1976) of Santa Cruz, California, USA obtained his BA in Mathematics from the University of California in Santa Cruz on 11 Jun 1988 at the age of 11 years 8 months.

Ganesh Sittampalam (b. 1979) of Surbiton, Surrey became Britain's youngest undergraduate when he started a BSc mathematics degree course at the University of Surrey at the age of 11 years 8 months in October 1990.

Youngest doctorate On 13 Apr 1814 the mathematician Carl Witte of Lochau was made a Doctor of Philosophy of the University of Giessen, Germany when aged 12.

School Oldest in Britain The title of the oldest existing school in Britain is contested. It is claimed that King's School in Canterbury, Kent was a foundation of St Augustine, some time between his arrival in Kent in AD 597 and his death c. 604. Cor Tewdws (College of Theodosius) at Llantwit Major, South Glamorgan, reputedly burnt down in AD 446, was refounded, after a lapse of 62 years, by St Illtyd in 508, and flourished into the 13th century. Winchester College was founded in 1382. Lanark Grammar School claims to have been referred to in a papal bull drawn up in 1183 by Lucius III.

Largest In 1988/89 Rizal High School, Pasig, Manila, Philippines had an enrolment of 16 458 regular students, although by the school year 1990/91 the number had declined to 15 947.

The school with the most pupils in Great Britain was Banbury Comprehensive, Oxon with 2767 in the 1975 summer term. In 1990/91 Exmouth Community College, Devon had the most pupils, with 2036.

The highest enrolment in Scotland has been at Our Lady's Roman Catholic High School, Motherwell, Lanarkshire, with a peak of 2317 in August 1977. The highest enrolment in 1990/91 was at Holyrood School, Glasgow, Strathclyde, with 1716 pupils.

The total in the Holy Child School, Belfast, Northern Ireland reached 2752 in 1973 before the school was split up. The highest enrolment in 1989/90 was 2519 at St Louise's Comprehensive College, Belfast.

Most expensive The annual cost of keeping a pupil at the Gstaad International School, Gstaad, Switzerland (founded 1974) in 1988/89 was FF200 000 (£21 600). The school is run by Alain Souperbiet, its founder.

In the academic year 1991/92 St Andrew's Private Tutorial Centre, Cambridge (co-founders W.A. Duncombe and C.T. Easterbrook) charges £13 230 for full-time science students (predominantly individual tuition plus accommodation).

Oldest PTA The parent–teacher association with the earliest known foundation date in Britain is that for Lawrence Sheriff School, Rugby, Warks, formed in 1908.

Most schools The greatest documented number of schools attended by a pupil is 265, by Wilma Williams, now Mrs R.J. Horton, from 1933–43 when her parents were in show business in the USA.

Most O and A levels Since 1965 Dr Francis L. Thomason of Hammersmith, London has accumulated 70 O and O/A levels, 16 A levels and 1 S level, making a total of 87, of which 36 have been in the top grade. A.F. Prime, a prisoner in HM Open Prison, Sudbury, Suffolk accumulated a total of 1 S level, 14 A levels and 34 O levels between 1968 and 1982. Environmental difficulties tend to make study harder in prison than elsewhere.

The highest number of top-grade A levels attained at one sitting is seven, by Stephen Murrell of Crown Woods School, Eltham, London in June 1978, out of eight passes. Robert Pidgeon (b. 7 Feb 1959) of St Peter's School, Bournemouth, Dorset secured 13 O level passes at grade A at one sitting in the summer of 1975, and subsequently passed three A levels at grade A and two S levels with firsts. Nicholas Barberis achieved a total of 27 top grades while at Eltham College, London, passing 20 O/AO levels and 7 A levels, all at grade A, between 1984 and 1988.

Youngest A level pass Ganesh Sittampalam (b. February 1979) of Surbiton, Surrey is the youngest person to have passed an A level, achieving grade A in both Mathematics and Further Mathematics in June 1988, when aged 9 years 4 months.

Youngest headmaster The youngest headmaster of a major public school was Henry Montagu Butler (b. 2 Jul 1833), appointed Headmaster of Harrow School on 16 Nov 1859 at the age of 26 years 137 days. His first term in office began in January 1860.

Most durable don Dr Martin Joseph Routh (1755–1854) was President of Magdalen College, Oxford from April 1791 for 63 years 8 months, until his death in his 100th year on 22 Dec 1854. He had previously been a Fellow for 16 years and was thus a don for a span of 79 years.

Most durable Fellow Tressilian Nicholas (1888–1989) was a Fellow of Trinity College, Cambridge for a total of 76 years, from 1912 to 1918 and 1919 until his death in 1989.

Most durable teachers David Rhys Davies (1835–1928) taught as a pupil teacher and subsequently a teacher and headmaster for a total of 76 years. Most of his teaching was done at Talybont-on-Usk School, near Brecon, Powys (1856–79) and at Dame Anna Child's School, Whitton, Powys. The teaching career of Col. Ernest Achey Loftus (1884–1987) spanned a total of 73 years. He started teaching in May 1901 in York, and in 1953, four years after retiring, went out to Africa. There he served as an assistant master in schools in Kenya, Malawi and finally Zambia, retiring as the world's oldest civil servant at the age of 91 years 38 days on 18 Feb 1975. Elsie Marguerite Touzel (1889–1984) of Jersey, Channel Islands began her teaching career aged 16 in 1905 and taught at various schools in Jersey until her retirement 75 years later on 30 Sep 1980.

Highest endowment The greatest single gift in the history of higher education has been $125 million, to Louisiana State University by C.B. Pennington in 1983.

Religions

Oldest Human burial, which has religious connotations, is known from *c.* 60 000 BC among *Homo sapiens neanderthalensis* in the Shanidar cave, northern Iraq.

Largest Religious statistics are necessarily only approximate. The test of adherence to a religion varies widely in rigour, while many individuals, particularly in the East, belong to two or more religions.

Christianity is the world's prevailing religion, with some 1 711 897 000 adherents in 1989, or 33·0 per cent of the world's population. In 1989 there were 890 907 000 Roman Catholics, or 17·5 per cent of the world's population in the same year. The largest non-Christian religion is Islam (Muslim) with some 880 555 000 followers in 1988.

In the UK the Anglicans comprise members of the Established Church of England, the Dis-established Church in Wales, the Episcopal Church in Scotland and the Church of Ireland. The Church of England has 2 provinces (Canterbury and York), 44 dioceses, 10 480 full-time diocesan clergymen and 13 155 parishes (end of 1990). In Scotland the largest membership is that of the Church of Scotland (12 synods, 46 presbyteries), which had 804 468 members at 31 Dec 1989.

Largest clergies The world's largest religious organization is the Roman Catholic Church, with 144 cardinals, 738 archbishops, 3224 bishops, 401 930 priests and 893 418 nuns in 1989.

Jews The total of world Jewry is estimated to be 18·2 million. The highest concentration is in the USA, with 5 944 000. The total in Israel is 3 537 000. The total of British Jewry is 330 000 of whom 201 000 are in London and 11 000 in Glasgow, the largest concentration in Scotland. The total in Tokyo, Japan is only 750.

PLACES OF WORSHIP

Earliest Many archaeologists are of the opinion that the decorated Upper Palaeolithic caves of Europe (*c.* 30 000–10 000 BC) were used as places of worship or religious ritual. Claims have been made that the El Juyo cave, northern Spain contains an actual shrine, dated to *c.* 12 000 BC. The oldest surviving Christian church in the world is a converted house in Qal'at es Salihiye (formerly Douro-Europos) in eastern Syria, dating from AD 232.

Oldest Great Britain The earliest Christian church in the UK was at Colchester, Essex and was built *c.* AD 320. Its ruins can still be seen next to the modern police station. The oldest surviving ecclesiastical building in the UK is a 6th-century cell built by St Brendan in AD 542 on Eileachan Naoimh (pronounced 'Noo'), Garvelloch Islands, Argyllshire. The church in Great Britain with the oldest origins is St Martin's Church in Canterbury, Kent. It was

built in AD 560 on the foundations of a first-century Roman temple. The chapel of St Peter on the Wall, Bradwell-on-Sea, Essex was built from AD 654–660. The oldest church in Ireland is the Gallerus Oratory, built c. AD 750 at Ballyferriter, near Kilmalkedar, Co. Kerry. Britain's oldest nunnery is St Peter and Paul Minster, on the Isle of Thanet, Kent. It was founded c. AD 748 by the Abbess Eadburga of Bugga. The oldest Roman Catholic church is St Etheldreda, Ely Place, Holborn, London, founded in 1251. The oldest non-conformist chapel is the thatched chapel at Horningsham, Wilts, dated 1566.

Largest temple The largest religious structure ever built is Angkor Wat ('City Temple'), enclosing 162·6 ha *402 acres* in Cambodia (formerly Kampuchea), southeast Asia. It was built to the Hindu god Vishnu by the Khmer King Suryavarman II in the period 1113–50. Its curtain wall measures 1280 × 1280 m *4199 × 4199 ft* and its population, before it was abandoned in 1432, was 80 000. The whole complex of 72 major monuments, begun c. AD 900, extends over 24 × 8 km *15 × 5 miles*.

The largest Buddhist temple in the world is Borobudur, near Jogjakarta, Indonesia, built in the 8th century. It is 31·5 m *103 ft* tall and 123 m *403 ft* square.

The largest Mormon temple is the Salt Lake Temple, Utah, USA, dedicated on 6 Apr 1893, with a floor area of 23 505 m² *253 015 ft²* or *5·8 acres*.

Largest cathedral The world's largest cathedral is the cathedral church of the Diocese of New York, St John the Divine, with a floor area of 11 240 m² *121 000 ft²* and a volume of 476 350 m³ *16 822 000 ft³*. The cornerstone was laid on 27 Dec 1892, and work on the Gothic building was stopped in 1941. Work restarted in earnest in July 1979. In New York it is referred to as 'St John the Unfinished'. The nave is the longest in the world at 183·18 m *601 ft* in length, with a vaulting 37·79 m *124 ft* in height.

The cathedral covering the largest area is that of Santa Mariá de la Sede in Sevilla

■ **Fastest elected Pope**

(Seville), Spain. It was built in Spanish Gothic style between 1402 and 1519, and is 126·18 m *414 ft* long, 82·60 m *271 ft* wide and 30·48 m *100 ft* high to the vault of the nave.

The largest cathedral in the British Isles is the Cathedral Church of Christ in Liverpool. It was built in modernized Gothic style, and work was begun on 18 Jul 1904; it was finally consecrated on 25 Oct 1978 after 74 years (cf. Exeter Cathedral, 95 years). Half a million stone blocks and 12 million bricks were used in its construction and the actual cost was some £6 million. The building encloses 9687 m² *104 275 ft²* and has an overall length of 193·85 m *636 ft*. The Vestey Tower is 100·88 m *331 ft* high. It contains the highest vaulting in the world — 53·34 m *175 ft* maximum at undertower, and the highest Gothic arches ever built, being 32·61 m *107 ft* at apexes.

Smallest The smallest church in the world designated as a cathedral is that of the Christ Catholic Church, Highlandville, Missouri, USA. It was consecrated in July 1983. It measures 4·26 × 5·18 m *14 × 17 ft* and has seating for 18 people.

The smallest cathedral in use in the UK is Cumbrae Cathedral (the Cathedral of the diocese of the Isles) at Millport on the isle of Cumbrae, Strathclyde, which was built in 1849–51. The nave measures only 12·19 × 6·09 m *40 × 20 ft* and the total floor area is 197·3 m² *2124 ft²*.

Largest church The largest church in the world is the Basilica of St Peter, built between 1506 and 1614 in the Vatican City, Rome, Italy. Its length, including the walls of the apse and façade, is 218·7 m *717 ft 6 in*. The area is 23 000 m² *247 572 ft²*. The inner diameter of the famous dome is 42·56 m *139 ft 8 in* and its centre is 119·88 m *393 ft 4 in* high. The external height is 136·57 m *448 ft 1 in*. Taller, although not as tall as the cathedral in Ulm, Germany (see 'Tallest spire'), is the Basilica of Our Lady of Peace

(Notre Dame de la Paix) at Yamoussoukro, Côte d'Ivoire, completed in 1989. Including its golden cross, it is 158 m *519 ft* high.

The elliptical basilica of St Pie X at Lourdes, France, completed in 1957 at a cost of £2 million, has a capacity of 20 000 under its giant span arches and a length of 200 m *656 ft*.

The largest church in the UK is the Collegiate Church of St Peter in Westminster, usually referred to as Westminster Abbey, which was built between AD 1050–1745. Its maximum length is 161·5 m *530 ft*, the breadth across the transept 61·87 m *203 ft* and the internal height 30·98 m *101 ft 8 in*. The largest parish church is the Parish Church of the Most Holy and Undivided Trinity at Kingston-upon-Hull, Humberside covering 2530 m² *27 235 ft²* and with an external length and width of 87·7 × 37·7 m *288 × 124 ft*. It is also believed to be the country's oldest brick building serving its original purpose, dating from *c*. 1285. Both the former Cathedral of St Mungo, Glasgow and Beverley Minster, Humberside are now used as parish churches. The largest school chapel is that of Lancing College, W Sussex. It is 45·7 m *150 ft* high and has a capacity of 600.

Longest The crypt of the underground Civil War Memorial Church in the Guadarrama Mountains, 45 km *28 miles* from Madrid, Spain, is 260 m *853 ft* in length. It took 21 years (1937–58) to build, at a

reported cost of £140 million, and is surmounted by a cross 150 m *492 ft* tall.

Smallest church The world's smallest church is the chapel of Santa Isabel de Hungría, in Colomares, a monument to Christopher Columbus at Benalmádena, Málaga, Spain. It is an irregular shape and has a total floor area of 1·96 m² *21⅛ ft²*.

The smallest church in Great Britain is St Gobban's Church in Portbradden, Co. Antrim. It measures 3·7 × 2·0 m *12 ft 1½ in × 6 ft 6 in*. The smallest church in use in England is Bremilham Church, Cowage Farm, Foxley, near Malmesbury, Wilts which measures 3·65 × 3·65 m *12 × 12 ft* and is used for service once a year. The smallest complete medieval English church in regular use is that at Culbone, Somerset, which measures 10·66 × 3·65 m *35 × 12 ft*. The smallest Welsh chapel is St Trillo's Chapel, Rhôs-on-Sea (Llandrillo-yn-Rhos), Clwyd, measuring only 3·65 × 1·83 m *12 × 6 ft*. The smallest chapel in Scotland is St Margaret's, Edinburgh, measuring 5·02 × 3·20 m *16½ × 10½ ft*, giving a floor area of 16·09 m² *173¼ ft²*.

Largest synagogue The largest synagogue in the world is the Temple Emanu-El on Fifth Avenue at 65th Street, New York City, USA. The temple, completed in September 1929, has a frontage of 45·72 m *150 ft* on Fifth Avenue and 77·11 m *253 ft* on 65th Street. The sanctuary proper can accommodate 2500 people, and the adjoining Beth-El Chapel seats 350. When all the facilities are

in use, more than 6000 people can be accommodated.

The largest synagogue in Great Britain is the Edgware Synagogue, Barnet, London, completed in 1959, with seating for 1630. That with the highest registered membership is Ilford Synagogue, London with 2210 in June 1989.

Largest mosque The largest mosque is Shah Faisal Mosque, near Islamabad, Pakistan. The total area of the complex is 18·97 ha *46·87 acres*, with the covered area of the prayer hall being 0·48 ha *1·19 acres*. It can accommodate 100 000 worshippers in the prayer hall and the courtyard, and a further 200 000 people in the adjacent grounds.

Tallest minaret The tallest minaret in the world is that of the Great Hassan II Mosque, Casablanca, Morocco, measuring 175·6 m *576 ft*. The cost of construction of the mosque was £218 million. Of ancient minarets the tallest is the Qutb Minar, south of New Delhi, India, built in 1194 to a height of 72·54 m *238 ft*.

Tallest and oldest pagoda The world's tallest pagoda is the Phra Pathom Chedi at Nakhon Pathom, Thailand, which was built for King Mongkut between 1853 and 1870. It rises to 115 m *377 ft*. The oldest pagoda in China is Sung-Yo Ssu in Honan, built with 15 12-sided storeys in AD 523. The 99·3 m *326 ft* tall Shwedagon Pagoda, Yangon (formerly Rangoon), Myanmar

■ **Largest church**
The largest church in the world is the Basilica of St Peter, built between 1506 and 1614 in the Vatican City, Rome, Italy. Its length, including the walls of the apse and façade, is 218·7 m 717 ft 6 in. The area is 23 000 m² 247 572 ft². (Photo: Spectrum)

Singing

Acharya Prem Bhikshuji (d. 18 Apr 1970) started chanting the Akhand Rama-Dhoon at Jamnagar, Gujarat, India on 31 Jul 1964 and devotees were still continuing in May 1990.

(formerly Burma) is built on the site of a 8·2 m *27 ft* tall pagoda of 585 BC.

Sacred object The sacred object with the highest intrinsic value is the 15th-century gold Buddha in Wat Trimitr Temple in Bangkok, Thailand. It is 3·04 m *10 ft* tall and weighs an estimated 5½ tonnes. At the March 1991 price of £203 per fine ounce, its intrinsic worth was £20·2 million. The gold under the plaster exterior was found only in 1954.

Longest nave The longest nave in the UK is that of St Albans Cathedral, which is 86·86 m *285 ft* long. The central tower of Liverpool's Anglican Cathedral (internal overall length 193·85 m *636 ft*) interrupts the nave with an undertower space.

Tallest spire The tallest cathedral spire in the world is that of the Protestant Cathedral of Ulm in Germany. The building is early Gothic and was begun in 1377. The tower, in the centre of the west façade, was not finally completed until 1890 and is 160·90 m *528 ft* high. The world's tallest church spire is that of the Chicago Temple of the First Methodist Church on Clark Street, Chicago, Illinois, USA. The building consists of a 22-storey skyscraper (erected in 1924) surmounted by a parsonage at 100·5 m *330 ft*, a 'Sky Chapel' at 121·92 m *400 ft* and a steeple cross at 173·12 m *568 ft* above street level.

The highest spire in Great Britain is that of the church of St Mary, called Salisbury Cathedral, Salisbury, Wilts. The Lady Chapel was built in the years 1220–25 and the main fabric of the cathedral was finished and consecrated in 1258. The spire was added later, *ante* 1305, and reaches a height of 123·13 m *404 ft*. The central spire of Lincoln Cathedral, which was completed *c*. 1307 and fell in 1548, was 160·02 m *525 ft* tall.

Stained glass *Oldest* Pieces of stained glass dated before AD 850, some possibly even to the 7th century, excavated by Prof. Rosemary Cramp, were set into a window of that date in the nearby St Paul's Church, Jarrow, Co. Durham. The oldest complete stained glass in the world represents the Prophets in a window of the Cathedral of Augsburg, Germany, dating from the second half of the 11th century. The oldest datable stained glass in the UK is represented by a figure of St Michael in All Saints Church, Dalbury, Derbys of the late 11th century.

Largest The largest stained-glass window is that of the Resurrection Mausoleum in Justice, Illinois, USA, measuring 2079 m² *22 381 ft²* in 2448 panels, completed in 1971. Although not one continuous window, the Basilica of Our Lady of Peace (Notre Dame de la Paix) at Yamoussoukro, Côte d'Ivoire contains a number of stained-glass windows covering a total area of 7432 m² *80 000 ft²*. The tallest stained glass is the 41·14 m *135 ft* high back-lit glass mural installed in 1979 in the atrium of the Ramada Hotel, Dubai.

The largest single stained-glass window in Great Britain is the east window in Gloucester Cathedral measuring 21·94 × 11·58 m *72 × 38 ft*, set up to commemorate the Battle of Crécy (1346), while the largest area of stained glass comprises the 128 lights, totalling 2322 m² *25 000 ft²*, in York Minster.

Brasses The world's oldest monumental brass is that commemorating Bishop Yso von Wölpe in the Andreaskirche, Verden, near Hanover, Germany, dating from 1231. An engraved coffin plate of St Ulrich (died

973), laid in 1187, was found buried in the Church of SS Ulrich and Afra, Augsburg, Germany in 1979.

The oldest brass in Great Britain is of Sir John D'Abernon (died 1277) at Stoke D'Abernon, near Leatherhead, Surrey, dating from *c*. 1320. A dedication brass dated 24 Apr 1241 in Ashbourne Church, Derbys has been cited as the earliest arabic writing extant in Britain.

CHURCH PERSONNEL

There are more than 2000 'registered' saints, of whom around two-thirds are either Italian or French. Britain's first Christian martyr was St Alban, executed *c*. AD 209. The first US-born saint was Mother Elizabeth Ann Bayley Seton (1774–1821), canonized on 14 Sep 1975.

Most rapidly canonized The shortest interval that has elapsed between the death of a saint and his or her canonization was in the case of St Peter of Verona, Italy, who died on 6 Apr 1252 and was canonized 337 days later on 9 Mar 1253. For the other extreme of 857 years, see table of Popes and Cardinals.

Bishopric *Longest tenure* The longest tenure of any Church of England bishopric is 57 years in the case of the Rt Rev. Thomas Wilson, who was consecrated Bishop of Sodar and Man on 16 Jan 1698 and died in office on 7 Mar 1755. Of English bishoprics, the longest tenures — if one excludes the unsubstantiated case of Aethelwulf, reputedly Bishop of Hereford from 937 to 1012 — are those of 47 years by Jocelin de Bohun of Salisbury (1142–89) and Nathaniel Crew or Crewe of Durham (1674–1721).

Bishop *Oldest* The oldest serving bishop (excluding suffragans and assistants) in the Church of England as at April 1991 was the Rt Rev. Eric Kemp, Bishop of Chichester, who was born on 27 Apr 1915.

The oldest Roman Catholic bishop in recent years has been Bishop Angelo Teutonico, formerly Bishop of Aversa, Italy (b. 28 Aug 1874), who died aged 103 years 276 days on 31 May 1978. He had celebrated mass about 24 800 times. Bishop Herbert Welch of the United Methodist Church, who was elected a Bishop for Japan and Korea in 1916, died on 4 Apr 1969 aged 106.

Youngest The youngest bishop of all time was HRH the Duke of York and Albany, the second son of George III, who was elected Bishop of Osnabrück, through his father's influence as Elector of Hanover, at the age of 196 days on 27 Feb 1764. He resigned after 39 years' enjoyment. The youngest serving bishop (excluding suffragans and assistants) in the Church of England is the Rt Rev. David Hope, Bishop of Wakefield, who was born on 14 Apr 1940. When suffragans and assistants are counted, the youngest is the Rt Rev. John Hind, Suffragan Bishop of Horsham, who was born on 19 Jun 1945.

Oldest parish priest Father Alvaro Fernandez (8 Dec 1880–6 Jan 1988) served as a parish priest at Santiago de Abres, Spain from 1919 until he was 107 years old. The oldest Anglican clergyman, Rev. Clement Williams (b. 30 Oct 1879), died aged 106 years 3 months on 3 Feb 1986. He lined the route at Queen Victoria's funeral and was ordained in 1904.

Longest service Rev. K.M. Jacob (b. 10 Jul 1880) was made a deacon in the Marthoma Syrian Church of Malabar in

Kerala, southern India in 1897. He served his church until his death on 28 Mar 1984, 87 years later.

The longest Church of England incumbency on record is one of 75 years 357 days by Rev. Bartholomew Edwards, Rector of St Nicholas, Ashill, Norfolk from 1813 to 1889. There is some doubt as to whether Rev. Richard Sherinton was installed at Folkestone from 1524 or 1529 to 1601. If the former is correct it would surpass the Edwards record (see above). The parish of Farrington, Hants had only two incumbents in a period of 122 years: Rev. J. Benn (28 Mar 1797 to 1857) and Rev. T.H. Massey (1857 to 5 Apr 1919). From 1675 to 1948 the incumbents of Rose Ash, Devon were from eight generations of the family of Southcomb.

Longest-serving chorister John Love Vokins (1890–1989) was a chorister for 92 years. He joined the choir of Christ Church, Heeley, Sheffield, S Yorks in 1895 and that of St Michael's, Hathersage, Derbys, 35 years later, and was still singing in 1987.

Oldest warden Having become a chorister in 1876 at the age of nine, Thomas Rogers was appointed vicar's warden in 1966 at Montacute, Somerset, aged 99.

Sunday school Sunday schools were established by Congregationalists in Neath and Tirdwyncyn, Wales in 1697.

F. Otto Brechel (1890–1990) of Mars, Pennsylvania, USA completed 88 years (4576 Sundays) of perfect attendance at Church School at three different churches in Pennsylvania — the first from 1902 to 1931, the second from 1931 to 1954, and the third from 1954 onwards.

Largest and smallest parishes The smallest parish in the UK is The Scares, which consists of rocky islets in Luce Bay with an area of 0·44 ha *1·10 acres* and is included in Wigtown, Dumfries & Galloway. The largest parish is Kilmonivaig in Inverness-shire, with an area of 108 145·46 ha *267 233·03 acres*. The parishes of Sturston and Tottington, in Norfolk, both have nil populations, in areas of 781 ha *1929·9 acres* and 1313 ha *3244·4 acres* respectively.

Oldest parish register The oldest part of any parish register surviving in England contains entries from the summer of 1538. There is a sheet from that of Alfriston, E Sussex recording a marriage on 10 Jul 1504, but this is among entries from 1547. Scotland's oldest surviving register is that for Anstruther-Wester, Fife, with burial entries from 1549.

Largest crowds The greatest recorded number of human beings assembled with a common purpose was an estimated 15 million at the Hindu festival of Kumbh mela, which was held at the confluence of the Yamuna (formerly the Jumna), the Ganges and the invisible 'Saraswathi' at Allahabad, Uttar Pradesh, India on 6 Feb 1989. (See also 'Largest funerals').

Largest funerals The funeral of the charismatic C.N. Annadurai (died 3 Feb 1969), Madras Chief Minister, was attended by 15 million people, according to a police estimate. The queue at the grave of the Russian chansonnier and guitarist Vladimir Visotsky (died 28 Jul 1980), stretched for 10 km *6·2 miles*. The longest funeral in Britain was probably that of Vice-Admiral Viscount Nelson on 9 Jan 1806. Ticket-holders were seated in St Paul's Cathedral by 8:30 a.m. Many were unable to leave until 9 p.m.

Elements

All known matter in, on and beyond the Earth is made up of chemical elements. It is estimated that there are 10^{87} electrons in the known Universe. The total of naturally-occurring elements is 94, comprising, at ordinary temperatures, two liquids, 11 gases and 81 solids (including 72 metals). The so-called 'fourth state' of matter is plasma, when negatively charged electrons and positively charged ions are in flux, 99 per cent of all visible matter is in this form.

SUB-NUCLEAR PARTICLES

As of April 1990 the existence was accepted of three gauge bosons, six leptons and 136 hadron multiplets (77 meson multiplets and 59 baryon multiplets), representing the eventual discovery of 256 particles and an equal number of anti-particles.

Heaviest The heaviest particle accepted is the neutral gauge boson, the Z°, of mass 91·18 GeV and lifetime 2.64×10^{-25} sec, which was discovered in May 1983 by the UA1 Collaboration, CERN, Geneva, Switzerland. Precision determinations of these values indicates that there are only three 'families' of quarks and leptons. The theoretical masses of the graviton (the as yet unobserved gravitational gauge boson), the photon, and the three neutrino leptons should all be zero. Current experimental limits are less than 7.6×10^{-67} g for the graviton, less than 5.3×10^{-60} g for the photon, and less than 10 eV (less than 1.8×10^{-32} g) for the electron neutrino.

The heaviest hadron accepted is the upsilon (11020) meson of mass 11·02 GeV and lifetime 8.3×10^{-24} sec, which consists of a bottom/anti-bottom quark combination and which was discovered in October 1984 by two groups using the Electron Storage Ring facilities at Cornell University, Ithaca, New York, USA.

Lightest The lightest hadron is the neutral pion meson of mass 134·974 MeV and lifetime 8.4×10^{-17} sec which was discovered in September 1949 at the University of California Radiation Laboratory, Berkeley, California, USA. It consists of a 'linear combination' of up/anti-up and down/anti-down quarks.

Quarks The lightest quark is the 'up' with a short-range or current mass of 6 MeV and a long-range mass of 350 MeV

whilst the heaviest is the as yet unobserved 'top' quark with a predicted mass of 140 GeV.

Most and least stable The 'Grand Unified Theory' of the weak, electromagnetic, and strong forces predicts that the proton will not be stable but experiments indicate that the lifetime of the most likely decay mode (to a positron and a neutral pion) has a lower limit of 3.1×10^{32} years, which is over 40 times longer than the maximum lifetime predicted by the theory.

The shortest-lived hadrons are the two baryons N(2220) and N(2600), both with lifetimes 1.6×10^{-24} sec (but see Z° lifetime above).

Newest Of the seven new particles accepted in April 1990 the most recently discovered are the neutral charmed meson $D_2^*(2460)^{\circ}$ of mass 2459 MeV and lifetime 3.5×10^{-23} sec discovered in September 1988 by the Tagged Photon Spectrometer Collaboration at Fermilab, Fermi National Accelerator Laboratory, Batavia, Illinois, USA, and the neutral charmed strange xi baryon Ξ_c°, of mass 2473 MeV and lifetime 1.1×10^{-22} sec discovered in November 1988 at the CLEO detector of the Electron Storage Ring facilities, Cornell University, Ithica, New York, USA.

CHEMICAL EXTREMES

Smelliest substance The most evil of over 17 000 smells so far classified must be a matter of opinion, but ethyl mercaptan (C_2H_5SH) and butyl seleno-mercaptan (C_4H_9SeH) are pungent claimants, each with a smell reminiscent of a combination of rotting cabbage, garlic, onions, burnt toast and sewer gas.

Most expensive perfume Retail prices tend to be fixed with an eye to public relations rather than levels solely dictated by the market cost of ingredients and packaging. The Chicago-based firm Jōvan marketed from March 1984 a cologne called Andron, which contains a trace of the attractant pheromone androstenol, which costs $2750 per oz.

Most potent poison The rickettsial disease Q-fever, can be instituted by a *single* organism, though it is fatal in only 1 in 1000 cases. About 10 organisms of *Francisella tularenesis* (formerly *Pasteurella tularenesis*) can institute tularaemia, variously called alkali disease, Francis disease or deerfly fever. This is fatal in upwards of 10 cases in 1000.

Most powerful nerve gas VX, 300 times more toxic than phosgene ($COCl_2$) used in World War I, was developed at the Chemical Defence Experimental Establishment, Porton Down, Wilts in 1952. Patents were applied for in 1962 and published in February 1974 showing it to be ethyl S-2-diisopropylaminoethylmethylphosphonothiolate. The lethal dosage is 10 mg-minute/m³ airborne or 0·3 mg orally.

Most absorbent substance The US Department of Agriculture Research Service announced on 18 Aug 1974 that 'H-span' or Super Slurper composed of one half starch derivative and one fourth each of acrylamide and acrylic acid can, when treated with iron, retains water 1300 times its own weight.

Finest powder The ultimate is solid helium, which was first postulated to be a monatomic powder as early as 1964.

Most lethal man-made chemical TCDD (2,3,7,8 tetrachlorodibenzo-p-dioxin), the most deadly of the 75 known dioxins, is admitted to be 150 000 times

more deadly than cyanide at 3.1×10^{-9} moles/kg .

Most refractory substance Tantalum carbide TaC $_{0.88}$ which melts at 3990°C *7214°F.*

Least dense substance These are the silica aerogels in which tiny spheres of bonded silicon and oxygen atoms are joined into long strands separated by pockets of air. In February 1990 the lightest of these aerogels with a density of only 0·005 g/cm³ *5 oz/ft³* was produced at the Lawrence Livermore Laboratory, California, USA. The main use will be in Space to collect micrometeroids and the debris present in comets' tails.

Highest superconducting temperature In March 1988 bulk superconductivity with a transition to zero resistance at $-148°C$ *$-234°F$* was obtained at the IBM Almaden Research Center, San Jose, California, USA for a mixed oxide of thallium, calcium, barium and copper - $Tl_2Ca_2Ba_2Cu_3O_x$.

Strongest acid and alkaline solutions Normal solutions of strong acids such as perchloric acid $HClO_4$ and strong alkalis such as sodium hydroxide NaOH, potassium hydroxide KOH and tetramethylammonium hydroxide $N(CH_3)_4OH$, tend towards pH values of 0 and 14 respectively. However this scale is inadequate for describing the 'superacids' the strongest of which is estimated to be an 80 per cent solution of antimony pentafluoride in hydrofluoric acid (fluoroantimonic acid HF : SbF_5). The acidity function, H_0, of this solution has not been measured but even a 50 per cent solution has an acidity function of -30 so that this acid mixture is a quintillion (10^{18}) times stronger than concentrated sulphuric acid.

Sweetest substance Talin from arils of katemfe (*Thaumatococcus Daniellii*) discovered in West Africa is 6150 times as sweet as a one per cent sucrose solution.

Most magnetic substance Neodymium iron boride $Nd_2Fe_{14}B$ with a maximum energy product (the highest energy that a magnet can supply when operating at a particular operating point) of up to 280 kJ/m³.

The 109 Elements

Commonest Extraterrestrial Hydrogen (H) accounts for 90 per cent of all known matter in the Universe and 70·68 per cent by mass in the Solar System.

Earth's lithosphere Oxygen (0) at 46·40 per cent by weight.

Atmosphere Nitrogen (N) at 78·08 per cent by volume (75·52 per cent by mass).

There are 94 naturally occuring elements while to date a further 15 transuranic elements (elements 95 to 109) have been claimed, of which 10 are undisputed. By 1984 6 845 000 chemical compounds had been produced from these elements, of which some 65 000 were in common use.

Rarest (of the 94) Earth's lithosphere Only 0·16 g *0·0056 oz* of astatine (At) is present in the Earth's crust, of which the isotope astatine 215 (At 215) (discovered by B. Karlik and T. Bernert of Austria in 1943) accounts for only 4·5 nanograms *1.6×10^{-10} oz.*

Atmosphere Radon (Rn) at 6×10^{-20} parts per million by volume. This is only 2·4 kg *5·3 lb* overall but concentration of this radioactive gas in certain granitic areas has been blamed for a number of cancer deaths. The total amount of radon in

the Earth's crust available to replenish the atmosphere is estimated to be 160 tonnes.

Density *Solid* The least dense element at room temperature is the metal lithium (Li) at 0·5334 g/cm³ *0·01927 lb/in³*, although the density of solid hydrogen at its melting point of −259·192°C is only 0·0871 g/cm³ *0·00315 lb/in³*. The densest solid at room temperature is osmium (Os) at 22·59 g/cm³ *0·8161 lb/in³*.

Gas At NTP (Normal Temperature and Pressure, 0°C and one atmosphere) the lightest gas is hydrogen (H) at 0·00008989 g/cm³ *0·005612 lb/ft³*. The heaviest gas is radon (Rn) at 0·01005 g/cm³ *0·6274 lb/ft³*.

Melting/boiling point *Highest* Metallic tungsten (W) melts at 3420°C *6188°F* and boils at 5860°C *10580°F*. On the assumption that graphite transforms to carbyne forms above 2300°C, *4172°F* then the non-metal with the highest melting and boiling points would be carbon (C) at 3530°C *6386°F* and 3870°C *6998°F* respectively. However, this is disputed, an alternative suggestion is that graphite remains stable at high temperatures, sublimes directly to vapour at 3720°C *6728°F* and cannot be obtained in a liquid form unless the temperature exceeds 4430°C (8006°F) and the pressure 100 atm *10 MPa*.

Lowest Helium (He) cannot be obtained as a solid atmospheric pressure, the minimum pressure being 24·985 atm *2·532 MPa* which occurs at a temperature of −272·375°C *−458·275°F*. The boiling point of helium is −268·928°C *−452·070°F*. Monatomic hydrogen (H) is expected to be a non-liquifiable superfluid gas. The metal with the lowest melting and boiling points is mercury (Hg) at −38·829°C *−37·892°F* and 356·62°C *673·92°F* respectively.

Thermal expansion At room temperature the metal with the highest expansion is caesium (Cs), at 94 × 10⁻⁶ per deg. C, while the diamond allotrope of carbon (C) has the lowest expansion at 1·0 × 10⁻⁶ per deg.C.

Hardest substance The carbon (C) allotrope diamond has a Knoop value of 8400.

Most ductile 1 oz of gold (Au) can be drawn to 43 miles or (1 g to *2·4 km*).

Highest tensile strength Boron at (B) 5·7 GPa *8·3×10⁵ lb/in²* (redetermined at the Technical Research Centre of Finland).

Purest In April 1978 P.V.E. McClintock of the University of Lancaster, reported success in obtaining the isotope helium 4 (He 4) with impurity levels at less than two parts in 10¹⁵.

Most expensive For commercially available elements, californium (Cf) was sold in 1970 for $10 per microgram.

Newest The discovery of element 108 or unniloctium (Uno) (provisional IUPAC name) was announced in April 1984 by G. Münzenberg *et al.* and was based on the observations of only three atoms at the Gesellschaft für Schwerionenforschung (GSI), Darmstadt, Germany. A less substantiated claim was made in June of the same year by Yu.Ts. Oganessian *et al.* of the Joint Institute for Nuclear Research, Dubna, USSR. The single atom of unnilennium (Une) produced at GSI on 29 Aug 1982 counts as the highest atomic number (109) and the heaviest atomic mass (266) obtained; a tentative Soviet claim to have

detected element 110 or unnunnillium (Uun) with a probable mass of 272 has not been substantiated.

Isotopes *Most* 36 each for both xenon (Xe) (9 stable isotopes identified by F.W. Aston (UK) 1920–22 and 27 radioactive identified 1939–81) and caesium (Cs) (1 stable identified by Aston in 1921 and 35 radioactive identified 1935–83).

Least Three confirmed isotopes for hydrogen (H) including two stable (identified by Aston in 1920 (protium) and by H.C. Urey, F.G. Brickwedde and G.M. Murphy (USA) in 1931 (deuterium)) and one radioactive (tritium) first identified by M.L.E Oliphant, P. Harteck and Lord Rutherford (UK) in 1934 but characterized as a radioactive isotope by L.W. Alvarez and R. Cornog (USA) in 1939.

Most stable The most stable radioactive isotope is the double-beta decaying tellurium 128 (Te 128), with a half-life of 1·5 × 10²⁴ years. It was first identified as being naturally-occuring by F.W. Aston (UK) in 1924 and confirmed as being the longest-living by E.C. Alexander Jr, B. Srinivasan and O.K. Manuel (USA) in 1968. The alpha-decay record is 8 × 10¹⁵ years for samarium 148 (Sm 148) and the beta-decay record is 9 × 10¹⁵ years for cadmium 113 (Cd 113). Both isotopes were identified as being naturally occuring by Aston in 1933 and 1924 respectively, while proof of their radioactivity was first obtained by T.R. Wilkins and A.J. Dempster (USA) in 1938 for Sm 148 and by D.E. Watt and R.N. Glover (UK) in 1961 for Cd 113.

Least stable Lithium 5 (Li5), with a lifetime of 4·4 × 10⁻²² sec—first characterized by E.W. Titterton and T.A. Brinkley (Australia/UK) in 1950.

Liquid range Based on the differences between melting and boiling points, the element with the shortest liquid range is the inert gas neon (Ne) at only 2·542 degrees (from −248·594°C *−415·469°F* to −246·052°C *−410·894°F*) while that with the longest liquid range is the radioactive transuranium element neptunium (Np) at 3453 degrees (from 637°C *1179°F* to 4090°C *6215°F*). However based on the true range of liquids from their melting points to their critical points, then the shortest range is for helium (He) at 5·195 degrees (from absolute zero −273·15°C *−459·67°F*), and the largest range is for tungsten (W) at 10 200 degrees (from 3 420°C to 13 620°C *6 188°F to 24 548°F*).

Toxic The most stringent restriction placed on a non-radioactive element is for beryllium (Be), with a threshold limit value in air of only 2 micrograms/m³. For radioactive isotopes, which occur naturally or are produced in nuclear installations and have ecologically significant half-lives (i.e. in excess of six months), the severest restriction in air is placed on Thorium 228 (Th228) or Radiothorium—first observed by O. Hahn (Germany) in 1905 at 2·4 × 10⁻¹⁶ grams/m³ (equivalent radiation intesity 0·0074 becquerel/m³). The severest restriction in water is placed on radium 228 (Ra228 or mesothorium 1 discovered by Hahn in 1907) at 1·1 × 10⁻¹³ grams/litre (equivalent radiation intensity 1·1 becquerel/litre).

Physical Extremes

Smallest optical prism Researchers at the National Institute of Standards and

Technology laboratories in Boulder, Colorado, USA have created a glass prism with sides 0·004 mm *0·001 in* barely visibile to the naked eye. This should find application in fibre optics research and instrumentation.

Highest temperature Those produced in the centre of a thermonuclear fusion bomb are of the order of 300 000 000 – 400 000 000° C. Of controllable temperatures, the highest effective laboratory figure reported is 200 million degrees C achieved in the Tokamak Fusion Test Reactor at the Princeton Plasma Physics Laboratory, Princeton, New Jersey, USA in June 1986.

Lowest temperature The absolute zero of temperature, 0 K, on the Kelvin scale corresponds to −273·15°C or −459·67°F. The lowest temperature reached is 2 × 10⁻⁹ Kelvin, i.e. two billionths of a degree above absolute zero. This was achieved at the Low Temperature Laboratory, Helsinki University of Technology, Finland in a nuclear demagnetization device by a team led by Prof. Olli V. Lounasmaa, including Dr Pertii Hakonen of Helsinki University and Dr Shi Yin of Michigan State University, USA and was announced in October 1989.

Smallest thermometer Dr Frederich Sachs, a biophysicist at the State University of New York at Buffalo, USA, has developed an ultra-microthermometer for measuring the temperature of single living cells. The tip is one micron in diameter, about one fiftieth the diameter of a human hair.

Largest barometer A water barometer 12 m *39 ft* in height was constructed in 1987 by Bert Bolle, curator of the Barometer Museum, Maartensdijk, Netherlands, where the instrument is situated.

Highest pressures A sustained laboratory pressure of 1·70 megabars (170 GPa *11 000 tons force/in²*), was achieved in the giant hydraulic diamond-faced press at the Carnegie Institution's Geophysical Laboratory, Washington, DC, USA and reported

Heaviest magnet

Is that in the Joint Institute for Nuclear Research at Dubna, near Moscow, USSR for the 10 GeV synchrophasotron measuring 60 m *196 ft* in diameter, and weighing 36 000 tonnes.

Smallest microphone

Prof. Ibrahim Kavrak of Bogazici University, Istanbul, Turkey developed a microphone for a new technique of pressure measurement in fluid flow in 1967. It has a frequency response of 10 Hz–10 KHz and measures 1·5 × 0·76 mm *0·06 × 0·03 in.*

Longest echo

The longest echo in any building is one of 15 sec following the closing of the door of the Chapel of the Mausoleum, Hamilton, Lanarkshire, built 1840–55.

Loudest noise

The loudest in a laboratory has been 210 dBA, or 400 000 acoustic watts, reported by NASA from a 14·63 m *48 ft* steel and concrete test bed for the Saturn V rocket static with 18·3 m *60 ft* deep foundations, at Marshall Space Flight Center, Huntsville, Alabama, USA in October 1965. Holes could be bored in solid material by this means, and the audible range was in excess of 161 km *100 miles*.

Highest note

A 'laser' beam striking a sapphire crystal at the Massachusetts Institute of Technology, Cambridge, Massachusetts, USA in September 1964 generated a note of 60 gigahertz.

in June 1978. This laboratory announced solid hydrogen achieved at 57 kilobars pressure on 2 Mar 1979. If created, metallic hydrogen is expected to be silvery white but soft, with a density of 1·1 g/cm³ *0·04 lb/in³*. The pressure required for the transition is estimated by H. K. Mao and P. M. Bell to be 1 megabar at 25° C *77° F*. Using dynamic methods and impact speeds of up to 29000 km/h *18 000 mph*, momentary pressures of 75 000 000 atmospheres 7000 GPa *490 000 tons/in²* were reported from the US in 1958.

Highest velocity The highest velocity at which any solid visible object has been projected is 150 km/sec *93 miles/sec* in the case of a plastic disc at the Naval Research Laboratory, Washington, DC, USA reported in August 1980.

Finest balance The Sartorius Model 4108, manufactured in Göttingen, Germany, can weigh objects of up to 0·5 g *0·018 oz* to an accuracy of 0·01 µg or 1 × 10⁻⁸ g, (3·5 × 10⁻¹⁰ oz) equivalent to little more than one sixtieth of the weight of the ink on this full stop.

Largest bubble chamber The $7 million installation, completed in October 1973 at Weston, Illinois, USA, is 4·57 m *15 ft* in diameter. It contains 33 000 litres *7259 gal*, of liquid hydrogen at a temperature of −247° C *−413° F* and has a superconducting magnet of 3 tesla.

Fastest centrifuge Ultra-centrifuges were invented by Theodor Svedberg (b. 30 Aug 1884) (Sweden) in 1923.

The highest man-made rotary speed ever achieved and the fastest speed of any earthbound object is 7250 km/h *4500 mph* by a swirling tapered 15·2 cm *6 in* carbon fibre rod in a vacuum at Birmingham University, reported on 24 Jan 1975.

Finest cut The $13 million large optics diamond turning machine at the Lawrence Livermore National Laboratory, California, USA was reported in June 1983 to be able to sever a human hair 3000 times lengthwise.

Most powerful electric current If fired simultaneously, the 4032 capacitors comprising the Zeus capacitor at the Los Alamos Scientific Laboratory, New Mexico, USA would produce, for a few microseconds, twice as much current as that generated elsewhere on Earth.

Hottest flame The hottest is carbon subnitride (C_4N_2), which at one atm can produce a flame calculated to reach 4988°C *9010°F*.

Highest measured frequency The highest *directly* measured is a visible yellow-green light at 520·2068085 terahertz (a terahertz being a million million hertz or cycles per second) for the o-component of the 17–1 P (62) transition line of iodine 127.

The highest measured frequency determined by precision metrology is a green light at 582·491703 terahertz for the b 21 component of the R(15) 43–0 transition line of iodine 127. However, with the decision on 20 Oct 1983 by the Conférence Générale des Poids et Mesures (CGPM) to define exactly the metre (m) in terms of the velocity of light (c) such that 'the metre is the length of the path travelled by light in vacuum during a time interval of 1/299 792 458 of a second' then frequency (f) and wavelength (λ) are exactly interchangeable through the relationship $f\lambda = c$.

Lowest friction The lowest coefficient of static and dynamic friction of any solid is 0·04, in the case of polytetrafluoroethylene [$-CF_2-CF_2-$]$_n$, called PTFE–

equivalent to wet ice on wet ice. It was first manufactured in quantity by E.I. du Pont de Nemours & Co. Inc. in 1943, and is marketed from the USA as Teflon.

In the centrifuge at the University of Virginia, USA a 13·60 kg *30 lb* rotor magnetically supported has been spun at 1000 rev/sec in a vacuum of 10⁻⁶ mm of mercury pressure. It loses only one revolution per second per day, thus spinning for years.

Smallest hole A hole of 40 Å (4 × 10⁻⁶ mm) was shown visually using a JEM 100C electron microscope and Quantel Electronics devices at the Department of Metallurgy, Oxford on 28 Oct 1979. To find such a hole is equivalent to finding a pinhead in a haystack with sides of 1·93 km *1·2 miles*.

An electron microscope beam on a sample of sodium beta-alumina at the University of Illinois, USA, in May 1983 accidentally bored a hole 2 × 10⁻⁹ m in diameter.

Most powerful laser beams The first illumination of another celestial body was achieved on 9 May 1962, when a beam of light was successfully reflected from the Moon by the use of a laser (light amplification by stimulated emission of radiation) attached to a 121·9 cm *48 in* telescope at the Massachusetts Institute of Technology, Cambridge, Massachusetts, USA. The spot was estimated to be 6·4 km *4 miles* in diameter on the Moon. The device was propounded in 1958 by the American Dr Charles Hard Townes (b. 1915). Such a flash for 1/5000th of a second can bore a hole through a diamond by vaporization at 10 000° C *18 032°F*, produced by 2 × 10²³ photons. The 'Shiva' laser was reported at the Lawrence Livermore Laboratory, California, USA to be concentrating 2·6 × 10¹³ watts into a pinhead-sized target for 9·5 × 10⁻¹¹ sec in a test on 18 May 1978.

Brightest light The brightest artificial sources are 'laser' pulses generated at the US Los Alamos National Laboratory, New Mexico, announced in March 1987 by Dr Robert Graham. An ultra-violet flash lasting 1 picosecond (1 × 10⁻¹² sec) is intensified to an energy of 5 × 10¹⁵ watts.

The most powerful searchlight ever developed was one produced during World War II by the General Electric Company Ltd at the Hirst Research Centre in Wembley, London. It had a consumption of 600 kW and gave an arc luminance of 46 500 candelas/cm² *300 000 candles/in²* and a maximum beam intensity of 2 700 000 000 candles from its parabolic mirror (diameter 3·04 m *10 ft*).

Of continuously burning sources, the most powerful is a 313 kW high-pressure argon arc lamp of 1 200 000 candle-power, completed by Vortek Industries Ltd of Vancouver, British Columbia, Canada in March 1984.

Shortest light pulse Charles Z. Shank and colleagues of the AT & T Laboratories in New Jersey, USA achieved a light pulse of 8 femtoseconds (8 × 10⁻¹⁵ sec), announced in April 1985. The pulse comprised only four or five wavelengths of visible light.

Largest electromagnet The world's largest electromagnet is part of the L3 detector, another experiment on LEP (large electron–ponitron collider). The octagonal shaped magnet consists of 6400 tons of low carbon steel yoke and 1100 tons of aluminium coil. The yoke elements, welded pieces of up to 30 tons each, were manufactured in the Soviet Union. The coil was manufactured in a modular technique

in Switzerland and consists of 168 turns welded together to form an eight-sided frame. Thirty thousand ampéres of current flow through the aluminium coil to creat a uniform magnetic field of 5 kilogauss. The magnet is higher than a four-storey building with a volume of approximately 12 × 12 ×12 m *39 × 39 × 39 ft*. The total weight of the magnet, including the frame, coil and inner support tube is 7810 tons. The L3 magnet is composed of more metal than the Eiffel Tower.

Magnetic fields The strongest continuous field strength achieved was a total of 35·3±0·3 teslas at the Francis Bitter National Magnet Laboratory, Massachusetts Institute of Technology, USA on 26 May 1988, employing a hybrid magnet with holmium pole pieces. This had the effect of enhancing the central magnetic field generated in the heart and brain.

The weakest magnetic field measured is one of 8 × 10⁻¹⁵ tesla in the heavily shielded room at the same laboratory. It is used by Dr David Cohen for research into the very weak magnetic field generated in the heart and brain.

Most powerful microscope The scanning tunnelling microscope (STM) invented at the IBM Zürich research laboratory in 1981 has the magnifying ability of 100 million and is capable of resolving down to one hundredth the diameter of an atom (3 × 10⁻¹⁰ m). The fourth generation of the STM now being developed is said to be 'about the size of a finger tip'.

By using field ion microscopy the tips of probes of scanning tunnelling microscopes have been shaped to end in a single atom — the last three layers constituting the world's smallest man-made pyramid, consisting of 7, 3 and 1 atoms. It was announced in January 1990 that D.M. Eigler and E.K. Schweizer of the IBM Almaden Research Center, San Jose, California, USA had used an STM to move and re-position single atoms of xenon on a nickel surface in order to spell out the initials 'IBM'.

Most powerful particle accelerator The 2 km *1·25 miles* diameter proton synchroton at the Fermi National Accelerator Laboratory near Batavia, Illinois, USA is the highest energy 'atom-smasher' in the world. On 14 May 1976 an energy of 500 giga electron volts (5 × 10¹¹) was achieved for the first time. On 13 Oct 1985 a centre of mass energy of 1·6 TeV (1·6 × 10¹¹ electron volts) was achieved by colliding beams of protons and anti-protons. This involves 1000 superconducting magnets maintained at a temperature of −268·8⁰ C *−452⁰ F* by means of the world's largest, 4500 litre *990 gal*, per hour helium liquefying plant, which began operating on 18 Apr 1980.

On 16 Aug 1983 the US Department of Energy set up a study for the $6 billion super superconductivity collider (SSC) 1995 with two 20 TeV proton and anti-proton colliding beams with a diameter of 83·6 km *52 miles* at Waxahachie, Texas, USA. White House approval was announced on 30 Jan 1987. On 6 Aug 1990 the cost estimate was put at $11 700 million compared with a $9 900 million estimate in November 1988.

Largest scientific instrument The largest scientific instrument so far is the 26·66 km *16·57 mile* circumference electron-positron storage ring 'LEP' at CERN, which began operations on 13 Aug 1989. The tunnel 3·8 m *12·46 ft* in diameter, runs between 50 and 150 m *164 x 492 ft* under the earth's surface, and is accessible through 18 vertical shafts. Over 60 000 tons of technical equipment have been installed in the tunnel and its eight underground work zones. It is intended to be a 'Z° factory' producing up to 10 000 of these neutral weak gauge bosons every day in order to obtain a deeper understanding of the sub-atomic nature of matter. The aim is that by 1992 the electron and positron beams will have energies of 96 GeV each.

Sharpest objects and smallest tubes
The sharpest objects yet made are glass micropipette tubes used in intracellular work on living cells. Techniques developed and applied by Prof. Kenneth T. Brown and Dale G. Flaming of the Department of Physiology, University of California, San Francisco, USA achieved by 1977 bevelled tips with an outer diameter of 0·02 µm and an 0·01 µm inner diameter.

The latter is smaller than the smallest known nickel tubing by a factor of 340 and is 6500 times thinner than a human hair.

Highest vacuum
Those obtained at the IBM Thomas J. Watson Research Center, Yorktown Heights, New York, USA in October 1976 in a cryogenic system with temperatures down to $-269\,°C\ -452\,°F$. This is equivalent to depopulating (baseball-sized) molecules from 1 m–80 km apart or from 1 yard– 50 miles.

Lowest viscosity
The California Institute of Technology first announced on 1 Dec 1957 that there was no measurable viscosity, i.e. perfect flow, in liquid helium II, which exists at temperatures close to absolute zero ($-273·15\,°C\ -459·67\,°F$).

Highest voltage
The highest-ever potential difference obtained in a laboratory has been $32 \pm 1·5$ million volts by the National Electrostatics Corporation at Oak Ridge, Tennessee, USA on 17 May 1979.

Numbers

In dealing with large numbers, scientists use the notation of 10 raised to various powers to eliminate a profusion of noughts. For example, 19 160 000 000 000 miles would be written $1·916 \times 10^{13}$ miles. Similarly, a very small number, for example 0·000 015 432 4 of a gram, would be written $1·543\,24 \times 10^{-5}$. Of the prefixes used before numbers the smallest is 'yocto' symbol y, of power 10^{-24} and the largest is 'yotta', symbol Y, of power 10^{24}. Both are based on the Greek octo, eight (for the eighth power of 10^3).

Highest numbers
The highest lexicographically accepted named number in the system of successive powers of ten is the centillion, first recorded in 1852. It is the hundredth power of a million, or 1 followed by 600 noughts. The number 10^{100} is designated a googol. The term was suggested by the nine-year old nephew of Dr Edward Kasner (USA). Ten raised to the power of a googol is described as a googolplex. Some conception of the magnitude of such numbers can be gained when it is said that the number of electrons in some models of the observable Universe does not exceed 10^{87}. The highest named number outside the decimal notation is the Buddhist *asankhyeya*, which is equal to 10^{140} and mentioned in Jain works of *c.* 100 BC. The highest number ever used in a mathematical proof is a bounding value published in 1977 and known as Graham's number. It concerns bi-chromatic hypercubes and is

inexpressible without the special 'arrow' notation, devised by Knuth in 1976, extended to 64 layers.

Prime numbers
A prime number is any positive integer (excluding unity 1) having no integral factors other than itself and unity, e.g. 2, 3, 5, 7 or 11. The lowest prime number is thus 2. The highest *known* prime number is $391\,581 \times 2^{216\,193} -1$ discovered on 6 Aug 1989 by a team known as the 'Amdahl Six'. The number contains 65 087 digits and was found on an Amdahl 1200 supercomputer in Santa Clara, California, USA. The 'team' also discovered the largest known twin primes, $1\,706\,595 \times 2^{11235} -1$ and $1\,706\,595 \times 2^{11235} + 1$. The lowest non-prime or composite number (excluding 1) is 4.

Perfect numbers
A number is said to be perfect if it is equal to the sum of its divisors other than itself, e.g. $1 + 2 + 4 + 7 + 14 = 28$. The lowest perfect number is 6 $(=1 + 2 + 3)$. The highest known, and the 31st so far discovered, is $(2^{216091} -1) \times 2^{216090}$. It is a consequence of the largest Mersenne prime (also the second largest prime known) being $2^{216091} -1$.

Newest mathematical constant
The study of turbulent water, the weather and other chaotic phenomena has revealed the existence of a new universal constant, the Feigenbaum number, named after its discoverer, Michell J Feigenbaum (US). It is equal to approximately $4·669\,201\,609\,102\,990$.

Most-proved theorem
A book published in 1940 contained 370 different proofs of Pythagoras' theorem including one by President Garfield of the United States.

Longest proof
The proof of the classification of all finite simple groups is spread over more than 14 000 pages in nearly 500 papers in mathematical journals, contributed by more than 100 mathematicians over a period of more than 35 years.

Oldest mathematical puzzle
dates from 1650 BC. This is an English version:

As I was going to St Ives, I met a man with seven wives. Every wife had seven sacks, every sack had seven cats. Every cat has seven kits. Kits, cats, sacks and wives, how many were going to St Ives?

Largest claimed accurate number in physics
Sir Arthur Eddington announced in 1938 that there are exactly 15 747 724 136 275 002 577 605 653 961 181 555 468 044 717 914 527 116 709 366 231 425 076 185 631 031 296 protons in the Universe, and the same number of electrons. Unfortunately for Eddington, no one else accepted his over-precise calculation, which is now discredited.

Most prolific mathematician
Leonard Euler (Switzerland) (1707–83) was so prolific that his papers were still being published for the first time more than 50 years after his death. His collected works have been printed bit by bit since 1910 and will eventually occupy more than 75 large quarto volumes.

Greatest mathematical prodigy
Blaise Pascal (1623–62), the French philo-

Quietest place
The 'dead room' ($10·67 \times 8·53$ m *35 × 28 ft*) in the Bell Telephone System laboratory at Murray Hill, New Jersey, USA, is the most anechoic room in the world, eliminating 99·98 per cent of reflected sound.

Most innumerate

The Nambiquara of the north-west Matto Grosso of Brazil lack any system of numbers. They do, however, have a verb which means 'they are alike'.

Ice-core drilling

The deepest borehole in ice was drilled at the Vostok station (Central Antarctica) by specialists of the Leningrad Mining Institute in September 1989, when a depth of 2540 m *8333 ft* was achieved. The 18th Expedition drilled the deepest 'dry' borehole (without antifreeze) in 1972, which reached 952·5 m *3125 ft*.

sopher and mathematician, discovered Pascal's theorem at the age of 16.

Largest prize ever offered Dr Paul Wolfskell left prize money in his will for the first person to solve the last therorem of Pierre Fermat (1601–65). This prize was worth 100 000 deutschmarks in 1908. As a result of inflation, the prize is now just over 10 000 deutschmarks.

Longest computer computation for a yes–no answer The twentieth Fermat number, $2^{2^{20}} + 1$, was tested on a CRAY–2 supercomputer in 1986 to see if it was a prime number. After 10 days of calculation the answer was no.

Most accurate and most inaccurate version of 'pi' In 1989 the greatest number of decimal places to which *pi* (π) has been calculated is 1 011 196 691 by David and Gregory Chudnovsky at Columbia University, New York, USA. The calculation was performed twice on an IBM 3090 mainframe and on a CRAY=2 supercomputer, and the results matched.

Places 762–767 comprise six consecutive '9's.

In 1853 William Shanks published his calculation of π to 707 decimal places, all calculated by hand. Ninety–two years later, in 1945, it was discovered that the last 180 digits were in fact all incorrect.

In 1897 the General Assembly of Indiana enacted in Bill No. 246 stating that *pi* was *de jure* 4.

Earliest measures The earliest known measure of weight is the *beqa* of the Amratian period of Egyptian civilization *c.* 3800 BC, found at Naqada, Egypt. The weights are cylindrical, with rounded ends and weigh from 188·7–211·2 g *6·65–7·45 oz*.

The unit of length used by the megalithic tomb-builders in north-western Europe *c.* 3500 BC appears to have been 82·90 ± 0·09 cm *2·72 ± 0·003 ft*. This was deduced by Prof. Alexander Thom (1894–1985) in 1966.

Time measure Owing to variations in the length of a day, which is estimated to be increasing irregularly at an average rate of about a millisecond per century due to the Moon's tidal drag, the second has been redefined. Instead of being 1/86 400th part of a mean solar day, it has, since 1960, been reckoned as 1/31 556 925 9747th part of the solar (or tropical) year at AD 1900, January 0·12 hr, Ephemeris time. In 1958 the second of Ephemeris time was computed to be equivalent to 9 192 631 770 ± 20 cycles of the radiation corresponding to the transition of caesium 133 atoms when unperturbed by exterior fields. The greatest diurnal change recorded has been 10 milliseconds on 8 Aug 1972, due to the most violent solar storm recorded in 370 years of observations.

The accuracy of the caesium beam frequency standard approaches eight parts in 10^{14}, compared to two parts in 10^{13} for the methane-stabilized helium-neon laser and six parts in 10^{13} for the hydrogen maser.

The longest measure of time is the *kalpa* in Hindu chronology. It is equivalent to 4320 million years. In astronomy a cosmic year is the period of rotation of the Sun around the centre of the Milky Way galaxy, i.e. 225 million years. In the Late Cretaceous Period of *c.* 85 million years ago the Earth rotated faster, resulting in 370·3 days per year while in Cambrian times *c.* 600 million years ago there is evidence that the year extended over 425 days.

MINE RECORDS

EARLIEST *World* ● 41 250 BC ± 1600 Lion Cavern, Haematite (red iron ore) at Ngwenya, Hhohho, Swaziland.
GB ● 3390 BC ± 150 Flint at Church Hill, Findon, W. Sussex.

DEEPEST *World*[1] ● 3777 m *12 391 ft* (*2·34 miles*) Gold, Western Deep Levels (temp 55°C *131°F*) at Carletonville, South Africa.
GB ● 1315 m *4314 ft* Coal, Plodder Seam, Bickershaw Colliery at Leigh, Lancs.
GB ● 1097 m *3600 ft* Tin, Williams Shaft at Dolcoath (1910) near Camborne, Cornwall.

FASTEST DRILLING
The most footage drilled in one month is 10 477m *34 574 ft* of a hole drilled during June 1988 by Harkins & Company Rig Number 13 while drilling four wells in McMullen County, Texas, USA.

COPPER *Deepest open pit* ● 800 m *2625 ft* Bingham Canyon (begun 1906), Location near Salt Lake City, Utah, USA.
Largest underground ● 573 km *356 miles* tunnels, San Manuel Mine, Magma Copper Co in Arizona, USA.

LEAD *Largest* ● >10 per cent of world output Viburnum Trend in south-east Missouri, USA.

GOLDMINING *Area* ● >51 per cent of world output, 38 mines of the Witwatersrand Discovery, South Africa, in 1886.

GOLD *Largest World*[2] ● 4900 ha *12 100 acres* East Rand Proprietary Mines Ltd at Boksburg, Transvaal, South Africa.
Largest, GB ● 120 000 fine oz (1854–1914), Clogau, St David's (discovered 1836) at Gwynedd, Wales.

Richest ● 49·4 million fine oz, Crown Mines (all-time yield) in Transvaal, South Africa.

IRON *Largest* ● 20 300 million tonnes *19 995 million tons* rich ore Lebedinsky (45–65% ore), Kursk region, USSR.

PLATINUM *Largest* ● 28 tonnes per annum, Rustenburg Platinum Mines Group, Rustenburg Platinum, Mine Location Western Transvaal, South Africa.

TUNGSTEN *Largest* ● 2000 tonnes per day, Union Carbide Mount Morgan mine, near Bishop, California, USA.

URANIUM *Largest* ● 5000 tons of uranium oxide, Rio Tinto Zinc open cast pit at Rössing, Namibia, South West Africa.

SPOIL DUMP *Largest, World* ● 275 million yd³ *210 million m³* New Cornelia Tailings at Ten Mile Wash, Arizona, USA.
Largest, GB ● 141 ha *348 acre* 12 million m³, Allerton Tip, near Castleford, West Yorks.

QUARRY *Largest, World* ● 7·21 km² *2·81 miles²*. 3355 million tonnes *3700 million short tons* extracted. Bingham Canyon, Utah, USA.
Largest, GB ● 150 m *500 ft* deep, 2·6 km *1·6 mile* circumference, Old Delabole Slate Quarry (since *c.* 1570), Cornwall.

COAL, OPEN CAST MINE ● 325 m deep 1130 ft 21 km² *8 mile²* area Fortuna-Garsdorf (lignite) (begun 1955), near Bergheim, West Germany.

COAL MINE *Oldest, UK* ● *c.* 1822 founded by William Stobart at Wearmouth, near Sunderland, Tyne and Wear.

[1] *Sinking began in Jun 1957. Scheduled to reach 3880 m 12 730 ft by 1992 with 14 000 ft or 2·65 miles regarded as the limit. No. 3 vertical ventilation shaft is the world's deepest shaft at 2948·9 m 9675 ft. This mine requires 128 050 tonnes 130 000 tons of air per day and refrigeration which uses the energy it would take to make 37 000 short tons of ice. An underground shift comprises 11 150 men. The deepest exploratory coal mining shaft is one reaching 6700 ft 2042 m near Thorez in the Ukrainian Donbas field, USSR in August 1983.*

[2] *The world's most productive gold mine may be Muruntau, Kyzyl Kum, Uzbekistan, USSR. According to one Western estimate it produces 80 tonnes of gold in a year. It has been estimated that South Africa has produced in 96 years (1886–1982) 36 400 tons or more than 31 per cent of all gold mined since 3900 BC.*

Borings and Mines

Deepest Man's deepest penetration into the Earth's crust is a geological exploratory drilling near Zapolarny, Kola peninsula, USSR, begun on 24 May 1970. By mid-1991 depth of 12 124 m *39 776 ft* was surpassed. The eventual target of 15 000 m *49 212 ft* is expected in 1995. The drill bit is mounted on a turbine driven by a mud pump. The temperature at 12 km *7·45 miles* was already 210° C *229° F*. The West Germans announced the test drilling of the Erbendorf hole, Upper Bavaria on 9 Oct 1986. The planned depth of the £150 million project is 14 km *8·6 miles or 45 900 ft*.

Ocean drilling The deepest recorded drilling into the sea bed by the *Glomar Challenger* of the US Deep Sea Drilling Project is one of 1740 m *5709 ft* off northwest Spain in 1976.

The deepest site is now 7034 m *23 077 ft* below the surface on the western wall of the Marianas Trench in the Pacific Ocean.

The deepest drilling in the North Sea is in 795·8 m *2611 ft* of water on 11–12 Jun 1986 by the British-built *Sovereign Explorer*, a propulsion-assisted semisubmersible drilling unit operated by Scotdrill Offshore Co.

Aberdeen, and contracted to Chevron Petroleum.

Oil fields In 1990 the world's largest oil producer was the USSR, dropping 4–5 per cent on the 1989 figure of 121·5 million barrels per day, followed by the USA with 7·5 million; the UK was sixth, with 2·27 million barrels.

The world's largest oil field is the Ghawar field, Saudi Arabia, developed by ARAMCO, which measures 240 × 35 km *150 × 22 miles*.

The area of the designated parts of the UK Continental shelf as at mid-1989 was 651 650 km² *252 000 miles²* with proven and probable reserves of 1330 million tonnes, of oil and 634 000 million m³ *22 400 000 million ft³* of gas.

Gas was first discovered in the West Sole Field in October 1965 and oil in commercial quantities in the Forties Field (Block 21/10) at 2098 m *6883 ft* beneath the sea from the drilling rig *Sea Quest* on 18 Sep 1970, though a small gas field was discovered near Whitby, N Yorks in 1937.

The most productive field is BP's Forties Field, which on 3 Apr 1989 became the first oil field in western Europe to produce a total of 2 billion barrels of oil and natural gas liquids. Production peaked for the UK's 32 oil fields at 127·5 million tonnes.

Oil refineries The world's largest refinery is the Amerada Hess refinery in St Croix, US Virgin Islands, producing on average 383 000 barrels per day in 1990.

UK The largest oil refinery in the United Kingdom is the Esso Refinery at Fawley, near Southampton, Hants. Opened in 1921 and much expanded in 1951, it has a capacity of 15·6 million tonnes per year. Together with the associated chemical plant, the total investment on the 1295 ha *3200 acre* site is in excess of £2·07 billion on a replacement cost basis.

The area occupied by the Shell Stanlow Refinery at Ellesmere Port, Cheshire, founded in 1922 and now with a capacity of 18 million tonnes per year, is 810 ha *2000 acres.*

Gas deposits The largest gas deposit in the world is at Urengoi, USSR, with an eventual production of 261 600 million yd³ *200 000 million m³* per year through six pipelines from proved reserves of 9 155 600 million yd³ *7 000 000 million m³*. The trillionth (10^{12}) cubic metre was produced on 23 Apr 1986.

Oil platforms *Heaviest* The world's heaviest oil platform is the *Gullfaks C* in the North Sea, built and operated by the Norwegian oil company Statoil. The platform is of the Condeep type, with a steel deck and modules on top of a concrete gravity base. Total dry weight of the £1·3 billion structure is 846 tonnes. Total height is 380 m *115·82 ft.* The gravity base was built by Norwegian Contractors, Stavanger and the deck by Aker, Stord.

Tallest The world's tallest production platform stands in water 536·44m *1760 ft* deep about 160·93 km *100 miles* off the Louisiana coast, USA. It is operated by Conoco and co-owned by Conoco, Texas and Occidental Petroleum.

Gusher The greatest wildcat ever recorded blew at Alborz No. 5 well, near Qum, Iran on 26 Aug 1956. The uncontrolled oil gushed to a height of 52 m *170 ft* at 120 000 barrels per day at a pressure of 62 055 kPa *9000 lb/in².* It was closed after 90 days' work by B. Mostofi and Myron Kinley of Texas.

The Lake View No. 1 gusher in California, USA on 15 Mar 1910 may have yielded 125 000 barrels in its first 24 hours.

Oil spills The slick from the Mexican marine blow-out beneath the drilling rig *Ixtoc I* in the Gulf of Campeche, Gulf of Mexico, on 3 Jun 1979 reached 640 km *400 miles* by 5 Aug 1979. It was eventually capped on 24 Mar 1980 after a loss of 3 000 000 barrels *535 000 tonnes.*

The *Exxon Valdez* (Capt Joseph Hazelwood) in Prince William Sound, Alaska, USA struck a reef on 24 Mar 1989 spilling 10 million gallons of crude slick spread over 6 733 km² *2 600 miles².*

The worst oil spill in history was of 236 000 tonnes of oil from two supertankers, *Atlantic Empress* and *Aegean Captain*, when they collided off Tobago on 19 Jul 1979.

The worst oil spill in British waters was from the 118 285 dwt *Torrey Canyon* which struck the Pollard Rock off Land's End on 18 Mar 1967 resulting in a loss of 106 000 tons of oil.

Flare The greatest gas fire was that which burnt at Gassi Touil in the Algerian Sahara from noon on 13 Nov 1961 to 9:30 a.m. on 28 Apr 1962. The pillar of flame rose 137 m *450 ft* and the smoke 182 m *600 ft.* It was

eventually extinguished by Paul Neal ('Red') Adair (b. 1916) of Houston, Texas, USA, using 245 kg *550 lb* of dynamite. His fee was understood to be about $1 000 000 plus expenses.

Water well The world's deepest water bore is the Stensvad Water Well 11-W1 of 2231 m *7320 ft* drilled by the Great Northern Drilling Co. Inc. in Rosebud County, Montana, USA in October–November 1961. The Thermal Power Co. geothermal steam well begun in Sonoma County, California, USA in 1955 is down to 2752 m *9029 ft.*

UK The deepest well in Great Britain is a water-table well 866 m *2842 ft* deep in the Staffordshire coal measures at Smestow, 8 km *5 miles* south-west of Wolverhampton, W Mids.

The deepest artesian well in Britain is that at the White Heather Laundry, Stonebridge Park, Brent, London, bored in 1911 to a depth of 678 m *2225 ft.*

The deepest known hand-dug well is one dug to a depth of 391·6 m *1285 ft* between 1858 and March 1862 on the site of Fitzherbert School, Woodingdean, Brighton, Sussex.

Power

Steam engines *Oldest* The oldest steam engine in working order is the 1812 Boulton & Watt 26-hp, 1066 mm *42 in* bore beam engine on the Kennet and Avon Canal at Great Bedwyn, Wilts. It was restored by the Crofton Society in 1971 and still runs periodically.

Largest The largest single-cylinder steam engine ever built was that designed by Matthew Loam of Cornwall and made by the Hayle Foundry Co. in 1849 for land draining at Haarlem, Netherlands. The cylinder was 3·65 m *12 ft* in diameter each stroke, also of 3·65 m *12 ft*, lifted 61 096 l *13 440 gal* of water.

Most efficient The most efficient steam engine recorded was Taylor's engine built by Michael Loam for United Mines,

Gwennap, Cornwall in 1840. It registered only 1·7 lb of coal per horsepower per hour.

Largest power plant Currently, the most powerful installed power station is the Grand Coulee, Washington State, USA, with 7·4 million kW/hr (ultimately 10 830 MW), which began operating in 1942.

The $11-billion Itaipu power station on the Paraná River by the Brazil-Paraguay border began generating power formally on 25 Oct 1984 and will attain 13 320 kW from 18 turbines. Construction began in 1975 with a workforce approaching 28 000.

The power station with the greatest installed capacity in Great Britain is Drax, N Yorks, with five of its 660 MW sets yielding 3300 MW in mid-1986. The sixth set was operational in 1987. A 3300 MW oil-fired installation is under construction on the Isle of Grain, Kent.

The 1880 MW underground pumped storage scheme at Dinorwic, Gwynedd is the largest in Europe, with a head of 530 m *1739 ft* and a capacity of 390 m³/sec *13 770 ft³/sec.* The £425 million plant was completed in 1984 with a capacity of 1681 MW.

Earliest atomic pile The world's first atomic pile was built in a disused doubles squash court at Stagg Field, University of Chicago, Illinois, USA. It went 'critical' at 3:25 p.m. on 2 Dec 1942.

Nuclear power station The first nuclear power station producing electricity was the EBR-1 in the USA on 20 Dec 1951.

The world's largest nuclear power station with 10 reactors and an output of 9096 MW is the station in Fukushima, Japan.

Britain's earliest was Calder Hall (Unit 1), Cumbria opened on 27 Aug 1956.

Nuclear reactor The largest single nuclear reactor in the world is the 1450 MW (net) reactor at the Ignalina station, Lithuania, USSR, put on full power in January 1984.

The largest under construction is the CHOOZ-B1 reactor in France. Work began

a net annual output of 544 million kW. The 804 m *2 640 ft* barrage contains 24 turbo alternators.

The $1000-million Passamaquoddy project for the Bay of Fundy in Maine, USA, and New Brunswick, Canada remains a project. The $46 million pilot Annapolis River project for the Bay of Fundy was begun in 1981.

Largest boiler The largest boilers ever designed were those ordered in the United States from Babcock & Wilcox (USA), with a capacity of 1330 MW, so involving the evaporation of 4 232 000 kg *9 330 000 lb* of steam per hour.

The largest installed in the United Kingdom are five 660 MW units for the Drax Power Station, designed and constructed by Babcock & Wilcox.

Largest generator Generators in the 2 000 000 kW (or 2000-MW) range are now in the planning stages both in the UK and the USA.

The largest operational is a turbo-generator of 1450 MW (net) being installed at the Ignalina atomic power station in Lithuania, USSR.

Turbines The largest hydraulic turbines are those rated at 815 000 kW (equivalent to 1·1 million hp), 9·7 m *32 ft* in diameter with a 407 tonnes runner and a 317·5 tonnes shaft installed by Allis-Chalmers at the Grand Coulee Third Powerplant, Washington State, USA.

Pump The world's largest reversible pump-turbine is that made by Allis-Chalmers for the Bath County project, Virginia, USA. It has a maximum rating of 457 MW as a turbine and maximum operating head of 393 m *1 289 ft*. The impeller/runner diameter is 6349 mm *20 ft 9 in*, with a synchronous speed of 257·1 rpm.

Gas The largest gas turbine is type GT 13 E from BBC Brown Boveri AG, with a maximum output of 140 MW. The first machine is being installed in Holland in order to increase the general output of a 500 MW steam-powered plant (Hemweg 7) by more than 46 per cent.

The smallest self-sustaining gas turbine is one with 5 cm *2 in* compressor and turbine wheels built by Geoff Knights of London. It has an operating speed of 50 000 RPM.

Battery *Largest* The 10 MW lead-acid battery at Chino, California, USA has a design capacity of 40 MW/h. It will be used at an electrical sub-station for levelling peak demand loads. This $13 million project is a co-operative effort by Southern California Edison Co. Electric Power Research Institute, and International Lead Zinc Research Organization Inc.

Longest-lasting The zinc foil and sulphur dry-pile batteries made by Watlin and Hill of London in 1840 have powered ceaseless tintinnabulation inside a bell jar at the Clarendon Laboratory, Oxford since that year.

Largest gasworks The flow of natural gas from the North Sea is diminishing the manufacture of gas by the carbonization of coal and the reforming process using petroleum derivatives. Britain's largest ever gasworks, covering 120 ha *300 acres*, were at Beckton, Newham, east London.

Currently, the largest gasworks in the UK are the Breakwater Works at Oreston, Plymouth, Devon, which opened in 1966–7 and cover an area of 7·6 ha *19 acres*. They convert complex hydrocarbons into methane and produce 1 415 850 m³ *50 million ft³* per day.

on site in July 1982 and the first reactor is scheduled for operation in 1991 with a net capacity of 1457 MW.

Fusion power Tokamak-7, the experimental thermonuclear apparatus, was declared in January 1982 by USSR academician Velikhov to be operating 'reliably for months on end'. An economically viable thermonuclear reactor is not anticipated until 'about 2030'.

The recent temperature attained in the Joint European Torus (JET) at Culham, Oxon was 100 million° C *(180 million° F)* on 10 Oct 1988.

Solar power plant The largest solar furnace in the world is LUZ. Located in the Mojave Desert, 140 miles northeast of Los Angeles, USA, it is currently operating the world's nine largest solar electric generating systems (SEGS) which account for more than 92 per cent of the the world's solar electricity. LUZ is now producing 354 MW. SEGS IX is the second phase in a six-plant, $1·5 billion solar development programme due for completion in 1994 which will bring the total to 675 MW.

The $30 million thermal solar energy system at the Packerland Packing Co. Bellevue Plant, Green Bay, Wisconsin, USA, completed in January 1984, comprises 9750 *1·21 × 2·43 m 4 × 8 ft* collectors covering 28 985 m² *7·16 acres*. It will yield up to 8000 million BTUs a month.

Tidal power station The world's first major station is the Usine marémotrice de la Rance, officially opened on 26 Nov 1966 on the Rance estuary in the Golfe de St Malo, Brittany, France. It was built in five years at a cost of 420 million francs, and has

Biggest black-out The greatest power failure in history struck seven northeastern US states and Ontario, Canada on 9–10 Nov 1965. About 30 million people in 207 200 km² *80 000 miles²* were plunged into darkness. Only two were killed.

Windmill The earliest recorded windmills are those used for grinding corn in Iran in the 7th century AD.

The earliest date attributed to a windmill in England is 1185 for one at Weedley, near Hull, Humberside.

The oldest Dutch mill is the tower-mill at Zeddam, Gelderland, built c. 1450.

The oldest working mill in England is the post-mill at Outwood, near Redhill, Surrey, built in 1665, though the Ivinghoe Mill in Pitstone Green Farm, Bucks, dating from 1627, has been restored.

The post-mill in North Ronaldsay, Orkney Islands operated until 1905.

The Netherlands' largest is the Dijkpolder in Maasland, built in 1718. The sails measure 29 m *95 ¾ ft* from tip to tip.

Tallest The De Noord windmill in Schiedam, Netherlands at 33·33 m *109 ft 4 in* is the tallest in Europe.

The tallest windmill still standing in Britain is the nine-storey Sutton Mill, Norfolk, built in 1853, which (before being struck by lightning in 1941) had sails 22·2 m *73 ft* in diameter with 216 shutters.

Largest The world's first 3000 kW wind generator was the 150 m *492 ft* tall turbine, built by Grosse Windenergie–Anlage which was set up in 1982 on the Friesian coast of Germany.

The £12 million 3000-kW aerogenerator LS-1 with 60 m *196 ft 10 in* blades on a 37 m *121 ft* tall tower on Burgar Hill, Evie, Orkney built by Taylor Woodrow was switched on in a gale on 10 Nov 1987. It will generate about 9 million kW/h per annum, enough for 2000 average houses.

The $14·2 million GEC MOD-5A installation on the north shore of Oahu, Hawaii will produce 7300 kW when the wind reaches 51·5 km/h *32 mph* with 122 m *400 ft* rotors. Installation was started in March 1984.

Water mill There has been a water-powered corn-mill at Priston Mill near Bath, Avon since pre-Norman times. The earliest recorded is dated AD 931.

Tidal Mill On 12 Nov 1989 the Eling Tide Mill, Hants attained 16 hr 7 min rotation of the waterwheel in one day. It is the only surviving mill in the world harnessing the power of the tide for regular production of wholemeal flour.

Engineering

Oldest machinery The earliest mechanism still in use is the *dâlu*—a water-raising instrument known to have been in use in the Sumerian civilization, which originated c. 3500 BC in lower Iraq. The *dâlu* is thus even earlier than the saqiyas on the Nile.

The oldest piece of machinery (excluding clocks) operating in the United Kingdom is the snuff mill driven by a water-wheel at Wilson & Co. Sharrow Mill in Sheffield, S Yorks. It is known to have been operating in 1797 and more probably since 1730.

Blast furnace The world's largest blast

furnace has an inner volume of 5245 m³ *185 224 ft³* and a 14·9 m *49 ft* diameter hearth at ZBF at the Oita Works, Kyūshū, Japan, completed in October 1976 with 4 380 000 tonnes annual capacity.

Catalytic cracker The world's largest catalytic cracker is Exxon's Bayway Refinery plant at Linden, New Jersey, USA, with a fresh feed rate of 19 077 000 litres *5 040 000 US gal* per day.

Concrete pumping The world record distance for pumping ready mixed concrete without a relay pump is 1520 m *4 986 ft*, set on the Lake Chiemsee, Bavaria sewage tunnels project in the summer of 1989.

Conveyor belt The world's longest single-flight conveyor belt is one of 29 km *18 miles* in Western Australia installed by Cable Belt Ltd of Camberley, Surrey.

Great Britain's longest is also by Cable Belt and 8·9 km *5 ½ miles* underground at Longannet power station in Fife.

The world's longest multi-flight conveyor was one of 100 km *62 miles* between the phosphate mine near Bucraa and the port of El Aiún, Morocco, built by Krupps and completed in 1972. It had 11 flights of 9–11 km *5·6–6·8 miles* and was driven at 4·5 m/sec *10·06 mph*. It has since been closed down.

Most powerful crane The most powerful cranes are the two aboard the semi-submersible vessel *Micoperi 7000* (190 m *623·35 ft* in length and 89 m *292 ft* in breadth) operated by Officine Meccaniche Reggiane designed by American Hoist & Derrick Company, built by Monfalcone, Gorizia, Italy and launched 15 Dec 1986. Each has a capacity of 7000 tonnes. In tandem they can lift 14 000 tonnes. In its first six months of operation it achieved a record lift of 5 700 tonnes.

Gantry crane The 28·14 m *92·3 ft* wide Rahco (R.A. Hanson Disc Ltd) gantry crane at the Grand Coulee Dam Third Powerplant was tested to lift a load of 2232 tonnes in 1975. It lowered a 1789 tonnes generator rotor with an accuracy of 0·8 mm *1·32 in*.

Tallest mobile crane The 810 tonnes Rosenkranz K10001, with a lifting capacity of 1 000 tonnes, and a combined boom and jib height of 202 m *663 ft*, is carried on 10 trucks each limited to a length of 23·06 m *75 ft 8 in* and an axle weight of 118 tonnes. It can lift 30 tonnes to a height of 160 m *525 ft*.

The Taklift 4 craneship of the Smit International fleet based in Rotterdam, Netherlands has boom and jib height of 95 m *312 ft*.

Most powerful diesel engines Five 12RTA84 type diesel engines have been constructed by Sulzer Brothers of Winterthur, Switzerland, for container ships built for the American President Lines. Each 12 cylinder power unit gives a maximum continuous output of 41 920 kW *57 000 bhp* at 95 rev/min. The first of these ships, the *President Truman*, was handed over in April 1988 and the most recent in September of that year.

Most powerful rocket engine The most powerful rocket engine was built in the USSR by Scientific Industrial Corporation of Energetic Engineering during 1980. The engine has a thrust of 806 000 kg *1 776 895 lb* in open space and a thrust of 740 000 kg *1 631 393 lb* at the Earth surface. The RD-170 has a turbopump of 190 MW and burns liquid oxygen and kerosene.

Dragline The Ural Engineering Works (named after Ordzhonikidze) in Sverd-

lovsk, USSR, completed in March 1962, has a dragline known as the ES-25(100), with a boom of 100 m *328 ft*, and a bucket with a capacity of 24 m³ *31·5 yd³*.

The world's largest walking dragline is 'Big Muskie', the Bucyrus-Erie 4250W with an all-up weight of 12 000 tonnes and a bucket capacity of 168 m³ *220 yd³* on a 94·4 m *310 ft* boom. This is the largest mobile land machine and is now operating on the Central Ohio Coal Co. Muskingum site in Ohio, USA.

The largest dragline excavator in Britain is 'Big Geordie', the Bucyrus-Erie 1550W, 6250 gross hp, weighing 3000 tonnes with a forward mast 48·7 m *160 ft* high. On open-cast coal workings at Butterwell, Northumberland in September 1975 it proved able to strip 100 tonnes of overburden in 65 sec with its 49·7 m³ *65 yd³* bucket on a 80·7 m *265 ft* boom. It is owned by Derek Crouch (Contractors) Ltd of Peterborough, Cambs.

Earthmover The giant wheeled loader developed for open-air coal mining in Australia by SMEC, a consortium of 11 manufacturers in Tokyo, Japan, is 16·8 m *55·1 ft* in length, weighs 180 tonnes and its rubber tyres are 3·5 m *11·5 ft* in diameter. The bucket has a capacity of 19 m³ *671 ft³*.

Escalator The term was registered in the USA on 28 May 1900 but the earliest 'Inclined Escalator' was installed by Jesse W. Reno on the pier at Coney Island, New York, USA in 1896.

The first installation in Britain was at Harrods department store, London in November 1898.

The longest escalators in Britain are the

four in the Tyne Tunnel, Tyne & Wear and installed in 1951. They measure 58·7 m *192 ft 8 in* between combs with a vertical lift of 25·9 m *85 ft* and a step speed of up to 2·7 km/h *1·7 mph*.

The escalators on the Leningrad underground, USSR at Lenin Square have 729 steps and a vertical rise of 59·68 m *195 ft 9½ in*.

The world's longest *ride* is on the four-section outdoor escalator at Ocean Park, Hong Kong, which has an overall length of 227 m *745 ft* and a total vertical rise of 115 m *377 ft*.

The world's longest 'moving sidewalks' are those installed in 1970 in the Neue Messe Centre, Dusseldorf, Germany, which measure 225 m *738 ft* between comb plates.

The longest in Great Britain which is called a 'Travelator', is the 110·3 m *362 ft 2 in* long Dunlop Starglide at London's Heathrow Airport Terminal 3, installed in March–May 1970.

The ultimate in absurdity to weary shoppers can be found at the Shopping Mall at Kawasaki-shi, Japan. It has a vertical

■ **Most powerful rocket engine**
Built in 1980 the RD–170 rocket engine was used with the Energia *and* Zenit *rockets to take the* Buran *shuttle into low Earth orbit or spaceships to Mars. It has a turbopump of 190 MW which burns liquid oxygen and kerosene.*

■ **Most powerful diesel engine**
The President Polk *one of five 12RTA84 type container ships with the most powerful diesel engines, constructed by Sulzer Brothers of Switzerland. Each 12 cylinder power units gives a maximum continuous output of 41 920 kW 57 000 bhp.*
(Photo: Sulzer)

ENGINEERING

Escalator riding
The record distance travelled on a pair of 'up' and 'down' escalators is 214·34 km *133·18 miles*, by David Beattie and Adrian Simons at Top Shop, Oxford Street, London from 17–21 Jul 1989. They each completed 7032 circuits.

Top spinning
The duration record for spinning a clock-balance wheel by unaided hand is 5 min 26·8 sec by Philip Ashley, 16, of Leigh, Lancs on 20 May 1968.

The record using 91·4 cm *36 in* of string with a 205·5 g *7¼ oz* top is 58 min 20 sec, by Peter Hodgson at Southend-on-Sea, Essex on 4 Feb 1985.

A team of 25 from the Mizushima Plant of Kawasaki Steel Works in Okayama, Japan spun a giant top 2 m *6 ft 6¾ in* tall and 2·6 m *8 ft 6¼ in* in diameter, weighing 360 kg *793·6 lb*, for 1 hr 21 min 35 sec on 3 Nov 1986.

height of 83·4 cm *32·83 in* and was installed by Hitachi Ltd.

Excavator The world's largest excavator is the 13 000 tonnes bucket wheel excavator being assembled at the open-cast lignite mine at Hambach, Germany, with a rating of 200 000 m² *260 000 yd²* per 20 hr working day. It is 210 m *690 ft* in length and 82 m *269 ft* tall. The wheel is 67·88 m *222 ft* in circumference with 5 m *6·5 yd²* buckets.

Forging The largest forging on record is one of a 204·4 tonnes *450 600 lb*, 16·76 m *55 ft* long generator shaft for Japan, forged by the Bethlehem Steel Corporation of Pennsylvania, USA in October 1973.

Fork lift truck Kalmar LMV of Sweden manufactured in 1985 ten counterbalanced fork lift trucks capable of lifting loads up to 80 tonnes at a load centre of 2300 mm *90·5 in*. They were built to handle the large-diameter pipeline in the Libyan Great Man-made River Project.

Lathe The largest is the 38·4 m *126 ft* long 416·2 tonnes giant lathe built by Waldrich Siegen of Germany in 1973 for the South African Electricity Supply Commission at Rosherville. It has a capacity for 300 tonnes work pieces and a swing-over beds of 5 m *16 ft 5 in* in diameter.

Greatest lift The heaviest lifting operation in engineering history was the raising of the entire 1·6 km *0·745 mile* long offshore Ekofisk complex in the North Sea, owing to subsidence of the sea bed. The complex consists of eight platforms weighing some 40 000 tonnes. During 17–18 Aug 1987 it was raised 6·5 m *21 ft 4 in* by 122 hydraulic jacks requiring a computer-controlled hydraulic system developed and supplied by the Dutch Mannesmann-Texroth company: Hydraudyne Systems & Engineering bv of Boxtel, Netherlands.

Slowest machine A nuclear environmental machine for testing stress corrosion has been developed by Nene Instruments of Wellingborough, Northants that can be controlled at a speed as slow as one million millionth of a millimetre per minute, or one metre *3·28 ft* in about 2000 million years.

Nut The largest nuts ever made weigh 4·74 tonnes each with an outside diameter of 132 cm *52 in* and a 63·5 cm *25 in* thread. Known as 'Pilgrim Nuts', they are manufactured by Pilgrim Moorside Ltd of Oldham, Lancs for use on the columns of a large forging press.

Oil tank The largest oil tanks ever constructed are the five ARAMCO 1 ½-million-barrel storage tanks at Ju'aymah, Saudi Arabia. They are 21·94 m *72 ft* tall with a diameter of 117·6 m *386 ft* and were completed in March 1980.

Passenger lift The fastest domestic passenger lifts in the world are the express lifts to the 60th floor of the 240 m *787·4 ft* tall 'Sunshine 60' building, Ikebukuro, in Tokyo, Japan, completed 5 Apr 1978. They were built by Mitsubishi Corporation and operate at a speed of 609·6 m/min *2 000 ft/min* or 36·56 km/h *22·72 mph*.

Much higher speeds are achieved in the winding cages of mine shafts. A hoisting shaft 2072 m *6 800 ft* deep, owned by Western Deep Levels Ltd in South Africa, winds at speeds of up to 65·2 km/h *40·9 mph* (1095 m/min *3 595 ft/min*). Otitis-media (popping of the ears) presents problems even above 16 km/h *10 mph*.

The longest lift in the United Kingdom is one 283·4 m *930 ft* long inside the BBC television tower at Bilsdale, West Moor, N Yorks, built by J.L. Eve Construction. It

runs at 39·6 m/min *130 ft/min*. The longest fast lifts are the two 15-passenger cars in the British Telecom Tower, London, which travel 164 m *540 ft* at up to 304 m/min *1000 ft/min*.

Pipelines *Earliest* The world's earliest pipeline, of 5 cm *2 in* diameter cast iron, laid at Oil Creek, Pennsylvania, USA in 1863 was torn up by Luddites.

The longest crude oil pipeline in the world is the Interprovincial Pipe Line Co. installation from Edmonton, Alberta, Canada to Buffalo, New York State, USA, a distance of 2856 km *1 775 miles*. Along the length of the pipe, 13 pumping stations maintain a flow of 31 367 145 litres *6 900 000 gal* of oil per day.

The eventual length of the Trans-Siberian pipeline will be 3732 km *2 319 miles*, running from Tuimazy through Omsk and Novosibirsk to Irkutsk. The first 48 km *30 mile* section was opened in July 1957.

Gas The world's longest submarine pipeline is that of 425 km *264 miles* for natural gas from the Union Oil platform to Rayong, Thailand, opened on 12 Sep 1981.

The longest North Sea pipeline is the Ekofisk–Emden line covering 418 km *260 miles* and completed in July 1975.

The deepest North Sea pipeline is that from the Cormorant Field to Firths Voe, Shetland, at 162 m *530 ft*.

The longest natural gas pipeline in the world is the Trans-Canada pipeline, which by 1974 had 9099 km *5 654 miles* of pipe up to 106·6 cm *42 in* in diameter.

The Tyumen–Chelyabinsk–Moscow Brandenburg gas pipeline runs for 4330 km *2 690 miles*.

The large-calibre Urengoi-Nzhgorod line to Western Europe, begun in November 1982, covers 4451 km *2 765 miles* and was completed on 25 Jul 1983. It has a capacity of 32 000 million m³ *42 000 million yd³* per annum.

Water The world's longest water pipeline runs a distance of 563 km *350 miles* to the Kalgoorlie goldfields from near Perth in Western Australia. Engineered in 1903, the system has since been extended five-fold by branches.

Most expensive The world's most expensive pipeline is the Alaska pipeline running 1284 km *798 miles* from Prudhoe Bay to Valdez. On completion of the first phase in 1977, it had cost at least $6 billion. The pipe is 1·21 m *48 in* in diameter and will eventually carry up to 2 million barrels of crude oil per day.

Press The world's two most powerful production machines are forging presses in the USA. The Loewy closed-die forging press, in a plant leased from the US Air Force by the Wyman-Gordon Company at North Grafton, Massachusetts weighs 9469 tonnes and stands 34·79 m *114 ft 2 in* high, of which 20·1 m *66 ft* is sunk below the operating floor. It has a rated capacity of 44 600 tonnes and became operational in October 1955.

The other similar press is at the plant of the Aluminum Company of America in Cleveland, Ohio, USA.
In January 1986 ASEA's QUINTUS department delivered a sheet metal forming press to BMW AG, Munich, Germany. This press, which is the largest in the world in terms of forming pressure and press force is a QUINTUS fluid cell press with a press force of 106 000 tonnes. The Bêché & Grohs

counter-blow forging hammer, manufactured in Germany, is rated at 60 000 tonnes.

The most powerful press in Great Britain is the closed-die forging and extruding press installed in 1967 at the Cameron Iron Works, Livingston, West Lothian. The press is 28 m *92 ft* tall (8·2 m *27 ft* below ground) and exerts a force of 30 000 tonnes.

Printer The world's fastest printer is the Radiation Inc. electro-sensitive system at the Lawrence Radiation Laboratory, Livermore, California, USA. High-speed recording of up to 30 000 lines per minute, each containing 120 alphanumeric characters, is attained by controlling electronic pulses through chemically-impregnated recording paper which is rapidly moving under closely-spaced fixed styluses. It can thus print the Bible (773 692 words) in 65 seconds; 3306 times as fast as the world's fastest typist.

Radar installation The largest of the three installations in the US Ballistic Missile Early Warning System (BMEWS) is that near Thule, in Kalaallit Nunaat (Greenland), 1498 km *931 miles* from the North Pole. It was completed in 1960 at a cost of $500 million.

Its sister stations are one at Cape Clear, Alaska, USA, which was completed in 1961 and the $115 million radar installation at Fylingdales Moor, N Yorks which was completed in June 1963.

The largest scientific radar installation is the 84 000 m² *21 acre* ground array at Jicamarca, Peru.

Ropes The largest rope ever made was a coir fibre launching rope with a circumference of 119 cm *47 in* made in 1858 for the British liner *Great Eastern* by John and Edwin Wright of Birmingham, W Mids. It consisted of four strands, each of 3780 yarns. The longest fibre rope ever made without a splice was one of 18·29 km *11·36 miles* of 16·5 cm *6½ in* circumference manila by Frost Brothers (now British Ropes Ltd) in London in 1874.

The strongest cable-laid wire rope strop made is one 394 mm *15 ½ in* in diameter with a breaking strain of 7028 tonnes, and manufactured by ScanRope Ltd of Norway. The sling was used to lift the steel jacket for the Veslefrikk Offshore Field in the Norwegian sector in 1989.

Ropeway or téléphérique The longest ropeway in the world is the Compagnie Minière de l'Ogooué, or COMILOG, installation built in 1959–62 for the Moanda manganese mine in Gabon, which extends 76 km *47·2 miles*. It has 858 towers and 2800 buckets, with 155 km *96·3 miles* of wire rope running over 6000 idler pulleys.

The highest and longest passenger-carrying aerial ropeway in the world is the Teleférico Mérida (Mérida téléphérique) in Venezuela, from Mérida City (1639·5 m *5379 ft*) to the summit of Pico Espejo (4763·7 m *15 629 ft*), a rise of 3124 m *10 250 ft*. The ropeway is in four sections, involving three car changes in the 12·8 km *8 mile* ascent in one hour. The fourth span is 3069 m *10 070 ft* in length. The two cars work on the pendulum system—the carrier rope is locked and the cars are hauled by means of three pull ropes powered by a 230 hp 233 cv motor. They have a maximum capacity of 45 persons and travel at 9·7 m/sec *32 ft/sec* (35·08 km/h *21·8 mph*).

The longest single-span ropeway is the 4114 m *13 500 ft* span from the Coachella Valley to Mt San Jacinto (3298 m *310 821 ft*), California, USA, inaugurated on 12 Sep 1963.

Britain's longest cabin lift is that at Llandudno, opened in June 1969. It has 42 cabins with a capacity of 1000 people per hour and is 1621 m *5320 ft* in length.

Shovel The Marion 6360 has a reach of 72·16 m *236·75 ft*, a dumping height of 46·63 m *153 ft* and a bucket capacity of 180 yd³ *4860 ft³*. Manufactured in 1964 by the Marion Power Shovel Co. Ohio, USA, it weighs 11 million kg *24 250 000 lb* and uses 20 electric motors that generate 45 000 hp to operate its 67·2 m *220·5 ft* long boom arm. It is operated for open-cast coal mining near Percy in Illinois, USA by the Arch Mineral Corporation.

Snow-plough blade A blade measuring 9·83 m *32 ft 3 in* in length was designed and constructed by the Thomas Sedgwick Construction Co.Inc. of Syracuse, New York, USA for use at Hancock International Airport. With a 15·24 cm *6 in* snowfall the plough can push away 6 499 m³ *8500 yd³* of snow in one hour.

Transformer The world's largest single-phase transformers are rated at 1 500 000 kVA, of which eight are in service with the American Electric Power Service Corporation. Of these, five stepdown from 765 to 345 kV.

Britain's largest transformers are those rated at 1 000 000 kVA built by Hackbridge & Hewittic, Walton-on-Thames, Surrey, first commissioned for the CEGB in October 1968.

Transmission lines The longest span between pylons of any power line in the world is that across the Sogne Fjord, Norway, between Rabnaberg and Fatlaberg. Supplied in 1955 by Whitecross of Warrington, Cheshire, and projected and erected by A.S. Betonmast of Oslo as part of the high-tension power cable from Refsdal power station at Vik, it has a span of 4888 m *16 040 ft* and a weight of 12 tonnes. In 1967 two further high-tensile steel/aluminium lines 4878 m *16 006 ft* long, and weighing 33 tonnes, manufactured by Whitecross and BICC, were erected here.

The longest in Britain are the 1618 m *5310 ft* lines built by J.L. Eve across the Severn, with main towers each 148 m *488 ft* high.

Highest The world's highest are those across the Straits of Messina, Italy with towers of 205 m *675 ft* (Sicily side) and 224 m *735 ft* (Calabria) and 3627 m *11 900 ft* apart.

The highest lines in Britain are those made by BICC at West Thurrock, Essex, which cross the Thames estuary suspended from 192 m *630 ft* tall towers at a minimum height of 76 m *250 ft*, with a 130 tonne breaking load. They are 1371 m *4500 ft* apart.

Highest voltages The highest voltages now carried are 1 330 000 volts for 1970 km *1224 miles* on the DC Pacific Inter-tie in the USA. The Ekibastuz DC transmission lines in Kazakhstan, USSR are planned to be 2400 km *1490 miles* long with 1 500 000 volt capacity.

Valve The world's largest valve is the 9·75 m *32 ft* diameter, 170 tonne butterfly valve designed by Boving & Co. Ltd of London for use at the Arnold Air Force Base engine test facility in Tennessee, USA.

Wire ropes The longest wire ropes in the world are the four made at British Ropes Ltd, Wallsend, Tyne & Wear, each measuring 24 000 m *14·9 miles*. The ropes are 35 mm *1·3 in* in diameter, weigh 108·5 tonnes each and were ordered by the CEGB for use in the construction of the 2000 MW cross-Channel power cable.

The thickest ever manufactured are spliced crane strops from wire ropes 28·2 cm *11 ¼ in* thick with 2392 individual wires made in March 1979 by British Ropes Ltd of Doncaster at Willington Quay, also Tyne & Wear, and designed to lift loads of up to 3000 tonnes.

The suspension cables on the Seto Grand Bridge, Japan, completed in 1988, are 104 cm *41 in* in diameter.

The heaviest ever wire ropes (four in number) are each of 130 tonnes, made for the twin shaft system of Western Deep Levels gold mine, South Africa by Haggie Rand Ltd of Johannesburg.

Wind tunnels The world's largest wind tunnel is that of the NASA Ames Research Center in Mountain View, Palo Alto, California, USA. The new tunnel 12 × 24 m *40 × 80 ft* was opened on 11 Dec 1989 and powered by six 22 500 hp motors enabling a best speed of 555 km/h *345 mph*.

Time Pieces

Largest sundial The world's largest sundial is the Samrat Yantra, with gnomon height of 27 m *88·5 ft* and a vertical height of 36 m *118 ft*. It was built in 1724 at Jaipur, India.

On 1 Mar 1991 the Walt Disney World Co. in Orlando, Florida, USA unveiled the largest cylindrical sundial measuring 36·5 m *120 ft* high, 37·18 m *122 ft* in diameter at the base. The sundial was designed by Arata Isozaki of Tokyo, Japan.

Most accurate time measurer The most accurate time-keeping devices are the twin atomic hydrogen masers installed in 1964 in the US Naval Research Laboratory, Washington, DC, USA. They are based on the frequency of the hydrogen atom's transition period of 1 420 450 751 694 cycles/sec. This enables an accuracy to within 1 sec in 1 700 000 years.

Clock Oldest The earliest mechanical clock that is, is one with an escapement—it was completed in China in AD 725 by I Hsing and Liang Lingtsan.

The oldest surviving working clock in the world is the faceless clock dating from 1386, or possibly earlier, at Salisbury Cathedral, Wilts, which was restored in 1956, having struck the hours for 498 years and ticked more than 500 million times. Earlier dates, ranging back to c. 1335, have been attributed to the weight-driven clock in Wells Cathedral, Somerset, but only the iron frame is original.

A model of Giovanni de Dondi's heptagonal astronomical clock of 1348–64 was completed in 1962.

Largest The world's most massive clock is the astronomical clock in the Cathedral of St Pierre, Beauvais, France, constructed between 1865 and 1868. It contains 90 000 parts and is 12·1 m *40 ft* high, 6·09 m *20 ft* wide and 2·7 m *9 ft* deep.

The Su Sung clock, built in China at K'aifeng in 1088–92, had a 20·3 tonnes bronze armillary sphere for 1·52 tonnes of water. It was removed to Beijing (formerly Peking) in 1126 and was last known to be working in its 12·1 m *40 ft* high tower in 1136.

Another large clock is 'Timepiece', which measures 15·54 × 15·54 × 15·54 m *51 × 51 × 51 ft*. It is suspended over five storeys in the atrium of the International Square building in Washington, DC, USA. Computer driven and accurate to within 1/100th of a second, it weighs 2 tonnes. It is lit by 122 m *400 ft* of neon tube lighting and requires 460 m *1500 ft* of cable and wiring. Twelve tubes at its base light up to tell the hour and the minute. The clock, designed by the sculptor John Safer, also indicates when the sun is at its zenith in 12 international cities.

The largest clock in the United Kingdom is that on the Royal Liver Building, Liverpool (built 1908–11), with dials 7·62 m *25 ft* in diameter and four minute hands each 4·26 m *14 ft* long. The mechanism and dials weigh 22 tons and are 67 m *220 ft* above street level.

Clock faces The world's largest is that of the floral clock 21 m *68 ft 10 ¾ in* in diameter, manufactured by Seiko for the Koryu Fujisho Co. and installed in June 1988 inside the Rose Building in the city of Hokkaido, Japan. The large hand of the clock is 8·5 m *27 ft 10 ½ in* long.

The digital, electronic, two-sided clock which revolves on top of the Texas Building in Fort Worth, Texas, USA, has dimensions of 13·4 × 13·4 × 8·5 m *44 × 44 × 28 ft*.

The largest vertical outdoor clock face is the octagonal Colgate clock in Jersey, New Jersey, USA, with a diameter of 15·24 m *50 ft* and a minute hand 8·31 m *27 ft 3 in* in length. In 1989 it was dismantled from the position it had occupied since 1908 at the top of the company's factory, which is being redeveloped. It is planned to relocate it at another site.

Four-faced Tallest The tallest four-faced clock in the world is that of the Williamsburgh Savings Bank in Brooklyn, New York City, USA. It is 131 m *430 ft* above street level.

Largest The largest four-faced clock in the world is that on the building of the Allen-Bradley Co. of Milwaukee, Wisconsin, USA. Each face has a diameter of 12·28 m *40 ft 3 ½ in* with a minute hand 6·09 m *20 ft* in overall length.

Most accurate mechanical The Olsen clock, completed for Copenhagen Town Hall, Denmark in December 1955, has more than 14 000 units, and took 10 years to make; the mechanism functions in 570 000 different ways. The celestial pole motion will take 25 753 years to complete a full circle and is the slowest-moving designed mechanism in the world. The clock is accurate to 0·5 sec in 300 years—50 times more accurate than the previous record.

Most expensive The highest price paid for any clock is £880 000 for a Thomas Tompion (1639–1713) unrecorded miniature longcase, known as a 'night clock' at Christie's, London on 6 Jul 1989.

Watch Oldest The oldest portable clockwork time-keeper is one made of iron by Peter Henlein in Nürnberg (Nüremberg), Bavaria, Germany, c. 1504.

The earliest wrist-watches were those of Jacquet-Droz and Leschot of Geneva, Switzerland, dating from 1790.

Largest The largest watch was a 'Swatch' 162 m *531 ft 6 in* long and 20 m *65 ft 7 ½ in* in diameter, made by D. Tomas Feliu, which was set up on the Bank of Bilbao building, Madrid, Spain from 7–12 Dec 1985.

The Eta 'watch' on the Swiss pavilion at Expo 86 in Vancouver, British Columbia,

Longest stoppage of 'Big Ben'
The longest stoppage of the clock in the House of Commons clock tower, London since the first tick on 31 May 1859 has been 13 days, from noon on 4 April to noon on 17 Apr 1977. In 1945 a host of starlings slowed the minute hand by 5 minutes.

Pendulum
The longest pendulum in the world is 22·5 m *73 ft 9 ¾ in* on the water-mill clock installed by the Hattori Tokeiten Co. in the Shinjuku NS building in Tokyo, Japan in 1983.

Morse

The highest recorded speed at which anyone has received Morse Code is 75·2 words per min — over 17 symbols per sec. This was achieved by Ted R. McElroy of the USA in a tournament at Asheville, North Carolina, USA on 2 Jul 1939.

The highest speed recorded for hand key transmitting is 175 symbols a minute by Harry A. Turner of the US Army Signal Corps at Camp Crowder, Missouri, USA on 9 Nov 1942.

Thomas Morris, a GPO operator, is reputed to have been able to send at 39–40 wpm *c.* 1919, but this is not verifiable.

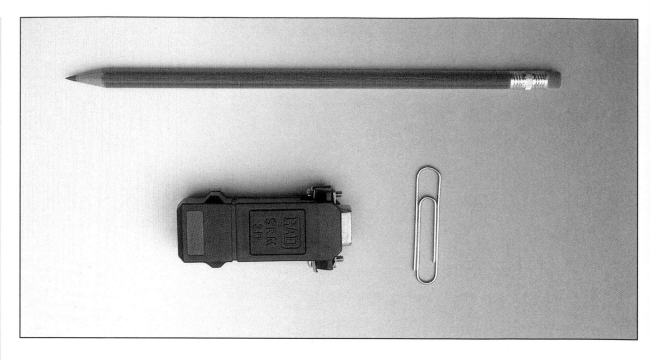

Canada from May–October weighed 35 tonnes and stood 24·3 m *80 ft* high.

Smallest The smallest watches are those produced by Jaeger le Coultre of Switzerland. They are equipped with a 15-jewelled movement measure just over 1·2 cm *½ in* long and 0·476 cm *3/16 in* in width. Movement and case together weigh under 7 g *0·25 oz*.

Astronomical The entirely mechanical Planetarium Copernicus, made by Ulysse Nardin of Switzerland, is the only wristwatch that indicates the time of day, the date, the phases of the Moon, and the astronomical position of the Sun, Earth, Moon and the planets known in Copernicus' day. It also represents the Ptolemaic universe showing the astrological 'aspects' at any given time.

Most expensive The record price paid for a watch is £16 004 392 at Habsbury Feldman, Geneva, Switzerland on 9 Apr 1989 for a Patek Philippe 'Calibre '89' with 1728 separate parts.

Excluding watches with jewelled cases, the most expensive standard man's pocket watch is Heaven at Hand, known to the connoisseurs as the Packard and made in 1922 by Patek Philippe for the American automobile magnate James Packard. The timepiece is the most outstanding example of a 'complicated' pocket watch in the world and was bought back by Patek Philippe in September 1988 for £750 000. To satisfy Packard's eccentric demands, Patek Philippe created a perfect celestial chart in enamel on the watch in gold casing to show the heavens as they moved over Packard's hometown of Warren, Ohio, USA—in fact exactly as he could see them from his bedroom window.

Computers

Earliest The earliest programmable electronic computer was the 1500-valve Colossus formulated by Prof. Max H.A. Newman (1897–1985) and built by T.H. Flowers. It was run in December 1943 at Bletchley Park, Bucks to break the German coding machine Enigma. It arose from a concept published in 1936 by Dr Alan Math-

ison Turing (1912–54) in his paper *On Computable Numbers with an Application to the* Entscheidungsproblem. Colossus was declassified on 25 Oct 1975.

The world's first stored-programme computer was the Manchester University Mark I, which incorporated the Williams storage cathode ray tube (patented 11 Dec 1946). It ran its first program, by Prof. Tom Kilburn (b. 1921), for 52 min on 21 Jun 1948.

Computers were greatly advanced by the invention of the point-contact transistor by John Bardeen and Walter Brattain announced in July 1948, and the junction transistor by R.L. Wallace, Morgan Sparks and Dr William Bradford Shockley (1910–89) in early 1951.

The concept of the integrated circuit, which has enabled micro-miniaturisation, was first published on 7 May 1952 by Geoffrey W.A. Dummer (b. 1909) in Washington, DC, USA.

The invention of the microcomputer was attributed to a team led by M.E. Hoff, Jr of Intel Corporation with the production of the microprocessor chip '4004' in 1969–71. On 17 July 1990 however printing was accorded to Gilbert Hyatt (b. 1938), who devised a single chip microcomputer at Micro Computer Inc. of Van Nuys, Los Angeles in 1968–71, with the award of US Patent No. 4942516.

Most powerful and fastest The world's most powerful and fastest computer is the liquid-cooled CRAY-2, named after Seymour R. Cray of Cray Research Inc. Minneapolis, Minnesota, USA. Its memory has a capacity of 256 million 64-bit words, resulting in a capacity of 32 million bytes of main memory. (NB: a 'byte' is a unit of storage comprising eight 'bits' which are collectively equivalent to one alphabetic symbol or two numericals). It attains speeds of 250 million floating point operations per second.

The most powerful British computer is the International Computer's Distribution Array Processor—the ICL DAP.

Sandia National Laboratory, New Mexico, USA on 18 Mar 1988 announced a 'massively parallel' hypercube computer with 1024 parallel processors, which, by breaking down problems into parts for simultaneous solution, proved 1019 times

faster than a conventional mainframe computer.

In May 1988 NEC (Nippon Electric Co.) announced a £1·6 billion research programme to attain a fifth generation computer able to read handwriting and understand speech in many languages, and incorporating super conduction and Josephson functions.

Computer company The world's largest computer firm is International Business Machines (IBM) Corporation of New York, USA. At December 1990 assets were $87·6 billion and gross income was $69 billion. It has 373 816 employees worldwide and 789 046 stockholders.

Smallest modem Modems are devices that allow electron signals to be transmitted over large distances by MOdulating the signal at one end, and DEModulating the signal back to its original form at the destination. The smallest is the SRM-3A which is 61 mm *2·4 in* long, 31 mm *1·2 in* wide, and 19·8 mm *0·8 in* high, and weighs 31 g *1·1 oz*. It is currently manufactured by RAD Data Communications Ltd of Tel Aviv, Israel.

Smallest word processor The Easi-Text 1350 was introduced by Minimicro of Huntington, N Yorks, in April 1986. It is based on the Sharp PC-1350 computer which measures 182 × 72 × 16 mm *7·2 × 2·8 × 0·6 in*, and the entire system, including an A4-size Epson P-80 printer, fits into an executive briefcase.

Megabits The megabit barrier was broken in February 1984, with the manufacture of a 1024K-bit integrated circuit the size of a drawing pin head and as thin as a human hair, by four Japanese companies: Hitachi, NEC, NTT Atsugi Electrical Communications and Toshiba. Toshiba announced that manufacture of an 80-picosecond LSI (large scale integration) chip of gallium arsenide had started in 1985–6.

Fastest transistor A transistor capable of switching 230 000 million times per second was announced by Illinois State University, USA on 5 Oct 1986.

Telecommunications

Telephones There were approximately

423 618 819 telephones in the world at 1 Jan 1989. The country with the greatest number was the United States, with 118 400 662.

This compares with the British Telecom figure of 26 million (December 1990) (6th largest in the world to the USA, Japan, USSR, Germany and France), or 418 per 1000 people.

The territory reported to have the fewest reported telephone lines is Pitcairn Island, with 24.

The city with the most telephones in the world is Tokyo, Japan with 5 511 000. The greatest number of calls made in any country is in the United States with 421 822 million per annum.

Longest telephone cable The world's longest submarine telephone cable is ANZCAN, which runs for 15 151 km *9415 miles* (8181 nautical miles) from Port Alberni, Canada to Auckland, New Zealand and Sydney, Australia via Fiji and Norfolk Island. It cost some US$ 379 million and was inaugurated by HM Queen Elizabeth II in November 1984.

Longest terrestrial call A telephone call around the world, over an estimated 158 845 km *98 700 miles*, was made on 28 Dec 1985 from, and back to, the Royal Institution, London, during one of the Christmas lectures given by David Pye, Prof. of Zoology, Queen Mary College, London. The international telecommunications 'rule', that only one communication satellite be used at a time, was suspended for the demonstration so that both geostationary Intelsats, one over the Indian Ocean and one over the Pacific, could be employed. The two 'telephonists', Anicka Russell and Alison Risk, experienced a delay in their conversation of 530 milliseconds.

Largest and smallest telephones The world's largest operational telephone was exhibited at a festival on 16 Sep 1988 to celebrate the 80th birthday of Centraal Beheer, an insurance company based in Apeldoorn, Netherlands. It was 2·74 m *8 ft 1 in* high and 6·06 m *19 ft 11 in* long, and weighed 3·5 tonnes. The handset, being 7·14 m *23 ft 5 in* long, had to be lifted by crane in order to make a call.
The smallest operational telephone was created by Jeff Smith of GTE Northwest, Everett, Washington State, USA in 1988 and measured 10·48 × 1·90 × 3·81 cm *4 ⅛ × ¾ × 1½ in*.

Busiest telephone exchange GPT (GEC Plessey Telecommunications Ltd) demonstrated the ability of the 'System X' telephone exchange to handle 1 558 000 calls in an hour through one exchange at Beeston, Nottingham on 27 Jun 1989.

Largest switchboard The world's biggest switchboard is that in the Pentagon, Washington, DC, USA, with 25 000 lines handling over 200 000 calls per day through 160 934 km *100 000 miles* of telephone cable.

Facsimile machine *Largest* The largest facsimile machine is manufactured by WideCom Group Inc of Ontario, Canada. 'Wide Fax' has scanning and printing facilities to 60·96 cm *24 in*.

Smallest The world's smallest facsimile machine is capable of sending and receiving A4-size documents, together with an error correction mode. The RICOH PF-1 portable measures 27·94 × 17·78 × 5·08 cm *11 × 7 × 2 in* and weighs 5·5 lb.

Optical fibre The longest distance at which signals have been transmitted without repeaters is 251·6 km *156·3 miles* at the British Telecom research laboratory at Martlesham Heath, Suffolk in February 1985. The laser wavelength was 1525 nm and the rate was 35 megabits/sec.

Telescopes

Earliest It is not known when the first telescopes were made. The refractive properties of lenses were certainly known in ancient times, and spectacles were in use in the 13th century. Roger Bacon (*c.* 1214–92) in England wrote extensively about lenses, and claims have been made on behalf of various others, notably the Elizabethan scientists Diggs and Dee. Leonardo da Vinci (1452–1519) is said to have used some sort of reflecting device to 'make the Moon seem larger', though this is not fully authenticated. It is very probable that the first telescope actually constructed was a refractor made by H. Lippershey in Holland in 1608. The first astronomical observations with telescopes were made shortly afterwards, notably in 1609 by Thomas Harriot, who even drew a telescopic map of the Moon—though the first really systematic telescopic observations were made by Galileo from January 1610.

The first reflecting telescope was made by Isaac Newton, and was presented to the Royal Society in 1671 and thought to have been constructed in 1668 or 1669.

Largest reflector The largest single-mirror telescope now in use is the 6 m *19 ft 8 in* reflector sited on Mount Semirodriki, near Zelenchukskaya in the Caucasus Mountains, USSR, at an altitude of 2080 m *6830 ft* and was completed in 1976. It has never come up to expectations, partly because it is not set up on a really good observing site. The largest satisfactory single-mirror telescope is the 508 cm *200 in* Hale reflector at Mount Palomar, California, USA. Though the Hale was completed in 1948, it is now much more efficient than it was, as it is used with electronic devices which are more sensitive than photographic plates. The CCD (Charged-Coupled Device) increases the sensitivity by a factor of around 100.

Metal-Mirror A 183 cm *72 in* reflector was made by the third Earl of Rosse, and set up at Birr Castle, Republic of Ireland in 1845. The mirror was of speculum metal (an alloy of copper and tin). With it, Lord Rosse discovered the spiral forms of the galaxies. It was last used in 1909.

The largest British reflector is the 420 cm *165·35 in* William Herschel completed in 1987; it is set up at the Los Muchachos Observatory on La Palma, Canary Isles. Also at La Palma is the 256 cm *100·78 in* Issac Newton telescope, transferred there from its old site at Herstmonceux in Sussex.

Largest partially completed telescope The Keck telescope on Mauna Kea, Hawaii, USA now being constructed will have a 1000 cm *393·70 in* mirror, made up of 36 segments fitted together to produce the correct curve. Each segment is 183 cm *72 in* in aperture. An active support system holds each segment in place, and ensures that the images produced are brought to the same focus. The first image of the spiral galaxy 1232 was obtained on 24 Nov 1990, when nine of the segments were in place. It has been estimated that all the segments will be in place by the end of 1991, and that the first regular observational programmes will begin in 1992.

Multiple-mirror The MMT (Multiple-Mirror telescope) at the Whipple Observatory at Mount Hopkins, Arizona, USA uses six 183 cm *600·3 in* mirrors together, giving a light-grasp equal to a single 447 cm *176 in* mirror. There are, however, considerable operational problems.

Largest planned The largest telescope of the century should be the VLT (Very Large Telescope) being planned by the European Southern Observatory. It will consist of four 8 m *26·24 ft* telescopes working together, providing a light-grasp equal to a single 16 m *52·50 ft* mirror. The chosen site is Paranal, Northern Chile, well to the north of the La Silla Observatory. It is hoped to have the first units working by 1995, and the complete telescope by 2000.

Infrared The largest infrared telescope is the UKIRT (United Kingdom Infrared Telescope) on Mauna Kea, Hawaii, USA it has a 374 cm *147 in* mirror. It is however, so

■ **Widest facsimile**
With a scanning and printing width of up to 60·96 cm 24 in this facsimile machine is manufactured by WideCom Group Inc. Ontario, Canada.
(Photos: Mel Loynd)

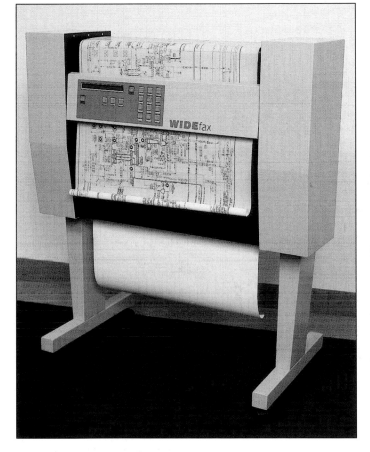

Planetaria

The ancestor of the modern planetarium is the rotatable Gottorp Globe, built by Andreas Busch in Denmark about 1660. It was 10·54 m *34·6 ft* in circumference, weighed nearly 3 ½ tonnes and is now preserved in Leningrad, USSR. The stars were painted on the inside. The first modern planetarium was opened 1923 at Jena, Germany; it was designed by Walther Bauersfelt of the Carl Zeiss company.

The world's largest planetarium is in Miyazaki, Japan, completed on 30 Jun 1987. The dome has a diameter of 27 m *88 ft 7 in.*

First telescope to use active optics

Active optics involves automatic correction of the mirror curve as the telescope is moved around. It gives a great increase in resolution. The first major telescope to use active optics was the New Technology Telescope (NTT) at La Silla in the Atacama Desert of northern Chile, the observing site of the ESO (European Southern Observatory). The NTT like all modern telescopes has an altazimuth mount, and is probably the most effective ground-based telescope in use in the world today. It will shortly incorporate adaptive optics which involves compensating the shape of the mirror for minor short-term variations in the atmosphere.

good that it can be used for visual work as well as infrared.

Southern The largest southern telescope is the 401 cm *157·87 in* reflector at Cerro Tololo in the Atacama Desert, northern Chile. The Anglo-Australian Telescope (AAT) at Siding Spring in New South Wales has a 389 cm *153·14 in* mirror.

Sub-millimetre The James Clark Maxwell telescope on Mauna Kea, Hawaii, USA has a 15 m *49·21 ft* paraboloid primary, and is used for studies of the sub-millimetre part of the electromagnetic spectrum (0·3–1·0 mm *0·01–0·03 in*). It does not produce a visual image.

Solar The McMath solar telescope at Kitt Peak, Arizona, USA has a 2·1 m *6·88 ft* primary mirror; the light is sent to it via a 32° inclined tunnel from a coelostat (rotatable mirror) at the top end. Extensive modifications to it are now being planned.

Largest refractor A 18·90 m *62 ft* long 101·6 cm *40 in* refractor completed in 1897 is situated at the Yerkes Observatory, Williams Bay, Wisconsin, USA and belongs to the University of Chicago, Illinois, although nearly 100 years old it is still in full use on clear nights. A larger refractor measuring 150 cm *59·05 in* was built in France and shown at the Paris Exhibition in 1900. It was a failure and was never used for scientific work.

Britain's largest refractor is the 71·12 cm *28 in* Great Equatorial Telescope of 1893 installed in the Old Royal Observatory, Greenwich, south-east London.

Largest radio dish Radio waves from the Milky Way were first detected by Karl Jansky of Bell Telephone Laboratories, Holmdel, New Jersey, USA in 1931 when he was investigating 'static' with an improvised 30·48 m *100 ft* aerial. The only purpose-built radio telescope built before the outbreak of the war in 1939 was made by an amateur, Grote Reber, who detected radio emissions from the Sun. The diameter of the dish was 9·5 m *31·16 ft*.

The first really large 'dish' was the 76·2 m *250 ft* telescope at Jodrell Bank, Cheshire, now known as the Lovell Telescope, completed in 1957. It is part of the MERLIN network, which includes other dishes in various parts of Britain.

The world's largest fully-steerable dish is the 100 m *328 ft* diameter, 3048 tonnes, assembly at the Max Planck Institute for Radio Astronomy of Bonn in the Effelsberger Valley, Germany; it was completed in 1971.

Largest radio installation The largest radio installation is the Australian Telescope which includes dishes at Parkes 64 m (*210 ft*), Siding Spring 22 m (*72 ft*) and Culgoora 22 m (*72 ft*). There are also links with tracking stations at Usuada and Kashima, Japan, and with the TDRS (Tracking and Data Relay Satellite) which is in a geosynchronous orbit. This is equivalent to a radio Telescope with an effective diameter of 2·16 Earth diameters 27 523 km *17 102 miles*.

The VLA (Very Large Array) of the US National Science Foundation is Y-shaped, with each arm 20·9 km *13 miles* long and with 27 mobile antennae (each of 25 m *82 ft* diameter) on rails. It is 80 km *50 miles* west of Socorro in the Plains of San Augustin, New Mexico, USA. It was completed on 10 Oct 1980.

Observatory Oldest The oldest building extant is the 'Tower of the Winds' used by Andronichus of Cyrrhus in Athens, Greece *c.* 100 BC, and equipped with sundials and clepsydra.

Highest The high-altitude observatory at Denver, Colorado, USA is at 4297 m *14 100 ft* and was opened in 1973. The main instrument is a 60·48 cm *24 in* reflector. It is slightly higher than the observatory at the summit of Mauna Kea, in Hawaii 4194 m *13 760 ft*.

Lowest The lowest 'observatory' is at Homestake Mine, South Dakota, USA, where the 'Telescope' is a tank of cleaning fluid (perchioroethylene), which contains chlorine, and can trap neutrinos from the Sun. The installation is 1·7 km *1·56 miles* below ground level, in the shaft of a goldmine; the detector has to be at this depth, as otherwise the experiments would be confused by cosmic rays. The Homestake

Observatory has been operating since 1964 and has provided results of tremendous value, as the solar neutrinos are far less numerous than had been predicted by theory - a result amply confirmed by other neutrino detectors in Japan and the USSR.

First space This was the orbiting solar observatory 0504 launched on 18 Oct 1967.

Largest Schmidt telescope A Schmidt telescope is invaluable in astronomy, as it uses a spherical mirror with a correcting plate and can cover a very wide field with a single exposure. The largest is the 2 m *6·56 ft* instrument at the Karl Schwarzschild Observatory at Tautenberg, Germany. It has a clear aperture of 134 cm *53 in* with a 200 cm *78·7 in* mirror, focal length 4 m *13·12 ft*. It was brought into use in 1960. Next in size is the Palomar Schmidt at the Palomar Observatory, California, USA with a clear aperture of 126 cm *49·5 in* and a 183 cm *72 in* mirror, operational in 1948.

Space telescope Largest The largest is the $1·55 billion NASA Edwin P. Hubble Space Telescope of 11 tonnes and 13·1 m *43 ft* in overall length with a 240 cm *94·5 in* reflector. It was placed in orbit at 613 km *381 miles* altitude aboard a US space shuttle on 24 April 1990. When it had been launched, it was found to have a defective mirror, because of a mistake in the original construction–giving serious problems of spherical aberration. It is hoped to effect repair in the future. Nevertheless it is doing excellent work in some areas of research in which it can out-perform any ground base telescope.

Rocketry and Missiles

Earliest uses War rockets, propelled by gun-powder (charcoal-saltpetre-sulphur), were described by Tseng Kung Liang of China in 1042. This early form of rocket became known in Europe by 1258.

The pioneer of military rocketry in Britain was Col. Sir William Congreve, Bt, MP (1772–1828), Comptroller of the Royal

PROGRESSIVE ROCKET ALTITUDE RECORDS

HEIGHT MILES	KM	ROCKET	PLACE	LAUNCH DATE
0·71	1·14	A 7·62 cm *3 in* rocket	Hackney, London, England	April 1750
1·24	2	Reinhold Tiling[1] (Germany) solid fuel rocket	Osnabruck, Germany	April 1931
3·04	4·87	GIRD-X semi-liquid fuel (USSR)	Moscow, USSR	Nov 1933
52·46	84·42	A4 rocket (Germany)[2]	Peenemünde, Germany	3 Oct 1942
c. 85	*c.* 136	A.4 rocket (Germany)[2]	Heidelager, Poland	early 1944
118	190	A4 rocket (Germany)[2]	Heidelager, Poland	mid 1944
244	392·6	V2/WAC Corporal (2-stage) Bumper No. 5 (USA)	White Sands, New Mexico, USA[3]	24 Feb 1949
682	1097	Jupiter C (USA)	Cape Canaveral, Florida, USA	20 Sep 1956
>800	>1300	ICBM test flight R-7 (USSR)	Tyuratam, USSR	21 Aug 1957
>2700	>4345	Farside No. 5 (4-stage) (USA)	Eniwetok Atoll	20 Oct 1957
70 700	113 770	Pioneer 1-B Lunar Probe (USA)	Cape Canaveral, Florida, USA	11 Oct 1958
215 300 000*	346 480 000	Luna I or Mechta (USSR)	Tyuratam, USSR	2 Jan 1959
242 000 000*	389 450 000	Mars I (USSR)	USSR	1 Nov 1962
3 666 000 000[4]	5 900 000 000	Pioneer 10 (USA)	Kennedy Space Center, Cape Canaveral, Florida, USA	2 Mar 1972

* Apogee in solar orbit.
[1] There is some evidence that Tiling may shortly afterwards have reached 9500 m 5·90 miles with a solid-fuel rocket at Wangerooge, East Friesian Islands, Germany.
[2] Soviet sources believe that a maximum altitude of 94 km 58·4 was reached in this period. The A4 was latterly referred to as the V2 rocket, a code for second revenge weapon (vergeltungswaffe) following upon the V1 'flying bomb'.
[3] The V2/WAC of 392·66 km 244 miles may have been exceeded during the period 1950-56 to the time of the Jupiter C flight, as the Soviets reported in 1954 that a rocket had reached 386 km 240 miles at an unspecified date.
[4] Distance on crossing Pluto's orbit on 17 Oct 1986. Pioneer 11 and Voyager 2 are also leaving the solar system.

Laboratory, Woolwich, London and Inspector of Military Machines. His '6 lb rocket' was developed to a range of 1825 m *2000 yd* by 1805 and first used by the Royal Navy against Boulogne, France on 8 Oct 1806.

The first launching of a liquid-fuelled rocket (patented 14 Jul 1914) was by Dr Robert Hutchings Goddard (1882–1945) of the USA, at Auburn, Massachusetts, USA, on 16 Mar 1926, when his rocket reached an altitude of 12·5 m *41 ft* and travelled a distance of 56 m *184 ft*.

The USSR's earliest rocket was the semi-liquid-fuelled GIRD-IX (Gruppa Izucheniya Reaktivnogo Dvizheniya), begun in 1931 and tested on 17 Aug 1933.

Highest velocity The first space vehicle to achieve the Third Cosmic velocity sufficient to break out of the Solar System was *Pioneer 10*. The Atlas SLV-3C launcher with a modified Centaur D second stage and a Thiokol Te-364-4 third stage left the Earth at an unprecedented 51 682 km/h *32 114 mph* on 2 Mar 1972.

However, the fastest escape velocity from Earth achieved was 54 614 km/h[m[m[*34 134 mph*, achieved by the ESA *Ulysses* spacecraft, powered by an IUS–Pam upper stage after deployment from the Space Shuttle Discovery on 18 Oc 1989, en route to a solar polar orbit via Jupiter.
Mariner 10 reached a recorded Solar System speed of 211 126 km/h (*131 954 mph*) as it passed Mercury in September 1974 but the highest speed of approximately 252 800 km/h (*158 000 mph*) is recorded by the NASA-German *Helios B* solar probe each time it reaches the perihelion of its

solar orbit. Sister spaceship *Helios A* will also exceed *Mariner* 10's velocity. (See Closest approach to the Sun)

Most powerful rocket The USSR's NI booster first launched from Baikonur on 21 Feb 1969 had a thrust of 4620 tonnes. It exploded at takeoff + 70 secs. The USSR's current booster *Energya*, first launched on 15 May 1987 from the Baiknour Cosmodrome, when fully loaded weighs 2400 tonnes and has a thrust of over 4000 tonnes. It is capable of placing 140 tonnes into low Earth orbit and measures 59 m *193·56 ft* tall with a maximum diameter of 16 m *52·5 ft*. It comprises a core stage powered by four liquid oxygen and hydrogen engines - the first cryogenic units flown by the Russians. There are also four strap-on boosters powered by single RD 170 engines burning liquid oxygen and kerosene.

Closest approach to the Sun by a rocket The research spacecraft *Helios B* approached within 43·4 million km *27 million miles* of the Sun, carrying both US and West German instrumentation, on 16 Apr 1976. (See Highest velocity.)

Remotest man-made object *Pioneer 10*, launched from Cape Canaveral, Florida, USA, crossed the mean orbit of Pluto on 17 Oct 1986 being then at a distance of 5900 million km *3·670 billion miles*. In AD 34 593 it will make its nearest approach to the star *Ross 248*, 10·3 light-years distant. *Voyager 1*, travelling faster, will surpass *Pioneer 10* in remoteness from the Earth. *Pioneer 11* and *Voyager 2* are also leaving the solar system.

S*pace Flight*

The physical laws controlling the flight of artificial satellites were first propounded by Sir Isaac Newton (1642–1727) in his *Philosophiae Naturalis Principia Mathematica* ('Mathematical Principles of Natural Philosophy'), begun in March 1686 and first published in July 1687.

The first artificial satellite was successfully put into orbit at an altitude of 228·5/946 km *142·588 miles* and a velocity of more than 28 565 km/h *17 750 mph* from the Baikonur Cosmodrome at Tyuratam, 275 km *170 miles* east of the Aral Sea and 250 km *155·34* miles south of the town of Baikonour on the night of 4 Oct 1957. This spherical satellite *Sputnik 1* ('Fellow Traveller') officially designated 'Satellite 1957 Alpha 2', weighing 83·6 kg *184·3 lb*, with a diameter of 58 cm *22·8 in*, and its lifetime is believed to have been 92 days, ending on 4 Jan 1958. The 29·5 m *96 ft 8 in* SS–6 launcher was designed under the direction of former Gulag prisoner Dr Sergey Pavlovich Korolyov (1907–66).

Earliest manned satellite The earliest manned space flight ratified by the world governing body, the Fédération Aéronautique Internationale (FAI, founded 1905), was by Cosmonaut Flight Major (later Col.) Yuri Alekseyevich Gagarin (1934–68) in *Vostok 1* on 12 Apr 1961.

Details filed showed take-off to be from the Baikonur Cosmodrome at 6:07 a.m. GMT

SPACE FLIGHT

and the landing near Smelovka, near Engels, in the Saratov region, USSR, 108 minutes later. Col. Gagarin landed separately from his spacecraft, by parachute after ejecting as planned, as did all the Vostok pilots. The flight time of the capsule is not recorded.

The maximum altitude during *Vostok I's* 40 868·6 km *25 394·5 miles* flight was listed at 327 km *203·2 miles*, with a maximum speed of 28 260 km/h *17 560 mph*.

Col. Gagarin, invested a Hero of the Soviet Union and awarded the Order of Lenin and the Gold Star Medal, was killed in a jet plane crash near Moscow on 27 Mar 1968.

First woman in space
The first woman to orbit the Earth was Junior Lt (now Lt-Col. Eng) Valentina Vladimirovna Tereshkova (b. 6 Mar 1937), who was launched in *Vostok 6* from Tyuratam, USSR, at 9:30 a.m. GMT on 16 Jun 1963, and landed at 8:16 a.m. on 19 June, after a flight of 2 days 22 hr 50 min, during which she completed over 48 orbits (1 971 000 km *1 225 000 miles*) and passed momentarily within 4·8 km *3 miles* of *Vostok 5*.

Space fatalities
The greatest published number to perish in any of the 140 attempted space flights to December 1990 is seven (five men and two women) aboard the *Challenger* 51L on 28 Jan 1986, when an explosion occurred 73 sec after lift-off, at a height of 14 326 m *47 000 ft*. Four people, all Soviet, have been killed during actual spaceflight, Vladimir Komarov of *Soyuz 1* on 24 Apr 1967 which crashed on landing and the un-spacesuited Georgi Dobrovolsky, Viktor Patsayev and Vladislav Volkov who died when their *Soyuz 11* spacecraft depressurized during the re-entry on 29 Jun 1971.

First 'walk' in space
Lt-Col (now Maj Gen) Aleksey Arkhipovich Leonov (b. 20 May 1934) from *Voskhod 2* was the first person to engage in EVA 'extra-vehicular activity' on 18 Mar 1965. Capt. Bruce McCandless II (b. 8 Jun 1937 USN), from the space shuttle *Challenger*, was the first to engage in untethered EVA, at an altitude of 264 km *164 miles* above Hawaii, on 7 Feb 1984. His MMU (Manned Manoeuvering Unit) back-pack cost. $15 million to develop. The first woman to perform an EVA was Svetlana Savitskaya from *Soyuz T12*/*Salyut 7* on 25 Jul 1985.

Astronaut Oldest
The oldest astronaut of the 242 people in space was Vance DeVoe Brand (b. 9 May 1931) (USA), aged 59 while on the space shuttle mission aboard the STS 35 *Columbia* on 2 Dec 1990. The oldest woman was Shannon Lucid (USA) aged 46 years on space shuttle mission STS 34 *Atlantis* on 18 Oct 1989.

Youngest The youngest has been Major (later Lt-Gen.) Gherman Stepanovich Titov (b. 11 Sep 1935), who was aged 25 years 329 days when launched in *Vostok 2* on 6 Aug 1961. The youngest woman in space was Valentina Tereshkova, 26. (See First woman in space.)

Longest and shortest manned space flight
The longest manned flight was by Col. Vladimir Georgeyevich Titov (b. 1 Jan 1947) and Flight Engineer Musa Khiramanovich Manarov (b. 22 Mar 1951) launched to the Mir space station aboard *Soyuz TM4* on 21 Dec 1987, landed, in *Soyuz TM6* (with French cosmonaut Jean–Loup Chretien), at a secondary recovery site near Dzhezkazgan, Kazakhstan, USSR, on 21 Dec 1988, after a space flight lasting 365 days 22 hr 39 min 47 sec. The shortest manned Flight was made by Cdr Alan Shepard, USN aboard *Mercury Redstone 3* on 5 May 1961. His sub-orbital mission lasted 15 min 28 sec.

The most experienced space traveller is Musa Manarov who clocked up 500 days on two spaceflights in 1977–8 and 1990–1 on 14 Apr 1991. At the end of his *Soyuz TM11* mission on 20 May 1991 he will have clocked up 534 days in space.

Most journeys
Capt. John Watts Young (b. 24 Sep 1930) (USN ret.) completed his sixth space flight on 8 Dec 1983, when he relinquished command of *Columbia* STS 9/Spacelab after a space career of 34 days 19 hr 41 min 53 sec.

Largest crew
The most crew on a single space mission number eight. This included one female and was launched on space shuttle STS 61A, *Challenger* 9, the 22nd shuttle mission, on 30 Oct 1985, carrying the West German Spacelab D1 laboratory. The mission, commanded by Hank Warren Hartsfield, lasted 7 days 44 min 51 sec.

Most in space
The greatest number of people in space at any one time has been 12, seven Americans aboard the space shuttle *Columbia* STS 35, two Soviets aboard the Mir space station and two Soviets and a Japanese journalist aboard *Soyuz TM11* from 2–10 Dec 1990.

Lunar conquest
Neil Alden Armstrong (b. Wapakoneta, Ohio, USA of Scottish [via Ireland] and German ancestry, on 5 Aug 1930), command pilot of the *Apollo 11* mission, became the first man to set foot on the Moon, on the Sea of Tranquillity, at 02:56 and 15 sec GMT on 21 Jul 1969. He was followed out of the lunar module *Eagle* by Col. Edwin Eugene Aldrin, Jr, USAF (b. Montclair, New Jersey, USA of Swedish, Dutch and British ancestry, on 20 Jan 1930), while the command module *Columbia* piloted by Lt.Col. Michael Collins, USAF (b. Rome, Italy, of Irish and pre-Revolutionary American ancestry, on 31 Oct 1930) orbited above.

Eagle landed at 20:17 and 42 sec GMT on 20 July and lifted off at 17:54 GMT on 21 July, after a stay of 21 hr 36 min. *Apollo 11* had blasted off from Cape Canaveral, Florida, USA at 13:32 GMT on 16 July and was a culmination of the US space programme which, at its peak, employed 376 600 people and attained in 1966–67 a record budget of $5·9 billion.

Altitude The greatest altitude attained by man was when the crew of the *Apollo 13*

were at apocynthion (i.e. their furthest point 254 km *158 miles* above the lunar surface, and 400 187 km *248 655 miles* above the Earth's surface at 1:21 a.m. BST on 15 Apr 1970. The crew were Capt. James Arthur Lovell, Jr, USN (b. Cleveland, Ohio, 25 Mar 1928), Fred Wallace Haise, Jr (b. Biloxi, Missouri, 14 Nov 1933) and John L. Swigert (1931–82).

The greatest altitude attained by a woman is 531 km *330 miles* by Kathryn Sullivan (b. Paterson, New Jersey 3 Oct 1951) during her flight on STS 31 on 24 Apr 1990.

Speed The fastest speed at which humans have travelled is 39 897 km/h *24 791 mph* when the command module of *Apollo 10* carrying Col.(now Brig. Gen.) Thomas Patten Stafford, USAF (b. Weatherford, Oklahoma, 17 Sep 1930), and Cdr Eugene Andrew Cernan (b. Chicago, Illionois 14 Mar 1934) and Cdr (now Capt.) John Watts Young, USN (b. San Francisco, California, 24 Sep 1930), reached this maximum value at the 121·9 km *400 000 ft* altitude interface on its trans-Earth return flight on 26 May 1969.

The highest speed recorded by a woman is 28 582 km/h *17 864 mph* by Kathryn Sullivan at the start of re-entry at the end of the STS 31 *Discovery* Shuttle mission on 29 Apr 1990. The highest recorded by a Soviet space traveller was 28 115 km/h *17 470 mph* by Junior Lt (now Lt-Col.) Valentina Vladimirovna Tereshkova-Nikolayev of the USSR in *Vostok 6* on 16 Jun 1983 although, because of orbital injection of Soyuz spacecraft occurs at marginally lower altitude, it is probable that Tereshkova's speed was exceeded twice by Svetlana Savistkaya aboard Soyuz TM7 and TM12 on 19 Aug 1982 and 17 Jul 1984.

Longest spacewalk
The longest spacewalk was the second lunar EVA by Eugene Cernan and Jack Schmitt on *Apollo 17* which lasted 7 hr 37 min. The longest recorded spacewalk in Earth orbit was made outside space shuttle *Discovery* STS 511 in September 1985 lasting 7 hr 20 min by James van Hoften and Bill Fisher, although this may have been exceeded by *Soyuz TM9's* Anatoli Solovyov and Alexander Balandin during an EVA outside the Mir space station on 1 Jul 1990.

First extra-terrestrial vehicle
The first wheeled vehicle landed on the Moon was the unmanned *Lunokhod I* which began its Earth-controlled travels on 17 Nov 1970. It moved a total of 10·54 km *6·54 miles* on gradients up to 30° in the Mare Imbrium and did not become non-functioning until 4 Oct 1971.

The lunar speed and distance record was set by the unmanned *Apollo 16* Rover, with 18 km/h *11·2 mph* downhill and 33·8 km *22·4 miles*.

Heaviest and largest space objects
The heaviest object orbited is the Saturn V third stage with *Apollo 15* (spacecraft), which, prior to trans-lunar injection into parking orbit, weighed 140 512 kg *138·29 tons*. The 200 kg *442 lb* US RAE (Radio Astronomy Explorer) B, or *Explorer 49*, launched on 10 Jun 1973 had, however, antennae 415 m *1500 ft* from tip to tip.

Most expensive project
The total cost of the US manned space programme up to and including the 28 Apr 1991 was *Discovery* space shuttle mission, it has been estimated to be $76 982 400 000. The first 15 years of the USSR space programme, from 1958 to September 1973, have been estimated to have cost $45 billion. The cost of the NASA shuttle programme was $42·8 billion which included the launch of *Discovery*.

■ Space project
The Apollo Programme has been estimated to have cost $25 541 400 000. This picture, taken from Apollo 15, is of the Earth seen rising over the horizon of the Moon. (Photo: NASA)

Building and Structures

Brick carrying

The greatest distance achieved for carrying a 4·08 kg *9 lb* brick in a nominated ungloved hand in an uncradled downward pincher grip is 99·37 km *61¾ miles*, by Reg Morris of Walsall, W Mids on 16 Jul 1985.

The women's record for a 4·422 kg *9 lb 12 oz* brick is 36·2 km *22½ miles*, by Wendy Morris of Walsall, W Mids on 28 Apr 1986.

The British women's record for a 2·97 kg *6 lb 9 oz* smooth-sided brick is 9·6 km *6 miles*, by Karen Stevenson of Wallasey, Merseyside on 17 Aug 1984.

Bricklaying

Tony Gregory of Horndon on the Hill, Essex laid 747 bricks, each weighing 2·00 kg *4·41 lb*, in 60 min at Grays, Essex on 18 Apr 1987. This was achieved in accordance with the rules of the Brick Development Association and the Guild of Bricklayers.

Hod carrying

Russell Bradley of Worcester carried bricks totalling 207 kg *456 lb 6 oz* up a ladder of the minimum specified length of 3·65 m *12 ft* on 28 Jan 1991 at Worcester City Football Club.

He also carried bricks with a total weight of 260·4 kg *574·1 lb* in a 48 kg *105·8 lb* hod a distance of 5 m *16 ft 5 in* on the flat before ascending a runged ramp to a height of 2·13 m *7 ft* at Worcester Rugby Club on 17 Mar 1991.

EARLIEST STRUCTURES

World The earliest known human structure is a rough circle of loosely piled lava blocks found on the lowest cultural level at the Lower Palaeolithic site at Olduvai Gorge in Tanzania, revealed by Dr Mary Leakey in January 1960. The structure was associated with artifacts and bones on a work-floor, dating from *c.* 1 750 000 BC.

The earliest evidence of *buildings* yet discovered is that of 21 huts with hearths or pebble-lined pits and delimited by stake-holes found in October 1965 at the Terra Amata site in Nice, France, thought to belong to the Acheulian culture of *c.* 400 000 years ago. Excavation carried out between 28 Jun and 5 Jul 1966 revealed one hut with palisaded walls with axes of 15 m *49 ft* and 6 m *20 ft*. The remains of a stone tower 6·1 m *20 ft* high originally built into the walls of Jericho have been excavated and are dated to 5000 BC. The foundations of the walls themselves have been dated to as early as 8350 BC.

The oldest free-standing structures in the world are now believed to be the megalithic temples at Mgarr and Skorba in Malta. With those at Ggantija in Gozo, they date from *c.* 3250 BC.

Great Britain Twelve small stone clusters, associated with broken bones and charcoal in stratum C of the early Palaeolithic site at Hoxne, near Eye, Suffolk may be regarded as Britain's earliest structural remains, dated *c.* 250 000 BC.
On the Isle of Jura, Argyll, a hearth consisting of three linked stone circles has been dated to the Mesolithic period 6013 ± 200 BC.
Remains of the earliest dated stone habitations structures and cooking pit were discovered at Culverwell, Isle of Portland, Dorset. They date to 5 200 ± 135 BC (Mesolithic). In December 1990 the discovery was reported of house-like structures at Romsey, Hants datable to *c.* 4800 BC

Ireland The earliest known evidence of human occupation dates from the *Mesolithic* period *c.* 7500 BC at the Carrowmore site in Co. Sligo. Ireland became enisled or separated from Great Britain *c.* 9050 BC. Nearby there are megalithic burials dating from 3800 ± 80 BC. The great Neolithic passage grave of Neugrange in the Boyne Valley of Ireland has now been dated to *c.* 3100 BC, the oldest in Europe of its kind.
The earliest surviving piece of Roman building is the bottom 4·25 m *14 ft* of their beacon at Dover, Kent dating from the First century AD.

Buildings for Working

Construction project The Madinat Al-Jubail Al-Sinaiyah project in Saudi Arabia is believed to be the largest public works project in modern times. Construction started in 1976 for the industrial city covering 10 146 m² *250 705 acres*. At the peak of construction, nearly 52 000 workers were employed, representing 62 nationalities. The total earth dredging and moving volume has reached 270 million m³, enough to construct a belt around the Earth at the equator 7 × 1 m *23 × 3·3 ft* high.

The seawater cooling system is believed to be the world's largest canal system, bringing 10 million m³ *353 million ft³* of seawater per day to cool the industrial establishment.

The London Docklands development has been described as 'the world's largest commercial development'. The cost in 1991 was estimated at about £7 billion.

Industrial The largest multi-level industrial building is the 15 level building developed for warehouse and container freight at Terminal 3, Port of Kwaichung, Hong Kong by Asia Terminals Ltd. The building measures 276 × 292 m *905·5 × 958 ft* and 109·5 m *359·25 ft* high. It has a total floor area of 866 000 m² *932 851·4 ft²* and a cubic capacity of 5 850 000 m³ *2 065 896 ft³*. The entire area in each floor of the building is directly accessible by 14 m *45·92 ft* long container trucks and the complex comprises 26·8 km *16·6 miles* of roadway and 2610 container truck parking bays.

Commercial The greatest ground area covered by any commercial building in the world under one roof is the flower auction building of the Co-operative VBA (Verenigde Bloemenveilingen Aalsmeer) Aalsmeer, Netherlands, with dimensions of 776 × 631 m *2546 × 2070 ft*. The original floor surface of 343 277 m² *84·82 acres* was extended in 1986 to 368 477 m² *91·05 acres*.

The largest building in Britain is the Ford Parts Centre at Daventry, Northants, which measures 602 × 237 m *1975 × 778 ft* or 14·86 ha *36·7 acres*. It was opened on 6 Sep 1972 and cost nearly £8 million. It employs 1600 people and is fitted with 14 000 fluorescent lights.

The assembly plant with the largest cubic capacity in the world is the Boeing Co. main assembly plant at Everett, Washington State, USA, completed in 1968, with a capacity of 5·6 million m³ *200 million ft³*.

Scientific The most capacious scientific building is the Vehicle Assembly Building (VAB) at Complex 39, the selected site for the final assembly and launching of the Apollo Moon space craft on the Saturn V rocket, at the John F. Kennedy Space Center on Merritt Island, Cape Canaveral, Florida, USA. Construction began in April

THE WORLD'S TALLEST STRUCTURES
PROGRESSIVE RECORDS

HEIGHT m	ft	STRUCTURE	LOCATION	MATERIAL	BUILDING OR COMPLETION DATES
62	*204*	Djoser step pyramid (earliest pyramid)	Saqqâra, Egypt	Tura limestone casing	*c.* 2650 BC
91·7	*300·8*	Pyramid of Meidum	Meidum, Egypt	Tura limestone casing	*c.* 2600 BC
101·1	*331·6*	Snefru Bent pyramid	Dahshûr, Egypt	Tura limestone casing	*c.* 2600 BC
104	*342*	Snefru North Stone pyramid	Dahshûr, Egypt	Tura limestone casing	*c.* 2600 BC
146·5	*480·9 [1]*	Great Pyramid of Cheops (Khufu)	El Gizeh, Egypt	Tura limestone casing	*c.* 2580 BC
160	*525 [2]*	Lincoln Cathedral, central tower	Lincoln, England	lead sheathed wood	*c.* 1307–1548
149	*489 [3]*	St Paul's Cathedral spire	City of London, England	lead sheathed wood	1315–1561
141	*465*	Minster of Notre Dame	Strasbourg, France	Vosges sandstone	1420–1439
153	*502 [4]*	St Pierre de Beauvais spire	Beauvais, France	lead sheathed wood	–1568
144	*475*	St Nicholas Church	Hamburg, Germany	stone and iron	1846–1847
147	*485*	Rouen Cathedral spire	Rouen, France	cast iron	1823–1876
156	*513*	Köln Cathedral spires	Cologne, Germany	stone	–1880
169	*555 [5]*	Washington Monument	Washington, DC, USA	stone	1848–1884
300·5	*985·9 [6]*	Eiffel Tower	Paris, France	iron	1887–1889
318	*1046*	Chrysler Building	New York City, USA	steel and concrete	1929–1930
381	*1250 [7]*	Empire State Building	New York City, USA	steel and concrete	1929–1930
479	*1572*	KWTV Television Mast	Oklahoma City, USA	steel	November 1954
490	*1610 [8]*	KSWS Television Mast	Roswell, New Mexico, USA	steel	December 1956
493	*1619*	WGAN Television Mast	Portland, Maine, USA	steel	September 1959
510	*1676*	KFVS Television Mast	Cape Girardeau, Missouri, USA	steel	June 1960
533	*1749*	WTVM & WRBL Television Mast	Columbus, Georgia, USA	steel	May 1962
533	*1749*	WBIR-TV Mast	Knoxville, Tennessee, USA	steel	September 1963
547	*1794*	Ostankinskayatv Tower	Moscow, USSR	steel	1967
628	*2063*	KTHI-TV Mast	Fargo, North Dakota, USA	steel	November 1963
646·38	*2120·6*	Warszawa Radio Mast	Plock, Poland	galvanized steel	22 Jul 1974

[1] *Original height. With loss of pyramidion (topmost stone) height now 137 m 449 ft 6 in.*
[2] *Fell in a storm.*
[3] *Struck by lightning and destroyed 4 June 1561.*
[4] *Fell April 1573, shortly after completion.*
[5] *Sinking at a rate of 0·0047 ft per annum or 12·7 cm 5 in since 1884.*
[6] *Original height. With addition of TV antenna in 1957, now 320·75 m 1052 ft.*
[7] *Original height. With addition of TV tower on 1 May 1951, now 449 m 1472 ft. Exterior is clad in limestone from the Empire Quarry, Indiana.*
[8] *Fell in gale in 1960.*

1963 by the Ursum Consortium. It is a steel-framed building measuring 218 m *716 ft* in length, 158 m *518 ft* in width and 160 m *525 ft* high. The building contains four bays, each with its own door 140 m *460 ft* high. Its floor area is 31 911 m² *343 500 ft²* and its capacity is 3 666 500 m³ *129 482 000 ft³*. The building was 'topped out' on 14 Apr 1965, the cost then amounting to $108 700 000.

Administrative The largest ground area covered by any office building is that of the Pentagon, in Arlington, Virginia, USA. Built to house the US Defense Department's offices, it was completed on 15 Jan 1943 and cost an estimated $83 million. Each of the outermost sides is 281 m *921 ft* long and the perimeter of the building is about 1405 m *4609·58 ft*. Its five storeys enclose a floor area of 604 000 m² *6 500 000 ft²*. The corridors total 27 km *17 miles* in length and there are 7748 windows to be cleaned. Twenty-nine thousand people work in the building, which has over 44 000 telephones connected by 257 500 km *160 000 miles* of cable. Two hundred and twenty staff handle 280 000 calls a day. Two restaurants, six cafeterias, ten snack bars and a staff of 675 form the catering department.

Office The complex with the largest rentable space are the World Trade Center in New York City, USA with a total of 406 000 m² *4 370 000 ft²* in each of the twin towers of which the taller Tower Two (formerly B) is 415·22 m *1362 ft 3 ¼ in* high. The tip of the TV antenna on Tower One is 521·2 m *1710 ft* above street level and is thus 91 cm *3 ft* taller than the antennae on top of the Sears Tower (see below).

The largest single open plan office in the United Kingdom is that of British Gas West Midlands at Solihull, Warks built by Spooners (Hull) Ltd in 1962. It now measures 230 × 49 m *753 × 160 ft*, and can accommodate 2125 clerical and managerial staff.

Rentals According to *World Rental Levels* by Richard Ellis of London, the highest rents in the world for prime offices, are in Tokyo, Japan at £104.67 (*$176.89*) per ft² p.a. (December 1990). With added service charges and rates this is increased to £113.75 (*$192.24*) per ft².

A typical apartment in the commercial and residential Kioicho building in Akasaka, Japan costs over $17 000 per month — payable 10 months in advance!

TALLEST

The tallest office building in the world is the Sears Tower, national headquarters of Sears, Roebuck & Co. in Wacker Drive, Chicago, Illinois, USA, with 110 storeys rising to 443 m *1454 ft*. Its gross area is 408 760 m² *4·4 million ft²*. Construction was started in August 1970 and it was 'topped out' on 4 May 1973, having surpassed the World Trade Center in New York City in height at 2:35 p.m. on 6 Mar 1973 with the first steel column reaching to the 104th storey. The addition of two TV antennae brought the total height to 520·29 m *1707 ft*. The building's population is 16 700, served by 103 elevators and 18 escalators. It has 16 000 windows.

Europe The tallest building in Europe is the Messeturm (Fair Tower) in Frankfurt, Germany completed in October 1990. The 70-storey office building is 256·5 m *841 ft 6 in* high.

UK The Canary Wharf tower at London Docklands overtook the National Westminster tower block by 60·96 m *200 ft* when

it was 'topped out' in November 1990. The tallest of the three towers is the 50-storey 243·8 m *800 ft* high tower, resembling a steel obelisk designed by Ceasar Pelli (US), consists of nearly 16 000 pieces of steel and weighs almost 27 000 tonnes.

SHALLOWEST

The shallowest commercial building is the 1·8 m *6 ft* wide, 30 m *100 ft* long Sam Kee Building at 8 West Pender, Vancouver, Canada. It was erected in 1912.

HABITATIONS

Greatest altitude The highest inhabited buildings in the world are those in the Indo-Tibetan border fort of Bāsisi by the Māna Pass (Lat. 31° 04'N, Long. 79° 24'E) at *c*. 5988 m *19 700 ft*.

In April 1961, however, a three-room dwelling was discovered at 6600 m *21 650 ft* on Cerro Llullaillaco 6723 m *22 057 ft*, on the Argentine–Chile border, believed to date from the late pre-Columbian period *c*.1480. A settlement on the T"e-li-mo trail in southern Tibet is sited at an altitude of 6019 m *19 800 ft*.

Northernmost The Danish scientific station set up in 1952 in Pearyland, northern Kalaallit Nunaat (Greenland) is over 1450 km *900 miles* north of the Arctic Circle. Eskimo hearths dated to before 1000 BC were discovered in Pearyland in 1969. Polar Eskimos were discovered in Inglefield Land, north-west Greenland in 1818.

The USSR's drifting research station 'North Pole 15' passed within 2·8 km *1 ¼ miles* of the North Pole in December 1967.

The most northerly continuously inhabited place is the Canadian Department of National Defense outpost at Alert on Ellesmere Island, Northwest Territories in Lat. 82° 30' N, Long. 62° W, set up in 1950.

Southernmost The most southerly permanent human habitation is the United States' Amundsen–Scott South Polar Station, completed in 1957 and replaced in 1975.

EMBASSIES AND CIVIC BUILDINGS

Largest The USSR embassy on Bei Xiao Jie, Beijing, China, in the north-eastern corner of the northern walled city, occupies the whole 18·2 ha *45 acre* area of the old Orthodox Church Mission (established 1728), now known as the *Bei guan*. It was handed over to the USSR in 1949.

The largest in Great Britain is the United States embassy in Grosvenor Square, London. The Chancery Building alone, completed in 1960, has 600 rooms for a staff of 700 on seven floors, with a usable floor area of 236 895 m² *2 550 000 ft²*.

EXHIBITION CENTRES

Largest The International Exposition Center in Cleveland, Ohio, USA, the world's largest, is situated on a 70·8 ha *175 acre* site adjacent to Cleveland Hopkins International Airport in a building which measures 232 250 m² *2·5 million ft²*. An indoor terminal provides direct rail access and parking for 10 000 cars.

UK The National Exhibition Centre, Birmingham, opened in February 1976, consists of five halls which interconnect covering 87 180 m² *938·397 ft²* with a volume of 1 168 466 m³ *41·26 million ft³*.

SHOPPING CENTRES

The world's first shopping centre was built in 1896 at Roland Park, Baltimore, Maryland, USA.

The world's largest centre is the $1·1 billion West Edmonton Mall in Alberta, Canada, which was opened on 15 Sep 1981 and completed four years later. It covers 483 080 m² *5·2 million ft²* on a 49 ha *121 acre* site and encompasses 828 stores and services as well as 11 major department stores. Parking is provided for 20 000 vehicles for more than 500 000 shoppers per week.

The world's largest wholesale merchandise mart is the Dallas Market Center on Stemmons Freeway, Dallas, Texas, USA, with nearly 864 000 m² *9·3 million ft²* in eight buildings. The complex covers 60 ha *150 acres* and houses some 3400 permanent showrooms displaying merchandise of more than 26 000 manufacturers. The Center attracts 600 000 buyers each year to its 38 annual markets and trade shows.

The largest shopping complex in Europe is the MetroCentre in Gateshead, Tyne & Wear. The site covers an area of 54·63 ha *135 acres* housing 340 retail units (including the largest single-storey branch of Marks and Spencer at 17 279 m² *186 000 ft²*), giving a gross selling area of 204 380 m² *2·2 million ft²*. The complex also includes a leisure centre, 10-screen cinema, a 28-lane bowling alley, parking for 12 000 cars and its own purpose-built British Rail station.

■ **Highest rentals**
High-rise rents at the commercial and residential Kioicho building in Akasaka, Japan are over $17 000 per month — payable 10 months in advance! (Photo: Gamma/Wada)

Sand castle

The tallest sand castle on record, using hands, buckets and shovels, was 5·33 m *17 ft 6 in* high and was made by Pacific Northwest Sandshapers at Harrison Hot Springs, British Columbia, Canada on 14–15 Apr 1990.

The longest sand castle was 8·37 km *5·2 miles* long, and was made by staff and pupils of Ellon Academy, near Aberdeen, Grampian on 24 Mar 1988.

Britain's largest covered city centre shopping complex is Manchester's Arndale Centre, which has a floor area of 209 000 m² *2 246 200 ft²* (gross retail area of 110 270 m² *1 187 000 ft²*) including a car park for 1800 cars. The centre was completed in 1979 after three years' work and was the first such centre in Europe with its own radio station, called 'Centre Sound' Radio.

The longest mall in the world is part of the £40 million shopping centre at Milton Keynes, Bucks. It measures 650 m *2133 ft*.

INDUSTRIAL STRUCTURES

Tallest chimneys The Ekibastuz, USSR coal power-plant No. 2 stack is 420 m *1377 ft* tall and was built at a cost of 7·89 million roubles. It was started on 15 Nov 1983 and completed on 15 Oct 1987 by Soviet Building Division of the Ministry of Energy. The diameter tapers from 44 m *144·35 ft* at the base to 14·2 m *46·58 ft* at the top. It weighs 60 000 tonnes and became operational in 1991.

The world's most massive chimney is one of 350 m *1148 ft* at Puentes de Garcia Rodriguez, north-west Spain, built by M.W. Kellog Co. It contains 15 570 m³ *20 600 yd³* of concrete and 1315 tonnes of steel and has an internal volume of 189·720 m³ *6·7 million ft³*.

Europe's tallest chimney serves the Zasavje thermo-power plant in Trboulje, Yugoslavia and was completed at a height of 360 m *1181 ft* on 1 Jun 1976.

The tallest chimney in Great Britain is one of 259 m *850 ft* at Drax Power Station, N Yorks, begun in 1966 and 'topped out' on 16 May 1969. It has an untapered diameter of 26 m *85 ft* and has the greatest capacity of any chimney. The architects were Clifford Tee & Gale of London.

The oldest known industrial chimney in Britain is the Stone Edge chimney, near Chesterfield, Derbys, built to a height of 16·76 m *55 ft ante* 1771.

Cooling towers The largest is that adjacent to the nuclear power plant at Uentrop, Germany, which is 179·8 m *590 ft* tall, completed in 1976.

The largest in the United Kingdom are of the Ferrybridge and Didcot type and measure 114 m *374 ft* tall and 91 m *300 ft* across the base.

HANGARS

Largest Hangar 375 ('Big Texas') at Kelly Air Force Base, San Antonio, Texas, USA, completed on 15 Feb 1956, has four doors each 76·2 m *250 ft* wide, 18·28 m *60 ft* high and weighing 608 tonnes. The high bay area measures 609·6 × 91·4 × 27·4 m *2000 × 300 × 90 ft* and is surrounded by a 17·8 ha *44 acre* concrete apron.

The largest hangar building in the United Kingdom is the Britannia assembly hall at the former Bristol Aeroplane Company's works at Filton, Avon, now part of British Aerospace. The overall width of the hall is 321 m *1054 ft* and the overall depth of the centre bay is 128 m *420 ft*. It encloses a floor area of 3·0 ha *7 ½ acres*. The cubic capacity of the hall is 934 000 m³ *33 000 000 ft³*. The building was begun in April 1946 and completed by September 1949. (See also Largest Doors.)
Delta Airlines' jet base on a 56·6 ha *140 acre* site at Hartsfield International Airport, Atlanta, Georgia, USA has 14·5 ha *36 acres* roof area.

GLASSHOUSE

Largest Britain's biggest greenhouse complex is that adjacent to the power station at Drax, N Yorks, which yields some 5000 tonnes of fruit a year. The area under glass covers 144·836 m² *37·78 acres*.

GRAIN ELEVATOR

Largest The single-unit elevator operated by the C-G-F Grain Co. at Wichita, Kansas, USA consists of a triple row of storage tanks, 123 on each side of the central loading tower or 'head house'. The unit is 828 m *2 717 ft* long and 30 m *100 ft*

wide. Each tank is 37 m *120 ft* high, with an inside diameter of 9 m *30 ft* giving a total storage capacity of 7·3 million hl *20 000 000 bushels* of wheat.

The world's largest collection of elevators are the 23 at Thunder Bay, Ontario, Canada, on Lake Superior. They have a total capacity of 37·4 million hl *103·9 million bushels*.

SEWAGE WORKS

Largest The West-Southwest Treatment Plant, opened in 1940 on a site of 203 ha *501 acres* in Chicago, Illinois, USA, serves an area containing 2 940 000 people. It treated an average of 3160 million litres *835 million US gal* of waste per day in 1973 and the capacity of its sedimentation and aeration tanks is 1 280 000 m³ *1·6 million yd³*.

The largest full treatment works in Britain and probably in Europe is the Beckton Works, east London, which serves a 2 966 000 population and handles a daily flow of 941 million litres *207 million gal* in a tank capacity of 21 400 m³ *757 000 ft³*.

WOODEN BUILDING

Largest The two US Navy airship hangars built in 1942–3 at Tillamook, Oregon, USA are now used by the Louisiana-Pacific Corporation as a sawmill. They measure 304·8 m *1000 ft* long, 51·8 m *170 ft* high at the crown and 90·22 m *296 ft* wide at the base.

What is believed to be the oldest complete wooden building in England was discovered in December 1986 in the Fenlands, Cambs. It measures 8 × 2 m *26·2 × 6·65 ft* and was a burial chamber of the Neolithic period c. 3000 BC.

AIR-SUPPORTED BUILDING

Largest The octagonal Pontiac Silverdome Stadium, Michigan, USA measures 159 m *522 ft* wide and is 220 m *722 ft* long. It has a capacity for 80 600. The air pressure is 34·4 kPa *5 lb/in²* supporting the 4 ha *10 acre* translucent 'Fiberglas' roofing. The structural engineers were Geiger-Berger Associates of New York City, USA.

The largest standard size air hall is one 262 m *860 ft* long, 42·6 m *140 ft* wide and 19·8 m *65 ft* high. One was first sited at Lima, Ohio, USA, made by Irvin Industries of Stamford, Connecticut, USA.

Buildings for Living

WOODEN BUILDINGS

Oldest The oldest extant wooden buildings in the world are those comprising the Pagoda, Chumanar Gate and Temple of Horyu (Horyu-ji) at Nara, Japan, dating from c. AD 670 and completed in 715. The wood used wa from 1000-year-old Hinoki trees. The nearby Daibutsuden, built in 1704–11, once measured 87 × 46·75 × 51 m *285·4 × 153·3 × 167·3 ft*.
The dimensions now are 57·3 × 50·4 × 48·6 m *188 × 165·3 × 159·4 ft*.

CASTLES

Earliest The castle at Gomdan, in the Yemen, originally had 20 storeys and dates from before AD 100.

The oldest stone castle extant in Great Britain is Richmond Castle, N Yorks, built c. 1075.

The oldest castle in the Irish Republic is

Ferrycarrig near Wexford, dating from *c.* 1180.

The oldest castle in Northern Ireland is Carrickfergus Castle, Co. Antrim, which dates from before 1210.

Largest The largest inhabited castle in the world is the royal residence of Windsor Castle at Windsor, Berks. It is primarily of 12th century construction and is in the form of a waisted parallelogram measuring 576 × 164 m *1890 × 540 ft.*

The total area of Dover Castle in Kent, however, covers 13·75 ha *34 acres,* with a width of 335·2 m *1100 ft* and a curtain wall of 550 m *1800 ft,* or if underground works are taken in, 700 m *2300 ft.* The overall dimensions of Carisbrooke Castle, Isle of Wight 110 × 137 m *450 × 360 ft,* become 411 × 251 m *1350 × 825 ft* if its earthworks are included.

The most capacious of all Irish castles is Carrickfergus (see above) but that with the most extensive fortifications is Trim Castle, Co. Meath, built *c.* 1205 with a curtain wall 443 m *1455 ft* long.

The largest castle in Scotland is Edinburgh Castle with a major axis of 402 m *1320 ft* and measuring 1025 m *3360 ft* along its perimeter wall including the Esplanade.

Forts The largest ancient castle in the world is Hradčany Castle, Prague, Czechoslovakia, originating in the 9th century. It is an oblong irregular polygon with an axis of 570 m *1870 ft* and an average tranverse diameter of 128 m *420 ft* it has a surface area of 7·28 ha *18 acres.*

Fort George, Ardersier, Inverness-shire, Scotland, built in 1748–69, measures 640 m *2100 ft* in length and has an average width of 189 m *620 ft.* The total site covers 17·2 ha *42 ½ acres.*

Thickest walls Urnammu's city walls at Ur (now Muqayyar, Iraq), destroyed by the Elamites in 2006 BC, were 27 m *88 ft* thick and made of mud brick.

The walls of the Great Tower or Donjon of Flint Castle, Clwyd, built in 1277–80, are 7 m *23 ft* thick.

PALACES

Largest The Imperial Palace (Gu gong) in the centre of Beijing, the northern capital of China, covers a rectangle 960 × 750 m *1050 × 820 yd,* an area of 72 ha *177·9 acres.* The outline survives from the construction of the third ming Emperor, Yung Lo (1402–24), but due to constant rearrangements most of the intra-mural buildings are 18th-century. These consist of five halls and 17 palaces, of which that occupied by the last empress until 1924 was the Palace of Accumulated Elegance (*Chu xia gong*).

The Palace of Versailles, 23 km *14 miles* south-west of Paris, has a façade with 375 windows, 580 m *634 yd* in length. The building, completed in 1682 for Louis XIV, occupied over 30 000 workmen under Jules Hardouin-Mansert (1646–1708).

Residential The palace (Istana Nurul Iman) of HM the Sultan of Brunei in the capital Bandar Seri Begawan completed in January 1984 at a reported cost of £300 million, is the largest in the world, with 1788 rooms and 257 lavatories. The underground garage accommodates the Sultan's 110 cars.

UK The largest palace in the United Kingdom in royal use is Buckingham Palace, London, so named after its site, bought in 1703 by John Sheffield, the 1st

Duke of Buckingham and Normanby (1648–1721). Buckingham House was reconstructed in the Palladian style between 1825 and 1836, following the design of John Nash (1752–1835). The 186 m *610 ft* long East Front was built in 1846 and

refaced in 1912. The Palace, which stands in 15·8 ha *39 acres* of garden, has 600 rooms including a ballroom 34 m *111 ft* long.

The largest-ever royal palace is Hampton Court, Middx, acquired by Henry VIII from Cardinal Wolsey in 1525 and greatly

Pole sitting

Modern records do not, in fact, compare with that of St Simeon the Younger (*c.* AD 521–97), called Stylites, a monk who spent his last 45 years up a stone pillar on the Hill of Wonders, near Antioch, Syria.

The 'standards of living' at the top of poles can vary widely. Mellissa Sanders lived in a shack measuring 1·8 m × 2·1 m *6 ft × 7 ft* at the top of a pole in Indianapolis, Indiana, USA from 26 Oct 1986–24 Mar 1988, a total of 516 days.

Pat Bowen stayed in a barrel (maximum capacity 682 litres *150 gal*) at the top of a pole 5·48 m *18 ft* high outside the Bull Hotel, Ludlow, Shrops for 40 days 1 hr from 28 May–7 Jul 1986.

House of cards

The greatest number of storeys achieved in building freestanding houses of standard playing cards is 68, to a height of 3·9 m *12 ft 10 in,* built by John Sain, 15, of South Bend, Indiana, USA in May 1984.

BUILDINGS FOR LIVING

enlarged by him and later by William III, Queen Anne and George I, whose son George II was its last resident monarch. It covers 1·6 ha *4 acres* of a 270·7 ha *669 acre* site.

Largest moat From plans drawn by French sources it appears that those which surround the Imperial Palace in Beijing (see above) measure 49 m *54 yd* wide and have a total length of 3290 m *3600 yd*. In all, the city's moats total 38 km *23 ½ miles*.

HOTELS

Largest The $290 million Excalibur Hotel/Casino, Nevada, USA built on a 47·3 ha *117 acre* site, was opened in April 1990. Comprising 4032 de luxe rooms and employing 4000 staff, the facilities include seven themed restaurants and a total of 11 food outlets throughout the hotel/casino.

The Hotel Rossiya in Moscow opened in 1967 with 3200 rooms, but owing to its proportion of dormitory accommodation, it is not now internationally listed among the largest hotels. The Izmailovo Hotel complex, opened in July 1980 for the XXIInd Olympic Games in Moscow was designed to accommodate 9500 people.

Great Britain The greatest sleeping capacity of any hotel in Great Britain is 1859 (914 bedrooms) in the London Forum Hotel, Cromwell Road, London, which has a staff of 419 and was opened in 1973.

The Regent Hotel, Royal Leamington Spa, Warks, when first opened in 1819 with 100 bedrooms and one bathroom was then claimed to be the largest in the world.

The largest hotel is the Grosvenor House Hotel, Park Lane, London, which was opened in 1929. It is eight storeys high, covering 1 ha *2 ½ acres* and caters for more than 100 000 visitors per year in 470 rooms. The Great Room is the largest single hotel room measuring 55 × 40 m *181 × 131 ft* with a height of 7 m *23 ft*. Banquets for 1500 are frequently held there.

Hoteliers Following its acquisition of Holiday Inns North America in February 1990, Bass plc, the UK's top brewing company, also became the world's largest hotel operator. The company now owns, manages and franchises 1697 hotels totalling 326 388 rooms in 50 countries. (See Brewers.)

Britain's largest hotel and catering group is Trusthouse Forte, with over 830 hotels world-wide. It employs 84 000 staff in the UK, and 16 000 overseas and had a turnover of £2·6 billion in 1990/91.

Largest lobby The lobby at the Hyatt Regency, San Francisco, USA, is 106·6 m *350 ft* long, 48·7 m *160 ft* wide, and at 51·8 m *170 ft* is the height of a 17-storey building.

Tallest Measured from the street level of its main entrance to the top, the 226·1 m *741·9 ft* tall 73-storey Westin Stamford in Raffles City, Singapore was 'topped out' in March 1985. The $235 million hotel is operated by Westin Hotel Co. and owned by Raffles City Pte Ltd. However, their Detroit Plaza measured from the rear entrance level, is 227·9 m *748 ft* tall.

Britain's tallest hotel is the 27-storey 132·24 m *380 ft* tall London Forum Hotel (see above).

Smallest Punta Grande Hotel, Las Puntas, Hierro Island, Tenerife in the Canaries has a total area of 600 m² *6459 ft²*. There are four double bedrooms looking on to a small terrace, a lounge, a bar-restaurant and a solarium. Reconstructed in 1987, the building is more than 150 years old.

Narrowest The Star Hotel in Moffat, Dumfries & Galloway, Scotland, the narrowest detached hotel, is only 6·1 m *20 ft* wide. The eight-bedroom hotel, which has two bars, is owned by Douglas and Monica House and Tim and Allison Leighfield.

Most remote Garvault Hotel, by Kinbrace, Sutherland, Scotland is claimed to be the most isolated in mainland Britain, being some 25·7 km *16 miles* from its nearest competitor at Forsinard, also in Sutherland.

Most expensive The Penthouse Suite in the Fairmont Hotel, San Francisco, California, USA can be rented for $6 000 per night, plus taxes. The price includes a round-the-clock butler and maid, and airport limousine service. The suite was built in 1927 atop the Fairmont's main building. It has an immense drawing-room with grand piano, dining-room accommodating up to 50, a two-storey circular library with the celestial constellation in gold on a domed ceiling, a games room, three bedrooms and four bathrooms with 24-carat gold-plated fittings.

Great Britain The Royal Suite of the Hotel Intercontinental, London, costs £1200 per day (incl. VAT).

Most mobile The three-storey brick Hotel Fairmount (built 1906) in San Antonio, Texas, USA, which weighed 1451 tonnes, was moved on 36 dollies with pneumatic tyres over city streets approximately five blocks and over a bridge, which had to be reinforced. The move by Emmert International of Portland, Oregon, USA took four days, 30 Mar–2 Apr 1985, and cost $650 000.

Spas Spas are named after the watering place in the Liège province of Belgium, where hydropathy was developed from 1626.

The largest measured, by number of available hotel rooms, is Vichy, Allier, France, with 14 000 rooms.

The highest French spa is Barèges, Hautes-Pyrénées, at 1240 m *4068 ft* above sea level.

HOUSING

Largest estate In the United Kingdom the 675 ha *1670 acre* Becontree Estate is on a site of 1214 ha *3000 acres* in Barking and Redbridge, London, and was built between 1921 and 1929. The total number of homes is 26 822, with an estimated population of nearly 90 000.

New towns Of the 32 set up in Great Britain, that with the largest eventual planned population is Milton Keynes, Bucks, with a projected 210 000 for 1992.

Largest house *World* The 250-room Biltmore House in Asheville, North Carolina, USA is owned by George and William Cecil, grandsons of George Washington Vanderbilt II (1862–1914). The house was built between 1890 and 1895 in an estate of 48 160 ha *119 000 acres*, at a cost of $4·4 million; it currently has 4856 ha *12 000 acres*.

Most expensive The most expensive private house ever built is the Hearst Ranch at San Simeon, California, USA. It was built from 1922–39 for William Randolph Hearst (1863–1951), at a total cost of more than $30 million. It has more than 100 rooms, a 32 m *104 ft* long heated swimming pool, a 25 m *83 ft* long assembly hall and a garage for 25 limousines. The house required 60 servants to maintain it.

Great Britain The house with the most rooms is Knole, near Sevenoaks, Kent, believed to have had 365 rooms, one for each day of the year, and now in the care of the National Trust. It is built round seven courtyards, the total depth from front to back being about 120 m *400 ft*. Thomas Bourchier, Archbishop of Canterbury (1454–86), bought the estate in 1456 and commenced building. Sir Thomas Sackville, Earl of Dorset put the finishing touches between 1603–8.

Smallest house In Britain the 19th-century fisherman's cottage at The Quay, Conwy, Gwynedd, has a 182 cm *72 in* frontage, is 309 cm *122 in* high, and is 254 cm *100 in* front to back. It has two tiny rooms and a staircase.

The narrowest known house frontage is of 119·38 cm *47 in* at 50 Stuart Street, Millport, Great Cumbrae, Strathclyde, Scotland.

Largest non–palatial residence St Emmeram Castle, Regensburg, Germany, valued at more than $177 million, contains 517 rooms with a floor space of 21 460 m² *231 000 ft²*. Only 95 rooms are personally used by the family of the late Prince Johannes von Thurn und Taxis.

UK Wentworth Woodhouse, near Rotherham, S Yorks, formerly the seat of the Earls Fitzwilliam, is now privately owned by Wensley Haydon-Baillie. The main part of the house, built over 300 years ago, has more than 240 rooms with over 1000 windows, and its principal façade is 183 m *600 ft* long.

The royal residence Sandringham House, Norfolk has been reported to have had 365 rooms before the demolition of 73 surplus rooms in 1975.

The largest house in Republic of Ireland is Castletown in Co. Kildare, owned by the Hon. Desmond Guinness. It is the headquarters of the Irish Georgian Society.

Scotland's largest house is Hopetoun House, West Lothian, built between 1696

and 1756 with a west façade 206 m *675 ft* long.

Oldest in Britain Eastry Court near Sandwich, Kent dates from AD 603. Some of the original timbers and stone infill still survive behind its present Georgian façade.

Inhabited The *aula* or hall of Barton Manor, Nyetimber, Pagham, W Sussex includes structures from the Saxon times *c.* 800 AD.

Most visited stately home In Great Britain in 1990 Warwick Castle, near Stratford-on-Avon, Warks, received 685 000 visitors. Built by the Beauchamp family, it dates from the 14th century.

Oldest Barracks Collins Barracks, formerly the Royal Barracks, Dublin, Republic of Ireland, were completed in 1704 and still in use.

FLATS

Tallest The 218 m *716 ft* Metropolitan Tower on West 57 Street, New York, USA is of 78 storeys, of which the upper 48 are residential.

The tallest purely residential block of flats is Lake Point Tower, Chicago, Illinois, USA which has 879 units consisting of 70 storeys and stands 194·88 m *639·4 ft* high.

Great Britain The tallest residential block in Great Britain is Shakespeare Tower in the Barbican in the City of London, which has 116 flats on 44 storeys and rises to a height of 127·77 m *419 ft 2 ½ in* above the street. The first of the three Barbican towers was 'topped out' in May 1971.

Largest The private blocks which form the Barbican Estate in the City of London, with 2011 flats, occupy a 16 ha *40 acre* site with covered parking space for 2000 cars. The architects were Chamberlain, Powell and Son.

The largest council block is Hyde Park, Sheffield, Yorks with 1300 flats in 18 storeys. It was completed in 1964.

Buildings for Entertainment

STADIUM

Largest The open Strahov Stadium in Prague, Czechoslovakia was completed in 1934 and can accommodate 240 000 spectators for mass displays of up to 40 000 Sokol gymnasts.

Football The Maracaña Municipal Stadium in Rio de Janeiro, Brazil, has a normal capacity of 205 000, of whom 155 000 can be seated. A crowd of 199 854 was accommodated for the World Cup final between Brazil and Uruguay on 16 Jul 1950. A dry moat, 2·13 m *7 ft* wide and more than 1·5 m *5 ft* deep, protects players from spectators and vice versa.

Britain's most capacious football stadium is Hampden Park, Glasgow, Scotland opened on 31 Oct 1903 its record attendance was 149 547 on 17 Apr 1937. The present licensed limit is 74 400.

Covered The Azteca Stadium, Mexico City, opened in 1968, has a capacity of 107 000. Nearly all seats are under cover.

The largest covered stadium in Great Britain is the Empire Stadium, Wembley, Middx, opened in April 1923. It was the

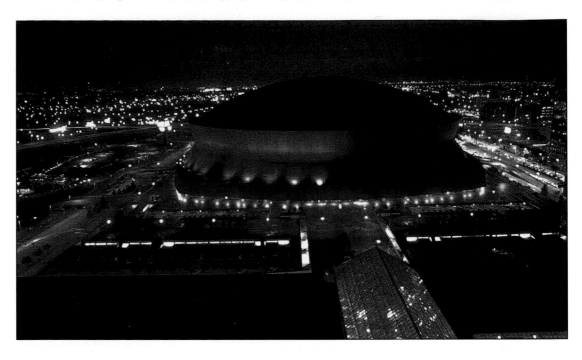

scene of the 1948 Olympic Games and the final of the 1966 World Cup. In 1962–3 the capacity under cover was increased to 100 000 of whom 45 000 can be seated. The original cost was £1 250 000.

Retractable roof The world's largest covers the 54 000 seating capacity sky dome of the Toronto Blue Jays baseball team's new stadium near the CN Tower, Toronto, Canada completed in June 1989. The diameter is 207 m *679 ft*.

Indoor The $173 million 83·2 m *273 ft* tall Superdome in New Orleans, Louisiana, USA covering 5·26 ha *13 acre* 83·2 m *273 ft* high, was completed in May 1975. Its maximum seating capacity for conventions is 97 365 or 76 791 for football. Box suites rent for $35 000 excluding the price of admission. A gondola with six 7·92 m *25·98 ft* TV screens produces instant replay.

Largest roof The transparent acryl glass 'tent' roof over the Munich Olympic Stadium, Germany measures 84 997·9 m² *914 940 ft²* in area, resting on a steel net supported by masts.

The roof of longest span in the world is the 207·2 m *680 ft* diameter of the Louisiana Superdome in New Orleans, Louisiana, USA. The major axis of the elliptical Texas Stadium completed in 1971 at Irving, Texas, is, however, 240 m *787 ft 4 in*.

Amusement resort *Largest* Disney World is set in 11 332 ha *28 000 acres* of Orange and Osceola counties, 32 km *20 miles* south-west of Orlando in central Florida, USA. It was opened on 1 Oct 1971 after a $400 million investment.

Most attended Disneyland, Anaheim, California, USA (opened 1955) received its 250-millionth visitor on 24 Aug 1985 at 9:52 a.m. Disneyland welcomed its 300-millionth visitor in 1989.

Largest pleasure beach Virginia Beach, Virginia, USA has 45 km *28 miles* of beach front on the Atlantic and 16 km *10 miles* of estuary frontage. The area embraces 600 km² *255 miles²* with 134 hotels and motels.

The most visited pleasure beach in Britain is at Blackpool, Lancs and attracts 6 ½ million visitors annually.

Piers *Origins* The origin of piers goes back to the origin of man-made harbours.

That at Caesarea reputedly had the first free-standing breakwaters in 13 BC. However, it is possible that the structures associated with the 'great harbours' of the ancient world in Crete, Alexandria and Carthage pre-date this.

Longest The longest pleasure pier in the world is Southend Pier at Southend-on-Sea, Essex. It is 2·15 km *1·34 miles* in length and it was first opened in August 1889, with final extensions made in 1929. In 1949–50 the pier had a peak 5·75 million visitors. The pier railway closed in October 1978, and reopened on 2 May 1986.

Great Britain The earliest date attributed to a seaside 'jetty' is 1560 at Great Yarmouth, Norfolk; it was replaced by a new structure in 1808 which was washed away in 1953. The Old Pier, at Weymouth, Dorset dates back to 1812.

Most piers The resort with the most piers was Atlantic City, New Jersey, USA with seven, though currently only five remain: the Garden Pier (1912), Million Dollar (1906) now called Shops on Ocean One, Auditorium (1900), now the Steeplechase, Steel (1898) and Applegates (1883), now known as Central.

In Great Britain only Blackpool, Lancs now has three—North, Central and South.

FAIRS

Earliest The earliest major international fair was the Great Exhibition of 1851 in the Crystal Palace, Hyde Park, London, which in 141 days attracted 6 039 195 admissions.

Largest The site of the Louisiana Purchase Exposition at St Louis, Missouri, USA covered 514·66 ha *1271·76 acres* and there was an attendance of 19 694 855. The 1904 Olympic Games were also staged

Big wheel The original Ferris Wheel, named after its constructor George W. Ferris (1859–96), was erected in 1893 at the Midway, Chicago, Illinois, USA at a cost of $385 000. It was 76 m *250 ft* in diameter, 240 m *790 ft* in circumference, weighed 1087 tonnes and carried 36 cars each seating 60 people, making a total of 2160 passengers. The structure was removed in 1904 to St Louis, Missouri, USA and was eventually sold as scrap for $1800.

In 1897 a Ferris Wheel with a diameter of

■ **Longest roof span**
The Louisiana Superdome, USA has the longest roof span in the world with a diameter of 207·2 m 680 ft. It was the venue for the 1990 Superbowl XXIV. (Photo: All Sport, USA-/Rosato)

taurant chain is operated by McDonald's Corporation of Oak Brook, Illinois, USA founded in 1955 by Ray A. Kroc (1902–84) after buying out the brothers Dick and 'Mac' McDonald, pioneers of the fast-food drive-in. By April 1991 McDonald's licensed and owned 12 000 restaurants in 53 countries. Their largest outlet, and the first in the USSR, opened in Moscow on 31 Jan 1990, when 630 specially-trained local staff were faced with 20 000 Muscovites queueing for their first taste of *Big Mak* at the 700-seater restaurant. World-wide sales in 1990 were $18·7 billion.

Fish and chip restaurant The world's largest fish and chip shop is Harry Ramsden's at White Cross, Guiseley, W Yorks, with 140 staff serving 1 million customers per year, who consume 213 tonnes of fish and 356 tonnes of potatoes. On 30 Oct 1988, between 11:30 a.m. and 10:00 p.m., Harry Ramsden's celebrated their Diamond Jubilee by serving 10 182 servings of fish and chips at 1928 prices.

PUBLIC HOUSES

Oldest There are various claimants to the title of the Great Britain's oldest inn. A foremost claimant is 'The Fighting Cocks', at St Albans, Herts an 11th-century structure on an eighth-century site. The timber frame of the Royalist Hotel, Digbeth Street, Stow-on-the-Wold, Glos has been dated to even earlier it was 'The Eagle and the Child' in the 13th century and known to exist in AD 947. An origin as early as AD 560 has been claimed for 'Ye Olde Ferry Boat Inn' at Holywell, Cambs. There is some evidence that it antedates the local church, built in 980, but documents are not earlier than AD 1100. The 'Bingley Arms', Bardsey, near Leeds, W Yorks, restored and extended in 1738, existed as the 'Priest's Inn', according to Bardsey Church records of AD 905.

The oldest Irish pub is 'Grace Neill's Bar', Donaghadee, Co. Down, built in 1611. An inn has stood on the site of the 'Brazen Head Inn', Lower Bridge Street, Dublin, Republic of Ireland since the late 12th century. The present structure dates from 1668.

Largest World The largest beer-selling establishment in the world is the 'Mathäser', Bayerstrasse 5, Munich, Germany, where the daily sale reaches 48 000 litres *84 470 pts*. It was established in 1829, demolished in World War II and rebuilt by 1955. It now seats 5500 people.

The beer-consumption at the Dube beer halls in the Bantu township of Soweto, Johannesburg, South Africa may, however, be higher on some Saturdays when the average daily consumption of 27 280 litres *48 000 pts* is far exceeded.

Great Britain The largest public house in Great Britain is the 'Downham Tavern', Downham Way, Bromley, Kent, built in 1930. Two large bars (counter length 13·7 m *45 ft*) accommodate 1000 customers with 18–20 staff.

Smallest The 'Lakeside Inn', The Promenade, Southport, Merseyside, measured by floor area, is 6·7 × 4·87 m *22 × 16 ft* and 4·57 m *15 ft* in height. The ground floor of 'The Nutshell', Bury St. Edmunds, Suffolk is 4·82 × 2·28 m *15 ft 10 in × 7 ½ ft*.

'The Smiths Arms', Godmanstone, Dorset has external dimensions of 12·04 × 3·5 m *39 ½ × 11 ½ ft* and is 3·65 m *12 ft* in height.

The pub with the smallest bar room is the 'Dove Inn', Upper Mall, Chiswick, London measuring 127 × 239 cm *4 ft 2 in × 7 ft*

■ **Largest diameter Ferris wheel**

Cosmoclock 21 is 100 m 328 ft in diameter and 105 m 344·88 ft high. The 60 arms holding the gondalas serve as a second hand for the clock and light up one by one per second of every minute.

Largest harem

The Winter Harem of the Grand Seraglio at Topkapi, Istanbul, Turkey was completed in 1589 and has 400 rooms. By the time of Abdul Hamid II was deposed in 1909 the number of *carge* 'those who serve' had dwindled from 1200 to 370 odalisques, with 127 eunuchs.

86·5 m *284 ft* was erected for the Earl's Court Exhibition, London. It had ten 1st-class and 30 2nd-class cars.

The largest diameter wheel now operating is the Cosmoclock 21 at Yokohama City, Japan. It is 105 m *344·48 ft* high and 100 m *328 ft* in diameter, with 60 gondolas each with eight seats. With such features as illumination by laser beams and acoustic effects by sound synthesizers, the 60 arms holding the gondolas, each serve as a second hand for the 13 m *42·65 ft* long electric clock mounted at the hub.

Roller coaster The maximum speeds claimed for switchbacks, scenic railways or roller coasters have long been exaggerated for commercial reasons.

Longest The longest roller coaster in the world is *The Beast* at Kings Island near Cincinnati, Ohio, USA. The run of 2·25 km *1·40 miles* incorporates 243·8 m *800 ft* of tunnels and a 540-degree banked helix.

Highest vertical drop The $8 million Magnum XL-200, opened in May 1989 at Cedar Point Park, Sandusky, Ohio, USA has a vertical drop of 59·37 m *194·8 ft* on which a speed of 115·86 km/h *72 mph* is reached. Cedar Point has nine coasters, making its total more than any other Park.

Tallest The tallest is the *Moonsault Scramble* at the Fujikyu Highland Park, near Kawaguchi Lake, Japan, opened on 24 Jun 1983. It is 70 m *230 ft* tall.

Wooden The latest design of Curtis D. Summers, who has already designed over 30 wooden coasters, is the *Texas Giant* at Six Flags over Texas, Arlington, Texas, USA. At its highest point it is 43·58 m *143 ft*, with a top speed of up 100 km/h *62 mph*. It carries 28 passengers.

Tallest looping At its highest point 57·30 m *188 ft* above the ground the *Viper* at Six Flags Magic Mountain, Valencia, California, USA sends riders upside-down seven times over a 1167·38 m *3830 ft* track.

Longest slide The Bromley Alpine Slide on Route 11 in Peru, Vermont, USA, has a length of 1402 m *4600 ft* and a vertical drop of 250 m *820 ft*.

Night club's Earliest night club (*boîte de nuit*) was 'Le Bal des Anglais' at 6 rue des Anglais, Paris, France. Established in 1843, it closed *c.* 1960.

Largest Gilley's Club (formerly Shelly's), built in 1955, was extended in 1971 on Spencer Highway, Houston, Texas, USA, with a seating capacity of 6000 under one roof covering 1·6 ha *4 acres*.

In the more classical sense the largest night club in the world is The Mikado in the Akasaka district of Tokyo, Japan, with a seating capacity of 2000. Binoculars are essential to an appreciation of the floor show.

Lowest The Minus 206 in Tiberias, Israel, on the shores of the Sea of Galilee, is 206 m *676 ft* below sea level. An alternative candidate is the oft-raided 'Outer Limits', opposite the Cow Palace, San Francisco, California, USA. It has been called 'The Most Busted Joint' and 'The Slowest to Get the Message'.

Restaurants Earliest The Casa Botin was opened in 1725 in Calle de Cuchilleros 17, Madrid, Spain.

Largest The Tump Nak restaurant in Bangkok, Thailand consists of 65 adjoining houses built on 4 ha *10 acres*. A thousand waiters are available to serve the 3000 potential customers.

Highest The highest restaurant in the world is in the Chacaltaya ski resort, Bolivia, at 5340 m *17 519 ft*.

The highest in Great Britain is the Ptarmigan Observation Restaurant at 1112 m *3650 ft* above sea level on Cairngorm, (1244 m *4084 ft*) near Aviemore, Invernessshire, Scotland.

Restaurateurs The world's largest res-

10 in. Another contender is the 'Earl Grey', Quenington, Glos whose measurements are 3·73 × 2·89 m *12 ¼ ft × 9 ½ ft.* The floor area of the public bar at the Highfield Hall of Residence, Southampton, Hants measures 8·21 m² *88·37 ft²*.

Most remote The Old Forge public house at Inverie, Knoydart, Inverness-shire is 32·18 km *20 miles* by ferry and 38·62 km *24 miles* 'as the crow flies' due to no roads into or out of Knoydart from its nearest contender.

Tallest bar Humperdink's Seafood and Steakhouse Bar at Dallas, Texas, USA is 7·69 m *25 ft 3 in* high with two levels of shelving containing over 1000 bottles. The lower level has four rows of shelves approximately 12 m *40 ft* across and can be reached from floor level. If an order has to be met from the upper level, which has five rows of shelves, it is reached by climbing a ladder.

Longest bars The world's longest permanent bar is the 103·6 m *340 ft* long bar in 'Lulu's Roadhouse', Kitchener, Ontario, Canada, opened on 3 Apr 1984. The 'Bar at Erickson's', on Burnside Street, Portland, Oregon, USA in its heyday (1883–1920) possessed a bar measuring 208·48 m *684 ft* which ran continuously around and across the main saloon measuring 208·48 m *684 ft*. The chief bouncer, Edward 'Spider' Johnson, had an assistant named 'Jumbo' Reilly who weighed 23 st and was said to resemble 'an ill-natured orang-utan'. Beer was five cents for 16 fluid ounces. Temporary greater length bars have been erected.

The longest bar in Great Britain with beer pumps is the Long Bar at the Cornwall Coliseum Auditorium at Carlyon Bay, St Austell, Cornwall, measuring 31·8 m *104 ¼ ft* and having 34 dispensers.

The longest bar in a pub is of 31·77 m *104 ⅓ ft* in length, at 'The Horse Shoe', Drury Street, Glasgow, Scotland.

The Grandstand Bar at Galway Racecourse, Republic of Ireland, completed in 1955, measures 64 m *210 ft.*

Longest pub name 'The Old Thirteenth Cheshire Astley Volunteer Rifleman Corps Inn' in Astley Street, Stalybridge, Manchester has 55 letters. The contrived name of 'Bertie Belcher's Brighton Brewery Company at the Hedgehog and Hogshead–it's really in Hove, actually', has 83 letters and another contender recently opened in Fulham Road, London is 'Henry J. Bean's But His Friends, Some of Whom Live Down This Way, All Call Him Hank Bar and Grill,' with 74 letters.

Shortest name In Great Britain the shortest name was the 'X' at Westcott, Cullompton, Devon but in October 1983 the name was changed to the 'Merry Harriers'.

Commonest name There are probably about 630 called the 'Red Lion'. Arthur Amos of Bury St Edmunds, Suffolk, has recorded 21 516 names for pubs since 1938. On his death in June 1986, his son John took over the collection, which now numbers 25 095.

Highest In Great Britain the 'Tan Hill Inn' is 528 m *1732 ft* above sea level. It is just in N Yorks on the moorland road between Reeth, N Yorks and Brough, Cumbria. The 'Snowdon Summit' licensed bar and cafeteria is, when open, the highest at 1085 m *3560 ft.*

Most visits Stanley House of Totterdown, Bristol has visited 3311 differently named pubs in Britain by means of public transport only, from 1969 to March 1990.

Jimmy Young of Better Pubs Ltd, claims to have visited 23 752 different pubs up to 20 Apr 1989.

The Blackcountry Ale Tairsters of Tipton, W Mids, Peter Hill, Joseph Hill, Rob Jones and John Drew have visited 3400 different public houses touring by car the coast line and every county and region of mainland Great Britain. The visits were all made in their spare time in aid of local hospital funds between 2 Nov 1984 and 26 May 1990.

Towers and Masts

TALLEST STRUCTURES

World The tallest structure in the world, the guyed Warszawa Radio mast at Konstantynow, 96 km *60 miles* north-west of the capital of Poland, is 646·38 m *2120 ⅔ ft* tall or more than four-tenths of a mile. It was completed on 18 Jul 1974 and put into operation on 22 Jul 1974. It was designed by Jan Polak and weighs 550 tonnes. The mast is so high that anyone falling off the top would reach their terminal velocity and hence cease to be accelerating before hitting the ground. Work was begun in July 1970 on this tubular steel construction, with its 15 steel guy ropes. It recaptured for Europe, after 45 years, a record held in the USA since the Chrysler Building surpassed the Eiffel Tower in 1929.

The tallest structure in the Great Britain is the Independent Television Commission's mast north of Horncastle, Lincs, completed in 1965 to a height of 385 m *1265 ft* with 2·13 m *7 ft* added by meteorological equipment installed in September 1967. It serves Yorkshire TV and weighs 210 tonnes.

TALLEST TOWERS

The tallest self-supporting tower (as opposed to a guyed mast) in the world is the $44 million CN Tower in Metro Center, Toronto, Canada, which rises to 553·34 m *1 815 ft 5 in.* Excavation began on 12 Feb 1973 for the erection of the 130 000 tonnes reinforced, post-tensioned concrete structure, which was 'topped out' on 2 Apr 1975. The 416-seat restaurant revolves in the Sky Pod at 347·5 m *1140 ft*, from which the visibility extends to hills 120 km *74 ½ miles* distant. Lightning strikes the top about 200 times (30 storms) per annum.

The tallest tower built before the era of television masts is the Eiffel Tower in Paris, France, designed by Alexandre Gustav Eiffel (1832–1923) for the Paris Exhibition and completed on 31 Mar 1889. It was 300·51 m *985 ft 11 in* tall, now extended by a TV antenna to 320·75 m *1052 ⅓ ft*, and weighs 7340 tonnes. The maximum sway in high winds is 12·7 cm *5 in.* The whole iron edifice, which has 1792 steps, took 2 years, 2 months and 2 days to build and cost 7 799 401 francs 31 centimes.

The tallest self-supported tower in Great Britain is the 329·18 m *1080 ft* tall Independent Broadcasting Authority transmitter at Emley Moor, W Yorks, completed in September 1971. The structure, which cost £900 000, has an enclosed room at the 263·65 m *865 ft* level and weighs with its foundations more than 15 000 tonnes.

The tallest tower of the pre-television era was the New Brighton Tower of 171·29 m *562 ft* built on Merseyside in 1897–1900 and dismantled in 1919–21.

Bridges

Oldest Arch construction was understood by the Sumerians as early as 3200 BC and a reference exists to a Nile bridge in 2650 BC.

The oldest surviving datable bridge in the world is the slab stone single-arch bridge over the River Meles in Izmir (formerly Smyrna) Turkey, which dates from *c.* 850 BC.

The clapper bridges of Dartmoor and Exmoor (e.g. the Tarr Steps over the River Barle, Exmoor, Somerset) are thought to be of prehistoric types although none of the existing examples can be certainly dated. They are made of large slabs of stone placed over boulders.

The Romans built stone bridges in England and remains of these have been found at Corbridge, Northumberland, dating to the 2nd century AD, and at Chesters, Northumberland and Willowford, Cumbria. Remains of a very early wooden bridge have been found at Aldwinkle, Northants.

LONGEST

Cable suspension The world's longest bridge span is the main span of the Humber Estuary Bridge, Humberside, at 1410 m *4626 ft.* Work began on 27 Jul 1972, after a decision announced on 22 Jan 1966. The towers are 162·5 m *533 ft 1 ⅝ in* tall from datum and are 36 mm *1 ⅜ in* out of parallel to allow for the curvature of the Earth. Including the Hessle and the Barton side spans, the bridge stretches 2220 m or *1·37 miles.* It was structurally completed on 18 Jul 1980 at a cost of £96 million and was opened by H M the Queen on 17 Jul 1981. Tolls range between 70 pence for motorcycles and £10·90 for heavy vehicles; pedestrians and pedal cyclists are toll free.

The Akashi-Kaikyo road bridge linking Honshū and Shikoku, Japan was started in 1988 and completion is planned for 1998.

■ Tallest structure
The tallest structure in the world is the guyed Warszawa Radio mast at Konstantynow, Poland. It is 646·8 m 2120 ⅔ ft high.

BRIDGES

130

The main span will be 1990 m *6528 ft* in length with an overall suspended length with side spans totalling 3910 m *12 828 ft*. Two towers will rise 297 m *974·40 ft* above water level, and the two main supporting cables will be 1 100 mm in diameter, making both dimensions a world record.

The Seto-Ohashi double-deck road and rail bridge linking Kojima, Honshu with Sakaide, Shikoku, Japan opened on 10 Apr 1988 at a cost of £4·9 billion and 17 lives. The tolls for cars are £24 each way for the 3·6 m *12 ft* spans and viaducts. The Minami Bisan-seto Bridge on this link has the world's longest suspension bridge span 1 100 m *3 609 ft* for combined road/railway traffic.

The longest cable-stayed bridge span in the world is the 490 m *1608 ft* Ikuchi Bridge in Japan between Honshu and Shikoku on the Onomichi-Imabari Route, completed in 1991.

The Tatara Bridge on the Onomichi-Imabari Route, Japan, is due for completion in 1999, and will be the leading long-span cable-stayed bridge in the world, with a main span of 890 m *2920 ft*.

UK The United Kingdom's leading long-span cable-stayed bridge will be the second

Severn Bridge, Bristol, Avon, due for completion in 1996, with a main span of 456 m *1 496 ft*.

Cantilever The Quebec Bridge (Pont de Québec) over the St Lawrence River in Canada has the longest cantilever truss span of any in the world 549 m *1800 ft* between the piers and 987 m *3239 ft* overall. It carries a railway track and two carriageways. Begun in 1899, it was finally opened to traffic on 3 Dec 1917 at a cost of 87 lives, and Cdn$22·5 million.

Great Britain's longest is the Forth Bridge. Its two main spans are 521 m *1710 ft* long. It carries a double railway track over the Firth of Forth 47·5 m *156 ft* above the water level. Work commenced in November 1882 and the first test trains crossed on 22 Jan 1890 after an expenditure of £3 million. It was officially opened on 4 Mar 1890. Of the 4500 workers who built it, 57 were killed in various accidents. To commemorate the centenary of the Forth Bridge HRH Prince Edward on 7 Oct 1990 switched on the ScottishPower floodlights. Consisting of over 1000 lights they illuminate the bridge from span to span. Over 40·23 km *25 miles* of cable were laid, making the structure the biggest illuminated bridge in the world.

Steel arch The longest is the New River

Gorge bridge, near Fayetteville, West Virginia, USA, completed in 1977, with a span of 518·2 m *1700 ft*.

The longest in Great Britain is the Runcorn–Widnes bridge, Cheshire opened on 21 Jul 1961, with a span of 329·8 m *1082 ft*.

Floating The longest is the Second Lake Washington Bridge, Evergreen, Seattle, Washington State, USA. Its total length is 3839 m *12 596 ft* and its floating section measures 2291 m *7518 ft*. It was built at a total cost of $15 million and completed in August 1963.

Covered The longest is that at Hartland, New Brunswick, Canada, measuring 390·8 m *1282 ft* overall, completed in 1899.

Railway The longest is the Huey P. Long Bridge, Metairie, Louisiana, USA, with a railway section 7 km *4·35 miles* in length and a longest span of 241 m *790 ft*. It was completed on 16 Dec 1935.

Britain's is the second Tay Bridge 3552 m *11 653 ft*, across the Firth of Tay at Dundee, Scotland, opened on 20 Jun 1887. Of the 85 spans, 74 length 3136 m *10 289 ft* are over the waterway.

The 878 brick arches of the former London

–Greenwich Railway viaduct between London Bridge and Deptford Creek, built in 1836, extend for 6· km *3 ¾ miles.*

Longest bridging The Second Lake Pontchartrain Causeway was completed on 23 Mar 1969, joining Lewisburg and Mandeville, Louisiana, USA. It has a length of 38 422 m *126 055 ft.* It cost $29·9 million and is 69 m *228 ft* longer than the adjoining First Causeway completed in 1956.

Longest railway viaduct The longest railway viaduct in the world is the rock-filled Great Salt Lake Railroad Trestle, carrying the Southern Pacific Railroad 19 km *11·85 miles* across the Great Salt Lake, Utah, USA. It was opened as a pile and trestle bridge on 8 Mar 1904, but converted to rock fill in 1955–60.

Stone arch The longest stone arch bridge is the 1161 m *3810 ft* long Rockville Bridge north of Harrisburg, Pennsylvania, USA, with 48 spans containing 196 000 tonnes of stone. It was completed in 1901.

The longest stone arch span is the Planen Bridge in Germany at 89·9 m *295 ft.*

UK The longest in the United Kingdom is the Grosvenor Bridge at Chester, Cheshire (60·96 m *200 ft*) completed in 1830, and at the time of its construction the largest such span in the world.

Widest The widest long-span bridge is the 502·9 m *1650 ft* Sydney Harbour Bridge, Australia (48·8 m *160 ft* wide). It carries two electric overhead railway tracks, eight lanes of roadway and a cycle and footway. It was officially opened on 19 Mar 1932.

The Crawford Street Bridge in Providence, Rhode Island, USA has a width of 350 m *1148 ft.*

The River Roch is bridged for a distance of 445 m *1460 ft* where the culvert passes through the centre of Rochdale, Manchester and this is sometimes claimed to be a breadth.

Cycleway bridge The longest cycleway bridge is over the 17 railway tracks of Cambridge Station, Cambs. It has a tower 35 m *114·82 ft* high and two 50 m *164 ft* long approach ramps, and is 237·6 m *779·52 ft* in length.

HIGHEST

The highest bridge in the world is over the Royal Gorge of the Arkansas River in Colorado, USA, and is 321 m *1053 ft* above the water level. It is a suspension bridge with a main span of 268 m *880 ft* and was constructed in six months, ending on 6 Dec 1929.

The tallest multispan cantilever construction in the United Kingdom is over the Dee bridge on the A483 Newbridge Bypass, Clwyd. It is 57·3 m *188 ft* high. The Crumlin viaduct (60·96 m *200 ft*) held the United Kingdom record between 1857 until its demolition in 1966.

Railway The highest railway bridge in the world is the Mala Rijeka viaduct of Yugoslav Railways at Kolasin on the Belgrade–Bar line. It is 198 m *650 ft* high and was opened on 1 Jun 1976. It consists of steel spans mounted on concrete piers.

The highest railway bridge in Great Britain is the Ballochmyle viaduct over the river Ayr, Ayrshire, Scotland built 51·5 m *169 ft* over the river bed in 1846–48. At that time it had the world's longest masonry railway arch span of 55·16 m *181 ft.*

Road The road bridge at the highest altitude in the world, 5602 m *18 380 ft*, is the

30 m *98·4 ft* long Bailey Bridge designed and constructed by Lt.Col. S.G. Vombatkere and an Indian Army team in August 1982 near Khardung-La, in Ladakh, India.

AQUEDUCTS

Longest ancient The greatest of ancient aqueducts was the aqueduct of Carthage in Tunisia, which ran 141 km *87·6 miles* from the springs of Zaghouan to Djebel Djougar. It was built by the Romans during the reign of Publius Aelius Hadrianus (AD 117–138). In 1895, 344 arches still survived. Its original capacity has been calculated at 31·8 million litres *7 million gal* per day.

The triple-tiered aqueduct Pont du Gard, built in AD 19 near Nîmes, France, is 48 m *157 ft* high.

The tallest of the 14 arches of the Aguas Livres aqueduct, built in Lisbon, Portugal, in 1784 is 65 m *213 ¼ ft* .

Longest modern The world's longest aqueduct, in the non-classical sense of water conduit, excluding irrigation canals, is the California State Water Project aqueduct, completed in 1974, with a length of 1329 km *826 miles*, of which 619 km *385 miles* is canalized.

The longest bridged aqueduct in Great Britain is the Ponteysyllte in Clwyd on the Llangollen Canal. It is 307 m *1007 ft* long, and has 19 arches up to 36 m *118 ft* high above low water on the Dee. Designed by Thomas Telford (1757–1834), it was opened in 1805. It is still in use today by pleasure craft.

Canals

Earliest Relics of the oldest canals in the world, dated by archaeologists c.4000 BC, were discovered near Mandali, Iraq early in 1968.

The earliest canals in Britain were first cut by the Romans. In the Midlands the 17 km *11 mile* long Fossdyke Canal between Lincoln and the river Trent at Torksey was built in about AD 120 and was scoured in 1122. It is still in use today.

Though the Exeter Canal was cut as early as 1564–66, the first wholly artificial major navigation canal in the United Kingdom was the 29·7 km *18 ½ mile* long canal with 14 locks from Whitecoat Point to Newry, Northern Ireland, opened on 28 Mar 1742.

The Sankey Navigation Canal in Lancashire, 12·8 km *8 miles* in length, with 10 locks, was opened in November 1757.

Longest The longest canal of the ancient world was the Grand Canal of China from Beijing to Hangzhou. It was begun in 540 BC and not completed until 1327, by which time it extended (including canalized river sections) for 1781 km *1107 miles.* The estimated workforce c. AD 600 reached 5 million on the Pien section. Having been allowed by 1950 to silt up to the point that it was nowhere more than 1·8 m *6 ft* deep, it is now, however, plied by vessels of up to 2000 tonnes .

The Beloye More (White Sea) Baltic Canal from Belomorsk to Povenets, in the USSR, is 227 km *141 miles* long and has 19 locks. It was completed with the use of forced labour in 1933. It cannot accommodate ships of more than 5 m *16 ft* in draught.

The world's longest big-ship canal is the Suez Canal linking the Red and Mediter-

ranean Seas, opened on 16 Nov 1869 but inoperative from June 1967 to June 1975. The canal was planned by the French diplomatist Comte Ferdinand de Lesseps (1805–94) and work began on 25 Apr 1859. The workforce consisted of 8213 men and 368 camels. It is 161·9 km *100·6 miles* in length from Port Said lighthouse to Suez Roads, and 60 m *197 ft* wide.

The largest vessel to transit the Suez Canal has been SS *Settebello*, of 322 446 tonnes (length 338·43 m *1110·3 ft*; beam 57·35 m *188·1 ft* at a maximum draught of 22·35 m *73·3 ft*). This was southbound in ballast on 6 Aug 1986. USS *Shreveport* transited southbound on 15–16 Aug 1984 in a record 7 hr 45 min.

Canals and river navigations in Great Britain amount to approximately 5630 km *3 500 miles* with a further 160 km *100 miles* being restored. Of this total 4000 km *2500 miles* are inter-linked.

Busiest The busiest ship canal is the Kiel Canal linking the North Sea with the Baltic Sea in Germany. Over 45 000 transits were recorded in 1987.

Next comes the Suez Canal, with over 20 000 transits, and third the Panama Canal, with over 10 000.

Busiest in terms of tonnage of shipping using it is the Suez Canal, with nearly 440 million grt.

Longest artificial seaway The St Lawrence Seaway is 304 km *189 miles* in length along the New York State–Ontario border from Montreal to Lake Ontario. It enables ships up to 222 m *728 ft* long and 8 m *26·2 ft* draught (some of which are of 26 400 tonnes) to sail 3769 km *2342 miles* from the North Atlantic up the St Lawrence estuary and across the Great Lakes to Duluth, Minnesota, USA. The project, begun in 1954, cost $470 million and the seaway was opened on 25 Apr 1959.

Longest irrigation The Karakumsky Kanal stretches 1200 km *745·66 miles* from Haun-Khan to Ashkhabad, Turkmenistan, USSR. The 'navigable' length in 1991 will be 800 km *497 miles.*

LOCKS

Largest The Berendrecht lock, which links the river Scheldt with docks at the port of Antwerp, Belgium, is the largest sea lock in the world. First used in April 1989, it has a length of 500 m *1640·41 ft*, a width of 68 m *223 ft* and a sill level of 13·50 m *44·29 ft.* Each of its four sliding lock gates weighs 1500 tonnes. The total cost of construction was approximately BFr 12 000 million.

The largest and deepest lock in the United Kingdom is the Royal Portbury Entrance Lock, Bristol, which measures 366 × 42·7 m *1200 × 140 ft* and has a depth of 20·2 m *66 ft.* It was opened in August 1977.

Deepest The Zaporojie on the Dnieperbug Canal, USSR can raise or lower barges at 39·2 m *128 ft.*

Highest rise and longest flight The world's highest lock elevator overcomes a head of 68·58 m *225 ft* at Ronquières on the Charleroi–Brussels Canal, Belgium. The two 236-wheeled caissons, each able to carry 1370 tonnes, take 22 minutes to cover the 1432 m *4698 ft* long inclined plane.

The highest rise of any boat-carrying plane in Britain was the 68·6 m *225 ft* of the 285 m *935 ft* long Hobbacott Down plane on the Bude Canal, Cornwall.

The longest flight of locks in the United

Coal shovelling

The record for filling a 508 kg *1120 lb* hopper with coal is 29·4 sec, by Piet Groot at the Inangahua A and P Show, New Zealand on 1 Jan 1985.

Kingdom is on the Worcester and Birmingham Canal at Tardebigge, Hereford & Worcester, where in a 4 km *2 ½ mile* stretch there are the Tardebigge (30 locks) and Stoke (six locks) flights which together drop the canal 78·9 m *259 ft*.

The flight of locks on the Huddersfield Narrow Canal, (closed in 1944), on the 11·6 km *7 ¼ mile* stretch to Marsden from Huddersfield numbered 42.

Largest cut The Corinth Canal, Greece opened in 1893, was 6342 km *3940 miles* long, 8 m *26·24 ft* deep, with an average depth of cutting of 306 m *1003 ft* over some 4·2 km *26 miles*, and an extreme depth of 459 m *1505 ft*. The Gaillard Cut (known as 'the Ditch') on the Panama Canal is 82 m *270 ft* deep between Gold Hill and Contractor's Hill with a bottom width of 152 m *500 ft*. In one day in 1911 as many as 333 trains each carrying 363 tonnes of earth left this site.

Dams

Earliest The earliest known dams were those uncovered by the British School of Archaeology in Jerusalem in 1974 and at Jawa in Jordan. These stone-built earthen dams are dated to c. 3200 BC.

Most massive Measured by volume, the earth and rock-filled Pati dam on the Paraná river, Argentina has a volume of 238 180 000 m³ *311 527 000 yd ³*. It is 174·9 km *108·6 miles* in length and 36 m *118 ft* high. This will be surpassed in volume by the Syncrude Tailings dam in Canada with 540 million ³ *706 million yd ³*.

The most massive dam in Britain is the Northumbrian Water Authority's Kielder dam, a 52 m *170 ft* high earth embankment

measuring 1140 m *3740 ft* in length and 5 300 000 m ³ *6 932 000 yd ³*.

Britain has longer low dams or barrages of the valley cut-off type, notably the Hanningfield dam, Essex, built from July 1952 to August 1956 to a length of 2088 m *6850 ft* and a height of 19·7 m *64 ½ ft*.

Largest concrete The Grand Coulee dam on the Columbia River, Washington State, USA was begun in 1933 and became operational on 22 Mar 1941. It was finally completed in 1942 at a cost of $56 million. It has a crest length of 1272 m *4173 ft* and is 167 m *550 ft* high and 8 092 000 m ³ *10 585 000 yd ³* of concrete were used in its construction. It weighs approximately 19 595 000 tonnes.

Highest The highest will be the 335 m *1098 ft* high Rogunskaya earth-filled dam across the river Vakhsh, Tadzhikistan, USSR, with a crest length of only 602 m *1975 ft* and a volume of 71 million m³ *3·002 billion ft ³*. Preparations for building started in 1976, and construction began in March 1981. The completion date is set for early 1992.

Meanwhile the tallest dam completed is the 300 m *984 ft* high Nurek dam, USSR, of 58 million m³ *2·05 billion ft³* volume.

The rock-fill Llyn Brianne dam, Dyfed is Great Britain's highest dam, reaching 91 m *298 ½ ft* in November 1971. It became operational on 20 Jul 1972.

Longest The 41 m *134 ½ ft* high Yacyreta–Apipe dam across the Paraná on the Paraguay–Argentina border will extend for 69·6 km *43·24 miles*. It is due for completion in 1992.

The Kiev dam across the Dnieper, Ukraine, USSR completed in 1964, has a crest length of 412 km *256 miles*. The Chapeton Dam under construction on the Parana River, Argentina will have a crest length of

224 km *139 miles* and is due to be completed in 1996.

In the early 17th century an impounding dam of moderate height was built in Lake Hungtze, Jiangsu, China, of a reputed length of 100 km *62 miles*.

The longest sea dam in the world is the Afsluitdijk stretching 32·5 km *20·195 miles* across the mouth of the Zuider Zee in two sections of 2·499 km *1·553 miles* (mainland of North Holland to the Isle of Wieringen) and 30 km *18·641 miles* from Wieringen to Friesland. It has a sea-level width of 89 m *293 ft* and a height of 7·5 m *24 ft 7 in*.

Strongest On completion, this will be the 245 m *803·8 ft* high Sayano-Shushenskaya Sam on the River Yenisey, USSR, which is designed to bear a load of 18 million tonnes from a fully-filled reservoir of 31 300 million m³ *41 000 million yd ³* capacity.

Largest reservoir The most voluminous man-made reservoir is the Bratskoe reservoir, on the Angara river in Siberia, USSR with a volume of 169·3 km³ *5978.74 ft ³* and an area of 5470 km² *2 111·967 miles²*. It extends for 599 km *372 miles* in length with a width of 33 km *21 miles*. It was filled in 1961–67.

The world's largest artificial lake measured by surface area is Lake Volta, Ghana, formed by the Akosombo dam, completed in 1965. By 1969 the lake had filled to an area of 8482 km² *3275 miles ²*, with a shoreline 7250 km *4500 miles* in length.

The completion in 1954 of the Owen Falls Dam near Jinja, Uganda, across the northern exit of the White Nile from the Victoria Nyanza marginally raised the level of that natural lake by adding 204·8 km³ and technically turned it into a reservoir with a surface area of 6·9 million ha *17 169 920 acres*.

The $4-billion Tucurui dam in Brazil of 64·3 million m³ had, by 1984, converted the Tocantins River into a 1900 km *1180 mile* long chain of lakes.

The most capacious reservoir in Britain is Kielder Water in the North Tyne Valley, Northumberland, which filled to 2000 million hl *44 000 million gal* from 15 Dec 1980 to mid 1982, and which acquired a surface area of 1086 ha *2684 acres* and a perimeter of 43·4 km *27 miles* to become England's second largest lake.

The largest wholly artificial reservoir in Great Britain is the Queen Mary reservoir, built between August 1914 and June 1925 at Littleton, near Staines, Surrey, with an available storage capacity of 369·6 million litres *8130 million gal* and a water area of 286 ha *707 acres*. The length of the perimeter embankment is 6329 m *20 766 ft*.

Rutland Water has a lesser capacity (124 106 million litres *27 300 million gal*) and a lesser perimeter (38·6 km *24 miles*) but a greater surface area of 1254 ha *3100 acres*.

The deepest reservoir in Europe is Loch Morar, Inverness-shire, Scotland, with a maximum depth of 310 m *1017 ft*.

Largest polder (reclaimed land)
Of the five great polders in the old Zuider Zee, Netherlands, the largest will be the Markerwaard, of 60 300 ha *149 000 acre* (603 km² *232·8 miles ²*). Work on the 106 km *66 mile* long surrounding dyke was begun in 1957. The water area remaining after the erection of the 1927–32 dam (32 km *20 miles* in length) is called IJsselmeer, which will have a final area of 1262·6 km² *487 ½ miles ²*.

Largest levees
The most massive ever built are the Mississippi levees, begun in 1717 but vastly augmented by the US Federal Government after the disastrous floods of 1927. These extend for 2787 km *1732 miles* along the main river from Cape Girardeau, Missouri, USA to the Gulf of Mexico and comprise more than 765 million m³ *1000 million yd ³* of earthworks. Levees on the tributaries comprise an additional 3200 km *2000 miles*.

Tunnels

LONGEST

Water-supply tunnel
The longest tunnel of any kind is the New York City West Delaware water-supply tunnel, begun in 1937 and completed in 1944. It has a diameter of 4·1 m *13 ½ ft* and runs for 168·9 km *105 miles* from the Rondout reservoir into the Hillview reservoir, on the border of Yonkers and New York City, USA.

The UK's longest is the Kielder Water tunnel system. These tunnels have been driven through the rock to link the Tyne Valley and the Wear Valley. A pipe then passes under the river Wear and the tunnel then proceeds to link up with the Tees Valley. The system is 32·18 km *20·2 miles* in length.

The London ring (water) main under construction since 1986, will be 76 km *47·2 miles* in length.

Rail
The 53·85 km *33·46 mile* long Seikan rail Tunnel was bored 240 m *787 ft* beneath sea level and 100 m *328 ft* below the sea bed of the Tsugaru Strait between Tappi Saki, Honshū, and Fukushima, Hokkaidō, Japan. Tests started on the sub-aqueous

section (23·3 km *14 ½ miles*) in 1964 and construction in June 1972. It was holed through on 27 Jan 1983 after a loss of 34 lives. The cost by the completion of tunnelling after 20 years 10 months in March 1985 and subsequent maintenance to February 1987 was £2 995 million. The first test run took place on 13 Mar 1988.

Proposals for a Brenner Base Tunnel between Innsbruck, Austria and Italy envisage a rail tunnel between 58–63 km *36–39 miles* long. *31·03 miles.*

Great Britain's longest main-line railway tunnel is the Severn Tunnel 7 km *4 miles*, linking Avon and Gwent, constructed with 76 400 000 bricks between 1873 and 1886.

Continuous subway
The Moscow Metro underground railway line from Medvedkovo to Bittsevsky is *c.* 37·9 km *23·55 miles* long and was completed in early 1990.

Road tunnel
The 16·32 km *10·14 mile* long two-lane St Gotthard road tunnel from Göschenen, Switzerland to Airolo, Italy opened to traffic on 5 Sep 1980. Nineteen lives were lost during its construction, begun in autumn 1969, at a cost of SWF 686 million.

The longest road tunnel in the United Kingdom is the Mersey (Queensway) Tunnel, joining Liverpool and Birkenhead, Merseyside. It is 3·43 km *2·13 miles* long, or 4·62 km *2·87 miles* including branch tunnels. Work commenced in December 1925 and it was opened by HM King George V on 18 Jul 1934. The total cost was £7¾ million. The 11 m *36 ft* wide four-lane roadway carries nearly 7 ½ million vehicles a year. The first tube of the second Mersey (Kingsway) Tunnel was opened on 24 Jun 1971, with the breakthrough of the second in 1972.

Largest
The largest diameter road tunnel in the world is that blasted through Yerba Buena Island, San Francisco, California, USA. It is 23 m *76 ft* wide, 17 m *56 ft* high and 165 m *540 ft* long. More than 90 million vehicles pass through on its two decks every year.

Hydro-electric irrigation
The 82·9 km *51 ½ mile* long Orange–Fish Rivers tunnel, South Africa, was begun in 1967 at an estimated cost of £60 million. The boring was completed in April 1973. The lining to a minimum thickness of 23 cm *9 in* will give a completed diameter of 5·33 m *17 ½ ft*.

The Majes dam project in Peru involves 98 km *60·9 miles* of tunnels for hydro-electric and water-supply purposes. The dam is at 4200 m *13 780 ft* altitude.

Sewerage
The Chicago TARP (Tunnels and Reservoir Plan) in Illinois, USA involves 193 km *120 miles* of sewerage tunnelling. The Viikinmäki Central Treatment Plant in Helsinki, Finland is the world's first major waste-water plant to be built underground. It will involve the excavation of nearly 1 million m³ *35 314 ft³* of rock before its completion in 1993.

Bridge-tunnel
The Chesapeake Bay bridge-Tunnel, extends 28·40 km *17·65 miles* from Eastern Shore, Virginia Peninsula to Virginia Beach, Virginia, USA. It cost $200 million and was completed after 42 months. It opened to traffic on 15 Apr 1964.

The longest bridged section is Trestle C (7·34 km *4·56 miles* long) and the longest tunnel is the Thimble Shoal Channel Tunnel (1·75 km *1·09 miles*).

Longest and largest canal-tunnel
The Rove tunnel on the Canal de Marseille au Rhône in the south of France was completed in 1927 and is 7120 m *23 359 ft* long, 22 m *72 ft* wide and 11·4 m *37 ft* high. Built to be navigated by sea-going ships, it was closed in 1963 following a collapse of the structure and has not been re-opened.

Great Britain
The longest canal tunnel in Great Britain is the Standedge (more properly Stanedge) Tunnel in W Yorks on the Huddersfield Narrow Canal, built from 1794 to 4 Apr 1811. It measures 5·21 km *3 miles* in length and was closed on 21 Dec 1944. However, it is currently undergoing restoration.

The British canal system contained 84 tunnels exceeding 27·4 m *90 ft*, of which 48 are still open. The longest of these is the 2·79 km *1·73 miles* long Blisworth tunnel on the Grand Union Canal in Northamptonshire.

Oldest navigable
The Malpas tunnel on the Canal du Midi in south-west France was completed in 1681 and is 161 m *528 ft* long. Its completion enabled vessels to navigate from the Atlantic Ocean to the Mediterranean Sea via the river Garonne to Toulouse and the Canal du Midi to Sete.

Specialized Structures

Advertising signs Highest
The highest are the four Bank of Montreal logos at the top of the 72-storey 285 m *935 ft* tall First Canadian Place, Toronto, Canada. Each sign, built by Claude Neon Industries Ltd, measures 6·09 × 6·70 m *20 × 22 ft* and was lifted by helicopter.

The most conspicuous sign ever erected was the electric Citroën sign on the Eiffel Tower, Paris. It was switched on on 4 Jul 1925, and could be seen 38 km *24 miles* away. It was in six colours with 250 000 lamps and 90 km *56 miles* of electric cables. The letter 'N' which terminated the name 'Citroën' between the second and third levels measured 20·8 m *68 ft 5 in* in height and was dismantled in 1936.

Neon The longest is the letter 'M'

The Channel Tunnel

The Channel Tunnel, an electric railway under the English Channel is being constructed as a joint Anglo-French project at an estimated cost of £7·7 billion. It is the largest single civil engineering project undertaken this century in Europe and will provide the first fixed links between the railway and road systems of Britain and the Continent. Non-stop through trains, operated by the national railways, will carry passengers and freight. Motorcars, coaches and lorries will be carried on shuttle trains and run on a continuous loop line between Cheriton, near Folkestone, Kent and Sangatte near Calais, France. The system will consist of three bored tunnels - two main tunnels each carrying a single railway track and a central tunnel containing essential services such as electricity, ventilation and drainage. Some 37 km *23 miles* will be under the sea and the journey will take about 35 minutes. The project is due for completion in 1993.

■**First channel tunnel scheme** *Right: Albert Mathieu-Favier's idea was a scheme of two tunnels. This picture depicts the one to carry horse-drawn vehicles.*

TUNNEL HISTORY

For nearly 200 years engineers have put forward various schemes for the building of a Channel Tunnel. The first person to conceive the idea was a Frenchman Albert Mathieu-Favier, a mining engineer, who in 1802 suggested horse-drawn vehicles, with candles for lighting and air shafts for ventilation. In 1851 Hector Horeau put forward the idea of an iron tube to rest on the sea bed. In 1867 Thomé de Gamond exhibited a version at the Universal Exhibition of Paris, but unfortunately other projects such as the Suez Canal, the London underground and St Gotthard alpine tunnel were being constructed and the channel tunnel was once more put into the background. From then on wars and financial objections intervened.

The project eventually got under way when Prime Minister Margaret Thatcher and President Mitterrand signed a Treaty on 12 Feb 1986, agreeing to the conditions under which the tunnel was to be built and operated. Excavation commenced on 1 Jul 1987, and on 30 Oct 1990 the two countries linked with a British bore hole 5·08 cm *2 in* in diameter.

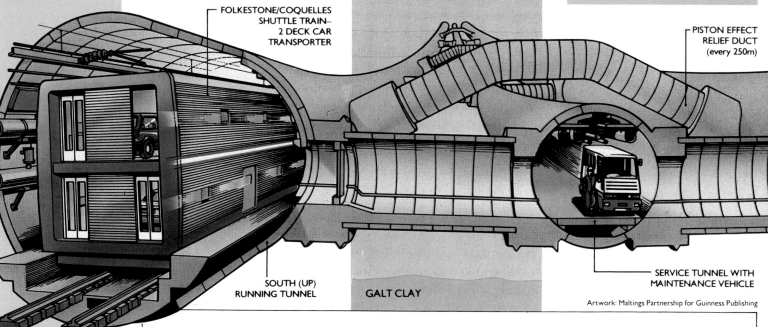

THE ENGLISH CHANNEL

SEA BED

GREY CHALK

CHALK MARL

GALT CLAY

FOLKESTONE/COQUELLES SHUTTLE TRAIN– 2 DECK CAR TRANSPORTER

PISTON EFFECT RELIEF DUCT (every 250m)

SOUTH (UP) RUNNING TUNNEL

SERVICE TUNNEL WITH MAINTENANCE VEHICLE

Artwork: Maltings Partnership for Guinness Publishing

Above: an artist's impression of a typical cross section of the Channel Tunnel and shuttle train. (Locomotive and Loader Wagon not shown)

Right: a three dimensional map (end to end) of the route from the M20 motorway Folkestone, Kent to Sangatte, France (which is not to scale).

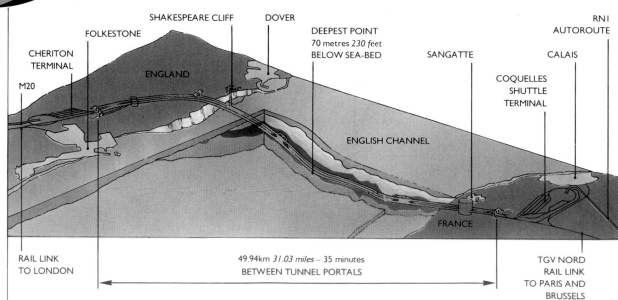

CHERITON TERMINAL

FOLKESTONE

SHAKESPEARE CLIFF

DOVER

M20

ENGLAND

DEEPEST POINT 70 metres *230 feet* BELOW SEA-BED

SANGATTE

ENGLISH CHANNEL

FRANCE

RN1 AUTOROUTE

CALAIS

COQUELLES SHUTTLE TERMINAL

RAIL LINK TO LONDON

49.94km *31.03 miles* – 35 minutes BETWEEN TUNNEL PORTALS

TGV NORD RAIL LINK TO PARIS AND BRUSSELS

installed on the Great Mississippi River Bridge is 548·6 m *1800 ft* and comprises 200 high-intensity lamps.

The largest neon sign measures 64 × 16·7 m *210 × 55 ft* and was built for Marlboro cigarettes at Hung Hom, Kowloon, Hong Kong in May 1986. It contains 10 668 m *35 000 ft* of neon tubing and weighs approximately 114·7 tonnes .

An interior-lit fascia advertising sign in Clearwater, Florida, USA completed by the Adco Sign Corp in April 1983 measured 356·17 m *1168 ft 6 ½ in* in length.

Hoarding The world's largest hoarding is Bassat Ogilvy Promotional Campaigns for FordEspana, measuring 145 m *475 ft 9 in* in length and 24 m *78 ft 9 in* in width. It is sited at Plaza de Toros Monumental de Barcelona, Barcelona, Spain.

UK The UK's largest is 86·56 × 25 m *284 × 82 ft* produced by Heritage Hampers. It is sited on the roof of Ayresome Park, Middlesbrough Football Club stand, N Yorks.

Illuminated The world's longest illuminated sign measures 60 m × 20 m *196 ft 7½ in × 65·6 ft*. It is illuminated by 62 400 W metal-halide projectors and was erected by Abudi Signs Industry Ltd of Israel.

UK The UK's longest illuminated sign is the name VOLVO LEX measuring 57·930 m *190 ft 1 in*. It was installed by Herbert & Sons Signs Ltd of Surrey at Lex, a Volvo dealer in Edgware Road, Colindale, London NW9.

Animated The world's most massive is that outside the Circus Circus Hotel, Reno, Nevada, USA, and is named Topsy the Clown. It is 38·7 m *127 ft* tall and weighs over 40·8 tonnes, with 2·25 km *1·4 miles* of neon tubing. His smile measures 4·26 m *14 ft* across.

Longest Airborne Reebok International Ltd of Massachusetts, USA flew a banner from a single seater plane which read 'Reebok Totally Beachin'. The banner measured 15·24 m *50 ft* in height and 30·48 m *100 ft* in length, and was flown from 13–16 and 20–23 Mar 1990 for four hours each day.

Barn The longest tithe barn in Britain is one measuring 81 m *268 ft* long at Wyke Farm, near Sherborne, Dorset.

The Ipsden Barn, Oxon, is 117 m *385 ½ ft* long but 9 m *30 ft* wide 1074 m² *11 565 ft²*.

Bonfire The largest was constructed in Espel, in the Noordoost Polder, Netherlands. It stood 27·87 m *91 ft 5 in* high with a base circumference of 84·40 m *276 ft 11 in* and was lit on 19 Apr 1987.

Great Britain's largest was the Coronation bonfire at the top of Arrowthwaite Brows, Whitehaven, Cumbria, lit in 1902 with 812 tonnes of timber, and 4546 litres *1000 gal* each of petroleum and tar. It was octagonal in shape and built to a height of 36·67 m *120 ft*, with a base circumference of 47·2 m *155 ft* tapering to 6·1 m *20 ft*.

Breakwater The world's longest breakwater is that which protects the Port of Galveston, Texas, USA. The granite South Breakwater is 10·85 km *6·74 miles* in length.

Great Britain's longest is the North Breakwater at Holyhead, Anglesey, which is 2·395 km *1·48 miles* in length and was completed in 1873.

Buildings demolished by explosives The largest has been the 21-storey Traymore Hotel, Atlantic City, New Jersey,

Demolition work
Fifteen members of the Black Leopard Karate Club demolished a seven-room wooden farmhouse west of Elnora, Alberta, Canada in 3 hr 18 min by foot and empty hand on 13 Jun 1982.

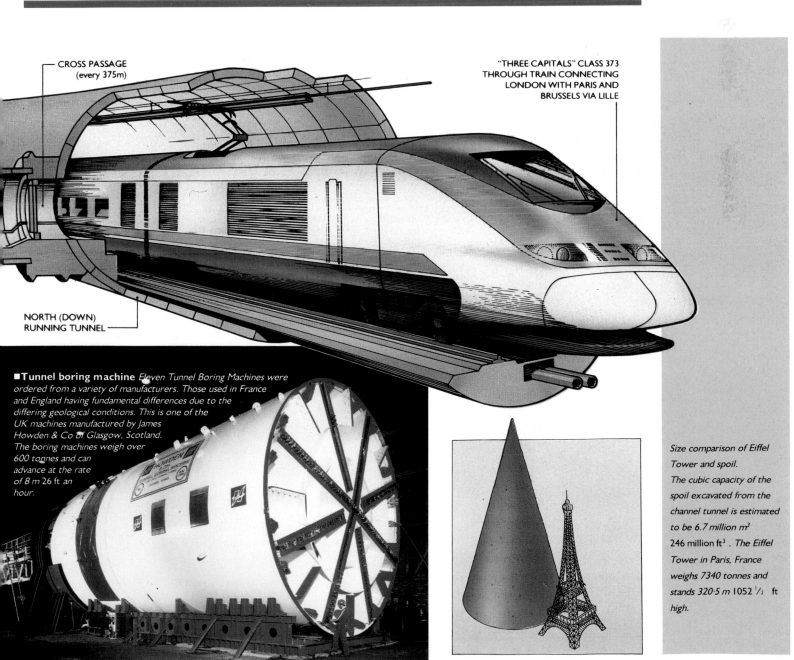

— CROSS PASSAGE (every 375m)

"THREE CAPITALS" CLASS 373 THROUGH TRAIN CONNECTING LONDON WITH PARIS AND BRUSSELS VIA LILLE

NORTH (DOWN) RUNNING TUNNEL

■**Tunnel boring machine** *Eleven Tunnel Boring Machines were ordered from a variety of manufacturers. Those used in France and England having fundamental differences due to the differing geological conditions. This is one of the UK machines manufactured by James Howden & Co of Glasgow, Scotland. The boring machines weigh over 600 tonnes and can advance at the rate of 8 m 26 ft an hour.*

Size comparison of Eiffel Tower and spoil. The cubic capacity of the spoil excavated from the channel tunnel is estimated to be 6.7 million m³ 246 million ft³ . The Eiffel Tower in Paris, France weighs 7340 tonnes and stands 320.5 m 1052 ½ ft high.

Grave digging

It is recorded that Johann Heinrich Karl Thieme, sexton of Aldenburg, Germany, dug 23 311 graves during a 50-year career. In 1826 his understudy dug *his* grave.

■ **Lighthouse**
The lights with the greatest range are those on the Empire State Building, New York City, USA. Each of the four lights has a candlepower of 450 000 000 and can be seen at 130 km 80 miles from the ground and 490 km 300 miles from the air. (Photo: Images)

USA on 26 May 1972 by Controlled Demolition Inc. of Towson, Maryland. This 600-room hotel had a cubic capacity of 181 340 m³ *6 495 500 ft³*.

The tallest chimney ever demolished by explosives was the Matla Power Station chimney, Kriel, South Africa, on 19 Jul 1981. It stood 275 m *902 ft* and was brought down by the Santon (Steeplejack) Co. Ltd of Greater Manchester.

Great Britain On 14 Oct 1990 Controlled Demolition Group Ltd of Leeds successfully demolished eight blocks of high rise flats at Kersal Vale, Salford, Manchester. The total cubic capacity of the tower blocks was 155 000 m³ *5 473 736 ft³*.

Cemetery Largest Rookwood Necropolis, New South Wales, Australia is the largest cemetery covering an area of 295 ha *728 acres*, with over 575 536 interments. It has been in continuous use since 1867.

Great Britain's largest is Brookwood Cemetery, Brookwood, Surrey, owned by the London Necropolis Co. It is 200 ha *500 acres* in extent and has more than 225 000 interments.

Tallest The permanently illuminated Memorial Cemiterio Ecumencio, Šao Paulo, Brazil is 10-storeys high, occupying an area of 18 000 m² *4·448 acres*. When full, the final capacity will be 20 000.

Tallest columns The thirty-six 27·43 m *90 ft* tall fluted pillars of Vermont marble in the colonnade of the Education Building, Albany, New York State, USA. Their base diameter is 1·98 m *6 ½ ft*.

The tallest load-bearing stone columns in the world are those measuring 21 m *69 ft* in the Hall of Columns of the Temple of Amun at Karnak, opposite Thebes on the Nile, the ancient capital of Upper Egypt. They were built in the 19th dynasty in the reign of Rameses II *c.* 1270 BC.

Crematorium The largest crematorium in the world is at the Nikolo-Arkhangelskoye Cemetery, east Moscow, USSR with seven twin cremators of British design, completed in March 1972. It has several Halls of Farewell for atheists.

The oldest crematorium in Great Britain was built in 1879 at Woking, Surrey. The first cremation took place there on 26 Mar 1885, the practice having been found legal after the cremation of Iesu Grist Price on Caerlan Fields, Llantrisant, Mid Glamorgan on 13 Jan 1884.

Dome The largest is the Louisiana Superdome, New Orleans, USA which has a diameter of 207·26 m *680 ft*.

The largest dome of ancient architecture is that of the Pantheon, built in Rome in AD 112, with a diameter of 43 m *142 ½ ft*.

Britain's largest is that of the Bell Sports Centre, Perth, Scotland, with a diameter of 67 m *222 ft*. It was designed by D.B. Cockburn and constructed in Baltic whitewood by Muirhead & Sons Ltd of Grangemouth, Central, Scotland.

Doors Largest The four doors in the Vehicle Assembly Building near Cape Canaveral, Florida, USA have a height of 140 m *460 ft*.

Great Britain's largest are those of the Britannia Assembly Hall, at Filton airfield, Avon. The doors are 315 m *1035 ft* in length and 20 m *67 ft* high, divided into three bays each 105 m *345 ft* across.

The largest simple hinged door in Great Britain is that of Ye Old Bull's Head, Beaumaris, Anglesey, which is 3·35 m *11 ft* wide and 3·96 m *13 ft* high.

Heaviest The heaviest is that of the laser target room at Lawrence Livermore National Laboratory, California, USA. It weighs 326·5 tonnes, is up to 2·43 m *8 ft* thick and was installed by Overly.

Oldest Great Britain's oldest are those of Hadstock Church, near Saffron Walden, Essex, which date from *c.* 1040 AD and exhibit evidence of Danish workmanship.

Largest dry dock With a maximum shipbuilding capacity of 1 200 000 tons dwt, the Daewoo Okpo No. 1 Dry Dock, Koje Island in South Korea measures 530 m *1738·84 ft* long by 131 m *430 ft* wide and was completed in 1979. The dock gates, 14 m *46 ft* high and 10 m *32·8 ft* thick at the base, are the world's most massive.

Britain's largest is the Belfast Harbour Commission and Harland & Wolff building dock in Belfast. It was excavated by Wimpey to a length of 556 m *1825 ft* and a width of 93 m *305 ft* and can accommodate tankers of 1 million tons dwt. Work was begun on 26 Jan 1968 and completed on 30 Nov 1969 and involved the excavation of 306 000 m³ *400 000 yd³* of soil.

Largest earthworks The largest prior to the mechanical era were the Linear Earth Boundaries of the Benin Empire in the Bendel state of Nigeria. Their existance was first reported in 1900 and partially surveyed in 1967. In April 1973 it was estimated by Patrick Darling that the total length of the earthworks was probably between 6400–12 800 km *4000 and 8000 miles*, with the amount of earth moved estimated at 380–460 million m³ *500–600 million yd³*.

The greatest prehistoric earthwork in Britain is Wansdyke, originally Wodensdic, which ran 138 km *86 miles* from Portishead, Avon to Inkpen Beacon and Ludgershall, south of Hungerford, Berks. It was built by the Belgae as their northern boundary.

The most extensive single-site earthwork is the Dorset Cursus near Gussage St Michael, 8 km *5 miles* south-west of Cranborne, dating from *c.* 1900 BC. The workings are 9·7 km *6 miles* in length, involving an estimated 191 000 m³ *250 000 yd³* of excavations.

The largest of the Celtic hill-forts is Mew Dun, or Maiden Castle, 3 km *2 miles* south west of Dorchester, Dorset. It covers 46·5 ha *115 acres* and was abandoned shortly after AD 43.

Fence Longest The dingo-proof wire fence enclosing the main sheep areas of Australia is 1·8 m *6 ft* high, 30 cm *1 ft* underground and stretches for 5531 km *3437 miles*. The Queensland state government discontinued full maintenance in 1982.

Tallest The world's tallest fences are security screens 20 m *65·6 ft* high erected by Harrop-Allin of Pretoria, South Africa in

SEVEN WONDERS OF THE WORLD

The Seven Wonders of the World were first designated by Antipater of Sidon in the 2nd century BC. They included the Pyramids of Giza, built by three Fourth Dynasty Egyptian Pharaohs: Khwfw (Khufu or Cheops), Kha-f-Ra (Khafre, Khefren or Chepren) and Menkaure (Mycerinus) near El Giza (El Gizeh), south-west of El Qâhira (Cairo) in Egypt.

THE GREAT PYRAMID

The 'Horizon of Khufu' was finished under Rededef *c.* 2580 BC. Its original height was 146·5 m *480 ft 11 in* (now, since the loss of its topmost stones and the pyramidion, reduced to 137 m *449 ft 6 in*) with a base line of 230 m *756 ft*, thus covering slightly more than 5 ha *13 acres*. It has been estimated that a permanent work force of 4000 required 30 years to manoeuvre into position the 2 300 000 limestone blocks averaging 2 ½ tonnes each, totalling about 5 840 000 tonnes and a volume of 2 568 000m³ *90 700 000 ft³*. Some blocks weigh 15 tons. A costing exercise published in December 1974 indicated that the work would require 405 men 6 years at a cost of $1·13 billion.

FRAGMENT REMAINS OF:

The Temple of Artemis (Diana) of the Ephesians, built *c.* 350 BC at Ephesus, Turkey (destroyed by the Goths in AD 262).
The Tomb of King Mausolus of Caria, at Halicarnassus, now Bodrum, Turkey, *c.* 325 BC.

NO TRACE REMAINS OF:

The Hanging Gardens of Semiramis, at Babylon, Iraq *c.* 600 BC; The statue of Zeus (Jupiter), by Phidias (5th century BC) at Olympia, Greece (lost in a fire at Istanbul) in marble, gold and ivory and 12 m *40 ft* tall; the figure of the god Helios (Apollo), a 35 m *117 ft* tall statue sculptured 292–280 BC, by Chares of Lindus (destroyed by an earthquake in 224 BC).

The world's earliest lighthouse, 122 m *400 ft* tall built by Sostratus of Cnidus (*c.* 270 BC) as a pyramid shaped tower of white marble, on the island of Pharos (Greek, *pharos*=lighthouse), off the coast of El Iskandariya (Alexandria), Egypt (destroyed by earthquake in AD 1375).

November 1981 to protect fuel depots and refineries at Sasolburg from terrorist rockets.

Tallest flagpole Erected outside the Oregon Building at the 1915 Panama-Pacific International Exposition in San Francisco, California, USA, and trimmed from a Douglas fir, the flagpole stood 91 m *299 ft 7 in* in height and weighed 47 tonnes.

The tallest unsupported flagpole in the world is the 85·95 m *282 ft* tall steel pole weighing 54 430 kg *120 000 lb*, which was erected on 22 Aug 1985 at the Canadian Expo 86 exhibition in Vancouver, British Columbia which supports a gigantic ice hockey stick 62·5 m *205 ft* in length. Sherrold Haddad of Flag Chevrolet Oldsmobile Ltd was instrumental in moving and reconstructing the flagpole where it has been relocated at the company's premises in 104th Avenue, Surrey, British Columbia.

Great Britain's tallest flagpole is a 68 m *225 ft* tall Douglas fir staff at Kew, Richmond-upon-Thames, Surrey. Cut in Canada, it was shipped across the Atlantic and towed up the river Thames on 7 May 1958, to replace the old 65 m *214 ft* tall staff erected in 1919.

Tallest fountain The tallest is the fountain at Fountain Hills, Arizona, USA built, at a cost of $1·5 million for McCulloch Properties Inc. At full pressure of 26·3 kg/cm² *375 lb/in²* and at a rate of 26 500 litres/min *5828 imp. gal/min*, the 170 m *560 ft* tall column of water weighs more than 8 tonnes. The nozzle speed achieved by the three 600 hp pumps is 236 km/h *146·7 mph*.

Britain's tallest is the Emperor Fountain at Chatsworth, Bakewell, Derbys. When first tested on 1 Jun 1844, it attained the then unprecedented height of 79 m *260 ft*. Since the war it has not been played to more than 76 m *250 ft* and rarely beyond 55 m *180 ft*.

Largest gasholder The largest gasholders are at Fontaine L'Eveque, Belgium, where disused mines have been adapted to store up to 500 million m³ *17 650 million ft³* of gas at ordinary pressure.

Probably the largest conventional gasholder is that at Wien-Simmering, Vienna, Austria, completed in 1968, with a height of 84 m *275 ft* and a capacity of 300 000 m³ *10·59 million ft³*.

Great Britain's largest was at the East Greenwich Gas Works No. 2 Holder was built in 1891 with an original capacity for 346 000 m³ *12 200 000 ft³*. As constructed its capacity was 252 000 m³ *8·9 million ft³* with a water tank 92 m *303 ft* in diameter and a full inflated height of 45 m *148 ft*. The record is now held by No. 1 holder built in 1885 (capacity 243 500 m³ *8·6 million ft³*) has a height of 61 m *200 ft*.

The River Tees Northern Gas Board's 361 m *1186 ft* deep underground storage in use since January 1959, has a capacity of 9300 m³ *330 000 ft³*.

Longest deep-water jetty The Quai Hermann du Pasquier at Le Havre, France, with a length of 1524 m *5000 ft*, is part of an enclosed basin and has a constant depth of water of 9·8 m *32 ft* on both sides.

Lamp-post The tallest lighting columns are the four made by Petitjean & Clé of Troyes, France and installed by Taylor Woodrow at Sultan Qaboos Sports Complex, Muscat, Oman. They stand 63·5 m *208 ft 4 in* high.

Lighthouse Tallest The 106 m *348 ft* steel tower near Yamashita Park in Yokohama, Japan has a power of 600 000 candelas and a visibility range of 32 km *20 miles*.

Bishop Rock, Isles of Scilly measures 47·8 m *156·8 ft* high to its helipad.

The tallest Scottish lighthouse is the 42·3 m *139 ft* tall North Ronaldsay lighthouse, Orkney Islands.

Most Powerful The lighthouse in Great Britain with the most powerful light is the shorelight at Strumble Head, near Fishguard, Dyfed, Wales It has an intensity of 6 000 000 candelas.

Greatest range The lights with the greatest range are those 332 m *1089 ft* above the ground on the Empire State Building, New York City, USA. Each of the four-arc mercury bulbs has a rated candlepower of 450 000 000, visible 130 km *80 miles* away on the ground and 490 km *300 miles* away from aircraft.

Remotest The remotest lighthouse is Sule Skerry, 56 km *35 miles* off shore and 72 km *45 miles* north-west of Dunnet Head, Highland.

The remotest in the Republic of Ireland is

Blackrock, 14 km *9 miles* off the Mayo coast.

Marquee Largest A marquee covering an area of 17 500 m² *188 368 ft²* (1·7 ha *4·32 acres*) was erected by the firm of Deuter from Augsburg, Germany for the 1958 'Welcome Expo' in Brussels, Belgium.

Great Britain Great Britain's was one made by Piggot Brothers in 1951 and used by the Royal Horticultural Society at their annual show (first held in 1913) in the grounds of the Royal Hospital in Chelsea, London. It measured 94 × 146 m *310 × 480 ft* and consisted of 30 km *18 ¾ miles* of 91 cm *36 in* wide canvas covering a ground area of 13 820 m² *148 800 ft²*.

The largest single-unit tent in Britain covers a ground area of more than 12 000 m² *129 170 ft²* and was manufactured by Clyde Canvas Ltd of Edinburgh, Scotland.

Manor Marquees Ltd, of Maidstone, Kent, erected a 143 m *470 ft* long marquee in one lift on 16 May 1987.

The Offshore Europe 1983 exhibition at Bridge of Don, Aberdeenshire, Scotland was housed in 15 contiguous air tents covering 6·91 acres *28 400 m²*.

Maypole The tallest reported and erected in England was one of Sitka spruce 32·12 m *105 ft 7 in* tall, put up in Pelynt, Cornwall on 1 May 1974.

The permanent pole at Paganhill, near Stroud, Glos, is 27·43 m *90 ft* tall.

Maze The oldest datable representation of a labyrinth is that on a clay tablet from Pylos, Greece *c.*1200 BC.

The world's largest hedge maze is that at Longleat, near Warminster, Wilts, designed for Lord Weymouth by Greg Bright, which has 2·72 km *1·69 miles* of paths flanked by 16 180 yew trees. It was opened on 6 Jun 1978 and measures 116 × 57 m *381 × 187 ft*.

'Il Labirinto' at Villa Pisani, Stra, Italy, in which Napoleon was 'lost' in 1807, had 6·4 km *4 miles* of pathways.

Britain's oldest surviving hedge maze is at Hampton Court Palace, East Molesey, Surrey. It was designed by George London and Henry Wise in 1690 and measures 67·66 × 24·99 m *222 × 82 ft*.

Menhir The tallest found is the 380 tonnes Grand Menhir Brisé, now in four pieces, which originally stood 22 m *72 ft* high at Locmariaquer, Brittany, France. Recent research suggests a possible 22·8 m *75 ft* high menhir, in three pieces, weighing 250 tonnes, also at Locmariaquer.

Great Britain's tallest is one of 7·6 m *25 ft* at Rudston, Humberside.

Monuments Tallest The stainless-steel Gateway to the West arch in St Louis, Missouri, USA, completed on 28 Oct 1965 to commemorate the westward expansion after the Lousiana Purchase of 1803 is a sweeping arch spanning 192 m *630 ft* and rising to the same height of 192 m *630 ft*. It cost $29 million. It was designed in 1947 by the Finnish-American architect Eero Saarinen 1910–61.

Tallest column Constructed from 1936–39, at a cost of $1·5 million, the tapering column which commemorates the Battle of San Jacinto (21 Apr 1836), on the bank of the San Jacinto River near Houston, Texas, USA, is 173 m *570 ft* tall, 14 m *47 ft* square at the base, and 9 m *30 ft* square

Largest fumigation

Carried out during the restoration of the Mission Inn complex in Riverside, California, USA on 28 Jun–1 Jul 1987 to rid the buildings of termites, the fumigation was performed by Fume Masters Inc. of Riverside. Over 350 tarpaulins were used each weighing up to 160 kg *350 lb* and the operation involved completely covering the 6500 m² *70 000 ft²* site and buildings—domes, minarets, chimneys and balconies, some of which exceeded 30 m *100 ft* in height.

Garbage dump

Reclamation Plant No. 1, Fresh Kills, Staten Island, New York, USA, opened in March 1974, is the world's largest sanitary landfill. In its first four months of operation 457 000 tonnes of refuse from New York City carried by 700 barges was dumped on the site.

Largest revolving globe

The 30 tonnes 10 m *32·81 ft* in diameter sphere called 'Globe of Peace' was built in five years by Orfeo Bartolucci from Apecchio, Pesaro, Italy.

Kitchen

An Indian government field kitchen set up in April 1973 at Ahmadnagar, Maharashtra, a famine area, daily provided 1·2 million subsistence meals.

The Djoser step pyramid at Saqqâra, Egypt was constructed by Imhotep the architect and astrologer and chief minister to Djoser c. 2686–2613 BC. It is the oldest monument of hewn stone known to the world. The pyramid consists of six steps and attains a height of 62 m 204 ft. The Great Sphinx of Egypt, one of the wonders of ancient Egyptian architecture, is here seen next to the pyramids of Giza. (Photos: Spectrum)

■ Snowman
Standing 20·40 m 66·92 ft high Fubukukun (the Blizzardman) was built by 30 villagers from Sumon, Niigata, Japan.

2494 m *8182 ft*, south-east of Malatya, eastern Turkey. This measures 59·8 m *197 ft* tall and covers 3 ha *7·5 acres*.

Europe's largest is Silbury Hill, 9·7 km *6 miles* west of Marlborough, Wilts, which involved the moving of an estimated 681 000 tonnes of chalk, at a cost of 18 million man-hours to make a cone 39 m *130 ft* high with a base of 2 ha *5 ½ acres*. Prof. Richard Atkinson who was in charge of the 1968 excavations showed that it is based on an innermost central mound, similar to contemporary round barrows, and it is now dated to 2745 ± 185 BC.

The largest long barrow in England is that inside the hill-fort at Maiden Castle near Dorchester, Dorset (see Largest earthwork). It originally had a length of 548 m *1800 ft* and had several enigmatic features such as a ritual pit with pottery, limpet shells and animal bones.

The longest long barrow containing a megalithic chamber is that at West Kennet (*c*. 2200 BC), near Silbury, Wilts, measuring 117 m *385 ft* in length.

Naturist resort *Oldest* The oldest resort is Der Freilichtpark, Klingberg, Germany, established in 1903.

100 000 people each year visit the centre Helio-Marin at Cap d'Agde, southern France, which covers 90 ha *222 acres*. The appellation 'nudist camp' is deplored by naturists.

Largest standing obelisk (monolithic) The 'skewer' or 'spit' (from the Greek *obeliskos*) of Tuthmosis III brought from Aswan, Egypt by Emperor Constantius in the spring of AD 357 was repositioned in the Piazza San Giovanni in Laterane, Rome on 3 Aug 1588. Once 36 m *118·1 ft* tall, it now stands 32·81 m *107·6 ft* and weighs 455 tonnes.

The unfinished obelisk, probably commissioned by Queen Hatshepsut *c*.1490 BC, at Aswan, Egypt is 41·75 m *136·8 ft* in length and weighs 1 168 tonnes.

The longest time an obelisk has remained *in situ* is that still at Heliopolis, near Cairo, erected by Senusret I *c*.1750 BC.

Tallest The world's tallest obelisk is the Washington Monument in Washington, D.C, USA. Situated in a 42·89 ha *106 acre* site and standing 169·3 m *555 ft 5 ⅛ in* in heigh it was built to honour George Washington (1732–99), the first President of the United States.

The United Kingdom's tallest is Cleo-

at the observation tower, which is surmounted by a star weighing 199·6 tonnes. It is built of concrete with buff limestone, and weighs 31 888 tonnes.

Great Britain's largest megalithic prehistoric monument and largest existing henge are the 11·5 ha *28 ½ acre* earthworks and stone circles of Avebury, Wilts, 'rediscovered' in 1646. The earliest calibrated date in the area of this Neolithic site is *c*. 4200 BC. The work is 365 m *1200 ft* in diameter with a 12 m *40 ft* ditch around the perimeter. It required an estimated 15 million man-hours of work.

The henge of Durrington Walls, Wilts, obliterated by road building, had a diameter of 472 m *1550 ft*. It was built *c*.2500 BC and required some 900 000 man-hours.

The largest trilithons exist at Stonehenge, to the south of Salisbury Plain, Wilts, with single sarsen blocks weighing over 45 tonnes and requiring over 550 men to drag them up a 9 degree gradient. The earliest stage of the construction of the ditch has been dated to 2800 BC. Whether Stonehenge, which required some 30 million man-years, was built as a place of worship, sky worship, as a lunar calendar, an eclipse-predictor or a navigation school, is still debated.

The newest scheduled ancient monuments are a hexagonal pillbox and 48 concrete tank-traps south of Christchurch, Dorset, built in World War II and protected since 1973.

Largest artificial mound The gravel mound built as a memorial to the Seleucid King Antiochus I (reigned 69–34 BC) stands on the summit of Nemrud Dagi

patra's Needle on the Embankment, London, which at 20·88 m *68 ft 5 in* is the world's 11th tallest. It weighs 189·35 tonnes. It was towed up the Thames from Egypt on 21 Jan 1878 and positioned on 13 September.

Longest piers The Dammam Pier, Saudi Arabia, on the Persian Gulf, with an overall length of 10·93 km *6·79 miles*, was begun in July 1948 and completed on 15 Mar 1950. The area was subsequently developed by 1980 into the King Abdul Aziz Port, with 39 deep-water berths. The original causeway, much widened, and the port extend for 12·8 km *7·95 miles*.

Great Britain's longest is the Bee Ness Jetty, completed in 1930, which stretches 2500 m *8200 ft* along the west bank of the river Medway, 8·8 km *5 ½ miles* below Rochester, at Kingsnorth, Kent.

Longest covered promenade The Long Corridor in the Summer Palace in Beijing is a covered promenade running for 728 m *2388·45 ft*. It is built entirely of wood and divided by crossbeams into 273 sections. These crossbeams, as well as the ceiling and side pillars have over 10 000 paintings of famous Chinese landscapes, episodes from folk tales and flowers and birds.

Pyramid *Largest* The largest pyramid, and the largest monument ever constructed, is the Quetzalcóatl at Cholula de Rivadabia, 101 km *63 miles* south-east of Mexico City. It is 54 m *177 ft* tall and its base covers an area of nearly 18·2 ha *45 acres*. Its total volume has been estimated at 3 300 000 m³ *4 300 000 yd³* compared with 2·5 million m³ *3 360 000 yd³* for the Pyramid of Khufu or Cheops (see Seven Wonders of the World).

The largest known single block comes from the Third Pyramid (Pyramid of Mycerinus) and weighs 290 tonnes.

Oldest The Djoser Step Pyramid at Saqqâra, Egypt, constructed by Imhotep to a height of 62 m *204 ft*, and originally with a Tura limestone casing and dates from *c.* 2900 BC.

The oldest New World pyramid is that on the island of La Venta in south-eastern Mexico built by the Olmec people *c.* 800 BC. It stands 30 m *100 ft* tall with a base dimension of 128 m *420 ft*.

Scaffolding The largest free-standing scaffolding is believed to be that erected for the restoration of the Goldstone antenna in California, USA. It was 51·8 m *170 ft* high, 21·3 m *70 ft* deep and went 54·8 m *180 ft* around the circumference of the structure.

UK The UK's tallest was 52·36 m *171 ft 9 in* high erected around the statue of the Albert Memorial in Kensington, London. It was free-standing and cladded and could resist wind forces of up to 90 mph.

Scarecrow The tallest scarecrow built was 'Stretch II', constructed by the Speers family of Paris, Ontario, Canada and a crew of 15 at the Paris Fall Fair on 2 Sep 1989. It measured 31·56 m *103 ft 6 ¾ in* in height.

Snow and ice constructions A snow palace 26·5 m *87 ft* high, one of four structures which together spanned 214·2 m *702·7 ft*, was unveiled on 7 Feb 1987 at Asahikawa City, Hokkaidō Japan.

The world's largest ice construction was the ice palace built in January 1986, using 9 000 blocks of ice, at St Paul, Minnesota, USA during the Winter Carnival. Designed by Ellerbe Associates Inc., it stood 39·24 m *128 ft 9 in* high—the equivalent of a 13-storey building.

Snowman The tallest was (Fubukikun, the Blizzard Man), built by villagers of Sumon and Niigata, Japan between March and April 1990, which stood 20·40 m *66·92 ft* tall.

Longest stairway The service staircase for the Niesenbahn funicular near Spiez, Switzerland rises to 2365 m *7759 ft*. It has 11 674 steps and a bannister.

The stone-cut T'ai Chan temple stairs of 6600 steps in the Shandong Mountains, China ascend 1428 m *4700 ft*.

The tallest spiral staircase is on the outside of the chimney Bobila Almirall located in Angel Sallent in Terrasa, Barcelona, Spain. Built by Mariano Masana i Ribas in 1956 it is 63·2 m *207·34 ft* high and has 217 steps.

The longest spiral staircase is one 336·2 m *1103 ft* deep with 1520 steps installed in the Mapco–White–County Coal Mine, Carmi, Illinois, USA by Systems Control Inc. in May 1981.

The longest stairs in Great Britain are those from the transformer gallery to the surface, 324 m *1065 ft*, in the Cruachan Power Station, Argyll, Scotland. They have 1420 steps and the plant's work-study unit allows 27 min 41·4 sec for the ascent.

Statue *Longest* Near Bamiyan, Afghanistan there are the remains of the recumbent Sakya Buddha, built of plastered rubble, which was 'about 305 m' *1 000 ft* long and is believed to date from the 3rd or 4th century AD.

Tallest A full-figure statue, that of 'Motherland', an enormous pre-stressed concrete female figure on Mamayev Hill, outside Volgograd, USSR, was designed in 1967 by Yevgeny Vuchetich, to commemorate victory in the Battle of Stalingrad (1942–3). The statue from its base to the tip of the sword clenched in her right hand measures 82·30 m *270 ft*.

The statue of Maitreya is carved out of a single piece of white sandalwood tree. It stands 26 m *85·30 ft* high and is located in north-west of Beijing at the Lama Temple (Yonghegong) built in 1649. The Imperial Court took two years to carve the statue in the Pavilion House of Ten Thousand Fortunes and finished the project in 1750.

Tallest swing A glider swing 9·14 m *30 ft* high was constructed by Kenneth R. Mack, Langenburg, Saskatchewan, Canada for Uncle Herb's Amusements. The swing is capable of taking its four sides 7·62 m *25 ft* off the ground.

Largest tidal river barrier The Thames Barrier at Woolwich, London has nine piers and 10 gates. There are six rising sector gates 61 m *200 ft 1 ½ in* wide and four falling radial gates 31·5 m *103 ft 4 in* wide. The site was chosen in 1971. It was opened by HM the Queen on 8 May 1984.

Largest tomb The Mount Li tomb, belonging to Zheng, the first emperor of China, dates to 221 BC and is situated 40 km *25 miles* east of Xianyang. The two walls surrounding the grave measure 2173 × 974 m *7129 × 3195 ft* and

■ **Tallest wooden statue**
This magnificent statue of Maitreya is carved out of a single white sandalwood tree standing 26 m 85.30 ft high. It is situated in the Pavilion House of Ten Thousand Fortunes of the Lama Temple north-west of Beijing. (Photo: Beijing Tourist Office)

Window cleaning
Keith Witt of Amarillo, Texas, USA cleaned three standard 1079 × 1194 mm *42½ × 47 in* office windows with a 300 mm *11.8 in* long squeegee and 9 litres *1.98 gal* of water in 10.50 sec on 21 Jan 1990. The record was achieved at the International Window Cleaning Association convention at Orlando, Florida, USA.

■ **Largest waterwheel**
The Mohammadieh Noria wheel at Hamah, Syria has a wheel diameter of 40 m 131 ft. (Photo: Explorer)

685 × 578 m *2247 × 1896 ft*. Several pits in the tomb contained a vast army of an estimated 8000 life-size terracotta soldiers.

A tomb housing 180 000 World War II dead on Okinawa, Japan was enlarged in 1985 to accommodate another 9000 bodies thought to be buried on the island.

Totem pole A 52.73 m *173 ft* tall pole was raised on 6 Jun 1973 at Alert Bay, British Columbia, Canada. It tells the story of the Kwakiutl and took 36 man-weeks to carve.

Vats Largest The largest wooden wine cask in the world is the Heidelberg Tun, completed in 1751, in the cellar of the Friedrichsbau, Heidelberg, Germany. Its capacity is 1855 litres *40 790 gal*.

'Strongbow', used by H. P. Bulmer Ltd, the English cider-makers of Hereford, measures 19.65 m *64½ ft* in height and 23.0 m *75½ ft* in diameter, with a capacity of 74 099 litre *1 630 000 gal*.

Oldest The world's oldest is that in use since 1715 at Hugel et Fils (founded 1639) Riquewihr, Haut-Rhin, Germany by 12 generations of the family.

Longest wall The Great Wall of China has a main-line length of 3460 km *2150 miles*— nearly three times the length of Britain. Completed during the reign of Qin Shi Huangdi (221–210 BC), it has a further 2860 km *1780 miles* of branches and spurs. Its height varies from 4.5–12 m *15–39 ft* and it is up to 9.8 m *32 ft* thick. It runs from Shanhaikuan, on the Gulf of Bohai, to Yumenkuan and Yang-guan and was kept in repair up to the 16th century. Some 51.5 km *32 miles* of the wall have been destroyed since 1966 and part of the wall was blown up to make way for a dam in July 1979. It was reported in October 1990 that after 2 years of struggle Lin Yu-tian became the first to walk its entire length and that the average pedometer readings indicated a length of 5500 km *3415 miles*.

The longest of the Roman walls in Britain was the 4.5–6 m *15–20 ft* tall Hadrian's Wall, built AD 122–26. It crossed the Tyne-Solway isthmus for 118 km *73½ miles* from Bowness-on-Solway, Cumbria, to Wallsend-on-Tyne, Tyne & Wear, and was abandoned in AD 383.

Indoor waterfall The tallest indoor waterfall measures 34.74 m *114 ft* in height and consists of 2743 m² *2525 ft²* of marble. It is situated in the lobby of Greektown's International Center Building, Detroit, Michigan, USA.

Water tower The Union at New Jersey, USA, built in 1965, rises to a height of 64 m *210 ft*, with a capacity of 113 650 litres *250 000 gal*. The tower is owned and operated by the Elizabethtown Water Co.

Largest waterwheel The Mohammadieh Noria wheel at Hamah, Syria has a diameter of 40 m *131 ft* and dates from Roman times.

Britain's largest is the 15.36 m *50 ft 5 in* diameter wheel built in 1870 at Caernarfon, Gwynedd, Wales. It worked until 1925 and is 1.52 m *5 ft* in width. It is exhibited and can be seen working at the Welsh Slate Museum, Dinorwic, Llanberis, Gwynedd.

The Lady Isabella wheel at Laxey, Isle of Man is the largest in the British Isles. It was built for draining a lead mine. Completed on 27 Sep 1854 it has been disused since 1929. It has a circumference of 69 m *228 ft*, a diameter of 22 m *72½ ft* and an axle weighing 9 tonnes.

Largest window The largest sheet of glass ever manufactured was one of 50 m² *538.2 ft²*, or 20 m *65 ft 7 in* by 2.5 m *8 ft 2¼ in*, exhibited by the Saint Gobin Co. in France at the *Journées Internationales de Miroiterie* in March 1958.

The largest single windows in the world are those in the Palace of Industry and Technology at Rondpoint de la Défense, Paris, France, with an extreme width of 218 m *715.2 ft* and a maximum height of 50 m *164 ft*.

The largest sheet of tempered (safety) glass ever processed was one made by P.T. Sinar Rasa Kencana of Jakarta, Indonesia, which measures 7 m *22.96 ft* long by 2.14 m *7.02 ft* wide and is 12 mm thick.

The United Kingdom record for Pilkington of St Helens, Merseyside is a sheet of 2.5 × 15.2 m *8 ft 2¼ in × 49 ft 10½ in* made for the Festival of Britain in 1951.

Largest wine cellar The cellars at Paarl, those of the Ko-operative Wijnbouwers Vereeniging, known as KWV, near Cape Town, in the centre of the wine-growing district of South Africa, cover an area of 10 ha *25 acres* and have a capacity of 136 million litres *30 million gal*.

The Cienega Winery of the Almaden Vineyards in Hollister, California, USA covers 1.6 ha *4 acres* and can house 37 300 oak barrels containing 1.83 million gallons of wine.

Ziggurat The largest zigguarat (from the Assyrian *ziqqurati*, = summit, height) ever built was that of the Elamite King Untas, *c.* 1250 BC. known as the Ziggurat of Choga Zanbil, 30 km *18.6 miles* from Haft Tepe, Iran. The outer base was 105 × 105 m *344 × 344 ft* and the fifth 'box' 28 × 28 m *91.8 × 91.8 ft*, nearly 50 m *164 ft* above.

The largest partially surviving ziggurat is the Ziggurat of Ur (now Muquyyar, Israel) with a base 61 × 45.7 m *200 × 150 ft*, built to three storeys and surmounted by a summit temple. The first and part of the second storeys now survive to a height of 18 m *60 ft*. It was built in the reign of Ur-nammu (*c.* 2113–2096 BC).

Transport

Ships

EARLIEST SEA-GOING BOATS

Aborigines are thought to have been able to cross the Torres Strait from New Guinea to Australia, then at least 70 km *43 ½ miles* across, as early as 55 000 BC. They are believed to have used double canoes.

The earliest surviving 'vessel' is a pine-wood dug-out found in Pesse, Netherlands and dated to *c.* 6315 ± 275 BC and now in the Provincial Museum, Assen.

The earliest representation of a boat is disputed between possible rock art outlines of Mesolithic skin-boats in Høgnipen, Norway (*c.* 8000–7000 BC); Minateda,

Spain (7000–3000 BC), and Kobystan, USSR (8000–6000 BC).

A 45 cm *18 in* long paddle was found at the Star Carr site, N Yorks, discovered in 1948. It has been dated to *c.* 7600 BC and is now in the Cambridge Museum of Archaeology.

The oldest surviving boat is a 8·2 m *27 ft* long 0·76 m *2 ½ ft* wide wooden eel-catching canoe discovered at Tybrind Vig on the Baltic island of Fünen, which is dated to *c.* 4490 BC.

The oldest surviving prehistoric boat in Britain was found in 1984 on Hasholme Hall Farm, Holme-on-Spalding Moor, North Humberside. It is 2300 years old and is 13·71 m *45 ft* long. It will require special conservation until the late 1990s.

The oldest shipwreck ever found is one of a Cycladic trading vessel located off the islet

of Dhókós, near the Greek island of Hydra, reported in May 1975 and dated to 2450 BC ± 250.

A wreck about 2400 years old is currently being excavated in the crater of a live volcano off the northern coast of Sicily. The cargo includes large quantities of classical Greek pottery.

Earliest power Marine propulsion by steam engine was first achieved when in 1783 the Marquis Jouffroy d'Abbans (1751 –1832) ascended a reach of the river Saône near Lyon, France, in the 180 tonnes paddle steamer *Pyroscaphe*.

The tug *Charlotte Dundas* was the first successful power-driven vessel. She was a stern paddle-wheel steamer built for the Forth and Clyde Canal in 1801–2 by William Symington (1763–1831), using a

MARINE CIRCUMNAVIGATION RECORDS

(Compiled by Nobby Clarke and Richard Boehmer)

Strictly speaking, a circumnavigation involves someone passing through a pair of antipodal points. Of the records listed below, only those with an asterisk against them are actually known to have met this requirement. A non-stop circumnavigation is entirely self-maintained; no water supplies, provisions, equipment or replacements of any sort may be taken aboard en route. Vessel may anchor, but no physical help may be accepted apart from passing mail or messages.

CATEGORY	VESSEL	SKIPPER	START	FINISH
* FIRST	*Victoria* Expedition of Fernão de Magalhães (Ferdinand Magellan)	Juan Sebastián de Elcano or del Cano (d. 1526) and 17 crew	Seville 20 Sep 1519	San Lucar 6 Sep 1522 30 700 nm
* FIRST BRITISH	*Golden Hind* (ex *Pelican*) 100 tons	Francis Drake (*c.* 1540–96) (Knighted 4 Apr 1581)	Plymouth 13 Dec 1577	26 Sep 1580
FIRST WOMAN	*Etoile* (Storeship for Bougainville's *La Boudeuse*)	Crypto-female valet of M. de Commerson, named Jeanne Baret	St Malo 1766	1769 (revealed as female on Hawaii)
FIRST FORE-AND-AFT RIGGED VESSEL	*Union* 98 tons (sloop)	John Boit Junior, aged 19–21, (US) and 22 crew	Newport, RI 1794 (via Cape Horn westabout)	Newport, RI 1796
FIRST YACHT	*Nancy Dawson* (schooner)	Robert Shedden (British) and crew (died in Mexico, 1849)	Thames 1847	Thames 1850
* FIRST SOLO	*Spray* 11·2 m *36 ft 9 in* gaff yawl	Capt Joshua Slocum, 51, (US) (a non-swimmer)	Newport, RI, via Magellan Straits 24 Apr 1895	3 Jul 1898 46 000 nm
FIRST MOTOR BOAT	*Speejacks* 29·9 m *98 ft*	Albert Y. Gowen (US) plus wife and crew	New York City 1921	New York City 1922
* FIRST SUBMERGED	*Triton* Nuclear submarine	Capt Edward L. Beach USN plus 182 crew	New London, Connecticut 16 Feb 1960	10 May 1960 84 days 19 hr, 36 300 nm
* FIRST MULTIHULL	*Rehu Moana* 12·2 m *40 ft* catamaran cutter	David Lewis (New Zealander)	Plymouth 23 May 1964	27 Jul 1967 660 days + 500 days in port, 41 609 nm
* FIRST NON-STOP SOLO W–E	*Suhaili* 9·87 m *32·4 ft* Bermudan ketch	Robin Knox-Johnston (British)	Falmouth 14 Jun 1968	22 Apr 1969 (312 days)
* FIRST SOLO MULTIHULL	*Victress* 12·2 m *40 ft* Bermudan ketch	Nigel Tetley (British) (b. South Africa)	Plymouth 16 Sep 1968 (W–E via Cape Horn)	21 May 1969 (trimaran sank after circumnavigation was completed)
* FIRST NON-STOP SOLO E–W	*British Steel* 18 m *59 ft* ketch	Chay Blyth (British)	Hamble River, Hants 18 Oct 1970	6 Aug 1971 (292 days)
* FIRST WOMAN SOLO	*Express Crusader* 16·15 m *53 ft* cutter	Dame Naomi James (New Zealander)	Dartmouth 9 Sep 1977	Dartmouth 8 Jun 1978 265 sailing days + 7 days in port
FIRST SOLO IN BOTH DIRECTIONS (via Cape Horn)	*Ocean Bound* 12·5 m *41 ft* Bermudan sloop	David Scott Cowper (British)	Plymouth 1979 (W–E) Plymouth 1981 (E–W)	Plymouth 1980 Plymouth 1982
FIRST SOLO ROUND THREE TIMES (same yacht)	*Tarmin* 7·5 m *24 ft 7 in* Bermudan sloop	John Sowden (US)	Various ports 1966, 1974, 1983	1970, 1977, 1986
FIRST BY NORTH-WEST PASSAGE	*Mabel E. Holland* 12·8 m *42 ft* motor lifeboat	David Scott Cowper (British)	Newcastle-upon-Tyne 14 Jul 1986	Newcastle-upon-Tyne 24 Sep 1990 (approx. 260 days motoring)
FASTEST SAIL NON-STOP W–E Solo in monohull	*Ecureuil d'Aquitaine II* 18·3 m *60 ft* ULDB cutter	Titouan Lamazou (French)	Les Sables (VGC) 26 Nov 1989	Les Sables (via 5 capes) 16 Mar 1990 109 days 8 hr 48 min 50 sec (205·7 mpd)
* FASTEST SAIL WITH STOPS W–E Solo in multihull	*Un Autre Regard* 22·9 m *75 ft* trimaran	Olivier de Kersauson (French)	Brest 28 Dec 1988	Brest (via 5 capes and 2 stops) 5 May 1989 125 d 19 h 32 m 33 s + 2 days in port
FASTEST SAIL WITH STOPS W–E Solo in monohull	*Groupe Sceta* 18·3 m *60 ft* ULDB sloop	Christophe Auguin (French)	Newport, RI (BOC) 15 Sep 1990	Newport, RI (via 3 capes and 3 stops) 23 Apr 1991 120 d 22 h 36 m 35 s + 98 d 14 h 34 m 47 s in port
* FASTEST SAIL WITH STOPS W–E Non-solo in monohull	*UBS Switzerland* 24·4 m *80 ft* IOR sloop	Pierre Fehlmann (Swiss)	Portsmouth (WRWR) 28 Sep 1985	Portsmouth (via 4 capes and 3 stops) 9 May 1986 117 d 14 h 31 m 42 s + 105 d 5 h 49 m 58 s in port
FASTEST SAIL WITH STOP W–E Clippership	*James Baines* 81·1 m *266 ft* 3-masted ship	Charles McDonnell (British)	Liverpool 10 Dec 1854	Liverpool (via Melbourne) 20 May 1855 133 days + 28 days in port
FASTEST SAIL WITH STOPS E–W Solo in monohull	*Ocean Bound* 12·5 m *41 ft* Bermudan sloop	David Scott Cowper (British)	Plymouth 22 Sep 1981	Plymouth (via 5 capes and 3 stops) 17 May 1982 221 days + 16 days in port

Eduard Roditi, author of *Magellan of the Pacific*, advances the view that Magellan's slave, Enrique, was the first circumnavigator. He had been purchased in Malacca and it was shown that he already understood the Filipino dialect Vizayan, when he reached the Philippines from the east. He 'tied the knot' off Limasawa on 28 Mar 1521. ULDB = Ultra-light displacement boat. VGC = Vendée Globe Challenge Race. BOC = British Oxygen Corp. Challenge Around Alone Race. IOR = International Offshore Rule. WRWR = Whitbread Round World Race. All mileages are nautical miles.

double-acting condensing engine constructed by James Watt (1736–1819).

The screw propeller was invented and patented by a Kent farmer, Sir Francis Pettit Smith (1808–71), on 31 May 1836 (British Patent No. 7104).

The world's oldest active paddle steamer and continuously operated as such is *Skibladner*, which has plied Lake Mjøsa, Norway since 1856. She was built in Motala, Sweden and has had two major refits.

Oldest vessel The oldest British vessel afloat, the training ship *Foudroyant*, for many years a familiar sight lying at her moorings in Portsmouth Harbour, Hampshire was built of teak at Bombay in 1817 as HMS *Trincomalee*. In use as a seamanship training ship since 1897, the *Foudroyant* was moved from Portsmouth, to Hartlepool, Cleveland in 1987 to undergo repairs and restoration as a typical naval frigate of the Nelson era. When the work is completed the *Foudroyant* will be displayed in a specially constructed dry-dock at Hartlepool.

Oldest active The world's oldest active ocean-going ship is the *MV Doulos* (Greek for 'servant'), built in 1914 in the USA and first named *Medina*. She is currently operating as an international Educational and Christian service vessel with approximately 300 crew, staff and passengers on board from 30 different nations.

Earliest turbine The *Turbinia*, built in 1894 at Wallsend-on-Tyne, Tyne & Wear, to the design of the Hon. Sir Charles Parsons (1854–1931), was 30·48 m *100 ft* long and of 45·2 tonnes displacement with machinery consisting of three steam turbines totalling about 2000 shp. At her first public demonstration in 1897 she reached 34·5 knots *63·9 km/h* and is now preserved at Newcastle upon Tyne.

WARSHIPS

Largest battleships The largest battleships in active service are the USS *Missouri* and USS *Wisconsin*, 270 m *887 ft* long with a full load displacement of 58 000 tonnes. Both were first commissioned in 1944, and following major refits were recommissioned in 1986 and 1988 respectively. Each has nine 16 inch guns which were used for shore bombardment during the Gulf War in early 1991. The 16 inch projectiles of 1225 kg *2700 lb* can be fired a distance of 39 km *23 miles*.

Two other ships of the same class, USS *New Jersey* and USS *Iowa* are now in reserve; *New Jersey* last saw action off Lebabon in 1983–4.

The Japanese battleships *Yamato* (completed on 16 Dec 1941 and sunk south-west of Kyūshū, Japan by US planes on 7 Apr 1945) and *Musashi* (sunk in the Philippine Sea by 11 bombs and 16 torpedoes on 24 Oct 1944) were the largest battleships ever commissioned, each with a full load displacement of 73 977 tonnes. With an overall length of 263 m *863 ft*, a beam of 38·7 m *127 ft* and a full load draught of 10·8 m *35 ½ ft*, they mounted nine 460 mm *18·1 in* guns in three triple turrets. Each of the guns weighed 164·6 tonnes and was 22·8 m *75 ft* in length, firing a 1451 kg *3200 lb* projectile.

Britain's largest ever and last battleship was HMS *Vanguard* (1944–60) with a full load displacement of 52 245 tonnes and an overall length of 248·1 m *814 ft*. She had eight 15 in guns, which were originally mounted in the battlecruisers *Courageous*

and *Glorious* in 1917. Completed too late for service in World War II, *Vanguard* spent much of her time in the Home Fleet's Training Squadron. She was broken up at Faslane, Strathclyde in 1960.

Smallest Royal Navy warship The Attacker Class Fast Patrol boats, built by Allday in 1983–4, have an overall length of 20 m *65·6 ft* and a displacement of 34 tonnes. HMS *Attacker*, one of five of these vessels, is operated by students of the Universities of Glasgow and Strathclyde for training. Under her commander, Lt Commander A.G.C. Black, she visited a total of 24 ports in the Clyde Estuary between 10 a.m. on 11 Nov 1988 and 11 a.m. on 12 November.

Earliest surviving 'Ironclad' HMS *Warrior*, open to the public at Portsmouth, Hants, in her restored state since 1987, was built on the Thames at Blackwall in 1860. Constructed of iron and teak, she was powered by a 932 kW *1 250 hp* steam engine as well as a full rig of sails. After her withdrawal from service the *Warrior* performed various static roles, latterly spending 50 years as an oil depot pontoon at Milford Haven. She was presented to the Maritime Trust in 1979, but was transferred to a separate Trust in 1983. After the completion of extensive restoration work at Hartlepool, Cleveland she was towed to Portsmouth.

Fastest warship The hovercraft, the 23·7 m *78 ft* long 100 tonnes US Navy test vehicle SES-100B achieved a speed of 91·9 knots *105·8 mph*. (See fastest hovercraft.)

Fastest destroyer The highest speed attained by a destroyer was 45·25 knots (*83·42 km/h*) by the 2830 tonnes French destroyer *Le Terrible* in 1935. She was built in Blainville, France and powered by four Yarrow small tube boilers and two Rateau geared turbines, giving 100 000 shp. She was removed from the active list at the end of 1957.

AIRCRAFT CARRIERS

Largest The warships with the largest full load displacement in the world are the Nimitz class US Navy aircraft carriers USS

Nimitz, Dwight D. Eisenhower, Carl Vinson, Theodore Roosevelt and *Abraham Lincoln* at 98 386 tons. They are 332·9 m *1092 ft* in length overall, with 1·82 ha *4 ½ acres* of flight deck, and have a speed well in excess of 30 knots *56 km/h* from their four nuclear-powered 260 000 shp geared steam turbines. They have to be refuelled after about 1 450 000 km *900 000 miles* of steaming. Their complement is 5986.

The Royal Navy's largest fighting ship is the aircraft carrier HMS *Ark Royal*, commissioned 1 Nov 1985. She has a 167·6 m *550 ft* long flight deck and is 209·3 m *685·8 ft* long overall, and has a top speed of 28 knots being powered by four Rolls Royce Olympus TM3B gas turbines delivering 94 000 shp.

SUBMARINES

Largest The world's largest submarines are of the USSR Typhoon class. The launch of the first at the secret covered shipyard at Severodvinsk in the White Sea, USSR was announced by NATO on 23 Sep 1980. They are believed to have a dived displacement of 26 500 tonnes, to measure 170 m *557·6 ft* overall and to be armed with 20 SS NX 20 missiles with a 8895 km *4800* nautical mile range, each with seven warheads. By late 1987 two others built in Leningrad were operational, each deploying 140 warheads.

The largest submarines ever built for the Royal Navy are the four atomic-powered nuclear vessels *Resolution, Repulse, Renown* and *Revenge*, R class boats with a surface displacement of 7620 tonnes and a dived displacement of 8 500, a length of 129·5 m *425 ft*, a beam of 10 m *33 ft* and a draught of 9·1 m *30 ft*.

The longest submarine patrol ever spent dived and unsupported is 111 days by HM Submarine *Warspite* (Cdr J.G.F. Cooke RN) in the South Atlantic from 25 Nov 1982 to 15 Mar 1983. She sailed 57 085 km *30 804 nautical miles*.

Fastest The Russian Alfa class nuclear-powered submarines have a reported maximum speed of 45 knots *83·4 km/h* plus. With use of titanium alloy, they are believed to be able to dive to 762 m *2500 ft*. A US spy

■ **Aircraft carrier**
The USS Dwight D.
Eisenhower *is one of four
of the world's largest full
load displacement
warships at* 100 846 *tons.
The flight deck covers*
1·82 ha 4 ½ *acres. This
view was taken at Monaco.*
(Photo: US Navy)

Most landings
The greatest number on
an aircraft carrier in one
day was 602, achieved by
Marine Air Group 6 of
the United States Pacific
Fleet Air Force aboard
the USS *Matanikau* on 25
May 1945 between 8 a.m.
and 5 p.m.

satellite over Leningrad's naval yard on 8 Jun 1983 showed they were being lengthened and are now 79·3 m *260·1 ft* long.

Deepest The US Navy deep submergence vessel *Sea Cliff* (DSV 4) 30 tons, commissioned in 1973, reached in March 1985 a depth of 6 000 m *20 000 ft*.

PASSENGER LINERS

Largest The largest and the longest is the *Norway* of 76 000 grt and 315·53 m *1035 ft 7 ½ in* in overall length, with a capacity of 2400 passengers. She was built as the *France* in 1961 and renamed after purchase in June 1979 by Knut Kloster of Norway. She is normally employed on cruises in the Caribbean and is based at Miami, USA. Work undertaken during an extensive refit, including two new decks during the autumn of 1990 increased the *Norway's* tonnage to 76 000 grt.

The RMS *Queen Elizabeth* (finally 82 998 but formerly 83 673 gross tons), of the Cunard fleet, was the largest passenger vessel ever built and had the largest displacement of any liner in the world. She had an overall length of 314 m *1031 ft*, was 36 m *118 ft 7 in* in breadth and was powered by steam turbines which developed 168 000 hp. Her last passenger voyage ended on 15 Nov 1968. In 1970 she was removed to Hong Kong to serve as a floating marine university and renamed *Seawise University*. She was burnt out on 9 Jan 1972 when three *simultaneous* outbreaks of fire strongly pointed to arson. The gutted hull had been cut up and removed by 1978. *Seawise* was a pun on the owner's initials— C.Y. Tung (1911–82).

Britain's largest liner is RMS *Queen Eliza-*

beth 2 at 66 451 gross tons and with an overall length of 293 m *963 ft*, completed for Cunard Line in 1968. She set a 'turn round' record of 5 hr 47 min at New York City, USA on 21 Nov 1983. Her original steam turbine machinery was replaced with diesel electric units in April 1987. She is the last large passenger liner to be regularly employed on transatlantic service between Southampton, Hants and New York, USA.

TANKERS

Largest The *Happy Giant*, formerly the *Seawise Giant*, was 564 739 tonnes deadweight. She was 485·45 m *1504 ft* long overall, with a beam of 68·86 m *225 ft 11 in*, and has a draught of 24·61 m *80 ft 9 in*. She was lengthened by Nippon Kokan in 1980 by adding an 81 m *265 ft 8 in* midship section. She was attacked by Iraqi Mirage jets off Larak Island in the Persian Gulf on 22 Dec 1987 and was severely damaged in another attack on 14 May 1988. Despite this damage, she has been bought by an owner in Norway, and is to be returned to service after refitting in South Korea. A new diesel engine in place of her steam turbines will result in her deadweight tonnage being reduced to approximately 420 000.

The largest tanker and ship of any kind in service is the 555 051 tonnes deadweight *Hellas Fos*, a steam turbine tanker built in 1979. Of 254 583 grt and 227 801 nrt, she is managed by the Bilinder Marine Corporation of Athens.

CARGO VESSELS

Largest The largest ship carrying dry cargo is the Norwegian ore carrier *Berge Stahl* of 364 767 tonnes deadweight built in

South Korea for the Norwegian owner Sig Bergesen. It has a length of 343 m *1125 ft*, a beam measuring 63·5 m *208 ft* and was launched on 5 Nov 1986.

The largest British ore/oil carriers (registered in the Isle of Man) are Lombard North Wheelease Ltd *Rapana* and *Rimula* built in Sweden in 1973 and 1974 of 227 400 tonnes dwt, with lengths of 332·77 m *1091 ft 9 in*.

Largest whale factory The USSR's *Sovietskaya Ukraina* (32 034 gross tons) with a summer deadweight of 46 738 tonnes was completed in October 1959. She is 217·8 m *714 ½ ft* in length and 25·8 m *84 ft 7 in* in the beam.

Barges The world's largest RoRo (roll-on, roll-off) ships are four *El Rey* class barges of 16 700 tons and 176·78 m *580 ft* in length. They were built by the FMC Corp of Portland, Oregon, USA and are operated by Crowley Maritime Corp of San Francisco, USA between Florida, USA and Puerto Rico with tri-level lodging of up to 376 truck-trailers.

Container ship *Earliest* Shipborne containerization began in 1955 when the tanker *Ideal X* was converted by Malcolm McLean (USA). She carried containers only on deck.

Largest The 12 built for United States Lines in Korea in 1984–5 are capable of carrying 4482 TEU containers) with a gross tonnage of 57 075. They were named *American Alabama, California, Illinois, Kentucky,* etc. Following the financial collapse of United States Lines, the fleet was sold and the 12 ships now have such names as *Sea-Land Atlantic, Achiever, Commitment,*

TRANSATLANTIC AND TRANSPACIFIC MARINE RECORDS

(Compiled by Nobby Clarke and Richard Boehmer)

CATEGORY	VESSEL	SKIPPER	START	FINISH	DURATION
FIRST CRUISE	Lively 140-ton Brig	Shuttleworth (British) guests and 25 crew	UK 1783 Hudson Bay	Florida UK 1784	420 days
FIRST SOLO SAILING E–W	15-ton gaff sloop	Josiah Shackford (US)	Bordeaux, France, 1786	Surinam (Guiana)	35 days
FIRST ROWING	Ship's boat c. 6·1 m 20 ft	John Brown and 5 British deserters from garrison	St Helena 10 Jun 1799	Belmonte, Brazil (fastest-ever row)	28 days (83 mpd)
FIRST MULTIHULL (raft)	Non Pareil 7·62 m 25 ft	John Mikes and 2 crew (US)	New York 1868	Southampton	51 days
FIRST SOLO SAILING W–E	Centennial 6·09 m 20 ft	Alfred Johnson (US)	Shag Harbor, Maine, 1876	Wales	46 days
FIRST MOTOR-BOAT	Abiel Abbott Low 11·58 m 38 ft (engine: 10hp kerosene)	William C. Newman (US) Edward (son)	New York 1902	Falmouth	36 days (83·3 mpd)
FIRST WOMAN SOLO W–E	lugger 5·5 m 18 ft	Gladys Gradeley (US)	Nova Scotia 1903	Hope Cove, Devon	60 days
FIRST WOMAN SOLO E–W	Felicity Ann 7·01 m 23 ft	Ann Davison (British)	Las Palmas 20 Nov 1952	Dominica 1953	65 days
FIRST SOLO ROWING E–W	Britannia 6·70 m 22 ft	John Fairfax (British)	Las Palmas 20 Jan 1969	Ft Lauderdale, Florida 19 Jul 1969	180 days
FIRST SOLO ROWING W–E	Super Silver 6·1 m 20 ft	Tom McClean (Irish)	St John's, Newfoundland 1969	Black Sod Bay, Ireland 27 Jul 1969	70·7 days
FIRST OUTBOARD	Trans-Atlantic 7·92 m 26 ft (2·65 hp Evinrudes)	Al Grover (US) Dante (son)	St Pierre, Newfoundland 1985 (via Azores)	Lisbon	34 days (88 mpd approx.)
FIRST ROW BOTH DIRECTIONS	QE III 5·87 m 19 ft 10 in	Don Allum (British)	Canaries 1986 St John's, Newfoundland	Nevis Ireland 1987	114 days 77 days
YOUNGEST SOLO SAILING	Sea Raider 10·67 m 35 ft	David Sandeman (British) (17 years 176 days)	Jersey, Channel Islands 1976	Newport, Rhode Island	43 days
OLDEST SOLO SAILING	Tawny Pipit 7·62 m 25 ft	Stefan Szwarnowski (British) (76 years 165 days)	New Jersey 2 Jun 1989	Bude 13 Aug 1989	72 days
YOUNGEST SOLO ROWING	Finn Again 6·25 m 20 ft 6 in	Sean Crowley (British) (25 years 306 days)	Halifax, Nova Scotia, 17 Jun 1988	Co. Galway, 21 Sep 1988	95 days 22 hr
OLDEST SOLO ROWING	Khaggavisana 6·02 m 19¾ ft	Sidney Genders (British) (51 years)	Penzance, Cornwall, 1970	Miami, Florida via Antigua	160 days 8 hr
FASTEST POWER W–E	Gentry Eagle 33·5 m 110 ft	Tom Gentry (US)	Ambrose Light Tower 13:49 BST 24 Jul 1989	Bishop Rock Light 03:56 BST 27 Jul 1989	2 days 14 hr 7 min 47 sec (45·7 knots smg)
FASTEST SAIL W–E Non-solo in multihull	Jet Services 5 22·9 m 75 ft catamaran sloop	Serge Madec (French)	Ambrose Light Tower 2 Jun 1990	Lizard Lighthouse 9 Jun 1990	6 days 13 hr 3 min 32 sec (18·4 knots smg)
FASTEST SAIL W–E Non-solo in monohull	Phocea 74·0 m 243 ft ULDB schooner	Philippe Morinay (French)	Ambrose Light Tower 26 Jun 1988	Lizard Lighthouse 3 Jul 1988	8 days 3 hr 29 min (14·8 knots smg)
FASTEST SAIL W–E Solo in multihull	Pierre Ier 18·3 m 60 ft trimaran sloop	Florence Arthaud (French)	Ambrose Light Tower 24 Jul 1990	Lizard Lighthouse 3 Aug 1990	9 days 21 hr 42 min (12·2 knots smg)
FASTEST SAIL W–E Clipper ship	Red Jacket 76·5 m 251 ft 3-masted ship	Asa Eldridge (US)	Sandy Hook, New Jersey 11 Jan 1854	Liverpool Bar 23 Jan 1854	12 days (approx. 260 mpd av.)
FASTEST SAIL E–W Non-solo in multihull	Elf Aquitaine III 18·3 m 60 ft trimaran sloop	Jean Maurel (French)	Plymouth 10 Jun 1990	Newport, Rhode Island 21 Jun 1990	10 days 23 hr 15 min (11·0 knots smg)
FASTEST SAIL E–W Non-solo in monohull	Allied Bank 18·3 m 60 ft ULDB sloop	John Martin (South African)	Plymouth 10 Jun 1990	Newport, Rhode Island 26 Jun 1990	15 days 13 hr 40 min (7·8 knots smg)
FASTEST SAIL E–W Solo in multihull	Fleury Michon (IX) 18·3 m 60 ft trimaran	Philippe Poupon (French)	Plymouth (STAR) 5 Jun 1988	Newport, Rhode Island 15 Jun 1988	10 days 9 hr 15 min 9 sec (11·6 knots smg)
FASTEST SAIL E–W Solo in monohull	Thursday's Child 18·3 m 60 ft ULDB cutter	Warren Luhrs (US)	Plymouth (STAR) 2 Jun 1984	Newport, Rhode Island 19 Jun 1984	16 days 22 hr 27 min (7·1 knots smg)
FASTEST SAIL E–W Clipper ship	Andrew Jackson 67·1 m 220 ft 3-masted ship	W.S. Johnson (US)	Liverpool 3 Nov 1860	New York 18 Nov 1860	15 days (approx. 210 mpd av.)
FIRST RAFT shore to shore	La Balsa 12·8 m 42 ft (balsa logs)	Vital Alsar (Spanish) and 3 crew	Guayaquil, Ecuador 1970	Mooloolaba Australia	160 days
FIRST ROWING	Britannia II 10·66 m 35 ft	John Fairfax (British) Sylvia Cook (British)	San Francisco 26 Apr 1971	Hayman I., Australia 22 Apr 1972	362 days
FIRST ROWING SOLO	Hele-on-Britannia 9·75 m 32 ft	Peter Bird (British)	San Francisco 23 Aug 1982	Gt Barrier Reef, Australia 14 Jun 1983	294 days 14 480 km 9000 miles
FASTEST SAIL CALIFORNIA–HAWAII Non-solo in multihull	Aikane X-5 19·1 m 63 ft catamaran	Rudy Choy (US)	Los Angeles 17 Aug 1989	Honolulu 24 Aug 1989	6 days 22 hr 41 min 12 sec (13·3 knots smg)
FASTEST SAIL CALIFORNIA–HAWAII Non-solo in monohull	Merlin 20·4 m 67 ft ULDB sloop	Bill Lee (US)	Los Angeles (TransPac) 2 Jul 1977	Honolulu 10 Jul 1977	8 days 11 hr 1 min 45 sec (11·0 knots smg)
FASTEST SAIL CALIFORNIA–HAWAII Solo in multihull	Bullfrog Sunblock 12·2 m 40 ft trimaran	Ian Johnston (Australian)	San Francisco (SoloTP) 14 Jun 1986	Kauai 24 Jun 1986	10 days 10 hr 3 min 43 sec (8·5 knots smg)
FASTEST SAIL CALIFORNIA–HAWAII Solo in monohull	Intense 9·1 m 30 ft ULDB sloop	Bill Strange (US)	San Francisco (SoloTP) 25 Jun 1988	Kauai 7 Jul 1988	11 days 15 hr 21 min (7·6 knots smg)
FASTEST SAIL CALIFORNIA–JAPAN	Pen Duick V 10·7 m 35 ft sloop	Eric Tabarly (French)	San Francisco 15 Mar 1969	Tokyo 24 Apr 1969	39 days 15 hr 44 min (4·66 knots smg)

N.B.—The earliest single-handed Pacific crossings were achieved East–West by Bernard Gilboy (US) in 1882 in the 5·48 m 18 ft double-ender Pacific to Australia, and West–East by Fred Rebel (Latvia) in the 5·48 m 18 ft Elaine, (from Australia) and Edward Miles (US) in the 11·2 m 36¼ ft Sturdy II (from Japan) both in 1932, the latter via Hawaii. ULDB = Ultra-light displacement boat. All mileages are nautical miles. STAR is a transatlantic race. smg = speed made good.

OTHER MARINE RECORDS

(Compiled by Richard Boehmer)

CATEGORY	VESSEL	SKIPPER	START	FINISH	DURATION
LONGEST TIME AND DISTANCE NON-STOP BY SAIL	*Parry Endeavour* 13·92 m *44 ft* Bermudan sloop	Jon Sanders (Australian)	Fremantle 25 May 1986	Fremantle 13 Mar 1988	(71 000 nm in 658 days) (4·5 knots)
GOLD RUSH ROUTE Fastest multihull	*Great American* 18·3 m *60 ft* trimaran	Georgs Kolesnikovs (Canadian)	New York 10 Mar 1989	San Francisco 26 May 1989	76 days 23 hr 20 min (7·36 knots smg)
GOLD RUSH ROUTE Fastest monohull	*Thursday's Child* 18·3 m *60 ft* ULDB cutter	Warren Luhrs (US)	New York 24 Nov 1988	San Francisco 12 Feb 1989	80 days 18 hr 39 min (includes 3-day stop)
GOLD RUSH ROUTE Fastest clipper ship	*Flying Cloud* 70 m *229 ft* 3-masted ship	Josiah Creesy (US)	New York 21 Jan 1854	San Francisco 20 Apr 1854	88 days 19 hr (approx. 155 mpd av.)
BRITISH TEA ROUTE Fastest solo in multihull	*Elle & Vire* 18·3 m *60 ft* trimaran	Philippe Monnet (French)	off Foo Chow 8 Dec 1989	London 13 Feb 1990	67 days 10 hr 26 min 5 sec (8·40 knots smg)
BRITISH TEA ROUTE Fastest clipper ship	*Zingra*	W. Gould	Shanghai 26 Dec 1863	Liverpool 20 Mar 1864	85 days (approx. 165 mpd av.)
AROUND AUSTRALIA Fastest multihull	*Steinlager I* 18·3 m *60 ft* trimaran	Peter Blake (New Zealander)	Sydney (AA) 8 Aug 1988	Sydney (7 stops) 13 Oct 1988	33 days 17 hr 42 min 7 sec (+ 32 days in port)
AROUND AUSTRALIA Fastest monohull	*NBL Technovator* 16·2 m *53 ft* ULDB sloop	Peter Neale (Australian)	Sydney (AA) 8 Aug 1988	Sydney (7 stops) 18 Oct 1988	45 days 3 hr 35 min 23 sec (+ 25 days in port)
AROUND BRITISH ISLES Fastest power	*Ilan Voyager* 21·3 m *70 ft* trimaran	Mark Pridie (British)	Brighton 9 May 1989	Brighton 12 May 1989	3 days 0 hr 42 min (21·6 knots smg)
AROUND BRITISH ISLES Fastest multihull	*Saab Turbo* 22·9 m *75 ft* catamaran	François Boucher (French)	Plymouth (RB & I) 18 Jun 1989	Plymouth (4 stops) 3 Jul 1989	7 days 7 hr 30 min (+ 8 days in port)
AROUND BRITISH ISLES Fastest monohull	*Voortreckker II* 18·3 m *60 ft* ULDB sloop	Bertie Reed (South African)	Plymouth (RB & I) 10 Jul 1982	Plymouth (4 stops) 29 Jul 1982	10 days 16 hr 10 min (+ 8 days in port)
ROUND THE HORN 50–50 Fastest sailing ship	*Brenhilda* length unknown, barque	James Learmont (British)	49° 50′ S 65° 05′ W noon 9 Jul 1902	50° 20′ S 75° 44′ W noon 14 Jul 1902	5 days 1 hr
BEST DAY'S RUN Non-solo in multihull	*Jet Services 5* 18·3 m *60 ft* catamaran sloop	Serge Madec (French)	42·638° N 62·626° W 22:22 GMT 3 Jun 1990	45·750° N 51·480° W 21:58 GMT 4 Jun 1990	514·01 nm (GCD)/23 hr 36 min (21·8 knots smg)
BEST DAY'S RUN Non-solo in monohull	*Phocea* 74·0 m *243 ft* ULDB schooner	Philippe Morinay (French)	during transatlantic record run in 1988		490 nm/24 hr (20·4 knots smg)
BEST DAY'S RUN Non-solo in monohull, < 200 ft	*Fortuna Extra Lights* 23·5 m *77 ft* ULDB sloop	Jose Santana (Spanish)	48° 11′ S 70° 15′ E 13:38 GMT 16 Nov 1989	45° 35′ S 79° 23′ E 13:16 GMT 17 Nov 1989	405·4 nm (GCD)/23 hr 38 min (17·2 knots smg)
BEST DAY'S RUN Solo in multihull	*Laiterie Mont St Michel* 18·3 m *60 ft* trimaran	Olivier Moussy (French)	50° 13′ N 11° 30′ W 18:18 GMT 6 Jun 1988	48° 18′ N 23° 30′ W 21:17 GMT 7 Jun 1988	430·8 nm (GCD)/24 hr (18·0 knots smg)
BEST DAY'S RUN Solo in monohull	*Generali Concorde* 18·3 m *60 ft* sloop	Alain Gautier (French)	50·300° S 42·550° E 15:39 GMT 2 Dec 1990	51·800° S 50·617° E 15:16 GMT 3 Dec 1990	317·1 nm (GCD)/23 hr 37 min (13·43 knots smg)
BEST DAY'S RUN Clipper ship	*Champion of the Seas* 76·8 m *252 ft* 3-masted ship	Alex Newlands (British)	47° 01′ S 88° 31′ E noon 11 Dec 1854	49° 58′ S 99° 15′ E noon 12 Dec 1854	461·5 nm (GCD)/23 hr 17 min (19·8 knots smg)
BEST DAY'S RUN Sailboard	*Fanatic board* Gaastra sail	Françoise Canetos (French)	Sète, France 13 Jul 1988	14 Jul 1988	227 nm/24 hr (9·46 knots smg)
ENGLISH CHANNEL 2 X Fastest multihull	*Fleury Michon (VIII)* 22·9 m *75 ft* trimaran	Philippe Poupon (French)	Calais Dec 1986	Calais via Dover Dec 1986	2 hr 21 min 57 sec (18·6 knots smg)
ENGLISH CHANNEL 2 X Fastest sailboard	*Hi Fly Board* Gaastra sail	Pascal Maka (French)	Cape Blanc-Nez 1985	Cape Gris-Nez via Dover 1985	1 hr 59 min 57 sec (18·5 knots smg)
ONE NAUTICAL MILE Fastest sail	*Crédit Agricole (II)* 22·6 m *74 ft* catamaran	Philippe Jeantot (French)	Martinique January 1985		2 min 13 sec (27·1 knots smg)
500 METRES Fastest	*Naish sailboard* with ART sail	Pascal Maka (French)	Saintes Maries de-la-Mer, France 27 Feb 1990		22·65 sec (42·91 knots)
500 METRES Fastest sailboat	*Longshot* 6·3 m *20 ft 9 in* trifoiler	Russell Long (US)	Lethbridge, Canada 12 Oct 1990		26·17 sec (37·14 knots)

ULDB = Ultra-light displacement boat. AA = Around Australia Race. RB & I = Round Britain & Ireland Race. GCD = Great circle distance. smg = speed made good. All mileages are nautical miles.

Riveting

The world record for riveting is 11 209 in 9 hr, by John Moir at the Workman Clark Ltd shipyard, Belfast in June 1918. His peak hour was his 7th, with 1409 rivets, an average of nearly 23½ per min.

Integrity, etc. while others have the prefix 'Nedlloyd' (*Nedlloyd Holland*) or the suffix 'Bay' (*Galveston Bay*). Their new owners have decided to limit their capacity to 3456 TEU in normal operation.

American President Lines has built five ships in Germany, *President Adams*, *President Jackson*, *President Kennedy*, *President Polk* and *President Truman*, which are termed post-Panamax, being the first container vessels too large for transit of the Panama Canal. They are 275·14 m *902·69 ft* in length and 39·41 m *129·29 ft* in beam; the maximum beam for the Panama transit is 32·3m *105·97 ft*. These vessels have a quoted capacity of 4300 TEU; they have in fact carried in excess of this in normal service.

Most powerful tugs The *Nikolay Chiker* and *SB–134*, commissioned in April–May 1989, and built by Hollming Ltd of Sweden for V/O Sudoiport, USSR, are of 24 480 hp and 250 tons bollard pull at full power They are 99 m *324·80 ft* long and 19·45 m *63·81 ft* wide.

Largest car ferries The world's largest car and passenger ferry is the 58 376 grt *Silja Serenade* which entered service between Stockholm and Helsinki in 1990 and is operated by the Silja Line. She is 203 m *666 ft* long and 31·5 m *103·34 ft* wide, and can carry 2500 passengers and 450 cars.

Fastest The fastest is the 24 065 grt gas-turbine powered *Finnjet*, built in 1977, operates in the Baltic between Helsinki, Finland and Travemunde, Germany and is capable of exceeding 30 knots.

Largest rail ferry The operating area of the biggest international rail ferries *Klaipeda*, *Vilnius*, *Mukran* and *Greifswald* is in the Baltic sea, between the ports of Klaipeda, Lithuania, USSR and Mukran, Germany. Consisting of two-decks 190·50 m *625 ft* in length, 91·86 m *301·4 ft* in breadth and 11 700 tons deadweight were built in Wismar, Germany. Each of them can lift 103 rail cars of standard 14·83 m *48·65 ft* length and weighing up to 84 tons. The ferries can cover a distance of 506 km *273 nautical miles* in 17 hours.

Largest propeller The largest propeller ever made is the triple-bladed screw of 11 m *36 ft 1 in* diameter made by Kawasaki Heavy Industries, Japan delivered on 17 Mar 1982 for the 208 739 dwt bulk carrier *Hoei Maru* (now renamed *New Harvest*).

Largest hydrofoil The 64·6 m *212 ft* long *Plainview* (314 tonnes full load) naval hydrofoil was launched by the Lockheed Shipbuilding and Construction Co. at Seattle, Washington State, USA on 28 Jun 1965. She has a service speed of 92 km/h *57·2 mph*.

Three 165-ton Supramar PTS 150 Mk III hydrofoils carry 250 passengers at 40 knots *74 km/h* across the Öre Sound between Malmö, Sweden and Copenhagen, Denmark. They were built by Westermoen Hydrofoil Ltd of Mandal, Norway.

River boat The world's largest inland boat is the 116 m *382 ft Mississippi Queen*, designed by James Gardner of London. The vessel was commissioned on 25 Jul 1976 in Cincinatti, Ohio, USA and is now in service on the Mississippi river.

Most powerful icebreakers The most powerful purpose-built icebreaker is the 25 375 tonnes 140 m *460 ft* long *Rossiya*, powered by 55·95 kW *75 000 hp* nuclear engines, built in Leningrad, USSR and completed in 1985.

A 74·6 kW *100 000 hp* 194 m *636 ft* long Polar icebreaker of the Class 8 type was ordered by the Canadian Government in October 1985. Its cost was $Can 500 million.

The largest *converted* icebreaker was the 306·9 m *1007 ft* long SS *Manhattan* (43 000 shp), which was converted by the Humble Oil Co. into a 152 407 tonnes icebreaker. She made a double voyage through the North-West Passage in arctic Canada from 24 August to 12 Nov 1969.

The North-West Passage was first navigated by Roald Engebereth Gravning Amundsen (Norway) (1872–1928) in the sealing sloop *Gjøa* in 1906.

Yacht *Most expensive* The fitting-out of the 143·2 m *470 ft* Saudi Arabian royal yacht *Abdul Aziz*, built in Denmark, was completed on 22 Jun 1984 at Vospers Yard, Southampton, Hants. It was estimated in September 1987 to be worth more than $100 million.

Longest The private (non-Royal) yacht is the 85·9 m *282 ft Nabila* which originally cost some $29 million. She was sold in September 1987 by the Sultan of Brunei to New York property dealer Donald Trump (b. 1946) for close to this price and renamed *Trump Princess*. Her original owner was Adnan Kashoggi, who installed a helicopter pad and an operating theatre.

Most powerful dredger The 142·7 m *468·4 ft* long *Prins der Nederlanden* of 10 586 grt can dredge 20 000 tonnes of sand from a depth of 35 m *115 ft* via two suction tubes in less than an hour.

Wooden ship *Heaviest* The *Richelieu*, 101·70 m *333 ⅔ ft* long and of 8662 tonnes was launched in Toulon, France on 3 Dec 1873.

HM battleship *Lord Warden*, completed in 1869, displaced 8060 tonnes.

Longest The longest ever built was the New York–built *Rochambeau* (1867–72), formerly *Dunderberg*, which measured 115 m *377 ft 4 in* overall.

It should be noted that the biblical length of Noah's Ark was 300 cubits or, at 45·7 cm *18 in* to a cubit, 137 m *450 ft*.

Largest human powered The giant ship *Tessarakonteres* a three-banked catamaran galley with 4000 rowers, built for Ptolemy IV *c.* 210 BC in Alexandria, Egypt,

measured 128 m *420 ft* with up to eight men to an oar of 38 cubits (17·5 m *57 ft*) in length.

Longest canoe The 35·7 m *117 ft* long Kauri wood Maori war canoe *Nga Toki Matawhaorua* 20·3 tonnes was shaped with adzes at Kerikeri Inlet, New Zealand in 1940. The crew numbered 70 or more.

The 'Snake Boat' *Nadubhagóm* 41·1 m *135 ft* long from Kerala, southern India has a crew of 109 rowers and nine 'encouragers'.

Light vessels The earliest station still marked by a light vessel is the Newarp in the North Sea, off Great Yarmouth, Norfolk established in 1791. A Nore light vessel was first placed in the Thames estuary in 1732. *Note:* In 1989 all Trinity House manned light vessels around the United Kingdom were withdrawn and then replaced by unmanned beacons or unmanned light vessels.

SAILING SHIPS

Largest The largest vessel ever built in the era of sail was the *France II* (5806 gross tons), launched at Bordeaux, France in 1911. The *France II* was a steel-hulled, five-masted barque (square-rigged on four masts and fore and aft rigged on the aftermost mast). Her hull measured 127·4 m *418 ft* overall. Although principally designed as a sailing vessel with a stump topgallant rig, she was also fitted with two auxiliary engines; however these were removed in 1919 and she became a pure sailing vessel. She was wrecked off New Caledonia on 13 Jul 1922.

The only seven-masted sailing schooner ever built was the 114·4 m *375·6 ft* long *Thomas W. Lawson* (5218 gross tons) built at Quincy, Massachusetts, USA in 1902 and wrecked off the Isles of Scilly, Cornwall on 15 Dec 1907. (See Largest junks below.)

Largest in service The largest now in service is the 109 m *357 ft Sedov*, built in 1921 in Kiel and used for training in the USSR. She is 14·6 m *48 ft* in width, with a displacement of 6300 gross registered tonnage, and sail area of 4192 m² *45 123 ft²*.

The world's only surviving First Rate Ship-of-the-Line is the Royal Navy's 104-gun battleship HMS *Victory*, laid down at Chatham, Kent on 23 Jul 1759 and constructed from the wood of some 2200 oak trees. She bore the body of Admiral Nelson from Gibraltar to Portsmouth, Hants arriving 44 days after serving as his victorious flagship at the Battle of Trafalgar on 21 Oct 1805. In 1922 she was moved to No.2 dock, Portsmouth—site of the world's oldest graving dock. The length of her cordage (both standing and running rigging) is 30·77 km *19·12 miles*.

Oldest active The oldest active square-rigged sailing vessel in the world is the restored SV *Maria Asumpta*, (formerly the *Ciudad de Inca*), built near Barcelona, Spain in 1858. She is 38 m *125 ft* overall of 127 gross registered tonnage. She was restored in 1981–2 and is used for film work, promotional appearances at regattas and sail training. She is operated by The Friends of *Maria Asumpta* of Lenham, Maidstone, Kent.

Longest The longest is the 187 m *613 ft* long French built *Club Med 1* with five aluminium masts. The 762 m² *2 500 ft²* polyester sails are computer-controlled. She is operated as a Caribbean cruise vessel for 425 passengers for Club Med. With her small sail area and powerful engines she is really a motor-sailer.

Largest junks The largest on record was the sea-going *Cheng Ho*, flagship of Admiral Cheng Ho's 62 treasure ships, of *c.* 1420, with a displacement of 3150 tonnes and a length variously estimated up to 164 m *538 ft*. She is believed to have had nine masts.

A river junk 110 m *361 ft* long, with treadmill-operated paddle-wheels, was recorded in AD 1161.

In *c.* AD 280 a floating fortress 182·8 m *600 ft* square, built by Wang Chün on the Yangtse river, took part in the Chin-Wu river war. Present-day junks do not, even in the case of the Chiangsu traders, exceed 51·8 m *170 ft* in length.

Longest day's run under sail Calculated for any commercial vessel under sail, the longest day's run was one of 461·5 nautical miles by the clipper *Champion of the Seas* (2722 registered tons) of the Liverpool Black Ball Line, running before a north-westerly gale in the south Indian Ocean under the command of Capt. Alex Newlands in 1854. The elapsed time between the fixes was 23 hr 17 min, giving an average of 19·8 knots.

Largest sails Sails are known to have been used for marine propulsion since 3500 BC. The largest spars ever carried were those in HM Battleship *Temeraire*, completed at Chatham, Kent, on 31 Aug 1877. She was broken up in 1921. The fore and main yards measured 35 m *115 ft* in length. The foresail contained 1555 m *5100 ft* of canvas, weighing 2·03 tonnes and the total sail area was 2322 m² *25 000 ft²*.

HM Battleship *Sultan* was ship-rigged when completed at Chatham, Kent on 10 Oct 1871 and carried 3168 m² *34 100 ft²* of sails plus 1421 m² *15 300 ft²* of stunsails. She was broken up in 1946.

Tallest mast The *Velsheda*, a J class sailing vessel, is the tallest known single masted yacht in the world. Measured from heel fitting to the mast truck, she is 51·59 m *169 ¼ ft* in height. Built in 1933, the second of the four British J-class yachts, she is unusual in that she was the only one ever built that was not intended to race for the America's Cup. With a displacement of 145 tonnes, she supports a sail area of 7 500 ft² *16 140 ft²*.

Largest wreck The 312 186 deadweight tonnage VLCC (very large crude carrier) *Energy Determination* blew up and broke in two in the Straits of Hormuz on 12 Dec 1979. Her full value was $58 million.

The largest wreck removal was carried out in 1979 by Smit Tak International, who removed the remains of the French tanker *Betelgeuse*, 120 000 tons, from Bantry Bay, Republic of Ireland, within 20 months.

Most massive collision The closest approach to an irresistible force striking an immovable object occurred on 16 Dec 1977, 35 km *22 miles* off the coast of southern Africa, when the tanker *Venoil* (330 954 dwt) struck her sister ship *Venpet* (330 869 dwt).

OCEAN CROSSINGS

Earliest Atlantic The earliest crossing of the Atlantic by a power vessel, as opposed to an auxiliary-engined sailing ship, was a 22 day voyage begun in April 1827, from Rotterdam, Netherlands, to the West Indies, by the *Curaçao*. She was a 38·7 m *127 ft* wooden paddle boat of 438 tons, built as the *Calpe* in Dover, Kent in 1826 and purchased by the Dutch Government for the West Indian mail service.

■ **Fastest Atlantic crossing by the largest catamaran**
Under the rules of the Hales Trophy or 'Blue Riband' for Atlantic crossings, Hoverspeed Great Britain set the highest average speed at 36·966 knots between the Nantucket Light Buoy and Bishop Rock Lighthouse on 20–23 Jun 1990. She was launched in Tasmania on 28 Jan 1990 and made the record crossing during delivery to Hoverspeed. When in regular service between Dover and Calais/Boulogne she will be able to carry 450 passengers and 80 cars. (Photo: Gamma/Rossi)

The earliest Atlantic crossing entirely under steam (with intervals for desalting the boilers) was by HMS *Rhadamanthus*, from Plymouth, Devon to Barbados in 1832.

The earliest crossing under continuous steam power was by the condenser-fitted packet ship *Sirius*, 714 tonnes from Queenstown (now Cóbh) Republic of Ireland to Sandy Hook, New Jersey, USA, in 18 days 10 hr, from 4–22 Apr 1838.

Fastest Atlantic Under the rules of the Hales Trophy or 'Blue Riband', which recognize the highest average speed rather than the shortest duration, the record is held by *Hoverspeed Great Britain* with an average speed of 36·966 knots between the Nantucket Light Buoy and Bishop Rock Lighthouse on 20–23 Jun 1990. However, although she is a passenger vessel, *Hoverspeed Great Britain* is not intended for the North Atlantic, and traditionalists still feel that the Blue Riband should be held by the vessel making the best passge in regular liner service.

That distinction goes to the liner *United States* (then 51 988, now 38 216 gross tons), former flagship of the United States Lines. On her maiden voyage between 3–7 Jul 1952 from New York, USA to Le Havre, France and Southampton, Hants, she averaged 35·39 knots, *65·95 km/h* for three days 10 hr 40 min (6:36 p.m. GMT, 3 July to 5:16 a.m., 7 July) on a route of 5465 km *2949 nautical miles* from the Ambrose light vessel to the Bishop Rock lighthouse, Isles of Scilly, Cornwall. During this run, on 6–7 July, she steamed the greatest distance ever covered by any ship in a day's run (24 hr)— 1609 km *868 nautical miles*, hence averaging 36·17 knots *67·02 km/h*. The maximum speed attained from her 240 000 shaft horsepower engines was 38·32 knots *71·01 km/h* in trials on 9–10 Jun 1952.

Fastest Pacific The fastest crossing from Yokohama to Long Beach, California, USA (4840 nautical miles *8960 km*) took 6 days 1 hr 27 min (30 Jun–6 Jul 1973) by the container ship *Sea-Land Commerce* 50 315 tons, at an average speed of 33·27 knots *61·65 km/h*.

Fastest Channel crossing The English Channel was crossed by a commercial ferry in 52 min 49 sec from Dover, Kent to Calais, France by Townsend Thoresen's *Pride of Free Enterprise* in a near gale of Force 7 on 9 Feb 1982.

Water speed The highest speed ever achieved on water is an estimated *300 knots 556 km/h* by Kenneth Peter Warby (b. 9 May 1939) on the Blowering Dam Lake, New South Wales, Australia on 20 Nov 1977 in his unlimited hydroplane *Spirit of Australia*.

The official world water speed record is *277·57 knots 514·389 km/h* set on 8 Oct 1978 by Warby on Blowering Dam Lake.

Fiona, Countess of Arran (b. 1918) drove her 4·57 m *15 ft* three-point hydroplane *Stradag* (Gaelic 'The Spark') to the first world water speed record for electrically propelled powerboats at a speed of 83·64 km/h *51·973 mph*, at the National Water Sports Centre, Holme Pierrepoint, Nottingham, on 22 Nov 1989.

MERCHANT SHIPPING

Total The world total of merchant shipping, excluding vessels of less than 100 gross tonnage, sailing vessels and barges, was 423 627 198 gross tonnage on 1 Jul 1990.

Shipbuilding World-wide production completed in 1990 was 15·9 million gross tonnage of ships, excluding sailing ships, non-propelled vessels and vessels of less than 100 gross tonnage.

The figures for the USSR, Romania and the People's Republic of China are incomplete.

Japan completed 6·8 million gross tonnage (43 per cent of the world total) in 1990.

The world's leading shipbuilder in 1990 was Hyundai of South Korea, which completed 35 ships of 1·8 million gross tonnage.

Physically, the largest shipyard in the United Kingdom is Harland and Wolff of Queen's Island, Belfast, whose dry dock can accommodate up to 1 million tonnes deadweight. United Kingdom completions totalled 130 650 gross tonnage in 1990.

Biggest owner The largest ship owners are the Japanese NYK Group whose fleet of owned vessels totals 12 821 406 dwt tons.

Largest fleet The largest merchant fleet in the world at mid-1990 was that under the flag of Liberia with a fleet totalling 54 699 564 gross tonnage.

The UK figure for mid-1990 was 1998 ships of 6 716 325 gross tonnage.

PORTS

Largest The largest port in the world is the Port of New York and New Jersey, USA. The port has a navigable waterfront of 1215 km *755 miles* (474 km *295 miles* in New Jersey), stretching over 238 km² *92 miles²*. A total of 261 general cargo berths and 130 other piers gives a total berthing capacity of 391 ships at any one time. The total warehousing floor space is 170·9 ha *422·4 acres*.

Busiest The world's busiest port and largest artificial harbour is Rotterdam-Europoort in the Netherlands, which covers 100 km² *38 miles²*, with 122·3 km *76 miles* of quays. It handled 292 million tonnes of sea-going cargo in 1989 an increase of about 7 per cent on its 1988 figure.

Although the port of Singapore handled less tonnage, in terms of numbers of ships it was busier, with 36 000 ships calling there during 1988.

HOVERCRAFT (skirted air-cushion vehicles)

Earliest The ACV (air-cushion vehicle) was first made a practical proposition by Sir Christopher Sydney Cockerell (b. 4 Jun 1910), a British engineer who had the idea in 1954, published his Ripplecraft report 1/55 on 25 Oct 1955 and patented it on 12 Dec 1955.

The earliest patent relating to air-cushion craft was applied for in 1877 by John I. Thornycroft (1843–1928) of Chiswick, London, and the Finn Toivo Kaario developed the idea in 1935.

The first flight by a hovercraft was made by the 4 tonne Saunders-Roe SR-N1 at Cowes, Isle of Wight on 30 May 1959. With a 680 kg *1500 lb* thrust Viper turbojet engine, this craft reached 68 knots *126 km/h* in June 1961.

The first hovercraft public service was run across the Dee estuary, Scotland by the 60 knot *111 km/h* 24-passenger Vickers-Armstrong VA-3 between July and September 1962.

Largest The SRN4 Mk III, a British-built civil hovercraft weighs 305 tons and can accommodate 418 passengers and 60 cars. It is 56·38 m *185 ft* in length, and is powered by four Bristol Siddeley Marine Proteus engines, giving a maximum speed in excess of the scheduled permitted cross-Channel operating speed of 65 knots.

Fastest The world's fastest warship a hovercraft, is the 23·7 m *78 ft* long 100 tonnes US Navy test vehicle SES-100B. She reached a world record 91·9 knots *105·8 mph* on 25 Jan 1980 on the Chesapeake Bay Test Range, Maryland, USA. As a result of the success of this test craft, a 3000 tonnes US Navy Large Surface Effect Ship (LSES) was built by Bell Aerospace under contract from the Department of Defense in 1977–81.

Longest journey The longest hovercraft journey was one of 8047 km *5000 miles*, by the British Trans-African Hovercraft Expedition, under the leadership of David Smithers, through eight West African countries in a Winchester class SRN6, between 15 Oct 1969 and 3 Jan 1970.

Cross-Channel The fastest scheduled crossing of the Channel was achieved by an SRN 4 Mark II Mountbatten class Hovercraft, operated by Hoverspeed, on 1 Sep 1984, when *The Swift* completed the Dover-Calais run in 24 min 8·4 sec.

Highest The highest altitude reached by a Hovercraft was on 11 Jun 1990 when *Neste Enterprise* and her crew of ten reached the navigable source of the Yangtze river, China at 4983 m *16 050 ft*.

The greatest altitude at which a hovercraft is operating is on Lake Titicaca, Peru, where since 1975 an HM2 Hoverferry has been hovering 3811 m *12 506 ft* above sea level.

Road Vehicles

COACHING

Before the widespread use of tarred road surfaces from 1845, coaching was slow and hazardous. The zenith was reached on 13 Jul 1888 when J. Selby Esq. drove the *Old Times* coach 173 km *108 miles* from London to Brighton and back with eight teams and 14 changes in 7 hr 50 min, to average 22·19 km/h *13·79 mph*. Four-horse carriages could maintain a speed of 34 km/h *21⅓ mph* for nearly an hour.

The *Border Union* stage coach, built *c.* 1825, ran four in hand from Edinburgh to London (632 km *393 miles*). When it ceased in 1842, due to competition from railways, the allowed schedule was 42 hr 23 min to average better than 14·9 km/h *9 ¼ mph*.

The record for changing a team of four horses by a team of 12 ostlers is 21·32 sec, set at Donnington Race Circuit, Leics, on 9 Aug 1990, for the Norwich Union Charity Mail Coach team led by driver John Parker.

The longest horse-drawn procession was a cavalcade of 68 carriages which measured 'nose to tail' 920 m *3018 ft*, organized by the Spies Travelling Company of Denmark on 7 May 1986. It carried 810 people through the woods around Copenhagen to celebrate the coming of spring.

MOTOR CARS

The number of vehicles constructed worldwide in 1989 was 485 607 800, of which 35 057 630 were motor cars.

The UK production figure for 1989 was 1 505 019.

The world's largest manufacturer of motor vehicles and parts (and the largest manufacturing company) is General Motors Corporation of Detroit, Michigan, USA. The company has on average 761 400 employees and revenues for 1990 were $126 billion producing 5 571 905 vehicles.

The largest British manufacturer is the Rover Group plc, which produced 501 300 vehicles in 1990 and had sales of £3·8 billion, of which £1·2 billion were overseas sales. The company produced four out of every 10 cars built in Britain and accounted for nearly half of the number of cars exported from the UK.

Largest plant The largest single motor car plant in the world is the Volkswagenwerk at Wolfsburg, Germany, with 61 000 employees and a capacity for 4100 vehicles daily. The factory buildings cover an area of 150 ha *371 acres* and the whole plant covers 760 ha *1878 acres*, with 70 km *43·5 miles* of rail sidings.

Salesmanship The all-time record for automobile sales in units sold individually is 1425 in 1973 by Joe Girard of Detroit, Michigan, USA. His lifetime total of one-at-a-time selling was 13 001 sales, all retail, with a record 174 in a month and he averaged six sales per day.

Earliest automobiles *Model* The earliest automobile of which there is a record is a two-foot-long steam-powered model constructed by Ferdinand Verbiest (died 1687), a Belgian Jesuit priest, and described in his *Astronomia Europaea*. His model of 1668 was possibly inspired either by Giovanni Branca's description of a steam turbine, published in his *La Macchina* in 1629, or by Nan Huai-Jen (writings on 'fire carts') in the Chu dynasty (*c.* 800 BC).

Passenger-carrying The earliest full-scale automobile was the first of two military steam tractors, completed at the Paris Arsenal in 1769 by Nicolas-Joseph Cugnot (1725–1804). This reached 3·6 km/h *2 ¼ mph*. Cugnot's second, larger tractor, completed in May 1771, today survives in the Conservatoire Nationale des Arts et Métiers in Paris.

The world's first passenger-carrying automobile was a steam-powered road vehicle carrying eight passengers and built by Richard Trevithick (1771–1833). It first ran on 24 Dec 1801 in Camborne, Cornwall.

Internal combustion The Swiss Isaac de Rivaz (died 1828) built a carriage powered by his 'explosion engine' in 1805. The first practical internal combustion engined vehicle was that built by the Londoner Samuel Brown (Brit. Pat. No. 5350,

FASTEST CARS

CATEGORY	KM/H	MPH	CAR	DRIVER	PLACE	DATE
JET ENGINED official	1019·4	*633·468*	Thrust 2	Richard Noble (GB)	Black Rock Desert, Nevada, USA	4 Oct 1983
ROCKET ENGINED official	1001·473	*622·287*	Blue Flame	Gary Gabelich (USA)	Bonneville, Utah, USA	23 Oct 1970
unofficial*	1190·377	*739·666*	Budweiser Rocket	Stan Barrett (USA)	Edwards Air Force Base, California, USA	17 Dec 1979
WHEEL DRIVEN turbine	690·909	*429·311*	Bluebird	Donald Campbell (UK)	Lake Eyre, Australia	17 Jul 1964
multi piston engine	673·516	*418·504*	Goldenrod	Robert Summers (USA)	Bonneville, Utah, USA	12 Nov 1965
single piston engine	640·446	*397·996*	Speed O Motive	Al Teague (USA)	Bonneville, Utah, USA	9 Nov 1989

* This published speed of Mach 1·0106 is *not* officially sanctioned by the USAF whose Digital Instrumented Radar was not calibrated or certified. The radar information was *not* generated by the vehicle directly but by an operator aiming the dish by means of a TV screen. To claim a speed to 6 significant figures appears quite unsustainable.

Registrations

The world's first plates were introduced by the Paris police in 1893.

Registration plates were introduced in Britain in 1903.

The original A1 plate was secured by the 2nd Earl Russell (1865–1931) for his 12 hp Napier. This plate, willed in September 1950 to Trevor T. Laker of Leicester, was sold in August 1959 for £2500 in aid of charity.

Licence plate No. 8 was sold at a Hong Kong government auction for HK$5 million on 13 Feb 1988 to Law Ting-pong, a textile manufacturer. The number 8 is considered a lucky number.

Longest car

A 30·48 m *100 ft* long 26-wheeled limo was designed by Jay Ohrberg of Burbank, California, USA. It has many features, including a swimming pool, diving board and a king-sized water bed. It is designed to drive as one piece or it can be changed to bend in the middle. Its main purpose is for use in films and exhibitions.

■ Heaviest car

The heaviest car in production today is the Soviet-built ZIL-41047. It weighs 3335 kg 7 352 lb can carry seven passengers comfortably and uses a gallon of petrol every 13 miles 20·92 km. (Photo: Gamma/Brissaud)

25 Apr 1826), whose 2·9 kW *4 hp* two-cylinder atmospheric gas 88 litre engined carriage climbed Shooters Hill, Blackheath, Kent in May 1826.

Britain's continuous motoring history started in November 1894 when Henry Hewetson drove his imported Benz Velo in the south-eastern suburbs of London.

The first successful petrol-driven car, the Motorwagen, built by Karl-Friedrich Benz (1844–1929) of Karlsruhe, Germany, ran at Mannheim, in late 1885. It was a 230 kg *3 cwt* three-wheeler reaching 13–16 km/h *8–10 mph*. Its single-cylinder engine (bore 91·4 mm *3·6 in*, stroke 160 mm *6·3 in*) delivered 0·63 kW *0·85 hp* at 400 rpm. It was patented on 29 Jan 1886. Its first 1 km *1·62 mile* road test was reported in the local newspaper, the *Neue Badische Landeszeitung*, of 4 Jun 1886, under the heading 'Miscellaneous'.

FASTEST CARS

Land speed The *official* one-mile land-speed record is 1019·467 km/h *633·468 mph*, set by Richard Noble (b. 1946) on 4 Oct 1983 over the Black Rock Desert, Nevada, USA in his 17 000 lb thrust Rolls-Royce Avon 302 jet-powered *Thrust 2*, designed by John Ackroyd (see also table).

The highest reputed land speed record in one direction is 1190·377 km/h *739·666 mph* or Mach 1·0106 by Stan Barrett (USA) in the *Budweiser Rocket*, a rocket-engined three-wheeled car, at Edwards Air Force Base, California, USA on 17 Dec 1979 (see also table).

The highest land speed attained in Britain is 424·74 km/h *263·92 mph* by Richard Noble in *Thrust* at Greenham Common, Berks on 25 Sep 1980.

The highest land speed recorded by a woman is 843·323 km/h *524·016 mph* by Mrs Kitty Hambleton, *née* O'Neil (USA) in the 48 000-hp rocket-powered three-wheeled SM1 *Motivator* over the Alvard Desert, Oregon, USA on 6 Dec 1976. Her official two-way record was 825·126 km/h *512·710 mph* and she probably touched 965 km/h *600 mph* momentarily.

Diesel engined The prototype 3 litre Mercedes C 111/3 attained 327·3 km/h *203·3 mph* in tests on the Nardo Circuit, southern Italy on 5–15 Oct 1978, and in April 1978 averaged 314·462 km/h *195·398 mph* for 12 hours, so covering a world record 3773·55 km *2399·76 miles*.

Rocket-powered sleds The highest speed recorded on ice is 399·00 km/h *247·93 mph* by *Oxygen*, driven by Sammy Miller (b. 15 Apr 1945) on Lake George, New York, USA on 15 Feb 1981.

Electric car The land speed record for an electric car over a distance of 1 km flying start was achieved by Christopher Sleath of Market Harborough, Leics with a speed of 62·18 mph, at Bruntingthorpe Training Ground, Leics on 25 Jun 1990.

The land speed record was last broken in an electric car by Camille Jenatzy in *La Jamais Contente* in April 1899 with a speed of 65·79 mph over a flying kilometer in one direction. Ninety years later this was beaten by D. J. S Lambert in a replica of the original car with a speed of 67·62 mph, at RAF Elvington, N Yorks on 25 Mar 1989.

Steam car On 19 Aug 1985 Robert E. Barber broke the 79-year-old record for a steam car No. 744 *Steamin' Demon*, built by the Barber-Nichols Engineering Co. which reached 234·33 km/h *145·607 mph* at Bonneville Salt Flats, Utah, USA.

Road cars Various de-tuned track cars have been licensed for road use but are not normal production models.

Lamborghini asserted a speed of 325 km/h *202 mph* for their Diablo at the Nardo Test Track, Italy, reported in March 1990.

The highest road-tested acceleration reported is 0–96·5 km/h *0–60 mph* in 3·98 sec for a Ferrari F-40 owned by Nick Mason and driven by Mark Hales of *Fast Lane* magazine at Millbrook, Beds on 9 Feb 1989.

The fastest lap on a UK circuit by a production car was achieved by a Ferrari Testarossa at 275·19 km/h *171 mph* with a peak speed of 280·01 km/h *174 mph* at Millbrook, Beds on 12 Dec 1988. The car was driven by Howard Lees of *Autocar & Motor* Magazine.

LARGEST CARS

Of cars produced for private use, the largest was the Bugatti 'Royale' type 41, known in Britain as the 'Golden Bugatti', of which only six were assembled at Molsheim, France by the Italian Ettore Bugatti. First built in 1927, this machine has an eight-cylinder engine of 12·7 litres capacity, and measures over 6·7 m *22 ft* in length. The bonnet is over 2 m *7 ft* long.

Largest engines The largest car ever used was the 'White Triplex', sponsored by J.H. White of Philadelphia, Pennsylvania,

USA. Completed early in 1928, after two years' work, the car weighed about 4·06 tonnes and was powered by three Liberty V12 aircraft engines with a total capacity of 81188 cc, developing 1119 kW *1500 bhp* at 2000 rpm. It was used to break the world speed record but crashed at Daytona, Florida, USA on 13 Mar 1929.

Most powerful *Production car* The highest engine capacity of a production car was 13·5 litres, for the US Pierce-Arrow 6–66 Raceabout of 1912–18, the US Peerless 6–60 of 1912–14 and the Fageol of 1918.

The most powerful current production car is the Cizeta V16T, which develops 388 kW *520 bhp*.

Heaviest The heaviest car in production today (up to twenty-five made annually) appears to be the Soviet-built Zil–41047 limousine with a 3·88 m *12·72 ft* wheel-base. It weighs 3335 kg *7 352 lb*. The 'stretched' Zil (four to five made annually) and used by President Mikail Gorbachev weighs 6 tonnes and is made of three-inch armour-plated steel. The eight-cylinder, 7-litre engine guzzles fuel at the rate of 6 miles to the gallon.

MISCELLANEOUS CARS

Highest mileage The highest recorded mileage for a car was 1 906 879 km *1 184 880 miles* by August 1978 for a 1957 Mercedes 180 D owned by Robert O'Reilly of Olympia, Washington State, USA. Its subsequent fate is unknown.

Longest in production The Morgan 4/4 celebrated its 55th birthday on 27 Dec 1990. Built by the Morgan Motor Car Co. of Malvern, Hereford & Worcester (founded 1910), there is still a six to eight-year waiting list.

Among mass-production models, the Volkswagen 'Beetle' date from 1938.

The 'Beetle' production now exceeds 20·8 million, the Mexican's still produce it.

Britain's champion seller has been the Mini, designed by Sir Alec Issigonis (1906–88), which originally sold for £496 19s 2d in August 1959.

Lightest Louis Borsi of London has built and driven a 9·5 kg *21 lb* car with a 2·5 cc engine. It is capable of 25 km/h *15 mph*.

MOST EXPENSIVE

Special The most expensive car ever built was the US Presidential 1969 Lincoln Continental Executive delivered to the US Secret Service on 14 Oct 1968. It has an overall length of 6·56 m *21 ft 6·3 in* with a 4·06 m *13 ft 4 in* wheel-base and with the addition of 2·03 tonnes of armour plate, weighs 5·443 tonnes (5443 kg *12 000 lb*). The estimated cost of research, development and manufacture was $500 000, but it is rented at $5000 per annum. Even if all four tyres were shot out it can travel at 80 km/h *50 mph* on inner rubber-edged steel discs.

In March 1979 Carriage House Motor Cars of New York, USA completed four years' work on converting a 1973 Rolls-Royce, including lengthening it by 76·2 cm *30 in*. The price tag was $500 000.

Standard The most expensive list-price British standard car is the Rolls-Royce eight-cylinder 6750 cc Phantom VI, quoted at £350 000 (including tax). More expensive are custom-built models.

The unrivalled collector of Rolls-Royces was Bhagwan Shree Rajneesh (Osho) (born Chandra Mohan Jain) (1931–90), the Indian mystic of Rajneeshpuram, Oregon, USA. His disciples bestowed 93 of these

upon him before his deportation in November 1985.

Used Although higher prices have been reported for sales by private treaty, the greatest price paid at a public auction was £6·4 million (including commission) for a 1962 Ferrari 250 GTO sold by Sothebys on 22 May 1990 at Monte Carlo, Monaco. It was bought by Hans Thulin (Sweden).

Most inexpensive The cheapest car of all time was the 1922 Red Bug Buckboard, built by the Briggs & Stratton Co. of Milwaukee, Wisconsin, USA, listed at $150–$125. It had a 1·57 m *62 in* wheel-base and weighed 111 kg *245 lb*. Early models of the King Midget cars were sold in kit form for self-assembly for as little as $100 in 1948.

In May 1991 the cheapest listed new car in Britain was for the Polish FSO 1300 at £3166.

DRIVING

Round the world The fastest circumnavigation embracing more than an equator's length of driving (41 967 km *26 078 road miles*) is one of 39 days 23 hr 35 min. Driving two Rover 827Si Saloon cars, six members (three male and three female) of the Transworld Venture organized by the Royal Army Ordnance Corps left the Tower of London on 13 May and returned to the same place on 22 Jun 1990. On their epic journey they travelled through six continents and covered 25 countries. The distance covered was 40 534·7 km *25 187·8 miles*.

Amphibious circumnavigation The only circumnavigation by an amphibious vehicle was by Ben Carlin (Australia) (died 7 Mar 1981) in the amphibious jeep, *Half-Safe*. He completed the last leg of the Atlantic crossing (the English Channel) on 24 Aug 1951. He arrived back in Montreal, Canada on 8 May 1958, having completed a circumnavigation of 62 765 km *39 000 miles* over land and 15 450 km *9600 miles* by sea and river. He was accompanied on the transatlantic stage by his ex-wife Elinore (USA) and on the long trans-Pacific stage (Tokyo to Anchorage, Alaska) by Broye Lafayette De-Mente (b. Missouri, 1928).

One-year duration record The greatest distance ever covered in one year is 573 029 km *354 257 miles* by two Opel Rekord 2-litre passenger sedans, both of which covered this distance between 18 May 1988 and the same date in 1989 without any major mechanical breakdowns. The vehicles were manufactured by the Delta Motor Corporation, Port Elizabeth, South Africa, and were driven on tar and gravel roads in the Northern Cape by a team of company drivers from Delta. The entire undertaking was monitored by the Automobile Association of South Africa.

Trans-Americas Garry Sowerby (Canada), with Tim Cahill (USA) as co-driver and navigator, drove a 1988 GMC Sierra K3500 four-wheel-drive pick-up truck powered by a 6·2 litre V8 Detroit diesel engine from Ushuaia, Tierra del Fuego, Argentina to Prudhoe Bay, Alaska, USA, a distance of 23 720 km *14 739 miles*, in a total elapsed time of 23 days 22 hr 43 min from 29 Sep to 22 Oct 1987. The vehicle and team were surface freighted from Cartagena, Colombia to Balboa, Panama so as to by-pass the Darien Gap.

The Darién Gap was first traversed by the Land-Rover *La Cucaracha Carinosa* (The Affectionate Cockroach) of the Trans-Darién Expedition 1959–60, crewed by former SAS man Richard E. Bevir (UK) and engineer Terence John Whitfield (Australia). They left Chepo, Panama on 3 Feb 1960 and reached Quibdó, Colombia on 17 June, averaging 201 m *220 yd* per hour of indescribable difficulty.

Cape to London The record time for the 18 787 km *11 674 mile* road route from Cape Town, South Africa to London is 14 days 19 hr 26 min, set by husband and wife team Brig John and Dr Lucy Hemsley from 8–22 Jan 1983 in a Range Rover. Apart from the Channel crossing they were the first to drive entirely overland from Cape Town, to London.

British counties June Laird (driver-/leader) together with Jim Laird of Buxton, Derbys and Robert Nottger of Pitlochry, Scotland (drivers) completed a tour of the 72 counties of the United Kingdom, covering a distance of 4131·2 km *2582 miles* in the

Car wrecking
The greatest number of cars wrecked in a stunting career is 1997 to 1 Jun 1990 by Dick Sheppard of Gloucester.

Ramp jumping
The longest ramp jump in a car, with the car landing on its wheels and being driven on, is 70·73 m *232 ft*, is by Jacqueline De Creed (*née* Creedy) in a 1967 Ford Mustang at Santa Pod Raceway, Beds on 3 Apr 1983.

Driving tests
The record for persistence in taking the Department of Transport's driving test is held by Mrs Git Kaur Randhawa (b. 7 Feb 1937) of Hayes, Middlesex, who triumphed at her 48th attempt, after more than 330 lessons, on 19 Jun 1987.

The world's easiest tests have been those in Egypt, in which the ability to drive 6 m *19·64 ft* forward and the same in reverse has been deemed sufficient. In 1979 it was reported that accurate reversing between two rubber traffic cones had been added. 'High cone attrition' soon led to the substitution of white lines.

record time of 97 hr 35 min. Their journey commenced on 21 Jul 1989 at Lerwick, Shetland Islands and finished on 25 Jul 1989 at Stornoway, Lewis.

Around Ireland
June and Tony Laird (drivers) together with Jim Laird (navigator), all of Buxton, Derbys drove around the 32 counties of northern and southern Ireland in a time of 17 hr 57 min on 3–4 Aug 1990, covering a distance of 1149·04 km *714 miles* an average speed of 39·78 mph.

Round Britain economy
A diesel-powered Ford 1800 Fiesta was driven by Anne Gotto, Monica Fisher and John Taylor around a 5853 km *3637 mile* course from 30 September to 5 Oct 1990 returning a fuel consumption of 38·796 km/litre *93·746 mpg*.

Petrol consumption
An experimental Japanese vehicle achieved the equivalent of 2269 lm/litre *6409 mpg* in the Shell Mileage Marathon at Silverstone, Northants on 30 Jun 1988.

Most economical
Amongst production cars available in the United Kingdom both Citroen AX 14DTR and the Daihatsu Charade Diesel Turbo could make this claim. The Department of Transport figures are: Citroen 54·3 mpg (urban cycle), 78·5 mpg (steady 56 mph), 56.5 mpg (steady 75 mph); Daihatsu 57.6 mpg (urban cycle) 78·5 mpg (steady 56 mph), 49·6 (steady 75 mph). (*Because of current standard practice metric figures have not been added*). On 9 Aug 1989 motoring writer Stuart Bladon drove a Citroen AX 14DTR a distance of 180·26 km *112·01 miles* using one gallon of fuel driving on the M11 Motorway in a test run arranged by Lucas Diesel Systems.

Longest fuel range
The greatest distance driven without refuelling on a single fuel fill in a standard vehicle (185·1 litre *40·7 gal* carried in factory optional twin fuel tanks) is 2315·9 km *1438·2 miles* by a 1990 Toyota LandCruiser diesel pick-up. Driven by Ewan Kennedy and Ray Barker with Ian Lee (observer) from Perth, Western Australia to Port Augusta, South Australia in 31 hr 51 min in September 1990, the average speed was 72·7 km/h *45·2 mph*, giving 35·3 mpg *8·0 litres/100km*.

Mountain driving
Vehicles have been driven up Ben Nevis, Inverness-shire, Scotland (1343 m *4406 ft*) on six occasions. The record times are 7 hr 23 min (ascent) and 1 hr 55 min (descent) by George F. Simpson in an Austin 7 on 6 Oct 1928. Henry Alexander accomplished the feat twice in May 1911 (Model T Ford) and on 13 Sep 1928 (Model A Ford).

The most recent ascent was on 11 Sep 1987 when two Suzuki four-wheel ATV Quad Runner vehicles drove from Old Inverlochy Castle to the summit in 2 hr 21 min. They were driven by Jerome Fack of Wadebridge, Cornwall, Paul Hunt of Egham, Surrey, David Kirke of London and Rod Shand of Fort William, Scotland.

Driving in reverse
Charles Creighton (1908–70) and James Hargis of Maplewood, Missouri, USA drove their Model A Ford 1929 roadster in reverse from New York, USA 5375 km *3340 miles* to Los Angeles, California, from 26 Jul–13 Aug 1930 without once stopping the engine. They arrived back in New York in reverse on 5 September, so completing 11 555 km *7180 miles* in 42 days.

The highest average speed attained in any non-stop reverse drive exceeding 800 km *500 miles* was achieved by Gerald Hoagland, who drove a 1969 Chevrolet Impala 806·2 km *501 miles* in 17 hr 38 min at Chemung Speed Drome, New York, USA on 9–10 Jul 1976, to average 45·72 km/h *28·41 mph*.

Brian 'Cub' Keene and James 'Wilbur' Wright drove their Chevrolet Blazer 14 533 km *9031 miles* in 37 days (1 Aug–6 Sep 1984) through 15 US states and Canada. Though it was prominently named 'Stuck in Reverse', law enforcement officers in Oklahoma refused to believe it and insisted they drove in reverse reverse, i.e. forwards, out of the state.

Battery-powered vehicle
Robert Dodds and Ian Pridding with the support of the Pontllanfraith Rotary Club travelled 1479 km *919 miles* from John o' Groats, Highland to Land's End, Cornwall in a Sinclair C5 in 80 hr 47 min from 18–21 May 1987.

David Turner and Tim Pickhard of Turners of Boscastle Ltd, Cornwall, travelled 1408 km *875 miles* from Land's End to John o' Groats in 63 hours in a Freight Rover Leyland Sherpa powered by a Lucas electric motor from 21–23 Dec 1985.

Two-side-wheel driving
Car Bengt Norberg (b. 23 Oct 1951) of Äppelbo, Sweden drove a Mitsubishi Colt GTi-16V on two side wheels non-stop for a distance of 310·391 km *192·873 miles* in a time of 7 hr 15 min 50 sec. He also achieved a distance of 44·805 km *30·328 miles* in 1 hr at Rattvik Horse Track, Sweden on 24 May 1989.

Sven-Erik Söderman (b. 26 Sep 1960) achieved a speed of 164·38 km/h *102·14 mph* over a 100 m flying start on the two wheels of a Opel Kadette at Mora Siljan airport, Dalecarlia, Sweden on 2 Aug 1990. Söderman also broke the 1000 m flying kilometre at 152·96 km/h *95·04 mph* at the same venue on 24 Aug 1990.

Truck Sven-Erik Söderman of Sweden drove a Daf 2800 7·5 ton truck on two wheels for a distance of 9·5 km *5·90 miles* at Mora Siljan airport, Delecarlia, Sweden on 10 Nov 1990.

Bus Bobby Ore (b. Jan 1949) drove a double-decker bus a distance of 246 m *810 ft* on two-wheels at North Weald airfield, Essex on 21 May 1988.

Wheelie
Steve Murty drove a Multi-Part Skytrain truck on its rear wheels for 412·5 m *1353 ⅓ ft* at Mondello Park, Co. Kildare, Republic of Ireland on 23 Aug 1987. The 60-ton truck was powered by a 373 kW *500 bhp* Cummins turbo-charged 14-litre engine and had a ZF-Ecomat 600 hp five-speed automatic gearbox.

Most durable driver
The Goodyear Tire and Rubber Co. test driver Weldon C. Kocich drove 5 056 470 km *3 141 946 miles* from 5 Feb 1953 to 28 Feb 1986, so averaging 153 226 km *95 210 miles* per year.

Oldest driver
Roy M. Rawlins (b. 10 Jul 1870) of Stockton, California, USA was warned for driving at 152 km/h *95 mph* in a 88·5 km/h *55 mph* zone in June 1974. On 25 Aug 1974 he was awarded a California State licence valid until 1978, but Mr Rawlins died on 9 Jul 1975, one day short of his 105th birthday.

Mrs Maude Tull of Inglewood, California, USA, who took to driving aged 91 after her husband died, was issued a renewal on 5 Feb 1976 when aged 104.

Britain's oldest known drivers have been Benjamin Kagan (1878–1988) of Leeds and Rev. Albert Thomas Humphrey (1886–1988) from Pawlett, near Bridgwater, Somerset, both drove up to the age of 102.

The greatest age at which a man has first passed the Department of Transport driving test has been 89 years 2 months by David Coupar (b. 9 Feb 1898) on 4 Mar 1987 in Perth, Perthshire.

The oldest woman to pass was Mrs Gerty Edwards Land (b. 9 Sep 1897) on 27 Apr 1988 in Colne, Lancs. She was aged 90 years 229 days.

Currently Britain's oldest known driver is John Roland Powers (b. 19 Apr 1891) of Westwood Heath, Warks, who was still driving when he celebrated his 100th birthday in April.

The holder of the earliest driving licence to be issued in Britain was Mr Reginald 'Gerry' Bond (1889–1989) of Bournemouth, Dorset, whose first licence was dated October 1907.

Youngest driver
Instances of drivers under the age of 17 have been recorded in HM Armed Forces. Mrs P.L.M. Williams (b. 3 Feb 1926), now of Risca, Gwent, as Private Patterson in the ATS drove a 5-ton truck in 1941 aged 15.

Stephen Andrew Blackbourn of Lincoln, Lincs having passed his driving test on his 17th birthday, went on to pass the advanced test less than five hours later on 20 Feb 1989. His brother Mark previously held the record.

SERVICES

Car parks
The world's largest is the West Edmonton Mall, Edmonton, Alberta, Canada, which can hold 20 000 vehicles. There are overflow facilities on an adjoining lot for 10 000 more cars.

The largest parking area in Great Britain is that for 15 000 cars and 200 coaches at the National Exhibition Centre, Birmingham (see p.123).

Britain's highest-capacity underground car park is under the Victoria Centre, Nottingham, with space for 1650 cars, opened in June 1972.

Garage
The largest private garage is one of two storeys built outside Bombay for the private collection of 176 cars owned by Pranlal Bhogilal (b. 1939).

The KMB Overhaul Centre, operated by the Kowloon Motor Bus Co. (1933) Ltd, Hong Kong, is the world's largest multi-storey service centre. Purpose built for double decker buses, its four floors occupy in excess of 47·000 m² *11·6 acres*.

Filling stations
The largest concentration of pumps are 204—96 of them Tokheim Unistar (electronic) and 108 Tokheim Explorer (mechanical)—in Jeddah, Saudi Arabia.

The highest filling station in the world is at Leh, Ladakh, India, at 3658 m *12 001 ft*, operated by the Indian Oil Corporation.

The largest filling station of the 20 016 in the United Kingdom is the Esso service area on the M4 at Leigh Delamere, Wilts, opened on 3 Jan 1972. It has 48 petrol and diesel pumps and extends over 17·4 ha *43 acres*.

The commonest brand of petrol in the United Kingdom is Shell, with 2886 retail outlets. The oldest of the 46 motorway service stations is Watford Gap on the M1, opened on 2 Nov 1959.

Tow The longest on record was one of 7658 km *4759 miles* from Halifax, Nova Scotia to Canada's Pacific coast, when Frank J. Elliott and George A. Scott of Amherst, Nova Scotia, Canada persuaded 168 passing motorists in 89 days to tow their Model T Ford (in fact engineless) to win a $1000 bet on 15 Oct 1927.

After his 1969 MGB, broke down in the vicinity of Moscow, USSR, the late Eddie McGowan of Chipping Warden, Oxforshire was towed a distance 2343 km *1456 miles* from Moscow to West Berlin on a 2 m *7 ft* single nylon tow rope from 12–17 Jul 1987.

Tyres *Largest* The world's largest ever manufactured were by the Goodyear Tire & Rubber Co. for giant dumper trucks. They measure 3·65 m *12 ft* in diameter, weigh 5670 kg *12 500 lb* and cost $74 000. A tyre 5·18 m *17 ft* in diameter is believed to be the limitation of what is practical.

Fattest The widest tyre in normal production is the Pirelli P Zero with 335/35 ZR 17 dimensions.

Skid marks The longest recorded on a public road have been those 290 m *950 ft* long left by a Jaguar car involved in an accident on the M1 near Luton, Beds, on 30 Jun 1960. Evidence given in the subsequent High Court case *Hurlock* v. *Inglis et al.* indicated a speed 'in excess of 160 km/h *100 mph*' before the application of the brakes'.

The skid marks made by the jet-powered *Spirit of America*, driven by Norman Craig Breedlove, after the car went out of control at Bonneville Salt Flats, Utah, USA, on 15 Oct 1964, were nearly 9·6 km *6 miles* long.

VEHICLES

Land *Largest* The most massive auto-motive land vehicle is 'Big Muskie', the 10 890 tonnes mechanical shovel built by Bucyrus Erie for the Musk mine. It is 148·43 m *487 ft* long, 46·02 m *151 ft* wide and 67·66 m *222 ft* high, with a grab capacity of 325 tons.

Longest The Arctic Snow Train owned by the world-famous wire-walker Steve McPeak (USA) has 54 wheels and is 174·3 m *572 ft* long. It was built by R. G. Le Tourneau Inc. of Longview, Texas, USA for the US Army. Its gross train weight is 400 tons, with a top speed of 32 km/h *20 mph*, and it was driven by a crew of six when used as an 'overland train' for the military. McPeak undertook all repairs including every punctured wheel single-handed in often sub-zero temperatures in Alaska. It generates 4 680 shaft horsepower and has a fuel capacity of 29 648 litres *6522 gal.*

Largest ambulance The world's largest are the 18 m *59 ft 0 ½ in* long articulated Alligator Jumbulances Marks VI, VII, VIII and IX, operated by the ACROSS Trust to convey the sick and handicapped on holidays and pilgrimages across Europe. They are built by Van Hool of Belgium with Fiat engines, cost £200 000 and carry 44 patients and staff.

Crawler The most massive vehicle ever constructed is the Marion eight-caterpillar crawler used for conveying Saturn V rockets to their launch pads at Cape Canaveral, Florida, USA. It measures 40 × 34·7 m *131 ft 4 in × 114 ft* and the two built cost $12·3 million. The loaded train weight is 8165 tonnes .

The windscreen wiper blades are 106 cm *42 in* long and are the world's largest.

Buses *Earliest* The first municipal motor omnibus service in the world was inaugurated on 12 Apr 1903 and ran between Eastbourne railway station and Meads, E Sussex.

Longest The longest are the articulated buses, with 121 passenger seats and room also for 66 'strap-hangers', built by the Wayne Corporation of Richmond, Indiana, USA for use in the Middle East. They are 23·16 m *76 ft* long and weigh 10 870 kg *10·72 ton.*

The longest rigid single bus is 14·96 m *49 ft* long and carries 69 passengers. It was built by Van Hool of Belgium.

Largest fleet The 6580 single-decker buses in Rio de Janeiro, Brazil make up the world's largest bus fleet.

Of the London fleet of 4803 buses, 4120 are double-deckers.

Longest route The longest regularly scheduled bus route is operated by 'Across Australia Coach Lines', who inaugurated a regular scheduled service between Perth and Brisbane on 9 Apr 1980. The route is 5455 km *3389 miles* long, taking 75 hr 55 min.

The longest route in Great Britain is 1089 km *677 miles* between Plymouth, Devon and Aberdeen, Scotland. The No. 806 service is operated jointly by Western National Ltd and Northern Scottish Omnibuses Ltd, each company allocating coaches on alternate days.

Caravans *Largest* The largest two-wheeled two-storey caravan was built in 1990 by H.E Sheik Hamad Bin Hamdan Al Nahyan of Abu Dhabi, United Arab Emirates. It is 20 m *66 ft* long, 12 m *39·37 ft* wide and weighs 120 tons. There are eight bedrooms and bathrooms and four garages and water storage for 24 000 litres *5 279 gal.*

Longest journey The continuous motor caravan journey of 231 288 km *143 716 miles* by Harry B. Coleman and Peggy Larson in a Volkswagen Camper from 20 Aug 1976 to 20 Apr 1978 took them through 113 countries.

Fastest The world speed record for a caravan is 201·02 km/h *124·91 mph* by an Alpha 14 towed by a Le Mans Aston Martin V8 saloon driven by Robin Hamilton, at RAF Elvington, N Yorks on 14 Oct 1980.

Dumper truck The world's largest is the Terex Titan 33–19 manufactured by General Motors Corporation and now in operation at Westar Mine, British Columbia, Canada. It has a loaded weight of 548·6 tonnes *539·9 tons* and a capacity of 317·5 tonnes. When tipping its height is 17·06 m *56 ft*. The 16-cylinder engine delivers 2462 kW *3300 hp*. The fuel tank holds 5904·6 litres *1300 gal.*

Fire engines The world's most powerful fire appliance is the 641·5 kW *860 hp* eight-wheel Oshkosh firetruck used for aircraft fires. It can discharge 190 000 litres *41 600 gal* of foam through two turrets in just 150 sec. It weighs 60 tonnes.

Fastest The fastest on record is the

PROGRESSIVE SPEED RECORDS

Speed km/h	mph	Person and Vehicle	Place	Date
40	*25*	Sledging	Heinola, Finland	c.6500 BC
55	*35*	Horse-riding	Anatolia, Turkey	c.1400 BC
70	*45*	Mountain Sledging	Island of Hawaii (now USA)	ante AD 1500
80	*50*	Ice Yachts (earliest patent)	Netherlands	AD 1600
95	*56·75*	Grand Junction Railway 2–2–2: *Lucifer*	Madeley Banks, Staffs, England	13 Nov 1830
141·3	*87·8*	Tommy Todd, downhill skier	La Porte, California, USA	March 1873
144·8	*90·0*	Midland Railway 4–2–2 2·36 m *7 ft 9 in* single	Ampthill, Bedford, England	March 1897
210·2	*130·61*	Siemens & Halske electric engine	Marienfeld-Zossen, near Berlin	27 Oct 1903
c.257·5	*c.150*	Frederick H. Marriott (*fl.* 1957) Stanley Steamer *Wogglebug*	Ormond Beach, Florida, USA	26 Jan 1907
339	*210·64*	Sadi Lecointe (France) Nieuport-Delage 29	Villesauvage, France	25 Sep 1924
668·2	*415·2*	Flt Lt (Later Wing Cdr) George Hedley Stainforth AFC *Supermarine S.6B*	Lee-on-Solent, England	29 Sep 1931
1004	*623·85*	Flugkapitan Heinz Dittmar Me. 163V–1	Peenemunde, Germany	2 Oct 1941
1078	*670*	Capt Charles Elwood Yeager, USAF Bell XS–1	Muroc Dry Lake, California, USA	14 Oct 1947
1556	*967*	Capt Charles Elwood Yeager, USAF Bell XS–1	Muroc Dry Lake, California, USA	26 Mar 1948
4675·1	*2905*	Maj Robert M. White, North American X–15	Muroc Dry Lake, California, USA	7 Mar 1961
c.28 260	*c.17 560*	Flt Maj Yuriy Alekseyevich Gagarin, *Vostok I*	Earth orbit	12 Apr 1961
38 988	*24 226*	Col Frank Borman, USAF, Capt James Arthur Lovell, Jr, USN, Maj William A. Anders, USAF *Apollo VIII*	Trans-lunar injection	21 Dec 1968
897	*24 790·8*	Cdrs Eugene Andrew Cernan and John Watts Young, USN and Col Thomas P. Stafford, USAF *Apollo X*	Re-entry after lunar orbit	26 May 1969

A complete progressive table comprising entries from prehistoric times to date was published in the 1977 edition.

ROAD VEHICLES

Lawn mowers

The widest gang mower in the world is the 5 ton 18·28 m *60 ft* wide 27-unit 'Big Green Machine' used by the turf farmer Jay Edgar Frick of Monroe, Ohio, USA. It mows an acre in 60 sec.

The longest drive on a lawn mower was 4882 km *3034 miles*, when Ian Ireland of Harlow, Essex drove an Iseki SG15 between Harlow, and Southend Pier, Essex from 13 Aug to 7 Sep 1989. He was assisted by members of 158 Round Table, Luton, Beds and raised over £15 000 in aid of the Leukaemia Research Fund.

A 12-hour run-behind record of 169·13 km *105·1 miles* was set at Wisborough Green, W Sussex on 28–29 Jul 1990 by the 'Doctor's Flyers' team.

The greatest distance covered in the annual 12-hour Lawn Mower Race (under the rules of the British Lawn Mower Racing Association) is 460·259 km *286 miles* by Andy, Barry and Trevor Stemp at Wisborough Green, W Sussex on 30–31 Jul 1988.

Pedal car

The record from Marble Arch, London to the Arc de Triomphe, Paris, France, including a Channel crossing by ferry, is 23 hr 21 min 27 sec, for a distance of 400·7 km *249 miles*, by six members of Lea Manor High School and Community College, Luton, Beds on 27–28 May 1989.

Snowmobile

Tony Lenzini of Duluth, Minnesota, USA drove his 1986 Arctic Cat Cougar snowmobile a total of 11 604·6 km *7211 miles* in 60 riding days between 28 Dec 1985 and 20 Mar 1986.

Jaguar XJ12 'Chubb Firefighter', which on 2 Nov 1982 atttained a speed of 210·13 km/h *130·57 mph* in tests when servicing the *Thrust 2* land-speed record trials. (See Fastest cars - Land speed.)

Karting The highest mileage recorded in 24 hours on a closed indoor circuit by a four-man team is 835·9773 km 3833 laps of a 218·1 m *238·5 yd* track at Silvia Park, Auckland, New Zealand on 1–2 Sep 1990. The 5-hp 144 cc Honda engined kart was driven by Andrew Hill, Harry and Matt Redward and Rhodri Griffiths.

The greatest distance recorded in a 48-hour marathon is 2730 km *1696·3 miles* by Denis Wedes, Stephen Mantle, Len Nicholson and Janice Bennett, driving a Yamaha RC100SE kart powered by a KT100J 100 cc engine at Mount Sugarloaf Circuit, Newcastle, New South Wales, Australia on 25–27 Mar 1983.

The highest mileage of the 100 cc non-gearbox solo six-hour record is 313·51 km *194·81 miles* by Emily Newman at Rye House Raceway, Hoddesdon, Herts on 25 Jul 1986.

Solar powered The highest speed attained by a solely solar-powered land vehicle is 78·37 km/h *48·71 mph* by Molly Brennan driving the General Motors *Sunraycer* at Mesa, Arizona, USA on 24 Jun 1988. The highest speed of 135 km/h *83·88 mph* using solar/battery power was achieved by Star Micronics solar car *Solar star* driven by Manfred Hermann on 5 Jan 1991 at Richmond RAAF Base, Richmond NSW, Australia.

Taxis The largest taxi fleet is that in Mexico City, with 60 000 'normal' taxis, *pesaros* (communal fixed route taxis) and *settas* (airport taxis).

Currently there are 16 190 taxis and 20 926 taxi-drivers in London.

The longest fare on record is one of 22 000 km *13 670 miles* with the meter running, at a cost of £31 446. Ned Kelly and Dr John Morgan accompanied by taxi-drivers Guy Smith and Kanelli Tsiros, left London on 19 Aug 1988 and arrived in Sydney, Australia on 27 Oct 1988. The journey was part of the Australian Bicentenary celebrations and a sum of A$350 000 was raised for children's charities in Ireland, the United Kingdom, Singapore and Australia.

Charles Kerslake (b. 27 Jun 1895) held a London Metropolitan cab licence from February 1922 until his retirement in May 1988.

Tractor The world's largest tractor is the $459 000 US Department of Agriculture Wide Tractive Frame Vehicle completed by Ag West of Sacramento, California in June 1982. It measures 10·05 m *33 ft* between its wheels, which are designed to run on permanent paths, and weighs 22·22 tonnes .

Marathon Ronald Smiley of Dublin drove a tractor around Ireland a distance of 5580 km *3467·7 miles* from 4–23 Jul 1990 in aid of GORTA.

Trams *Longest journey* The longest now possible is from Krefeld St Tönis to Witten Annen Nord, Germany. With luck at the eight inter-connections, the 105·5 km *65·5 mile* trip can be achieved in 5 ½ hours.

By early 1991 Leningrad, USSR had the most extensive tramway system with 2402 cars on 64 routes with 690·6 km *429·13 miles* of tracks.

The only tramway system in Great Britain until the £43 million Greater Manchester Rapid Transit System opens is at Blackpool, Lancs.

The Glasgow system was scrapped in 1962 and that in London in 1952.

Oldest In revenue service are motor cars 1 and 2 of the Manx Electric Railway, dating from 1893.

Trolleybuses The last trolleybus in Britain, owned by Bradford Corporation, ran in 1972. Plans have been made to reintroduce trolleybuses by both West and South Yorks Passenger Transport Executives.

Most powerful truck A 1987 Ford LTL 9000 truck, owned and driven by Ken Warby of Cincinnati, Ohio, USA, is equipped with a General Electric J 79 tuned to produce 88 950 N *20 000 lbf* of thrust. Weighing 4·4 tonnes, it has achieved 338·27 km/h *210·2 mph* in 7·7 sec over a quarter-mile standing start.

Wrecker The world's most powerful wrecker is the Twin City Garage and Body Shop's 20·6 tonnes, 10·9 m *36 ft* long International M6-23 'Hulk' 1969 stationed at Scott City, Missouri, USA. It can lift in excess of 295 tonnes on its short boom.

LOADS

Heaviest load On 14–15 Jul 1984 John Brown Engineers & Contractors BV moved the Conoco Kotter Field production deck with a roll-out weight of 3805 tonnes for the Continental Netherlands Oil Co. of Leidsenhage, Netherlands.

The heaviest road load moved in the United Kingdom has been a 1305 tonnes module for the semi-submersible drilling rig *Ocean Alliance 2002*. It measured 21 m *70 ft* high by 30·5 m *100 ft* long by 27·4 m *90 ft* wide and was drawn by four tractor units. It covered a total of 0·8 km *0·49 miles* of public road on its journey from the River Tees to the River Clyde on 5 Nov 1985.

Longest The longest item moved by road was an high-pressure steel gas storage vessel 83·8 m *275 ft* long and weighing 233 tonnes transported to a new site at Beckton gasworks in east London on 10 Jul 1985. The overall train length was 99 m *325 ft*.

The longest item moved has been a 91·210 m *299·05 ft* horizontal bridge-like structure for use in an aircraft hangar. It weighed 62 tonnes and was transported to the paint spraying facility at Stansted airport, London on 29 Nov 1990. The overall train length was 101·12 m *331·54 ft*, the steel structure was built and erected by Fabriweld Ltd (Ireland).

MODEL CAR

Non-stop duration A Scalextric Jaguar XJ8 ran non-stop for 866 hr 44 min 54 sec and covered a distance of 2850·39 km *1771·2 miles* from 2 May to 7 Jun 1989. The event was organized by the Rev. Bryan G. Apps, MA and church members of Southbourne, Bournemouth, Dorset.

24 hour Slot car racing Under the rules of the B.S.C.R.A (British Slot Car Racing Association) a 24 hour world record was set for 1/32 scale car. On 5–6 Jul 1986 the North London Society of Model Engineers team at the ARRA club in Southport, Merseyside achieved a distance of 492·364 km *305·949 miles*, 11 815 laps of the track driving a Rondeau M482C Group C Sports car, built by Ian Fisher.

MOTORCYCLES

Earliest The earliest internal combustion-engined motorized bicycle was a wooden-framed machine built at Bad Cannstatt in October–November 1885 by

Gottlieb Daimler (1834–1900) of Germany and first ridden by Wilhelm Maybach (1846–1929). It had a top speed of 19 km/h *12 mph* and developed 0·373 kW *one-half of one horsepower* from its single-cylinder 264 cc four-stroke engine at 700 rpm. Known as the 'Einspur', it was lost in a fire in 1903.

The first motorcycles of entirely British production were the 1046-cc Holden flat-four and the 2¾ hp Clyde single both produced in 1898.

The earliest factory which made motorcycles in quantity was opened in 1894 by Heinrich and Wilhelm Hildebrand and Alois Wolfmüller at Munich, Germany. In its first two years this factory produced over 1000 machines, each having a water-cooled 1488 cc twin-cylinder four-stroke engine developing about 2·5 bhp at 600 rpm—the highest capacity motorcycle engine ever put into production.

Fastest production road machine The 112 kW *151 hp* 1-litre Kawasaki Tu Atara YB6 EI has a road-tested top speed of 300 km/h *186 mph*.

Fastest racing machine There is no satisfactory answer to the identity of the fastest track machine other than to say that the current Honda, Suzuki and Yamaha machines have all been geared to attain speeds marginally in excess of 300 km/h *186·4 mph* under race conditions.

Highest speeds Official world speed records must be set with two runs over a measured distance made in opposite directions within a time limit—1 hr for FIM records and 2 hr for AMA records.

Donald A. Vesco (USA) (b. 8 Apr 1939), riding his 21 ft *6·4 m* long *Lightning Bolt* streamliner, powered by two 1016 cc Kawasaki engines on Bonneville Salt Flats, Utah, USA on 28 Aug 1978 set AMA and FIM absolute records with an overall average of 512·733 km/h *318·598 mph* and had a fastest run at an average of 513·165 km/h *318·865 mph*.

The highest speed achieved over two runs in the UK is 308·82 km/h *191·891 mph* by Roy Francis Daniel (b. 7 Dec 1938) on his 998 cc supercharged twin-engined RDS Triumph at Elvington, N Yorks on 29 Jul 1978. His average time for the 402·33 m *440 yd* was 4·69 sec.

The world record for 1 km *1093·6 yd* from a standing start is 16·68 sec by Henk Vink (b. 24 Jul 1939) (Netherlands) on his supercharged 984 cc four-cylinder Kawasaki, at Elvington airfield, N Yorks on 24 Jul 1977. The faster run was made in 16·09 sec.

The world record for 402.33 m *1320 ft* from a standing start is 8·805 sec by Henk Vink on his supercharged 1132 cc four-cylinder Kawasaki at Elvington airfield, N Yorks on 23 Jul 1977. The faster run was made in 8·55 sec.

The fastest time for a single run over 440 yd from a standing start is 7·08 sec by Bo O'Brechta (USA) riding a supercharged 1200 cc Kawasaki-based machine at Ontario, California, USA in 1980.

The highest terminal velocity recorded at the end of a 440 yd run from a standing start is 321·14 km/h *199·55 mph* by Russ Collins (USA) at Ontario, California, USA on 7 Oct 1978.

Most expensive The Japanese Bimota Tesi ID 906 is the most expensive road-going motorcycle available in the United Kingdom. Priced at £25 500, it has an electronically fuel-injected Yamaha engine in a rectangular section alloy frame.

Longest Les Nash of Coventry, W Mids constructed a 'self made' 3500 cc machine with a Rover V-8 engine. It measures 3·81 × 1·22 m *12 ft 6 in × 4 ft* and weighs more than 500 lb *½ ton*. It is street legal.

Smallest Magnor Mydland of Norway has constructed a motorcycle with a wheelbase of 120 mm *4·72 in*, a seat height of 148 mm *5·82 in* and with wheels 38 mm *1·49 in* for the front and 49 mm *3·39 in* for the back in diameter. He rode a distance of 570 m *1870 ft* reaching a speed of 11·6 km/h *7·2 mph*.

Simon Timperley and Clive Williams of Progressive Engineering Ltd, Ashton-under-Lyne, Lancs designed and constructed a motorcycle with a wheel-base of 10·79 cm *4·25 in*, a seat height of 9·52 cm *3¾ in* and with a wheel diameter of 1·90 cm *0·75 in* for the front and 2·41 cm *0·950 in* for the back. Simon rode the bike a distance of 1 m *3·2 ft*, reaching a speed of 3·2 km/h *2 mph*.

Duration The longest time a motor scooter, a Kinetic Honda DX 100 cc, has been kept in non-stop motion is 1001 hrs ridden by Har Parkash Rishi, Amarjeet Singh and Navjot Chadha. They covered a distance of 30 965 km *49 831 miles* at Traffic Park, Pune, Maharashtra, India between 22 Apr–3 Jun 1990.

Biggest pyramid The White Helmets, of the Royal Signals Motorcycle Display Team, successfully achieved an eight-bike, 36-man pyramid for 300 m *328 yd* on 2 Sep 1986. They also achieved a 13-man pyramid, held together by muscle and determination only, with no straps, harnesses or any other aids, mounted on three motorcycles which travelled a distance of 1 km *0·8 mile* in 2 min 6·6 sec at Catterick airfield, N Yorks on 30 Sep 1988.

Backwards riding Steering a motor-cycle facing backwards from the top of a 3·3 m *10 ft* ladder, over a continuous period of 1 hr 30 min Signalman Dewi Jones of the Royal Signals White Helmets, covered a distance of 33 km *20·505 miles* at Catterick airfield, N Yorks on 30 Nov 1988.

Wheelie Distance Yasuyuki Kudoh at the Japan Automobile Research Institute, Tsukuba City, Ibaragi-pref, Japan on 5 May 1991 covered 331 km *205·7 miles* non-stop on the rear wheel of his Honda TLM 220 R 216 cc motorcycle.

Speed The highest speed attained on a back wheel is 241 km/h *150 mph* by Steve Burns on 3 Jul 1989 at Bruntingthorpe Proving Ground, Leics on his Suzuki GXS 1100 engine Spondon 1425 turbo.

Two-wheel sidecar riding Graham John Martin drove a distance of 320·1 km *198·9 miles* on a Yamaha XS 1100 cc bike in a time of 3 hr 5 min at Gerotek Test Track, Pretoria, South Africa on 21 Aug 1988.

Most on one machine The record for the most people on a single machine is, all 46 members of the Illawarra Mini Bike Training Club, New South Wales, Australia. They rode on a 1000 cc motorcycle and travelled a distance of 1 mile *1·609 km* on 11 Oct 1987.

Oldest motorcyclist Arthur Merrick Cook (b. 13 Jun 1895) still regularly rides his Suzuki 125 GS Special motorcycle every day.

BICYCLES

Earliest The first design for a machine propelled by cranks and pedals with connecting rods has been attributed to Leonardo da Vinci (1452–1519), or one of his pupils, c. 1493.

The earliest such design actually built was in 1839–40 by Kirkpatrick Macmillan (1810–78) of Dumfries, Scotland. The machine is now in the Science Museum, Kensington, London.

The first practical bicycle was the *vélocipède* built in March 1861 by Pierre Michaux and his son Ernest of rue de Verneuil, Paris, France.

In 1870, James Starley of Coventry, W. Midlands constructed the first 'penny-farthing' or Ordinary bicycle. It had wire-spoked wheels for lightness and was available with an optional-speed gear.

Bicycle parade The greatest participation is one involving 30 000 cyclists (2·75 per cent of the population of Puerto Rico at San Juan on 17 Apr 1988). It was organized by TV personality 'Pacheco' Joaquín Monserrat.

Trishaw The longest trishaw parade on record was when 177 trishaw pedlars rode in single file in Penang, Malaysia on 23 Nov 1986.

Longest The longest true tandem bicycle ever built (i.e. without a third stabilizing wheel) is one of 20·4 m *66 ft 11 in* for 35 riders built by Pedaalstompers Westmalle of Belgium. The riders covered c .60 m *195 ft* in practice on 20 Apr 1979. The machine weighs 1100 kg *2425 lb*.

Terry Thessman of Pahiatua, New Zealand designed and built a bike measuring 22·24 m *72·96 ft* long and weighing 154·2 kg *340 lb*. It was ridden by four riders a distance of 246 m *807 ft* on 27 Feb 1988.

Smallest Jacques Puyoou of Pau, Pyrénées-Atlantiques, France has built a tandem of 36 cm *14·1 in* wheel diameter, which has been ridden by him and Madame Puyoou.

Largest The largest bicycle as measured by the front-wheel diameter is 'Frankencycle', built by Dave Moore of Rosemead, California, USA and first ridden by Steve Gordon of Moorpark, California, on 4 Jun 1989. The wheel diameter is 3·048 m *10 ft* and it is 11 ft 2 in high.

HPVs Fastest land The world speed records for human-powered vehicles (HPVs) 200 m flying start (single rider) are 105·383 km/h *65·484 mph* by Fred Markham at Mono Lake, California, USA on 11 May 1986 and 101·25 km/h *62·92 mph* (multiple riders) by Dave Grylls and Leigh Barczewski at the Ontario Speedway, California, on 4 May 1980. The one-hour standing start (single rider) is held by Pat Kinch, riding *Kingcycle Bean*, averaging a speed of 75·57 km/h *46·96 mph* on 8 Sep 1990 at Millbrook Proving Ground, Bedford.

A British 200 m record was set by S. Poulter in *Poppy Flyer*, in 9·10 sec at Greenham Common, Berks on 2 Aug 1981.

Water cycle The men's 2000 m record (single ride) is 20·66 km/h *12·84 mph* by Steve Hegg in *Flying Fish* at Long Beach, California, USA on 20 Jul 1987.

Endurance From 10–21 Jul 1983, 24 students of City and Guilds College, London drove an HPV round Great Britain on a 5914 km *3675 mile* route to average 23·19 km/h *14·41 mph*.

Wheelie A duration record of 5 hr 12 min 33 sec was set by David Robilliard at the Beau Sejour Leisure Centre, St Peter Port, Guernsey, Channel Islands on 28 May 1990.

Unicycles Tallest The tallest unicycle ever mastered is one 31·01 m *101 ft 9 in* tall ridden by Steve McPeak (with a safety wire

suspended by an overhead crane) for a distance of 114·6 m *376 ft* in Las Vegas, USA in October 1980. The freestyle riding (i.e. without any safety harness) of ever taller unicycles must inevitably lead to serious injury or fatality.

Smallest Peter Rosendahl of Las Vegas, Nevada, USA rode a unicycle with a wheel diameter of 7·58 cm *2·988 in* in a radius of 1·21 m *4 ft* for 30 sec at Circus Circus Hotel, Las Vegas, Nevada, USA on 4 Aug 1990.

Endurance Deepak Lele of Maharashtra, India unicycled 6378 km *3963 miles* from New York to Los Angeles, USA from 6 Jun–25 Sep 1984.

Mike Day, 21, of Manchester and Michel Arets, (b. 9 Sep 1959) of Maidstone, Kent unicycled 1450 km *901 miles* from Land's End, Cornwall to John o' Groats, Highland from 27 Aug to 10 Sep 1986 in 14 days 12 hr 41 min.

Takayuki Koike of Kanagawa, Japan set a unicycle record for 160·9 km *100 miles* in 6 hr 44 min 21·84 sec on 9 Aug 1987.

Backwards Peter Rosendahl of Nevada, USA rode his 60·96 cm *24 in* wheel unicycle backwards for a distance of 74·75 km *46·7 miles* in 9 hr 25 min on 19 May 1990.

Sprint Peter Rosendahl of Las Vegas, Nevada, USA, at the Wet 'N Wild Show, Las Vegas, USA on 1 Jul 1990 set a sprint record from a standing start over 100 m *(328 ft)* in 12·74 secs and the flying start for same distance in 12·43 secs.

Roads

Road mileages The country with the greatest length of road is the United States (all 50 states), with 6 260 177 km *3·89 million miles* of graded roads.

Great Britain has 380 256 km *236 287 miles* of road, including 2999 km *1864 miles* of motorway.

■ **Unicyle records**
Peter Rosendahl of Nevada, USA currently holds four unicycle records; smallest rideable, backwards distance, fastest sprint from standing and flying starts.

Ramp jumping
The longest distance ever achieved for motorcycle long-jumping is 74·98 m *246 ft*, by Todd Seeley at a World of Wheels show in Tampa, Florida, USA on 28 Feb 1988.

Wall of death
The greatest endurance feat on a 'wall of death' was 6 hr 7 min 38 sec, by Hugo Dabbert (b. Hildesheim, Germany on 24 Sep 1938) at Rüsselsheim on 14 Aug 1980. He rode 6841 laps on the 10 m *32·8 ft* diameter wall on a Honda CM 400T, averaging 35·2 km/h *21·8 mph* for the 214·8 km *133·4 miles*.

Penny-farthing
The record for riding from John o' Groats, Highland to Land's End, Cornwall on Ordinary bicycles, more commonly known in the 1870s as 'penny-farthings', is 9 days 6 hr 52 min by police officer Clive Flint of Manchester, from 2–10 Jun 1984.

Underwater tricycling
A team of 32 divers pedalled a distance of 187·7 km *116·66 miles* in 75 hr 20 min on a standard tricycle at Diver's Den, Santa Barbara, California, USA on 16–19 Jun 1988 to raise money for the Muscular Dystrophy Association.

Britain's longest uninterrupted dual carriageway is from Plymouth to Exeter (A38) and then by the M5 and M6, A74, M74, M73 amd M80 for a total of 829 km *515 miles* ending at Dunblane Fourways Restaurant, Stirling, Scotland.

Trackway Oldest The oldest known trackway in England is the Sweet Way in the Somerset Levels. New evidence found in 1990 indicates that the road was built from trees felled in the winter of 3807–3806 BC.

The oldest in the Republic of Ireland are near Lanesborough, Co. Longford, where prehistoric tracks made of oak and ash logs which have been radiocarbon dated to *c.*

2500–2300 BC have been discovered at Corlea and Derryoghill bogs.

Longest motorable road The Pan-American Highway, from north-west Alaska, USA to Santiago, Chile, thence eastward to Buenos Aires, Argentina and terminating in Brasilia, Brazil is over 24 140 km *15 000 miles* in length. There remains a gap known as the Tapon del Darién in Panama and another at the Atrato Swamp, Colombia.

Great Britain The longest designated road in Great Britain is the A1 from London to Edinburgh, of 650 km *404 miles*.

The longest Roman roads were Watling Street, from Dubrae (Dover), 346 km *215 miles* through Londinium (London) to Viroconium (Wroxeter), and Fosse Way, which ran 350 km *218 miles* from Lindum (Lincoln) through Aquae Sulis (Bath) to Isca Dumnoniorum (Exeter).However, a 16 km *10 mile* section of Fosse Way between Ilchester and Seaton remains indistinct.

Highest roads The highest trail in the world is a 13 km *8 mile* stretch of the Kang-ti-suu between Khaleb and Hsin-chi-fu, Tibet, which in two places exceeds 6080 m *20 000 ft*.

The highest carriageable road in the world is one 1180 km *733·2 miles* long between Tibet and south-western Sinkiang, China completed in October 1957, which takes in passes of altitudes up to 5632 m *18 480 ft* above sea level.

Europe Europe's highest pass (excluding the Caucasian passes) is the Col de Restefond (2802 m *9193 ft*), completed in 1962, with 21 hairpins bends between Jausiers and Saint Etienne-de-Tinée, France. It is usually closed between early October and early June.

The highest motor road in Europe is the Pico de Veleta in the Sierra Nevada, southern Spain. The shadeless climb of 36 km *22·4 miles* brings the motorist to 3469 m *11 384 ft* above sea level and became, on completion of a road on its southern side in 1974, arguably Europe's highest 'pass'.

The highest road in the United Kingdom is the A6293 unclassified tarmac private extension at Great Dun Fell, Cumbria (847 m *2780 ft*), leading to a Ministry of Defence and Air Traffic Control installation. A permit is required to use it.

The highest public classified road in England is the A689 at Killhope Cross (626 m *2056 ft*) on the Cumbria–Durham border near Nenthead.

The highest classified road in Scotland is the A93 road over the Grampians through Cairnwell, a pass between Blairgowrie, Perthshire and Braemar, Aberdeenshire, which reaches a height of 670 m *2199 ft*. An estate track exists to the summit of Ben a'Bhuird 2276 m *3860 ft* in Grampian.

The highest classified road in Wales is the Rhondda Afan inter-valley road (A4107), which reaches 533 m *1750 ft* 4 km *2½ miles* in height east of Abergwynfi, Mid Glamorgan.

The highest motorway in Great Britain is the trans-Pennine M62, which, at the Windy Hill interchange, reaches an altitude of 371 m *1220 ft*. Its Dean Head cutting is the deepest roadway cutting in Europe, at 55·7 m *183 ft*.

Lowest roads The lowest road is along the Israeli shores of the Dead Sea at 393 m *1290 ft* below sea level.

The world's lowest 'pass' is Rock Reef Pass, Everglades National Park, Florida, USA, which is 91 cm *3 ft* above sea level.

The lowest surface roads in Great Britain are just below sea level in the Holme Fen area of Cambridgeshire.

Widest roads The widest in the world is the Monumental Axis, running for 2·4 km *1½ miles* from the Municipal Plaza to the Plaza of the Three Powers in Brasilia, the capital of Brazil. The six-lane boulevard was opened in April 1960 and is 250 m *820·2 ft* wide.

The San Francisco–Oakland Bay Bridge Toll Plaza has 23 lanes (17 west-bound) serving the bridge in Oakland, California, USA.

The only instance of 17 carriageway lanes side by side in Britain occurs on the M61 at Linnyshaw Moss, Worsley, Greater Manchester.

Traffic volume The most heavily travelled stretch of road is Route 10 Junction Route 13.80 Los Angeles, Normandie Avenue Interchange, California, USA, with a peak-hour traffic volume of 18 000 vehicles.

The territory with the highest traffic density in the world is Hong Kong. By 1 Jan 1987 there were 300 000 motor vehicles on 1395 km *867 miles* of serviceable roads, giving a density of 4·14 m *4·53 yd* per vehicle.

The comparative figure for the United Kingdom in 1984 was 19·60 m *21·44 yd*.

The greatest traffic density at any one point in Great Britain is at Hyde Park Corner, London. The flow (including the underpass) for 24 hours in 1990 was 240 000 vehicles.

Bridge The world's busiest bridge is the Howrah Bridge across the river Hooghly in Calcutta, India. In addition to 57 000 vehicles per day it carries an incalculable number of pedestrians across its 457 m *1500 ft* long 21·9 m *72 ft* wide span.

The busiest bridge in Great Britain is the Severn Bridge, on 1 May 1989 76 162 vehicles crossed over it. The busiest Thames bridge is Twickenham Bridge, with a 24-hr average of 62 000 vehicles.

Motorway Britain's busiest and most heavily travelled motorway is the M25 with the section between junctions 13 (Staines) and 14 (Heathrow) being the worst with an average traffic flow of 168 000 vehicles over a 24 hr period.

Longest traffic jams The longest ever reported was that of 16 Feb 1980, which stretched northwards from Lyon 176 km *109·3 miles* towards Paris, France. A record traffic jam was reported for 1½ million cars crawling bumper-to-bumper over the East-West German border on 12 Apr 1990.

The longest traffic jams in Britain were two of 64·3 km *40 miles*: on the M1 from Junction 13 (Milton Keynes) to Junction 18 (Rugby) on 5 Apr 1985, and on the M6 between Charnock Richard and Carnforth, Lancs on 17 Apr 1987 involving 200 000 people and a tailback of 50 000 cars and coaches.

The longest traffic jam on the M25 was on 17 Aug 1988 with 35·40 km *22 miles* of solid traffic, with a tailback from midway between junction 9 (Leatherhead) and junction 8 (Reigate).

Most complex interchange The most complex interchange on the British road system is that at Gravelly Hill, north of Birmingham on the Midland Link Motorway section of the M6, opened on 24 May 1972. Popularly known as 'Spaghetti Junction', it includes 18 routes on six levels (together with a diverted canal and river), which consumed 26 000 tonnes of steel, 250 000 tonnes of concrete and 300 000 tonnes of earth, and cost £8·2 million.

Longest ring-road Work on the M25 six lane London Orbital Motorway, 195·5 km *121½ miles* long commenced in 1972 and completed on 29 Oct 1986 at an estimated cost of £909 million, or £8 million per mile. The first circumnavigation was by Terence Whelan, editor of *Ideal Home*, and Peter Cracknell (navigator).

Longest viaduct The longest elevated road viaduct on the British road system is the 4779 km *2·97 mile* Gravelly Hill to Castle Bromwich section of the M6 in the West Midlands. It was completed in May 1972.

Street Longest The longest designated street in the world is Yonge Street, running north and west from Toronto, Canada. The first stretch, completed on 16 Feb 1796, ran 55·783 km *34 miles*. Its official length, now extended to Rainy River on the Ontario-Minesota border, is 1896·2 km *1178·3 miles*.

Narrowest The world's narrowest street is in the village of Ripatransone in the Marche region of Italy. It is called Vicolo della Virilita ('Virility Alley') and is 43 cm *16·9 in* wide.

Shortest The title of 'The Shortest Street in the World' is claimed by Bacup in Lancashire, where Elgin Street, situated by the old market ground, measures just 5·18 m *17 ft*.

Steepest The steepest street in the world is Baldwin Street, Dunedin, New Zealand, which has a maximum gradient of 1 in 1·266.

Britain's steepest motorable road is the unclassified Chimney Bank at Rosedale Abbey, N Yorks which is signposted '1 in 3'. The county surveyor states it is 'not quite' a 33 per cent gradient. Unclassified road No. 149 at Ffordd Penllech, Harlech which is narrow and twisting, is at its steepest gradient 1 in 2·92.

The longest steep hill on any classified road in the United Kingdom is the Bealach na Ba ('The Pass of the Cattle') on the road from Kishorn to Applecross in Highland. In 9·6 km *6 miles* this single-track road rises from sea level to 626 m *2054 ft*, with gradients of 1 in 4 and several hairpin bends. A sign warns that it is not suitable for 'inexperienced drivers'.

Milestone Britain's oldest milestone *in situ* is a Roman stone dating from AD 150 on the Stanegate, at Chesterholme, near Bardon Mill, Northumberland.

Longest ford The longest ford in any classified road in England is in Violet's Lane, north of Furneux Pelham, Herts, which measures 903 m *987½ yd* in length.

Square Largest Tiananmen 'Gate of Heavenly Peace' Square in Beijing, described as the navel of China, covers 39·6 ha *98 acres*.

The Maiden e Shah in Isfahan, Iran extends over 8·1 ha *20·1 acres*.

Great Britain The largest square in Great Britain is the 2·82 ha *6·99 acre* Ladbroke Square (open to residents only), constructed in 1842–5, while Lincoln's Inn Fields covers 2·76 ha *6·84 acres*.

Oldest The oldest London square is Lincoln's Inn Fields, dating to the mid-17th century.

Railways

TRAINS

Earliest Wagons running on wooden rails were used for mining as early as 1550 at Leberthal, Alsace, and in Britain for conveying coal from Strelley to Wollaton near Nottingham from 1604–15, and at Broseley Colliery, Shrops, in October 1605.

Richard Trevithick built his first steam locomotive for the 914 mm *3 ft* gauge iron plateway at Coalbrookdale, Shrops, in 1803, but there is no evidence that it ran. His second locomotive drew wagons in which men rode on a demonstration run at Penydarren, Mid Glamorgan on 22 Feb 1804, but it broke the plate rails.

The earliest commercially successful steam locomotive worked in 1812 on the Middleton Colliery Railway to Leeds, Yorks, and was authorized by Britain's first Railway Act on 9 Jun 1758.

The first permanent public railway to use steam traction was the Stockton & Darlington, from its opening on 27 Sep 1825 from Shildon to Stockton via Darlington, in Cleveland. The 7 tonne *Locomotion* could pull 48 tonnes at a speed of 24 km/h *15 mph*. It was designed and driven by George Stephenson (1781–1848).

The first regular steam passenger service was inaugurated over a one-mile section (between Bogshole Farm and South Street in Whitstable, Kent) on the 10·05 km *6¼ mile* Canterbury & Whitstable Railway on 3 May 1830, hauled by the engine *Invicta*.

The first practical electric railway was Werner von Siemens' oval metre gauge demonstration track, about 300 m *984 ft* long, at the Berlin Trades Exhibition on 31 May 1879.

Fastest The world's fastest speed with passengers in a non-railed vehicle is 400·7 km/h *249 mph* by the Maglev (magnetic levitation) MLU-001 test train over the 7 km *4·3 mile* long JNR experimental track at Miyazaki, Japan on 4 Feb 1987.

The highest speed recorded on any national rail system is 515 km/h *320 mph* by the French SNCF high-speed train TGV (Train à Grande Vitesse) between Courtalain and Tours on 18 May 1990. It was brought into service on 27 Sep 1981. By September 1983 it had reduced its scheduled time for the Paris–Lyon run of 425 km *264 miles* to 2 hours exactly, so averaging 212·5 km/h *132 mph*.

The highest speed ever ratified for a steam locomotive was 201·16 km/h *125 mph* over 402 m *440 yd* by the LNER 4-6-2 No. 4468 *Mallard* (later numbered 60022), which hauled seven coaches weighing 243 tonnes gross down Stoke Bank, near Essendine, between Grantham, Lincs, and Peterborough, Cambs, on 3 Jul 1938. Driver Joseph Duddington was at the controls with Fireman Thomas Bray. The engine suffered some damage.

British Rail inaugurated their HST (High Speed Train) daily services between London–Bristol and South Wales on 4 Oct 1976. The electric British Rail APT-P (Advanced Passenger Train-Prototype) attained 261 km/h *162 mph* between Glasgow and Carlisle on its first revenue-earning run on 7 Dec 1981. It covered the 644 km *400 miles* from Glasgow to London in 4¼ hr, but was subsequently withdrawn from service because of technical problems.

British Rail set a new world speed record for diesel traction on 1 Nov 1987, when a special train testing the prototype SIG bogies for the Mk IV InterCity coaches reached 238·9 km/h *148·4 mph* between Darlington and York, with two InterCity 125 power cars.

Design of the 140 mph *237 km/h* Class 91 Electra locomotive, tested in July 1988, calls for an eventual schedule for the 632 km *393 miles* London–Edinburgh route of 3½ hr, to average 180·6 km/h *112·28 mph*. One locomotive reached 260 km/h *162 mph* between Grantham and Peterborough on 18 Sep 1989.

Longest non-stop Steam Locomotive No. 4472, *Flying Scotsman* completed a non-stop run, hauling 535 tonnes, between Parkes and Broken Hill in New South Wales, Australia on 6 Aug 1989. The total distance covered was 679·12 km *422 miles* in a time of 9 hr 25 min 15 sec.

Longest non-stop The longest run on British Rail without any advertised stop is by the Euston to Inverness InterCity Sleeper between Watford Junction and Perth, a distance of 781·5 km *446·5 miles* which takes 11 hr 01 min.

Most powerful The world's most powerful steam locomotive, measured by tractive effort, was No. 700, a triple-articulated or triplex with 2-8-8-8-4 wheels, and six-cylinder engine built by the Baldwin Locomotive Works in 1916 for the Virginian Railway, USA. It had a tractive force of 75 434 kg *166 300 lb* when working compound and 90 520 kg *199 560 lb* when working simple.

RAILWAYS

Smallest model railway

The most miniature model railway ever built is one of 1:1000 scale by Jean Damery (b. 1923) of Paris, France. The engine runs on a 4½ volt battery and measures 7·9 mm *5/16 in* overall.

Spike driving

In the World Championship Professional Spike Driving Competition held at the Golden Spike National Historic Site in Utah, USA, Dale C. Jones, 49, of Lehi, Utah, USA drove six 7-in railroad spikes in a time of 26·4 sec on 11 Aug 1984. He incurred no penalty points under the official rules.

Probably the heaviest train ever hauled by a single engine was one of 15 545 tonnes made up of 250 freight cars stretching 2·5 km *1·6 miles* by the *Matt H. Shay* (No. 5014), a 2-8-8-8-2 engine, which ran on the Erie Railroad from May 1914 until 1929.

On 16 Feb 1986, a single locomotive, No. 59001, one of five diesels built by General Motors and privately owned by quarry company Foster Yeoman of Merehead, Somerset, hauled a 4639 tonnes train, the heaviest on record in Britain, during trials on Savernake Bank, Wilts.

Greatest load The world's strongest rail carrier, with a capacity of 807 tonnes is the 336 tonnes 36-axle 'Schnabel' 92 m *301 ft 10 in* long built for a US railway by Krupp, Germany in March 1981.

The heaviest load carried by British Rail was a 37·1 m *122 ft* long boiler drum weighing 279 tonnes which was carried from Immingham Dock to Killingholme, Humberside in September 1968.

The heaviest load ever moved on rails is the 10 860 tonnes Church of the Virgin Mary (built in 1548 in the village of Most, Czechoslovakia), in October–November 1975, because it was in the way of coal workings. It was moved 730 m *800 yd* at 0·002 km/h *0·0013 mph* over four weeks, at a cost of £9 million.

Freight trains The world's longest and heaviest freight train on record with the largest number of wagons recorded, made a run on the 1065 mm *3 ft 6 in* gauge Sishen–Saldanha railway in South Africa on 26–27 Aug 1989. The train consisted of 660 wagons each loaded to 105 tons gross, a tank car and a caboose, moved by nine 50 kV electric and seven diesel-electric locomotives distributed along the train. The train was 7·302 km *4½ miles* long and weighed 69 393 tons excluding locomotives. It travelled a distance of 861 km *535 miles* in 22 hr 40 min.

British Rail's heaviest freight train began its regular run on 16 Sep 1983 from Mer-

ehead Quarry, Somerset to Acton, West London, with 3300 tonnes of limestone in 43 wagons and hauled by two engines, the total length of the train being nearly 800 m *½ mile*. Since February 1986 this has been hauled by a single '59' class diesel. (See Most powerful above.)

The longest regular freight train journey on British Rail is the twice-weekly china clay train from Burgullow, Cornwall to Irvine, Scotland, a round trip of 1834 km *1140 miles*, hauled by the same pair of diesel locomotives throughout.

TRACKS

Longest The world's longest run is one of 9438 km *5864½ miles* on the Trans-Siberian line from Moscow to Nakhodka, USSR, in the Soviet Far East. There are 97 stops on the journey, which takes 8 days 4 hr 25 min.

The 3145 km *1954 mile* Baikal–Amur (BAM) main line (USSR), begun with forced labour in 1938, was restarted in 1974 and put into service on 27 Oct 1984. A total of 382 million m³ *13 500 million ft³* of earth had to be moved and 3901 bridges built in this £8000 million project.

Longest straight The Commonwealth Railways Trans-Australian line over the Nullarbor Plain, from Mile 496 between Nurina and Loongana, Western Australia to Mile 793 between Ooldea and Watson, South Australia, is 478 km *297 miles* dead straight, although not level.

The longest straight on British Rail is the 29 km *18 miles* between Barlby Junction and Brough, N Yorks on the 'down' line from Selby to Kingston-upon-Hull, Humberside.

Widest and narrowest gauge The widest in standard use is 1·676 m *5 ft 6 in*. This width is used in Spain, Portugal, India, Pakistan, Bangladesh, Sri Lanka, Argentina and Chile.

The narrowest gauge on which public services are operated is 260 mm *10¼ in* on the Wells Harbour (1·12 km *0·7 mile*) and the

Wells Walsingham Railways (6·5 km *4 miles*) in Norfolk.

Highest line At 4817 m *15 806 ft* above sea level, the standard gauge (1435 mm *4 ft 8½ in*) track on the Morococha branch of the Peruvian State Railways at La Cima is the highest in the world.

The highest point on the British Rail system is at Drumochter Pass on the Perthshire-Inverness border, where the track reaches an altitude of 452 m *1484 ft* above sea-level.

The highest railway in Britain is the Snowdon Mountain Railway, which rises from Llanberis, Gwynedd to 1064 m *3493 ft* above sea-level, just below the summit of Snowdon (*Yr Wyddfa*). It has a gauge of 800 mm *2 ft 7 ½ in*.

Lowest line The world's lowest is in the Seikan Tunnel between Honshu and Hokkaido, Japan. The rails are 240 m *786 ft* below the Tsugaro Straits. The tunnel was opened on 13 Mar 1988 and is 53·8 km *33·4 miles* long.

On British Rail, the Severn Tunnel is 43·8 m *144 ft* below sea level.

Steepest gradient The world's steepest standard-gauge gradient by adhesion is 1:11, between Chedde and Servoz on the metre-gauge SNCF Chamonix line, France.

The steepest sustained adhesion-worked gradient on a main line in the United Kingdom is the 3·2 km *2 mile* Lickey incline of 1:37·7, just southwest of Birmingham.

From the tunnel bottom to James Street, Liverpool, on the former Mersey Railway, there is a stretch of 1:27; from the re-opened Thameslink tunnel to London Blackfriars station there is a stretch of 1:29 and between Folkestone Junction and Harbour, Kent, 1·6 km *1 mile* of 1:30.

Slightest gradient The slightest gradient posted on the British Rail system is one indicated as 1:14 400 between Pirbright Junction and Farnborough, Hants. This could be described alternatively as England's most obtuse summit.

Busiest system The railway carrying the largest number of passengers is the East Japan Railway Co. which in 1989 carried 14 660 000 passengers daily. Among articles lost in 1989 were 377 712 umbrellas, 141 200 clothing items, 143 761 books and stationery items, 4359 accessories and 89 799 purses.

Greatest length of railway The country with the greatest length of railway is the United States with 296 489 km *184 235 miles* of track.

The farthest anyone can get from a railway on the mainland island of Great Britain is 155·6 km *97·3 miles* by road in the case of Southend, Mull of Kintyre, Scotland.

The number of journeys made on British Rail in the 12 months to 31 Mar 1990 was 746 400 million (average 44·6 km *27·74 miles*) compared with the peak year of 1957, when 1101 million journeys (average 33 km *20·51 miles* were made.

RAIL TRAVEL

Calling all stations Alan M. Witton of Chorlton, Manchester visited every open British Rail station (2362) in a continuous tour for charity of 26 703 km *16 592 ¾ miles* in 452 hr 26 ½ min from 13 Jul–28 Aug 1980.

Colin M. Mulvany and Seth N. Vafiadis of west London visited every open British Rail station (2 378) embracing also the Tyne & Wear, Glasgow and London underground systems (333 stations) for charity in 31 days 5 hr 8 min 58 sec. They travelled over 24 989 km *15 527·6 miles* to average 61·2 km/h *38·05 mph* from 4 Jun–5 Jul 1984.

Four points of the compass Ronald Carter and his son Jonathan (13) of Whitkirk, Leeds traversed the extreme points of the compass for stations in Great Britain—Thurso (north), Lowestoft, Suffolk (east), Penzance, Cornwall (south) and Arisaig, Scotland (west) in 47 hr 38 min from 31 May–2 Jun 1990.

Most miles in 7 days Jonathan Carter and his mother Norma, of Whitkirk, Leeds travelled 18 597·875 km *11 556½ miles* using a British Rail 7-day Rover ticket from 23–30 Jun 1990.

Most miles in 24 hours The greatest distance travelled on British Rail in 24 hours (without duplicating any part of the journey) is 2710·06 km *1684 miles* by Jonathan and Norma Carter of Whitkirk, Leeds and Matthew Clarke of Bradford, N Yorks on 26–27 Oct 1990.

Longest journey In the course of some 73 years commuting by British Rail from Kent to London, Ralph Ransome of Birchington travelled an equivalent of an estimated 39 times round the world. He retired early, aged 93, on 5 Feb 1986.

Irish rail travel John Byrne of Dublin, Republic of Ireland travelled the length of the entire Irish rail system–Iarnród Éireann in connection with the Cheeverstown Rail Marathon from Dublin to Dublin in 3 days 14 hr 50 min on 21–24 Sep 1987.

John Byrne and Lisa Shelley covered the entire passenger rail networks of Iarnród Éireann and Northern Ireland Railways in 4 days 2 hr 47 min from 4–8 Jul 1988.

Most countries in 24 hours The number of countries travelled through entirely by train in 24 hours is 10, by Aaron Kitchen on 16–17 Feb 1987. His route started in Yugoslavia and continued through Austria, Italy, Liechtenstein, Switzerland, France, Luxemburg, Belgium and the Netherlands, arriving in West Germany 22 hr 42 min later.

Handpumped railcars A speed of 20·51 mph for a 300 m *984 ft* course was achieved by Gold's Gym, Surrey, British Columbia, Canada at the Annual World Championship Handcar Races, Port Moodby, British Columbia with their five-man team (one pusher, four pumpers) in a time of 32·71 sec on 2 Jul 1986.

STATIONS

Largest The world's largest is Grand Central Terminal, Park Avenue and 42nd Street, New York City, USA, built from 1903–13. It covers 19 ha *48 acres* on two levels with 41 tracks on the upper level and 26 on the lower. On average more than 550 trains and 180 000 people per day use it.

The largest railway station in extent on the British Rail system is the 16-platform Clapham Junction, London, extending over 11·22 ha *27¾ acres*, with a total platform face of 3243 m *10 682 ft*.

The station with the largest number of platforms is Waterloo, London (9·9 ha *24½ acres*), which has 19 main and two Waterloo and City Line platforms, with a total face of 4347 m *14 272 ft*.

Victoria Station (8·80 ha *21¾ acres*) has, however, a total face length of 5213 m *17 102 ft* for its 16 platforms.

Oldest Liverpool Road Station, Greater Manchester was first used on 15 Sep 1830.

Part of the original station is now a museum.

Busiest The busiest railway junction in the world is Clapham Junction, London, on the Southern Region of British Rail, with an average of 2200 trains passing through each 24 hours. All trains from Waterloo and all the Brighton line trains from Victoria pass through.

Highest The Condor station in Bolivia at 4786 m *15 705 ft* on the metre gauge Rio Mulato to Potosi line is the highest in the world.

The highest passenger station on British Rail is Corrour, Inverness-shire, Scotland at an altitude of 410·5 m *1347 ft* above sea level.

Waiting-rooms The world's largest waiting-rooms are the four in Beijing Station, Chang'an Boulevard, Beijing, China, opened in September 1959, with a total standing capacity of 14 000.

Platforms The longest railway platform in the world is the Kharagpur platform, West Bengal, India, which measures 833 m *2733 ft* in length.

The State Street Center subway platform on 'The Loop' in Chicago, Illinois, USA measures 1066 m *3500 ft* in length.

The longest in the British Rail system is the 602·69 m *1977 ft 4 in* long platform at Gloucester, Glos.

The two platforms comprising the New Misato railway station on the Musashino line, Saitama, Japan are 300 m *984 ft* apart and are connected by a bridge.

UNDERGROUND RAILWAYS

Most extensive The subway with most stations in the world is the New York City Metropolitan Transportation Authority subway, USA (first section opened on 27 Oct 1904). The network covers 372·93 km *231·73 route miles* and 5 million passengers per day in 1990. The 469 stations are closer set than those of the London Underground.

London The earliest (first section between Farringdon Street and Edgware Road opened 10 Jan 1863) and one of the most extensive underground or rapid transit railway systems of the 67 in the world is the London Underground, with 409 km *254 miles* of route, of which 135 km *85 miles* is bored tunnel and 32 km *20 miles* is 'cut and cover'. The whole system is operated by a staff of 19 000 serving 272 stations. The 478 trains comprising 3908 cars carried 765 million passengers in 1989–90.

The greatest depth is 67·4 m *221 ft* at Holly Bush Hill, Hampstead on the Northern Line. The longest journey without a change is on the Central Line from Epping to West Ruislip—54·9 km *34·1 miles*.

Travelling The record for touring the 272 stations of the London Underground, including Heathrow Terminal 4 station which opened on 12 Apr 1986, is 18 hr 41 min 41 sec set by a team of five: Robert A. Robinson, Peter D. Robinson, Timothy J. Robinson, Timothy J. Clark and Richard J. Harris, on 30 Jul 1986.

Moscow metro The record transit on 9 Dec 1988 (all 123 named stations) was 9 hr 39 min 50 sec by Peter Altman of Edgware, Middx and Miss Jackie Smith of Bobblestock, Herefordshire.

Busiest The world's busiest metro system is that in Greater Moscow, USSR, with as many as 3·3 billion passengers per year. There are 141 stations (18 of which have more than one name, being transfer

stations) and 226.7 km *140 miles* of track. The 5 kopek fare has just been increased to 15 kopeks for the first time since the Metro first went into operation in 1935.

Aircraft

The use of the Mach scale for aircraft speeds was introduced by Prof. Ackeret of Zürich, Switzerland. The Mach number is the ratio of the velocity of a moving body to the local velocity of sound. This ratio was first employed by Dr Ernst Mach (1838–1916) of Vienna, Austria in 1887. Thus Mach 1·0 equals 1224·67 km/h *760·98 mph* at sea level at 15°C *59°F*, and is assumed, for convenience, to fall to a constant 1061·81 km/h *659·78 mph* in the stratosphere, i.e. above 11 000 m *36 089 ft*.

EARLIEST FLIGHTS

The first controlled and sustained power-driven flight occurred near the Kill Devil Hill, Kitty Hawk, North Carolina, USA at 10:35 a.m. on 17 Dec 1903, when Orville Wright (1871–1948) flew the 12-hp chain-driven *Flyer I* for a distance of 36·5 m *120 ft* at an airspeed of 48 km/h *30 mph*, a ground speed of 10·9 km/h *6·8 mph* and an altitude of 2·5–3·5 m *8–12 ft* for about 12 seconds, watched by his brother Wilbur (1867–1912), four men and a boy. Both brothers, from Dayton, Ohio, were bachelors because, as Orville put it, they had not the means to 'support a wife as well as an aeroplane'. The *Flyer* is now in the National Air and Space Museum at the Smithsonian Institution, Washington DC, USA.

The first hop by a man-carrying aeroplane entirely under its own power was made when Clément Ader (1841–1925) of France flew in his *Eole* for about 50 m *164 ft* at Armainvilliers, France on 9 Oct 1890. It was powered by a lightweight steam engine of his own design, which developed about 15 kW *20 hp*.

The earliest 'rational design' for a flying machine, according to the Royal Aeronautical Society, was that published by Emanuel Swedenborg (1688–1772) in Sweden in 1717.

Great Britain The first officially recognized flight in the British Isles was made by the US citizen Samuel Franklin Cody (1861–1913) who flew 423 m *1390 ft* in his own biplane at Farnborough, Hants on 16 Oct 1908.

Horatio Frederick Phillips (1845–1924) almost certainly covered 152 m *500 ft* in his *Phillips II* 'Venetian blind' aeroplane at Streatham, Surrey in 1907.

The first Briton to fly was George Pearson Dickin (1881–1909), a journalist from Southport, Lancs as a passenger with Wilbur Wright at Auvour, France on 3 Oct 1908.

The first resident British citizen to fly in Britain was J.T.C. Moore-Brabazon (later Lord Brabazon of Tara) (1884–1964), with three short but sustained flights from 30 Apr–2 May 1909.

Cross-Channel The earliest crossing was made on Sunday, 25 Jul 1909 when Louis Blériot (1872–1936) of France flew his *Blériot XI* monoplane, powered by a 23-hp Anzani engine, 41·8 km *26 miles* from Les Baraques, France to Northfall Meadow, near Dover Castle, Kent in 36½ minutes, after taking off at 4:41 a.m.

Jet-engined Proposals for jet propulsion date back to Capt. Marconnet (1909) of

Supersonic flight

The first was achieved on 14 Oct 1947 by Capt. (later Brig Gen) Charles ('Chuck') Elwood Yeager (b. 13 Feb 1923), over Edwards Air Force Base, Muroc, California, USA in a Bell XS-1 rocket plane ('Glamorous Glennis' named for Yeager's wife) at Mach 1·015 (1078 km/h *670 mph*) at an altitude of 12 800 m *42 000 ft*. The XS-1 is now in the National Air and Space Museum at the Smithsonian Instutution, Washington, DC, USA.

The first British aircraft to attain Mach 1 in a dive was the de Havilland D.H.108 tail-less research aircraft on 9 Sep 1948, piloted by John Derry (killed 1952).

Solar powered

The *Solar Challenger*, designed by a team led by Dr Paul MacCready, was flown for the first time entirely under solar power on 20 Nov 1980. On 7 Jul 1981, piloted by Steve Ptacek (USA), the *Solar Challenger* became the first aircraft of this category to achieve a crossing of the English Channel. Taking off from Pontoise-Cormeilles, Paris, France the 262·3 km *163 mile* journey to Manston, Kent was completed in 5 hr 23 min at a maximum altitude of 3353 m *11 000 ft*. The aircraft has a wing span of 14·3 m *47 ft*.

France, and Henri Coanda (1886–1972) of Romania, and to the turbojet proposals of Maxime Guillaume in 1921.

The earliest tested run was that of British Power Jets' experimental WU1 (Whittle Unit No.1) on 12 Apr 1937, invented by Flying Officer (later Air Commodore) Sir Frank Whittle (b. 1 Jun 1907), who had applied for a patent on jet propulsion in 1930.

The first flight by an aeroplane powered by a turbojet engine was made by the Heinkel He 178, piloted by Flug Kapitän Erich Warsitz, at Marienehe, Germany on 27 Aug 1939. It was powered by a Heinkel He S3b engine weighing 378 kg *834 lb* (as installed with long tailpipe) designed by Dr Hans 'Pabst' von Ohain and first tested in August 1937.

The first British jet flight of 17 mins was made by Flt Lt P. E. G. 'Jerry' Sayer (killed 1942) in the Gloster-Whittle E.28/39 (wing span 8·84 m *29 ft*, length 7·70 m *25 ft 3 in*) fitted with an 390 kg *860 lb* s. t. Whittle W-1 engine at Cranwell, Lincs on 15 May 1941. The maximum speed was c. 560 km/h *350 mph*. This aircraft (W4041/G) is now in the Science Museum, London.

Trans-Atlantic The first crossing of the North Atlantic by air was made by Lt-Cdr (later Rear Admiral) Albert Cushion Read (1887–1967) and his crew (Stone, Hinton, Rodd, Rhoads and Breese) in the 84 knots (*155 km/h*) US Navy/Curtiss flyingboat NC-4 from Trepassey Harbor, Newfoundland, Canada via the Azores, to Lisbon, Portugal from 16–27 May 1919. The whole flight of 7591 km *4717 miles*, originating from Rockaway Air Station, Long Island, New York, USA on 8 May, required 53 hr 58 min, terminating at Plymouth, Devon on 31 May. The Newfoundland-Azores flight of 1930 km *1200 miles* took 15 hr 18 min at 81·7 knots (*151·4 km/h*).

Non-stop The first non-stop transatlantic flight was achieved 18 days later. The pilot, Capt John Williams Alcock (1892 –1919), and navigator, Lt Arthur Whitton Brown (1886–1948) left Lester's field, St John's, Newfoundland, Canada at 4:13 p.m. GMT on 14 Jun 1919, and landed at Derrygimla bog near Clifden, Co. Galway, Republic of Ireland at 8:40 a.m. GMT, 15 June, having covered a distance of 3154 km *1960 miles* in their Vickers Vimy, powered by two 360-hp Rolls-Royce Eagle VIII engines. Both men were created civil KBEs on 21 Jun 1919, when Alcock was aged 26 years 227 days, and they shared a *Daily Mail* prize of £10 000.

Solo The first transatlantic solo flight was achieved by Capt. (later Brig.) Charles Augustus Lindbergh (1902–74) who took off in his 220 hp Ryan monoplane *Spirit of St Louis* at 12:52 p.m. GMT on 20 May 1927 from Roosevelt Field, Long Island, New York, USA. He landed at 10:21 p.m. GMT on 21 May 1927 at Le Bourget Airfield, Paris, France. His flight of 5810 km *3610 miles* lasted 33 hr 29½ min and he won a prize of $25 000. The *Spirit of St Louis* is now in the National Air and Space Museum at the Smithsonian Institution, Washington, DC, USA.

Most flights Between March 1948 and his retirement on 1 Sep 1984 Flight Service Manager Charles M. Schimpf logged a total of 2 880 Atlantic crossings—a rate of 6·4 per month.

Trans-Pacific The first non-stop flight was by Maj Clyde Pangborn and Hugh Herndon in the Bellanca cabin monoplane *Miss Veedol*. They took off from Sabishiro

Beach, Japan and covered the distance of 7335 km *4558 miles* to Wenatchee, Washington State, USA in 41 hr 13 min from 3–5 Oct 1931. (For earliest crossing, see Circumnavigational flights.)

Circumnavigational flights Strict circumnavigation of the globe requires the plane to pass through two antipodal points, thus covering a minimum distance of 40 007·89 km *24 859·75 miles*.

Earliest The earliest such flight, of 42 398 km *26345 miles*, was by two US Army Douglas DWC amphibians in 57 'hops' between 6 April and 28 Sep 1924, beginning and ending at Seattle, Washington State, USA. The *Chicago* was piloted by Lt Lowell H. Smith and Lt Leslie P. Arnold, and the *New Orleans* by Lt Erik H. Nelson and Lt John Harding.

Fastest The fastest flight under the FAI (Fédération Aéronatique Internationale) rules, which permit flights that exceed the length of the Tropic of Cancer or Capricorn (36 787·599 km *22 858·754 miles*), was that of the 37 216 km *23 125 miles* eastabout flight of 36 hr 54 min 15 sec by the Boeing 747SP *'Friendship One'* (Capt. Clay Lacy) from Seattle, Washington State, USA with 141 passengers from 28–30 Jan 1988. The plane reached 1292 km/h *803 mph* over the Atlantic and refuelled only in Athens, Greece and T'ai-pei, Taiwan.

First without refuelling Dick Rutan and Jeana Yeager, in their specially constructed aircraft *Voyager*, designed by Dick's brother Burt Rutan, flew from Edwards Air Force Base, California, USA from 14–23 Dec 1986. Their flight took 9 days 3 min 44 sec and they covered a distance of 40 212·139 km *2 4 986·655 miles* averaging 186·1 km/h *115·64 mph*. The plane, with a wing span of 33·77 m *1108·8 ft* was capable of carrying 5636 litres *1240 gal* of fuel weighing 4052 kg *8934 lb*. It took over two years to construct. The pilot flew in a cockpit measuring 1·7 × 0·54 m *5·6 × 1·8 ft* and the off-duty crew member occupied a cabin 2·3 × 0·6 m *7 ½ × 2 ft*. *Voyager* is now in the National Air and Space Museum at the Smithsonian Institution, Washing, DC, USA.

First circum-polar Capt. Elgen M. Long, 44, achieved the first circum-polar flight in a Piper Navajo from 5 Nov–3 Dec 1971. He covered 62 597 km *38 896 miles* in

215 flying hours. The cabin temperature sank to −40° C −40°F over Antarctica.

First single-engined flight Richard Norton, an American airline captain, and Calin Rosetti, head of satellite navigation systems at the European Space Agency, made the first single-engined circum-polar flight in a Piper PA-46-310P Malibu. This began and finished at Le Bourget airport, Paris, France, from 21 Jan–15 Jun 1987. They travelled 55 266 km *34 342 miles* in a flying time of 185 hr 41 min.

Largest wing span The aircraft with the largest wing span ever constructed is the $40-million Hughes H.4 Hercules flyingboat ('Spruce Goose'). She was raised 21·3 m *70 ft* into the air in a test run of 914 m *1000 yd*, piloted by Howard Hughes (1905–76), off Long Beach Harbor, California, USA on 2 Nov 1947, but after this she never flew again. The eight-engined 193 tonnes aircraft has a wing span of 97·51 m *319 ft 11 in* and a length of 66·64 m *218 ft 8 in*. In a delicate engineering feat she was moved bodily by the Goldcoast Corporation, aided by the US Navy barge crane YD-171, on 22 Feb 1982 to her final resting place 9·6 km *6 miles* across the harbour under a 126·5 m *415 ft* diameter, clear–span aluminium dome, the world's largest.

Among current aircraft, the Soviet Antonov An-124 has a span of 73·3 m *240 ft 5 ¾ in*, and the Boeing 747-400 one of 64·92 m *213 ft*.

A modified six-engine version of the An–124, known as An–225 and built to carry the Soviet space shuttle *Buran*, has a wing span of 88·4 m *290 ft* (see Heaviest below).

The $34-million Piasecki Heli-Stat, comprising a framework of light-alloy and composite materials, to mount four Sikorsky SH-34J helicopters and the envelope of a Goodyear ZPG-2 patrol airship, was exhibited on 26 Jan 1984 at Lakehurst, New Jersey, USA. Designed for use by the US Forest Service and designated Model 94-37J Logger, it had an overall length of 104·55 m *343 ft* and was intended to carry a payload of 21·4 tons. It crashed on 1 Jul 1986.

Heaviest The aircraft with the highest standard maximum take-off weight is the Antonov An–225 *Myira* (Dream) at 508 tonnes. The aircraft lifted a payload of

156 300 kg *344 579 lb* to a height of 12 410 m *40 715 ft* on 22 Mar 1989. This flight was achieved by Capt. Alexander Galunenko with his crew of seven pilots. The flight was made along the route Kiev-Leningrad-Kiev without landing at a range of 2100 km *1305 miles* and lasted 3 hr 47 min.

Electric plane The MB-E1 is the first electrically propelled aircraft. A Bosch 8-kW *10·7 hp* motor is powered by Varta FP25 nickel-cadmium 25 Ah batteries. The aircraft, with a wing span of 12 m *39·4 ft*, is 7 m *23 ft* long and weighs 400 kg *882 lb*. It was designed by the model aircraft constructor Fred Militky (USA) and made its maiden flight on 21 Oct 1973.

Ultralight On 3 Aug 1985 Anthony A. Cafaro (b. 30 Nov 1951) flew a ultralight aircraft (max weight 111 kg *245 lb*, maximum speed 104·6 km/h *65 mph*, fuel capacity 18·93 litre *5 US gal*) single-seater Gypsy Skycycle for 7 hr 31 min at Dart Field, Mayville, New York, USA. Nine fuel 'pick-ups' were completed during the flight.

Smallest The smallest plane ever flown is the *Bumble Bee Two*, designed and built by Robert H. Starr of Arizona, USA. It is 2·64 m *8 ft 10 in* long, with a wing span of 1·68 m *5 ft 6 in*, and weighed 179·62 kg *396 lb* empty. The highest speed attained was 305·8 km/h *190 mph*. On 8 May 1988 it flew to a height of approximately 121·9 m *400 ft*, crashed, and was totally destroyed.

The smallest jet is the 450 km/h *280 mph* *Silver Bullet*, weighing 196 kg *432 lb*, with a 5·18 m *17 ft* wing span, built by Bob Bishop (USA).

Bombers *Heaviest* The eight-jet swept-wing Boeing B-52H Stratofortress, which has a maximum take-off weight of 220 tonnes, has a wing span of 56·38 m *185 ft* and is 48·02 m *157 ft 6 ¾ in* in length. It has a speed of over 1046 km/h *650 mph*. The B-52 can carry 12 SRAM thermonuclear short-range attack missiles or 24, 340 kg *750 lb* bombs under its wings and eight more SRAMs or 84, 226 kg *500 lb* bombs in the fuselage.

The ten-engined Convair B-36J, weighing 185 tonnes, had a greater wing span at 70·10 m *230 ft*, but it is no longer in service. Its top speed was 700 km/h *435 mph*.

Fastest The world's fastest operational bombers include the French Dassault Mirage IV, which can fly at Mach 2·2 (2333 km/h *1450 mph*) at 11 000 m *36 000 ft*.

The American variable-geometry or 'swing-wing' General Dynamics FB-111A has a maximum speed of Mach 2·5, and the Soviet swing-wing Tupolev Tu-22M, known to NATO as 'Backfire', has an estimated over-target speed of Mach 2·0 but could be as fast as Mach 2·5.

Largest airliner The highest capacity jet airliner is the Boeing 747 'Jumbo Jet', first flown on 9 Feb 1969. It can carry from 385 to more than 500 passengers and has a maximum speed of 969 km/h *602 mph*. Its wing span is 59·64 m *231·8 ft* and its length 70·7 m *195·7 ft*. It entered service on 22 Jan 1970. The first 747-400 entered service with Northwest Airlines on 26 Jan 1988; it has a wing span of 64·92 m *213 ft*, a range exceeding 12 875 km *8000 miles* can carry 422 passengers. In the 747-300, theoretical accommodation is available for 516 passengers seated 10-abreast in the main cabin plus up to 69 in the stretched upper deck.

A stretched version of the McDonnell Douglas MD-11 airliner was being studied, with accommodation for 515 passengers in the main cabin and up to 96 in a lower 'panorama deck' forward of the wing. This has given way to the MD-12, proposed in early 1990.

The greatest passenger load recorded was one of 306 adults, 328 children and 40 babies (total 674) from cyclone-devastated Darwin to Sydney, New South Wales, Australia on 29 Dec 1974.

The largest ever British aircraft was the experimental Bristol type 167 Brabazon, which had a maximum take-off weight of 131·4 tonnes, a wing span of 70·10 m *230 ft* and a length of 53·94 m *177 ft*. This eight-engined aircraft first flew on 4 Sep 1949. The four-jet Super VC10, the last design constructed by Vickers, weighed 149·5 tons and had a wing span of 44·55 m *146 ft 10 in*.

Fastest airliner The supersonic BAC/Aérospatiale Concorde, first flown on 2 Mar 1969, with a designed capacity of 128 passengers, cruises at up to Mach 2·2 (2333 km/h *1450 mph*). It has a maximum take-off weight of 185 065 kg *408 000 lb*. It flew at Mach 1·05 on 10 Oct 1969, exceeded Mach 2 for the first time on 4 Nov 1970, and became the first supersonic airliner used on passenger services on 21 Jan 1976. In service with Air France and British Airways, Concorde has been laid out for 100 passengers. The New York–London record is 2 hr 55 min 15 sec, set on 14 Apr 1990.

Most capacious The Aero Spacelines Super Guppy has a cargo hold with a usable volume of 1410 m³ *49 790 ft³* and a maximum take-off weight of 79·38 tonnes. Its wing span is 47·62 m *156 ft 3 in* and its length 43·05 m *141 ft 3 in*. Its cargo compartment is 33·17 m *108 ft 10 in* long with a cylindrical section 7·62 m *25 ft* in diameter.

The Soviet Antonov An–124 *Ruslan* has a cargo hold with a usable volume of 1014 m³ *35 800 ft³* and a maximum take-off weight of 405 tonnes. It is powered by four Lotarev D-18T turbofans giving a cruising speed of up to 850 km/h *528 mph* at 12 000 m *39 370 ft* and a range of 4500 km *2796 miles*. A special-purpose heavy-lift version of the An-124, known as An-225 *Myira* Dream, has been developed with a stretched fuselage providing as much as 1 190 m³ *42 000 ft³* usable volume. A new wing centre section carries an additional two engines, providing an estimated total 310 000 lb thrust. Having flown first on 21 Dec 1988, the aircraft was used to carry the Soviet space shuttle *Buran* for the first time on 13 May 1989 when it was airborne for 13 hr 13 min.(See heaviest above.)

Soviet manufacturer Antonov and British charter company Air Foyle claim a record for heaviest commerical air cargo movement following carriage of three tranformers weighing 43 tonnes each and other equipment a total of 133·485 tonnes from Barcelona, Spain to Noumea, New Caledonia, between 10–14 Jan 1991. Antonov and Soviet State airline Aeroflot carried a one-piece newsprint press weighing 55 tonnes from Helsinki, Finland to Melbourne, Australia in November 1989 on behalf of forwarding agent Röhlig Australia. Total payload was 122 tonnes.

Largest propeller The largest ever used was the 6·9 m *22 ft 7 ½ in* diameter Garuda propeller, fitted to the Linke-Hofmann R II built in Breslau, Germany (now Wroclaw, Poland) which flew in 1919. It was driven by four 193 kW *260 hp* Mercedes engines and turned at only 545 rpm.

Most flights by propeller-driven aircraft A Convair CV-580 turboprop airliner was reported in April 1991 to have achieved 139 368 flights. Exact age was not announced, but even if it were the first such airframe the figure equates to more than nine flights a day since 1952.

Most flights by jet airliner A survey of ageing airliner or so-called 'geriatric jets' in *Flight International* magazine for April 1990 reported a McDonnell Douglas DC-9 which had logged 90 914 flights in less than 21 years. This equates to ten flights a day and 11 daily flights at weekends, but after allowing for 'downtime' for maintenance the real daily average is higher.

Scheduled flights *Longest* The non-stop flights of United Airlines and Qantas, Los Angeles, USA to Sydney, Australia is 14 hr 50 min in a Boeing 747SP, a journey of over 12 050 km *7487 miles*.

The longest delivery flight by a commercial jet is 18 104·6 km *11250 miles* from London to Sydney, Australia by the Qantas Boeing 747-400 *Longreach*, using 179 500 kg *176·6 tons* of specially formulated Shell Jet A-1 high-density fuel, in 20 hr 9 min on 16–17 Aug 1989. It is the first time this route has been completed non-stop by an airliner.

A Boeing 767-200ER flight from Seattle, USA to Nairobi, Kenya on 8–9 Jun 1990 was the subject of claims for speed and endurance records and is likely to be the longest delivery flight by a twin-engined commercial jet. The Royal Brunei Airlines Boeing 767 flew 14 890 km *8 040 nautical miles* great-circle distance in 18 hr 29 min, consuming 74·2 tons of fuel.

Shortest The shortest scheduled flight is by Loganair between the Orkney Islands of Westray and Papa Westray which has been flown with Britten-Norman Islander twin-engined 10-seat transports since September 1967. Though scheduled for 2 minutes, in favourable wind conditions it has been accomplished in 58 sec by Capt. Andrew D. Alsop. The check-in time for the 2 min flight is 20 min.

United Airlines provides the shortest scheduled flight by jet, by Boeing 727 between San Francisco and Oakland, California, USA. There are three daily return flights, the time averages 5 minutes for the 19·3 km *12 mile* journey.

Most flights in 24 hours Brother Michael Bartlett of London an 'Eccentric Globetrotter' made 42 scheduled passenger flights with Heli Transport of Nice, Southern France between Nice, Sophia Antipolis, Monaco and Cannes in 13 hr 33 min on 13 Jun 1990.

Fastest intercontinental scheduled airline GB Airways have, since 1931, been operating a scheduled service from Gibraltar in Europe to Tangier in Africa on an almost daily basis. The flight by Pilatus Britten-Norman Trislander averages 30 min and covers a distance of 60 km *37 miles*.

HIGHEST SPEED

Official record The airspeed record is 3529·56 km/h *2193·167 mph*, by Capt. Eldon W. Joersz and Maj George T. Morgan, Jr, in a Lockheed SR-71A near Beale Air Force Base, California, USA over a 25 km *15 ½ mile* course on 28 Jul 1976.

Air-launched record The fastest fixed-wing aircraft in the world was the US North American Aviation X-15A-2, which flew for the first time (after modification from the X-15A) on 25 Jun 1964 powered by a liquid oxygen and ammonia rocket propulsion system. Ablative materials on the airframe enabled it to withstand a temperature of 3 000°F. The landing speed was momentarily 389·1 km/h *242 mph*. The

Stowaway
The most rugged stowaway was Socarras Ramirez, who escaped from Cuba on 4 Jun 1969 by stowing away in an unpressurized wheel well in the starboard wing of a Douglas DC8. The aircraft, belonging to Iberian Airlines, was on a flight from Havana, Cuba to Madrid, Spain, a distance of 9010 km *5600 miles*.

Wing walking
Roy Castle, host of the BBC TV *Record Breakers* programme, flew on the wing of a Boeing Stearman aeroplane for 3 hr 23 min on 2 Aug 1990, taking off from Gatwick, W Sussex and landing at Le Bourget, near Paris, France.

John O'Groats-Land's End
The record time for an End to End' over Great Britain where supersonic overflying is banned is 46 min 44 sec by a McDonnell F-4K Phantom (Wing-Cdr John Brady and Flt. Lt Mike Pugh) on 24 Feb 1988.

Round the world
The fastest time for a circumnavigation on scheduled flights is 44 hr 6 min by David J. Springbett (b. 2 May 1938) of Taplow, Bucks. His route took him from Los Angeles, California, USA eastabout via London, Bahrain, Singapore, Bangkok, Manila, Tokyo and Honolulu from 8–10 Jan 1980 over a 37 124 km *23 068 mile* course.

12 EC countries
On 13 Jun 1989 Michael Hamlin and Robert Noortman of Hamlin Jet Ltd flew a Cessna Citation *Biz Jet One* a distance of 5954·41 km *3700 miles*. They landed at 12 different landing strips of the 12 EC countries in a time of 18 hrs 55 min.

Paris–London

The fastest time to travel the 344 km *214 miles* from central Paris, France, to central London (BBC TV centre) is 38 min 58 sec by David Boyce of Stewart Wrightson (Aviation) Ltd on 24 Sep 1983. He travelled by motorcycle and helicopter to Le Bourget; Hawker Hunter jet (piloted by the late Michael Carlton) to Biggin Hill, Kent; and by helicopter to the TV centre car park.

London–New York

The record from central London to downtown New York City, USA by helicopter and Concorde, is 3 hr 59 min 44 sec and the return 3 hr 40 min 40 sec, set by David J. Springbett and David Boyce on 8–9 Feb 1982.

■ Largest airport

The Khalid International airport outside Riyadh, Saudi Arabia covers an area of 221 km² 86 miles². It also has the world's tallest control tower at 74 m 243 ft. (Photos: Gamma-/Guenet)

highest speed attained was 7274 km/h *4520 mph* (Mach 6·7) when piloted by Maj William J. Knight, USAF (b. 1930), on 3 Oct 1967.

An earlier version piloted by Joseph A. Walker (1920–66) reached 107 960 m *354 200 ft* also over Edwards Air Force Base, California, USA on 22 Aug 1963. The programme was suspended after the final flight of 24 Oct 1968.

US NASA Rockwell International space shuttle orbiter *Columbia* commanded by Cdr John W. Young, USN and piloted by Robert L. Crippen was launched from the Kennedy Space Center, Cape Canaveral, Florida, USA on 12 Apr 1981 after expenditure of $9·9 billion since 1972. *Columbia* broke all records in space by a fixed-wing craft, with 26 715 km/h *16 600 mph* at main engine cut-off. After re-entry from 122 km *400 000 ft*, experiencing temperatures of 2160° C *3920° F*, she glided home weighing 97 tonnes, and with a landing speed of 347 km/h *216 mph*, on Rogers Dry Lake, California, USA on 14 Apr 1981.

Under a new FAI (Fédération Aéronautique Internationale) Category P for erospacecraft, *Columbia* is holder of the current absolute world record for

duration—10 days 7 hr 47 min 23 sec to main touchdown when launched on its sixth mission, STS 9 Spacelab 1, with six crewmen, on 28 Nov 1983. Space shuttle orbiter *Challenger* was destroyed soon after launch from Cape Canaveral on 28 Jan 1986 (see Chapter 4).

Orbiter *Atlantis* holds the shuttle altitude record of 515 km *320 miles* achieved on 3 Oct 1985 on its maiden flight STS 51J.

The greatest mass lifted by the shuttle and placed in orbit was 118 697 kg *261 679 lb* by orbiter *Discovery* on STS 51A, launched on 8 Nov 1984.

Fastest jet The USAF Lockheed SR-71, a reconnaissance aircraft, is the world's fastest jet (see official record, above). First flown on 22 Dec 1964, it was reportedly capable of attaining an altitude ceiling of close to 30 480 m *100 000 ft*. It has a wing span of 16·94 m *55·6 ft* and a length of 32·73 m *107·4 ft* and weighs 75·9 tons *170 000 lb* at take-off. Its reported range at Mach 3 was 4800 km *2982 miles* at 24 000 m *78 750 ft*. At least 30 are believed to have been built when the plane was retired by the US Air Force.

It was reported on 15 Jan 1988 that the US Air Force was developing secretly a Mach 5

6115 km/h *3800 mph* high altitude (above 30 480 m *100 000 ft*) stealth aircraft.

Fastest combat jet The fastest combat jet is the USSR Mikoyan MiG-25 fighter (NATO code name 'Foxbat'). The reconnaissance 'Foxbat-B' has been tracked by radar at about Mach 3·2 (3395 km/h *2110 mph*). When armed with four large underwing air-to-air missiles known to NATO as 'Acrid', the fighter 'Foxbat-A' is limited to Mach 2·8 (2969 km/h *1845 mph*). The single-seat 'Foxbat-A' has a wing span of 13·95 m *45 ft 9 in*, is 3·82 m *278 ft 2 in* long and has an estimated maximum take-off weight of 37 421 kg *82 500 lb*.

Fastest biplane The fastest is the Italian Fiat CR42B, with a 753 kW *1010 hp* Daimler-Benz DB601A engine, attained 520 km/h *323 mph* in 1941. Only one was built.

Fastest piston-engined aircraft The fastest speed is for a cut-down privately-owned Hawker Sea Fury which attained 836 km/h *520 mph* in level flight over Texas, USA, in August 1966. It was piloted by Mike Carroll (killed 1969) of Los Angeles, USA.

The FAI accredited record for a piston-engined aircraft is 832·12 km/h *517·055 mph* over Mojave, California, USA by Frank Taylor (USA) in a modified North American P-51D Mustang powered by a 3000 hp *2 237 kW* Packard Merlin, over a 25 km *15 ½ mile* course on 30 Jul 1983.

Fastest propeller-driven aircraft The Soviet Tu-114 turboprop transport achieved a recorded speed of 877·212 km/h *545·076 mph* carrying heavy payloads over measured circuits. It is developed from the Tupolev Tu-95 bomber, known to NATO as the 'Bear', and has four 14 795 hp *11 033 kw* engines.

The turboprop-powered Republic XF-84H prototype US Navy fighter which flew on 22 Jul 1955 had a top *design* speed of 1078 km/h *670 mph*, but was abandoned.

McDonnell Douglas expected its projected MD-91X, powered by counter-rotating multi-bladed fans, to cruise at about Mach 0·78 814 km/h *514 mph*. In tests during 1987–8 with an MD-80 experimentally fitted with a General Electric GE36 engine driving two fans (in place of one of the two standard Pratt & Whitney JT8D turbofans) a maximum speed of Mach 0·865 was attained.

Fastest transatlantic flight The flight record is 1 hr 54 min 56·4 sec by Maj James V. Sullivan, 37, and Maj Noel F. Widdifield, 33, flying a Lockheed SR-71A eastwards on 1 Sep 1974. The average speed, slowed by refuelling by a KC-135 tanker aircraft, for the New York–London stage of 5570·80 km *3461·53 miles* was 2908·026 km/h *1806·963 mph*.

The solo record (Gander to Gatwick) is 8 hr 47 min 32 sec by Capt. John J.A. Smith in a Rockwell 685 on 12 Mar 1978.

Fastest climb Heinz Frick of British Aerospace took a Harrier GR5 powered by a Rolls-Royce 11-61 Pegasus engine from a standing start to 12 000 m *39 370 ft* in 126·63 sec at the Rolls-Royce flight test centre, Bristol, Avon on 15 Aug 1989.

Aleksandr Fedotov (USSR) in a Mikoyan E 266M (MiG-25) aircraft established the fastest time to height record on 17 May 1975, reaching 30 000 m *98 425 ft* in 4 min 11·7 sec after take off.

Duration The record is 64 days 22 hr 19 min 5 sec, set by Robert Timm and John

Cook in the Cessna 172 *Hacienda*. They took off from McCarran Airfield, Las Vegas, Nevada, USA just before 3:53 p.m. local time on 4 Dec 1958 and landed at the same airfield just before 2:12 p.m. on 7 Feb 1959. They covered a distance equivalent to six times round the world, refuelling without landing.

AIRPORTS

Largest The £2·1 billion King Khalid international airport outside Riyadh, Saudi Arabia covers an area of 221 km² *86 miles ²*. It was opened on 14 Nov 1983. It also has the world's largest control tower, 74 m *243 ft* in height.

The Hajj Terminal at the £2·8 billion King Abdul-Aziz airport near Jeddah, Saudia Arabia is the world's largest roofed structure, covering 1·5 km² *370 acres*.

The present six runways and five terminal buildings of Dallas/Fort Worth airport, Texas, USA are planned to be extended to nine runways, 13 terminals, 260 gates, with an ultimate capacity for 150 million passengers.

The world's largest airport terminal is Hartsfield Atlanta international airport, Georgia, USA, opened on 21 Sep 1980, with floor space covering 20·43 ha *50 ½ acres*. It has 146 gates handling 48 024 566 passengers in 1990, but has capacity for 75 million.

The new airport planned for Denver, Colorado, USA is expected to occupy an area of 116·5 km² *45 miles ²*. Completion of Phase 1, involving five runways, was scheduled for mid-1993. Initially, the new airport will have 94 gates - fewer (but larger) than the 110 at the existing Stapleton Airport which it replaces. Cost was put at least $2·6 billion.

UK Seventy airline companies from 61 countries operate scheduled services into Heathrow airport, London (1197 ha *2958 acres*). Between 1 January–31 Dec 1990 there were 390 485 air transport movements, including 344 841 passenger flights, handled by a staff of 51 400 employed by the various companies, government departments and Heathrow Airport Ltd, a subsidiary of BAA plc.

The total number of passengers, both incoming and outgoing, was 39 610 550 including transit passengers.

The most flights handled by Heathrow in a day was 1 232 on 6 Jul 1990 and the largest number of passengers handled in a day was 153 722 on 2 Sep 1990. A record 12 446 passengers were handled in one hour (11–12 a.m. GMT) on 31 Jul 1988.

The Airport's busiest single hour for passenger flights was 7–8 p.m on 15 Mar 1990 when 90 flights were handled using two active runways.

Busiest The Chicago international airport, O'Hare Field, Illinois, USA, with a total of 59 130 007 passengers and 780 658 operation movements in the year 1989. This represents a take-off or landing every 40·4 sec around the clock.

Heathrow Airport, London, handles more international traffic than any other, having 31 525 476 international passengers in 1989. Gatwick Airport, London is now the second busiest international airport with 19 870 000 passengers.

In terms of freight operations, New York City's Kennedy international airport handled 1 072 600 tonnes in 1988, while Tokyo international airport at Narita handled 1 018 600 tonnes of international freight.

Non-airline airport Among airports served by very few airlines, Van Nuys in southern California, USA is the busiest. In 1989, the airport saw 492 936 movements, of which less than one per cent were by scheduled airline, which averages more than 55 non-airline take-offs or landings per hour throughout the year.

The busiest landing area ever has been Bien Hoa Air Base, South Vietnam, which handled approximately 1 000 000 take-offs and landings in 1970.

Helipad The world's largest helipad is An Khe, South Vietnam. The heliport at Morgan City, Louisiana, USA, one of a string used by helicopters flying energy-related offshore operations into the Gulf of Mexico, has pads for 46 helicopters.

Landing fields Highest The highest is La Sa (Lhasa) airport, People's Republic of China, at 4363 m *14 315 ft*.

Lowest The lowest landing field is El Lisan on the east shore of the Dead Sea, 360 m *1180 ft* below sea level, but during World War II BOAC Short C-class flying boats, operated from the surface of the Dead Sea at 394 m *1292 ft* below sea level.

The lowest international airport is Schiphol, Amsterdam, Netherlands, at 4·5 m *15 ft* below sea level.

Farthest and nearest to city or capital The airport farthest from the city centre it allegedly serves is Viracopos, Brazil, which is 96 km *60 miles* from São Paulo. Gibraltar airport is a mere 800 m *880 yd* from the city centre.

AIRLINES

Busiest The country with the busiest airlines system is the United States, where the total number of passengers for air carriers in domestic operations in 1990 was 964 114 000.

United Kingdom airlines flew 705 424 000 km *438 330 086 miles* and carried 100 553 068 passengers on all services, excluding air taxi operations, in 1989.

On 31 Mar 1990 British Airways operated a fleet of 224 aircraft. Staff employed on airline activities totalled 50 320, and 24 238 000 passengers were carried in 1989–90 on 550 000 km *341 754 miles* of unduplicated routes.

Largest The USSR state airline Aeroflot, so named since 1932, was instituted on 9 Feb 1923. It operates 1650 aircraft over 1 000 000 km *620 000 miles* of routes, employs 500 000 people and carried 132 million passengers and 3 million tonnes of freight in 1989. Seventy per cent of its routes are international; it serves 160 passenger and five cargo routes outside the country, making regular flights to 99 countries. Its domestic network covers 3600 towns.

Oldest Koninklijke-Luchtvaart-Maatschappij NV (KLM), the national airline of the Netherlands, opened its first scheduled service (Amsterdam–London) on 17 May 1920, having been established on 7 Oct 1919.

Delag (Deutsche Luftschiffahrt AG) was founded at Frankfurt am Main, Germany on 16 Nov 1909 and started a scheduled airship service in June 1910.

Chalk's International Airline has been flying amphibious planes from Miami, Florida, USA to the Bahamas since July 1919. Albert 'Pappy' Chalk flew from 1911–75.

Aerospace company The world's largest aerospace company is Boeing of Seattle, Washington, USA, with 1990 sales of $27·6 billion and a workforce of 160 000 world-wide. Cessna Aircraft Company of Wichita, Kansas, USA had total sales of $600·9 million in 1989. The company has produced more than 177 000 aircraft since Clyde Cessna's first was built in 1911.

HELICOPTERS

Earliest Leonardo da Vinci (1452–1519) proposed the idea of a helicopter-type craft, although it is known that the French had built helicopter toys before this time.

Igor Sikorsky built a helicopter in Russia in 1909, but the first practical machine was the Focke-Achgellis, first flown in 1936.

Fastest Under FAI rules, the world's speed record for helicopters was set by Trevor Eggington, who averaged 400·87 km/h *249·09 mph* over Somerset on 11 Aug 1986 in a Westland Lynx company demonstrator helicopter.

Largest The Soviet Mil Mi-12 (NATO code-name 'Homer'), also known as the V-12, is powered by four 6,500 hp *4847 kW* turboshaft engines and has a span of 67 m *219 ft 10 in* over its rotor tips, with a length of 37·00 m *121 ft 4 ½ in*. It weighs 103·3 tonnes.

Highest altitude The record for helicopters is 12 442 m *40 820 ft* by an Aérospatiale SA315B Lama, over France on 21 Jun 1972.

The highest recorded landing has been at 7000 m *23 000 ft*, below the south-east face of Everest in a rescue sortie in May 1971.

Longest hover Doug Daigle, Brian Watts and Dave Meyer of Tridair Helicopters, together with Rod Anderson of Helistream, Inc. of California, USA maintained a continuous hovering flight in a 1947 Bell B model for 50 hr 50 sec between 13–15 Dec 1989.

Circumnavigation H. Ross Perot and Jay Coburn, both of Dallas, Texas, USA, made the first helicopter circumnavigation in *Spirit of Texas* on 1–30 Sep 1982.

The first solo round-the-world flight in a helicopter was completed by Dick Smith (Australia) on 22 Jul 1983. Taking-off from and returning to the Bell Helicopter facility at Fort Worth, Texas, USA, in a Bell Model 206L, *LongRanger III*, his unhurried flight began on 5 Aug 1982 and covered a distance of 56 742 km *35 258 miles*.

AUTOGYROS

Earliest The autogyro or gyroplane, a rotorcraft with an unpowered rotor turned by the airflow in flight, preceded the practical helicopter with an engine-driven rotor.

Juan de la Cierva (Spain), designed the first successful gyroplane with his model C.4 (commercially named an 'Autogiro') which flew at Getafe, Spain on 9 Jan 1923.

Speed, altitude and distance records Wing-Cdr Kenneth H. Wallis (GB) holds the straight-line distance record of 874·32 km *543·27 miles* set in his WA-116F autogyro on 28 Sep 1975 with a non-stop flight from Lydd, Kent to Wick, Highland.

On 20 Jul 1982, flying from Boscombe Down, Wilts, he established a new autogyro altitude record of 5643·7 m *18 516 ft* in his WA-121/Mc.

Wing-Cdr Wallis also flew his WA-116, with

a 72-hp McCulloch engine, to a record speed of 193·9 km/h *120 ½ mph* over a 3 km *1·86 mile* straight course on 18 Sep 1986.

It was reported that on 8 Apr 1931, Amelia Earhart (USA) reached a height in excess of 5791 m *19 000 ft* in an autogyro at Pitcairn Aviation Field, Pennsylvania, USA.

FLYING-BOAT

Fastest The fastest flying-boat ever built was the Martin XP6M-1 Seamaster, the US Navy four-jet-engined minelayer flown in 1955–9, with a top speed of 1040 km/h *646 mph*. In September 1946 the Martin JRM-2 Mars flying-boat set a payload record of 30 992 kg *68 327 lb*.

The official flying-boat speed record is 912 km/h *566·69 mph*, set up by Nikolay Andreyevskiy and crew of two in a Soviet Beriev M-10, powered by two AL-7 turbojets, over a 15–25 km *9·3–15 ½ mile* course on 7 Aug 1961.

The M-10 holds all 12 records listed for jet-powered flying-boats, including an altitude record of 14 962 m *49 088 ft* set by Georgiy Buryanov and crew over the Sea of Azov, USSR on 9 Sep 1961.

AIRSHIPS

Earliest The earliest flight in an airship was by Henri Giffard from Paris in his steam-powered coal-gas airship 2500 m³ *88 300 ft³* in volume and 43·8 m *144 ft* long, on 24 Sep 1852.

The earliest British airship was a 566 m³ *20 000 ft³* craft, 22·8 m *75 ft* long built by Stanley Spencer. Her maiden flight was from Crystal Palace, London on 22 Sep 1902.

Largest Rigid The largest was 213·9-tonnes German *Graf Zeppelin II* (LZ 130),

with a length of 245 m *803·8 ft* and a capacity of 199 981 m³ *7 062 100 ft³*. She made her maiden flight on 14 Sep 1938 and in May and August 1939 made radar spying missions in British air space. She was dismantled in April 1940. Her sister ship *Hindenburg* was 1·70 m *5·6 ft* longer.

The largest British airship was the R101 built by the Royal Airship Works, Cardington, Beds, which first flew on 14 Oct 1929. She was 236·8 m *777 ft* in length and had a capacity of 155 995 m³ *5 508 800 ft³*. She crashed near Beauvais, France, killing 48 of those aboard, on 5 Oct 1930.

Non-rigid The largest ever constructed was the US Navy ZPG 3-W, which had a capacity of 42 937 m³ *1 516 300 ft³*, was 122·9 m *403 ft* long and 25·93 m *85·1 ft* in diameter, and had a crew of 21. She first flew on 21 Jul 1958, but crashed into the sea in June 1960.

Hot-air The world altitude record of 3159 m *10 365 ft* is held by the Cameron D-38 hot-air airship flown at Cunderdin, Western Australia, on 27 Aug 1982. It was flown by R.W. Taaffe (Australia).

Oscar Lindstrom in a Colt AS 56 Hotair airship achieved a distance and duration record of 93·033 km *57·8 miles* in a time of 3 hr 41 min 55 sec, from Stockholm to Tobo, Sweden on 20 Mar 1988.

Greatest passenger load The most people ever carried in an airship was 207, in the US Navy *Akron* in 1931. The transatlantic record is 117, by the German *Hindenburg* in 1937.

The largest airship currently certificated for the public transport of passengers (13) is the 59 m *193·6 ft* long non-rigid Skyship 600 series of 666 m³ *235 400 ft³* capacity, built by Airship Industries.

Distance records The FAI accredited straight-line distance record for airships is 6384·5 km *3967·1 miles*, set up by the German *Graf Zeppelin*, captained by Dr Hugo Eckener, between 29 Oct–1 Nov 1928.

From 21–25 Nov 1917 the German Zeppelin L59 flew from Yambol, Bulgaria, to south of Khartoum, Sudan, and returned to cover a minimum of 7250 km *4500 miles*.

Duration record The longest recorded flight by a non-rigid airship (without refuelling) is 264 hr 12 min by a US Navy Goodyear-built ZPG-2 class ship (Cdr J.R. Hunt, USN) from South Weymouth Naval Air Station, Massachusetts, USA from 4–15 Mar 1957, landing back at Key West, Florida, USA after having flown 15 205 km *9448 miles*.

BALLOONING

Earliest The earliest recorded ascent was by a model hot-air balloon invented by Father Bartolomeu de Gusmão (*né* Lourenço) (1685–1724), which was flown indoors at the Casa da India, Terreiro do Paço, Portugal on 8 Aug 1709.

Distance record The record distance travelled by a balloon is 8382·54 km *5208·68 miles*, by the Raven experimental helium-filled balloon *Double Eagle V* (capacity 11 300 m³ *399·053 ft³*) from 9–12 Nov 1981. The journey stated from Nagashima, Japan and ended at Covello, California, USA. The crew for this first manned balloon crossing of the Pacific Ocean were Ben L. Abruzzo, 51, Rocky Aoki, 43 (Japan), Ron Clark, 41, and Larry M. Newman, 34.

Ex-USAF Col. Joe Kittinger (see also Parachuting) became the first man to complete a solo transatlantic crossing by balloon. Accomplished in the 3000 m³ *105944 ft³* helium-filled balloon *Rosie O'Grady* between 14 and 18 Sep 1984, Kittinger lifted off from Caribou, Maine, USA and completed a distance of approximately 5701 km *3543 miles* before landing at Montenotte, Italy 86 hours later.

The first balloon crossing of the North Atlantic was made from 12–17 Aug 1978 (137 hr 6 min) in the gas balloon *Double Eagle II*, crewed by Ben L. Abruzzo, Maxie L. Anderson and Larry M. Newman.

Highest Unmanned The highest altitude attained by an unmanned balloon was 51 815 m *170 000 ft* by a Winzen balloon of 1·35 million m³ *47·8 million ft³* launched at Chico, California, USA in October 1972.

Manned The greatest altitude reached in a manned balloon is an unofficial 37 735 m *123 800 ft* by Nicholas Piantanida (1933–66) of Bricktown, New Jersey, USA, from Sioux Falls, South Dakota on 1 Feb 1966. He landed in a cornfield in Iowa but did not survive.

The official record (closed gondola) is 34 668 m *113 740 ft* by Cdr Malcolm D. Ross, USNR and the late Lt-Cdr Victor A. Prother, USN in an ascent from the deck of USS *Antietam* over the Gulf of Mexico on 4 May 1961 in a balloon of 339 804 m³ *12 million ft³*.

Owing to an oversight, Keith Lang and Harold Froelich, scientists from Minneapolis, USA, ascended in an open gondola and without the protection of pressure suits to an altitude of 12·84 km *42 150 ft*, just under 8 miles, on 26 Sep 1956. During their 6 ½-hour flight, at maximum altitude and without goggles, they observed the Earth and measured a temperature of −57·7°C *−72° F*.

Largest The largest balloons ever built have an inflatable volume of 2 million m³ *70 million ft³* and stand 300 m *1000 ft* tall. They are unmanned. The manufacturers are Winzen Research Inc. Minnesota, USA.

Hot-air The modern revival of this form of ballooning began in the USA in 1961, and the first World Championships were held in Albuqerque, New Mexico, USA on 10–17 Feb 1973.

Mass ascent The greatest mass ascent of hot-air balloons from a single site took place when 128 participants at the Ninth Bristol International Balloon Festival at Ashton Court, Bristol, Avon took off within 1 hour on 15 Aug 1987.

Atlantic crossing Richard Branson (GB) with his pilot Per Lindstrand (GB), were the first to cross the Atlantic in a hot-air balloon, from 2–3 Jul 1987. They ascended from Sugarloaf, Maine, USA and covered the distance of 4947 km *3075 miles*, to Limavady, Co. Londonderry in 31 hrs 41 min.

Pacific crossing Richard Branson and Per Lindstrand also crossed the Pacific in the *Virgin Otsuka Pacific Flyer* from the southern tip of Japan to Lac la Matre, Yukon north-western Canada on 15–17 Jan 1991 in a 73 624 m³ *2·6 million ft³* hot-air balloon (the largest ever flown) to set FAI records for duration (46 hrs 15 min) and distance (great circle 7671·9 km *4768 miles*). Unofficial world best performance were additionally set for the fastest speed from take-off to landing of 237 km/h *147 mph*. A speed of 385 km/h *239 mph* was sustained over one hour.

Altitude Per Lindstrand (GB) achieved the altitude record of 19 811 m *64 996 ft* in a Colt 600 hot-air balloon over Laredo, Texas, USA on 6 Jun 1988.

The FAI endurance and distance record for a gas and hot-air balloon is 96 hr 24 min and 3339·086 km *2074·817 miles* by *Zanussi*, crewed by Donald Allan Cameron (GB) and Maj. Christopher Davey (GB), which failed by only 166 km *103 miles* to achieve the first balloon crossing of the Atlantic on 30 Jul 1978.

Highest most passengers *Miss Champagne*, a balloon of 73 625 m³ *2·6 million ft³* capacity, was built by Tom Handcock of Portland, Maine, USA. Tethered, it rose to height of 12·25 m *50 ft* with 61 passengers on board on 19 Feb 1988.

The Dutch balloonist Henk Brink made an unthethered flight of 200 m *656 ft* in the 24 000 m³ *850 000 ft³ Nashua Number One* carrying a total of 50 passengers and crew. The flight, on 17 Aug 1988, lasted 25 min, commenced from Lelystad airport, Netherlands, and reached an altitude of 100 m *328 ft*.

PERSONAL AVIATION RECORDS

Oldest and youngest passengers Airborne births are reported every year.

The oldest person to fly has been Mrs Jessica S. Swift (b. Anna Stewart, 17 Sep 1871), aged 110 years 3 months, from Vermont to Florida, USA in Dec 1981.

The oldest Briton to fly is Charlotte Hughes of Marske-by-the-Sea, Hartlepool, Cleveland (b. 1 Aug 1877). She was given a flight on Concorde to New York on 4 Aug 1987. She returned four days later.

Most experienced passenger Edwin A. Shackleton of Bristol, Avon has flown as

a passenger in 392 different types of aircraft. His first flight was in March 1943 in D.H. Dominie R9548; other aircraft have included helicopters, gliders, microlights, gas and hot air ballons.

Pilots *Youngest* The youngest age at which anyone has ever qualified as a military pilot is 15 years 5 months in the case of Sgt Thomas Dobney (b. 6 May 1926) of the RAF. He had overstated his age (14 years) on entry.

Wholly untutored, James A. Stoodley aged 14 years 5 months took his 13-year-old brother John on a 29-minute joy ride in an unattended US Piper Cub trainer aircraft near Ludgershall, Wilts in December 1942.

Oldest The world's oldest pilot is Ed McCarty (b. 18 Sep 1885) of Kimberley, Idaho, USA, who in 1979 was flying his rebuilt 30-year-old Ercoupe, at the age of 94.

The oldest British pilot is Air Commodore Harold 'Daddy' Probyn (b. 8 Dec 1891), who first flew with the RFC in 1916 and last flew on 8 Dec 1983 a Rheims Rocket No. 5Y AYF in Kenya.

Longest serving military pilot Sqn Ldr N.E. Rose, AFC(RAF Retd) (b. 30 May 1924) flew military aircraft without a break from 1942–89 achieving 11 539 hours of

flying in 54 different types of aircraft. He first learnt to fly in a Tiger Moth in Southern Rhodesia then flew Hurricanes in World War II. He last flew with the RAF in a Chipmunk of No. 10 Air Experience Flight.

Longest interval between transatlantic flights Wing-Cdr A.G. Evenden first flew the Atlantic as a crew member of the British R34 the first airship to cross the Atlantic, between 2–6 Jul 1919. Sixty years later on 2 Jul 1979 he made the crossing in Concorde.

Most flying hours *Pilot* John Edward Long (b. 10 Nov 1915) (USA) between 1 May 1933 and 7 Sep 1989 totalled 53 290 hr 5 min logged flights as a pilot— more than six years airborne.

Passenger The record as a supersonic passenger is held by Fred Finn, who made his 687th Concorde crossing in February 1991 he commutes regularly from New Jersey, USA to London. In April 1991 he became the first passenger to achieve 10 million miles.

Since September 1970 Maisie Muir of Orkney, Scotland has flown over 8000 times with Loganair in connection with her work duties at the Royal Bank of Scotland.

Longest air ticket
A 12 m *39 ft 4 ½ in* ticket was issued for $4500 to M. Bruno Leunen of Brussels, Belgium in December 1984 for a 85 623 km *53 203 mile* trip on 80 airlines with 109 stopovers.

Most to jump from a balloon
On 5 Apr 1990, 12 members of the Red Devils Free Fall Parachute Team in one flight, together made a jump from a Cameron A210, hot air balloon over Bath, Avon, at a height of 1828 m *6 000 ft*.

PARACHUTING RECORDS

It is estimated that the human body reaches 99 per cent of its low-level terminal velocity after falling 573 m *1880 ft*, which takes 13–14 sec. This is 188–201 km/h *117–125 mph* at normal atmospheric pressure in a random posture, but up to 298 km/h *185 mph* in a head-down position.

FIRST ● Tower[1] ● Louis-Sébastien Lenormand (1757–1839), quasi-parachute, Montpellier, France, 1783.
Balloon ● André-Jacques Garnerin (1769–1823), 680 m *2230 ft* Monceau Park, Paris, France, 22 Oct 1797.
Aircraft ● *Man*: 'Captain' Albert Berry, an aerial exhibitionist, St Louis, Missouri, USA, 1 Mar 1912. *Woman*: Mrs Georgina 'Tiny' Broadwick (b. 1893), Griffith Park, Los Angeles, USA, 21 Jun 1913.

LONGEST DURATION FALL ● Lt Col Wm H. Rankin, USMC, 40 min due to thermals, North Carolina, USA, 26 Jul 1956.

LONGEST DELAYED DROP ● World ● *Man*: Capt Joseph W. Kittinger[2], 25 816 m *84 700 ft 16·04 miles*, from balloon at 31 333 m *102 800 ft*, Tularosa, New Mexico, USA, 16 Aug 1960. *Woman*: E. Fomitcheva (USSR) 14 800 m *48 556 ft*, over Odessa, USSR, 26 Oct 1977.
Over UK ● *Man (Civilian)*: M. Child, R. McCarthy, 10 180 m *33 400 ft* from balloon at 10 851 m *35 600 ft*, Kings Lynn, Norfolk, 18 Sep 1986. *Woman (Civilian)*: Francesca Gannon and Valerie Slattery, 6520 m *21 391 ft* from aircraft at 7600 m *24 934 ft*, Netheravon, Wilts, 11 Mar 1987. *Group*: S/Ldr J. Thirtle AFC, Fl Sgt A. K. Kidd AFM, Sgts L. Hicks (d. 1971), P. P. Keane AFM BEM, K. J. Teesdale AFM, 11 943 m *39 183 ft* from aircraft at 12 613 m *41 383 ft*, Boscombe Down, Wilts, 16 Jun 1967.

MID-AIR RESCUE ● Earliest ● Miss Dolly Shepherd (1886–1983) brought down Miss Louie May on her single 'chute from balloon at 3350 m *11 000 ft*, Longton, Staffs, 9 Jun 1908.
Lowest ● Gregory Robertson saved Debbie Williams (unconscious), collision at 2750 m *9000 ft*, pulled her ripcord at 1065 m *3500 ft*—10 secs from impact, Coolidge, Arizona, USA, 18 Apr 1987.

HIGHEST ESCAPE ● Flt Lt J. de Salis, RAF and Fg Off P. Lowe, RAF, 17 068 m *56 000 ft*, Moynash, Derby, 9 Apr 1958.
Lowest ● S/Ldr Terence Spencer DFC, RAF, 9–12 m *30–40 ft*, Wismar Bay, Baltic, 19 Apr 1945.

HIGHEST LANDING ● Ten USSR parachutists[3], 7133 m *23 405 ft*, Lenina Peak, USSR May 1969.

MOST SOUTHERLY ● T/Sgt Richard J. Patton (d. 1973), Operation Deep Freeze, South Pole, 25 Nov 1956.
MOST NORTHERLY ● Dr Jack Wheeler (US); pilot Capt Rocky Parsons, −31·6° C *−25° F*, in Lat. 90° 00' N, 15 Apr 1981.

CROSS-CHANNEL (LATERAL FALL) ● Sgt Bob Walters with three soldiers and two Royal Marines, 35·4 km *22 miles* from 7600 m *25 000 ft*, Dover, Kent to Sangatte, France, 31 Aug 1980.

TOTAL SPORT PARACHUTING DESCENTS ● *Man*: Roch Charmet (France, d. 20 Feb 1989), 14 650, various locations, *Woman*: Valentina Zakoretskaya (USSR), 8000, over USSR, 1964–September 1980.

24-HOUR TOTAL ● Dale Nelson (USA), 301 (in accordance with United States Parachute Association rules), Pennsylvania, USA, 26–27 May 1988.

MOST TRAVELLED ● Kevin Seaman from a Cessna Skylane (pilot Charles E. Merritt), 19 611 km *12 186 miles*, jumps in all 50 US States, 26 Jul–15 Oct 1972.

HEAVIEST LOAD ● US Space Shuttle *Columbia*, external rocket retrieval, 80 ton capacity, triple array, each 36·5 m *120 ft* diameter, Atlantic, off Cape Canaveral, Florida, USA, 12 Apr 1981.

HIGHEST STACK ● 24, The Royal Marine Free Fall Display Team, Dunkeswell, Devon, 20 Aug 1986.

LARGEST FREE FALL FORMATION ● World: 144, held for 8·8 sec, from 4876 m *16 000 ft*, Quincy, Illinois, USA, 11 Jul 1988. UK: 60, held for 4 sec, from 4572 m *15 000 ft*, Peterborough, Cambs, 8 Jun 1989.

OLDEST ● *Man*; Edwin C. Townsend (d. 7 Nov 1987), 89 years, Vermillion Bay, Louisiana, USA, 5 Feb 1986. *Woman*; Mrs Sylvia Brett (GB), 80 years 166 days, Cranfield, Beds, 23 Aug 1986.

LONGEST FALL WITHOUT PARACHUTE ● World ● Vesna Vulovic (Yugoslavia), air hostess in DC-9 which blew up at 10 160 m *33 330 ft* over Serbska Kamenice, Czechoslovakia, 26 Jan 1972.
UK ● Flt-Sgt Nicholas Stephen Alkemade (d. 22 Jun 1987), from blazing RAF Lancaster bomber, at 5485 m *18 000 ft* over Germany (near Oberkürchen), 23 Mar 1944.

[1] *The king of Ayutthaya, Siam in 1687 was reported to have been diverted by an ingenious athlete parachuting with two large umbrellas. Faustus Verancsis is reputed to have descended in Hungary with a framed canopy in 1617.*

[2] *Maximum speed in rarefied air was 1006 km/h 625·2 mph at 27 430 m 90 000 ft—marginally supersonic.*

[3] *Four were killed.*

AIRCRAFT

■ **Human powered flight**
Kanellos Kanellopoulos pedalled his way 4·5 m 15 ft above the waves to cross from Crete to the island of Santorini, a distance of 119 km 74 miles in a time of 2 hr 49 min. (Photo: Gamma-/Macrakis)

Most flying records
Brendan O'Brien of Croydon, Surrey holds 201 point to point speed records as verified by the FAI (*Federation Aeronautique Internationale*) flying a Fournier RF4 single-seater single-engined plane on the 2 Jul 1985.

Plane pulling
Dave Gauder single-handedly pulled Concorde 12·19 m *40 ft* across the tarmac at Heathrow Airport, London on 11 Jun 1987.

Most planes flown James B. Taylor, Jr (1897–1942) flew 461 different types of powered aircraft during his 25 years as an active experimental test and demonstration pilot for the US Navy and a number of American aircraft manufacturing companies. The planes flown included the most advanced military fighter and attack aircraft of their day. He was one of the few pilots of the 1920s and 1930s qualified to perform terminal velocity dives. During one dive in 1939, he may have become the first pilot in history to fly faster than 500 mph and live.

Human-powered flight The first man-powered Channel crossing was achieved on 12 Jun 1979 by Bryan Allen (USA) in the *Gossamer Albatross*, designed by Dr Paul MacCready. The 35·82 km *22·26 mile* flight from Folkestone, Kent to Cap Gris Nez, France set the duration record of 2 hr 49 min.

The Daedalus Project, centred on the Massachusetts Institute of Technology, achieved its goal of human-powered flight from Crete to the island of Santorini 119 km *74 miles* distant on 23 Apr 1988, when Kanellos Kanellopoulos (b. 25 Apr 1957) averaged 29·7 km/h *18·5 mph* in his 34·1 m *112 ft* wing span machine.

MODEL AIRCRAFT

Altitude, speed and duration
Maynard L. Hill (USA), flying radio-controlled models, established the world record for altitude of 8208 m *26 929 ft* on 6 Sep 1970, and on 4 Jul 1983 set a closed-circuit distance record of 765 km *1231 miles*.

The free-flight speed record is 343·92 km/h *213·70 mph* by V. Goukoune and V. Myakinin (both USSR), with a radio-controlled model at Klementyevo, USSR on 21 Sep 1971.

The record duration flight is one of 32 hr 7 min 40 sec by Eduard Svoboda (Czecho-

slovakia), flying a radio-controlled glider on 23–24 Aug 1980.

An indoor model with a rubber motor designed by J. Richmond (USA) set a duration record of 52 min 14 sec on 31 Aug 1979.

Largest glider In January 1990 *Eagle III*, a radio controlled glider weighing 14·5 lb with a wing span of 9·80 m *32 ft 6 in* was designed and constructed by Carlos Reńe Tschen and Carlos Reńe Tschen Jr of Colonia San Lázaro, Guatemala.

Cross-Channel The first model helicopter flight was achieved by a 5 kg *11 lb* model Bell 212, radio controlled by Dieter Zeigler for 52 km *32 miles* between Ashford, Kent and Ambleteuse, France on 17 Jul 1974.

Smallest The smallest to fly is one weighing 0·1 g *0·004 oz* powered by attaching a horsefly and designed by insectonaut Don Emmick of Seattle, Washington State, USA. On 24 Jul 1979 one flew for 5 minutes at Kirkland, Washington State.

Paper aircraft The flight duration record for a paper aircraft is 16·89 sec by Ken Blackburn in the Reynolds Coliseum, N Carolina State University, USA on 29 Nov 1983.

The indoor record with a 3·65 m *12 ft* ceiling is 1 min 33 sec set in the Fuji TV studios, Tōkyō, Japan on 21 Sep 1980.

A paper plane was reported and witnessed to have flown 2 km *1 ¼ miles* by 'Chick' C.O. Reinhart from a tenth-storey office window at 60 Beaver Street, New York City, USA across the East River to Brooklyn in August 1933, helped by a thermal from a coffee-roasting plant.

An indoor distance of 58·82 m *193 ft* was recorded by Tony Felch at the La Crosse Center, Wisconsin, USA on 21 May 1985.

Largest The largest flying paper aeroplane with a wing span of 4·89 m *16 ft 4 in* was constructed by pupils of Pendleton Heights High School, Indiana, USA and

flown on 24 May 1990. It was launched from a 3·04 m *10 ft* high platform and flown for a distance of 25·92 m *85 ft 3 in*.

KITE FLYING

The following records are all recognized by *Kite Lines* magazine:–

Longest The longest kite flown was 1034·45 m *3394 ft* in length. It was made and flown by Michel Trouillet and a team of helpers at Nîmes, France on 18 Nov 1990.

Largest The largest kite flown was one of 553 m² *5952 ft²*. It was first flown by a Dutch team on the beach at Scheveningen, Netherlands on 8 Aug 1981.

Highest The classic record height of 9740 m *31 955 ft* was reached by a train of eight kites over Lindenberg, Germany on 1 Aug 1919.

The altitude record for a single kite is 3801 m *12 471 ft*, in the case of a kite flown by Henry Helm Clayton and A.E. Sweetland at the Blue Hill Weather Station, Milton, Massachusetts, USA on 28 Feb 1898.

Fastest The fastest speed attained by a kite was 193 km/h *120 mph* for a kite flown by Pete DiGiacomo at Ocean City, Maryland, USA on 22 Sep 1989.

Greatest lift The greatest lift by a single kite was one of 330·21 kg *728 lb*, achieved by a kite flown by G. William Tyrrell, Jr, also at Ocean City, Maryland, USA on 23 Sep 1984.

Most on a single line The greatest number of kites flown on a single line is 11 284, by Sadao Harada and a team of helpers at Sakurajima, Kagoshima, Japan on 18 Oct 1990.

Longest duration The longest recorded flight is one of 180 hr 17 min by the Edmonds Community College team at Long Beach, Washington State, USA from 21–29 Aug 1982. Managing the flight of the J-25 parafoil was Harry N. Osborne.

COMMERCE

Greatest auction
The largest-ever auction was of the Hughes Aircraft Co. for $5 billion by General Motors of Detroit, Michigan, USA on 5 Jun 1985.

Greatest barter deal
The biggest barter in trading history was 36 million barrels of oil, valued at £900 million, exchanged for 10 Boeing 747s destined for the Royal Saudi Airline in July 1984.

Jumble sale
The Cleveland Convention Center, Ohio, USA White Elephant Sale (instituted 1933) on 18–19 Oct 1983 raised $427 935·21. The greatest amount of money raised at a one-day sale is $170 139·76 at the 56th one-day rummage sale organized by the Winnetka Congregational Church, Illinois, USA on 12 May 1988.

Britain's largest jumble sale was Jumbly '79, sponsored by *Woman's Own*, at Alexandra Palace, London from 5–7 May 1979 in aid of the Save the Children Fund. The attendance was 60 000 and the gross takings in excess of £60 000.

Brickworks
The largest brickworks in the world is the London Brick Co. Ltd plant at Stewartby, Beds. Established in 1898, the site now covers 90 ha *221 acres* and has a weekly production capacity of 10·5 million bricks and brick equivalent.

Commerce

Oldest industry The oldest known industry is flint knapping, involving the production of chopping tools and hand axes, dating from 2·5 million years ago in Ethiopia. The earliest evidence of trading in exotic stone and amber dates from c. 28 000 BC in Europe. Agriculture is often described as 'the oldest industry in the world', whereas in fact there is no firm evidence yet that it was practised before c. 11 000 BC.

Oldest company The Faversham Oyster Fishery Co. is referred to in the Faversham Oyster Fishing Act of 1930 as existing 'from time immemorial', i.e. in English law, from before 1189.

Stora Kopparbergs Bergslags of Falun, Sweden's oldest industrial enterprise, has been in continuous operation since the 11th century. It is first mentioned in historical records in the year 1288, when a Swedish bishop bartered an eighth share in the enterprise. Originally concerned with the mining and processing of copper, it is today the largest privately-owned power producer in Sweden. The Royal Mint has origins going back to AD 287. The Oxford University Press celebrated a 500th anniversary in 1978 not of itself, but of the earliest origin of printing in Oxford in 1478.

The Shore Porters' Society of Aberdeen, Grampian, a haulier, shipping and warehouse partnership, is known to have been established before 4 Jun 1498. The Whitechapel Bell Foundry of Whitechapel Road, east London has been in business since c. 1570. It has indirect successions through Master Founder Thomas Mears II since 1810 and via Rudhalls of Gloucester, back to 1270. John Brooke & Sons Holdings Ltd, spinners and clothiers of Huddersfield, W Yorks, has been run by the same family since 1541. The present directors, brothers E.L.M. and M.R.H. Brooke, are of the 16th generation. The first bill of adventure, signed by the English East India Co., was dated 21 Mar 1601.

Largest companies The first company to have assets in excess of $1 billion was the United States Steel (now USX) Corporation of Pittsburgh, Pennsylvania, with $1·5 billion at the time of its creation by merger in 1902.

The largest manufacturing company in the world in terms of assets, sales and employees is currently General Motors Corporation of Detroit, Michigan, USA, with operations throughout the world. Apart from its core business of motor vehicles and components, it produces defence and aerospace materials and provides computer and communication services. Its total revenue in 1990 was $126 billion and assets at 31 Dec 1990 were valued at $180 billion. The company's total 1990 payroll was $28·8 billion to an average 761 400 employees. Dividends paid in 1990 were $1·9 billion.

UK The net assets of Shell Transport and Trading Co. plc at 31 Dec 1990 were £11·2 billion, mainly comprising its 40 per cent share in the net assets of the Royal Dutch Shell Group of companies which stood at £28·5 billion. Group companies employ some 137 000 staff. Shell Transport was formed in 1897 by Marcus Samuel (1853–1927), later the 1st Viscount Bearsted. The biggest British manufacturing company is Imperial Chemical Industries (ICI) plc, which had assets of £11 billion at 1 Jan

1991. Its staff and payroll averaged 132 100 during the year. The company, which has more than 400 UK and overseas subsidiaries, was formed on 7 Dec 1926 by the merger of four concerns — British Dyestuffs Corporation Ltd; Brunner, Mond & Co. Ltd; Nobel Industries Ltd and United Alkali Co. Ltd. The first chairman was Sir Alfred Moritz Mond (1868–1930), later the 1st Lord Melchett.

Largest employer The world's largest employer is Indian Railways, with 1 646 704 staff at 31 Mar 1990. The United Kingdom's National Health Service employed a total of 1 223 000 staff (excluding general practitioners) at 30 Sep 1989.

Greatest sales The first company to surpass the $1 billion mark in annual sales was the United States Steel (now USX) Corporation of Pittsburgh, Pennsylvania in 1917. There are now 570 corporations with sales exceeding $1 billion, including 272 from the United States. The *Fortune* 500 List of leading industrial corporations at April 1991 is headed by the General Motors Corporation of Detroit, Michigan, USA, with sales of $126 billion for 1990. Britain's highest sales figure was achieved in 1989 by British Petroleum (BP) at £29 billion, representing profits of £2 billion compared with £3·9 billion in 1987/88.

Sales per unit area Richer Sounds plc, the electrical goods retail chain, topped the *Retail Rankings* table for sales based on square footage of selling space in 1990. Sales at their busiest outlet at London Bridge Walk reached £17 340 per square foot.

Greatest profit The greatest net profit ever made by a corporation in 12 months is $7·6 billion by American Telephone and Telegraph Co. (AT&T) from 1 Oct 1981 to 30 Sep 1982.

Greatest loss The Argentine-government owned oil company Yacimientos Petrolíferos (YPF) was reported to have made a trading loss of $4·6 billion in 1983. The loss for the National Coal Board (now British Coal) in the tax year ending 31 Mar 1985 was £2·2 billion.

Take-overs The highest bid in a corporate take-over was $21 billion for RJR Nabisco Inc., the tobacco, food and beverage company, by the Wall Street leveraged buyout firm Kohlberg Kravis Roberts, who offered $90 a share on 24 Oct 1988. By 1 Dec 1988 the bid, led by Henry Kravis, had reached $109 per share to aggregate $25 billion.

UK The largest bid ever made for a British company is £13 billion for BAT Industries on 11 Jul 1989 by Hoylake, led by Sir James Goldsmith, Jacob Rothschild and Kerry Packer. Hanson Trust won control of Consolidated Gold Fields (founded 1897) on 7 Aug 1989 with a bid of £3·5 billion.

Bankruptcies Rajendra Sethia (b. 1950) was arrested in New Delhi, India on 2 Mar 1985 on charges including criminal conspiracy and forgery. He had been declared bankrupt by the High Court in London on 18 Jan 1985, when Esal Commodities was said to be in debt for a record £170 million. His personal debts were estimated at £140 million. William G. Stern (b. 1936) of London, a US citizen since 1957, who set up the Wilstar Group Holding Co. in the London property market in 1971, was declared bankrupt for £104 million in February 1979. This figure rose to £143 million by February 1983. He was discharged for £500 000 suspended for 2½ years on 28 Mar 1983.

The number of UK companies declared bankrupt or plunged into liquidation in 1990 reached a record 24 442, with receiverships totalling 2634. The construction, property and retail sectors were the worst hit.

Companies The number of companies registered in Great Britain at 31 Mar 1991 was 1 186 448, of which 11 650 were public limited companies and the balance private.

Accountants The world's largest firm of accountants and management consultants is KPMG Peat Marwick McLintock, whose world-wide fee income totalled $5·36 billion at 30 Sep 1990. The company had 77 300 employees in 802 offices at 31 Mar 1991.

Banks The International Bank for Reconstruction and Development (founded on 27 Dec 1945 and known as the World Bank) is the world's largest multilateral development bank. Based in Washington, DC, USA, the bank had an authorized share capital of $171·4 billion at 31 Dec 1988. There were 151 members with a subscribed capital of $102 billion at 31 Dec 1988, at which time the World Bank also had unallocated reserves and accumulated net income of $9·2 billion. The International Monetary Fund (IMF), also in Washington, DC, had 155 members with total quotas of $131 billion as at February 1991.

The world's biggest commercial bank is the Dai-Ichi Kangyo Bank Ltd of Japan, with assets on 31 Mar 1989 of $414·1 billion. The bank with most branches is the State Bank of India, which had 12 462 outlets on 1 Jan 1991 and assets of £22 billion.

Britain's oldest independent bank is C. Hoare & Co., founded in 1672 by Richard Hoare, a goldsmith, in London. Child & Co. of Fleet St, although now part of the Royal Bank of Scotland, can trace its origins back to 1584 when its founder William Wheeler became formally apprenticed as a goldsmith. The bank with the largest network in the United Kingdom is the National Westminster, with consolidated total assets of £116·2 billion and 3066 branches at 31 Dec 1989.

Building societies The world's biggest lender is the Japanese government-controlled House Loan Corporation. The biggest building society in the world is the Halifax Building Society of Halifax, W Yorks. Established in 1853, it had total assets of £54 billion in 1990 and lending in that year was £9·6 billion. The Society has 17 651 employees and 2352 offices.

Chemists The largest chain of chemist stores in the world is Rite Aid Corporation of Shiremanstown, Pennsylvania, USA which, in 1989, had 2353 branches throughout the United States. The Walgreen Co. of Deerfield, Illinois, USA has fewer shops, but a larger volume of sales, totalling $5·3 billion in 1989.

Britain's largest chain of pharmacies is Boots the Chemists, which had 1050 retail stores at April 1991. The firm was founded by Jesse Boot (1850–1931), later the 1st Baron Trent.

Department stores Woolworth Corporation now operates more than 8700 general stores world-wide. Frank Winfield Woolworth opened his first store, 'The Great Five Cent Store', in Utica, New York, USA on 22 Feb 1879. The net income for 1990 was $317 million.

The world's largest department store is R.H. Macy & Co. Inc. at Herald Square, New York City, USA. It covers 20·3 ha *50·5 acres* and employs 14 000 staff handling

400 000 items. Total sales for the company's 150 stores in 1990 were $7·3 billion. Rowland Hussey Macy's sales on his first day at his fancy goods store on 6th Avenue, on 27 Oct 1858, were recorded as $11·06.

The largest department store in the United Kingdom is Harrods Ltd of Knightsbridge, London, named after Henry Charles Harrod (1800–85), who opened a grocery in Knightsbridge Village in 1849. It has a total selling floor space of 9 ha *22 acres*, with 50 lifts and 36 flights of stairs and escalators, employs 4000–5500 people depending on the time of year, and achieved record sales of over £312 million in the year ending 1 Feb 1987. The record for a day is £7 million in the January 1987 sale. Nearly £13 million was taken over the first four days of the 1990 January sale, with £45 million taken over the entire January sale period.

Longest wait for a sale Kevin Mellish (b. 2 Aug 1948) queued for a carpet reduced in price by more than 86 per cent for 20 days outside Arding and Hobbs, Clapham, London, from 7 to 27 Dec 1986.

Employment agency Blue Arrow became the world's largest employment group when, on 5 Sep 1987, it bid successfully for the US company Manpower, at £825 million.

Insurance The company with the highest volume of insurance in force in the world is the Metropolitan Life Insurance Co. of New York City, USA, with $908·6 billion at year end 1990. The Prudential Insurance Company of America of Newark, New Jersey has the greatest volume of consolidated assets, totalling $169 billion at 31 Dec 1990. The largest single association in the world is the Blue Cross and Blue Shield Association, the US-based hospital insurance organization. It had a membership of 71 million on 31 Dec 1990, and benefits paid out in 1990 totalled $55·9 billion.

The largest life assurance group in the United Kingdom is the Prudential Corporation plc, whose total assets at 1 Jan 1991 were £36·5 billion.

The largest life assurance policy ever issued was for $100 million, bought by a major US entertainment corporation on the life of a leading US entertainment industry figure. The policy was sold in July 1990 by Peter Rosengard of London and was placed by Shel Bachrach of Albert G. Ruben & Co. Inc. of Beverly Hills, California, USA and Richard Feldman of the Feldman Agency, East Liverpool, Ohio with nine insurance companies to spread the risk. The highest payout on a single life was reported on 14 Nov 1970 to be some $18 million to Linda Mullendore, widow of an Oklahoma, USA rancher. Her murdered husband had paid $300 000 in premiums in 1969.

The largest ever marine insurance loss was approximately $836 million for the Piper Alpha Oil Field in the North Sea. On 6 Jul 1988 a leak from a gas compression chamber underneath the living quarters ignited and triggered a series of explosions which blew Piper Alpha apart. Of the 232 people on board, only 65 survived. The largest sum claimed for consequential losses is £890 million against owning, operating and building corporations and Claude Phillips resulting from the 66 million gallon oil spill from MT *Amoco Cadiz* on the Brittany coast on 16 Mar 1978.

Law firms The world's largest law firm is Baker & McKenzie, employing 1560 lawyers, 490 of whom are partners, in 31 coun-

tries at 1 May 1991. The firm was founded in Chicago, Illinois, USA in 1949.

Paper company The world's largest producer of paper, fibre and wood products is International Paper of Purchase, New York, USA, with sales in 1990 of $12·9 billion. The company employs 69 000 workers.

The largest uncoated wood-free paper machine in the United Kingdom is the PM6 at the New Thames Paper Co. in Kemsley, near Sittingbourne, Kent, which has a capacity of over 160 000 tonnes per year. The paper manufacturing and converting complex covers an area of 60·7 ha *150 acres*.

Pharmaceuticals The world's largest pharmaceutical company is Johnson & Johnson of New Brunswick, New Jersey, USA. The company employed a workforce of 82 200, generating sales of $11·2 billion in 1990. Total assets at year end were $9·5 billion. Britain's largest pharmaceutical turnover in 1989/90 was by Glaxo, with sales totalling £2·8 billion.

Public relations The world's largest public relations firm is Burson Marsteller. Based in New York, USA, the company had a net fee income of $154·3 million in 1988. Hill and Knowlton Inc. has most offices world-wide, with 68, including one in Beijing, China.

Retailer The largest retailing firm in the world is Sears, Roebuck and Co. (founded by Richard Warren Sears in North Redwood, Minnesota, USA in 1886) of Chicago, Illinois, USA. World-wide revenues were $31·6 billion in the year ending 31 Dec 1989, when Sears Merchandise Group had 847 retail stores, 1731 sales offices and 1769 independent catalogue merchants in the United States. Total assets stood at $2·5 billion.

Steel companies From data available, the world's largest producer of steel is believed to be the Nippon Steel Corporation of Japan, which produced 28·765 million tonnes of crude steel in 1990. It employs 54 062 workers.

The Pohang works of the Pohang Iron & Steel Co. Ltd (POSCO) of South Korea produced 9 million tonnes of crude steel in 1988, the highest amount produced by a single integrated works.

Economics

MONETARY AND FINANCIAL

Largest budget The greatest governmental expenditure ever made by any country has been $1251·7 billion by the US government for the fiscal year 1990. The highest-ever revenue figure was $1031·3 billion in the same US fiscal year.

The greatest fiscal surplus ever was $8 419 469 844 in the United States in 1947/48. The worst deficit was the $221·1 billion in the US fiscal year 1986.

The greatest general UK government expenditure is £212·7 billion planned for the fiscal year 1990/1. The highest general government receipts are expected to be £218·6 billion for the same fiscal year. The public sector borrowing requirement, at a peak of £12 519 million in 1980/81, had been converted into a debt repayment of £14 524 million by 1988/89.

Foreign aid The greatest donor of foreign aid has been the United States — the total net foreign aid given by its

government between 1 Jul 1945 and 1 Jan 1990 was $300·8 billion. The country receiving most US aid in 1989 was Egypt, with $2085 million. US foreign aid began with $50 000 to Venezuela for earthquake relief in 1812.

Least taxed The sovereign countries with the lowest income tax in the world are Bahrain, Brunei, Kuwait and Qatar, where the rate, regardless of income, is nil. No tax is levied on the Sarkese (inhabitants of Sark) in the Channel Islands, or on the inhabitants of Tristan da Cunha.

Highest taxation rates The country with the most confiscatory taxation is Norway, where in January 1974 the Labour Party and Socialist Alliance abolished the 80 per cent limit. Some 2000 citizens were then listed in the *Lignings Boka* as paying more than 100 per cent of their taxable income. The shipping magnate Hilmar Reksten (1897–1980) was assessed at 491 per cent.

In the UK until 1979 the former top earned and unearned rates were 83 per cent and 98 per cent. The standard rate of tax was reduced to 25 per cent and the higher rate to 40 per cent in the 1988 Budget. The all-time record was set in 1967/68, when a 'special charge' of up to 9s. (45p) in the £ additional to surtax brought the top rate to 27s 3d in the £ (or 136 per cent) on investment income.

Balance of payments (current account) The record deficit for any country for a fiscal year is $143·7 billion in 1987 by the USA. The record surplus is $87·0 billion in 1987 by Japan.

The most favourable current balance of payments figure for the UK has been a surplus of £6748 million in 1981 (best quarter January–March, with a surplus of £2935 million). The worst figure was a deficit of £19 904 million in 1989 (worst quarter July–September, with a deficit of £6097 million).

Highest tax demands The highest recorded personal tax demand is one for $336 million on 70 per cent of the estate of Howard Hughes. The highest disclosed UK personal income tax demand raised is one for £5 371 220 against international merchant banker Nicholas van Hoogstraten, then aged 34, for 1981.

Highest and lowest rates in Great Britain Income tax was first introduced in Great Britain in 1799 for incomes above £60 per annum. It was discontinued in 1815, only to be reintroduced in 1842 at the rate of 7d (2·91p) in the £. It was at its lowest at 2d (0·83p) in the £ in 1875, gradually climbing to 1s 3d (6·24p) by 1913. From April 1941 until 1946 the record peak of 10s (50p) in the £ was maintained to assist in the financing of the war effort.

National debt The largest national debt of any country in the world is that of the United States, where the gross federal public debt of the federal government surpassed the trillion (10^{12}) dollar mark on 30 Sep 1981. By the end of 1989 it had reached $2857·4 billion, with net interest payments on the debt of $169·1 billion.

The national debt in Great Britain was less than £1 million during the reign of James II in 1687. It was £197 300 million or £3448 per person in March 1989. This, placed in a pile of brand new £5 notes, would be 3945·96 km *2452·02 miles* in height.

Most foreign debt The country most heavily in overseas debt in early 1990 was the United States, with $675 billion,

Toyshop
The world's biggest toyshop is Hamleys, founded in 1760 in Holborn, London and moved to Regent Street, London W1 in 1901. Its selling space covers 4180 m² *45 000 ft²* on six floors, and over 400 staff are employed during the Christmas season.

■ Highest incomes
The largest incomes derive from the collection of royalties per barrel by rulers of oil-rich sheikhdoms who have not formally revoked personal entitlement. Shaikh Zayid ibn Sultan an-Nuhayan (b. 1918), Head of State of the United Arab Emirates, arguably has title to some $9000 million of the country's annual gross national product. (Photo: Gamma/Maous)

although the size of its debt is small relative to its economic strength. Among developing countries, Brazil has the highest foreign debt, with $123 billion at the end of 1990.

Gross national product The country with the largest gross national product is the United States, which, having reached $3 trillion ($3 \times 10^{12}$) in 1981, was running at $5234 billion at the end of the fiscal year 1989. The GNP of the UK at factor cost in 1989 was £437 182 million.

National wealth The richest territory as listed in the 1990 *World Bank Atlas* ranking is Switzerland, which in 1988 had an average gross national product (GNP) per capita of $27 370. The USA, which had held the lead from 1910 to 1973, was sixth. The UK stood 20th, with $12 850. It has been estimated that the value of all physical assets in the USA on 1 Jan 1983 was $12·5 trillion ($12·5 \times 10^{12}$) per capita. The latest estimated figure for private wealth in the UK is £1 172 000 million or £53 000 per household.

Poorest country Mozambique had the lowest GNP per capita in 1988, with $100, although there are several sovereign countries for which the *World Bank Atlas* is not able to include data.

Gold reserves The country with the greatest monetary gold reserves is the United States, whose Treasury had 261·93 million fine oz of the world's 938·95 million fine oz on hand at the end of 1989. Valued at $400 per fine oz, these amounts would translate to $104 772 million and $375 580 million respectively. The United States Bullion Depository at Fort Knox, 48 km *30 miles* south-west of Louisville, Kentucky, USA, has been the principal federal depository of US gold since December 1936. Gold is stored in 446 000 standard mint bars of 12·4414 kg *400 troy ounces* measuring 17·7 × 9·2 × 4·1 cm *7 × 3⅝ × 1⅝ in*. Gold's peak price was $850 on 21 Jan 1980.

The UK's gold reserves at the end of 1989 totalled 18·99 million fine oz.

Minimum lending rate The highest-ever figure for the British bank rate (since 13 Oct 1972, the minimum lending rate) was 17 per cent from 15 Nov 1979 to 3 Jul 1980.

The longest period without a change was the 12 years 13 days from 26 Oct 1939 to 7 Nov 1951, during which time the rate stayed at 2 per cent. This lowest-ever rate had been first attained on 22 Apr 1852.

Worst inflation The world's worst inflation occurred in Hungary in June 1946, when the 1931 gold pengö was valued at 130 million trillion ($1·3 \times 10^{20}$) paper pengös. Notes were issued for 'Egymillard billion' (one milliard billion or 10^{21}) pengös on 3 Jun and withdrawn on 11 Jul 1946. Vouchers for 1000 billion billion (10^{27}) pengös were issued for taxation payment only. On 6 Nov 1923 the circulation of Reichsbank marks reached 400 338 326 350 700 000 000 and inflation was 755 700 millionfold on 1913 levels. The country with the worst inflation in 1990 was Nicaragua, where the rate was 13 500 per cent.

The UK's worst rate in a year was for August 1974 to August 1975, when inflation ran at a rate of 26·9 per cent. The increase in the Tax and Price Index (allowing for tax reliefs) was 8·1 per cent for the 12 months to June 1990. The largest 12 month increase in the TPI (extrapolated) was 31·9 per cent, also recorded in August 1975.

Least inflation The country with the least inflation over a year in recent times was Equatorial Guinea, which had a rate of −17·8 per cent in 1986.

WEALTH AND POVERTY ━━━

The comparison and estimation of extreme personal wealth are beset with intractable difficulties. Quite apart from reticence and the element of approximation in the valuation of assets, as Jean Paul Getty (1892–1976) once said: 'If you can count your millions you are not a billionaire.' The term millionaire was invented *c.* 1740 and billionaire (in the original American sense of one thousand million) in 1861. The earliest dollar centi-millionaire was Cornelius Vanderbilt (1794–1877), who left $100 million in 1877. The earliest billionaires were John Davison Rockefeller (1839–1937); Henry Ford (1863–1947) and Andrew William Mellon (1855–1937). In 1937, the last year in which all three were alive, a billion US dollars were worth £205 million, but

that amount of sterling would today have a purchasing power exceeding £5000 million.

Richest men Much of the wealth of the world's monarchs represents national rather than personal assets. The least fettered and most monarchical is HM Sir Muda Hassanal Bolkiah Mu'izzaddin Waddaulah (b. 15 Jul 1946) of Brunei. He appointed himself Prime Minister, Finance and Home Affairs Minister on 1 Jan 1984. *Fortune* magazine reported in September 1990 that his fortune was $25 billion.

Forbes magazine estimated in its issue of 23 Jul 1990 that Yoshiaki Tsutsumi (b. 1934) of Japan was the world's richest man, with assets of $16 billion. He heads Japan's Seibu Railway Group, and his empire includes golf courses, hotels and ski resorts.

Forbes magazine reported in its issue of 22 Oct 1990 that the richest man in the United States is John Kluge of Charlottesville, Virginia, with a personal fortune of $5·6 billion. Aged 76, Kluge is chairman of Metromedia. His $500 million estate in Charlottesville was described in *Town & Country* magazine as 'the most lavish of the century'.

The richest man in Great Britain is reputed to be the 6th Duke of Westminster (b. 22 Dec 1951), whose assets were estimated in April 1991 to be worth £3·7 billion. (See also 'Richest women', below.)

Richest women The title of the world's wealthiest woman has been wrongly conferred upon the recluse Hideko Osano (b. 1930), widow since October 1986 of the Japanese tycoon Kenji Osano. The US press first estimated her wealth at $25 billion. In fact much of her husband's wealth was diverted from her.

HM the Queen is asserted by some to be the wealthiest woman, and *The Sunday Times* estimated in April 1991 that she had assets worth £7·0 billion. However, few of her assets under the perpetual succession of the Crown are either personal or disposable.

The largest fortune proved in the will of a woman in the UK was one of £92 814 057 net by Dorothy de Rothschild (1895–1988), matriarch of the leading family in world Jewry.

The cosmetician Madame C.J. Walker (*née* Sarah Breedlove) (b. Delta, Louisiana, USA on 23 Dec 1867, died 1919) is reputed to have become the first self-made millionairess. She was an uneducated Negro orphan whose fortune was founded on a hair straightener.

Richest families It has been tentatively estimated that the combined value of the assets nominally controlled by the Du Pont family of some 1600 members may be of the order of $150 000 million. The family arrived in the USA from France on 1 Jan 1800. Capital from Pierre Du Pont (1730–1817) enabled his son Eleuthère Irénée Du Pont to start his explosives company in the United States.

Youngest millionaires The youngest person ever to accumulate a million dollars was the American child film actor Jackie Coogan (1914–84), co-star with Sir Charles Chaplin (1889–1977) in *The Kid*, made in 1920.

The youngest millionairess was Shirley Temple (b. Santa Monica, California, USA on 23 Apr 1928), formerly Mrs John Agar, Jr, now Mrs Charles Black, who accumulated wealth exceeding $1 000 000 before

she was 10. Her childhood acting career spanned the years 1934 to 1939.

Highest incomes The largest incomes derive from the collection of royalties per barrel by rulers of oil-rich sheikhdoms who have not formally revoked personal entitlement. Shaikh Zayid ibn Sultan an-Nuhayan (b. 1918), Head of State of the United Arab Emirates, arguably has title to some $9000 million of the country's annual gross national product.

Greatest wills The highest-valued will ever proved in the UK was worth £118 221 949 net, left by the 6th Marquess of Cholmondeley (1919–90). He was the former Lord Great Chamberlain, and as such was known to the public as the figure who walked backwards in front of the Queen at the State Opening of Parliament.

On 29 Apr 1985 the estate of Sir Charles Clore (1904–79) was agreed by a court hearing at £123 million. The Inland Revenue initially claimed £84 million in duties, but settled for £67 million.

The greatest will proved in Ireland was that of the 1st Earl of Iveagh (1847–1927), who left £13 486 146.

Largest dowry The largest recorded dowry was that of Elena Patiño, daughter of Don Simón Iturbi Patiño (1861–1947), the Bolivian tin millionaire, who in 1929 bestowed £8 000 000 from a fortune at one time estimated to be worth £125 000 000.

Greatest miser If meanness is measurable as a ratio between expendable assets and expenditure then Henrietta (Hetty) Howland Green (*née* Robinson) (1835–1916), who kept a balance of over $31 400 000 in one bank alone, was the all-time world champion. Her son had to have his leg amputated because of her delays in finding a *free* medical clinic. She herself ate cold porridge because she was too thrifty to heat it. Her estate proved to be worth $95 million.

Return of cash The largest amount of cash ever found and returned to its owners was $500 000, discovered by Lowell Elliott, 61, on his farm at Peru, Indiana, USA. It had been dropped in June 1972 by a parachuting hijacker. Jim Priceman, 44, assistant cashier at Doft & Co. Inc., returned an envelope containing $37·1 million in *negotiable* bearer certificates found outside 110 Wall Street to A.G. Becker Inc. of New York, USA on 6 Apr 1982. In announcing a reward of $250 Beckers were acclaimed as 'being all heart'.

Greatest bequests The greatest bequest in the lifetime of a billionaire was that of Ryoichi Sasakawa, chairman of the Japanese Shipbuilding Industry Foundation, who made total donations of 644 699 912 000 yen ($5 160 452 000) in the years 1962–88.

The largest single bequest in the history of philanthropy was the art collection belonging to the American publisher Walter Annenberg, which was worth $1 billion. He announced on 12 Mar 1991 that he would be leaving the collection to the Metropolitan Museum of Art in New York City, USA.

The largest single cash bequest was the $500 million gift, announced on 12 Dec 1955, to 4157 educational and other institutions by the Ford Foundation (established 1936) of New York, USA.

The greatest benefactions of a British millionaire were those of William Richard Morris, later the Viscount Nuffield (1877–

1963), which totalled more than £30 million between 1926 and his death on 22 Aug 1963.

Highest salary It was reported by the US government that Michael Milken, the 'junk bond king' at Drexel Burnham Lambert Inc., was paid $550 million in salary and bonuses in 1987. (See also 'Fines', p. 93.)

Britain's highest-paid man is William Brown, an insurance broker with Walsham Brothers, whose salary for 1989 was reported to be £8 136 274.

Highest fees The highest-paid investment consultant in the world is Harry D. Schultz, who operates from Monte Carlo and Zurich, Switzerland. His standard consultation fee for 60 minutes is $2400 on weekdays and $3400 at weekends. Most popular are the five-minute phone consultations at $200 (i.e. $40 a minute). His 'International Harry Schultz Letter', instituted in 1964, sells at $50 per copy. A life subscription costs $2400.

Golden handshake *Business Week* magazine reported in May 1989 that the largest golden handshake ever given was one of $53·8 million, to F. Ross Johnson, who left RJR Nabisco as chairman in February 1989.

In the UK, Robert Noonan was reported on 25 Apr 1989 to stand to receive £2 270 000 in a pay-off under the £82 million terms of a bid for Marler Estates, of which he was chairman, by Conrad Holdings.

PAPER MONEY

Earliest Paper money was an invention of the Chinese, first tried in AD 812 and prevalent by AD 970. The world's earliest banknotes (*banco-sedler*) were issued in Stockholm, Sweden in July 1661, the oldest survivor being one of five dalers dated 6 Dec 1662. The oldest surviving printed Bank of England note is one for £555 to bearer, dated 19 Dec 1699, measuring 11·4 × 19·6 cm *4½ × 7½ in.*

Largest and smallest The largest paper money ever issued was the one-kwan note of the Chinese Ming Dynasty issue of 1368–99, which measured 22·8 × 33·0 cm *9 × 13 in.* In October 1983 one sold for £340. The smallest national note ever issued was the 10-bani note of the Ministry of Finance of Romania, in 1917. It measured (printed area) 27·5 × 38 mm *1·09 × 1·49 in.* Of German *Notgeld*, the smallest were the 1–3 pfg notes of Passau (1920–21), measuring 18 × 18·5 mm *0·70 × 0·72 in.*

Highest values The highest-value notes in circulation are US Federal Reserve $10 000 banknotes, bearing the head of Salmon P. Chase (1808–73). It was announced in 1969 that no further notes higher than $100 would be issued, and only 345 $10 000 bills remain in circulation or unretired. The highest value ever issued by the US Federal Reserve System is a note for $100 000, bearing the head of Woodrow Wilson (1856–1924), which is only used for transactions between the Federal Reserve and the Treasury Department.

Two Bank of England notes for £1 million still exist, dated before 1812, but these were used only for internal accounting. There are also two Treasury £1 million notes dating from 1948 in existence, one of which was sold to the dealer Brian Dawson for £23 100 at Christie's, London on 9 Oct 1990.

The highest-value notes in Great Britain which have been *issued* are £1000 notes, first printed in 1725, discontinued on 22 Apr 1943 and withdrawn on 30 Apr 1945. At least

16 of these notes were still unretired up to January 1991. Of these, perhaps 10 are in the hands of collectors or dealers.

Lowest values The lowest-value (and the lowest-denomination) legal tender banknote is the one-sen (or 1/100th of a rupiah) Indonesian note. Its exchange value in early 1991 was more than 350 000 to the £.

The lowest-denomination Bank of England notes ever printed were the black on pale blue half-crown (now 12½ p) notes in 1941, signed by the late Sir Kenneth Peppiatt. Very few examples have survived and they are now valued at not less than £750.

Highest circulation The highest ever Bank of England note circulation in the UK was £18 412 million worth on 21 Dec 1990 — equivalent to a pile 368·23 km *228·82 miles* high in new £5 notes.

Most expensive The record price paid for a single lot of banknotes was £240 350 (including buyer's premium) by Richard Lobel, on behalf of a consortium, at Phillips, London on 14 Feb 1991. The lot consisted of a cache of British military notes which were found in a vault in Berlin, Germany, and contained more than 17 million notes.

Banknote collection Colin Dealey of Berkhamsted, Herts has accumulated banknotes from 178 different countries in three years since he started collecting in 1988.

CHEQUES AND COINS

Largest The greatest amount paid by a single cheque in the history of banking was £1 425 000 000. Issued on 11 Jul 1989 and signed by D Gareth Jones, Abbey National Building Society Treasurer and Assistant General Manager, and Jonathan C Nicholls, Abbey National Building Society

Coin balancing
Hiem Shda of Kiriat Mozkien, Israel stacked a pyramid of 847 coins on the edge of a coin free-standing vertically on the base of a coin which was on a table on 30 Jul 1989.

Coin snatching
The greatest number of 10p pieces clean-caught from being flipped from the back of a forearm into the same downward palm is 248, by Stuart May of Petersfield, Hants on 20 Mar 1991.

ECONOMICS

■ **Most expensive coin**
The record price paid for an individual coin is $1 500 000, for this US 1907 Double Eagle Ultra High Relief $20 gold coin. It was sold by MTB Banking Corporation of New York, USA to a private investor on 9 Jul 1990. (Photos: MTB Banking)

Line of coins

The most valuable line of coins was made up of 662 353 US quarters to a value of $165 788. It was 16·12 km *10 miles 5 ft 7 in* long and was laid at Central City Park, Atlanta, Georgia, USA on 16 Mar 1985. The most valuable line of coins laid in Britain was the 'Golden Mile' laid at the Town Hall at Romford, Essex on 22 Apr 1990 under the supervision of Pauline Obee, assisted by volunteers from Havering-atte-Bower, Essex. It was made of £1 coins and had a value of £71 652. A carpet of 1 945 223 Belgian one-franc coins (21 mm *0·83 in* in diameter) and thus with a total length of 40·85 km *25·38 miles* was laid in Geel, Belgium by members of Mepp-Stegeta on 25 Jun 1988. The longest line of coins laid in Britain was 23·55 km *14·63 miles* long, achieved by friends and pupils of Brumby Comprehensive School, Scunthorpe, South Humberside with 1·3 million 1p coins on 29 Mar 1987.

Assistant Treasurer, the cheque represented a payment from the expiring Abbey National Building Society in favour of the newly created Abbey National plc. A larger one, for $4 176 969 623·57, was drawn on 30 Jun 1954, although this was an internal US Treasury cheque.

Collection — record price The highest price ever paid for a coin collection was $25 235 360 for the Garrett family collection of US and colonial coins, which had been donated to Johns Hopkins University, Baltimore, Maryland, USA. The sales were made at a series of four auctions held on 28–29 Nov 1979 and 25–26 Mar 1981 at the Bowers & Ruddy Galleries in Wolfeboro, New Hampshire, USA. The collection was put together by members of the Garrett family between 1860 and 1942.

Hoards The most valuable hoard of coins was one of about 80 000 aurei in Brescello near Modena, Italy in 1714, believed to have been deposited *c.* 37 BC. The largest deliberately buried hoard ever found was the Brussels hoard of 1908 containing *c.* 150 000 coins.

The largest accidental hoard on record was the 1715 Spanish Plate Fleet, which sank off the coast of Florida, USA. A reasonable estimate of its contents would be some 60 million coins, of which about half were recovered by Spanish authorities shortly after the event. Of the remaining 30 million pieces, perhaps 500 000 have been recovered by modern salvors. The other 29½ million coins are, presumably, still on the bottom of the sea, awaiting recovery.

The record in terms of weight is 43 tonnes of gold, from the White Star Liner HMS *Laurentic*, which was mined in 40·2 m *132 ft* of water off Fanad Head, Donegal, Ireland in 1917. 3191 of the 3211 gold ingots have been recovered since then by the Royal Navy, Cossum Diving Syndicate and Consortium Recovery Ltd.

Largest mint The largest mint in the world is that of the US Treasury. It was built from 1965–69 on Independence Mall, Philadelphia and covers 4·65 ha *11½ acres*,

COINS

——— OLDEST ———
World: c. 630 BC electrum staters of King Gyges of Lydia, Turkey[1]. *British: c.* 95 BC Westerham-type gold stater (51 known)[2].

——— EARLIEST DATED ———
World: Samian silver tetradrachm struck in Zankle (now Messina), Sicily, dated year 1, viz 494 BC — shown as 'A'. *Christian Era:* MCCXXXIIII (1234) Bishop of Roskilde coins, Denmark (6 known). *British:* 1539 James V of Scotland gold 'bonnet piece'. *Earliest English:* 1548 Edward VI gold ten shillings (MDXLVIII).

——— HEAVIEST ———
World: 19·71 kg *43 lb 7¼ oz* Swedish 10-daler copper plate 1644[3]. *British:* 121·1 g *4·27 oz* Shrewsbury silver pound of 1644, the heaviest of the Charles I silver pounds from the English Civil War[4].

——— LIGHTEST ———
World: 0·002 g *14 000 to the oz* nepalese silver ¼ jawa *c.* 1740. *British:* 2·66 grains *180 to the oz* Henry VIII 2nd coinage silver farthings (1526–42).

——— MOST EXPENSIVE ———
World: $3 190 000 for the King of Siam Proof Set, a set of 1804 and 1834 US coins which had once been given to the King of Siam, purchased by Iraj Sayah and Terry Brand at Superior Galleries, Beverly Hills, California, USA on 28 May 1990. Included in the set of nine coins was the 1804 silver dollar, which had an estimated value of about $2 000 000. The record price paid for an individual coin is $1 500 000, for the US 1907 Double Eagle Ultra High Relief $20 gold coin, sold by MTB Banking Corporation of New York, USA to a private investor on 9 Jul 1990. *British:* £124 300 (including buyer's premium) bid for a Victoria gothic crown in gold (2 known), at a joint auction between Spink & Son, London and the Taisei Stamp and Coin Co., in Tokyo, Japan on 3 Jul 1988.

——— RAREST ———
There are believed to be a large number of 'singletons' throughout the world.

---

[1] Chinese uninscribed 'spade' money of the Chou Dynasty has been dated to *c.* 550 BC.

[2] Bellovaci-type gold staters circulated as early as *c.* 130 BC, which were struck in northern France and not in Britain.

[3] The largest coin-like medallion was completed on 21 Mar 1986 for the World Exposition in Vancouver, British Columbia, Canada, Expo 86 — a $1 000 000 gold piece. Its dimensions were 95·25 cm *37·5 in* diameter and 19·05 mm *¾ in* thick, and it weighed 166 kg *365 lb 15 oz* or 5337 oz (troy) of gold.

[4] The heaviest current British coin is the 39·94 g *1·4066 oz* gold £5 piece.

---

with an annual production capacity on a three-shift seven-day week of 15 billion coins. One new high-speed stamping machine can produce coins at a rate of 40 000 per hour.

Charity fund-raising The 'Sport Aid' event, conceived by Chris Long and organ-

ized by Bob Geldof, took place in 277 cities on 25 May 1986 and raised a world-wide figure of over £67 million. Twenty million runners took part in the races in 78 countries.

The greatest recorded amount raised by a charity walk or run is (Can)$24·7 million by Terry Fox (1958–81) of Canada who, with an artificial leg, ran from St John's, Newfoundland to Thunder Bay, Ontario in 143 days from 12 Apr–2 Sep 1980. He covered 5373 km *3339 miles*.

LABOUR

Oldest trade union The oldest of the 73 trade unions affiliated to the Trades Union Congress (founded 1868) is the Educational Institute of Scotland (EIS), founded in Edinburgh on 18 Sep 1847, with 46 489 members.

Largest trade union The world's largest union is Professionalniy Soyuz Rabotnikov Agro-Promyshlennogo Kompleksa (Agro-Industrial Complex Workers' Union) in the Soviet Union, with 36 634 613 members at 1 Jan 1990.

The largest union in the UK is the Transport and General Workers' Union (TGWU), with 1 270 776 members at 1 Jan 1990. Its peak membership was 2 086 281 in 1979.

Smallest trade union The ultimate in small unions was the Jewelcase and Jewellery Display Makers Union (JJDMU), founded in 1894. It was dissolved on 31 Dec 1986 by its general secretary, Charles Evans. The motion was seconded by Fergus McCormack, its only surviving member.

Longest name The union with the longest name is the International Association of Marble, Slate and Stone Polishers, Rubbers and Sawyers, Tile and Marble Setters' Helpers and Marble Mosaic and Terrazzo Workers' Helpers, or the IAMSSPRSTMSHMMTWH of Washington, DC, USA.

Earliest labour dispute A labour dispute concerning monotony of diet and working conditions was recorded in 1153 BC in Thebes, Egypt. The earliest recorded strike was one by an orchestra leader named Aristos from Greece, in Rome *c.* 309 BC. The dispute concerned meal breaks.

Largest labour dispute The most serious single labour dispute in the UK was the General Strike of 4–12 May 1926, called by the Trades Union Congress in support of the Miners' Federation. During the nine days of the strike 1 580 000 people were involved and 14 220 000 working days were lost. In the year 1926 as a whole a total of 2 750 000 people were involved in 323 different labour disputes and the working days lost during the year amounted to 162 300 000, the highest figure ever recorded.

A total of 4 128 000 working days were lost in all industries and services in 1989, involving 727 000 workers and 701 stoppages. Most days were lost in the public administration, sanitary services and education group, with 2 237 000.

Longest strike The world's longest recorded strike ended on 4 Jan 1961, after 33 years. It concerned the employment of barbers' assistants in Copenhagen, Denmark. The longest recorded major strike was that at the plumbing fixtures factory of the Kohler Co. in Sheboygan, Wisconsin, USA, between April 1954 and October 1962. The strike is alleged to have cost the United Automobile Workers' Union about $12 000 000 to sustain.

Britain's most protracted national strike was called by the National Union of Mineworkers from 8 Mar 1984 to 5 Mar 1985. HM Treasury estimated the cost to be £2625 million or £118·93 per household.

Highest unemployment The highest recorded percentage unemployment in Great Britain was on 23 Jan 1933, when the total of unemployed persons on the Employment Exchange registers was 2 903 065, representing 22·8 per cent of the insured working population. The peak figure for the post-war period in the UK has been 12·3 per cent (3 407 729) on 9 Jan 1986, falling to 5·5 per cent on 14 Jun 1990.

Lowest unemployment In December 1973 in Switzerland (population 6·6 million), the total number of unemployed was reported to be 81. The lowest recorded peacetime level of unemployment in Britain was 0·9 per cent on 11 Jul 1955, when 184 929 persons were registered. The peak figure for the employed labour force in the UK has been 27 433 000 in September 1990.

Working career The longest working life has been that of 98 years by Mr Izumi (see p. 67) who began work goading draft animals at a sugar mill at Isen, Tokunoshima, Japan in 1872. He retired as a sugar cane farmer in 1970 aged 105.

The longest working life recorded in the UK was that of Susan O'Hagan (1802–1909) who was in domestic service with three generations of the Hall family of Lisburn, near Belfast, Co. Antrim for 97 years from the age of 10 to light duties at 107.

The longest recorded industrial career in one job in Britain was that of Miss Polly Gadsby, who started work with Archibald Turner & Co. of Leicester at the age of nine. In 1932, after 86 years' service, she was still at her bench wrapping elastic at the age of 95. Theodore C. Taylor (1850–1952) served 86 years with J.T. & J. Taylor of Batley, W Yorks including 56 years as chairman. The longest serving chairman (appointed July 1926) of any board of directors was Mrs Mary Henrietta Anne Moody (b. 7 Apr 1881) of Mark & Moody Ltd, printers and booksellers of Stourbridge, W Mids. She had completed 59 years at the time of her death on 5 Aug 1985. Edward William Beard (1878–1982), a builder of Swindon, Wilts retired in October 1981 after 85 years with the firm he had founded in 1896. Commissioner Catherine Bramwell-Booth (b. 20 Jul 1883, died 4 Oct 1987) had been serving the Salvation Army since 1903. Richard John Knight (b. 20 Apr 1881) was company secretary to seven companies at the time of his death on 12 Nov 1984, aged 103 years.

Working week A case of a working week of 142 hours (with an average each day of 3 hr 42 min 51 sec for sleep) was recorded in June 1980 by Dr Paul Ashton, 32, the anaesthetics registrar at Birkenhead General Hospital, Merseyside. He described the week in question as 'particularly bad but not untypical'. Some non-consultant doctors are contracted to work 110 hours a week or be available for 148 hours. Some contracts for fully salaried university lecturers call for a three-hour week or a 72-hour year spread over 24 weeks.

ASSOCIATION

Oldest club Britain's oldest gentlemen's club is White's, St James's, London, opened c. 1697 by Francis White (died 1711) as a Chocolate House. It moved to its present site in 37 St James's in 1755. It has been described as an 'oasis in a desert of democracy'. Britain's oldest known dining club is the Charterhouse School Founder's Day Dinner, held annually on 12 December. London clubland's most senior member is Sir Walter Howard, who was born in 1888 and joined the United Oxford and Cambridge University Club in 1912.

ENERGY CONSUMPTION

To express the various forms of available energy (coal, liquid fuels and water power etc., but omitting vegetable fuels and peat), it is the practice to convert them all into terms of coal.

The highest consumption in the world is in the US Virgin Islands, with an average of 30 350 kg *597·4 cwt* per person per annum. The highest in a sovereign country is 21 881 kg *430·7 cwt* per person in Qatar. The UK average was 5940 kg *116·9 cwt* per person in 1989. The lowest average is 13 kg *28·6 lb* per person, most recently recorded in Bhutan in 1987.

STOCK EXCHANGES

The oldest Stock Exchange of the 138 listed throughout the world is that of Amsterdam, Netherlands, founded in 1602 with dealings in printed shares of the United East India Company of the Netherlands in the Oude Zijds Kapel. The largest in trading volume in 1990 was Tokyo, with $1450 billion, ahead of New York City with $957 billion and London with $608·5 billion.

Most bargains The highest number of equity bargains in one day on the London Stock Exchange was 114 973 on 22 Oct 1987. The record for a year is 13 021 337 bargains in the year ending 31 Dec 1987. There were 7158 securities listed at 31 Mar 1991 (cf. the 9749 peak in June 1973). Their total nominal value was £400·7 billion (gilt-edged £118·7 billion), with a market value of £2195·2 billion (gilt-edged £121·2 billion).

Trading volume The busiest session on the London market was on 20 May 1987, when 1·3 billion shares were traded.

FT-SE 100 index The highest closing figure for the FT-SE 100 share index was 2545·3 on 5 Apr 1991, after a gain of 20·8 points. The index closed above 2500 for the first time on 14 Mar 1991 at 2500·6, a gain of 52·4 points. The highest ever trading level was 2552·1, reached briefly on 5 Apr 1991. The greatest rise in a day has been 142·2 points to 1943·8 on 21 Oct 1987 and the greatest fall in a day was 250·7 to 1801·6 on 20 Oct 1987. The lowest closing figure was 986·9 on 23 Jul 1984.

US records The highest index figure on the Dow Jones Industrial average (instituted 8 Oct 1896) of selected stocks at the close of a day's trading was 3027·50 on 31 May 1991, a rise of 27·05 points on the day. This was the first time the index had closed above 3000 points, although it had edged past the 3000 barrier for the first time on Friday 13 Jul 1990 after a strong run.

The record day's trading was 608 148 710 shares on 20 Oct 1987. The old record trading volume in a day on the New York Stock Exchange of 16 410 030 shares on 29 Oct 1929, the 'Black Tuesday' of the famous 'crash', was unsurpassed until April 1968. The Dow Jones Industrial average, which reached 381·71 on 3 Sep 1929, plunged 30·57 points on 29 Oct 1929, on its way to the Depression's lowest point of 41·22 on 2 Jul 1932. The largest decline in a day, 508 points (22·6 per cent), occurred on 19 Oct 1987. The total lost in security values from 1 Sep 1929 to 30 Jun 1932 was $74 billion. The greatest paper loss in a year was $210 billion in 1974. The record daily increase of 69·89 on 3 Apr 1986 was most recently bettered on 21 Oct 1987 with a rise of 186·84 points to 2027·85. The largest stock trade in the history of the New York Exchange was a 48 788 800-share block of Navistar International Corporation stock at $10 in a $487 888 000 transaction on 10 Apr 1986. The highest price paid for a seat on the New York Stock Exchange was $1·15 million in 1987. The lowest 20th-century price was $17 000 in 1942. The market value of stocks listed on the New York Stock Exchange reached an all-time high of $3200 billion at the end of March 1991.

Most valued companies The market capitalization of Nippon Telegraph and Telephone (NTT) was quoted as $87·4 bil-

Largest Flotation

The £5·2 billion sale of the 12 UK electricity companies sparked off 12·75 million applications, generating 5·7 million shareholders. First day trading on 11 Dec 1990 closed with Manweb producing the highest premium — 66p on the 100p partly paid price of 240p. (Artwork: Maltings Partnership for Guinness Publishing)

COMPANY	PREMIUM	SHARES TRADED (millions)
Manweb	+ 66p	27
South Wales Electricity	+ 64p	22
Yorkshire Electricity	+ 59 ½p	39
Norweb	+ 52p	40
East Midlands Electricity	+ 50 ½p	44
Southern Electric	+ 50p	50
SWEB	+ 50p	25
Eastern Electricity	+ 48p	56
MEB	+ 44p	36
Northern Electric	+ 42 ½p	23
LEB	+ 42p	39
Seeboard	+ 42p	20

KEY

■ Nominal share value (100p)

■ Shares traded (increments of 5 million)

■ Premiums after first day's trading (5p increments)

(Artwork: Maltings Partnership for Guinness Publishing)

■ Most expensive stamps

Relative to their total face value, the most expensive stamps ever produced were the 1847 1d and 2d Mauritius 'Post Office' stamps. J Barnard was paid ten guineas (£10·50) for engraving the die and printing 500 of each. Thus the production costs far outweighed the revenue from sales, as the total face value of the 1000 stamps was only £6·25. (Photo: Gamma)

Stamp licking

John Kenmuir of Hamilton, Strathclyde licked and affixed 393 stamps in 4 min at the BBC TV studios on 26 Sep 1990, later shown on the *Record Breakers* programme.

---

lion at September 1990, falling from $112·2 billion in the preceding three-month period.

The greatest aggregate market value of any corporation at year end was £74·99 billion for International Business Machines (IBM) Corporation on 31 Dec 1990. Britain's most valued company is British Telecommunications (BT), whose market capitalization was £20·9 billion at 31 Mar 1991.

The market value of the American Telephone and Telegraph Co. (AT&T), formerly the company with the greatest assets, on 31 Dec 1983 was $59·4 billion, held among 3 million ordinary shareholders. A total of 20 109 shareholders attended the AGM in April 1961, thereby setting a world record.

The largest rights issue in Britain was one of £921 million by Barclays Bank, announced on 7 Apr 1988.

Smallest company equity Britain's smallest ever company was Frank Davies Ltd, incorporated on 22 Aug 1924 with a ½ d share capital divided into two ¼ d shares. Converting to decimal coinage (£0·002 divided into two shares of £0·001), it was finally dissolved in 1978 without ever having increased its share capital.

Largest flotation The largest ever flotation in stock-market history was the £5·2 billion sale of the 12 UK regional electricity companies to 5·7 million shareholders. The offer was heavily oversubscribed, with a total of 12·75 million applications processed.

The earlier flotation of British Gas plc had an equity offer which produced the higher sum of £7·75 billion, but to only 4·5 million shareholders. Allotment letters were dispatched on 15 Dec 1986.

Highest par value The highest denomination of any share quoted in the world is a single share in Moeara Enim Petroleum Corporation, worth £42 846 (*164 000 Dutch florins*) on 17 Aug 1989.

Greatest personal loss The highest recorded personal paper losses on stock values were incurred by Ray A. Kroc (1902–84), former chairman of McDonald's Corporation, amounting to $65 million on 8 Jul 1974 (see Restaurateurs).

Largest investment house The largest securities company in the USA, and

---

formerly the world's largest partnership, with 124 partners before becoming a corporation in 1959, is Merrill Lynch, Pierce, Fenner & Smith Inc. (founded 6 Jan 1914) of New York. Its parent, Merrill Lynch and Co. Inc., had $68 billion in assets under management at April 1991, held $356 billion in client assets and employed about 39 000 staff in 510 offices world-wide.

Names The longest name on the British Index of Company Names is The Australian Academy of the Humanities for the Advancement of Scholarship in Language, Literature, History, Philosophy and the Fine Arts, a company incorporated by Royal Charter.

The longest name on the Index registered under the Companies Acts is The Liverpool and Glasgow Association for the Protection of Commercial Interest as Respects Wrecked and Damaged Property Ltd, company number 15147. The shortest names on the Index are G Ltd, H Ltd, M Ltd, Q Ltd, U Ltd, X Ltd and Y Ltd.

POSTAL SERVICES

Largest mail The country with the largest mail in the world is the United States, whose population posted 161·6 billion letters and packages in the year ending 30 Sep 1989, when the US Postal Service employed 763 743 people, with the world's largest civilian vehicle fleet of 182 533 cars and trucks.

The UK total was 15 293 million letters and 196·3 million parcels in the year ending 31 Mar 1990. The record day was 17 Dec 1990 with 119·6 million items, when Christmas cards coincided with share certificates following the flotation of the 12 regional electricity distribution companies.

Switzerland takes first place in the average number of letters and packages which each person posts during one year. The figure was 655 in 1988. The UK figure was 271 per head in 1989.

Postal addresses The practice of numbering houses began on the Pont Notre Dame, Paris, France in 1463. The highest-numbered house in Britain is No. 2679 Stratford Road, Hockley Heath, W Mids, owned since 1977 by Mr and Mrs Malcolm Aldridge. The highest-numbered house in Scotland is No. 2631 London Road, Mount Vernon, Glasgow, which has been owned since 1986 by Mr and Mrs Norman Brown.

Oldest pillar boxes The first orthodox system of roadside posting-boxes was established in 1653 in Paris, France to facilitate the interchange of correspondence in the city. They were erected at the intersection of main thoroughfares and were emptied three times a day.

A cast iron posting box dating from *c.* 1690 was found at the White Hart coaching inn, Spilsby, Lincs in January 1988. The oldest pillar box still in service in the British Isles is one dating from 8 Feb 1853 in Union Street, St Peter Port, Guernsey, Channel Islands. It was cast by John Vaudin in Jersey and was restored to its original maroon livery in October 1981. The oldest box in mainland Britain is at Barnes Cross, Holwell (postally in Bishop's Caundle), Dorset, dating from probably later in 1853. The oldest in the Republic of Ireland is a hexagonal-roofed pillar box in Kent Railway Station, Glanmire, Co. Cork, dating from 1857.

Post offices The country with the greatest number of post offices is India, with 144 829 in 1988. In the same year there were 21 030 post offices in the UK, the oldest of which is at Sanquhar, Dumfries & Galloway, first referred to in 1763. The northernmost post office in the British Isles is at Haroldswick, Unst, Shetland Islands and the most southerly is at Samarès, Jersey, Channel Islands. The highest post office in England is at Flash, Staffs at 462.6 m *1518 ft.* The longest post office counter in Britain was one of 56.38 m *185 ft* with 33 positions when opened in 1962 at Trafalgar Square, London. Currently the longest is at George Square, Glasgow, Strathclyde which is 47.8 m *157 ft* long with 22 positions.

Agriculture

Origins It has been estimated that about 21 per cent of the world's land surface is cultivable and that only 7.6 per cent is actually under cultivation.

Evidence adduced in 1971 from Nok Nok

Tha and Spirit Cave, Thailand tends to confirm that plant cultivation was part of the Hoabinhian culture *c.* 11 000 BC, but it is still likely that hominids (humans and their human-like ancestors) probably survived for 99.93 per cent of their known history without cultivating plants or domesticating animals. A village site found near Nineveh, Iraq and dated provisionally to 9000 BC shows evidence of agricultural practices. The earliest evidence for maize cultivation comes from samples taken of sediments in Lake Ayauchi, near the Rio Santiago tributary of the Amazon, which were dated to at least 5300 years ago. Rice was grown in China by *c.* 5000 BC at Hemudu, near Shanghai.

It has been suggested that reindeer (*Rangifer tarandus*) may have been domesticated as early as 18 000 BC, but definite proof is still lacking. The earliest known animals domesticated for food were probably descendants of the wild goats or Bezoar (*Capra aegagrus = hircus*), which were herded at Asiah, Iran *c.* 7700 BC. Sheep (*Ovis aries*) have been dated to *c.* 7200 BC at Argissa Magula in Thessaly, Greece, and pigs (*Sus domestica*) and cattle (*Bos primigenius = taurus*) to *c.* 7000 BC at the same site.

The earliest definite date for the horse (*Equus caballus*) is *c.* 4350 BC from Dereiska, Ukraine, USSR, but crib-biting evidence from southern France indicates that horses may have been tethered earlier than 30 000 BC. The oldest evidence for the possible domestic use of camels (*Camelus*) came from the site at Sihi, Saudi Arabia, where a jawbone has been carbon-dated to *c.* 7200–7100 BC.

Chickens were domesticated before 6000 BC in Indochina and had spread to north China by 5900–5400 BC, as shown by radiocarbon dating from a Neolithic site at Peiligan, near Zhengzou, and also at Cishan and Beixin. Chickens did not reach Britain until *c.* 150 BC.

FISHERIES

United Nations Food and Agricultural Organization figures for 1988 showed the world's leading fishing nation to be Japan, with a total catch of 11.9 million tonnes, followed by the USSR (11.3 million tonnes), China (10.3 million tonnes), perhaps surprisingly, Peru (6.6 million tonnes) and the United States (5.9 million tonnes). The figure for the United Kingdom was 909 600 tonnes, and the total world-wide was 97.9 million tonnes.

The record for a single trawler is £278 798 from a 37 897-tonne catch by the Icelandic vessel *Videy* at Hull, Humberside on 11 Aug 1987. The greatest catch ever recorded from a single throw is 2471 tonnes by the purse seine-net boat M/S *Flømann* from Hareide, Norway in the Barents Sea on 28 Aug 1986. It was estimated that more than 120 million fish were caught in this shoal.

REAL ESTATE

Landowners The world's largest landowner is the United States Government, with a holding of 295 million ha *728 million acres*, which represents an area 12 times larger than the United Kingdom. It has been suggested that the Soviet Government constitutionally owns all the land in the entire country, with the exception, perhaps, of that on which foreign embassies stand — a total of about 22 402 200 km² *8 649 500 miles²*.

The world's largest private landowner is reputed to be International Paper Co. of

Purchase, New York, USA with 3.64 million ha *9 million acres* at its disposal.

British Isles Great Britain's largest landholder is currently the Forestry Commission (instituted 1919), with 898 000 ha *2.2 million acres*. The individual with the largest known acreage is the 9th Duke of Buccleuch (b. 1923), who owns 136 035 ha *336 000 acres*. The United Kingdom's greatest-ever private landowner was George Granville Sutherland-Leveson-Gower, 3rd Duke of Sutherland (1828–92), who owned 550 000 ha *1.4 million acres* in 1883.

The longest tenure is that by St Paul's Cathedral, London of land at Tillingham, Essex, given by King Ethelbert before AD 616.

Prices The most expensive piece of property ever recorded, the land around the central Tokyo retail food store Mediya Building in the Ginza district, was quoted in October 1988 by the Japanese National Land Agency at 33.3 million yen per m² (then equivalent to $248 000).

■ **Most expensive property**
The Ginza district of Toyko, Japan, where the rent can reach $248 000 per m², and a parking space costs $2 million extra in rental. (Photo: Images)

Combine harvesting

On 8 Aug 1989 Philip Baker of West End Farm, Merton, Bicester, Oxon harvested 165·6 tonnes of wheat in eight hours using a Massey Ferguson MF 38 combine. On 9 Aug 1990 an international team from CWS Agriculture, led by estate manager Ian Hanglin, harvested 358·09 tonnes of wheat in eight hours from 44 ha *108·72 acres* at Cockayne Hatley Estate, Sandy, Beds. The equipment consisted of a Claas Commandor 228 combine fitted with a Shelbourne Reynolds SR 6000 stripper head.

Ploughing

The world championship (instituted 1953) has been staged in 18 countries and won by competitors from 12 nations. The United Kingdom has been the most successful country, with 10 championships. The only person to take the title three times is Hugh B. Barr of Northern Ireland, in 1954–56.

The fastest recorded time for ploughing one acre *0·405 ha* to UK Society of Ploughmen rules is 9 min 49·88 sec by Joe Langcake at Hornby Hall Farm, Brougham, Penrith, Cumbria on 21 Oct 1989. He used a Case IH 7140 Magnum tractor and Kverneland four-furrow plough.

The greatest area ploughed with a six-furrow plough to a depth of 22·86 cm *9 in* in 24 hours is 70 ha *173 acres*. This was achieved by Richard Gaisford and Peter Gooding of Wiltshire Young Farmers, using a Case IH tractor and Lemken plough, at Manor Farm, Pewsey, Wilts on 25–26 Sep 1990.

The record price per acre for agricultural land in Great Britain is £12 000 for a site at Elm Road, March, Cambs sold by J. Collingwood & Son of March on 31 Dec 1973.

FARMS

Earliest The earliest dated British farming site is Neolithic and is enclosed within the Iron-Age hill fort at Hembury, Devon, excavated during 1934–35 and now dated to 4210–3990 BC.

Largest The largest farms in the world are *kolkhozy* (collective farms) in the USSR. These have been reduced in number from 235 500 in 1940 to 26 900 in 1988 and represent a total cultivated area of 169·2 million ha *417·6 million acres*. Units of over 25 000 ha *60 000 acres* are not uncommon.

The pioneer farm owned by Laucidio Coelho near Campo Grande, Mato Grosso, Brazil *c.* 1901 covered 8700 km² *3358 miles²* and supported 250 000 head of cattle at the time of the owner's death in 1975.

British Isles The United Kingdom has 18 889 715 ha *46 677 000 acres* of farmland on nearly 240 300 holdings and the largest farms are Scottish hill farms in the Grampians. The largest arable holding is farmed by the Earl of Iveagh at Elveden, Suffolk, where 4500 ha *11 000 acres* are farmed on an estate covering 9000 ha *25 500 acres*, the greater part of which was formerly derelict land. The production in 1990 included 8350 tonnes of grain and 48 800 tonnes of sugar beet. Other vegetable crops, including potatoes, peas and carrots, produced a yield of over 11 000 tonnes. The livestock includes 1000 ewes and 6215 pigs.

Foot-and-mouth disease This first appeared in Great Britain at Stratford, east London in August 1839. The worst outbreak of the disease in Britain was that in Shropshire from 25 Oct 1967 to 25 Jun 1968, when there were 2364 outbreaks and 429 632 animals were slaughtered, at a direct and consequential loss of £150 million. The outbreak of 1871, when farms were much smaller, affected 42 531 farms.

Cattle station The world's largest cattle station is the Anna Creek station of South Australia owned by the Kidman family. It covers 30 000·5 km² *11 600 miles²* and is thus 23 per cent of the size of England. The biggest component is Strangway, at 14 000 km² *5500 miles²*.

Until 1915 the Victoria River Downs Station in Northern Territory, Australia had an area of 90 650 km² *35 000 miles²*, which is equivalent to the combined area of England's 20 largest counties.

Cow shed The longest cow shed in Britain is that of the Yorkshire Agricultural Society at Harrogate, N Yorks. It is 139 m *456 ft* long and can cater for 686 cows. The National Agricultural Centre at Kenilworth, Warks, completed in 1967, can house 782 animals.

Chicken ranch The Croton Egg Farm in Ohio, USA has 4·8 million hens laying some 3·7 million eggs daily.

Community garden The largest such project is that operated by the City Beautiful Council and the Benjamin Wegerzyn Garden Center at Dayton, Ohio, USA. It comprises 1173 allotments, each measuring 74·5 m² *812 ft²*.

Hop farm The world's leading hop growers are John I. Haas Inc., with farms in Idaho, Oregon and Washington, USA, Tasmania, Australia and Kent, covering a total net area of 2089 ha *5163 acres*. The largest field covers 694 ha *1715 acres* near Toppenish, Washington, USA.

Mushroom farm The world's largest mushroom farm is owned by Moonlight Mushrooms Inc. and was founded in 1937 in a disused limestone mine near Worthington, Pennsylvania, USA. The farm employs over 1000 people who work in a maze of underground galleries 177 km *110 miles* long, producing over 26 tonnes of mushrooms per year. The French annual consumption is unrivalled at 3·17 kg *7 lb* per person.

Piggery The world's largest piggery is the Sljeme unit in Yugoslavia, which is able to process 300 000 pigs per year.

Sheep station The largest sheep station in the world is Commonwealth Hill, in the north-west of South Australia. It grazes between 60 000 and 70 000 sheep, along with 24 000 uninvited kangaroos, in an area of 10 567 km² *4080 miles²* enclosed by 191 km *119 miles* of dog-proof fencing. The head count on Sir William Stevenson's 16 579 ha *40 970 acre* Lochinver station in New Zealand was 110 460 on 1 Jan 1991.

The largest sheep move on record occurred when 27 horsemen moved a flock of 43 000 sheep 64 km *40 miles* from Barcaldine to Beaconsfield station, Queensland, Australia in 1886.

Turkey farm The world's largest turkey farm is that of Bernard Matthews plc at Great Witchingham, Norfolk, where 2600 staff tend 9 million turkeys.

CROP PRODUCTION

Barley The total amount of land farmed for barley production in the 1990/91 season was estimated to be 73·2 million ha *18 million acres*, giving a total production of 181·5 million tonnes and an average yield of 2·48 tonnes/ha. The world's leading grower of barley is the USSR, which is estimated to produce 57 million tonnes from about 26 million ha *64·2 million acres*.

A yield of 12·2 tonnes/ha of winter barley was achieved on 2 Aug 1989 by farmers Stockton Park Leisure Ltd, Chirnside, Borders from 21·29 ha *52·6 acres*.

Cotton The total area of land used for cotton production in 1990/91 was estimated to be 33·6 million ha *83 million acres*, giving a total production of 87 million bales weighing 217·72 kg *480 lb* each. The leading cotton producer is China, with figures estimated at 20·5 million such bales from 5·5 million ha *13·6 million acres*.

Maize The total amount of land used for growing maize in 1990/91 was 128·2 million ha *316·8 million acres*, producing an estimated 472 million tonnes, of which 88 million tonnes was produced by China from an estimated 21 million ha *51·9 million acres*.

Oats The world-wide production of oats in 1990/91 was an estimated 42·8 million tonnes harvested from about 21·6 million ha *53·4 million acres*, most of which, 17·5 million tonnes, is produced by the USSR from some 10·5 million ha *26 million acres*.

Potatoes Roger Southwell harvested 205·65 tonnes of potatoes in four hours from an area of 2·46 ha *6·07 acres* at Watermill Farm, Northwold, Norfolk on 1 Nov 1989. The machinery used was made by Standen Engineering Ltd of Ely, Cambs.

Rice About half of the world's population, including virtually the whole of East Asia, is totally dependent on rice as the staple food. The total amount of land used for rice production is 146·8 million ha *362·7 million acres*, with India leading on the area farmed, at 42·2 million ha *104·3 million*

acres. The world's leading producer, however, is China with estimated yields of 185 million tonnes from 32·7 million ha *80·8 million acres*. The largest wild-rice (*Zizania aquatica*) farm in the world is that of Clearwater Rice Inc. at Clearbrook, Minnesota, USA, covering 809 ha *2000 acres*. In 1986 it yielded 261 727 kg *577 000 lb*, the largest amount to date.

Wheat An estimated 230·3 million ha *569 million acres* of land is used for wheat production world-wide, giving a yield of 590·1 million tonnes. The leading grower is the USSR, which produces 108 million tonnes from about 47·5 million ha *117·4 million acres*.

The largest single fenced field of wheat measured 14 160 ha *35 000 acres* and was sown in 1951 south-west of Lethbridge, Alberta, Canada. The British record yield is 13·99 tonnes/ha harvested from 17·49 ha *43·24 acres*, by Gordon Rennie of Clifton Mains, Newbridge, Lothian in 1981.

Baling A rick comprising 40 400 bales of straw was built between 22 Jul and 3 Sep 1982 by Nick and Tom Parsons, and a gang of eight, at Cuckoo Pen Barn Farm, Birdlip, Glos. The completed bale measured 45·7 × 9·1 × 18·2 m *150 × 30 × 60 ft* high and weighed some 711 tonnes. The team baled, hauled and ricked 24 200 bales in seven consecutive days from 22–29 July. Svend Erik Klemmensen of Trustrup, Djursland, Denmark baled 200 tonnes of straw in 9 hr 54 min using a Hesston 4800 baling machine on 30 Aug 1989.

LIVESTOCK PRICES

Note: Some exceptionally high livestock auction prices are believed to result from collusion between buyer and seller to raise the ostensible price levels of the breed concerned. Others are marketing and publicity exercises bearing little relation to true market prices.

Cattle The highest price ever paid was $2·5 million for the beefalo (a ⅜ bison, ⅜ Charolais, ¼ Hereford) 'Joe's Pride', sold by D.C. Basalo of Burlingame, California, USA to the Beefalo Cattle Co. of Calgary, Canada on 9 Sep 1974.

UK A 14-month-old Canadian Holstein bull 'Pickland Elevation B. ET' was bought by Premier Breeders of Stamfordham, Northumberland for £233 000 in September 1982. The highest price paid for a bull in Britain is 60 000 guineas (£63 000) for 'Lindertis Evulse', an Aberdeen-Angus owned by Sir Torquil and Lady Munro of Lindertis, Kirriemuir, Angus. The bull was bought by the late James R. Dick of Black Watch Farms on 5 Feb 1963. It failed a fertility test in August 1963 when 20 months old, thus becoming the world's most expensive piece of beef.

Cow The highest price paid for a cow is $1·3 million for a Holstein at auction in East Montpelier, Vermont, USA in 1985.

The British record is £33 600 for 'Ullswater Beatexus 8th', a British Friesian sold to the British Livestock Embryo Syndicate of Royston, Herts by Sir Keith and Lady Showering of West Horrington, Wells, Somerset on 9 May 1981.

Goat On 25 Jan 1985 an Angora buck bred by Waitangi Angoras of Waitangi, New Zealand was sold to Elliott Brown Ltd of Waipu, New Zealand for NZ$140 000.

Horse The highest price paid for a draught horse is $47 000 by C.G. Good of Ogden, Iowa, USA (see page 30) for the seven-year-old Belgian stallion 'Farceur' at Cedar Falls, Iowa on 16 Oct 1917.

A Welsh mountain pony stallion named 'Coed Cock Bari' was sold to an Australian bidder in Wales in September 1978 for 21 000 guineas (£22 050).

Pig The highest price ever paid for a pig is $56 000 for a cross-bred barrow named 'Bud', owned by Jeffrey Roemisch of Hermleigh, Texas, USA and bought by E.A. 'Bud' Olson and Phil Bonzio on 5 Mar 1983.

The British record is 3300 guineas (£3465) paid by Malvern Farms for a Swedish Landrace gilt 'Bluegate Ally 33rd', owned by the Davidson Trust, in a draft sale at Reading, Berks on 2 Mar 1955.

Sheep The highest price ever paid for a sheep is A$450 000 by Willogoleche Pty Ltd for the Collinsville stud 'JC&S 43' at the 1989 Adelaide Ram Sales in South Australia. The British record is £32 000 for a Scottish Blackface lamb ram 'Old Sandy' sold by Michael Scott at Lanark, Strathclyde on 14 Oct 1988.

Wool The highest price ever paid for wool is A$3008·5 per kg greasy for a bale of Tasmania superfine at the wool auction in Tasmania, Australia on 23 Feb 1989 by Fujii Keori Ltd of Osaka, Japan — top bidders since 1973.

CATTLE

As of 1989 the world's leading producer of cattle was India, with 269·2 million head. However, the leading producer of milk in 1989 was the USSR, with a total of 108·5 million tonnes.

Largest The heaviest breed of cattle is the Chianini, which was brought to the Chiana Valley in Italy from the Middle East in pre-Roman times. Four types of the breed exist, the largest of which is the Val di Chianini, found on the plains and low hills of Arezzo and Sienna. Mature bulls average 1·73 m *5 ft 8 in* at the forequarters and weigh 1300 kg *2865 lb* (cf. 850 kg *1873 lb* for cows), but Chianini oxen have been known to attain heights of 1·9 m *6 ft 2¾ in.* The sheer expense of feeding such huge cattle has put the breed under threat of extinction in Italy, but farmers in North America, Mexico and Brazil are still enthusiastic buyers of the breed.

A Holstein–Durham cross named 'Mount Katahdin', exhibited by A.S. Rand of Maine, USA from 1906–10, frequently weighed 2267 kg *5000 lb.* He stood 1·88 m *6 ft 2 in* at the shoulder, had a 3·96 m *13 ft* girth and died in a barn fire c. 1923.

UK Great Britain's largest breed of heavyweight cattle is the South Devon, mature bulls measuring up to 1·55 m *5 ft 1 in* at the withers and weighing about 1250 kg *2755 lb* (cows 1·35 m *4 ft 5 in* and 675 kg *1488 lb*). The heaviest example on record weighed 1678 kg *3700 lb.*

The British record for any breed is the 2032 kg *4480 lb* of 'The Bradwell Ox', owned by William Spurgin of Orpland Farm, Bradwell-on-Sea, Essex. In 1830, when six years old, this colossus measured 4·57 m *15 ft* from nose to tail and had a maximum girth of 3·35 m *11 ft.* The famous Shorthorn 'Durham' or 'Wonderful Ox', bred by Charles and Robert Colling of Teeswater, Yorks, weighed 1727 kg *3808 lb* at the age of 10. It was slaughtered in 1807 after dislocating a hip. The 'Airedale Heifer' of East Riddlesdon, near Keighley, S Yorks weighed 1197·5 kg *2640 lb* (c. 1820) and was 3·62 m *11 ft 10½ in* long.

Smallest The smallest breed of domestic cattle is the Ovambo of Namibia. Mature bulls and cows average 225 kg *496 lb* and 160 kg *353 lb* respectively. The smallest

British breed is the Miniature Dexter. Mature bulls weigh 450 kg *992 lb* and stand 1·1 m *3 ft 3⅓ in* at the withers. In May 1984 a height of 86·3 cm *34 in* was reported for an adult Miniature Dexter cow named 'Mayberry', owned by R. Hillier of Church Farm, South Littleton, Evesham, Worcs.

Oldest 'Big Bertha', a Dremon owned by Jerome O'Leary of Blackwatersbridge, Co. Kerry, Republic of Ireland, was born on 17 Mar 1944. (See also Most prolific.)

Most prolific On 25 Apr 1964 it was reported that a cow named 'Lyubik' had given birth to seven calves in Mogilev, USSR. Five short-lived and one stillborn calf were recorded from a Friesian at Te Puke, North Island, New Zealand on 27 Jul 1980. A case of five live calves at one birth was reported in 1928 by T.G. Yarwood of Manchester.

The lifetime breeding record is 39 in the case of 'Big Bertha' (b. 17 Mar 1944), a Dremon owned by Jerome O'Leary of Blackwatersbridge, Co. Kerry, Republic of Ireland. (See also Oldest.)

'Soender Jylland's Jens', a Danish black-and-white bull, left 220 000 surviving progeny by artificial insemination when he was put down at the age of 11 in Copenhagen in September 1978. 'Bendalls Adema', a Friesian bull, died at the age of 14 in Clondalkin, Dublin, Republic of Ireland on 8 Nov 1978, having sired an estimated 212 000 progeny by artificial insemination.

Birthweights The heaviest recorded live birthweight for a calf is 102 kg *225 lb* from a British Friesian cow at Rockhouse Farm, Bishopston, Swansea, W Glam in 1961. On 28 May 1986 a Holstein cow owned by Sherlene O'Brien of Simitar Farms, Henryetta, Oklahoma, USA gave birth to a perfectly formed stillborn calf weighing 122·4 kg *270 lb.* The sire was an Aberdeen-Angus bull which had 'jumped the fence'.

Lightest The lowest live birthweight recorded for a calf is 8 kg *17 lb 10 oz* for a bull (breed not identified) born on Jan van Rensberg's farm at Kankus, Orange Free State, South Africa in August 1972. It stood 40 cm *15 ¾ in* at the hindquarters and measured 55 cm *21½ in* overall.

Milk yields The highest recorded world lifetime yield of milk is 211 025 kg *465 224 lb* by the unglamorously named cow No. 289 owned by M.G. Maciel & Son of Hanford, California, USA, to 1 May 1984. The greatest yield from any British cow was that by 'Winton Pel Eva 2', owned by John Waring of Glebe House, Kilnwick, near Pocklington, Humberside, with 165 000 kg *363 759 lb.*

The greatest recorded yield for one lactation (maximum 365 days) is 25 247 kg *55 661 lb* in 1975 by the Holstein 'Beecher Arlinda Ellen', owned by Mr and Mrs Harold L. Beecher of Rochester, Indiana, USA. 'Oriel Freda 10' (b. 21 Feb 1978), a Friesian owned by the Mellifont Abbey Trust of Collon, Co. Louth, Republic of Ireland produced 21 513 kg *47 427½ lb* in 305 days in 1986.

The British lactation record (305 days) was set by 'Michaelwood Holm Emoselle 25' (b. 1 Aug 1973), a Friesian owned by Mick and Linda Holder of Aylesmore Farm, Newent, Glos with 19 400 kg *42 769 lb* in 1984–5. (See also Butterfat yields.)

The highest reported milk yield in a day is 109·3 kg *241 lb* by 'Urbe Blanca' in Cuba on or about 23 Jun 1982.

Butterfat yields The world record lifetime yield is 7425 kg *16 370 lb* by the US

Holstein 'Breezewood Patsy Bar Pontiac' in 3979 days. The British record butterfat yield in a lifetime is 5518 kg *12 166 lb* from 123 865 kg *273 072 lb* at 4·45 per cent by the Ayrshire cow 'Craighead Welma', owned by W. Watson Steele.

The world record for 365 days is 1418 kg *3126 lb* by 'Roybrook High Ellen', a Holstein owned by Yashuhiro Tanaka of Tottori, Japan. The British record for 365 days is 852 kg *1878 lb* by 'Michaelwood Holm Emoselle 25'. This cow went on to milk for a total of 395 days in her eighth lactation, producing an incredible 1012 kg *2231 lb* of butterfat. She also holds the British record for butterfat yield in one day, at 4·53 kg *10 lb.* (See also Milk yields.)

Cheese The oldest and most primitive cheeses are the Arabian *kishk*, made of the dried curd of goats' milk. Today there are 450 named cheeses in 18 major varieties, but many are merely named after different towns and differ only in shape or the method of packing. France has 240 varieties. The world's biggest producer of cheese is the United States, with a factory production of 2·2 million tonnes in 1980.

The most active cheese-eaters are the people of France, with an annual average in 1983 of 19·8 kg *43·6 lb* per person. Britain's cheese consumption, where 67 per cent is Cheddar, was 7·87 kg *16·02 lb* per head in 1988. Britain's most costly cheese is Lanark Blue, which is obtainable from some shops for £7·50 per lb.

GOATS

Largest The largest goat ever recorded was a British Saanen named 'Mostyn Moorcock', owned by Pat Robinson of Ewyas Harold, Hereford & Worcester, which reached a weight of 181·4 kg *400 lb* (shoulder height 111·7 cm *44 in* and overall length of 167·6 cm *66 in*). He died in 1977 at the age of four.

Smallest Some pygmy goats weigh only 15–20 kg *33–44 lb.*

Oldest The oldest goat on record is a Toggenburg feral cross named 'Hongi' (b. August 1971), belonging to April Koch of Glenorchy, near Otago, New Zealand, which was still alive in mid-March 1989 aged 17 years 8 months. The oldest goat currently living in Britain is 'Emmahazelina' (b. 20 Apr 1972), a British Toggenburg, owned by Michael C. Johnston of Farrington, Blandford Forum, Dorset.

Most prolific According to the British Goat Society, at least one or two cases of quintuplets are recorded annually out of the 10 000 goats registered, but some breeders only record the females born.

On 14 Jan 1980 a nanny named 'Julie', owned by Galen Cowper of Nampah, Idaho, USA, gave birth to septuplets, but they all died, including the mother.

Milk yields The highest recorded milk yield for any goat is 3499 kg *7714 lb* in 365 days by 'Osory Snow-Goose', owned by Mr and Mrs G. Jameson of Leppington, New South Wales, Australia, in 1977.

'Snowball', the goat owned by Don Papin of Tipton, California, USA, lactated continuously for 12 years 10 months between 1977 and 1989.

PIGS

The world's leading producer of hogs in 1989 was China, with 342 220 000 head.

Largest The heaviest pig ever recorded was a Poland–China hog named 'Big Bill', who was so obese that his belly dragged

Chicken and turkey plucking

Ernest Hausen (1877 –1955) of Fort Atkinson, Wisconsin, USA died undefeated after 33 years as champion. On 19 Jan 1939 he was timed at 4·4 sec for plucking a chicken.

Vincent Pilkington of Cootehill, Co. Cavan, Republic of Ireland killed and plucked 100 turkeys in 7 hr 32 min on 15 Dec 1978. His record for a single turkey is 1 min 30 sec, set on RTE Television in Dublin on 17 Nov 1980.

Sheep survival

On 24 Mar 1978 Alex Maclennan found one ewe still alive after he had dug out 16 sheep buried in a snowdrift for 50 days near the River Skinsdale on Mrs Tyser's Gordonbush Estate in Sutherland, Highland after the great January blizzard. The sheep's hot breath creates air-holes in the snow, and the animals gnaw their own wool for protein.

A Merino wether lost in the Benambra State Forest, New South Wales, Australia for five years produced 24·5 kg *54 lb* of wool from a fleece 45·7 cm *18 in* long.

Fine spinning

The longest thread of wool, hand-spun and plied to weigh 10 g *0·35 oz*, was one with a length of 553·03 m *1815 ft 3 in*, achieved by Julitha Barber of Bull Creek, Western Australia, Australia at the International Highland Spin-In, Bothwell, Tasmania on 1 Mar 1989.

Sheep to shoulder

At the International Wool Secretariat Development Centre, Ilkley, W Yorks, a team of eight using commercial machinery produced a jumper — from shearing sheep to the finished article — in 2 hr 28 min 32 sec on 3 Sep 1986.

along the ground. 'Bill' weighed an astonishing 1157·5 kg *2552 lb* just before he was put down after suffering a broken leg in an accident en route to the Chicago World Fair for exhibition in 1933. Other statistics included a shoulder height of 1·52 m *5 ft* and a length of 2·74 m *9 ft*. At the request of his owner, W.J. Chappall, this prized possession was mounted and put on display in Weekly County, Tennessee, USA until 1946, when he was acquired by a travelling carnival. On the death of the carnival's proprietor his family allegedly donated 'Big Bill' to a museum, but no trace has been found of him since.

UK The heaviest pig ever bred in Britain was a specimen of the now extinct Rudgewick, which weighed about 453 kg *1000 lb* at the age of two years. In 1798 a weight of 739·3 kg *1630 lb* was recorded for a boar bred in Middlesex. Another, bred at Godstone, Surrey, weighed 660·4 kg *1456 lb* in 1805. The only other British breed of pig known to exceed 635 kg *1400 lb* was the Gloucester Old Spot. One huge boar bred by Joseph Lawton of Astbury, Cheshire (and possibly owned by Joseph Bradbury of Little Hay Wood, Staffs) weighed 639·5 kg *1410 lb* in 1774. It stood 1·43 m *4 ft 8¼ in* at the shoulder and was 2·94 m *9 ft 8 in* long.

Smallest The smallest breed of pig is the Mini Maialino, developed by Stefano Morini of St Golo d'Enza, Italy, after 10 years of experimentation with Vietnamese pot-bellied pigs. The piglets weigh 400 g *14 oz* at birth and 9 kg *20 lb* at maturity.

Most prolific A breeding sow will live 12 years or more before it is slaughtered, but the maximum potential lifespan is 20 years. The highest recorded number of piglets in one litter is 34, farrowed on 25–26 Jun 1961 by a sow owned by Aksel Egedee of Denmark. In February 1955 a Wessex sow belonging to E.C. Goodwin of Paul's Farm, Leigh, near Tonbridge, Kent also had a litter of 34, of which 30 were stillborn. A litter of 32 piglets (eight stillborn) was farrowed in February 1971 by a British Saddleback owned by R. Spence of Toddington, Glos.

The highest number of live births in Britain is 30 from a White Wessex sow reported by W. Ives of Dane End Fruit Farm, near Ware, Herts in September 1979.

A Large White owned by H.S. Pedlingham farrowed 385 pigs in 22 litters from December 1923 to September 1934. During the period 1940–52 a Large Black sow belonging to A.M. Harris of Lapworth, Warks farrowed 26 litters. A Newsham Large White × Landrace sow of Meeting House Farm, Staintondale, near Scarborough, N Yorks had farrowed 189 piglets (seven stillborn) in nine litters up to 22 Mar 1988. Between 6 May 1987 and 9 Feb 1988 she gave birth to 70 piglets.

Birthweights The average birthweight for a piglet is 1·36 kg *3 lb*. A Hampshire × Yorkshire sow belonging to Rev. John Schroeder of Mountain Grove, Missouri, USA farrowed a litter of 18 on 26 Aug 1979. Five were stillborn, including one male which weighed 2·38 kg *5 lb 4 oz*.

The highest recorded weight for a piglet at weaning (eight weeks) is 36·7 kg *81 lb* for a boar, one of a litter of nine farrowed on 6 Jul 1962 by the Landrace gilt 'Manorport Ballerina 53rd', *alias* 'Mary', and sired by a Large White named 'Johnny' at Kettle Lane Farm, West Ashton, Trowbridge, Wilts.

In Nov 1957 a total weight of 514·3 kg *1134 lb* was reported at weaning for a litter of 18 piglets farrowed by an Essex sow

owned by B. Ravell of Seaton House, Thorugumbald, Hull, Humberside.

POULTRY

Chicken Largest The heaviest breed of chicken is the White Sully developed by Grant Sullens of West Point, California, USA by crossing and recrossing large Rhode Island Reds with other varieties. One monstrous rooster named 'Weirdo' reportedly weighed 10 kg *22 lb* in January 1973 and was so aggressive that he killed two cats and crippled a dog which ventured too close. The heaviest chicken is currently a White Ross 1 rooster named 'Bruno', owned by John Steele of Kirkhills Farms, Boyndie, Grampian. On 4 Jul 1989 this outsized bird recorded a weight of 10·02 kg *22 lb 1 oz*.

Most prolific The highest authenticated rate of egg-laying is by a White Leghorn, hen No. 2988, which laid 371 eggs in 364 days in an official test conducted by Prof. Harold V. Biellier ending on 29 Aug 1979 at the College of Agriculture, University of Missouri, USA. The British record is 353 eggs in 365 days in a national laying test at Milford, Surrey in 1957 by a Rhode Island Red 'Wonderful Lady', owned by W. Lawson of Welham Grange, Retford, Notts.

The highest recorded annual average per bird for a flock is 313 eggs in 52 weeks from 1000 Warren-Stadler SSL layers (from 21 weeks of age), owned by Eric Savage of White Lane Farm, Albury, Surrey in 1974–75.

Largest and smallest egg The heaviest egg reported is one of 454 g *16 oz*, with double yolk and double shell, laid by a White Leghorn at Vineland, New Jersey, USA on 25 Feb 1956. The largest recorded was one of 'nearly 12 oz' for a five-yolked egg measuring 31 cm *12¼ in* around the long axis and 22·8 cm *9 in* around the short, laid by a Black Minorca at Mr Stafford's Damsteads Farm, Mellor, Lancs in 1896.

An egg measuring 20·5 mm × 15·5 mm *0·8 × 0·6 in* was laid on 15 Jan 1991 by a hen owned by David Kay of Chippenham, Wilts.

Most yolks The highest claim for the number of yolks in a hen's egg is nine, reported by Diane Hainsworth of Hainsworth Poultry Farms, Mount Morris, New York, USA in July 1971, and also from a hen in Kirgizya, USSR in August 1977.

Flying 'Sheena', a barnyard bantam owned by Bill and Bob Knox, flew 192·07 m *630 ft 2 in* at Parkesburg, Pennsylvania, USA on 31 May 1985.

Duck An Aylesbury duck belonging to Annette and Angela Butler of Princes Risborough, Bucks laid 457 eggs in 463 days, including an unbroken run of 375 in as many days. The duck died on 7 Feb 1986. Another duck of the same breed owned by Edmond Walsh of Gormanstown, Co. Kildare, Republic of Ireland laid eggs every year right up to her 25th birthday. She died on 3 Dec 1978 aged 28 yr 6 months.

SHEEP

Largest The largest sheep ever recorded was a Suffolk ram named 'Stratford Whisper 23H', which weighed 247·2 kg *545 lb* and stood 1·09 m *43 in* tall in March 1991. It is owned by Joseph and Susan Schallberger of Boring, Oregon, USA.

Smallest The smallest breed of sheep is the Soay, which is now confined to the island of Hirta in the St Kilda group, Outer Hebrides. Adults weigh on average 25–27·2 kg *55–60 lb*.

Most prolific A case of eight lambs at a birth was reported by D.T. Jones of Priory Farm, Gwent in June 1956 and also by Ken Towse of Buckton, near Bridlington, Humberside in March 1981, but none lived.

A Border Leicester × Merino sheep owned by Roger Saunders gave birth to 4 ram and 3 ewe live lambs at Strathdownie, Victoria, Australia on 19 Jun 1984. Seven live lambs (4 rams and 3 ewes) were also reported for a Finn × Targhoe ewe owned by Elsward Meine of Crookston, Minnesota, USA on 24 Mar 1980. Pedigree Cambridge ewe No. 8125AP, owned by Peter Adorian, gave birth to seven live lambs weighing 19·05 kg *42 lb* at Gibbons Mill Farm, Billingshurst, W Sussex on 19 Mar 1990, and a Welsh mule owned by Dennis and Martin Swain of Holt Farm, Sherborne, Dorset also gave birth to seven live lambs, on 2 Jan 1991.

Birthweights The highest recorded birthweight for a lamb is 17·2 kg *38 lb* at Clearwater, Sedgwick County, Kansas, USA in 1975, but neither lamb nor ewe survived. Another lamb of the same weight was born on 7 Apr 1975 on the Gerald Neises Farm, Howard, South Dakota, USA but died soon afterwards.

On 13 Apr 1990 it was reported that a Kent ewe had given birth to a live lamb weighing 17·2 kg *28 lb* on the Belton estate, near Grantham, Lincs, farmed by Les Baker.

A four-year-old Suffolk ewe owned by Gerry H. Watson of Augusta, Kansas, USA gave birth to two live sets of triplets on 30–31 Jan 1982. The total weight of the lambs was 22·4 kg *49½ lb*. The greatest combined birthweight for lambs in Britain is 21·1 kg *43½ lb* for live quadruplets produced on 20 Feb 1990 by a Friezland × Exmoor Horn owned by John and Margaret Sillick of South Stursdon Farm, Bude, Cornwall.

The lowest live birthweight recorded for a lamb is 1·02 kg *2 lb 4 oz* for a ram named 'Tiny', born in April 1980 and owned by Jeanette Fox of Daisy Bank Farm, Barthomley, Cheshire. It was nursed to full health.

Oldest A crossbred sheep owned by Griffiths & Davies of Dolclettwr Hall, Taliesin, near Aberystwyth, Dyfed gave birth to a healthy lamb in the spring of 1988 at the grand old age of 28, after lambing successfully more than 40 times. She died on 24 Jan 1989 just one week before her 29th birthday.

Shearing The highest speed for sheep shearing in a working day was that recorded by Alan McDonald, who machine-sheared 805 lambs in nine hours (an average of 89·4) at Waitanguru, New Zealand on 20 Dec 1990. Peter Casserly of Christchurch, New Zealand achieved a solo blade (i.e. hand-shearing) record of 353 lambs in nine hours on 13 Feb 1976.

UK The British record set under National Shearing Competitions Committee rules (nine hours, sheep caught by shearers) is 1869 by the four-man team of William Workman, Ian Matthews, Howell Havard and Philip Evans at Pant Farm, Merthyr Cynog, Powys on 30 Jun 1990. Philip Evans also set a new solo record of 535 at this contest.

The record for lambs is 973 by Robert Bull and Barry Godsell at Winchelsea Beach, E Sussex on 17 Jun 1989, when Robert Bull also set the solo record of 517. In a 24-hour shearing marathon, Alan MacDonald and Keith Wilson machine-sheared 2220 sheep at Warkworth, Auckland Province, New Zealand on 26 Jun 1988. Godfrey Bowen of New Zealand sheared a Cheviot ewe in 46 sec at the Royal Highland Show held at Dundee, Tayside in June 1957.

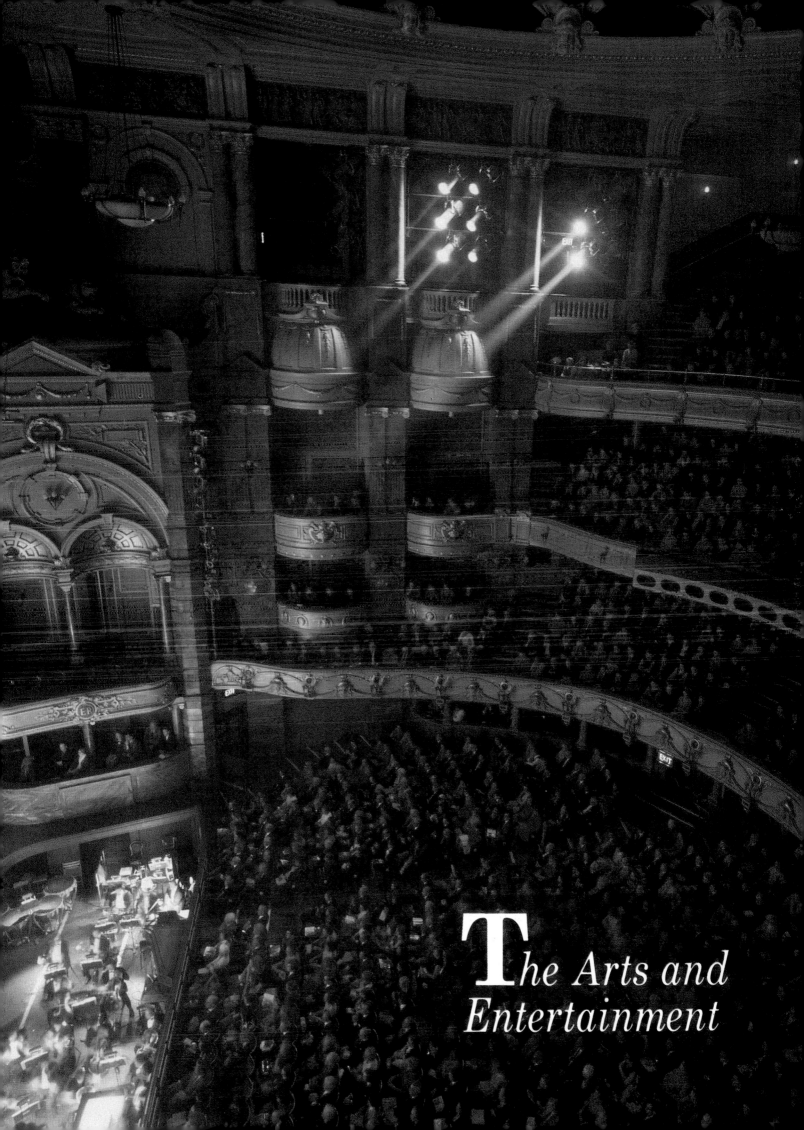

The Arts and Entertainment

PAINTING

Largest poster

A poster measuring 12 500 m² *134 550 ft²*, painted by 30 000 inhabitants of Miyazaki, Japan to celebrate the annual Himuka-no-Saiten Festival, was unveiled on 17 Mar 1990.

Finest paint brush

The finest standard brush sold is the 000 in Series 7 by Winsor and Newton known as a 'triple goose'. It is made of 150–200 Kolinsky sable hairs weighing 15 mg *0·000529 oz.*

Sand sculpture

The longest sand sculpture ever made — with the sculpture meticulously carved — was the 16 812 m *55 154 ft 6 in* long sculpture named 'The GTE Directories Ultimate Sand Castle' built by more than 8000 volunteers at Myrtle Beach, South Carolina, USA on 4 Jul 1990. The tallest was the 'Invitation to Fairyland', which was 17·12 m *56 ft 2 in* high, and was built by 2000 local volunteers at Kaseda, Japan on 26 Jul 1989 under the supervision of Gerry Kirk of Sand Sculptors International of San Diego and Shogo Tashiro of Sand Sculptors International of Japan.

Painting

Origins Evidence of Palaeolithic art was first found in 1833 at Veyrier, 5 km *3 miles* south-west of Geneva, Switzerland, when François Mayor (1779–1854) found two harpoon-like objects decorated with geometric figures. Recently discovered pieces of bone bearing geometric engraved marks from an Old Stone Age site at Bilzingsleben, near Erfurt, Germany could possibly be the world's oldest examples of art. They are dated to c. 350 000 years ago.

The oldest known dated examples of representational art come from La Ferrassie, near Les Eyzies in the Périgord, France, in layers dated to c. 25 000 BC. Blocks of stone were found with engraved animals and female symbols; some of the blocks also had symbols painted in red ochre.

Pieces of ochre with ground facets have been found at Lake Mungo, New South Wales, Australia in a context *ante* 30 000 BC, but there is no evidence to show whether these were used for body-painting or pictorial art.

Largest The largest-ever painting measures 6727·56 m² *72 437 ft²* after allowing for shrinkage of the canvas. It is made up of brightly coloured squares superimposed by a 'Smiley' face and was painted by students of Robb College at Armidale, New South Wales, Australia, aided by local schoolchildren and students from neighbouring colleges. The canvas was completed by its designer, Australian artist Ken Done, and unveiled at the University of New England at Armidale on 10 May 1990.

'Old Master' The largest 'Old Master' is *Il Paradiso*, by Jacopo Robusti, *alias* Tintoretto (1518–94), and his son Domenico (1565–1637) on the east wall of the Sala del Maggior Consiglio in the Palazzo Ducale (Doge's Palace) in Venice, Italy between 1587 and 1590. The work is 22 m *72 ft 2 in* long, 7 m *22 ft 11½ in* high and contains some 350 human figures.

UK The oval painting *Triumph of Peace and Liberty* by Sir James Thornhill (1676–1734) on the ceiling of the Painted Hall in the Royal Naval College, Greenwich measures 32·3 × 15·4 m *106 × 51 ft* and took 20 years (1707–27) to complete.

Auction The largest painting ever auctioned was Carl Larsson's *Midvinterblot*, painted in Stockholm, Sweden from 1911 to 1915 and sold at Sotheby's, London on 25 Mar 1988 for £880 000 to the Umeda Gallery of Japan. The painting measured 13·4 × 2·7 m *44 × 9 ft.*

Most valuable The 'Mona Lisa' (*La Gioconda*) by Leonardo da Vinci (1452–1519) in the Louvre, Paris, France was assessed for insurance purposes at $100 million for its move to Washington, DC, USA and New York City for exhibition from 14 Dec 1962 to 12 Mar 1963. However, insurance was not concluded because the cost of the closest security precautions was less than that of the premiums. It was painted c. 1503–07 and measures 77 × 53 cm *30·5 × 20·9 in.* It is believed to portray either Mona (short for Madonna) Lisa Gherardini, the wife of Francesco del Giocondo of Florence, or Constanza d'Avalos, coincidentally nicknamed La Gioconda, mistress of Giuliano de Medici. King Francis I of France bought the painting for his bathroom in 1517 for 4000 gold florins, or 15·3 kg *92 oz* of gold.

Most prolific painter Pablo Diego José Francisco de Paula Juan Nepomuceno Crispin Crispiano de la Santisima Trinidad Ruiz y Picasso (1881–1973) of Spain was the most prolific of all painters in a career which lasted 78 years. It has been estimated that Picasso produced about 13 500 paintings or designs, 100 000 prints or engravings, 34 000 book illustrations and 300 sculptures or ceramics. His lifetime *oeuvre* has been valued at £500 million.

Oldest RA The oldest Royal Academician was (Thomas) Sidney Cooper, who died on 8 Feb 1902 aged 98 yr 136 days. He exhibited 266 paintings over the record span of 69 consecutive years (1833–1902).

Youngest RA Mary Moser (later Mrs Hugh Lloyd, 1744–1819) was elected on the foundation of the Royal Academy in 1768 at the age of 24.

Youngest exhibitor The youngest exhibitor at the Royal Academy of Arts Annual Summer Exhibition was Lewis Melville 'Gino' Lyons (b. 30 Apr 1962). His *Trees and Monkeys* was painted on 4 Jun 1965, submitted on 17 Mar 1967 and exhibited to the public on 29 Apr 1967.

Largest galleries The world's largest art gallery is the Winter Palace and the neighbouring Hermitage in Leningrad, USSR. One has to walk 24 km *15 miles* to visit each of the 322 galleries, which house nearly 3 million works of art and objects of archaeological interest.

The Georges Pompidou National Centre for Art and Culture, Beauborg opened in Paris, France in 1977 with 17 700 m² *183 000 ft²* of floor space.

Most heavily endowed The J. Paul Getty Museum at Malibu, California, USA was established with an initial £700 million budget in January 1974 and now has an annual budget of £104 million for acquisitions to stock its 38 galleries.

MURALS

Earliest The earliest known murals on man-made walls are the clay relief leopards at Çatal Hüyük in southern Anatolia, Turkey, discovered by James Malaart at level VII in 1961 and dating from c. 6200 BC.

Largest A mural on the 23-storey Vegas World Hotel, Las Vegas, Nevada, USA covers an area of 8866·56 m² *95 442 ft².* A mural covering an area of 1668·7 m² *17 963 ft²* is painted on the walls of the Royal Liverpool Children's Hospital, Alder Hey, Liverpool, Merseyside.

MOSAICS

Largest The world's largest mosaic is on the walls of the central library of the Universidad Nacional Autónoma de Mexico in Mexico City. Of the four walls, the two largest measure 1203 m² *12 949 ft²*, and the scenes on each represent the pre-Hispanic past.

UK The largest Roman mosaic in Britain is the Woodchester Pavement, Glos of c. AD 325, excavated in 1793 and now recovered with protective earth. It measured 14·3 m² *47 ft²* and comprised 1·6 million tesserae. A total reconstruction carried out by Robert and John Woodward of Stroud, Glos was completed in June 1987.

HIGHEST PRICES

Most expensive painting Following the collapse of Australian tycoon Alan Bond's business empire in 1989, he was forced to part with Vincent Van Gogh's *Irises*, which he had bought in 1987 for a then record price of $53·9 million. The sale followed reports that Sotheby's had loaned Mr Bond $27 million towards the purchase, a practice which the auction house has subsequently reviewed. *Irises* was re-sold to the Getty Museum for an undisclosed sum in April 1990. On 15 May 1990 this record was shattered again when another Van Gogh, *Portrait of Dr Gachet*, was sold within three minutes for $82·5 million at Christie's, New York, USA. The painting depicts Van Gogh's physician and was completed only weeks before the artist's suicide in 1890. The new owner was subsequently identified as Ryoei Saito, Japan's second-largest paper manufacturer.

UK The highest auction price for a painting by a British artist is £10·78 million paid for John Constable's (1776–1837) *The Lock* (1824) at Sotheby's, London on 14 Nov 1990. The buyer was Baron Hans Heinrich Thyssen-Bornemisza, a director of Sotheby's.

Miniature The record price is £352 000, paid by the Alexander Gallery of New York, USA at Christie's, London on 7 Nov 1988 for a 54 mm *2⅛ in* high miniature of George Washington. It was painted by the Irish-American miniaturist John Ramage (c. 1748–1802) in 1789.

20th-century painting The record bid at auction for a 20th-century painting is $47·8 million for a self-portrait by Picasso (1881–1973), *Yo Picasso* (1901), at Sotheby's, New York, USA on 9 May 1989.

Living artist The highest price paid at auction for a work by a living artist is $20·68 million (*£13 million*) for *Interchange*, an abstract by the American painter Willem de Kooning (b. Rotterdam, Netherlands, 1904) at Sotheby's, New York on 8 Nov 1989. Painted in 1955, it was bought by the Japanese company Mountain Tortoise.

UK The highest price paid for any painting by a living artist born in the United Kingdom was $6·27 million for *Triptych May–June* by Francis Bacon (b. 1909 in Dublin, Republic of Ireland, then part of the United Kingdom), sold on 2 May 1989 at Sotheby's, New York, USA.

Print The record price for a print at auction was £561 600 for a 1655 etching of *Christ Presented to the People* by Rembrandt (1606–69) at Christie's, London on 5 Dec 1985. It was sold by the Chatsworth Settlement Trustees.

Drawing The highest price ever paid for a drawing is $8·36 million (*£4·27 million*) for the pen-and-ink scene *Garden of Flowers*, drawn by Vincent Van Gogh at Arles, France in 1888 and sold at Christie's, New York on 14 Nov 1990 to an anonymous buyer.

Poster The record price for a poster is £62 000 for an advertisement for the 1902 Vienna Exhibition by Koloman Moser (1868–1918), sold at Christie's, London on 1 Apr 1985.

Sculpture

Earliest A piece of ox rib found in 1973 at Pech de l'Aze, Dordogne, France in an early Middle Palaeolithic layer of the Riss glaciation of c. 105 000 BC has several engraved lines on one side, thought to be possibly intentional. A churingo or curved ivory plaque rubbed with red ochre from the Middle Palaeolithic Mousterian site at

Tata, Hungary has been dated to 100 000 BC by the thorium/uranium method.

The earliest known examples of sculpture date from the Aurignacian culture of *c.* 28 000–22 000 BC and include the so-called 'Venus' figurines from Austria and the numerous figurines from northern Italy and central France. A carving in mammoth ivory from the Magdalenian culture (*c.* 11–17 000 years ago) of a horse measuring 6·3 cm *2½ in* was found in the Vogelherd cave in south-west Germany.

British Isles The earliest example of an engraving found in Britain is of a horse's head on a piece of rib-bone from Robin Hood Cave, Creswell Crag, Derbys. It dates from the Upper Palaeolithic period of *c.* 15 000–10 000 BC. The earliest Scottish rock carving, from Lagalochan, Argyll, Strathclyde, dates from *c.* 3000 BC. Geometric carvings on the tomb at Newgrange, Co. Meath, Republic of Ireland are of a similar age.

Most expensive The record price paid for a sculpture at auction is £6·82 million at Sotheby's, London on 7 Dec 1989 for a bronze garden ornament, *The Dancing Faun*, made by the Dutch-born sculptor Adrien de Vries (1545/6–1626). London dealer Cyril Humpris bought the figure from an unnamed Brighton, W Sussex couple who had paid £100 for it in the 1950s and in whose garden it had stood unremarked for 40 years.

The highest price paid for the work of a sculptor during his lifetime is $1 265 000 given at Sotheby's, New York, USA on 21 May 1982 for the 190·5 cm *75 in* long elmwood *Reclining Figure* by Henry Moore (1898–1986).

Largest The mounted figures of Jefferson Davis (1808–89), Gen. Robert Edward Lee (1807–70) and Gen. Thomas Jonathan (Stonewall) Jackson (1824–63) cover 0·5 ha *1·33 acres* on the face of Stone Mountain, near Atlanta, Georgia, USA. They are 27·4 m *90 ft* high. Roy Faulkner was on the mountain face for 8 years 174 days with a thermo-jet torch, working with the sculptor Walker Kirtland Hancock and other helpers, from 12 Sep 1963 to 3 Mar 1972.

The largest scrap-metal sculpture was built by Sudhir Deshpande of Nashik, India and unveiled in February 1990. Named *Powerful*, the colossus weighs 27 tonnes and stands 17 m *55¾ ft* tall.

Ground figures In the Nazca Desert, 300 km *185 miles* south of Lima, Peru there are straight lines (one more than 11·2 km *7 miles* long), geometric shapes and outlines of plants and animals drawn on the ground some time between 100 BC and AD 600 for an uncertain but probably religious, astronomical or even economic purpose by an as yet imprecisely identified civilization. They were first detected from the air *c.* 1928 and have been described as the world's longest works of art.

Hill figures In August 1968 a 100 m *330 ft* tall figure was found on a hill above Tarapacá, Chile.

UK The largest human hill carving in Britain is the 'Long Man' of Wilmington, E Sussex, at 68 m *226 ft* in length. The oldest of all 'White Horses' in Britain is the Uffington horse in Oxfordshire, dating from the late Iron Age (*c.* 150 BC) and measuring 114 m *374 ft* from nose to tail and 36 m *120 ft* high.

Antiques

All prices quoted are inclusive of the

buyer's premium. The oldest firm of art auctioneers in the world is the Stockholms Auktionsverk of Sweden, which was established on 27 Feb 1647. Christie's of London held their first art auction in 1766. The largest firm is the Sotheby Group of London and New York, founded in 1744 although trading until 1778 was primarily in books. Sotheby's turnover in 1989 was a record $2·9 billion and their New York sales set a single series record of $360·4 million York in May 1990.

Art nouveau The highest auction price for any piece of art nouveau is $1·78 million (*£1·1 million*) for a standard lamp in the form of three lotus blossoms by the Daum Brothers and Louis Majorelle of France, sold at Sotheby's, New York, USA on 2 Dec 1989.

Blanket The most expensive blanket was a Navajo Churro hand-spun serape of *c.* 1852 sold for $115 500 at Sotheby's, New York, USA on 22 Oct 1983.

Carpet In 1946 the Metropolitan Museum in New York City, USA privately paid $1 million for the 8·07 × 4·14 m *26·5 × 13·6 ft* Anhalt Medallion carpet made in Tabriz or Kashan, Persia (now Iran) *c.* 1590. The highest price paid at auction for a carpet is £384 230 for a Louis XV Savonnerie at Christie's, Monaco in June 1989.

Ceramics The highest auction price for any ceramic is £3·74 million for a Chinese Tang dynasty (AD 681–907) horse sold by the British Rail Pension Fund and bought by a Japanese dealer at Sotheby's, London on 12 Dec 1989. The horse was stolen from a warehouse in Hong Kong on 14 November, but was recovered on 2 December in time for the sale.

Chamber pot A 935 g *33 oz* silver pot, made by David Willaume and engraved for the 2nd Earl of Warrington, sold for £9500 at Sotheby's, London on 14 Jun 1984.

Cigarette card The most valuable card is one of the six known baseball series cards

of Honus Wagner, who was a non-smoker, which was sold at Sotheby's, New York, USA for $451 000 on 22 Mar 1991. The buyers were Bruce McNall, owner of the Los Angeles Kings ice hockey club, and team member Wayne Gretzky, the game's most successful player.

Doll The highest price paid at auction for a doll is £90 200 for a 1909 bisque Kämmer and Reinhardt doll at Sotheby's, London on 16 Feb 1989. It was bought by Mme Dina Vierny, who had planned to open a Museum of Childhood in France.

Furniture The highest price ever paid for a single piece of furniture is £8·58 million (*$15·1 million*) at Christie's, London on 5 Jul 1990 for the 18th-century Italian 'Badminton Cabinet' owned by the Duke of Beaufort. It was bought by Barbara Piasecka Johnson of Princeton, New Jersey, USA. The highest price paid for an item of English furniture was £1·1 million at Christie's, London on 6 Jul 1989 for a George III ormolu-mounted mahogany dressing and writing commode, attributed to John Channon and made *c.* 1760.

Glass The auction record is £520 000 for a Roman glass cage-cup of *c.* AD 300, measuring 17·78 cm *7 in* in diameter and 10·16 cm *4 in* in height, sold at Sotheby's, London on 4 Jun 1979 to Robin Symes.

Gold plate The record for any gold artifact is £950 400 for the 22-carat font made by Paul Storr to the design of Humphry Repton in 1797. It was sold at Christie's, London by Lady Anne Cavendish-Bentinck and bought by Armitage of London on 11 Jul 1985.

Guns The highest price ever paid for a single gun is £125 000 given by the London dealers F. Partridge for a French flintlock fowling piece made for Louis XIII *c.* 1615 and attributed to Pierre le Bourgeoys of Lisieux, France (died 1627). This piece was included in the collection of the late William Goodwin Renwick (US) sold by Sotheby's, London on 21 Nov 1972. It is now in the

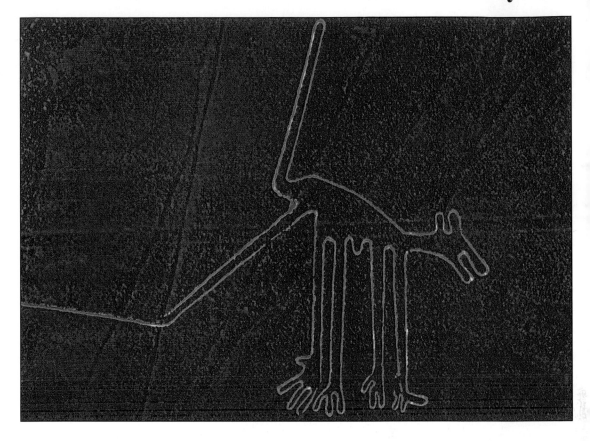

■ **Ground figures**
This computer-enhanced picture of an unidentified animal shows just one of the unexplained geometric shapes drawn in the Nazca Desert of Peru between 100 BC and AD 600. (Photo: Images)

Icon
The record price for an icon is $150 000 paid at Christie's, New York, USA on 17 Apr 1980 for the *Last Judgement* (from the George R. Hann collection, Pittsburgh, Pennsylvania), made in Novgorod, USSR in the 16th century.

Auctioneering
The longest one-man auction on record is one of 60 hr, conducted by Reg Coates at Gosport, Hants from 9–11 Sep 1988.

Metropolitan Museum of Art, New York City, USA. A .45 calibre Colt single-action army revolver, Serial No. 1 from 1873, was sold for $242 000 at Christie's, New York, USA on 14 May 1987.

Helmet The highest price ever paid for an item of headgear is $66 000 by the Alaska State Museum at an auction in New York City, USA in November 1981 for a native North American Tlingit Kiksadi ceremonial frog helmet dating from *c*. 1600.

Jade The highest price ever paid for an item in jade is $2 042 857 (*£1 087 452*) at Christie's, Geneva, Switzerland on 12 May 1988 for a jade, ruby and diamond necklace.

Jewellery The world's largest jewellery auction, which included a Van Cleef and Arpels 1939 ruby and diamond necklace, realized £31 380 197 when the collection belonging to the Duchess of Windsor (1896–1986) was sold at Sotheby's, Geneva, Switzerland on 3 Apr 1987.

The highest auction price for individual items of jewellery is £3·1 million for two, pear-shaped diamond drop earrings of 58·6 and 61 carats bought and sold anonymously at Sotheby's, Geneva on 14 Nov 1980.

Musical box The highest price paid for a musical box is £20 900 for a Swiss example made for a Persian prince in 1901 and sold at Sotheby's, London on 23 Jan 1985.

Playing cards The highest price for a deck of playing cards is $143 352 paid by the Metropolitan Museum of Art, New York City, USA at Sotheby's, London on 6 Dec 1983.

Scientific instrument The highest auction price paid for a scientific instrument is £385 000 for a 34·29 cm *13½ in* Dutch gilt-brass astrolabe of 1559 by Walter Arsenius at Christie's, London on 6 Dec 1983.

Silver The record for a single piece of English silver is £1 485 000 for the 'Maynard' sideboard dish made by the Huguenot silversmith Paul de Lamerie in 1736, which was sold at Christie's, London on 22 May 1991. The Dunham Massey sconces, a set of six George II wall sconces made by Peter Archambo in London in 1730, were sold to London dealer Armitage for £1 155 000 at Sotheby's, London on 3 May 1990.

Snuff box The highest price paid for a snuff box is £764 826 at Christie's, Geneva, Switzerland on 11 Nov 1986 for a pale-green chrysoprase and diamond gold box once owned by Frederick the Great of Prussia.

Spoons A set of 13 Henry VIII Apostle spoons owned by Lord Astor of Hever was sold for £120 000 on 24 Jun 1981 at Christie's, London. A Wiener Werkstätte spoon made by Josef Hoffmann of Austria *c*. 1905 was sold at Sotheby's, London for £17 600 on 28 Apr 1983.

Sword The highest price paid for a sword is £823 045 for the Duke of Windsor's Royal Navy officer's sword (presented to him by King George V in 1913) at Sotheby's, Geneva, Switzerland on 3 Apr 1987.

Tapestry The highest auction price for a tapestry is £638 000, paid by Swiss dealer Peter Kleiner at Christie's, London on 3 Jul 1990 for a fragment of a rare Swiss example woven near Basle in the 1430s. The tapestry was in the Benedictine Abbey at Muri until 1840 before descending through the Vischer family.

Teddy bear The highest price paid for a Teddy bear at auction is £55 100. The dual-plush brown bear made by Steiff of Germany *c*. 1920 was bought at Sotheby's, London on 19 Sep 1989 by dealer James Fox.

Thimble The record auction price for a thimble is £8000 paid by London dealer Winifred Williams at Christie's, London on 3 Dec 1979 for a Meissen dentil-shaped porcelain piece dated *c*. 1740.

Toys The most expensive antique toy, and the first to fetch $1 million, was sold privately by London dealers Mint & Boxed to an unnamed European in mid-1990. The work is a hand-painted tin plate replica of the 'Charles' hose reel, a piece of fire-fighting equipment pulled by two firemen, measuring 381 mm × 584 mm *15 × 23 in* and built *c*. 1870 by George Brown & Co. of Forestville, Connecticut, USA.

The highest price paid for a single toy soldier is £3375 for a uniformed scale figure of Hitler's deputy, Rudolf Hess, made by the Lineol company of Brandenburg, Germany as part of a line discontinued in 1941. The figure was among several sold by the Danish auction house Boyes in London on 23 Apr 1991. An extremely rare 70 mm *2¾ in* scale figure of the Colonel-in-Chief of the Welsh Guards was sold for £1200 at Phillips, London on 9 Sep 1987.

Typewriter The highest price paid for an antique machine is £9900 for an 1890 black enamel Guhl & Harbeck at Christie's, London on 10 Aug 1989.

Walking stick The highest auction price for a walking stick is $24 200 at Sotheby's, New York, USA in 1983 for an octagonal, whale-ivory nobbed stick decorated by Scrimshanders in 1845.

Language

Earliest The ability to speak is believed to be dependent upon physiological changes in the height of the larynx between *Homo erectus* and *Homo sapiens sapiens* as developed *ante* 45 000 BC. The discovery of a hyoid bone (from the base of the tongue) from a cave site on Mt Carmel, Israel shows that Neanderthal man was capable of speech 60 000 years ago.

Oldest English words It was first suggested in 1979 that languages ancestral to English and to Latvian (both Indo-European) split *c*. 3500 BC. According to researches completed in 1989, about 40 words of a pre-Indo-European substratum survive in English, e.g. apple (apal), bad (bad), gold (gol) and tin (tin).

Commonest language Today's world total of languages and dialects still spoken is about 4–5000, some 845 of which come from India.

The language used by more people than any other is Mandarin, spoken by an estimated 68 per cent of China's population, and hence by about 770 million people in 1990. The so-called national language (*Guóyǔ*) is a standardized form of northern Chinese (*Běifānghuà*) as spoken in the Beijing area. This was alphabetized into *zhùyīn fùhào* of 37 letters in 1913 by Wa Chih-hui (1865–1953). On 11 Feb 1938 the *Hanyu-Pinyin-Fang'an* system, which is a phonetic pronunciation guide, was introduced.

The next most commonly spoken language, and the most widespread, is English, with an estimated 330 million native speakers and nearly twice as many using it as a second or third language.

British Isles There are eight indigenous languages older than English still in use in the United Kingdom. These are: (1) *Welsh* (Cymraeg), a branch of Brythonic Celtic. In Gwynedd 61 per cent of the population speak it. (2) *Cornish* (Kernewek), also Brythonic but closer to Breton. The last monoglot speaker was probably Dolly Pentreath (died in Mousehole, 1777). In the current revival there are some 100 fluent speakers and 200 students. (3) *Scots Gaelic* (Gaidhlig), a branch of Goidelic Celtic spoken by up to 85 per cent of people in the Western Isles. (4) *Irish* (Gaelige) is the first official language of the Irish Republic, although only 4·5 per cent of the population use it daily. An estimated 45 000 people have a knowledge of it in Northern Ireland. (5) *Manx* (Gaelg). The last native speaker was Edward Madrill (1877–1974) and today some 60 people have learnt to speak it fluently. (6) *Channel Isles patois*. Some 10 000 people (13 per cent) speak *Jerriais* in Jersey; 6000 (11 per cent) *Guernesiais* in Guernsey, and less than 100 (16 per cent) *Sercqiais* in Sark. *Auregnais* became extinct in Alderney *c*. 1952. (7) *Sheldru* or

Shelta (known also as The Cant) is spoken by an estimated 25 000 travellers. Some scholars believe it has its origins in Pictish. (8) *Romani* (Romnimos) has been spoken by travellers since the 15th century and originates from northern India. *Puri* (pure) *jib* as opposed to *pogadi* (broken) is still spoken by about 350 Romani, mostly in north central Wales.

Most languages The former Australian territory of Papua New Guinea has, owing to its many isolated valleys, the greatest concentration of separate languages in the world, with more than 10 per cent of the world's total of 4–5000.

Most complex The following extremes of complexity have been noted: Chippewa, the North American Indian language of Minnesota, USA, has the most verb forms, with up to 6000; Haida, the North American Indian language, has the most prefixes, with 70; Tabassaran, a language of Daghestan, USSR, uses the most noun cases (48), while Inuit uses 63 forms of the present tense and simple nouns have as many as 252 inflections.

The 40-volume *Chung-wén Tà Tz'u-tiĕn* Chinese dictionary lists 49 905 characters. The fourth tone of 'i' has 84 meanings, varying as widely as 'dress', 'hiccough' and 'licentious'. The written language provides 92 different characters of 'i⁴'. The most complex written character in Chinese is that representing *xiè*, consisting of 64 strokes and meaning 'talkative'. The most complex in current use is *nang*, with 36 strokes, meaning 'a blocked-up nose'.

Least irregular verbs Esperanto was first published by its inventor Dr Ludwig Zamenhof (1859–1917) of Warsaw in 1887 without irregular verbs and is now estimated (by text book sales) to have a million speakers. The even earlier interlanguage Volapük, invented by Johann Martin Schleyer (1831–1912), also has absolutely regular configuration. The Turkish language has a single irregular verb — *olmak*, meaning 'to be'.

Most irregular verbs According to *The Morphology and Syntax of Present-day English* by Prof. Olu Tomori, English has 283 irregular verbs, 30 of which are merely formed with prefixes.

Rarest sounds The rarest speech sound is probably that written 'ř' in Czech, which occurs in very few languages and is the last sound mastered by Czech children. In the southern Bushman language !xo there is a click articulated with both lips, which is written ⊙. In some contexts the 'l' sound in the Arabic word *Allah* is pronounced uniquely in that language.

Commonest sound No language is known to be without the vowel 'a' (as in the English 'father').

Greatest linguist If the yardstick of ability to speak with fluency and reasonable accuracy is maintained, it is doubtful whether any human being could uphold fluency in more than 20–25 languages concurrently or achieve fluency in more than 40 in a lifetime.

The world's greatest linguist is believed to be George Campbell (b. 9 Aug 1912), who is retired from the BBC Overseas Service where he worked with 54 languages. Powell Alexander Janulus (b. 1939) has worked with 41 languages in the Provincial Court of British Columbia, Vancouver, Canada.

In terms of oral fluency, the most multilingual living person is Derick Herning of Lerwick, Shetland, whose command of 22

languages earned him victory in the inaugural 'Polyglot of Europe' contest held in Brussels, Belgium in May 1990.

The 1975 edition of *Who's Who in the United Nations* listed 'only' 19 languages for Georges Schmidt (1914–90), Chief of the UN Terminology Section in 1965–71, because he was then unable to find time to 'revive' his former fluency in 12 others.

Historically, the greatest linguists have been proclaimed as Prof. Rask (1787–1832) of Denmark, Sir John Bowring (1792–1872) and Dr Harold Williams of New Zealand (1876–1928), who were all fluent in 28 languages, and Cardinal Mezzofanti (1774–1849) of Italy (fluent in 26 or 27).

ALPHABET

Earliest The earliest example of alphabetic writing has been found at Ugarit (now Ras Sharma), Syria, dated to c. 1450 BC. It comprised a tablet of 32 cuneiform letters.

Oldest letter The letter 'O' is unchanged in shape since its adoption in the Phoenician alphabet c. 1300 BC.

Newest letters The newest letters to be added to the English alphabet are 'j' and 'v', which are of post-Shakespearean use c. 1630. Formerly they were used only as variants of 'i' and 'u'. There are 65 alphabets now in use world-wide.

Longest The language with most letters is Cambodian, with 72 (including some without any current use).

Shortest Rotokas of central Bougainville Island, Papua New Guinea has least letters, with 11 (a, b, e, g, i, k, o, p, ř, t and u).

Most and least consonants The language with most distinct consonantal sounds is that of the Ubykhs in the Caucasus, with 80–85, and that with the least is Rotokas, which has only six consonants.

The English word 'latchstring' contains six consecutive consonants, but the Georgian word *gvprtskvnis* ('he is feeling us') has eight separately pronounced consonants.

Most and least vowels The language with the most vowels is Sedang, a central Vietnamese language with 55 distinguish-

able vowel sounds, and that with the least is the Caucasian language Abkhazian with two. Cauaiauaia in Angola has nine consecutive vowel letters. The name of a language in Pará state, Brazil consists solely of seven vowels — *uoiauai*, and the Estonian word *jäääärne*, meaning 'the edge of the ice', has the same four consecutively.

Smallest letters In April 1990 the letters IBM were etched into a nickel crystal by an instrument called a scanning tunnelling microscope to form a corporate logo measuring 1·27 nm (10⁻⁹) long. It took physicists Donald Eigler and Erhard Schweizer at IBM's Almaden Research Center in San Jose, California, USA 22 hr to drag the 35 xenon atoms across the bumpy nickel surface, which had been chilled to near absolute zero. Their creation flew apart when the temperature rose above −228·89°C −380°F. In February 1991 it was announced that scientists at the Hitachi Central Research Laboratory in Tokyo, Japan had used the same technique at room temperature to etch sulphur atoms on molybdenum-disulphide into the message 'PEACE '91 HCRL'.

WORDS

Longest Lengthy concatenations and some compound or agglutinative words or nonce words are or have been written in the closed-up style of a single word, e.g. the 182-letter fricassee of 17 sweet and sour ingredients in Aristophanes' comedy *The Ecclesiazusae* in the 4th century BC. A compound 'word' of 195 Sanskrit characters (which transliterates into 428 letters in the Roman alphabet) describing the region near Kanci, Tamil Nadu, India appears in a 16th-century work by Tirumalāmbā, Queen of Vijayanagara.

English The longest real word in the *Oxford English Dictionary* is *floccipaucinihilipilification* (it is alternatively hyphenated with an 'n' in place of the 'p' as the seventh letter), with 29 letters, meaning 'the action of estimating as worthless', which was first used in 1741, and later by Sir Walter Scott (1771–1832).

The longest factitious word in the *Oxford English Dictionary* is *pneumonoultramicro-*

Vocabulary
The English language contains about 490 000 words plus another 300 000 technical terms, the most in any language but it is doubtful if any individual uses more than 60 000. UK residents who have undergone a full 16 years of education use perhaps 5000 words in speech and up to 10 000 words in written communications. The membership of the International Society for Philosophical Enquiry (no admission for IQs below 148) have an average vocabulary of 36 250 words. Shakespeare employed a vocabulary of c. 33 000 words.

■ **Most expensive toy**
This hand-decorated tin plate 'Charles' fire-hose reel, made by Brown & Co. of Forestville, Connecticut, USA c. 1870, became the first $1-million antique toy when it was sold privately in 1990 by dealers Mint & Boxed of London. (Photo: Caroline Neville Associates)

LANGUAGE

LONGEST WORDS

JAPANESE[1]	Chi-n-chi-ku-ri-n (12 letters) *a very short person (slang)*
SPANISH	Superextraordinarisimo (22) *extraordinary*
FRENCH	Anticonstitutionnellement (25) *anticonstitutionally*
CROATIAN	Prijestolonasljednikovica (25) *wife of an heir apparent*
ITALIAN	Precipitevolissimevolmente (26) *as fast as possible*
PORTUGUESE	Inconstitucionalissimamente (27) *with the highest degree of unconstitutionality*
ICELANDIC	Haecstaréttarmálaflutningsmaôur (29) *supreme court barrister*
RUSSIAN	Ryentgyenoelyektrokardiografichyeskogo (33 Cyrillic letters, transliterating as 38) *of the X-ray electrocardiographic*
HUNGARIAN	Megszentségtelenithetetlenségeskedéseitekért (44) *for your unprofanable actions*
DUTCH[4]	Kindercarnavalsoptochtvoorbereidingswerkzaamheden (49) *preparation activities for a children's carnival procession*
MOHAWK[2]	Tkanuhstasrihsranuhwe'tsraaksahsrakaratattsrayeri' (50) *the praising of the evil of the liking of the finding of the house is right*
TURKISH[4]	Cekoslovakyalılastırabilemediklerimizlerdenmisiniz (50) *'are you not of that group of persons that we were said to be unable to Czechoslovakianise?'*
GERMAN[3,4]	Donaudampfschiffahrtselectrizitaetenhauptbetriebswerkbau- unterbeamtengesellschaft (80) *The club for subordinate officials of the head office management of the Danube steamboat electrical services (name of a pre-war club in Vienna)*
SWEDISH[4]	Nordöstersjökustartilleriflygspaningssimulatoranläggningsmateriel- underhållsuppföljningssystemdiskussionsinläggsförberedelse- arbeten (130) *Preparatory work on the contribution to the discussion on the maintaining system of support of the material of the aviation survey simulator device within the north-east part of the coast artillery of the Baltic*

[1] Patent applications sometimes harbour long compound 'words'. An extreme example is one of 13 kana (Japanese syllabary) which transliterates to the 40-letter Kyûkitsûrohekimenfuchakunenry-ôsekisanryô meaning 'the accumulated amount of fuel condensed on the wall face of the air intake passage'.
[2] Lengthy concatenations are a feature of Mohawk.
[3] The longest dictionary word in everyday usage is Rechtsschutzversicherungsgesellschaften (39) meaning 'insurance companies which provide legal protection'.
[4] Agglutinative words are limited only by imagination and are not found in standard dictionaries. The first 100-letter such word was published in 1975 by the late Eric Rosenthal in Afrikaans.

Most succinct word

The most challenging word for any lexicographer to define briefly is the Fuegian (southernmost Argentina and Chile) word *mamihlapinatapai*, meaning 'looking at each other hoping that either will offer to do something which both parties desire but are unwilling to do'.

Most synonyms

The condition of being inebriated has more synonyms than any other condition or object. Delacourt Press of New York City, USA has published a selection of 1224 from 2241 compiled by Paul Dickson of Garrett Park, Maryland, USA. This selection does, however, have some surprising omissions.

scopicsilicovolcanoconiosis (or -*koniosis*), which has 45 letters and allegedly means 'a lung disease caused by the inhalation of very fine silica dust'. *Webster's Third International Dictionary* lists among its 450 000 entries *pneumonoultramicroscopicsilicovolcanoconiosises* (47 letters), the plural of this term. The medical term *hepaticocholangiocholecystenterostomies* (with 39 letters) refers to the surgical creations of new communications between gallbladders and hepatic ducts and between intestines and gall-bladders.

The longest regularly formed English word is *praetertranssubstantiationalistically* (37 letters), used by Mark McShane in his 1963 novel *Untimely Ripped*. The longest words in common use are *disproportionableness* and *incomprehensibilities* (21 letters). *Interdenominationalism* (22 letters) is found in *Webster's Dictionary*, and hence *interdenominationalistically* (28 letters) is perhaps permissible.

Longest palindromes
The longest known palindromic word is *saippuakivikauppias* (19 letters), which is Finnish for 'a dealer in lye' (caustic soda). The longest in English is *tattarrattat*, with 12 letters, which appears in the *Oxford English Dictionary*. Some baptismal fonts in Greece and Turkey bear the circular 25-letter inscription NIΨON ANOMHMATA MH MONAN OΨIN, meaning 'wash (my) sins not only (my) face'. This appears at St Mary's Church, Nottingham, St Paul's, Woldingham, Surrey and other churches.

Longest scientific name
The systematic name for *deoxyribonucleic acid* (DNA) of the human mitochondria contains 16 569 nucleotide residues and is thus *c.* 207 000 letters long. It was published in key form in *Nature* on 9 Apr 1981.

Longest anagrams
The longest non-scientific English words which can form anagrams are the 19-letter transpositions *representationalism* and *misrepresentational*. The longest scientific transposals are *hydroxydesoxycorticosterone* and *hydroxydeoxycorticosterones*, with 27 letters.

Longest abbreviation
The initials S.K.O.M.K.H.P.K.J.C.D.P.W.B., which stand for the Syarikat Kerjasama Orang-orang Melayu Kerajaan Hilir Perak Kerana Jimat Cermat Dan Pinjam-meminjam Wang Berhad, make up the longest known abbreviation. This is the Malay name for The Cooperative Company of the Lower State of Perak Government's Malay People for Money Savings and Loans Ltd, in Teluk Anson, Perak, West Malaysia (formerly Malaya). The abbreviation for this abbreviation is Skomk. The 55-letter full name of Los Angeles (El Pueblo de Nuestra Señora la Reina de los Angeles de Porciuncula) is abbreviated to L.A., or 3·63 per cent of its length.

Longest acronym
The acronym NIIOMTPLABOPARMBETZHELBET-RABSBOMONIMONKONOTDTEKH-STROMONT, with 56 letters (54 in Cyrillic) in the *Concise Dictionary of Soviet Terminology*, is the world's longest. It means 'the laboratory for shuttering, reinforcement, concrete and ferroconcrete operations for composite-monolithic and monolithic constructions of the Department of the Technology of Building-assembly operations of the Scientific Research Institute of the Organization for building mechanization and technical aid of the Academy of Building and Architecture of the USSR'.

Commonest words and letters
The most frequently used words in written English are, in descending order of frequency: the, of, and, to, a, in, that, is, I, it, for and as. The most commonly used in conversation is 'I'. The commonest letter is 'e'. More words begin with the letter 's' than any other, but the most commonly *used* initial letter is 't' as in 'the', 'to', 'that' or 'there'.

Most meanings
The most overworked word in English is 'set', which Dr Charles Onions of Oxford University Press gave 58 noun uses, 126 verbal uses and ten as a participial adjective.

PERSONAL NAMES

Earliest
The earliest personal name which has survived is seemingly that of a predynastic king of Upper Egypt *ante* 3050 BC, who is indicated by the hieroglyphic sign for a scorpion. It has been suggested that the name should be read as Sekhen. The earliest known name of any resident of Britain is Divitiacus, King of the Suessiones, the Gaulish ruler of the Kent area *c.* 100 BC under the name Prydhain. Scotland, unlike England, was never fully conquered by the Roman occupiers (AD 43–410). Calgacus (b. *c.* AD 40), who led the final resistance in Scotland, was the earliest native whose name has been recorded.

Longest pedigree
The only non-royal English pedigree that can with certainty show a clear pre-Conquest descent is that of the Arden family. Shakespeare's mother was a Mary Arden. It is claimed on behalf of the Clan Mackay that their clan can be traced to Loarn, the Irish invader of southwest Pictland, now Argyll, *c.* AD 501.

Longest personal name
The longest name appearing on a birth certificate is that of Rhoshandiatellyneshiaunneveshenk Koyaanfsquatsiuty Williams, born to Mr and Mrs James Williams in Beaumont, Texas, USA on 12 Sep 1984. On 5 Oct 1984 the father filed an amendment which expanded his daughter's first name to 1019 letters and the middle name to 36 letters.

Most Christian names
Laurence Watkins (b. 9 Jun 1965) of Auckland, New Zealand claims a total of 2310 Christian names, added by deed poll in 1991 after official opposition by the Registrar and a prolonged court battle. John and Margaret Nelson of Chesterfield, Derbys gave their daughter Tracy (b. 13 Dec 1985) a total of 139 other Christian names. In November 1986 the Registrar agreed to accommodate the names on a document separate from the birth certificate. The great-great-grandson of Carlos III of Spain, Don Alfonso de Borbón y Borbón (1866–1934), had 94 Christian names, several of which were lengthened by hyphenation.

Shortest
The commonest single-letter surname is 'O', prevalent in Korea but with 52 examples in US telephone books (1973–81) and 12 in Belgium. This name causes most distress to those concerned with the prevention of cruelty to computers. Every other letter, except 'Q', has been traced in US telephone books (used as a surname) by A. Ross Eckler.

British Isles
There exist among the 47 million names on the Department of Social Security index six examples of a one-letter surname — 'A', 'B', 'J', 'N', 'O' and 'X'. The Christian name 'A' has been used for five generations in the Lincoln Taber family of Fingringhoe, Essex.

Commonest family name
The Chinese name Chang is borne, according to estimates, by between 9·7 and 12·1 per cent of the Chinese population, so indicating even on the lower estimate that there are at least some 104 million Changs — more than the entire population of all but seven of the 171 sovereign countries of the world. The commonest surname in the English-speaking world is Smith. The most recent published count showed 659 050 nationally insured Smiths in Great Britain, of whom 10 102 were plain John Smith and another 19 502 were John (plus one or more given names) Smith. Including uninsured persons there were over 800 000 Smiths in England and Wales alone, of whom 81 493 were called A. Smith. It is no secret that by 1984 there were some 90 000 Singhs in Britain — the name means 'in secret'.

'Macs'
There are estimated to be 1 600 000 persons in Britain with M', Mc or Mac (Gaelic genitive of 'son') as part of their surname. The commonest of these is Macdonald, which accounts for about 55 000 of the Scottish population.

PLACE-NAMES

Earliest
The world's earliest known place-names are pre-Sumerian, e.g. Kish, Ur and the now lost Attara, and therefore earlier than *c.* 3600 BC. The earliest recorded British place-name is Belerion, the Penwith peninsula of Cornwall, referred to as such by Pytheas of Massilia *c.* 308 BC. The name Salakee (meaning 'tin island') on St Mary's, Scilly Isles is, however, arguably of a pre-Indo-European substrate. There are reasons to contend that Leicester (Ligora Castrum in Roman times) contains an element reflecting its founding by the western Mediterranean navigators, the Ligurians, as early as *c.* 1200 BC. The earliest distinctive name for what is now known as Great

Britain was Albion, used by Himilco c. 500 BC. The oldest name among England's 46 counties is Kent, first mentioned in its Roman form of Cantium (from the Celtic *canto*, meaning a rim, i.e. a coastal district), from the circumnavigation by Pytheas of Massilia. The earliest mention of England is the form *Angelcymn*, which appeared in the *Anglo-Saxon Chronicle* in AD 880.

Longest The official name for Bangkok, the capital city of Thailand, is Krungthep Mahanakhon. However, the full name is Krungthep Mahanakhon Bovorn Ratanakosin Mahintharayutthaya Mahadilokpop Noparatratchathani Burirom Udomratchanivetmahasathan Amornpiman Avatarnsathit Sakkathattiyavisnukarmprasit, with 167 letters. In its most scholarly transliteration it emerges with 175 letters.

The longest place-name currently in use in the world is Taumatawhakatangihangakoauauotamateaturipukakapikimaungahoronukupokaiwhenuakitanatahu, which is the unofficial 85-letter version of the name of a hill (305 m *1002 ft* above sea level) in the Southern Hawke's Bay district of North Island, New Zealand. The Maori translation means 'The place where Tamatea, the man with the big knees, who slid, climbed and swallowed mountains, known as landeater, played his flute to his loved one'.

British Isles The longest place-name in the United Kingdom is the concocted 58-letter version of Llanfairpwllgwyngyllgogerychwyrndrobwllllantysiliogogogoch, which is translated as 'St Mary's Church by the pool of the white hazel trees, near the rapid whirlpool, by the red cave of the Church of St Tysilio'. This is the name used for the reopened (April 1973) village railway station in Anglesey, Gwynedd and was coined by a local bard, Y Bardd Cocos (John Evans, 1827–95) as a hoax. The *official* name consists of only the first 20 letters. The longest Welsh place-name listed in the Ordnance Survey Gazetteer is Lower Llanfihangel-y-Creuddyn (26 letters), a village near Aberystwyth, Dyfed. For commercial rather than toponymic reasons the proprietors of the Fairbourne Steam Railway, near Barmouth, Gwynedd have posted a 67-letter name on a station board 19·5 m *64 ft* long. It reads 'Gorsafawddachaidraigddanheddogleddollonpenrhynarefrdraethceredigion', though the 'll' should read 'l' making 66 letters, or 65 if 'ch' is regarded as a single letter.

England The longest single-word (unhyphenated) place-name in England is Blakehopeburnhaugh (18 letters), a hamlet between Byrness and Rochester in Northumberland. The nearby Cottonshopeburnfoot (19 letters) is locally rendered as one word, but not by the Ordnance Survey. The village of North Leverton with Habblesthorpe, Notts has 30 letters, while the hyphenated Sutton-under-Whitestonecliffe, N Yorks has 27 letters on the Ordnance Survey, but with the insertion of 'the' and the dropping of the final 'e' it has 29 letters in the Post Office list. The longest parish name is Saint Mary le More and All Hallows with Saint Leonard and Saint Peter, Wallingford (68 letters) in Oxfordshire, formed on 5 Apr 1971.

Scotland The longest single-word place-name in Scotland is Coignafeuinternich in Inverness-shire. Kirkcudbrightshire (also 18 letters) became merged into Dumfries & Galloway on 16 May 1975.

A hill in the Loch More area, just north of Aultanrynie, Highland is named Meallan Liath Coire Mhic Dhubhghaill (32 letters).

Republic of Ireland The longest place-name in Ireland is Muckanaghederdauhaulia (22 letters), 6 km *4 miles* from Costello in Camus Bay, Co. Galway. The name means 'soft place between two seas'.

Shortest The shortest place-names in the world are the French village of Y (population 143), so named since 1241, the Danish village Å on the island Fyn, the Norwegian village of Å (pronounced 'Aw'), the Swedish place Å in Vikholandet, U in the Caroline Islands, Pacific Ocean, and the Japanese town of Sosei, which is alternatively called Aioi or O. There was once a place called '6' in West Virginia, USA.

British Isles The shortest place-names in Britain are the two-lettered Ae (population 199 in 1961), Dumfries & Galloway; Oa on the island of Islay, Strathclyde, and Bu on Wyre, Orkney Islands. In Gaelic the name of the island of Iona is I. In the Shetland Islands there are skerries called Ve and two stacks called Aa. The River E flows into the southern end of Loch Mhór, Inverness-shire, and O Brook flows on Dartmoor, Devon. The shortest place-name in the Republic of Ireland is Ta (or Lady's Island) Lough, a sea inlet on the coast of Co. Wexford. Tievelough in Co. Donegal is also called Ea.

Most spellings The spelling of the Dutch town of Leeuwarden has been recorded in 225 versions since AD 1046.

Bromesberrow, Hereford & Worcs is recorded in 161 spellings since the 10th century as reported by local historian Lester Steynor.

Literature

Earliest The earliest written language discovered has been on Yangshao culture pottery from Paa-t'o, near Xi'an (Sian) in the Shaanxi (Shensi) province of China found in 1962. This bears proto-characters for the numbers 5, 7 and 8 and has been dated to 5000–4000 BC. The earliest dated pictographs are on clay tablets from Nippur, southern Iraq, from one of the lowest excavation levels equivalent to Uruk V/VI and dated in 1979 to c. 3400 BC. Tokens or tallies from Tepe Asiab and Ganji-I-Dareh Tepe in Iran have, however, been dated to 8500 BC. The oldest surviving printed work is the Dharani scroll or *sutra* from wooden printing blocks found in the foundations of the Pulguk Sa pagoda, Kyŏngju, South Korea on 14 Oct 1966. It has been dated to no later than AD 704. Paper dated to between 71 BC and AD 21, i.e. 100 years earlier than the previous presumed date for paper's invention, has been found in north-west China. The oldest medical literature, a small clay tablet in the Sumerian script from Nippur (now in Iraq), is dated to c. 2100 BC. It is now in the University Museum of Philadelphia, Pennsylvania, USA and gives details of various ointments and plasters made of crushed turtle shell, nagasi plant, salt and mustard. Beer formed an ingredient of some of the ointments.

British Isles The earliest known piece of writing from the British Isles (c. AD 630) is a fragment of Irish uncial script in an ecclesiastical history sold for £75 000 by the Folger Shakespeare Library, Washington, DC, USA to the British Rail Pension Fund at Sotheby's, London on 25 Jun 1985. Fragments of Roman wooden writing tablets found in the 1970s at Vindolandia near Newcastle upon Tyne have been shown to make up the earliest known substantial written records in British history. These contain letters and a quotation from the Roman poet Virgil (70–19 BC) and are dated to c. AD 100. The earliest known manuscript written in Britain is a bifolium of Eusebius' *Historia Ecclesiastica* from c. AD 625, possibly from the Jarrow library.

Oldest mechanically printed It was claimed in November 1973 that a 28-page book of Tang dynasty poems at Yonsei University, Korea was printed from metal type c. 1160. It is widely accepted that the earliest mechanically printed full-length book was the 42-line per page Gutenberg Bible, printed in Mainz, Germany, c. 1454 by Johann Henne zum Gensfleisch zur Laden, called 'zu Gutenberg' (c. 1398–1468). Work on watermarks published in 1967 indicates a copy of a surviving printed 'Donatus' Latin grammar was made from paper of c. 1450. The earliest exactly dated printed work is the Psalter completed on 14 Aug 1457 by Johann Fust (c. 1400–66) and Peter Schöffer (1425–1502), who had been Gutenberg's chief assistant. The earliest printing by William Caxton (c. 1422–91), though undated, would appear to be *The Recuyel of the Historyes of Troye* in Cologne in late 1473 to spring 1474.

Largest book The 'thickest' printed book on record was produced by Peter Troendle of Basle, Switzerland. It has a cover size of only 5 ×4·5 cm *2 × 1⅘ in* but is 2·75 m *9 ft* thick.

Smallest book The smallest marketed bound printed book is one printed on 22 gsm paper measuring 1 mm × 1 mm *1/25 × 1/25 in*, comprising the children's story *Old King Cole!* and published in 85 copies in March 1985 by The Gleniffer Press of Paisley, Strathclyde. The pages can be turned (with care) only by the use of a needle.

Largest publication The 1112-volume set of *British Parliamentary Papers* was published by the Irish University Press in 1968–72. A complete set weighs 3·3 tonnes , costs £50 000 and would take six years to read at ten hours per day. The production involved the death of 34 000 Indian goats and the use of £15 000 worth of gold ingots. The total print is 500 sets and the price per set in 1987 was £49 500. The entire Buddhist scriptures are inscribed on 729 marble slabs measuring 1·5 × 1·06 m *5 × 3½ ft* housed in 729 stupas in the Kuthodaw Pagoda, south of Mandalay, Myanmar (formerly Burma). They were incised in 1860–68.

In 1990 The British Library published its *General Catalogue of Printed Books to 1975* on a set of three CD-ROMs, priced at £9000. Alternatively, readers can spend six months scanning 178 000 catalogue pages in 360 volumes.

Largest dictionary Deutsches Wörterbuch, started by Jacob and Wilhelm Grimm in 1854, was completed in 1971 and consists of 34 519 pages and 33 volumes costing DM 5 425 in 1988.

The Dictionary of Chinese Characters (Sichuan and Huber) in eight volumes will contain 20 million characters when completed in 1989.

The largest English-language dictionary is the 20-volume *Oxford English Dictionary*, with 21 728 pages. The first edition, edited by Sir James Murray, was published between 1884 and 1928. A first Supplement of 964 pages appeared in 1932, and a second one in four volumes, edited by R. W. Burchfield, between 1972 and 1986. Work on the second edition, prepared by J. A.

■ **Who's Who**
Yehudi Menuhin (b. 22 Apr 1916), who, at the age of 15, became the youngest non-hereditary entrant in Who's Who.
(Photo: Syndication International)

Debating

Students at University College, Dublin, Republic of Ireland debated the motion that 'Every Dog should have its Day' for 503 hr 45 min, from 16 Nov–7 Dec 1988.

Literary luncheons

Inaugurated by Christina Foyle in October 1930 at the Old Holborn Restaurant, London, attendances were over 1500 at the Grosvenor House, Park Lane, London at lunches for Mistinguett (1873–1956) and Dr Edvard Benes (1884–1948) in 1938.

Simpson and E. S. C. Weiner, began in 1984 and the work involved represented 500 years. Published in March 1989, it defines a total of 616 500 word-forms, with 2 412 400 illustrative quotations and approximately 350 million letters and figures. Now computerised, the dictionary required 625 million bytes to store the text in machine-readable form. The longest entry in the second edition is that for the verb *set*, with over 75 000 words of text. The greatest outside contributor has been Marghanita Laski (1915–88), who provided a reputed 250 000 quotations from 1958 until her death.

The *New Grove Dictionary of Music and Musicians*, edited by Stanley Sadie (b. 30 Oct 1930) and published in 20 volumes by Macmillan in February 1981, contains over 22 million words and 4500 illustrations and is the largest specialist dictionary.

Longest novel The longest novel of note ever published is *Les hommes de bonne volonté* by Louis Henri Jean Farigoule (1885–1972), alias Jules Romains, of France, in 27 volumes in 1932–46. The English version *Men of Good Will* was published in 14 volumes in 1933–46 as a 'novel-cycle'. The 4959-page edition published by Peter Davies Ltd has an estimated 2 070 000 words, excluding the 100-page index. The novel *Tokuga-Wa Ieyasu* by Sohachi Yamaoka has been serialised in Japanese daily newspapers since 1951. Now completed, it will require nearly 40 volumes.

Earliest encyclopaedias The earliest known encyclopaedia was compiled by

Speusippus (*post* 408–c. 338 BC), a nephew of Plato, in Athens *c.* 370 BC. The earliest encyclopaedia compiled by a Briton was *Liber exerptionum* by the Scottish monk Richard (d. 1173) at St Victor's Abbey, Paris *c.* 1140.

Largest encyclopaedia The largest encyclopaedia ever compiled was the *Yung-lo ta tien* (the great thesaurus of the Yung-lo reign) of 22 937 manuscript chapters (370 still survive) in 11 095 volumes. It was written by 2000 Chinese scholars in 1403–08. Currently, the largest encyclopaedia is *La Enciclopedia Universal Ilustrada Europeo-Americana* (J. Espasa & Sons, Madrid and Barcelona) totalling 105 000 pages with an annual supplement since 1935 comprising 165·2 million words. The number of volumes in the set in August 1983 was 104, and the price $2325.

The most comprehensive English-language encyclopaedia is *The New Encyclopaedia Britannica*, first published in Edinburgh, Lothian in December 1768. A group of booksellers in the United States acquired reprint rights in 1898 and completed ownership in 1899. The current 32-volume 15th edition contains 32 330 pages and 44 million words from more than 4000 contributors. It is now edited in Chicago, Illinois, USA.

Longest index The tenth collective index of *Chemical Abstracts*, completed in June 1983, contains 23 948 253 entries in 131 445 pages and 75 volumes and weighs 172·3 kg *380 lb*.

Who's Who The longest entry in *Who's Who* (founded 1848) was that of the Rt Hon. Sir Winston Leonard Spencer Churchill (1874–1965), who appeared in 67 editions from 1899 (18 lines) and had 211 lines by the 1965 edition. Currently, the longest entry in its wider format is that of Barbara Cartland, the romantic novelist, with 143 lines. Apart from those who qualify for inclusion by hereditary title, the youngest entrant has been Sir Yehudi Menuhin (b. New York City, USA, 22 Apr 1916), the concert violinist, who first appeared in the 1932 edition at the age of 15.

MAPS

Oldest A clay tablet depicting the river Euphrates flowing through northern Mesopotamia, Iraq dates to *c.* 2250 BC. The earliest printed map in the world is one of western China dated to 1115. The earliest surviving product of English map-making is the Anglo-Saxon *Mappa Mundi*, known as the Cottonian manuscript, from the late 10th century. The earliest printed map of Britain was Ptolemy's outline printed in Bologna, Italy in 1477.

Largest A giant relief map of California *Paradise in Panorama* by Reuben Hall, measuring 13·7 × 5·48 m *45 × 18 ft* and weighing 39 tonnes, was displayed in the Ferry Building, San Francisco, USA from 1924–60. It required 29 man-years and $147 000 to build and is now stored at the Hamilton Air Force Base in Novato, California.

HIGHEST PRICES

Book The highest price paid for any book is £8·14 million for the 226-leaf manuscript *The Gospel Book of Henry the Lion, Duke of Saxony* at Sotheby's, London on 6 Dec 1983. The book, which measures 34·3 × 25·4 cm *13½ × 10 in*, was illuminated *c.* 1170 by the monk Herimann at Helmershansen Abbey, Germany with 41 full-page illustrations and was bought by Hans Kraus for the Hermann Abs consortium.

The highest price ever paid for a printed book is $5·39 million for an Old Testament (Genesis to the Psalms) of the Gutenberg Bible printed in 1455 in Mainz, Germany. It was bought by Tokyo booksellers Maruzen Co. Ltd at Christie's, New York, USA on 22 Oct 1987. The most expensive new book is the reproduction of the full set of ornithological prints *The Birds of America* by John James Audubon (1785–1851), published by Abbeville Press, at $15 000.

Broadsheet The highest price ever paid for a broadsheet was $1 595 000 for one of the 23 known copies of the United States *Declaration of Independence*, printed by John Dunlap in Philadelphia, Pennsylvania, USA in 1776 by Samuel T. Freeman & Co. and sold to Ralph Newman of Chicago, Illinois on behalf of an undisclosed client at Sotheby's, New York on 3 Mar 1990.

Manuscript The highest price ever paid for a manuscript is £2·97 million by London dealers Quaritch at Sotheby's, London on 29 Nov 1990 for the 13th-century *Northumberland Bestiary*, a colourful and highly illustrated encyclopaedia of real and imaginary animals. The book was sold by the Duchess of Northumberland, whose family had owned it for over 200 years.

Musical The auction record for a musical manuscript is £2 585 000 paid by London dealer James Kirkman at Sotheby's, London on 22 May 1987 for a 508-page, 21·6 × 16·5 cm *8½ × 6½ in* bound volume of nine complete symphonies in Mozart's hand. The record price paid for a single musical manuscript is £880 000 for the autograph copy of Schumann's first (and only complete) piano concerto at Sotheby's, London on 22 Nov 1989. This record was equalled when Mozart's 14-page autograph manuscript of the *Fantasia in C minor* and *Sonata in C minor* (K475 and K457) for solo piano was sold at Sotheby's, London on 21 Nov 1990.

Atlas The highest price paid for an atlas is £340 000 for a Gerardus Mercator atlas of Europe *c.* 1571, sold at Sotheby's, London on 13 Mar 1979.

BIBLE

Oldest The earliest biblical texts are from two silver amulets found under the Scottish Church, Jerusalem in 1979 bearing Numbers Ch. 6 v. 22–27 and dated to *c.* 587 BC. In 1945 various papyrus texts were discovered at Nag Hammodi, Egypt, including gnostic gospels or secret books (apocrypha) ascribed to Thomas, James, John, Peter and Paul. They were buried *c.* 350 AD but the originals are thought to have been written *c.* AD 120–150. The oldest known Bible is the *Codex Vaticanus* written in Greek *ante* AD 350 and preserved in the Vatican Museum, Rome. The earliest complete Bible printed in English was edited by Miles Coverdale, Bishop of Exeter (*c.* 1488–1569) while he was living in Antwerp, Belgium and printed in 1535. William Tyndale's New Testament in English was, however, printed in Cologne and Worms, Germany in 1525. John Wyclife's first manuscript translation dates from 1382, but was not published until 1850.

Longest and shortest book The longest book in the Authorised Version (King James) of the Bible is the Book of Psalms, and the longest book including prose is the Book of the Prophet Isaiah, with 66 chapters. The shortest is the Third Epistle of John, which has only 294 words in 14 verses. The Second Epistle of John has only 13 verses but 298 words.

Longest and shortest psalm Of the 150 psalms, the longest is the 119th, with 176 verses, and the shortest is the 117th, with two verses.

Longest and shortest verse The shortest verse in the Authorised Version of the Bible is verse 35 of Chapter 11 of the Gospel according to St John, consisting of the two words 'Jesus wept'. The longest is verse 9 of Chapter 8 of the Book of Esther, which extends to a 90-word description of the Persian empire.

Total letters and words The total number of letters in the Bible is 3 566 480. The total number of words depends on the method of counting hyphenated words, but is usually given as between 773 692 and 773 746. According to Colin McKay Wilson of the Salvation Army, the word 'and' appears 46 227 times.

Longest name The longest actual name in English-language bibles is the 18-letter Maher-shalal-hash-baz, the symbolic name of the second son of Isaiah (Isaiah 8: 1 and 3). The caption of Psalm 22, however, contains a Hebrew title sometimes rendered as Al-Ayyeleth Hash-Shahar (20 letters).

DIARIES AND LETTERS

Longest-kept diary Col. Ernest Loftus of Harare, Zimbabwe began his daily diary on 4 May 1896 at the age of 12 and continued it until his death on 7 Jul 1987 aged 103 years 178 days, a total of 91 years. Alisa Morris of New York City, USA has a diary which comprises an estimated 15 million words in 238 volumes to date. The diary of T. C. Baskerville of Chorlton cum Hardy, Greater Manchester, maintained since August 1939, comprises an estimated 5·9 million words in 169 volumes occupying 36 500 pages.

Most letters Uichi Noda, former Vice Minister of Treasury and Minister of Construction in Japan, during his overseas trips, wrote 1307 letters to his bedridden wife Mitsu from July 1961 until her death in March 1985. The letters contain 5 million characters and have been published in 25 volumes totalling 12 404 pages. The Rev. Canon Bill Cook and his fiancée (later his wife) Helen of Diss, Norfolk exchanged 6000 love letters during their 4½ year separation from March 1942–May 1946.

Longest letter to an editor The *Upper Dauphin Sentinel* of Pennsylvania, USA published a letter of 25 513 words over eight issues from August to November 1979, written by John Sultzbaugh of Lykens, Pennsylvania.

Most letters to an editor David Green, author and solicitor of Castle Morris, Dyfed, had his 128th letter published in the main correspondence columns of *The Times* on 10 Apr 1991. His record year was 1972, when 12 of his letters were published.

Shortest correspondence The shortest correspondence on record was that between Victor Marie Hugo (1802–85) and his publishers, Hurst & Blackett, in 1862. The author was on holiday and anxious to know how his new novel *Les Misérables* was selling. He wrote '?' and received the reply '!'.

The shortest letter to *The Times* comprised the single abbreviated symbol 'Dr²?' in the interrogative from R.S. Cookson of London on 30 Jul 1984 in a correspondence on the correct form of recording a plurality of academic doctorates. On 8 Jan 1986 a letter was sent to *The Times* by a seven-year-old girl from the Isle of Man. It read 'Sir, Yours

faithfully Caroline Sophia Kerenhappuch Parkes'. The brief epistle was intended to inform readers of her unusual name, Kerenhappuch, mentioned in a letter the previous week from Rev. John Ticehurst on the subject of uncommon 19th-century names.

Most personal mail The highest confirmed amount of mail received by any private citizen in a year is 900 000 letters by the baseball star Henry Louis 'Hank' Aaron (b. 1934), reported by the US Postal Department in June 1974. About a third were letters of hate engendered by his bettering of George Herman 'Babe' Ruth's career record for home runs set in 1927. (See Baseball.)

Pen pals The longest sustained correspondence on record is one of 75 years from 11 Nov 1904 between Mrs Ida McDougall of Tasmania, Australia and Miss R. Norton of Sevenoaks, Kent until Mrs McDougall's death on 24 Dec 1979.

AUTOGRAPHS AND SIGNATURES

Earliest The earliest surviving examples of autographs are those made by scribes on cuneiform clay tablets from Tell Abu Salābīkh, Iraq, dated to the early Dynastic III A, c. 2600 BC. A scribe named 'a-du' has added 'dub-sar' after his name, which translated means 'Adu, scribe'. The earliest surviving signature is that of the scribe Amen-'aa, held in the Leningrad Museum, USSR and dated to the Egyptian Middle Kingdom, which began c. 2130 BC.

UK A signum exists for William I (the Conqueror) from c. 1070. The earliest English sovereign whose handwriting is known to have survived is Edward III (1327–77). The earliest full signature extant is that of Richard II, dated 26 Jul 1386. The Magna Carta does not bear even the mark of King John (reigned 1199–1216), but carries only his seal affixed on 19 Jun 1215.

Most expensive The highest price ever paid on the open market for a single signed autograph letter has been $360 000 on 29 Oct 1986 at Sotheby's, New York, USA for a letter of 1818 by Thomas Jefferson condemning prejudice against Jews. It was sold by Charles Rosenbloom of Pittsburgh, Pennsylvania, USA. The highest price paid for an autograph letter signed by a living person is $12 500 at the Hamilton Galleries on 22 Jan 1981 for a letter from President Ronald Reagan praising Frank Sinatra.

Rarest and most valuable Only one example of the signature of Christopher Marlowe (1564–93) is known. It is in the Kent County Archives on a will of 1583. It is estimated that a seventh Shakespearean signature, should it ever come to light, would realize more than £1 million at auction. The only known document which bears 10 US presidential signatures is a letter sent by President F.D. Roosevelt to Richard C. Corbyn, then of Dallas (now of Amarillo), Texas, USA dated 26 Oct 1932. It was subsequently signed by Herbert Hoover, Harry Truman, General Eisenhower, Gerald Ford, Lyndon Johnson, Jimmy Carter, Ronald Reagan and George Bush. Nixon's first signature was signed with an auto-pen but he later re-signed it.

AUTHORS

Most prolific The champion of the goose quill era was Józef Ignacy Kraszewski (1812–87) of Poland, who produced more than 600 volumes of novels and historical works. A lifetime output of 72–75 million

words has been calculated for Charles Harold St John Hamilton, alias Frank Richards (1876–1961), the creator of Billy Bunter. In his peak years (1915–26) he wrote up to 80 000 words a week for the boys' school weeklies *Gem* (1907–39), *Magnet* (1908–40) and *Boys' Friend*. Soho Tokutomi (1863–1957) wrote the history *Kinsei Nippon Kokuminshi* in 100 volumes of 42 468 pages and 19 452 952 letters in 35 years.

Most novels The greatest number of novels published is 904 by Kathleen Lindsay (Mrs Mary Faulkner) (1903–73) of Somerset West, Cape Province, South Africa. She wrote under two other married names and eight pen names. Baboorao Arnalkar (b. 9 Jun 1907) of Maharashtra State, India published 1092 short mystery stories in book form and several non-fiction books between 1936 and 1984.

After receiving a probable record 743 rejection slips, the British novelist John Creasey (1908–73), under his own name and 25 *noms de plume*, had 564 books totalling more than 40 million words published from 1932 to his death. The British authoress with the greatest total of full-length titles was Ursula Harvey Bloom (Mrs A.C.G. Robinson, formerly Mrs Denham-Cookes, 1892–1984), who reached 560 in 1976, starting in 1924 with *The Great Beginning* and including the best-sellers *The Ring Tree* (novel) and *The Rose of Norfolk* (non-fiction). Enid Mary Blyton (Mrs Darrell Waters, 1898–1968) completed 700 children's stories, many of them brief, with 59 in 1955. Her books have been translated into about 40 languages.

Most textbooks Britain's most successful writer of textbooks is ex-schoolmaster Ronald Ridout (b. 23 Jul 1916) who, since 1948, has had 515 titles published, with sales of 91·35 million. His *First English Workbook* has sold 5·6 million copies.

Greatest advance The greatest advance paid for any book is $5 million for *Whirlwind* to James Clavell at auction in New York City, USA on 11 Jan 1986 by William Morrow & Co. and Avon Books. On 5 May 1988 Mary Higgins Clark (USA) signed a contract for $10·1 million for four novels and a book of short stories. It was reported on 19 Aug 1988 that Jackie Collins had signed an £8·7 million contract for three books for Simon & Schuster. On 9 Feb 1989 horror writer Stephen King was reported to have scooped a £26 million advance for his next four books.

On 11 Jul 1990 it was reported that Jeffrey Archer had signed a deal worth between $20 and $30 million with HarperCollins for two unwritten novels and a collection of short stories. The contract was also said to include film, television and audio rights.

Top-selling It was announced on 13 Mar 1953 that 672 058 000 copies of the works of Stalin (Yózef Vissarionovich Dzhugashvili, 1879–1953) had been sold or distributed in 101 languages.

The world's top-selling writer of fiction is Dame Agatha Christie (née Miller, later Lady Mallowan, 1890–1976), whose 78 crime novels have sold an estimated 2 billion copies in 44 languages. Her famous Belgian detective, Hercule Poirot, features in 33 books and 56 stories, while his English counterpart, Miss Marple, has appeared in 12 books and 20 stories. Agatha Christie also wrote 19 plays and six romantic novels under the pseudonym Mary Westmacott. All 78 novels were re-issued to commemorate the centenary of her birth in 1990,

Longest literary gestation

The standard German dictionary *Deutsches Wörterbuch* was begun by the brothers Grimm (Jacob and Wilhelm, 1785–1863 and 1786–1859 respectively) in 1854 and finished in 1971. *Acta Sanctorum*, begun by Jean Bolland in 1643, arranged according to saints' days, reached the month of November in 1925 and an introduction for December was published in 1940.

Oxford University Press received back their proofs of *Constable's Presentments* from the Dugdale Society in December 1984. They had been sent out for correction 35 years earlier in December 1949.

Slowest seller

The accolade for the world's slowest-selling book (known in US publishing as slooow sellers) probably belongs to David Wilkins' translation of the New Testament from Coptic into Latin, published by Oxford University Press (OUP) in 1716 in 500 copies. Selling an average of one each 20 weeks, it remained in print for 191 years.

Overdue books

The record for an un-returned and overdue library book was set when a book in German on the Archbishop of Bremen, published in 1609, was borrowed from Sidney Sussex College, Cambridge by Colonel Robert Walpole in 1667–68. It was found by Prof. Sir John Plumb in the library of the then Marquess of Chol-mondeley at Houghton Hall, Norfolk and returned 288 years later. No fine was exacted.

and in 1989 Harper & Row paid £5·6 million (*$9·6 million*) for the rights to 33 titles. Royalty earnings are estimated to be worth £2·5 million per year.

The top-selling writer is currently Dame Barbara Cartland with global sales of over 600 million for 540 titles published in 25 languages. She has averaged 23 titles per year for the last 16 years and, in 1988, received *La Medaille de Vermeil de la Ville de Paris* for sales in France, which have now reached over 30 million. She was made a Dame of the Order of the British Empire by HM The Queen in the 1991 New Year's Honours List for services to literature and the community. An estimated 600 million copies of the works of Belgian novelist Georges Simenon (1903–89) have been sold in 47 languages.

Biography Georges Simenon (1903–89) wrote 22 autobiographical books from 1972. The longest biography in publishing history is that of Sir Winston Churchill by his son Randolph (4832 pages), continued after Randolph Churchill's death by Martin Gilbert (17 811 pages), comprising to date some 9 694 000 words.

Most rejections The greatest recorded number of publishers' rejections for a manuscript is 242 to date for the 150 000-word *World Government Crusade*, written in 1966 by Gilbert Young (b. 1906) of Bath, Avon. The record for rejections before publication of a work is 176 (and non-acknowledgement from many other publishers) in the case of Bill Gordon's *How Many Books Do You Sell in Ohio?* from October 1983 to November 1985. The record was then spoiled by Mr Gordon's rejection of a written offer from Aames-Allen.

Oldest The oldest author in the world was Alice Pollock (*née* Wykeham-Martin, 1868–1971) of Haslemere, Surrey, whose first book *Portrait of My Victorian Youth* was published in March 1971 when she was aged 102 years 8 months. The oldest living author is Griffith R. Williams of Llithfaen, Gwynedd, whose autobiography *Cofio Canrif* was published on his 102nd birthday on 5 Jun 1990.

Youngest Poet Laureate Laurence Eusden (1688–1730) 'received the bays' on 24 Dec 1718 at the age of 30 years and 3 months.

Oldest Poet Laureate The greatest age at which a poet has succeeded is 73 in the case of William Wordsworth (1770–1850) on 6 Apr 1843. The longest-lived Laureate was John Masefield, who died on 12 May 1967 aged 88 years 345 days. The longest any poet has worn the laurel is 41 years 322 days in the case of Alfred (later the 1st Lord) Tennyson (1809–92), who was appointed on 19 Nov 1850 and died in office on 6 Oct 1892.

Longest poem The lengthiest poem ever published has been the Kirghiz folk epic *Manas*, which appeared in printed form in 1958 but which has never been translated into English. According to the *Dictionary of Oriental Literatures*, this three part epic runs to about 500 000 lines. Short translated passages appear in *The Elek Book of Oriental Verse*. Roger Brien's (b. Montreal, 1910) *Prométhée—dialogue des vivants et des morts* runs to 456 047 lines, written from 1964–81. Brien has written another 497 000 lines of French poetry in over 90 published works.

The longest poem ever written in the English language is one on the life of King Alfred by John Fitchett (1766–1838) of Liverpool, Merseyside, which ran to

129 807 lines and took 40 years to write. His editor, Robert Riscoe, added the concluding 2585 lines.

In contrast to these, the 24-line Kamassian poem *Lament* is the only known literary work in this Samoyed language (distantly related to Hungarian), spoken in the Sayan Mountains near Lake Baikal, Siberia, USSR but on the verge of extinction. This little poem is chronicled in the Hungarian publication *Ancient Cultures of the Uralian Peoples* and is printed in International Phonetics because Kamassian has no written form of its own.

Most successful poem *If* by Rudyard Kipling (1865–1936), first published in 1910, has been translated into 27 languages and, according to Kipling, 'anthologized to weariness'.

HIGHEST PRINTINGS

The world's most widely distributed book is the Bible, which has been translated into 318 languages, and portions of it into a further 1628 languages. This compares with 222 languages for the works of Lenin. It has been estimated that between 1815 and 1975 some 2·5 billion copies of the Bible were printed, of which 1·5 billion were handled by Bible Societies. Since 1976 combined global sales of Today's English Version (*Good News*) New Testament and Bible (which is copyright of the Bible Societies) have exceeded 111·3 million copies. Apart from the King James version (averaging some 13 million copies printed annually), there are at least 14 other copyrights on other versions of the Bible. The oldest publisher of Bibles is the Cambridge University Press, which began with the Geneva version in 1591.

It has been reported that 800 million copies of the red-covered booklet *Quotations from the Works of Mao Tse-tung* were sold or distributed between June 1966, when possession became virtually mandatory in China, and September 1971, when its promoter Marshal Lin Piao died in an air crash.

It is believed that in the United States, Van Antwerp Bragg & Co. printed some 60 million copies of the 1879 edition of *The McGuffey Reader*, compiled by Henry Vail in the pre-copyright era for distribution to state schools.

The total disposal through non-commercial channels by Jehovah's Witnesses of *The Truth that Leads to Eternal Life*, published by the Watchtower Bible and Tract Society of New York City, USA on 8 May 1968, has reached 107 073 279 in 117 languages to date. The highest print order for a work of fiction in the UK was 3 million by Penguin Books Ltd for their paperback edition of *Lady Chatterley's Lover*, by D.H. (David Herbert) Lawrence (1885–1930). Total world-wide sales to May 1991 were 4 867 312 copies.

BEST-SELLING BOOKS

Excluding versions of the Bible, the world's all-time best-selling book is *The Guinness Book of Records*, first published in October 1955 by the Guinness Brewery and edited by Norris Dewar McWhirter (b. 12 Aug 1925) and his twin brother Alan Ross McWhirter (killed 27 Nov 1975). Global sales in 39 languages surpassed 65 million by the end of 1990. Surveys have shown that 42–54 per cent of book-buying households in the UK own at least one copy of the book.

Best-seller lists The longest duration on the *New York Times* best-seller list

(founded 1935) has been for *The Road Less Traveled* by M. Scott Peck, which on 2 Oct 1988 had its 258th week on the lists. *The Country Diary of an Edwardian Lady* by Edith Holden (1871–1920) held the No. 1 position in *The Sunday Times* best-seller list (which excludes books published annually) for 64 weeks. Its global sales in 13 languages are in excess of 3 million copies to date.

Fiction The novel with the highest sales has been *Valley of the Dolls* (first published March 1966) by Jacqueline Susann (Mrs Irving Mansfield) (1921–74), with a world-wide total of 28 712 000 to 30 Mar 1987. In the first six months the publishers Bantam sold 6·8 million copies. Alistair Stuart MacLean (1922–87) wrote 30 books, 28 of which each sold over a million copies in the United Kingdom alone. His books have been translated into 28 languages and 13 have been filmed. It has been estimated that a MacLean novel is purchased every 18 seconds. *The Cruel Sea* by Nicholas Monsarrat (1910–79), published in 1951, reached sales of 1·2 million in its original edition.

PUBLISHERS AND PRINTERS

Oldest publisher Cambridge University Press has a continuous history of printing and publishing since 1584. The University received Royal Letters Patent to print and sell 'all manner of books' on 20 Jul 1534. In 1978 the Oxford University Press (OUP) celebrated the 500th anniversary of the printing of the first book in the City of Oxford in 1478. This was before OUP itself was in existence.

Most prolific publisher At its peak in 1989, Progress Publishers (founded 1931 as the Publishing Association of Foreign Workers in the USSR) of Moscow, USSR produced over 750 titles in 50 languages annually.

The UK published a record 66 619 book titles in 1989, of which a record 16 394 were reprints and new editions. In terms of new titles per annum, Britain's most prolific publisher in 1989 was Oxford University Press with 1922.

Largest publisher The world's largest publishing company is Time Warner Inc. of New York, USA. It has 35 000 employees and revenue from its books and magazines totalled $2·9 billion in 1990.

Fastest publisher A thousand bound copies of Sir Frederick Mason's village history *Ropley—Past and Present* were produced in 12 hr 26 min from raw disk by publishers Scriptmate Editions in conjunction with printers Scan Laser Ltd.

Largest printer The largest printers in the world are believed to be R.R. Donnelley & Sons Co. of Chicago, Illinois, USA. The company, founded in 1864, has nearly 100 manufacturing facilities, offices, service centres and subsidiaries world-wide, turning out $3·5 billion worth of work per year. The largest printer under one roof is the United States Government Printing Office (founded 1861) in Washington, DC, USA. Encompassing 13·92 ha *34·4 acres* of floor space, the central office processes an average of 1954 print orders daily, and uses 4 500 tonnes of paper annually. The Super-intendent of Documents sells approximately $75·7 million worth of United States government publications every year and maintains an inventory of over 16 500 titles in print. It receives 5600 mail orders each day.

Largest print order The initial print order for the 1990–91 Automobile Association *Members' Handbook* was 6 153 000 copies. Stacked one on top of the other, the pile would be seven times the height of Mt Everest. The total print since 1908 is 97 673 000 and it is currently printed by web offset by Petty & Sons Ltd of Leeds, W Yorks and Jarrolds Printing Ltd of Norwich, Norfolk. The aggregate print of *The Highway Code* (instituted 1931) reached 109 539 339 at May 1990, with 2 million copies printed between April 1989 and May 1990.

Bookshops The bookshop with most titles and the longest shelving (48 km *30 miles*) in the world is W. & G. Foyle Ltd of London. Established in 1904 in a small shop in Islington, the company is now at 113–119 Charing Cross Road. The shop covers a site measuring 7044 m² *75 825 ft²*. The most capacious individual bookstore in terms of area is the Barnes & Noble Bookstore at 105 Fifth Ave at 18th Street, New York City, USA. It covers 14 330 m² *154 250 ft²* and has 20·71 km *12·87 miles* of shelving.

LIBRARIES AND MUSEUMS

Earliest One of the earliest known collections of archival material was that of King Ashurbanipal held at Nineveh, Iraq (668–627 BC). He had clay tablets referring to events and personages as far back as the Dynasty of Agode, *c.* 23rd century BC.

Largest library The United States Library of Congress (founded on 24 Apr 1800) in Washington, DC, USA contains 97·5 million items, including 27·6 million volumes and pamphlets. The buildings house 33·67 ha *83·2 acres* of floor space and 941·4 km *585 miles* of shelving. The largest non-statutory library in the world is the New York Public Library (founded 1895) in New York City, USA, with a floor space of 48 800 m² *525 276 ft²* and 141·6 km *88 miles* of shelving, plus an underground extension with the capacity for an additional 148 km *92 miles*. Its collection, including the contents of 82 branch libraries, embraces 13 887 774 volumes, 18 349 585 manuscripts and 381 645 maps.

UK The largest library in the United Kingdom is the British Library, dispersed among 19 buildings in London and a 24·3 ha *60 acre* site at Boston Spa, W Yorks, with a total staff of some 2500. The Library contains over 18 million volumes. Stock increases involve over 12·8 km *8 miles* of new shelving annually. The Newspaper Library at Colindale, north London, opened in 1932, has 583 000 volumes and parcels comprising 70 000 different titles on 35·4 km *22 miles* of shelving. The Document Supply Centre in West Yorks (shelf capacity 157·7 km *98 miles*) runs the largest library inter-lending operation in the world; it handles annually over 3 million requests from other libraries (UK and overseas) for items they do not hold in stock. The National Sound Archive holds 1 million discs and 62 000 hours of recorded tape. The largest public reference library in Europe is the extended Mitchell Library in Glasgow, Strathclyde. It has a floor area of 50 000 m² *538 200 ft²*, or 4·9 ha *12·3 acres*, and an ultimate capacity for 4 million volumes.

Oldest museum The world's oldest extant museum is the Ashmolean in Oxford, built between 1679 and 1683 and named after the collector Elias Ashmole (1617–92). Among its attractions is an exhibition of historic scientific instruments, housed there since 1924.

Largest museum The US Smithsonian Institution comprises 14 museums with 6000 employees, and contains over 137 million items. The American Museum of Natural History in New York City, USA was founded in 1869 and comprises 22 interconnected buildings. The buildings of the Museum and the Planetarium contain 139 350 m² *1·5 million ft²* of floor space, accommodating more than 30 million artifacts and specimens. Its exhibits are viewed by more than 3 visitors each year.

The largest and most visited museum in the United Kingdom is the British Museum (founded in 1753), which was opened to the public in 1759. The main building in Bloomsbury, London was begun in 1823 and has a total floor area of 8·7 ha *21·5 acres*. In 1990, 5 079 472 people passed through its doors.

Most popular The highest attendance for any museum is that at the Smithsonian's National Air and Space Museum, Washington, DC, USA, opened in July 1976. The record-setting day on 14 Apr 1984 required the doors to be temporarily closed with an attendance of over 118 437.

NEWSPAPERS

Oldest A copy has survived of a news pamphlet published in Cologne, Germany in 1470. The oldest existing newspaper in the world is the Swedish official journal *Post och Inrikes Tidningar*, founded in 1645 and published by the Royal Swedish Academy of Letters. The oldest existing commercial newspaper is the *Haarlems Dagblad/Oprechte Haarlemsche Courant*, published in Haarlem, Netherlands. First issued as the *Weeckelycke Courante van Europa* on 8 Jan 1656, a copy of issue No. 1 survives.

UK The newspaper with the earliest origins is *Berrow's Worcester Journal* (originally the *Worcester Post Man*), published in Worcester. It was traditionally founded in 1690 and has appeared weekly since June 1709. No complete file exists. The earliest date of foundation for any British newspaper published under the same title is the *Stamford Mercury*, printed since 1712 and traditionally even since 1695. The *London Gazette* (originally the *Oxford Gazette*) was first published on 16 Nov 1665. The oldest Sunday newspaper is *The Observer*, first issued on 4 Dec 1791. The earliest known edition of the Belfast-based *News Letter* was dated 6 Mar 1738 and has been a daily since 1855. The *Daily Universal Register* was founded in 1785 and changed its name to *The Times* in 1788.

Largest The most massive single issues of a newspaper have been of the *Sunday New York Times*, which by August 1987 had reached 6·35 kg *14 lb*, with a prediction that 7·7 kg *17 lb* was a probability. The largest page size ever used has been 130 × 89 cm *51 × 35 in* for *The Constellation*, printed in 1859 by George Roberts as part of the 4 July celebrations in New York City, USA. The *Worcestershire Chronicle* was the largest British newspaper, and a surviving issue of 16 Feb 1859 measures 82 × 57 cm *32¼ × 22½ in*.

Smallest The smallest original page size was the 7·6 × 9·5 cm *3 × 3¾ in* of the *Daily Banner* (25 cents per month) of Roseberg, Oregon, USA, issues of which, dated 1 and 2 Feb 1876, survive. The *Answers to Correspondents* published by Carr & Co. of London in 1888 measured 9 × 11 cm *3½ × 4½ in*. The British Library Newspaper Library contains the *Watford News and Advertiser* of 1 Apr 1899, which measures 7·5 × 10 cm *2·9 × 3·9 in*.

Most expensive Britain's most expensive papers are the *Observer* and *The Sunday Times* at 70p — more than double the price of the 1955 *Guinness Book of Records*.

Most The US published 1642 English-language daily newspapers at 1 Feb 1989, with a combined net paid circulation of 62·7 million copies per day. The peak year for US newspapers was 1910, when there were 2202. The leading newspaper readers in the world are the people of Sweden, where 580 newspapers are sold for each 1000 people, compared with the UK figure of 410.

Longest editorship Sir Etienne Dupuch (b. 16 Feb 1899) of Nassau, Bahamas was editor-in-chief of *The Tribune* from 1 Apr 1919 to 1972, and has been contributing editor to the present time, entering his 73rd year as an editor on 1 Apr 1991. The longest editorship of any UK national newspaper was that of 57 years by C. P. (Charles Prestwich) Scott (1846 –1932) of the *Manchester Guardian* (the *Guardian* from 1959), who occupied the post from the age of 26 in 1872 until his retirement in 1929.

Most durable feature Eric Hardy of Liverpool is in his 64th year as a regular natural history contributor to the *Daily Post* of Liverpool, with a weekly 'Countryside' feature. Albert E. Pool (b. 1909) was a part-time journalist for the *Lincolnshire and South Humberside* (formerly *Hull*) *Times* from March 1923 until the demise of the paper on 26 Jul 1985.

Most syndicated columnist In 1987 Ann Landers (*née* Eppie Lederer, b. 4 Jul 1918) appeared in over 1200 newspapers, with an estimated readership of 90 million. Her only serious rival was 'Dear Abby' (Mrs Pauline Phillips), her identical twin sister based in Beverly Hills, California, USA.

CIRCULATION

Earliest million The first newspaper to achieve a circulation of 1 million copies was *Le Petit Journal*, published in Paris, France, which reached this figure in 1886, when selling at 5 centimes. The *Daily Mail* first reached a million on 2 Mar 1900.

Highest The highest circulation for any newspaper in the world is that for *Komsomolskaya Pravda* (founded 1925), the Soviet youth paper, which had a peak daily circulation of 21 975 000 copies in May 1990. The eight-page weekly newspaper *Argumenty i Fakty* (founded 1978) of Moscow, USSR attained a figure of 33 431 100 copies in May 1990. It has an estimated readership of over 100 million.

UK The *News of the World* has attained peak sales of 9 million copies and had an estimated readership of over 19 million. The paper first appeared on 1 Oct 1843 and passed the million mark in 1905. The latest sales figure is 4 791 701 copies per issue (March 1991), with an estimated readership of 13 577 000. The highest net sale of any daily newspaper in the United Kingdom is that of *The Sun*, founded in London in 1964. The latest sales figure is 3 745 958 (March 1991), with an estimated readership of 10 107 000.

Most read The national newspaper which achieves the closest to a saturation circulation is the *Sunday Post*, established in Glasgow, Strathclyde in 1914. In 1989 its estimated readership in Scotland of 2 213 000 represented 54 per cent of the entire population aged 15 and over. The *Arran Banner* (founded March 1974) has a

Fastest crossword solution

The fastest recorded time for completing *The Times* crossword under test conditions is 3 min 45 sec by Roy Dean of Bromley, Kent in the BBC *Today* radio studio on 19 Dec 1970. Dr John Sykes won *The Times/Collins Dictionaries* championship 10 times between 1972 and 1990, when he solved each of the four puzzles in an average time of 8 min and beat the field by a record margin of 9½ min on 8 Sep at the Hilton hotel, London. He set a championship best time of 4 min 28 sec in 1989.

Slowest solution

In May 1966 *The Times* of London received an announcement from a Fijian woman that she had just succeeded in completing their crossword No. 673 in the issue of 4 Apr 1932. As disclosed by her husband, D.T. Lloyd in a letter to *The Times* on 8 Feb 1990, the woman was stationed in Fiji as the wife of a Civil Servant, and far from being fiendishly difficult, the puzzle was in an edition which was used to wrap a parcel and had subsequently lain uncompleted for 34 years.

Bottle orchestra

In an extraordinary display of oral campanology, the Brighton Bottle Orchestra — Terry Garoghan and Peter Miller — performed a musical medley on 444 Gordon's gin bottles at the Brighton International Festival, E Sussex on 21 May 1991. It took 18 hours to tune the bottles, and about 10 times the normal rate of puff (90 breaths/min) to play them.

Double bass

Sixteen musicians from Blandford, Dorset played a double bass simultaneously in a rendition of Strauss' *Perpetuum Mobile* on 6 Jun 1989.

readership of 97+ per cent on Britain's seventh largest offshore island.

PERIODICALS

Oldest The oldest continuing periodical in the world is *Philosophical Transactions of the Royal Society*, published in London, which first appeared on 6 Mar 1665. The bi-monthly *Gospel Magazine* has been published since 1766. Curtis's *Botanical Magazine* has been in continuous publication since 1 Feb 1787 as several 'parts' a year forming a series of continuously numbered volumes. Britain's oldest weekly periodical is *The Lancet*, first published in 1823. The *Scots Magazine* began in January 1739, ran until 1826 and has been produced since 1924 with only three breaks.

Largest circulations The peak circulation of any weekly periodical has been that of the US *TV Guide* which, in 1974, became the first magazine to sell a billion copies in a year. The world's highest circulation magazine is currently *Modern Maturity* of the US, with a figure in January–July 1988 of 17 924 783. In its 39 basic international editions, *Reader's Digest* (established February 1922) circulates 28 million copies monthly in 15 languages, including a US edition of more than 16·25 million copies and a UK edition (established 1939) of 1 527 560 copies (ABC July–December 1989). *Parade*, the US syndicated colour magazine, is distributed with 338 newspapers every Sunday. The circulation at July 1991 was 35·4 million.

UK Before the deregulation of the listings market in March 1991, the highest circulation of any periodical is Britain was that of the *Radio Times* (instituted on 28 Sep 1923). Average weekly sales for July–December 1989 was 3 037 129 copies, with a readership of 9 031 000. The highest sales figure for any issue was 11 037 139 copies for the 1989 Christmas edition. *TV Times* averaged sales of 2 944 737 in the period July–December 1989, with an estimated readership of 9 215 000.

Weightiest The heaviest magazine ever published was the February/March 1990 issue of the US Conde Nast publication *Bride's*, which ran to 1034 hernia-inducing pages.

Annual *Old Moore's Almanack* has been published annually since 1697, when it first appeared as a broadsheet produced by Dr Francis Moore (1657–1715) of Southwark, London to advertise his 'physiks'. The annual sale certified by its publishers, W. Foulsham & Co. Ltd of Slough, Berks, is 1 million copies and its aggregate sale is estimated to be in excess of 108 million.

CROSSWORDS

Earliest Opinions differ on what constitutes a true crossword as distinct from other forms of word puzzle, but the earliest contender is considered to be a 25-letter acrostic of Roman provenance discovered on a wall in Cirencester, Glos in 1868. Another contender is an example of 'blended squares', which appeared in the women's magazine *The People's Home Journal* in September 1904. The modern crossword is believed to have evolved from Arthur Wynne's 'Word Cross', published in the Sunday *New York World* on 21 Dec 1913. The first crossword published in a British newspaper was one furnished by C.W. Shepherd in the *Sunday Express* of 2 Nov 1924.

Largest published crossword In July 1982 Robert Turcot of Québec, Canada compiled a crossword comprising of 82 951 squares. It contained 12 489 clues across, 13 125 down and covered 3·55 m² *38·28 ft²*.

Most durable compilers The most prolific compiler is Roger F. Squires of Ironbridge, Shrops, who compiles 42 published puzzles single-handedly each week. His total output to September 1991 was over 37 500 crosswords, and his millionth clue was published in the *Daily Telegraph* on 6 Sep 1989. Adrian Bell (1901–1980) of Barsham, Suffolk contributed a record 4520 crosswords to *The Times* from 2 Jan 1930 until his death.

ADVERTISING

The world's highest newspaper advertising rate is 41·55 million yen for a full page in the morning edition and 32·37 million yen for the evening edition of the *Yomiuri Shimbun* of Tokyo (April 1989). The highest ever price for a single page was $527 400, for a four-colour back cover in *Parade* (circulation 35·4 million per week) in July 1991. The record for a four-colour inside page is $451 000 in *Parade*, with a black-and-white page costing $365 000.

The advertising revenue from the November 1982 US edition of *Reader's Digest* was a peak $14 716 551. The highest expenditure ever incurred on a single advertisement in a periodical is $3 851 684 by Walt Disney Productions, celebrating Mickey Mouse's 60th birthday, on 7 Nov 1988 in *Time* magazine.

The rate for a single page in the *News of the World SunDay* magazine is £28 500, and £57 000 for a centre spread (April 1990). The highest rate in Britain is a two-page colour spread in *The Sunday Times*, which cost £125 000 in April 1991.

The largest advertising group in the world is WPP Group plc of London. *Advertising Age* lists the group's billings for 1990 at $18·1 billion. The largest agency is Dentsu Inc. of Tokyo, Japan, with billings for 1990 quoted as $9·7 billion by *Advertising Age*. The world's leading advertiser is Unilever plc, the soap and cosmetics group, with spending of $1·74 billion in 1989.

Most durable advertiser The Jos Neel Co., a clothing store in Macon, Georgia, USA (founded 1880) has run an 'ad' in the *Macon Telegraph* every day in the upper left corner of page 2 since 22 Feb 1889 or 35 760 times to March 1987.

Music

Whistles and flutes made from perforated phalange bones have been found at Upper Palaeolithic sites of the Aurignacian period (*c.* 25 000–22 000 BC) at Istallóskö, Hungary and in Moldova, USSR. The world's earliest surviving musical notation dates from *c.* 1800 BC. A heptatonic scale deciphered from a clay tablet by Dr Duchesne-Guillemin in 1966–67 was found at a site in Nippur, Sumer, now Iraq. An Assyrian love song, also *c.* 1800 BC, to an Ugaritic god from a tablet of notation and lyric was reconstructed for an 11-string lyre at the University of California, Berkeley, USA on 6 Mar 1974. Musical history can, however, be traced back to the 3rd millennium BC, when the yellow bell (*huang chung*) had a recognized standard musical tone in Chinese temple music.

The human voice Before this century the extremes were a staccato E in *alt altissimo* (e^{iv}) by Ellen Beach Yaw (US) (1869–1947) in Carnegie Hall, New York City, USA on 19 Jan 1896, and an A_1 (55 Hz [cycles per sec]) by Kasper Foster (1617–73).

Madeleine Marie Robin (1918–60), the French operatic coloratura, could produce and sustain the B above high C in the Lucia mad scene in Donizetti's *Lucia di Lammermoor*. Since 1950 singers have achieved high and low notes far beyond the hitherto accepted extremes. However, notes at the bass and treble extremities of the register tend to lack harmonics and are of little musical value. Ivan Rebroff, the German bass, has a voice extending easily over four octaves from a low F to a high F, one and a quarter octaves above C.

The highest note put into song is G^{iv} first occurring in Mozart's *Popoli di Tessaglia*. The lowest vocal note in the classical repertoire is in Mozart's *Die Entführung aus dem Serail* in Osmin's aria which calls for a low D (73·4 Hz).

INSTRUMENTS

Earliest piano The earliest pianoforte in existence is one built in Florence, Italy in 1720 by Bartolommeo Cristofori (1655–1731) of Padua, and now preserved in the Metropolitan Museum of Art, New York City, USA.

Grandest piano The grandest grand piano was one of 1·25 tonnes and 3·55 m *11 ft 8 in* in length made by Chas H. Challen & Son Ltd of London in 1935. The longest bass string measured 3·02 m *9 ft 11 in*, with a tensile strength of 30 tonnes.

Most expensive piano The highest price ever paid for a piano was $390 000 at Sotheby's, New York, USA on 26 Mar 1980 for a Steinway grand of *c.* 1888 sold by the Martin Beck Theatre. It was bought by a non-pianist.

Smallest piano The smallest playable piano is a ⅛ th scale model of a 1910 Knabe. This 'baby' instrument measures just 19·05 × 8·57 × 16·5 cm *7½ × 3⅜ × 6½ in* and was built by Emil J. Cost.

Largest organ The largest and loudest musical instrument ever constructed is the now only partially functional Auditorium Organ in Atlantic City, New Jersey, USA. Completed in 1930, this heroic instrument had two consoles (one with seven manuals and another movable one with five), 1477 stop controls and 33 112 pipes, ranging in tone from 4·7 mm *⅕ in* to the 19·5 m *64 ft* tone. It had the volume of 25 brass bands, with a range of seven octaves. The world's largest fully functional organ is the six manual 30 067 pipe Grand Court Organ installed in the Wanamaker Store, Philadelphia, Pennsylvania, USA in 1911 and enlarged between then and 1930. It has a 19·5 m *64 ft* tone gravissima pipe. The world's most powerful electronic organ is Robert A. Nye's 7000-watt 'Golden Spirit' organ, designed by Henry N. Hunsicker. It has 700 speakers and made its public concert debut in Trump's Castle, Atlantic City, New Jersey, USA on 9 Dec 1988.

The world's largest church organ is that in Passau Cathedral, Germany. It was completed in 1928 by D.F. Steinmeyer & Co. and has 16 000 pipes and five manuals. The chapel organ at West Point US Military Academy, New York, USA has, since 1911, been expanded from 2406 to 18 200 pipes. The largest organ in Great Britain is that completed in Liverpool Anglican Cathedral on 18 Oct 1926, with two five-manual consoles, only one of which is now in use, and 9704 speaking pipes (originally 10 936) ranging from tones 1·9 cm to 9·75 m *¾ in* to *32 ft*.

Organ stop The Ophicleide stop of the Grand Great in the Solo Organ in the Atlantic City Auditorium (see left) is operated by a pressure of water 24 kPa *3½ lb/in²* and has a pure trumpet note of ear-splitting volume, more than six times the volume of the loudest locomotive whistles.

Largest pan pipes The world's largest pan pipes were created by Simon Desorgher and Lawrence Casserley and consist of five contra-bass pipes, each 100 mm in diameter with lengths of 4790 mm, 4160 mm, 3606 mm, 3104 mm and 2666 mm, respectively and five bass pipes of 50 mm diameter with lengths of 2395 mm, 2080 mm, 1803 mm, 1522 mm and 1333 mm. Their first public appearance was at Jubilee Gardens, London on 9 Jul 1988.

Most durable musicians Elsie Maude Stanley Hall (1877–1976) gave piano recitals for 90 years, giving her final concert in Rustenburg, Transvaal, South Africa aged 97. The longest international career in the history of western music was crowned by Mieczyslaw Horszowski (b. Poland, July 1892) with a recital given at the Wigmore Hall, London on 4 Jun 1991, three weeks before his 99th birthday. He played before Emperor Franz-Joseph in Vienna, Austria in 1899. Norwegian pianist Reidar Thommesen (1889–1986) played over 30 hours a week in theatre cafés when a nonagenarian. Charles Bridgeman (1779–1873) of All Saints Parish Church, Hertford, who was appointed organist in 1792, was still playing 81 years later in 1873.

The world's oldest active musician is Violet Loader (b. 9 Nov 1889) of Lymington, Hants, who has been the regular organist at the church of Our Lady of Mercy and St Joseph in Lymington since 1924. This record is very nearly matched by Yiannis Pipis (b. 25 Nov 1889) of Nicosia, Cyprus, who has been a professional Folkloric violinist since 1912. Rolland S. Tapley retired as a violinist from the Boston Symphony Orchestra after reputedly playing for an unrivalled 58 years from February 1920 to 27 Aug 1978.

Largest brass instrument The largest recorded brass instrument is a tuba standing 2·28 m *7½ ft* tall, with 11·8 m *39 ft* of tubing and a bell 1 m *3 ft 4 in* across. This contrabass tuba was constructed for a world tour by the band of American composer John Philip Sousa (1854–1932), *c.* 1896–98. It is now owned by a circus promoter in South Africa.

Largest stringed instrument The largest movable stringed instrument ever constructed was a pantaleon with 270 strings stretched over 4·6 m² *50 ft²* used by George Noel in 1767. The greatest number of musicians required to operate a single instrument was the six required to play the gigantic orchestrion, known as the Apollonican, built in 1816 and played until 1840. The largest playable guitar in the world is 5·82 m *19·09 ft* tall and was built by the Narrandera Country Music Association of New South Wales, Australia in 1989.

Most expensive guitar A Fender Stratocaster belonging to the legendary rock guitarist Jimi Hendrix (1942–70) was sold by his former drummer Mitch Mitchell to an anonymous buyer for £198 000 at Sotheby's, London on 25 Apr 1990.

Largest double bass A double bass measuring 4·26 m *14 ft* tall was built in 1924 in Ironia, New Jersey, USA by Arthur K. Ferris, allegedly on orders from the Archangel Gabriel. It weighed 590 kg *1301 lb* with a sound box 2·43 m *8 ft* across, and had leathern strings totalling 31·7 m *104 ft*. Its low notes could be felt rather than heard.

Most valuable 'cello The highest ever auction price for a violoncello is £682 000 paid at Sotheby's, London on 22 Jun 1988 for a Stradivarius known as 'The Cholmondeley', which was made in Cremona, Italy *c.* 1698.

Most valuable violin The record for a violin, or any instrument, is £902 000 (*$1·7 million*) for the 1720 'Mendelssohn' Stadivarius, named after the German banking family who were descendants of the composer. It was sold to a mystery buyer at Christie's, London on 21 Nov 1990.

The 'Alard violin made by Stradivarius (1644–1737) was confirmed by Jacques Français to have been sold by private treaty by W. E. Hill for $1·2 million (*£770 000*) to a Singaporean buyer in 1982.

Largest drum A drum with a 3·96 m *13 ft* diameter was built by the Supreme Drum Co., London and played at the Royal Festival Hall, London on 31 May 1987.

Largest drum kit A drum kit consisting of 81 pieces — 45 drums, including six bass drums, 15 cymbals, five temple blocks, two triangles, two gongs, two sets of wind chimes, one solid bar chime, six assorted cowbells, a drum set tambourine, a vibra slap and an icebell, is owned by Darreld MacKenzie of Calgary, Alberta, Canada.

Longest alphorn An alphorn 47 m *154 ft 8 in* long (excluding mouthpiece) weighing 103 kg *227 lb* was completed by Swiss-born Peter Wutherich, of Boise, Idaho, USA in December 1989. The bell diameter is 62 cm *24½ in* and the sound takes 105·7 milliseconds to emerge from the bowl after entry into the mouthpiece.

Highest and lowest notes The extremes of orchestral instruments (excluding the organ) range between a handbell tuned to g^v (6272 cycles/sec) and the sub-contrabass clarinet, which can reach C_{11}, or 16·4 cycles/sec. The highest note on a standard pianoforte is c^v (4186 cycles/sec), which is also the violinist's limit. In 1873 a sub-double bassoon able to reach $B_{111}\pm$ or 14·6 cycles/sec was constructed but no surviving specimen is known. The extremes for the organ are g^{vi} (the sixth G above middle C) (544 cycles/sec) and C_{111} (8·12 cycles/sec), obtainable from 1·9 cm *¾ in* and 19·5 m *64 ft* pipes respectively.

SONGS

Oldest The *shaduf* chant has been sung since time immemorial by irrigation workers on the man-powered, pivoted-rod bucket raisers of the Nile water mills (or *saqiyas*) in Egypt.

The oldest known harmonized music performed today is the English song *Sumer is icumen in*, which dates from *c.* 1240.

National anthems The oldest national anthem is the *Kimigayo* of Japan, the words

Bell ringing

Eight bells have been rung to their full 'extent' (40 320 unrepeated changes of Plain Bob Major) only once without relays. This took place in a bell foundry at Loughborough, Leics, beginning at 6:52 a.m. on 27 Jul 1963 and ending at 12:50 a.m. on 28 July, after 17 hr 58 min. The peal was composed by Kenneth Lewis of Altrincham, Manchester and the eight ringers were conducted by Robert B. Smith of Marple, Manchester. Theoretically it would take 37 years 355 days to ring 12 bells (maximus) to their full extent of 479 001 600 changes.

■ One-man band

Rory Blackwell of Starcross, Devon succeeded in playing 108 different instruments (19 melody and 89 percussion) simultaneously on 29 May 1989.

of which date from the 9th century, whilst the oldest music belongs to the anthem of the Netherlands. The anthem of Greece constitutes the first two verses of the Solomos poem, which has 158 stanzas. The shortest anthems are those of Japan, Jordan and San Marino, each with only four lines. Of the 11 wordless national anthems, the oldest is that of Spain, dating from 1770.

Top songs The most frequently sung songs in English are *Happy Birthday to You* (based on the original *Good Morning to All*), by Kentucky Sunday School teachers Mildred Hill and Patty Smith Hill of New York, USA (written in 1893 and under copyright from 1935 to 2010); *For He's a Jolly Good Fellow* (originally the French *Malbrouk*), known at least as early as 1781, and *Auld Lang Syne* (originally the Strathspey *I Fee'd a Lad at Michaelmass*), some words of which were written by Robert Burns (1759–96). *Happy Birthday* was sung in space by the Apollo IX astronauts on 8 Mar 1969.

Top-selling sheet music Sales of three non-copyright pieces are known to have exceeded 20 million, namely *The Old Folks at Home* by Stephen Foster (1855), *Listen to the Mocking Bird* (1855) and *The Blue Danube* (1867).

Of copyright material, the two top sellers are *Let Me Call You Sweetheart* (1910, by Whitson and Friedman) and *Till We Meet Again* (1918, by Egan and Whiting), each with some 6 million copies sold by 1967.

Other huge sellers have been *St Louis Blues, Stardust* and *Tea for Two*.

Songwriters The songwriters responsible for the most number one singles are John Lennon (1940–80) and Paul McCartney (b. 18 Jun 1942). McCartney is credited as writer on 32 number one hits in the US to Lennon's 26 (with 23 co-written), whereas Lennon authored 29 UK number ones to McCartney's 28 (25 co-written). Mike Stock, Matt Aitken and Pete Waterman are the most successful team of songwriter/producer/singers in Britain, with 13 of their 106 titles to May 1990 reaching

number one. Benny Andersson and Bjorn Ulvaeus, formerly of the Swedish group ABBA, have written ten UK number one hits. In the United States Barry Gibb of the Bee Gees has written or co-written 16 number ones. The most successful female songwriter in the US is Carole King (b. Carole Klein, 9 Feb 1942) with eight number ones, and in the UK it is Madonna with seven.

HYMNS

Earliest There are more than 950 000 Christian hymns in existence.

The music and parts of the text of a hymn in the *Oxyrhynchus Papyri* from the 2nd century are the earliest known hymnody.

The earliest exactly datable hymn is the *Heyr Himna Smióur* (*Hear, the Maker of Heaven*) from 1208 by the Icelandic bard and chieftain Kolbeinn Tumason (1173–1208).

Longest The *Hora novissima tempora pessima sunt; vigilemus* by Bernard of Cluny (mid 12th century) runs to 2966 lines.The *Hora novissima tempora pessima sunt; vigilemus* by Bernard of Cluny (mid 12th century) runs to 2966 lines. In English the longest is *The Sands of Time are Sinking* by Anne Ross Cousin (*née* Cundell, 1824–1906), which is in full 152 lines, though only 32 lines appear in the Methodist Hymn Book.

Most prolific hymnists Mrs Frances (Fanny) Jane van Alstyne (*née* Crosby, 1820–1915) of the US wrote 8500 hymns and is reputed to have knocked off one hymn in 15 minutes. Charles Wesley (1707–88) wrote about 6000 hymns. The works of John Mason Neale (1818–66) appear 56 times in the 7th (1950) edition of *Hymns Ancient and Modern*.

BELLS

Oldest The tintinnabulum found in the Babylonian Palace of Nimrod in 1849 by Mr (later Sir) Austen Henry Layard (1817–94) dates from *c*. 1100 BC. The oldest known tower bell is one in Pisa, Italy dated MCVI (1106).

UK The oldest bell in Great Britain is the fragile hand bell known as the Black or Iron Bell of St Patrick, which has been to dated *c*. AD 450. The oldest tower bell in Great Britain is one of 50 kg *1 cwt* at St Botolph, Hardham, Sussex, still in use but dated *ante* 1100. The oldest inscribed bell is the Gargate bell at Caversfield church, Oxon, which is dated *c*. 1200–1210.

The oldest *dated* bell in England is one hanging in Lissett church, near Bridlington, Humberside discovered in October 1972 to bear the date MCCLIIII (1254).

Heaviest The Tsar Kolokol, cast by Russian brothers I.F. and M.I. Motorin on 25 Nov 1735 in Moscow, weighs 202 tonnes, measures 6·6 m *22 ft* in diameter and 6·14 m *20 ft* high and its greatest thickness is 60 cm *24 in*. The bell was cracked in a fire in 1737 and a large fragment, weighing about 11·5 tonnes, was broken from it. The bell has stood, unrung, on a platform in the Kremlin in Moscow since 1836 with the broken section alongside. The heaviest bell still in use is the Mingun bell, weighing 92 tonnes with a diameter of 5·09 m *16 ft 8½ in* at the lip, in Mandalay, Myanmar (formerly Burma). The bell is struck by a teak boom from the outside. It was cast at Mingun late in the reign of King Bodawpaya (1782–1819). The heaviest swinging bell in the world is the Petersglocke in the south-west tower of Cologne Cathedral, Germany, cast in 1923 with a diameter of 3·40 m *11 ft 1¾ in* weighing 25·4 tonnes.

UK The heaviest bell hung in Great Britain is 'Great Paul' in the south-west tower of St Paul's Cathedral, London, cast in 1881. It weighs 17 tonnes, has a diameter of 2·9 m *9 ft 6½ in* and sounds note E-flat. 'Big Ben', the hour bell in the clock tower of the House of Commons, was cast in 1858 and weighs 13·8 tonnes. It is the most broadcast bell in the world and is note E.

Peals A ringing peal is defined as a diatonic 'ring' of five or more bells hung for full-circle change ringing. Of 5500 rings so hung, only 70 are outside the British Isles. The heaviest ring in the world is that of 13 bells cast in 1938–39 for the Anglican Cathedral in Liverpool, Merseyside. The total bell weight is 16·8 tonnes, of which Emmanuel, the tenor bell note A, weighs 4·2 tonnes.

Largest carillon The largest carillon (minimum of 23 bells) in the world is the Laura Spelman Rockefeller Memorial Carillon in Riverside Church, New York City, USA, with 74 bells weighing 103·6 tonnes. The bourdon, giving the note lower C, weighs 18·6 tonnes. Cast in England with a diameter of 3·09 m *10 ft 2 in*, this is the largest *tuned* bell in the world.

UK The carillon in St Nicholas Church, Aberdeen, Grampian consists of 48 bells, the total weight of which is 25·8 tonnes. The bourdon bell weighs 4·6 tonnes and is the note G-sharp.

ORCHESTRAS

Oldest The first modern symphony orchestra — basically four sections consisting of woodwind, brass, percussion and bowed string instruments — was founded at the court of Duke Karl Theodor at Mannheim, Germany in 1743. The oldest existing symphony orchestra, the Gewandhaus Orchestra of Leipzig, Germany, was also established in 1743. Originally known as the Grosses Concert and later as the Liebhaber-Concerte, its current name dates from 1781.

Largest On 17 Jun 1872, Johann Strauss

the younger (1825–99) conducted an orchestra of 987 pieces supported by a choir of 20 000, at the World Peace Jubilee in Boston, Massachusetts, USA. The number of first violinists was 400. On 4 Nov 1990 a 1500-piece orchestra consisting of 13 youth orchestras from Mexico and Venezuela gave a full concert, including works by Handel, Tchaikovsky, Beethoven and Dvorak, under the baton of Mexican conductor Fernando Lozano at the Magdalena Mixhiuca Sports Centre, Mexico City.

Largest band The most massive band ever assembled was one of 20 100 bandsmen at the Ullevaal Stadium, Oslo, Norway from Norges Musikkorps Forbund bands on 28 Jun 1964.

One-man band Rory Blackwell, aided by his double left-footed perpendicular percussion-pounder, plus his three-tier right-footed horizontal 22-pronged differential beater, and his 12-outlet bellow-powered horn-blower, played 108 different instruments (19 melody and 89 percussion) simultaneously in Dawlish, Devon on 29 May 1989. He also played 314 instruments in a single rendition in 1 min 23·07 sec, again at Dawlish, on 27 May 1985.

Largest marching band The largest marching band was one of 4524, including 1342 majorettes, under the direction of Danny Kaye (1913–87) at Dodger Stadium, Los Angeles, California, USA on 15 Apr 1985.

Musical march The longest recorded musical march was one of 68·4 km *42·5 miles* at Wheeling, West Virginia, USA by the Wheeling Park High School Marching Band on 21 Oct 1989. Of the 69 members who started, 31 managed to complete the march, in 14 hr 53 min.

Most successful bands The Black Dyke Mills Band has won the most British Open Brass Band Championship titles (instituted 1853) — 22 from 1862 to 1974, including three consecutive wins in 1972–74. The most successful pipe band is the Shotts & Dykehead Caledonian Pipe Band, with their 10th world title in August 1980.

Conductors The Austrian conductor Herbert von Karajan (1908–89), principal conductor of the Berlin Philharmonic Orchestra for 35 years before his retirement from the position shortly before his death, was the most prolific conductor ever, having made over 800 recordings of all the major works. Despite a reputation for being temperamental, Karajan had also led the Philharmonia of London, the Vienna State Opera and La Scala Opera of Milan. The 1991–92 season was the Cork Symphony Orchestra's 58th under the baton of Dr Aloys Fleischmann. Sir Georg Solti (b. 22 Oct 1912), the Hungarian-born former principal conductor of the Chicago Symphony Orchestra, has won a record 29 Grammy awards for his recordings. (See also Grammy awards.)

Largest choir Excluding 'sing alongs' by stadium crowds, the greatest choir is one of 60 000, which sang in unison as a finale of a choral contest among 160 000 participants in Breslau, Germany on 2 Aug 1937.

ATTENDANCES

Classical An estimated 800 000 attended a free open-air concert by the New York Philharmonic conducted by Zubin Mehta, on the Great Lawn of Central Park, New York, USA on 5 Jul 1986, as part of the Statue of Liberty Weekend.

Rock/pop festival Estimating the size of audiences at open-air events where no admission is paid is often left to the police, media reporters, promoters and publicity agents. Estimates therefore vary widely and there is no way to check the accuracy of claims. The best claim is believed to be 725 000 for Steve Wozniak's 1983 US Festival in San Bernadino, California. The Woodstock Music and Art Fair held on 15–17 Aug 1969 at Bethel, New York, USA is thought to have attracted an audience of 300–500 000. The attendance at the 3rd Pop Festival at East Afton Farm, Freshwater, Isle of Wight on 30 Aug 1970 was claimed by its promoters, Fiery Creations, to be 400 000.

Solo performer The largest *paying* audience ever attracted by a solo performer was an estimated 180–184 000 in the Maracaña Stadium, Rio de Janeiro, Brazil to hear Paul McCartney (b. 1942) on 2 Apr 1990. Jean-Michel Jarre, the *son et lumière* specialist, entertained an estimated audience of 2 million in Paris, France at a free concert for Bastille day in 1990. His London Dockland show of 8 Oct 1988 set a British record of 80 000 (in a downpour).

Most successful concert tour The Rolling Stones 1989 'Steel Wheels' North American tour earned an estimated £185 million ($310 million) and was attended by 3·2 million people in 30 cities.

Wembley Stadium Michael Jackson sold out seven nights at Wembley Stadium in the summer of 1988. The Stadium has a capacity of 72 000 so a total of 504 000 people saw Jackson perform on 14, 15, 16, 22, 23 Jul and 26, 27 Aug 1988.

Largest concert On 21 Jul 1990 Potsdamer Platz, straddling East and West Berlin, was the site of the largest single rock concert in terms of participants and organisation ever staged. Roger Waters' production of Pink Floyd's 'The Wall' involved 600 people performing on a stage measuring 168 × 25 m *551 × 82 ft* at its

■ **Largest concert**
Pink Floyd's The Wall *comes tumbling down in front of 200 000 people in the re-unified Potsdamer Platz, Berlin, Germany on 21 Jul 1990. A total of 600 performers were involved in the spectacle. (Photo: Gamma)*

Bell ringing

The greatest number of peals (minimum of 5000 changes, all in tower bells) rung in a year is 303, by Colin Turner of Abingdon, Oxon in 1989. The late George E. Fearn rang 2666 peals from 1928 to May 1974. Matthew Lakin (1801–1899) was a regular bell-ringer at Tetney Church near Grimsby, Humberside for 84 years.

MUSIC

■ **Highest-paid pianist**
Ignace Jan Paderewski
(1860-1941), concert
pianist and former Prime
Minister of Poland, earned
$500 000 in a single season
in 1922–23. (Photo: Hulton
Picture Library)

Singing

The longest recorded choir singing marathon is one of 80 hr 32 min, by the Danville High School Contemporaires Swing Choir, Danville, Illinois, USA from 8–12 Feb 1991.

Longest silence

The longest interval between the known composition of a major composer and its performance in the manner intended is from 3 Mar 1791 until 9 Oct 1982 (over 191 years), in the case of Mozart's *Organ Piece for a Clock*, a fugue fantasy in F minor (K 608), arranged by the organ builders Wm Hill & Son and Norman & Beard Ltd at Glyndebourne, E Sussex.

Worst singer

While no agreement exists as to the identity of history's greatest singer, there is unanimity on the worst. The excursions of the soprano Florence Foster Jenkins (1868–1944) into lieder and even high coloratura culminated on 25 Oct 1944 in her sell-out concert at the Carnegie Hall, New York City, USA. The diva's (already high) high F was said to have been made higher in 1943 by a crash in a taxi. It is one of the tragedies of musicology that Madame Jenkins' *Clavelitos*, accompanied by Cosme McMoon, was never recorded for posterity.

Clapping

The duration record for continuous clapping (sustaining an average of 160 claps per min, audible at 109·7 m *360 ft*) is 58 hr 9 min by V. Jeyaraman of Tamil Nadu, India from 12–15 Feb 1988.

highest point. An estimated 200 000 people gathered for the symbolic building and demolition of a wall made of 2500 styrofoam blocks.

COMPOSERS

Most prolific The most prolific composer of all time was probably Georg Philipp Telemann (1681–1767) of Germany. He composed 12 complete sets of services (one cantata every Sunday) for a year, 78 services for special occasions, 40 operas, 600 to 700 orchestral suites, 44 Passions, plus concertos and chamber music. The most prolific symphonist was Johann Melchior Molter (c. 1695–1765) of Germany who wrote 169. Franz Joseph Haydn (1732–1809) of Austria wrote 108 numbered symphonies, many of which are regularly played today.

Most rapid Among composers of the classical period the most prolific was Wolfgang Amadeus Mozart (1756–91) of Austria, who wrote c. 1000 operas, operettas, symphonies, violin sonatas, divertimenti, serenades, motets, concertos for piano and many other instruments, string quartets, other chamber music, masses and litanies, of which only 70 were published before he died aged 35. His opera *La Clemenza di Tito* (1791) was written in 18 days, and three symphonic masterpieces, *Symphony No. 39 in E flat major*, *Symphony No. 40 in G minor* and the *Jupiter Symphony No. 41 in C major*, were reputedly written in the space of 42 days in 1788. His overture *Don Giovanni* was written in full score at one sitting in Prague in 1787 and finished on the day of its opening performance.

Longest symphony The longest of all single classical symphonies is the orchestral symphony No. 3 in D minor by Gustav Mahler (1860–1911) of Austria. This work, composed in 1896, requires a contralto, a women's and a boys' choir in addition to a full orchestra. A full performance requires 1 hr 40 min, of which the first movement alone takes between 30 and 36 min. The Symphony No. 2 (the Gothic), composed from 1919–22 by William Havergal Brian (1876–1972), was played by over 800 performers (four brass bands) in the Victoria Hall, Hanley, Staffs on 21 May 1978 (conductor Trevor Stokes). A recent broadcast required 1 hr 45½ min. Brian wrote an even vaster work based on Shelley's 'Prometheus Unbound' lasting 4 hr 11 min, but the full score has been missing since 1961. The symphony *Victory at Sea* written by Richard Rodgers and arranged by Robert Russell Bennett for NBC TV in 1952 lasted 13 hours.

Longest piano composition The longest continuous non-repetitious piano piece ever published has been *The Well-Tuned Piano* by La Monte Young, first presented by the Dia Art Foundation at the Concert Hall, Harrison St, New York, USA on 28 Feb 1980. The piece lasted 4 hr 12 min 10 sec.

Symphonic Variations, composed in the 1930s for piano and orchestra by the British born Kaikhosru Shapurji Sorabji (1892–1988) on 500 pages of close manuscript in three volumes, would last for six hours at the prescribed tempo.

PERFORMERS

Highest-paid pianist Wladziu Valentino Liberace (1917–87) earned more than $2 million each 26-week season, with a peak of $138 000 for a single night's performance at Madison Square Garden, New York City in 1954. The highest-paid classical con-

cert pianist was Ignace Jan Paderewski (1860–1941), Prime Minister of Poland (1919–20), who accumulated a fortune estimated at $5 million, of which $500 000 was earned in a single season in 1922–23. The *nouveau riche* wife of a US industrialist once required him to play in her house behind a curtain. For concerts, Artur Rubinstein (1887–1982) between 1937 and 1976, commanded 70 per cent of the gross from his concerts.

Most successful singer Of great fortunes earned by singers, the highest on record are those of Enrico Caruso (1873–1921), the Italian tenor, whose estate was about $9 million, and the Italian-Spanish coloratura soprano Amelita Galli-Curci (1889–1963), who received about $3 million. The Irish tenor Count John Francis McCormack (1884–1945) gave up to ten concerts to capacity audiences in a single season in New York.

David Bowie drew a fee of $1·5 million for a single show at the US Festival in Glen Helen Regional Park, San Bernardino County, California, USA on 26 May 1983. The four-man rock band Van Halen attracted a matching fee. The total attendance at Michael Jackson's world tour, Sep 1987–Dec 1988, brought in a tour gross revenue in excess of $124 million.

Largest contract It was reported on 21 Mar 1991 that Michael Jackson (b. 29 Aug 1958) had signed a 15-year contract worth £500 million (*$890 million*) with the Sony Corporation of Japan for a series of music, television and film projects. Not wishing to be left out, in the same month Michael's sister Janet signed a deal with Virgin Records reportedly worth $32 million for as few as two albums.

Singer's pulling power In 1850, up to $653 was paid for a single seat at the US concerts of Johanna ('Jenny') Maria Lind (1820–87), the 'Swedish nightingale'. She had a range from g to e^{111}, of which the middle register is still regarded as unrivalled.

Fastest rapper Daddy Freddy rapped 528 syllables in 60 sec at the Guinness World of Records Exhibition in the Empire State Building, New York City, USA on 24 May 1991.

OPERA

Longest The longest of commonly performed operas is *Die Meistersinger von Nürnberg* by Wilhelm Richard Wagner (1813–83) of Germany. A normal uncut performance of this opera as performed by the Sadler's Wells company between 24 Aug and 19 Sep 1968 entailed 5 hr 15 min of music. *The Heretics* by Gabriel von Wayditch (1888–1969), a Hungarian-American, is orchestrated for 110 pieces and lasts 8½ hr.

Shortest The shortest opera published was *The Deliverance of Theseus* by Darius Milhaud (1892–1972), first performed in 1928, which lasted for 7 min 27 sec.

Longest aria The longest single aria, in the sense of an operatic solo, is Brünnhilde's immolation scene in Wagner's *Götterdämmerung*. A well-known recording of this has been precisely timed at 14 min 46 sec.

Largest opera houses The Metropolitan Opera House, Lincoln Center, New York City, USA completed in September 1966 at a cost of $45·7 million, has a capacity of 3800 seats in an auditorium 137 m *451 ft* deep. The stage is 71 m *234 ft* wide and 44·5 m *146 ft* deep. The tallest opera house is one housed in a 42-storey building on Wacker Drive in Chicago, Illinois, USA. The Teatro della Scala (La Scala) in Milan, Italy shares with the Bolshoi Theatre in Moscow, USSR the distinction of having the greatest number of tiers. Each has six, with the topmost being nicknamed the *Galiorka* by Russians.

Youngest opera singers Ginetta Gloria La Bianca, born in Buffalo, New York State, USA on 12 May 1934, sang Rosina in *The Barber of Seville* at the Teatro dell'Opera, Rome, Italy on 8 May 1950 aged 15 years 361 days, having appeared as Gilda in *Rigoletto* at Velletri 45 days earlier. Ginetta La Bianca was taught by Lucia Carlino and managed by Angelo Carlino.

Oldest opera singer The tenor Giovanni Martinelli sang Emperor Altoum in *Turandot* in Seattle, Washington State, USA on 4 Feb 1967 when aged 81. Danshi Toyotake (b. 1 Aug 1891) has been singing *Musume Gidayu* for 91 years.

BALLET

Fastest 'entrechat douze' In the *entrechat* (a vertical spring from the fifth position with the legs extended crisscrossing at the lower calf), the starting and finishing position each count as one, such that in an *entrechat douze* there are *5* crossings and uncrossings. This was performed by Wayne Sleep for the BBC *Record Breakers* programme on 7 Jan 1973. He was in the air for 0·71 sec.

Grands jetés On 28 Nov 1988, Wayne Sleep completed 158 grands jetés along the length of Dunston Staiths, Gateshead, Tyne & Wear in 2 min.

Most turns The greatest number of spins called for in classical ballet choreography is 32 *fouettés rond de jambe en tournant* in *Swan Lake* by Pyotr Ilyich Chaykovskiy (Tchaikovsky) (1840–93). Miss Rowena Jackson (later Chatfield) (b. Invercargill, New Zealand, 1925) achieved 121 such turns at her class in Melbourne, Victoria, Australia in 1940.

Most curtain calls The greatest recorded number of curtain calls ever received is 89 by Dame Margot Fonteyn de Arias (née Margaret Evelyn Hookham (1919–91) and Rudolf Hametovich Nureyev (born on a train near Irkutsk, USSR, 17 Mar 1938) after a performance of *Swan Lake* at the Vienna Staatsoper, Austria in October 1964.

Largest cast The largest number of ballet dancers used in a production in Britain has been 2000 in the London Coster Ballet of 1962, directed by Lillian Rowley, at the Royal Albert Hall, London.

Dancing

Marathon dancing must be distinguished from dancing mania, or tarantism, which is a pathological condition. The worst outbreak of the latter was at Aachen, Germany in July 1374, when hordes of men and women broke into a frenzied and compulsive choreomania in the streets. It lasted for many hours until injury or complete exhaustion ensued.

Largest and longest dances An estimated 25 000 people attended a 'Moonlight Serenade' outdoor evening of dancing to the music of the Glenn Miller Orchestra in Buffalo, New York, USA on 20 Jul 1984. An estimated total of 20 000 dancers took part in a single dance with one caller at the National Square Dance Convention at Louisville, Kentucky, USA on 26 Jun 1983.

The most taxing marathon dance staged as a public spectacle was one by Mike Ritof and Edith Boudreaux, who logged 5148 hr 28½ min to win $2000 at Chicago's Merry Garden Ballroom, Belmont and Sheffield, Illinois, USA from 29 Aug 1930 to 1 Apr 1931. Rest periods were progressively cut from 20 to 10 to 5 to nil minutes per hour, with 10-inch steps and a maximum of 15 seconds for closure of eyes.

Will Kemp in 1599 Morris-danced his way from London to Norwich in 9 days.

'Rosie Radiator' (Rose Marie Ostler) led an ensemble of 14 dancers through the streets of San Francisco, California, USA on 18 Jul 1987, covering a distance of 12·5 km *7¾ miles*.

Ballroom The world's most successful professional ballroom dancing champions have been Bill and Bobbie Irvine, who won 13 world titles between 1960 and 1968. The oldest competitive ballroom dancer was Albert J. Sylvester (1889–1989) of Corsham, Wilts who retired at the age of 94.

Conga The longest recorded conga was the Miami Super Conga, held in conjunction with Calle Ocho — a party to which Cuban-Americans invite the rest of Miami for a celebration of life together. Held on 13 Mar 1988, the conga consisted of 119 986 people. The longest in Britain comprised a 'snake' of 8659 people from the South-Eastern Region of the Camping and Caravanning Club of Great Britain and Ireland. It took place on 4 Sep 1982 at Brands Hatch, Kent.

Country dancing The most complex Scottish country dance ever held was a 256-some reel, choreographed by Ian Price, which took place on 24 Apr 1988 in Vancouver, Canada.

Flamenco The fastest flamenco dancer ever measured is Solero de Jerez, aged 17, who in Brisbane, Australia in September 1967 attained 16 heel taps per second, in an electrifying routine.

Limbo The lowest height for a bar (flaming) under which a limbo dancer has passed is 15·25 cm *6 in* off the floor, by Dennis Walston, alias King Limbo, at Kent, Washington State, USA on 2 Mar 1991. Junior J. Renaud (b. 7 Jun 1954) became the first Official World Limbo Champion at the inaugural International Limbo Competition on 19 Feb 1974 at Port of Spain, Trinidad.

The record for a performer on roller skates is 13·33 cm *5¼ in*, first achieved by Denise Culp of Rock Hill, South Carolina, USA on 22 Jan 1984. This has since been equalled by Tracey O'Callaghan on 2 Jun 1984 and Sandra Siviour on 30 Mar 1985, both at Bexley North, New South Wales, Australia, Jessie Ball on 27 Jun 1985 at Beverley Hills, New South Wales and Kelly Foley on 22 May 1987, Magdalena Petrik and Meegan Anderson, both on 13 Apr 1988, and Michelle Boyle, Donna Bray and Jessica McLeish on 21 May 1988, all at Parramatta, New South Wales. On 28 Jun 1988 Erika Howell of Brunswick, Georgia, USA equalled this height, as did Kellie Boyle at Burwood, New South Wales on 9 Aug 1989, Bahar (Jenny) Sonmez at Gosford, New South Wales on 26 Nov 1989 and Lindee Watmough, also at Gosford, on 30 Sep 1990.

Tap The fastest *rate* ever measured for tap dancing is 32 taps per second by Stephen Gare of Sutton Coldfield, W Mids, at the Grand Hotel, Birmingham, W Mids on 28 Mar 1990. Roy Castle, host of the BBC TV *Record Breakers* programme, achieved one million taps in 23 hr 44 min at the Guinness World of Records exhibition, London on 31 Oct–1 Nov 1985. The greatest-ever assemblage of tap dancers in a single routine numbered 5271 outside Macy's Store in New York City, USA on 12 Aug 1990.

Recorded sound

Origins The gramophone (phonograph) was first conceived by Charles Cros (1842–88), a French poet and scientist, who described his idea in sealed papers deposited in the French Academy of Sciences on 30 Apr 1877. However, the realization of a practical device was first achieved by Thomas Alva Edison (1847–1931) of the USA. The first successful wax cylinder machine was constructed by his mechanic, John Kruesi, on 4–6 Dec 1877, demonstrated on 7 Dec and patented on 19 Feb 1878. The horizontal disc was introduced by Emile Berliner (1851–1929) and first demonstrated in Philadelphia on 18 May 1888.

Earliest recordings The earliest voice recording is believed to be a speech made by Lord Stanley of Preston, Governor-General of Canada, during the opening of the Toronto Industrial Exhibition on 11 Sep 1888. Copies of this speech are held in the National Sound Archive, London.

Tape recording Magnetic recording was invented by Valdemar Poulsen (1869–1942) of Denmark with his steel wire Telegraphone in 1898 (US Pat. No. 661619). Fritz Pfleumer (German Patent 500900) introduced tape in 1928. Tapes were first used at the Blattner Studios, Elstree, Herts in 1929. Plastic tapes were devised by BASF of Germany in 1932–35, but were not marketed until 1950 by Recording Associates of New York.

Oldest records The BBC record library contains over 1 million records. The oldest records in the library are white wax cylinders dating from 1888. The world's largest private collection is believed to be that of Stan Kilarr (b. 1915) of Klamath Falls, Oregon, USA, with some 500 000. The earliest commercial disc recording was manufactured in 1895.

Smallest functional record Six titles of 33·3 mm *1⁵/₁₆ in* diameter were recorded by HMV's studio at Hayes, Middx on 26 Jan 1923 for Queen Mary's Dolls' House. Some 92 000 of these miniature records were pressed including 35 000 of *God Save The King* (Bb 2439).

Earliest jazz records *Indiana* and *The Dark Town Strutters Ball* were recorded for the Columbia label in New York on or about 30 Jan 1917, by the Original Dixieland Jazz Band, led by Dominick (Nick) James La Rocca (1889–1961). This was released on 31 May 1917. The first

Most curtain calls
On 24 Feb 1988 Luciano Pavarotti received 165 curtain calls and was applauded for 1 hr 7 min after singing the part of Nemorino in Gaetano Donizetti's *L'elisir d'amore* at the Deutsche Oper in Berlin, Germany.

Longest operatic encore
The longest encore listed in the *Concise Oxford Dictionary of Opera*, was of the entire opera Cimarosa's *Il Matrimonio Segreto* at its première in 1792. This was at the command of the Austro-Hungarian Emperor Leopold II (reigned 1790–92).

Dancing dragon
The longest dancing dragon, created by schoolchildren and volunteers from St Helens, Merseyside in June and July 1989, was 300·23 m *985 ft* long. It was made from foil, paper, bamboo and cane and decorated with scales. Five hundred people then brought it to life in dance as part of the Mayor's Carnival in St Helens on 30 Jul 1989.

Square dance calling
Alan Covacic called for 26 hr 2 min for the Wheelers and Dealers Square Dance Club at RAF Halton, Aylesbury, Bucks from 18–19 Nov 1988.

Phonographic identification
Dr Arthur B. Lintgen (b. 1932) of Rydal, Pennsylvania, USA, has an as yet unique and proven ability to identify the music on phonograph records purely by visual inspection without hearing a note.

RECORDED SOUND

Record store

HMV opened the world's largest record store at 150 Oxford Street, London on 24 Oct 1986. Its trading area measures 3408 m² *36 684 ft²*.

jazz record to be released was the ODJB's *Livery Stable Blues* (recorded 26 Feb), backed by *The Dixie Jass Band One-Step* (recorded 26 Feb), released by Victor on 7 Mar 1917.

Most successful singer The most successful singer is Madonna (Madonna Louise Veronica Ciccone, b. 16 Aug 1959). Her album *True Blue*, with sales of over 11 million, was number one in an unprecedented 28 countries. At May 1990 she had achieved a total of 17 UK Top Ten hits, with *Vogue* making her seventh No. 1 single. In 1986 she became the first woman to top both the singles and albums charts, and her albums *Like a Virgin* (1985), and *True Blue* (1986) include 5 Top Five singles.

Most successful solo recording artist No independently audited figures have ever been published for Elvis Aron Presley (1935–77). In view of Presley's world-wide tally of over 170 major hits on singles and over 80 top-selling albums from 1956 continuing after his death, it may be assumed that it was he who must have

succeeded Bing Crosby as the top-selling solo artist of all time. On 9 Jun 1960 the Hollywood Chamber of Commerce presented Harry Lillis (alias Bing) Crosby Jr (1904–77) with a platinum disc to commemorate the alleged sale of 200 000 000 records from the 2600 singles and 125 albums he had recorded. On 15 Sep 1970 he received a second platinum disc when Decca claimed a sale of 300 650 000 discs. No independently audited figures of his global lifetime sales have ever been published and figures are considered exaggerated.

Most successful group The singers with the greatest sales of any group have been The Beatles. This group from Liverpool, Merseyside comprised George Harrison (b. 25 Feb 1943), John Ono (formerly John Winston) Lennon (b. 9 Oct 1940–killed 8 Dec 1980), James Paul McCartney (b. 18 Jun 1942) and Richard Starkey, alias Ringo Starr (b. 7 Jul 1940). The all-time Beatles sales by May 1985 have been estimated by EMI at over 1000 million discs and tapes. All four ex-Beatles sold

many million further records as solo artists. Since their break-up in 1970, it is estimated that the most successful group in the world in terms of record sales is the Swedish foursome ABBA (Agnetha Faltskog, Anni-Frid Lyngstad, Bjorn Ulvaeus and Benny Andersson), who had total sales of over 215 million discs and tapes by May 1985.

All-girl group The most successful all-girl group in the history of the UK singles chart is Bananarama. Between 1982 and 1988 the group, comprising Keren Woodward, Sarah Dallin and Siobhan Fahey, scored 15 consecutive hits on their own, and a further two in partnership with the Funboy Three. Fahey left the group to pursue a solo career after marrying Eurythmics' Dave Stewart in 1988, and was replaced by Jacqui O'Sullivan.

Earliest golden discs The first actual golden disc was one sprayed by RCA Victor for the US trombonist and band-leader Alton 'Glenn' Miller (1904–44) for his *Chattanooga Choo Choo* on 10 Feb 1942. The first actual piece eventually to aggregate a total sale of a million copies was of performances by Enrico Caruso (b. Naples, Italy, 1873, d. 2 Aug 1921) of the aria *'Vesti la giubba'* ('On with the Motley') from the opera *I Pagliacci* by Ruggiero Leoncavallo (1858–1919), the earliest version of which was recorded with piano on 12 Nov 1902. The first single recording to surpass the million mark was Alma Gluck's *Carry Me Back to Old Virginny* on the Red Seal Victor label on the twelve-inch *30·48 cm* single faced (later backed) record No. 74420.

Most golden discs The only *audited* measure of gold, platinum and multi-platinum singles and albums within the United States is certification by the Recording Industry Association of America (RIAA), introduced on 14 Mar 1958. Out of the 2582 RIAA awards made to 1 Jan 1985, The Beatles, with 47 (plus one with Billy Preston) have most for a group.

Paul McCartney has 27 more awards outside the group and with Wings (including one with Stevie Wonder and one with Michael Jackson). The most awards to an individual is 56 to Elvis Presley (1935–77), spanning the period 1958 to 1 Jan 1986. Globally, however, Presley's total of million-selling singles has been authoritatively placed at 80 world-wide.

Most recordings In what is believed to be the largest ever recording project devoted to a single composer, 180 compact discs containing the complete set of authenticated works by Mozart were produced by Philips Classics for release in 1990–91 to commemorate the bicentenary of the composer's death. The complete set comprises over 200 hours of music and would occupy 2 m *6½ ft* of shelving. In the period between February 1987 and August 1989, Genesis P. Orridge and his band Psychic TV released 14 live albums on Temple Records. The albums are part of a series of 23.

Biggest sellers (Singles) The greatest seller of any gramophone record to date is *White Christmas* by Irving Berlin (b. Israel Bailin, 1888–1989), recorded by Bing Crosby on 29 May 1942. It was announced on Christmas Eve 1987 that North American sales alone reached 170 884 207 copies by 30 Jun 1987.

The highest claim for any 'pop' record is an unaudited 25 million for *Rock Around the Clock*, copyrighted in 1953 by James E. Myers under the name Jimmy DeKnight and the late Max C. Freedmann and recorded on 12 Apr 1954 by Bill Haley (1927–1981) and his Comets.

The top-selling British record of all time is *I Want to Hold Your Hand* by The Beatles, released in 1963, with world sales of over 13 million. The top selling single of all time in the UK is *Do They Know It's Christmas*, written and produced by Bob Geldof and Midge Ure, with 3·6 million copies sold by May 1987 with a further 8·1 million world-wide. The profits were in aid of the Ethiopian Famine Relief Fund and are now estimated to be over £90 million.

The only female solo artist to have a million-selling single in the UK is Jennifer Rush, whose single *The Power of Love* was certified in 1985. The best-selling female duet in the UK is *I Know Him So Well* by Elaine Page and Barbara Dickson with sales of over 820 000 to May 1987.

Biggest sellers (Albums) The best-selling album of all time is *Thriller* by Michael Jackson (b. Gary, Indiana, USA 29 Aug 1958), with global sales of over 40 million copies to date.

The best-selling album by a group is Fleetwood Mac's *Rumours* with over 25 million copies sold to date. The best-selling classical album is *In Concert*, with global sales of 5 million copies to date. It was recorded by operatic heavyweights José Carreras, Placido Domingo and Luciano Pavarotti at the 1990 World Cup Finals in Rome, Italy.

The best selling album by a British group is *Dark Side of the Moon* by Pink Floyd, with sales audited at 19·5 million to December 1986. The best-selling album in Britain is Dire Straits' *Brothers in Arms*, with over three million sold by May 1988.

The best-selling album by a woman is *True Blue* by Madonna, which had sold almost 17 million copies by October 1990. *Whitney Houston* by Whitney Houston, released in 1985, and with sales of over 14 million copies, is the best-selling debut album of all time.

The best-selling movie soundtrack is *Saturday Night Fever*, with sales of over 30 million to date.

The charts (US Singles) Singles record charts were first published by *Billboard* on 20 Jul 1940, when the No. 1 record was *I'll Never Smile Again* by Tommy Dorsey (1905–56). *Near You* by Francis Craig stayed at the No. 1 spot for 17 weeks in 1947.

The Beatles have had the most No. 1 hits (20), Conway Twitty the most Country No. 1s (35) and Aretha Franklin the most Rhythm and Blues No. 1s (20). Aretha Franklin is also the female solo artist with the most million-selling singles, with 14 between 1967 and 1973. Elvis Presley has had the most hit singles on *Billboard*'s Hot 100 — 149 from 1956 to May 1990.

Bing Crosby's *White Christmas* spent a total of 72 weeks in the chart between 1942 and 1962, while *Tainted Love* by Soft Cell stayed on the chart for 43 *consecutive* weeks from January 1982.

The charts (US Albums) *Billboard* first published an album chart on 15 Mar 1945 when the No. 1 was *King Cole Trio* featuring Nat 'King' Cole (1919–65). *South Pacific* was No. 1 for 69 weeks (non-consecutive) from May 1949. *Dark Side of the Moon* by Pink Floyd enjoyed 730 weeks on the *Billboard* charts to April 1989.

The Beatles have had the most No. 1 albums

(15), Elvis Presley was the most successful male soloist (9), and Simon and Garfunkel the top duo with three. Elvis Presley has also had the most hit albums (94 from 1956 to April 1989).

The woman with the most No. 1 albums (6), and most hit albums in total (40 between 1963 and April 1989), is Barbra Streisand, 30 of whose albums have been certified gold (500 000 sales) or platinum (1 million sales) by the RIAA, making her the best-selling female singer of all time.

The charts (UK Singles) Singles record charts were first published in Britain on 14 Nov 1952 by *New Musical Express*. *I Believe* by Frankie Laine (b. 30 Mar 1913) held the No. 1 position for 18 weeks (non-consecutive) from April 1953, with *Rose Marie* by Slim Whitman (b. 20 Jan 1924) the consecutive record holder with 11 weeks from July 1955.

The longest stay has been the 122 weeks of *My Way* by Francis Albert Sinatra (b. 12 Dec 1915) in ten separate runs from 2 Apr 1969 to 1972. The record for most consecutive weeks on the chart is 56 weeks for Engelbert Humperdinck's *Release Me* from 26 Jan 1967.

The Beatles and Elvis Presley hold the record for most No. 1 hits with 17 each, with Presley having an overall record of 106 hits in the UK singles chart from 1956 to May 1987.

The charts (UK Albums) The first British album chart was published on 8 Nov 1958 by *Melody Maker*. The first No. 1 LP was the film soundtrack *South Pacific*, which held the position for a record 70 consecutive weeks and eventually achieved a record 115 weeks at No. 1. The album with the most total weeks on chart is *Rumours* by Fleetwood Mac with 420 weeks by May 1988.

The recording of Vivaldi's *Four Seasons* by Nigel Kennedy and the English Chamber Orchestra topped the classical chart for over one year following its release on 25 Sep 1989.

The Beatles have had the most No. 1 albums — 12, and Elvis Presley the most hit albums — 91.

The youngest female soloist to have a No. 1 album in Britain is Kylie Minogue (b. Melbourne, Australia, 28 May 1968), who was 20 years old when her debut album *Kylie* topped the chart in July 1988. Kylie also holds the record for the best-ever start to a singles chart career, with her first 10 singles reaching the Top 5.

Fastest-selling The fastest-selling non-pop record of all time is *John Fitzgerald Kennedy — A Memorial Album*, recorded on 22 Nov 1963, the day of President Kennedy's assassination. The recording sold 4 million copies at 99 cents in six days (7–12 Dec 1963), thus ironically beating the previous speed record set by the satirical LP *The First Family* in 1962–63. The fastest-selling British record is the Beatles' double album *The Beatles*, with 'nearly 2 million' in its first week in November 1968.

Advance sales The greatest advance sale for a single world-wide is 2·1 million for *Can't Buy Me Love* by the Beatles. Released on 21 Mar 1964, it also holds the British record of 1 million jointly with another Beatles single, *I Want to Hold Your Hand*, released on 29 Nov 1963. The UK record for advance sales of an album is 1·1 million for *Welcome to the Pleasure Dome*, the debut album by Frankie Goes To Hollywood, released in 1984.

Fastest live recording to retail A limited edition of Midge Ure's *Dear God* single, including two live tracks *All Fall Down* and *Strange Brew* on the B-side, was delivered to retail 81 hrs 15 min after the live performance at The Venue, Edinburgh on 21 Nov 1988, at which the tracks were recorded.

Most song titles — DJ challenge Disc-jockey John Murray of Kirkcaldy, Fife played 37 song titles from two decks in two minutes on the BBC *Record Breakers* programme broadcast on 16 Nov 1990.

Compact discs Announced by Philips in 1978 and introduced by the same company in 1982, the compact disc (CD) increasingly challenges the LP and cassette as a recording medium. The first CD to sell a million copies world-wide was Dire Straits' *Brothers in Arms* in 1986. It subsequently topped a million sales in Europe alone, including over 250 000 in Britain.

Theatre

Oldest Theatre in Europe has its origins in Greek drama performed in honour of a god, usually Dionysus. The earliest amphitheatres date from the 5th century BC. The first stone-built theatre in Rome erected in 55 BC could accommodate 40 000 spectators.

Oldest indoor theatre The oldest indoor theatre in the world is the Teatro Olimpico in Vicenza, Italy. Designed in the Roman style by Andrea di Pietro, alias Palladio (1508–80), it was begun three months before his death and finished by his pupil Vicenzo Scamozzi (1552–1616) in 1583. It is preserved today in its original form.

UK The earliest London theatre was James Burbage's 'The Theatre', built in 1576 near Finsbury Fields, London. In 1989 archaeologists found the remains of the Elizabethan Rose theatre at Bankside in Southwark; it was built in 1587 by Philip Henslowe. The oldest theatre still in use in Great Britain is The Royal in Bristol, Avon. The foundation stone was laid on 30 Nov 1764, and the theatre was opened on 30 May 1766 with a 'Concert of Musick and a Specimen of Rhetorick'. The City Varieties Music Hall, Leeds was a singing room in 1762 and so claims to outdate the Theatre Royal. Actors had the legal status of rogues and vagabonds until the passing of the Vagrancy Act in 1824. The oldest amateur dramatic society is the Old Stagers inaugurated in Canterbury, Kent in 1841. They have performed in every year except the years of World Wars I and II.

Largest The world's largest building used for theatre is the National People's Congress Building (*Ren min da hui tang*) on the west side of Tiananmen Square, Beijing, China. It was completed in 1959 and covers an area of 5·2 ha *12·9 acres*. The theatre seats 10 000 and is occasionally used as such, as in 1964 for the play *The East is Red*.

The highest-capacity purpose-built theatre is the Perth Entertainment Centre, Western Australia, completed at a cost of A$8·3 million in November 1976. It contains 8003 seats and the stage area covers 1148 m² *12 000 ft²*.

Smallest The smallest regularly operating professional theatre in the world is the Piccolo in Juliusstrasse, Hamburg, Germany. It was founded in 1970 and has a maximum capacity of 30 seats.

Gladiatorial combat

Emperor Trajan of Rome (AD 98–117) staged a display involving 4941 pairs of gladiators over 117 days. Publius Ostorius, a freedman, survived 51 combats in Pompeii.

Longest chorus line

A record 369 dancers, including some Tiller Girls and several British TV personalities, fill the studio for the finale of the BBC Record Breakers programme, broadcast on 14 Dec 1990. (Photo: BBC Record Breakers)

Largest amphitheatre The Flavian amphitheatre or Colosseum of Rome, Italy, completed in AD 80, covers 2 ha *5 acres* with a capacity of 87 000. It has a maximum length of 187 m *612 ft* and a maximum width of 175 m *515 ft*.

Largest stage The largest stage in the world is in the Ziegfeld Room, Reno, Nevada, USA with 53·6 m *176 ft* passerelle, three main lifts each capable of raising 1200 show girls (65·3 tonnes), two 19·1 m *62½ ft* circumference turntables and 800 spotlights.

Longest runs The longest continuous run of any show in the world is *The Mousetrap* by Dame Agatha Christie. This thriller opened on 25 Nov 1952 at the Ambassadors Theatre, London (capacity 453) and moved after 8862 performances to the St Martin's Theatre next door on 25 Mar 1974. The 16 000th performance was on 6 May 1991, and the box office has grossed £19 million from more than 9 million attenders. The Vicksburg Theater Guild, Mississippi, USA has been playing the melodrama *Gold in the Hills* by J. Frank Davis discontinuously but every season since 1936.

Revue The greatest number of performances of any theatrical presentation is 47 250 (to April 1986) in the case of *The Golden Horseshoe Revue*, a show staged at Disneyland Park, Anaheim, California, USA. It started on 16 Jul 1955, closed on 12 Oct 1986 after being seen by 16 million people. The main performers were Fulton Burley, Dick Hardwick (who replaced Wally Boag who had appeared from the opening day until his retirement in 1983) and Betty Taylor, who played as many as five houses a day in a routine that lasted 45 minutes.

Broadway *A Chorus Line* opened on 25 Jul 1975 and closed on 28 Apr 1990 after a record run of almost 15 years and 6137 performances. It was created by Michael Bennet (1943–87).

Musical shows The off-Broadway musical show *The Fantasticks* by Tom Jones and Harvey Schmidt opened on 3 May 1960, and the total number of performances to 6 Jun 1991 is 12 897 at the Sullivan Street Playhouse, Greenwich Village, New York, USA.

UK The longest-running musical show ever performed in Britain was *The Black and White Minstrel Show*, later *Magic of the Minstrels*. The aggregate but discontinuous number of performances was 6464 with a total attendance of 7 794 552. The show opened at the Victoria Palace, London on 25 May 1962 and closed on 4 Nov 1972. It reopened for a season in June 1973 at the New Victoria and finally closed on 8 Dec 1973.

London Cats surpassed *Jesus Christ Superstar* on its eighth birthday at the New London Theatre, Drury Lane on 12 May 1989 (3358 performances) when it was being played in ten centres simultaneously. The aggregate gross was estimated at £250 million.

Comedy The British record for long-running comedy is held by *No Sex Please We're British* by Anthony Marriott and Alistair Foot and presented by John Gale, which opened at the Strand Theatre on 3 Jun 1971, transferred to the Duchess Theatre on 2 Aug 1986 and finally ended its run on 5 Sep 1987 after 17 years and 6761 performances. Its director Allan Davis had his name in lights from the start.

Christmas seasons The record for the longest run of consecutive Christmas seasons at the same theatre is held by *The Sooty Show*. It has been running annually at The Mayfair Theatre, London since 1966.

Shortest runs The shortest run on record was that of *The Intimate Revue* at the Duchess Theatre, London, on 11 Mar 1930. Anything which could go wrong did. With scene changes taking up to 20 min apiece, the management scrapped seven scenes to get the finale on before midnight. The run was described as 'half a performance'. The musical *Bernadette*, written by Gwyn and Maureen Hughes and starring Natalie Wright, closed on 14 Jul 1990 after just 24 days and 35 performances (including previews) at the Dominion Theatre, London.

The greatest loss sustained by a theatrical show was by the Royal Shakespeare Company's musical *Carrie*, which closed after five performances on Broadway on 17 May 1988 at a cost of $7 million. *King*, the musical about Martin Luther King, incurred a loss of £3 million in a six week run ending on 2 Jun 1990, thus matching the London record losses of *Ziegfeld* in 1988.

One-man shows The longest run of one-man shows is 849, by Victor Borge (b. Copenhagen, 3 Jan 1909) in his *Comedy in Music* from 2 Oct 1953 to 21 Jan 1956 at the Golden Theater, Broadway, New York City, USA. The world aggregate record for one-man shows is 1700 performances of *Brief Lives* by Roy Dotrice (b. Guernsey, 26 May 1923), including 400 straight at the Mayfair Theatre, London ending on 20 Jul 1974. He was on stage for more than 2½ per per performance of this 17th-century monologue and required 3 hr for make-up and 1 hr for removal of make-up, so aggregating 40 weeks in the chair.

Most durable performers Kanmi Fujiyama (b. 1929) played the lead role in 10 288 performances by the comedy company Sochiku Shikigeki from November 1966 to June 1983. Lore Noto co-starred in 6438 performances of *The Fantasticks*, the world's longest-running musical, between December 1970 and June 1986. (See Musical shows.) David Raven played Major Metcalfe in *The Mousetrap* on 4575 occasions between 22 Jul 1957 and 23 Nov 1968. Dame Anna Neagle (1904–86) played the lead role in *Charlie Girl* at the Adelphi Theatre, London for 2062 of 2202 performances between 15 Dec 1965 and 27 Mar 1971. She played the role a further 327 times in 327 performances in Australasia. Jack Howarth (1896–1984) was an actor on the stage and in television for 76 years from 1907 until his last appearance after 23 years as Albert Tatlock in *Coronation Street* on 25 Jan 1984. Frances Etheridge has played Lizzie, the housekeeper, in *Gold in the Hills* more than 660 times over a span of 47 years since 1936. (See Longest runs).

Advance sales The musical *Miss Saigon*, produced by Cameron Mackintosh and starring Jonathan Pryce and Lea Salonga, opened on Broadway in April 1991 after generating record advance sales of $36 million. Its move from London had been under threat because of a row over the cast for the American production.

Most roles The greatest recorded number of theatrical, film and television roles is 3385, from 1951 to March 1989 by Jan Leighton.

Most theatrical roles Kanzaburo Nakamura (b. July 1909) performed in 806 Kabuki titles from November 1926 to January 1987. As each title in this classical Japanese theatrical form lasts 25 days, he therefore played 20 150 performances.

Shakespeare The first all-amateur company to have staged all 37 plays was The Southsea Shakespeare Actors, Hants (founded 1947) in October 1966 when, under K. Edmonds Gateley, they presented *Cymbeline*. The longest play is *Hamlet* with 4042 lines and 29 551 words. Of Shakespeare's 1277 speaking parts the longest is Hamlet with 11 610 words.

Longest chorus line The longest professional chorus line in performing history numbered up to 120 in some of the early Ziegfeld's Follies. In the finale of *A Chorus Line* on the night of 29 Sep 1983, when it broke the record as the longest-running Broadway show ever, 332 top-hatted 'strutters' performed on stage. An even tighter squeeze was achieved by 369 dancers in a specially-choreographed routine per-

formed on the BBC *Record Breakers* programme broadcast on 14 Dec 1990.

Highest cabaret fee Dolly Parton received up to $400 000 per live concert. Johnny Carson's fee for the non-televised Sears Roebuck Centenary Gala in October 1984 was set at $1 million.

Ice shows Holiday on Ice Production Inc., founded by Morris Chalfen in 1945, stages the world's most costly live entertainment, with up to seven productions playing simultaneously in several of 75 countries. By 8 Mar 1988 the show had been seen by 250 million spectators. The total skating and other staff exceeds 900. Hazel Wendy Jolly (b. 1933) appeared in the Wembley Winter Pantomime for 27 years until her retirement in 1980.

Arts festival The world's largest arts festival is the annual Edinburgh Festival Fringe (instituted in 1947). In 1990, 537 groups gave 9504 performances of 1103 shows between 12 August and 1 September. Prof. Gerald Berkowitz of Northern Illinois University attended a record 145 separate performances at the 1979 Festival from 15 Aug–8 Sep.

Fashion shows The most prolific producer of fashion shows is Adalene Ross Riley of San Francisco, California, USA with a total of over 4721 to April 1989.

The greatest distance covered by female models on a catwalk is 114·4 km *71·1 miles*, by Roberta Brown and Lorraine McCourt at Parke's Hotel, Dublin, Republic of Ireland from 19–21 Sep 1983. Male model Eddie Warke covered a further 19·1 km *11·9 miles* on the catwalk. The compère was Marty Whelan of Radio 2.

Beauty contests The first international beauty contest was staged by P.T. Barnum (with the public to be the judges) in the USA in June 1855.

The world's largest annual beauty pageants are the Miss World and Miss Universe contests (inaugurated in 1951 and 1952 respectively). The most successful country in the latter contest has been the USA, with winners in 1954, 1956, 1960, 1967, 1980 and 1982. The greatest number of countries represented in the Miss Universe contest was 81 in 1983. The country which has produced the most winners in the Miss World contest is the United Kingdom, with five. They were Rosemarie Frankland (1961); Ann Sidney (1964); Lesley Langley (1965); Helen Morgan (1974), who resigned, and Sarah-Jane Hutt (1983). The maximum number of contestants was 84 in November 1988. The shortest reign as Miss World was 18 hr, by Miss Germany (Gabriella Brum) in 1980.

Circus

The world's largest permanent circus is Circus Circus, Las Vegas, Nevada, USA, opened on 18 Oct 1968 at a cost of $15 million. It covers an area of 11 984 m² *129 000 ft²*, covered by a tent-shaped flexiglass roof 27·43 m *90 ft* high.

The largest travelling circus is the Gold Unit of Ringling Bros. and Barnum & Bailey Circus. It seats 7000 people and is 120 × 60 × 20 m *394 × 197 × 66 ft*. It was first used for a show at Sapporo, Japan on 1 Jul 1988.

The largest circus crowd comprised 52 385 people who attended a performance of 'The Greatest Show on Earth' at the Superdome

in New Orleans, Louisiana, USA on 14 Sep 1975.

Flying trapeze Downward circles or 'muscle grinding' — 1350 by Sarah Denu (aged 14) (US) Madison, Wisconsin, USA, 21 May 1983. Single-heel hang on swinging bar, Angela Revelle (Angelique), Australia, 1977.

Highest aerial act Ian Ashpole (b. 15 Jan 1956) of Ross-on-Wye, Hereford & Worcester performed a trapeze act suspended from a hot-air balloon between St Neots, Cambs and Newmarket, Suffolk at 5004·8 m *16 420 ft* on 16 May 1986.

Triple twisting double somersault Tom Robin Edelston to catcher John Zimmerman, Circus World, Florida, USA on 20 Jan 1981.

Full twisting triple and the quadruple Vazquez Troupe. Miguel Vazquez to catcher Juan Vazquez at Ringling Bros, Amphitheater, Chicago, Illinois, USA in November 1981. On 20 Sep 1984 he performed a triple somersault in a layout position (no turn) to catcher Juan Vazquez at the Sports Arena, Los Angeles, California, USA.

Triple back somersault with 1½ twists Terry Cavaretta Lemus (now Mrs St Jules) at Circus Circus, Las Vegas, Nevada, USA in 1969.

Teeter board A seven-person high perch pyramid was established by the Bulgarian 'Kehaiovi Troupe' at the Tower Circus, Blackpool, Lancs on 16 Jul 1986. It was finished off with a leap from the top by 13-year old member Magdelena.

Trampoline Septuple twisting back somersault to bed and quintuple twisting back somersault to shoulders by Marco Canestrelli to Belmonte Canestrelli at Madison Square Garden, New York, USA on 5 Jan and 28 Mar 1979. Richard Tison (France) performed a triple twisting triple back somersault for television near Berchtesgaden, Germany on 30 Jun 1981.

Flexible pole Double full twisting somersault to a 5·08 cm *2 in* diameter pole by Roberto Tabak (aged 11) in Sarasota, Florida, USA in 1977. Triple full twisting somersault by Corina Colonelu Mosoianu (aged 13) at Madison Square Garden, New York, USA on 17 Apr 1984.

Human pyramid (or tuckle) Twelve (3 high) supported by a single understander. Weight 771 kg *1700 lb* or *121·4 stone* by Tahar Douis of the Hassani Troupe at BBC TV Pebble Mill Studio, Birmingham on 17 Dec 1979.

Nine high by top-mounter Josep-Joan Martínez Lozano, aged 10, of the Colla Vella dels Xiquets, 12 m *39 ft* tall on 25 Oct 1981 in Valls, Spain.

Oldest clown Charlie Rivel (b. José Andreu, Spain, 1896) performed for 82 years, making his first public appearance when he was three years old in 1899. He died in 1983 at the age of 87.

Human cannonball The first human cannonball was Emilio Onra *né* Maîtrejean at Cirque d'Hiver, Paris, France on 21 Nov 1875. The record distance a human has been hired from a cannon is 53·3 m *175 ft*, in the case of Emanuel Zacchini, son of the pioneer Hugo Zacchini, in the Ringling Bros. and Barnum & Bailey Circus, Madison Square Gardens, New York City, USA in 1940. His muzzle velocity has been estimated at 86·9 km/h *54 mph*. On his retirement the management were fortunate in finding that his daughter Florinda was of the same calibre.

An experiment on Yorkshire TV on 17 Aug 1978 showed that when Miss Sue Evans, 17, was fired, she was 9·5 mm *⅜ in* shorter on landing.

Lion-taming The greatest number of lions mastered and fed in a cage by an unaided lion-tamer was 40, by 'Captain' Alfred Schneider in 1925. Clyde Raymond Beatty handled more than 40 'cats' (lions and tigers) simultaneously. Beatty (b. Bainbridge, Ohio, USA, 10 Jun 1903, died Ventura, California, USA, 19 Jul 1965) was the featured attraction at every show he appeared in for more than 40 years. He insisted upon being called a lion-trainer. More than 20 lion-tamers have died of injuries since 1900.

Stilt-walking The fastest stilt-walker on record is Masaharu Tatsushiro, who covered 100 m *328 ft* on 30·48 cm *1 ft* high stilts in 14·15 sec in Tokyo, Japan on 30 Mar 1980.

Over a long distance, the fastest is M. Garisoain of Bayonne, France, who in 1892 walked the 8 km *4·97 miles* from Bayonne to Biarritz on stilts in 42 min, an average speed of 11·42 km/h *7·10 mph*.

The greatest distance ever walked on stilts is 4804 km *3008 miles*, from Los Angeles, California, USA to Bowen, Kentucky, USA by Joe Bowen from 20 Feb–26 Jul 1980.

In 1891 Sylvain Dornon stilt-walked from Paris, France to Moscow, USSR via Vilno in 50 stages, covering 2945 km *1830 miles*. Another source gives his time as 58 days. Either way, although Bowen's distance was greater, Dornon walked at a much higher speed.

Even with a safety or Kirby wire, very high stilts are *extremely* dangerous — 25 steps are deemed to constitute 'mastery'. The tallest stilts ever mastered measured 12·36 m *40 ft 6½ in* from ground to ankle; they were used by Eddy Wolf ('Steady Eddy') of Loyal, Wisconsin, USA to walk a distance of 27 steps without touching his safety handrail wires at Yokohama Dreamland Park, Yokohama, Japan on 9 Mar 1986. The stilts were of aluminium and weighed 25 kg *55 lb* each.

The heaviest stilts ever mastered weighed 25·4 kg *56 lb* each, and were used by Joe Long (b. Kenneth Caesar), who has suffered five fractures, at the BBC Television Centre, London on 8 Dec 1978. They were 7·31 m *24 ft* high.

Photography

CAMERAS

Earliest The earliest veiled reference to a photograph on glass taken in a camera was in a letter dated 19 Jul 1822 from Joseph Nicéphore Niépce (1765–1833), a French scientist. It was a photograph of a copper engraving of Pope Pius VII taken at Gras, near Chalon-sur-Saône, France, and it was rediscovered in London in February 1952 by the photo-historian Helmut Gernsheim after six years' research. The earliest photograph taken in England was one of a diamond-paned window in Laycock (or Lacock) Abbey, Wilts taken in August 1835 by William Henry Fox Talbot MP (1800–77), the inventor of the negative-positive process. The negative of this was donated to the Science Museum, London in 1937 by his grand-daughter Matilda. The world's earliest aerial photograph was taken in 1858 by Gaspard Félix Tournachon (1820–1910), *alias* Nadar, from a balloon

Fastest film production

The shortest time ever taken to make a feature-length film from scripting to screening is 13 days for *The Fastest Forward*, produced by Russ Malkin and directed by John Gore. It was given a gala première on 27 May 1990 at the Dominion Theatre, London.

High diving

Col. Harry A. Froboess (Switzerland) jumped 120 m *394 ft* into the Bodensee from the airship *Graf Hindenburg* on 22 Jun 1936.

The greatest height reported for a dive into an air bag is 99·36 m *326 ft* by stuntman Dan Koko, who jumped from the top of Vegas World Hotel and Casino on to a 6·1 × 12·2 × 4·2 m *20 × 40 × 14 ft* target on 13 Aug 1984. His impact speed was 141 km/h *88 mph*.

Kitty O'Neil dived 54·8 m *180 ft* from a helicopter over Devonshire Downs, California, USA on 9 Dec 1979 on to an air cushion measuring 9·14 × 18·28 m *30 × 60 ft* for a TV film stunt.

Most portrayed character

The character most frequently recurring on the screen is Sherlock Holmes, created by Sir Arthur Conan Doyle (1859–1930). The Baker Street sleuth has been portrayed by some 72 actors in over 204 films since 1900.

The character most often portrayed in horror films is Count Dracula, created by the Irish writer Bram Stoker (1847–1912). Representations of the Count or his immediate descendants outnumber those of his closest rival, Frankenstein's creation, by 160 to 112.

near Villacoublay, on the outskirts of Paris, France.

Largest The largest and most expensive industrial camera ever built is the 27 tonne Rolls Royce camera now owned by BPCC Graphics Ltd of Derby commissioned in 1956. It measures 2·69 m *8 ft 10 in* high, 2·51 m *8¼ ft* wide and 14·02 m *46 ft* in length. The lens is a 160 cm *63 in* f 16 Cooke Apochromatic and the bellows were made by Camera Bellows Ltd of Birmingham, W Mids. A pinhole camera was created from a standard Portakabin unit measuring 10·4 × 2·9 × 2·64 m *34 × 9½ × 9 ft* by photographers John Kippen and Chris Wainwright at the National Museum of Photography, Film and Television at Bradford, W Yorks on 25 Mar 1990. The unit produced a direct positive measuring 10·2 × 1·8 m *33 × 6 ft*.

Largest lens The National Museum of Photography, Film and Television, Bradford, W Yorks has the largest lens on display, made by Pilkington Special Glass Ltd, St Asaph, Clwyd. Its dimensions are: focal length 8·45 m *333 in*, diameter 1·372 m *54 in*, weight 215 kg *474 lb*. Its focal length enables writing on the museum's walls to be read from a distance of 12·19 m *40 ft*.

Smallest Apart from cameras built for intra-cardiac surgery and espionage, the smallest that has been marketed is the circular Japanese 'Petal' camera, with a diameter of 2·9 cm *1·14 in* and a thickness of 1·65 cm *0·65 in*. It has a focal length of 12 mm *0·47 in*. An Edwardian field camera was designed and built by William Pocklington of Ascot, Berks in 1989, with bellows made by Camera Bellows Ltd. When mounted on its tripod, the replica stands 150 mm *5·9 in* high, with a body measuring 34 × 34 × 50 mm *1·3 × 1·3 × 1·9 in* with bellows extended (34 × 34 × 19 mm *1·3 × 1·3 × 0·75 in* when closed). Fitted with a reversing back for landscape and portrait format, the camera produces pictures measuring 20 × 17 mm *0·78 × 0·67 in*.

Fastest A camera built for research into high-power lasers by the Blackett Laboratory of Imperial College of Science and Technology, London registered images at a rate of 33 billion frames per sec. The fastest production camera is currently the Imacon 675, made by Hadland Photonics Ltd of Bovingdon, Herts, at up to 600 million frames per sec.

Most expensive The most expensive complete range of camera equipment in the world is that of the Nikon Corporation of Tokyo, Japan, who marketed in May 1991 their complete range of 26 cameras with 84 lenses and 617 accessories at a total cost of £133 278.78 excluding VAT.

The highest auction price paid for a camera is £26 400 for a Leica R6 sold at Christie's, London on 9 Nov 1989 to De Liugi Garibaldi.

Longest negative On 1 Jul 1988 Christopher Creighton of Port Hope, Ontario, Canada, using a 24 in focal length Turner-Reich lens, fitted to a Kodak 8 Cirkut camera, made a portrait of an estimated 1500 inhabitants of Port Hope, achieving a 355 degree view in a single shot. The resulting negative measured 362 × 19·7 cm *11 ft 10½ in × 7¾ in*.

Most expensive photograph The platinum print *Roses, Mexico* taken by Tina Modotti in 1925 was sold at Sotheby's, New York, USA on 17 Apr 1991 for a record $165 000.

Cinema

FILMS

The earliest motion pictures ever taken were by Louis Aimé Augustin Le Prince (1842–90). He was attested to have achieved dim moving outlines on a whitewashed wall at the Institute for the Deaf, Washington Heights, New York, USA as early as 1885–87. The earliest surviving film (sensitised 53·9 mm *2⅛ in* wide paper roll) is from his camera, patented in Britain on 16 Nov 1888, taken in early October 1888 of the garden of his father-in-law, Joseph Whitley, in Roundhay, Leeds, W Yorks at 10–12 frames per sec.

The first commercial presentation of motion pictures was at Holland Bros' Kinetoscope Parlor at 1155 Broadway, New York City, USA on 14 Apr 1894. Viewers could see five films for 25 cents or 10 for 50 cents from a double row of Kinetoscopes developed by William Kennedy Laurie Dickson (1860–1935), assistant to Thomas Alva Edison (1847–1931), in 1889–91. The earliest publicly presented film on a *screen* was *La Sortie des Ouvriers de l'Usine Lumière*, probably shot in August or September 1894 in Lyon, France. It was exhibited at 44 rue de Rennes, Paris, France on 22 Mar 1895 by the Lumière brothers, Auguste Marie Louis Nicholas (1862–1954) and Louis Jean (1864–1948).

Earliest 'talkie' The earliest sound-on-film motion picture was achieved by Eugene Augustin Lauste (1857–1935), who patented his process on 11 Aug 1906 and produced a workable system using a string galvanometer in 1910 at Benedict Road, Stockwell, London. The earliest public presentation of sound on film was by the Tri-ergon process at the Alhambra cinema, Berlin, Germany on 17 Sep 1922.

Largest output India's production of feature-length films was a record 948 in 1990 and its annual output has exceeded 700 every year since 1979.

Most expensive film At the time of its release in July 1991, *Terminator 2: Judgement Day*, was reported to have cost Carolco Pictures a blockbusting $104 million, plus print and advertising costs of about $20 million. Its star, Arnold Schwarzenegger, was believed to have received a fee of $15 million for this sequel.

Least expensive full-length feature film The total cost of production for the 1927 film *The Shattered Illusion*, by Victorian Film Productions, was £300. It took 12 months to complete and included spectacular scenes of a ship being overwhelmed by a storm.

Most expensive film rights The highest price ever paid for film rights was $9·5 million announced on 20 Jan 1978 by Columbia for *Annie*, the Broadway musical by Charles Strouse starring Andrea McCardle, Dorothy Loudon and Reid Shelton.

Longest film The longest commercially-released film was Rainer Werner Fassbinder's 15 hr 21 min epic *Berlin Alexanderplatz*, which was shown in full at the Vista cinema, Hollywood, California, USA on 6–7 Aug 1983 with a two-hour break for dinner. At 15 hr 40 min, the slightly longer *Heimat* (1984) was shown throughout Germany and in London, but over two days at weekend screenings.

Highest box office gross The box office gross champion is Steven Spielberg's *ET: The Extra-Terrestrial*, released on 11 Jun 1982, which had grossed over $700 million (including videos) by December 1989. Its UK television premiere on Christmas day 1990 attracted 17·5 million viewers. On 24 Jun 1989 *Batman* (Warner Brothers) grossed $14·6 million for a single-day record. The highest ever opening day gross was also scored by *Batman* on 23 Jun 1989 with takings of $13·1 million.

In January 1991 UIP's *Ghost*, starring Patrick Swayze, Demi Moore and Oscar-winner Whoopi Goldberg, became the highest-ever grossing film in the UK, with box office takings of £20·7 million.

Largest loss Michael Cimino's 1980 production *Heaven's Gate* took $1·5 million in North American rentals against an estimated negative cost of $44 million and a total cost, including distribution and overheads, of $57 million.

Highest earnings Jack Nicholson stood to receive up to $60 million for playing 'The Joker' in Warner Brothers' $50 million *Batman*, through a percentage of the film's receipts in lieu of a fee.

The highest-paid actresses are Barbra Streisand, with $6 million for *Prince of Tides* and Meryl Streep (b. Summit, New Jersey, USA, 1949), who received $4 million for both *Out of Africa* and *Heartburn*.

Stuntman Dar Robinson was paid $100 000 for the 335 m *1100 ft* leap from the CN Tower, Toronto, Canada in November 1979 for *High Point*. His parachute opened just 91 m *300 ft* above the ground. He died 21 Nov 1986 aged 39.

Longest series still continuing Japan's *Tora-San* films have now stretched from *Tora-San I* in August 1969 to *Tora-San XL* in 1988, with Kiyoshi Atsumi (b. 1929) starring in each for Shochiku Co.

Largest number of extras It is believed that over 300 000 extras appeared in the funeral scene of Sir Richard Attenborough's *Gandhi* (1982).

Largest studios The largest complex of film studios in the world is that at Universal City, Los Angeles, California, USA. The back lot contains 573 buildings and there are 34 sound stages on the 170 ha *420 acre* site.

Largest studio stage The world's largest studio stage is the 007 stage at Pinewood Studios, Bucks. It was designed by Ken Adam and Michael Brown and built in 1976 for the James Bond film *The Spy Who Loved Me*. It measures 102 × 42 × 12 m *336 × 139 × 41 ft*, and accommodated 4·54 million litres *1·2 million gallons* of water, a full-scale 600 000-ton oil tanker and three nuclear submarines.

Largest film set The largest film set ever built was the 400 × 230 m *1312 × 754 ft* Roman Forum designed by Veniero Colosanti and John Moore for Samuel Bronston's production of *The Fall of the Roman Empire* (1964). It was built on a 22·25 ha *55 acre* site outside Madrid, Spain. 1100 workmen spent seven months laying the surface of the Forum with 170 000 cement blocks, erecting 6705 m *22 000 ft* of concrete stairways, 601 colums and 350 statues, and constructing 27 full-size buildings.

Longest directorial career The directorial career of King Vidor (1894–1982) lasted for 66 years, beginning with the two-reel comedy *The Tow* (1914) and culminating in another short, a documentary called *The Metaphor* (1980).

Oldest director Joris Ivens (b. Netherlands, 1898) directed the Franco-Italian co-production *Le Vent* in 1988 at the age of 89. He made his directorial debut with the Dutch film *De Brug* in 1928.

Most durable performers The record for the longest screen career is held by the German actor Curt Bois (b. 1900), who made his debut in *Mutterliebe* at the age of nine and whose recent films include *Der Himmel über Berlin* (1987). The American actress Helen Hayes (b. 10 Oct 1900) first appeared on screen at the age of 10 in *Jean and the Calico Doll*, but much of her later work has been on television. The most enduring stars of the big screen are French actor Charles Vanel (b. 1892), who marked his 75th anniversary as a film actor in *Les Saisons du Plaisir* (1988), and Lillian Gish (b. 14 Oct 1893) — although her birthdate is usually given as 1896. She made her debut in *An Unseen Enemy* (1912) and most recently appeared in *The Whales of August* (1987).

Most generations of screen actors in a family There are four generations of screen actors in the Redgrave family. Roy Redgrave (1872–1922) made his screen debut in 1911 and continued to appear in Australian films until 1920. Sir Michael Redgrave married actress Rachel Kempson and their two daughters Vanessa and Lynn and son Corin all went into films. Vanessa's two daughters Joely and Natasha and Corin's daughter Jemma are already successful actresses with, films such as *Wetherby*, *A Month in the Country* and *The Dream Demon* to their respective credit.

Costumes The largest number of costumes used for any one film was 32 000 for the 1951 film *Quo Vadis*. Elizabeth Taylor changed costume 65 times in *Cleopatra* (1963). The costumes were designed by Irene Sharaff and cost $130 000.

Most expensive Constance Bennett's sable coat in *Madam X* was valued at $50 000. The most expensive costume designed and made specially for a film was Edith Head's mink and sequins dance costume worn by Ginger Rogers in *Lady in the Dark*. It cost Paramount $35 000. The ruby slippers worn by Judy Garland in the 1939 film *The Wizard of Oz* were sold on 2 Jun 1988 to a mystery buyer at Christie's, New York, USA for $165 000.

Longest screen kiss The most prolonged osculatory marathon in cinematic history is one of 185 sec by Regis Toomey and Jane Wyman (later Mrs Ronald Reagan, b. 4 Jan 1914) in *You're in the Army Now* released in 1940.

Oscar winners Walter (Walt) Elias Disney (1901–66) has won more 'Oscars' — the awards of the United States Academy of Motion Picture Arts and Sciences, instituted on 16 May 1929 and named after Oscar Pierce of Texas, USA — than any other person. The count comprises 20 statuettes and 12 other pla-

ques and certificates, including posthumous awards.

The only person to win four Oscars in a starring role is Miss Katharine Hepburn (b. Hartford, Connecticut, USA, 8 Nov 1909) for *Morning Glory* (1932–3), *Guess Who's Coming to Dinner* (1967), *The Lion in Winter* (1968) and *On Golden Pond* (1981). The awards were made in 1934, 1968, 1969 and 1982 respectively. She has been nominated 12 times.

Eight performers have won two Oscars in starring roles (the year the award was presented is given in each case) — Ingrid Bergman in 1945 and 1956, Marlon Brando (1955 and 1973), Gary Cooper (1942 and 1953), Jane Fonda (1972 and 1979), Dustin Hoffman (1980 and 1989), Vivien Leigh (1940 and 1952), Frederic March (1933 and 1947) and Spencer Tracy in 1938 and 1939. Edith Head (1907–81) won eight individual awards for costume design.

The youngest ever winner was Shirley Temple (b. 23 Apr 1928), who received an honorary Oscar when aged five. The oldest recipients, George Burns (b. 20 Jan 1896) for *The Sunshine Boys* in 1976 and Jessica Tandy (b. 7 Jun 1909) for *Driving Miss Daisy* in 1990, were both 80 at the time of the presentation, although Miss Tandy was the elder of the two.

The film with most awards has been *Ben Hur* (1959) with 11. That with the highest number of nominations was *All About Eve* (1950) with 14. It won six (Best Supporting

■ **Longest screen career**

Lillian Gish (b. 14 Oct 1893) in her screen debut in D.W. Griffith's silent classic An Unseen Enemy *(1912), made 75 years before her most recent screen appearance in* The Whales of August *(1987). Also featured is her sister, Dorothy (1898–1968), with whom Lillian made her stage debut at the age of five. (Photo: National Film Archive)*

Brain of Britain quiz

The youngest person to become 'Brain of Britain' on BBC radio was Anthony Carr of Anglesey, Gwynedd in 1956 at the age of 16. The oldest contestant has been the author and translator Hugh Merrick (1898–1980) in his 80th year in August 1977.

The record score is 35 by the 1981 winner Peter Barlow of Richmond, Surrey and Peter Bates of Taunton, Somerset who won the title in 1984.

Actor: George Sanders; Best Picture, Best Costume Design; Edith Head, Charles Le Maire, Best Director; Joseph L. Mankiewicz, Best Sound Recording, Best Screenplay; Joseph L. Mankiewicz).

Most versatile personalities The only three performers to have won Oscar, Emmy, Tony and Grammy awards have been Helen Hayes (b. 1900) in 1932–1976; Richard Rodgers (1902–1979), composer of musicals, and Rita Moreno (b. 1931) in 1961–1977. Barbra Streisand received Oscar, Grammy and Emmy awards in addition to a special 'Star of the Decade' Tony award.

Most honoured entertainer The most honoured entertainer in history is Bob Hope (né Leslie Townes Hope, Eltham, London, 29 May 1903). He has been uniquely awarded the USA's highest civilian honours — the Medal of Freedom (1969); Congressional Gold Medal (1963); Medal of Merit (1966); Distinguished Public Service Medal (1973); Distinguished Service Gold Medal (1971) and is also an (1976) and was appointed Hon. Brigadier of the US Marine Corps. He also has 44 honorary degrees.

CINEMAS

Earliest The earliest structure designed and exclusively used for exhibiting projected films is believed to be one erected at the Atlanta Show, Georgia, USA in October 1895 to exhibit C.F. Jenkins' phantoscope. The earliest attempt at establishing a cinema in Britain was made by Birt Acres, whose Kineopticon opened at 2 Piccadilly Mansions at the junction of Piccadilly Circus and Shaftesbury Avenue, London on 21 Mar 1896. After only a few weeks, the cinema was gutted by fire.

Largest The largest cinema in the world is the Radio City Music Hall, New York City, USA, opened on 27 Dec 1932 with 5945 (now 5874) seats. In recent years it has specialized in screening premieres and major revivals. Kinepolis, the first eight screens of which opened in Brussels, Belgium in 1988, is the world's largest

cinema complex. It has 24 screens and a total seating capacity of 7000. The Odeon, Leicester Square, London has 1983 seats.

Most and least cinemas The country with the largest number of cinemas in relation to population is San Marino, with one cinema for every 3190 inhabitants (a total of seven). In comparison, the USA has one cinema for every 11 000 inhabitants and the UK has one cinema for every 45 000 inhabitants.

Highest cinema-going The Chinese Ministry of Culture reported in September 1987 that there were 21 billion cinema attendances in 1986 — or nearly 21 per person per annum. The UK admissions in 1990 were provisionally estimated at 98·8 million, or 1·9 million people per week.

Biggest screen The permanently installed cinema screen with the largest surface area is one of 29·30 × 21·48 m *96 × 70½ ft* in the Keong Emas Imax Theatre, Taman Mini Park, Jakarta, Indonesia opened on 20 Apr 1984. It was made by Harkness Screens Ltd at Borehamwood, Herts. A temporary screen measuring 90·5 × 10 m *297 × 33 ft* was used at the 1937 Paris Exposition.

Most films seen Gwilym Hughes of Dolgellau, Gwynedd has seen 20 064 films at the cinema to date. He saw his first film in 1953 while in hospital.

Radio

The earliest patent for telegraphy without wires (wireless) was received by Dr Mahlon Loomis (1826–86) of the United States. It was entitled 'Improvement in Telegraphy' and was dated 20 Jul 1872 (US Pat. No. 129 971). He in fact demonstrated only potential differences on a galvanometer between two kites 22 km *14 miles* apart in Loudoun County, Virginia, USA in October 1866.

Earliest patent The first patent for a system of communication by means of

electro-magnetic waves, numbered No. 12039, was granted on 2 Jun 1896 to the Italian-Irish Marchese Guglielmo Marconi (1874–1937). A public demonstration of wireless transmission of speech was, however, given in the town square of Murray, Kentucky, USA in 1892 by Nathan B. Stubblefield. He died destitute on 28 Mar 1928. The first permanent wireless installation was set up at The Needles on the Isle of Wight, Hants by Marconi's Wireless Telegraph Co. Ltd in November 1897.

Earliest broadcast The world's first advertised broadcast was made on 24 Dec 1906 by the Canadian-born Prof. Reginald Aubrey Fessenden (1868–1932) from the 128 m *420 ft* mast of the National Electric Signalling Company at Brant Rock, Massachusetts, USA. The transmission included Handel's *Largo*. Fessenden had achieved the broadcast of speech as early as November 1900 but this was highly distorted.

The first experimental broadcasting transmitter in Great Britain was set up at the Marconi Works in Chelmsford, Essex in December 1919. It broadcast a news service in February 1920, but the earliest regular broadcast was made from the Marconi transmitter '2MT' at Writtle, Essex on 14 Feb 1922.

Transatlantic transmissions The earliest claim to have received wireless signals (the letter S in Morse Code) across the Atlantic was made by Marconi, George Stephen Kemp and Percy Paget from a 10 kW station at Poldhu, Cornwall to Signal Hill, St John's, Newfoundland, Canada, at 12:30 p.m. on 12 Dec 1901. Human speech was first heard across the Atlantic in November 1915 when a transmission from the US Navy station at Arlington, Virginia was received by US radio-telephone engineers on the Eiffel Tower in Paris, France.

Earliest radio-microphones The radio-microphone, which was in essence also the first 'bug', was devised by Reg Moores (GB) in 1947 and first used on 76 MHz in the ice show *Aladdin* at Brighton Sports Stadium, E Sussex in September 1949.

Longest BBC national broadcast The reporting of the Coronation of Queen Elizabeth II on 2 Jun 1953 began at 10:15 a.m. and finished at 5:30 p.m., after 7 hr 15 min.

Longest continuous broadcast Radio Telefís Éireann transmitted an unedited reading of *Ulysses* by James Joyce (1882–1941) for 29 hr 38 min 47 sec on 16–17 Jul 1982.

Topmost prize Mary Buchanan, 15, on WKRQ, Cincinnati, USA, won a prize of $25 000 for 40 years (viz. $1 million) on 21 Nov 1980.

Most durable programmes *Rambling with Gambling*, the early morning WOR-NY programme, began in March 1925 and has been continued by three generations of the Gambling family.

BBC The longest-running BBC radio series is *The Week's Good Cause*, which began on 24 Jan 1926. The St Martin-in-the-Fields Christmas appeal by Canon Geoffrey Brown on 14 Dec 1986 raised a record £138 039. *Daily Service* began with an experimental broadcast on 2 Jan 1928 but it was transmitted only on Daventry 5XX. By December 1929 it was broadcast from all BBC transmitters.

The longest-running record programme is *Desert Island Discs* which began on 29 Jan

1942 and on which programme only one guest, Arthur Askey (1900–82), has been stranded a fourth time (on the 1572nd show on 20 Dec 1980). The programme was originally presented by its creator, Roy Plomley who died on 28 May 1985 having presented 1791 editions. It is now presented by former newsreader, Sue Lawley.

The longest-running solo radio feature is *Letter from America* by (Alfred) Alistair Cooke, Hon. KBE (b. Salford 20 Nov 1908), first broadcast on 24 Mar 1946. That on his 80th birthday was No. 2074. The original broadcaster of the series was Raymond Gram Swing.

The longest-running radio serial is *The Archers*, created by Godfrey Baseley and first broadcast on 1 Jan 1951, thereby celebrating its 40th anniversary on 1 Jan 1991. The Post Office issued a Commemorative Cover to coincide with the 10 000th episode broadcast on 26 May 1989. The only role which has been played without interruption from the start is that of Philip Archer by Norman Painting (b. Leamington Spa, Warks, 23 Apr 1924).

Most assiduous radio ham The late Richard C. Spenceley of KV4AA at St Thomas, Virgin Islands built his contacts (QSOs) to a record level of 48 100 in 365 days in 1978.

Most stations The country with the greatest number of radio broadcasting stations is the United States, where there were 9512 authorised broadcast stations as at April 1985 made up of both AM (amplitude modulation) and FM (frequency modulation).

Highest listening The peak recorded listenership on BBC Radio was 30 million on 6 Jun 1950 for the boxing match between Lee Savold (US) and Bruce Woodcock (GB) (b. Doncaster, S Yorks, 1921). Surveys carried out in 90 countries showed that, in 1990, the global estimated audience for the BBC World Service, broadcast in 38 languages, was 120 million regular listeners — greater than the combined listenership of Voice of America, Radio Moscow and *Deutsche Welle*. This is, however, a conservative estimate because figures are unavailable for several countries, including China, Cuba, Myanmar (formerly Burma), Iran, Afganistan and Vietnam.

Highest response The highest recorded response from a radio show occurred on 27 Nov 1974 when, on a 5-hr talk show on WCAU, Philadelphia, Pennsylvania, USA, astrologer Howard Sheldon registered a call count of 388 299 on the *Bill Corsair Show*.

Television

Invention The invention of television, the instantaneous viewing of distant objects by electrical transmissions, was not an act but a process of successive and interdependent discoveries.

The first commercial cathode ray tube was introduced in 1897 by Karl Ferdinand Braun (1850–1918), but was not linked to 'electric vision' until 1907 by the Russian Prof. Boris Rosing (disappeared 1918) in St Petersburg (Leningrad). A.A. Campbell Swinton (1863–1930) published the fundamentals of television transmission on 18 Jun 1908 in a brief letter to *Nature* entitled 'Distant Electric Vision'.

The earliest public demonstration of television was given on 27 Jan 1926 by John Logie Baird (1888–1946) of Scotland, using a

development of the mechanical scanning system patented by Paul Gottlieb Nipkow (1860–1940) on 6 Jan 1884. He had achieved the transmission of a Maltese Cross over 3·05 m *10 ft* at 8 Queen's Arcade, Hastings, E Sussex, by February 1924 and the first facial image (of William Taynton, 15) at 22, Frith Street, London on 30 Oct 1925. Taynton had to be bribed with 2s 6d. Baird launched his first television 'service' via a BBC transmitter on 30 Sep 1929 and marketed the first sets, Baird Televisors, at 26 guineas in May 1930. A patent application for the Iconoscope had been filed on 29 Dec 1923 by Dr Vladimir Kosma Zworykin (1889–1982) but was not issued until 20 Dec 1938. Kenjiro Takayanagi (b. 20 Jan 1899) succeeded in transmitting a 40-line electronic picture on 25 Dec 1926 with a Braun cathode ray tube and a Nipkow disc at Hamamatsu Technical College, Japan.

Earliest service Public transmissions on 30 lines were made from 22 Aug 1932–11 Sep 1935. It has been estimated that 6×10^{15} electrons traverse a television tube each second. A television station in Berlin, Germany made a low-definition (180-line) transmission from 22 Mar 1935, but the transmitter burnt out in August that year. The world's first high-definition (i.e. 405 lines) television broadcasting service was opened from Alexandra Palace, London on 2 Nov 1936, when there were about 100 sets in the United Kingdom. The chief engineer was Douglas Birkinshaw.

Transatlantic transmission On 9 Feb 1928 the image of J.L. Baird and of a Mrs Howe was transmitted from Station 2 KZ at Coulsdon, Surrey to Station 2 CVJ, Hartsdale, New York, USA. The earliest transatlantic transmission by satellite was achieved at 1 a.m. on 11 Jul 1962 via the active satellite *Telstar 1* from Andover, Maine, USA to Pleumeur Bodou, France. The picture was of Frederick R. Kappell, chairman of the American Telephone and Telegraph Co. (AT&T), which owned the satellite. The first 'live' broadcast was made on 23 Jul 1962 and the first woman to appear was the *haute couturière* Ginette Spanier, director of Balmain, the next day.

Longest telecast The longest pre-scheduled telecast on record was a continuous transmission for 163 hr 18 min by

GTV 9 of Melbourne, Australia, covering the Apollo XI moon mission from 19–26 Jul 1969.

The longest continuous TV transmission under a single director was a student production on WOCC TV3 at Otterbein College, Westerville, Ohio, USA transmitted over 48 hr 3 min on 17–19 Feb 1990 under the direction of Ben Kehoe.

Earliest video-tape recording Alexander M. Poniatoff first demonstrated video-tape recording known as Ampex (his initials plus 'ex' for excellence) in 1956.

The earliest demonstration of a home video recorder was on 24 Jun 1963 at the BBC News Studio at Alexandra Palace, London of the Telcan, developed by Norman Rutherford and Michael Turner of the Nottingham Electronic Valve Co.

Most durable shows The world's most durable TV show is NBC's *Meet the Press*, first transmitted on 6 Nov 1947 and weekly since 12 Sep 1948, originated by Lawrence E. Spivak, who appeared weekly as either moderator or panel member until 1975. Since 1949 over 150 000 individual episodes of the TV show *Bozo the Clown*, by Larry Harmon Pictures, have been aired daily on 150 stations in the US and abroad.

UK *Andy Pandy* was first transmitted on 11 Jul 1950 but consisted of repeats of a cycle of 26 shows until 1970. *Come Dancing* was first transmitted on 29 Sep 1950 but is seasonal. *Sooty* was first presented on BBC by its deviser Harry Corbett (1918–89) in 1952. In 1968, *Sooty* moved to Thames Television and when Harry retired in 1975, the show was continued his son Matthew, who still handles the puppets today. *The Good Old Days* ran from 20 Jul 1953 to 31 Dec 1983. Barney Colehan produced all 244 programmes.

The *BBC News* was inaugurated in vision on 5 Jul 1954. Richard Baker read the news from 1954 to Christmas 1982. Of current affairs programmes BBC's weekly *Panorama* was first transmitted on 11 Nov 1953 but has summer breaks, whereas Granada's *What the Papers Say* was transmitted weekly from 5 Nov 1956 until September 1988 when it moved to Channel 4. It has been broadcast on BBC2 since 16 Mar 1990.

■ **Highest listening**
The newsroom of the BBC World Service. Surveys of 90 countries show that at least 120 million listeners tuned in regularly in 1990 — more than the combined audience of Voice of America, Radio Moscow and Deutsche Welle. (Photo: BBC)

Fastest video production

Tapes of the Royal Wedding of HRH Prince Andrew and Miss Sarah Ferguson on 23 Jul 1986 were produced by Thames Video Collection. Live filming ended with the departure of the honeymoon couple from Chelsea Hospital by helicopter at 4:42 p.m. The first fully edited and packaged VHS tapes were purchased 5 hr 41 min later by Fenella Lee and Lucinda Burland of West Kensington at the Virgin Megastore in Oxford Street, London at 10:23 p.m.

'Mastermind' records

This annual BBC quiz series with 64 initial contenders began on 11 Sep 1972. Jennifer Keaveney (on 'The life and work of E. Nesbit') scored a record 40 points in a 1986 semi-final and equalled this score when she won the 1986 final with 'The life and works of Elizabeth Gaskell'. Mary Elizabeth Raw ('The life and reign of Charles I') also scored 40 points in the first programme of the 1989 series.

Most takes

The highest number of 'takes' for a TV commercial is 28 in 1973 by Pat Coombs, the comedienne. Her explanation was 'Every time we came to the punch line I just could not remember the name of the product'.

■ Largest TV screen

The main feature at the Tsukuba International Exposition '85, near Tokyo, Japan was the Sony JumboTRON, measuring 40 × 25 m 131 × 82 ft. A remote control is recommended, as the screen is best viewed from a distance of about 50–500 m 165–1650 ft, although it can be seen from over 0·8 km ¹/₂ mile away.

(Photo: Spectrum)

The monthly *Sky at Night* has been presented by Patrick Moore without a break or a miss since 24 Apr 1957.

The longest-running domestic drama serial is Granada's *Coronation Street* which ran twice weekly from 9 Dec 1960 until 20 Oct 1989, after which viewers were treated to a third weekly episode. William Roache has played Ken Barlow without a break since the outset, including an appearance in the 2000th episode broadcast on 24 Aug 1990.

Most sets The global total of homes with television surpassed 500 million in 1987, led by the USA with 89·13 million. However, on 15 Feb 1988 the new China News Agency announced that China's number of TV viewers had risen to 600 million from 100 million sets. There are 8250 TV transmitting stations world-wide, 1241 of which are in the USA. There are 364 TV sets per 1000 people in the USA, compared with 348 in Sweden and 330 in Britain. The USA had, by March 1991, 92·8 million TV households, with 50·24 million on cable TV. The number of homes with colour sets was 8·3 million (97 per cent) by January 1989. More than 60 per cent of the total homes own two or more TV sets.

The proportion of households in Great Britain with colour sets was 93 per cent in 1989. Just over half (51 per cent) of all households had two or more sets. The number of licences in force was 19 545 830 at 31 Mar 1991, of which 18 110 617 were for colour sets. The number of monochrome licences continues to decline in line with the trend towards colour viewing and at 31 Mar 1991 there were only 1 435 213 black-and-white licences in force.

TV watching In June 1988 it was reported that the average US child sees at least 26 000 murders on TV by his or her 18th birthday. Between the ages of 2 and 11 the average viewing time is 31 hours 52 minutes per week. In 1988 the average British person watched 25 hr 21 min of television per week.

Greatest audience The estimated global audience for the 1990 World Cup finals played in Italy from 8 June to 8 July was 31 billion. An estimated 2·5 billion viewers tuned into the live and recorded transmissions of the XXIIIrd Olympic Games in Los Angeles, California, USA from 27 Jul to 13 Aug 1984. The American Broadcasting Co. (ABC) airing schedule comprised 187½ hours of coverage on 56 cameras. The estimated viewership for the 'Live Aid' concerts organised by Bob Geldof and Bill Graham, via a record 12 satellites, was 1·6 billion, or nearly one third of the world's population. The *Muppet Show* is the most widely viewed programme in the world, with an estimated audience of 235 million in 106 countries at August 1989.

The programme which attracted the highest ever viewership was the *Goodbye, Farewell and Amen* final episode of M*A*S*H (the acronym for Mobile Army Surgical Hospital 4077) transmitted by CBS on 28 Feb 1983 to 60·3 per cent of all households in the United States. It was estimated that some 125 million people tuned in, taking a 77 per cent share of all viewing.

The biggest audience for a single broadcast on British television is 25·21 million for the England *v.* West Germany World Cup semi-final match on 4 Jul 1990. An aggregate audience of 39 million was estimated to have watched the wedding of TRH the Prince and Princess of Wales in London on 29 Jul 1981.

Most expensive production The *Winds of War*, a seven-part Paramount

World War II saga aired by ABC, was the most expensive ever TV production costing $42 million over 14 months' shooting. The final episode on 13 Feb 1983 attracted a rating of 41 per cent of the total number of viewers, and a share of 56 per cent share of total sets turned on that were tuned in.

Largest contracts John William Carson (b. 23 Oct 1925), the host of *The Tonight Show*, has a contract with NBC reportedly calling for annual payment of $5 million for his one-hour evening shows aired four times weekly. The highest-paid current affairs or news performer is Dan Rather of CBS, who reportedly signed an $8 million contract for five years from 1982. Marie Osmond signed a contract worth $7 million for seven hours of transmission, paid by NBC on 9 Mar 1981. The figure includes talent and production costs.

UK The largest contract in British television was one of a reported £9 million, inclusive of production expenses, signed by Tom Jones (b. Thomas Jones Woodward, 7 Jun 1940) of Treforest, Mid Glam in June 1968 with ABC-TV of the United States and ATV in London for 17 one-hour shows per annum from January 1969 to January 1974.

Highest-paid entertainer The highest-paid TV performer is currently the US comedian Bill Cosby, who was reported in the October 1990 issue of *Forbes* magazine to have earned an estimated $115 million for 1989 and 1990. A survey in the *National Enquirer* published in February 1988 contended that the royalty income of Paul McCartney was running at $41 million per annum and that his estimated personal fortune was $560 million.

Largest TV prizes On 24 Jul 1975 WABC-TV, New York City, USA transmitted the first televised Grand Tier draw of the State Lottery, in which the winner took the grand prize of $1 million. This was, however, taxable.

Most successful telethon The world record for a telethon is $78 438 573 in pledges in 21½ hours by the 1989 Jerry Lewis Labor Day Telethon on 4 Sep.

The Comic Relief '89 Appeal, the second 'Red Nose Day' hosted by comedians Lenny Henry and Griff Rhys-Jones, raised £26 660 145. The *ITV Telethon '90*, hosted by Michael Aspel, raised £24 127 917 in 27 hours over the May Bank Holiday.

Biggest sale The greatest number of episodes of any TV programme ever sold has been 1144 episodes of *Coronation Street* by Granada Television to CBKST Saskatoon, Saskatchewan, Canada, on 31 May 1971. This constituted 20 days 15 hr 44 min continuous viewing. A further 728 episodes

(Jan 1974–Jan 1981) were sold to CBC in August 1982.

Most prolific scriptwriter The most prolific television writer in the world is the Rt Hon. Lord Willis (b. 13 Jan 1918). Since 1949 he has created 41 series, including the first seven years and 2·25 million words of *Dixon of Dock Green*, which ran on BBC television from 1955 to 1976, 36 stage plays and 39 feature films. He has had 26 plays produced and his total output is since 1942 estimated to be 19·8 million words.

TV producer Aaron Spelling (b. 1928) has produced more than 1770 TV episodes totalling 2250 hours of air time, as well as 207½ hours of TV movies and eight feature films. The total 2467 broadcast hours is equal to 3688 km *2292 miles* of film and, projected 24 hours a day, it would take just 3½ months to screen it all. The average American TV is turned on six hours per day. At this rate, Spelling has produced enough film to last 374 days.

Highest TV advertising rates The highest television advertising rate is $800 000 per 30 sec for ABC network prime-time slot during the transmission of Super Bowl XXV on 27 Jan 1991. In the United Kingdom the maximum cost for a peak-time (8–11:30 p.m.) weekday 60-sec slot on Thames Television was £104 000 + VAT in April 1991. The longest run was 7 min 10 sec by Great Universal Stores on TV-am's *Good Morning Britain* for £100 000 on 20 Jan 1985.

Commercial records It was reported in March 1988 that Pepsi Cola had paid Michael Jackson £7 million to do four TV commercials for them.

Largest and smallest sets The Sony JumboTRON colour TV screen at the Tsukuba International Exposition '85 near Tokyo in March 1985 measured 24·3 m × 45·7 m *80 ft × 150 ft*. The largest cathode ray tubes for colour sets are 94 cm *37 in* models manufactured by Mitsubishi Electric of Japan.

The Seiko TV-Wrist Watch launched on 23 Dec 1982 in Japan has a 30·5 mm *1·2 in* screen and weighs only 80 g *2·8 oz*. Together with the receiver unit and headphones, the entire black and white system, costing 108 000 yen, weighs only 320 g *11·3 oz*. The smallest single-piece set is the Casio-Keisanki TV-10 weighing 338 g *11·9 oz* with a 6·85 cm *2·7 in* screen, launched in Tokyo in July 1983. The smallest available colour set is the liquid crystal display (LCD) Japanese Epson launched in 1985, with overall dimensions of 7·6 × 17·1 × 2·8 cm *3 × 6¾ × 1⅛ in*. Including batteries and its 52 800 crystals it weighs only 453 g *16 oz*.

Human
Achievements

Endurance and Endeavour

Most travelled The world's most travelled men are Parke G. Thompson, from Akron, Ohio, USA and Giorgio Ricatto, from Turin, Italy, both of whom have visited all of the 171 sovereign countries and 59 of the 60 non-sovereign or other territories (see Countries, p. 78). Both men have yet to go to the Heard and McDonald Islands, an island group in the southern Indian Ocean. The most travelled couple are Robert and Carmen Becker of East Northport, New York, USA, both of whom have visited 169 of the 171 sovereign countries (the exceptions being Afghanistan and Iraq) and 53 of the 60 non-sovereign or other territories.

The most travelled man in the horseback era was believed to be the Methodist preacher Bishop Francis Asbury (b. Handsworth, W Mids, 1745), who travelled 424 850 km *264 000 miles* in North America between 1771 and 1815. During this time he preached some 16 000 sermons and ordained nearly 3000 ministers.

Most isolated The farthest any human has been removed from his nearest living fellow human is 3596·4 km *2233·2 miles* in the case of the Command Service Module pilot Alfred M. Worden on the US *Apollo 15* lunar mission of 30 Jul–1 Aug 1971.

Longest walks The first person reputed to have 'walked round the world' is George Matthew Schilling (USA) from 3 Aug 1897 to 1904, but the first verified achievement was by David Kunst (b. 1939, USA) from 20 Jun 1970 to 5 Oct 1974.

Tomas Carlos Pereira (b. Argentina, 16 Nov 1942) spent 10 years, from 6 Apr 1968 to 8 Apr 1978, walking 48 000 km *29 825 miles* around five continents. Steven Newman of Bethel, Ohio, USA spent four years, from 1 Apr 1983 to 1 Apr 1987, walking 36 200 km *22 500 miles* around the world, covering 20 countries and five continents.

Rick Hansen (b. Canada, 1957), who was paralysed from the waist down in 1973 as a result of a motor accident, wheeled his wheelchair over 40 074·06 km *24 901·55 miles* through four continents and 34 countries. He started his journey from Vancouver on 21 Mar 1985 and arrived back there on 22 May 1987.

George Meegan (b. 2 Oct 1952) from Rainham, Kent walked 30 431 km *19 019 miles* from Usuaia, the southern tip of South America, to Prudhoe Bay in northern Alaska, taking 2426 days from 26 Jan 1977 to 18 Sep 1983. He thus completed the first traverse of the western hemisphere.

Sean Eugene Maguire (USA; b. 15 Sep 1956) walked 11 791 km *7327 miles* from the Yukon River, north of Livengood, Alaska to Key West, Florida in 307 days, from 6 Jun 1978 to 9 Apr 1979. The trans-Canada (Halifax to Vancouver) record walk of 6057 km *3764 miles* is 96 days by Clyde McRae, aged 23, from 1 May to 4 Aug 1973. John Lees (b. 23 Feb 1945) of Brighton, E Sussex walked 4628 km *2876 miles* across the USA from City Hall, Los Angeles, California to City Hall, New York in 53 days 12 hr 15 min

(averaging 86·49 km *53·75 miles* a day) between 11 April and 3 Jun 1972.

Great Britain Vera Andrews set a record for the longest continuous walk in Britain, when she covered a total distance of 11 777 km *7318 miles* between 2 Jan and 24 Dec 1990, taking in all of the British Gas showrooms. She started and finished at her home town of Clacton-on-Sea, Essex. The longest such walk by a man is one of 11 341 km *7047 miles* around the British coast by Ron Bullen of Binbrook, Lincs from 1 Apr 1986 to 7 Feb 1987.

North Pole conquest The claims of the two Arctic explorers Dr Frederick Albert Cook (1865–1940) and Cdr (later Rear-Ad.) Robert Edwin Peary (1856–1920), of the US Naval Civil Engineering branch, to have reached the North Pole lack positive proof, and several recent surveys have produced conflicting conclusions. On excellent pack ice and modern sledges, Wally Herbert's 1968–9 expedition (see Arctic crossing, below) attained a best day's route mileage of 37 km *23 miles* in 15 hr. Cook (see above) claimed 41·8 km *26 miles* twice, while Peary claimed a surely unsustainable average of 61 km *38 miles* over eight consecutive days.

The first people definitely to have reached the North Pole at ground level — the exact point Lat. 90° 00′ 00″ N (± 300 metres) — were Pavel Afanasyevich Geordiyenko, Pavel Kononovich Sen'ko, Mikhail Mikhaylovich Somov and Mikhail Yemel'yenovich Ostrekin (all USSR), on 23 Apr 1948. They arrived and departed by air.

The earliest indisputable attainment of the North Pole by surface travel over the sea-ice took place at 3 p.m. (Central Standard Time) on 19 Apr 1968, when expedition leader Ralph Plaisted (US), accompanied by Walter Pederson, Gerald Pitzel and Jean Luc Bombardier, reached the pole after a 42-day trek in four skidoos (snowmobiles). Their arrival was independently verified 18 hr later by a US Air Force weather aircraft. The party returned by aircraft.

Naomi Uemura (1941–84), the Japanese explorer and mountaineer, became the first person to reach the North Pole in a solo trek across the Arctic ice cap at 4:45 a.m. GMT on 1 May 1978. He had travelled 725 km *450 miles*, setting out on 7 Mar from Cape Edward, Ellesmere Island in northern Canada. He averaged nearly 13 km *8 miles* per day with his sled *Aurora* drawn by 17 huskies. He also left by aircraft.

Dr Jean-Louis Etienne, aged 39, was the first to reach the Pole solo and without dogs, on 11 May 1986 after 63 days. On 20 Apr 1987 Fukashi Kazami, aged 36, of Tokyo, Japan reached the North Pole from Ward Hunt Island, northern Canada in 44 days, having started on his 250 cc motorcycle on 8 March. Both left by aircraft.

The first woman to set foot on the North Pole was Mrs Fran Phipps on 5 Apr 1971. Galina Aleksandrovna Lastovskaya (b. 1941) and Lilia Vladislavovna Minina (b. 1959) were crew members of the USSR atomic icebreaker *Arktika*, which reached the Pole on 17 Aug 1977.

South Pole conquest The first men to cross the Antarctic Circle (Lat. 66° 33′ S) were the 193 crew members of the *Resolution* (462 tons) (Capt. James Cook, RN (1728–79) and *Adventure* (336 tons) (Lt Tobias Furneaux) on 17 Jan 1773 at 39° E. The first person known to have sighted the Antarctic ice shelf was Capt. Thaddeus Thaddevich Bellingshausen (Russia) (1778–1852) on 27 Jan 1820 from the vessel *Vostock* accompanied by *Mirnyy*. The first people known to have sighted the mainland of the continent were Capt. William Smith (1790–1847) and Master Edward Bransfield, RN, in the brig *Williams*. They saw the peaks of Trinity Land three days later, on 30 Jan 1820.

The South Pole (alt. 2779 m *9186 ft* on ice and 102 m *336 ft* bedrock) was first reached at 11 a.m. on 14 Dec 1911 by a Norwegian party of five men led by Capt. Roald Engebereth Gravning Amundsen (1872–1928), after a 53-day march with dog sledges from the Bay of Whales, to which he had penetrated in the vessel *Fram*. Subsequent calculations showed that Olav Olavson Bjaaland and Helmer Hanssen probably passed within 400–600 m *1310–1970 ft* of the exact location of the South Pole. The other two members were Sverre H. Hassell (died 1928) and Oskar Wisting (died 1936).

The first woman to set foot on Antarctica was Mrs Karoline Mikkelsen on 20 Feb 1935. It was not until 11 Nov 1969 that a woman stood at the South Pole. On that day Lois Jones, Eileen McSaveney, Jean Pearson, Terry Lee Tickhill (all US), Kay Lindsay (Australia) and Pam Young (NZ) arrived by air at Amundsen-Scott station and walked to the exact point from there.

First to see both Poles The first people to see both Poles were Amundsen (see above) and Oskar Wisting when they flew aboard the airship *Norge* over the North Pole on 12 May 1926, having previously been to the South Pole on 14 Dec 1911.

First to visit both Poles Dr Albert Paddock Crary (US) (1911–87) reached the North Pole in a Dakota aircraft on 3 May 1952. On 12 Feb 1961 he arrived at the South Pole by Sno Cat on a scientific traverse party from the McMurdo Station.

First to walk to both Poles The first man to walk to both the North and the South Pole was Robert Swan (b. 1956). He led the three-man Footsteps of Scott expedition, which reached the South Pole on 11 Jan 1986, and three years later headed the eight-man Icewalk expedition, which arrived at the North Pole on 14 May 1989.

Arctic crossing The first crossing of the Arctic sea-ice was achieved by the British Trans-Arctic Expedition, which left Point Barrow, Alaska on 21 Feb 1968 and arrived at the Seven Island archipelago north-east of Spitzbergen 464 days later, on 29 May 1969. This involved a haul of 4699 km *2920 statute miles* with a drift of 1126 km *700 miles*, compared with the straight-line distance of 2674 km *1662 miles*. The team comprised Wally Herbert (leader), 34, Major Ken Hedges, RAMC, 34, Allan Gill, 38, and Dr Roy Koerner (glaciologist), 36, and 40 huskies. The only crossing achieved in a single season was that by Fiennes and Burton (see Polar circumnavigation, below) from Alert via the North Pole to the Greenland Sea in open snowmobiles. Both reached the North Pole and returned by land.

Antarctic crossing The first surface crossing of the Antarctic continent was completed at 1:47 p.m. on 2 Mar 1958, after a trek of 3473 km *2158 miles* lasting 99 days from 24 Nov 1957, from Shackleton Base to Scott Base via the Pole. The crossing party of 12 was led by Dr (now Sir) Vivian Ernest Fuchs (b. 11 Feb 1908). The 4185 km *2600 mile* trans-Antarctic leg from Sanae to Scott Base of the 1980–82 Trans-Globe Expedition was achieved in 67 days, from 28 Oct 1980 to 11 Jan 1981, having reached the South Pole on 15 Dec 1980. The three-man party on snowmobiles comprised Sir Ranulph Fiennes, Bt (b. 1944), Oliver Shepard and Charles Burton.

Polar circumnavigation The first polar circumnavigation was achieved by Sir Ranulph Fiennes, Bt and Charles Burton of the British Trans-Globe Expedition, who travelled south from Greenwich (2 Sep 1979), via the South Pole (15 Dec 1980) and the North Pole (10 Apr 1982), and back to Greenwich, arriving on 29 Aug 1982 after a 56 325 km *35 000 mile* trek.

Longest sledge journeys The longest totally self-supporting polar sledge journey ever made was one of 1738 km *1080 miles* from west to east across Greenland (now Kalaallit Nunaat) from 18 Jun to 5 Sep 1934 by Capt. M. Lindsay (later Sir Martin Lindsay of Dowhill) (1905–81), Lt Arthur S. T. Godfrey, RE (later Lt-Col., killed 1942), Andrew N. C. Croft (later Col.), and 49 dogs. The Ross Sea Party of ten (three died) sledged over 3220 km *2000 miles* in 300 days from 6 May 1915. The International Trans-Antarctic Expedition (six members) sledged a distance of some 3700 km *2300 miles* in 117 days from 7 Nov 1989 (Patriot Hills) to 3 Mar 1990 (Mirnyy). The journey had started at Seal Nunataks on 27 Jul 1989, but the dogs accompanying the expedition were flown out from Patriot Hills to South America for a period of rest before returning to the Antarctic. The expedition was supported by aircraft throughout its duration.

Greatest ocean descent The record ocean descent was achieved in the Challenger Deep of the Marianas Trench, 400 km *250 miles* south-west of Guam in the Pacific Ocean, when the Swiss-built US Navy bathyscaphe *Trieste*, manned by Dr Jacques Piccard (Switzerland) (b. 1914) and Lt Donald Walsh, USN reached a depth of 10 916 m *35 813 ft* at 1:10 p.m. on 23 Jan 1960 (see p. 11). The pressure of the water was 1183 kgf/cm² *16 883 lbf/in²* and the temperature 3° C *37·4° F*. The descent took 4 hr 48 min and the ascent 3 hr 17 min.

Deep-diving records The record depth for the extremely dangerous activity of breath-held diving is 107 m *351 ft* by Angela Bandini (Italy) off Elba, Italy on 3 Oct 1989. She was under water for 2 min 46 sec.

The record dive with scuba (self-contained under-water breathing apparatus) is 133 m *437 ft* by John J. Gruener and R. Neal Watson (US) off Freeport, Grand Bahama on 14 Oct 1968. For women it is 105·16 m *345 ft* by Marty Dunwoody (US) off Bimini, Bahama Islands on 20 Dec 1987.

The record dive utilizing gas mixtures (nitrogen, oxygen and helium) was a simulated dive of 685·8 m *2250 ft* in a dry chamber by Stephen Porter, Len Whitlock and Erik Kramer at Duke University Medical Center in Durham, North Carolina, USA on 3 Feb 1981, in a 43-day trial in a sphere of 2·43 m *8 ft*.

A team of six divers (four Comex and two French Navy) descended and worked efficiently during a period of six days to a depth of 520 m *1706 ft* off Marseilles, France, as part of the Hydra VIII operation in the spring of 1988. This involved the use of 'hydreliox', a synthetic breathing mixture containing a high percentage of hydrogen. Arnaud de Nechaud de Feral performed a saturation dive of 73 days from 9 Oct–21 Dec 1989 in a hyperbaric chamber simulating a depth of 300 m *985 ft*, as part of the Hydra IX operation carried out by Comex at Marseilles, France. He was breathing 'hydrox', a mixture of hydrogen and oxygen.

Deepest underwater escapes The deepest underwater rescue ever achieved was of the *Pisces III*, in which Roger R. Chapman (28), and Roger Mallinson (35), were trapped for 76 hours when it sank to 480 m *1575 ft*, 240 km *150 miles* south-east of Cork, Republic of Ireland on 29 Aug 1973. It was hauled to the surface on 1 September by the cable ship *John Cabot* after work by *Pisces V*, *Pisces II* and the remote-control recovery vessel US CURV. The greatest depth from which an actual escape without any equipment has been made is 68·58 m *225 ft*, by Richard A. Slater from the rammed submersible *Nekton Beta* off Catalina Island, California, USA on 28 Sep 1970. The record for an escape with equipment was by Norman Cooke and Hamish Jones on 22 Jul 1987. During a naval exercise they escaped from a depth of 183 m *601 ft* from the submarine HMS *Otus* in Bjornefjorden, off Bergen, Norway. They were wearing standard suits with a built-in lifejacket, from which air expanding during the ascent passes into a hood over the escaper's head.

Deepest salvage The greatest depth at which salvage has been successfully carried out is 5029 m *16 500 ft*. The bathyscaphe *Trieste II* (Lt-Cdr Mel Bartels, USN) was used to attach cables to an 'electronic package' on the sea bed 645 km *400 miles* north of Hawaii on 20 May 1972.

The deepest salvage operation ever achieved with divers was on the wreck of HM cruiser *Edinburgh*, sunk on 2 May 1942 in the Barents Sea off northern Norway, inside the Arctic Circle, in 244·7 m *803 ft* of water. Over 32 days (from 17 Sep–7 Oct 1981), 12 divers dived on the wreck in pairs, using a bell from the *Stephaniturm* (1446 tonnes), under the direction of former RN officer Michael Stewart. A total of 460 gold ingots (the only 100 per cent salvage to date) was recovered, John Rossier being the first person to touch the gold.

Greatest penetration into the earth The deepest penetration made into the ground by human beings is in the

Best man
The world champion 'best man' is Ting Ming Siong, from Sibu, Sarawak, in Malaysia, who officiated for the 658th time since 1976 in April 1991.

Youngest married
It was reported in 1986 that an 11-month-old boy was married to a 3-month-old girl in Bangladesh to end a 20-year feud between two families over a disputed farm.

Longest engagement
The longest engagement on record was between Octavio Guillen and Adriana Martinez. They finally took the plunge after 67 years in June 1969 in Mexico City. Both were then aged 82.

Most married
Ralph and Patsy Martin of Quartzsite, Arizona, USA have married each other a total of 51 times, their first wedding having been in 1960. Richard and Carole Roble of South Hempstead, New York, USA have also married each other 51 times, with their first wedding being in 1969. Both couples have chosen different locations each time.

Western Deep Levels Mine at Carletonville, Transvaal, South Africa, where a record depth of 3581 m *11 749 ft* was attained on 12 Jul 1977. The virgin rock temperature at this depth is 55° C *131° F*.

Shaft-sinking record The one-month (31 days) world record is 381·3 m *1251 ft* for a standard shaft 7·92 m *26 ft* in diameter at Buffelsfontein Mine, Transvaal, South Africa, in March 1962.

The British record of 131·2 m *430 ft* for a shaft 7·92 m *26 ft* in diameter was set in No. 2 Shaft of the NCB's Whitemoor Mine near Selby, N Yorks in 31 days (15 Nov–16 Dec 1982).

Most marriages The greatest number of marriages contracted by one person in the monogamous world is 27 by former Baptist minister Glynn 'Scotty' Wolfe (b. 25 Jul 1908) of Blythe, California, USA, who first married in 1927. His latest wife is Daisy Delgado (b. 29 Dec 1970), a Filipino from Liloan, Cebu. His total number of children is, he believes, 41.

The greatest number of monogamous marriages by a woman is 21 by Linda Lou Essex of Anderson, Indiana, USA. She has been married to 15 different men since 1957, divorcing the last one in 1988.

The record for bigamous marriages is 104 by Giovanni Vigliotto, one of many aliases used by either Fred Jipp (b. New York City, 3 Apr 1936) or Nikolai Peruskov (b. Siracusa, Sicily, 3 Apr 1929) during 1949–81 in 27 US states and 14 other countries. Four victims were aboard one ship in 1968 and two in London. On 28 Mar 1983 in Phoenix, Arizona, USA he received 28 years for fraud and six for bigamy, and was fined $336 000.

In Britain, the only woman to contract eight legal marriages is Olive Joyce Wilson of Marston Green, Birmingham, W Mids. She has consecutively been Mrs John Bickley; Mrs Don Trethowan; Mrs George Hundley; Mrs Raymond Ward; Mrs Harry Latrobe; Mrs Leslie Harris; Mrs Ray Richards, and is now Mrs John Grassick. All were divorced except Mr Hundley, who died.

Oldest bride and bridegroom The oldest recorded bridegroom has been Harry Stevens, aged 103, who married Thelma Lucas, 84, at the Caravilla Retirement Home, Wisconsin, USA on 3 Dec 1984. The oldest recorded bride is Minnie Munro, aged 102, who married Dudley Reid, 83, at Point Clare, New South Wales, Australia on 31 May 1991.

The British record was set by Sir Robert Mayer (1879–1985), who married Jacqueline Noble, 51, in London on 10 Nov 1980 when aged 101 years. Mrs Winifred Clark (b. 13 Nov 1871) became Britain's oldest recorded bride when she married Albert Smith, 80, at St Hugh's Church, Cantley, S Yorks the day before her 100th birthday.

Longest marriage The longest recorded marriages were both of 86 years. Sir Temulji Bhicaji Nariman and Lady Nariman, who were married from 1853 to 1940, were cousins and the marriage took place when both were aged five. Sir Temulji (b. 3 Sep 1848) died, aged 91 years 11 months, in August 1940 at Bombay, India. Lazarus Rowe (b. Greenland, New Hampshire, USA in 1725) and Molly Webber were recorded as marrying in 1743. He died first in 1829, also after 86 years of marriage.

The British record is for a marriage of 82 years between James Frederick Burgess (b. 3 Mar 1861, died 27 Nov 1966) and his wife

Sarah Ann, *née* Gregory (b. 11 Jul 1865, died 22 Jun 1965). They were married on 21 Jun 1883 at St James's, Bermondsey, London.

Golden weddings The greatest number of golden weddings in a family is 10, the six sons and four daughters of Joseph and Sophia Gresl of Manitowoc, Wisconsin, USA all celebrating golden weddings between April 1962 and September 1988, and the six sons and four daughters of George and Eleonora Hopkins of Patrick County, Virginia, USA all celebrating their golden weddings between November 1961 and October 1988.

The British record is seven, the three sons and four daughters of Mr and Mrs J. Stredwick of East Sussex all celebrating their golden weddings between May 1971 and April 1981.

Mass ceremony The largest mass wedding ceremony was one of 6516 couples officiated over by Sun Myung Moon (b. 1920) of the Holy Spirit Association for the Unification of World Christianity at a factory near Seoul, South Korea on 30 Oct 1988.

Most expensive wedding The wedding of Mohammed, son of Shaik Rashid Bin Saeed Al Maktoum, to Princess Salama in Dubai in May 1981 lasted sevn days and cost an estimated £22 million. It was held in a purpose-built stadium for 20 000 people.

Oldest divorced On 2 Feb 1984 a divorce was granted in Milwaukee, Wisconsin, USA to Ida Stern, aged 91, and her husband Simon, 97. The British age record for divorce is 101 years, held by Harry Bidwell of Brighton, E Sussex. He was divorced on 21 Nov 1980 from a younger wife.

Banquets It was estimated that some 30 000 guests attended a military feast given at Radewitz, Poland on 25 Jun 1730 by King August II (1709–33).

The greatest number of people served indoors at a single sitting was 18 000 municipal leaders at the Palais de l'Industrie, Paris, France on 18 Aug 1889.

At the wedding of cousins Menachem Teitelbaum and Brucha Sima Melsels at Uniondale, Long Island, New York City, USA on 5 Dec 1984, the attendance of the Satmar sect of Hasidic Jews was estimated to be 17–20 000.

The most expensive menu ever served was for the main banquet at the Imperial Iranian 2500th Anniversary gathering at Persepolis in October 1971. The feast, which lasted 5½ hours, comprised quails' eggs stuffed with Iranian caviar, a mousse of crayfish tails in Nantua sauce, stuffed rack of roast lamb, a main course of roast peacock stuffed with *foie gras*, fig rings and raspberry sweet champagne sherbet. The wines included *Château Lafite-Rothschild* 1945 at £40 (now £235) per bottle from Maxime's, Paris.

Dining out The world champion for eating out is Fred E. Magel of Chicago, Illinois, USA, who since 1928 has dined out 46 000 times in 60 countries as a restaurant grader. He claims that the restaurant which served the largest helpings was Zehnder's Hotel, Frankenmuth, Michigan, USA. Mr Magel's favourite dishes are South African rock lobster and mousse of fresh English strawberries.

The greatest altitude at which a formal meal has been held is 6768 m *22 205 ft*, at the top of Mt Huascaran, Peru, when nine members of the Ansett Social Climbers from Sydney, Australia scaled the moun-

tain on 28 Jun 1989 with a dining table, chairs, wine and three-course meal. At the summit they put on top hats, thermal black ties and balldresses for their dinner party, which was marred only by the fact that the wine turned to ice.

Party-giving The International Year of the Child children's party in Hyde Park, London on 30–31 May 1979 was attended by the royal family and 160 000 children.

The world's biggest birthday party was attended by an estimated 35 000 people at Louisville, Kentucky, USA on 8 Sep 1979 to celebrate the 89th birthday of Col. Harland Sanders, the founder of Kentucky Fried Chicken. The largest in Britain was attended by an estimated 10 000 people on 5 Aug 1989 at Douglas, Isle of Man. The party was held to mark the 50th birthday of Trevor Baines, a well-known local businessman.

The largest Christmas party ever staged was that thrown by the Boeing Co. in the 65 000-seat Kingdome, Seattle, Washington State, USA. The party was held in two parts on 15 Dec 1979, and a total of 103 152 people attended.

During St Patrick's week of 11–17 Mar 1985, Houlihan's Old Place hosted St Pat's Parties at the 48 Kansas City, Missouri based Gilbert/Robinson restaurants, for a total of 206 854 documented guests.

Lecture fees Dr Ronald Dante was paid $3 080 000 for lecturing students on hypnotherapy at a two-day course held in Chicago, USA on 1–2 Jun 1986. He was teaching for 8 hours each day, and thus earned $192 500 per hour.

Longest pension Miss Millicent Barclay was born on 10 Jul 1872, three months after the death of her father, Col. William Barclay, and became eligible for a Madras Military Fund pension to continue until her marriage. She died unmarried on 26 Oct 1969, having drawn the pension for every day of her life of 97 years 3 months.

Medical families The four sons and five daughters of Dr Antonio B. Vicencio of Los Angeles, California, USA all qualified as doctors during the period 1964–82. Eight sons of John Robertson of Benview, Dumbarton, Strathclyde graduated as medical doctors between 1892 and 1914. The Maurice family of Marlborough, Wilts have had the same medical practice for six generations since 1792.

Miscellaneous Endeavours

It is intended to continue the process of phasing out the record categories in the 'Human Achievements' chapter where the duration of the event is the only criterion for inclusion. If you are planning an attempt on an endurance marathon you should contact us at a very early stage to check whether that category is likely to be retained in future editions of the book.

Accordion playing Ted Larkin, alias 'The Great Garibaldi', played an accordion for 90 hr from 4–8 Jun 1991 at the Elephant and Castle Shopping Centre, London.

Bag carrying In the greatest non-stop bag carrying feat, 50·8 kg *1 cwt* of household coal in an open bag was carried 54·7 km *34 miles* by Neil Sullivan, 37, of Small Heath, Birmingham, in 12 hr 45 min on 24 May 1986.

The record for the 1012·5 m *1107·2 yd* course at the annual Gawthorpe, W Yorks race is 4 min 6 sec by David Jones on 1 Apr 1991.

Barrel rolling The record for rolling a full 36-gallon metal beer barrel over a measured mile is 8 min 7·2 sec, by Phillip Randle, Steve Hewitt, John Round, Trevor Bradley, Colin Barnes and Ray Glover of Haunchwood Collieries Institute and Social Club, Nuneaton, Warks on 15 Aug 1982. A team of 10 rolled a 63½ kg *140 lb* barrel 240·35 km *150 miles* in 30 hr 31 min in Chlumčany, Czechoslovakia on 27–28 Oct 1982.

Barrow pushing The heaviest loaded one-wheeled barrow pushed for a minimum 60·96 level metres *200 level feet* was one loaded with bricks weighing a gross 3·753 tonnes *8275 lb*. It was pushed a distance of 74·06 m *243 ft* by John Sarich at London, Ontario, Canada on 19 Feb 1987.

Barrow racing The fastest time attained in a 1·6 km *1 mile* wheelbarrow race is 4 min 48·51 sec, by Piet Pitzer and Jaco Erasmus at the Transvalia High School, Vanderbijlpark, South Africa on 3 Oct 1987. Brothers-in-law Malcolm Shipley and Adrian Freebury pushed each other from John o' Groats to Land's End for charity in 30 days from 28 Jul–26 Aug 1980.

Bath tub racing The record for a 57·9 km *36 mile* bath tub race is 1 hr 22 min 27 sec, by Greg Mutton at the Grafton Jacaranda Festival, New South Wales, Australia on 8 Nov 1987. Tubs are limited to 1·90 m *75 in* and 4·5 kW *6 hp* motors. The greatest distance for paddling a hand-propelled bath tub in 24 hr is 145·6 km *90½ miles*, by 13 members of Aldington Prison Officers Social Club, near Ashford, Kent on 28–29 May 1983.

Baton twirling The greatest number of complete spins done between tossing a baton into the air and catching it is 10 by Donald Garcia, on the BBC *Record Breakers* programme on 9 Dec 1986.

The record for women is seven, by Lisa Fedick on the same programme, Joanne Holloway, at the UK National Baton Twirling Association Championships in Paignton, Devon on 29 Oct 1987 and Rachel Hayes on 18 Sep 1988, also later shown on the BBC *Record Breakers* programme.

Bed making The pair record for making a bed with 1 blanket, 2 sheets, an undersheet, an uncased pillow, 1 counterpane and 'hospital' corners is 17·3 sec, by Sister Sharon Stringer and Nurse Michelle Benkel of the Royal Masonic Hospital, London on 19 Sep 1990, shown on BBC TV's *Record Breakers* programme.

The record time for one person to make a bed is 28·2 sec, by Wendy Wall, 34, of Hebersham, Sydney, Australia on 30 Nov 1978.

Bed pushing The longest recorded push of a normally sessile object is of 5204 km *3233 miles 1150 yd*, in the case of a wheeled hospital bed by a team of nine employees of Bruntsfield Bedding Centre, Edinburgh from 21 Jun–26 Jul 1979.

Bed race The record time for the annual Knaresborough Bed Race (established 1966) in N Yorks is 12 min 9 sec for the 3·27 km *2 mile 63 yd* course crossing the River Nidd by the Vibroplant team on 9 Jun 1990. The course record for the 16·09 km *10 mile* Chew Valley Lake race (established 1977) in Avon is 50 min, by the Westbury Harriers' three-man bed team.

Beer keg lifting Tommy Gaskin raised a keg of beer weighing 62·5 kg *137·79 lb* above his head 656 times in the space of 6 hr at Newry, Co. Down on 28 Oct 1989.

Beer mat flipping Dean Gould of Felixstowe, Suffolk flipped and caught a pile of 102 mats (1·2 mm thick 490 gsm wood pulp board) through 180 degrees in Hamburg, Germany on 18 Mar 1988.

Beer stein carrying Barmaid Rosie Schedelbauer covered a distance of 15 m *49 ft 2½ in* in 4 sec with five full steins in each hand in a televised contest at Königssee, Germany on 29 Jun 1981.

Brick lifting Russell Bradley of Worcester lifted 30 bricks laid side by side off a table, raising them to chest height and holding them there for two seconds on 17 Nov 1990. The greatest weight of bricks lifted was also by Russell Bradley on the

same day, when he succeeded in lifting 26 far heavier bricks weighing a total of 86 kg *189 lb 9 oz*, again holding them for two seconds.

Bubble David Stein of New York City, USA created a 15·24 m *50 ft* long bubble on 6 Jun 1988. He made the bubble using a bubble wand, washing-up liquid and water.

Bubble-gum blowing The greatest reported diameter for a bubble-gum bubble under the strict rules of this highly competitive activity is 55·8 cm *22 in*, by Susan Montgomery Williams of Fresno, California, USA in June 1985.

The British record is 42 cm *16½ in* by Nigel Fell, 13, from Derryaghy, Co. Antrim in November 1979. This was equalled by John Smith of Willingham, Cambs on 25 Sep 1983.

Catapulting The greatest recorded distance for a catapult shot is 415 m *1362 ft* by James M. Pfotenhauer, using a patented 5·22 m *17 ft 1½ in* Monarch IV Supershot and a 53-calibre lead musket ball on Ski Hill Road, Escanaba, Michigan, USA on 10 Sep 1977.

Cigar box balancing Bruce Block balanced 213 cigar boxes (without modification) on his chin for 9·2 sec at the Guinness World of Records exhibition, London

■ **Bed race**
The record time for the annual Knaresborough Bed Race (established 1966) in N Yorks is 12 min 9 sec for the 3·27 km 2 mile 63 yd course. It was set by the Vibroplant team on 9 Jun 1990. This picture shows the drama of negotiating the River Nidd.

■ **Bubble**
David Stein of New York City, USA created a 15·24 m 50 ft long bubble on 6 Jun 1988. He made the bubble using a bubble wand, washing-up liquid and water. (Photo: Gelman & Gray/Lowry)

■ **Cigar box balancing**

■ **Field to loaf**
The fastest time for producing 13 loaves (a baker's dozen) from growing wheat is 23 min 49 sec, by Tendring Hundred Farmers' Club and bakers from Read Woodrow Ltd at St Osyth, Essex on 16 Aug 1990.

on 5 Nov 1990, later shown on the BBC *Record Breakers* programme.

Crate climbing Neville Stokes stacked 29 beer crates in a single column and climbed up them to a height of 7·37 m *24 ft 2 in* at Sowerby Bridge, West Yorks on 27 Aug 1990.

Crawling The longest continuous voluntary crawl (progression with one or other knee in unbroken contact with the ground) on record is 45·87 km *28½ miles*, by Reg Morris of Walsall, W Mids on 29 Jul 1988. The crawl took place on a measured course 2·41 km *1½ miles* long. It took 9 ½ hr and 19 laps of the track to gain the record. Over a space of 15 months ending on 9 Mar 1985, Jagdish Chander, 32, crawled 1400 km *870 miles* from Aligarh to Jamma, India to propitiate his favourite Hindu goddess, Mata.

Drumming Four hundred separate drums were played in 31·78 sec by Rory Blackwell at Finlake Country Park, Chudleigh, Devon on 30 May 1988.

Ducks and drakes (stone skipping) The record is 29 skips (14 plinkers and 15 pitty-pats), by Arthur Ring, 69, at Midway Beach, California, USA on 4 Aug 1984 and Jerdone 'Jerry' McGhee, 42, at Wimberley, Texas, USA on 18 Nov 1986.

Egg and spoon racing Dale Lyons of Meriden, W Mids ran 48·1 km *29·9 miles* while carrying a dessert spoon with a fresh egg on it in 4 hr 18 min on 23 Apr 1990.

Escapology A manufacturer of straitjackets acknowledges that an escapologist 'skilled in the art of bone and muscle

manipulation' could escape from a standard jacket in seconds. There are, however, methods by which such circumvention can itself be circumvented. Nick Janson of Benfleet, Essex has escaped from handcuffs locked on him by more than 1400 different police officers since 1954.

Faux pas If measured by financial consequence, the greatest *faux pas* on record was that of the young multi-millionaire James Gordon Bennett (1841–1918), committed on 1 Jan 1877 at the family mansion of his demure fiancée, one Caroline May, in Fifth Avenue, New York, USA. Bennett arrived in a two-horse cutter late and obviously in wine. By dint of intricate footwork, he gained the portals to enter the withdrawing room, where he was the cynosure of all eyes. He mistook the fireplace for a plumbing fixture more usually reserved for another purpose. The May family broke the engagement and Bennett was obliged to spend the rest of his foot-loose and fancy-free life based in Paris with the resultant non-collection of millions of dollars in tax by the US Treasury.

Field to loaf The fastest time for producing 13 loaves (a baker's dozen) from growing wheat is 23 min 49 sec, by Tendring Hundred Farmers' Club and bakers from Read Woodrow Ltd at St Osyth, Essex on 16 Aug 1990.

Grape catching The greatest distance at which a grape thrown from level ground has been caught in the mouth is 99·82 m *327 ft 6 in* by Paul J. Tavilla at East Boston, Massachusetts, USA on 27 May 1991. It was thrown by James Deady.

Guitar playing The fastest guitar playing ever was by Rick Raven (b. Gary Clarke), who played 5400 notes in a minute at the Jacobean Nite Club, Stockport, Greater Manchester on 27 Apr 1989.

Handbell ringing The longest recorded handbell ringing recital has been one of 60 hr 3 min, by 12 handbell ringers of Ecclesfield School, Sheffield, S Yorks from 21–23 Oct 1989.

Hitch-hiking The title of world champion hitch-hiker is claimed by Bill Heid of Allen Park, Michigan, USA who since 1964 has obtained free rides of 579 510 km *360 100 miles*.

The hitch-hiking record for the 1406 km *874 miles* from Land's End, Cornwall to John o' Groats, Highland is 17 hr 8 min by Martin Clark and Graham Beynon of Guildford, Surrey on 14–15 Sep 1987. The fastest time recorded for the round trip is

39 hr 28 min by Alan Carter of Gloucester from 14–16 May 1991.

Hop-scotch The greatest number of games of hop-scotch successfully completed in 24 hr is 307 by Ashrita Furman of Jamaica, New York, USA in Zürich, Switzerland on 5–6 Apr 1991.

Human centipede The largest 'human centipede' to move 30 m *98 ft 5 in* (with ankles firmly tied together) consisted of 1148 students and staff of University College Dublin, Republic of Ireland as part of UCD Science Day on 20 Feb 1991. Not one single person fell over in the course of the walk.

Kissing Alfred A.E. Wolfram of New Brighton, Minnesota, USA kissed 8001 women in 8 hr at the Minnesota Rennaissance Festival on 15 Sep 1990.

Knitting The world's most prolific hand-knitter of all time has been Mrs Gwen Matthewman of Featherstone, W Yorks. She attained a speed of 111 stitches per min in a test at Phildar's Wool Shop, Central Street, Leeds, W Yorks on 29 Sep 1980. Her technique has been filmed by the world's only Professor of Knitting — a Japanese.

Knot-tying The fastest recorded time for tying the six Boy Scout Handbook Knots (square knot, sheet bend, sheep shank,

■ **Field to loaf**

clove hitch, round turn and two half hitches, and bowline) on individual ropes is 8·1 sec by Clinton R. Bailey, Sr, 52, of Pacific City, Oregon, USA on 13 Apr 1977.

Land rowing The greatest distance covered by someone on a land rowing machine is 5278·5 km *3280 miles* by Rob Bryant of Fort Worth, Texas, USA, who 'rowed' across the USA. He left Los Angeles, California on 2 Apr 1990, reaching Washington, DC on 30 July.

Leap-frogging The greatest distance covered was 1429·2 km *888·1 miles* by 14 members of the class of 1988 of Hanover High School, in Hanover, New Hampshire, USA, who started leap-frogging on 10 Jun 1988 and stopped 189 hr 49 min later, on 18 Jun 1988.

Litter collection The greatest number of volunteers involved in collecting litter in one location on one day is 18 413, along the coastline of Florida, USA on 22 Sep 1990 as part of the Center for Marine Conservation's National Beach Cleanup programme.

Log rolling The record number of International Championships won is 10, by Jubiel Wickheim of Shawnigan Lake, British Columbia, Canada, between 1956 and 1969. At Albany, Oregon, USA on 4 Jul 1956 Wickheim rolled on a 35·5 cm *14 in* log against Chuck Harris of Kelso, Washington State, USA for 2 hr 40 min before losing. The youngest international log-rolling champion is Cari Ann Hayer (b. 23 Jun 1977), who won her first championship on 15 Jul 1984 at Hayward, Wisconsin, USA.

Merry-go-round The greatest distance travelled on a merry-go-round is 3962 km *2462 miles* by 14 people at the Mississippi–Alabama State Fair, Meridian, USA from 21 Sep–7 Oct 1990.

Milk bottle balancing The greatest distance walked by a person continuously balancing a full pint milk bottle on the head is 70·3 km *43·7 miles* around a track at a park in New York City, USA by Ashrita Furman on 12 Aug 1990.

Milk crate balancing Frank Charles balanced 24 milk crates, with a total weight of 33·6 kg *74 lb*, on his chin for 19 sec at Leyton Youth Centre, London on 30 Jul 1988.

Musical chairs The largest game on record was one starting with 8238 participants, ending with Xu Chong Wei on the last chair, which was held at the Anglo-Chinese School, Singapore on 5 Aug 1989.

Needle threading The record number of times that a strand of cotton has been threaded through a number 13 needle (eye 12·7 mm × 1·6 mm *1/2 in × 1/16 in*) in 2 hr is 7238, set by Brajesh Shrivastava at Gautam Nagar, Bhopal, India on 12 Dec 1990.

Oyster opening The record for opening oysters is 100 in 2 min 20·07 sec, by Mike Racz in Invercargill, New Zealand on 16 Jul 1990.

Pogo stick jumping The greatest number of jumps achieved is 130 077, by Gary Stewart in Reading, Ohio, USA on 8–9 Mar 1985. Ashrita Furman of Jamaica, New York, USA set a distance record of 21·02 km *13·06 miles* in 5 hr 23 min on 15 Sep 1989 in New York City, USA.

Pram pushing The greatest distance covered in pushing a pram in 24 hr is 563·62 km *350·23 miles* by 60 members of the Oost-Vlanderen branch of Amnesty International at Lede, Belgium on 15 Oct 1988. A

ten-man team from the Royal Marines School of Music, Deal, Kent, with an adult 'baby', covered a distance of 437·2 km *271·7 miles* in 24 hr from 22–23 Nov 1990.

Riding in armour The longest recorded ride in armour is one of 334·7 km *208 miles* by Dick Brown, who left Edinburgh, Lothian on 10 Jun 1989 and arrived in his home town of Dumfries, Dumfries & Galloway four days later. His total riding time was 35 hr 25 min.

Ring pull chain The longest ring pull chain was 40·25 km *30 miles* long, and consisted of 2 067 692 ring pulls. The chain, which weighed 0·75 tonne, was made between February and May 1990 and was shown on 28 May 1990 on the ITV *Telethon '90* programme.

Rope slide The greatest distance recorded in a rope slide is from the top of Blackpool Tower, Lancs — a height of 138·66 m *454 ft 11 in* — to a fixed point 373·33 m *1120 ft* from the base of the tower. Set up by the Royal Marines, the rope was descended on 8 Sep 1989 by Sgt Alan Heward and Cpl Mick Heap of the Royal Marines, John Herbert of Blackpool Tower, and Cheryl Baker and Roy Castle of the BBC *Record Breakers* programme. The total length descended was 366·4 m *1202 ft*.

Shorthand The highest recorded speeds ever attained under championship conditions are 300 words per min (99·64 per cent accuracy) for five minutes and 350 wpm (99·72 per cent accuracy, that is, two insignificant errors) for two minutes by Nathan Behrin (US) in tests in New York in December 1922. Behrin (b. 1887) used the Pitman system, invented in 1837. Morris I. Kligman, official court reporter of the US Court House, New York has taken 50 000 words in 5 hr (a sustained rate of 166·6 wpm). Rates are much dependent upon the nature, complexity and syllabic density of the material. Mr G.W. Bunbury of Dublin, Ireland held the unique distinction of writing at 250 wpm for 10 minutes on 23 Jan 1894. Mr Arnold Bradley achieved a speed of 309 wpm without error using the Sloan-

Duployan system, with 1545 words in 5 minutes in a test in Walsall, W Mids on 9 Nov 1920.

Spitting Randy Ober of Bentonville, Arkansas, USA spat a tobacco wad 14·50 m *47 ft 7 in* at the Calico 5th Annual Tobacco Chewing and Spitting Championships, held north of Barstow, California on 4 Apr 1982. The record for projecting a water-melon seed is 20·96 m *68 ft 9¼ in* by Lee Wheelis at Luling, Texas, USA on 24 Jun 1989. The greatest recorded distance for a cherry stone is 22·14 m *72 ft 7½ in*, by Rick Krause at Eau Claire, Michigan, USA on 2 Jul 1988.

String ball, largest The largest ball of string on record is one of 3·88 m *12 ft 9 in* in diameter, 12·19 m *40 ft* in circumference and weighing 10 tonnes, amassed by Francis A. Johnson of Darwin, Minnesota, USA between 1950 and 1978.

Talking (After-dinner speeches) The longest recorded after-dinner speeches both lasted 46 hr 10 min, and were given by Charles Garavan and Shaymus Kennedy in separate locations at University College Dublin, Republic of Ireland from 5–7 Dec 1990. Historically the longest recorded after-dinner speech before *unsuspecting* victims was one of 3 hr by Rev. Henry Whitehead (died March 1896) at the Rainbow Tavern, Fleet Street, London on 16 Jan 1874.

Tightrope walking The greatest 19th-century tightrope walker was Jean-François Gravelet, alias Charles Blondin (1824–97), of France, who made the earliest crossing of the Niagara Falls on a 76 mm *3 in* rope, 335 m *1100 ft* long, 48·75 m *160 ft* above the Falls on 30 Jun 1859. He also made a crossing with Harry Colcord pick-a-back on 15 Sep 1860. Though other artistes still find it difficult to believe, Colcord was his agent.

The oldest wirewalker was 'Professor' William Ivy Baldwin (1866–1953), who crossed the South Boulder Canyon, Colorado, USA on a 97·5 m *320 ft* wire with a 38·1 m *125 ft* drop on his 82nd birthday on 31 Jul 1948.

■ **Merry-go-round**
The greatest distance travelled on a merry-go-round is 3962 km 2462 miles by 14 people at the Mississippi–Alabama State Fair, Meridian, Mississippi, USA from 21 Sep–7 Oct 1990. Most of the record holders are in this picture at the scene of their successful attempt.

Litter bin
The world's largest litter bin was made by Glasdon UK Ltd of Blackpool, Lancs for 'Spring Clean Day' on 29 Mar 1990. The 5·64 m *18 ft 6 in* tall replica of their standard 'Topsy' bin has a capacity of 26 000 litres *5719 gal.*

Armour
The highest auction price paid for a suit of armour was £1 925 000, by B.H. Trupin on 5 May 1983 at Sotheby's, London for a suit made in Milan by Giovanni Negroli in 1545 for Henri II of France. It came from the Hever Castle Collection in Kent.

Condiment, rarest
The world's most prized condiment is Cà Cuong, a secretion recovered in minute amounts from beetles in North Vietnam. Owing to war conditions, the price had risen to $100 per 28 g *1 oz* before supplies virtually ceased in 1975.

Dish
The largest item on any menu in the world is roasted camel, prepared occasionally for Bedouin wedding feasts. Cooked eggs are stuffed into fish, the fish stuffed into cooked chickens, the chickens stuffed into a roasted sheep's carcass and the sheep stuffed into a whole camel.

The world tightrope endurance record is 185 days, by Henri Rochatain (b. 1926) of France, on a wire 120 m *394 ft* long, 25 m *82 ft* above a supermarket in Saint Etienne, France from 28 Mar–29 Sep 1973. His ability to sleep on the wire has left doctors puzzled.

Ashley Brophy of Neilborough, Victoria, Australia walked 11·57 km *7·18 miles* on a wire 45 m *147·64 ft* long and 10 m *32·81 ft* above the ground at the Adelaide Grand Prix, Australia on 1 Nov 1985 in 3½ hr.

Steve McPeak (b. 21 Apr 1945) of Las Vegas, Nevada, USA ascended the 46·6 mm *1·83 in* diameter Zugspitzbahn cable on the Zugspitze, Germany for a vertical height of 705 m *2313 ft* in three stints aggregating 5 hr 4 min on 24, 25 and 28 Jun 1981. The maximum gradient over the stretch of 2282 m *7485 ft* was more than 30 degrees.

The greatest drop over which anyone has walked on a tightrope is 3150 m *10 335 ft*, above the French countryside, by Michel Menin of Lons-le-Saunier, France, on 4 Aug 1989.

Typewriting The world duration record for typewriting on an electric machine is 264 hr, set by Violet Gibson Burns at the Royal Easter Show, Sydney, Australia from 29 Mar–9 Apr 1985. The longest duration in a typing marathon on a manual machine is 142 hr 50 min, by M. Kanagasundaram of Dindigul, India, from 25–31 Jul 1990. His marathon consisted of nearly 916 000 strokes.

Les Stewart of Mudjimba Beach, Queensland, Australia has typed the numbers 1 to 685 000 in *words* on 13 590 quarto sheets as of 5 Mar 1991. His target is to become a 'millionaire'.

The highest recorded speeds attained with a ten-word penalty per error on a manual machine are:

Five Min: 176 wpm net Mrs Carole Forristall Waldschlager Bechen at Dixon, Illinois, USA on 2 Apr 1959. One Hour: 147 wpm net Albert Tangora (US) (Underwood Standard), 22 Oct 1923.

The official hour record on an electric typewriter is 9316 words (40 errors) on an IBM machine, giving a net rate of 149 words per min, by Margaret Hamma, now Mrs Dilmore (US), in Brooklyn, New York, USA on 20 Jun 1941. In an official test in 1946, Stella Pajunas, now Mrs Garnard, attained a rate of 216 words in a minute on an IBM machine.

Mary Ann Morel (South Africa) set a numerical record at the CABEX '85 Exhibition in Johannesburg, South Africa on 6 Feb 1985 by typing spaced numbers from 1 to 781 in 5 min.

Unsupported circle The highest recorded number of people who have demonstrated the physical paradox of all being seated without a chair is an unsupported circle of 10 323 employees of the Nissan Motor Co. at Komazawa Stadium, Tokyo, Japan on 23 Oct 1982. The British record is 7402 participants at Goodwood Airfield, W Sussex on 25 May 1986, as part of a Sport Aid event.

Whip cracking The longest stock whip ever 'cracked' is one of 42·67 m *140 ft* (excluding the handle), wielded by Gary Brophy at Adelaide, Australia on 1 Nov 1985.

Writing, minuscule In 1926 an account was published of Alfred McEwen's pantograph record in which the 56-word version of the Lord's Prayer was written by diamond point on glass in the space of 0·04 × 0·02 mm *0·0016 × 0·0008 in.*

Frederick C. Watts of Felmingham, Norfolk demonstrated for photographers on 24 Jan 1968 his ability, without mechanical or optical aid, to write the Lord's Prayer 34 times (9452 letters) within the size of a definitive UK postage stamp, viz. 21·33 × 18·03 mm *0·84 × 0·71 in.*

Pan Xixing of Wuxi, China wrote 'True friendship is like sound health, the value of which is seldom known until it be lost (Proverb)' twice on a human hair in March 1990.

Surendra Apharya of Jaipur, India succeeded in writing 1314 characters (names of various countries, towns and regions) on a single grain of rice on 28 Feb 1991.

Yo-yo A yo-yo was a toy in Grecian times and is depicted on a bowl dated 450 BC. It was also a Filipino jungle fighting weapon recorded in the 16th century, weighing 1·81 kg *4 lb* with a 6 m *20 ft* thong. The word means 'come-come'. Though illustrated in a book in 1891 as a bandalore, the craze did not begin until Donald F. Duncan of Chicago, Illinois, USA initiated it in 1926. The most difficult modern yo-yo trick is the 'whirlwind', incorporating both inside and outside horizontal loop-the-loops. The individual continuous endurance record is 130 hr 13 min, by Jason Stremble and Scott Fletcher at Variety Village, Scarborough, Ontario, Canada from 17–22 Jul 1989.

'Fast' Eddy McDonald of Toronto, Canada completed 21 663 loops in 3 hr on 14 Oct 1990 at Boston, Massachusetts, USA, having previously set a 1 hr speed record of 8437 loops at Cavendish, Prince Edward Island, Canada on 14 Jul 1990.

Juggling

8 clubs (flashed) Anthony Gatto (US), 1989.

7 clubs (juggled) Albert Petrovski (USSR), 1963; Sorin Munteanu (Romania), 1975; Jack Bremlov (Czechoslovakia), 1985; Albert Lucas (US), 1985; Anthony Gatto (US), 1988.

8 plates Enrico Rastelli (Italy), 1896–1931; Albert Lucas (US), 1984.

10 balls Enrico Rastelli (Italy), 1896–1931; Albert Lucas (US), 1984.

12 rings (flashed) Albert Lucas (US), 1985.

11 rings (juggled) Albert Petrovski (USSR), 1963–6; Eugene Belaur (USSR), 1968; Sergei Ignatov (USSR), 1973.

7 flaming torches Anthony Gatto (US), 1989.

Bounce juggling Tim Nolan (US), 10 balls, 1988.

Basketball spinning Bruce Crevier (US), 15 basketballs (whole body), 1991.

Ball spinning (on one hand) François Chotard (France), 9 balls, 1990.

Duration: 5 clubs without a drop 45 min 2 sec, Anthony Gatto (US), 1989.

Duration: 3 objects without a drop Jas Angelo (GB), 8 hr 57 min 31 sec, 1989.

7 ping-pong balls with mouth Tony Ferko (Czechoslovakia), 1987.

Pirouettes with 3 cigar boxes Kris Kremo (Switzerland) (quadruple turn with 3 boxes in mid-air), 1977.

5 balls inverted Bobby May (US), 1953.

Most objects aloft 821 jugglers kept 2463 objects in the air simultaneously, each person juggling at least three objects, 1990.

3 objects while running (joggling) Owen Morse (US), 100 m in 11·68 sec, 1989 and 400 m in 57·32 sec, 1990. Albert Lucas (US), 110 m hurdles in 20·36 sec and 400 m hurdles in 1 min 10·37 sec, 1989. Owen Morse, Albert Lucas, Tuey Wilson and John Wee (all US), 1·6 km *1 mile* relay in 3 min 57·38 sec, 1990. Kirk Swenson (US), 1·6 km *1 mile* in 4 min 43 sec, 1986 and 5 km *3·1 miles* in 16 min 55 sec, 1986. Ashrita Furman (US), marathon—42·195 km *26 miles 385 yd*—in 3 hr 22 min 32·5 sec, 1988 and 80·5 km *50 miles* in 8 hr 52 min 7 sec, 1989.

5 objects while running (joggling) Owen Morse (US), 100 m in 13·8 sec, 1988. Bill Gillen (US), 1·6 km *1 mile* in 7 min 41·01 sec, 1989 and 5 km *3·1 miles* in 28 min 11 sec, 1989.

Food

Apple pie The largest apple pie ever baked was that made by ITV chef Glynn Christian in a 12 × 7 m *40 × 23 ft* dish at Hewitts Farm, Chelsfield, Kent from 25–27 Aug 1982. Over 600 bushels of apples were included in the pie, which weighed 13·66 tonnes *30 115 lb*. It was cut by Rear-Admiral Sir John Woodward.

Banana split The longest banana split ever created measured 7·32 km *4·55 miles* in length, and was made by residents of Selinsgrove, Pennsylvania, USA on 30 Apr 1988.

Barbecue The record attendance at a one-day barbecue was 35 072, at the Iowa State Fairgrounds, Des Moines, Iowa, USA on 21 Jun 1988. The greatest meat consumption ever recorded at a one-day barbecue was at the same event — 9131 kg *20 130 lb* of pork consumed in 5 hr. The greatest quantity of meat consumed at any barbecue was 9576 kg *21 112 lb* of beef at the Sertoma Club Barbecue, New Port Richey, Florida, USA, from 7–9 Mar 1986.

Cakes The largest cake ever created weighed 58·08 tonnes *128 238 lb 8 oz*, including 7·35 tonnes *16 209 lb* of icing. It was made to celebrate the 100th birthday of Fort Payne, Alabama, USA, and was in the shape of Alabama. The cake was prepared by a local bakery, EarthGrains, the first cut being made by 100-year old resident Ed Henderson on 18 Oct 1989. The tallest cake was 30·85 m *101 ft 2½ in* high, created by Beth Cornell and her team of helpers at the Shiawassee County Fairgrounds, Michigan, USA. It consisted of 100 tiers and was completed on 5 Aug 1990. The Alimentarium, a museum of food in Vevey, Switzerland, has on display the world's oldest which was sealed and 'vacuum-packed' in the grave of Pepionkh, who lived in Ancient Egypt around 2200 BC. The 11 cm *4·3 in* wide cake has sesame on it and honey inside, and was possibly made with milk.

Cheese The largest cheese ever created was a cheddar of 18 171 kg *40 060 lb*, made on 13–14 Mar 1988 at Simon's Specialty Cheese, Little Chute, Wisconsin, USA. It was subsequently taken on tour in a specially designed, refrigerated 'Cheesemobile'.

■ **Lasagne**
The largest lasagne was one weighing 1637·3 kg 3609·6 lb, and measuring 15·24 × 1·52 m 50 × 5 ft. It was made by Andreano Rossi of Dolmio, second from the left, and a team of helpers at the Royal Dublin Society Spring Show in Dublin, Republic of Ireland on 11 May 1990. On the right is Tony Cascarino, the Republic of Ireland footballer, who attended the event shortly before going out to play in the World Cup in Italy. (Photo: Masterfoods Ltd)

Noodle making

Mark Pi of the China Gate Restaurant, Columbus, Ohio, USA made 4096 noodle strings from a single piece of noodle dough in 1 min on 7 Nov 1990, representing a speed of more than 68 noodles per second. The attempt was subsequently shown on the BBC *Record Breakers* programme.

Omelette making

The greatest number of two-egg omelettes made in 30 min is 427, by Howard Helmer at the International Poultry Trade Show held at Atlanta, Georgia, USA on 2 Feb 1990.

Pancake tossing

The greatest number of times a pancake has been tossed in 2 min is 281, by Judith Aldridge in the Merry Hill shopping centre at Dudley, W Mids on 27 Feb 1990.

Winkling

Kevin O'Connor picked 50 shells (with a straight pin) in 2 min 42 sec at Brighton, E Sussex on 5 Aug 1990.

Cherry pie The largest cherry pie on record weighed 17 118·78 kg *37 740·65 lb* and contained 16 692·11 kg *36 800 lb* of cherry filling. It measured 6·1 m *20 ft* in diameter, and was baked by members of the Oliver Rotary Club at Oliver, British Columbia, Canada on 14 Jul 1990.

Chocolate model The largest chocolate model was one weighing 1800 kg *3968·3 lb*, of the 1992 Olympic Centre, Barcelona, Spain. It was made by Gremi Provincial de Pastissería, Confitería i Bollería school, Barcelona in November 1985 and measured 10 m × 5 m × 73 cm *32 ft 9¹/₂ in × 16 ft 4³/₄ in × 2 ft 4³/₄ in.*

Christmas pudding The largest was one of 1390 kg *3064·42 lb*, made by employees of Herbert Adams in Kensington, Victoria, Australia. They started preparing it on 16 Nov 1987 and finished the decorating on 9 Dec 1987.

Cocktail The largest cocktail on record was a 'Cabanas Surprise' of 2104·2 litres *462·9 gal*, made by Sun City Cabanas at Sun City, Bophuthatswana, South Africa on 2 Mar 1991.

Doughnut The largest doughnut ever made was lemon-filled and weighed 952·1 kg *2099 lb*, with a diameter of 6·7 m *22 ft*. It was baked by Ed Sanderson at Crystal River, Florida, USA on 10 Dec 1988.

Easter eggs The heaviest Easter egg ever made was one weighing 3430 kg *7561 lb 13½ oz*, 3·04 m *10 ft* high, by Siegfried Berndt at Macopa Patisserie, Leicester, and completed on 7 Apr 1982. An egg 5·78 m *18 ft 11½ in* tall was constructed by Tobler Suchard of Bedford on 10 Apr 1987.

Food, most expensive The most expensive food (as opposed to spice) is

First Choice Black Périgord truffle (*Tuber melanosporum*), which is sold at Harrods in London for £17·50 per 12·5 g *0·44 oz* jar. However, in January 1985 in the Hafr El-Baten market, Riyadh, Saudi Arabia local truffles sold for SR 5000 for 3 kg, equivalent to £50·16 for 12·5 g.

Fruit, most expensive John Synnott of Ashford, Co. Wicklow, Republic of Ireland sold 453 g *1 lb* of strawberries (a punnet of 30 berries) for £530 or £17·70 a berry on 5 Apr 1977. The buyer was restaurateur Leslie Cooke, at an auction by Walter L. Cole Ltd in the Dublin Fruit Market.

Haggis The largest haggis (encased in eight ox stomach linings) on record weighed 285·8 kg *630 lb* and was made for the ASDA Superstore, Corby, Northants by David A. Hall Ltd of Broxburn, Lothian on 6 Nov 1986.

Hamburger The largest hamburger on record was one of 2503 kg *5520 lb*, made at the Outgamie County Fairgrounds, Seymour, Wisconsin, USA on 5 Aug 1989.

Ice-cream sundae The largest ice-cream sundae was one weighing 24 908·8 kg *54 914·8 lb*, made by Palm Dairies Ltd under the supervision of Mike Rogiani in Edmonton, Alberta, Canada on 24 Jul 1988. It consisted of 20 270·7 kg *44 689·5 lb* of ice-cream, 4394·4 kg *9688·1 lb* of syrup and 243·7 kg *537·2 lb* of topping.

Jelly The world's largest jelly, a 35 000 litre *7700 gal* water-melon flavoured pink jelly made by Paul Squires and Geoff Ross, worth $14 000, was set at Roma Street Forum, Brisbane, Queensland, Australia on 5 Feb 1981 in a tank supplied by Pool Fab.

Kebab The longest kebab ever was one 324·9 m *1065 ft 11 in* long, made by George Psarias of the Olive Tree Greek Restaurant, Rodley, Leeds, W Yorks on 26 Aug 1990.

Lasagne The largest lasagne was one weighing 1637·3 kg *3609·6 lb* and measuring 15·24 × 1·52 m *50 × 5 ft*. It was made by Andreano Rossi of Dolmio and a team of helpers at the Royal Dublin Society Spring Show in Dublin, Republic of Ireland on 11 May 1990.

Loaf The longest loaf on record was a Rosca de Reyes 1064 m *3491 ft 9 in* long, baked at the Hyatt Regency Hotel in Guadalajara, Mexico on 6 Jan 1991. If a consumer of the 'Rosca', or twisted loaf, finds the embedded doll, that person has to host the Rosca party (held annually at Epiphany) the following year.

The largest pan loaf ever baked weighed 1435 kg *3163 lb 10 oz* and measured 3 × 1·25 × 1·1 m *9 ft 10 in × 4 ft 1 in × 3 ft 7 in*, by staff of Sasko in Johannesburg, South Africa on 18 Mar 1988.

Lollipop The world's largest ice lollipop was one of 3211 kg *7080 lb*, constructed by students and staff at Lawrence University, Appleton, Wisconsin, USA on 17 Feb 1990. The largest 'regular' lollipop weighed 1007·3 kg *2220·5 lb 11 oz* and was made by Stephen Spring and James Alexandrou of Lolly Pops/Johnson's Confectionery at Darling Harbour, Sydney, Australia on 18–19 Aug 1990.

Meat pie The largest meat pie on record weighed 9030 kg *19 908 lb* and was the 9th in the series of Denby Dale, W Yorks pies. It was baked on 3 Sep 1988 to mark the bicentenary of Denby Dale pie-making, the

Yard of ale

Peter Dowdeswell of Earls Barton, Northants drank a yard of ale (1·42 litres *2½ pints*) in 5·0 sec at RAF Upper Heyford, Oxon on 4 May 1975.

Wine tasting

The largest ever reported was that staged by the Wine Institute at the St Francis Hotel, San Francisco, California, USA on 17 Jul 1980, with 125 pourers, 90 openers and a consumption of 3000 bottles.

■ Smallest bottles

The smallest bottles of liquor now sold are of White Horse Scotch Whisky, which stand just over 5 cm 2 in high and contain 1·3 ml 22 minims. A mini case of 12 bottles costs about £7.00, and measures 5·3 × 4·8 × 3·4 cm 2 1/16 × 1 7/8 × 1 5/16 in. (Photo: Guinness Publishing/Cumbrae Supply Company).

first one in 1788 having been made to celebrate King George III's return to sanity. The fourth (Queen Victoria's Jubilee, 1887) went a bit 'off' and had to be buried in quicklime.

Milk shake The largest milk shake was a chocolate one of 7160·8 litres *1575·2 gal*, made by the Smith Dairy Products Co. at Orrville, Ohio, USA on 20 Oct 1989.

Mince pie The largest mince pie recorded was one of 1025 kg *2260 lb*, measuring 6·09 × 1·52 m *20 × 5 ft*, baked at Ashby-de-la-Zouch, Leics on 15 Oct 1932.

Omelette The largest omelette in the world had an area of 123 m² *1324 ft²* and was made in a skillet 12·52 m *41 ft 1 in* in diameter. It was cooked by staff and pupils of the Municipal School for Special Education at Opwijk, Belgium on 10 Jun 1990.

Paella The largest paella measured 16 m *52 ft 6 in* in diameter and was made by Josep Gruges ('Pepitu') on 25 Aug 1987 in the Playa de Aro, Gerona, Spain. The ingredients included 3700 kg *8140 lb* of rice, 3000 kg *6600 lb* of meat, 1500 kg *3300 lb* of mussels, 700 kg *1540 lb* each of beans and peppers, 200 kg *440 lb* of garlic and 400 litres *88 gal* of oil. The paella was eaten by 40 000 people who washed it all down with 8000 bottles of Catalan champagne.

Pancake The largest pancake was 10·03 m *32 ft 11 in* in diameter and 2·6 cm *1 in* deep, and weighed 1300 kg *2866 lb*. It was made and flipped at Dijkerhoek, Holten, Netherlands on 13 May 1990.

Pastry The longest pastry in the world was an apple strudel 615·11 m *2018 ft 2 in* in length, made by Port Macquarie College of Technical and Further Education at Port Macquarie, New South Wales, Australia on 30 Sep 1990.

Pizza The largest pizza ever baked was one measuring 37·4 m *122 ft 8 in* in diameter, made at Norwood Hypermarket, Norwood, South Africa on 8 Dec 1990.

Popcorn The largest box of popcorn contained 107·38 m³ *3791·8 ft³* of popped corn. It measured 9·75 × 9·75 m *32 × 32 ft* and was filled by the 1990 marketing block

class at Fresno State University, California, USA from 25–28 Apr 1990. The average depth was 1·13 m *3 ft 8½ in*.

Salami The longest salami on record was one 18·7 m *61 ft 3½ in* long with a circumference of 61 cm *24 in*, weighing 545·4 kg *1202·5 lb*, made by the Kutztown Bologna Co., Pennsylvania, USA and displayed at the Lebanon Bologna Fest in Kutztown on 11–13 Aug 1989.

Sausage The longest continuous sausage on record was one of 21·12 km *13·125 miles*, made at the premises of Keith Boxley at Wombourne, near Wolverhampton, W Mids in 15 hr 33 min on 18–19 Jun 1988.

Spice, most expensive Prices for wild ginseng (root of *Panax quinquefolium*) from the Chan Pak Mountain area of China, thought to have aphrodisiac qualities, were reported in November 1979 to be as high as $23 000 per ounce in Hong Kong. Total annual shipments from Jilin Province do not exceed 4 kg *140 oz* a year. A leading medical journal in the USA has likened its effects to 'corticosteroid poisoning'.

Spice, 'hottest' The hottest of all spices is claimed to be siling labuyo from the Philippines. The chili pepper or capsicum known as tepin, of south-west USA, comes in pods 7 mm *⅜ in* in diameter. A single dried gram will produce detectable 'heat' in 31 kg *68·3 lb* of bland sauce.

Stick of rock The mightiest piece was a stick weighing more than 305 kg *673·5 lb*, 3·6 m *12 ft* long and 40·6 cm *16 in* thick, made by the Carshalton Confectionery Co. of St Annes-on-Sea, Lancs on 21 May 1987.

Strawberry bowl The largest bowl of strawberries ever picked had a net weight of 2191·7 kg *4832 lb*. The strawberries were picked at Walt Furlong's farm at New Ross, Co. Wexford, Republic of Ireland during the Enniscorthy Strawberry Fair on 9 Jul 1989.

Sweets The largest sweet on record was a marzipan chocolate weighing 1850 kg *4078·5 lb*, made at the Ven International Fresh Market, Diemen, Netherlands on 11–13 May 1990.

Trifle The largest sherry trifle on record was one weighing 3128·05 kg *6896 lb*, including 91 litres *20 gal* of sherry, made on 26 Sep 1990 by students of Clarendon College of Further Education, Nottingham.

Yorkshire pudding The largest Yorkshire pudding was one measuring 9·14 × 3·66 m *30 × 12 ft* (33·44 m² *360 ft²*). It was made by a team from the Army Catering Corps of the Prince of Wales' Own Regiment of Yorkshire at Skipsea, Humberside on 8 Apr 1990.

Drink

As from 1 Jan 1981 the strength of spirits has been expressed only in terms of percentage volume of alcohol at 20° C. Absolute or '100 per cent volume' alcohol was formerly expressed as 75·35° over proof, or 75·35° OP. In the USA proof is double the actual percentage of alcohol by volume at 15·6° C *60° F*, so that absolute alcohol is 200 per cent proof spirit. 'Hangovers' are said to be aggravated by the presence of such toxic congenerics as amyl alcohol ($C_5H_{11}OH$).

Beer Strongest Roger & Out brewed at the Frog & Parrot in Sheffield, S Yorks, from a recipe devised by W.R. Nowill and G.B. Spencer, has an alcohol volume of 16·9 per cent. It was first brewed in July 1985 and has been on sale ever since. The strongest lager is Samichlaus Dark 1987, brewed by Brauerei Hürlimann of Zürich, Switzerland. It is 14·93 per cent alcohol by volume at 20° C.

Bottles Largest A bottle 2·11 m *6 ft 11 in* tall and 1·64 m *5 ft 4½ in* in circumference was displayed at the Laidley Tourist Festival, in Queensland, Australia on 2 Sep 1989. The bottle was filled with 418·25 litres *92 gal* of Laidley Gold, a wheat beer only available in Laidley.

The largest bottles normally used in the wine and spirit trade are the Jeroboam (equal to 4 bottles of champagne or, rarely, of brandy, and from 5–6½ bottles of claret according to whether blown or moulded) and the double magnum (equal, since *c.* 1934, to 4 bottles of claret or, more rarely, red Burgundy). A complete set of champagne bottles would consist of a quarter bottle, through the half bottle, bottle, magnum, Jeroboam, Rehoboam, Methuselah, Salmanazar and Balthazar, to the Nebuchadnezzar, which has a capacity of 16 litres *28·14 pt*, and is equivalent to 20 bottles.

A bottle containing 33·7 litres of Château Lalande Sourbet 1985, equal in volume to almost 45 standard wine bottles, was auctioned on 10 Oct 1989 in Copenhagen, Denmark.

Martell Cognac is available in a range of 21 bottle sizes from 30 ml *0·05 pt* to 3·78 litres *6·65 pt*.

Smallest The smallest bottles of liquor now sold are of White Horse Scotch Whisky, which stand just over 5 cm *2 in* high and contain 1·3 ml *22 minims*. A mini case of 12 bottles costs about £7.00, and measures 5·3 × 4·8 × 3·4 cm *2 1/16 × 1 7/8 × 1 5/16 in*. The distributors are Cumbrae Supply Co., Linwood, Strathclyde.

Brewers The oldest brewery in the world is the Weihenstephan Brewery, Freising, near Munich, Germany, founded in AD 1040.

The largest single brewing organization in the world is Anheuser-Busch Inc. of St Louis, Missouri, USA, with 12 breweries

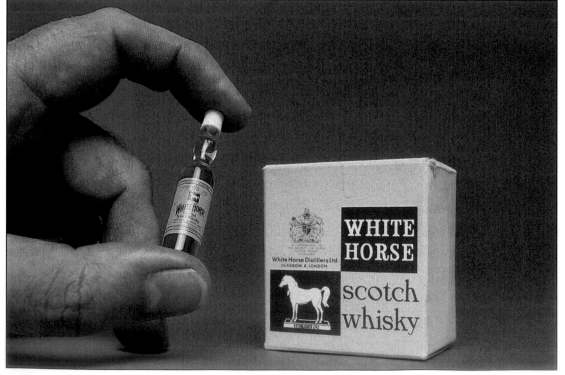

in the United States. In 1990 the company sold 10·2 billion litres *2·2 billion gal*, the greatest annual volume ever produced by a brewing company. The company's St Louis plant covers 40·5 ha *100 acres* and has an annual capacity of 1·5 billion litres *336 million gal*. The largest brewery on a single site is Coors Brewing Co. of Golden, Colorado, USA, where 2·27 billion litres *499 million gal* were produced in 1990.

The largest brewing company in the United Kingdom, with over 22 per cent of the UK beer market, is Bass plc, which has 6785 public houses and 645 off-licences. The company has net assets of £3·6 billion, controls 13 breweries and has 100 000 employees. Its turnover for the year ending 30 Sep 1989 was £4 billion. (See Hoteliers, Chapter 6).

Distillers The world's largest distilling company is the Seagram Co. Ltd, of Canada, with sales in the year ending 31 Jan 1991 totalling $6·1 billion. The group employs about 17 700 people.

The largest blender and bottler of Scotch whisky is United Distillers, the spirits company of Guinness plc, at their Shieldhall plant in Glasgow, which has the capacity to fill an estimated 144 million bottles of Scotch a year. This is equivalent to approximately 109 million litres *24 million gal*, most of which is exported. The world's best-selling brands of Scotch and gin, Johnnie Walker Red Label and Gordon's, are both products of United Distillers.

Old Bushmills Distillery, Co. Antrim, licensed in 1608, claims to have been in production in 1276.

Most alcoholic drinks During independence (1918–40) the Estonian Liquor Monopoly marketed 98 per cent potato alcohol (196 proof US). In 31 US states Everclear, 190 proof or 95 per cent volume alcohol, is marketed by the American Distilling Co. 'primarily as a base for home-made cordials'. Royal Navy rum, introduced in 1655, was 40° OP (79 per cent volume) before 1948, but was later reduced to 4·5° UP (under proof) or 46 per cent volume. The daily rum ration for Royal Navy sailors was abolished on 31 Jul 1970. Full-strength British Navy Pusser's Rum is currently distributed by I.D.V. (UK) Ltd of Harlow, Essex. The Royal New Zealand Navy still issues Navy rum at 4·5 under proof and is the only navy in the world that does so.

Spirits Most expensive The most expensive spirit is Springbank 1919 Malt Whisky, which is sold at Harrods in London for £6500 (including VAT) per bottle.

Vintners The world's oldest champagne firm is Ruinart Père et Fils, founded in 1729. The oldest cognac firm is Augier Frères & Cie, established in 1643.

Wine Oldest Evidence of wine dating from c. 3500 BC was detected at Godin Tepe, Iran in early 1991. Excavations there revealed the remains of a Sumerian jar containing a large red stain. This was analysed, and the results showed the presence of tartaric acid, a chemical naturally abundant in grapes.

The oldest bottle of wine to have been sold at auction was a bottle of 1648 Johannisberger, which was bought by Scharlachberg brandy distillery for 19 720 DM (including buyer's premium) through Weichmann auctioneers at Wiesbaden, Germany in December 1981. At the time the sum paid was equivalent to £4085.

Most expensive £105 000 was paid for a bottle of 1787 Château Lafite claret, sold to

Christopher Forbes (US) at Christie's, London on 5 Dec 1985. The bottle was engraved with the initials of Thomas Jefferson (1743–1826), 3rd President of the United States — 'Th J' — a factor which greatly affected the bidding. In November 1986 its cork, dried out by exhibition lights, slipped. Although the wine has not been tasted, it is assumed to be undrinkable as a result.

The record price for a half bottle of wine is FF180 000 (£18 000), for a 1784 Château Margaux, also bearing the initials of Thomas Jefferson, which was sold by Christie's at Vinexpo in Bordeaux, France on 26 Jun 1987.

The record price for a glass of wine is FF4000 (£410), for the first glass of Beaujolais Nouveau 1990 released in Beaune, in the wine region of Burgundy, France. It was bought by Bernard Repolt and Philip Holzberg at Pickwick's, a British pub in Beaune, on 15 Nov 1990.

Auction The largest single sale of wine was conducted by Christie's of London on 10–11 Jul 1974 at Quaglino's Ballroom, London, when 2325 lots comprising 432 000 bottles realized £962 190.

Soft drinks Pepsico of Purchase, New York, USA topped the *Fortune 500* table for beverage companies in April 1991, with total sales for 1990 of $17·8 billion, compared with $10·4 billion for the Coca-Cola Company of Atlanta, Georgia. Coca-Cola is, however, the world's most popular soft drink, with sales in 1990 of over 471 million drinks per day, representing an estimated 45 per cent of the world market.

Mineral water The world's largest mineral water firm is Source Perrier, near Nîmes, France, with an annual production of more than 2·5 billion bottles, of which 1·1 billion now come from Perrier. The French drink about 72 litres *152 pints* of mineral water per person per year.

Manufactured Articles

Collections: Because of the infinite number of objects it is possible to collect, we can only include a small number of claims which reflect proven widespread interest.

We are more likely to consider claims for items accumulated on a personal basis over

a significant period of time, made through appropriate established and recognized societies, as these are often better placed to comment authoritatively in record terms.

Amplifier The largest working guitar amplifier is 2·75 m *9·04 ft* high, weighs 325·68 kg *718 lb* and houses 32 25·4 cm *10 in* speakers driven by 600 W of all tube power. However, it can handle 1400 W output. This Ampeg Mega SVT Bass Amp System was unveiled at the NAMM EXPO in Chicago, Illinois, USA by St Louis Music of St Louis, Missouri.

Basket The world's biggest basket is a hand-woven maple example which measures 14·63 × 7·01 × 5·79 m *48 × 23 × 19 ft*. It was made by the Longaberger Company of Dresden, Ohio, USA in 1990.

Beds In Bruges, Belgium, Philip, Duke of Burgundy had a bed 3·81 m *12½ ft* wide and 5·79 m *19 ft* long erected for the perfunctory *coucher officiel* ceremony with Princess Isabella of Portugal in 1430.

The largest bed in Great Britain is the Great Bed of Ware, dating from c. 1580, from the Crown Inn, Ware, Herts and now preserved in the Victoria and Albert Museum, London. It is 3·26 m wide, 3·37 m long and 2·66 m tall *10 ft 8½ in × 11 ft 1 in × 8 ft 9 in*. The largest bed marketed in the United Kingdom was the Super Size Diplomat bed, which measured 2·74 × 2·74 m *9 × 9 ft*, from The London Bedding Centre, Sloane Street. It costs more than £4000.

A promotional 1·5 tonne, 6 × 4·40 m *19 ft 8 in × 14 ft 5 in* pinewood bed accommodating 39 people was exhibited by a French company in August 1986.

Beer cans Beer cans date from a test marketing by Krueger Beer of Newark, New Jersey, USA at Richmond, Virginia in 1935. The largest collection has been made by John F. Ahrens of Mount Laurel, New Jersey, USA, who has nearly 15 000 different cans. A Rosalie Pilsner can sold for $6000 in the USA in April 1981. A collection of 2502 unopened bottles and cans of beer from 103 countries was bought for A$25 000 by the Downer Club ACT of Australia at the Australian Associated Press Financial Markets Annual Charity Golf Tournament on 23 Mar 1990.

Beer labels (Labology) Jan Solberg of Oslo, Norway has amassed 348 000 different labels from around the world to date. The greatest collection of different British beer labels is 30 722 owned by Keith Osborne, Hon. Sec. of the Labologists'

Champagne cork flight

The longest flight of a cork from an untreated and unheated bottle 1·22 m *4 ft* from level ground is 54·18 m *177 ft 9 in*, reached by Prof. Heinrich Medicus at the Woodbury Vineyards, New York, USA on 5 Jun 1988.

Beer tankard

The largest tankard was made by the Selangor Pewter Co. of Kuala Lumpur, Malaysia and unveiled on 30 Nov 1985. It measures 198·7 cm *6½ ft* in height and has a capacity of 2796 litres *615 gal*.

Bottle cap pyramid

A pyramid consisting of 263 810 crown bottle caps was constructed by 12 students of Nanyang Technological Institute, Singapore from 10–17 Jun 1990. Between 2 April and 10 May 1990, 16 members of the Belgian army based in Lüdenscheid, Germany constructed a hexagonal-based pyramid consisting of 276 681 crown caps.

Can construction

A scale-model stadium-shaped structure consisting of 2 million empty beverage cans was built in Verona, Italy by 150 members of AVIS–AIDO with the cooperation of Rail (producers of aluminium cans). It was completed on 1 Dec 1989 after 18 000 hours of work.

Knitted blanket

The world's largest blanket was made by the people of Perth, Western Australia in a joint venture between the Living Stone Foundation Inc. and Radio 6PR. Comprising hand-knitted, machine-knitted and crocheted sections, it measured 2599 m² *27 976 ft²* and was unveiled on 6 Aug 1989.

Greetings cards

Craig Shergold of Carshalton, Surrey was reported to have collected a record 33 million get-well cards by May 1991. Jarrod Booth of Salt Spring Island, British Columbia, Canada had a collection of 205 120 Christmas cards in February 1990.

■ Most finely-woven carpet

The 'Hereke Treasure' carpet, made for Ozipek Halicilik A.S. of Hereke, Turkey and now owned by Gandhara Carpet Japan Co. Ltd of Tokyo, contains 576 knots per cm² 3716 per in² and was woven by five women over a period of five years. (Photo: Gandhara Carpet Japan Co. Ltd)

Society (founded by Guinness Exports Ltd in 1958). His oldest is one of *c.* 1846 from A.B. Walker & Co. of Warrington, Cheshire.

Beer mats (Tegestology) The world's largest collection of beer mats is owned by Leo Pisker of Vienna, Austria, who has collected 135 480 different mats from 154 countries to date. The largest collection of British mats to date is 59 250, owned by Timothy Stannard of Birmingham, W Mids.

Bottle caps Since 1950 Helge Friholm (b. 1909) of Søborg, Denmark has amassed 67 330 different bottle caps from 170 countries.

Bottle collections George E. Terren of Southboro, Massachusetts, USA had a collection of 29 508 miniature bottles of distilled spirit and liquor at 1 Mar 1988. David L. Maund of Upham, Hants has amassed a collection of 8732 unduplicated miniature Scotch whisky bottles. Over the past 30 years he has also collected 323 different miniature Guinness bottles.

The world's greatest collection of unduplicated whisky bottles is one of 4800 assembled by Edoardo Giaccone at his *whiskyteca* in Salo, Lake Garda, Italy. The largest reported collection of spirits and liqueurs is 2890 unduplicated bottles collected by Ian Boasman at Bistro French, Preston, Lancs by February 1990.

Ted Shuler of Germantown, Tennessee, USA has a collection of 2401 different bottled beers, including specimens from 99 countries.

Candles A candle 24·38 m *80 ft* high and 2·59 m *8½ ft* in diameter was exhibited at the 1897 Stockholm Exhibition by the firm of Lindahls. The overall height was 38·70 m *127 ft.* A candle constructed by Enham Industries at the Charlton Leisure Centre, Andover, Hants on 2 Jul 1989 measured 30·99 m *101·7 ft* in height.

Cards The world's largest greeting card was produced by seven members of Oceanway PTA, Jacksonville, Florida, USA. It measured 11·35 × 16·69 m *37 ft 3 in × 54 ft 9 in* and was delivered by the United States Postal Service to Oceanway Seventh Grade Center on 21 Apr 1989. The largest greeting card delivered by the Royal Mail in the UK measured 36·5 × 3·6 m *120 × 12 ft.* It was sent by comedian Les Dawson to Quadrant

(Royal Mail Catering Services) in celebration of their first birthday on 21 Sep 1989.

Carpets and rugs The earliest carpet known is a Seythian woollen pile-knotted carpet measuring 1·8 m² *6 ft²* and dating from the 4th–3rd centuries BC. It was discovered by the Russian archaeologist Sergey Ivanovich Rudenko in 1947 in the Pazyryk Valley in southern Siberia and is now preserved in the Hermitage Museum in Leningrad, USSR.

Of ancient carpets, the largest was a gold-enriched silk carpet of Hashim (dated AD 743) of the Abbasid caliphate in Baghdad, Iraq. It is reputed to have measured 54·86 × 91·44 m *180 × 300 ft.* On 13 Feb 1982 a 4851 m² *52 225 ft²* red carpet was laid by the Allied Corporation from Radio City Music Hall to the New York Hilton along the Avenue of the Americas, New York City, USA.

The most finely-worked carpet known is one having 576 knots per cm² *3716/in².* It was made by five women, selected from 3000 weaving specialists, for Ozipek Halicilik A.S. of Hereke, Turkey. The project took five years to complete and the finished product, named 'Hereke Treasure', was sold to Gandhara Carpet Japan Ltd, Tokyo in March 1988. The most magnificent carpet ever made was the Spring carpet of Khusraw made for the audience hall of the Sassanian palace at Ctesiphon, Iraq. It was made of silk and gold thread, encrusted with emeralds, and measured about 650 m² *7000 ft².* It was cut up as booty by looters in AD 635 and from the known realization value of the pieces must have had an original value of some £100 million.

Chair An enlarged version, 16·25 m *53 ft 4 in* tall, of the chair George Washington sat in while presiding at the Constitutional Convention was made by the NSA and brought to Washington, DC, USA for the 1989 Inauguration.

Chandeliers The world's largest set of chandeliers was created by the Kookje Lighting Co. Ltd of Seoul, Korea. It is 12 m *39 ft* high, weighs 10·67 tonnes and has 700 bulbs. Completed in November 1988, it occupies three floors of the Lotte Chamshil Department Store in Seoul. Britain's largest chandelier measures 9·1 m *30 ft* and is in the Chinese Room at the Royal Pavi-

lion, Brighton, E Sussex. It was made in 1818 and weighs 1 tonne.

Cheque The world's largest cheque was made by the Christmas Cracker Project and measured 16 × 8 m *52 ½ × 26 ft.* The £50 cheque, representing 'One million hours of time and energy', was presented in London on 28 Sep 1990.

Christmas cracker The largest functional cracker ever constructed was one measuring 42·67 m *140 ft* in length and 2·13 m *7 ft* in diameter. It was made by the Industrial Society and pulled at their London offices on 21 Dec 1990.

Cigarettes World production in 1985 was 9873 billion cigarettes. The people of China were estimated to consume 1576 billion cigarettes in 1989. In Senegal 80 per cent of urban males smoke. The peak consumption in the United Kingdom was 3230 cigarettes per adult in 1973. In 1990 98·325 billion cigarettes were sold, 42 per cent of adult males and 33 per cent of women were smokers, averaging 99 manufactured cigarettes per week. Of the 151 brands most recently analysed for the Department of Health, the one with highest tar/nicotine content is Capstan Full Strength, with 24/2·4 mg per cigarette. Silk Cut Ultra Low King Size is the only brand listed with less than 4/0·3 mg per cigarette. In the Philippines there is a brand with a 71 mg nicotine content per cigarette. The oldest brand still available on the British market is Wills Woodbine, introduced in 1888.

The longest cigarettes ever marketed were Head Plays, each 27·9 cm *11 in* long and sold in packets of five in the United States in about 1930 to save tax. The shortest were Lilliput cigarettes, each 31·7 mm *1¼ in* long and 3 mm *⅛ in* in diameter, made in Great Britain in 1956.

The world's largest collection of cigarettes is owned by Robert E. Kaufman of New York, USA. To date he has 8390 different cigarettes made in 173 countries and territories. The oldest brand represented is Lone Jack, made in the USA *c.* 1885. Both the longest and shortest (see above) are represented.

Cigarette cards The earliest known tobacco card is 'Vanity Fair', dated 1876 and issued by Wm S. Kimball & Co. of Rochester, New York, USA. The earliest British example appeared *c.* 1883 in the form of a calendar issued by Allen & Ginter, of Richmond, Virginia, USA trading from Holborn Viaduct, the City of London. The largest known collection is that of Edward Wharton-Tigar (b. 1913) of London, with more than 1 million cigarette and trade cards in about 45 000 sets. This collection has been accepted as a bequest by the British Museum, where it will eventually be available for public study.

Cigarette lighters The Leaders Lighthouse Table Lighter is made in 18-ct gold and is designed in the shape of a lighthouse set on an island base of amethyst which alone weighs 50 kg *1 cwt.* The lighthouse itself weighs 1600 g *51·4 oz troy* and the windows on its stem are also of amethyst. Priced at £37 500, it was sold by Alfred Dunhill, St James's, London in 1986.

Frans Van der Heijden of Vlijmen, Netherlands has collected a total of 13 515 different lighters to date.

Cigarette packets The earliest surviving cigarette packet is a Finnish Petit Canon packet for 25, made by Tollander & Klärich in 1860, from the Ventegodt Collection. The rarest is the Latvian 700-year anniversary (1201–1901) Riga packet,

believed to be unique, from the same collection. The largest verified private collection was one of 62 837 from over 150 countries, owned by Vernon Young of Farnham, Surrey.

Cigars The largest cigar ever made measures 5·095 m *16 ft 8½ in* in length and weighs 262 kg *577 lb 9 oz*. Its construction took 243 hours and used 3330 full tobacco leaves. It was made by Tinus Vinke and Jan Weijmer in February 1983 and is in the Tobacco Museum in Kampen, Netherlands. The largest marketed cigar in the world is the 35·5 cm *14 in* Valdez Emperador made by Fábrica de Puros Santa Clara of San Andrés Tuxtla, Veracruz, Mexico and exclusively distributed by Tabacos San Andrés.

Credit cards The largest collection of valid credit cards to date is one of 1265 (all different) owned by Walter Cavanagh (b. 1943) of Santa Clara, California, USA. The cost of acquisition to 'Mr Plastic Fantastic' was nil, and they are worth more than $1·6 million in credit. They are kept in the world's longest wallet — 76·2 m *250 ft* in length weighing 15·87 kg *35 lb*.

Dress A wedding outfit created by Helene Gainville with jewels by Alexander Reza is believed to be worth $7 301 587·20 precisely. The dress is embroidered with diamonds mounted on platinum and was unveiled in Paris, France on 23 Mar 1989. A robe made for Emperor Field-Marshal Jean-Bédel Bokassa with a 11·8 m *39 ft* long train was encrusted with 785 000 pearls and 1 220 000 crystal beads by Guiselin of Paris, and cost £77 125. It was for his coronation at Bangui, Central African Empire (now Republic) on 4 Dec 1977. (See also Shoes.)

The world's longest wedding dress train measured 52·2 m *171 ft 3 in* and was made by Agnès Remaud of La Roche-sur-Yon, France. The British record was 29·8 m *97 ft 7 ¾* long and was made by Margaret Riley of Thurnby Lodge, Leics for the blessing of the marriage of Diane and Steven Reid in Thurmaston, Leics on 6 May 1990.

Egg The largest and most elaborate jewelled egg stands 70 cm *2 ft* tall and was fashioned from 16·8 kg *37 lb* of gold studded with 20 000 pink diamonds. Designed by London jeweller Paul Kutchinsky, the Argyle Library Egg took six British craftsmen 7000 man-hours to create and has a price tag of £7 million. It was unveiled on 30 Apr 1990 before going on display at the Victoria and Albert Museum, London.

Fabrics The oldest surviving fabric, discovered from Level VI A at Çatal Hüyük, Turkey, has been radiocarbon dated to 5900 BC. The most expensive fabric is vicuña cloth manufactured by Fujii Keori Ltd of Osaka, Japan, retailing at 1 million yen (£4450) per metre in January 1988. The finest denier nylon yarn ever produced is the 5 denier produced by Nilit Ltd of Tel Aviv, Israel and used by Pretty Polly for women's hosiery in the UK. The sheerest stockings normally available are 9 denier. A hair from the average human head is about 50 denier.

Fan An intricately carved wooden fan measuring 3·3 m *10·9 ft* when unfolded and 1·8 m *6 ft* high was completed by Wang Xianbao of Shanghai, China in January 1987.

Fireworks The largest firework ever produced was Universe I Part II, exploded for the Lake Toya Festival in Hokkaido, Japan on 15 Jul 1988. The 700 kg *1543 lb* shell was 139 cm *54·7 in* in diameter and burst to a diameter of 1200 m *3937 ft*. The longest firecracker display was produced

by the Johor Tourism Department, the United Malaysian Youth Movement and Mr Yap Seng Hock, and took place on 20 Feb 1988 at Pelangi Garden, Johor Bahru, Johor, Malaysia. The total length of the display was 5723·3 m *18 777 ft* and it consisted of 3 338 777 firecrackers and 666 kg *1468 lb* of gunpowder. It burned for 9 hr 27 min.

Flags The study of flags is known as vexillology from the Latin *vexillum*, a flag, and was coined by Whitney Smith of Winchester, Massachusetts, USA. The oldest known flag is one dated to *c.* 3000 BC found in 1972 at Khabis, Iran. It is of metal and measures 23 × 23 cm *9 × 9 in* and depicts an eagle, two lions, a goddess, three women and a bull.

The largest flag in the world, one of the Republic of China presented to the city of Kaohsiung, Taiwan by Unichamps Inpe'l Corporation on 9 Apr 1989, measured 126 × 84 m *413 × 275½ ft* and weighed 820 kg *1807·7 lb*. The largest Union Flag (or Union Jack) was one displayed at the Royal Tournament, Earl's Court, London in July 1976. This flag measured 73·15 × 32·91 m *240 × 108 ft*, weighed more than a tonne and was made by Form 4Y at Bradley Rowe School, Exeter, Devon. The largest flag *flown* from a flagstaff is a Brazilian national flag measuring 70 × 100 m *229 ft 8 in × 328 ft 1 in* in Brasilia.

Football The world's largest football measures 2·36 m *7¾ ft* in diameter, weighs 36·28 kg *80 lb* and has 8640 stitches requiring 129·54 m *425 ft* of thread. It was made by Mitre Sports of Huddersfield, W Yorks and it is hoped that the football will eventually be signed by all the Football League Clubs in Britain.

Glass The most priceless example of the art of glass-making is usually regarded as the Portland Vase, which dates from late in the first century BC or first century AD. It was made in Italy, and was in the possession of the Barberini family in Rome from at least 1642. It was eventually bought by the Duchess of Portland in 1792 but was smashed while in the British Museum by William Lloyd on 7 Feb 1845.

The thinnest glass, type D263, has a minimum thickness of 0·035 mm *0·00137 in* and a maximum thickness of 0·055 mm *0·0021 in*. It is made by Deutsche Spezialglas AG of Grünenplan, Germany for use in electronic and medical equipment.

Gold The gold coffin of the Pharaoh Tutankhamun (14th century BC), discovered by Howard Carter on 16 Feb 1923 in the Valley of the Kings, western Thebes, Egypt, weighed 110·4 kg *243 lb*. The subsequent exhibition at the British Museum from 30 Mar–30 Dec 1972 attracted 1 656 151 people (of whom 45·7 per cent bought catalogues), resulting in a profit of £657 731·22.

Hammock A 44·4 m *145½ ft* long hammock was woven by members of the Åboland Crafts Guild of Pargas, Finland in July 1988. The completed hammock was suspended between large oak trees and accommodated 21 people.

Jigsaw puzzles The earliest jigsaws were made as 'dissected maps' by John Spilsbury (1739–69) in Russell Court, off Drury Lane, London *c.* 1762.

The world's largest jigsaw puzzle measures 920·22 m² *9905·5 ft²* and consists of 187 220 pieces. It was made by Robert Longstaff Workshops of Longworth, Oxon for the Family Heart Association and was assembled on 22–26 Oct 1990 at Harrow Leisure Centre, London. A puzzle consisting of

204 484 pieces was made by students of the Gravenvoorde in Almelo, Netherlands on 25 May–1 Jun 1991. The completed article measured 96·25 m² *1036 ft²*.

Custom-made Stave puzzles of 2640 pieces, created by Steve Richardson of Norwich, Vermont, USA, cost $8680 in March 1991.

Kettle The largest antique copper kettle was one standing 0·9 m *3 ft* high with a 1·8 m *6 ft* girth and a 90 litre *20 gal* capacity, built in Taunton, Somerset, for the hardware merchants Fisher and Son *c.* 1800.

Knife The penknife with the greatest number of blades is the Year Knife made by cutlers Joseph Rodgers & Sons, of Sheffield, S Yorks, whose trademark was granted in 1682. The knife was made in 1822 with 1822 blades, and a blade was added every year until 1973 when there was no further space. It was acquired by Britain's largest hand-tool manufacturers, Stanley Works (Great Britain) Ltd of Sheffield, in 1970.

Lantern A 3·7 m *12 ft 1¾ in* high lantern with a 12 m *39 ft 4 in* circumference was made on 29 Apr 1989 by members of the Lotus Lantern International Buddhist Centre and staff of the Seoul Hilton International Hotel, South Korea.

Lego tower The tallest Lego tower, 18·15 m *59 ½ ft* high, was built in Tel Aviv,

Garden gnome
The earliest recorded garden gnome was one placed in the rockery at Lamport Hall, Northants in 1847 by Sir Charles Isham, Bt (1819–1903), who believed they were real people.

Quilt

The world's largest patchwork quilt was made by 7000 citizens of North Dakota, USA for the state's 1989 centennial. It measured 25·9 × 40·8 m *85 × 134 ft.* The largest patchwork quilt in the UK measures 15·24 × 28·3 m *50 ft 4 in × 92 ft 9½ in* and was completed on 14 Aug 1990 by residents of Anchor Housing Association sheltered schemes throughout the country.

Knitted scarf

The longest scarf ever knitted measured an amazing 32 km 3·9 m *20 miles 13 ft.* It was knitted by residents of Abbeyfield Houses for the Abbeyfield Society of Potters Bar, Herts and was completed on 29 May 1988.

Typewriters

The first patent for a typewriter was by Henry Mill in 1714, but the earliest known working machine was made by Pellegrine Turri of Italy in 1808.

Wooden bowl

A one-piece bowl made of monkeypod wood was crafted by Dan Cunningham in Kamuela, Hawaii, USA in September 1990. The bowl, which took 2978 hours to complete, stands 2 m *6 ft 7 in* tall, measures 5·5 m *18 ft 1 in* in circumference and weighs 340 kg *750 lb.*

Yo-yo

The largest yo-yo ever constructed was one measuring 1·82 m *6 ft* in diameter made by the woodwork class of Shakamak High School in Jasonville, Indiana, USA. It weighed 372 kg *820 lb* and was launched from a 48·76 m *160 ft* crane on 29 Mar 1990, when it 'yo-yoed' 12 times.

Israel in May 1990 and consisted of 221 560 bricks. The tallest tower in Britain was 15·01 m *49 ft 2⅞ in* high and was built in the forecourt of Waterloo Station, London on 29–30 Oct 1985.

Matchbox labels The oldest matchbox label of accepted provenance is that of Samuel Jones *c.* 1830. The greatest British prize is a Lucifer & Congreve label of *c.* 1835. The finest collection of trademark labels (excluding any pub/bar or other advertising labels) consists of some 280 000 pieces collected by the phillumenist Robert Jones of Indianapolis, USA. Teiichi Yoshizawa (b. 1904) of Chiba-Ken, Japan has amassed 712 118 matchbox labels (including advertising labels) from 150 countries since 1925.

Matchstick The longest matchstick, made by Stichting at Tegelen, Netherlands on 25 Jun 1988, measured 18·80 m *61 ft 8 in*, weighed 1000 kg *2204 lb* and burnt for 6 hr 45 min 1 sec.

Needles Needles made of bone have been found in sites of the Upper Palaeolithic Aurignacian period in France dated *c.* 28 000–24 000 BC. The longest needle is one 185·5 cm *6 ft 1 in* long made by George Davies of Thomas Somerfield, Bloxwich, W Mids for stitching on mattress buttons lengthways. One is preserved in the National Needle Museum at Forge Mill, Redditch, Hereford & Worcester.

Paper clip An iron paper clip measuring 7 m *23 ft* and weighing 600 kg *1328 lb* was made by O. Mustad & Son of Norway. It was unveiled on 9 Oct 1989 at the Norwegian School of Management in Sandvika in honour of Johan Våler, pioneer of the paper clip in 1899.

Pens The most expensive writing pen is the 5003.002 Caran D'Ache 18-carat solid gold Madison slimline ballpoint pen, incorporating white diamonds of 6.35 carats, exclusively distributed by Jakar International Ltd of London. Its recommended retail price in 1992 is £23 950 (including VAT). A Japanese collector paid 1·3 million French francs in February 1988 for the Anémone fountain pen made by Réden of France. It was encrusted with 600 precious stones, including emeralds, amethysts, rubies, sapphires and onyx, and took skilled craftsmen over a year to complete.

The world's leading pen is the BiC Crystal, made by the BiC organization, with daily global sales of 14 million. More than 600 000 are sold daily in the UK, containing enough ink to draw a line around the Earth 37 times.

Photographs with stars Barbara Ann Thomas of Fredericksburg, Virginia, USA has had her photograph taken with 206 Hollywood stars. Husband John acts as photographer while they holiday at film locations in Hollywood, Los Angeles, California, USA.

Piggy bank A piggy bank measuring 2·31 × 3·61 m *7½ × 12 ft* with a capacity of 7·2 m³ *254·25 ft³* was made by Mercian Housing Association Ltd in May 1990.

Pistol In December 1983 it was reported that Ray Bily owned an initialled gold pistol made for Hitler which was valued at $375 000 for insurance purposes. The pistol with the largest magazine capacity is the .22LR M.100P with 103 rounds of continuous firepower, manufactured by Calico, Bakersfield, California, USA.

Postcards Deltiology is claimed to be the third largest collecting hobby, next only to stamps and coins. Austria issued the first cards in 1869, followed by Britain in 1872. The highest price paid for a postcard was $4400 for one of the five known Mucha Waverly Cycle cards. It was sold by Susan Brown Nicholson of Lisle, Illinois, USA in September 1984.

Pottery The largest thrown vase on record is one measuring 5·345 m *17½ ft* in height (including a 1·30 m *4¼ ft* tall lid) weighing 600 kg *1322 lb 12 oz.* It was completed on 1 Jun 1991 by Faiarte Ceramics of Rustenberg, South Africa. The Chinese ceramic authority Chingwah Lee of San Francisco, California was reported in August 1978 to have valued a unique 99 cm *39 in* Kang Hxi four-sided vase, then in a bank vault in Phoenix, Arizona, USA, at $60 million.

Shoes James Smith, founder of James Southall & Co. of Norwich, Norfolk, introduced sized shoes in 1792. The firm began making 'Start-rite' children's shoes in 1923. The largest shoes ever sold, excluding those made for cases of elephantiasis, are a pair size 42 built for the giant Harley Davidson of Avon Park, Florida, USA.

Emperor Bokassa of the Central African Empire (now Republic) commissioned pearl-studded shoes from the House of Berluti of Paris, France at a cost of $85 000 for his self-coronation on 4 Dec 1977. (See also Dress.)

The most expensive marketed shoes are mink-lined golf shoes with 18-carat gold embellishments and ruby-tipped spikes made by Stylo Matchmakers International of Northampton, which retail for $18 500 (£10 800) per pair. A pair of women's cream kid and braid high-heeled slap-soled shoes of *c.* 1660 were sold by Lord Hereford at Sotheby's, London in September 1987 to Sonia Bata for £21 000. An export licence was reportedly refused on 20 Jun 1988.

Silver The largest single pieces of silver are a pair of water jugs of 242·7 kg *10 408 troy oz* made in 1902 for the Maharaja of Jaipur (1861–1922). They are 160 cm *5 ft 3 in* tall, with a circumference of 2·48 m *8 ft 1½ in*, and have a capacity of 8182 litres *1800 gal.* They are now in the City Palace, Jaipur, India. The silversmith was Gorind Narain.

Sofa The longest standard sofa manufactured for the market is the Augustus Rex, 3·74 m *12¼ ft* in length, made by Dodge & Son of Sherborne, Dorset. In April 1990 a 6·63 m *21 ft 9 in* long jacquard fabric sofa with an estimated value of $8000 was specially manufactured by Mountain View Interiors of Collingwood, Ontario, Canada. In April 1987 a 4·77 m *15 ft 6 in* black suede sofa was specially manufactured by Kingcome Sofas of London at their Devon workshops.

Stuffed toy, longest A snake measuring 83·52 m *274 ft* and weighing 70 kg *154·3 lb* was made in a total of 60 hours by members of Brettell Lane Day Centre, Amblecote, W Mids in February 1990.

Suit EVA suits made for extra-vehicular activity, worn by Space Shuttle crews since 1982, have a unit cost of $3·4 million.

Table The longest table was set up in Pesaro, Italy on 20 Jun 1988 by the US Libertas Scavolini basketball team. It was 3070 m *3357 yd* in length and was used to seat 12 000 people.

Table cloth The world's largest table cloth is 457·81 m *1502 ft* long, 1·37 m *4½ ft* wide and was made by the Sportex division of Artex International in Highland, Illinois, USA on 17 Oct 1990. The UK record table cloth is 300·5 m *328·6 yd* long and 1·83 m *6 ft* wide, made of damask by Tonrose Ltd of Manchester in June 1988.

Tapestry The earliest known examples of tapestry-woven linen are three pieces from the tomb of the Egyptian pharaoh Thutmose IV, dated to 1483–1411 BC.

The largest tapestry ever woven is the *History of Irak*, with an area of 1242·1 m² *13 370·7 ft².* It was designed by the Yugoslavian artist Frane Delale and produced by the Zivtex Regeneracija Workshop in Zabok, Yugoslavia. Completed in 1986, the tapestry now adorns the wall of an amphitheatre in Baghdad, Iraq. Britain's largest single piece of tapestry is *Christ in Glory*, measuring 22·77 × 11·59 m *74 ft 8 in × 38 ft* and designed by Graham Vivian Sutherland (1903–80) for an altar-hanging in Coventry Cathedral, W Midlands. It cost £10 500, weighs just over 1 tonne and was delivered from Pinton Frères of Felletin, France—where it had occupied 12 weavers for over two years—on 1 Mar 1962 in time for the consecration of the cathedral on 25 May.

The famous Bayeux *Telle du Conquest, dite tapisserie de la reine Mathilde*, a hanging measuring 49·5 cm *19½ in* wide and 70·40 m *231 ft* in length, depicts events of 1064–66 in 72 scenes and was probably worked in Canterbury, Kent *c.* 1086. It was 'lost' for 2½ centuries from 1476 until 1724.

The *Overlord* embroidery of 34 panels, each measuring 2·43 × 0·91 m *8 × 3 ft*, commissioned by Lord Dulverton (b. 1915) from the Royal School of Needlework in London, was completed in 1979 after 100 man-years of work and is 12·49 m *41 ft* longer than the Bayeux. It has the largest area of any embroidery—75·8 m² *816 ft².* An uncompleted embroidery, 20·3 cm *8 in* deep and 407·82 m *1338 ft* long, of scenes from C.S. Lewis's *Narnia* children's stories has been worked by Margaret S. Pollard of Truro, Cornwall to the order of Michael Maine.

Tartan The earliest evidence of tartan is the so-called Falkirk tartan, found stuffed in a jar of coins in Bells Meadow, Falkirk, Central. It is of a dark and light brown pattern and dates from *c.* AD 245. The earliest reference to a specific named tartan is to a Murray tartan in 1618, although Mackay tartan was probably worn earlier. There are 2179 tartans known to The Tartans Museum at the headquarters of the Scottish Tartans Society in Comrie, Perth, Tayside. HRH The Prince of Wales is eligible to wear 11, including the Balmoral, which has been exclusive to the royal family since 1852.

Time capsule The world's largest time capsule is the Tropico Time Tunnel of 283 m³ *10 000 ft³* in a cave in Rosamond, California, USA. It was sealed by the Kern Antelope Historical Society on 20 Nov 1966 and is intended for opening in AD 2866.

Wallet The most expensive wallet ever made is a platinum-cornered, diamond-studded crocodile creation by Louis Quatorze of Paris, France and Mikimoto of Tokyo, Japan, selling in September 1984 at £56 000.

Zip-fastener The world's longest zip-fastener was laid around the centre of Sneek, Netherlands on 5 Sep 1989. The brass zipper, made by Yoshida (Netherlands) Ltd, was 2851 m *9353·56 ft* long and consisted of 2 565 900 teeth.

Sports
and Games

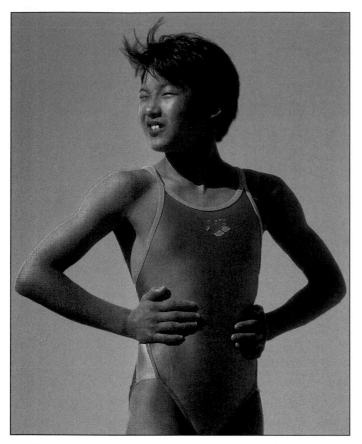

■ **Youngest world champion**

■ **Youngest world champion**

Fu Mingxia (China) won the women's world title for platform diving at Perth, Australia on 4 Jan 1991, at the age of 12 years. (Photo: All-Sport/S. Bruty)

■ **Oldest world champion**

Fred Davis (b. 14 Feb 1913) won the world professional billiards title, aged 67, in June 1980. Here he is seen in action in the 1991 World Masters, still a player to be reckoned with at the age of 78.

(Photo: All-Sport/H. Boylan)

■ **Previous page**

Soviet pole vaulter Rodion Gataullin. (Photo: Empics)

General Records

Origins Sport stems from the time when self-preservation ceased to be the all-consuming human preoccupation. Archery, although a hunting skill in Mesolithic times (by c. 8000 BC), did not become an organized sport until later, possibly as early as c. 1150 BC, as an archery competition is described in Homer's *Iliad*, and certainly by c. AD 300, among the Genoese. The earliest dated evidence is c. 2750–2600 BC for wrestling. Ball games by girls depicted on Middle Kingdom murals at Beni Hasan, Egypt have been dated to c. 2050 BC.

Fastest The fastest speed reached in a non-mechanical sport is in sky-diving, in which a speed of 298 km/h *185 mph* is attained in a head-down free-falling position, even in the lower atmosphere. In delayed drops speeds of 1005 km/h *625 mph* have been recorded at high, rarefied altitudes.

The fastest projectile speed in any moving ball game is c. 302 km/h *188 mph* in pelota. This compares with 273 km/h *170 mph* (electronically timed) for a golf ball driven off a tee.

Largest playing field For any ball game, the largest playing field is 12·4 acres *5 ha* for polo, or a maximum length of 300 yd *274 m* and a width, without side boards, of 200 yd *182 m*. With boards the width is 160 yd *146 m*.

Twice a year in the Parish of St Columb Major, Cornwall, a game called hurling (not to be confused with the Irish game) is played on a 'pitch', which consists of the entire parish, approximately 25 square miles *64·7 km²*.

World record breakers *Youngest* The youngest at which anybody has broken a non-mechanical world record is 12 yr 298 days for Gertrude Caroline Ederle (USA) (b. 23 Oct 1906) with 13 min 19·0 sec for women's 880 yd freestyle swimming at Indianapolis, USA on 17 Aug 1919.

Oldest Gerhard Weidner (West Germany) (b. 15 Mar 1933) set a 20-mile walk record on 25 May 1974, aged 41 yr 71 days, the oldest to set an official world record, open to all ages, recognized by an international governing body. Lee Chin-yong (South Korea) (b. 15 Aug 1925) was 62 yr 273 days when he broke the consecutive chins record on 14 May 1988.

Most prolific Between 24 Jan 1970 and 1 Nov 1977 Vasiliy Alekseyev (USSR) (b. 7 Jan 1942) broke 80 official world records in weightlifting.

Champion *Youngest* The youngest successful competitor in a world title event was a French boy, whose name is not recorded, who coxed the Netherlands' Olympic pair at Paris on 26 Aug 1900. He was not more than ten and may have been as young as seven.

Fu Mingxia (China) won the women's world title for platform diving at Perth, Australia on 4 Jan 1991, at the age of 12 years.

The youngest individual Olympic winner was Marjorie Gestring (USA) (b. 18 Nov 1922), who took the springboard diving title at the age of 13 yr 268 days at the Olympic Games in Berlin on 12 Aug 1936.

Oldest Fred Davis (b. 14 Feb 1913) won (and retained) the world professional billiards title in 1980, aged 67.

Youngest international The youngest at which any person has won international honours is aged eight in the case of Joy Foster, the Jamaican singles and mixed doubles table tennis champion in 1958.

British Diver Beverley Williams (b. 5 Jan 1957) was 10 yr 268 days old when she competed against the USA at Crystal Palace, London on 30 Sep 1967.

Oldest competitor at major games William Edward Pattimore (b. 1 Mar 1892) competed for Wales at bowls at the 1970 Commonwealth Games in Edinburgh at the age of 78, the oldest competitor at such an international event open to competitors of all ages.

Britain's oldest Olympian was Hilda Lorna Johnstone (1902–90) who was 70 yr 5 days when she was placed twelfth in the Dressage competition at the 1972 Olympic Games.

The second edition of the Guinness Encyclopedia of Sports Records & Results (Peter Matthews and Ian Morrison), published in October 1990, contains further sports records and champions.

Most versatile Charlotte 'Lottie' Dod (1871–1960) won the Wimbledon singles tennis title five times between 1887 and 1893, the British Ladies' Golf Championship in 1904, an Olympic silver medal for archery in 1908, and represented England at hockey in 1899. She also excelled at skating and tobogganing.

Mildred 'Babe' Zaharias (*née* Didrikson) (1914–56) (USA) won two gold medals (80 m hurdles and javelin) and a silver (high jump) at the 1932 Olympic Games. She set world records at those three events in 1930–2. She was an All-American basketball player for three years and set the world record for throwing the baseball 90·22 m *296 ft*. Switching to golf she won the US Women's Amateur title in 1946 and the US Women's Open in 1948, 1950 and 1954. She also excelled at several other sports.

Charles Burgess Fry (GB) (1872–1956) was perhaps the most versatile male sportsman at the highest level. On 4 Mar 1893 he equalled the world long jump record of 7·17 m *23 ft 6½ in.* He represented England *v.* Ireland at soccer (1901) and played first-class rugby for the Barbarians. His greatest achievements, however, were at cricket, where he headed the English batting averages in six seasons and captained England in 1912. He was also an excellent angler and tennis player.

Longest reign Jacques Edmond Barre (France) (1802–73) was a world champion for 33 years (1829–62) at real tennis.

Although archer Alice Blanche Legh (1855–1948) did not compete every year, she was a British champion for a span of 41 years (1881–1922), during which she won 23 national titles, the last when she was aged 67.

Largest contract In March 1990, the National Football League concluded a deal worth $3640 million for four years' cover-

■ **Oldest world champion**

age of American Football by the five major TV and cable networks, ABC, CBS, NBC, ESPN and TBS. This represented $26·1 million for each League team in the first year, escalating to $39·1 million in the fourth.

Largest crowd The greatest number of live spectators for any sporting spectacle is the estimated 2 500 000 who have lined the route of the New York Marathon. However, spread over three weeks, it is estimated that more than 10 000 000 see the annual *Tour de France* cycling race.

Olympic The total attendance at the 1984 Summer Games was given as 5 797 923 for all sports, including 1 421 627 for soccer and 1 129 465 for track and field athletics.

Single sporting venue 'More than 400 000' travel to the annual *Grand Prix d'Endurance* motor race on the Sarthe circuit near Le Mans, France.

Stadium A crowd of 199 854 attended the Brazil *v.* Uruguay soccer match, in the Maracaña Municipal Stadium, Rio de Janeiro, Brazil on 16 Jul 1950.

Most participants On 15 May 1988 an estimated 110 000 (including unregistered athletes) ran in the Examiner Bay to Breakers 12·2 km *7·6 mile* race in San Francisco, California, USA. (Fields now *c.* 70 000.)

The 1988 Women's International Bowling Congress Championship tournament attracted 77 735 bowlers for the 96-day event held 31 March–4 July at Reno/Carson City, Nevada, USA.

Worst disasters In recent history, the stands at the Hong Kong Jockey Club racecourse collapsed and caught fire on 26 Feb 1918, killing an estimated 604 people.

During the reign of Antoninus Pius (AD 138–161), 1112 spectators were quoted as being killed when the upper wooden tiers in the Circus Maximus, Rome collapsed during a gladiatorial combat.

Britain On 15 Apr 1989, 95 people were killed and 170 injured, at the Leppings Lane end of Hillsborough Stadium, Sheffield, S Yorks, through overcrowding just after the start of the FA Cup semi-final between Liverpool and Nottingham Forest.

Aerobatics

Origins The first aerobatic 'manoeuvre' is generally considered to be the sustained inverted flight in a Bleriot of Célestin-Adolphe Pégoud (1889–1915), at Buc, France on 21 Sep 1913, but Lt Capt. Petr Nikolayevich Nesterov (1887–1914), of the Imperial Russian Air Service, performed a loop in a Nieuport Type IV monoplane at Kiev, USSR on 27 Aug 1913.

World Championships Held biennially since 1960 (except 1974), scoring is based on a system originally devised by Col. José Aresti of Spain. The competition consists of two compulsory and a free programme.

The men's team competition has been won a record six times by the USSR. Petr Jirmus (Czechoslovakia) is the only man to become world champion twice, in 1984 and 1986. Betty Stewart (USA) won the women's competition in 1980 and 1982. Lyubov Nemkova (USSR) won a record five medals: first in 1986, second in 1982 and 1984 and third in 1976 and 1978. The oldest ever world champion has been Henry Haigh (USA) (b. 12 Dec 1924), aged 63 in 1988.

British The only medal achieved by Britain has been a bronze in the team event at Kiev, USSR in 1976.

The highest individual placing by a Briton is fourth by Neil Williams (1935–77) in 1976.

Inverted flight The duration record is 4 hr 9 min 5 sec by John 'Hal' McClain in a Swick Taylorcraft on 23 Aug 1980 over Houston International Raceways, Texas, USA.

Loops Joann Osterud achieved 208 outside loops in a 'Supernova' Hyperbipe over North Bend, Oregon, USA on 13 Jul 1989. On 21 Jun 1980, R. Steven Powell performed 2315⅝ inside loops in a Bellanca Decathalon over Almont, Michigan.

Brian Lecomber completed 180 consecutive inside loops in a Jaguar Extra 230 on 29 Jul 1988 over Plymouth, Devon.

American Football

Origins American football, a direct descendant of the British games of soccer and rugby, evolved at American universities in the 19th century. The first match under the Harvard Rules was played by Harvard against McGill University of Montreal at Cambridge, Massachusetts, USA on 15 May 1874. The Intercollegiate Football Association was founded in November 1876. The professional game dates from August 1895 when Latrobe played Jeanette at Latrobe, Pennsylvania, USA. The American Professional Football Association was formed on 17 Sep 1920. This became the National Football League (NFL) on 24 Jun 1922. The American Football League (AFL) was formed in 1960; the NFL and AFL merged in 1970.

NFL RECORDS

Championships The Green Bay Packers won a record 11 NFL titles, 1929–31, 1936, 1939, 1944, 1961–2, 1965–7.

Most consecutive wins The record is 18 by: the Chicago Bears (twice), 1933–4 and 1941–2; the Miami Dolphins, 1972–3; and the San Francisco 49ers, 1988–9. The most consecutive games without defeat is 25 by Canton (22 wins and 3 ties) in 1921–3.

Most games played George Blanda (b. 17 Sep 1927) played in a record 340 games in a record 26 seasons in the NFL, (Chicago Bears 1949–58, Baltimore Colts 1950, Houston Oilers 1960–66 and Oakland Raiders 1967–75). The most consecutive games played is 282 by Jim Marshall (Cleveland Browns 1960 and Minnesota Vikings 1961–79).

Longest run from scrimmage Tony Dorsett (b. 7 Apr 1954) scored on a touchdown run of 99 yd for the Dallas Cowboys *v.* the Minnesota Vikings on 3 Jan 1983.

Longest pass completion A pass completion of 99 yd has been achieved on six occasions and has always resulted in a

NFL RECORDS

MOST POINTS

Career	2002	George Blanda (Chicago Bears, Baltimore Colts, Houston Oilers, Oakland Raiders), 1949–75.
Season	176	Paul Hornung (Green Bay Packers), 1960.
Game	40	Ernie Nevers (Chicago Cardinals) v. Chicago Bears, 28 Nov 1929.

MOST TOUCHDOWNS

Career	126	Jim Brown (Cleveland Browns), 1957–65.
Season	24	John Riggins (Washington Redskins), 1983.
Game	6	Ernie Nevers (Chicago Cardinals) v. Chicago Bears, 28 Nov 1929
		William 'Dub' Jones (Cleveland Browns) v. Chicago Bears, 25 Nov 1951
		Gale Sayers (Chicago Bears) v. San Francisco 49ers, 12 Dec 1965.

MOST YARDS GAINED RUSHING

Career	16 726	Walter Payton (Chicago Bears), 1975–88.
Season	2105	Eric Dickerson (Los Angeles Rams), 1984.
Game	275	Walter Payton (Chicago Bears) v. Minnesota Vikings, 20 Nov 1977.

MOST YARDS GAINED RECEIVING

Career	13 089	Steve Largent (Seattle Seahawks), 1976–90.
Season	1746	Charley Hennigan (Houston Oilers), 1961.
Game	336	Willie 'Flipper' Anderson (Los Angeles Rams) v. New Orleans Saints, 26 Nov 1989.

MOST YARDS GAINED PASSING

Career	47 003	Fran Tarkenton (Minnesota Vikings, New York Giants), 1961–78.
Season	5084	Dan Marino (Miami Dolphins), 1984.
Game	554	Norm Van Brocklin (Los Angeles Rams) v. New York Yanks, 28 Sep 1951.

MOST PASSES COMPLETED

Career	3686	Fran Tarkenton (Minnesota Vikings, New York Giants), 1961–78.
Season	378	Dan Marino (Miami Dolphins), 1986.
Game	42	Richard Todd (New York Jets) v. San Francisco 49ers, 21 Sep 1980.

PASS RECEPTIONS

Career	819	Steve Largent (Seattle Seahawks), 1976–90.
Season	106	Art Monk (Washington Redskins), 1984.
Game	18	Tom Fears (Los Angeles Rams) v. Green Bay Packers, 3 Dec 1950.

FIELD GOALS

Career	373	Jan Stenerud (Kansas City Chiefs, Green Bay Packers, Minnesota Vikings), 1967–85.
Season	35	Ali Haji-Sheikh (New York Giants), 1983.
Game	7	Jim Bakken (St Louis Cardinals), v. Pittsburgh Steelers, 24 Sep 1967.
		Rich Karlis (Minnesota Vikings) v. Los Angeles Rams, 5 Nov 1989.
Longest	63	Tom Dempsey (New Orleans Saints) v. Detroit Lions, 8 Nov 1970.

■ **Most successful passer**

■ **Longest run from scrimmage**

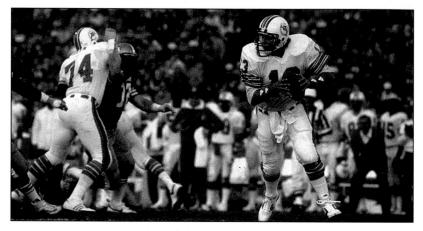

■ **Most pass completions**

■ Most successful passer

In a 17-year career with the Minnesota Vikings and the New York Giants, Fran Tarkenton passed for a NFL record total of 47 003 yards. Not suprisingly he also holds the record for the greatest number of passes completed, 3686. (Photo: Sports Illustrated)

■ Longest run from scrimmage

Tony Dorsett scored on a touchdown run of 99 yd for the Dallas Cowboys v. the Minnesota Vikings on 3 Jan 1983. (Photo: All-Sport (USA)/Stewart)

■ Most pass completions

Despite completing a Super Bowl record 29 passes, Dan Marino of the Miami Dolphins still ended up on the losing side against the San Francisco 49ers in Super Bowl XIX. (Photo: All-Sport (USA))

touchdown. The most recent was a pass from Ron Jaworski (b. 23 Mar 1951) to Mike Quick (b. 14 May 1959) of the Philadelphia Eagles against the Atlanta Falcons on 10 Nov 1985.

SUPER BOWL

First held in 1967 between the winners of the NFL and the AFL. Since 1970 it has been contested by the winners of the National and American Conferences of the NFL.

The most wins is four by the Pittsburgh Steelers, 1975–6, 1979–80; and by the San Francisco 49ers, 1982, 1985, 1989–90.

The highest team score and record victory margin was when the San Francisco 49ers beat the Denver Broncos 55–10 at New Orleans, Louisiana on 28 Jan 1990.

The highest aggregate score was in 1979 when Pittsburgh beat the Dallas Cowboys 35–31.

In their 42–10 victory over the Denver Broncos on 31 Jan 1988, the Washington Redskins scored a record 35 points in the second quarter.

OTHER RECORDS

Highest team score Georgia Tech, Atlanta, Georgia scored 222 points, including a record 32 touchdowns, against Cumberland University, Lebanon, Tennessee (nil) on 7 Oct 1916.

In Britain The premier competition is the Coca-Cola Bowl (formerly the Budweiser Bowl) which was inaugurated in 1986. It has been won twice by the London Ravens, 1986 and 1987, and by the Manchester Spartans, 1989 and 1990.

Highest score The East Kent Cougars, based in Folkestone, beat the Maidstone

SUPER BOWL GAME & CAREER RECORDS

POINTS	18	Roger Craig (San Francisco 49ers)	1985
		Jerry Rice (San Francisco 49ers)	1990
Career	24	Franco Harris (Pittsburgh Steelers)	1975–6, 1979–80
		Roger Craig (San Francisco 49ers)	1985, 1989–90
		Jerry Rice (San Francisco 49ers)	1989–90
TOUCHDOWNS	3	Roger Craig (San Francisco 49ers)	1985
		Jerry Rice (San Francisco 49ers)	1990
Career	4	Franco Harris (Pittsburgh Steelers)	1975–6, 1979–80
		Roger Craig (San Francisco 49ers)	1985, 1990
		Jerry Rice (San Francisco 49ers)	1990
TOUCHDOWN PASSES	5	Joe Montana (San Francisco 49ers)	1990
Career	11	Joe Montana (San Francisco 49ers)	1982, 1985, 1989–90
YARDS GAINED RUSHING	204	Timmy Smith (Washington Redskins)	1988
Career	354	Franco Harris (Pittsburgh Steelers)	1975–6, 1979–80
YARDS GAINED PASSING	357	Joe Montana (San Francisco 49ers)	1989
Career	1142	Joe Montana (San Francisco 49ers)	1982, 1985, 1989–90
YARDS GAINED RECEIVING	215	Jerry Rice (San Francisco 49ers)	1989
Career	364	Lynn Swann (Pittsburgh Steelers)	1975–6, 1979–80
PASSES COMPLETED	29	Dan Marino (Miami Dolphins)	1985
Career	83	Joe Montana (San Francisco 49ers)	1982, 1985, 1989–90
PASS RECEPTIONS	11	Dan Ross (Cincinnati Bengals)	1982
		Jerry Rice (San Francisco 49ers)	1989
Career	20	Jerry Rice (San Francisco 49ers)	1989–90
FIELD GOALS	4	Don Chandler (Green Bay Packers)	1968
		Ray Wersching (San Francisco 49ers)	1982
Career	5	Ray Wersching (San Francisco 49ers)	1982, 1985
MOST VALUABLE PLAYER	3	Joe Montana (San Francisco 49ers)	1982, 1985, 1990

M20's, 148–6 at Mote Park, Maidstone, Kent on 15 May 1988.

Angling

Oldest existing club The Ellem fishing club was formed by a number of Edinburgh and Berwickshire gentlemen in

Scotland in 1829. Its first annual general meeting was held on 29 Apr 1830.

Largest single catch The largest officially ratified fish ever caught on a rod was a man-eating great white shark (*Carcharodon carcharias*) weighing 1208 kg *2664 lb* and measuring 5·13 m *16 ft 10 in* long, caught on a 58 kg *130 lb* test line by Alf Dean at Denial Bay, near Ceduna, South Australia on 21 Apr 1959. A great

WORLD RECORDS; FRESHWATER AND SALTWATER
A selection of All-Tackle records ratified by the International Game Fish Association as at 1 Jan 1991

Species	Weight lb oz	kg	Name of Angler	Location	Date	
BARRACUDA, GREAT	83 0	37·64	K. J. W. Hackett	Lagos, Nigeria	13 Jan	1952
BASS, EUROPEAN	20 11	9·40	Jean Baptiste Bayle	Saintes Maries de la Mer, France	6 May	1986
BASS, LARGEMOUTH	22 4	10·09	George W. Perry	Montgomery Lake, Georgia, USA	2 Jun	1932
BASS, SMALLMOUTH	11 15	5·41	David L. Hayes	Dale Hollow Lake, Kentucky, USA	9 Jul	1955
BASS, STRIPED	78 8	35·60	Albert R. McReynolds	Atlantic City, New Jersey, USA	21 Sep	1982
BLUEFISH	31 12	14·40	James M. Hussey	Hatteras, North Carolina, USA	30 Jan	1972
BONEFISH	19 0	8·61	Brian W. Batchelor	Zululand, South Africa	26 May	1962
CATFISH, FLATHEAD	91 4	41·39	Mike Rogers	Lewisville, Texas, USA	28 Mar	1982
COD, ATLANTIC	98 12	44·79	Alphonse J. Bielevich	Isle of Shoals, New Hampshire, USA	8 Jun	1969
DOLPHIN	87 0	39·46	Manuel Salazar	Papagallo Gulf, Costa Rica	25 Sep	1976
HALIBUT, PACIFIC	356 8	161·70	Gregory C. Olsen	Juneau, Alaska, USA	8 Nov	1986
JACK, CREVALLE	54 7	24·69	Thomas F. Gibson Jr	Port Michel, Gabon	15 Jan	1982
JEWFISH	680 0	308·44	Lynn Joyner	Fernandina Beach, Florida, USA	20 May	1961
MACKEREL, KING	90 0	40·82	Norton I. Thomton	Key West, Florida, USA	16 Feb	1976
MARLIN, BLACK	1560 0	707·61	Alfred C. Glassell Jr	Cabo Blanco, Peru	4 Aug	1953
MARLIN, BLUE (Atlantic)	1282 0	581·51	Larry Martin	St Thomas, Virgin Islands	6 Aug	1977
MARLIN, BLUE (Pacific)	1376 0	624·14	Jay Wm de Beaubien	Kaaiwi Point, Kona Coast, Hawaii, USA	31 May	1982
MARLIN, STRIPED	494 0	224·10	Bill Boniface	Tutukaka, New Zealand	16 Jan	1986
MARLIN, WHITE	181 14	82·50	Evandro Luiz Coser	Vitoria, Brazil	8 Dec	1979
MUSKELLUNGE	69 15	31·72	Arthur Lawton	St Lawrence River, New York, USA	22 Sep	1957
PIKE, NORTHERN	55 1	25·00	Lothar Louis	Lake of Grefeern, Germany	16 Oct	1986
SAILFISH (Atlantic)	128 1	58·10	Harm Steyn	Luanda, Angola	27 Mar	1974
SAILFISH (Pacific)	221 0	100·24	C. W. Stewart	Santa Cruz Island, Ecuador	12 Feb	1947
SALMON, ATLANTIC	79 2	35·89	Henrik Henriksen	Tana River, Norway		1928
SALMON, CHINOOK	97 4	44·11	Les Anderson	Kenia River, Alaska, USA	17 May	1985
SALMON, COHO	33 4	15·08	Jerry Lifton	Pulaski, New York, USA	27 Sep	1989
SHARK, HAMMERHEAD	991 0	449·50	Allen Ogle	Sarasota, Florida, USA	30 May	1982
SHARK, MAKO	1115 0	505·76	Patrick Guillanton	Black River, Mauritius	16 Nov	1988
SHARK, PORBEAGLE	465 0	210·92	Jorge Potier	Padstow, Cornwall, England	23 Jul	1976
SHARK, THRESHER	802 0	363·80	Dianne North	Tutukaka, New Zealand	8 Feb	1981
SHARK, TIGER	1780 0	807·40	Walter Maxwell	Cherry Grove, S. Carolina, USA	14 Jun	1964
SHARK, WHITE	2664 0	1208·38	Alfred Dean	Ceduna, South Australia	21 Apr	1959
SNAPPER, CUBERA	121 8	55·11	Mike Hebert	Cameron, Louisiana, USA	5 Jul	1982
SNOOK	53 10	24·32	Gilbert Ponzi	Parasmina Ranch, Costa Rica	18 Oct	1978
STURGEON, WHITE	468 0	212·28	Joey Pallotta III	Benicia, California, USA	9 Jul	1983
SWORDFISH	1182 0	536·15	L. Marron	Iquique, Chile	17 May	1953
TARPON	283 0	128·36	M. Salazar	Lake Maracaibo, Venezuela	19 Mar	1956
TROUT, BROOK	14 8	6·57	Dr W. J. Cook	Nipigon River, Ontario, Canada	Jul	1916
TROUT, BROWN	35 15	16·30	Eugenio Cavaglia	Nahuel Huapi, Argentina	16 Dec	1952
TROUT, LAKE	65 0	29·48	Larry Daunis	Great Bear Lake, NWT, Canada	8 Aug	1970
TROUT, RAINBOW	42 2	19·10	David Robert White	Bell Island, Alaska, USA	22 Jun	1970
TUNA, BIGEYE (Pacific)	435 0	197·31	Dr Russel V. A. Lee	Cabo Blanco, Peru	17 Apr	1957
TUNA, BLUEFIN	1496 0	679·00	Ken Fraser	Aulds Cove, Nova Scotia, Canada	26 Oct	1979
TUNA, YELLOWFIN	388 12	176·35	Curt Wiesenhutter	San Benedicto Island, Mexico	1 Apr	1977
WAHOO	155 8	70·53	William Bourne	San Salvador, Bahamas	3 Apr	1990
WALLEYE	25 0	11·34	Mabry Harper	Old Hickory Lake, Tennessee, USA	1 Apr	1960

white shark weighing 1537 kg *3388 lb* was caught by Clive Green off Albany, Western Australia on 26 Apr 1976 but will remain unratified as whale meat was used as bait.

The biggest ever rod-caught fish by a British angler is a 620 kg *1366 lb* great white shark, by Vic Samson at The Pales, South Australia on 8 Apr 1989.

In June 1978 a great white shark measuring 6·2 m *20 ft 4 in* in length and weighing over 2268 kg *5 000 lb* was harpooned and landed by fishermen in the harbour of San Miguel, Azores.

The largest marine animal killed by *hand* harpoon was a blue whale 29·56 m *97 ft* in length, by Archer Davidson in Twofold Bay, New South Wales, Australia in 1910. Its tail flukes measured 6·09 m *20 ft* across and its jaw bone 7·11 m *23 ft 4 in*.

The largest fish ever taken underwater was an 804 lb *364 kg* giant black grouper or jewfish by Don Pinder of the Miami Triton Club, Florida, USA in 1955.

The British spear-fishing record is 89 lb *40·36 kg* for an angler fish by James Brown (Weymouth Association Divers) in 1969.

World Freshwater Championship
The *Confédération Internationale de la Pêche Sportive* (CIPS) championships were inaugurated as European championships in 1953 and recognized as World championships in 1957.

France won the European title in 1956 and 12 world titles between 1959 and 1990. Robert Tesse (France) took the individual title a record three times, 1959–60, 1965.

The record weight (team) is 34·71 kg *76·52 lb* in 3 hr by West Germany on the Neckar at Mannheim, Germany on 21 Sep 1980. The individual record is 16·99 kg *37·45 lb* by Wolf-Rüdiger Kremkus (West Germany) at Mannheim on 20 Sep 1980. The most fish caught is 652 by Jacques Isenbaert (Belgium) at Dunajvaros, Yugoslavia on 27 Aug 1967.

British Championship
The National Angling Championship (instituted 1906) has been won seven times by Leeds (1909–10, 1914, 1928, 1948–9, 1952).

James H. R. Bazley (Leeds) won the individual title twice (1909, 1927). Since 1972 the event has been split into divisions. Eddie Townsin (Cambridge) won the national title in 1967 and Division 4 in 1982; Charlie Hibbs (Leigh) won Division 2 in 1974 and 1984.

The record catch is 34·72 kg *76 lb 9 oz* by David Burr (Rugby) in the Huntspill, Somerset in 1965. The largest single fish caught in the Championships is a carp of 6·41 kg *14 lb 2 oz* by John C. Essex on 13 Sep 1975 on the River Nene, Peterborough.

The highest points score by Division 1 team champions is 91·9 % by the Nottingham Federation in 1990.

Casting The longest freshwater cast ratified under ICF (International Casting Federation) rules is 175·01 m *574 ft 2 in* by Walter Kummerow (West Germany), for the Bait Distance Double-Handed 30 g event held at Lenzerheide, Switzerland in the 1968 Championships. The British national record is 148·78 m *488 ft 1 in* by Andy Dickison on the same occasion.

At the currently contested weight of 17·7 g, known as 18 g Bait Distance, the longest Double-Handed cast is 139·31 m *457 ft ½ in* by Kevin Carriero (USA) at Toronto, Canada on 24 Jul 1984. The British national records are: Fixed spool reel, 138·79 m *455 ft 3 in* by Hugh Newton at Peterborough, Cambs on 21 Sep 1985; and Multiplier reel, 108·97 m *357 ft 6 in* by James Tomlinson at Torrington, Devon on 27 Apr 1985.

The longest Fly Distance Double-Handed cast is 97·28 m *319 ft 1 in* by Wolfgang Feige (West Germany) at Toronto, Canada on 23 Jul 1984. Hywel Morgan set a British national record of 91·22 m *299 ft 2 in* at Torrington, Devon on 27 Apr 1985.

The UK Surfcasting Federation record (150 g *5¼ oz* weight) is 257·32 m *844 ft 3 in* by Neil Mackellow at Peterborough, Cambs on 1 Sep 1985.

IGFA world records
The International Game Fish Association (IGFA) recognizes world records for a large number of species of game fish (both fresh and saltwater). Their thousands of categories include all-tackle, various line classes and tippet classes for fly fishing. New records recognized by the IGFA reached an annual peak of 1074 in 1984.

The heaviest freshwater category recognized is for the sturgeon — record weight of 212·28 kg *468 lb* caught by Joey Pallotta on 9 Jul 1983 off Benicia, California, USA.

Fish fight
The longest recorded individual fight with a fish is 32 hr 5 min by Donal Heatley (New Zealand) (b. 1938) with a Black marlin (estimated length 6 m *20 ft* and weight 680 kg *1500 lb*) off Mayor Island off Tauranga, North Island, New Zealand on 21–22 Jan 1968. It towed the 12 tonne launch 80 km *50 miles* before breaking the line.

Fly fishing
World fly fishing championships were inaugurated by the CIPS in 1981. The most team titles is four by Italy, 1982–4, 1986. The first British winner was Henry Anthony 'Tony' Pawson (b. 22 Aug 1921) at Salamanca, Spain in 1984. He also played amateur soccer for England and captained Oxford University at cricket. His son John won the title in 1988.

BRITISH RECORDS—NATIONAL COARSE FISH
As recognized by the National Association of Specialist Anglers

Species	Weight lb	oz	dr	kg	Name of Angler	Location	Date
BLEAK		4	4	0·12	B. Derrington	River Monnow, Wye Mouth	1982
BREAM, COMMON	16	6	–	7·43	Anthony Bromley	Private water, Staffs	1986
BREAM, SILVER		15	–	0·425	D. E. Flack	Grime Spring, Lakenheath, Suffolk	1988
CARP	51	8	–	23·36	C. Yates	Redmire Pool, Herefordshire	1980
CARP, CRUCIAN	5	10	8	2·56	G. Halls	Lake near Kings Lynn, Norfolk	1976
CARP, GRASS	16	1	–	7·28	J. P. Buckley	Horton Fishery, Berks	1990
CATFISH (WELS)	43	8	–	19·73	R. J. Bray	Wilstone Reservoir, Tring, Herts	1970
CHUB	8	4	–	3·74	G. F. Smith	Royalty Fishery, Hampshire Avon	1913
DACE	1	4	–	0·57	J. L. Gasson	Little Ouse, Thetford, Norfolk	1960
EEL	11	2	–	5·04	S. Terry	Kingfisher Lake, Ringwood, Hants	1978
GUDGEON		5	–	0·141	D. Hall	River Nadder, Salisbury, Wilts	1990
PERCH	5	9	–	2·52	J. Shayler	Private water, Kent	1985
PIKE	45	6	–	20·58	Gareth Edwards	Llandefgfedd Reservoir, Pontypool, Gwent	1990
ROACH	4	3	–	1·89	R. N. Clarke	Dorset Stour	1990
RUDD	4	8	–	2·04	Rev. E. C. Alston	Thetford, Norfolk	1933
RUFFE		5	4	0·148	R. J. Jenkins	West View Farm, Cumbria	1980
TENCH	14	3	–	6·43	Philip Gooriah	Wraysbury No.1 Reservoir	1987
WALLEYE	11	12	–	5·33	F. A. Adams	The Delph, Welney, Norfolk	1934
ZANDER	18	8	–	8·39	D. Litton	Cambridge stillwater	1988

FRESHWATER GAME FISH
As recognized by the National Anglers' Council

Species	Weight lb	oz	dr	kg	Name of Angler	Location	Date
SALMON	64	–	–	29·03	Miss G. W. Ballantine	River Tay, Scotland	1922
TROUT, AMERICAN BROOK	5	13	8	2·65	A. Pearson	Avington Fishery, Hants	1981
TROUT, BROWN	19	9	4	8·88	J. A. F. Jackson	Loch Quioch, Inverness	1978
TROUT, RAINBOW	24	2	13	10·96	J. Moore	Pennine Trout Fishery, Littleborough, Lancs	1990
TROUT, SEA	22	8	–	10·20	S. Burgoyne	River Leven	1989

ted the Pa–pingo Shoot since 1488. The world governing body is the *Fédération Internationale de Tir à l'Arc* (FITA), founded in 1931.

Highest championship scores The highest scores achieved in either a World or Olympic championship for Double FITA rounds are: men, 2617 points (possible 2880) by Darrell Owen Pace (USA) (b. 23 Oct 1956) and Richard Lee McKinney (USA) (b. 20 Oct 1963) at Long Beach, California, USA on 21–22 Oct 1983; and women, 2683 points by Kim Soo-nyung (South Korea) (b. 5 Apr 1971) at Seoul, South Korea on 27–30 Sep 1988.

British records York round – possible 1296 pts: Single round, 1184 Steven Hallard (b. 22 Feb 1965) at Cheshire Championships on 5 Aug 1989; Double round, 2254 Steven Hallard at Lichfield, Staffs 8–9 Aug 1987.

Hereford (Women) – possible 1296 pts: Single round, 1202 Pauline Edwards (b. 23 Apr 1949) at Bucks County Championships on 1 Sep 1985; Double round, 2380 Joanne Franks (later Edens) (b. 1 Oct 1967) at the British Target Championships on 8 Sep 1987.

FITA round (Men): Single round, 1314 Steven Hallard; Double round, 2616 Steven Hallard, both at Lausanne, Switzerland in July 1989

■ **Highest championship score**
Darrell Owen Pace (USA) achieved a men's Double FITA rounds record of 2617 points (possible 2880) at Long Beach, California, USA on 21–22 Oct 1983. (Photo: All-Sport (USA)/Duffy)

Archery

Origins Though the earliest pictorial evidence of the existence of bows is seen in the Mesolithic cave paintings in Spain, archery as an organized sport appears to have developed in the 3rd century AD. Competitive archery may however date back to the 12th century BC. The oldest archery body in the British Isles is the Society of Archers in Yorkshire, formed on 14 May 1673, though the Society of Kilwinning Archers, in Scotland, has contes-

World Archery Records — Single FITA rounds

Event	Points	Name and Country	Possible	Year
		MEN		
FITA	1352	Vladimir Yesheyev (USSR)	1440	1990
90 m	330	Vladimir Yesheyev (USSR)	360	1990
70 m	344	Hiroshi Yamamoto (Japan)	360	1990
50 m	345	Richard McKinney (USA)	360	1982
30 m	357	Takayoshi Matsushita (Japan)	360	1986
Final	345	Vladimir Yesheyev (USSR)	360	1990
Team	3963	USSR (Stanislav Zabrodskiy, Vadim Shikarev, Vladimir Yesheyev)	4320	1989
Final	1005	South Korea (Kim Sun-bin, Yang Chang-hoon, Park Jae-pyo)	1080	1990
		WOMEN		
FITA	1370	Lee Eun-kyung (South Korea)	1440	1990
70 m	341 *	Kim Soo-nyung (South Korea)	360	1990
60 m	347	Kim Soo-nyung (South Korea)	360	1989
50 m	337	Lee Eun-kyung (South Korea)	360	1990
30 m	357	Joanne Edens (GB)	360	1990
Final	346	Kim Soo-nyung (South Korea)	360	1990
Team	4025	South Korea (Kim Soo-nyung, Wang Hee-nyung, Kim Kyung-wook)	4320	1989
Final	1010	South Korea (Kim Soo-nyung, Wang Hee-nyung, Kim Kyung-wook)	1080	1989

* unofficial

Indoor Double FITA rounds at 25 m

	Points	Name and Country	Possible	Year
MEN	591	Erwin Verstegen (Holland)	600	1989
WOMEN	592	Petra Ericsson (Sweden)	600	1991

Indoor FITA round at 18 m

	Points	Name and Country	Possible	Year
MEN	591	Vladimir Yesheyev (USSR)	600	1989
WOMEN	587	Denise Parker (USA)	600	1989

FITA round (Women): Single round, 1306 Pauline Edwards at the Cheshire Championships in August 1989; Double round, 2591 A. Williamson (b. 3 Nov 1971) at Belgian FITA Star on 5 Jun 1989.

World Championships The most titles won by a man is four by Hans Deutgen (Sweden) (1917–89) in 1947–50 and by a woman is seven by Janina Spychajowa-Kurkowska (Poland) (b. 8 Feb 1901) in 1931–4, 1936, 1939 and 1947. The USA has a record 14 men's and 8 women's team titles.

Oscar Kessels (Belgium) (1904–68) participated in 21 world championships.

Olympic Games Hubert van Innis (Belgium) (1866–1961) won six gold and three silver medals at the 1900 and 1920 Olympic Games.

British Championships The most titles is 12 by Horace Alfred Ford (1822–80) in 1849–59 and 1867, and 23 by Alice Blanche Legh (1855–1948) in 1881, 1886–92, 1895, 1898–1900, 1902–9, 1913 and 1921–2. Miss Legh was inhibited from winning from 1882 to 1885 – because her mother was champion – and for four further years 1915–18 because there were no Championships during World War I.

24 hours – target archery The highest recorded score over 24 hours by a pair of archers is 76 158 during 70 Portsmouth Rounds (60 arrows per round at 20 yd at 60 cm FITA targets) by Simon Tarplee and David Hathaway at Evesham, Worcs on 1 Apr 1991. During this attempt Simon Tarplee set an individual record of 38 500.

FLIGHT SHOOTING

CROSSBOW: 1871·84 m *2047 yd 2 in*, Harry Drake (USA) (b. 7 May 1915), 'Smith Creek' Flight Range near Austin, Nevada, USA, 30 Jul 1988.
UNLIMITED FOOTBOW: 1854·40 m *1 mile 268 yd*, Harry Drake, Ivanpah Dry Lake, California, USA, 24 Oct 1971.
RECURVE BOW: *Men*; 1222·01 m *1336 yd 1 ft 3 in*, Don Brown (USA), 'Smith Creek' Flight Range, 2 Aug 1987. *Women*; 950·39 m *1039 yd 1 ft 1 in*, April Moon (USA), Wendover, 13 Sep 1981.
CONVENTIONAL FOOTBOW: *Men*; 1410·87 m *1542 yd 2 ft 10 in*, Harry Drake, Ivanpah Dry Lake, 6 Oct 1979. *Women*; 1018·48 m *1113 yd 2 ft 6 in*, Arlyne Rhode (USA) (b. 4 May 1936), Wendover, Utah, USA, 10 Sep 1978.
COMPOUND BOW: *Men*; 1060·55 m *1159 yd 2 ft 6 in*, Bert McCune Jnr (USA), 'Smith Creek' Flight Range, 2 Aug 1987. *Women* (25 kg); 826·73 m *904 yd 4 in*, April Moon (USA), 'Smith Creek' Flight Range, 5 Oct 1989.
BROADHEAD FLIGHT UNLIMITED COMPOUND BOW: *Men*; 678·53 m *742 yd 2 in*, Jesse Morehead (USA), Wendover, 24 Jun 1990. *Women*; 440·01 m *481 yd 4 in*, April Moon (USA), Salt Lake City, Utah, USA, 29 Jun 1989.

Athletics

The earliest evidence of organized running was at Memphis, Eygpt *c.* 3800 BC. The earliest accurately dated Olympic Games was in July 776 BC, at which celebration Coroibos won the foot race. The oldest surviving measurements are a long jump of 7·05 m *23 ft 1 ½ in* by Chionis of Sparta in *c.* 656 BC and a discus throw of 100 cubits (about 46·30 m *152 ft*) by Protesilaus.

Fastest speed An analysis of split times at each 10 metres in the 1988 Olympic Games 100 m final in Seoul on 24 Sep 1988 won by Ben Johnson (Canada) in 9·79 (average speed 36·77 km/h *22·85 mph* but later disallowed as a world record due to his positive drugs test for steroids) from Carl Lewis (USA) 9·92, showed that both Johnson and Lewis reached a peak speed (40 m–50 m and 80 m–90 m respectively) of 0·83 sec for 10 m, i.e. 43·37 km/h *26·95 mph*. In the women's final Florence Griffith-Joyner was timed at 0·91 sec for each 10 m from 60 m–90 m, i.e. 39·56 km/h *24·58 mph*.

Highest jump above own head The greatest height cleared above an athlete's own head is 59 cm *23¼ in* by Franklin Jacobs (USA) (b. 31 Dec 1957), 1·73 m *5 ft 8 in* tall, who jumped 2·32 m *7 ft 7¼ in* at New York, USA, on 27 Jan 1978. The greatest height cleared by a woman above her own head is 32 cm *12¾ in* by Yolanda Henry (USA) (b. 2 Dec 1964), 1·68 m *5 ft 6 in* tall, who jumped 2·00 m *6 ft 6¾ in* at Seville, Spain on 30 May 1990.

Most Olympic titles The most Olympic gold medals won is ten (an absolute Olympic record) by Raymond Clarence Ewry (USA) (1874–1937) in the standing high, long and triple jumps in 1900, 1904, 1906 and 1908.

Women The most gold medals won by a woman is four shared by: Francina 'Fanny' E. Blankers-Koen (Netherlands) (b. 26 Apr 1918) with 100 m, 200 m, 80 m hurdles and 4 × 100 m relay, 1948; Elizabeth 'Betty'

Cuthbert (Australia) (b. 20 Apr 1938) with 100 m, 200 m, 4 × 100 m relay, 1956 and 400 m, 1964; and Bärbel Wöckel (*née* Eckert) (GDR) (b. 21 Mar 1955) with 200 m and 4 × 100 m relay in 1976 and 1980.

Most wins at one Games The most gold medals at one celebration is five by Paavo Johannes Nurmi (Finland) (1897–1973) in 1924; 1500 m, 5000 m, 10 000 m cross-country, 3000 m team and cross-country team. The most at individual events is four by Alvin Christian Kraenzlein (USA) (1876–1928) in 1900: 60 m, 110 m hurdles, 200 m hurdles and long jump.

Most Olympic medals The most medals won is 12 (nine gold and three silver) by Paavo Nurmi (Finland) in the Games of 1920, 1924 and 1928.

Women The most medals won by a woman athlete is seven by Shirley Barbara de la Hunty (*née* Strickland) (Australia) (b. 18 Jul 1925) with three gold, one silver and three bronze in the 1948, 1952 and 1956 Games. A re-read of the photo-finish indicates that she finished third, not fourth, in the 1948 200 metres event, thus unofficially increasing her medal haul to eight. Irena Szewinska (*née* Kirszenstein) (Poland) (b. 24 May 1946) won three gold, two silver and two bronze in 1964, 1968, 1972 and 1976, and is the only woman athlete to win a medal in four successive Games.

Most Olympic titles *British* The most gold medals won by a British athlete (excluding tug of war and walking, *q.v.*) is two by: Charles Bennett (1871–1949)

■ **First 20-footer**
Sergey Bubka (USSR) has set a remarkable 26 world records indoors and out (to June 1991) and was the first pole vaulter to surpass 20 feet when he cleared 6·10 m indoors at San Sebastian, Spain on 15 Mar 1991. (Photo: All-Sport/G. Mortimore)

225

■ All-round talent
Jackie Joyner-Kersee (USA) (b. 3 Mar 1962) accumulated a world record 7291 points for the heptathlon at the 1988 Olympic Games at Seoul, South Korea on 23–24 September. In the javelin, she threw 45·66 m 149 ft 9 in which contributed 776 points. (Photo: All-Sport (USA)/Duffy)

(1500 m and 5000 m team, 1900); Alfred Edward Tysoe (1874–1901) (800 m and 5000 m team, 1900); John Thomas Rimmer (1879–1962) (4000 m steeplechase and 5000 m team, 1900); Albert George Hill (1889–1969) (800 m and 1500 m, 1920); Douglas Gordon Arthur Lowe (1902–81) (800 m 1924 and 1928); Sebastian Newbold Coe (b. 29 Sep 1956) (1500 m 1980 and 1984) and Francis Morgan 'Daley' Thompson (b. 30 Jul 1958) (decathlon 1980 and 1984). Daley Thompson was also world champion at the decathlon in 1983.

Most Olympic medals *British* The most medals won by a British athlete is four by Guy Montagu Butler (1899–1981) gold for the 4 × 400 m relay and silver for 400 m in 1920 and bronze for each of these events in 1924, and by Sebastian Coe, who also won silver medals at 800 m in 1980 and 1984. Three British women athletes have won three medals: Dorothy Hyman (b. 9 May 1941) with a silver (100 m, 1960) and two bronze (200 m, 1960 and 4 × 100 m relay, 1964), Mary Denise Rand (now Toomey, *née* Bignal), (b. 10 Feb 1940) with a gold (long jump), a silver (pentathlon) and a bronze (4 × 100 m relay), all in 1964 and Kathryn Jane Cook (*née* Smallwood) (b. 3 May 1960), all bronze – at 4 × 100 m relay 1980 and 1984, and at 400 m in 1984.

Olympic champions *Oldest and youngest* The oldest athlete to win an Olympic title was Irish-born Patrick Joseph 'Babe' McDonald (*né* McDonnell) (USA) (1878–1954) who was aged 42 yr

WORLD RECORDS *WOMEN*

World outdoor records for the women's events scheduled by the International Amateur Athletic Federation. Fully automatic electric timing is mandatory for all events up to 400 metres.

RUNNING

	min sec	Name and country	Place	Date	
100 metres	10·49	Delorez Florence Griffith Joyner (USA) (b. 21 Dec 1959)	Indianapolis, Indiana, USA	16 Jul	1988
200 metres	21·34	Delorez Florence Griffith Joyner (USA)	Seoul, South Korea	29 Sep	1988
400 metres	47·60	Marita Koch (GDR) (b. 18 Feb 1957)	Canberra, Australia	6 Oct	1985
800 metres	1:53·28	Jarmila Kratochvílová (Czechoslovakia) (b. 26 Jan 1951)	Münich, Germany	26 Jul	1983
1000 metres	2:30·6	Tatyana Providokhina (USSR) (b. 26 Mar 1953)	Podolsk, USSR	20 Aug	1978
1500 metres	3:52·47	Tatyana Kazankina (USSR) (b. 17 Dec 1951)	Zürich, Switzerland	13 Aug	1980
1 mile	4:15·61	Paula Ivan (Romania) (b. 20 Jul 1963)	Nice, France	10 Jul	1989
2000 metres	5:28·69	Maricica Puică (Rumania) (b. 29 Jul 1950)	Crystal Palace, London	11 Jul	1986
3000 metres	8:22·62	Tatyana Kazankina (USSR)	Leningrad, USSR	26 Aug	1984
5000 metres	14:37·33	Ingrid Kristiansen (*née* Christensen) (Norway) (b. 21 Mar 1956)	Stockholm, Sweden	5 Aug	1986
10 000 metres	30:13·74	Ingrid Kristiansen (Norway)	Oslo, Norway	5 Jul	1986

HURDLING

100 metres (2' 9" *84 cm*)	12·21	Yordanka Donkova (Bulgaria) (b. 28 Sep 1961)	Stara Zagora, Bulgaria	20 Aug	1988
400 metres (2' 6" *76 cm*)	52·94	Marina Styepanova (*née* Makeyeva) (USSR) (b. 1 May 1950)	Tashkent, USSR	17 Sep	1986

RELAYS

4 × 100 metres	41·37	GDR	Canberra, Australia	6 Oct	1985
		(Silke Gladisch (now Möller), Sabine Rieger (now Günther), Ingrid Auerswald (*née* Brestrich), Marlies Göhr (*née* Oelsner))			
4 × 200 metres	1:28·15	GDR	Jena, Germany	9 Aug	1980
		(Marlies Göhr (*née* Oelsner), Romy Müller (*née* Schneider), Bärbel Wöckel (*née* Eckert), Marita Koch)			
4 × 400 metres	3:15·17	USSR	Seoul, South Korea	1 Oct	1988
		(Tatyana Ledovskaya, Olga Nazarova, Maria Pinigina (*née* Kulchunova), Olga Bryzgina (*née* Vladykina))			
4 × 800 metres	7:50·17	USSR	Moscow, USSR	5 Aug	1984
		(Nadezha Olizarenko (*née* Mushta), Lyubov Gurina, Lyudmila Borisova, Irina Podyalovskaya)			

FIELD EVENTS

	m	ft	in					
High Jump	2·09	6	10¼	Stefka Kostadinova (Bulgaria) (b. 25 Mar 1965)	Rome, Italy		30 Aug	1987
Long Jump	7·52	24	8¼	Galina Chistyakova (USSR) (b. 26 Jul 1962)	Leningrad, USSR		11 Jun	1988
Triple Jump	14·95	49	1	Inessa Kravets (USSR) (b. 5 Oct 1966)	Moscow, USSR		10 Jun	1991
Shot 4 kg *8 lb 13 oz*	22·63	74	3	Natalya Lisovskaya (USSR) (b. 16 Jul 1962)	Moscow, USSR		7 Jun	1987
Discus 1 kg *2 lb 3·27 oz*	76·80	252	0	Gabriele Reinsch (GDR) (b. 23 Sep 1963)	Neubrandenburg, Germany		9 Jul	1988
Javelin 600 g *24·74 oz*	80·00	262	5	Petra Felke (GDR) (b. 30 Jul 1959)	Potsdam, Germany		9 Sep	1988

HEPTATHLON

7291 points		Jacqueline Joyner-Kersee (USA) (b. 3 Mar 1962)	Seoul, South Korea	23–24 Sep	1988

(100 m hurdles 12·69 sec; High Jump 1·86 m *6 ft 1¼ in*; Shot 15·80 m *51 ft 10 in*; 200 m 22·56 sec; Long Jump 7·27 m *23 ft 10 in*; Javelin; 45·66 m *149 ft 9 in*; 800 m 2 min 08·51 sec)

WORLD RECORDS MEN

World outdoor records for the men's events scheduled by the International Amateur Athletic Federation. Fully automatic electric timing is mandatory for events up to 400 metres.

RUNNING	min sec	Name and country	Place	Date
100 metres	9·90*	Leroy Russell Burrell (USA) (b. 21 Feb 1967)	New York, USA	14 Jun 1991
200 metres	19·72A	Pietro Mennea (Italy) (b. 28 Jun 1952)	Mexico City, Mexico	12 Sep 1979
400 metres	43·29	Harry Lee 'Butch' Reynolds Jr (USA) (b. 8 Aug 1964)	Zürich, Switzerland	17 Aug 1988
800 metres	1:41·73	Sebastian Newbold Coe (GB) (b. 29 Sep 1956)	Florence, Italy	10 Jun 1981
1000 metres	2:12·18	Sebastian Newbold Coe (GB)	Oslo, Norway	11 Jul 1981
1500 metres	3:29·46	Saïd Aouita (Morocco) (b. 2 Nov 1959)	West Berlin, Germany	23 Aug 1985
1 mile	3:46·32	Steven Cram (GB) (b. 14 Oct 1960)	Oslo, Norway	27 Jul 1985
2000 metres	4:50·81	Saïd Aouita (Morocco)	Paris, France	16 Jul 1987
3000 metres	7:29·45	Saïd Aouita (Morocco)	Cologne, Germany	20 Aug 1989
5000 metres	12:58·39	Saïd Aouita (Morocco)	Rome, Italy	22 Jul 1987
10 000 metres	27:08·23	Arturo Barrios (Mexico) (b. 12 Dec 1963)	Berlin, Germany	18 Aug 1989
20 000 metres	56:55·6	Arturo Barrios (Mexico)	La Flèche, France	30 Mar 1991
25 000 metres	1 hr 13:55·8	Toshihiko Seko (Japan) (b. 15 Jul 1956)	Christchurch, New Zealand	22 Mar 1981
30 000 metres	1 hr 29:18·8	Toshihiko Seko (Japan)	Christchurch, New Zealand	22 Mar 1981
1 hour	21 101 m 13·111 miles	Arturo Barrios (Mexico)	La Flèche, France	30 Mar 1991

* Ben Johnson (Canada) (b. 30 Dec 1961) ran 100 m in 9·79 sec at Seoul, South Korea on 24 Sep 1988, but was subsequently disqualified on a positive drugs test for steroids. He later admitted to having taken drugs over many years, and this invalidated his ratified 9·83 sec at Rome, Italy on 30 Aug 1987.
A This record was set at high altitude—Mexico City 2240 m 7349 ft. Best mark at low altitude: 200 m: 19·75 sec, Frederick Carleton 'Carl' Lewis (USA) (b. 1 Jul 1961), Indianapolis, Indiana, USA, 19 Jun 1983 and Joseph Nathaniel 'Joe' DeLoach (USA) (b. 5 Jun 1967) at Seoul, South Korea on 28 Sep 1988.

HURDLING

	min sec		Place	Date
110 metres (3' 6" 106 cm)	12·92	Roger Kingdom (USA) (b. 26 Aug 1962)	Zürich, Switzerland	16 Aug 1989
400 metres (3' 0" 91·4 cm)	47·02	Edwin Corley Moses (USA) (b. 31 Aug 1955)	Koblenz, Germany	31 Aug 1983
3000 metres steeplechase	8:05·35	Peter Koech (Kenya) (b. 18 Feb 1958)	Stockholm, Sweden	4 Jul 1989

RELAYS

	min sec		Place	Date
4 × 100 metres	37·79	France	Split, Yugoslavia	1 Sep 1990
		(Max Morinière, Daniel Sangouma, Jean-Charles Trouabal, Bruno Marie-Rose)		
4 × 200 metres	1:19·38	Santa Monica Track Club (USA)	Koblenz, Germany	23 Aug 1989
		(Daniel Everett, Leroy Burrell, Floyd Wayne Heard, Carl Lewis)		
4 × 400 metres	2:56·16A	United States	Mexico City, Mexico	20 Oct 1968
		(Vincent Edward Matthews, Ronald John Freeman II, George Lawrence James, Lee Edward Evans)		
	2:56·16	United States	Seoul, South Korea	1 Oct 1988
		(Daniel Everett, Steven Earl Lewis, Kevin Bernard Robinzine, Harry Lee 'Butch' Reynolds)		
4 × 800 metres	7:03·89	Great Britain	Crystal Palace, London	30 Aug 1982
		(Peter Elliott, Garry Peter Cook, Steven Cram, Sebastian Coe)		
4 × 1500 metres	14:38·8	West Germany	Cologne, Germany	17 Aug 1977
		(Thomas Wessinghage, Harald Hudak, Michael Lederer, Karl Fleschen)		

FIELD EVENTS

	m	ft in		Place	Date
High Jump	2·44	8 0	Javier Sotomayor (Cuba) (b. 13 Oct 1967)	San Juan, Puerto Rico	29 Jul 1989
Pole Vault	6·08	19 11½	Sergey Bubka (USSR) (b. 4 Dec 1963)	Moscow, USSR	9 Jun 1991
Long Jump	8·90A	29 2½	Robert Beamon (USA) (b. 29 Aug 1946)	Mexico City, Mexico	18 Oct 1968
Triple Jump	17·97	58 11	William Augustus 'Willie' Banks (USA) (b. 11 Mar 1956)	Indianapolis, USA	16 Jun 1985
Shot 7·26 kg 16 lb	23·12	75 10¼	Eric Randolph 'Randy' Barnes (USA) (b. 16 Jun 1966)	Los Angeles, California, USA	20 May 1990
Discus 2 kg 4 lb 6·55 oz	74·08	243 0	Jürgen Schult (GDR) (b. 11 May 1960)	Neubrandenburg, Germany	6 Jun 1986
Hammer 7·26 kg 16 lb	86·74	284 7	Yuriy Georgiyevich Sedykh (USSR) (b. 11 Jun 1955)	Stuttgart, Germany	30 Aug 1986
Javelin 800 g 28·22 oz	96·96†	318 1	Seppo Räty (Finland) (b. 27 Apr 1962)	Punkalaidun, Finland	2 Jun 1991

A Set at high altitude; the low altitude best: 8·79 m 28 ft 10 in, Carl Lewis at Indianapolis, Indiana, USA on 19 Jun 1983.
† With the new javelin, which has the centre of gravity moved back, introduced in 1986. The best performance with the old javelin was 104·80 m 343 ft 10 in by Uwe Hohn (GDR) (b. 16 Jul 1962) at East Berlin, Germany on 20 Jul 1984.

DECATHLON

8847 points ..... Francis Morgan 'Daley' Thompson (GB) (b. 30 Jul 1958) ..... Los Angeles, California, USA ..... 8–9 Aug 1984
(1st day: 100 m 10·44 sec, Long Jump 8·01 m 26 ft 3½ in, Shot Put 15·72 m 51 ft 7 in, High Jump 2·03 m 6 ft 8 in, 400 m 46·97 sec)
(2nd day: 110 m Hurdles 14·33 sec, Discus 46·56 m 152 ft 9 in, Pole Vault 5·00 m 16 ft 4¾ in, Javelin 65·24 m 214 ft 0 in, 1500 m 4:35·00 sec)

26 days when he won the 25·4 kg 56 lb weight throw at Antwerp, Belgium on 21 Aug 1920. The oldest female champion was Lia Manoliu (Romania) (b. 25 Apr 1932) aged 36 yr 176 days when she won the discus at Mexico City on 18 Oct 1968. The youngest gold medallist was Barbara Pearl Jones (USA) (b. 26 Mar 1937) who at 15 yr 123 days was a member of the winning 4 × 100 m relay team, at Helsinki, Finland on 27 Jul 1952. The youngest male champion was Robert Bruce Mathias (USA) (b. 17 Nov 1930) aged 17 yr 263 days when he won the decathlon at the London Games on 5–6 Aug 1948.

The oldest Olympic medallist was Tebbs Lloyd Johnson (1900–84), aged 48 yr 115 days when he was third in the 1948 50 000 m walk. The oldest woman medallist was Dana Zátopková (b. 19 Sep 1922) aged 37 yr 348 days when she was second in the javelin in 1960.

World Championships Quadrennial World Championships, distinct from the Olympic Games, were inaugurated in 1983, when they were held in Helsinki, Finland. The most medals won is six gold by Frederick Carleton 'Carl' Lewis (b. 1 Jul 1961), gold at 100 m, long jump and 4 × 100 m relay in 1983 and the latter two also in 1987, when he added the 100 m gold as Ben Johnson was stripped of his title by the IAAF in 1989 following his admission of drug taking. Lewis has also won six Olympic golds, four in 1984 and two in 1988.

World record breakers Oldest and youngest For the greatest age at which anyone has broken a world record under IAAF jurisdiction see General Records. The female record is 36 yr 139 days for Marina Styepanova (née Makeyeva) (USSR) (b. 1 May 1950) with 52·94 sec for the 400 m hurdles at Tashkent, USSR on 17 Sep 1986. The youngest individual record breaker is Wang Yan (China) (b. 9 Apr 1971) who set a women's 5000 m walk record at age 14 yr 334 days with 21 min 33·8 sec at Jian, China on 9 Mar 1986. The youngest male is 17 yr 198 days Thomas Ray (GB) (1862–1904) when he pole-vaulted 3·42 m 11 ft 2¾ in on 19 Sep 1879 (prior to IAAF ratification).

Most records in a day Jesse Owens (USA) (1913–80) set six world records in 45 min at Ann Arbor, Michigan on 25 May 1935 with a 9·4 sec 100 yd at 3:15 p.m., a 8·13 m 26 ft 8¼ in long jump at 3:25 p.m., a 20·3 sec 220 yd (and 200 m) at 3:45 p.m. and a 22·6 sec 220 yd low hurdles (and 200 m) at 4 p.m.

Most national titles Great Britain The most national senior titles won by an

Longest career
Duncan McLean (1884–1980) of Scotland set a world age (92) record of 100 m in 21·7 sec in August 1977, over 73 years after his best ever sprint of 100 yd in 9·9 sec in South Africa in February 1904.

WORLD INDOOR RECORDS

Track performances around a turn must be made on a track of circumference no longer than 200 metres.

MEN
RUNNING

	min:sec	Name and country	Place	Date
50 metres	5·61*	Manfred Kokot (GDR) (b. 3 Jan 1948)	East Berlin, Germany	4 Feb 1973
	5·61*	James Sanford (USA) (b. 27 Dec 1957)	San Diego, California, USA	20 Feb 1981
60 metres	6·48*	Leroy Russell Burrell (USA) (b. 21 Feb 1967)	Madrid, Spain	13 Feb 1991
200 metres	20·36	Bruno Marie-Rose (France) (b. 20 May 1965)	Liévin, France	22 Feb 1987
400 metres	45·05	Thomas Schönlebe (GDR) (b. 6 Aug 1965)	Sindelfingen, Germany	5 Feb 1988
	45·05 ±	Danny Everett (USA) (b. 1 Nov 1966)	Stuttgart, Germany	4 Feb 1990
800 metres	1:44·84	Paul Ereng (Kenya) (b. 22 Aug 1967)	Budapest, Hungary	4 Mar 1989
1000 metres	(2:16·4 officially) 2:16·62	Robert Druppers (Netherlands) (b. 29 Apr 1962)	The Hague, Netherlands	20 Feb 1988
1500 metres	3:34·16	Noureddine Morceli (Algeria) (b. 20 Feb 1970)	Seville, Spain	28 Feb 1991
1 mile	3:49·78	Eamonn Coghlan (Ireland) (b. 21 Nov 1952)	East Rutherford, New Jersey, USA	27 Feb 1983
3000 metres	7:39·2	Emiel Puttemans (Belgium) (b. 8 Oct 1947)	West Berlin, Germany	18 Feb 1973
5000 metres	13:20·4	Suleiman Nyambui (Tanzania) (b. 13 Feb 1953)	New York, USA	6 Feb 1983
50 metres hurdles	6·25	Mark McKoy (Canada) (b. 10 Dec 1961)	Kobe, Japan	5 Mar 1986
60 metres hurdles	7·36‡	Gregory 'Greg' Foster (USA) (b. 4 Aug 1958)	Los Angeles, USA	16 Jan 1987
	7·37	Roger Kingdom (USA) (b. 26 Aug 1962)	Piraeus, Greece	8 Feb 1989

* Ben Johnson (Canada) (b. 30 Dec 1961) ran 50 m in 5·55 sec at Ottawa, Canada on 31 Jan 1987 and 60 m in 6·41 at Indianapolis, USA on 7 Mar 1987, but these were invalidated due to his admission of having taken drugs over many years, following his disqualification at the 1988 Olympics.
± not recognised as run all the way in lanes and IAAF rules specify breaking from lanes after two turns.
‡ adjudged by observers to have been with a rolling start, but officially ratified.

RELAYS

	min:sec		Place	Date
4 × 200 metres	1:22·11	United Kingdom	Glasgow, Strathclyde	3 Mar 1991
		(Linford Christie, Darren Braithwaite, Ade Mafe, John Regis)		
4 × 400 metres	3:03·05	Germany	Seville, Spain	10 Mar 1991
		(Rico Lieder, Jens Carlowitz, Karsten Just, Thomas Schönlebe)		

WALKING

	min:sec		Place	Date
5000 metres	18:11·41u	Ronald Weigel (GDR) (b. 8 Aug 1959)	Vienna, Austria	13 Feb 1988
	18:23·55	Mikhail Shchennikov (USSR) (b. 26 Dec 1967)	Seville, Spain	10 Mar 1991

u not officially recognised.

FIELD EVENTS

	m	ft in	Name and country	Place	Date
High Jump	2·43	7 11½	Javier Sotomayor (Cuba) (b. 13 Oct 1967)	Budapest, Hungary	4 Mar 1989
Pole Vault	6·12	20 1	Sergey Bubka (USSR) (b. 4 Dec 1963)	Grenoble, France	23 Mar 1991
Long Jump	8·79	28 10¼	Fredrick Carleton 'Carl' Lewis (USA) (b. 1 Jul 1961)	New York, USA	27 Jan 1984
Triple Jump	17·76	58 3¼	Michael Alexander Conley (USA) (b. 5 Oct 1962)	New York, USA	27 Feb 1987
Shot	22·66	74 4¼	Eric Randolph 'Randy' Barnes (USA) (b. 16 Jun 1966)	Los Angeles, California, USA	20 Jan 1989

HEPTATHLON

		Name and country	Place	Date
HEPTATHLON	6285 points	Christian Plaziat (France) (b. 28 Oct 1963)	Nogent-sur-Oise, France	10–11 Feb 1990

(60 m 6·78 sec; Long jump, 7·45 m; Shot, 14·42 m; High jump, 2·13 m; 60 m hurdles, 7·98 sec; Pole vault, 4·90 m; 1000 m 2:47·24)

WOMEN
RUNNING

	min:sec	Name and country	Place	Date
50 metres	6·11†	Marita Koch (GDR) (b. 18 Feb 1957)	Grenoble, France	2 Feb 1980
60 metres	7·00	Nelli Cooman-Fiere (Netherlands) (b. 6 Jun 1964)	Madrid, Spain	23 Feb 1986
200 metres	22·24	Merlene Ottey (Jamaica) (b. 10 May 1960)	Seville, Spain	10 Mar 1991
400 metres	49·59	Jarmila Kratochvílová (Czechoslovakia) (b. 26 Jan 1951)	Milan, Italy	7 Mar 1982
800 metres	1:56·40	Christine Wachtel (GDR) (b. 6 Jan 1965)	Vienna, Austria	13 Feb 1988
1000 metres	2:34·8	Brigitte Kraus (GDR) (b. 12 Aug 1956)	Dortmund, Germany	19 Feb 1978
1500 metres	4:00·27	Doina Melinte (Romania) (b. 27 Dec 1956)	East Rutherford, New Jersey, USA	9 Feb 1990
1 mile	4:17·14	Doina Melinte (Romania)	East Rutherford, New Jersey, USA	9 Feb 1990
3000 metres	8:33·82	Elly van Hulst (Netherlands) (b. 9 Jun 1957)	Budapest, Hungary	4 Mar 1989
5000 metres	15:13·72	Uta Pippig (Germany) (b. 7 Sep 1965)	Stuttgart, Germany	10 Feb 1991
50 metres hurdles	6·58	Cornelia Oschkenat (GDR) (b. 29 Oct 1961)	Berlin, Germany	20 Feb 1988
60 metres hurdles	7·69	Lyudmila Narozhilenko (USSR) (b. 21 Apr 1964)	Chelyabinsk, USSR	4 Feb 1990

† Angella Issajenko (née Taylor) (Canada) (b. 28 Sep 1958) ran 6·06 at Ottawa, Canada on 31 Jan 1987. This was accepted as a world record, but subsequently invalidated when she admitted steroid usage.

RELAYS

	min:sec		Place	Date
4 × 200 metres	1:32·55	S. C. Eintracht Hamm (West Germany)	Dortmund, Germany	19 Feb 1988
		(Helga Arendt, Silke-Beate Knoll, Mechthild Kluth, Gisela Kinzel)		
4 × 400 metres	3:27·22	Germany	Seville, Spain	10 Mar 1991
		(Sandra Seuser, Katrin Schreiter, Annet Hesselbarth, Grit Breuer)		

WALKING

	min:sec		Place	Date
3000 metres	11:50·90	Beate Anders (GDR) (b. 4 Feb 1968)	Seville, Spain	9 Mar 1991

FIELD EVENTS

	m	ft in	Name and country	Place	Date
High jump	2·06	6 9	Stefka Kostadinova (Bulgaria) (b. 25 Nov 1965)	Piraeus, Greece	20 Feb 1988
Long jump	7·37	24 2¼	Heike Dreschler (GDR) (b. 16 Dec 1964)	Vienna, Austria	13 Feb 1988
Triple jump	14·45	47 5	Galina Chistyakova (USSR) (b. 26 Jul 1962)	Lipetsk, USSR	29 Jan 1989
Shot	22·50	73 10	Helena Fibingerová (Czechoslovakia) (b. 13 Jul 1959)	Jablonec, Czechoslovakia	19 Feb 1988

PENTATHLON

		Name and country	Place	Date
PENTATHLON	4705	Liliana Nastase (Romania) (b. 1 Aug 1962)	Sofia, Bulgaria	25 Feb 1990

(60 m hurdles 8·19 sec; High jump 1·72 m; Shot 13·71 m; Long jump 6·77 m; 800 m 2:16·60)

---

athlete is 30 by Judith Miriam Oakes (b. 14 Feb 1958) at the shot (10 WAAA outdoor, 12 WAAA indoor, 8 UK titles), 1977–91. The greatest number of senior AAA titles (excluding those in tug of war events) won by one athlete is 14 individual and one relay title by Emmanuel McDonald Bailey (Trinidad) (b. 8 Dec 1920), 1946–53. The most won outdoors in a single event is 13 by Denis Horgan (Ireland) (1871–1922) in the shot, 1893–1912. 13 senior titles was also won by: Michael Anthony Bull (b. 11 Sep 1946) at pole vault, eight indoor and five out, and by Geoffrey Lewis Capes (b. 23 Aug 1949) at shot, six indoor and seven out.

The greatest number of WAAA outdoor titles won by one athlete is 14 by Suzanne Allday (née Farmer) (b. 26 Nov 1934) with seven each at shot and discus between 1952 and 1962. She also won two WAAA indoor shot titles.

■ **World record**

Most international appearances
The greatest number of international matches contested for any nation is 89 by shot-putter Bjørn Bang Andersen (b. 14 Nov 1937) for Norway, 1960–81.

The greatest number of full Great Britain international appearances (outdoors and indoors) is 73 by Verona Marolin Elder (*née* Bernard) (b. 5 Apr 1953), mostly at 400 m, from 1971 to 1983. The men's record is 67 by shot-putter Geoff Capes, 1969–80. At pole vault and decathlon Mike Bull had 66 full internationals or 69 including the European Indoor Games, before these were official internationals. The most outdoors is 61 by hammer thrower Andrew Howard Payne (b. South Africa, 17 Apr 1931) from 1960 to 1974.

Oldest and youngest internationals
The oldest full Great Britain international was Hector Harold Whitlock (1903–85) at 50 km walk at the 1952 Olympic Games, aged 48 yr 218 days. The oldest woman was Christine Rosemary Payne (*née* Charters, now Chimes) (b. 19 May 1933) at discus in the Great Britain *v.* Finland match on 26 Sep 1974, aged 41 yr 130 days. The youngest man was high jumper Ross Hepburn (b. 14 Oct 1961) *v.* the USSR on 26 Aug 1977, aged 15 yr 316 days, and the youngest woman was Janis Walsh (b. 28 Mar 1960) *v.* Belgium (indoor) at 60 m

and 4 × 200 m relay on 15 Feb 1975, aged 14 yr 324 days.

Longest winning sequence
Iolanda Balas (Romania) (b. 12 Dec 1936) won a record 140 consecutive competitions at high jump from 1956 to 1967. The record at a track event is 122 at 400 metres hurdles by Edwin Corley Moses (USA) (b. 31 Jul 1955) between his loss to Harald Schmid (West Germany) (b. 29 Sep 1957) at Berlin, Germany on 26 Aug 1977 and that to Danny Lee Harris (USA) (b. 7 Sep 1965) at Madrid, Spain on 4 Jun 1987.

'End to end'
The fastest confirmed run from John o' Groats to Land's End is 10 days 15 hr 27 min by Donald Alexander Ritchie (GB) (b. 6 Jul 1944) from 1–12 Apr 1989. A faster 10 days 3 hr 30 min was claimed by Fred Hicks (GB) for 1410 km *876 miles* on 20–30 May 1977. The fastest by a women is 13 days 17 hr 42 min by walker Ann Sayer (see Walking). A relay team of 10 from Vauxhall Motors A.C. covered the distance in 76 hr 58 min 29 sec from 31 May–3 Jun 1990.

Longest running race
The longest races ever staged were the 1928 (5507 km *3422 miles*) and 1929 (5898 km *3665 miles*) trans-continental races from New York City to Los Angeles, California, USA. The Finnish-born Johnny Salo (1893–1931) was the winner in 1929 in 79 days, from

31 March to 18 June. His elapsed time of 525 hr 57 min 20 sec (averaging 11·21 km/h *6·97 mph*) left him only 2 min 47 sec ahead of Englishman Pietro 'Peter' Gavuzzi (1905–81).

The longest race staged annually is Australia's Westfield Run from Paramatta, New South Wales to Doncaster, Victoria (Sydney to Melbourne). The distance run has varied slightly, but the record time is by Yiannis Kouros (Greece) (b. 13 Feb 1956), 5 days 2 hr 27 min 27 sec in 1989, when the distance was 1060 km *658 miles*.

Longest runs
The longest run by an individual is one of 17 918 km *11 134 miles* around the USA, by Sarah Covington-Fulcher (USA) (b. 14 Feb 1962) starting and finishing in Los Angeles, California, 21 Jul 1987–2 Oct 1988. Robert J Sweetgall (USA) (b. 8 Dec 1947) ran 17 027 km *10 608* around the perimeter of the USA starting and finishing in Washington, DC, Oct 1982–15 Jul 1983. Ron Grant (Australia) (b. 15 Feb 1943) ran around Australia, 13 383 km *8316 miles* in 217 days 3 hr 45 min, 28 Mar–31 Oct 1983. Max Telford (New Zealand) (b. Hawick, 2 Feb 1955) ran 8224 km *5110 miles* from Anchorage, Alaska to Halifax, Nova Scotia, in 106 days 18 hr 45 min from 25 Jul to 9 Nov 1977.

The fastest time for the cross-America run is 46 days 8 hr 36 min by Frank Giannino Jr (USA) (b. 1952) for the 4989 km *3100 miles* from San Francisco to New York from 1 Sep–17 Oct 1980. The women's trans-America record is 69 days 2 hr 40 min by Mavis Hutchinson (South Africa) (b. 25 Nov 1942) from 12 Mar–21 May 1978.

Greatest mileage
Douglas Alistair Gordon Pirie (GB) (b. 10 Feb 1931), who set five world records in the 1950s, estimated that he had run a total distance of 347 600 km *216 000 miles* in 40 years to 1981.

Dr Ron Hill (b. 21 Sep 1938), the 1969 European and 1970 Commonwealth marathon champion, has not missed a day's training since 20 Dec 1964. His meticulously compiled training log shows a total of 198 048 km *123 065 miles* from 3 Sep 1956 to 17 May 1991. He has finished 114 marathons, all sub 2:52 and has raced in 52 nations.

■ **Long distance bests**

■ **World record**
Bruno Marie-Rose celebrates bringing the French 4 × 100 metres team to European Championship victory at Split, Yugoslavia on 1 Sep 1990. He and team-mates, Max Morinière, Daniel Sangouma and Jean-Charles Troubal had further cause for celebration as they had set a new world record of 37·79 sec. (Photo: All-Sport/G. Mortimore)

Backwards running
Anthony 'Scott' Weiland, 27, ran the Detroit marathon backwards in 4 hr 7 min 54 sec on 13 Oct 1982. Donald Davis (USA) (b. 10 Feb 1960) ran 1 mile backwards in 6 min 7·1 sec at the University of Hawaii on 21 Feb 1983. Ferdie Ato Adoboe (Ghana) ran 100 yd backwards in 12·8 sec (100 m in 14·0 sec) at Amherst, Massachusetts, USA on 28 Jul 1983.

Arvind Pandya of India ran backwards across America, Los Angeles to New York, in 107 days, 18 Aug–3 Dec 1984. He also ran backwards from John o' Groats to Land's End, *940 miles* in 26 days 7 hr, 6 Apr–2 May 1990.

■ **Long distance bests**
Seen here during his 10 000 metres record run at Berlin in 1989, Arturo Barrios (Mexico) (b. 12 Dec 1963) has recently set long distance bests for 20 000 metres and the hour. Both records were set at La Flèche, France on 30 Mar 1991. (Photo: All-Sport/B. Martin)

ATHLETICS

UNITED KINGDOM (NATIONAL) RECORDS MEN

RUNNING

	min sec	Name	Place	Date	
100 metres	9·97	Linford Christie (b. 10 Apr 1960)	Seoul, South Korea	24 Sep	1988
200 metres	20·09	Linford Christie	Seoul, South Korea	28 Sep	1988
400 metres	44·50	Derek Antony Redmond (b. 3 Sep 1965)	Rome, Italy	1 Sep	1987
800 metres	1:41·73	Sebastian Newbold Coe (b. 29 Sep 1956)	Florence, Italy	10 Jun	1981
1000 metres	2:12·18	Sebastian Newbold Coe	Oslo, Norway	11 Jul	1981
1500 metres	3:29·67	Steven Cram (b. 14 Oct 1960)	Nice, France	16 Jul	1985
1 mile	3:46·32	Steven Cram.	Oslo, Norway	27 Jul	1985
2000 metres	4:51·39	Steven Cram.	Budapest, Hungary	4 Aug	1985
3000 metres	7:32·79	David Robert Moorcroft (b. 10 Apr 1953)	Crystal Palace, London	17 Jul	1982
5000 metres	13:00·41	David Robert Moorcroft	Oslo, Norway	7 Jul	1982
10 000 metres	27:23·06	Eamonn Thomas Martin (b. 9 Oct 1958)	Oslo, Norway	2 Jul	1988
20 000 metres	57:28·7	Carl Edward Thackery (b. 14 Oct 1962)	La Flèche, France	31 Mar	1990
25 000 metres	1 hr 15:22·6	Ronald Hill.	Bolton, Lancashire	21 Jul	1965
30 000 metres	1 hr 31:30·4	James Noel Carroll Alder (b. 10 Jun 1940)	Crystal Palace, London	5 Sep	1970
1 hour	12 miles 1268 yd *20 472m*	Ronald Hill.	Leicester	9 Nov	1968

HURDLING

	min sec	Name	Place	Date	
110 metres	13·08	Colin Ray Jackson (b. 18 Feb 1967)	Auckland, New Zealand	28 Jan	1990
400 metres	47·92	Kriss Kezie Uche Chukwu Duru Akabusi (b. 28 Nov 1958)	Split, Yugoslavia	29 Aug	1990
3000 metres Steeplechase	8:07·96	Mark Robert Rowland (b. 7 Mar 1963)	Seoul, South Korea	30 Sep	1988

RELAYS

	min sec	Name	Place	Date	
4 × 100 metres	37·98	National Team: Darren Braithwaite, John Paul Lyndon Regis, Marcus Adam, Linford Christie.	Split, Yugoslavia	1 Sep	1990
4 × 200 metres	1:21·29	National Team: Marcus Adam, Adeoye Mafe, Linford Christie, John Paul Lyndon Regis	Birmingham	23 Jun	1989
4 × 400 metres	2:58·22	National Team: Paul David Saunders, Kriss Akabusi, John Regis, Roger Anthony Black	Split, Yugoslavia	1 Sep	1990
4 × 800 metres	7:03·89	National Team: Peter Elliott, Gary Peter Cook, Steven Cram, Sebastian Newbold Coe	Crystal Palace, London	30 Aug	1982
4 × 1500 metres	14:56·8	National Team: Alan David Mottershead, Geoffrey Michael Cooper, Stephen John Emson, Roy Wood	Bourges, France	24 Jun	1979

FIELD EVENTS

	m	ft	in	Name	Place	Date	
High Jump	2·34	7	8¼	Dalton Grant (b. 8 Apr 1966)	Gateshead, Tyne & Wear	28 Aug	1989
(Indoors)	2·35	7	8½	Dalton Grant	Budapest, Hungary	4 Mar	1989
Pole Vault	5·65	18	6½	Keith Frank Stock (b. 18 Mar 1957)	Stockholm, Sweden	7 Jul	1981
Long Jump	8·23	27	0	Lynn Davies (b. 20 May 1942)	Bern, Switzerland	30 Jun	1968
Triple Jump	17·57A	57	7¾	Keith Leroy Connor (b. 16 Sep 1957)	Provo, Utah, USA	5 Jun	1982
Shot 7·26 kg *16 lb*	21·68	71	1½	Geoffrey Lewis Capes (b. 23 Aug 1949)	Cwmbran, Gwent	18 May	1980
Discus 2 kg *4 lb 6·55 oz*	64·32†	211	0	William Raymond Tancred (b. 6 Aug 1942)	Woodford, Essex	10 Aug	1974
Hammer 7·26 kg *16 lb*	77·54	254	5	Martin Girvan (b. 17 Apr 1960)	Wolverhampton, West Midlands	12 May	1984
Javelin 800 g *28·22 oz*	90·98	298	6	Stephen James Backley (b. 12 Feb 1969)	Stockholm, Sweden	2 Jul	1990

A *Record set at high altitude, best at low altitude: 17·41 m 57 ft 1¼in by John Herbert (b. 20 Apr 1962) at Kobe, Japan on 2 Sep 1985.*

† *William Raymond Tancred threw 64·94 m 213 ft 1in at Loughborough, Leicestershire on 21 Jul 1974 and Richard Charles Slaney (b. 16 May 1956) threw 65·16 m 213 ft 9 in at Eugene, Oregon, USA on 1 Jul 1985 but these were not ratified.*

DECATHLON

		Name	Place	Date
8847 points		Francis Morgan 'Daley' Thompson (GB) (b. 30 Jul 1958)	Los Angeles, California, USA	8–9 Aug 1984

(1st day: 100 m 10·44 sec, Long Jump 8·01 m *26 ft 3½in*, Shot Put 15·72 m *51 ft 7 in*, High Jump 2·03 m *6 ft 8 in*, 400 m 46·97 sec)

(2nd day: 110 m Hurdles 14·33 sec, Discus 46·56 m *152 ft 9 in*, Pole Vault 5·00 m *16 ft 4¾in*, Javelin 65·24 m *214 ft 0 in*, 1500 m 4:35·00 sec)

Highest marathon The highest start to a marathon is for the biennially-held Everest Marathon, first run on 27 Nov 1987. It begins at Gorak Shep, 5212 m *17 100 ft* and ends at Namche Bazar, 3444 m *11 300 ft*. The fastest time to complete this race is 3 hr 59 min 4 sec by Jack Maitland in 1989.

The greatest competitive distance run in a year is 8855 km *5502 miles* by Malcolm Campbell (GB) (b. 17 Nov 1934) in 1985.

1000 hours Ron Grant (Australia) ran 3 km within an hour, every hour, for 1000 consecutive hours at New Farm Park, Brisbane, Queensland, Australia from 6 Feb–20 Mar 1991.

Mass relay records The record for 100 miles *160·9 km* by 100 runners from one club is 7 hr 53 min 52·1 sec by Baltimore Road Runners Club, Towson, Maryland, USA on 17 May 1981. The women's record is 10 hr 47 min 9·3 sec on 3 Apr 1977 by the San Francisco Dolphins Southend Running Club, USA. The record for 100 × 100 m is 19 min 14·19 sec by a team from Antwerp at Merksem, Belgium on 23 Sep 1989.

The longest relay ever run was 16 936 km *10 524 miles* by 2660 runners at Trondheim, Norway from 26 Aug–20 Oct 1985. Twenty members of the Melbourne Fire Brigade ran 15 059 km *9357 miles* around Australia on Highway No. 1 in 43 days 23 hr 58 min, 10 Jul–23 Aug 1983. The most participants is

4800, 192 teams of 25, in the Batavierenrace, 167·2 km *103·89 miles* from Nijmegen to Enschede, Netherlands on 23 Apr 1983. The greatest distance covered in 24 hours by a team of ten is 450·978 km *280·232 miles* by Oxford Striders RC at East London, South Africa on 5–6 Oct 1990.

Highland Games The weight and height of cabers (Gaelic *cabar*) vary considerably. Extreme values are 7·62 m *25 ft* and 127 kg *280 lb*. The Braemar caber (5·86 m *19 ft 3 in* and 54·4 kg *120 lb*) in Grampian was untossed from 1891 until 1951 when it was tossed by George Clark (1907–86). The best authentic mark recorded for throwing the 56 lb weight for height, using one hand only is 5·23 m *17 ft 2 in* by Geoffrey Lewis Capes (b. 23 Aug 1949) at Lagos, Nigeria on 5 Dec 1982. The best throw recorded for the Scots hammer is 46·08 m *151 ft 2 in* by William Anderson (b. 6 Oct 1938) at Lochearnhead on 26 Jul 1969.

MARATHON

The marathon is run over a distance of

42·195 km *26 miles 385 yd*. This distance was that used for the race at the 1908 Olympic Games, run from Windsor to the White City stadium, and which became standard from 1924. The marathon (of 40 km) was introduced to the 1896 Olympic Games to commemorate the legendary run of Pheidippides (or Philippides) from the battlefield of Marathon to Athens in 490 BC. The 1896 Olympic marathon was preceded by trial races that year. The first Boston marathon, the world's longest-lasting major marathon, was held on 19 Apr 1897 at 39 km *24 miles 1232 yd* and the first national marathon championship was that of Norway in 1897.

The first championship marathon for women was organized by the Road Runners Club of America on 27 Sep 1970.

Fastest It should be noted that courses may vary in severity. The following are the best times recorded, all on courses whose distance has been verified.

The world records are: (men) 2 hr 6 min 50 sec by Belayneh Dinsamo (Ethiopia) (b.

—— UNITED KINGDOM (NATIONAL) RECORDS *WOMEN* ——

RUNNING

	Min sec	Name and country	Place	Date
100 metres	11·10	Kathryn Jane Smallwood (now Cook) (b. 3 May 1960)	Rome, Italy	5 Sep 1981
200 metres	22·10	Kathryn Jane Cook (*née* Smallwood)	Los Angeles, California, USA	9 Aug 1984
400 metres	49·43	Kathryn Jane Cook (*née* Smallwood)	Los Angeles, California, USA	6 Aug 1984
800 metres	1:57·42	Kirsty Margaret McDermott (now Wade) (b. 6 Aug 1962)	Belfast, Northern Ireland	24 Jun 1985
1000 metres	2:33·70	Kirsty Margaret McDermott (now Wade)	Gateshead, Tyne and Wear	9 Aug 1985
1500 metres	3:59·96	Zola Budd (b. 26 May 1966)	Brussels, Belgium	30 Aug 1985
1 mile	4:17·57	Zola Budd	Zürich, Switzerland	21 Aug 1985
2000 metres	5:29·58	Yvonne Carol Grace Murray (b. 4 Oct 1964)	Crystal Palace, London	11 Jul 1986
3000 metres	8:28·83	Zola Budd	Rome, Italy	7 Sep 1985
5000 metres	14:48·07	Zola Budd	Crystal Palace, London	26 Aug 1985
10000 metres	31:06·99	Elizabeth McColgan (*née* Lynch (b.24 May 1964)	Oslo, Norway	2 Jul 1988

RELAYS

		Name and country	Place	Date
4 × 100 metres	42·43	National Team: Heather Regina Hunte (now Oakes), Kathryn Jane Smallwood (now Cook), Beverley Lanita Goddard (now Callender), Sonia May Lannaman	Moscow, USSR	1 Aug 1980
4 × 200 metres	1:31·57	National Team; Donna-Marie Louise Hartley (*née* Murray), Verona Marolin Elder (*née* Bernard), Sharon Colyear (now Danville), Sonia May Lannaman	Crystal Palace, London	20 Aug 1977
4 × 400 metres	3:24·78	National Team: Sally Janet Jane Gunnell, Jennifer Elaine Stoute, Patricia Beckford, Linda Keough	Split, Yugoslavia	1 Sep 1990
4 × 800 metres	8:23·8	National Team: Joan Florence Allison (*née* Page), Sheila Janet Carey (*née* Taylor), Patricia Barbara Lowe (now Cropper), Rosemary Olivia Stirling (now Wright)	Paris, France	2 Oct 1971

HURDLING

	Min sec	Name and country	Place	Date
100 metres	12·82	Sally Jane Janet Gunnell (b. 29 Jul 1966)	Zürich, Switzerland	17 Aug 1988
400 metres	54·03	Sally Jane Janet Gunnell	Seoul, South Korea	28 Sep 1988

FIELD EVENTS

	m	ft	in	Name and country	Place	Date
High Jump	1·95	6	4 3/4	Diana Clare Elliot (now Davies) (b. 7 May 1961)	Oslo, Norway	26 Jun 1982
Long Jump	6·90	22	7 3/4	Beverly Kinch (b. 14 Jan 1964)	Helsinki, Finland	14 Aug 1983
Triple Jump	13·34	43	9	Michelle Griffith (b. 6 Oct 1971)	Crystal Palace	15 Jun 1991
Shot 4 kg *8 lb 13 oz*	19·36	63	6 1/4	Judith Miriam Oakes (b. 14 Feb 1958)	Gateshead, Tyne and Wear	14 Aug 1988
Discus 1 kg *2 lb 3·27 oz*	67·48	221	5	Margaret Elizabeth Ritchie (b. 6 Jul 1952)	Walnut, California, USA	26 Apr 1981
Javelin 600 g *21·16 oz*	77·44	254	1	Fatima Whitbread (b. 3 Mar 1961)	Stuttgart, Germany	28 Aug 1986

HEPTATHLON

		Name and country	Place	Date
6623 points		Judy Earline Veronica Simpson (*née* Livermore) (b. 14 Nov 1960)	Stuttgart, Germany	29–30 Aug 1986

(100 m hurdles 13·05 sec; High Jump 1·92 m *6 ft 3 1/2 in*; Shot 14·75 m *48 ft 4 in*; 200 m 25·09 sec; Long Jump 6·56 m *21 ft 6 1/4 in*; Javelin 40·92 m *134 ft 3 in*; 800 m 2 min 11·70 sec)

28 Jun 1965) at Rotterdam, Netherlands on 17 Apr 1988 and (women) 2 hr 21 min 6 sec by Ingrid Kristiansen (*née* Christensen) (Norway) (b. 21 Mar 1956) at London on 21 Apr 1985.

The British records are: (men) 2 hr 7 min 13 sec by Stephen Henry Jones (b. 4 Aug 1955) at Chicago, Illinois, USA on 20 Oct 1985 and (women) 2 hr 25 min 56 sec by Véronique Marot (b. 16 Sep 1955) at London on 23 Apr 1989.

Most competitors The record number of confirmed finishers in a marathon is 24 953 from 26 500 starters in the London marathon on 22 Apr 1990. A record 105 men ran under 2 hr 20 min and 46 under 2 hr 15 min in the World Cup marathon at London on 21 Apr 1991, and a record 6 men ran under 2 hr 10 min at Fukuoka, Japan on 4 Dec 1983 and at London on 23 Apr 1989. A record 9 women ran under 2 hr 30 min in the first Olympic marathon for women at Los Angeles, USA on 5 Aug 1984.

Most run by an individual Thian K. 'Sy' Mah (Canada) (1926–88) ran 524 marathons of 26 miles 385 yd or longer from 1967 to his death in 1988. He paced himself to take 3½ hr each run.

Three in three days The fastest combined time for three marathons in three days is 8 hr 22 min 31 sec by Raymond Hubbard (Belfast 2 hr 45 min 55 sec, London 2 hr 48 min 45 sec and Boston 2 hr 47 min 51 sec) on 16–18 Apr 1988.

Oldest finishers The oldest man to complete a marathon was Dimitrion Yordanidis (Greece), aged 98, in Athens, Greece on 10 Oct 1976. He finished in 7 hr 33 min. Thelma Pitt-Turner (New Zealand) set the women's record in August 1985, completing the Hastings, New Zealand marathon in 7 hr 58 min at the age of 82.

WALKING ————

Most Olympic medals Walking races have been included in the Olympic events since 1906. The only walker to win three gold medals has been Ugo Frigerio (Italy) (1901–68) with the 3000 m in 1920, and 10 000 m in 1920 and 1924. He also holds the record of most medals with four (he won the bronze medal at 50 000 m in 1932), a total shared with Vladimir Stepanovich Golubnichiy (USSR) (b. 2 Jun 1936), who won gold medals for the 20 000 m in 1960 and 1968, the silver in 1972 and the bronze in 1964.

The best British performance has been two gold medals by George Edward Larner (1875–1949) for the 3500 m and the 10 miles in 1908, but Ernest James Webb (1872 –1937) won three medals, being twice 'walker up' to Larner and finishing second in the 10 000 m in 1912.

Most titles Four-time Olympian, Ronald Owen Laird (b. 31 May 1938) of the New York AC, USA, won a total of 65 US national titles from 1958 to 1976, plus four Canadian Championships.

The greatest number of UK national titles won by a British walker is 27 by Vincent Paul Nihill (b. 5 Sep 1939) from 1963 to 1975.

Longest race The Paris–Colmar, until 1980 Strasbourg–Paris, event in France (instituted 1926 in the reverse direction), now about 524 km *325 miles*, is the world's longest annual race walk.

The fastest performance is by Robert Pietquin (Belgium) (b. 1938) who walked 507 km *315 miles* in the 1980 race in 60 hr 1 min 10 sec (after deducting 4 hr compulsory stops). This represents an average speed of 8·45 km/h *5·25 mph*. Roger Quéméner (France) has won a record seven times, 1979, 1983, 1985–9. The first woman to complete the race was Annie van der Meer (Netherlands) (b. 24 Feb 1947), who was 10th in 1983 in 82 hr 10 min.

'End to end' The fastest Land's End to John o' Groats walk is 12 days 3 hr 45 min

■ **Most participants**

Throughout the 1980s, the record for the most runners in a marathon regularly alternated between those held in London and New York. The latter reached a peak of 24 588 in 1989 when course records were set by Juma Ikangaa (Tanzania), 2:08:01 and Ingrid Kristiansen (Norway), 2:25:30. The picture shows the runners streaming across the Verrazano-Narrows Bridge. (Photo: All-Sport (USA)/L. Jeffrey)

Walking on hands

The distance record for walking on hands is 1400 km *871 miles*, by Johann Hurlinger of Austria, who walked from Vienna to Paris in 1900. Shin Don-mok of South Korea completed a 50 m *54·68 yd* inverted sprint in 17·44 sec on 14 Nov 1986. A four-man relay team of David Lutterman, Brendan Price, Philip Savage and Danny Scannell covered 1·6 km *1 mile* in 24 min 48 sec on 15 Mar 1987 at Knoxville, Tennessee, USA.

Walking on water

Rémy Bricka of Paris, France 'walked' across the Atlantic Ocean on skis 4·2 m *13 ft 9 in* long in 1988. Leaving Tenerife, Canary Islands on 2 Apr 1988, he covered 5636 km *3502 miles*, arriving at Trinidad on 31 May 1988.

■ **Most world badminton titles**

Yang Yang is one of three Chinese players to have won two singles world titles. Here he celebrates winning the 1989 All-England championships. (Photo: All-Sport)

■ **Most participants**

ROAD WALKING WORLD — BEST PERFORMANCES —

It should be noted that severity of road race courses and the accuracy of their measurement may vary, sometimes making comparisons of times unreliable.

MEN

20 km: 1 hr 18 min 13 sec, Pavol Blazek (Czechoslovakia) (b. 9 Jul 1958) at Hildesheim, Germany on 16 Sep 1990.
30 km: 2 hr 2 min 41 sec, Andrey Perlov (USSR) (b. 12 Dec 1961) at Leningrad, USSR on 5 Aug 1989.
50 km: 3 hr 37 min 41 sec, Andrey Perlov (USSR) at Leningrad, USSR on 5 Aug 1989.

WOMEN

10 km: 41 min 30 sec, Kerry Ann Saxby (Australia) (b. 2 Jun 1961) at Canberra, Australia on 27 Aug 1988.
20 km: 1 hr 29 min 40 sec, Kerry Saxby at Värnamo, Sweden on 13 May 1988.

BRITISH BESTS

MEN

20 km: 1 hr 22 min 03 sec, Ian Peter McCombie (b. 11 Jan 1961) at Seoul, South Korea on 23 Sep 1988.
30 km: 2 hr 7 min 56 sec, Ian Peter McCombie at Edinburgh, Lothian on 27 Apr 1986.
50 km: 3 hr 51 min 37 sec, Christopher Lloyd Maddocks (b. 28 Mar 1957) at Burrator, Devon on 28 Oct 1990.

WOMEN

10 km: 45 min 42 sec, Lisa Martine Langford (b. 15 Mar 1967) at New York, USA on 3 May 1987.

for 1426·4 km *886·3 miles* by WO2 Malcolm Barnish of the 19th Regiment, Royal Artillery from 9–21 Jun 1986. The women's record is 13 days 17 hr 42 min by Ann Sayer (b. 16 Oct 1936), 20 Sep–3 Oct 1980. The Irish 'end to end' record over the 644 km *400·2 miles* from Malin Head, Donegal to Mizen Head, Cork is 5 days 22 hr 30 min, set by John 'Paddy' Dowling (b. 15 Jun 1929) on 18–24 Mar 1982.

24 hours The greatest distance walked in 24 hr is 226·432 km *140 miles 1229 yd* by Paul Forthomme (Belgium) on a road course at Woluwe, Belgium on 13–14 Oct 1984. The best by a woman is 202·3 km *125·7 miles* by Annie van der Meer at Rouen, France on 30 Apr–1 May 1984 over a 1·185–km lap road course.

Backwards walking The greatest ever exponent of reverse pedestrianism has been Plennie L. Wingo (b. 24 Jan 1895) who completed his 12 875 km *8000 mile* transcontinental walk from Santa Monica, California, USA to Istanbul, Turkey from 15 Apr 1931 to 24 Oct 1932. The 24 hr distance record is 153 km *95 miles* by Anthony Thornton (USA) in Minneapolis, Minnesota, USA in 1989.

Badminton

Origins A similar game was played in

China in the 2nd millennium BC. The modern game may have evolved *c.*1870 at Badminton Hall in Avon, the seat of the Dukes of Beaufort, or from a game played in India. The first modern rules were codified in Pune in 1876.

World Championships (instituted 1977) A record five titles have been won by Park Joo-bong (South Korea), men's doubles 1985 and 1991 and mixed doubles 1985, 1989 and 1991. Three Chinese players have won two individual world titles: men's singles: Yang Yang 1987 and 1989; women's singles: Li Lingwei 1983 and 1989; Han Aiping 1985 and 1987. The most wins at the men's International Championship for the Thomas Cup (instituted 1948) is eight by Indonesia (1958, 1961, 1964, 1970, 1973, 1976, 1979 and 1984).

The most wins at the women's International Championship for the Uber Cup (instituted 1956) is five by Japan (1966, 1969, 1972, 1978 and 1981).

All-England Championships For long the most prestigious championships, they were instituted in 1899. A record eight men's singles were won by Rudy Hartono Kurniawan (Indonesia) (b. 18 Aug 1948), in 1968–74 and 1976. The greatest number of titles won (including doubles) is 21 by George Alan Thomas (1881–1972) between 1903 and 1928. The women's singles were won ten times by Judy Hashman (*née*

ULTRA LONG DISTANCE WORLD RECORDS

TRACK (Men)

Event	hr:min:sec	Name	Place	Date
50 km	2:48:06	Jeff Norman (GB)	Timperley, Manchester	7 Jun 1980
50 miles	4:51:49	Don Ritchie (GB)	Hendon, London	12 Mar 1983
100 km	6:10:20	Don Ritchie (GB)	Crystal Palace, London	28 Oct 1978
100 miles	11:30:51	Don Ritchie (GB)	Crystal Palace, London	15 Oct 1977
200 km	15:11:10†	Yiannis Kouros (Greece)	Montauban, France	15–16 Mar 1985
200 miles	27:48:35	Yiannis Kouros (Greece)	Montauban, France	15–16 Mar 1985
500 km	60:23:00	Yiannis Kouros (Greece)	Colac, Australia	26–29 Nov 1984
500 miles	105:42:09	Yiannis Kouros (Greece)	Colac, Australia	26–30 Nov 1984
1000 km	136:17:00	Yiannis Kouros (Greece)	Colac, Australia	26 Nov–1 Dec 1984

	kilometres			
24 hours	283·600	Yiannis Kouros (Greece)	Montauban, France	15–16 Mar 1985
48 hours	452·270	Yiannis Kouros (Greece)	Montauban, France	15–17 Mar 1985
6 days	1023·200	Yiannis Kouros (Greece)	Colac, Australia	26 Nov–1 Dec 1984

ROAD (Men)
Where superior to track bests and run on properly measured road courses.

	hr:min:sec			
50 km	2:43:38	Thompson Magawana (South Africa)	Claremont–Kirstenbosch	12 Apr 1988
50 miles	4:50:21	Bruce Fordyce (South Africa)	London–Brighton	25 Sep 1983
1000 miles	10d 10hr 30min 35sec	Yiannis Kouros (Greece)	New York, USA	21–30 May 1988

	kilometres			
24 hours	286·463	Yiannis Kouros (Greece)	New York, USA	28–29 Sep 1985
6 days	1028·370	Yiannis Kouros (Greece)	New York, USA	21–26 May 1988

TRACK (Women)

	hr:min:sec			
15 km	49:44·0	Silvana Cruciata (Italy)	Rome, Italy	4 May 1981
20 km	1:06:55·5	Rosa Mota (Portugal)	Lisbon, Portugal	14 May 1983
25 km	1:29:30	Karolina Szabo (Hungary)	Budapest, Hungary	23 Apr 1988
30 km	1:47:06	Karolina Szabo (Hungary)	Budapest, Hungary	23 Apr 1988
50 km	3:36:58	Ann Franklin (GB)	Barry, South Glamorgan	9 Mar 1986
50 miles	6:17:30†	Monika Kuno (West Germany)	Vogt, Germany	8–9 Jul 1983
100 km	8:01:01	Monika Kuno (West Germany)	Vogt, Germany	8–9 Jul 1983
100 miles	14:29:44	Ann Trason (USA)	Santa Rosa, USA	18–19 Mar 1989
200 km	19:28:48	Eleanor Adams (GB)	Melbourne, Australia	19–20 Aug 1989
200 miles	39:09:03	Hilary Walker (GB)	Blackpool, Lancashire	5–6 Nov 1988
500 km	77:53:46	Eleanor Adams (GB)	Colac, Australia	13–15 Nov 1989
500 miles	134:01:59	Eleanor Adams (GB)	Colac, Australia	13–19 Nov 1989

	kilometres			
1 hour	18·084	Silvana Cruciata (Italy)	Rome, Italy	4 May 1981
24 hours	240·169	Eleanor Adams (GB)	Melbourne, Australia	19–20 Aug 1989
48 hours	366·512	Hilary Walker (GB)	Blackpool, Lancashire	5–7 Nov 1988
6 days	883·631	Sandra Barwick (New Zealand)	Campbelltown, Australia	18–24 Nov 1990

†Timed on one running watch only.

ROAD (Women)
Where run on properly measured road courses.

	hr:min:sec			
30 km	1:38:27	Ingrid Kristiansen (Norway)	London	10 May 1987
50 km	3:08:13	Frith van der Merwe (South Africa)	Claremont-Kirstenbosch	25 Mar 1989
50 miles	5:40:18	Ann Trason (USA)	Houston, USA	23 Feb 1991
100 km	7:18:57	Birgit Lennartz (West Germany)	Hanua, Germany	28 Sep 1989
100 miles	13:55:02	Ann Trason (USA)	Queens, New York	16–17 Sep 1989
200 km	19:22:05	Ann Trason (USA)	Queens, New York	16–17 Sep 1989
(indoors)	19:00:31	Eleanor Adams (GB)	Milton Keynes	3–4 Feb 1990
1000 miles	14d 20hr 18min 24sec	Suprabha Schecter (USA)	New York, USA	20 Sep–5 Oct 1989

It should be noted that road times must be assessed with care as course conditions can vary considerably.

TRACK WALKING—*WORLD RECORDS*

The International Amateur Athletic Federation recognises men's records at 20 km, 30 km, 50 km and 2 hours, and women's at 5 km and 10 km.

Event	Time hr:min:sec	Name, country and date of birth	Place	Date
MEN				
10 km	38:02·60	Jozef Pribilinec (Czechoslovakia) (b. 6 Jul 1960)	Banská Bystrica, Czechoslovakia	30 Aug 1985
20 km	1:18:40·0	Ernesto Canto (Mexico) (b. 18 Oct 1959)	Fana, Norway	5 May 1984
30 km	2:03:56·5	Thierry Toutain (France) (b. 14 Feb 1962)	Héricourt, France	24 Mar 1991
50 km	3:41:38·4	Raul Gonzalez (Mexico) (b. 29 Feb 1952)	Fana, Norway	25 May 1979
1 hour	15 447 m	Jozef Pribilinec (Czechoslovakia)	Hildesheim, Germany	6 Sep 1986
2 hours	29 090 m	Thierry Toutain (France)	Héricourt, France	24 Mar 1991
WOMEN				
3 km	11:51·26	Kerry Ann Saxby (Australia) (b. 2 Jun 1961)	Melbourne, Australia	7 Feb 1991
5 km	20:07·52	Beate Anders (GDR) (b. 4 Feb 1968)	Rostock, Germany	23 Jun 1990
10 km	41:56·23	Nadezhda Ryashkina (USSR) (b. 1967)	Seattle, Washington, USA	24 Jul 1990

■ **Most world badminton titles**

Longest rallies
In the men's singles final
of the 1987 All-England
Championships between
Morten Frost (Denmark)
and Icuk Sugiarto (Indo-
nesia) there were two
successive rallies of over
90 strokes.

Most shuttles
In the final of the Indian
National Badminton
Championships 1986,
when Syed Modi beat
Vimal Kumar 15–12,
15–12, 182 shuttles were
used in the 66-minute

Devlin) (USA) (b. 22 Oct 1935) in 1954,
1957–8, 1960–4, 1966–7. She also equalled
the greatest number of titles won of 17 by
Meriel Lucas (later Mrs King Adams) from
1899 to 1910.

Shortest game In the 1969 Uber Cup in
Tokyo, Japan, Noriko Takagi (later Mrs
Nakayama) (Japan) beat Poppy
Tumengkol (Indonesia) in 9 min.

Baseball

Origins Rev. Thomas Wilson, of Maidstone, Kent, England, wrote disapprov-
ingly of baseball being played on Sundays.
The probable evolution of the game from
the traditional English game of rounders
was refuted by a commission established by
Albert G. Spalding (1850–1915) in 1907.
They determined that the first rules of
baseball had been drawn up by Abner
Doubleday (1819–93) in Cooperstown, New
York in 1839 but this is not now accepted by
baseball historians as accurate. Traditionally he laid out the first baseball field
for a game played by miltary cadets. The
National Baseball Hall of Fame was
dedicated in Cooperstown on 12 Jun 1939 as
part of the celebrations of the centennial of
the US national game. The basic rules for
the modern game were formulated by
Alexander Cartwright Jr (1820–92) in 1845
and the first match under the Cartwright
rules was played on 19 Jun 1846 in
Hoboken, New Jersey when the New York
Nine beat a team from the sport's first
organized club, the New York Knicker-
bockers, 23–1 in four innings. There are

two major leagues in the USA, the National
League of Professional Base Ball Clubs
(NL) formed on 2 Feb 1876 at the Grand
Central Hotel, New York, and the Ameri-
can League (AL) formed on 28 Jan 1901.

WORLD SERIES

Origins Played annually betwen the winners of the National League and the American League, the World Series was first
staged unofficially in 1903, and officially
from 1905. The most wins is 22 by the New
York Yankees between 1923 and 1978 from
a record 33 series appearances for winning
the American League titles between 1921
and 1981. The most National League titles
is 19 by the Dodgers—Brooklyn 1890–1957,
Los Angeles 1958–88.

Most valuable player The only men to
have won this award twice are: Sanford
'Sandy' Koufax (b. 30 Dec 1935) (Los
Angeles, NL 1963, 1965), Robert 'Bob'
Gibson (b. 9 Nov 1935) (St. Louis NL, 1964,
1967) and Reginald Martinez 'Reggie'
Jackson (b. 18 May 1946) (Oakland AL
1973, New York AL, 1977).

Attendance The record attendance for a
series is 420 784 for the six games when the
Los Angeles Dodgers beat the Chicago
White Sox 4–2 between 1 and 8 Oct 1959.
The single game record is 92 706 for the fifth

game of this series at the Memorial
Coliseum, Los Angeles on 6 Oct 1959.

MAJOR LEAGUE

Most games played Peter Edward
'Pete' Rose (b. 14 Apr 1941) played in a
record 3562 games with a record 14 053 at
bats for Cincinnati NL 1963–78 and 1984–6,
Philadelphia NL 1979–83, Montreal NL
1984. Henry Louis 'Lou' Gehrig (1903–41)
played in 2130 successive games for the
New York Yankees (AL) from 1 Jun 1925 to
30 Apr 1939.

Most home runs *Career* Henry
Louis 'Hank' Aaron (b. 5 Feb 1934) holds
the major league career record with 755
home runs; 733 for the Milwaukee
(1954–65) and Atlanta (1966–74) Braves in
the National League and 22 for the Milwaukee Brewers (AL) 1975–6. On 8 Apr
1974 he had bettered the previous record of
714 by George Herman 'Babe' Ruth (1895
–1948). Ruth hit his home runs from 8399
times at bat, the highest home run percentage of 8·5%. Joshua Gibson (1912–47) of
Homestead Grays and Pittsburgh Craw-
fords, Negro League clubs, achieved a
career total of nearly 960 homers including
an unofficial record season's total of 75 in
1931.

WORLD SERIES RECORDS
AL American League, NL National League

Most series played......................14	Lawrence Peter 'Yogi' Berra (New York, AL) 1947–63	
Most series played by pitcher ...11	Edward Charles 'Whitey' Ford (New York, AL)..................1950–64	
Most home runs in a game..........3	George Herman 'Babe' Ruth (New York, AL)............6 Oct 1926	
	3	George Herman 'Babe' Ruth (New York, AL)............9 Oct 1928
	3	Reginald Martinez Jackson (New York, AL)............ 18 Oct 1977
Runs batted in 6	Robert C. Richardson (New York, AL)............8 Oct 1960	
Strikeouts.....................................17	Robert Gibson (St Louis, NL)............2 Oct 1968	
Perfect game (9 innings)	Donald James Larson (New York, AL) v Brooklyn............8 Oct 1956	

US MAJOR LEAGUE RECORDS
AL American League
NL National League

BATTING

AVERAGE, Career, ·366 Tyrus Raymond Cobb (Detroit AL, Philadelphia AL) 1905–28. **Season**, ·438 Hugh Duffy (Boston NL) 1894.

RUNS, Career, 2245 Tyrus Raymond Cobb 1905–28. **Season**, 192 William Robert Hamilton (Phildelphia NL) 1894.

HOME RUNS, Career[*1], 755 Henry 'Hank' Aaron (Milwaukee NL, Atlanta NL, Milwaukee AL) 1954–76. **Season**, 61 Roger Eugene Maris (New York NL) 1961.

RUNS BATTED IN, Career, 2297 Henry 'Hank' Aaron 1954–76. **Season**, 190 Lewis Rober 'Hack' Wilson (Chicago NL) 1930. **Game**, 12 James LeRoy Bottomley (St Louis NL) 16 Sep 1924. **Innings**, 7 Edward Cartwright (St Louis AL) 23 Sep 1890.

BASE HITS, Career, 4256 Peter Edward Rose (Cincinnati NL, Philadelphia NL, Montreal NL, Cincinnati NL) 1963–86. **Season**, 257 George Harold Sisler (St Louis AL) 1920.

TOTAL BASES, Career, 6856 Henry 'Hank' Aaron 1954–76. **Season**, 457 George Herman 'Babe' Ruth (New York AL) 1921.

HITS, Consecutive, 12 Michael Franklin 'Pinky' Higgins (Boston AL) 19–21 Jun 1938; Walter 'Moose' Dropo (Detroit AL) 14–15 Jul 1952.

CONSECUTIVE GAMES BATTED SAFELY, 56 Joseph Paul DiMaggio (New York AL) 15 May–16 Jul 1941.

STOLEN BASES, Career[*2], 939 Rickey Henley Henderson (Oakland AL) 1979–91. **Season**, 130 Rickey Henderson 1982.

CONSECUTIVE GAMES PLAYED[*3], 2130 Henry Louis 'Lou' Gehrig (New York AL) 1 Jun 1925–30 April 1939.

PITCHING

GAMES WON, Career, 511 Denton True 'Cy' Young (Cleveland NL, St Louis NL, Boston AL, Cleveland, Boston NL) 1890–1911. **Season**, 60 Charles Gardner Radbourn (Providence NL) 1884.

CONSECUTIVE GAMES WON, 24 Carl Owen Hubbell (New York NL) 1936–7.

SHUTOUTS, Career, 110 Walter Perry Johnson (Washington AL) 1907–27. **Season**, 16 George Washington Bradley (St Louis NL) 1876; Grover Cleveland Alexander (Philadelphia NL) 1916.

STRIKEOUTS, Career, 5400 Lynn Nolan Ryan (New York NL, California AL, Houston NL, Texas AL) 1966–91. **Season**, 383 Lynn Nolan Ryan (California AL) 1973. (513 Matthew Aloysius Kilroy (Baltimore AA) 1886). **Game (9 innings)**, 20 Roger Clemens (Boston AL) v. Seattle 29 Apr 1986.

NO-HIT GAMES, Career, 7 Lynn Nolan Ryan 1973–91.

EARNED RUN AVERAGE, Season, 0·90 Ferdinand Schupp (140 inns) (New York NL) 1916; 0·96 Hubert 'Dutch' Leonard (222 inns) (Boston AL) 1914; 1·12 Robert Gibson (305 inns) (St Louis NL) 1968.

Japanese League records that are superior to those in the US major leagues;
[1] *868 Sadaharu Oh (Yomiuri) 1959–80.*
[2] *1059 Yutaka Fukumoto (Hankyu) 1969–87.*
[3] *2215 Sachio Kinugasa (Hiroshima) 1970–87.*

Season The US major league record for home runs in a season is 61 by Roger Eugene Maris (1934-85) for New York Yankees in 162 games in 1961. 'Babe' Ruth hit 60 in 154 games in 1927 for the New York Yankees. The most official home runs in a minor league season is 72 by Joe Bauman of Roswell, New Mexico in 1954.

Game The most home runs in a major league game is four, first achieved by Robert Lincoln 'Bobby' Lowe (1868–1951) for Boston v. Cinncinnati on 30 May 1894. The feat had been achieved a further ten times since then.

Consecutive games The most consecutive games hitting home runs is eight by Richard Dale Long (b. 6 Feb 1926) for Pittsburgh (NL), 19–28 May 1956 and by Donald Arthur Mattingly (b. 21 Apr 1961) for New York (AL), July 1987.

Most games won by a pitcher
Denton True 'Cy' Young (1876–1955) had a record 511 wins and a record 749 complete games from a total of 906 games and 815 starts in his career for Cleveland NL 1890–8, St Louis NL 1899–1900, Boston AL 1901–08, Cleveland AL 1909–11 and Boston NL 1911. He pitched a record total of 7357 innings. The career record of most games pitching is 1070 by James Hoyt Wilhem (b. 26 Jul 1923) for a total of nine teams between 1952 and 1969; he set the career record with 143 wins by a relief pitcher. The season's record is 106 games pitched by Michael Grant Marshall (b. 15 Jan 1943) for Los Angeles (NL) in 1974.

Most consecutive games won by a pitcher
Carl Owen Hubell (1903–88) pitched for the New York Yankees to win 24 consecutive games, 16 in 1936 and 8 in 1937.

Most consecutive hits
Michael Franklin 'Pinky' Higgins (1909–69) had 12 consecutive hits for Boston (AL) 19–21 Jun 1938. This was equalled by Walter 'Moose' Droppo (b. 30 Jan 1923) for Detroit (AL) 14–15 Jul 1952. Joseph Paul DiMaggio (b. 25 Nov 1914) hit in a record 56 consecutive games for New York in 1941; he was 223 times at bat, with 91 hits, scoring 16 doubles, 4 triples and 15 home runs.

Most consecutive scoreless games
Orel Leonard Hershiser IV (b. 16 Sep 1958) pitched a record 59 consecutive shutout innings from 30 Aug to 28 Sep 1988.

Perfect game
A perfect nine innings game, in which the pitcher allows no hits, no runs and does not allow a man to reach first base, was first achieved by John Lee Richmond (1857–1929) for Worcester against Cleveland in the NL on 12 Jun 1880. There have been 13 subsequent perfect games over nine innings, but no pitcher has achieved this feat more than once. On 26 May 1959 Harvey Haddix Jr. (b. 18 Sep 1925) for Pittsburgh pitched perfect game for 12 innings against Milwaukee in the National League, but lost in the 13th.

Cy Young award
Awarded annually from 1956 to the outstanding pitcher on the major leagues, the most wins is three: National League: George Thomas Seaver (b. 17 Nov 1944) (New York) 1969, 1973, 1975; Stephen Norman Carlton (b. 22 Dec 1944) (Philadelphia) 1977, 1980, 1982. American League: Sanford Koufax (b. 30 Dec 1935) (Los Angeles) 1963, 1965–6; James Alvin Palmer (b. 15 Oct 1945) (Baltimore) 1973, 1975–6.

Youngest player
Frederick Joseph Chapman (1872–1957) pitched for Philadelphia in the American Association at 14 yr 239 days on 22 Jul 1887, but did not play again.

■ Versatility
With his selection for the Pro Bowl at American football in 1990, Bo Jackson of the Los Angeles Raiders became the first man ever to have combined this with All-Star selection at baseball. He plays baseball for the Kansas City Royals and is seen in action for the Raiders, ironically, against the Kansas City Chiefs. (Photos: All-Sport (USA)/J. Rettaliatta and All-Sport/S. Dunn)

Longest home run
In a minor league game at Emeryville Ball Park, California, USA on 4 Jul 1929, Roy Edward 'Dizzy' Carlyle (1900–56) hit a home run measured at 188·4 m *618 ft.*

In 1919 'Babe' Ruth hit a 178·9 m *587 ft* homer in a Boston Red Sox v. New York Giants exhibition match at Tampa, Florida, USA.

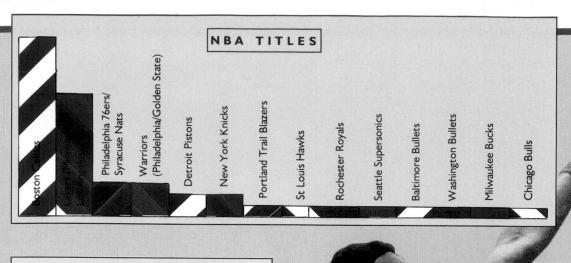

NBA TITLES

Boston Celtics · Lakers/Minneapolis/Los Angeles · Philadelphia 76ers/Syracuse Nats · Warriors (Philadelphia/Golden State) · Detroit Pistons · New York Knicks · Portland Trail Blazers · St Louis Hawks · Rochester Royals · Seattle Supersonics · Baltimore Bullets · Washington Bullets · Milwaukee Bucks · Chicago Bulls

'WILT' CHAMBERLAIN

Year	Points	Year	Points
1960	† * 2707	1967	† 1956
1961	* 3033	1968	† 1992
1962	* 4029	1969	1664
1963	* 3586	1970	328
1964	* 2948	1971	1696
1965	* 2534	1972	1213
1966	† * 2649	1973	1084

* = Season's leading scorer

† = NBA Most Valuable Player for the season

This building was the unlikely setting for the first ever game of basketball in mid-December 1891, in Springfield, Massachusetts, USA.

MICHAEL JORDAN

Year	Points
1985	2313
1986	408
1987	* 3041
1988	† * 2868
1989	* 2633
1990	* 2752
1991	† * 2580

* = Season's leading scorer

† = NBA Most Valuable Player for the season

NCAA DIVISION I MEN'S CHAMPIONSHIP RECORDS

The National Collegiate Athletic Association (NCAA) is the principal administrator of organized collegiate sports in the United States. The NCAA basketball tournament was first held in 1939. Currently 64 teams are selected to compete in the play off tournament, with the semi-finals and final, "the final four" held at one site. The "final four" is one of the premier events of the American sports calender.

TEAM RECORDS

Most wins 10 UCLA 1964-65, 1967-73, 1975
Most points 103 UNLV (v. Duke) 1990 (Championship game)
Most points 149 Loyola Marymount 1990 (Tournament game) (v. Michigan)

INDIVIDUAL RECORDS

Most points 44 Bill Walton, UCLA 1973 (Championship game) (v. Memphis State)
Most points 61 Austin Carr, Notre Dame 1970 (Tournament game) (v. Ohio State)
Most points 184 Glen Rice, Michigan 1989 (Tournament season) (6 games)
Most points 358 Elvin Hayes, Houston (Tournament career) (13 games) 1966-68

Source: NCAA

KAREEM ABDUL-JABBAR

Year	Points
1970	2361
1971	† * 2596
1972	† * 2822
1973	2292
1974	† 2191
1975	1949
1976	† 2275
1977	† 2152
1978	1600
1979	1903
1980	† 2034
1981	2095
1982	1818
1983	1722
1984	1717
1985	1735
1986	1846
1987	1366
1988	1165
1989	748

* = Season's leading scorer
† = NBA Most Valuable Player for the season

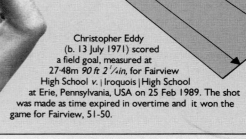

LONGEST GOAL

Christopher Eddy
(b. 13 July 1971) scored
a field goal, measured at
27·48m *90 ft 2¼in*, for Fairview
High School *v.* | Iroquois | High School
at Erie, Pennsylvania, USA on 25 Feb 1989. The shot
was made as time expired in overtime and it won the
game for Fairview, 51-50.

OLYMPIC TITLES

MEN

USA
Yugoslavia

WOMEN

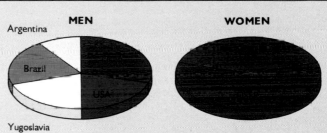

WORLD CHAMPIONSHIP TITLES

MEN

Argentina
Brazil
USA
Yugoslavia

WOMEN

100 Years of Basketball

Dr James A. Naismith
inventor of
basketball

First basketball team
including James Naismith
(right in centre row)

Longest throw

Glen Edward Gorbous (b. Canada 8 Jul 1930) threw 135·88 m *445 ft 10 in* on 1 Aug 1957.

Mildred Ella 'Babe' Didrikson (later Mrs Zaharias) (USA) (1914–56) threw 90·2 m *296 ft* at Jersey City, New Jersey, USA on 25 Jul 1931.

Fastest base runner

The fastest time for circling bases is 13·3 sec by Ernest Evar Swanson (1902–73) at Columbus, Ohio, USA in 1932, at an average speed of 29·70 km/h *18·45 mph.*

Fastest pitcher

Lynn Nolan Ryan (then of the California Angels) (b. 31 Jan 1947) was measured to pitch at 162·3 km/h *100·9 mph* at Anaheim Stadium, California, USA on 20 Aug 1974.

Basketball shooting skill

The greatest goal-shooting demonstration has been by Ted St Martin of Jacksonville, Florida, USA who, on 25 Jun 1977, scored 2036 consecutive free throws. Also at Jacksonville, he scored 90 out of 97 attempts in 5 minutes on 24 Feb 1990. On 14 Dec 1990, Jeff Liles scored 224 out of 237 attempts in 10 minutes at Southern Nazarene University, Bethany, Oklahoma, USA. These speed records were both achieved with one ball and one rebounder.

In 24 hours Fred Newman scored 20 371 free throws from a total of 22 049 taken (92·39 per cent) at Caltech, Pasadena, California, USA on 29–30 Sep 1990.

Steve Bontrager (USA) (b. 1 Mar 1959) of Polycell Kingston scored 21 points in a minute from seven positions in a demonstration for BBC TV's *Record Breakers* on 29 Oct 1986.

The youngest major league player of all time was the Cincinnati pitcher Joseph Henry Nuxhall (b. 30 Jul 1928), who played one game in June 1944, aged 15 yr 314 days. He did not play again in the NL until 1952. The youngest player to play in a minor league game was Joe Louis Reliford (b. 29 Nov 1939) who played for the Fitzgerald Pioneers against Statesboro Pilots in the Georgia State League, aged 12 yr 234 days on 19 Jul 1952.

Oldest player Leroy Robert 'Satchel' Paige (1906–82) pitched for Kansas City A's (AL) at 59 years 80 days on 25 Sep 1965.

Record attendances The all-time season record for attendances for both leagues is 55 173 597 in 1989. The record for an individual league is 30 331 417 for the American League in 1990 and this included an individual team record of 3 885 284 for the home games of the Toronto Blue Jays.

An estimated 114 000 spectators watched a game between Australia and an American Services team in a demonstration event during the Olympic Games at Melbourne on 1 Dec 1956.

Basketball

Origins The game of 'Pok-ta-Pok' was played in the 10th century BC, by the Olmecs in Mexico, and closely resembled basketball in its concept. 'Ollamalitzli' was a variation of this game played by the Aztecs in Mexico as late as the 16th century. If the solid rubber ball was put through a fixed stone ring the player was entitled to the clothing of all the spectators. Modern basketball (which may have been based on the German game *Korbball*) was devised by the Canadian-born Dr James A. Naismith (1861–1939) at the Training School of the International YMCA College at Springfield, Massachusetts, USA in mid-December 1891. The first game played under modified rules was on 20 Jan 1892. The International Amateur Basketball Federation (FIBA) was founded in 1932; it has now dropped the word Amateur from its title.

Most titles *Olympic* The USA has won nine men's Olympic titles. From the time the sport was introduced to the Games in 1936 until 1972 they won 63 consecutive matches in the Olympic Games until they lost 50–51 to the USSR in the disputed Final match in Munich. They won eighth and ninth titles in 1976 and 1984.

The women's title was won by the USSR in 1976 and 1980 and by the USA in 1984 and 1988.

World The USSR has won most titles at both the men's World Championships (instituted 1950) with three (1967, 1974 and 1982) and women's (instituted 1953) with six (1959, 1964, 1967, 1971, 1975 and 1983). Yugoslavia have also won three men's world titles: 1970, 1978 and 1990.

European The most wins in the European Nations Championships for men is 14 by the USSR, and in the women's event 20, also by the USSR, winning all but the 1958 championship since 1950, in this biennial contest.

The most European Champions Cup (instituted 1957) wins is seven by Real Madrid, Spain 1964–5, 1967–8, 1974, 1978 and 1980. The women's title has been won 18 times by Daugawa, Riga, Latvia, USSR between 1960 and 1982.

English The most English National Championship titles (instituted 1936) have been won by London Central YMCA, with eight wins in 1957–8, 1960, 1962–4, 1967 and 1969.

The English National League title has been won seven times by Crystal Palace 1974, 1976–8, 1980 and 1982–3. In the 1989/90 season Kingston won all five domestic trophies; the Carlsberg League and Championship play-offs, the Coca-Cola National Cup, NatWest Trophy and WIBC. The English Women's Cup (instituted 1965) has been won a record eight times by the Tigers, 1972–3, 1976–80 and 1982.

Highest score In a senior international match Iraq scored 251 against Yemen (33) at New Delhi in November 1982 at the Asian Games.

The highest in a British Championship is 125 by England v. Wales (54) on 1 Sep 1978. England beat Gibraltar 130–45 on 31 Aug 1978.

US College The NCAA aggregate record is 331 when Loyola Marymount Lions (181) beat US International Gulls (150) on 31 Jan 1989. The single team score was surpassed in a match between the same teams on 6 Jan 1991, won by Loyola 186–140.

The highest score in a US college match is 210 by Essex County (Community) College when beating Englewood Cliffs College (67) on 20 Jan 1979.

United Kingdom The highest score recorded in a match is 250 by the Nottingham YMCA Falcons v. Mansfield Pirates at Nottingham on 18 Jun 1974. It was a handicap competition and Mansfield received 120 points towards their total of 145.

The highest score in a senior National League match is 174 by Chiltern Fast Break v. Swindon Rakers (40) on 13 Oct 1990.

The highest in the National Cup is 157 by Solent Stars v. Corby (57) on 6 Jan 1990.

Individual Mats Wermelin, age 13 (Sweden), scored all 272 points in a 272–0 win in a regional boys' tournament in Stockholm, Sweden on 5 Feb 1974.

The record score by a woman is 156 points by Marie Boyd (now Eichler) of Central HS, Lonaconing, Maryland, USA in a 163–3 defeat of Ursaline Academy, Cumbria on 25 Feb 1924.

The highest score by a British player is 124 points by Paul Ogden for St Albans School, Oldham (226) v. South Chadderton (82) on 9 Mar 1982.

The highest individual score in a league match in Britain is 108 by Lewis Young for Forth Steel in his team's 154–74 win over Stirling in the Scottish League Division One at Stirling on 2 Mar 1985.

The record in an English National League (Div. One) or Cup match is 73 points by Terry Crosby (USA) for Home Spare Bolton in his team's 120–106 defeat by Cottrills Manchester Giants at Altrincham, Cheshire on 26 Jan 1985; by Billy Hungrecker in a semi-final play-off for Worthing v. Plymouth at Worthing, W Sussex on 20 Mar 1988; and by Renaldo Lawrence for Stevenage in his team's 113–102 win against Gateshead on 30 Dec 1989.

NATIONAL BASKETBALL ASSOCIATION (USA)

Origins The Amateur Athletic Union (AAU) organized the first national tournament in the USA in 1897. The first professional league was the National Basketball League (NBL), founded in 1898, but this league only lasted two seasons. The American Basketball League was formed in 1925, but declined and the NBL was refounded in 1937. This organization merged with the Basketball Association of America in 1949 to form the National Basketball Association (NBA). Boston Celtics have won a record 16 NBA titles, 1957, 1959–66, 1968–9, 1974, 1976, 1981, 1984, 1986.

Highest score The highest aggregate score in an NBA match is 370 when the Detroit Pistons (186) beat the Denver Nuggets (184) at Denver on 13 Dec 1983. Overtime was played after a 145–145 tie in regulation time. The record in regulation time is 318, when Denver Nuggets beat San Antonio Spurs 163–155 at Denver on 11 Jan 1984. The most points in a half is 107 by Phoenix Suns in the first half against Denver on 11 Nov 1990. The most points in a quarter is 58 (fourth) by Buffalo at Boston on 20 Oct 1972.

Individual scoring Wilton Norman 'Wilt' Chamberlain (b. 21 Aug 1936) set an NBA record with 100 points for Philadelphia v. New York at Hershey on 2 Mar 1962. This included a record 36 field goals and 28 free throws (from 32 attempts) and a record 59 points in a half (the second). The free throws game record was equalled by Adrian Dantley (b. 28 Feb 1956) for Utah v. Houston at Las Vegas on 5 Jan 1984. The most points scored in an NBA game in one quarter is 33 (second) by George Gervin for San Antonio v. New Orleans on 9 Apr 1978.

Most games Kareem Abdul-Jabbar (formerly Ferdinand Lewis Alcindor) (b. 16 Apr 1947) took part in a record 1560 NBA regular season games over 20 seasons, totalling 57,446 minutes played, for the Milwaukee Bucks, 1969–75, and the Los Angeles Lakers, 1975–89. He also played a record 237 play-off games. The most successive games is 906 by Randy Smith for Buffalo, San Diego, Cleveland and New York from 18 Feb 1972 to 13 Mar 1983. The record for playing complete games in one season is 79 by Wilt Chamberlain for Philadelphia in 1962, when he was on court for a record 3882 minutes. Chamberlain went through his entire career of 1045 games without fouling out.

Most points Kareem Abdul-Jabbar set NBA career records with 38 887 points, including 15 837 field goals in regular season games, and 5762 points, including 2356 field goals in play-off games. The previous record holder, Wilt Chamberlain, had an average of 30·1 points per game for his total of 31 419 for Philadelphia 1959–62, San Francisco 1962–5, Philadelphia 1964–8 and Los Angeles 1968–73. He scored 50 or more points in 118 games, including 45 in 1961/2 and 30 in 1962/3 to the next best career total of 17. He set season's records for points and scoring average with 4029 at 50·1 per game, and also for field goals, 1597, for Philadelphia in 1961/2. The highest career average for players exceeding 10 000 points is 32·6 by Michael Jordan (b. 17 Feb 1963), 16 596 points in 509 games for the Chicago Bulls, 1984–91. Jordan also holds the career scoring average record for play-offs at 34·6, 2425 points in 70 games 1984–91.

Winning margin The greatest winning margin in an NBA game was the 63 points by which Los Angeles 162, beat Golden State, 99, on 19 Mar 1972.

Winning streak Los Angeles Lakers won a record 33 NBA games in succession from 5 Nov 1971 to 7 Jan 1972, as during the 1971/2 season they won a record 69 games with 13 losses.

Youngest and oldest player The youngest NBA player has been Bill Willoughby (b. 20 May 1957), who made his début for Atlanta Hawks on 23 Oct 1975 at 18 yr 156 days. The oldest NBA regular player was Kareem Abdul-Jabbar, who made his last appearance for the Los Angeles Lakers at 42 yr 59 days old in 1989.

Tallest player Tallest in NBA history has been Manute Bol (Sudan) (b. 16 Oct 1962) of the Washington Bullets and Golden State Warriors at 7 ft 6 ¾ in. He made his pro début in 1985.

OTHER RECORDS

Most points The records for the most points scored in a college career are (women): 4061, Pearl Moore of Francis Marion College, Florence, South Carolina, USA, 1975–9; (men): 4045 by Travis Grant for Kentucky State, USA in 1969–72.

In the English National League, Ian Day (b. 16 May 1953) scored 3456 points in 203 games, 1973–84.

Tallest players Suleiman Ali Nashnush (b. 1943) was reputed to be 2·45 m *8 ft* when he played for the Libyan team in 1962. Aleksandr Sizonenko of Kuibyshev Stroitel and USSR is 2·39 m *7 ft 10 in* tall. The tallest woman player was Iuliana Larionovna Semenova (USSR) (b. 9 Mar 1952) at a reported 2·18 m *7 ft 2 in* and weighing 127 kg *281 lb*.

British Christopher Greener of London Latvians was 2·29 m *7 ft 6¼ in* and made his international debut for England *v.* France on 17 Dec 1969.

Longest goal Christopher Eddy (b. 13 Jul 1971) scored a field goal, measured at 27·48 m *90 ft 2¼ in*, for Fairview High School *v.* Iroquois High School at Erie, Pennsylvania, USA on 25 Feb 1989. The shot was made as time expired in overtime and it won the game for Fairview, 51–50.

British A distance of 23·10 m *75 ft 9½ in* is claimed by David Tarbatt (b. 23 Jan 1949) of Altofts Aces *v.* Harrogate Demons at Featherstone, W Yorks on 27 Jan 1980.

Billiards

Origins The earliest recorded mention of billiards was in France in 1429, and Louis XI, King of France 1461–83, is reported to have had a billiard table. The first recorded public billiards room in England was the Piazza, Covent Garden, London, in the early part of the 19th century. Rubber cushions were introduced in 1835 and slate beds in 1836.

Most titles *World* The greatest number of World Championships (instituted 1870) won by one player is eight by John Roberts Jr (GB) (1847–1919) in 1870 (twice), 1871, 1875 (twice), 1877 and 1885 (twice). The record for world amateur titles is four by Robert James Percival Marshall (Australia) (b. 10 Apr 1910) in 1936, 1938, 1951 and 1962.

Britain The greatest number of United Kingdom professional titles (instituted 1934) won is seven (1934–9 and 1947) by Joe Davis (1901–78), who also won four world titles (1928–30 and 1932). The greatest number of English Amateur Championships (instituted 1888) won is 15 by Norman Dagley (b. 27 Jun 1930) in 1965–6, 1970–5, 1978–84. The record number of women's titles is eight by Vera Selby (b. 13 Mar 1930), 1970–8. Uniquely, Norman

Dribbling
Peter del Masto (USA) dribbled a basketball without 'travelling' from near Lee to Provincetown, Massachusetts, a distance of 426·8 km *265·2 miles*, from 12–25 Aug 1989.

Bob Nickerson of Gallitzin, Pennsylvania and Dave Davlin of Garland, Texas, USA are the only people to have successfully demonstrated the ability to dribble four basketballs simultaneously.

Billiards
Walter Lindrum made an unofficial 100 break in 27·5 sec in Australia on 10 Oct 1952. His official record is 100 in 46·0 sec set in Sydney, Australia in 1941.

Youngest champion
The youngest winner of the world professional title is Mike Russell (b. 3 Jun 1969), aged 20 yr 49 days, when he won at Leura, Australia on 23 Jul 1989.

Dagley has won the English Amateur Championships (as above), World Amateur Championships (1971, 1975), United Kingdom Professional Championship (1987) and World Professional Championship (1987).

Highest breaks Tom Reece (1873–1953) made an unfinished break of 499 135, including 249 152 cradle cannons (two points each) in 85 hr 49 min against Joe Chapman at Burroughes' Hall, Soho Square, London between 3 Jun and 6 Jul 1907. This was not recognized because press and public were not continuously present.

The highest certified break made by the anchor cannon is 42 746 by William Cook (England) from 29 May to 7 Jun 1907.

The official world record under the then baulk-line rule is 1784 by Joe Davis in the United Kingdom Championship on 29 May 1936.

Walter Albert Lindrum (Australia) (1898–1960) made an official break of 4137 in 2 hr 55 min against Joe Davis at Thurston's on 19–20 Jan 1932, before the baulk-line rule was in force.

Davis had an unofficial personal best of 2502 (mostly pendulum cannons) in a

match against Tom Newman (England) (1894–1943) in Manchester in 1930.

The highest break recorded in amateur competition is 1149 by Michael Ferreira (India) at Calcutta, India on 15 Dec 1978.

Under the more stringent 'two pot' rule, restored on 1 Jan 1983, the highest break is Ferreira's 962 unfinished in a tournament at Bombay, India on 29 Apr 1986.

3 CUSHION

Origins This pocketless variation dates back to 1878. The world governing body, the *Union Mondiale de Billiard* (UMB), was formed in 1928.

Most titles William F. Hoppe (USA) (1887–1959) won 51 billiards championships in all forms spanning the pre- and post-international era from 1906 to 1952.

UMB Raymond Ceulemans (Belgium) (b. 12 Jul 1935) has won 19 world three-cushion championships (1963–73, 1975–80, 1983, 1985).

BAR BILLIARDS

Scoring rates Keith Sheard scored 28 530 in 19 min 5 sec in a league game at the Crown and Thistle, Headington, Oxford on 9 Jul 1984. Sheard scored 1500 points in a

BOARD GAMES

Backgammon

Alan Malcolm Beckerson (b. 21 Feb 1938) devised a game of just 16 throws in 1982.

Most chess moves

The Master game with most moves on record was one of 269 moves, when Ivan Nikolić drew with Goran Arsović in a Belgrade, Yugoslavia tournament, on 17 Feb 1989. It took a total of 20 hr 15 min.

Domino stacking

David Coburn successfully stacked 291 dominoes on a single supporting domino on 19 Aug 1988 in Miami, Florida, USA.

Domino toppling

The greatest number set up single-handed and toppled is 281 581 out of 320 236 by Klaus Friedrich, 22, at Fürth, Germany on 27 Jan 1984. The dominoes fell within 12 min 57·3 sec, having taken 31 days (10 hr daily) to set up.

Thirty students at Delft, Eindhoven and Twente Technical Universities in the Netherlands set up 1 500 000 dominoes representing all of the European Community member countries. Of these, 1 382 101 were toppled by one push on 2 Jan 1988.

Solitaire

The shortest time taken to complete the game is 13·22 sec by Dorothy Clark at Williamwood High School, Clarkston, Glasgow on 10 Mar 1989.

Biggest board game

The world's biggest board game was a version of the game, Goose, and was organized by 'Jong Nederland'. It stretched for 638 m *697 yd* and was played by 1631 participants at Someren, Netherlands on 16 Sep 1989.

minute on BBC TV's *Record Breakers* on 23 Sep 1986.

The highest score in 24 hours by a team of five is 1 754 730 by Les Green, Ricard Powell, Kevin Clark, Mick Lingham and Curt Driver of The Shipwrights Arms, Chatham, Kent on 26–27 May 1990.

Board Games

BACKGAMMON

Origins Forerunners of the game have been traced back to a dice and a board game found in excavations at Ur, dated to 3000 BC. Later the Romans played a game remarkably similar to the modern one. The name 'backgammon' is variously ascribed to Welsh 'little battle', or Saxon 'back game'.

CHESS

Origins The game is believed to have originated in ancient India under the same name as the four traditional army divisions, Chaturanga (literally 'four-corps'). The name chess is derived from the Persian word *shah* (a king or ruler). The earliest written reference is from the Middle Persian Chatrang Namak (c. AD 590–628). The oldest pieces identified as chesspieces were found at Nashipur, datable to c.AD 900. It reached Britain in c. 1255. The *Fédération Internationale des Echecs* (FIDE) was established in 1924.

World Championships World champions have been officially recognized since 1886. The longest undisputed tenure was 26 yr 337 days by Dr Emanuel Lasker (1868–1941) of Germany, from 1894 to 1921.

The women's world championship title was held by Vera Francevna Stevenson-Menchik (USSR, later GB) (1906–44) from 1927 until her death, and was successfully defended a record seven times.

Team The USSR has won the biennial men's team title (Olympiad) a record 18 times between 1952 and 1990, and the women's title 11 times from its introduction in 1957 to 1986.

Youngest Gary Kimovich Kasparov (USSR) (b. 13 Apr 1963) won the title on 9 Nov 1985 at 22 yr 210 days.

Maya Grigoryevna Chiburdanidze (USSR) (b. 17 Jan 1961) won the women's title in 1978 when only 17.

Oldest Wilhelm Steinitz (Austria, later USA) (1836–1900) was 58 yr 10 days when he lost his title to Lasker on 26 May 1894.

Most active Anatoliy Yevgenyevich Karpov (USSR) (b. 23 May 1951) in his tenure as champion, 1975–85, averaged 45·2 competitive games per year, played in 32 tournaments and finished first in 26.

Most British titles The most British titles have been won by Dr Jonathan Penrose (b. 7 Oct 1933) with ten titles in 1958–63, 1966–9.

Rowena Mary Bruce (*née* Dew) (b. 15 May 1919) won 11 women's titles between 1937 and 1969.

Grand Masters The youngest individual to qualify as an International Grand Master is Robert James 'Bobby' Fischer (USA) (b. 9 Mar 1943), aged 15 yr 185 days on 10 Sep 1958. The youngest Briton to qualify is Michael Adams (b. 17 Nov 1971), aged 17 yr 216 days on 21 Jul 1989.

The first British player to attain official International Grand Master status was

Anthony John Miles (b. 23 Apr 1955), on 24 Feb 1976.

Highest rating The highest rating ever attained on the officially adopted Elo System is 2800 by Gary Kasparov (USSR) at the end of 1989.

The highest-rated woman player is Judit Polgar (Hungary) (b. 25 Jul 1976), currently at 2540 but has achieved a peak rating of 2555.

The top British player on the Elo list is Nigel David Short (b. 1 Jun 1965) who reached a peak rating of 2665 in mid-1988.

The top British woman is Susan Kathryn Arkell (*née* Walker) (b. 28 Oct 1965) who reached a peak of 2355 on 1 Jul 1988.

Least games lost by a world champion José Raúl Capablanca (Cuba) (1888–1942) lost only 34 games (out of 571) in his adult career, 1909–39. He was unbeaten from 10 Feb 1916 to 21 Mar 1924 (63 games) and was world champion 1921–7.

Slowest moves The slowest reported moving (before time clocks were used) in an official event is reputed to have been by Louis Paulsen (Germany) (1833–91) against Paul Charles Morphy (USA) (1837–84) at the first American Chess Congress, New York on 29 Oct 1857. The game ended in a draw on move 56 after 15 hours of play of which Paulsen used c. 11 hours.

Grand Master Friedrich Sämisch (Germany) (1896–1975) ran out of the allotted time (2 hr 30 min for 45 moves) after only 12 moves, in Prague, Czechoslovakia, in 1938.

The slowest move played, since time clocks were introduced, was at Vigo, Spain in 1980 when Francisco R. Torres Trois (b. 3 Sep 1946) took 2 hr 20 min for his seventh move v. Luis M. C. P. Santos (b. 30 Jun 1955).

Most opponents The record for most consecutive games played is 663 by Vlastimil Hort (Czechoslovakia, later Germany) (b. 12 Jan 1944) over 32½ hours at Porz, Germany on 5–6 Oct 1984. He played 60–120 opponents at a time, scoring over 80 per cent wins and averaging 30 moves per game. He also holds the record for most games simultaneously, 201 during 550 consecutive games of which he only lost ten, in Seltjarnes, Iceland on 23–24 Apr 1977.

Eric G. J. Knoppert (Netherlands) (b. 20 Sep 1959) played 500 games of 10-minute chess against opponents averaging 2002 on the Elo scale on 13–16 Sep 1985. He scored 413 points (1 for win, ½ for draw), a success rate of 82·6 per cent.

DRAUGHTS

Origins Draughts, known as checkers in North America, is believed to have originated on the French/Spanish border in the 12 th century, when backgammon men were placed on a chessboard and moved as in the well-known game of the time, *alquerque*. The earliest book on the game was by Antonio Torquemada of Valencia, Spain in 1547.

World champions Walter Hellman (USA) (1916–75) won a record eight world titles during his tenure as world champion 1948–75. Dr Marion Tinsley (USA) (b. 3 Feb 1927), the current world champion, has been internationally undefeated in match-play from 1947 to 1990.

British titles The British Championship (biennial) was inaugurated in 1886 and has been won six times by Samuel Cohen (1905–72), 1924, 1927, 1929, 1933, 1937 and 1939. John McGill (b. 1936) won six Scottish titles between 1959 and 1974.

William Edwards (b. 28 Jan 1915) of Abercynon, Wales won the English open title on a record five successive occasions – 1979, 1981, 1983, 1985 and 1987.

In 1986, Andrew Knapp (b. 19 Oct 1966), on his first attempt, became at 19 yr 322 days the youngest ever winner of the English Amateur Championship (instituted 1910).

Youngest and oldest national champion Asa A. Long (b. 20 Aug 1904) became the youngest US national champion, aged 18 yr 64 days, when he won in Boston, Massachusetts, USA on 23 Oct 1922. He became the oldest, aged 79 yr 334 days, when he won his sixth title in Tupelo, Mississippi, USA on 21 Jul 1984. He was also world champion 1934–8.

Most opponents Major H. Roy White played a record 222 games simultaneously, winning 221 and drawing 1, at the Canadian Forces Base, Cornwallis, Nova Scotia, Canada on 27 Oct 1990.

The largest number of opponents played without a defeat or draw is 172 by Nate Cohen of Portland, Maine, USA at Portland on 26 Jul 1981. This was not a simultaneous attempt, but consecutive play over a period of four hours.

Newell W. Banks (1887–1977) played 140 games simultaneously, winning 133 and drawing seven, in Chicago, Illinois in 1933. His playing time was 145 min, so averaging about one move per sec. In 1947 he played blindfolded for 4 hr per day for 45 consecutive days, winning 1331 games, drawing 54 and losing only two, while playing six games at a time.

Longest and shortest games In competition the prescribed rate of play is not less than 30 moves per hour with the average game lasting about 90 min. In 1958 a game between Dr Marion Tinsley (USA) and Derek Oldbury (GB) lasted 7 hr 30 min (played under the 5-minutes-a-move rule).

The shortest possible game is one of 20 moves composed by Alan Malcolm Beckerson (GB) in 1977.

SCRABBLE®

Origins The crossword game was invented by Alfred M. Butts in 1931 and was developed, refined and trademarked as Scrabble® Crossword Game by James Brunot in 1948.

Highest scores The highest competitive game score is 1049 by Phil Appleby (b. 9 Dec 1957) in June 1989. His opponent scored 253 and the margin of victory, 796 points, is also a record.

His score included a single turn of 374 for the word 'OXIDIZERS'. The highest competitive single turn score recorded, however, is 392 by Dr Saladin Karl Khoshnaw (of Kurdish origin) in Manchester in April 1982. He laid down 'CAZIQUES', which means 'native chiefs of West Indian aborigines'.

Most titles British National Championships were instituted in 1971. Philip Nelkon (b. 21 Jul 1956) has won a record three times, 1978, 1981 and 1990.

Bobsleigh and Tobogganing

BOBSLEDDING

Origins The oldest known sledge is dated c. 6500 BC and came from Heinola, Finland.

240

The first known bobsleigh race took place at Davos, Switzerland in 1889. The International Federation of Bobsleigh and Tobogganing was formed in 1923, followed by the International Bobsleigh Federation in 1957.

Most titles The Olympic four-man bob title (instituted 1924) has been won five times by Switzerland (1924, 1936, 1956, 1972 and 1988).

The USA (1932, 1936), Switzerland (1948, 1980), Italy (1956, 1968), West Germany (1952, 1972) and GDR (1976, 1984) have won the Olympic two-man bob (instituted 1932) event twice.

The most gold medals won by an individual is three by Meinhard Nehmer (GDR) (b. 13 Jun 1941) and Bernhard Germeshausen (GDR) (b. 21 Aug 1951) in the 1976 two-man, 1976 and 1980 four-man events.

The most medals won is six (two gold, two silver, two bronze) by Eugenio Monti (Italy) (b. 23 Jan 1928), 1956 to 1968.

The only British victory was at two-man bob in 1964 by the Hon. Thomas Robin Valerian Dixon (b. 21 Apr 1935) and Anthony James Dillon Nash (b. 18 Mar 1936).

World and Olympic The world four-man bob title (instituted 1924) has been won 19 times by Switzerland (1924, 1936, 1939, 1947, 1954–7, 1971–3, 1975, 1982–3, 1986–90) including their five Olympic victories.

Italy won the two-man title 14 times (1954, 1956–63, 1966, 1968–9, 1971 and 1975).

Eugenio Monti was a member of eleven world championship crews, eight two-man and three four-man in 1957–68.

TOBOGGANING

Origins The word toboggan comes from the Micmac American Indian word *tobaakan*. The St Moritz Tobogganing Club, Switzerland, founded in 1887, is the oldest toboggan club in the world. It is notable for being the home of the Cresta Run, which dates from 1884, and for the introduction of the one-man skeleton racing toboggan.

Cresta Run The course is 1212·25 m *3977 ft* long with a drop of 157 m *514 ft* and the record is 50·91 sec (av. 85·72 km/h *53·26 mph*) by Franco Gansser (Switzerland) (b. 2 May 1945) on 22 Feb 1987. On 20 Jan 1991 Christian Bertschinger (Switzerland) (b. 8 Feb 1964) set a record from Junction (890 m *2920 ft*) of 41·45 sec.

The greatest number of wins in the Grand National (instituted 1885) is eight by the 1948 Olympic champion Nino Bibbia (Italy) (b. 15 Mar 1922) in 1960–4, 1966, 1968 and 1973; and by Franco Gassner in 1981, 1983–6, 1988–9 and 1991. The greatest number of wins in the Curzon Cup (instituted 1910) is eight by Bibbia in 1950, 1957–8, 1960, 1962–4, and 1969. The only men to have won the four most important races (Curzon Cup, Brabazon Trophy, Morgan Cup and Grand National) in one season are, Bruno Bischofberger (1972), Paul Felder (1974), Nico Baracchi (1982) and Franco Gansser (1988), all of Switzerland.

LUGEING

In lugeing the rider adopts a sitting, as opposed to a prone, position. Official international competition began at Klosters, Switzerland in 1881. The first European championships were at Reichenberg, Ger-

many in 1914 and the first World Championships at Oslo, Norway in 1953. The International Luge Federation was formed in 1957. Lugeing became an Olympic sport in 1964.

Most titles The most successful riders in the World Championships have been Thomas Köhler (GDR) (b. 25 Jun 1940), who won the single-seater title in 1962, 1964 (Olympic), 1965 and 1967 and shared the two-seater title in 1967 and 1968 (Olympic), and Hans Rinn (GDR) (b. 19 Mar 1953), Olympic champion two-seater 1976 and 1980 and world champion at single-seater 1973 and 1977, two-seater 1977 and 1980.

Margit Schumann (GDR) (b. 14 Sep 1952) has won five women's titles, 1973–5, 1976 (Olympic) and 1977.

Steffi Walter (*née* Martin) (GDR) (b. 17 Sep 1962) became the first rider to win two Olympic single-seater luge titles, with victories at the women's event in 1984 and 1988.

Fastest speed The highest recorded, photo-timed speed is 137·4 km/h *85·38 mph* by Asle Strand (Norway) at Tandådalens Linbana, Sälen, Sweden on 1 May 1982.

Bowling (Tenpin)

Origins The ancient German game of nine-pins (*Heidenwerfen* – knock down pagans) was exported to the United States in the early 17th century. In 1841 the Connecticut State Legislature prohibited the game and other states followed. Eventually a tenth pin was added to evade the ban; but there is some evidence of ten pins being used in Suffolk about 200 years ago.

Highest 24-hour bowling score

A team of six scored 202 015 at Verdes Tropicana at West Palm Beach, Florida, USA on 24–25 Aug 1990. This total included an individual 24 hr record of 44 695 by Mike Cernobyl.

■ **Largest attendance**
Muhammad Ali (l) and Leon Spinks (r) square up to each other during their WBA World Heavyweight title fight at the Superdome, New Orleans on 15 Sep 1978. The fight attracted a crowd of 63 350, the largest for an indoor fight. Ali won on points and regained the world title for a record third time. (Photo: All-Sport (USA))

The first body to standardize rules was the American Bowling Congress (ABC), established in New York on 9 Sep 1895.

World Championships The World (*Fédération Internationale des Quilleurs*) Championships were instituted for men in 1954 and for women in 1963.

The highest pinfall in the individual men's event is 5963 (in 28 games) by Ed Luther (USA) at Milwaukee, Wisconsin, USA on 28 Aug 1971.

For the current schedule of 24 games the men's record is 5261 by Richard Clay 'Rick' Steelsmith (b. 1 Jun 1964) and women's record is 4894 by Sandra Jo Shiery (USA), both at Helsinki, Finland in June 1987.

Highest scores The highest individual score for three sanctioned games (possible 900) is 899 by Thomas Jordan (USA) (b. 27 Oct 1966) at Union, New Jersey, USA on 7 Mar 1989.

The record by a woman is 864 by Jeanne Maiden (b. 10 Nov 1957) at Tacoma, Washington, USA on 23 Nov 1986.

The maximum 900 for a three-game series was achieved by Glenn Richard Allison (b. 22 May 1930) at the La Habra Bowl in Los Angeles, California, USA on 1 Jul 1982, but this was not recognized by the ABC due to the oiling patterns on the boards. It has been recorded five times in unsanctioned games – by Leon Bentley at Lorain, Ohio, USA on 26 Mar 1931; by Joe Sargent at Rochester, New York, USA in 1934; by Jim Murgie in Philadelphia, Pennsylvania, USA on 4 Feb 1937; by Bob Brown at Roseville Bowl, California, USA on 12 Apr 1980 and by John Strausbaugh at York, Pennsylvania, USA on 11 Jul 1987. Such series must have consisted of 36 consecutive strikes (i.e. all pins down with one ball).

The record for consecutive strikes in sanctioned match play is 33, first achieved by John Pezzin (b. 1930) at Toledo, Ohio, USA on 4 Mar 1976.

The highest number of sanctioned 300 games is 42 (to June 1991) by Robert Learn Jr (b. 11 Apr 1962) of Erie, Pennsylvania, USA; the women's record is 17 by Jeanne Maiden.

The highest average for a season attained in sanctioned competition is 245·63 by Doug Vergouven of Harrisonville, Montana, USA in 1989/90. The women's record is 232 by Patty Ann of Appleton, Wisconsin, USA in 1983/4.

Great Britain The British record for a three-game series is 806 by Philip Anthony Scammell (b. 8 May 1962) at Worthing, W Sussex on 26 Sep 1986. Army Sergeant Michael Langley scored 835 at S.H.A.P.E., Belgium on 15 Apr 1985. The three-game series record for a woman player is 740 by Elizabeth Cullen at the Astra Bowl, RAF Brize Norton, Oxon on 15 Mar 1983.

The maximum score for a single game of 300 has been achieved on several occasions. The first man to do so was Albert Kirkham (b. 1931) of Burslem, Staffs on 5 Dec 1965. The first woman was Georgina Wardle (b. 24 Jul 1948) at the Sheffield Bowl, S Yorks on 20 Jan 1985. The first person to achieve the feat twice is Patrick Duggan (b. 26 May 1944), in 1972 and 1986, both at Bexleyheath Bowl, Kent.

PBA records Earl Roderick Anthony (b. 27 Apr 1938) was the first to win $1 million and won a record 41 PBA titles to 1990.

The season's record earnings is $298 237 by Mike Aulby (b. 25 Mar 1960) in 1989. The career record is $1 996 201 by Marshall Holman (b. 29 Sep 1954) to the end of 1990.

Largest bowling centre The Fukuyama Bowl, Osaka, Japan has 144 lanes. The Tokyo World Lanes Centre, Japan, now closed, had 252 lanes.

Bowls

OUTDOOR

Origins Whilst bowling games date back some 7000 years, the game of bowls in recognizable form can be traced back to the 13th century in England. The Southampton Town Bowling was formed in 1299. A green dating back to 1294 is claimed by the Chesterfield Bowling Club. After falling into disrepute, the game was rescued by the bowlers of Scotland who, headed by William W. Mitchell (1803–84), framed the modern rules in 1848–9.

World Championships (instituted 1966) The only man to win two or more singles titles is David John Bryant (England) (b. 27 Oct 1931), who won in 1966, 1980 and 1988. With the triples 1980, and the Leonard trophy 1984 and 1988, he has won six World Championship gold medals.

At Johannesburg, South Africa in February 1976, the South African team achieved an unprecedented clean sweep of all four titles plus the team competition (Leonard Trophy).

The Leonard Trophy has been won twice by England, 1980 and 1988 and by Scotland, 1972 and 1984.

Elsie Wilke (New Zealand) won two women's singles titles, 1969 and 1974.

Two Australian women have won three gold medals: Merle Richardson: fours 1977, singles and pairs 1985; and Dorothy Roche: triples 1985 and 1988, fours 1988.

English and British Championships The record number of English Bowls Association (founded 8 Jun 1903) championships is 16 won or shared by David Bryant, including six singles (1960, 1966, 1971–3, 1975), three pairs (1965, 1969, 1974), three triples (1966, 1977, 1985) and four fours championships (1957, 1968, 1969 and 1971). He has also won seven British Isles titles (four singles, one pairs, one triple, one fours) in the period 1957–86. 1987.

The youngest ever EBA singles champion was David A. Holt (b. 9 Sep 1966) at 20 yr 346 days in 1987.

Highest score In an international bowls match, Swaziland beat Japan by 63–1 during the World Championships at Melbourne, Australia on 16 Jan 1980.

Most eights Freda Ehlers and Linda Bertram uniquely scored three consecutive eights in the Southern Transvaal pairs event at Johannesburg, South Africa on 30 Jan 1978.

Most international appearances By any bowler is 78 by Syd Thompson (b. 29 Aug 1912) for Ireland, 1947–73 and David Bryant for England, 1958–87. Bryant also had 50 indoor caps.

The youngest bowler to represent England was Gerard Anthony Smyth (b. 29 Dec 1960) at 20 yr 196 days on 13 Jul 1981.

INDOOR

The English Indoor Bowling Association became an autonomous body in 1971. Prior to that it was part of the English Bowling Association.

Championships David Bryant has won the World Indoor singles (instituted 1979) three times, 1979–81 and with Tony Allcock (b. 11 Jun 1955) has won the pairs (instituted 1986) five times, 1986–7, 1989–91. The English National Singles title (instituted 1960) has been won most often by David Bryant with nine wins between 1964 and 1983.

The youngest EIBA singles champion, John Dunn (b. 6 Oct 1963), was 17 yr 117 days when he won in 1981.

Highest score Joan Eggleton, Brenda King, Maureen Smith and Patricia Bain of Eastbourne & District Indoor Bowls Club beat a four from Egerton Park, 59–2 over 21 ends at Eastbourne, E Sussex on 7 Feb 1989.

The greatest 'whitewash' is 55–0 by C. Hammond and B. Funnell against A. Wise

and C. Lock in the second round of the EIBA National Pairs Championships on 17 Oct 1983 at The Angel, Tonbridge, Kent.

Boxing

Origins Boxing with gloves was depicted on a fresco, from the Isle of Thera, Greece, which has been dated to 1520 BC. The earliest prize-ring code of rules was formulated in England on 16 Aug 1743 by the champion pugilist Jack Broughton (1704–89), who reigned from 1734 to 1750. Boxing, which had in 1867 come under the Queensberry Rules formulated for John Sholto Douglas, 8th Marquess of Queensberry (1844–1900), was not established as a legal sport in Britain until after the ruling, *R. v. Roberts and Others*, of Mr Justice Grantham, following the death of Billy Smith (Murray Livingstone) due to a fight on 24 Apr 1901.

Longest fights The longest recorded fight with gloves was between Andy Bowen of New Orleans (1867–94) and Jack Burke at New Orleans, Louisiana, USA on 6–7 Apr 1893. It lasted 110 rounds, 7 hr 19 min (9:15 p.m.–4:34 a.m.), and was declared a no contest (later changed to a draw). Bowen won an 85-round bout on 31 May 1893.

The longest bare-knuckle fight was 6 hr 15 min between James Kelly and Jack Smith at Fiery Creek, Dalesford, Victoria, Australia on 3 Dec 1855.

The greatest number of rounds was 276 in 4 hr 30 min when Jack Jones beat Patsy Tunney in Cheshire in 1825.

Shortest fights There is a distinction between the quickest knock-out and the shortest fight. A knock-out in 10½ sec (including a 10 sec count) occurred on 23 Sep 1946, when Al Couture struck Ralph Walton while the latter was adjusting a gum shield in his corner at Lewiston, Maine, USA. If the time was accurately taken it is clear that Couture must have been more than half-way across the ring from his own corner at the opening bell.

The shortest fight on record appears to be one in a Golden Gloves tournament at Minneapolis, Minnesota, USA on 4 Nov 1947, when Mike Collins floored Pat Brownson with the first punch and the contest was stopped, without a count, 4 sec after the bell.

The shortest world title fight was 45 sec, when Lloyd Honeyghan (b. 22 Apr 1960) beat Gene Hatcher in an IBF welterweight bout at Marbella, Spain on 30 Aug 1987. Some sources also quote the Al McCoy (1894–1966) first round knockout of George Chip in a middleweight contest on 7 Apr 1914 as being in 45 sec.

The shortest ever heavyweight world title fight was the James J. Jeffries (1875–1953) –Jack Finnegan bout at Detroit, USA on 6 Apr 1900, won by Jeffries in 55 sec.

The shortest ever British title fight was one of 40 sec (including the count), when Dave Charnley knocked out David 'Darkie' Hughes in a lightweight championship defence in Nottingham on 20 Nov 1961.

Eugene Brown, on his professional debut, knocked out Ian Bockes of Hull at Leicester on 13 Mar 1989. The fight was officially stopped after '10 seconds of the first round'. Bockes got up after a count of six but the referee stopped the contest.

Most British titles The most defences of a British heavyweight title is 14 by

'Bombardier' Billy Wells (1889–1967) from 1911 to 1919.

The only British boxer to win three Lonsdale Belts outright was heavyweight Henry William Cooper (b. 3 May 1934). He retired after losing to Joe Bugner (b. Hungary, 13 Mar 1950), having held the British heavyweight title from 12 Jan 1959 to 28 May 1969 and from 24 Mar 1970 to 16 Mar 1971.

The fastest time to win a Lonsdale Belt, for three successive championship wins, is 161 days by Carl Crook (b. 10 Nov 1963) at lightweight, 14 Nov 1990–24 Apr 1991.

The longest time for winning a Lonsdale Belt outright is 8 yr 236 days by Kirkland Laing (b. 20 Jun 1954), 4 Apr 1979–26 Nov 1987.

Tallest The tallest boxer to fight professionally was Gogea Mitu (b. 1914) of Romania in 1935. He was 2·33 m *7 ft 4 in* and weighed 148 kg *327 lb.*

John Rankin, who won a fight in New Orleans, Louisiana, USA in November 1967, was reputedly also 2·33 m *7 ft 4 in.*

Jim Culley, 'The Tipperary Giant', who fought as a boxer and wrestled in the 1940s is also reputed to have been 2·33 m *7 ft 4 in.*

Most fights without loss Edward Henry (Harry) Greb (USA) (1894–1926) was unbeaten in a sequence of 178 bouts, but these included 117 'no decision', of which five were unofficial losses, in 1916–23.

Of boxers with complete records, Packey McFarland (USA) (1888–1936) had 97 fights (5 draws) in 1905–15 without a defeat.

Pedro Carrasco (Spain) (b. 7 Nov 1943) won 83 consecutive fights from 22 April 1964 to 3 Sep 1970, drew once and had a further nine wins before his loss to Armando Ramos in a WBC lightweight contest on 18 Feb 1972.

Most knock-outs The greatest number of finishes classed as 'knock-outs' in a career (1936–63) is 145 (129 in professional bouts) by Archie Moore (USA) (b. Archibald Lee Wright, 13 Dec 1913 or 1916).

The record for consecutive KO's is 44 by Lamar Clark (USA) (b. 1 Dec 1934) from 1958 to 11 Jan 1960. He knocked out six in one night (five in the first round) at Bingham, Utah, USA on 1 Dec 1958.

Largest purse The total purse for the world heavyweight fight between Mike Gerard Tyson (USA) (b. 30 Jun 1966) and Michael Spinks (USA) (b. 22 Jul 1956) at Convention Hall, Atlantic City, New Jersey, USA on 27 Jun 1988, was estimated as at least $35·8 million, $22 m for Tyson and $13·8 m for Spinks, who was knocked out after 1 min 31 sec of the first round.

Attendances *Highest* The greatest paid attendance at any boxing fight has been 120 757 (with a ringside price of $27·50) for the Tunney *v.* Dempsey world heavyweight title fight at the Sesquicentennial Stadium, Philadelphia, Pennsylvania, USA on 23 Sep 1926.

The indoor record is 63 350 at the Ali *v.* Leon Spinks (b. 11 Jul 1953) fight in the Superdome, New Orleans, Louisiana, USA on 15 Sep 1978.

The British attendance record is 82 000 at the Len Harvey *v.* Jock McAvoy fight at White City, London on 10 Jul 1939.

The highest non-paying attendance is 135 132 at the Tony Zale *v.* Billy Pryor fight at Juneau Park, Milwaukee, Wisconsin, USA on 16 Aug 1941.

Lowest The smallest attendance at a world heavyweight title fight was 2434, at the Cassius (Muhammad Ali) Clay *v* Sonny Liston fight at Lewiston, Maine, USA on 25 May 1965.

WORLD HEAVYWEIGHT

Earliest title fight Long accepted as the first world heavyweight title fight, with gloves and 3-min rounds, was that between John Lawrence Sullivan (1858–1918) and 'Gentleman' James John Corbett (1866–1933) in New Orleans, Louisiana, USA on 7 Sep 1892. Corbett won in 21 rounds. However the fight between Sullivan, then the world bare-knuckle champion, and Dominick F. McCafferey in Chester Park, Cincinnati, Ohio on 29 Aug 1885 was staged under Queensberry Rules with the boxers wearing gloves over six rounds. The referee Billy Tait left the ring without giving a verdict, but when asked two days later said that Sullivan had won.

Reign *Longest* Joe Louis (USA) (b. Joseph Louis Barrow, 1914–81) was champion for 11 years 252 days, from 22 Jun 1937, when he knocked out James Joseph Braddock in the eighth round at Chicago, Illinois, USA, until announcing his retirement on 1 Mar 1949. During his reign Louis made a record 25 defences of his title.

Shortest 83 days for WBA champion James 'Bonecrusher' Smith (USA) (b. 3 Apr 1955), 13 Dec 1986 to 7 Mar 1987, and for Ken Norton (USA) (b. 9 Aug 1945), recognized by the WBC as champion from 18 Mar–9 Jun 1978. Tony Tucker (USA) (b. 28 Dec 1958) was IBF champion for 64 days, 30 May–2 Aug 1987.

Most recaptures Muhammad Ali is the only man to regain the heavyweight championship twice. Ali first won the title on 25 Feb 1964, defeating Sonny Liston. He defeated George Foreman on 30 Oct 1974, having been stripped of the title by the world boxing authorities on 28 Apr 1967. He won the WBA title from Leon Spinks on 15

■ **Longest-lived**
Jack Sharkey (b. Joseph Paul Cukoschay, 26 Oct 1902) is the longest-lived world heavyweight champion, surpassing the previous record of 87 yr 341 days, held by Jack Dempsey (1895–1983), on 3 Oct 1990. Sharkey won the title on 21 Jun 1932 defeating Max Schmeling on points, but lost in his first defence to the 'Ambling Alp', Primo Carnera, on 29 Jun 1933.
(Photo: Hulton Picture Library)

BOXING

Heaviest
Primo Carnera (Italy) (1906–67), the 'Ambling Alp', who won the title from Jack Sharkey in New York City, USA on 29 Jun 1933, scaled 118 kg *260½ lb* for this fight but his peak weight was 122 kg *270 lb*. He had an expanded chest measurement of 137 cm *54 in* and the longest reach at 217 cm *85½ in* (fingertip to fingertip).

Lightest heavyweight
Robert James 'Bob' Fitzsimmons (1863–1917), from Helston, Cornwall weighed 75 kg *167 lb*, when he won the title by knocking out James J. Corbett at Carson City, Nevada, USA on 17 Mar 1897.

Canoe raft
A raft of 376 kayaks and canoes, organized by the People's Association Youth Movement, was held together by hands only, while free floating for 30 seconds, on the Johor Strait at Sembawang, Singapore on 26 Jun 1990.

Sep 1978, having previously lost to him on 15 Feb 1978.

Undefeated Rocky Marciano (b. Rocco Francis Marchegiano) (1923–69) is the only world champion at *any weight* to have retired having won every fight of his entire professional career (1947–56); and 43 of his 49 fights were by knock-outs or stoppages.

Oldest Jersey Joe Walcott (USA) (b. Arnold Raymond Cream, 31 Jan 1914) was 37 yr 168 days, when he knocked out Ezzard Mack Charles (1921–75) on 18 Jul 1951 in Pittsburgh, Pennsylvania, USA. He was also the oldest holder at 38 yr 236 days, losing his title to Rocky Marciano on 23 Sep 1952.

Youngest Mike Tyson (USA) was 20 yr 144 days when he beat Trevor Berbick (USA) to win the WBC version at Las Vegas, Nevada, USA on 22 Nov 1986. He added the WBA title when he beat James 'Bonecrusher' Smith on 7 Mar 1987 at 20 yr 249 days. He became universal champion on 2 Aug 1987 when he beat Tony Tucker (USA) for the IBF title.

Tallest There is uncertainty as to the tallest world champion. Ernest Terrell (USA) (b. 4 Apr 1939), WBA champion 1965–67, was reported to be 1·98 m *6 ft 6 in*. Slightly higher figures had been given for earlier champions, but, according to measurements by the physical education director of the Hemingway Gymnasium, Harvard University, Cambridge, Massachusetts Primo Carnera was 1·966 m *6 ft 5·4 in*, although widely reported and believed to be up to 2·04 m *6 ft 8½ in*. Jess Willard (1881–1968), who won the title in 1915, often stated to be 1·99 m *6 ft 6¼ in*, was in fact 1·96 m *6 ft 5¼ in*.

Shortest Tommy Burns, world champion from 23 Feb 1906 to 26 Dec 1908, stood 1·70 m *5 ft 7 in* and weighed between 76–81 kg *168–180 lb*.

WORLD CHAMPIONS Any

Reign Longest The Joe Louis heavyweight duration record of 11 yr 252 days stands for all divisions.

Shortest Tony Canzoneri (USA) (1908–59) was world light-welterweight champion for 33 days, 21 May to 23 Jun 1933, the shortest period for a boxer to have won and lost the world title in the ring.

Youngest Wilfred Benitez (b. New York, 12 Sep 1958) of Puerto Rico, was 17 yr 176 days when he won the WBA light welterweight title in San Juan, Puerto Rico on 6 Mar 1976.

Oldest Archie Moore, who was recognized as a light heavyweight champion up to 10 Feb 1962 when his title was removed, was then believed to be between 45 and 48.

Longest career Bob Fitzsimmons had a career of over 31 years from 1883 to 1914. He had his last world title bout on 20 Dec 1905 at the age of 42 yr 208 days. Jack Johnson (USA) (1878–1946) also had a career of over 31 years, 1897–1928.

Longest fight The longest world title fight (under Queensberry Rules) was that between the lightweights Joe Gans (1874–1910), of the USA, and Oscar Matthew 'Battling' Nelson (1882–1954), the 'Durable Dane', at Goldfield, Nevada, USA on 3 Sep 1906. It was terminated in the 42nd round when Gans was declared the winner on a foul.

Most different weights The first to have won world titles at four weight categories was Thomas Hearns (USA) (b. 18 Oct 1958), WBA welterweight in 1980, WBC

super welterweight in 1982, WBC light heavyweight in 1987 and WBC middleweight in 1987. He added a fifth weight division when he won the super middleweight title recognized by the newly created World Boxing Organization (WBO) on 4 Nov 1988, and he won his sixth title, the WBA light-heavyweight title, on 3 Jun 1991.

Winning titles recognized by the two senior authorities, the WBA and WBC, Sugar Ray Leonard (USA) (b. 17 May 1956) won world titles at his fourth and fifth weight categories, when he beat Donny Lalonde (Canada) on 7 Nov 1988, to annex both WBC light heavyweight and super middleweight titles. He had previously won the WBC welterweight in 1979 and 1980, WBA junior middleweight in 1981 and WBC middleweight in 1987.

The only man to hold world titles at three weights *simultaneously* was Henry 'Homicide Hank' Armstrong (USA) (1912–88), at featherweight, lightweight and welterweight from August to December 1938. In recent years there has been a proliferation of weight categories and governing bodies but Armstrong was undisputed world champion at widely differing weights which makes his achievement all the more remarkable.

Most recaptures The only boxer to win a world title five times at one weight is 'Sugar' Ray Robinson (USA) (b. Walker Smith Jr, 1921–89), who beat Carmen Basilio (USA) in the Chicago Stadium on 25 Mar 1958, to regain the world middleweight title for the fourth time.

Dennis Andries (b. Guyana, 5 Nov 1953) became the first British boxer to regain a world title twice when he won the WBC light-heavyweight title on 28 Jul 1990.

The record number of title bouts in a career is 37, of which 18 ended in 'no decision', by three-time world welterweight champion Jack Britton (USA) (1885–1962) in 1915–22. The record containing no 'no decision' contests is 27 (all heavyweight) by Joe Louis between 1937–50.

Greatest weight difference When Primo Carnera (Italy) 122 kg *270 lb* fought Tommy Loughran (USA) 83 kg *184 lb* for the world heavyweight title at Miami, Florida, USA on 1 Mar 1934, there was a weight difference of 39 kg *86 lb* between the two fighters. Carnera won the fight on points.

Greatest 'tonnage' The greatest 'tonnage' recorded in any fight is 317 kg *700 lb* when Claude 'Humphrey' McBride (Oklahoma), 154 kg *340 lb*, knocked out Jimmy Black (Houston), who weighed 163 kg *360 lb* in the third round at Oklahoma City on 1 Jun 1971.

The greatest 'tonnage' in a world title fight was 221·5 kg *488 ¾ lb*, when Carnera, then 117·5 kg *259 ½ lb* fought Paolino Uzcudun (Spain) 104 kg *229 ¼ lb* in Rome, Italy on 22 Oct 1933.

Most knock-downs in title fights Vic Toweel (South Africa) (b. 12 Jan 1929) knocked down Danny O'Sullivan of London 14 times in ten rounds in their world bantamweight fight at Johannesburg on 2 Dec 1950, before the latter retired.

Twins When Khaokor Galaxy (Thailand) won the WBA bantamweight title on 8 May 1988, he and his twin brother, Khaosai, were the first twins ever to be world boxing champions. Khaosai Galaxy had been WBA super flyweight champion since 21 Nov 1984.

AMATEUR

Most Olympic titles Only two boxers have won three Olympic gold medals: southpaw László Papp (Hungary) (b. 25 Mar 1926), middleweight 1948, light-middleweight 1952 and 1956; and Teofilo Stevenson (Cuba) (b. 23 Mar 1952), heavyweight 1972, 1976 and 1980.

The only man to win two titles in one celebration was Oliver L. Kirk (USA), who won both bantam and featherweight titles in St Louis, Missouri, USA in 1904, but he needed only one bout in each class.

Another record that will stand forever is that of the youngest Olympic boxing champion: Jackie Fields (*né* Finkelstein) (USA) (b. 9 Feb 1908) who won the 1924 featherweight title at 16 years 162 days. The minimum age for Olympic boxing competitors is now 17.

Oldest gold medallist Richard Kenneth Gunn (GB) (1871–1961) won the Olympic featherweight gold medal on 27 Oct 1908 in London aged 37 yr 254 days.

World Championships Two boxers have won three world championships (instituted 1974): Teofilo Stevenson (Cuba), heavyweight 1974, 1978 and superheavyweight 1986, and Adolfo Horta (Cuba) (b. 3 Oct 1957) bantam 1978, feather 1982 and lightweight 1986.

Most British titles The greatest number of ABA titles won by any boxer is eight by John Lyon (b. 9 Mar 1962) at light-flyweight 1981–4 and at flyweight 1986–9.

Alex 'Bud' Watson (b. 27 May 1914) of Leith, Scotland won the Scottish heavyweight title in 1938, 1942–3, and the light-heavyweight championship 1937–9, 1943–5 and 1947, making ten in all. He also won the ABA light-heavyweight title in 1945 and 1947.

Longest span The greatest span of ABA title-winning performances is that of the heavyweight Hugh 'Pat' Floyd (b. 23 Aug 1910), who won in 1929 and gained his fourth title 17 years later in 1946.

Canoeing

The acknowledged pioneer of canoeing as a modern sport was John Macgregor (1825–92), a British barrister, in 1865. The Canoe Club was formed on 26 Jul 1866.

Most titles Olympic Gert Fredriksson (Sweden) (b. 21 Nov 1919) won a record six Olympic gold medals, 1948–60. He added a silver and a bronze for a record eight medals.

The most by a woman is three by Lyudmila Iosifovna Pinayeva (*née* Khvedosyuk) (USSR) (b. 14 Jan 1936), 1964–72 and Birgit Schmidt (*née* Fischer) (GDR) (b. 25 Feb 1962), one in 1980 and two in 1988.

The most gold medals at one Games is three by Vladimir Parfenovich (USSR) (b. 2 Dec 1958) in 1980 and by Ian Ferguson (New Zealand) (b. 20 Jul 1952) in 1984.

World Including the Olympic Games a women's record 22 titles have been won by Birgit Schmidt, 1978–88.

The men's record is 13 by Gert Fredriksson, 1948–60, Rüdiger Helm (GDR) (b. 6 Oct 1956), 1976–83, and Ivan Patzaichin (Romania) (b. 26 Nov 1949), 1968–84.

The most individual titles by a British canoeist is four by Richard Fox (b. 5 Jun

1960) at K1 slalom in 1981, 1983, 1985 and 1989. Fox also won four gold medals at K1 team, between 1981 and 1987.

Highest speed The Hungarian four-man kayak Olympic champions in 1988 at Seoul, South Korea covered 1000 m in 2 min 58·54 sec in a heat. This represents an average speed of 20·16 km/h *12·53 mph*.

In this same race the Norwegian four achieved a 250 m split of 42·08 sec between 500 m and 750 m for a speed of 21·39 km/h *13·29 mph*.

Longest journey Father and son Dana and Donald Starkell paddled from Winnipeg, Manitoba, Canada by ocean and river to Belem, Brazil, a distance of 19 603 km *12 181 miles* from 1 Jun 1980 to 1 May 1982. All portages were human powered.

Without portages or aid of any kind the longest is one of 9820 km *6102 miles* by Richard H. Grant and Ernest 'Moose' Lassy circumnavigating the eastern USA via Chicago, New Orleans, Miami, New York and the Great Lakes from 22 Sep 1930 to 15 Aug 1931.

English Channel The singles record crossing is 3 hr 33 min 47 sec by Andrew William Dougall Samuel (b. 12 Jul 1937) of Glasgow, from Shakespeare Bay, Dover to Wissant, France on 5 Sep 1976.

The doubles record is 2 hr 28 min 18 sec by Shaun Rice (Ireland) and Colin Simpkins (South Africa) in a K2 on 19 Jul 1986 from Shakespeare Bay, Dover to Cap Gris Nez, France.

North Sea On 22–23 Jun 1986, a team of five in the 'Canadian Club Challenge' paddled K1s from Zeebrugge, Belgium to Felixstowe, Suffolk, over 177 km *110 miles* across open sea, in 28 hr 56 min 12 sec.

Loch Ness The fastest time from Fort Augustus to Lochend (36·5 km *22·7 miles*) is 2 hr 58 min 48 sec by Colin Simpkins (South Africa) in a Jaguar K1 on 26 Jul 1987.

River Rhine The fastest time, solo and unsupported, is 10 days 12 hr 9 min by Frank Palmer, 15–25 May 1988. The supported team record is 7 days 23 hr 31 sec by the RAF Laarbruch Canoe Club, led by Andy Goodsell, 17–24 May 1989. The 'Rhine Challenge', as organized by the International Long River Canoeists Club, begins from an official marker post in Chur, Switzerland and ends at Willemstad, Netherlands, a distance of 1149 km *714 miles*.

Longest race The Canadian Government Centennial Voyageur Canoe Pageant and Race from Rocky Mountain House, Alberta to the Expo 67 site at Montreal, Quebec was 5283 km *3283 miles*. Ten canoes represented Canadian provinces and territories. The winner of the race, which took from 24 May to 4 Sep 1967, was the Province of Manitoba canoe *Radisson*.

24 hours Zdzislaw Szubski paddled 252·9 km *157·1 miles* in a Jaguar K1 canoe on the Vistula River, Wloclawek to Gdansk, Poland on 11–12 Sep 1987.

Women Lydia Formentin paddled 156·4 km *97·2 miles* on the Swan River, Western Australia in 1979.

Flat water Thomas J. Mazuzan paddled, without benefit of current, 199·53 km *123·98 miles* on the Barge Canal, New York State, USA on 24–25 Sep 1986.

Open sea Randy Fine (USA) paddled

194·1 km *120·6 miles* along the Florida coast on 26–27 Jun 1986.

Greatest lifetime distance Fritz Lindner of Berlin, Germany, totalled 103 444 km *64 278 miles* from 1928 to 1987.

Highest altitude In September 1976 Dr Michael Leslie Jones (1951–78) and Michael Hopkinson of the British Everest Canoe Expedition canoed down the River Dudh Kosi, Nepal from an altitude of 5334 m *17 500 ft*.

Eskimo rolls Ray Hudspith (b. 18 Apr 1960) achieved 1000 rolls in 34 min 43 sec at the Elswick Pool, Newcastle upon Tyne on 20 Mar 1987. He completed 100 rolls in 3 min 7·25 sec at Killingworth Leisure Centre, Tyne and Wear on 3 Mar 1991.

Randy Fine (USA) completed 1796 continuous rolls at Biscayne Bay, Miami, Florida, USA on 8 Jun 1991.

'Hand rolls' Colin Hill achieved 1000 rolls in 31 min 55·62 sec at Consett, Co. Durham on 12 Mar 1987. He also achieved 100 rolls in 2 min 39·2 sec at Crystal Palace, London on 22 Feb 1987. He completed 3700 continuous rolls at Durham City Swimming Baths, Co. Durham on 1 May 1989.

Card Games

CONTRACT BRIDGE

Origins Bridge (a corruption of Biritch, a now obsolete Russian word whose meanings include 'declarer') is thought either to be of Levantine origin, similar games having been played there in the early 1870s, or to have come from India.

Auction bridge was invented *c.* 1902. The contract principle, present in several games (notably the French game *Plafond*, *c.* 1917), was introduced to bridge by Harold Stirling Vanderbilt (USA) (1884–1970) on 1 Nov 1925 during a Caribbean voyage aboard the SS *Finland*. It became a world-wide craze after the USA v. Great Britain challenge match between Romanian-born Ely Culbertson (1891–1955) and Lt-Col Walter Thomas More Buller (1887–1938) at Almack's Club, London in September 1930. The USA won the 200-hand match by 4845 points.

Biggest tournament The Epson World Bridge Championship, held on 7 Jun 1991, was contested by almost 90 000 players playing the same hands at centres in 95 countries.

Most world titles The World Championship (Bermuda Bowl) has been won a record 13 times by Italy's Blue Team (*Squadra Azzura*), 1957–59, 1961–63, 1965–67, 1969, 1973–75 and by the USA, 1950–51, 1953–54, 1970–71, 1976–77, 1979, 1981, 1983, 1985, 1987. Italy also won the team Olympiad in 1964, 1968 and 1972. Giorgio Belladonna (b. 7 Jun 1923) was in all the Italian winning teams.

The USA have a record five wins in the women's world championship for the Venice Trophy: 1974, 1976, 1978, 1987 and 1989, and three women's wins at the World Team Olympiad: 1976, 1980 and 1984.

Most hands In the 1989 Bermuda Bowl in Perth, Australia Marcel Branco and Gabriel Chagas, both of Brazil, played a record 752 out of a possible 784 boards.

Most master points In the latest ranking list based on Master Points awarded by the World Bridge Federation during the last ten years, the leading players in the

world are (men) Robert Hamman (b. 1938) of Dallas, Texas, USA with 597 and (women) Sandra Landy (GB) with 284. The all-time leading Master Point winner was Giorgio Belladonna (Italy) with 1821¼ points. The world's leading woman player is Jacqui Mitchell (USA) with 347 points.

Barry Crane of Los Angeles, California, USA led the American Contract Bridge League rankings from 1968 to his murder in 1985. He amassed a record total of 35 137·6 Master Points. The current leader is Paul Soloway with 34 953 to June 1991. The most master points scored in a year is 3270 by Grant Baze (USA) in 1984.

The first man to win 10 000 Master Points was Oswald Jacoby (USA) (1902–84) in October 1967. He had been a member of the winning World Championship team in 1935 and on 4 Dec 1983 became the oldest member of a winning team of a major open team championship, in the Curtis Reisinger Trophy.

Rika 'Rixi' Markus (Austria, later GB) (b. 27 Jun 1910) has won numerous titles during an illustrious career and became the first woman World Grand Master in 1974.

Youngest life master Joel Wooldridge (b. 19 Jul 1979) of Buffalo, New York became the world's youngest ever Life Master on 2 Dec 1990 at 11 yr 135 days.

The youngest ever woman Master is Patricia Thomas (b. 10 Oct 1968) at 14 yr 28 days in 1982.

CRIBBAGE

Origins The invention of the game (once called Cribbidge) is credited to the English dramatist Sir John Suckling (1609–42).

Rare hands Four maximum 29 point hands have been achieved by William E. Johnson of Waltham, Massachusetts, USA, 1974–81 and by Mrs Mary Matheson of Springhill, Nova Scotia, Canada, 1974–85. Paul Nault of Athol, Massachusetts, USA had two such hands within eight games in a tournament on 19 Mar 1977.

Most points in 24 hours The most points scored by a team of four, playing singles in two pairs, is 111 201 by Christine and Elizabeth Gill, Jeanette MacGrath and Donald Ward at Grannie's Healin' Hame, Embo, Highland Region on 2–3 May 1987.

Cricket

Origins The earliest evidence of a game similar to cricket is from a drawing depicting two men playing with a bat and ball dated *c.* 1150. The game was played in Guildford, Surrey, at least as early as 1550. The earliest major match of which the full score survives was one in which a team representing England (40 and 70) was beaten by Kent (53 and 58 for 9) by one wicket at the Artillery Ground in Finsbury, London on 18 Jun 1744. Cricket was played in Australia as early as 1803. The first international match was played between Canada and the USA in 1844. Fifteen years later those countries were host to the first English touring team. The first touring team to visit England was an Australian Aborigine XI in 1868.

BATTING RECORDS Teams

Highest innings Victoria scored 1107 runs in 10 hr 30 min against New South Wales in an Australian Sheffield Shield match at Melbourne on 27–28 Dec 1926.

INDIVIDUAL RECORDS
FIRST-CLASS AND TEST CAREER

		Name	Team	Year
		BATTING		
MOST RUNS	First-Class 61 237	Sir John Berry 'Jack' Hobbs (1882–1963) (av. 50·65)	Surrey/England	1905–34
	Test 10 122	Sunil Manohar Gavaskar (b. 10 Jul 1949) (av. 51·12)	India (125 Tests)	1971–87
MOST CENTURIES	First-Class 197	Sir Jack Hobbs (in 1315 innings)	Surrey/England	1905–34
	Test 34	Sunil Gavaskar (in 214 innings)	India	1971–87
HIGHEST AVERAGE	First-Class 95·14	Sir Donald George Bradman (b. 28 Aug 1908)	NSW/South Australia/Australia	1927–49
		(28 067 runs in 338 innings, including 43 not outs)		
	Test 99·94	Sir Donald Bradman (6996 runs in 80 innings)	Australia (52 Tests)	1928–48
		BOWLING		
MOST WICKETS	First-Class 4187	Wilfred Rhodes (1877–1973) (av. 16·71)	Yorkshire/England	1898–1930
	Test 431	Sir Richard John Hadlee (b. 3 Jul 1951) (av. 22·29)	New Zealand (83 Tests)	1973–90
LOWEST AVERAGE	Test 10·75	George Alfred Lohmann (1865–1901) (112 wkts)	England (18 Tests)	1886–96
(min 15 wkts)				
		WICKET-KEEPING		
MOST DISMISSALS	First-Class 1649	Robert William Taylor (b. 17 Jul 1941)	Derbyshire/England	1960–88
	Test 355	Rodney William Marsh (b. 11 Nov 1947)	Australia (96 Tests)	1970–84
MOST CATCHES	First-Class 1473	Robert Taylor	Derbyshire/England	1960–88
	Test 343	Rodney Marsh	Australia	1970–84
MOST STUMPINGS	First-Class 418	Leslie Ethelbert George Ames (1905–90)	Kent/England	1926–51
	Test 52	William Albert Stanley Oldfield (1894–1976)	Australia (54 Tests)	1920–37
		FIELDING		
MOST CATCHES	First-Class 1018	Frank Edward Woolley (1887–1978)	Kent/England	1906–38
	Test 130	Allan Robert Border (b. 27 Jul 1955)	Australia (125 Tests)	1978–91

IN A FIRST-CLASS SEASON IN ENGLAND

	Name	Team	Year
	BATTING		
MOST RUNS 3816	Denis Charles Scott Compton (b. 23 May 1918) (av. 90·85)	Middlesex/England	1947
MOST CENTURIES 18	Denis Compton (in 50 innings with 8 not outs)	Middlesex/England	1947
HIGHEST AVERAGE 115·66	Sir Donald Bradman (2429 runs in 26 innings, with 5 not outs)	Australians	1938
	BOWLING		
MOST WICKETS 304	Alfred Percy 'Tich' Freeman (1888–1965) (1976·1 overs) (av. 18·05)	Kent	1928
LOWEST AVERAGE 8·54	Alfred Shaw (1842–1907) (186 wkts)	Nottinghamshire	1880
(min 100 wkts)			
	WICKET-KEEPING		
MOST DISMISSALS 128	Leslie Ames (79 caught, 49 stumped)	Kent	1929
MOST CATCHES 96	James Graham Binks (b. 5 Oct 1935)	Yorkshire	1960
MOST STUMPINGS 64	Leslie Ames	Kent	1932
	FIELDING		
MOST CATCHES 78	Walter Reginald Hammond (1903–65)	Gloucestershire	1928

IN A TEST SERIES

	Name	Team	Year
	BATTING		
MOST RUNS 974	Sir Donald Bradman (av. 139·14)	Australia v. England (5 Tests)	1930
MOST CENTURIES 5	Clyde Leopold Walcott (b. 17 Jan 1926)	West Indies v. Australia (5 Tests)	1954–5
HIGHEST AVERAGE 563·00	Walter Reginald Hammond (563 runs, 2 inns, 1 not out)	England v. New Zealand (2 Tests)	1932–3
	BOWLING		
MOST WICKETS 49	Sydney Francis Barnes (1873–1967) (av. 10·93)	England v. South Africa (4 Tests)	1913–14
LOWEST AVERAGE 5·80	George Alfred Lohmann (35 wkts)	England v. South Africa (3 Tests)	1895–6
(min 20 wkts)			
	WICKET-KEEPING		
MOST DISMISSALS 28	Rodney Marsh (all caught)	Australia v. England (5 Tests)	1982–3
MOST STUMPINGS 9	Percy William Sherwell (1880–1948)	South Africa v. Australia (5 Tests)	1910–11
	FIELDING		
MOST CATCHES 15	Jack Morrison Gregory (1895–1973)	Australia v. England (5 Tests)	1920–21
	ALL-ROUND		
400 RUNS/ 30 WICKETS 475/34	George Giffen (1859–1927)	Australia v. England (5 Tests)	1894–5

Test England scored 903 runs for seven wickets declared in 15 hr 17 min, *v.* Australia at The Oval, London on 20, 22 and 23 Aug 1938.

County Championship Yorkshire scored 887 in 10 hr 50 min, *v.* Warwickshire at Edgbaston, Birmingham on 7–8 May 1896.

Lowest innings The traditional first-class record is 12 by Oxford University (who batted a man short) *v.* the Marylebone Cricket Club (MCC) at Cowley Marsh, Oxford on 24 May 1877, and by Northamptonshire *v.* Gloucestershire at Gloucester on 11 Jun 1907. However, 'The Bs' scored 6 in their second innings *v.* England at Lord's, London on 12–14 Jun 1810 in one of the major matches of that era.

Test 26 by New Zealand *v.* England at Auckland on 28 Mar 1955.

Aggregate for two innings 34 (16 and 18) by Border *v.* Natal in the South African Currie Cup at East London on 19 and 21 Dec

1959. In an early match, Leicestershire totalled 23 (15 and 8) *v.* Nottinghamshire (61) at Leicester on 25 Aug 1800.

Greatest victory A margin of an innings and 851 runs was recorded, when Pakistan Railways (910 for 6 wickets declared) beat Dera Ismail Khan (32 and 27) at Lahore on 2–4 Dec 1964.

In England England won by an innings and 579 runs (also the record for a Test) against Australia at The Oval on 20–24 Aug 1938 when Australia scored 201 and 123 with two men short in both innings. The most one-sided county match was when Surrey (698) defeated Sussex (114 and 99) by an innings and 485 runs at The Oval on 9–11 Aug 1888.

Most runs in a day Australia scored 721 all out (ten wickets) in 5 hr 48 min against Essex at Southchurch Park, Southend-on-Sea on 15 May 1948.

Test 588 at Old Trafford, Manchester on 27 Jul 1936 when England added 398 and India were 190 for 0 in their second innings by the close.

BATTING RECORDS *Individuals*

Highest innings Hanif Mohammad (b. 21 Dec 1934) scored 499 in 10 hr 35 min for Karachi against Balawalpur at Karachi, Pakistan on 8, 9 and 11 Jan 1959.

In England Archibald Campbell MacLaren (1871–1944) scored 424 in 7 hr 50 min for Lancashire *v.* Somerset at Taunton, Somerset on 15–16 Jul 1895.

Test Sir Garfield St Aubrun Sobers (b. 28 Jul 1936) scored 365 not out in 10 hr 14 min for West Indies *v.* Pakistan at Sabina Park, Kingston, Jamaica on 27 Feb–1 Mar 1958. The English Test record is 364 by Sir Leonard Hutton (1916–90) against Australia at The Oval on 20, 22 and 23 Aug 1938.

Longest innings Hanif Mohammad (Pakistan) batted for 16 hr 10 min for 337 runs against the West Indies at Bridgetown, Barbados on 20–23 Jan 1958. The English record is 13 hr 17 min by Len Hutton in his record Test score of 364 (see above).

Most runs off an over The first batsman to score 36 runs off a six ball over was Sir Garfield Sobers off Malcolm Andrew Nash (b. 9 May 1945) for Nottinghamshire *v.* Glamorgan at Swansea on 31 Aug 1968. His feat was emulated by Ravishankar Jayadritha Shastri (b. 27 May 1962) for Bombay *v.* Baroda at Bombay, India on 10 Jan 1985 off the bowling of Tilak Raj (b. 15 Jan 1960).

Playing in a Shell Trophy match for Wellington *v.* Canterbury at Christchurch on 20 Feb 1990, in a deliberate attempt to give away runs, Robert Howard Vance (b. 31 Mar 1955) bowled an over containing 22 balls, 17 of which were deliberate no-balls (the umpire losing count and declaring over one ball early!). From this over Lee Kenneth Germon (b. 4 Nov 1968) of Canterbury hit 70 runs, including eight sixes and five fours, Richard Petrie scored five runs including one four, and with two runs from no-balls off which no runs were hit, a total of 77 runs was conceded.

Most sixes in an innings John Richard Reid (b. 3 Jun 1928) hit 15 in an innings of 296, lasting 3 hr 40 min, for Wellington *v.* Northern Districts in a Plunket Shield match at Wellington, New Zealand on 14–15 Jan 1963.

Test Walter Hammond hit ten in his 336 not out for England *v.* New Zealand at Auckland on 31 Mar and 1 Apr 1933.

Triple hundred and hundred The only batsman to have scored a triple hundred and a hundred in the same match is Graham Alan Gooch (b. 23 Jul 1953) for England *v.* India at Lord's in 1990. He scored 333 in the first innings on 26–27 July and 123 in the second on 30 July for a record Test aggregate 456 runs.

Double hundreds The only batsman to score double hundreds in both innings is Arthur Edward Fagg (1915–77), who made 244 and 202 not out for Kent *v.* Essex at Colchester, Essex from 13–15 Jul 1938.

Sir Donald Bradman scored a career record 37 double hundreds, 1927–49.

Fastest scoring Cedric Ivan James 'Jim' Smith (1906–79) scored 50 in 11 min for Middlesex *v.* Gloucestershire at Bristol on 16 Jun 1938. He went on to score 66. A faster 50 was completed off 13 balls in 8 min (1:22 to 1:30 p.m.) in 11 scoring strokes by Clive Clay Inman (b. 29 Jan 1936) in an innings of 57 not out for Leicestershire *v.* Nottinghamshire at Trent Bridge, Nottingham on 20 Aug 1965, but full tosses were bowled to expedite a declaration.

Fastest 100 The fastest against genuine bowling was completed in 35 min off between 40 and 46 balls by Percy George Herbert Fender (1892–1985), in his 113 not out for Surrey *v.* Northamptonshire at Northampton on 26 Aug 1920. Thomas Masson Moody (Australia) (b. 2 Oct 1965) completed a century in 26 min off 36 balls

for Warwickshire *v.* Glamorgan at Swansea on 27 Jul 1990.

The hundred in fewest recorded deliveries was by David William Hookes (b. 3 May 1955) in 34 balls, in 43 min, for South Australia *v.* Victoria at Adelaide on 25 Oct 1982. In all he scored 107 from 40 balls in this the second innings, following 137 in the first innings. The fastest hundred in a major one-day competition was by Graham David Rose (b. 12 Apr 1964) off 36 balls for Somerset against Devon in the Nat West Trophy first round at Torquay on 27 Jun 1990.

The fastest Test hundred was one off 56 balls by Isaac Vivian Alexander Richards (b. 7 Mar 1952) for the West Indies *v.* England at St John's, Antigua on 15 Apr 1986. His final score was 110 in 81 minutes. Edwin Boaler Alletson (1884–1963) scored 189 runs in 90 min for Nottinghamshire *v.* Sussex at Hove on 20 May 1911. The most prolific scorer of hundreds in an hour or less was Gilbert Laird Jessop (1874–1955), with 14 between 1897 and 1913.

Fastest 200 Scored in 113 min by Ravi Shastri off 123 balls for Bombay *v.* Baroda at Bombay on 10 Jan 1985 (see most runs off an over). Clive Hubert Lloyd (b. 31 Aug 1944), for West Indians *v.* Glamorgan at Swansea on 9 Aug 1976, and Gilbert Jessop (286), for Gloucestershire *v.* Sussex at Hove on 1 Jun 1903, both scored 200 in 120 min. Lloyd received 121 balls, but the figure for Jessop is not known.

■ **Highest test aggregate**
In the first Test against India at Lord's in 1990, Graham Gooch (b. 23 Jul 1953) scored a record 456 runs. He scored 333 in the first innings on 26–27 July and 123 in the second on 30 July. It is also the only time a player has scored a triple hundred and a century in the same first-class match. (Photo: All-Sport/A. Murrell)

Most runs off a ball
Garry Chapman (partnered by Chris Veal) scored 17 (all run, with no overthrows) off a single delivery for Banyule against Macleod at Windsor Reserve, Victoria, Australia on 13 Oct 1990. Chapman had pulled the ball to mid-wicket where it disappeared into 25 cm *10 in* high grass. The unfortunate bowler was the aptly-named Mr Hyde.

The record in first-class cricket is ten by Albert Neilson Hornby (1847 –1925) off the bowling of James Street (1839–1906) for Lancashire *v.* Surrey at The Oval on 14 Jul 1873, a feat equalled by Samuel Hill Wood (later Sir Samuel Hill Hill-Wood) (1872–1949) off Cuthbert James Burnup (1875–1960) for Derbyshire *v.* MCC at Lord's on 26 May 1900.

Most runs off an over
H. Morley scored 62, nine sixes and two fours, off an eight-ball over from R. Grubb which had four no-balls, in a Queensland country match in 1968–9.

■ Fastest 100
On 26 Aug 1920 Percy Fender (1892–1985) scored a 100 in 35 min for Surrey v. Northants at Northampton. That remained the record in first-class cricket for 70 years until Australian Tom Moody, aided by full tosses and long hops to expedite a declaration, took just 26 min to hit a century off 36 balls for Warwickshire v. Glamorgan at Swansea on 27 Jul 1990. Fender, shown in RAF uniform in 1940, played in 13 Tests for England and was captain of Surrey, 1921–31. He was the oldest Test cricketer at the time of his death at the age of 92. (Photos: All-Sport and Hulton Picture Library)

Fastest 300 Completed in 181 min by Denis Compton, who scored 300 for the MCC *v.* North-Eastern Transvaal at Benoni, South Africa on 3–4 Dec 1948.

Slowest scoring The longest time a batsman has ever taken to score his first run is 1 hr 37 min by Thomas Godfrey Evans (b. 18 Aug 1920), before he scored 10 not out for England *v.* Australia at Adelaide on 5–6 Feb 1947. The longest innings without scoring is 87 min by Vincent Richard Hogg (b. 3 Jul 1952) for Zimbabwe-Rhodesia 'B' *v.* Natal 'B' at Pietermaritzburg in the South African Castle Bowl competition on 20 Jan 1980.

The slowest hundred on record is by Mudassar Nazar (b. 6 Apr 1956) for Pakistan *v.* England at Lahore on 14–15 Dec 1977. He required 9 hr 51 min for 114, reaching the 100 in 9 hr 17 min. The slowest double hundred is one of 12 hr 56 min (518 balls) by Don Sardha Brendon Priyantha Kuruppu (b. 5 Jan 1962) during an innings of 201 not out for Sri Lanka *v.* New Zealand at Colombo on 16–19 Apr 1987.

Highest partnership For any wicket is the fourth-wicket stand of 577 by Gulzar Mahomed (b. 15 Oct 1921), 319, and Vijay Samuel Hazare (b. 11 Mar 1915), 288, for Baroda *v.* Holkar at Baroda, India on 8–10 Mar 1947.

In England 555, for the first-wicket by Percy Holmes (1886–1971) (224 not out) and Herbert Sutcliffe (1894–1978) (313) for Yorkshire *v.* Essex at Leyton, Essex on 15–16 Jun 1932.

Test 467, for the third wicket by Martin David Crowe (b. 22 Sep 1962) (299) and Andrew Howard Jones (b. 9 May 1959) (186) for New Zealand *v.* Sri Lanka at Wellington on 3–4 Feb 1991.

BOWLING

Most wickets *In an innings* Only one bowler has taken all ten wickets in an innings on three occasions — Alfred 'Tich' Freeman of Kent, 1929–31. The fewest runs scored off a bowler taking all ten wickets is ten, off Hedley Verity (1905–43) for Yorkshire *v.* Nottinghamshire at Leeds on 12 Jul 1932. The only bowler to bowl out all ten was John Wisden (1826–84) for North *v.* South at Lord's in 1850.

In a match James Charles 'Jim' Laker (1922–86) took 19 wickets for 90 runs (9–37 and 10–53) for England *v.* Australia at Old Trafford from 27–31 Jul 1956.

Most consecutive wickets No bowler in first-class cricket has yet achieved five wickets with five consecutive balls. The nearest approach was that of Charles Warrington Leonard Parker (1882–1959) (Gloucestershire) in his own benefit match against Yorkshire at Bristol on 10 Aug 1922, when he struck the stumps with five successive balls but the second was called as a no-ball. The only man to have taken four wickets with consecutive balls more than once is Robert James Crisp (b. 28 May 1911) for Western Province *v.* Griqualand West at Johannesburg, South Africa on 24 Dec 1931 and against Natal at Durban, South Africa on 3 Mar 1934.

Patrick Ian Pocock (b. 24 Sep 1946) took five wickets in six balls, six in nine balls and seven in eleven balls for Surrey *v.* Sussex at Eastbourne, E Sussex on 15 Aug 1972. In his own benefit match at Lord's on 22 May 1907, Albert Edwin Trott (1873–1914) of Middlesex took four Somerset wickets with four consecutive balls and then later in the same innings achieved a 'hat trick'.

Most consecutive maidens Hugh Joseph Tayfield (b. 30 Jan 1929) bowled 16 consecutive eight-ball maiden overs (137 balls without conceding a run) for South Africa v. England at Durban on 25–26 Jan 1957. The greatest number of consecutive six-ball maiden overs bowled is 21 (131 balls) by Rameshchandra Gangaram 'Bapu' Nadkarni (b. 4 Apr 1932) for India v. England at Madras on 12 Jan 1964. Alfred Shaw (1842–1907) of Nottinghamshire bowled 23 consecutive 4-ball maiden overs (92 balls) for North v. South at Trent Bridge, Nottingham on 17 Jul 1876.

Most balls The most balls bowled in a match is 917 by Cottari Subbanna Nayudu (b. 18 Apr 1914), 6–153 and 5–275, for Holkar v. Bombay at Bombay on 4–9 Mar 1945. The most balls bowled in a Test match is 774 by Sonny Ramadhin (b. 1 May 1929) for the West Indies v. England, 7–49 and 2–179, at Edgbaston on 29 May–4 Jun 1957. In the second innings he bowled a world record 588 balls (98 overs).

Most expensive bowling The greatest number of runs hit off one bowler in an innings is 362, off Arthur Alfred Mailey (1886–1967) of New South Wales by Victoria at Melbourne on 24–28 Dec 1926. The most runs conceded by a bowler in a match is 428 by Cottari Subbanna Nayudu in the Holkar v. Bombay match above. The most runs conceded in a Test innings is 298 by Leslie O'Brien 'Chuck' Fleetwood-Smith (1910–71) for Australia v. England at The Oval on 20–23 Aug 1938.

ALL-ROUNDERS

The double The 'double' of 1000 runs and 100 wickets in the same season was performed a record number of 16 times by Wilfred Rhodes between 1903 and 1926. The greatest number of consecutive seasons in which a player has performed the 'double' is 11 (1903–13) by George Herbert Hirst (1871–1954), of Yorkshire and England. Hirst is also the only player to score 2000 runs (2385) and take 200 wickets (208) in the same season (1906).

Century on début and wicket with first ball Frederick William Stocks (b. 6 Nov 1918) of Nottinghamshire achieved the unique feat of scoring a century on his first-class début, v. Kent at Trent Bridge on 13 May 1946, and of taking a wicket with his first ball in first-class cricket, v. Lancashire at Old Trafford on 26 Jun 1946.

Test cricket The best all-round Test career record is that of Ian Terence Botham (b. 24 Nov 1955) with 5119 runs (av. 34·35), 376 wickets (av. 28·27) and 112 catches in 97 matches, 1977–89. Botham is the only player to score a hundred and take eight wickets in an innings in the same Test, with 108 and 8–34 for England v. Pakistan at Lord's on 15–19 Jun 1978. He scored a hundred (114) and took more than ten wickets (6–58 and 7–48) in a Test, for England v. India in the Golden Jubilee Test at Bombay on 15–19 Feb 1980. This feat was emulated by Imran Khan Niazi (b. 25 Nov 1952) with 117, 6–98 and 5–82 for Pakistan v. India at Faisalabad on 3–8 Jan 1983. Botham completed the double of 1000 runs and 100 wickets in the fewest Test matches (21) on 30 Aug 1979. Kapil Dev Nikhanj (India) (b. 6 Jan 1959) achieved his double in the shortest time span, 1 year 107 days, and at the youngest age, 21 yr 27 days, in his 25th Test. The double of 2000 runs and 200 wickets was achieved in fewest matches (42) by Botham and at the youngest age by Kapil Dev at 24 yr 68 days. The double of 3000 runs and 300 wickets was achieved in fewest matches, 71, by Botham and at the youngest age by Kapil Dev at 28 yr 1 day.

WICKET-KEEPING

Most dismissals *Innings* The most dismissals is eight (all caught) by Arthur Theodore Wallace 'Wally' Grout (1927–68) for Queensland v. Western Australia at Brisbane on 15 Feb 1960, David Edward East (b. 27 Jul 1959) for Essex v. Somerset at Taunton on 27 Jul 1985 and by Steven Andrew Marsh (b. 27 Jan 1961) for Kent v. Middlesex at Lord's on 31 May–1 Jun 1991. The most stumpings in an innings is six by Henry 'Hugo' Yarnold (1917–74) for Worcestershire v. Scotland at Broughty Ferry, Tayside on 2 Jul 1951. The Test record is seven (all caught) by Wasim Bari (b. 23 Mar 1948) for Pakistan v. New Zealand at Auckland on 23 Feb 1979, by Bob Taylor for England v. India at Bombay on 15 Feb 1980, and by Ian David Stockley Smith (b. 28 Feb 1957) for New Zealand v. Sri Lanka at Hamilton on 23–24 Feb 1991.

Match The most dismissals is 12 by: Edward Pooley (1838–1907), eight caught, four stumped, for Surrey v. Sussex at The Oval on 6–7 Jul 1868; nine caught, three stumped by both Donald Tallon (1916–84) for Queensland v. New South Wales at Sydney, Australia on 2–4 Jan 1939, and by Hedley Brian Taber (b. 29 Apr 1940) for New South Wales v. South Australia at Adelaide on 13–17 Dec 1968. The record for catches is 11 by: Arnold Long (b. 18 Dec 1940), for Surrey v. Sussex at Hove on 18 and 21 Jul 1964, by Rodney Marsh for Western Australia v. Victoria at Perth on 15–17 Nov 1975; by David Leslie Bairstow (b. 1 Sep 1951) for Yorkshire v. Derbyshire at Scarborough on 8–10 Sep 1982; by Warren Kevin Hegg (b. 23 Feb 1968) for Lancashire v. Derbyshire at Chesterfield on 9–11 Aug 1989; by Alec James Stewart (b. 8 Apr 1963) for Surrey v. Leicestershire at Leicester on 19–22 Aug 1989; and by Tim Neilsen for South Australia v. Western Australia on 15–18 Mar 1991. The most stumpings in a match is nine by Frederick Henry Huish (1869–1957) for Kent v. Surrey at The Oval on 21–23 Aug 1911. The Test record for dismissals is ten, all caught, by Bob Taylor for England v. India at Bombay, 15–19 Feb 1980.

FIELDING

Most catches *Innings* The greatest number of catches in an innings is seven, by Michael James Stewart (b. 16 Sep 1932) for Surrey v. Northamptonshire at Northampton on 7 Jun 1957; and by Anthony Stephen Brown (b. 24 Jun 1936) for Gloucestershire v. Nottinghamshire at Trent Bridge on 26 Jul 1966.

Match Walter Hammond held ten catches (four in the first innings, six in the second) for Gloucestershire v. Surrey at Cheltenham on 16–17 Aug 1928.

The most catches in a Test match is seven by Greg Chappell for Australia v. England at Perth on 13–17 Dec 1974; and by Yajurvindra Singh (b. 1 Aug 1952) for India v. England at Bangalore on 28 Jan–2 Feb 1977.

TEST CRICKET

Origins The first match, now considered as a Test, was played at Melbourne on 15–19 Mar 1877 between Australia and England, represented by James Lillywhite's touring party. Neither side was representative of their countries and indeed such was the case for many matches, now accepted as Tests, played over the next fifty years or so. The first Test match in England was against Australia at The Oval on 6–8 Sep 1880. Eight nations have played

Test cricket; Australia, England, India, New Zealand, Pakistan, South Africa, Sri Lanka and West Indies.

OTHER TEST RECORDS

Test appearances The most Tests played is 125 by Sunil Gavaskar (India), 1971–87 and Allan Robert Border (Australia) (b. 27 Jul 1955), 1978–91. Border's total includes a record 122 consecutive Tests matches. The English record for most Tests is 114 by Michael Colin Cowdrey (b. 24 Dec 1932) and David Ivon Gower (b. 1 Apr 1957), 1978–91; and for consecutive Tests is 65 by Alan Philip Eric Knott (b. 9 Apr 1946), 1971–7 and Ian Botham, 1978–84.

Longest match The lengthiest recorded cricket match was the 'timeless' Test between England and South Africa at Durban on 3–14 Mar 1939. It was abandoned after ten days (eighth day rained off) because the ship taking the England team home was due to leave. The total playing time was 43 hr 16 min and a record Test match aggregate of 1981 runs was scored.

Largest crowds The greatest attendance at a cricket match is about 394 000 for the Test between India and England at Eden Gardens, Calcutta on 1–6 Jan 1982. The record for a Test series is 933 513 for Australia v. England (five matches) in 1936–37. The greatest recorded attendance at a cricket match on one day was 90 800 on the second day of the Test between Australia and the West Indies at Melbourne on 11 Feb 1961. The English match record is 159 000 for England v. Australia at Headingley, Leeds on 22–27 Jul 1948, and the record for one day probably a capacity of 46 000 for Lancashire v. Yorkshire at Old Trafford on 2 Aug 1926. The English record for a Test series is 549 650 for the series against Australia in 1953. The highest attendance for a limited-overs game is 84 153 at the Benson and Hedges World Series Cup match between Australia and England at Melbourne on 23 Jan 1985.

Most successful Test captain Clive Hubert Lloyd (b. 31 Aug 1944) led the West Indies in a record 74 Test matches from 22 Nov 1974 to 2 Jan 1985. Of these, 36 were won, 12 lost and 26 were drawn. His team set records for most successive Test wins, 11 in 1984, and most Tests without defeat, 27, between losses to Australia in December 1981 and January 1985 (through injury Lloyd missed one of those matches, when the West Indies were captained by Vivian Richards).

ONE-DAY INTERNATIONALS

The first 'limited overs' international was played at Melbourne Cricket Ground on 5 Jan 1971 between Australia and England. The Prudential (now Texaco) Trophy series of one-day internationals began in England in 1972, matches being of 55 overs per side. The Benson and Hedges World Cup Series has been held annually in Australia since 1979–80.

World Cup The World Cup was held in England in 1975, 1979 and 1983, and in India and Pakistan in 1987. The West Indies are the only double winners, in 1975 and 1979. Matches were played at 60 overs per side (except at 50 overs in 1987).

One-day international records *Team* The highest innings score by a team is 360–4 (50 overs) by the West Indies v. Sri Lanka at Karachi, Pakistan on 13 Oct 1987. The lowest completed innings total is 45 by Canada v. England at Old Trafford on 14 Jun 1979. The largest victory margin is 232 by Australia v. Sri Lanka (323–2 to 91), at Adelaide, Australia on 28 Jan 1985.

Fastest bowler
The highest speed for a ball bowled by any bowler, measured electronically, is 160·45 km/h *99·7 mph* by Jeffrey Robert Thomson (Australia) (b. 16 Aug 1950) against the West Indies in December 1975.

Longest throw
A cricket ball (155 g *5½ oz*) was reputedly thrown 128·6 m *140 yd 2 ft* by Robert Percival, a left-hander, on Durham Sands racecourse on Easter Monday, 18 Apr 1882.

Most extras
The most extras conceded in a Test innings is 71 by the West Indies in Pakistan's 1st innings at Georgetown, Guyana on 3–4 Apr 1988. The figure consisted of 21 byes, 8 leg byes, 4 wides and 38 no-balls.

In a one-day international, the West Indies conceded 59 extras (8 byes, 10 leg byes, 4 no balls and 37 wides) against Pakistan at Brisbane on 7 Jan 1989.

Cricketing sons

The seven sons of Rev. Henry Foster, of Malvern, uniquely all played county cricket for Worcestershire between 1899 and 1934.

Successive sixes

Cedric Ivan James Smith (1906–79) hit nine successive sixes for a Middlesex XI v. Harrow and District at Rayner's Lane, Harrow in 1935. This feat was repeated by Arthur Dudley Nourse (1910–81) in a South African XI v. Military Police match at Cairo, Egypt in 1942–3. Nourse's feat included six sixes in one over.

Fastest scoring rate

In the match Royal Naval College, Dartmouth v. Seale Hayne Agricultural College in 1923, Kenneth Anderson Sellar (b. 11 Aug 1906) and Leslie Kenneth Allen Block (1906–80) were set to score 174 runs in 105 min but achieved this total in 33 min, so averaging 5·27 runs per min.

ENGLISH ONE–DAY RECORDS

GC/NWT : Gillette Cup (1963–1980); NatWest Trophy (1981–) (60-over matches).

SL (Sunday League) : John Player (1969–1986); Refuge Assurance (1987–) (40-over matches).

B & H : Benson & Hedges Cup (1972–) (55-over matches).

MOST WINS

GC/NWT 5, Lancashire 1970–2, 1975, 1990. **SL** 3, Kent 1972–3, 1976; Essex 1981, 1984–5; Hampshire 1975, 1978, 1986; Worcestershire 1971, 1987–8; Lancashire 1969–70, 1989. **B & H** 3, Kent 1973, 1976, 1978; Leicestershire 1972, 1975, 1985.

HIGHEST INNINGS TOTAL

GC/NWT 413–4 Somerset v. Devon, Torquay, 1990. **SL** 360–3 Somerset v. Glamorgan, Neath, 1990. **B & H** 366–4 Derbyshire v. Combined Universities, The Parks, Oxford, 1991.

LOWEST INNINGS TOTAL

GC/NWT 39 Ireland v. Sussex, Hove, 1985. **SL** 23 Middlesex v. Yorkshire, Headingley, 1974. **B & H** 50 Hampshire v. Yorkshire, Headingley, 1991.

HIGHEST INDIVIDUAL INNINGS

GC/NWT 206 Alvin Isaac Kallicharran (b. 21 Mar 1949), Warwickshire v. Oxfordshire, Edgbaston, 1984. **SL** 176 Graham Alan Gooch (b. 23 Jul 1953), Essex v. Glamorgan, Southend, 1983. **B & H** 198* Graham Gooch, Essex v. Sussex, Hove, 1982.

BEST INDIVIDUAL BOWLING

GC/NWT 8–21 Michael Anthony Holding (b. 16 Feb 1954), Derbyshire v. Sussex, Hove, 1988. **SL** 8–26 Keith David Boyce (b. 11 Oct 1943), Essex v. Lancashire, Old Trafford, 1971; Alan Ward (b. 10 Aug 1947) took 4 wickets in 4 balls, Derbyshire v. Sussex, Derby, 1970. **B & H** 7–12 Wayne Wendell Daniel (b. 16 Jan 1956), Middlesex v. Minor Counties (East), Ipswich, 1978.

MOST DISMISSALS IN INNINGS

GC/NWT 6, Robert William Taylor (b. 17 Jul 1941), Derbyshire v. Essex, Derby, 1981; Terry Davies (b. 25 Oct 1960), Glamorgan v. Staffordshire, Stone, 1986. **SL** 7, Bob Taylor, Derbyshire v. Lancashire, Old Trafford, 1975. **B & H** 8, Derek John Somerset Taylor (b. 12 Nov 1942), Somerset v. Combined Universities, Taunton, 1982.

RUNS IN CAREER

GC/NWT 1950, Dennis Leslie Amiss (b. 7 Apr 1943), Warwickshire 1963–87. **SL** 7040, Dennis Amiss, Warwickshire 1969–87. **B & H** 4156, Graham Gooch, Essex 1973–91.

WICKETS IN CAREER

GC/NWT 81, Geoffrey Graham Arnold (b. 3 Sep 1944), Surrey, Sussex 1963–80. **SL** 386, John Kenneth Lever (b. 24 Feb 1949), Essex 1969–89. **B & H** 149, John Lever, Essex 1972–89.

DISMISSALS IN CAREER

GC/NWT 66, Bob Taylor, Derbyshire 1963–84. **SL** 255, David Bairstow, Yorkshire 1972–90. **B & H** 122, David Bairstow, Yorkshire 1972–90.

* Not out

Individual The highest individual score is 189 not out by Isaac Vivian Alexander Richards (b. 7 Mar 1952) for the West Indies v. England at Old Trafford on 31 May 1984. The best bowling analysis is 7–51 by Winston Walter Davis (b. 18 Sep 1958) for the West Indies v. Australia at Headingley on 12 Jun 1983. The best partnership is 224 unbroken by Dean Mervyn Jones (b. 24 Mar 1961) and Allan Robert Border (b. 27 Jul 1955) for Australia v. Sri Lanka at Adelaide, Australia on 28 Jan 1985

Career The most matches played is 229 by Allan Border (Australia), 1979–91. The most runs scored is 6780 (av. 42·91) by Desmond Leo Haynes (West Indies) (b. 15 Feb 1956) in 182 matches, 1977–91. This total includes a record 16 centuries. The most wickets taken is 197 (av. 26·14) by Kapil Dev (India) in 163 matches, 1978–91. The most dismissals is 200 (181 ct, 19 st) by Peter Jeffrey Leroy Dujon (West Indies) (b. 28 Mar 1956) in 165 matches, 1981–91. Vivian Richards has taken a record 101 catches by a fielder in 187 games, 1975–91.

ENGLISH COUNTY

The greatest number of victories since 1890, when the Championship was officially constituted, has been by Yorkshire with 29 outright wins (the last in 1968), and one shared (1949). The record number of consecutive title wins is seven by Surrey from 1952 to 1958. The greatest number of appearances in County Championship matches is 763 by Wilfred Rhodes for Yorkshire between 1898 and 1930, and the greatest number of consecutive appearances is 423 by Kenneth George Suttle (b. 25 Aug 1928) of Sussex between 1954 and 1969. James Graham 'Jimmy' Binks (b. 5 Oct 1935) played in all 412 County Championship matches for Yorkshire between his debut in 1955 and his retirement in 1969.

OLDEST AND YOUNGEST

First-class The oldest player in first-class cricket was the Governor of Bombay, Raja Maharaj Singh (India) (1878–1959), aged 72 yr 192 days, when he batted, scoring 4, on the opening day of the match played on 25-27 Nov 1950 at Bombay for his XI v. Commonwealth XI. The youngest is reputed to be Alim-ud-din (Pakistan) (b. 15 Dec 1930) for Rajputna v. Baroda at Baroda, India on 26 Feb 1943, aged 12 yr 73 days. The oldest Englishman was Benjamin Aislabie (1774–1842) for MCC (of whom he was the secretary) v. Cambridge University at Lord's on 1 and 2 Jul 1841, when he was aged 67 yr 169 days. The youngest English first-class player was Charles Robertson Young (1852–?) for Hampshire v. Kent at Gravesend on 13 Jun 1867, aged 15 yr 131 days.

Test The oldest man to play in a Test match was Wilfred Rhodes, aged 52 yr 165 days, for England v. West Indies at Kingston, Jamaica on 12 April 1930. Rhodes made his Test debut in the last Test of William Gilbert Grace (1848–1915), who at 50 yr 320 days at Nottingham on 3 Jun 1899 was the oldest ever Test captain. The youngest Test captain was the Nawab of Pataudi (later Mansur Ali Khan) at 21 yr 77 days on 23 Mar 1962 for India v. West Indies at Bridgetown, Barbados. The youngest Test player was Mushtaq Mohammad (b. 22 Nov 1943), aged 15 yr 124 days, for Pakistan v. West Indies at Lahore on 26 March 1959. England's youngest player was Dennis Brian Close (b. 24 Feb 1931) aged 18 yr 149 days v. New Zealand at Old Trafford on 23 Jul 1949.

WOMEN'S CRICKET

Earliest The first recorded women's match took place at Gosden Common, Surrey on 26 Jun 1745. *Circa* 1807 Christina Willes is said to have introduced the round-arm bowling style. The first Test match was Australia v. England at Brisbane on 28–31 Dec 1934. The International Women's Cricket Council was formed in 1958.

Batting Individual The highest individual innings recorded is 224 not out by Mabel Bryant for Visitors v. Residents at Eastbourne, E Sussex in August 1901. The highest innings in a Test match is 193 by Denise Annetts (b. 30 Jan 1964), in 381 minutes, for Australia v. England at Collingham, Notts on 23–24 Aug 1987 in a four-day Test. With Lindsay Reeler (b. 18 Mar 1961), 110 not out, she added 309 for the third wicket, the highest Test partnership. The highest in a three-day Test is 189 (in 222 minutes) by Elizabeth Alexandra 'Betty' Snowball (1907–88) for England v. New Zealand at Christchurch, New Zealand on 16 Feb 1935.

Rachael Flint (*née* Heyhoe) (b. 11 Jun 1939) has scored the most runs in Test cricket with 1814 (av. 49·02) in 25 matches from December 1960 to July 1979.

Team The highest innings score by any team is 567 by Tarana v. Rockley, at Rockley, New South Wales, Australia in 1896. The highest Test innings is 525 by Australia v. India at Ahmedabad on 4 Feb 1984. The highest score by England is 503 for five wickets declared by England v. New Zealand at Christchurch, New Zealand on 16 and 18 Feb 1935. The most in a Test in England is 426 by India at Stanley Park, Blackpool, Lancs on 3–7 Jul 1986.

The lowest innings in a Test is 35 by England v. Australia at St Kilda, Melbourne, Australia on 22 Feb 1958. The lowest in a Test in England is 63 by New Zealand at Worcester on 5 Jul 1954.

Bowling Mary Beatrice Duggan (England) (1925–73) took a record 77 wickets (av. 13·49) in 17 Tests from 1949 to 1963. She recorded the best Test analysis with seven wickets for six runs for England v. Australia at St Kilda, Melbourne on 22 Feb 1958.

Rubina Winifred Humphries (b. 19 Aug 1915), for Dalton Ladies v. Woodfield SC, at Huddersfield, W Yorks on 26 Jun 1931, took all ten wickets for no runs. (She also scored all her team's runs.) This bowling feat was equalled by Rosemary White (b. 22 Jan 1938) for Wallington LCC v. Beaconsfield LCC in July 1962.

All-round Betty Wilson (Australia) (b. 1923) was the first Test player, man or woman, to score a century and take ten wickets in a Test match. She took 7–7, including a hat-trick, and 4–9 and scored exactly 100 in the second innings against England at St Kilda on 21–24 Feb 1958. Enid Bakewell (b. 18 Dec 1940) was the first English Test player, man or woman, to achieve this Test Match double. Playing against the West Indies at Edgbaston on 1–3 Jul 1979, she scored 112 not out and had match figures of 10–75.

World Cup Four women's World Cups have been staged. Australia won in 1978, 1982 and 1988 and England in 1973. The highest individual score in this series is 143 not out by Lindsay Reeler for Australia v. Netherlands at Perth, Australia on 29 Nov 1988.

MINOR CRICKET RECORDS

Highest individual innings In a Junior House match between Clarke's House (now Poole's) and North Town, at Clifton College, Bristol, 22–23, 26–28 Jun 1899, Arthur Edward Jeune Collins (1885–1914) scored an unprecedented 628 not out in 6 hr 50 min, over five afternoons' batting, carrying his bat through the innings of 836. The scorer, E. W. Pegler, gave the score as '628–plus or minus 20, shall we say'.

Highest partnership During a Harris Shield match in 1988 at Sassanian Ground, Bombay, India, Vinod Kambli (b. 18 Jan 1972) (349 not out) and Sachin Tendulkar (b. 24 Apr 1973) (326 not out) put on an unbeaten partnership of 664 runs for the third wicket for Sharadashram Vidyamandir v. St Xavier's High School.

Fastest individual scoring Stanley Keppel 'Shunter' Coen (South Africa) (1902–67) scored 50 runs (11 fours and one six) in 7 min for Gezira v. the RAF in 1942. The fastest hundred by a prominent player in a minor match was by Vivian Frank Shergold Crawford (1879–1922) in 19 min at Cane Hill, Surrey on 16 Sep 1899. Lindsay Martin scored 100 off 20 deliveries (13 sixes, 5 fours and 2 singles) for Rosewater v. Warradale on 19 Dec 1987. David Michael Roberts Whatmore (b. 6 Apr 1949) scored 210 (including 25 sixes and 12 fours) off 61 balls for Alderney v. Sun Alliance at Alderney, Channel Islands on 19 Jun 1983. His first 100 came off 33 balls and his second off 25 balls.

Bowling Nine wickets with nine consecutive balls were taken by: Stephen Fleming, for Marlborough College 'A' XI v. Bohally Intermediate at Blenheim, New Zealand in December 1967; and by Paul Hugo for Smithfield School v. Aliwal North, South Africa in February 1931. In the Inter-Divisional Ships Shield at Purfleet, Essex on 17 May 1924, Joseph William Brockley (b. 9 Apr 1907) took all ten wickets, clean bowled, for two runs in 11 balls – including a triple hat trick. Jennings Tune took all ten wickets, all bowled, for 0 runs in five overs for Cliffe v. Eastrington in the Howden and District League at Cliffe, Yorkshire on 6 May 1922.

In 1881 Frederick Robert Spofforth (1853–1926) at Bendigo, Victoria, Australia clean bowled all ten wickets in *both* innings. J. Bryant for Erskine v. Deaf Mutes in Melbourne on 15 and 22 Oct 1887, and Albert Rimmer for Linwood School v. Cathedral GS at Canterbury, New Zealand in December 1925, repeated the feat. In the 1910 season, H. Hopkinson, of Mildmay CC, London, took 99 wickets for 147 runs.

Maurice Hanes bowled 107 consecutive balls (17 overs and five balls) for Bedworth II v. A P Leamington II at Bedworth, Warks on 16 Jun 1979, without conceding a run.

Wicket-keeping Welihinda Badalge Bennett (b. 25 Jan 1933) caught four and stumped six batsmen in one innings, on 1 March 1953 for Mahinda College v. Galle CC, at the Galle Esplanade, Sri Lanka.

Fielding In a Wellington, New Zealand secondary schools 11-a-side match on 16 Mar 1974, Stephen Lane, 13, held 14 catches in the field (seven in each innings) for St Patrick's College, Silverstream v. St Bernard's College, Lower Hutt.

Croquet

Origins Its exact origins are obscure, but croquet was probably derived from the French game *Jeu de Mail* first mentioned in the 12th century. A game resembling croquet, possibly of foreign origin, was played in Ireland in the 1830s, and was introduced to Hampshire 20 years later. The first club was formed in the Steyne Gardens, Worthing, W Sussex in 1865.

Most championships The greatest number of victories in the Open Croquet Championships (instituted at Evesham, Worcestershire, 1867) is ten by John William Solomon (b. 22 Nov 1931) (1953, 1956, 1959, 1961, 1963–8). He also won ten Men's Championships (1951, 1953, 1958–60, 1962, 1964–5, 1971–2), ten Open Doubles (with Edmond Patrick Charles Cotter) (1954–5, 1958–9, 1961–5 and 1969) and one Mixed Doubles (with Freda Oddie) in 1954, making a total of 31 titles. Solomon has also won the President's Cup (instituted 1934, an invitation event for the best eight players) on nine occasions (1955, 1957–9, 1962–4, 1968 and 1971), and was Champion of Champions on all four occasions that that competition was run (1967–70).

G. Nigel Aspinall (b. 1946) has won the President's Cup a record 11 times, 1969–70, 1973–6, 1978, 1980, 1982, 1984–5.

Dorothy Dyne Steel (1884–1965), fifteen times winner of the Women's Championship (1919–39), won the Open Croquet Championship four times (1925, 1933, 1935–36). She had also five Doubles and seven Mixed Doubles for a total of 31 titles.

International trophy The MacRobertson International Shield (instituted 1925) has been won a record eight times by Great Britain, 1925, 1937, 1956, 1963, 1969, 1974, 1982 and 1990.

A record seven appearances have been made by John G. Prince (New Zealand) in 1963, 1969, 1975, 1979, 1982, 1986 and 1990; on his debut he was the youngest ever international at 17 yr 190 days.

Cross-country Running

Origins The earliest recorded international cross-country race took place over 14·5 km *9 miles 18 yd* from Ville d'Avray, outside Paris, France on 20 Mar 1898 between England and France (England won by 21 points to 69).

World Championships The inaugural International Cross-Country Championships took place at the Hamilton Park Racecourse, Scotland on 28 Mar 1903.

The greatest margin of victory is 56 sec or 356 m *390 yd* by John 'Jack' Thomas Holden (England) (b. 13 Mar 1907) at Ayr Racecourse, Strathclyde on 24 Mar 1934.

Since 1973 the events have been official world championships under the auspices of the International Amateur Athletic Federation.

Most wins The greatest number of team victories has been by England with 45 for men, 11 for junior men and seven for women.

The USA and USSR each has a record eight women's team victories.

The greatest team domination was by Kenya at Auckland, New Zealand on 26 March 1988. Their senior men's team finished eight men in the first nine, with a low score of 23 (six to score) and their junior men's team set a record low score, 11 (four to score) with six in the first seven.

The greatest number of men's individual victories is four by: Jack Holden (England) in 1933–35 and 1939; by Alain Mimoun-o-Kacha (France) (b. 1 Jan 1921) in 1949, 1952, 1954 and 1956; by Gaston Roelants (Belgium) (b. 5 Feb 1937) in 1962, 1967, 1969

and 1972 and by John Ngugi (Kenya) (b. 10 May 1962), 1986–89.

The women's race has been won five times by: Doris Brown-Heritage (USA) (b. 17 Sep 1942), 1967–71; and by Grete Waitz (*née* Andersen) (Norway) (b. 1 Oct 1953), 1978–81 and 1983.

Most appearances Marcel van de Wattyne (Belgium) (b. 7 Jul 1924) ran in a record 20 races, 1946–65.

The women's record is 16 by Jean Lochhead (Wales) (b. 24 Dec 1946), 1967–79, 1981, 1983–84.

English Championship The National Cross-Country Championship was inaugurated at Roehampton, London in 1877.

The most individual titles won is four by Percy H. Stenning (1854–92) (Thames Hare and Hounds) in 1877–80 and Alfred E. Shrubb (1878–1964) (South London Harriers) in 1901–4.

The most successful club in the team race has been Birchfield Harriers from Birmingham with 28 wins and one tie between 1880 and 1988.

The largest field was the 2195 finishers in the senior race in 1990 at Leeds, W Yorks on 24 Feb. In this race, a record 250 clubs scored by having six runners finish.

The most individual wins in the English women's championships is six by Lillian Styles, 1928–30, 1933–4 and 1937; the most successful team is Birchfield Harriers with 13 titles.

Curling

Origins Although a 15th-century bronze figure in the Florence Museum appears to be holding a curling stone, the earliest illustration of the sport was in one of the Flemish painter Pieter Bruegel's winter scenes c. 1560. The game was probably introduced into Scotland by Flemings in the 15th century. The earliest documented club is Muthill, Tayside, formed in 1739. Organized administration began in 1838 with the formation in Edinburgh of the Grand (later Royal) Caledonian Curling Club, the international legislative body until the foundation of the International Curling Federation in 1966 (became World Curling Federation in 1991). Curling was first played indoors in Montreal, Canada in 1807, and in Britain at Southport, Merseyside in 1878.

The USA won the first Gordon International Medal series of matches, between Canada and the USA, at Montreal in 1884. Curling has been a demonstration sport at the Olympic Games of 1924, 1932, 1964 and 1988. A specialized German version of the game was demonstrated in 1936.

Most titles Canada has won the men's World Championships (instituted 1959) 20 times, 1959–64, 1966, 1968–72, 1980, 1982–83, 1985–87, 1989–90.

The most Strathcona Cup (instituted 1903) wins is seven by Canada (1903, 1909, 1912, 1923, 1938, 1957, 1965) against Scotland.

The most women's World Championships (instituted 1979) is six by Canada (1980, 1984–87, 1989).

'Perfect' game Stu Beagle, of Calgary, Alberta, Canada, played a perfect game (48 points) against Nova Scotia in the Canadian Championships (Brier) at Fort William (now Thunder Bay), Ontario on 8 Mar 1960.

Largest field
The largest recorded field in any cross-country race was 11 763 starters (10 810 finished) in the 30 km *18·6 miles* Lidingöloppet, near Stockholm, Sweden on 3 Oct 1982.

Fastest game in curling
Eight curlers from the Burlington Golf and Country Club curled an eight-end game in 47 min 24 sec, with time penalties of 5 min 30 sec, at Burlington, Ontario, Canada on 4 Apr 1986, following rules agreed with the Ontario Curling Association. The time is taken from when the first rock crosses the near hogline until the game's last rock comes to a complete stop.

■ **Olympic gold**
Curling has been a demonstration sport at the Olympic Games of 1924, 1932, 1936 (when a specialized German version of the game was played), 1964 and 1988. In 1988 Canada won the women's title defeating Sweden in the final. (Photo: All-Sport (USA)/Leah)

Highest cycling
Canadians Bruce Bell, Philip Whelan and Suzanne MacFadyen cycled at an altitude of 6960 m *22 834 ft* on the peak of Mt Aconcagua, Argentina on 25 Jan 1991.

Bernice Fekete, of Edmonton, Alberta, Canada, skipped her rink to two consecutive eight-enders on the same ice at the Derrick Club, Edmonton on 10 Jan and 6 Feb 1973.

Two eight-enders in one bonspiel were scored at the Parry Sound Curling Club, Ontario, Canada from 6–8 Jan 1983.

Longest throw The longest throw of a curling stone was a distance of 175·66 m *576 ft 4 in* by Eddie Kulbacki (Canada) at Park Lake, Neepawa, Manitoba, Canada on 29 Jan 1989. The attempt took place on a specially prepared sheet of curling ice on frozen Park Lake, a record 1200 ft *365·76 m* long.

Largest bonspiel The largest bonspiel in the world is the Manitoba Curling Association Bonspiel held annually in Winnipeg, Canada. In 1988 there were 1424 teams of four men, a total of 5696 curlers, using 187 sheets of curling ice.

Largest rink The world's largest curling rink was the Big Four Curling Rink, Calgary, Alberta, Canada, opened in 1959 and closed in 1989. Ninety-six teams and 384 players were accommodated on two floors each with 24 sheets of ice.

Cycling

Origins The earliest recorded bicycle race was a velocipede race over 2 km *1·24 miles* at the Parc de St Cloud, Paris on 31 May 1868, won by Dr James Moore (GB) (1847–1935) (later Chevalier de la Légion d'Honneur).

Highest speed The highest speed ever achieved on a bicycle is 245·077 km/h *152·284 mph* by John Howard (USA) behind a wind-shield at Bonneville Salt Flats, Utah, USA on 20 Jul 1985. It should be noted that considerable help was provided by the slipstreaming effect of the lead vehicle.

The British speed record is 158·05 km/h *98·21 mph* over 200 metres by David Le Grys (b. 10 Aug 1955) on a closed section of the M42 at Alvechurch, Warks on 28 Aug 1985.

The greatest distance ever covered in one hour is 122·771 km *76 miles 504 yd* by Leon Vanderstuyft (Belgium) (1890–1964) on the Montlhéry Motor Circuit, France, on 30 Sep 1928, achieved from a standing start paced by a motorcycle.

The 24 hr record behind pace is 1958·196 km *1216·8 miles* by Michael Secrest at Phoenix International Raceway, Arizona on 26–27 Apr 1990.

Most titles *Olympic* The most gold medals won is three by Paul Masson (France) (1874–1945) in 1896, Francisco Verri (Italy) (1885–1945) in 1906; and Robert Charpentier (France) (1916–66) in 1936. Daniel Morelon (France) (b. 28 Jul 1944) won two in 1968, and a third in 1972; he also won a silver in 1976 and a bronze medal in 1964. In the 'unofficial' 1904 cycling programme, Marcus Latimer Hurley (USA) (1885–1941) won four events.

World World Championships are contested annually. They were first staged for amateurs in 1893 and for professionals in 1895.

The most wins at a particular event is ten by Koichi Nakano (Japan) (b. 14 Nov 1955), professional sprint 1977–86.

The most wins at a men's amateur event is seven by; Daniel Morelon (France), sprint 1966–67, 1969–71, 1973, 1975; and Leon Meredith (GB) (1882–1930), 100 km motor paced 1904–5, 1907–9, 1911, 1913.

The most women's titles is eight by Jeannie Longo (France) (b. 31 Oct 1958), pursuit 1986 and 1988–89; road 1985–87 and 1989 and points 1989.

British Beryl Burton, 25 times British all-round time trial champion (1959–83), won 72 individual road TT titles, 14 track pursuit titles and 12 road race titles to 1986.

Ian Hallam (b. 24 Nov 1948) won a record 25 men's titles, 1969–82.

Tour de France The world's premier stage race was first contested in 1903. Held over a three week period, the longest race ever staged was over 5743 km *3569 miles* in 1926. The greatest number of wins is five by Jacques Anquetil (France) (1934–1987),

1957, 1961–64; Eddy Merckx (Belgium) (b. 17 Jun 1945), 1969–72 and 1974; and Bernard Hinault (France) (b. 14 Nov 1954), 1978–79, 1981–82 and 1985.

The closest race ever was in 1989 when after 3267 km *2030 miles* over 23 days (1–23 Jul) Greg LeMond (USA) (b. 26 Jun 1960), who completed the Tour in 87 hr 38 min 35 sec, beat Laurent Fignon (France) (b. 12 Aug 1960) in Paris by only 8 sec.

The fastest average speed was 38·88 km/h *24·16 mph* by Pedro Delgado (Spain) (b. 15 Apr 1960) in 1988.

The longest ever stage was the 486 km from Les Sables d'Olonne to Bayonne in 1919. The most participants was 210 starters in 1986.

Tour of Britain (Milk Race) Four riders have won the Tour of Britain twice each – Bill Bradley (GB) (1959–60), Leslie George West (GB) (1965, 1967), Fedor den Hertog (Netherlands) (1969, 1971) and Yuriy Kashurin (USSR) (1979, 1982).

The closest race ever was in 1976 when after 1665·67 km *1035 miles* over 14 days (30 May–12 Jun) Bill Nickson (GB) (b. 30 Jan 1953) beat Joe Waugh (GB) by 5 sec.

The fastest average speed is 42·185 km/h *26·213 mph* by Joey McLoughlin (GB) (b. 3 Dec 1964) in the 1986 race (1714 km *1065 miles*).

Malcolm Elliott (b. 1 Jul 1961) won a record six stages in 1983 and had taken his total to 15 by 1987, after winning a record four in succession.

The longest Milk Race was in 1969 (2438·16 km *1515 miles*) although the longest ever Tour of Britain was in 1953 (2624·84 km *1631 miles* starting and finishing in London).

Six-day races The most wins in six-day races is 88 out of 233 events by Patrick Sercu (b. 27 Jun 1944), of Belgium, 1964–83.

Longest one-day race The longest single-day 'massed start' road race is the 551–620 km *342–385 miles* Bordeaux–Paris, France, event. Paced over all or part of the route, the highest average speed was in 1981 with 47·186 km/h *29·32 mph* by Herman van Springel (Belgium) (b. 14 Aug 1943) for 584·5 km *363·1 miles* in 13 hr 35 min 18 sec.

Land's End to John o' Groats The 'end to end' record for the 1363 km *847 miles* is 1 day 21 hr 2 min 19 sec by Andy Wilkinson on 29 Sep–1 Oct 1990.

The women's record is 2 days 6 hr 49 min by Pauline Strong on 28–30 Jul 1990.

Cross-America The trans-America solo records recognized by the Ultra-Marathon Cycling Association are: men, Paul Selon 8 days 8 hr 45 min; women, Susan Notorangelo 9 days 9 hr 9 min, both in the Race Across America, Costa Mesa, California to New York, 5000 km *3107 miles* in August 1989.

The trans-Canada record is 13 days 15 hr 4 min by Ronald J. Dossenbach of Windsor, Ontario, 6115 km *3800 miles* from Vancouver, BC to Halifax, Nova Scotia on 30 Jul–13 Aug 1988.

Daniel Buettner, Bret Anderson, Martin Engel and Anne Knabe cycled the length of the Americas, from Prudhoe Bay, Alaska, USA to the Beagle Channel, Ushuaia, Argentina from 8 Aug 1986–13 Jun 1987. They cycled a total distance of 24 568 km *15 266 miles*.

Endurance Thomas Edward Godwin (GB) (1912–75) in the 365 days of 1939 covered 120 805 km *75 065 miles* or an average of 330·96 km *205·65 miles* per day. He then completed 160 934 km *100 000 miles* in 500 days to 14 May 1940.

Jay Aldous and Matt DeWaal cycled 22 997 km *14 290 miles* on a round-the-world trip from This is the Place Monument, Salt Lake City, Utah, USA in 106 days, 2 Apr–16 Jul 1984.

Nicholas Mark Sanders (b. 26 Nov 1957) of Glossop, Derbys, circumnavigated the world (20 977·8 km *13 035 road miles*) in 78 days 3 hr 30 min between 5 Jul and 21 Sep 1985. He cycled 7728 km *4802 miles* around Britain in 22 days, 10 Jun–1 Jul 1984.

Cycle touring The greatest mileage amassed in a cycle tour was more than 643 700 km *402 000 miles* by the itinerant lecturer Walter Stolle (b. Sudetenland, 1926) from 24 Jan 1959 to 12 Dec 1976. He visited 159 countries starting from Romford, Essex.

From 1922 to 25 Dec 1973 Tommy Chambers (1903–84) of Glasgow, rode a verified total of 1 286 517 km *799 405 miles*.

Visiting every continent, John W. Hathaway (b. England, 13 Jan 1925) of Vancouver, Canada covered 81 300 km *50 600 miles* from 10 Nov 1974 to 6 Oct 1976. Veronica and Colin Scargill, of Bedford, travelled 29 000 km *18 020 miles* around the world on a tandem, 25 Feb 1974–27 Aug 1975.

The most participants in a bicycle tour was 31 678 in the 90 km *56 mile* London to Brighton Bike Ride on 19 Jun 1988.

The most participants in a tour in an excess of 1000 km is 2037 (from 2157 starters) for the Australian Bicentennial Caltex Bike Ride from Melbourne to Sydney from 26 Nov–10 Dec 1988.

CYCLO-CROSS

The greatest number of World Championships (instituted 1950) has been won by Eric de Vlaeminck (Belgium) (b. 23 Aug 1945) with the Amateur and Open in 1966 and six Professional titles in 1968–73.

British titles (instituted 1955) have been won most often by John Atkins (b. 7 Apr 1942) with five Amateur (1961–2, 1966–8), seven Professional (1969–75) and one Open title in 1977.

Three Peaks Martin Peters and Phil Smart of Stourbridge, cycled from sea level at Caernarvon, Gwynedd, via the peaks of

WORLD RECORDS

Records are recognized by the Union Cycliste Internationale (UCI) for both professionals and amateurs on open air and indoor tracks for a variety of distances at unpaced flying and standing starts and for motor-paced. In this list only the best are shown, with a † to signify those records set by a professional rather than an amateur.

OPEN–AIR TRACKS

MEN

Distance	hr:min:sec	Name and country	Venue	Date
Unpaced standing start				
1 km	1:02·091	Maic Malchow (GDR)	Colorado Springs, USA	28 Aug 1986
4 km	4:31·160	Gintautas Umaras (USSR)	Seoul, South Korea	18 Sep 1987
5 km	5:44·700	Gregor Braun (West Germany)†	La Paz, Bolivia	12 Jan 1986
10 km	11:39·720	Francesco Moser (Italy)†	Mexico City	19 Jan 1984
20 km	23:21·592	Francesco Moser (Italy)†	Mexico City	23 Jan 1984
100 km	2:09:11·312	Kent Bostick (USA)	Colorado, Springs, USA	13 Oct 1989
1 hour	51·15135 km	Francesco Moser (Italy)†	Mexico City	23 Jan 1984
Unpaced flying start				
200 metres	10·118	Michael Hübner (GDR)	Colorado Springs, USA	27 Aug 1986
500 metres	26·993	Rory O'Reilly (USA)	La Paz, Bolivia	23 Nov 1985
1 km	58·269	Dominguez Rueda Efrain (Colombia)†	La Paz, Bolivia	13 Dec 1986
Motor-paced				
50 km	35:21·108	Aleksandr Romanov (USSR)	Tbilisi, USSR	6 May 1987
100 km	1:10:29·420	Giovanni Renosto (Italy)†	Bassano del Grappa, Italy	16 Sep 1988
1 hour	85·067 km	Giovanni Renosto (Italy)†	Bassano del Grappa, Italy	16 Sep 1988

WOMEN

Unpaced standing start				
1 km	1:13·899	Zhou Lingmei (China)	Beijing, China	27 Sep 1990
3 km	3:38·190	Jeannie Longo (France)	Mexico City	5 Oct 1989
5 km	6:14·135	Jeannie Longo (France)	Mexico City	27 Sep 1989
10 km	12:59·435	Jeannie Longo (France)	Mexico City	1 Oct 1989
20 km	25:59·883	Jeannie Longo (France)	Mexico City	1 Oct 1989
100 km	2:28:26·259	Francesca Galli (Italy)	Milan, Italy	26 Oct 1987
1 hour	46·35270 km	Jeannie Longo (France)	Mexico City	1 Oct 1989
Unpaced flying start				
200 metres	11·383	Isabelle Gautheron (France)	Colorado Springs, USA	16 Aug 1986
500 metres	30·59	Isabelle Gautheron (France)	Cali, Colombia	14 Sep 1986
1 km	1:10·463	Erika Salumyae (USSR)	Tashkent, USSR	15 May 1984

Many of the above venues, such as La Paz, Colorado Springs, Cali and Mexico City, are at high altitude. The UCI recognises separate world records for the classic one-hour event at venues below 600 metres. These are: MEN 49·80193 km Francesco Moser on 3 Oct 1986, WOMEN 43·58789 km Jeannie Longo on 30 Sep 1986, both at Milan.

INDOOR TRACKS

MEN

Unpaced standing start				
1 km	1:02·576	Aleksandr Kirichenko (USSR)	Moscow, USSR	2 Aug 1989
4 km	4:28·900	Vyacheslav Yekimov (USSR)	Moscow, USSR	20 Sep 1986
5 km	5:40·872	Vyacheslav Yekimov (USSR)†	Moscow, USSR	26 Oct 1990
10 km	11:31·968	Vyacheslav Yekimov (USSR)	Moscow, USSR	7 Jan 1989
20 km	23:14·553	Vyacheslav Yekimov (USSR)	Moscow, USSR	3 Feb 1989
100 km	2:10:08·287	Beat Meister (Switzerland)	Stuttgart, Germany	22 Sep 1989
4 km team	4:10·877	USSR (Vyacheslav Yekimov, Dmitriy Nelyubin, Mikhail Orlov, Yevgeniy Berzin)	Moscow, USSR	4 Aug 1989
1 hour	50·644 km	Francesco Moser (Italy)	Stuttgart, Germany	21 May 1988
Unpaced flying start				
200 metres	10·099	Vladimir Adamashvili (USSR)	Moscow, USSR	6 Aug 1990
500 metres	26·649	Aleksandr Kirichenko (USSR)	Moscow, USSR	29 Oct 1988
1 km	57·260	Aleksandr Kirichenko (USSR)	Moscow, USSR	25 Apr 1989
Motor-paced				
50 km	32:56·746	Aleksandr Romanov (USSR)	Moscow, USSR	21 Feb 1987
100 km	1:05:58·031	Aleksandr Romanov (USSR)	Moscow, USSR	21 Feb 1987
1 hour	91·131 km	Aleksandr Romanov (USSR)	Moscow, USSR	21 Feb 1987

WOMEN

Unpaced standing start				
1 km	1:13·377	Erika Salumyae (USSR)	Moscow, USSR	21 Sep 1983
3 km	3:43·490	Jeannie Longo (France)	Paris, France	14 Nov 1986
5 km	6:22·713	Jeannie Longo (France)	Grenoble, France	2 Nov 1986
10 km	12:54·26	Jeannie Longo (France)	Paris, France	19 Oct 1989
20 km	26:51·222	Jeannie Longo (France)	Moscow, USSR	29 Oct 1989
100 km	2:24:57·618	Tea Vikstedt-Nyman (Finland)	Moscow, USSR	30 Oct 1990
1 hour	45·016 km	Jeannie Longo (France)	Moscow, USSR	29 Oct 1989
Unpaced flying start				
200 metres	11·164	Galina Yenyukhina (USSR)	Moscow, USSR	6 Aug 1990
500 metres	29·655	Erika Salumyae (USSR)	Moscow, USSR	6 Aug 1988
1 km	1:05·232	Erika Salumyae (USSR)	Moscow, USSR	31 May 1987

LONG DISTANCE BESTS (unpaced)

24 hr	830·79 km	Michael L. Secrest (USA)	Montreal, Canada	13–14 Mar 1985
1 000 km	32 hr 4 min	Herman de Munck (Belgium)	Keerbergen, Belgium	23–24 Sep 1983
1 000 miles	51:12:32	Herman de Munck (Belgium)	Keerbergen, Belgium	23–25 Sep 1983

Roller cycling

James Baker (USA) achieved a record speed of 246·5 km/h *153·2 mph* at El Con Mall, Tucson, Arizona, USA on 28 Jan 1989.

Darts speed

The fastest time taken to complete three games of 301, finishing on doubles, is 1 min 47 sec by Keith Deller on BBC TV's *Record Breakers* on 22 Oct 1985.

The record time for going round the board clockwise in 'doubles' at arm's length is 9·2 sec by Dennis Gower at the Millers Arms, Hastings, E Sussex on 12 Oct 1975 and 14·5 sec in numerical order by Jim Pike (1903–60) at the Craven Club, Newmarket, Suffolk in March 1944.

The record for this feat at the 9 ft *2·7 m* throwing distance, retrieving own darts, is 2 min 13 sec by Bill Duddy (b. 29 Sep 1932) at The Plough, Haringey, London on 29 Oct 1972.

Longest horse ride

Henry G. Perry, a stockman from Mollongghip, Victoria, Australia rode 22 565 km *14 021 miles* around Australia in 157 days, 1 May to 4 Oct 1985, with six horses.

Snowdon, Scafell Pike and Ben Nevis, to sea level Fort William, Highland in 63 hr 34 min, from 23–25 Jul 1989.

CYCLE SPEEDWAY

First mention of the sport is at Coventry in 1920 and it was first organized in 1945. The sport's governing body, the Cycle Speedway Council, was formed in 1973.

Most British Senior Team Championships (instituted 1950) is six by: Wednesfield, Wolverhampton (1974, 1976–8, 1981 and 1983); Offerton, Cheshire (1962, 1964–5, 1969, 1972–3); and Poole, Dorset (1982, 1984, 1987–90).

The most individual titles is four by Derek Garnett (b. 16 Jul 1937) (1963, 1965, 1968 and 1972); he also won the inaugural British Veterans' Championship in 1987.

Darts

Origins Darts can be dated from the use by archers of heavily weighted ten-inch throwing arrows for self-defence in close quarters fighting. The 'dartes' were used in Ireland in the 16th century and darts was played on the *Mayflower* by the Plymouth pilgrims in 1620. The modern game dates from at least 1896 when Brian Gamlin of Bury, Lancs, is credited with inventing the present numbering system on the board. The first recorded score of 180 was by John Reader at the Highbury Tavern in Sussex in 1902.

Most titles Eric Bristow (b. 25 Apr 1957) has most wins in the World Masters Cham-

---

DARTS SCORING RECORDS

24-HOUR

MEN (8 players) 1 722 249 by Broken Hill Darts Club at Broken Hill, New South Wales, Australia on 28–29 Sep 1985. **WOMEN** (8 players) 744 439 by a team from the Lord Clyde, Leyton, London on 13–14 Oct 1990. **INDIVIDUAL** 496 949 by Ian Brown at Lanark, Strathclyde on 1–2 Jul 1988. **BULLS AND 25s** (8 players) 510 625 by a team at the Kent and Canterbury Hospital Sports and Social Club, Canterbury on 20–21 Oct 1989.

10-HOUR

MOST TREBLES 3056 (from 7992 darts) by Paul Taylor at the Woodhouse Tavern, Leytonstone, London on 19 Oct 1985. **MOST DOUBLES** 3265 (from 8451 darts) by Paul Taylor at the Lord Brooke, Walthamstow, London on 5 Sep 1987. **HIGHEST SCORE** (retrieving own darts) 465 919 by Jon Archer and Neil Rankin at the Royal Oak, Cossington, Leics on 17 Nov 1990. **BULLS** (individual) 855 by Fred Carter (GB) at Accrington, Lancashire on 11 Jan 1987.

6-HOUR

MEN 210 172 by Russell Locke at the Hugglescote Working Mens Club, Coalville, Leics on 10 Sep 1989. **WOMEN** 99 725 by Karen Knightly at the Lord Clyde, Leyton, London on 17 Mar 1991.

MILLION AND ONE UP

MEN (8 players) 36 750 darts by the Jobby Crossan Select Team, St Eugenes Parish Hall, Derry, Northern Ireland on 12–13 Jun 1987. **WOMEN** (8 players) 70 019 darts by The Delinquents darts team at the Top George, Combe Martin, Devon on 11–13 Sep 1987.

---

pionship (instituted 1974) with five, 1977, 1979, 1981 and 1983–84, the World Professional Championship (instituted 1978) with five, 1980–81 and 1984–86, and the World Cup Singles (instituted 1977), four, 1983, 1985, 1987 and 1989.

Seven men have won the annual *News of the World* Individual Championship twice; most recently by Eric Bristow, 1983–84 and by Mike Gregory (b. 16 Dec 1956), 1987–88.

John Lowe (b. 21 Jul 1945) is the only other man to have won each of the four major titles: World Masters, 1976 and 1980; World Professional, 1979 and 1987; World Cup Singles, 1981; and *News of the World*, 1981.

World Cup The first World Cup was held at the Wembley Conference Centre, London in 1977.

England has a record six wins at this biennial tournament. Eric Bristow and John Lowe played on all six teams.

A biennial World Cup for women was instituted in 1983 and has been won three times by England.

Record prize John Lowe won £102 000 for achieving the first 501 scored with the minimum nine darts in a major event on 13 Oct 1984 at Slough in the quarter-finals of the World Match-play Championships. His darts were six successive treble 20s, treble 17, treble 18 and double 18.

Least darts Scores of 201 in four darts, 301 in six darts, 401 in seven darts and 501 in nine darts, have been achieved on various occasions.

Roy Edwin Blowes (Canada) (b. 8 Oct 1930) was the first person to achieve a 501 in nine darts, 'double-on, double-off', at the Widgeons pub, Calgary, Canada at 9 Mar 1987. His scores were: bull, treble 20, treble 17, five treble 20s and a double 20 to finish.

The lowest number of darts thrown for a score of 1001 is 19 by: Cliff Inglis (b. 27 May 1935) (160, 180, 140, 180, 121, 180, 40) at the Bromfield Men's Club, Devon on 11 Nov 1975 and Jocky Wilson (140, 140, 180, 180, 180, 131, Bull) at The London Pride, Bletchley, Bucks on 23 Mar 1989.

A score of 2001 in 52 darts was achieved by Alan Evans (b. 14 Jun 1949) at Ferndale, Mid Glam on 3 Sep 1976.

A score of 3001 in 73 darts was thrown by Tony Benson at the Plough Inn, Gorton, Manchester on 12 Jul 1986. Linda Batten (b. 26 Nov 1954) set a women's 3001 record of 117 darts at the Old Wheatsheaf, Enfield, London on 2 Apr 1986.

A total of 100 001 was achieved in 3732 darts by Alan Downie of Stornoway on 21 Nov 1986.

Equestrian Sports

Origins Evidence of horse-riding dates from a Persian engraving dated *c.* 3000 BC. Pignatelli's academy of horsemanship at Naples dates from the 16th century. The earliest jumping competition was at the Agricultural Hall, Islington, London, in 1869. Equestrian events have been included in the Olympic Games since 1912.

SHOW JUMPING

Olympic Games The most Olympic gold medals is five by Hans-Günter Winkler (West Germany) (b. 24 Jul 1926), four team in 1956, 1960, 1964 and 1972 and the individual Grand Prix in 1956. He also won team silver in 1976 and team bronze in 1968 for a record seven medals overall.

The most team wins in the Prix des Nations is six by Germany in 1936, 1956, 1960, 1964 and as West Germany in 1972 and 1988.

The lowest score obtained by a winner is no faults by Frantisek Ventura (Czechoslovakia) (1895–1969) on *Eliot*, 1928 and Alwin Schockemöhle (West Germany) (b. 29 May 1937) on *Warwick Rex*, 1976.

Pierre Jonquères d'Oriola (France) (b. 1 Feb 1920) uniquely won the individual gold medal twice, 1952 and 1964.

World Championships The men's World Championships (instituted 1953) have been won twice by Hans-Günter Winkler (West Germany) (1954–55) and Raimondo d'Inzeo (Italy) (b. 8 Feb 1925) (1956 and 1960).

The women's title (1965–74) was won twice by Jane 'Janou' Tissot (*née* Lefebvre) (France) (b. Saigon, 14 May 1945) on *Rocket* (1970 and 1974).

President's Cup The world team championship (instituted 1965) has been won a record 13 times by Great Britain, 1965, 1967, 1970, 1972–74, 1977–79, 1983, 1985–86, 1989.

World Cup Instituted in 1979, double winners have been Conrad Homfeld (USA) (b. 25 Dec 1951), 1980 and 1985; Ian Miller (Canada) (b. 6 Jan 1947), 1988–9; and John Whitaker (GB) (b. 5 Aug 1955), 1990–91.

King George V Gold Cup and Queen Elizabeth II Cup David Broome (b. 1 Mar 1940) has won the King George V Gold Cup (first held 1911) a record five times, 1960 on *Sunsalve*, 1966 on *Mister Softee*, 1972 on *Sportsman*, 1977 on *Philco*, 1981 on *Mr Ross* and 1991 on *Lannegan*.

The Queen Elizabeth II Cup (first held 1949), for women, has been won five times by his sister Elizabeth Edgar (b. 28 Apr 1943), 1977 on *Everest Wallaby*, 1979 on *Forever*, 1981 and 1982 on *Everest Forever*, 1986 on *Everest Rapier*.

The only horse to win both these trophies is *Sunsalve* in 1957 (with Elisabeth Anderson) and 1960.

Jumping records The official *Fédération Equestre Internationale* records are: high jump 2·47 m *8 ft 1¼ in* by *Huasó*, ridden by Capt. Alberto Larraguibel Morales (Chile) at Viña del Mar, Santiago, Chile on 5 Feb 1949; long jump over water 8·40 m *27 ft 6¾ in* by *Something*, ridden by André Ferreira (South Africa) at Johannesburg, South Africa on 25 Apr 1975.

The British high jump record is 2·32 m *7 ft 7¼ in* by the 16·2 hands *167 cm* grey gelding *Lastic* ridden by Nick Skelton (b. 30 Dec 1957) at Olympia, London on 16 Dec 1978.

On 25 Jun 1937, at Olympia, the Lady Wright (*née* Margery Avis Bullows) set the best recorded height for a British equestrienne on her liver chestnut *Jimmy Brown* at 2·23 m *7 ft 4 in*.

The greatest recorded height reached on bareback is 2·13 m *7 ft* by Michael Whitaker (b. 17 Mar 1960) on *Red Flight* at Dublin, Republic of Ireland on 14 Nov 1982.

THREE-DAY EVENT

Olympic Games and World Championships Charles Ferdinand Pahud de Mortanges (Netherlands) (1896–1971) won a record four Olympic gold medals, team 1924 and 1928, individual (riding *Marcroix*) 1928 and 1932, when he also won a team silver medal.

Bruce Oram Davidson (USA) (b. 13 Dec

1949) is the only rider to have won two world titles (instituted 1966), on *Irish Cap* in 1974 and *Might Tango* in 1978.

Richard John Hannay Meade (GB) (b. 4 Dec 1938) is the only British rider to win three gold medals – as an individual in 1972 with team titles in 1968 and 1972, all in the three-day event.

Badminton The Badminton Three-Day Event (instituted 1949) has been won six times by Lucinda Jane Green (*née* Prior-Palmer) (b. 7 Nov 1953), in 1973 (on *Be Fair*), 1976 (*Wide Awake*), 1977 (*George*), 1979 (*Killaire*), 1983 (*Regal Realm*) and 1984 (*Beagle Bay*).

Ian David Stark (GB) (b. 22 Feb 1954) became the first ever rider to ride first (*Sir Wattie*) and second (*Glenburnie*) in the same year at Badminton in May 1988.

DRESSAGE

Olympic Games and World Championships Germany (West Germany 1968–90) have won a record seven team gold medals, 1928, 1936, 1964, 1968, 1976, 1984 and 1988, and have most team wins, six, at the World Championships (instituted 1966). Dr Reiner Klimke (West Germany) (b. 14 Jan 1936) has won a record six Olympic golds (team 1964–88, individual, 1984). He also won individual bronze in 1976 for a record seven medals overall, and is the only rider to win two world titles, on *Mehmed* in 1974 and *Ahlerich* in 1982. Henri St Cyr (Sweden) (1904–79) won a record two individual Olympic gold medals, 1952 and 1956.

World Cup Instituted in 1986, the only double winner is Christine Stückelberger (Switzerland) (b. 22 May 1947) on *Gauguin de Lully* in 1987–88.

CARRIAGE DRIVING

World Championships were first held in 1972. Three team titles have been won by: Great Britain, 1972, 1974 and 1980; Hungary, 1976, 1978 and 1984; and the Netherlands, 1982, 1986 and 1988.

Two individual titles have been won by György Bárdos (Hungary), 1978 and 1980 and by Tjeerd Velstra (Netherlands), 1982 and 1986.

Fencing

Origins 'Fencing' (fighting with single sticks) was practised as a sport, or as a part of a religious ceremony, in Egypt as early as *c.* 1360 BC. The first governing body for fencing in Britain was the Corporation of Masters of Defence founded by Henry VIII before 1540, and fencing has been practised as sport, notably in prize fights, since that time. The modern foil was introduced in France as a practice weapon for the short court sword in the mid-17th century. In the late 19th century the épée was developed in France and the light fencing sabre in Italy.

Most titles *World* The greatest number of individual world titles won is five by Aleksandr Romankov (USSR) (b. 7 Nov 1953), at foil 1974, 1977, 1979, 1982 and 1983, but Christian d'Oriola (France) won four world foil titles, 1947, 1949, 1953–54 as well as two individual Olympic titles (1952 and 1956).

Five women foilists have won three world titles: Hélène Mayer (Germany) (1910–53), 1929, 1931, 1937; Ilona Schacherer-Elek (Hungary) (1907–88), 1934–35, 1951; Ellen Müller–Preis (Austria) (b. 6 May 1912),

1947, 1949–50; Cornelia Hanisch (West Germany) (b. 12 Jun 1952), 1979, 1981, 1985; and Anja Fichtel (West Germany) (b. 17 Aug 1968), 1986, 1988 and 1990. Of these only Ilona Schacherer-Elek also won two individual Olympic titles (1936 and 1948). The longest span for winning an individual world or Olympic title is 20 years by Aladár Gerevich (Hungary) (b. 16 Mar 1910) at sabre, 1935–55, who also had a 28 year span for winning Olympic team gold medals.

Olympic The most individual Olympic gold medals won is three by Ramón Fonst (Cuba) (1883–1959) in 1900 and 1904 (two) and by Nedo Nadi (Italy) (1894–1952) in 1912 and 1920 (two). Nadi also won three team gold medals in 1920 making five gold medals at one celebration, the record for fencing and then a record for any sport.

Edoardo Mangiarotti (Italy) (b. 7 Apr 1919) with six gold, five silver and two bronze, holds the record of 13 Olympic medals. He won them for foil and épée from 1936 to 1960.

The most gold medals by a woman is four (one individual, three team) by Yelena Dmitryevna Novikova (*née* Byelova) (USSR) (b. 28 Jul 1947) from 1968 to 1976, and the record for all medals is seven (two gold, three silver, two bronze) by Ildikó Sági (formerly Ujlaki, *née* Retjö) (Hungary) (b. 11 May 1937) from 1960 to 1976.

British Three British fencers have won individual world titles: Gwen Neligan (1906–72) at foil in 1933; Henry William Furze 'Bill' Hoskyns (b. 19 Mar 1931) at épée in 1958; and Allan Louis Neville Jay

■ **World Cup**
Since it was instituted in 1979, there have been three double winners and the most recent is John Whitaker (GB) (b. 5 Aug 1955) in 1990 and 1991. Here he is seen in action during the 1990 World Championships in Stockholm, when he won the individual silver medal.
(Photo: Pressens Bild Ab)

Between 1969 and 1991, John N. P. Watson, hunting correspondent to *Country Life*, hunted with 280 different packs of foxhounds, staghounds and harehounds in Britain, Ireland, USA and Europe.

Most postponements

The Scottish Cup tie between Inverness Thistle and Falkirk during the winter of 1978–9 was postponed a record 29 times due to weather conditions. Finally Falkirk won the game 4–0.

Fastest own goal

Torquay United's Pat Kruse (b. 30 Nov 1953) equalled the fastest goal on record when he headed the ball into his own net only 6 sec after kick-off v. Cambridge United on 3 Jan 1977.

Heaviest goalkeeper

The biggest goalkeeper in representative football was the England international Willie J. 'Fatty' Foulke (1874–1916), who stood 1·90 m *6 ft 3 in* and weighed 141 kg *22 st 3 lb*. His last games were for Bradford City, by which time he was 165 kg *26 st.* He once stopped a game by snapping the cross bar.

(b. 30 Jun 1931) at foil in 1959, when he also won silver in épée. The only British fencer to win an Olympic gold medal is Gillian Mary Sheen (now Donaldson) (b. 21 Aug 1928) in the 1956 foil.

A record three Olympic medals were won by Edgar Isaac Seligman (1867–1958) with silver medals in the épée team event in 1906, 1908 and 1912.

Bill Hoskyns has competed most often for Great Britain with six Olympic appearances, 1956–76.

Amateur Fencing Association titles The most won at one weapon is ten at women's foil by Gillian Sheen, 1949, 1951–8, 1960. The men's records are: foil, 7 by John Emyrs Lloyd (1908–1987) 1928, 1930–3, 1937–8; épée, 6 by Edward Owen 'Teddy' Bourne (b. 30 Sep 1948) 1966, 1972, 1974, 1976–8 and William Ralph Johnson (b. 3 Jun 1948) 1968, 1982, 1984–5, 1987, 1990; and sabre, 6 by Dr Roger F. Tredgold (1912–75) 1937, 1939, 1947–9, 1955.

Field Sports

HUNTING

Hunting the fox in Britain became popular from the second half of the 18th century, though it is mentioned very much earlier. Prior to that time hunting was confined principally to the deer and the hare.

Pack The Old Charlton Hunt (later the Goodwood) in West Sussex (now extinct), the Duke of Monmouth and Lord Grey of Werke at Charlton, Sussex, and the Duke of Buckingham in North Yorks owned packs which were entered to fox only, during the reign (1660–85) of Charles II.

Largest The pack with the greatest number of hounds has been the Duke of Beaufort's hounds maintained at Badminton, Avon since 1786. At times hunting six days a week, this pack once had 120 couples at hounds. It now meets four days a week.

Longest mastership The 10th Duke of Beaufort (1900–84) was Master of Foxhounds from 1924 until his death in 1984 and hunted his hounds on 3895 days from 1920–67.

Longest hunt The longest recorded hunt was one held by Squire Sandys which ran from Holmbank, northern Lancs to Ulpha, Cumbria, a total of nearly 80 miles *128 km* in reputedly only 6 hr, in January or February 1743.

The longest duration hunt was one of 10 hr 5 min by Charlton Hunt of W Sussex, which ran from East Dean Wood at 7:45 a.m. to a kill over 57¼ miles *92 km* away at 5:50 p.m. on 26 Jan 1738.

BEAGLING

Longest mastership Jean Bethel 'Betty' McKeever (*née* Dawes) (1901–90) was Master of the Blean Beagles in Kent from 1909 until her death. She was given her first pack by her father at the age of eight and remained the sole Master.

GAME SHOOTING

Record heads The world's finest head is the 23-pointer stag in the Maritzburg collection, Germany. The outside span is 191 cm *75½ in*, the length 120 cm *47½ in* and the weight 18·824 kg *41½ lb*.

The greatest number of points is probably 33 (plus 29) on the stag shot in 1696 by Frederick III (1657–1713), the Elector of Brandenburg, later King Frederick I of Prussia.

Largest tally to a single sportsman A record 556 813 head of game fell to the guns of the 2nd Marquess of Ripon (1852–1923) between 1867 and when he dropped dead on a grouse moor after shooting his 52nd bird on the morning of 22 Sep 1923. This figure included 241 234 pheasants, 124 193 partridge and 31 900 hares. (His game books are held by the gunmakers James Purdey and Sons.)

Thomas, the 6th Baron Walsingham (1843–1919), bagged 1070 grouse, a one-day record for a single gun, in Yorkshire on 30 Aug 1888.

Fives

ETON FIVES

A handball game against the buttress of Eton College Chapel was first recorded in 1825. New courts were built at Eton in 1840, the rules were codified in 1877, rewritten laws were introduced three times and last amended in 1981.

Most titles One pair has won the amateur championship (Kinnaird Cup) ten times – Brian C. Matthews (b. 15 Aug 1957) and John P. Reynolds (b. 9 Aug 1961), 1981–90. John Reynolds won an eleventh title with M. de Souza-Girao in 1991.

RUGBY FIVES

As now known, this game dates from *c.* 1850 with the first inter-public school matches recorded in the early 1870s. The Oxford v. Cambridge contest was inaugurated in 1925 and the Rugby Fives Association was founded in the home of Dr Edgar Cyriax (1874–1954), in Welbeck Street, London on 29 Oct 1927. The dimensions of the standard rugby fives court were approved by the Association in 1931.

Most titles The greatest number of Amateur Singles Championships (instituted 1932) ever won is 17 by Wayne Enstone (b. 12 Jun 1951) in 1973–8 and 1980–90.

The record for the Amateur Doubles Championship (instituted 1925) is 10 by David John Hebden (b. 30 Jun 1948) and Ian Paul Fuller (b. 25 May 1953) in 1980–85 and 1987–90.

The invitation World Championships were first held in 1983. On the first three occasions Wayne Enstone won the singles and Enstone and Steve Ashton the doubles.

Football (Association)

Origins A game with some similarities termed *Tsu-chu* was played in China in the 4th and 3rd centuries BC. One of the earliest references to the game in England is a Royal Proclamation by Edward II in 1314 banning the game in the City of London. The earliest clear representation of football is an Edinburgh print dated 1672–3. The game was standardized with the formation of the Football Association in England on 26 Oct 1863. The oldest club is Sheffield FC, formed on 24 Oct 1857. The oldest in the Football League is Notts County, founded in 1862. Eleven per side became standard in 1870.

PROFESSIONAL

Longest match The duration record for first-class fixtures is 3 hr 30 min (with interruptions), in the Copa Libertadores in Santos, Brazil, on 2–3 Aug 1962, when Santos drew 3–3 with Penarol FC of Montevideo, Uruguay.

The longest British match on record was one of 3 hr 23 min between Stockport County and Doncaster Rovers in the second leg of the Third Division (North) Cup at Edgeley Park, Stockport, Greater Manchester on 30 Mar 1946.

Longest unbeaten run Nottingham Forest were undefeated in 42 consecutive First Division matches from 20 Nov 1977 to 9 Dec 1978. In Scottish Football Glasgow Celtic were undefeated in 62 matches (49 won, 13 drawn), 13 Nov 1915–21 April 1917.

GOAL SCORING

Teams The highest score recorded in a first-class match is 36. This occurred in the Scottish Cup match between Arbroath and Bon Accord on 5 Sep 1885, when Arbroath won 36–0 on their home ground. But for the lack of nets and the consequent waste of retrieval time the score must have been even higher. Seven further goals were disallowed for offside.

The highest margin recorded in an international match is 17, when England beat Australia 17–0 at Sydney on 30 Jun 1951. This match is not listed by England as a *full* international. The highest in the British Isles was when England beat Ireland 13–0 at Belfast on 18 Feb 1882.

The highest score between English clubs in any major competition is 26, when Preston North End beat Hyde 26–0 in an FA Cup tie at Deepdale, Lancs on 15 Oct 1887. The biggest victory in an FA Cup final is six when Bury beat Derby County 6–0 at Crystal Palace on 18 Apr 1903, in which year Bury did not concede a single goal in their five Cup matches.

The highest score by one side in a Football League (First Division) match is 12 goals when West Bromwich Albion beat Darwen 12–0 at West Bromwich, W Mids on 4 Apr 1892; when Nottingham Forest beat Leicester Fosse by the same score at Nottingham on 21 Apr 1909; and when Aston Villa beat Accrington 12–2 at Perry Barr, W Mids on 12 Mar 1892.

The highest aggregate in League Football was 17 goals when Tranmere Rovers beat Oldham Athletic 13–4 in a Third Division (North) match at Prenton Park, Merseyside, on Boxing Day, 1935. The record margin in a League match has been 13 in the Newcastle United 13, Newport County 0 (Second Division) match on 5 Oct 1946 and in the Stockport County 13, Halifax 0 (Third Division (North)) match on 6 Jan 1934.

The highest number of goals by any British team in a professional league in a season is 142 in 34 matches by Raith Rovers (Scottish Second Division in the 1937/8 season. The English League record is 134 in 46 matches by Peterborough United (Fourth Division) in 1960/1.

Individual The most scored by one player in a first-class match is 16 by Stephan Stanis (*né* Stanikowski, b. Poland, 15 Jul 1913) for Racing Club de Lens v. Aubry-Asturies, in Lens, France, in a wartime French Cup game on 13 Dec 1942.

The record number of goals scored by one player in an international match is ten by Sofus Nielsen (1888–1963) for Denmark v. France (17–1) in the 1908 Olympics and by Gottfried Fuchs (1889–1972) for Germany who beat Russia 16–0 in the 1912 Olympic tournament (consolation event) in Sweden.

BRITISH GOAL-SCORING RECORDS

SCOTTISH CUP
13 John Petrie for Arbroath *v.* Bon Accord on 5 Sep 1885

FOOTBALL LEAGUE
10 Joe Payne (1914–77) for Luton Town *v.* Bristol Rovers (Div 3S) at Luton on 13 Apr 1936

FOOTBALL LEAGUE DIVISION ONE
7 Ted Drake (b. 16 Aug 1912) for Arsenal *v.* Aston Villa at Birmingham on 14 Dec 1935
James David Ross for Preston North End *v.* Stoke at Preston on 6 Oct 1888

FOOTBALL LEAGUE/LITTLEWOODS CUP
6 Frankie Bunn (b. 6 Oct 1962) for Oldham Athletic *v.* Scarborough at Oldham on 25 Oct 1989

FA CUP (PRELIMINARY ROUND)
10 Chris Marron for South Shields *v.* Radcliffe at South Shields on 20 Sep 1947

FA CUP
9 Edward 'Ted' MacDougall (b. 8 Jan 1947) for Bournemouth *v.* Margate (first round) at Bournemouth on 20 Nov 1971

SCOTTISH LEAGUE
8 James Edward McGrory (1904–82) for Celtic *v.* Dunfermline (Div 1) at Celtic Park, Glasgow on 14 Jan 1928

HOME INTERNATIONAL
6 Joe Bambrick (b. 3 Nov 1905) for Ireland *v.* Wales at Belfast on 1 Feb 1930

AMATEUR INTERNATIONAL
6 William Charles Jordan (1885–1949) for England *v.* France at Park Royal, London on 23 Mar 1908; Vivian John Woodward (1879–1954) for England *v.* Holland at Stamford Bridge, London on 11 Dec 1909; Harold A. Walden for Great Britain *v.* Hungary at Stockholm, Sweden on 1 Jul 1912

Most in a season The most goals in a League season is 60 in 39 games by William Ralph 'Dixie' Dean (1907–80) for Everton (First Division) in 1927/8 and 66 in 38 games by James Smith (1902–76) for Ayr United (Scottish Second Division) in the same season. With three more in Cup ties and 19 in representative matches Dean's total was 82.

Career Artur Friedenreich (Brazil) (1892–1969) scored an undocumented 1329 goals in a 43 year first-class football career. The most goals scored in a specified period is 1281 by Edson Arantes do Nascimento (Brazil) (b. 23 Oct 1940), known as Pelé, from 7 Sep 1956 to 10 Oct 1977 in 1363 games. His best year was 1959 with 126, and the *Milesimo* (1000th) came from a penalty for his club Santos in the Maracaña Stadium, Rio de Janeiro on 19 Nov 1969 when playing his 909th first-class match. He later added two more goals in special appearances. Franz 'Bimbo' Binder (b. 1 Dec 1911) scored 1006 goals in 756 games in Austria and Germany between 1930 and 1950.

The international career record for England is 49 goals by Robert 'Bobby' Charlton (b. 11 Oct 1937). His first was *v.* Scotland on 19 Apr 1958 and his last on 20 May 1970 *v.* Colombia.

The greatest number of goals scored in British first-class football is 550 (410 in Scottish League matches) by James McGrory of Glasgow Celtic (1922–38). The most scored in League matches is 434, for West Bromwich Albion, Fulham, Leicester City and Shrewsbury Town, by George Arthur Rowley (b. 21 Apr 1926) between 1946 and April 1965. Rowley also scored 32 goals in the F.A. Cup and one for England 'B'.

Fastest goals The fastest Football League goals on record were scored in 6 sec by Albert E. Mundy (b. 12 May 1926) (Aldershot) in a Fourth Division match *v.* Hartlepool United at Victoria Ground, Hartlepool, Cleveland on 25 Oct 1958, by Barrie Jones (b. 31 Oct 1938) (Notts County) in a Third Division match *v.* Torquay United on 31 Mar 1962, and by Keith Smith (b. 15 Sep 1940) (Crystal Palace) in a Second Division match *v.* Derby County at the Baseball Ground, Derby on 12 Dec 1964.

The fastest confirmed hat-trick is in 2½ minutes by Ephraim 'Jock' Dodds (b. 7 Sep 1915) for Blackpool *v.* Tranmere Rovers on 28 Feb 1942, and Jimmy Scarth (b. 26 Aug 1920) for Gillingham *v.* Leyton Orient in Third Division (Southern) on 1 Nov 1952. A hat-trick in 1 min 50 sec is claimed for Maglioni of Independiente *v.* Gimnasia y Escrima de la Plata in Argentina on 18 Mar 1973. John McIntyre (Blackburn Rovers) scored four goals in 5 min *v.* Everton at Ewood Park, Blackburn, Lancs on 16 Sep 1922. William 'Ginger' Richardson (West Bromwich Albion) scored four goals in 5 min from the kick-off against West Ham United at Upton Park on 7 Nov 1931. Frank Keetley scored six goals in 21 min in the second half of the Lincoln City *v.* Halifax Town league match on 16 Jan 1932. The international record is three goals in 3½ min by George William Hall (Tottenham Hotspur) for England against Ireland on 16 Nov 1938 at Old Trafford, Greater Manchester.

GOALKEEPING

The longest that any goalkeeper has succeeded in preventing any goals being scored past him in top-class competition is 1275 mins by Abel Resino of Athletico Madrid to 17 Mar 1991. The record in international matches is 1142 min for Dino Zoff (Italy), from September 1972 to June 1974.

The British club record in all competitive matches is 1196 min by Chris Woods (b. 14 Nov 1959) for Glasgow Rangers from 26 Nov 1986 to 31 Jan 1987.

THE FIFA WORLD CUP

The *Fédération Internationale de Football Association* (FIFA), which was founded on

■ **Longest clean sheet**
The longest that any goalkeeper has succeeded in preventing any goals being scored past him in top-class competition is 1275 mins by Abel Resino of Athletico Madrid to 17 Mar 1991. (Photo: AllSport/Richiardi)

FOOTBALL

■ **World Cup winner**
Franz Beckenbauer lifts the World Cup after West Germany's 2–1 victory over the Netherlands in 1974. In 1990 he became the first person to win the World Cup as a player and manager when West Germany beat Argentina, 1–0.

(Photos: All-Sport)

21 May 1904, instituted the first World Cup on 13 Jul 1930, in Montevideo, Uruguay. It is held quadrennially. Three wins have been achieved by Brazil 1958, 1962 and 1970; Italy 1934, 1938 and 1982; and West Germany 1954, 1974 and 1990. Brazil, uniquely, have taken part in all 14 finals tournaments.

Appearances Antonio Carbajal (Mexico) (b. 1923) is the only player to have appeared in five World Cup finals tournaments, keeping goal for Mexico in 1950, 1954, 1958, 1962 and 1966, playing 11 games in all. The most appearances in finals tournaments is 21 by: Uwe Seeler (West Germany) (b. 5 Nov 1936), 1958–70; and by Wladyslaw Zmuda (Poland) (b. 6 Jun 1954), 1974–86. Pelé is the only player to have been with three World Cup–winning teams, in 1958, 1962 and 1970. The youngest ever to play in the World Cup is Norman Whiteside, who played for Northern Ireland v. Yugoslavia aged 17 yr 42 days on 17 Jun 1982.

Goal scoring Just Fontaine (b. Marrakesh, Morocco, 18 Aug 1933) of France scored 13 goals in six matches in the final stages of the 1958 competition in Sweden. Gerd Müller (West Germany) (b. 3 Nov 1945) scored 10 goals in 1970 and four in 1974 for the highest aggregate of 14 goals. Fontaine, Jairzinho (Brazil) and Alcide Ghiggia (Uruguay) are the only three

players to have scored in every match in a final series. Jairzinho scored seven in six games in 1970 and Ghiggia, four in four games in 1950 .

The most goals scored in a final is three by Geoffrey Charles Hurst (b. 8 Dec 1941) for England v. West Germany on 30 Jul 1966. Three players have scored in two finals: Vava (real name Edwaldo Izito Neto) (Brazil) in 1958 and 1962, Pelé in 1958 and 1970; and Paul Breitner (West Germany) in 1974 and 1982.

The highest score in a World Cup match occurred in a qualifying match in Auckland on 15 Aug 1981 when New Zealand beat Fiji 13–0. The highest score during the final stages is 10, scored by Hungary in a 10–1 win over El Salvador at Elche, Spain on 15 Jun 1982. The highest match aggregate in the finals tournament is 12, when Austria beat Switzerland, 7–5, in 1954.

The best defensive record belongs to England, who in six matches in 1966 conceded only three goals.

OLYMPIC GAMES

The only country to have won the Olympic football title three times is Hungary in 1952, 1964 and 1968. The United Kingdom won the unofficial tournament in 1900 and the official tournaments of 1908 and 1912. The highest Olympic score is 17 by Denmark v. France 'A' (1) in 1908. A record 126 nations are taking part in qualifying for the 1992 tournament.

TOURNAMENT RECORDS

World Club Championship This club tournament was started in 1960 between the winners of the European Cup and the Copa Libertadores, the South American equivalent. The most wins is three by Peñarol, Uruguay in 1961, 1966 and 1982 and by Nacional, Uruguay in 1971, 1980 and 1988. Independiente, Argentina won in 1973 and 1984 and reached the final in 1975, but couldn't agree dates for the matches with Bayern Munich.

European Championship (Nations Cup) Held every four years from 1958. West Germany are the only country to have won twice, in 1972 and 1980. They also lost in the 1976 final, to Czechoslovakia.

European Champion Clubs Cup The European Cup for the league champions of the respective nations was approved by FIFA on 8 May 1955 and was

run by the European governing body UEFA (Union of European Football Associations) which came into being in the previous year. Real Madrid won the first final, and have won a record six times 1956–60, 1966. The highest score in a final was Real Madrid's 7–3 win over Eintracht Frankfurt at Hampden Park, Glasgow on 18 May 1960.

Glasgow Celtic became the first British club to win the Cup, beating Inter-Milan 2–1 in Lisbon, Portugal on 25 May 1967. They also became the first British club to win the European Cup and the two senior domestic tournaments (League and Cup) in the same season. Liverpool, winners in 1977, 1978, 1981 and 1984, have been the most successful British club and in 1983/4 emulated Celtic by also winning two domestic competitions – League and Milk Cup.

European Cup Winners Cup A tournament for national cup winners started in 1960/1. Barcelona have won a record three times, 1979, 1982 and 1989. Tottenham Hotspur were the first British club to win the trophy, when they set a record score for the final beating Atlético Madrid 5–1 in Rotterdam, Netherlands on 15 May 1963.

UEFA Cup Originally known as the International Inter-City Industrial Fairs Cup, this club tournament began in 1955. The first competition lasted three years, the second two years. In 1960/1 it became an annual tournament and since 1971/2 has been for the UEFA Cup. The most wins is three by Barcelona in 1958, 1960 and 1966. The first British club to win the trophy was Leeds United in 1968.

INTERNATIONAL CAPS

Oldest The oldest international has been William Henry 'Billy' Meredith (1874 –1958) (Manchester City and United) who played outside right for Wales v. England at Highbury, London on 15 Mar 1920 when aged 45 yr 229 days. He played internationally for a record span of 26 years (1895 –1920).

Youngest The youngest British international was Norman Whiteside, who played for Northern Ireland v. Yugoslavia at 17 yr 42 days on 17 Jun 1982.

England's youngest international was Duncan Edwards (1936–58) (Manchester United) v. Scotland at Wembley on 2 Apr 1955, at 18 yr 183 days. The youngest Welsh cap was John Charles (b. 27 Dec 1931) (Leeds United), v. Ireland at Wrexham on 8

BRITISH INTERNATIONAL APPEARANCES

ENGLAND 125, Peter Leslie Shilton (b. 18 Sep 1949) (Leicester City, Stoke City, Nottingham Forest, Southampton, Derby County) 1970–90.

NORTHERN IRELAND 119, Patrick A. Jennings (b. 12 Jun 1945) (Watford, Tottenham Hotspur, Arsenal) 1964–86.

SCOTLAND 102, Kenneth M. Dalglish (b. 4 Mar 1951) (Celtic, Liverpool) 1971–86.

WALES 72, Joseph P. 'Joey' Jones (b. 4 Mar 1955) (Wrexham, Liverpool, Chelsea, Huddersfield Town) 1972–86; Peter Nicholas (b. 10 Nov 1959) (Crystal Palace, Arsenal, Luton Town, Aberdeen, Chelsea, Watford) 1979–91.

REPUBLIC OF IRELAND 72, William 'Liam' Brady (b. 13 Feb 1956) (Arsenal, Juventus, Sampdoria, Internazionale, Ascoli, West Ham U) 1974–90

Mar 1950, aged 18 yr 71 days. Scotland's youngest international has been John Alexander Lambie (1868–1923) (Queen's Park), at 17 yr 2 days v. Ireland on 20 Mar 1886. The youngest for the Republic of Ireland was James Holmes (b. 11 Nov 1953) (Coventry City), at 17 yr 200 days v. Austria in Dublin on 30 May 1971.

Most international appearances

The greatest number of appearances for a national team is 150 by Hector Chumpitaz (Peru) (b. 12 Apr 1943) from 1963 to 1982. This includes all matches played by the national team. The record for full internationals against other national teams is 125 by Peter Shilton of England.

The most international appearances by a woman is 59 by Linda Curl (b. 1962) for England, 1977–90.

FA CHALLENGE CUP AND SCOTTISH FA CUP

Most wins The greatest number of FA Cup wins is eight by Tottenham Hotspur, 1901, 1921, 1961, 1962, 1967, 1981, 1982 and 1991 (nine appearances). The most appearances in the final is 11 by; Arsenal (5 wins), Everton (4), Newcastle United (6) and Manchester United (7). The most goals in a final is seven; in 1890 when Blackburn Rovers beat Sheffield Wednesday 6–1 and in 1953 when Blackpool beat Bolton Wanderers 4–3.

The greatest number of Scottish FA Cup wins is 29 by Celtic in 1892, 1899, 1900, 1904, 1907–8, 1911–12, 1914, 1923, 1925, 1927, 1931, 1933, 1937, 1951, 1954, 1965, 1967, 1969, 1971–2, 1974–5, 1977, 1980, 1985 and 1988–9.

Youngest player The youngest player in an FA Cup final was Paul Allen (b. 28 Aug 1962) for West Ham United v. Arsenal on 10 May 1980, aged 17 yr 256 days. Derek Johnstone (Rangers) (b. 4 Nov 1953) was 16 yr 11 months old when he played in the Scottish League Cup final against Celtic on 24 Oct 1970. The youngest goal scorer in the FA Cup final was Norman Whiteside (b. 7 May 1965) for Manchester United v. Brighton at 18 yr 19 days on 26 May 1983. The youngest player ever in the FA Cup competition was full back Andrew Awford (b. 14 Jul 1972) at 15 yr 88 days for Worcester City in a qualifying round tie at Borehamwood, Herts on 10 Oct 1987.

Most medals Three players have won five FA Cupwinners' medals: James Henry Forrest with Blackburn Rovers (1884–6, 1890–1); the Hon. Sir Arthur Fitzgerald Kinnaird KT with Wanderers (1873, 1877–8) and Old Etonians (1879, 1882); and Charles Harold Reynolds Wollaston with Wanderers (1872–3, 1876–8).

The most Scottish Cupwinners' medals won is eight by Charles Campbell (Queen's Park) in 1874–6, 1880–2, 1884 and 1886.

Longest tie The most protracted FA Cup tie in the competition proper was that between Stoke City and Bury in the third round, with Stoke winning 3–2 in the fifth meeting after 9 hr 22 min of play in January 1955. The matches were at Bury (1–1) on 8 Jan; Stoke-on-Trent on 12 Jan (abandoned after 22 min of extra time with the score 1–1); Goodison Park (3–3) on 17 Jan; Anfield (2–2) on 19 Jan; and finally at Old Trafford on 24 Jan. In the 1972 final qualifying round Alvechurch beat Oxford City after five previous drawn games (total playing time 11 hours).

FOOTBALL LEAGUE CUP

Instituted in 1960/1, the most wins is four by; Liverpool, 1981–4; and Nottingham Forest, 1978–9, 1989–90.

SCOTTISH LEAGUE CUP

Instituted in 1946/7, the most wins is 17 by Rangers between 1947 and 1990.

LEAGUE CHAMPIONSHIPS

The record number of successive national league championships is nine by: Celtic (Scotland) 1966–74; CSKA, Sofia (Bulgaria) 1954–62; and MTK Budapest (Hungary) 1917–25. The Sofia club holds a European post-war record of 26 league titles, including two under the name CFKA Sredets (re-named CSKA).

English The greatest number of League Championships (First Division) is 18 by Liverpool in 1901, 1906, 1922–3, 1947, 1964, 1966, 1973, 1976–7, 1979–80, 1982–4, 1986, 1988 and 1990. The record number of wins in a season is 33 from 42 matches by Doncaster Rovers in Third Division (North) in 1946/7. The First Division record is 31 wins from 42 matches by Tottenham Hotspur in 1960/1. In 1893/4 Liverpool won 22 and drew 6 in 28 Second Division games. They also won the promotion match. The most points in a season under the current scoring system is 102 from 46 matches by Swindon in the Fourth Division in 1985/6. Under the new system the First Division record would have been Liverpool's 98 in 1978/9, when they won 30 and drew 8 of their 42 matches.

'Double' The only FA Cup and League Championship 'doubles' are those of Preston North End in 1889, Aston Villa in 1897, Tottenham Hotspur in 1961, Arsenal in 1971 and Liverpool in 1986. Preston won the League without losing a match and the Cup without having a goal scored against them throughout the whole competition.

Scottish Glasgow Rangers have won the Scottish League Championship 41 times (one shared 1891) between 1891 and 1991. Their 76 points in the Scottish First Division in 1920/1 represents a record in any division.

Closest win In 1923/4 Huddersfield won the First Division Championship over Cardiff by 0·02 of a goal with a goal average of 1·81. The 1988/9 League Championship was decided by the fact that Arsenal had scored more goals (73 to 65) than Liverpool, after both teams finished level on points and goal difference.

PLAYERS

Most durable Peter Leslie Shilton (b. 18 Sep 1949) has made a record 1295 senior UK appearances, including a record 930 League appearances, 286 for Leicester City (1966–74), 110 for Stoke City (1974–7), 202 for Nottingham Forest (1977–82), 188 for Southampton (1982–7) and 144 for Derby County (1987–90), 82 FA Cup, 92 League Cup, 125 internationals, 13 Under-23, 4 Football League XI and 49 various European and other club competitons. Norman John Trollope (b. 14 Jun 1943) made 770 League appearances for one club, Swindon Town, between 1960 and 1980.

Transfer fees The highest transfer fee quoted for a player is 16 thousand million

■ **Most FA Cup wins**
Gary Mabbutt raises his arm in triumph after Des Walker's decisive own goal in the 1991 FA Cup Final. Tottenham Hotspur beat Nottingham Forest 2–1, to win the FA Cup for a record eighth time.
(Photo: All-Sport/S. Botterill)

Sent off!

In a Gancia Cup match at Waltham Abbey, Essex on 23 Dec 1973, the referee, Michael J. Woodhams, sent off the entire Juventus-Cross team and some club officials.

lira (£7·7 million) by Juventus for Roberto Baggio (b. 18 Feb 1967) from Fiorentina on 18 May 1990.

The record fee between two British clubs is £2·3 million (including VAT and other levies) paid by Manchester United to Middlesborough for Gary Pallister (b. 30 Jun 1965) on 28 Aug 1989. The highest transfer fee for a British player is the estimated £4·5 million paid by Olympique Marseille of France to Tottenham Hotspur for Chris Waddle (b. 14 Dec 1960) on 6 Jul 1989.

ATTENDANCES

Greatest crowds The greatest recorded crowd at any football match was 199 589 for the Brazil v. Uruguay World Cup match in the Maracaña Municipal Stadium, Rio de Janeiro, Brazil on 16 Jul 1950. The record attendance for a European Cup match is 136 505 at the semi-final between Glasgow Celtic and Leeds United at Hampden Park, Glasgow on 15 Apr 1970.

The British record paid attendance is 149 547 at the Scotland v. England international at Hampden Park, Glasgow on 17 Apr 1937. It is, however, probable that this total was exceeded (estimated 160 000) at the FA Cup final between Bolton Wanderers and West Ham United at Wembley Stadium on 28 Apr 1923, when the crowd spilled onto the pitch and the start was delayed 40 min until it was cleared. The counted admissions were 126 047.

The Scottish Cup record attendance is 146 433 when Celtic played Aberdeen at Hampden Park on 24 Apr 1937. The record attendance for a League match in Britain is 118 567 for Rangers v. Celtic at Ibrox Park, Glasgow on 2 Jan 1939.

The highest attendance at an amateur match has been 120 000 in Senayan Stadium, Jakarta, Indonesia on 26 Feb 1976 for the Pre-Olympic Group II final, North Korea v. Indonesia.

Smallest crowd The smallest crowd at a full home international was 2315 for Wales v. Northern Ireland on 27 May 1982 at the Racecourse Ground, Wrexham, Clwyd. The smallest paying attendance at a Football League fixture was for the Stockport County v. Leicester City match at Old Trafford, Manchester on 7 May 1921. Stockport's own ground was under suspension and the 'crowd' numbered 13 but an estimated 2000 gained free admission. When West Ham beat Castilla of Spain (5–1) in the European Cup Winners Cup at Upton Park, Greater London on 1 Oct 1980 and when Aston Villa beat Besiktas of Turkey (3–1) in the European Cup at Villa Park, Birmingham on 15 Sep 1982, there were no paying spectators due to disciplinary action by the European Football Union.

PENALTIES

The greatest number of penalty kicks taken to decide a cup game under the jurisdiction of the Football League occurred in a Freight Rover Trophy, Southern Section quarter-final between Aldershot and Fulham on 10 Feb 1987, at the Recreation Ground, Aldershot, Hants. After 90

minutes play the score was 1–1. A further 30 minutes of extra time produced no further scoring. It needed 28 penalty kicks, of which only seven were missed, before Aldershot won 11–10.

The record number of penalties awarded in a League match is five during the Crystal Palace v. Brighton & Hove Albion Second Division game on 27 Mar 1989. Palace missed three of their spot kicks and each side was successful once. Palace eventually won 2–1.

In the Cyprus First-Division match in which Omonia beat Olympiakos 6–4 in Nicosia on 15 February 1987, FIFA referee Stafanos Hadjistefanou awarded six penalties, three to each side, all of which were converted by George Savvides (Omonia) and Sylvester Vernon (Olympiakos).

OTHER MATCHES

Highest scores *Teams* Drayton Grange Colts beat Eldon Sports Reserves 49–0 in a Daventry and District Sunday League match at Grange Estate, Northants on 13 Nov 1988. Every member of the side including the goalkeeper scored at least one goal.

In an Under-14 League match between Midas FC and Courage Colts, in Kent, on 11 Apr 1976, the full-time score after 70 minutes play was 59–1. Top scorer for Midas was Kevin Graham with 17 goals. Courage had scored the first goal.

Needing to improve their goal 'difference' to gain promotion in 1979, Ilinden FC of Yugoslavia, with the collusion of the opposition, Mladost, and the referee, won their final game of the season 134–1. Their rivals for promotion won their match, under similar circumstances, 88–0.

Individual Dean Goodliff scored 26 goals for Deleford Colts v. Iver Minors in the Slough Boys Soccer Combination Under-14 League at Iver, Bucks in his team's 33–0 win on 22 Dec 1985. The women's record is 22 goals by Linda Curl of Norwich Ladies in a 40–0 league victory over Milton Keynes Reserves at Norwich on 25 Sep 1983.

Season The greatest number of goals in a season reported for an individual player in junior professional league football is 96 by Tom Duffy (b. 7 Jan 1937), for Ardeer Thistle FC, Strathclyde in 1960/1. Paul Anthony Moulden (b. 6 Sep 1967) scored 289 goals in 40 games for Bolton Lads Club in Bolton Boys Federation intermediate league and cup matches in 1981/2. An additional 51 goals scored in other tournaments brought his total to 340, the highest season figure reported in any class of competitive football for an individual. He made his Football League debut for Manchester City on 1 Jan 1986 and has played for the England Youth team.

Fastest goals *Individual* Wind-aided goals in 3 sec after kick-off have been scored by a number of players. Damian Corcoran (b. 25 Nov 1976) scored three goals within a minute for 7th Fulwood Cubs v. 4th Fulwood Cubs on 1 Feb 1987.

Own goal The fastest own goals on record have been in 5 sec 'scored' by Peter Johnson of Chesham United v. Wycombe Wanderers on 21 Feb 1976 and by John Smythe of Vernon Carus v. Duke Williams Reserves in March 1986.

Team The shortest time for a semi-professional team to score three goals from the start of a game is 122 sec by Burton Albion v. Redditch United in a Beazer

GLIDING

Homes League Premier Division match on 2 Jan 1989.

Longest ties In the Hertfordshire Intermediate Cup, London Colney beat Leavesden Hospital after 12 hr 41 min play and seven ties from 6 Nov to 17 Dec 1971.

Largest tournament The Metropolitan Police 5-a-side Youth Competition in 1981 attracted an entry of 7008 teams, a record for an FA sanctioned competition.

Most and least successful teams Winlaton West End FC, Tyne & Wear, completed a run of 95 league games without defeat between 1976 and 1980. Penlake Junior Football Club remained unbeaten for 153 games (winning 152 including 85 in succession) in the Warrington Hilden Friendly League from 1981 until defeated in 1986. Stockport United FC, of the Stockport Football League, lost 39 consecutive League and Cup matches, September 1976 to 18 Feb 1978.

Ball control Allan Abuto Nyanjong (Kenya) juggled a regulation soccer ball for 16 hr 27 min 52 sec non-stop with feet, legs and head without the ball ever touching the ground at the Hyatt Regency Crystal City, Arlington, Virginia, USA on 16 Jan 1988. The heading record is 7 hr 3 min 33 sec by Huh Nam Jin (South Korea) at Swiss Grand Hotel, South Korea on 29 Aug 1990. Jan Skorkovsky of Prague, Czechoslavakia kept a football up while he travelled a distance of 42·195 km *26·219 miles* for the Prague City Marathon in 7 hr 18 min 55 sec on 8 Jul 1990.

Gaelic Football

Origins The game developed from inter-parish 'free for all' with no time-limit, specific playing area or rules. The earliest reported match was Meath v. Louth, at Slane in 1712. Standardization came with the formation of the Gaelic Athletic Association in Thurles, Ireland on 1 Nov 1884.

All-Ireland Championships The greatest number of All-Ireland Championships won by one team is 30 by Ciarraidhe (Kerry) between 1903 and 1986.

The greatest number of successive wins is four by Wexford (1915–18) and Kerry twice (1929–32, 1978–81).

The most finals contested by an individual is ten, including eight wins by the Kerry players Pat Spillane, Paudie O'Shea and Denis Moran, 1975–76, 1978–82, 1984–86.

The highest team score in a final was when Dublin, 27 (5 goals, 12 points) beat Armagh, 15 (3 goals, 6 points) on 25 Sep 1977. The highest combined score was 45 points when Cork (26) beat Galway (19) in 1973. A goal equals three points.

The highest individual score in an All-Ireland final has been 2 goals, 6 points by Jimmy Keaveney (Dublin) v. Armagh in 1977, and by Michael Sheehy (Kerry) v. Dublin in 1979.

Largest crowd The record crowd is 90 556 for the Down v. Offaly final at Croke Park, Dublin in 1961.

Gambling

BINGO

Bingo is a lottery game which, as Keno, was developed in the 1880s from Lotto, whose origin is thought to be the 17th-century Italian game *tumbule*. It has long been known in the British Army (called Housey-Housey) and the Royal Navy (called Tombola). The winner was the first to complete a random selection of numbers from 1 to 90. The USA version called Bingo differs in that the selection is from 1 to 75.

Largest house The largest 'house' in Bingo sessions was 15 756 at the Canadian National Exhibition, Toronto on 19 Aug 1983. Staged by the Variety Club of Ontario Tent Number 28, there was total prize money of $C250 000 with a record one-game payout of $C100 000.

Earliest and latest Full House A 'Full House' call occurred on the 15th number by Norman A. Wilson at Guide Post Working Men's Club, Bedlington, Northumberland on 22 Jun 1978, by Anne Wintle of Brynrefrin, Mid Glam, on a coach trip to Bath on 17 Aug 1982 and by Shirley Lord at Kahibah Bowling Club, New South Wales, Australia on 24 Oct 1983.

'House' was not called until the 86th number at the Hillsborough Working Men's Club, Sheffield, S Yorks on 11 Jan 1982. There were 32 winners.

FOOTBALL POOLS

The winning dividend paid out by Littlewoods Pools in their first week in February 1923 was £2 12s 0d . In 1987/8 the three British Pools companies which comprise the Pool Promoters Association (Littlewoods, Vernons and Zetters) had a total record turnover of £661 165 000 of which Littlewoods contributed over 70 per cent.

Biggest win Two unnamed punters won c. £1·5 million each in November 1972 on the state-run Italian pools.

British The record individual payout, which is also the biggest ever prize paid in any British competition, is £1 698 077 paid by Littlewoods Pools to Capt. Ernest Hames of Maidstone, Kent for matches played on 8 Jun 1991.

The record double payout is £1 988 510 by Littlewoods on 13 Feb 1988 to John Clark of Bristol, Avon (£991 656) and an anonymous Strathclyde woman (£996 854). Littlewoods' record total payout for a single week is £3 462 139 on 17 Mar 1990.

HORSE RACING

Highest ever odds The highest secured odds were 1 670 759 to 1 by George Rhodes of Aldershot, Hants. For a 5p bet, with a 10 per cent bonus for the ITV Seven, less tax, he was paid £86 024.42 by the William Hill Organization on 30 Sep 1984.

Edward Hodson of Wolverhampton, W Mids landed a 3 956 748 to 1 bet for a 55p stake on 11 Feb 1984, but his bookmaker had a £3000 payout limit.

The world record odds on a 'double' are 31 793 to 1 paid by the New Zealand Totalisator Agency Board on a five shilling tote ticket on *Red Emperor* and *Maida Dillon* at Addington, Christchurch in 1951.

Greatest payout Anthony A. Speelman and Nicholas John Cowan (both Great Britain) won $1 627 084.40, after federal income tax of $406 768.00 was withheld, on a $64 nine-horse accumulator at Santa Anita racecourse, California, USA on 19 Apr 1987. Their first seven selections won and the payout was for a jackpot, accumulated over 24 days.

The largest payout by a British bookmaker is £250 016 by Ladbrokes, paid to a Mr.'X' for a combination tricast on 20 May 1989.

Biggest tote win The best recorded tote win was one of £341 2s 6d to 2s representing odds of 3410¼ to 1, by Catharine Unsworth of Blundellsands, Liverpool, Merseyside at Haydock Park on a race won by *Coole* on 30 Nov 1929. The highest odds in Irish tote history were £289.64 for a 10p unit on *Gene's Rogue* at Limerick on 28 Dec 1981.

Largest bookmaker The world's largest bookmaker is Ladbrokes with a turnover from gambling in 1988 of £2107 million and the largest chain of betting shops, 1986 in Great Britain and the Republic of Ireland at 1 Sep 1990, as well as 991 in Belgium and The Netherlands.

Gliding

Origins Research by Isadore William Deiches has shown evidence of the use of gliders in Ancient Egypt c. 2500–1500 BC. Emanuel Swedenborg (1688–1772) of Sweden made sketches of gliders c. 1714. The earliest man-carrying glider was designed by Sir George Cayley (1773–1857) and carried his coachman (possibly John Appleby) about 457 m *500 yd* across a valley in Brompton Dale, N Yorks in the summer of 1853.

Most titles The most World Individual Championships (instituted 1937) won is four by Ingo Renner (Australia) in 1976 (Standard class), 1983, 1985 and 1987 (Open).

British The British National Championship (instituted 1939) has been won eight times by Ralph Jones (b. 29 Mar 1936).

The first woman to win this title was Anne Burns (b. 23 Nov. 1915) of Farnham, Surrey on 30 May 1966.

Women's altitude records The women's single-seater world record for absolute altitude is 12 637 m *41 449 ft* by Sabrina Jackintell (USA) in an Astir GS on 14 Feb 1979.

The height gain record is 10 212 m *33 506 ft* by Yvonne Loader (New Zealand) at Omarama, New Zealand on 12 Jan 1988.

The British single-seater absolute altitude record is 10 550 m *34 612 ft* by Anne Burns in a Skylark 3B over South Africa on 13 Jan 1961, when she set a then world record and still a British record for height gain of 9119 m *29 918 ft*.

HANG GLIDING

Origins In the 11th century the monk, Eilmer, is reported to have flown from the 18·3 m *60 ft* tower of Malmesbury Abbey, Wilts. The earliest modern pioneer was Otto Lilienthal (1848–96) (Germany) with about 2500 flights in gliders of his own construction between 1891 and 1896. In the 1950s Prof. Francis Rogallo of the National Space Agency, USA, developed a flexible 'wing' from his space capsule re-entry researches.

World Championships The World Team Championships (officially instituted 1976) have been won most often by Great Britain (1981, 1985, 1989 and 1991).

WORLD RECORDS The *Fédération Aéronautique Internationale* recognizes world records for rigidwing, flexwing and multiplace flexwing. These records are the greatest in each category – all by flexwing gliders.

Bookings
In the local cup match between Tongham Youth Club, Surrey and Hawley, Hants, on 3 Nov 1969, the referee booked all 22 players including one who went to hospital, and one of the linesmen. The match, won by Tongham 2–0, was described by a player as 'a good, hard game'.

Glencraig United, Faifley, near Clydebank, had all 11 team members and two substitutes for their 2–2 draw against Goldenhill Boys' Club on 2 Feb 1975 booked in the dressing room *before* a ball was kicked. The referee, Mr Tarbet of Bearsen, took exception to the chant which greeted his arrival. It was not his first meeting with Glencraig.

Goalkeeping
Craig Manktelow (b. 5 Mar 1967) of Kawerau Electrical Services in New Zealand played 15 matches without conceding a goal, a total of 1350 min, from 6 May–19 Aug 1989.

Slot machines
The biggest beating handed to a 'one-armed bandit' was $6 814 823.48 by Cammie Brewer, 61, at the Club Cal-Neva, Reno, Nevada, USA on 14 Feb 1988.

Biggest lottery win
The biggest individual gambling win is $40 million by Mike Wittkowski in the Illinois State Lottery, announced on 3 Sep 1984. From $35 worth of 'Lotto' tickets bought by his family, the winning six numbers bring him $2 million for the next 20 years.

Largest casino
The Trump Taj Mahal, Atlantic City, New Jersey, USA which opened in April 1990 has a casino area of 11 100 m² *120 000 ft²*

GLIDING WORLD & BRITISH RECORDS
(*Single-seaters*)

DISTANCE		NAME	TYPE OF GLIDER	LOCATION	DATE
STRAIGHT DISTANCE	1460·8 km *907·7 miles*	Hans-Werner Grosse (West Germany)	ASW-12	Lübeck, Germany to Biarritz, France	25 Apr 1972
(British)	949·7 km *589·9 miles*	Karla Karel	LS-3	Australia	20 Jan 1980
DECLARED GOAL DISTANCE	1254·26 km *779·4 miles*	Bruce Drake (New Zealand)	Nimbus 2	Te Anau to Te Araroa, New Zealand	14 Jan 1978
		David Speight (New Zealand)	Nimbus 2	Te Anau to Te Araroa, New Zealand	14 Jan 1978
		S. H. 'Dick' Georgeson (New Zealand)	Nimbus 2	Te Anau to Te Araroa, New Zealand	14 Jan 1978
(British)	859·2 km *534 miles*	M. T. Alan Sands	Nimbus 3	Ridge soaring to Chilhowee, Va, USA	23 Apr 1986
GOAL AND RETURN	1646·68 km *1023·2 miles*	Tom Knauff (USA)	Nimbus 3	Williamsport, Pa to Knoxville, Tn, USA	25 Apr 1983
(British)	1127·68 km *700·72 miles*	M. T. Alan Sands	Nimbus 3	Lock Haven, Pa to Bluefield, Va, USA	7 May 1985
ABSOLUTE ALTITUDE	14 938 m *49 009 ft*	Robert R. Harris (USA)	Grob G102	California, USA	17 Feb 1986
(British)	11 500 m *37 729 ft*	H. C. Nicholas Goodhart	Schweitzer 1-23	California, USA	12 May 1955
HEIGHT GAIN	12 849 m *42 303 ft*	Paul Bikle (USA)	Schweitzer SGS1-23E	Mojave, California, USA	25 Feb 1961
(British)	10 065 m *33 022 ft*	David Benton	Nimbus 2	Portmoak, Scotland	18 Apr 1980

SPEED OVER TRIANGULAR COURSE

DISTANCE	KM/H	*MPH*	NAME	TYPE OF GLIDER	LOCATION	DATE
100 km	195·3	*121·35*	Ingo Renner (Australia)	Nimbus 3	Australia	14 Dec 1982
(British)	143·3	*88·99*	E. Paul Hodge	Standard Cirrus	Rhodesia	30 Oct 1976
300 km	169·49	*105·32*	Jean-Paul Castel (France)	Nimbus 3	South Africa	15 Nov 1986
(British)	146·8	*91·2*	Edward Pearson	Nimbus 3	S. W. Africa	30 Nov 1976
500 km	170·06	*105·67*	Beat Bunzli (Switzerland)	Nimbus 3	South Africa	18 Dec 1987
(British)	141·3	*87·8*	Bradley James Grant Pearson	ASW-20	South Africa	28 Dec 1982
750 km	158·40	*98·43*	Hans-Werner Grosse (West Germany)	ASW-22	Australia	8 Jan 1985
(British)	109·8	*68·2*	Michael R. Carlton	Kestrel 19	South Africa	5 Jan 1975
1000 km	145·32	*90·29*	Hans-Werner Grosse (West Germany)	ASW-17	Australia	3 Jan 1979
(British)	112·15	*69·68*	George Lee	ASW 20	Australia	25 Jan 1989
1250 km	133·24	*82·79*	Hans-Werner Grosse (West Germany)	ASW-17	Australia	9 Jan 1980
(British)	109·01	*67·73*	Robert L. Robertson	Ventus A	USA	2 May 1986

Highest shot, on Earth
Timothy J. Ayers played a shot from the summit of McKinley (6194 m *20 320 ft*), Alaska, USA on 23 May 1984.

Golf ball balancing
Lang Martin balanced seven golf balls vertically without adhesive at Charlotte, North Carolina, USA on 9 Feb 1980.

Biggest bunker
The world's biggest bunker (called a trap in the USA) is Hell's Half Acre on the 535 m *585 yd* seventh hole of the Pine Valley course, Clementon, New Jersey, USA, built in 1912 and generally regarded as the world's most trying course.

MEN Greatest distance in straight line and declared goal distance: 488·19 km *303·36 miles* Larry Tudor (USA), Wills Wing Hobbs Airpark, New Mexico to Elkhart, Kansas, 3 Jul 1990.

Height gain: 4343·4 m *14 250 ft* Larry Tudor (USA), Owens Valley, California, 4 Aug 1985.

Out and return distance: 310·302 km *192·818 miles* Larry Tudor (USA) and Geoffrey Loyns (GB), Owens Valley, 26 Jun 1988.

Triangular course distance: 168 km *104·4 miles* Hans Ulrich Bluimenthal, Markus Hangstangl and Sepp Singhammer (all West Germany), St. André-les-Alps, France, 9 Aug 1990.

WOMEN
Greatest distance: 291·31 km *181·02 miles* Kari Castle (USA), Hobbs Airpark, 1 Jul 1990.

Height gain: 3352 m *10 997 ft* Tover Buas-Hansen (Norway) and Keven Klinefelder (USA), Owens Valley, 6 Jul 1989.

Out and return distance: 292·83 km *181·48 miles* Kari Castle (USA), Hobbs Airpark, 3 Jul 1990. 131·96 km *81·99 miles* Tover Buas-Hansen, Owens Valley, 6 Jul 1989.

Declared goal distance: 212·50 km *132·04 miles* Liavan Mallin (Ireland), Owens Valley, 13 Jul 1989.

Triangular course distance: Jenney Ganderton (Australia), 106·7 km *66·3 miles*, Forbes, Australia, 23 Jan 1990.

BRITISH RECORDS The British record for distance is held by Geoffrey Loyns, 312·864 km *194·41 miles*, in Flagstaff, Arizona, USA on 11 Jun 1988.

The best in Britain is 244 km *151·62 miles* by Gordon Rigg from Lords Seat to Witham Friary, Somerset on 4 Jun 1989.

The British height gain record is 4145·33 m *13 600 ft* by Colin Rider at Wether Fell, N Yorks on 4 Jul 1987.

Greatest descent
John Bird piloted a hang glider from a height of 39 000 ft *11 887·2 m* when he was released from a hot-air balloon, to the ground, landing in Edmonton, Alberta, Canada on 29 Aug 1982. He touched down 80·4 km *50 miles* from his point of departure.

Golf

Origins Although a stained glass window in Gloucester Cathedral, dating from 1350, portrays a golfer-like figure, the earliest mention of golf occurs in a prohibiting law passed by the Scottish Parliament in March 1457 under which 'goff be utterly cryit doune and not usit'. The Romans had a cognate game called *paganica* which may have been carried to Britain before AD 400. The Chinese Nationalist Golf Association claims the game is of Chinese origin (*Ch'ui Wan* – the ball hitting game) in the 3rd or 2nd century BC. There were official ordinances prohibiting a ball game with clubs in Belgium and Holland from 1360. Gutta percha balls succeeded feather balls in 1848 and by 1902 were in turn succeeded by rubber-cored balls, invented in 1899 by Coburn Haskell (USA). Steel shafts were authorized in the USA in 1925 and in Britain in 1929.

Oldest club The oldest club of which there is written evidence is the Gentlemen Golfers (now the Honourable Company of Edinburgh Golfers) formed in March 1744 – ten years prior to the institution of the Royal and Ancient Club of St Andrews, Fife. However, the Royal Burgess Golfing Society of Edinburgh claims to have been founded in 1735.

Highest course The Tuctu Golf Club in Morococha, Peru, is 4369 m *14 335 ft* above sea level at its lowest point. Golf has, however, been played in Tibet at an altitude of over 4875 m *16 000 ft*.

Great Britain The nine hole course at Leadhills, Strathclyde is 457 m *1500 ft* above sea level.

Longest hole The longest hole in the world is the 7th hole (par-7) of the Sano Course, Satsuki GC, Japan, which measures 831 m *909 yd*.

The longest hole on a championship course in Great Britain is the sixth at Troon, Strathclyde, which stretches 528 m *577 yd*.

Largest green Probably the largest green in the world is that of the par-6 635 m *695 yd* fifth hole at International GC, Bolton, Massachusetts, USA, with an area greater than 2600 m² *28 000 ft²*.

Longest course The world's longest course is the par-77 7612 m *8325 yd* International GC (see also above) from the 'Tiger' tees, remodelled in 1969 by Robert Trent Jones.

Floyd Satterlee Rood used the United States as a course, when he played from the Pacific surf to the Atlantic surf from 14 Sep 1963 to 3 Oct 1964 in 114 737 strokes. He lost 3511 balls on the 5468 km *3397·7 mile* trail.

Longest drives In officially regulated long driving contests over level ground the greatest distance recorded is 400 m *437 yd 2 ft 4 in* by Jack L. Hamm (USA), at an altitude of 1609 m *5280 ft*, at Denver, Colorado, USA on 25 Oct 1989. The longest recorded drive at sea level is 375 m *411 yd* by Cary B. Schuman (USA) at the Navy Marine Golf Course, Oahu, Hawaii, USA on 7 May 1989.

On an airport runway Kelly Murray (Canada) drove a Wilson Ultra 432 ball 626·2 m *684·8 yd* at Fairmont Hot Springs, British Columbia, Canada on 25 Sep 1990.

The women's record is held by Helen Dobson (GB) who drove a Titleist Pinnacle 469·1 m *531 yd* at RAF Honnington, Suffolk on 31 Oct 1987.

The greatest recorded drive on an ordinary course is one of 471 m *515 yd* by Michael Hoke Austin (b. 17 Feb 1910) of Los Angeles, California, USA, in the US National Seniors Open Championship at Las Vegas, Nevada on 25 Sep 1974. Austin, 1·88 m *6 ft 2 in* tall and weighing 92 kg *210 lb* drove the ball to within a yard of the green on the par-4 412 m *450 yd* fifth hole of the Winterwood Course and it rolled 59 m *65 yd* past the flagstick. He was aided by an estimated 56 km/h *35 mph* tailwind.

A drive of 2414 m *2640 yd (1½ miles)* across ice was achieved by an Australian meteorologist named Nils Lied at Mawson Base, Antarctica in 1962.

MOST TITLES *World's major golf championships:*

Championship	Player		Titles	Years
The Open	Harry Vardon (1870–1937)		6	1896, 1898–9, 1903, 11, 14
The Amateur	John Ball (1861–1940)		8	1888, 90, 92, 94, 99, 1907, 1910, 12
US Open	Willie Anderson (1880–1910)		4	1901, 03–05
	Robert Tyre Jones Jr (1902–71)		4	1923, 26, 29–30
	William Ben Hogan (b. 13 Aug 1912)		4	1948, 50–51, 53
	Jack William Nicklaus (b. 21 Jan 1940)		4	1962, 67, 72, 80
US Amateur	Robert Tyre Jones Jr (1902–71)		5	1924–25, 27–8, 30
US PGA	Walter Charles Hagan (1892–1969)		5	1921, 24–7
	Jack William Nicklaus		5	1963, 71, 73, 75, 80
US Masters	Jack William Nicklaus		6	1963, 65–6, 72, 75, 86
US Women's	Elizabeth 'Betsy' Earle-Rawls (b. 4 May 1928)		4	1951, 53, 57, 60
Open	'Mickey' Wright (b. 14 Feb 1935)		4	1958–59, 61, 64
US Women's Amateur	Glenna C. Vare (*née* Collett) (b. 20 Jun 1903)		6	1922, 25, 28–30, 35
British Women's	Charlotte Cecilia Pitcairn Leitch (1891–1977)		4	1914, 20–21, 26
	Joyce Wethered (b. 17 Nov 1901) (Now Lady Heathcoat-Amory)		4	1922, 24–5, 29

Note: Nicklaus is the only golfer to have won 5 different major titles (The Open, US Open, Masters, PGA and US Amateur titles) twice and a record 20 all told (1959–86). In 1930 Bobby Jones achieved a unique 'Grand Slam' of the US and British Open and Amateur titles.

Arthur Lynskey claimed a drive of 182 m *200 yd* horizontal and 3200 m *2 miles* vertical off Pikes Peak, Colorado (4300 m *14 110 ft*) on 28 Jun 1968.

On the Moon the energy expended on a mundane 274 m *300 yd* drive would achieve, craters permitting, a distance of 1·6 km *1 mile*.

Longest putt The longest recorded holed putt in a major tournament was one of 26 m *86 ft* on the vast 13th green at the Augusta National, Georgia by Cary Middlecoff (USA) (b. 6 Jan 1921) in the 1955 Masters' Tournament.

Robert Tyre 'Bobby' Jones Jr, (1902–71) was reputed to have holed a putt in excess of 30 m *100 ft* at the fifth green in the first round of the 1927 Open at St Andrews.

Bob Cook (USA) sank a putt measured at 42·74 m *140 ft 2¾ in* on the 18th at St Andrews in the International Fourball Pro Am Tournament on 1 Oct 1976.

SCORES

Lowest 9 holes Nine holes in 25 (4, 3, 3, 2, 3, 3, 1, 4, 2) was recorded by A. J. 'Bill' Burke in a round in 57 (32 + 25) on the 5842 m *6389 yd* par-71 Normandie course at St Louis, Missouri, USA on 20 May 1970.

The tournament record is 27 by Mike Souchak (USA) (b. 10 May 1927) for the second nine (par-35), first round of the 1955 Texas Open (see 72 holes); Andy North (USA) (b. 9 Mar 1950) second nine (par-34), first round, 1975 BC Open at En-Joie GC, Endicott, New York; José Maria Canizares (Spain) (b. 18 Feb 1947), first nine, third round, in the 1978 Swiss Open on the 6228 m *6811 yd* Crans GC, Crans-sur-Seine; and Robert Lee (GB) (b. 12 Oct 1961) first nine, first round, in the Monte Carlo Open on the 5714 m *6249 yd* Mont Agel course on 28 Jun 1985.

Lowest 18 holes *Men* At least four players have played a long course (over 6000 m *6561 yd*) in a score of 58, most recently Monte Carlo Money (USA) (b. 3 Dec 1954), the par-72, 6041 m *6607 yd* Las Vegas Municipal GC, Nevada, USA on 11 Mar 1981.

Alfred Edward Smith (1903–85) achieved an 18-hole score of 55 (15 under par 70) on his home course of 3884 m *4248 yd* on 1 Jan 1936, scoring 4, 2, 3, 3, 4, 2, 4, 3, 4, 3 = 29 out, and 2, 3, 3, 3, 3, 2, 5, 4, 1 = 26 in.

The United States PGA Tournament record for 18 holes is 59 (30 + 29) by Al Geiberger (b. 1 Sep 1937) in the second round of the Danny Thomas Classic, on the 72-par 6628 m *7249 yd* Colonial GC course, Memphis, Tennessee on 10 Jun 1977.

Other golfers to have recorded 59 over 18 holes in major non-PGA tournaments include: Samuel Jackson 'Sam' Snead (b. 27 May 1912) in the third round of the Sam Snead Festival at White Sulphur Springs, West Virginia, USA on 16 May 1959; Gary Player (South Africa) (b. 1 Nov 1935) in the second round of the Brazilian Open in Rio de Janeiro on 29 Nov 1974; David Jagger (GB) (b. 9 Jun 1949) in a Pro-Am tournament prior to the 1973 Nigerian Open at Ikoyi GC, Lagos; and Miguel Martin (Spain) in the Argentine Southern Championship at Mar de Plata on 27 Feb 1987.

Women The lowest recorded score on an 18-hole course (over 5120 m *5600 yd*) for a woman is 62 (30 + 32) by Mary 'Mickey' Kathryn Wright (USA) (b. 14 Feb 1935) on the Hogan Park Course (par-71, 5747 m *6286 yd*) at Midland, Texas, USA, in November 1964, and by Janice Arnold (New Zealand) (31 + 31) at Coventry GC (5317 m *5815 yd*) on 24 Sep 1990.

Wanda Morgan (b. 22 Mar 1910) recorded a score of 60 (31 + 29) on the Westgate and Birchington GC course, Kent, over 18 holes (4573 m *5002 yd*) on 11 Jul 1929.

Great Britain The lowest score recorded in a first-class professional tournament on a course of more than 5486 m *6000 yd* in Great Britain is 61 (29 + 32), by Thomas Bruce Haliburton (1915–75) of Wentworth GC in the Spalding Tournament at Worthing, W Sussex in June 1952, and 61 (32 + 29) by Peter J. Butler (b. 25 Mar 1932) in the Bowmaker Tournament at Sunningdale, Berks on 4 Jul 1967.

Lowest 36 holes The record for 36 holes is 122 (59 + 63) by Sam Snead in the 1959 Sam Snead Festival on 16–17 May 1959.

Horton Smith (1908–63), twice US Masters Champion, scored 121 (63 + 58) on a short course on 21 Dec 1928 (see 72 holes).

The lowest score by a British golfer has been 124 (61 + 63) by Alexander Walter Barr 'Sandy' Lyle (b. 9 Feb 1958) in the Nigerian Open at the 5508 m *6024 yd* (par-71) Ikoyi GC, Lagos in 1978.

Lowest 72 holes The lowest recorded score on a first-class course is 255 (29 under par) by Leonard Peter Tupling (GB) (b. 6 Apr 1950) in the Nigerian Open at Ikoyi GC, Lagos in February 1981, made up of 63, 66, 62 and 64 (average 63·75 per round).

The lowest 72 holes in a US professional event is 257 (60, 68, 64, 65) by Mike Souchak in the 1955 Texas Open at San Antonio.

The 72 holes record on the European tour is 258 (64, 69, 60, 65) by David Llewellyn (b. 18 Nov 1951) in the Biarritz Open on 1–3 Apr 1988. This was equalled by Ian Woosnam (Wales) (b. 2 Mar 1958) (66, 67, 65, 60) in the Monte Carlo Open on 4–7 Jul 1990.

The lowest 72 holes in an open championship in Europe is 262 (67, 66, 66, 63) by Percy Alliss (GB) (1897–1975) in the 1932 Italian Open at San Remo, and by Lu Liang Huan (Taiwan) (b. 10 Dec 1935) in the 1971 French Open at Biarritz.

Kelvin D. G. Nagle (b. 21 Dec 1920) of Australia shot 261 in the Hong Kong Open in 1961.

The lowest for four rounds in a British first-class tournament is 262 (66, 63, 66 and 67) by Bernard Hunt in the Piccadilly Tournament on the par-68 5655 m *6184 yd* Wentworth East course, Virginia Water, Surrey on 4–5 Oct 1966.

Trish Johnson scored 242 (64, 60, 60, 58) (21 under par) in the Bloor Homes Eastleigh Classic at the Fleming Park Course (4025 m *4402 yd*) at Eastleigh, Hants on 22–25 Jul 1987.

Horton Smith scored 245 (63, 58, 61 and 63) for 72 holes on the 4297 m *4700 yd* course (par-64) at Catalina Country Club, California, USA, to win the Catalina Open on 21–23 Dec 1928.

Highest score It is recorded that Chevalier von Cittern went round 18 holes in 316, averaging 17·55 per hole, at Biarritz, France in 1888.

Steven Ward took 222 strokes for the 5680 m *6212 yd* Pecos course, Reeves County, Texas, USA on 18 Jun 1976, but he was aged only 3 years 286 days.

Hans Merell of Mogadore, Ohio took 19 strokes on the par-3 16th (203 m *222 yd*) during the third round of the Bing Crosby National Tournament at Cypress Point Club, Del Monte, California, USA on 17 Jan 1959.

Fastest rounds *Individual* With such variations in lengths of courses, speed records, even for rounds under par, are of little comparative value. The fastest round played when the golf ball comes to rest before each new stroke is 27 min 9 sec by James Carvill (b. 13 Oct 1965) at Warrenpoint Golf Course, Co. Down (18 holes, 5628 m *6154 yd*) on 18 Jun 1987.

Team Forty-eight players completed the 18-hole 6500 m *7108 yd* Kyalami course, near Johannesburg, South Africa in 9 min 51 sec on 23 Feb 1988 using only one ball. They scored 73!

Slowest rounds The slowest stroke-play tournament round was one of 6 hr 45 min taken by South Africa in the first round of the 1972 World Cup at the Royal Melbourne GC, Australia. This was a four-ball medal round; everything holed out.

Most holes in 24 hours *On foot* Ian Colston, 35, played 22 rounds and five holes (401 holes) at Bendigo GC, Victoria, Australia (par-73, 5542 m *6061 yd*) on 27–28 Nov 1971.

The British record is 360 holes by Antony J.

Most shots for one hole

A woman player in the qualifying round of the Shawnee Invitational for Ladies at Shawnee-on-Delaware, Pennsylvania, USA, *c.* 1912, took 166 strokes for the short 118 m *130 yd* 16th hole. Her tee shot went into the Binniekill River and the ball floated. She put out in a boat with her exemplary but statistically-minded husband at the oars. She eventually beached the ball 2·4 km *1½ miles* downstream but was not yet out of the wood. She had to play through one on the home run.

In a competition at Peacehaven, E Sussex in 1890, A. J. Lewis had 156 putts on one green without holing out.

The highest score for a single hole in the British Open is 21 by a player in the inaugural meeting at Prestwick in 1860.

Double figures have been recorded on the card of the winner only once, when Willie Fernie (1851–1924) scored a ten at Musselburgh, Lothian in 1883.

Ray Ainsley of Ojai, California, took 19 strokes for the par-4 16th hole during the second round of the US Open at Cherry Hills Country Club, Denver, Colorado on 10 Jun 1938. Most of the strokes were used in trying to extricate the ball from a brook.

World one-club record

Thad Daber (USA), with a 6-iron, played the 5520 m *6037 yd* Lochmore GC, Cary, North Carolina, USA in 70 to win the 1987 World One-club Championship.

Golf Majors

Ben Hogan (9)
Gary Player (9)
Walter Hagen (11)
Tom Watson (8)
Jack Nicklaus (total wins: 18)
Harry Vardon (7)
Arnold Palmer (7)
Bobby Jones (7)
Sam Snead (7)
Gene Sarazen (7)

Key   British Open   US Open   US PGA   US Masters

■ Most majors

These ten great golfers have won seven or more 'Majors' — US Masters, The Open, US Open, US PGA — and, as the feature shows, the greatest of these is Jack Nicklaus. He is the only golfer to have won each of these titles twice and he holds the record for the lowest four round total in both the US Masters and US Open.

Throwing the golf ball

The lowest recorded score for throwing a golf ball round 18 holes (over 5500 m *6000 yd*) is 82 by Joe Flynn (USA), 21, at the 5694 m *6228 yd* Port Royal course, Bermuda on 27 Mar 1975.

Most balls hit in one hour

The most balls driven in one hour, over 100 yds and into a target area, is 1536 by Noel Hunt at Shrigley Hall, Pott Shrigley, Cheshire on 2 May 1990.

Clark at Childwall GC, Liverpool on 18 Jul 1983.

David Brett of Stockport played 218 holes in 12 hours at Didsbury GC, Greater Manchester (par-70, 5696 m *6230 yd*) on 22 Jun 1990.

Using golf carts Charles Stock played 783 holes at Boston Hills GC, Hudson, Ohio, USA (9 holes, 2844 m *3110 yd*) on 20 Jul 1987.

Terry Zachary played 391 holes in 12 hours on the 6132 m *6706 yd* course at Connaught GC, Alberta, Canada on 16 Jun 1986.

Most holes played in a week Steve Hylton played 1128 holes at the Mason Rudolph GC (5541m *6060 yd*), Clarkesville, Tennessee, USA from 25–31 Aug 1980. Using a buggy for transport, Colin Young completed 1260 holes at Patshull Park GC (5863 m *6412 yd*), Pattingham, Shropshire from 2–9 Jul 1988.

CHAMPIONSHIP RECORDS

The Open (inaugurated 1860, Prestwick, Strathclyde) *First nine holes* 28 by Denis Durnian (b. 30 Jun 1950), at Royal Birkdale, Southport, Merseyside in the second round on 15 Jul 1983.

Any round 63 by: Mark Stephen Hayes (USA) (b. 12 Jul 1949) at Turnberry, Strathclyde on 7 Jul 1977; Isao Aoki (Japan) (b. 31 Aug 1942) at Muirfield, Lothian on 19 Jul 1980; Gregory John Norman (Australia) (b. 10 Feb 1955) at Turnberry on 18 Jul 1986; and Paul Broadhurst (GB) (b. 14 Aug 1965) at St Andrews, Fife on 21 Jul 1990.

First 36 holes Thomas Henry Cotton (1907–1987) at Royal St George's, Sandwich, Kent completed the first 36 holes in 132 (67+65) on 27 Jun 1934. This was equalled by Nicholas Alexander 'Nick' Faldo (GB) (b. 18 Jul 1957) (67, 65) and Greg Norman (Australia) (66, 66) at St Andrews on 19–20 Jul 1990. Faldo added a third round of 67 for a 54 holes record, 199.

Total aggregate 268 (68, 70, 65, 65) by Thomas Sturges Watson (USA) (b. 4 Sep 1949) at Turnberry in July 1977.

US Open (inaugurated in 1895) *Any round* 63 by: Johnny Miller (b. 29 Apr 1947) on the 6328 m *6921 yd* par-71 Oakmont Country Club course, Pennsylvania on 17 Jun 1973; by Jack Nicklaus and Tom Weiskopf (USA) (b. 9 Nov 1942) at Bal-

---

tusrol Country Club, Springfield, New Jersey, both on 12 Jun 1980.

First 36 holes 134 by: Jack Nicklaus (63, 71) at Baltusrol on 12–13 Jun 1980; and Tze-Chung Chen (Taiwan) (65, 69) at Oakland Hills, Birmingham, Michigan in 1985.

Total aggregate 272 (63, 71, 70, 68) by Jack Nicklaus (b. 21 Jan 1940) on the lower course (6414 m *7015 yd*) at Baltusrol Country Club, 12–15 Jun 1980.

US Masters (played on the 6382 m *6980 yd* Augusta National Golf Course, Georgia, first in 1934) *Any round* 63 by Nicholas Raymond Leige Price (Zimbabwe) (b. 28 Jan 1957) in 1986.

First 36 holes 131 (65, 66) by Raymond Loran Floyd (b. 4 Sep 1942) in 1976.

Total aggregate 271 by: Jack Nicklaus (67, 71, 64, 69) in 1965 and Raymond Floyd (65, 66, 70, 70) in 1976.

TEAM COMPETITONS

World Cup (formerly Canada Cup) The World Cup (instituted as the Canada Cup in 1953) has been won most often by the USA with 17 victories between 1955 and 1988.

The only men to have been on six winning teams have been Arnold Palmer (b. 10 Sep 1929) (1960, 1962–4, 1966–7) and Jack Nicklaus (1963–4, 1966–7, 1971 and 1973). Only Nicklaus has taken the individual title three times (1963–4, 1971).

The lowest aggregate score for 144 holes is 544 by Australia, Bruce Devlin (b. 10 Oct 1937) and Anthony David Graham (b. 23 May 1946), at San Isidro, Buenos Aires, Argentina from 12–15 Nov 1970.

The lowest individual score has been 269 by Roberto de Vicenzo (Argentina) (b. 14 Apr 1923), also in 1970.

Ryder Cup The biennial Ryder Cup professional match between the USA and Europe (British Isles or Great Britain prior to 1979) was instituted in 1927.

The USA have won 21 to 5 (with 2 draws) to 1989.

Arnold Palmer has the record of winning most Ryder Cup matches with 22 from 32 played, with two halved and 8 lost.

Christy O'Connor Sr (Ireland) (b. 21 Dec 1924) played in ten contests, 1955–73.

Walker Cup The series was instituted in 1921 (for the Walker Cup since 1922 and now held biennially).

The USA have won 28, Great Britain & Ireland 3 (in 1938, 1971 and 1989) and the 1965 match was tied.

Jay Sigel (USA) (b. 13 Nov 1943) has won a record 14 matches, with five halved and eight lost, 1977–89. Joseph Boynton Carr (GB&I) (b. 18 Feb 1922) played in ten contests, 1947–67.

Curtis Cup The biennial ladies' Curtis Cup match between the USA and Great Britain and Ireland was first held in 1932.

The USA have won 20 to 1990, GB & I four (1952, 1956, 1986 and 1988) and two matches have been tied.

Mary McKenna (GB & I) (b. 29 Apr 1949) played in a record ninth match in 1986, when for the first time she was on the winning team.

INDIVIDUAL RECORDS

Richest prize The greatest first place

GOLF

prize money ever won is $1 000 000 awarded annually from 1987 to 1990 to the winners of the Sun City Challenge, Bophuthatswana, South Africa; Ian Woosnam (Wales) was the first winner.

The greatest total prize money is $2 500 000 (including $450 000 first prize) for the Nabisco Championship of Golf at Hilton Head Island, South Carolina, USA on 26–29 Oct 1989.

Highest earnings *US PGA and LPGA circuits* The all-time professional money-winner is Tom Kite (USA) (b. 9 Dec 1949) with $6 689 127, to May 1991. He also holds the earnings record for a year on the US PGA circuit, $1 395 278 in 1989.

The record career earnings for a woman is by Pat Bradley (b. 24 Mar 1951) with $3 629 130 to 20 Jun 1991. The season's record is $863 578 by Beth Daniel in 1990.

European circuit Ian Woosnam (Wales) won a season's record £574 166 in European Order of Merit tournaments in 1990. The tour career earnings record is £2 126 096 by Severiano Ballesteros (Spain) at the end of 1990.

In all events world-wide in 1987 Ian Woosnam won £1 042 662.76.

Most tournament wins John Byron Nelson (USA) (b. 4 Feb 1912) won a record 18 tournaments (plus one unofficial) in one year, including a record 11 consecutively from 8 Mar to 4 Aug 1945.

Sam Snead from turning professional in 1934 won 84 official US PGA tour events, 1936–65.

The ladies' PGA record is 88 by Kathy Whitworth (b. 27 Sep 1939) from 1962 to 1985.

Biggest winning margin The greatest margin of victory in a major tournament is 21 strokes by Jerry Pate (USA) (b. 16 Sep 1953), who won the Colombian Open with 262 from 10–13 Dec 1981.

Cecilia Leitch won the Canadian Ladies' Open Championship in 1921 by the biggest margin for a major title, 17 up and 15 to play.

Youngest and oldest champions The youngest winner of The Open was Tom Morris Jr (1851–75) at Prestwick, Strathclyde in 1868 aged 17 yr 249 days.

The oldest Open champion was 'Old Tom' Morris (1821–1908), aged 46 yr 99 days when he won at Prestwick in 1867. Oldest this century has been the 1967 champion, Roberto de Vicenzo, at 44 yr 93 days.

The oldest US Open champion was Raymond Floyd (b. 4 Sep 1942) at 43 yr 284 days on 15 Jun 1986.

Youngest and oldest national champions Thuashni Selvaratnam (b. 9 Jun 1976) won the 1989 Sri Lankan Ladies Amateur Open Golf Championship, aged 12 yr 324 days, at Nuwara Eliya GC on 29 Apr 1989. Angela Uzelli (b. 1 Feb 1940) won the English Women's Championship, aged 50 yr 114 days, at Rye, E Sussex on 26 May 1990.

Most club championships Marjorie Edey (1913–81) was ladies champion at Charleswood GC, Winnipeg, Manitoba, Canada 36 times between 1937 and 1980.

The men's record is 34 by Bernard Charles Cusack (b. 24 Jan 1920), including 33 consecutively, at the Narembeen GC, Western Australia, between 1943 and 1982.

At different clubs, Peter Toogood (Australia) (b. 11 Apr 1930) has won 35 cham-

pionships: 2 at Huntingdale GC, Victoria, 5 at Riverside GC, 9 at Kingston Beach GC and 19 at Royal Hobart GC, all Tasmania.

The British record is 35 by Helen Gray at Todmorden GC, Lancs between 1952 and 1989.

Patricia Shepherd (b. 7 Jan 1940) won 30 consecutive championships at Turriff GC, Grampian, 1959–88.

HOLES IN ONE

Longest The longest straight hole ever holed in one shot was, appropriately, the tenth (408 m *447 yd*) at Miracle Hills GC, Omaha, Nebraska, USA by Robert Mitera (b. 1944) on 7 Oct 1965. Mitera stood 1·68 m *5 ft 6 in* tall and weighed 75 kg *165 lb* (11 st 11 lb). He was a two handicap player who normally drove 224 m *245 yd*. A 80 km/h *50 mph* gust carried his shot over a 265 m *290 yd* drop-off.

The longest 'dog-leg' hole achieved in one is the 439 m *480 yd* fifth at Hope Country Club, Arkansas, USA by L. Bruce on 15 Nov 1962.

The women's record is 359 m *393 yd* by Marie Robie on the first hole of the Furnace Brook GC, Wollaston, Massachusetts, USA on 4 Sep 1949.

The longest hole in one performed in the British Isles is the seventh (par-4, 359 m *393 yd*) at West Lancashire GC by Peter Richard Parkinson (b. 26 Aug 1947) on 6 Jun 1972.

Consecutive There are at least 18 cases of 'aces' being achieved in two consecutive holes, of which the greatest was Norman L. Manley's unique 'double albatross' on the par-4 301 m *330 yd* seventh and par-4 265 m *290 yd* eighth holes on the Del Valle Country Club course, Saugus, California, USA on 2 Sep 1964.

The first woman to record consecutive 'aces' was Sue Prell, on the 13th and 14th holes at Chatswood GC, Sydney, Australia on 29 May 1977.

The closest to achieving three consecutive holes in one were Dr Joseph Boydstone on the 3rd, 4th and 9th at Bakersfield GC,

California, USA, on 10 Oct 1962 and Rev. Harold Snider (b. 4 Jul 1900) who aced the 8th, 13th and 14th holes of the par-3 Ironwood course, Arizona, USA on 9 Jun 1976.

Youngest and oldest The youngest golfer recorded to have shot a hole-in-one is Coby Orr (5 years) of Littleton, Colorado on the 94 m *103 yd* fifth at the Riverside Golf Course, San Antonio, Texas, USA in 1975.

The British record was set by Mark Alexander, aged 6 yr 251 days, on the 99 m *109 yd* sixth at the Chessington Golf Centre, Greater London on 17 Sep 1989. The youngest girl to score an ace is Nicola Hammond, aged 10 yr 204 days on the 98 m *107 yd* third at Dereham GC, Norfolk on 17 June 1990.

The oldest golfers to have performed this feat are: (men) 99 yr 244 days Otto Bucher (Switzerland) (b. 12 May 1885) on the 100 m *130 yd* 12th at La Manga GC, Spain on 13 Jan 1985; (women) 95 yr 257 days Erna Ross (b. 9 Sep 1890) on the 102 m *112 yd* 17th at The Everglades Club, Palm Beach, Florida, USA on 23 Apr 1986.

The British records: (men) 92 yr 169 days Samuel Richard Walker (b. 6 Jan 1892) at the 143 m *156 yd* 8th at West Hove GC, E Sussex on 23 Jun 1984; (women) 90 yr 236 days Dorothy Huntley-Flindt (b. 19 Jun 1898) at the 102 m *112 yd* 13th at Barton-on-Sea GC, Hants on 10 Feb 1989.

The oldest player to score his age is C. Arthur Thompson (1869–1975) of Victoria, British Columbia, Canada, who scored 103 on the Uplands course of 5682 m *6215 yd* in 1973.

Greyhound Racing

Origins The first greyhound meeting was staged at Hendon, north London with a railed hare operated by a windlass, in September 1876. Modern greyhound racing originated with the perfecting of the mechanical hare by Owen Patrick Smith at Emeryville, California, USA, in 1919. St

Largest tournament The Volkswagen Grand Prix Open Amateur Championship in the United Kingdom attracted a record 321 238 (206 820 men and 114 958 women) competitors in 1984.

■ **Highest earnings** *Ian Woosnam (Wales) won a season's record £574 166 in European Order of Merit tournaments in 1990. Early in 1991 he became the world's number one and confirmed his position by immediately winning his first major, the US Masters. (Photo: All-Sport/S. Munday)*

THE WORLD

265

GYMNASTICS

Topmost tipster
In greyhound racing, Mark Sullivan of the *Sporting Life* forecast all 12 winners at Wimbledon on 21 Dec 1990.

Longest odds
Apollo Prince won at odds of 250–1 at Sandown GRC, Springvale, Victoria, Australia on 14 Nov 1968.

Gymnastics/ Aerobics display
The now discontinued Czechoslovak Spartakiad featured gymnastics displays by about 180 000 participants. Held at the Strahov Stadium, Prague until 1989, there were 200 000 spectators for each of the four days. On the six hectare infield there were markers for 13 824 gymnasts at a time.

Club swinging
Albert Rayner set a world record of 17 512 revolutions (4·9 per sec) in 60 min at Wakefield, W Yorks on 27 Jul 1981.

Petersburg Kennel Club, located in St Petersburg, Florida, USA, which opened on 3 Jan 1925, is the oldest greyhound track in the world still in operation on its original site. The earliest greyhound race behind a mechanical hare in the British Isles was at Belle Vue, Manchester on 24 Jul 1926.

Derby Two greyhounds have won the English Greyhound Derby (instituted 1927, now over 500 m *546 yd*) twice: *Mick the Miller* on 25 Jul 1929, when owned by Albert H. Williams, and on 28 Jun 1930 when owned by Mrs Arundel H. Kempton, and *Patricia's Hope* on 24 Jun 1972 when owned by Gordon and Basil Marks and Brian Stanley and 23 Jun 1973 when owned by G. & B. Marks and J. O'Connor.

The highest prize was £40 000 to *Slippy Blue* for the Derby on 23 Jun 1990.

The only greyhounds to win the English, Scottish and Welsh Derby 'triple' are *Trev's Perfection*, owned by Fred Trevillion, in 1947, *Mile Bush Pride*, owned by Noel W. Purvis, in 1959, and *Patricia's Hope* in 1972.

Grand National The only greyhound to have won the Grand National (instituted 1927 over 480 m *525 yd*, now 500 m *546 yd* and five flights) three times is *Sherry's Prince* (1967–78) owned by Mrs Joyce Mathews of Sanderstead, Surrey, in 1970–72.

Fastest greyhound The highest speed at which any greyhound has been timed is 67·14 km/h *41·72 mph* (374 m *410 yd* in 20·1 sec) by *The Shoe* on the then straight track at Richmond, New South Wales, Australia on 25 Apr 1968. It is estimated that he covered the last 91·44 m *100 yd* in 4·5 sec or at 73·14 km/h *45·45 mph*.

The highest speed recorded for a greyhound

in Great Britain is 62·97 km/h *39·13 mph* by *Beef Cutlet*, when covering a straight course of 457 m *500 yd* in 26·13 sec at Blackpool, Lancs, on 13 May 1933.

The fastest automatically timed speed recorded for a full four-bend race is 62·59 km/h *38·89 mph* at Brighton, E Sussex by *Glen Miner* on 4 May 1982 with a time of 29·62 sec for 515 m *563 yd*.

The fastest over hurdles is 60·58 km/h *37·64 mph* at Brighton by *Wotchit Buster* on 22 Aug 1978.

Most wins The most career wins is 143 by the American greyhound, *JR's Ripper* in 1982–6.

The most consecutive victories is 32 by *Ballyregan Bob*, owned by Cliff Kevern and trained by George Curtis from 25 Aug 1984 to 9 Dec 1986, including 16 track record times. His race wins were by an average of more than nine lengths.

Highest earnings The career earnings record is held by *Homespun Rowdy* with $297 000 in the USA, 1984–7.

The richest first prize for a greyhound race is $125 000 won by *Ben G Speedboat* in the Great Greyhound Race of Champions at Seabrook, New Hampshire, USA on 23 Aug 1986.

Gymnastics

Origins A primitive form of gymnastics was practised in ancient Greece and Rome during the period of the ancient Olympic Games (776 BC to AD 393) but Johann Friedrich Simon was the first teacher of modern gymnastics at Basedow's School, Dessau, Germany in 1776.

World Championships *Women* The greatest number of titles won in the World Championships (including Olympic Games) is 12 individual wins and five team by Larisa Semyonovna Latynina (b. 27 Dec 1934) of the USSR, between 1956 and 1964.

The USSR has won the team title on 19 occasions (ten world and nine Olympics).

Men Boris Anfiyanovich Shakhlin (USSR) (b. 27 Jan 1932) won ten individual titles between 1954 and 1964. He also had three team wins.

The USSR has won the team title a record eleven times (seven World Championships, four Olympics) between 1952 and 1989.

Youngest champions Aurelia Dobre (Romania) (b. 6 Nov 1972) won the women's overall world title at 14 yr 352 days on 23 Oct 1987. Daniela Silivas (Romania) revealed in 1990 that she was born on 9 May 1971, a year later than previously claimed, so that she was 14 yr 185 days when she won the gold medal for balance beam on 10 Nov 1985.

The youngest male world champion was Dmitriy Bilozerchev (USSR) (b. 17 Dec 1966) at 16 yr 315 days at Budapest, Hungary on 28 Oct 1983.

Olympics Japan (1960, 1964, 1968, 1972 and 1976) has won the men's team title most often. The USSR has won the women's title nine times (1952–80, 1988).

The most men's individual gold medals is six by: Boris Shakhlin (USSR), one in 1956, four (two shared) in 1960 and one in 1964; and Nikolay Yefimovich Andrianov (USSR) (b. 14 Oct 1952), one in 1972, four in 1976 and one in 1980.

Vera Caslavska-Odlozil (b. 3 May 1942) (Czechoslovakia) has won most individual

■ **Youngest champion**
Aurelia Dobre (Romania) (b. 6 Nov 1972) won the women's overall world title at 14 yr 352 days on 23 Oct 1987. Here she is seen in action on the balance beam for which she also won the individual title in 1987. (Photo: All-Sport (USA)/Martin)

gold medals with seven, three in 1964 and four (one shared) in 1968.

Larisa Latynina won six individual gold medals and was in three winning teams from 1956–64, making nine gold medals. She also won five silver and four bronze making 18 in all — an Olympic record.

The most medals for a male gymnast is 15 by Nikolay Andrianov (USSR), seven gold, five silver and three bronze from 1972–80.

Aleksandr Nikolayevich Dityatin (USSR) (b. 7 Aug 1957) is the only man to win a medal in all eight categories in the same Games, with three gold, four silver and one bronze at Moscow in 1980.

Highest score Nadia Comaneci (Romania) (b. 12 Nov 1961) was the first to achieve a perfect score (10·00) in the Olympics, and achieved seven in all at Montreal, Canada in July 1976.

British Championships The British Gymnastic Championship was won ten times by Arthur John Whitford (b. 2 Jul 1908) in 1928–36 and 1939. He was also in four winning teams. Wray 'Nik' Stuart (b. 20 Jul 1927) equalled the record of nine successive wins, 1956–64.

The women's record is eight by Mary Patricia Hirst (b. 18 Nov 1918) (1947, 1949–50 and 1952–6).

EXERCISES
SPEED AND STAMINA

Records are accepted for the most repetitions of the following activities within the given time span.

CHINS (CONSECUTIVE) 370 Lee Chin-yong (South Korea) (b. 15 Aug 1925) at Backyon Gymnasium, Seoul, South Korea on 14 May 1988.

CHINS ONE ARM (FROM A RING)—CONSE-CUTIVE 22 Robert Chisnall (b. 9 Dec 1952) at Queen's University, Kingston, Ontario, Canada on 3 Dec 1982. (Also 18 two-finger chins, 12 one-finger chins).

PARALLEL BAR DIPS—1 HOUR 3645 Simon Kent (GB) at Mablethorpe, Lincs on 29 Aug 1990.

PRESS-UPS (PUSH-UPS)—24 HOURS 37 350 Paddy Doyle (GB) at the Holiday Inn, Birmingham, W Mids on 1–2 May 1989.

PRESS-UPS (ONE ARM)—5 HOURS 7643 Paddy Doyle at the Albany Hotel, Birmingham, W Mids on 31 Jul 1990.

PRESS-UPS (FINGER TIP)—5 HOURS 6011 Vince Manson (GB) at HM Prison Albany, Newport, Isle of Wight on 25 Jul 1990.

PRESS-UPS (ONE FINGER)—CONSE-CUTIVE 100 Harry Lee Welch Jr at Durham, N. Carolina, USA on 31 Mar 1985.

SIT-UPS—24 HOURS 60 690 Louis Scripa Jr (USA) at Jack La Lanne's American Health & Fitness Spa, Sacramento, California, USA on 31 Aug–1 Sep 1990.

LEG RAISES—12 HOURS 41 788 Lou Scripa Jr at Jack La Lanne's American Health & Fitness Spa, Sacramento, California, USA on 2 Dec 1988.

SQUATS—1 HOUR 2550 Ashrita Furman (USA) at Philadelphia, Pennsylvania, USA on 3 Nov 1989.

SQUAT THRUSTS—1 HOUR 2998 Paul Wai Man Chung at the Chung Sze Kung Fu (HK) Association, Kowloon, Hong Kong on 14 Apr 1991.

BURPEES—1 HOUR 1551 Ashrita Furman at the Natural Physique Centre, New York, USA on 13 Mar 1990.

PUMMEL HORSE DOUBLE CIRCLES—CONSECUTIVE 75 by Lee Thomas (GB) on BBC television on 12 Dec 1985.

PRESS-UPS IN A YEAR Paddy Doyle achieved a documented 1 500 230 press-ups of which the 24-hour record was a part, from October 1988 to October 1989.

The most overall titles in Modern Rhythmic Gymnastics is by Sharon Taylor with five successive, 1977–81.

World Cup Gymnasts who have won two World Cup (instituted 1975) overall titles are three men: Nikolay Andrianov (USSR), Aleksandr Dityatin (USSR) and Li Ning (China) (b. 8 Sep 1963), and one woman: Marta Yevgenyevna Filatova (USSR) (b. 19 Jul 1961).

Youngest international Pasakevi 'Voula' Kouna (b. 6 Dec 1971) was aged 9 yr 299 days at the start of the Balkan Games at Serres, Greece on 1 Oct 1981, when she represented Greece.

Modern Rhythmic Gymnastics The most overall individual world titles in Modern Rhythmic Gymnastics is three by Maria Gigova (Bulgaria) in 1969, 1971 and 1973 (shared).

Bulgaria has a record eight team titles 1969, 1971, 1973, 1981, 1983, 1985, 1987 and 1989 (shared). Bianka Panova (Bulgaria) (b. 27 May 1960) won all four apparatus gold medals all with maximum scores, and won a team gold in 1987.

Marina Lobach (USSR) (b. 26 Jun 1970) won the 1988 Olympic title with perfect scores for all events.

Lilia Ignatova (Bulgaria) has won both the individual World Cup titles that have been held, 1983 and 1986.

Handball

Origins Handball was first played c. 1895 in Germany. It was introduced into the Olympic Games at Berlin in 1936 as an 11-a-side outdoor game, with Germany winning, but when re-introduced in 1972 it was an indoor game with seven-a-side, the standard team size since 1952.

The International Handball Federation was founded in 1946. The first international match was held at Halle/Saale on 3 Sep 1925, when Austria beat Germany 6–3.

Most championships Olympic The USSR has won four titles — men 1976 and 1988, women 1976 and 1980. Yugoslavia has also won two men's titles in, 1972 and 1984.

World Championships (instituted 1938) Romania has won four men's and three women's titles (two outdoor, one indoor) from 1956 to 1974. Three women's titles have also been won by the GDR 1971, 1975 and 1978 and the USSR 1982, 1986 and 1990.

European Champions' Cup Spartak of Kiev, USSR have won 13 women's titles between 1970 and 1988.

Vfl Gummersbach, West Germany have won a record five men's titles, 1967, 1970, 1971, 1974, 1983. They are also the only club team to win all three European trophies; European Champions' Cup, European Cup Winners' Cup and IHF Cup.

Highest score The highest score in an international match was recorded when the USSR beat Afghanistan 86–2 in the 'Friendly Army Tournament' at Miskolc, Hungary in August 1981.

Britain Most titles The most men's national championship titles is seven by Brentwood '72 (British Championship, 1974; English National League, 1979–83; British League, 1985).

The most women's titles is eight by Wakefield Metros (English National League, 1982–87; British League, 1988, 1990).

Highest score The highest score in a men's league match is by Glasgow University, who beat Claremont, 69–5 at Glasgow, Strathclyde in March 1984. The women's record match is Wakefield Metros 47–13 defeat of Ruislip Eagles at Featherstone, W Yorks on 25 Feb 1990.

Highest score by an individual Graham Hammond scored 29 for Wakefield (39) against Hull University (13) at Eccles Recreation Centre, in November 1990.

The women's record is 15 by Donna Hankinson (b. 24 Mar 1972) for Manchester United SSS (26) against Arcton (9) at Kirkby on 12 Nov 1989, Julie Wells (b. 9 Jan 1963) for Wakefield Metros (47) against Ruislip Eagles (13) at Featherstone, W Yorks on 25 Feb 1990, and Catherine Densmore for Halewood Town (23) against Ruislip Eagles (17) at Bristol, Avon on 25 May 1991.

Somersaults
Ashrita Furman performed 8341 forward rolls in 10 hr 30 min over 19·67 km *12 miles 390 yards* from Lexington to Charleston, Massachusetts, USA on 30 Apr 1986.

Shigeru Iwasaki (b. 1960) backwards somersaulted 50 m *54·68 yd* in 10·8 sec at Tokyo, Japan on 30 Mar 1980.

Static wall 'sit' (or Samson's Chair)
Paddy Doyle stayed in an unsupported sitting position against a wall for 4 hr 40 min at The Magnet Centre, Erdington, W Mids on 18 Apr 1990.

HARNESS RACING MILE RECORDS				
TROTTING		Horse (driver)	Place	Date
World	1:52·2	*Mack Lobell* (John Campbell)	Springfield, USA	21 Aug 1987
PACING				
World	1:48·4	*Matt's Scooter* (Michel Lachance)	Lexington, USA	23 Sep 1988
Race	1:49·6	*Nihilator* (William O'Donnell)	East Rutherford, USA	3 Aug 1985
	1:49·6	*Call For Rain* (Clint Albraith)	Lexington, USA	1 Oct 1988

Harness Racing

Origins Trotting races were held in Valkenburg, Netherlands in 1554. In England the trotting gait (the simultaneous use of the diagonally opposite legs) was known in the 16th century. The sulky first appeared in 1829. Pacers thrust out their fore and hind legs simultaneously on one side.

Most successful driver In North American harness racing history has been Herve Filion (b. 1 Feb 1940) of Québec, Canada, who had achieved 12 964 wins to 19 May 1991 including a record 814 wins in a year, 1989.

John D. Campbell (USA) (b. 8 Apr 1955) has the highest career earnings of $93 857 328 to 19 May 1991. This includes a year record of $11 622 778 in 1990 when he won 543 races.

Highest price For a pacer is $19·2 million for *Nihilator* who was syndicated by Wall Street Stable and Almahurst Stud Farm in 1984. The highest for a trotter is $6 million for *Mack Lobell* by John Erik Magnusson of Vislanda, Sweden in 1988.

Greatest winnings For any harness horse is $4 408 857 by the trotter *Ourasi* (France) (who won 32 races) to the end of 1990. The greatest amount won by a pacer is $3 225 653 by *Nihilator*, who won 35 of 38 races in 1984–5.

The single season records are $2 091 860 by pacer *Beach Towel* in 1990 and $1 878 798 by trotter *Mack Lobell* in 1987.

The largest ever purse was $2 161 000 for the Woodrow Wilson two-year-old race over 1 mile at the Meadowlands, New Jersey, USA on 16 Aug 1984. Of this sum a record $1 080 500 went to the winner *Nihilator*, driven by William O'Donnell (b. 4 May 1948).

Hockey

Origins A representation of two players with curved snagging sticks apparently in an orthodox 'bully' position was found in Tomb No. 17 at Beni Hasan, Egypt and has been dated to *c.* 2050 BC. There is a British reference to the game in Lincolnshire in 1277. The modern game evolved in south London in the 1860s.

An English Hockey Association was founded in 1875, but the current English men's governing body, the Hockey Association, was formed on 18 Jan 1886. The All-England Women's Hockey Association was founded in 1895.

The Fédération Internationale de Hockey was formed on 7 Jan 1924.

Most Olympic medals India was Olympic champion from the reintroduction of Olympic hockey in 1928 until 1960, when Pakistan beat them 1–0 at Rome. They had their eighth win in 1980. Of the seven Indians who have won three Olympic team gold medals, two have also won a silver medal — Leslie Walter Claudius (b. 25 Mar 1927), in 1948, 1952, 1956 and 1960 (silver), and Udham Singh (b. 4 Aug 1928), in 1952, 1956, 1964 and 1960 (silver).

A women's tournament was added in 1980, when Zimbabwe were the winners. The Netherlands won in 1984 and Australia in 1988.

World Cup The World Cup for men was first held in 1971, and for women in 1974. The most wins are, (men) three by Pakistan, 1971, 1978 and 1982; (women) five by the Netherlands, 1974, 1978, 1983, 1986 and 1990.

Champions' Trophy First held in 1978 and contested annually since 1980 by the top six men's teams in the world; the most wins is five, by Australia, 1983–5, 1989–90. The first women's Champions' Trophy was won by the Netherlands in 1987. South Korea won in 1989.

MEN

The first organized club was the Blackheath Rugby and Hockey Club founded in 1861. The oldest club with a continuous history is Teddington HC formed in the autumn of 1871. They played Richmond on 24 Oct 1874 and used the first recorded circle *versus* Surbiton at Bushey Park, London on 9 Dec 1876.

The first international match was the Wales *v.* Ireland match at Rhyl, Clwyd on 26 Jan 1895. Ireland won 3–0.

Highest international score The highest score was when India defeated the USA 24–1 at Los Angeles, California, USA in the 1932 Olympic Games.

The greatest number of goals in an international in Britain was when England defeated France 16–0 at Beckenham, Kent on 25 Mar 1922.

Most international appearances Heiner Dopp (b. 27 Jun 1956) represented West Germany 286 times between 1975 and 1990, indoors and out.

The most by a player from the British Isles is 228 by Richard Leman (b. 13 Jul 1959), 146 (106 outdoor, 52 indoor) for England and 70 for Great Britain, 1980–90. Harold David Judge (b. 19 Jan 1936) played a record 124 times for Ireland, 1957–78. The first player to achieve 100 international appearances for England was Norman Hughes (b. 30 Sep 1952) on 21 Sep 1986. The most indoor caps for England is 85 by Richard Clarke (b. 3 Apr 1952), 1976–87.

Greatest scoring feats The greatest number of goals scored in international hockey is 267 by Paul Litjens (Netherlands) (b. 9 Nov 1947) in 177 games.

M. C. Marckx (Bowden 2nd XI) scored 19 goals against Brooklands 2nd XI (score 23–0) on 31 Dec 1910. He was selected for England in March 1912 but declined due to business priorities. David Ashman has scored 1944 goals for Hampshire, Southampton, Southampton Kestrals and Hamble Old Boys (for whom he has scored 1785 goals a record for one club), 1958–91.

Fastest goal in an international John French scored 7 sec after the bully-off for England *v.* West Germany at Nottingham on 25 Apr 1971.

Greatest goalkeeping Richard James Allen (India) (b. 4 Jun 1902) did not concede a goal during the 1928 Olympic tournament and a total of only three in 1936.

Longest game The longest international game on record was one of 145 min (into the sixth period of extra time), when the Netherlands beat Spain 1–0 in the Olympic tournament at Mexico City on 25 Oct 1968.

Club matches of 205 min have twice been recorded: the Hong Kong Football Club beat Prison Sports Dept as the first to score in a 'sudden death' play-off after 2–2 at full time on 11 Mar 1979, and Gore Court beat

Hampstead in the first round of the English Club Championships in 1983.

WOMEN

The earliest women's club was East Molesey in Surrey formed c. 1887. Two ladies' hockey clubs, Wimbledon and Ealing, each founded one year later, are still in existence.

The first national association was the Irish Ladies' Hockey Union founded in 1894.

The All England Women's Hockey Association held its first formal meeting in Westminster Town Hall, London on 23 Nov 1895.

The first international match was an England v. Ireland game in Dublin in 1896. Ireland won 2–0.

Most international appearances Valerie Robinson made a record 144 appearances for England, 1963–84.

Highest scores The highest score in an international match was when England beat France 23–0 at Merton, Greater London on 3 Feb 1923.

In club hockey, Ross Ladies beat Wyeside, at Ross-on-Wye, Herefordshire 40–0 on 24 Jan 1929, when Edna Mary Blakelock (1904–89) scored a record 21 goals.

Highest attendance The highest attendance was 65 165 for the match between England and the USA at Wembley, London on 11 Mar 1978.

Horse Racing

Origins Horsemanship was an important part of the Hittite culture of Anatolia, Turkey dating from 1400 BC. The 33rd ancient Olympic Games of 648 BC in Greece featured horse racing. The earliest races recorded in England were those held in about AD 200 at Netherby, Cumbria between Arab horses imported by the Romans.

Largest prizes The highest prize money for a day's racing is $10 million for the Breeders' Cup series of seven races staged annually in the USA since 1984. Included each year is a record $3 million for the Breeders' Cup Classic.

Most runners The most horses in a race has been 66 in the Grand National on 22 Mar 1929. The record for the Flat is 58 in the Lincolnshire Handicap at Lincoln on 13 Mar 1948.

HORSES

Most successful The horse with the best win-loss record was *Kincsem*, a Hungarian mare foaled in 1874, who was unbeaten in 54 races (1876–79) throughout Europe, including the Goodwood Cup of 1878.

Longest winning sequence *Camarero*, foaled in 1951, was undefeated in 56 races in Puerto Rico from 19 Apr 1953 to his first defeat on 17 Aug 1955 (in his career to 1956, he won 73 of 77 races).

Career *Galgo Jr* (foaled 1928) won 137 of 159 starts in Puerto Rico between 1930 and 1936; in 1931 he won a record 30 races in one year.

Same race *Doctor Syntax* (foaled 1811) won the Preston Gold Cup on seven successive occasions, 1815–21.

Triple Crown winners The English Triple Crown (2000 Guineas, Derby, St Leger) has been won 15 times, most recently by *Nijinsky* in 1970. The fillies'

■ **Greatest winnings**

■ **Most successful horse racing trainer**

equivalent (1000 Guineas, Oaks, St Leger) has been won nine times, most recently by *Oh So Sharp* in 1985. Two of these fillies also won the 2000 Guineas: *Formosa* (in a dead-heat) in 1868 and *Sceptre* in 1902. The American Triple Crown (Kentucky Derby, Preakness Stakes, Belmont Stakes) has been achieved 11 times, most recently by *Affirmed* in 1978.

Greatest winnings The career earnings record is $6 679 242 by the 1987 Kentucky Derby winner *Alysheba* (foaled 1984) from 1986–8. The most prize money earned in a year is $4 578 454 by *Sunday Silence* (foaled 1986) in the USA in 1989. His total included $1 350 000 from the Breeders' Cup Classic and a $1 million bonus for the best record in the Triple Crown races: he won the Kentucky Derby and Preakness Stakes and was second in the Belmont Stakes. The leading money-winning mare is *Lady's Secret* (foaled 1982) with $3 021 325 in the

USA, 1984–7. The one race record is $2·6 million by *Spend A Buck* (foaled 1982) for the Jersey Derby, Garden State Park, New Jersey, USA on 27 May 1985, of which $2 million was a bonus for having previously won the Kentucky Derby and two preparatory races at Garden State Park.

Oldest winners The oldest horses to win on the Flat have been the 18-year-olds *Revenge* at Shrewsbury on 23 Sep 1790, *Marksman* at Ashford, Kent on 4 Sep 1826 and *Jorrocks* at Bathurst, Australia on 28 Feb 1851. At the same age *Wild Aster* won three hurdle races in six days in March 1919 and *Sonny Somers* won two steeplechases in February 1980.

World speed records The highest race speed recorded is 69·62 km/h *43·26 mph* by *Big Racket*, 20·8 sec for ¼ mile *409·26 m*, at Mexico City, Mexico on 5 Feb 1945. The 4-year-old carried 51·7 kg *114 lb*. The record

Most expensive horse

Enormous valuations placed on potential stallions may be determined from sales of a minority holding, but such valuations would, perhaps, not be reached on the open market. The most paid for a yearling is $13·1 m on 23 Jul 1985 at Keeneland, Kentucky, USA by Robert Sangster and partners for *Seattle Dancer*.

MAJOR RACE RECORDS

RACE (instituted)	RECORD TIME	MOST WINS			LARGEST FIELD
		Jockey	Trainer	Owner	
FLAT					
Derby (1780) 1 m 4 f 10 yd *2423 m* Epsom, Surrey	2 min 33·8 sec *Mahmoud* 1936 2 min 33·84 sec *Kahyasi* 1988 *	9—Lester Piggott 1954, 57, 60, 68, 70, 72, 76, 77, 83	7—Robert Robson 1793, 1802, 09, 10, 15, 17, 23 7—John Porter 1868, 82, 83, 86, 90, 91, 99 7—Fred Darling 1922, 25, 26, 31, 38, 40, 41	5—3rd Earl of Egremont 1782, 1804, 05, 07, 26 5—HH Aga Khan III 1930, 35, 36, 48, 52	34 (1862)
2000 Guineas (1809) 1 mile *1609 m* Newmarket, Suffolk	1 min 35·8 sec *My Babu* 1948 1 min 35·84 sec *Tirol* 1990 *	9—Jem Robinson 1825, 28, 31, 33, 34, 35, 36, 47, 48	7—John Scott 1842, 43, 49, 53, 56, 60, 62	5—4th Duke of Grafton 1820, 21, 22, 26, 27 5—5th Earl of Jersey 1831, 34, 35, 36, 37	28 (1930)
1000 Guineas (1814) 1 mile *1609 m* Newmarket	1 min 36·85 sec *Oh So Sharp* 1985	7—George Fordham 1859, 61, 65, 68, 69, 81, 83	9—Robert Robson 1818, 19, 20, 21, 22, 23, 25, 26, 27	8—4th Duke of Grafton 1819, 20, 21, 22, 23, 25, 26, 27	29 (1926)
Oaks (1779) 1 m 4 f 10 yd *2423 m* Epsom	2 min 34·21 sec *Time Charter* 1982	9—Frank Buckle 1797, 98, 99, 1802, 03, 05, 17, 18, 23	12—Robert Robson 1802, 04, 05, 07, 08, 09, 13, 15, 18, 22, 23, 25	6—4th Duke of Grafton 1813, 15, 22, 23, 28, 31	26 (1848)
St Leger (1776) 1 m 6 f 127 yd *2932 m* Doncaster, South Yorkshire	3 min 01·6 sec *Coronach* 1926 *Windsor Lad* 1934	9—Bill Scott 1821, 25, 28, 29, 38, 39, 40, 41, 46	16—John Scott 1827, 28, 29, 32, 34, 38, 39, 40, 41, 45, 51, 53, 56, 57, 59, 62	7—9th Duke of Hamilton 1786, 87, 88, 92, 1808, 09, 14	30 (1825)
King George VI and Queen Elizabeth Diamond Stakes (1951) 1 ½ miles *2414 m* Ascot, Berkshire	2 min 26·98 sec *Grundy* 1975	7—Lester Piggott 1965, 66, 69, 70, 74, 77, 84	5—Dick Hern 1972, 79, 80, 85, 89	2—Nelson Bunker Hunt 1973, 74	19 (1951)
Prix de l'Arc de Triomphe (1920) 2400 metres *1 mile 864 yd* Longchamp, Paris, France	2 min 26·3 sec *Trempolino* 1987	4—Jacques Doyasbère 1942, 44, 50, 51 4—Frédéric 'Freddy' Head 1966, 72, 76, 79 4—Yves Saint-Martin 1970, 74, 82, 84 4—Pat Eddery 1980, 85, 86, 87	4—Charles Semblat 1942, 44, 46, 49 4—Alec Head 1952, 59, 76, 81 4—François Mathet 1950, 51, 70, 82	6—Marcel Boussac 1936, 37, 42, 44, 46, 49	30 (1967)
VRC Melbourne Cup (1861) 3200 metres *1 mile 1739 yd* Flemington, Victoria, Australia	3 min 16·3 sec *Kingston Rule* 1990	4—Bobby Lewis 1902, 15, 19, 27 4—Harry White 1974, 75, 78, 79	8—Bart Cummings 1965, 66, 67, 74, 75, 77, 79, 90	4—Etienne de Mestre 1861, 62, 67, 78	39 (1890)
Kentucky Derby (1875) 1 ¼ miles *2012 m* Churchill Downs, Loiusville, USA	1 min 59·4 sec *Secretariat* 1973	5—Eddie Arcaro 1938, 41, 45, 48, 52 5—Bill Hartack 1957, 60, 62, 64, 69	6—Ben Jones 1938, 41, 44, 48, 49, 52	8—Calumet Farm 1941, 44, 48, 49, 52, 57, 58, 68	23 (1974)
Irish Derby (1866) 1 ½ miles *2414 m* The Curragh, Co. Kildare	2 min 28·8 sec *Tambourine* 1962	6—Morny Wing 1921, 23, 30, 38, 42, 46	6—Vincent O'Brien 1953, 57, 70, 77, 84, 85	5—HH Aga Khan III 1925, 32, 40, 48, 49	24 (1962)
JUMPING					
Grand National (1839) 4 ½ miles *7242 m* Aintree, Liverpool, Merseyside	8 min 47·8 sec *Mr Frisk* 1990	5—George Stevens 1856, 63, 64, 69, 70	4—Fred Rimell 1956, 61, 70, 76	3—James Machell 1873, 74, 76 3—Sir Charles Assheton-Smith 1893, 1912, 13 3—Noel Le Mare 1973, 74, 77	66 (1929)
Cheltenham Gold Cup (1924) 3 ¼ miles *5230 m* Cheltenham, Gloucestershire	6 min 23·4 sec *Silver Fame* 1951	4—Pat Taaffe 1964, 65, 66, 68	5—Tom Dreaper 1946, 64, 65, 66, 68	7—Dorothy Paget 1932, 33, 34, 35, 36, 40, 52	22 (1982)
Champion Hurdle (1927) 2 miles *3218 m* Cheltenham	3 min 50·7 sec *Kribensis* 1990	4—Tim Molony 1951, 52, 53, 54	5—Peter Easterby 1967, 76, 77, 80, 81	4—Dorothy Paget 1932, 33, 40, 46	24 (1964) 24 (1991)

* *Electronically timed*

for 1½ miles *2414 m* is 60·86 km/h *37·82 mph* by 3-year-old *Hawkster* (carrying 54·9 kg *121 lb*) at Santa Anita Park, Arcadia, California, USA on 14 Oct 1989 with a time of 2 min 22·8 sec.

JOCKEYS

Most successful William Lee 'Bill' Shoemaker (USA) (b. weighing 1·1 kg *2½ lb*, 19 Aug 1931), whose racing weight was 44 kg *97 lb* at 1·50 m *4 ft 11 in*, rode a record 8833 winners from 40 350 mounts from his first ride on 19 Mar 1949 and first winner on 20 Apr 1949 to his retirement on 3 Feb 1990. Laffit Pincay (b. 29 Dec 1946, Panama City) has earned a career record $154 659 844 from 1964 to the end of 1990.

The most races won by a jockey in a year is 597 from 2312 rides by Kent Desormeaux (b. 27 Feb 1970) in 1989. The greatest amount won in a year is 2 356 280 400 yen (c. $16 250 000 or a little less than £10 million) by Yutaka Take (b. 1969) in Japan in 1990. The greatest amount won in the USA in a year is $14 877 298 by José Adeon Santos (USA) (b. Chile, 26 Apr 1961) in 1988.

Wins The most winners ridden in one day is nine by Chris Wiley Antley (USA) (b. 6 Jan 1966) on 31 Oct 1987. They consisted of four in the afternoon at Aqueduct, New York, USA and five in the evening at The Meadowlands, New Jersey, USA.

One card The most winners ridden on one card is eight by six riders, most recently (and from fewest rides) by Pat Day from nine rides at Arlington, Illinois, USA on 13 Sep 1989.

Consecutive The longest winning streak

is 12 by: Sir Gordon Richards (1904–86) (one race at Nottingham on 3 Oct, six out of six at Chepstow on 4 Oct and the first five races next day at Chepstow) in 1933; and by Pieter Stroebel at Bulawayo, Southern Rhodesia (now Zimbabwe), 7 Jun–7 Jul 1958.

TRAINERS

Jack Charles Van Berg (USA) (b. 7 Jun 1936) has the greatest number of wins in a year, 496 in 1976. The career record is 5540 by Dale Baird (USA) (b. 17 Apr 1935) from 1962 to 1990. The greatest amount won in a year is $17 842 358 by Darrell Wayne Lukas (USA) (b. 2 Sep 1935) in 1988.

The only trainer to saddle the first five finishers in a championship race is Michael William Dickinson (b. 3 Feb 1950) of Dunkeswick, W Yorks in the Cheltenham Gold Cup on 17 Mar 1983; he won a record 12 races in one day, 27 Dec 1982.

OWNERS

The most lifetime wins by an owner is 4775 by Marion H. Van Berg (1895–1971) in North America in 35 years. The most wins in a year is 494 by Dan R. Lasater (USA) in 1974. The greatest amount won in a year is $5 858 168 by Ogden Phipps (USA) in 1988.

FLAT RACING

Most successful horses *Eclipse* (foaled 1764) still has the best win-loss record, being unbeaten in a career of 18 races between May 1769 and October 1770. The longest winning sequence is 21 races by *Meteor* (foaled 1783) between 1786 and 1788. The most races won in a season is 23 (from 34 starts) by three-year-old *Fisherman* in 1856. *Catherina* (foaled 1830) won a career record 79 out of 176 races, 1832–41. The most successful sire was *Stockwell* (foaled 1849) whose progeny won 1153 races (1858–76) and who in 1866 set a record of 132 races won.

The greatest amount ever won by an English-trained horse is £1 182 140 by the filly *Pebbles* (foaled 1981) in 1983–5. In 1985 she won a record £1 012 611 in one season, including the Breeders' Cup Turf in New York, USA.

The biggest winning margin in a Classic is 20 lengths by *Mayonaise* in the 1000 Guineas on 12 May 1859.

Since the introduction of the Pattern-race system in 1971, the most prolific British-trained winner of such races has been *Brigadier Gerard* (foaled 1968) with 13 wins, 1971–2.

Since the introduction in 1977 of official ratings in the International Classifications, the highest-rated horse has been *Dancing Brave* (foaled 1983) on 141 in 1986.

Most successful jockeys Sir Gordon Richards won 4870 races from 21 815 mounts from his first mount at Lingfield Park, Surrey on 16 Oct 1920 to his last at Sandown Park, Surrey on 10 Jul 1954. His first win was on 31 Mar 1921. In 1953, at his 28th and final attempt, he won the Derby, six days after his knighthood. He was champion jockey 26 times between 1925 and 1953 and won a record 269 races (from 835 rides) in 1947. Lester Keith Piggott (b. 5 Nov 1935) has won 4369 races in Great Britain, from 1948 to June 1991, but his global total exceeds 5200. The most prize-money won in a year is £2 903 976 by William Fisher Hunter Carson (b. 16 Nov 1942) in 1990.

The most Classic races won by a jockey is 29 by Lester Piggott from his first on *Never Say Die* in the 1954 Derby to the 1985 2000 Guineas on *Shadeed*. (Derby — 9, St Leger — 8, Oaks — 6, 2000 Guineas — 4, 1000 Guineas — 2.)

Most successful trainers The greatest number of wins in a season is 180 (from 446 starts) by Henry Richard Amherst Cecil (b. 11 Jan 1943) of Newmarket in 1987.

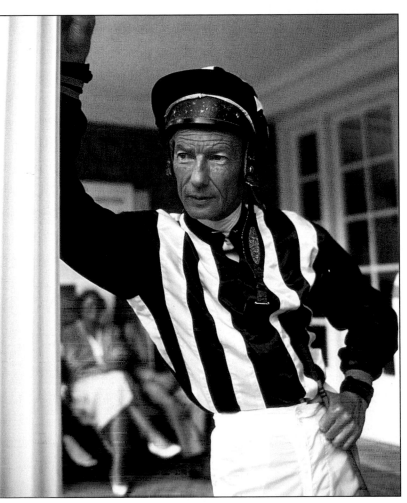

The record prize money earned in a season is £2 000 330 by Michael Ronald Stoute (b. 22 Oct 1945) of Newmarket in 1989; he set a record for world-wide earnings of £2 778 405 in 1986. The most Classics won by a trainer is 40 by John Scott (1794–1871) of Malton, Yorkshire between 1827 and 1863. James Croft (1787–1828) of Middle-

Hurling stroke

Hurling stroke

The greatest distance for a 'lift and stroke' is one of 117 m *129 yd* credited to Tom Murphy of Three Castles, Kilkenny, in a 'long puck' contest in 1906.

■ **Most wins by NHL goaltender**

Bernie Parent (b. 3 Apr 1945) of the Philadelphia Flyers achieved a record 47 wins in a season, with 13 losses and 12 ties, in 1973/4. The Flyers went on to win the Stanley Cup with Parent being awarded the Conn Smyth Trophy for most valuable player in the play-offs. The Flyers repeated their success the following year as did Parent making him one of only three players to win the Trophy twice. (Photo: Sports Illustrated/Tony Triolo)

ham, Yorkshire trained the first four horses in the St Leger on 16 Sep 1822. Alexander Taylor (1862–1943) of Manton, Wiltshire, was champion trainer in money won a record 12 times between 1907 and 1925. Henry Cecil has been champion in races won a record eight times since 1978.

Most successful owners H H Aga Khan III (1877–1957) was leading owner a record 13 times between 1924 and 1952. The record prize money won in a season is £2 243 755 by Sheikh Mohammed bin Rashid al Maktoum of Dubai (b. 1949) in 1990, when his horses won a record 176 races. The most Classics won is 20 by George Fitzroy, 4th Duke of Grafton (1760–1844) between 1813 and 1831 and by Edward Stanley, 17th Earl of Derby (1865–1948) between 1910 and 1945.

The Derby The greatest of England's five Classics is the Derby Stakes, inaugurated on 4 May 1780, and named after Edward Stanley, 12th Earl of Derby (1752–1834). The distance was increased in 1784 from a mile to 1½ miles and is now officially described as 1 mile 4 furlongs 10 yd *2423 m*. The race has been run at Epsom Downs, Surrey, except for the two war periods, when it was run at Newmarket, Cambs, and is for three-year-olds only. Since 1884 the weights have been: colts 57·2 kg *9 st*, fillies 54·9 kg *8 st 9 lb*. Geldings were eligible until 1904.

Largest and smallest winning margins *Shergar* won the Derby by a record 10 lengths in 1981. There have been two dead-heats: in 1828 when *Cadland* beat *The Colonel* in the run-off, and in 1884 between *St Gatien* and *Harvester* (stakes divided).

Longest and shortest odds Three winners have been returned at odds of 100–1: *Jeddah* (1898), *Signorinetta* (1908) and *Aboyeur* (1913). The shortest-priced winner

was *Ladas* (1894) at 2–9 and the hottest losing favourite was *Surefoot*, fourth at 40–95 in 1890.

Largest prize The richest prize on the British Turf was £355 000 for the Derby on 6 Jun 1990, won by *Quest for Fame*, and on 5 Jun 1991, won by *Generous*.

JUMPING

Most successful horses *Sir Ken* (foaled 1947), who won the Champion Hurdle in 1952–4, won a record 16 hurdle races in succession, April 1951 to March 1953. Three other horses have also won a record three Champion Hurdles; *Hatton's Grace* (foaled 1940) 1949–51; *Persian War* (foaled 1963) 1968–70; *See You Then* (foaled 1980) 1985–7. The greatest number of Cheltenham Gold Cup wins is five by *Golden Miller* (foaled 1927), 1932–6.

The greatest amount earned by a British jumper is £643 967 by *Desert Orchid* (foaled 1979) in 1983–91. The previous record holder, the mare *Dawn Run* (foaled 1978), uniquely won both the Champion Hurdle (1984) and Cheltenham Gold Cup (1986).

Most successful jockeys Peter Michael Scudamore (b. 13 Jun 1958) has won a career record 1374 races over jumps (from 6592 mounts) from 1978 to 1991.

The record number of wins in a season is 221 (from 663 rides) by Peter Scudamore in 1988/9. The most prize-money won in a season is £922 473 by Thomas Richard Dunwoody (b. 18 Jan 1964) in 1990/91. The most wins in a day is six by amateur Charles James Cunningham (1849–1906) at Rugby, Warks on 29 Mar 1881. The record number of successive wins is ten by: John Alnam 'Johnny' Gilbert (b. 26 Jul 1920), 8–30 Sep 1959; and by Philip Charles Tuck (b. 10 Jul 1956), 23 Aug–3 Sep 1986. The record number of championships is seven by: Gerald 'Gerry' Wilson (1903–68) 1933–8 and 1941; John Francome (b. 13 Dec 1952) (one shared) in 1976, 1979, 1981–5; and Peter Scudamore (one shared) in 1982, 1986–91.

Most successful trainers Martin Charles Pipe (b. 29 May 1945) became, in 1990/91, the first National Hunt trainer to win more than £1 million in prize money, ending the season with a total of £1 203 014. During this season he trained a record 230 winners from 782 starts. Frederick Thomas Winter (b. 20 Sep 1926) of Lambourn, Berks was champion trainer in money won a record eight times between 1971 and 1985. William Arthur Stephenson (b. 7 Apr 1920) of Leasingthorne, Co. Durham was champion trainer in races won a record 10 times between 1966 and 1977.

Grand National The first Grand National Steeple Chase may be regarded as the Grand Liverpool Steeple Chase of 26 Feb 1839 though the race was not given its present name until 1847. It became a handicap in 1843. Except for 1916–18, and 1941–5 the race has been run at Aintree, near Liverpool, over 30 fences.

Most wins The only horse to win three times is *Red Rum* (foaled 1965) in 1973, 1974 and 1977, from five runs. He came second in 1975 and 1976. *Manifesto* (foaled 1888) ran a record eight times (1895–1904). He won in 1897 and 1899, came third three times and fourth once.

Highest prize The highest prize and the richest ever over jumps in Great Britain was £90 970 won by *Seagram* on 6 Apr 1991.

Heaviest weight The highest weight ever carried to victory is 79·4 kg *12 st 7 lb* by

Cloister (1893), *Manifesto* (1899), *Jerry M.* (1912) and *Poethlyn* (1919).

Hurling

Origins A game of very ancient origin, hurling was included in the Tailteann Games (instituted 1829 BC). It only became standardized with the formation of the Gaelic Athletic Association in Thurles, Ireland on 1 Nov 1884. The Irish Hurling Union was formed on 24 Jan 1879.

Most titles *All-Ireland* The greatest number of All-Ireland Championships won by one team is 27 by Cork between 1890 and 1990. The greatest number of successive wins is four by Cork (1941–4).

Most appearances The most appearances in All-Ireland finals is ten shared by Christy Ring (Cork and Munster) and John Doyle (Tipperary). They also share the record of All-Ireland medals won with eight each. Ring's appearances on the winning side were in 1941–4, 1946 and 1952–4, while Doyle's were in 1949–51, 1958, 1961–2 and 1964–5. Ring also played in a record 22 inter-provincial finals (1942–63) and was on the winning side 18 times.

Highest and lowest scores The highest score in an All-Ireland final (60 min) was in 1989 when Tipperary 41 (4 goals, 29 points) beat Antrim (3 goals, 9 points). The record aggregate score was when Cork 39 (6 goals, 21 points) defeated Wexford 25 (5 goals, 10 points) in the 80-minute final of 1970. A goal equals three points. The highest recorded individual score was by Nick Rackard (Wexford), who scored 7 goals and 7 points against Antrim in the 1954 All-Ireland semi-final. The lowest score in an All-Ireland final was when Tipperary (1 goal, 1 point) beat Galway (nil) in the first championship at Birr in 1887.

Largest crowd The largest crowd was 84 865 for the All-Ireland final between Cork and Wexford at Croke Park, Dublin in 1954.

Ice Hockey

Origins There is pictorial evidence that a hockey-like game (*kalv*) was played on ice in the early 16th century in the Netherlands. The game was probably first played in North America on 25 Dec 1855 at Kingston, Ontario, Canada, but Halifax also lays claim to priority. The International Ice Hockey Federation was established in 1908. The British Ice Hockey Association was founded in 1913.

World Championships and Olympic Games World Championships were first held for amateurs in 1920 in conjunction with the Olympic Games, which were also considered as world championships up to 1968. From 1977 World Championships have been open to professionals. The USSR won 22 world titles between 1954 and 1990, including the Olympic titles of 1956, 1964 and 1968. They have a record seven Olympic titles with a further four, 1972, 1976, 1984 and 1988. The longest Olympic career is that of Richard Torriani (Switzerland) (1911–88) from 1928 to 1948. The most gold medals won by any player is three, achieved by USSR players Vitaliy Semyenovich Davydov, Anatoliy Vasilyevich Firssov, Viktor Grigoryevich Kuzkin and Aleksandr Pavlovich Ragulin in 1964, 1968 and 1972, and by

Vladislav Aleksandrovich Tretyak in 1972, 1976 and 1984.

Women The first world championships were won by Canada, who beat the USA 5–2, at Ottawa, Canada on 24 Mar 1990.

National Hockey League (NHL) It was founded on 22 Nov 1917 in Montreal, succeeding the National Hockey Association of Canada. The first league games were played on 19 Dec 1917. It is now contested by 21 teams, seven from Canada and 14 from the USA, divided into two divisions within two conferences: Adams and Patrick Divisions in the Wales Conference; Norris and Smythe Divisions in the Campbell Conference. At the end of the regular season 16 teams compete in the Stanley Cup play-offs to decide the NHL champion.

Stanley Cup The Stanley Cup was first presented in 1893 (original cost $48.67) by Lord Stanley of Preston, then Governor-General of Canada. From 1894 it was contested by amateur teams for the Canadian Championship. From 1910 it became the award for the winners of the professional league play-offs. It has been won most often by the Montreal Canadiens with 23 wins in 1916, 1924, 1930–31, 1944, 1946, 1953, 1956–60, 1965–6, 1968–9, 1971, 1973, 1976–9, 1986, from a record 31 finals. Henri Richard played on a record 11 winning teams for the Canadiens between 1956 and 1973. The longest Stanley Cup final game was settled after 115 min 13 sec, in the third period of overtime, when Edmonton Oilers beat Boston Bruins 3–2 on 15 May 1990.

Scoring records Wayne Gretzky (Edmonton and Los Angeles) has scored 299 points in Stanley Cup games, 93 goals and 206 assists, all are records. Gretzky scored a season's record 47 points (16 goals and a record 31 assists) in 1985. The most goals in a season is 19 by Reginald Joseph Leach (b. 23 Apr 1950) for Philadelphia in 1976 and Jari Kurri (Finland) (b. 18 May 1960) for Edmonton in 1985. Five goals in a Stanley Cup game were scored by Maurice Richard (b. 14 Aug 1924) in Montreal's 5–1 win over Toronto on 23 Mar 1944, by Darryl Glen Sittler for Toronto (8) *v.* Philadelphia (5) on 22 Apr 1976, by Reggie Leach for Philadelphia (6) *v.* Boston (3) on 6 May 1976, and by Mario Lemieux (b. 5 Oct 1965) for Pittsburgh (10) *v.* Philadelphia (7) on 25 Apr 1989. A record six assists in a game were achieved by Mikko Leinonen (b. 15 Jul 1955) for New York Rangers (7) *v.* Philadelphia (3) on 8 Apr 1982 and by Wayne Gretzky for Edmonton (13) *v.* Los Angeles (3) on 9 Apr 1987, when his team set a Stanley Cup game record of 13 goals. The most points in a game is eight by Patrik Sundström (Sweden) (b. 14 Dec 1961), three goals and five assists, for New Jersey (10) *v.* Washington (4) on 22 Apr 1988 and by Mario Lemieux, five goals and three assists, for Pittsburgh *v.* Philadelphia.

NHL RECORDS

Most games played Gordon 'Gordie' Howe (Canada) (b. 31 Mar 1928) played in a record 1767 regular season games (and 157 play-off games) over a record 26 seasons, from 1946 to 1971 for the Detroit Red Wings and in 1979/80 for the Hartford Whalers. He also played 419 games (and 78 play-off games) for the Houston Aeros and for the New England Whalers in the World Hockey Association (WHA) from 1973 to 1979, and a grand total of 2421 major league games.

Most goals and points *Career* The most goals scored in a season is 92 in the 1981/2 season by Wayne Gretzky for the Edmonton Oilers. He scored a record 215 points, including a record 163 assists in 1985/6. In 1981/2 in all games, adding Stanley Cup play-offs and for Canada in the World Championship, he scored 238 points (103 goals, 135 assists). The North American career record for goals is 1071 (including a record 801 in the NHL) by Gordie Howe in 32 seasons, 1946–80. He took 2204 games to achieve the 1000th goal, but Robert Marvin 'Bobby' Hull (b. 3 Jan 1939) (Chicago Black Hawks and Winnipeg Jets) scored his 1000th in his 1600th game on 12 Mar 1978.

Wayne Gretzky has the record for assists of 1424 and overall records for regular season and play-off games for assists, 1630 and total points, 2441 (2142 NHL, 299 Stanley Cup). His 811 goals (718 + 93) have come from 1075 games.

Game The North American major league record for most points scored in one game is ten by Jim Harrison (b. 9 Jul 1947) (three goals, seven assists) for Alberta, later Edmonton Oilers in a WHA match at Edmonton on 30 Jan 1973, and by Darryl Sittler (b. 18 Sep 1950) (six goals, four assists) for Toronto Maple Leafs *v.* Boston Bruins in an NHL match at Toronto on 7 Feb 1976.

The most goals in a game is seven by Joe Malone in Québec's 10–6 win over Toronto St. Patricks at Québec City on 31 Jan 1920. The most assists is seven by Billy Taylor for Detroit *v.* Chicago on 16 Mar 1947 and three times by Wayne Gretzky for Edmonton, *v.* Washington on 15 Feb 1980, *v.* Chicago on 11 Dec 1985, and *v.* Qubec on 14 Feb 1986.

Fastest goal Joseph Antoine Claude Provost (b. 17 Sep 1933) (Montreal Canadiens) scored after 4 sec *v.* Boston Bruins in the second period at Montreal on 9 Nov 1957, and this was repeated by Denis Joseph Savard (b. 4 Feb 1961) (Chicago Black Hawks) *v.* Hartford Whalers in the third period at Chicago on 12 Jan 1986. From the opening whistle, the fastest is 5 sec by Doug Smail (b. 2 Sep 1957) (Winnipeg Jets) *v.* St Louis Blues at Winnipeg on 20 Dec 1981, and by Bryan John Trottier (b. 17 Jul 1956) (New York Islanders) *v.* Boston Bruins at Boston on 22 Mar 1984. Canadian Bill Mosienko (b. 2 Nov 1921) (Chicago Black Hawks) scored three goals in 21 sec *v.* New York Rangers on 23 Mar 1952.

Goaltending Terry Sawchuk (1929–70) played a record 971 games as a goaltender, for Detroit, Boston, Toronto, Los Angeles and New York Rangers from 1950 to 1970. He achieved a record 435 wins (to 337 losses, and 188 ties) and had a record 103 career shutouts. Jacques Plante (1929–86), with 434 NHL wins surpassed Sawchuk's figure by adding 15 wins in his one season in the WHA for a senior league total of 449 from 868 games. Bernie Parent (b. 3 Apr 1945) achieved a record 47 wins in a season, with 13 losses and 12 ties, for Philadelphia in 1973/4.

Gerry Cheevers (b. 2 Dec 1940) (Boston Bruins) went a record 32 successive games without a defeat in 1971–2.

Team records Montreal Canadiens won a record 60 games and 132 points (with 12 ties) from 80 games played in 1976/7; their eight losses was also the least ever in a season of 70 or more games. The highest percentage of wins in a season was ·875% achieved by the Boston Bruins with 30 wins in 44 games in 1929/30. The longest undefeated run during a season, 35 games (25 wins and ten ties), was established by the Philadelphia Flyers from 14 Oct 1979 to 6 Jan 1980. The most goals scored in a season is 446 by the Edmonton Oilers in 1983/4, when they also achieved a record 1182 scoring points.

Game The highest aggregate score is 21 when Montreal Canadiens beat Toronto St Patrick's, 14–7, at Montreal on 10 Jan 1920, and Edmonton Oilers beat Chicago Black Hawks, 12–9, at Chicago on 11 Dec 1985. The single team record is 16 by Montreal Canadiens *v.* Québec Bulldogs (3), at Québec City on 3 Nov 1920.

The longest match was 2 hr 56 min 30 sec (playing time) when Detroit Red Wings beat Montreal Maroons 1–0 in the sixth period of overtime at the Forum, Montreal, at 2:25 a.m. on 25 Mar 1936. Norm Smith, the Red Wings goaltender, turned aside 92 shots for the NHL's longest single shutout.

OTHER RECORDS

British competitions The English National (later British) League Cham-

■ **Fastest hat-trick**

■ **Fastest hat-trick**
Three goals in 10 seconds was achieved by Jørgen Palmgren Erichsen for Frisk v. Holmen in a junior league match in Norway on 17 Mar 1991. Jørgen can be seen here with the players who assisted him (from right); Bjørn Erik Moksnes, John Are Hårstad-Evjen, Andres Bastiansen and Eric Thuv.

■ **Most speed skating titles**
Karin Kania (née Enke) (GDR) (b. 20 Jun 1961) has won a record five overall speed skating World Championships, in 1982, 1984, 1986–8. She has also won a record six overall titles at the World Sprint Championships 1980–81, 1983–4, 1986–7. (Photo: All-Sport (USA)/Loubat)

pionship (instituted 1935) has been won by the Wembley Lions four times, in 1936–7, 1952 and 1957 and by Streatham (later Redskins) in 1950, 1953, 1960 and 1982. Murrayfield Racers have won the Northern League (instituted 1966) seven times, 1970–72, 1976, 1979–80 and 1985. The Icy Smith Cup (first held 1966), the premier British club competition until 1981, was won by Murrayfield Racers nine times, 1966, 1969–72, 1975 and 1979–81. The British Championship (instituted 1982) (now Heineken Championship) has been won a record three times by Dundee Rockets, 1982–4 and by Durham Wasps, 1987–8, 1991. The Heineken League title has been won four times by Durham Wasps, 1985, 1988–9 and 1991. The 'Grand Slam' of Autumn Cup (now Norwich Union Cup), Heineken League and Heineken Championships has been won by Dundee Rockets (1983/4) and by Durham Wasps (1990/91). Cardiff Devils uniquely won the First and Premier Divisions in successive seasons, 1989–90.

Most goals Team The greatest number of goals recorded in a world championship match was when Australia beat New Zealand 58–0 at Perth on 15 Mar 1987.

British The highest score and aggregate in a British League match was set when Medway Bears beat Richmond Raiders 48–1 at Gillingham in a Second Division fixture on 1 Dec 1985, when Kevin Mac-Naught (Canada) (b. 23 Jul 1960) scored a record 25 points from seven goals and 18 assists.

The most individual goals scored in a senior game is 18 by Rick Smith (Canada) (b. 28 Aug 1964) in a 27–2 win for Chelmsford Chieftains against Sheffield Sabres in an English League match on 3 Mar 1991. Steve Moria (Canada) (b. 1960) achieved the highest number of assists, 13, for Fife Flyers at Cleveland on 28 Mar 1987. Rick Fera (Canada) (b. 1964) set British season's records of 165 goals and 318 points for Murrayfield Racers in 48 games in 1986/7. Tim Salmon (Canada) (b. 27 Nov 1964) achieved a season's record 183 assists in 47 games for Ayr Bruins in 1985/6. The highest career points for the Heineken

League is 1343 (588 goals, 755 assists) by Tony Hand (GB) (b. 15 Aug 1967) in 270 games to end of the 1990/91 season.

Fastest scoring In minor leagues, Per Olsen scored 2 seconds after the start of the match for Rungsted against Odense in the Danish First Division at Hørsholm, Denmark on 14 Jan 1990. Three goals in 10 seconds was achieved by Jørgen Palmgren Erichsen for Frisk v. Holmen in a junior league match in Norway on 17 Mar 1991. The Vernon Cougars scored five goals in 56 seconds against Salmon Arm Aces at Vernon, BC, Canada on 6 Aug 1982. The Kamloops Knights of Columbus scored seven goals in 2 min 22 sec v. Prince George Vikings on 25 Jan 1980.

Great Britain The fastest goal in the Heineken League was scored by Stephen Johnson for Durham Wasps after four seconds v. Ayr Bruins at Ayr, Strathclyde on 6

Nov 1983. Mark Salisbury (GB) (b. 4 Dec 1970) scored a hat-trick in 19 seconds for Basingstoke Beavers v. Telford Tigers on 26 Jan 1991. The fastest goal in a Heineken Championship final was scored after 27 sec by Jim Mollard for Murrayfield Racers against Cardiff Devils at Wembley on 22 Apr 1990. Cardiff eventually won the tie 6–5 on penalties, after a 6–6 tie in regulation time and 10 min overtime.

In an English Junior League (under-16) game Jonathan Lumbis scored a hat-trick in 13 seconds for Nottingham Cougars v. Peterborough Jets on 4 Nov 1984.

Ice Skating

Origins The earliest reference to ice skating is in early Scandinavian literature referring to the 2nd century though its origins are believed, on archaeological evidence, to be ten centuries earlier still. The earliest English account of 1180 refers to skates made of bone. The earliest skating club was the Edinburgh Skating Club formed in 1742.

The first recorded race was from Wisbech to Whittlesey, Cambs in 1763. The earliest artificial rink in the world was opened at the Baker Street Bazaar, Portman Square, London on 7 Dec 1842, although the surface was not of ice. The first artificial ice rink was opened in the King's Road, Chelsea, London on 7 Jan 1876.

The National Skating Association of Great Britain was founded in 1879. The International Skating Union was founded at Scheveningen, Netherlands in 1892.

FIGURE SKATING

Most titles *Olympic* The most Olympic gold medals won by a figure skater is three by: Gillis Grafström (Sweden) (1893–1938) in 1920, 1924 and 1928 (also silver medal in 1932); by Sonja Henie (Norway) (1912–69) in 1928, 1932 and 1936; and by Irina Konstantinovna Rodnina (USSR) (b. 12 Sep 1949) with two different partners in the Pairs in 1972, 1976 and 1980.

World The greatest number of men's individual world figure skating titles

■ **Most speed skating titles**

(instituted 1896) is ten by Ulrich Salchow (Sweden) (1877–1949), in 1901–5 and 1907–11. The women's record (instituted 1906) is also ten individual titles by Sonja Henie between 1927 and 1936. Irina Rodnina won ten pairs titles (instituted 1908), four with Aleksey Nikolayevich Ulanov (b. 4 Nov 1947), 1969–72, and six with her husband Aleksandr Gennadyevich Zaitsev (b. 16 Jun 1952), 1973–8. The most ice dance titles (instituted 1952) won is six by Lyudmila Alekseyevna Pakhomova (1946–86) and her husband Aleksandr Georgiyevich Gorshkov (USSR) (b. 8 Oct 1946), 1970–74 and 1976. They also won the first ever Olympic ice dance title in 1976.

British The most individual British titles are: (men) 11 by Jack Ferguson Page (1900–47) (Manchester SC) in 1922–31 and 1933; and (women) six by Magdalena Cecilia Colledge (b. 28 Nov 1920) (Park Lane FSC, London) in 1935–6, 1937 (two), 1938 and 1946. Page and Ethel Muckelt (1885–1953) won nine pairs titles, 1923–31. The most by an ice dance couple is six by Jayne Torvill (b. 7 Oct 1957) and Christopher Colin Dean (b. 27 Jul 1958), 1978–83.

Triple Crown Karl Schäfer (Austria) (1909–76) and Sonja Henie achieved double 'Grand Slams', both in the years 1932 and 1936. The only British skaters to win the 'Grand Slam' of World, Olympic and European titles in the same year are John Anthony Curry (b. 9 Sep 1949) in 1976 and the ice dancers Jayne Torvill and Christopher Dean in 1984.

Highest marks The highest tally of maximum six marks awarded in an international championship was 29 to Jayne Torvill and Christopher Dean (GB) in the World Ice Dance Championships at Ottawa, Canada on 22–24 Mar 1984. This comprised seven in the compulsory dances, a perfect set of nine for presentation in the set pattern dance and 13 in the free dance, including another perfect set from all nine judges for artistic presentation. They previously gained a perfect set of nine sixes for artistic presentation in the free dance at the 1983 World Championships in Helsinki, Finland and at the 1984 Winter Olympic Games in Sarajevo, Yugoslavia. In their career Torvill and Dean received a record total of 136 sixes.

The most by a soloist is seven: by Donald George Jackson (Canada) (b. 2 Apr 1940) in the World Men's Championship at Prague, Czechoslovakia in 1962; and by Midori Ito (Japan) (b. 13 Aug 1969) in the World Championships at Paris, France in 1989.

Most mid-air rotations Kurt Browning (Canada) (b. 18 Jun 1966) was the first to achieve a quadruple jump in competition — a toe loop in the World Championships at Budapest, Hungary on 25 Mar 1988. The first woman to do so was Suruya Bonaly (France) (b. 15 Dec 1973) in the Women's World Championships at Munich, Germany on 16 Mar 1991.

Largest rink The world's largest indoor ice rink is in the Moscow Olympic arena which has an ice area of 8064 m² *86 800 ft²*. The five rinks at Fujikyu Highland Skating Centre, Japan total 26 500 m² *285 243 ft²*.

SPEED SKATING

Most titles *Olympic* The most Olympic gold medals won in speed skating is six by Lidiya Pavlovna Skoblikova (b. 8 Mar 1939) of Chelyabinsk, USSR, in 1960 (two) and 1964 (four). The male record is by Clas Thunberg (Finland) (1893–1973) with five gold (including one tied), and also one silver and one tied bronze, in 1924 and 1928.

Eric Arthur Heiden (USA) (b. 14 Jun 1958) also won five gold medals, uniquely at one Games at Lake Placid, New York, USA in 1980.

World The greatest number of world overall titles (instituted 1893) won by any skater is five; by Oscar Mathisen (Norway) (1888–1954) in 1908–9 and 1912–14; and Clas Thunberg in 1923, 1925, 1928–9 and 1931. The most titles won in the women's events (instituted 1936) is five by Karin Kania (*née* Enke) (GDR) (b. 20 Jun 1961) in 1982, 1984, 1986–8. Kania also won a record six overall titles at the World Sprint Championships 1980–81, 1983–4, 1986–7. A record four men's sprint overall titles

have been won by Eric Heiden, 1977–80 and by Igor Zhelezovskiy (USSR), 1985–6, 1989 and 1991.

The record score achieved for the world overall title is 157·396 points by Johann-Olav Koss (Norway) at Heerenveen, Netherlands on 9–10 Feb 1991. The record low women's score is 171·630 points by Jacqueline Börner (GDR) at Calgary, Canada on 10–11 Feb 1990.

World Short-track Championships The most successful skater in these championships (instituted 1978) has been Sylvia Daigle (Canada) (b. 1 Dec 1962) women's overall champion in 1979, 1983 and 1989–90.

Barrel jumping on ice skates The official distance record is 8·99 m *29 ft 5 in* over 18 barrels, by Yvon Jolin at Terrebonne, Quebec, Canada on 25 Jan 1981. The women's record is 6·20 m *20 ft 4¼ in* over 11 barrels, by Janet Hainstock in Michigan, USA on 15 Mar 1980.

SPEED SKATING WORLD RECORDS

MEN

Metres	min sec	Name (Country)	Place	Date
500	36·45	Uwe-Jens Mey (GDR)	Calgary, Canada	14 Feb 1988
	36·23 u	Nick Thometz (USA)	Medeo, USSR	26 Mar 1987
1000	1:12·58 A	Pavel Pegov (USSR)	Medeo, USSR	25 Mar 1983
	1:12·58	Igor Zhelezovskiy (USSR)	Heerenveen, Netherlands	25 Feb 1989
	1:12·05 Au	Nick Thometz (USA)	Medeo, USSR	27 Feb 1987
1500	1:52·06	André Hoffmann (GDR)	Calgary, Canada	20 Feb 1988
3000	3:57·52	Johann-Olav Koss (Norway)	Heerenveen, Netherlands	13 Mar 1990
	3:56·65 Au	Sergey Martyuk (USSR)	Medeo, USSR	11 Mar 1977
5000	6:41·73	Johann-Olav Koss (Norway)	Heerenveen, Netherlands	9 Feb 1991
10 000	13:43·54	Johann-Olav Koss (Norway)	Heerenveen, Netherlands	10 Feb 1991

u *unofficial.* A *set at high altitude.*

WOMEN

Metres	min sec	Name (Country)	Place	Date
500	39·10	Bonnie Blair (USA)	Calgary, Canada	22 Feb 1988
1000	1:17·65	Christa Rothenburger (now Luding) (GDR)	Calgary, Canada	26 Feb 1988
1500	1:59·30 A	Karin Kania (*née* Enke) (GDR)	Medeo, USSR	22 Mar 1986
3000	4:10·80	Gunda Kleeman (Germany)	Calgary, Canada	9 Dec 1990
5000	7:14·13	Yvonne van Gennip (Netherlands)	Calgary, Canada	28 Feb 1988
10 000†	15:25·25	Yvonne van Gennip (Netherlands)	Heerenveen, Netherlands	19 Mar 1988

† *Record not officially recognized for this distance.*

WORLD SHORT TRACK SPEED SKATING RECORDS

MEN

Metres	min sec	Name (Country)	Place	Date
500	44·46	Orazio Fagone (Italy)	Budapest, Hungary	16 Jan 1988
1000	1:31·80	Tsutomu Kawasaki (Japan)	Amsterdam, Netherlands	18 Mar 1990
1500	2:22·21	T. Kawai (Japan)	Seoul, South Korea	31 Mar 1991
3000	5:04·24	Tatsuyoshi Ishihara (Japan)	Amsterdam, Netherlands	17 Mar 1985

WOMEN

Metres	min sec	Name (Country)	Place	Date
500	47·08	Zhang Yumei (China)	North Ryde, Australia	23 Mar 1991
1000	1:39·00	Li Yan (China)	Calgary, Canada	25 Feb 1988
1500	2:28·26	Eden Donatelli (Canada)	Seoul, South Korea	31 Mar 1991
3000	5:18·33	Maria Rosa Candido (Italy)	Budapest, Hungary	17 Jan 1988

BRITISH SHORT TRACK SPEED SKATING RECORDS

MEN

Metres	min sec	Name	Place	Date
500	44·80	Wilfred O'Reilly	Calgary, Canada	23 Feb 1988
1000	1:33·44	Wilfred O'Reilly	Calgary, Canada	24 Feb 1988
1500	2:29·43	Stuart Horsepool	Humberside	11 Feb 1990
3000	5:17·47	Wilfred O'Reilly	Chamonix, France	6 Apr 1986

WOMEN

Distance	min sec	Name	Place	Date
500	51·78	Kim Ferran	Brugge, Belgium	18 Mar 1984
1000	1:46·63	Nicky Bell	Chamonix, France	5 Apr 1986
1500	2:46·88	Amanda Worth	Tokyo, Japan	8 Apr 1983
3000	5:59·08	Amanda Worth	Richmond, London	1 Mar 1985

Longest skating jump

Robin John Cousins (GB) (b. 17 Aug 1957) achieved 5·81 m *19 ft 1 in* in an axel jump and 5·48 m *18 ft* with a back flip at Richmond Ice Rink, Surrey on 16 Nov 1983.

Largest ice yacht

The largest yacht was *Icicle*, built for Commodore John E. Roosevelt for racing on the Hudson River, New York in 1869. It was 21 m *68 ft 11 in* long and carried 99 m² *1070 ft²* of canvas.

Judo throws

The brothers Carl and Peter Udry completed 18 779 judo throwing techniques in a ten-hour period at Hendra Sports Field, Truro, Cornwall on 29 Aug 1987.

Marbles

The record for clearing the ring (between 1·75 and 1·9 m *5¾–6¼ ft* in diameter) of 49 marbles is 2 min 56 sec by the Black Dog Boozers of Crawley, W Sussex at BBC Television Centre, London for BBC Television's *Record Breakers* on 14 Sep 1987.

Microlighting Endurance

Eve Jackson flew from Biggin Hill, Kent to Sydney, Australia from 26 Apr 1986 to 1 Aug 1987. The flight took 279 hr 55 min and covered 21 950 km *13 639 miles*. From 1 Dec 1987 to 29 Jan 1988, Brian Milton (GB) flew from London to Sydney with a flying time of 241 hr 20 min and covered 21 968 km *13 650 miles*. Vijaypat Singhania (India) flew from Biggin Hill to Delhi, India, a distance of 8724 km *5420 miles* in 87 hr 55 min, from 18 Aug to 10 Sep 1988.

The first British skater to win the world title was Wilfred O'Reilly (b. 22 Aug 1964) at Sydney, Australia on 24 Mar 1991.

Longest race The 'Elfstedentocht' ('Tour of the Eleven Towns'), which originated in the 17th century, was held in the Netherlands from 1909–63, and again in 1985 and 1986, covering 200 km *124 miles 483 yd*. As the weather does not permit an annual race in the Netherlands, alternative 'Elfstedentocht' take place at suitable venues. These venues have included Lake Vesijärvi, near Lahti, Finland; Ottawa River, Canada and Lake Weissenssee, Austria. The record time for 200 km is: men, 5 hr 40 min 37 sec by Dries van Wijhe (Netherlands); and women, 5 hr 48 min 8 sec by Alida Pasveer (Netherlands), both at Lake Weissensee (altitude 1100 m *3609 ft*), Austria on 11 Feb 1989. Jan-Roelof Kruithof (Netherlands) won the race eight times, 1974, 1976–7, 1979–83. An estimated 16 000 skaters took part in 1986.

24 hours Martinus Kuiper (Netherlands) skated 546·650 km *339·681 miles* in 24 hr in Alkmaar, Netherlands on 12–13 Dec 1988.

Ice and Sand Yachting

Origins The sport originated in the Low Countries from the year 1600 (earliest patent granted) and along the Baltic coast. The earliest authentic record is Dutch, dating from 1768. Land or sand yachts of Dutch construction were first reported on beaches (now in Belgium) in 1595. The earliest international championship was staged in 1914.

Highest speeds The highest speed officially recorded is 230 km/h *143 mph* by John D. Buckstaff in a Class A stern-steerer on Lake Winnebago, Wisconsin, USA in 1938. Such a speed is possible in a wind of 115 km/h *72 mph*.

Sand The official world record for a sand yacht is 107 km/h *66·48 mph* set by Christian-Yves Nau (France) (b. 1944) in *Mobil* at Le Touquet, France on 22 Mar 1981, when the wind speed reached 120 km/h *75 mph*. A speed of 142·26 km/h *88·4 mph* was attained by Nord Embroden (USA) in *Midnight at the Oasis* at Superior Dry Lake, California, USA on 15 Apr 1976.

Judo

Origins Judo is a modern combat sport which developed out of an amalgam of several old Japanese martial arts, the most popular of which was ju-jitsu (jiu-jitsu), which is thought to be of Chinese origin. Judo has greatly developed since 1882, when it was first devised by Dr Jigoro Kano (1860–1938). The International Judo Federation was founded in 1951.

Most titles *World and Olympic* World Championships were inaugurated in Tokyo, Japan in 1956. Women's championships were first held in 1980 in New York, USA. Yashiro Yamashita (b. 1 Jun 1957) won nine consecutive Japanese titles 1977–85, four world titles; Over 95 kg 1979, 1981 and 1983, Open 1981, and the Olympic Open category in 1984. He retired undefeated after 203 successive wins, 1977–85. Two other men have won four world titles, Wilhelm Ruska (Netherlands)

(b. 29 Aug 1940), Over 93 kg 1967, 1971 and 1972 Olympic and Open titles, and Shozo Fujii (Japan) (b. 12 May 1950), Under 80 kg 1971, 1973 and 1975, Under 75 kg 1979. The only men to have won two Olympic gold medals are Wilhelm Ruska (Netherlands), Over 93 kg and Open in 1972; Peter Seisenbacher (Austria) (b. 25 Mar 1960), 86 kg 1984 and 1988; and Hitoshi Saito (Japan) (b. 2 Jan 1961), Over 95 kg 1984 and 1988. Ingrid Berghmans (Belgium) (b. 24 Aug 1961) has won a record six women's world titles (first held 1980): Open 1980, 1982, 1984 and 1986 and Under 72 kg in 1984 and 1989. She has also won three silver medals and a bronze. She also won the Olympic 72 kg title in 1988, when women's judo was introduced as a demonstration sport.

Karen Briggs (b. 11 Apr 1963) is the most successful British player, with four women's world titles, Under 48 kg in 1982, 1984, 1986 and 1989.

British The greatest number of titles (instituted 1966) won is nine by David Colin Starbrook (b. 9 Aug 1945) (6th dan): Middleweight 1969–70, Light-heavyweight 1971–5 and the Open division 1970–71. A record six titles in the women's events (instituted 1971) were won by Christine Gallie (*née* Child) (b. 1946) (6th dan): Heavyweight in 1971–5 and the Open division in 1973. Adrian Neil Adams (b. 27 Sep 1958) has the most successful international record of any British male player. He won two junior (1974 and 1977) and five senior (1979–80, 1983–5) European titles; four World Championships medals (one gold, one silver, two bronze) and two Olympic silver medals. He also won eight British senior titles.

Highest grades The efficiency grades in judo are divided into pupil (*kyu*) and master (*dan*) grades. The highest awarded is the extremely rare red belt *Judan* (10th dan), given to only 13 men so far. The Judo protocol provides for an 11th dan (*Juichidan*) who also would wear a red belt, a 12th dan (*Junidan*) who would wear a white belt twice as wide as an ordinary belt, and the highest of all, *Shihan* (ductor), but these have never been bestowed, save for the 12th dan to the founder of the sport Dr Jigoro Kano.

The highest British native Judo grade is 8th dan by Charles Stuart Palmer (b. 1930). Christine Gallie was awarded her 6th dan in 1983.

Jiu-Jitsu The World Council of Jiu-Jitsu Organization has staged World Championships biennially since 1984. The Canadian team has been the team winners on each occasion.

Karate

Origins Based on techniques devised from the 6th century Chinese art of Shaolin boxing (Kempo), Karate was developed by an unarmed populace in Okinawa as a weapon against armed Japanese oppressors *c.* 1500. Transmitted to Japan in the 1920s by Funakoshi Gichin, this method of combat was refined into karate and organized into a sport with competitive rules. The five major styles of karate in Japan are: *Shotokan, Wado-ryu, Goju-ryu, Shito-ryu* and *Kyokushinkai*, each of which places different emphasis on speed and power, etc. Other styles include *Sankukai, Shotokai* and *Shukokai*. *Wu shu* is a comprehensive term embracing all Chinese martial arts. *Kung fu* is one aspect of these arts popularized by the cinema.

The governing body for the sport in Britain is the Martial Arts Commission, and all the martial arts are represented.

World Championships Great Britain have won a record six world titles (instituted 1970) at the Kumite team event, 1975, 1982, 1984, 1986, 1988 and 1990. Two men's individual kumite titles have been won by: Pat McKay (GB) at Under 80 kg, 1982 and 1984; Emmanuel Pinda (France) at Open, 1984 and Over 80 kg, 1988 and Theirry Masci (France) at Under 70 kg, 1986 and 1988. Four women's kumite titles have been won by Guus van Mourik (Netherlands) at Over 60 kg, 1982, 1984, 1986 and 1988. Three individual kata titles have been won by men: Tsuguo Sakumoto (Japan) 1984, 1986 and 1988; women: Mie Nakayama (Japan) 1982, 1984 and 1986.

Top exponents The leading exponents among karateka are a number of 10th dans in Japan.

The leading exponents in the United Kingdom are 8th dans: Tatsuo Suzuki (*Wado-ryu*) (b. 27 Apr 1928), Keinosuke Enoeda (*Shotokan*) and Steve Arneil (*Kyokushinkai*).

Lacrosse

MEN

Origins The game is of American Indian origin, derived from the inter-tribal game *baggataway*, and was played before 1492 by Iroquois Indians in lower Ontario, Canada and upper New York State, USA. The French named it after their game of *chouler à la crosse*, known in 1381.

It was introduced into Great Britain in 1867. The English Lacrosse Union was formed in 1892.

Lacrosse was included in the Olympic Games of 1904 and 1908 and featured as an exhibition sport in the 1928, 1932 and 1948 Games.

Most titles *World* The USA has won five of the six World Championships, in 1967, 1974, 1982, 1986 and 1990. Canada won the other world title in 1978 beating the USA 17–16 after extra time — this was the first drawn international match.

English The English Club Championship (Iroquois Cup instituted 1890), has been won most often by Stockport with 17 wins between 1897 and 1989. The record score in a final is 33 by Stockport *v.* London University (4) on 9 May 1987.

Most international appearances The record number of international representations is 42 by Peter Daniel Roden (Mellor) (b. 8 Nov 1954) from 1976–90.

Highest scores The highest score in an international match is the USA's 32–8 win over England at Toronto, Canada in 1986.

England's highest score was their 19–11 win over Canada at Melbourne, Australia in August 1974.

Fastest scoring Rod Burns scored only 4 seconds into the game for South Manchester and Wythenshawe *v.* Sheffield University on 6 Dec 1975.

WOMEN

The first reported playing of lacrosse by women was in 1886. The game has evolved seperately from the men's game so that the rules now differ considerably.

The All-England Women's Lacrosse Association was formed in 1912.

World Championships / World Cup The first World Cup was held in 1982, and the USA have won twice, 1982 and 1989.

Most international appearances Vivien Jones played in 64 internationals (52 for Wales, 9 for the Celts and 3 for Great Britain), 1977–90. Caro Macintosh (b. 18 Feb 1932) played in 56 internationals (52 for Scotland and four for Great Britain).

Highest score The highest score by an international team was by Great Britain and Ireland with their 40–0 defeat of Long Island during their 1967 tour of the USA.

Marbles

Origins The name derives from the practice in the 18th century of making the ball from marble chips. However, marbles dates from ancient times and may have been a children's game in ancient Egypt, where pebbles or nuts were used. It was introduced into Britain by the Romans in the 1st century AD. It became a competitive sport under the British Marbles Board of Control at the Greyhound Hotel, Tinsley Green, Crawley, W Sussex in 1926.

Most championships The British Championship (established 1926) has been won most often by the Toucan Terribles with 20 consecutive titles (1956–75). Three founder members, Len Smith, Jack and Charlie Dempsey, played in every title win. They were finally beaten in 1976 by the Pernod Rams, captained by Len Smith's son, Paul. Len Smith (1917–90) won the individual title 15 times (1957–64, 1966, 1968–73) but lost in 1974 to his son Alan.

Microlighting

The *Fédération Aéronautique Internationale* has established two classes of aircraft for which records are accepted, C1 a/o and R 1-2-3, and the following are the overall best of the two classes (all in the C1 a/o class).

World records Distance in a straight line: 1627·78 km *1011·48 miles* Wilhelm Lischak (Austria), Volsau, Austria to Brest, France, 8 Jun 1988.

Altitude: 9189 m *30 147 ft* Eric S. Winton (Australia), Tyagarah Aerodrome, NSW, Australia, 8 Apr 1989.

Distance in a closed circuit: 2702·16 km *1679·09 miles* Wilhelm Lischak (Austria), Wels, Austria, 18 Jun 1988.

Speed over a 100 km closed circuit: 297·72 km/h *185 mph* C. T. Andrews (USA), 3 Aug 1982.

Speed over a 500 km closed circuit: 293·04 km/h *182 mph* C. T. Andrews (USA), 3 Aug 1982.

David Cook set a British altitude record of 8249 m *27 066 ft* on 28 Apr 1990 at Aldeburgh, Suffolk.

Modern Pentathlon & Biathlon

Points scored in riding, fencing, cross country and hence overall scores have no comparative value between one competition and another. In shooting and swimming (300 m) the scores are of record significance.

The Modern Pentathlon (Fencing, Swimming, Shooting, Running and Riding) was inaugurated into the Olympic Games at Stockholm in 1912. The Modern Pentathlon Association of Great Britain was formed in 1922. *L'Union Internationale de Pentathlon Moderne* (UIPM) was founded at Aldershot, Hants on 3 Aug 1948. The administration of Biathlon (cross-country skiing and shooting) was added in 1957, and the name modified accordingly, *L'Union Internationale de Pentathlon Moderne et Biathlon* (UIPMB).

MODERN PENTATHLON

Most titles *World* András Balczó (Hungary) (b. 16 Aug 1938) won the record number of world titles (instituted 1949), six individual and seven team. He won the world individual title in 1963, 1965–7 and 1969 and the Olympic title in 1972. His seven team titles (1960–70) comprised five world and two Olympic. The USSR has won a record 13 world and four Olympic team titles. Hungary has also won a record four Olympic team titles and ten world titles.

Women's World Championships were first held in 1981. Poland have won a record four women's world team titles: 1985, 1988, 1989 and 1990; Great Britain won three world titles and three World Cups, 1978–80, when this competition preceded the world championships. The only double individual champion has been Irina Kiselyeva (USSR), 1986–7.

Olympic The greatest number of Olympic gold medals won is three, by András Balczó, a member of the winning team in 1960 and 1968 and the 1972 individual champion. Lars Hall (Sweden) (b. 30 Apr 1927) has uniquely won two individual championships (1952 and 1956). Pavel Serafimovich Lednyev (USSR) (b. 25 Mar 1943) won a record seven medals (two team gold, one team silver, one individual silver, three individual bronze), 1968–80.

The best British performance is the team gold medal in 1976 by Jim Fox, Adrian Philip Parker and Daniel Nightingale. The best individual placing is fourth by Jeremy Robert 'Jim' Fox (b. 19 Sep 1941) in 1972 and Richard Lawson Phelps (b. 19 Apr 1961) in 1984.

Probably the greatest margin of victory was by William Oscar Guernsey Grut (Sweden) (b. 17 Sep 1914) in the 1948 Games, when he won three events and was placed fifth and eighth in the other two.

British The pentathlete with most British titles is Jim Fox, with ten (1963, 1965–8, 1970–74). Wendy Norman won a record seven women's titles, 1978–80, 1982, 1986–8.

BIATHLON

The biathlon, which combines cross-country skiing and rifle shooting, was first included in the Olympic Games in 1960, and World Championships were first held in 1958. Since 1984 there has been a women's World Championship and a women's biathlon will be contested at the 1992 Olympics.

Most titles *Olympic* Two Olympic individual titles have been won by: Magnar Solberg (Norway) (b. 4 Feb 1937), in 1968 and 1972; and by Franz-Peter Rötsch (GDR) (b. 19 Apr 1964) at both 10 km and 20 km in 1988. The USSR has won all six 4 × 7·5 km relay titles, 1968–88. Aleksandr Ivanovich Tikhonov (b. 2 Jan 1947) who was a member of the first four teams also won a silver in the 1968 20 km.

World Frank Ullrich (GDR) (b. 24 Jan 1958) has won a record six individual world titles, four at 10 km, 1978–81, including the 1980 Olympics, and two at 20 km, 1982–3.

Aleksandr Tikhonov was in ten winning USSR relay teams, 1968–80 and won four individual titles.

The Biathlon World Cup (instituted 1979) was won four times by Frank Ullrich, 1978 and 1980–82. He was second in 1979 and third in 1983.

Motorcycle Racing

Earliest race The first motorcycle race was held over a mile *1·6 km* on an oval track at Sheen House, Richmond, Surrey on 29 Nov 1897, won by Charles Jarrott (1877 –1944) on a Fournier. The oldest continuous motorcycle races in the world are the Auto-Cycle Union Tourist Trophy (TT) series, first held on the 25·44 km *15·81 mile* 'Peel' (St John's) course in the Isle of Man on 28 May 1907, and still run in the island on the 'Mountain' circuit.

Fastest circuits The highest average lap speed attained on any closed circuit is 257·958 km/h *160·288 mph* by Yvon du Hamel (Canada) (b. 1941) on a modified 903 cc four-cylinder Kawasaki Z1 at the 31-degree banked 4·02 km *2·5 mile* Daytona International Speedway, Florida, USA in March 1973. His lap time was 56·149 sec.

The fastest road circuit used to be Francorchamps circuit near Spa, Belgium, then 14·12 km *8·74 miles* in length. It was lapped in 3 min 50·3 sec (average speed 220·721 km/h *137·150 mph*) by Barry

■ **Two titles in a year** In 1985 Freddie Burdette Spencer (USA) (b. 20 Dec 1961), riding for Honda, became the first man ever to win the 250 cc and 500 cc titles in the same year. (Photo: All-Sport (USA)/M. Powell)

Stephen Frank Sheene (GB) (b. 11 Sep 1950) on a 495 cc 4-cylinder Suzuki during the Belgian Grand Prix on 3 Jul 1977. On that occasion he set a record time for this ten-lap (141·20 km *87·74 mile*) race of 38 min 58·5 sec (average speed 217·370 km/h *135·068 mph*).

United Kingdom The lap record for the outer circuit (4·453 km *2·767 miles*) at the Brooklands Motor Course, near Weybridge, Surrey (open between 1907 and 1939) was 80 sec (average speed 200·37 km/h *124·51 mph*) by Noel Baddow 'Bill' Pope (later Major) (GB) (1909–71) on a Brough Superior powered by a supercharged 996 cc V-twin '8-80' JAP engine developing 110 bhp, on 4 Jul 1939.

The fastest circuit in current use is that over public roads at Dundrod, Co. Antrim for the Ulster Grand Prix. Steve Hislop (Scotland) (b. 11 Jan 1962) set a lap record of 199·10 km/h *123·72 mph* and overall average speed of 195·50 km/h *121·46 mph* for the 'King of the Road' race on 11 Aug 1990.

Longest circuit The 60·72 km *37·73 mile* 'Mountain' circuit on the Isle of Man, over which the principal TT races have been run since 1911 (with minor amendments in 1920), has 264 curves and corners and is the longest used for any motorcycle race.

Most successful riders *World Championships* The most World Championship titles (instituted by the *Fédération Internationale Motocycliste* in 1949) won is 15 by Giacomo Agostini (Italy) (b. 16 Jun 1942), seven at 350 cc, 1968–74, and eight at 500 cc in 1966–72, 1975. He is the only man to win two World Championships in five consecutive years (350 cc and 500 cc titles 1968–72).

Angel Roldan Nieto (Spain) (b. 25 Jan 1947) won a record seven 125 cc titles, 1971–2, 1979, 1981–4 and he also won a record six titles at 50 cc, 1969–70, 1972, 1975–7. Klaus Enders (West Germany) (b. 1937) won six world side-car titles, 1967, 1969–70, 1972–4.

Agostini won 122 races (68 at 500 cc, 54 at 350 cc) in the World Championship series

between 24 Apr 1965 and 25 Sep 1977, including a record 19 in 1970, also achieved by Mike Hailwood in 1966.

In 1985 Freddie Burdette Spencer (USA) (b. 20 Dec 1961), riding for Honda, became the first man ever to win the 250 cc and 500 cc titles in the same year.

Most successful machines Japanese Yamaha machines won 40 World Championships between 1964 and 1990.

Tourist Trophy The record number of victories in the Isle of Man TT races is 14 by Stanley Michael Bailey Hailwood (1940–81) between 1961 and 1979. The first man to win three consecutive TT titles in two events was James A. Redman (Rhodesia) (b. 8 Nov 1931). He won the 250 cc and 350 cc events in 1963–5. Mike Hailwood won three events in one year, in 1961 and 1967, and this feat was repeated by William Joseph Dunlop (Ireland) (b. 25 Feb 1952) in 1985 and 1988; and by Steve Hislop in 1989 and 1991.

The Isle of Man TT circuit speed record is 198·72 km/h *123·48 mph* by Steve Hislop on 1 Jun 1991. He also set the race speed record 1 hr 52 min 10·6 sec for an average speed of 194·87 km/h *121·09 mph* to win the 1991 Senior TT on his 750 cc Honda.

Trials A record three World Trials Championships have been won by Yrjö Vesterinen (Finland), 1976–8; Eddie Lejeune (Belgium), 1982–4; Thierry Michaud (France), 1985–6 and 1988, and Jordi Tarres (Spain), 1987, 1989–90.

Moto-cross Joël Robert (Belgium) (b. 11 Nov 1943) won six 250 cc Moto-cross World Championships (1964, 1968–72). Between 25 Apr 1964 and 18 Jun 1972 he won a record fifty 250 cc Grand Prix. The youngest moto-cross world champion was Dave Strijbos (Netherlands) (b. 9 Nov 1968), who won the 125 cc title aged 18 yr 296 days on 31 Aug 1986. Eric Geboers (Belgium) has uniquely won all three categories of the Moto-Cross World Championships, at 125 cc in 1983, 250 cc in 1987 and 500 cc in 1988.

Youngest and oldest world champions Loris Capirossi (Italy) (b. 4 Apr 1973) is the youngest to win a World Cham-

pionship. He was 17 yr 165 days when he won the 125 cc title on 16 Sep 1990. The oldest was Hermann-Peter Müller (1909–76) of West Germany, who won the 250 cc title in 1955 aged 46.

Motor Racing

Earliest races There are various conflicting claims, but the first automobile race was the 323 km *201 mile* Green Bay to Madison, Wisconsin, USA run in 1878 won by an Oshkosh steamer. In 1887 Count Jules Félix Philippe Albert de Dion de Malfiance (1856–1946) won the *La Vélocipéde* 31 km *19·3 miles* race in Paris in a De Dion steam quadricycle in which he is reputed to have exceeded 59 km/h *37 mph*. The first 'real' race was from Paris to Bordeaux and back (1178 km *732 miles*) on 11–13 Jun 1895. The first to finish was Emile Levassor (1844–97) of France, in a Panhard-Levassor two-seater, with a 1·2-litre Daimler engine developing 3½ hp. His time was 48 hr 47 min (average speed 24·15 km/h *15·01 mph*). The first closed circuit race was held over five laps of a mile *1·6 km* dirt track at Narragansett Park, Cranston, Rhode Island, USA on 7 Sep 1896, won by A. H. Whiting, driving a Riker electric.

The oldest race in the world still regularly run, is the RAC Tourist Trophy, first staged on 14 Sep 1905, in the Isle of Man. The oldest continental race is the French Grand Prix, first held on 26–27 Jun 1906. The Coppa Florio, in Sicily, has been irregularly held since 1906.

Fastest circuits The highest average lap speed attained on any closed circuit is 403·878 km/h *250·958 mph* in a trial by Dr Hans Liebold (Germany) (b. 12 Oct 1926) who lapped the 12·64 km *7·85 mile* high-speed track at Nardo, Italy in 1 min 52·67 sec in a Mercedes-Benz C111-IV experimental coupé on 5 May 1979. It was powered by a V8 engine with two KKK turbochargers, with an output of 500 hp at 6200 rpm.

The fastest road circuit was the Francorchamps circuit near Spa, Belgium, then

14·10 km *8·76 miles* in length which was lapped in 3 min 13·4 sec (average speed 262·461 km/h *163·086 mph*) on 6 May 1973, by Henri Pescarolo (France) (b. 25 Sep 1942) driving a 2993-cc V12 Matra-Simca MS670 Group 5 sports car.

Fastest race The fastest race is the Busch Clash at Daytona, Florida, USA over 80·5 km *50 miles* on a 4 km *2½ mile* 31-degree banked track. In 1987 Bill Elliott (b. 8 Oct 1955) averaged 318·322 km/h *197·802 mph* in a Ford Thunderbird. Al Unser Jr set the world record for a 805 km *500 mile* race on 9 Aug 1990 when he won the Michigan 500A at an average speed of 305·2 km/h *189·7 mph*.

WORLD CHAMPIONSHIP GRAND PRIX MOTOR RACING —

Most successful drivers The World Drivers' Championship, inaugurated in 1950, has been won a record five times by Juan-Manuel Fangio (Argentina) (b. 24 Jun 1911) in 1951 and 1954–57. He retired in 1958, after having won 24 Grand Prix races (two shared) from 51 starts.

Alain Prost (France) (b. 24 Feb 1955) holds the records for both the most Grand Prix points in a career, 676·5 and the most Grand Prix victories, 44 from 175 races, 1980–91. The most Grand Prix victories in a year is eight by Ayrton Senna (Brazil) (b. 21 Mar 1960) in 1988. The most Grand Prix starts is 214 by Ricardo Patrese (Italy) (b. 17 Apr 1954) from 1977–91. The greatest number of pole positions is 56 by Ayrton Senna from 116 races (30 wins), 1985–91.

Oldest and youngest The youngest world champion was Emerson Fittipaldi (Brazil) (b. 12 Dec 1946) who won his first World Championship on 10 Sep 1972 aged 25 yr 273 days. The oldest world champion was Juan-Manuel Fangio who won his last World Championship on 4 Aug 1957 aged 46 yr 41 days.

The youngest Grand Prix winner was Bruce Leslie McLaren (1937–70) of New Zealand, who won the United States Grand Prix at Sebring, Florida on 12 Dec 1959, aged 22 yr 104 days. Troy Ruttman (USA) was 22 yr 80 days when he won the India-

napolis 500 on 30 May 1952, which was part of the World Championships at the time. The oldest Grand Prix winner (in pre-World Championship days) was Tazio Giorgio Nuvolari (Italy) (1892–1953), who won the Albi Grand Prix at Albi, France on 14 Jul 1946, aged 53 yr 240 days. The oldest Grand Prix driver was Louis Alexandre Chiron (Monaco) (1899–1979), who finished sixth in the Monaco Grand Prix on 22 May 1955, aged 55 yr 292 days. The youngest driver to qualify for a Grand Prix was Michael Christopher Thackwell (New Zealand) (b. 30 Mar 1961) at the Canadian GP on 28 Sep 1980, aged 19 yr 182 days.

Manufacturers Ferrari have won a record eight manufacturers' World Championships, 1961, 1964, 1975–7, 1979, 1982–3. Ferrari have 103 race wins in 476 Grands Prix, 1950–91.

The greatest dominance by one team since the Constructor's Championship was instituted in 1958 was by McLaren in 1988 when they won 15 of the 16 Grands Prix. Ayrton Senna had eight wins and three seconds, Alain Prost had seven wins and seven seconds. The McLarens, powered by Honda engines, amassed over three times the points of their nearest rivals, Ferrari. Excluding the Indianapolis 500 race, then included in the World Drivers' Championship, Ferrari won all seven races in 1952 and the first eight (of nine) in 1953.

Fastest race The fastest overall average speed for a Grand Prix race on a circuit in current use is 235·421 km/h *146·284 mph* by Nigel Mansell (GB) in a Williams-Honda at Zeltweg in the Austrian Grand Prix on 16 Aug 1987. The qualifying lap record was set by Keke Rosberg (Finland) at 1 min

■ **Most pole positions**
Ayrton Senna (Brazil) dominated the beginning of the 1991 season, winning each of the first four races. He began each race from pole position making his career total a record 56. Remarkably in a Formula One career which began in 1985, he has started nearly half of his Grand Prix races from the front. (Photo: All-Sport)

MOTOR RACING

05·59 sec, an average speed of 258·803 km/h *160·817 mph*, in a Williams-Honda at Silverstone in the British Grand Prix on 20 Jul 1985.

Closest finish The closest finish to a World Championship race was when Ayrton Senna (Brazil) in a Lotus beat Nigel Mansell (GB) in a Williams by 0·014 sec in the Spanish Grand Prix at Jerez de la Frontera on 13 Apr 1986. In the Italian Grand Prix at Monza on 5 Sep 1971, 0·61 sec separated winner Peter Gethin (GB) from the fifth placed driver.

BRITISH GRAND PRIX

First held in 1926 as the RAC Grand Prix, and held annually with the above name since 1949. The venues have been Aintree, Merseyside; Brands Hatch, Kent; Brooklands, Surrey; Donington, Leics and Silverstone, Northants.

Fastest speed The fastest race time is 1 hr 18 min 10·436 sec, average speed 235·405 km/h *146·274 mph*, when Alain Prost won in a McLaren at Silverstone on 21 Jul 1985.

Most wins The most wins by a driver is five by Jim Clark, 1962–5 and 1967, all in Lotus cars. Jim Clark and Jack Brabham (Australia) (b. 2 Apr 1926) have both won the race on three different circuits; Brands Hatch, Silverstone and Aintree. The most wins by a manufacturer is ten by Ferrari, 1951–4, 1956, 1958, 1961, 1976, 1978 and 1990.

LE MANS

The greatest distance ever covered in the 24-hour *Grand Prix d'Endurance* (first held on 26–27 May 1923) on the old Sarthe circuit at Le Mans, France is 5333·724 km *3314·222 miles* by Dr Helmut Marko (Austria) (b. 27 Apr 1943) and Gijs van Lennep (Netherlands) (b. 16 Mar 1942) in a 4907-cc flat-12 Porsche 917K Group 5 sports car, on 12–13 Jun 1971. The record for the greatest distance ever covered for the current circuit is 5332 km *3313·241 miles* (av. speed 221·63 km/h *137·718 mph*) by Jan Lammers (Holland), Johnny Dumfries and Andy Wallace (both GB) in a Jaguar XJR9 on 11–12 Jun 1988.

The race lap record (now 13·535 km *8·410 mile* lap) is 3 min 21·27 sec (average speed 242·093 km/h *150·429 mph*) by Alain Ferté (France) in a Jaguar XRJ-9 on 10 Jun 1989. Hans Stück (West Germany) set the practice lap record of 3 min 14·8 sec (av. speed 252·05 km/h *156·62 mph*) on 14 Jun 1985.

Most wins The race has been won by Porsche cars twelve times, in 1970–71, 1976–7, 1979, 1981–7. The most wins by one man is six by Jacques Bernard 'Jacky' Ickx (Belgium) (b. 1 Jan 1945), 1969, 1975–7 and 1981–2.

INDIANAPOLIS 500

The Indianapolis 500 mile *804 km* race (200 laps) was inaugurated in the USA on 30 May 1911. Three drivers have four wins: Anthony Joseph 'A.J.' Foyt Jr (USA) (b. 16 Jan 1935) in 1961, 1964, 1967 and 1977; Al Unser Sr (USA) (b. 29 May 1939) in 1970–71, 1978 and 1987; and Rick Mears (USA) (b. 3 Dec 1951) in 1979, 1984, 1988 and 1991. The record time is 2 hr 41 min (299·299 km/h *185·981 mph*) by Arie Luyendyk (Netherlands) driving a Lola-Chevrolet on 27 May 1990. The record average speed for four laps qualifying is 362·577 km/h *225·301 mph* by Emerson Fittipaldi (Brazil) in a Penske-Cheverolet on

13 May 1990. On the same day he set the one-lap record of 363·018 km/h *225·575 mph*. The track record is 367·728 km/h *228·502 mph* by Al Unser Jr (USA) on 11 May 1990. A. J. Foyt Jr has started a record 34 races, 1959–90 and Rick Mears has started from pole position a record six times, 1979, 1982, 1986, 1988–9 and 1991. The record prize fund is $7 009 150 and the individual prize record is $1 219 704 by Rick Mears, both in 1991.

NASCAR records Richard Lee Petty (USA) (b. 2 Jul 1937) won 200 NASCAR Winston Cup races in 1137 starts from 1958 to 26 May 1991. His best season was 1967 with 27 wins. Petty, on 1 Aug 1971, was the first driver to pass $1 million career earnings. The NASCAR career money record is $13 383 969 by Dale Earnhardt (b. 29 Apr 1952) to 2 Jun 1991. This includes a year's record $3 083 056 in 1990. Geoff Bodine (b. 18 Apr 1949) won 55 races in NASCAR Modified racing in 1978. Shawna Robinson (b. 30 Nov 1954) became the first woman to win a NASCAR race when she won an event in the NASCAR Dash Series at Asheville, North Carolina, USA on 10 Jun 1988.

RALLYING

The earliest long rally was promoted by the Parisian daily *Le Matin* in 1907 from Peking (now Beijing), China to Paris over about 12 000 km *7500 miles* on 10 Jun. The winner, Prince Scipione Borghese (1872–1927) of Italy, arrived in Paris on 10 Aug 1907 in his 40-hp Itala accompanied by his chauffeur, Ettore, and Luigi Barzini.

Longest The longest ever rally was the *Singapore Airlines* London–Sydney Rally over 31 107 km *19 329 miles* from Covent

Garden, London on 14 Aug 1977 to Sydney Opera House, won on 28 Sep 1977 by Andrew Cowan, Colin Malkin and Michael Broad in a Mercedes 280E. The longest held annually is the Safari Rally (first run in 1953 as the Coronation Rally, through Kenya, Tanzania and Uganda, but now restricted to Kenya). The race has covered up to 6234 km *3874 miles*, as in the 17th Safari held from 8–12 Apr 1971. It has been won a record five times by Shekhar Mehta (b. Kenya, 20 Jun 1945) in 1973, 1979–82.

The Paris–Dakar 92 rally between 25 Dec 1991 and 22 Jan 1992 is scheduled to be raced over about 12 700 km *7890 miles* from Paris to Cape Town. It will, however, no longer go near the Sénégalese capital.

Monte Carlo The Monte Carlo Rally (first run 1911) has been won a record four times by: Sandro Munari (Italy) (b. 27 Mar 1940) in 1972, 1975, 1976 and 1977; and Walter Röhrl (West Germany) (b. 7 Mar 1947) (with co-driver Christian Geistdorfer) in 1980, 1982–4, each time in a different car. The smallest car to win was an 851-cc Saab driven by Erik Carlsson (Sweden) (b. 5 Mar 1929) and Gunnar Häggbom (Sweden) (b. 7 Dec 1935) on 25 Jan 1962, and by Carlsson and Gunnar Palm on 24 Jan 1963.

Britain The RAC Rally (first held 1932) has been recognized by the FIA since 1957. Hannu Mikkola (Finland) (b. 24 May 1942) (with co-driver Arne Hertz) has a record four wins, in a Ford Escort, 1978–9 and an Audi Quatro, 1981–2.

World Championship Two World Drivers' Championships (instituted 1979) have been won by Walter Röhrl, 1980 and 1982, Juha Kankkunen (Finland) (b. 2 Apr 1959), 1986–7 and by Mikki Biasion (Italy) 1988–9. The most wins in World Championship races is 19 by Hannu Mikkola and Markku Alen (Finland) to the start of 1991. Lancia have won a record eight manufacturers' World Championships. The first winner of the women's World Championship, inaugurated in 1990, was Louise Aitken-Walker (GB).

DRAG RACING

Piston engined The official lowest elapsed time recorded by a piston-engined dragster from a standing start for 440 yd *402 m* is 4·897 sec by Joe Amato (USA) (b. 1944) at Gainesville, Florida on 24 Mar 1991. The highest terminal velocity reached at the end of a 440 yd run is 476·43 km/h *296·05 mph* by Gary Ormsby (USA) (b. 11 Nov 1941) in qualifying for the NHRA Heartlands Nationals at Topeka, Kansas, USA on 29 Sep 1990. The run was clocked at 4·881 sec but was not officially recognized. The lowest elapsed time for a woman is 4·962 sec by Shirley Muldowney (USA) (b. 1940) at Topeka on 29 Sep 1989. For a petrol-driven piston-engined car the lowest elapsed time is 7·184 sec by Darrell Alderman (USA) (b. 1949), driving a Dodge Daytona and the highest terminal velocity is 309·27 km/h *192·18 mph* by Warren Johnson (b. 1943) in a Oldsmobile Cutlass Supreme, both at Dallas, Texas on 13 Oct 1990. The lowest elapsed time for a petrol-driven piston-engined motorcycle is 7·697 sec by John Myers (USA) (b. 1958) at Gainesville, Florida, USA on 8 Mar 1990 and the highest terminal velocity is 283·99 km/h *176·47 mph* by John Mafaro (USA) (b. 1949) at Indianapolis on 4 Sep 1989.

Most wins The greatest number of wins in National Hot Rod Association national events is 80 by Bob Glidden in Pro Stock, 1973–91.

Highest speeds The most successful land speed record breaker was Sir Malcolm Campbell (GB) (1885–1948). He broke the official record nine times between 25 Sep 1924, with 235·216 km/h *146·157 mph* in a Sunbeam, and 3 Sep 1935, when he achieved 480·620 km/h *301·129 mph* in the Rolls Royce-engined *Bluebird*.

Mountaineering

Although bronze-age artifacts have been found on the summit of the Riffelhorn, Switzerland (2927 m *9605 ft*), mountaineering as a sport has a continuous history dating back only to 1854. Isolated instances of climbing for its own sake exist back to the 13th century. The Atacamenans built sacrificial platforms near the summit of Llullaillaco (6723 m *22 057 ft*) in late pre-Columbian times c. 1490.

The earliest recorded rock climb in the British Isles was of Stac na Biorrach, St Kilda (71·9 m *236 ft*) by Sir Robert Moray in 1698.

Mt Everest Everest (8863 m *29 078 ft*) was first climbed at 11:30 a.m. on 29 May 1953, when the summit was reached by Edmund Percival Hillary (b. 20 Jul 1919), of New Zealand, and Sherpa Tenzing Norgay (1914–86, formerly called Tenzing Khumjung Bhutia). The successful expedition was led by Col. (later Hon. Brigadier) Henry Cecil John Hunt (b. 22 Jun 1910) on 23 Apr 1979.

Most conquests Ang Rita Sherpa (b. 1947), with ascents in 1983, 1984, 1985, 1987, 1988 and 1990 has scaled Everest six times and all without the use of bottled oxygen.

Solo Reinhold Messner (Italy) (b. 17 Sep 1944) was the first to make the entire climb solo on 20 Aug 1980. Also Messner, with Peter Habeler (Austria) (b. 22 Jul 1942), made the first entirely oxygen-less ascent on 8 May 1978.

First Britons Douglas Scott (b. 29 May 1941) and Dougal Haston (1940–77) successfully completed the climb on 24 Sep 1975.

First woman Junko Tabei (Japan) (b. 22 Sep 1939) reached the summit on 16 May 1975.

Oldest Richard Daniel Bass (USA) (b. 21 Dec 1929) was aged 55 yr 130 days when he reached the summit on 30 Apr 1985.

Most successful expedition The Mount Everest International Peace Climb, a team of American, Russian and Chinese climbers, led by James W. Whittaker (USA), in 1990 succeeded in putting the greatest number of people on the summit, 20, from 7–10 May 1990.

Sea level to summit Timothy John Macartney-Snape (Australia) (b. 30 Apr 1963) traversed Mount Everest's entire altitude from sea level to summit. He set off on foot from the Bay of Bengal near Calcutta, India on 5 Feb 1990 and reached the summit on 11 May having walked approximately 1200 km *745 miles*.

All continents The first person to climb the highest mountain in each of the seven continents (Africa; Kilimanjaro 5895 m *19 340 ft*: Antarctica; Vinson Massif 5140 m *16 863 ft*: Asia; Everest 8863 m *29 078 ft*: Europe; El'brus 5642 m *18 510 ft*: North and Central America; McKinley 6194 m *20 320 ft*: South America; Aconcagua 6960 m *22 834 ft* and Australasia; Carstensz Pyramid 5030 m *16 502 ft*) was Patrick Morrow (Canada) (b. 18 Oct 1952). He completed the last of the seven mountains, with his successful conquest of Carstensz Pyramid on 7 May 1986.

Mountaineer Reinhold Messner was the first person to successfully scale all 14 of the world's mountains of over 8000 m *26 250 ft*, all without oxygen. With his ascent of Kanchenjunga in 1982, he became the first person to climb the world's three highest mountains, having earlier reached the summits of Everest and K2.

Greatest walls The highest final stage in any wall climb is that on the south face of Annapurna I (8091 m *26 545 ft*). It was climbed by the British expedition led by Christian John Storey Bonington (b. 6 Aug 1934) when from 2 Apr to 27 May 1970, using 5500 m *18 000 ft* of rope, Donald Whillans (1933–85) and Dougal Haston scaled to the

OLYMPIC RECORDS – ATHLETICS

MEN	min:sec	Name	Year
100 m	9·92	Carl Lewis (USA)	1988
200 m	19·75	Joe DeLoach (USA)	1988
400 m	43·86 a	Lee Evans (USA)	1968
800 m	1:43·00	Joaquim Cruz (Brazil)	1984
1500 m	3:32·53	Sebastian Coe (GB)	1984
5000 m	13:05·59	Saïd Aouita (Morocco)	1984
10 000 m	27:21·46	Brahim Boutayeb (Morocco)	1988
Marathon	2:09·21	Carlos Lopes (Portugal)	1984
3000 m Steeplechase	8:05·51	Julius Kariuki (Kenya)	1988
110 m hurdles	12·98	Roger Kingdom (USA)	1988
400 m hurdles	47·19	Andre Phillips (USA)	1988
4 × 100 m relay	37·83	USA	1984
4 × 400 m relay	2:56·16	USA	1968 a & 1988
20 km walk	1:19·57	Jozef Pribilinec (Czechoslovakia)	1988
50 km walk	3:38·29	Vyacheslav Ivanenko (USSR)	1988
	m		
High jump	2·38	Gennadiy Avdeyenko (USSR)	1988
Pole vault	5·90	Sergey Bubka (USSR)	1988
Long jump	8·90 a	Bob Beamon (USA)	1968
Triple jump	17·61	Khristo Markov (Bulgaria)	1988
Shot	22·47	Ulf Timmerman (GDR)	1988
Discus	68·82	Jürgen Schult (GDR)	1988
Hammer	84·80	Sergey Litvinov (USSR)	1988
Javelin	85·90 *	Jan Zelezny (Czechoslovakia)	1988
old	94·58	Miklós Németh (Hungary)	1976
Decathlon	8847 points	Daley Thompson (GB)	1984
WOMEN	min:sec		
100 m	10·62	Florence Griffith-Joyner (USA)	1988
	10·56 w	Florence Griffith-Joyner (USA)	1988
200 m	21·34	Florence Griffith-Joyner (USA)	1988
400 m	48·65	Olga Bryzgina (USSR)	1988
800 m	1:53·43	Nadezhda Olizarenko (USSR)	1980
1500 m	3:53·96	Paula Ivan (Romania)	1988
3000 m	8:26·53	Tatyana Samolenko (USSR)	1988
10 000 m	31:05·21	Olga Bondarenko (USSR)	1988
Marathon	2:24·52	Joan Benoit (USA)	1984
100 m hurdles	12·38	Yodanka Donkova (Bulgaria)	1988
400 m hurdles	53·17	Debbie Flintoff-King (Australia)	1988
4 × 100 m relay	41·60	GDR	1980
4 × 400 m relay	3:15·18	USSR	1988
	m		
High jump	2·03	Louise Ritter (USA)	1988
Long jump	7·40	Jackie Joyner-Kersee (USA)	1988
Shot	22·41	Ilona Slupianek (GDR)	1980
Discus	72·30	Martina Hellman (GDR)	1988
Javelin	74·68	Petra Felke (GDR)	1988
Heptathlon	7291 points	Jackie Joyner-Kersee (USA)	1988

* performance made in qualifying round.
a at high altitude, Mexico City 2240 m.
w wind-assisted.

OLYMPIC RECORDS – SWIMMING

MEN	min:sec		
50 m freestyle	22·14	Matt Biondi (USA)	1988
100 m freestyle	48·63	Matt Biondi (USA)	1988
200 m freestyle	1:47·25	Duncan Armstrong (Australia)	1988
400 m freestyle	3:46·95	Uwe Dassler (GDR)	1988
1500 m freestyle	14:58·27	Vladimir Salnikov (USSR)	1980
4 × 100 m freestyle relay	3:16·53	USA	1988
4 × 200 m freestyle relay	7:12·51	USA	1988
100 m backstroke	54·51	David Berkoff (USA)	1988
200 m backstroke	1:58·99	Rick Carey (USA)	1984
100 m breaststroke	48·63	Steve Lunquist (USA)	1984
200 m breaststroke	2:13·34	Victor Davis (Canada)	1984
100 m butterfly	53·80	Anthony Nesty (Surinam)	1988
200 m butterfly	1:56·94	Michael Gross (FRG)	1988
200 m individual medley	2:00·17	Tamás Darnyi (Hungary)	1988
400 m individual medley	4:14·75	Tamás Darnyi (Hungary)	1988
4 × 100 m medley relay	3:36·93	USA	1988

WOMEN			
50 m freestyle	25·49	Kristin Otto (GDR)	1988
100 m freestyle	54·79	Barbara Krause (GDR)	1980
200 m freestyle	1:57·65	Heike Freidrich (GDR)	1988
400 m freestyle	4:03·85	Janet Evans (USA)	1988
800 m freestyle	8:20·20	Janet Evans (USA)	1988
4 × 100 m freestyle relay	3:40·63	GDR	1988
100 m backstroke	1:00·86	Rica Reinisch (GDR)	1980
200 m backstroke	2:09·99	Krisztina Egerszegi (Hungary)	1988
100 m breaststroke	1:07·95	Tania Dangalakova (Bulgaria)	1988
200 m breaststroke	2:26·71	Silke Hörner (GDR)	1988
100 m butterfly	59·00	Kristin Otto (GDR)	1988
200 m butterfly	2:06·90	Mary T. Meagher (USA)	1984
200 m individual medley	2:12·59	Daniela Hunger (GDR)	1988
400 m individual medley	4:36·29	Petra Schneider (GDR)	1980
4 × 100 m medley relay	4:03·74	GDR	1988

Olympic Games

These records include the Games held at Athens in 1906.

The earliest celebration of the ancient Olympic Games of which there is a certain record is that of July 776 BC, when Coroibos, a cook from Elis, won the foot race, though their origin dates from perhaps as early as c. 1370 BC. The ancient Games were terminated by an order issued in Milan in AD 393 by Theodosius I, 'the Great' (c. 346–95), Emperor of Rome. At the instigation of Pierre de Fredi, Baron de Coubertin (1863–1937), the Olympic Games of the modern era were inaugurated in Athens on 6 Apr 1896. In 1992, the XVI Winter Games take place at Albertville, France from 8–23 February and the XXV Summer Games at Barcelona, Spain from 25 July–9 August.

Ever present Five countries have never failed to be represented at the 22 celebrations of the Summer Games: Australia, France, Greece, Great Britain and Switzerland (only contested the Equestrian events, held in Stockholm, Sweden, in 1956 and did not attend the Games in Melbourne). Of these only Great Britain has been present at all Winter celebrations as well.

Largest crowd The largest crowd at any Olympic site was 150 000 at the 1952 ski-jumping at the Holmenkollen, outside Oslo, Norway. Estimates of the number of spectators of the marathon race through Tokyo, Japan on 21 Oct 1964 ranged from 500 000 to 1 500 000. The total spectator attendance at Los Angeles in 1984 was given as 5 797 923 (see General Records).

Olympic Torch relay The longest journey of the torch within one country, was for the XV Olympic Winter Games in Canada in 1988. The torch arrived from Greece at St John's, Newfoundland on 17 Nov 1987 and was transported 18 060 km *11 222 miles* (8188 km *5088 miles* by foot, 7111 km *4419 miles* by aircraft/ferry, 2756 km *1712 miles* by snowmobile and 5 km *3 miles* by dogsled) until its arrival at Calgary on 13 Feb 1988.

Most medals In ancient Olympic Games victors were given a chaplet of wild olive leaves. Leonidas of Rhodos won 12 running titles 164–152 BC. The most individual gold medals won by a male competitor in the modern Games is ten by Raymond Clarence Ewry (USA) (1874–1937) (see Track and Field Athletics). The female record is seven by Vera Caslavska-Odlozil (Czechoslovakia) (see Gymnastics).

The most gold medals won by a British competitor is four by: Paul Radmilovic (1886–1968) in water polo, 1908, 1912 and 1920 and 4 × 200 m freestyle relay in 1908; and swimmer Henry Taylor (1885–1951) in 1906 and 1908. The Australian swimmer Iain Murray Rose, who won four gold medals, was born in Birmingham, W Mids on 6 Jan 1939.

The only Olympian to win four consecutive individual titles in the same event has been Alfred Adolph Oerter (USA) (b. 19 Sep 1936), who won the discus, in 1956–68. However, Raymond Clarence Ewry (USA) won both the standing long jump and the standing high jump at four games in succession, 1900, 1904, 1906 and 1908. This is if the Intercalated Games of 1906, which were staged officially by the International

OLYMPIC RECORDS – WEIGHTLIFTING

CLASS	LIFT	KG		
52 kg	Snatch	120	Sevdalin Marinov (Bulgaria)	1988
	Jerk	150	Sevdalin Marinov (Bulgaria)	1988
	Total	270	Sevdalin Marinov (Bulgaria)	1988
56 kg	Snatch	127·5	Oksen Mirzoyan (USSR)	1988
			Liu Shoubin (China)	1988
	Jerk	165	Oksen Mirozoyan (USSR)	1988
	Total	120	Oksen Mirozoyan (USSR)	1988
60 kg	Snatch	152·5	Naim Suleymanoğlü (Turkey)	1988
	Jerk	190	Naim Suleymanoğlü (Turkey)	1988
	Total	342·5	Naim Suleymanoğlü (Turkey)	1988
67·5 kg	Snatch	155	Israil Militosyan (USSR)	1988
	Jerk	195	Yanko Rusev (Bulgaria)	1980
	Total	342·5	Yanko Rusev (Bulgaria)	1980
75 kg	Snatch	167·5	Borislav Guidikov (Bulgaria)	1988
	Jerk	207·5	Borislav Guidikov (Bulgaria)	1988
	Total	375	Borislav Guidikov (Bulgaria)	1988
82·5 kg	Snatch	177·5	Yurik Vardanyan (USSR)	1988
	Jerk	222·5	Yurik Vardanyan (USSR)	1988
	Total	400	Yurik Vardanyan (USSR)	1988
90 kg	Snatch	187·5	Anatoliy Khrapatiy (USSR)	1988
	Jerk	225	Anatoliy Khrapatiy (USSR)	1988
	Total	412·5	Anatoliy Khrapatiy (USSR)	1988
100 kg	Snatch	190	Pavel Kuznyetsov (USSR)	1988
	Jerk	235	Pavel Kuznyetsov (USSR)	1988
	Total	425	Pavel Kuznyetsov (USSR)	1988
110 kg	Snatch	210	Yuriy Zakharevich (USSR)	1988
	Jerk	245	Yuriy Zakharevich (USSR)	1988
	Total	455	Yuriy Zakharevich (USSR)	1988
110 kg +	Snatch	212·5	Aleksandr Kurlovich (USSR)	1988
	Jerk	255	Vasiliy Alekseyev (USSR)	1976
	Total	462·5	Aleksandr Kurlovich (USSR)	1988

OLYMPIC RECORDS – ARCHERY

Double FITA rounds

Men	2616	Darrell Pace (USA)	1984
Women	2683	Kim Soo-nyung (South Korea)	1988

OLYMPIC RECORDS – SHOOTING

MEN

Small Bore rifle-prone	599	Li Ho-jun (North Korea)	1972
		plus four other men	1976–84
-3 positions	1181	Alister Allan (GB)	1988
Air rifle	594	Goran Maksimovis (Yugoslavia)	1988
Free pistol	581	Aleksandr Melentyev (USSR)	1980
Rapid-fire pistol	598	Afanasiy Kuzmin (USSR)	1988
Air pistol	590	Eric Buljung (USA)	1988
Running Game	591	Gennadiy Avramenko (USSR)	1988
		Tor Heiestad (Norway)	1988

WOMEN

Standard Rifle-3 positions	590	Silvia Sperber (FRG)	1988
Air rifle	395	Launi Meli (USA)	1988
		Irina Chilova (USSR)	1988
		Zhang Qiuping (China)	1988
Sport pistol	591	Nino Salukvadze (USSR)	1988
Air pistol	390	Nino Salukvadze (USSR)	1988

MIXED

Trap	199	Angelo Scalzone (Italy)	1972
Skeet	198	Yevgeniy Petrov (USSR)	1968
		plus seven other men	1968–88

OLYMPIC RECORDS – SPEED SKATING

MEN min:sec

500 m	36·45	Uwe-Jens Mey (GDR)	1988
1000 m	1:13·03	Nikolay Gulyayev (USSR)	1988
1500 m	1:52·06	André Hoffman (GDR)	1988
5000 m	6:44·63	Tomas Gustafsson (Sweden)	1988
10 000 m	13:48·20	Tomas Gustafsson (Sweden)	1988

WOMEN

500 m	39·10	Bonnie Blair (USA)	1988
1000 m	1:17·65	Christa Rothenburger (GDR)	1988
1500 m	2:00·68	Yvonne van Gennip (Netherlands)	1988
3000 m	4:11·94	Yvonne van Gennip (Netherlands)	1988
5000 m	7:14·13	Yvonne van Gennip (Netherlands)	1988

MOST MEDALS

The total medals, by nation, for all Olympic events (including those now discontinued).

Summer Games (1896–88)

	G	S	B	Total
USA	752	569	481	1802
USSR [1]	397	323	304	1024
Great Britain	172	221	206	599
Germany [2]	153	206	208	567
France	153	170	175	498
Sweden	132	142	167	441
GDR [3]	154	131	126	411
Italy	147	121	123	391
Hungary	125	112	137	374
Finland	97	75	110	282
Japan	87	75	82	244
Australia	71	67	87	225
Romania	55	64	82	201
Poland	40	56	95	191
Canada	39	62	73	174
Switzerland	41	63	58	162
Netherlands	43	46	65	154
Bulgaria	35	62	49	146
Czechoslovakia [4]	45	48	49	142
Denmark	25	50	49	124

Excludes medals won in Official Art competitions in 1912–48.

Winter Games (1924–88)

USSR [1]	79	57	59	195
Norway	54	60	54	168
USA	42	46	35	123
GDR [3]	39	36	35	110
Finland	33	43	34	110
Austria	28	38	32	98
Sweden	36	25	31	92
Germany [2]	26	26	23	75
Switzerland	23	25	25	73
Canada	14	12	18	44
Netherlands	13	17	12	42
France	13	10	16	39
Italy	14	10	9	33
Czechoslovakia [4]	2	8	13	23
Great Britain	7	4	10	21

[1] Includes Czarist Russia
[2] Germany 1896–1964, West Germany 1968–88
[3] GDR, East Germany, 1968–88
[4] Includes Bohemia

Olympic Committee, are included. Also Paul B. Elvström (Denmark) (b. 25 Feb 1928) won four successive gold medals at monotype yachting events, 1948–60, but there was a class change (1948 Firefly class, 1952–60 Finn class).

Swimmer Mark Andrew Spitz (USA) (b. 10 Feb 1950) won a record seven golds at one celebration, at Munich in 1972, including three in relays. The most won in individual events at one celebration is five by speed skater, Eric Arthur Heiden (USA) (b. 14 Jun 1958) at Lake Placid, New York, USA in 1980.

The only man to win a gold medal in both the Summer and Winter Games is Edward Patrick Francis Eagan (USA) (1898–1967) who won the 1920 light-heavyweight boxing title and was a member of the winning four-man bob in 1932. Christa Luding (née Rothenburger) (GDR) (b. 4 Dec 1959) became the first woman to win a medal at both the Summer and Winter Games when she won a silver in the cycling sprint event in 1988. She had previously won medals for speed skating, 500 m gold in 1984, and 1000 m gold and 500 m silver in 1988.

Gymnast Larisa Latynina (USSR) (b. 27 Dec 1934) won a record 18 medals and the men's record is 15 by Nikolay Andrianov (see Gymnastics). The record at one celebration is eight by gymnast Aleksandr Dityatin (USSR) (b. 7 Aug 1957) in 1980.

Youngest and oldest gold medallist The youngest ever winner was a French boy (whose name is not recorded) who coxed the Netherlands pair in 1900. He was 7–10 years old and he substituted for Dr Hermanus Brockmann, who coxed in the heats but proved too heavy. The youngest ever female champion was Marjorie Gestring (USA) (b. 18 Nov 1922, now Mrs Bowman), aged 13 yr 268 days, in the 1936 women's springboard event. Oscar Swahn was in the winning Running Deer shooting team in 1912 aged 64 yr 258 days and in this event was the oldest medallist, silver, at 72 yr 280 days in 1920.

Youngest and oldest British competitor The youngest competitor to represent Britain in the Olympic Games

was Magdalena Cecilia Colledge (b. 28 Nov 1920), aged 11 yr 73 days when she skated in the 1932 Games. The oldest was Hilda Lorna Johnstone (1902–90), aged 70 yr 5 days, in the equestrian dressage in the 1972 Games.

Longest span The longest span of an Olympic competitor is 40 years by: Dr Ivan Osiier (Denmark) (1888–1965) in fencing, 1908–32 and 1948; Magnus Konow (Norway) (1887–1972) in yachting, 1908–20, 1928 and 1936–48; Paul Elvström (Denmark) in yachting, 1948–60, 1968–72 and 1984–88; and Durward Randolph Knowles (Great Britain 1948, then Bahamas) (b. 2 Nov 1917) in yachting, 1948–72 and 1988. Raimondo d'Inzeo (b. 8 Feb 1925) competed for Italy in equestrian events at a record eight celebrations from 1948–76, gaining one gold, two silver and three bronze medals. This was equalled by Paul Elvström and Durward Knowles in 1988. The longest feminine span is 28 years by Anne Jessica Ransehousen (née Newberry) (USA) (b. 14 Oct 1938) in dressage, 1960, 1964 and 1988. Fencer Kerstin Palm (Sweden) (b. 5 Feb 1946) competed in a women's record seven celebrations, 1964–88.

The longest span of any British competitor is 32 years by Enoch Jenkins (1892–1984) who competed in clay pigeon shooting, 1920, 1924 and 1952. The longest feminine span is 20 years by Dorothy Jennifer Beatrice Tyler (née Odam) (b. 14 Mar 1920) who high-jumped from 1936–56. The record number of appearances for Great Britain is six by swimmer and water polo player Paul Radmilovic, 1906–28; and by fencer Bill Hoskyns from 1956–76.

Most participants
The greatest number of competitors at a Summer Games celebration is 8465 (6279 men, 2186 women), who represented a record 159 nations, at Seoul, South Korea in 1988. The greatest number at the Winter Games is 1428 (1113 men, 315 women) representing 57 countries, at Calgary, Canada in 1988.

■ **Most medals**
The most individual gold medals won at a single Olympic celebration is five by Eric Arthur Heiden (USA) (b. 14 Jun 1958) when he won all the speed skating events at Lake Placid, New York, USA in 1980. (Photo (opposite): All-Sport (USA)/Duffy)

Abseiling (or Rappeling)

Wilmer Pérez and Luis Aulestia set an abseiling or rappeling record of 1029 m *3376 ft* by descending from above the Angel Falls in Venezuela down to its base on 24 Aug 1989. The descent took 1¼ hr.

The longest descent down the side of a building is one of 267·6 m *878 ft* by David Griffiths and Phil Barber, who abseiled down the transmitting tower of National Transcommunications Ltd at Emley Moor, W Yorks in just over four minutes on 8 May 1991.

Human fly

The longest climb achieved on the vertical face of a building occurred on 26 Jun 1986 when Daniel Goodwin of California, USA climbed a record 342·9 m *1125 ft* up the outside of the 553·34 m *1815 ft 5 in* CN Tower in Toronto, Canada (the tallest self-supporting tower in the world) using neither climbing aids nor safety equipment.

Top to bottom

Clive Johnson and Les Heaton of 'Mountain Adventure' climbed the highest peaks and descended the deepest caves in each of England, Scotland and Wales in 16 hr 14 min from 16–18 Sep 1986.

summit. The longest wall climb is on the Rupal-Flank from the base camp at 3560 m *11 680 ft* to the South Point 8042 m *26 384 ft* of Nanga Parbat, a vertical ascent of 4482 m *14 704 ft*. This was scaled by the Austro-German-Italian expedition led by Dr Karl Maria Herrligkoffer (b. 13 Jun 1916) in April 1970.

Europe's greatest wall is the 2000 m *6600 ft* north face of the Eigerwand (Ogre wall) first climbed by Heinrich Harrer and Fritz Kasparek of Austria and Andreas Heckmair and Wiggerl Vörg of Germany from 21–24 Jul 1938. The north-east face of the Eiger had been climbed on 20 Aug 1932 by Hans Lauper, Alfred Zurcher, Alexander Graven and Josef Knubel. The greatest alpine solo climb was that of Walter Bonatti (Italy) (b. 22 Jun 1930) of the south west pillar of the Dru, Montenvers, now called the Bonatti Pillar, with five bivouacs in 126 hr 7 min from 17–22 Aug 1955.

The most demanding free climbs in the world are those rated at 5·13, the premier location for these being in the Yosemite Valley, California, USA.

The top routes in Britain are graded E7·7b, which relates closely to 5·13.

Highest bivouac Four Nepalese summiters bivouacked at more than 8800 m *28 870 ft* in their descent from the summit of Everest on the night of 23 Apr 1990. They were Ang Rita Sherpa, on his record breaking sixth ascent of Everest, Ang Kami Sherpa (b. 1952), Pasang Norbu Sherpa (b. 1963) and Top Bahadur Khatri (b. 1960).

Oldest Teiichi Igarashi (Japan) (b. 21 Sep 1886) climbed Mount Fuji (Fuji-yama) (3776 m *12 388 ft*) at the age of 99 years 302 days on 20 Jul 1986.

MOUNTAIN RACING

Mount Cameroon Reginald Esuke (Cameroon) descended from the summit 4095 m *13 435 ft* to Buea at 915 m *3002 ft* in 1 hr 2 min 15 sec on 24 Jan 1988, achieving a vertical rate of 51 m *167·5 ft* per min. Timothy Leku Lekunze (Cameroon) set the record for the race to the summit and back of 3 hr 46 min 34 sec on 25 Jan 1987, when the temperature varied from 35°C at the start to 0°C at the summit. The record time for the ascent is 2 hr 25 min 20 sec by Jack Maitland (GB) in 1988. The women's record for the race is 4 hr 42 min 31 sec by Fabiola Rueda (Colombia) (b. 26 Mar 1963) in 1989.

MOUNTAIN ENDURANCE RUNNING

British Three Peaks record The Three Peaks route from sea level at Fort William, Highland, to sea level at Caernarvon, via the summits of Ben Nevis, Scafell Pike and Snowdon, was walked by Arthur Eddleston (1939–84) (Cambridge H) in 5 days 23 hr 37 min from 11–17 May 1980. Peter and David Ford, David Robinson, Kevin Duggan and John O'Callaghan, of Luton and Dunstable, ran the distance in relay in 54 hr 39 min 14 sec from 7–9 Aug 1981. The fastest individual total time for climbing the three mountains is 4 hr 16 min by Joss Naylor from 8–9 Jul 1971.

On 24 Oct 1990 a team of 3 from the Royal Marines covered the distance in 7 hr 59 min, being transported between the peaks by helicopter. Their running time was 5 hr 25 min.

A total climbing time of 7 hr 47 min was achieved by Brian Stadden from 13–15 Aug 1982 for Five Peaks, adding the highest points in Northern Ireland—Slieve Donard

(852 m *2796 ft*) and in the Republic of Ireland—Carrauntoohil (1041 m *3414 ft*) to the Three Peaks.

Bob Graham The record for the round of 42 lakeland peaks covering a total distance of 99 km *62 miles* and 7900 m *26 000 ft* of ascent and descent, is 13 hr 54 min by Billy Bland, 34, on 19 Jun 1982. Ernest Roger Baumeister (b. 17 Dec 1941) (Dark Peak Fell Runners Club) ran the double Bob Graham Round in 46 hr 34½ min on 30 Jun–1 Jul 1979. The women's single round record is 19 hr 11 min by Hélène Diamantides on 12 Aug 1989.

24-hour records The Lakeland record is 76 peaks (ascents and descents of approximately 11 900 m *39 000 ft*) from Braithwaite achieved by Mark McDermott on 19–20 Jun 1988.

The Scottish record is 28 Munro (mountains over 914 m *3000 ft*) summits achieved by Jon Broxap on 30–31 Jul 1988. He covered 128 km *80 miles*, with 10 700 m *35 000 ft* of ascents and descents in 23 hr 20 min from Cluanie Inn.

Scottish 3000 ft peaks The Munros record for climbing and linking the 277 peaks (over 914 m *3000 ft* entirely on foot is 66 days 22 hr by Hugh Symonds (b. 1 Feb 1953). He covered 2198 km *1374 miles* and climbed 128 600 m *422 000 ft* between Ben Hope and Ben Lomond, 19 Apr–25 Jun 1990. He rowed to Skye, sailed to Mull and ran between all the other peaks.

Scottish 4000 ft peaks The record for traversing all eight 1219·2 m *4000 ft* peaks, a 136·79 km *85 mile* cross-country route from Glen Nevis to Glen More is 21 hr 39 min by Martin Stone on 4 Jul 1987.

Welsh 3000 ft peaks The record for traversing the 15 Welsh peaks of over 914 m *3000 ft* is 4 hr 19 min 56 sec, from Snowdon Summit to Foel Fras by Colin Donnelly on 11 Jun 1988.

Everest Base Camp to Kathmandu The record is 3 days 10 hr 8 min by Hélène Diamantides and Alison Wright, both 22, from 8–10 Oct 1987. They covered 288 km *180 miles*, climbed 9800 m *32 000 ft* and descended 14 000 m *46 000 ft*.

Multiple peaks Mick Cottam, Andrew Curson and Matthew Beresford, completed a climb of all 349 peaks in England over 609·6 m *2000 ft* (walking a distance of 647·76 km *402·5 miles*) from 21 Jul–11 Aug 1985.

Craig Caldwell took 377 days to cycle, walk and climb to the top of the 277 Munros and the 222 Corbetts (762–914 m *2500–3000 ft*) in Scotland, from February 1985–March 1986. In all he cycled 6682 km *4152 miles*, walked 4876 km *3030 miles* and climbed 252 542 m *828 491 ft*.

Netball

The game was invented in the USA in 1891 and introduced into England in 1895 by Dr Toles. The All England Women's Netball Association was formed in 1926. The oldest club in continuous existence is the Polytechnic Netball Club of London founded in 1907.

Most titles *World* Australia has won the World Championships (instituted 1963) a record five times, 1963, 1971, 1975, 1979 and 1983.

English The National Club's Championships (instituted 1966) have been won

eight times by Sudbury Netball Club (1968–70, 1971 (shared), 1973, 1983–5). Surrey has won the County Championships (instituted 1932) a record 19 times (1949–64, 1966, 1981; 1969 and 1986 (both shared)).

Most international appearances The record number of internationals is 100 by Jillean Hipsey of England, 1978–87.

Highest scores The World Tournament record score was in Auckland, New Zealand in 1975 when England beat Papua New Guinea 114 goals to 16. The record number of goals in the World Tournament is 402 by Judith Heath (England) (b. 1942) in 1971.

Orienteering

Origins The first indications of orienteering as a competitive sport have been found in the Swedish army (1888) and the Norwegian army (1895). The first civilian competition seems to have been organized on 31 Oct 1897 (with eight participants) by the sport club Tjalve, outside Oslo, Norway. In spite of a number of other small events up to 1910, the sport died out in Norway but in Sweden survived World War I. On 25 Mar 1919, the first large competition with more than 200 participants was organized in the forest of Nacka, outside Stockholm. From there the sport spread rapidly throughout Sweden and later (about 1925) to Finland, Norway and (especially post-1945) to other countries in Europe and elsewhere. The initiator was Major Ernst Killander, who is known as 'The Father of Orienteering'. World Championships were instituted in 1966. Annual British Championships were instituted in 1967 following the formation of the British Orienteering Federation.

Most titles *World* The men's relay has been won a record seven times by Norway, 1970, 1978, 1981, 1983, 1985, 1987 and 1989. Sweden have won the women's relay eight times, 1966, 1970, 1974, 1976, 1981, 1983, 1985 and 1989. Three women's individual titles have been won by Annichen Kringstad-Svensson (Sweden) (b. 15 Jul 1960), 1981, 1983 and 1985. The men's title has been won twice by: Åge Hadler (Norway) (b. 14 Aug 1944), in 1966 and 1972; Egil Johansen (Norway) (b. 18 Aug 1954), 1976 and 1978; and Øyvind Thon (Norway) (b. 25 Mar 1958), in 1979 and 1981.

British Geoffrey Peck (b. 27 Sep 1949) won the men's individual title a record five times, 1971, 1973, 1976–7 and 1979 as well as the over-35s title in 1985–6 and over-40s in 1989. Carol McNeill (b. 20 Feb 1944) won the women's title six times, 1967, 1969, 1972–6. She also won the over-35s title in 1984, 1985 and 1990, and the over-45s title in 1990.

Terry Dooris (b. 22 Sep 1926) of Southern Navigators has competed in all 25 British individual championships 1967–91, whilst Lorna Collett (b. 2 Sep 1922) of South Ribble OC competed in the 24 from 1967–90.

Most competitors The most competitors at an event in one day is 38 000 in the Ruf des Herbstes at Sibiu, Romania in 1982. The largest event is the five-day Swedish O-Ringen at Småland, which attracted 120 000 competitors in July 1983.

Ski orienteering Eight World Championships in ski orienteering have been held. Sweden have won the men's relay five times (1977, 1980, 1982, 1984, 1990) and

Finland have won the women's relay five times (1975, 1977, 1980, 1988, 1990).

Parachuting

Parachuting became a regulated sport with the institution of World Championships in 1951. A team title was introduced in 1954 and women's events were included in 1956.

Most titles *World* The USSR won the men's team title in 1954, 1958, 1960, 1966, 1972, 1976 and 1980, and the women's team title in 1956, 1958, 1966, 1968, 1972 and 1976. Nikolay Ushamyev (USSR) has won the individual title twice, 1974 and 1980.

British Sgt Ronald Alan 'Scotty' Milne (b. 5 Mar 1952) of the Parachute Regiment won the British title five times in 1976–7, 1979–81. Rob Colpus and Geoff Sanders each shared ten British titles for Relative Work parachuting, the 4-Way and 8-Way titles won by their team 'Symbiosis' in 1976–7, 1979, 1981–2.

Greatest accuracy At Yuma, Arizona, USA, in March 1978, Dwight Reynolds scored a record 105 daytime dead centres, and Bill Wenger and Phil Munden tied with 43 night time DCs, competing as members of the US Army team, the Golden Knights. With electronic measuring the official FAI record is 50 DCs by Aleksandr Aasmiae (USSR) at Fergana, USSR in October 1979 and by Linger Abdurakhmanov (USSR) at Fergana in 1988, when the women's record was set at 41 by Natalya Filinkova (USSR) in 1988.

The Men's Night Accuracy Landing record on an electronic score pad is 27 consecutive dead centres by Cliff Jones (USA) in 1981. The women's record is 21 by Inessa Stepanova (USSR) at Fergana in 1988.

Parascending Andrew Wakelin (GB) at Artesia Airport, New Mexico, USA on a Sorcerer 33 canopy on a 488 m *1600 ft* line on 1 Aug 1985 set records for distance: 7300 m *23 950 ft*, and height gain: 400 m *1312 ft*. The duration record is 21 min 8 sec by Pat Sugrue on a Paramount 9 in South Wales on 12 Apr 1986.

Nigel Horder scored four successive dead centres at the Dutch Open, Flevhof, Netherlands on 22 May 1983.

Pelota Vasca

Origins The game, which originated in Italy as *longue paume* and was introduced into France in the 13th century, is said to be the fastest of all ball games. The glove or *gant* was introduced c. 1840 and the *chistera* was invented by Jean 'Gantchiki' Dithurbide of Ste Pée, France. The *grand chistera* was invented by Melchior Curuchague of Buenos Aires, Argentina in 1888. The world's largest *frontón* (enclosed stadium) is the World Jaï Alaï at Miami, Florida, USA, which had a record attendance of 15 052 on 27 Dec 1975.

World Championships The *Federacion Internacional de Pelota Vasca* stage World Championships every four years (first in 1952). The most successful pair have been Roberto Elias and Juan Labat (Argentina), who won the *Trinquete Share* four times, 1952, 1958, 1962 and 1966. Labat won a record seven world titles in all. The most wins in the long court game *Cesta Punta* is three by Hamuy of Mexico, with two different partners, 1958, 1962 and 1966.

Longest domination The longest domination as the world's No. 1 player was enjoyed by Chiquito de Cambo (*né* Joseph Apesteguy) (France) (1881–1955) from the beginning of the century until succeeded in 1938 by Jean Urruty (France) (b. 19 Oct 1913).

Pétanque

The origins of pétanque or boules can be traced back over 2000 years, but it was not until 1945 that the *Fédération Française de Pétanque et Jeu Provençal* was formed, and subsequently the *Fédération Internationale* (FIPJP). The first recognized British club was formed on 30 Mar 1966 as the Chingford Club de Pétanque and the British Pétanque Association was founded in 1974.

World Championships Winner of the most World Championships (instituted 1959) has been France with ten titles to 1989. Two women's World Championships have been held in 1988 and 1990 and the winners were Thailand on both occasions.

Pigeon Racing

Origins Pigeon racing developed from the use of homing pigeons for carrying messages. The sport originated in Belgium from commercial services and the earliest long-distance race was from London to Antwerp in 1819, involving 36 pigeons.

Longest flights The official British duration record (into Great Britain) is 1887 km *1173 miles* in 15 days by *C.S.O.*, owned by Rosie and Bruce of Wick, in the 1976 Palamos Race. In the 1975 Palamos Race, *The Conqueror*, owned by Alan Raeside, homed to Irvine, Strathclyde, 1625 km *1010 miles*, in 43 hr 56 min. The greatest number of flights over 1000 miles flown by one pigeon is that of *Dunning Independence*, owned by D. Smith, which annually flew from Palamos to Dunning, Perthshire, 1662 km *1039 miles*, between 1978 and 1981.

The longest confirmed distances, flown in opposite directions, by a single pigeon were north from Rome, Italy, 1474·38 km *916·16 miles*, and south from The Faroes, 1178·82 km *732·5 miles*, by a dark cock, *GB83X 03693*, to the loft of Marley Westrop of Hitchin, Herts.

The greatest claimed homing flight by a pigeon was for one owned by the 1st Duke of Wellington (1769–1852). Released from a sailing ship off the Ichabo Islands, West Africa on 8 April, it dropped dead a mile from its loft at Nine Elms, Wandsworth, Greater London on 1 Jun 1845, 55 days later, having apparently flown an airline route of 8700 km *5400 miles*, but possibly a distance of 11 250 km *7000 miles* to avoid the Sahara Desert. In 1990 it was reported that a pigeon, owned by David Lloyd and George Workman of Nantyffyllon, Mid Glam, had completed a flight of 10 800 km *6750 miles* from its release at Lerwick, Shetland to Shanghai, China, possibly the longest non-homing flight ever. In both cases, however, the lack of constant surveillance makes it difficult to confirm that the pigeons completed the distances unaided.

Highest speeds In level flight in windless conditions it is very doubtful if any pigeon can exceed 96 km/h *60 mph*. The highest race speed recorded is one of 2952 m *3229 yd* per min (177·14 km/h *110·07 mph*) in the East Anglian Federation race from East Croydon, Surrey on 8 May 1965 when the 1428 birds were backed by a powerful south-south-west wind. The winner was owned by A. Vigeon & Son, Wickford, Essex.

The highest race speed recorded over a distance of more than 1000 km *621·37 miles* is 2224·5 m *2432·7 yd* per min (133·46 km/h *82·93 mph*) by a hen in the Central Cumberland Combine race over 1099·316 km *683 miles 147 yd* from Murray Bridge, South Australia to North Ryde, Sydney on 2 Oct 1971.

24-hour records The world's longest reputed distance in 24 hours is 1292 km *803 miles* (velocity 1394 m *1525 yd* per min) by E. S. Petersen's winner of the 1941 San Antonio R.C. event in Texas, USA.

The best 24-hr performance into the United Kingdom is 1165·3 km *724 miles 219 yd* by E. Cardno's *Mormond Lad*, on 2 Jul 1977, from Nantes, France to Fraserburgh, Grampian. Average speed was 1507 m *1648 yd* per min (90·41 km/h *56·18 mph*).

Career records Owned by R. Green, of Walsall Wood, W Mids, *Champion Breakaway* won 59 first prizes from 1972 to May 1979.

The greatest competitive distance flown is 32 318 km *20 082 miles* by *Nunnies*, a chequer cock owned by Terry Haley of Abbot's Langley, Herts.

Mass release The largest ever simultaneous release of pigeons was at Beachy Head near Eastbourne, E Sussex on 11 May 1991 when 42 500 birds were released for the Save The Children Fund Eastbourne Classic. The 300-mile race, organized by the Up North Combine, was won by Ray Hart of Withernsea, Hull.

Polo

Origins Polo can be traced to origins in Manipur state, India c. 3100 BC when it was played as *Sagol Kangjei*. It is also claimed to be of Persian origin, having been played as *Pulu c.* 525 BC. The game was introduced to British officers at Cachar by the Manipur Maharaja, Sir Chandrakirti Singh, and the earliest club was the Cachar Club (founded in 1859) in Assam, India. The oldest club still in existence is the Calcutta Polo Club (1862). The game was introduced into England from India in 1869 by the 10th Hussars at Aldershot, Hants and the earliest match was one between the 9th Lancers and the 10th Hussars on Hounslow Heath, Greater London in July 1871. The earliest international match between England and the USA was in 1886.

The game's governing body is the Hurlingham Polo Association, which drew up the first English rules in 1875.

Most titles The British Open Championship for the Cowdray Park Gold Cup (instituted 1956) has been won five times by Stowell Park, 1973–4, 1976, 1978 and 1980.

Highest handicap The highest handicap based on six 7½ min 'chukkas' is ten goals introduced in the USA in 1891 and in the UK and in Argentina in 1910. A total of 55 players have received ten-goal handicaps and there are four currently playing in Britain, two Mexicans and two Argentinians. The last (of six) ten-goal handicap players from the UK was Gerald Balding in 1939.

Pool potting speed

The record times for potting all 15 balls in a speed competition are: (men) 37·9 sec by Rob McKenna at Blackpool, Lancs on 7 Nov 1987 and (women) 44·5 sec by Susan Thompson at Shrublands Community Centre, Gorleston, Norfolk on 20 Apr 1990.

Cow pat tossing

The record distances in the country sport of throwing dried cow pats or 'chips' depend on whether or not the projectile may be 'moulded into a spherical shape'. The greatest distance achieved under the 'non-sphericalization and 100 per cent organic' rule (established in 1970) is 81·07 m *266 ft*, by Steve Urner at the Mountain Festival, Tehachapi, California, USA on 14 Aug 1981.

Boomerang throwing

The greatest number of consecutive two-handed catches is 801, by Stéphane Marguerite (France) on 26 Nov 1989 at Lyon, France.

The longest out-and-return distance is one of 134·2 m *440 ft 3 in* by Jim Youngblood (USA) on 12 Jun 1989 at Gaithersburg, Maryland, USA.

The longest flight duration (with self-catch) is one of 2 min 59·94 sec by Dennis Joyce (USA) at Bethlehem, Pennsylvania, USA on 25 Jun 1987.

John Flynn (USA) caught 70 boomerang throws in 5 min at Geneva, Switzerland on 20 Aug 1988.

The juggling record — the number of consecutive catches with two boomerangs, keeping at least one boomerang aloft at all times — is 136, also by John Flynn (USA) at Catskill, New York, USA on 1 Sep 1990.

The highest handicaps of current UK players is nine by Howard Hipwood (b. 24 Mar 1950). Claire J. Tomlinson of Gloucestershire attained a handicap of five, the highest ever by a woman, in 1986.

A match of two 40-goal teams has been staged on three occasions at Palermo, Buenos Aires, Argentina in 1975, in the USA in 1990 and Australia in 1991.

Pool

Pool or championship pocket billiards with numbered balls began to become standardized *c.* 1890. The greatest exponents were Ralph Greenleaf (USA) (1899–1950), who won the 'world' professional title 19 times (1919–37), and William 'Willie' Mosconi (USA) (b. 27 Jun 1913), who dominated the game from 1941 to 1956.

The longest consecutive run in an American straight pool match is 625 balls by Michael Eufemia at Logan's Billiard Academy, Brooklyn, New York, USA on 2 Feb 1960, although this was not officially recognized. The official best is 526 by Willie Mosconi at Sprinfield, Ohio, USA in March 1954. The greatest number of balls pocketed in 24 hr is 16 009 by Paul Sullivan at Selby, N Yorks on 8–9 Apr 1989.

Powerboat Racing

A petrol engine was first installed in a boat by Jean Joseph Etienne Lenoir (1822–1900) on the River Seine, Paris, France in 1865. Actual powerboat racing started in about 1900, the first prominent race being from Calais, France to Dover, Kent in 1903. International racing was largely established by the presentation of a Challenge Trophy by Sir Alfred Harmsworth in 1903. Thereafter, racing developed mainly as a 'circuit' or short, sheltered course type competition. Offshore or sea-passage races also developed, initially for displacement (non-planing) cruisers. Offshore events for fast (planing) cruisers began in 1958 with a 273 km *170 mile* passage race from Miami, Florida to Nassau, Bahamas. Outboard motor, i.e. the combined motor / transmission detachable propulsion unit type racing began in the USA in about 1920. Both inboard and outboard motor boat engines are mainly petrol fuelled, but since 1950 diesel (compression ignition) engines have appeared and are widely used in offshore sport.

Highest speeds The highest speed recorded by a propeller-driven boat is 368·52 km/h *229 mph* by *The Texan*, a Kurtis Top Fuel Hydro Drag boat, driven by Eddie Hill (USA) on 5 Sep 1982 at Chowchilla, California, USA. He also set a 440 yd *402 m* elapsed time record of 5·16 sec in this boat at Firebird Lake, Arizona, USA on 13 Nov 1983. The official American Drag Boat Association record is 360·29 km/h *223·88 mph* by *Final Effort*, a Blown Fuel Hydro boat driven by Robert T. Burns at Creve Coeur Lake, St Louis, Missouri, USA on 15 Jul 1985 over a ¼ mile *402 m* course.

The fastest speed recognized by the *Union Internationale Motonautique* for an outboard-powered boat is in Class (e): 285·83 km/h *177·61 mph* by P. R. Knight in a Chevrolet-engined Lautobach hull on Lake Ruataniwha, New Zealand in 1986. Robert F. Hering (USA) set the world Formula One record at 266·085 km/h

---

165·338 mph at Parker, Arizona, USA on 21 Apr 1986.

The fastest speed recognized for an offshore boat is 248·537 km/h *154·438 mph* for one way and 238·559 km/h *148·238 mph* for two runs by Tom Gentry (USA), in his 15 m *49 ft* catamaran, powered by four Gentry Turbo Eagle V8 Chevrolets on 8 Mar 1987.

The fastest speed recorded for a diesel (compression ignition) boat is 218·248 km/h *135·532 mph* by the hydroplane *Iveco World Leader*, powered by an Aifo-Fiat engine, driven by Carlo Bonomi at Venice, Italy on 4 Apr 1985.

Highest race speeds The highest speed recorded in an offshore race is 166·22 km/h *103·29 mph* by Tony Garcia (USA) in a Class I powerboat at Key West, Florida, USA in November 1983.

Longest races The longest offshore race has been the Port Richborough London to Monte Carlo Marathon Offshore international event. The race extended over 4742 km *2947 miles* in 14 stages from 10–25 Jun 1972. It was won by *H.T.S.* (GB) driven by Mike Bellamy, Eddie Chater and Jim Brooker in 71 hr 35 min 56 sec for an average of 66·24 km/h *41·15 mph*. The longest circuit race is the 24-hour race held annually since 1962 on the River Seine at Rouen, France.

Longest jetboat jumps The longest ramp jump achieved by a jetboat has been 36·57 m *120 ft* by Peter Horak (USA) in a Glastron Carlson CVX 20 Jet Deluxe with a 460 Ford V8 engine (take-off speed 88 km/h *55 mph*) for a documentary TV film, at Salton Sea, California, USA on 26 Apr 1980. The longest leap on to land is 38·7 m *172 ft* by Norm Bagrie (New Zealand) from the Shotover River on 1 Jul 1982 in the 1½ ton jetboat *Valvolene*.

Projectiles

Throwing The longest independently authenticated throw of any inert object heavier than air is 383·13 m *1257 ft*, for a flying ring, by Scott Zimmerman on 8 Jul 1986 at Fort Funston, California, USA.

Greatest distances achieved with other miscellaneous objects:

Brick .... 44·54 m *146 ft 1 in*
(standard 2·268 kg *5 lb* building brick)
Geoff Capes at Braybrook School, Orton Goldhay, Cambs on 19 Jul 1978.

Egg (fresh hen's) .... 96·90 m *317 ft 10 in*
(without breaking it)
Risto Antikainen to Jyrki Korhonen at Siilinjarvi, Finland on 6 Sep 1981.

Gumboot ('Wellie wanging', using a size 8 Challenger Dunlop boot)
Men .... 52·73 m *173 ft*
Tony Rodgers of Warminster, Wilts on 9 Sep 1978.

Women .... 39·60 m *129 ft 11 in*
Rosemary Payne at Cannon Hill Park, Birmingham on 21 Jun 1975.

Haggis .... 55·11 m *180 ft 10 in*
(minimum weight 680 g *1 lb 8 oz*)
Alan Pettigrew at Inchmurrin, Loch Lomond, Strathclyde on 24 May 1984.

Rolling pin .... 53·4 m *175 ft 5 in*
(907 g *2 lb*)
Lori La Deane Adams, 21, at Iowa State Fair, Iowa, USA on 21 Aug 1979.

Slinging .... 437·13 m *1434 ft 2 in*
(using a 129·5 cm *51 in* long sling and a 56·5 g *2 oz* stone)
Lawrence L. Bray at Loa, Utah, USA on 21 Aug 1981.

Racketball

Racquetball using a 12 m × 6 m *40 ft × 20 ft* court was invented in 1950 by Joe Sobek at the Greenwich YMCA, Connecticut, USA, originally as Paddle Rackets. The International Racquetball Association was founded in 1960 by Bob Kendler (USA). It changed its name in 1979 to the American Amateur Racquetball Association. In 1979 the International Amateur Racquetball Federation (IARF) was founded and staged its first World Championships in 1981.

World Championships Instituted in 1981 and held biennially since 1984, the USA has won all five IARF team titles, 1981, 1984, 1986 (tie with Canada), 1988 and 1990. The most singles titles won is two by: (men) Egan Inoue (USA), 1986 and 1990, and; (women) Cindy Baxter (USA), 1981 and 1986, and Heather Stupp (Canada), 1988 and 1990.

Racketball using a 9·75 m × 6·4 m *32 ft × 21 ft* court (as for squash) was introduced to Britain by Ian Wright in 1976. The British Racketball Association was formed and staged inaugural British National Championships in 1984. Three titles have been won at the women's event by Bett Dryhurst, 1985–7.

Rackets

There is record of the sale of a racket court at Southernhay, Exeter, Devon dated 12 Jan 1798. The game, which is of 17th-century origin, was played by debtors in the Fleet Prison, London in the middle of the 18th century, and an inmate, Robert Mackay, claimed the first 'world' title in 1820. The first closed court champion was Francis Erwood at Woolwich, London in 1860.

World Championships Of the 22 world champions since 1820, the longest reign is by Geoffrey Willoughby Thomas Atkins (b. 20 Jan 1927) who held the title, after beating the professional James Dear (1910–81) in 1954, until retiring, after defending it four times, in April 1972.

Most Amateur titles Since the Amateur Singles Championship was instituted in 1888 the most titles won by an individual is nine by Edgar Maximilian Baerlein (1879–1971) between 1903 and 1923. Since the institution of the Amateur Doubles Championship in 1890 the most shares in titles has been eleven by: David Sumner Milford (1905–84), between 1938 and 1959; and John Ross Thompson (b. 10 May 1918), between 1948 and 1966; they won ten titles together. Milford also won seven Amateur Singles titles (1930–51), an Open title (1936) and held the World title from 1937 to 1946. Thompson additionally won an Open Singles title and five Amateur Singles titles.

Real/Royal Tennis

The game originated as *jeu de paume* in French monasteries *c.* 1050. A tennis court

pionships in 1985 and 1987 were won by Judith Anne Clarke (Australia) (b. 28 Dec 1954).

British The Amateur Championship of the British Isles (instituted 1888) has been won 16 times by Howard Rea Angus (b. 25 Jun 1944) 1966–80 and 1982. He also won eight Amateur Doubles Championships with David Warburg (1923–1987), 1967–70, 1972–4 and 1976, and was world champion 1976–81.

Rodeo

Origins Rodeo, which developed from 18th-century *fiestas*, came into being in the early days of the North American cattle industry. The sport originated in Mexico and spread from there into the cattle regions of the USA. Steer wrestling came in with Bill Pickett (1870–1932) of Texas in 1900 and a bronc riding competition was held in Deer Trail, Colorado as early as 1869. Claims to the first held before paying spectators are many; The West of the Pecos Rodeo at Pecos, Texas, first held in 1883 was the earliest documented, organized rodeo competition and is now sanctioned by the Professional Rodeo Cowboys Association (PRCA), professional rodeo's largest organized association.

The largest rodeo in the world is the National Finals Rodeo, organized by the PRCA and Women's Professional Rodeo Association (WPRA). The top 15 money-earning cowboys in each of the six PRCA events and the top 15 WPRA barrel racers compete at the Finals. It was first held at Dallas, Texas, USA in 1959 and was held at Oklahoma City, Oklahoma for 20 years before moving to Las Vegas, Nevada in 1985. The 1989 Finals had a paid attendance of 165 467 for ten performances. In 1990 a record $2·3 million in prize money was offered for the event, staged in Las Vegas.

Most world titles The record number of all-around titles (awarded to the leading money winner in a single season in two or more events) in the PRCA World Championships is six by Larry Mahan (USA) (b. 21 Nov 1943) in 1966–70 and 1973, and, consecutively, 1974–9 by Tom Ferguson (b. 20 Dec 1950). Roy Cooper (b. 13 Nov 1955) has record career earnings of $1 239 256, 1975–90. Jim Shoulders (b. 13 May 1928) of Henrietta, Texas won a record 16 World Championships at four events between 1949 and 1959. The record figure for prize money in a single season is $213 772 by Ty Murray (b. 11 Oct 1969) in 1990. Lewis Feild (b. 28 Oct 1956) won a record $75 219 for one rodeo ($47 449 for saddle bronc riding and $27 770 for bareback riding) at the 1987 National Finals Rodeo, Las Vegas, Nevada, USA.

Youngest champions The youngest winner of a world title is Anne Lewis (b. 1 Sep 1958), who won the WPRA barrel racing title in 1968, at 10 years old. Ty Murray is the youngest cowboy to win the PRCA All-Around Champion title, aged 20, in 1989.

Time records Records for PRCA timed events, such as calf-roping and steer-wrestling, are not always comparable, because of the widely varying conditions due to the sizes of arenas and amount of start given the stock. The fastest time recorded for calf roping under the current PRCA rules is 6·7 sec by Joe Beaver (b. 13 Oct 1965) at West Jordan, Utah in 1986, and the fastest time for steer wrestling is 2·4 sec

Flying disc throwing (formerly Frisbee)

The World Flying Disc Federation distance records are: (men) 190·07 m *623 ft 7 in*, by Sam Ferrans (US) on 2 Jul 1988 at La Habra, California, USA; (women) 130·09 m *426 ft 10 in*, by Amy Bekken (US) on 25 Jun 1990 at La Habra, California, USA. The throw, run and catch records are: (men) 92·64 m *303 ft 11 in*, by Hiroshi Oshima (Japan) on 20 Jul 1988 at San Francisco, California, USA; (women) 60·02 m *196 ft 11 in*, by Judy Horowitz (US) on 29 Jun 1985 at La Mirada, California, USA. The 24-hour distance records for a pair are: (men) 583·20 km *362·4 miles*, by Leonard Muise and Gabe Ontiveros (US) on 21–22 Sep 1988 at Carson, California, USA; (women) 186·12 km *115·7 miles*, by Jo Cahow and Amy Berard (US) on 30–31 Dec 1979 at Pasadena, California, USA. The records for maximum time aloft are: (men) 16·72 sec, by Don Cain (US) on 26 May 1984 at Philadelphia, Pennsylvania, USA; (women) 11·75 sec, by Anni Kreml (US) on 21 Jul 1988 at San Francisco, California, USA.

is mentioned in the sale of the Hôtel de Nesle, Paris bought by King Philippe IV of France in 1308. The oldest of the surviving active courts in Great Britain is that at Falkland Palace, Fife built by King James V of Scotland in 1539.

Most titles *World* The first recorded world tennis champion was Clerge (France) *c.* 1740. Jacques Edmond Barre (France) (1802–73) held the title for a record 33 yr from 1829 to 1862. Pierre Etchebaster (1893–1980), a Basque, holds the record for the greatest number of successful defences of the title with eight between 1928 and 1952.

The first two Women's World Cham-

Top bull

The top bucking bull *Red Rock* dislodged 312 riders, 1980–88, and was finally ridden to the eight-second bell by Lane Frost (1963–89) (world champion bull rider 1987) on 20 May 1988. *Red Rock* had retired at the end of the 1987 season but still continued to make guest appearances.

Skateboarding

World championships have been staged intermittently since 1966. David Frank, 25, covered 435·3 km *270·5 miles* in 36 hr 43 min 40 sec in Toronto, Canada on 11–12 Aug 1985.

The highest speed recorded on a skateboard under USSA rules is 115·53 km/h *71·79 mph* on a course at Mt Baldy, California, USA in a prone position by Richard K. Brown, 33, on 17 Jun 1979.

The stand-up record is 86·01 km/h *53·45 mph* by John Hutson, 23, at Signal Hill, Long Beach, California, USA on 11 Jun 1978.

The high-jump record is 1·67 m *5 ft 5¾ in* by Trevor Baxter (b. 1 Oct 1962) of Burgess Hill, E Sussex at Grenoble, France on 14 Sep 1982.

At the 4th US Skateboard Association Championship, at Signal Hill on 25 Sep 1977, Tony Alva, 19, jumped 17 barrels (5·18 m *17 ft*).

by: James Bynum, at Marietta, Oklahoma, USA in 1955; Carl Deaton at Tulsa, Oklahoma in 1976; and Gene Melton at Pecatonica, Illinois in 1976. The fastest team roping time is 3·7 sec, by Bob Harris and Tee Woolman at Spanish Fork, Utah in 1986

Bull riding Jim Sharp (b. 6 Oct 1965) of Kermit, Texas became the first rider to ride all ten bulls at a National Finals Rodeo at Las Vegas in December 1988.

The highest score in bull riding was 98 points out of a possible 100 by Denny Flynn on *Red Lightning* at Palestine, Illinois, USA in 1979.

Saddle bronc riding The highest scored saddle bronc ride is 95 out of a possible 100 by Doug Vold at Meadow Lake, Saskatchewan, Canada in 1979. *Descent*, a saddle bronc owned by Beutler Brothers and Cervi Rodeo Company, received a record six PRCA saddle bronc of the year awards, 1966–9, 1971–2.

Bareback riding Joe Alexander of Cora, Wyoming, scored 93 out of a possible 100 at Cheyenne, Wyoming in 1974. *Sippin' Velvet*, owned by Bernis Johnson, has been awarded a record five PRCA bareback horse of the year titles between 1978 and 1987.

Roller Skating

The first roller skate was devised by Jean Joseph Merlin (1735–1803) of Huy, Belgium in 1760 but with disastrous results. James L. Plimpton of New York produced the present four-wheeled type and patented it in January 1863. The first indoor rink was opened in the Haymarket, London in about 1824.

Most titles *Speed* The most world speed titles won is 18 by two women: Alberta Vianello (Italy), eight track and ten road 1953–65; and Annie Lambrechts (Belgium), one track and 17 road 1964–81, at distances from 500 m to 10 000 m.

The most British national individual men's titles have been won by Michael Colin McGeogh (b. 30 Mar 1946) with 19 in 1966–85. Chloe Ronaldson (b. 30 Nov 1939) won 40 individual and 14 team women's senior titles from 1958 to 1985.

Figure The records for figure titles are: five by Karl Heinz Losch in 1958–9, 1961–2 and 1966; and four by Astrid Bader in 1965–8, both of West Germany. The most world pair titles is four by Dieter Fingerle (West Germany) in 1959, 1965–7 with two different partners and by John Arishita and Tammy Jeru (USA) 1983–86.

Speed skating The fastest speed put up in an official world record is 43·21 km/h *26·85 mph* when Luca Antoniel (Italy) (b. 12 Feb 1968) recorded 24·99 sec for 300 m on a road at Gujan Mestras, France on 31 Jul 1987. The women's record is 40·30 km/h *25·04 mph* by Marisa Canafoglia (Italy) (b. 30 Sep 1965) for 300 m on the road at Grenoble, France on 27 Aug 1987. The world records for 10 000 m on a road or track are: (men) 14 min 55·64 sec, Giuseppe de Persio (Italy) (b. 3 Jun 1959) at Gujan Mestras, France on 1 Aug 1988; (women) 15 min 58·022 sec, Marisa Canafogilia (Italy) at Grenoble, France on 30 Aug 1987.

Largest rink The greatest indoor rink ever to operate was located in the Grand Hall, Olympia, London. Opened in 1890 and

closed in 1912, it had an actual skating area of 6300 m² *68 000 ft²*. The current largest is the main arena of 3250 m² *34 981 ft²* at Guptill Roll-Arena, Boght Corner, New York, USA. The total rink area is 3844 m² *41 380 ft²*.

Endurance Theodore James Coombs (b. 1954) of Hermosa Beach, California, USA skated 8357 km *5193 miles* from Los Angeles, California to New York and back to Yates Center, Kansas from 30 May to 14 Sep 1979.

Land's End to John o' Groats Steve Fagan, 20, roller skated the distance, 1488 km *925 miles*, in 9 days 10 hr 25 min from 1–10 May 1984, averaging 157 km *98 miles* a day. The fastest time by a woman was 12 days 4 hr 15 min by Cheryl Fisher, 17, from 19 Sep–1 Oct 1987.

ROLLER HOCKEY

Roller hockey (previously known as rink hockey in Europe) was introduced to Britain as rink polo, at the old Lava rink, Denmark Hill, London in the late 1870s. The Amateur Rink Hockey Association was formed in 1908, and in 1913 became the National Rink Hockey (now Roller Hockey) Association. England won the first World Championships, 1936–9, since when Portugal has won most titles with 12 between 1947 and 1982. Portugal also won a record 16 European (instituted 1926) titles between 1947 and 1987.

Rowing

The Sphinx Stela of Amenhotep (Amonophis) II (1450–1425 BC) records that he *stroked* a boat for some three miles. The earliest established sculling race is the Doggett's Coat and Badge, which was first rowed on 1 Aug 1716 from London Bridge to Chelsea as a race for apprentices, and is still contested annually. Although rowing regattas were held in Venice in 1300 the first English regatta probably took place on the Thames by the Ranelagh Gardens, near Putney in 1775.

Most Olympic medals Six oarsmen have won three gold medals: John Brenden Kelly (USA) (1889–1960), father of the late HSH Princess Grace of Monaco, Single Sculls (1920) and Double Sculls (1920 and 1924); his cousin Paul Vincent Costello (USA) (b. 27 Dec 1894), Double Sculls (1920, 1924 and 1928); Jack Beresford, Jr (GB) (1899–1977), Single sculls (1924), Coxless Fours (1932) and Double Sculls (1936), Vyacheslav Nikolayevich Ivanov (USSR) (b. 30 Jul 1938), Single Sculls (1956, 1960 and 1964); Siegfried Brietzke (GDR) (b. 12 Jun 1952), Coxless Pairs (1972) and Coxless Fours (1976, 1980); and Pertti Karppinen (Finland) (b. 17 Feb 1953), Single Sculls (1976, 1980 and 1984).

World Championships World rowing championships distinct from the Olympic Games were first held in 1962, at first four yearly, but from 1974 annually, except in Olympic years.

The most gold medals won at World Championships and Olympic Games is eight at coxed pairs by the Italian brothers Giuseppe (b. 24 Jul 1959) and Carmine (b. 5 Jan 1962) Abbagnale, World 1981–2, 1985, 1987, 1989–90, Olympics 1984 and 1988. At women's events Jutta Behrendt (*née* Hahn) (GDR) (b. 15 Nov 1960) has won a record six golds.

The most wins at Single Sculls is five, by Peter-Michael Kolbe (West Germany) (b. 2

Aug 1953), 1975, 1978, 1981, 1983 and 1986, and by Pertti Karppinen, 1979 and 1985 with his three Olympic wins (above), and in the women's events by Christine Hahn (*née* Scheiblich) (GDR) (b. 31 Dec 1954), 1974–5, 1977–8 (and the 1976 Olympic title).

Boat Race The earliest University Boat Race, which Oxford won, was from Hambledon Lock to Henley Bridge on 10 Jun 1829. Outrigged eights were first used in 1846. In the 137 races to 1991, Cambridge won 69 times, Oxford 67 times and there was a dead heat on 24 Mar 1877.

The race record time for the course of 6·779 km *4 miles 374 yd* (Putney to Mortlake) is 16 min 45 sec by Oxford on 18 Mar 1984. This represents an average speed of 24·28 km/h *15·09 mph*. The smallest winning margin has been by a canvas by Oxford in 1952 and 1980. The greatest margin (apart from sinking) was Cambridge's win by 20 lengths in 1900.

Boris Rankov (Oxford, 1978–83) rowed in a record six winning boats. Susan Brown (b. 29 Jun 1958), the first woman to take part, coxed the winning Oxford boats in 1981 and 1982. Daniel Topolski coached Oxford to ten successive victories, 1976–85.

The tallest man ever to row in a University boat has been Gavin Stewart (Wadham, Oxford) (b. 25 Feb 1963) at 2·04 m *6 ft 8½ in* in 1987–8. The heaviest was Christopher Heathcote (b. March 1963), the Oxford No. 6, who weighed 110 kg *243 lb* in 1990. The lightest oarsman was the 1882 Oxford Stroke, Alfred Herbert Higgins, at 60 kg *9 st 6½ lb*. The lightest coxes, Francis Henry Archer (Cambridge) (1843–89) in 1862 and Hart Parker Vincent Massey (Oxford) (b. Canada, 30 Mar 1918) in 1939, were both 32·6 kg *5 st 2 lb*.

The youngest 'blue' ever was Matthew John Brittin (Cambridge) (b. 1 Sep 1968) at 18 yr 208 days, in 1986.

Head of the River A processional race for eights instituted in 1926, the Head has an entry limit of 420 crews (3780 competitors). The record for the course Mortlake–Putney (the reverse of the Boat Race) is 16 min 37 sec by the ARA National Squad in 1987.

Henley Royal Regatta The annual regatta at Henley-on-Thames, Oxon, was inaugurated on 26 Mar 1839. Since then the course, except in 1923, has been about 2112 m *1 mile 550 yd*, varying slightly according to the length of boat. In 1967 the shorter craft were 'drawn up' so all bows start level.

The most wins in the Diamond Challenge Sculls (instituted 1844) is six consecutively by Stuart A. Mackenzie (Australia and GB) (b. 5 Apr 1937), 1957–62. The record time is 7 min 23 sec by Vaclav Chalupa (Czechoslovakia) (b. 7 Dec 1967) on 2 Jul 1989. The record time for the Grand Challenge Cup (instituted 1839) event is 5 min 58 sec by Hansa Dortmund, West Germany on 2 Jul 1989.

Highest speed The highest recorded speed on non-tidal water for 2000 m *2187 yd* is by an American eight in 5 min 27·14 sec (22·01 km/h *13·68 mph*) at Lucerne, Switzerland on 17 Jun 1984. A crew from Penn AC, USA, was timed in 5 min 18·8 sec (22·58 km/h *14·03 mph*) in the FISA Championships on the River Meuse, Liège, Belgium on 17 Aug 1930.

24 hours The greatest distance rowed in 24 hours (upstream and downstream) by an eight is 209 km *130 miles* by members of the

Renmark Rowing Club, South Australia on 20–21 Apr 1984.

Cross-Channel Ivor Lloyd sculled across the English Channel in a record 3 hr 35 min 1 sec on 4 May 1983.

River Thames Malcom Knight, Simon Leifer and Kevin Thomas rowed the navigable length of the Thames, 299·14 km *185·88 miles*, from Lechlade Bridge, Glos to Southend Pier, Essex in 39 hr 27 min 12 sec in a skiff from 10–11 May 1988. The fastest time from Folly Bridge, Oxford to Westminster Bridge, London (180 km *112 miles*) is 14 hr 25 min 15 sec by an eight from Kingston Rowing Club on 1 Feb 1986.

Longest race The longest annual rowing race is the annual Tour du Lac Leman, Geneva, Switzerland for coxed fours (the five-man crew taking turns as cox) over 160 km *99 miles*. The record winning time is 12 hr 52 min by LAGA Delft, Netherlands on 3 Oct 1982.

International Dragon Boat Races Instituted in 1975 and held annually in Hong Kong, the fastest time achieved for the 640 metres *700 yd* course is 2 min 27·45 sec by the Chinese Shun De team on 30 Jun 1985. The best time for a British team was 2 min 36·40 sec by the Kingston Royals crew on 3 Jun 1990. Teams have 28 members — 26 rowers, one steersman and one drummer.

Rugby League

There have been four different scoring systems in Rugby League football. For the purpose of these records all points totals remain as they were under the system in operation at the time they were made.

The Northern Rugby Football Union was formed on 29 Aug 1895 at the George Hotel, Huddersfield, W Yorks. Twenty-one clubs from Yorkshire and Lancashire were present and all but one agreed to resign from the Rugby Union. Payment for loss of wages was the major cause of the break-away and full professionalism was allowed in 1898. A reduction in the number of players from 15 to 13 took place in 1906. The title 'Rugby Football League' was adopted in 1922.

World Cup There have been eight World Cup Competitions. Australia have most wins, with five, 1957, 1968, 1970, 1977 and 1988 as well as a win in the International Championship of 1975.

Most titles The Northern Rugby League was formed in 1901. The word 'Northern' was dropped in 1980. Wigan have won the League Championship a record 12 times (1909, 1922, 1926, 1934, 1946, 1947, 1950, 1952, 1960, 1987, 1990 and 1991).

In the Rugby League Challenge Cup (inaugurated 1896/7 season) a record 12 titles have been won by Wigan, 1924, 1929, 1948, 1951, 1958–9, 1965, 1985, 1988–91.

Since 1974 there have been five major competitions for RL clubs: Challenge Cup, League Championship, Premiership, Regal Trophy (formerly John Player Special Trophy) and County Cups. In 1990 these were officially called the 'Grand Slam' and as yet no club has achieved this. Wigan won four of these in one season, winning all but the Challenge Cup in 1986/7. In all major competitions since 1895 Wigan have a record 71 wins.

Three clubs have won all possible major Rugby League trophies in a season: Huns-

let, 1907/8 season, Huddersfield, 1914/15 and Swinton, 1927/8, all won the Challenge Cup, League Championship, County Cup and County League (now defunct).

HIGHEST SCORES

Senior match The highest aggregate score in a game where a senior club has been concerned was 121 points, when Huddersfield beat Swinton Park Rangers by 119 (19 goals, 27 tries) to 2 (one goal) in the first round of the Northern Union Cup on 28 Feb 1914. The highest score in League football is 102 points by Leeds *v.* Coventry (nil) on 12 Apr 1913. St Helens beat Carlisle 112–0 in the Lancashire Cup on 14 Sep 1986. In the Yorkshire Cup Hull Kingston Rovers beat Nottingham City 100–6 on 19 Aug 1990. The highest score in the First Division is 90 points by Leeds *v.* Barrow (nil) on 11 Feb 1990.

Challenge Cup Final The highest score in a Challenge Cup final is 38 points (8 tries, 7 goals) by Wakefield Trinity *v.* Hull (5) at Wembley, London on 14 May 1960. The record aggregate is 52 points when Wigan beat Hull 28–24 at Wembley on 4 May 1985. The greatest winning

margin was 34 points when Huddersfield beat St Helens 37–3 at Oldham, Greater Manchester on 1 May 1915.

International match The highest score in an international match is Australia's 70–8 defeat of Papua New Guinea in World Cup match at Wagga Wagga, Australia on 20 Jul 1988. Great Britain's highest score in an international is the 60–4 win over France at Headingley, Leeds, W Yorks on 16 Feb 1991.

Touring teams The record score for a British team touring Australasia is 101 points by England *v.* South Australia (nil) at Adelaide in May 1914. The record for a touring team in Britain is 92 (10 goals, 24 tries) by Australia against Bramley 7 (2 goals and 1 try) at the Barley Mow Ground, Bramley, near Leeds on 9 Nov 1921.

Most points Leigh scored a record 1436 points (258 tries, 199 goals, 6 drop goals) in the 1985/6 season, playing in 43 Cup and League games.

HIGHEST INDIVIDUAL SCORES

Most points, goals and tries in a game George Henry 'Tich' West (1882

–1927) scored 53 points (10 goals and a record 11 tries) for Hull Kingston Rovers (73) in a Challenge Cup tie v. Brookland Rovers (5) on 4 Mar 1905.

The record for a League match is 39 (5 tries, 12 goals) by Jimmy Lomas (1880–1960) in Salford's 78–0 win over Liverpool City on 2 Feb 1907.

The most goals in a Cup match is 22 kicked by James 'Jim' Sullivan (1903–77) for Wigan v. Flimby and Fothergill on 14 Feb 1925. The most goals in a League match is 15 by Michael Stacey (b. 9 Feb 1953) for Leigh v. Doncaster on 28 Mar 1976. The most tries in a League match is ten by Lionel Cooper (b. Australia, 1922–87) for Huddersfield v. Keighley on 17 Nov 1951.

Most points *Season and career* The record number of points in a season was 496 by Benjamin Lewis Jones (Leeds) (b. 11 Apr 1931), 194 goals, 36 tries, in 1956/7.

Neil Fox (b. 4 May 1939) scored 6220 points (2575 goals including 4 drop goals, 358 tries) in a senior Rugby League career from 10 Apr 1956 to 19 Aug 1979, consisting of 4488 for Wakefield Trinity, 1089 for five other clubs, 228 for Great Britain, 147 for Yorkshire and 268 in other representative games.

Most tries *Season and career* Albert Aaron Rosenfeld (1885–1970) (Hud-

dersfield), an Australian-born wing-threequarter, scored 80 tries in 42 matches in the 1913/14 season.

Brian Bevan (Australia) (1924–91), a wing-threequarter, scored 796 tries in 18 seasons (16 with Warrington, two with Blackpool Borough) from 1945 to 1964. He scored 740 for Warrington, 17 for Blackpool and 39 in representative matches.

Most goals *Season and career* The record number of goals in a season is 221, in 47 matches, by David Watkins (b. 5 Mar 1942) (Salford) in the 1972/3 season.

Jim Sullivan (Wigan) kicked 2867 goals in his club and representative career, 1921–46.

Most consecutive scores David Watkins (Salford) played and scored in every club game during seasons 1972/3 and 1973/4, contributing 41 tries and 403 goals — a total of 929 points, in 92 games.

Individual international records Jim Sullivan (Wigan) played in most internationals (60 for Wales and Great Britain, 1921–39), kicked most goals (160) and scored most points (329).

Michael Sullivan (no kin) (b. 12 Jan 1934) of Huddersfield, Wigan, St Helens, York and Dewsbury played in 51 international games for England and Great Britain and scored a record 45 tries, 1954–63.

Michael O'Connor (b. 30 Nov 1960) scored a record 30 points (4 tries, 7 goals) for Australia v. Papua New Guinea at Wagga Wagga, Australia on 20 Jul 1988.

Most Challenge Cup Finals Eric Batten (b. 13 Jun 1914) (Leeds, Bradford Northern and Featherstone Rovers) played in a record eight Challenge Cup finals, including wartime guest appearances, between 1941 and 1952 and was on four winning sides.

Andrew 'Andy' Gregory (b. 10 Aug 1961) has appeared in six Challenge Cup winning sides. He played for Widnes, 1981 and 1984, and for Wigan, 1988–91.

Youngest and oldest players Harold Spencer Edmondson (1903–82) played his first League game for Bramley at 15 yr 81 days. The youngest representative player was Harold Wagstaff (1891–1939) who played for Yorkshire at 17 yr 141 days, and for England at 17 yr 228 days.

The youngest player in a Cup final was Shaun Edwards (b. 17 Oct 1966) at 17 yr 201 days for Wigan when they lost 6–19 to Widnes at Wembley on 5 May 1984.

The youngest Great Britain international is Paul Newlove (b. 10 Aug 1971) who played in the first Test v. New Zealand on 21 Oct 1989 at Old Trafford, Greater Manchester, aged 18 yr 72 days. The oldest player for Great Britain was Jeffrey Grayshon (b. 4 Mar 1949) at 36 yr 250 days v. New Zealand at Elland Road, Leeds on 9 Nov 1985.

Most durable player The most appearances for one club is 774 by Jim Sullivan for Wigan, 1921–46. He played a record 928 first-class games in all. The longest continuous playing career is that of Augustus John 'Gus' Risman (b. 21 Mar 1911), who played his first game for Salford on 31 Aug 1929 and his last for Batley on 27 Dec 1954.

Keith Elwell (b. 12 Feb 1950) played in 239 consecutive games for Widnes from 5 May 1977 to 5 Sep 1982. In his career, 1972–85, he received a record 28 winners' or runners-up medals in major competitions.

Most and least successful teams Wigan won 31 consecutive league games from February 1970 to February 1971. Huddersfield were undefeated for 40 league and cup games in 1913/14. Hull is the only club to win all League games in a season, 26 in Division II 1978/9. Runcorn Highfield holds the record of losing 55 consecutive League games from 29 Jan 1989 to 27 Jan 1991. The run was ended with a 12–12 draw with Carlisle on 3 Feb 1991.

Record transfer fee Graham Steadman (b. 8 Dec 1961) became the costliest transferred player (from Featherstone Rovers to Castleford) on 7 Apr 1990 when he played for Great Britain against France. In June 1989 a Rugby League tribunal fixed the transfer fee at £145 000 plus another £25 000 if he achieved international status. John Gallagher (b. 29 Jan 1964), a New Zealand All Black, although born in London, joined Leeds on 21 May 1990. The five year contract was reported as being in the region of £300 000.

Greatest crowds The greatest attendance at any Rugby League match is 102 569 for the Warrington v. Halifax Challenge Cup final replay at Odsal Stadium, Bradford on 5 May 1954.

The record attendance for any international match is 70 204 for the First Test between Australia and England on the Sydney Cricket Ground on 6 Jun 1932. The highest international attendance in

Britain is 54 569 for the First Test between Great Britain and Australia at Wembley Stadium, London on 27 Oct 1990.

AMATEUR RUGBY LEAGUE

The British Amateur Rugby League Association (BARLA) was formed in 1973 'to foster, develop, extend and control amateur rugby league football in Great Britain'. Prior to that year the ultimate control of amateurs as well as professionals rested with the Rugby Football League. A National League was formed in 1986/7.

National Cup Pilkington Recreation (St Helens, Merseyside) have won the National Cup four times (1975, 1979, 1980, 1982). John McCabe (b. 26 Jan 1952) has played in a record five National Cup finals, winning on each occasion. He played for Pilkington Recreation in each of their four successes and captained Thatto Heath (St Helens, Merseyside) to victory in 1987.

Highest score *Major competitions* Humberside beat Carlisle by 138 points to nil in the second round of the National Inter-league Competition on 20 Oct 1984.

Most tries Simon Haughton (b. 10 Nov 1975) scored 130 tries, including nine in one game, from the prop-forward position for the Bingley under-14 side, W Yorks in the 1989/90 season.

Rugby Union

Records are determined in terms of present-day scoring values, i.e. a try at 4 points; a dropped goal, penalty or goal from a mark at 3 points; and a conversion at 2 points. The *actual* score, in accordance with whichever of the eight earlier systems was in force at the time, is also given, in parenthesis.

Although there are records of a game with many similarities to rugby dating back to the Roman occupation, the game is traditionally said to have originated from a breach of the rules of the football played in November 1823 at Rugby School by William Webb Ellis (later the Rev.) (c. 1807–72). This handling code of football evolved gradually and was known to have been played at Cambridge University in 1839. The Rugby Football Union was founded on 26 Jan 1871. The International Rugby Football Board (IRFB) was founded in 1886.

WORLD CUP

The inaugural World Cup was contested in Australia and New Zealand by 16 national teams in 1987. The final in Auckland on 20 Jun 1987 was won by New Zealand, who beat France 29–9. The highest team score was New Zealand's 74–13 victory over Fiji at Christchurch on 27 May 1987. They scored ten goals, two tries and two penalty goals. The individual match record was 30 (3 tries, 9 conversions) by Didier Camberabero (France) (b. 9 Jan 1961) v. Zimbabwe at Auckland on 2 Jun 1987. The leading scorer in the tournament was the New Zealand goal-kicker Grant James Fox (b. 6 Jun 1962), with 126 points.

INTERNATIONAL CHAMPIONSHIP

The International Championship was first contested by England, Ireland, Scotland and Wales in 1884. France first played in 1910.

Wales has won a record 21 times outright and tied for first a further 11 times to 1988. The most Grand Slams, winning all four

matches, is nine by England 1913–14, 1921, 1923–4, 1928, 1957, 1980 and 1991.

Highest team score The highest score in an International Championship match was set at Swansea on 1 Jan 1910 when Wales beat France 49–14 or 59–16 on present-day scoring values (8 goals, 1 penalty goal, 2 tries, to 1 goal, 2 penalty goals, 1 try).

Season's scoring Simon David Hodgkinson (b. 15 Dec 1962) scored a record 60 points (18 penalty goals, 3 conversions) in the four games of an International Championship series in 1991.

Individual match records John 'Jack' Bancroft (1879–1942) kicked a record nine goals (8 conversions and 1 penalty goal) for Wales v. France at Swansea on 1 Jan 1910. Simon Hodgkinson kicked a championship record seven penalty goals for England v. Wales at Cardiff on 19 Jan 1991.

HIGHEST TEAM SCORES

Internationals The highest score in any full international was when New Zealand beat Japan by 106–4 at Tokyo, Japan on 1 Nov 1987, although New Zealand did not award caps. France beat Paraguay 106–12 at Asuncion, Paraguay on 28 Jun 1988.

The highest aggregate score for any international match between the Four Home Unions is 69 when England beat Wales by 69 points (7 goals, 1 drop goal and 6 tries) to nil at Blackheath, London on 19 Feb 1881. (Note: there was no point scoring in 1881.) The highest aggregate score under the modern points system between IRFB members is 79, when Australia beat France 48–31 at Ballymore, Brisbane, Australia on 24 Jun 1990.

The highest score by any overseas side in an international in the British Isles is 53 points (7 goals, 1 drop goal and 2 tries) to nil when South Africa beat Scotland at Murrayfield, Edinburgh on 24 Nov 1951 (44–0).

Tour match The record score for any international tour match is 125–0 (17 goals, 5 tries and 1 penalty goal) (103–0) when New Zealand beat Northern New South Wales at Quirindi, Australia on 30 May 1962. The highest under scoring in use for the game is 117–6 for New Zealand's defeat of South Australia on 1 May 1974.

Match In Denmark, Comet beat Lindo by 194–0 on 17 Nov 1973. The highest British score is 174–0 by 7th Signal Regiment v. 4th Armoured Workshop, REME, on 5 Nov 1980 at Herford, Germany. Scores of over 200 points have been recorded in school matches, for example Radford School beat Hills Court 214 points (31 goals and 7 tries) to nil (200–0) on 20 Nov 1886. The highest score in the Courage Clubs Championship is 146–0 by Billingham against Hartlepool Athletic in a Durham/Northumberland Division 3 match at Billingham, Co. Durham on 3 Oct 1987.

Season The highest number of points accumulated in a season by a club is 1917 points (including a record 345 tries) in 47 games by Neath, West Glamorgan in 1988/9.

HIGHEST INDIVIDUAL SCORES

Internationals Phil Bennett (Wales) (b. 24 Oct 1948) scored 34 points (2 tries, 10 conversions, 2 penalty goals) for Wales v. Japan at Tokyo on 24 Sep 1975, when Wales won 82–6. The highest individual points score in any match between members of the

International Board is 26 by Allan Roy Hewson (b. 6 Jun 1954) (1 try, 2 conversions, 5 penalty goals and a drop goal) for New Zealand against Australia at Auckland on 11 Sep 1982.

Patrice Lagisquet (b. 4 Sep 1962) scored seven tries for France v. Paraguay on 28 Jun 1988. The most tries in an international match between IRFB members is five by George Campbell Lindsay (1863–1905) for Scotland v. Wales on 26 Feb 1887, and by Douglas 'Daniel' Lambert (1883–1915) for England v. France on 5 Jan 1907. Ian Scott Smith (Scotland) (1903–72) scored a record six consecutive international tries in 1925, comprising the last three v. France and two weeks later, the first three v. Wales. The most tries in an international career is 37 by David Ian Campese (b. 21 Oct 1962) for Australia, 1982–90.

A record eight penalty goals were kicked by Mark Andrew Wyatt (b. 12 Apr 1961) when he scored all Canada's points in their 24–19 defeat of Scotland at St John, New Brunswick, Canada on 25 May 1991.

Career In all internationals Micheal Patrick Lynagh (b. 25 Oct 1963) scored a record 564 points in 43 matches for Australia, 1984–90. Andrew Robertson Irvine (Heriots) (b. 16 Sep 1951) scored 301 points, a career record in inter-IRFB internationals, 273 for Scotland (including 12 v. Romania) and 28 for the British Lions, from 1973 to 1982.

Season The first-class season scoring record is 581 points by Samuel Arthur Doble (1944–77) of Moseley, in 52 matches in 1971/2. He also scored 47 points for England in South Africa out of season.

Andy Higgin (b. 4 Mar 1963) scored a record 28 drop goals in a season in first-class rugby, for the Vale of Lune in 1986/7.

Career William Henry 'Dusty' Hare (b. 29 Nov 1952) scored 7337 points in first-class games from 1971–89, comprising 1800 for Nottingham, 4427 for Leicester, 240 for England, 88 for the British Lions and 782 in other representative matches.

Most tries Alan John Morley (b. 25 Jun 1950) scored 473 tries in senior rugby in 1968–86 including 378 for Bristol, a record for one club. John Huins scored 85 tries in 1953–4, 73 for St Luke's College, Exeter and 12 more for Neath and in trial games.

Match Jannie van der Westhuizen scored 80 points (14 tries, 9 conversions, 1 dropped goal, 1 penalty goal) for Carnarvon (88) v. Williston (12) at North West Cape, South Africa on 11 March 1972.

In a junior house match in February 1967 at William Ellis School, Edgware, Greater London, between Cumberland and Nunn, 12-year-old Thanos Morphitis (b. 5 Mar 1954), contributed 90 points (13 tries and 19 conversions) (77) to Cumberland's winning score.

Most international appearances Cameron Michael Henderson Gibson (b. 3 Dec 1942) played in 69 internationals for Ireland, 1964–79, a record for matches between the seven member countries of the 'International Rugby Football Board' and France. Including 12 appearances for the British Lions, he played in a total of 81 international matches. William James 'Willie John' McBride (b. 6 Jun 1940) made a record 17 appearances for the British Lions, as well as 63 for Ireland.

Youngest international Edinburgh Academy pupils Ninian Jamieson Finlay (1858–1936) and Charles Reid (1864–1909) were both 17 yr 36 days old when they

MOST INTERNATIONAL APPEARANCES

Country	Caps	Player	Years
FRANCE	85	Serge Blanco (b. 31 Aug 1958)	1980–91
IRELAND	69	Cameron Michael Henderson Gibson (b. 3 Dec 1942)	1964–79
NEW ZEALAND	55	Colin Earl Meads (b. 3 Jun 1936)	1957–71
WALES	55†	John Peter Rhys 'JPR' Williams (b. 2 Mar 1949)	1969–81
AUSTRALIA	54	David Ian Campese (b. 21 Oct 1962)	1982–90
SCOTLAND	52	James Menzies 'Jim' Renwick (b. 12 Feb 1952)	1972–84
	52	Colin Thomas Deans (b. 3 May 1955)	1978–87
ENGLAND	43	Anthony Neary (b. 25 Nov 1948)	1971–80
	43	Rory Underwood (b. 19 Jun 1963)	1984–91
SOUTH AFRICA	38	Frederick Christoffel Hendrick Du Preez (b. 28 Nov 1935)	1960–71
	38	Jan Hendrik Ellis (b. 5 Jan 1943)	1965–76

* Gareth Owen Edwards (b. 12 Jul 1947) made a record 53 consecutive international appearances, never missing a match throughout his career for Wales, 1967–78. Willie John McBride also had 53 consecutive appearances during his 63 games for Ireland.

Note: The criteria used to decide which games are classed as full internationals vary between countries.

■ **Hong Kong Sevens**
This, the world's most prestigious international tournament for seven-a-side teams, was first held in 1976. The record of six wins is held by Fiji, 1977–8, 1980, 1984, 1990–91. Seen here in action is Fiji's Noa Nadruku, the 1991 tournament's leading try scorer with 10.
(Photo: All-Sport/R. Cheyne)

played for Scotland v. England in 1875 and 1881 respectively. However, as Finlay had one less leap year in his lifetime up to his first cap, the outright record must be credited to him. Daniel Brendan Carroll (1892–1956) was aged only 16 yr 149 days when he played for Australia in the 1908 Olympic Games rugby tournament — not considered to be a 'full' international.

County Championships The County Championships (instituted 1889) have been won most often by Gloucestershire with 15 titles (1910, 1913, 1920–22, 1930–32, 1937, 1972, 1974–6 and 1983–4). The most individual appearances is 104 by Richard Trickey (Sale) (b. 6 Mar 1945) for Lancashire between 1964 and 1978.

Club Championships The most outright wins in the RFU Club Competition (John Player Cup, 1971–87, now Pilkington Cup) is six by Bath, 1984–7, 1989–90. The highest team score (and aggregate) in the final is for Bath's 48–6 win over Gloucester in 1990. In the 1989 season Bath completed the double having won the English league title, the Courage Clubs Championship, which was founded in the 1987/8 season. The most wins in the Welsh Rugby Union Challenge Cup (Schweppes Welsh Cup, instituted 1971/2) is seven by Llanelli, 1973–6, 1985, 1988 and 1991. The highest team score in the final is 30 by Llanelli against Cardiff (7) in 1973. The highest aggregate is when Cardiff beat Newport 28–21 in 1986. The most wins in the Scottish League Division One (instituted 1973/4) is ten by Hawick between 1973 and 1986.

Seven-a-sides Seven-a-side rugby dates from 28 Apr 1883 when Melrose RFC Borders, in order to alleviate the poverty of a club in such a small town, staged a seven-a-side tournament. The idea was that of Ned Haig, the town's butcher.

Middlesex Seven-a-sides The Middlesex Seven-a-sides were inaugurated in 1926 and have been won a record 12 times by Harlequins, 1926–9, 1933, 1935, 1967, 1978, 1986–90.

Greatest crowd The record paying attendance is 104 000 for Scotland's 12–10 win over Wales at Murrayfield, Edinburgh on 1 Mar 1975.

Longest kicks The longest recorded successful drop goal is 82 m *90 yd* by Gerald Hamilton 'Gerry' Brand (b. 8 Oct 1906) for South Africa v. England at Twickenham, Greater London, on 2 Jan 1932. This was taken 6 m *7 yd* inside the England 'half', 50 m *55 yd* from the posts, and dropped over the dead ball line.

The place kick record is reputed to be 91 m *100 yd* at Richmond Athletic Ground, London, by Douglas Francis Theodore Morkel (1886–1950) in an unsuccessful penalty for South Africa v. Surrey on 19 Dec 1906. This was not measured until 1932. In the match Bridlington School 1st XV v. an Army XV at Bridlington, Humberside on 29 Jan 1944, Ernie Cooper (b. 21 May 1926), captaining the school, landed a penalty from a measured 74 m *81 yd* from the post with a kick which carried over the dead ball line. The record in an international was set at 64·22 m *70 yd 8½ in* by Paul Huw Thorburn (b. 24 Nov 1962) for Wales v. Scotland on 1 Feb 1986.

Fastest try The fastest try in an international game was when Herbert Leo 'Bart' Price (1899–1943) scored for England v. Wales at Twickenham on 20 Jan 1923 less than 10 sec after kick-off. The fastest try in any game was scored in 8 sec by Andrew Brown for Widden Old Boys v. Old Ashtonians at Gloucester on 22 Nov 1990.

Most successful team The Feilding senior 4ths of New Zealand played 108 successive games without defeat from 1984–9. The Chiltern mini rugby side, from their formation as an Under-8 side, played 213 games without defeat, 29 Sep 1985–8 Apr 1990.

WOMEN'S RUGBY

The first women's World Cup was contested by 12 teams in 1991, with the USA beating England 19–6 in the final at Cardiff, S Glam on 14 April.

Shinty

Origins Shinty (from the Gaelic *sinteag*, a bound) has roots reaching back more than 2000 years to the ancient game of *camanachd*, the sport of the curved stick, the diversion of the heroes of Celtic history and legend. It was effective battle training, exercising speed and co-ordination of eye and arm along with aggression and cool self-control. In spite of the break-up of the clan system in the Highlands of Scotland, the 'ball plays', involving whole parishes, without limit in number or time except the fall of night, continued in areas such as Lochaber, Badenoch and Strathglass. Whisky and the inspiration of the bagpipes were important ingredients of these occasions. The ruling body of this apparently ungovernable game was established in 1893 when the Camanachd Association was set up at Kingussie, Highland.

Most titles Newtonmore, Highland has won the Camanachd Association Challenge Cup (instituted 1896) a record 28 times, 1907–86. David Ritchie (b. 9 Jun 1944) and Hugh Chisholm (b. 14 Oct 1949) of Newtonmore, have won a record 12 winners' medals. In 1923 the Furnace Club, Argyll won the cup without conceding a goal throughout the competition.

In 1984 Kingussie Camanachd Club won all five senior competitions, including the Camanachd Cup final. This feat was equalled by Newtonmore in 1985.

Shooting

The Lucerne Shooting Guild (Switzerland) was formed c. 1466 and the first recorded shooting match was at Zurich in 1472.

Most Olympic medals Carl Townsend Osburn (USA) (1884–1966), in 1912, 1920 and 1924, won a record 11, five gold, four silver and two bronze. Six other marksmen have won five gold medals. The only marksman to win three individual gold medals has been Gudbrand Gudbrandsönn Skatteboe (Norway) (1875–1965) in 1906. Separate events for women were first held in 1984.

Bisley The National Rifle Association was instituted in 1859. The Queen's

(King's) Prize has been shot since 1860 and has only once been won by a woman, Marjorie Elaine Foster (1894–1974) (score 280) on 19 Jul 1930. Arthur George Fulton (1887–1972) won three times (1912, 1926, 1931). Both his father and his son also won the Prize.

The highest score (possible 300) for the final of the Queen's Prize is 295 by Lindsay Peden (Scotland) on 24 Jul 1982. The record for the Silver Medals is 150 (possible 150) by Martin John Brister (City Rifle Club) (b. 1951) and (Lord) John Swansea (b. 1 Jan 1925) on 24 Jul 1971. This was equalled by John Henry Carmichael (WRA Bromsgrove RC) on 28 Jul 1979 and Robert Stafford on 26 Jul 1980, with the size of the bullseyes reduced.

Small-bore The National Small-Bore Rifle Association, of Britain, was formed in 1901. The British team record (1966 target) is 1988/2000 by Lancashire in 1968–9 and London in 1980–81. The British individual small-bore rifle record for 60 shots prone is 600/600, first achieved by John Palin (b. 16 Jul 1934) in Switzerland in 1972. Richard Hansen shot 5000 consecutive bullseyes in 24 hr at Fresno, California, USA on 13 Jun 1929.

Clay pigeon Most world titles have been won by Susan Nattrass (Canada) (b. 5 Nov 1950) with six, 1974–5, 1977–9, 1981. The record number of clay birds shot in an hour is 3172 by Dan Carlisle (USA) at Norco, California, USA on 20 May 1990.

The maximum 200/200 was achieved by Ricardo Ruiz Rumoroso at the Spanish Clay Pigeon Championships at Zaragossa on 12 Jun 1983.

Noel D. Townend achieved the maximum 200 consecutive down-the-line targets at Nottingham and District Gun Club, Nottingham on 21 Aug 1983.

Highest score in 24 hours The Easingwold Rifle and Pistol Club team of John Smith, Edward Kendall, Phillip Kendall and Paul Duffield scored 120 242 points (averaging 95·66 per card) on 6–7 Aug 1983.

Skiing

The most ancient ski in existence was found well preserved in a peat bog at Hoting, Sweden, dating from c. 2500 BC. The earliest recorded military use of skiing was at the Battle of Isen, near Oslo, Norway in 1200. The Trysil Shooting and Skiing Club, founded in Norway in 1861, claims it is the world's oldest. The oldest ski competitions are the Holmenkøllen Nordic events which were first held in 1866. The first downhill races were staged in Australia in the 1850s. The International Ski Federation (FIS) was founded on 2 Feb 1924, succeeding the International Skiing Commission, founded at Christiania (Oslo), Norway on 18 Feb 1910.

The Ski Club of Great Britain was founded on 6 May 1903. The National Ski Federation of Great Britain was formed in 1964 and changed its name to the British Ski Federation in 1981.

Most titles World/Olympic Championships — Alpine The World Alpine Championships were inaugurated at Mürren, Switzerland, in 1931. The greatest number of titles won has been by Christel Cranz (b. 1 Jul 1914) of Germany, with seven individual — four slalom (1934, 1937–9) and three downhill (1935, 1937, 1939), and five combined (1934–5, 1937–9). She also won the gold medal for the Combined in the 1936 Olympics. The most won by a man is seven by Anton 'Toni' Sailer (Austria) (b. 17 Nov 1935), who won all four in 1956 (giant slalom, slalom, downhill and the non-Olympic Alpine combination) and the downhill, giant slalom and combined in 1958.

World/Olympic Championships — Nordic The first World Nordic Championships were those of the 1924 Winter Olympics in Chamonix, France. The greatest number of titles won is 11 by Gunde Svan (Sweden) (b. 12 Jan 1962), seven individual; 15 km 1989, 30km 1985 and 1991, 50 km 1985 and 1989, and Olympics, 15 km 1984, 50 km 1988: and four

Highest shinty scores

The highest Scottish Cup final score was in 1909 when Newtonmore beat Furnace 11–3 at Glasgow, Dr Johnnie Cattanach scoring eight hails or goals. In 1938 John Macmillan Mactaggart scored ten hails for Mid-Argyll in a Camanachd Cup match.

Bench rest shooting

The smallest group on record at 914 m *1000 yd* is 11·11 cm *4·375 in* by Earl Chronister with a ·30–378 Weatherby Mag at Williamsport, Pennsylvania, USA on 12 Jul 1987.

SHOOTING–INDIVIDUAL WORLD RECORDS

In 1986, the International Shooting Union (UIT) introduced new regulations for determining major championships and world records. Now the leading competitors undertake an additional round with a target sub-divided into tenths of a point for rifle and pistol shooting, and an extra 25 shots for trap and skeet. Harder targets have since been introduced and the table below shows the world records, as recognized by the UIT on 1 Jan 1991, for the 13 Olympic shooting disciplines, giving in brackets the score for the number of shots specified plus the score in the additional round.

MEN

FREE RIFLE 50 m 3 × 40 shots	1276·7	(1179 + 97·7)	Rajmond Debevec (Yugoslavia)	Zürich, Switzerland	5 Jun 1990
FREE RIFLE 50 m 60 shots prone	702·9	(599 + 103·8)	Vari Zsolt (Hungary)	Munich, Germany	2 Jun 1990
AIR RIFLE 10 m 60 shots	699·4	(596 + 103·4)	Rajmond Debevec (Yugoslavia)	Zürich, Switzerland	7 Jun 1990
FREE PISTOL 50 m 60 shots	671	(579 + 92)	Sergey Pyzhyanov (USSR)	Munich, Germany	30 May 1990
	671	(577 + 94)	Spas Koprinkov (Bulgaria)	Moscow, USSR	9 Aug 1990
RAPID-FIRE PISTOL 25 m 60 shots	891	(594 + 297)	Ralf Schumann (West Germany)	Munich, Germany	3 Jun 1989
AIR PISTOL 10 m 60 shots	695·1	(593 + 102·1)	Sergey Pyzhyanov (USSR)	Munich, Germany	13 Oct 1989
RUNNING GAME TARGET 50 m 30 + 30 shots	678	(582 + 96)	Jan Kermiet (Czechoslovakia)	Munich, Germany	12 Oct 1990

WOMEN

STANDARD RIFLE 50 m 3 × 20 shots	684·4	(589 + 95·4)	Vessela Letcheva (Bulgaria)	Munich, Germany	1 Jun 1990
AIR RIFLE 10 m 40 shots	499·4	(397 + 102·4)	Valentina Cherkasova (USSR)	Suhl, Germany	30 May 1987
SPORT PISTOL 25 m 60 shots	693	(593 + 100)	Nino Salukvadse (USSR)	Zagreb, Yugoslavia	13 Jul 1989
AIR PISTOL 10 m 40 shots	492·4	(392 + 100·4)	Lieslotte Breker (West Germany)	Zagreb, Yugoslavia	18 May 1989

OPEN

TRAP 200 targets	224	(200 + 24)	Jörg Damme (West Germany)	Moscow, USSR	18 Aug 1990
SKEET 200 targets	223	(198 + 25)	Valeriy Timokhin (USSR)	Tampere, Finland	15 Jun 1989
	223	(199 + 24)	Bruno Rosetti (Italy)	Zagreb, Yugoslavia	15 Jul 1989
	223	(199 + 24)	Ennio Falco (Italy)	Bologna, Italy	19 May 1990
	223	(198 + 25)	Ole Justesen (Denmark)	Suhl, Germany	27 May 1990

MOST OLYMPIC SKIING TITLES

MEN

ALPINE	3	Anton 'Toni' Sailer (Austria) (b. 17 Nov 1935)	Downhill, slalom, giant slalom, 1956
	3	Jean-Claude Killy (France) (b. 30 Aug 1943)	Downhill, slalom, giant slalom 1968
NORDIC	4[1]	Sixten Jernberg (Sweden) (b. 6 Feb 1929)	50 km 1956; 30 km 1960; 50 km and 4 × 10 km 1964
	4	Gunde Svan (Sweden) (b. 12 Mar 1962)	15 km and 4 × 10 km 1984; 50 km and 4 × 10 km 1988
	4	Thomas Wassberg (Sweden) (b. 27 Mar 1956)	15 km 1980; 50 km 1984; 4 × 10 km 1984, 1988
Ski-jumping	4	Matti Nykänen (Finland) (b. 17 Jul 1963)	70 m hill 1988; 90 m hill 1984, 1988; Team 1988

WOMEN

ALPINE	2	Andrea Mead-Lawrence (USA) (b. 19 Apr 1932)	Slalom, giant slalom 1952
	2	Marielle Goitschel (France) (b. 28 Sep 1945)	Giant slalom 1964; slalom 1968
	2	Marie-Thérèse Nadig (Switz) (b. 8 Mar 1954)	Downhill, giant slalom 1972
	2	Rosi Mittermaier (now Neureuther) (West Germany) (b. 5 Aug 1950)	Downhill, slalom 1976
	2[2]	Hanni Wenzel (Liechtenstein) (b. 14 Dec 1956)	Giant slalom, slalom 1980
	2	Vreni Schneider (Switzerland) (b. 26 Nov 1964)	Giant slalom, slalom 1988
NORDIC	4	Galina Kulakova (USSR) (b. 29 Apr 1942)	5 km, 10 km and 3 × 5 km relay 1972; 4 × 5 km relay 1976
(individual)	3	Marja-Liisa Hämäläinen (Finland) (b. 10 Aug 1955)	5 km, 10 km and 20 km 1984

[1] **Most medals** 9, Sixten Jernberg, four golds, three silver and two bronze
9, Raisa Smetanina, three gold, five silver and one bronze at women's Nordic skiing 1976–88.
[2] *Wenzel won a silver in the 1980 downhill and a bronze in the 1976 slalom for a record four medals in Alpine skiing.*

■ **All disciplines**
With a victory in a super-giant slalom event on 9 Dec 1990, Petra Kronberger (Austria) became the first woman to win World Cup races at all four disciplines. She is pictured at the 1991 World Championships, when she won the downhill gold medal.

relays; 4 × 10 km, 1987 and 1989, and Olympics, 1984 and 1988. The most titles won by a woman is nine by Galina Alekseyevna Kulakova (USSR) (b. 29 Apr 1942) five individual and four relay in 1970–78. The most medals is 22 by Raisa Petrovna Smetanina (USSR) (b. 29 Feb 1952) including six gold, 1974–91. Ulrich Wehling (GDR) (b. 8 Jul 1952) with the Nordic combined in 1972, 1976 and 1980, is the only skier to win the same event at three successive Olympics. The most titles won by a jumper is five by Birger Ruud (b. 23 Aug 1911) of Norway, in 1931–2 and 1935–7. Ruud is the only person to win Olympic

events in each of the dissimilar Alpine and Nordic disciplines. In 1936 he won the Ski-jumping and the Alpine downhill (which was not then a separate event, but only a segment of the Combined event).

World Cup The World Cup was introduced for Alpine events in 1967. The most individual event wins is 86 (46 giant slalom, 40 slalom from a total of 287 races) by Ingemar Stenmark (Sweden) (b. 18 Mar 1956) in 1974–89, including a men's record 13 in one season in 1978/9, of which 10 were part of a record 14 successive giant slalom wins from 18 Mar 1978, his 22nd birthday, to 21 Jan 1980. Franz Klammer (Austria) (b. 3

Dec 1953) won a record 25 downhill races, 1974–84. Annemarie Moser (*née* Pröll) (Austria) (b. 27 Mar 1953) won a women's record 62 individual event wins, 1970–79. She had a record 11 consecutive downhill wins from Dec 1972 to Jan 1974. Vreni Schneider (Switzerland) (b. 26 Nov 1964) won a record 13 events (and a combined) including all seven slalom events in the 1988/9 season. The Nations' Cup, awarded on the combined results of the men and women in the World Cup, has been won a record 13 times by Austria 1969, 1973–82, 1990–91.

Ski-jumping The longest ski-jump ever recorded is one of 194 m *636 ft* by Piotr Fijas (Poland) at Planica, Yugoslavia on 14 Mar 1987. The women's record is 110 m *361 ft* by Tiina Lehtola (Finland) (b. 3 Aug 1962) at Ruka, Finland on 29 Mar 1981. The longest dry ski-jump is 92 m *302 ft* by Hubert Schwarz (West Germany) at Berchtesgarten, Germany on 30 Jun 1981.

Highest speed The official world record, as recognized by the International Ski Federation for a skier, is 223·741 km/h *139·030 mph* by Michael Prufer (Monaco) and the fastest by a woman is 214·413 km/h *133·234 mph* by Tarja Mulari (Finland), both at Les Arcs, France on 16 Apr 1988. On the same occasion, Graham Wilkie (GB) (b. 21 Sep 1959) set a British men's record of 219·914 km/h *136·651 mph* and Patrick Knaff (France) set a one-legged record of 185·567 km/h *115·309 mph*.

On 18 Apr 1987, a British women's record was set by Divina Galica (b. 13 Aug 1944) at 191·99 km/h *119·30 mph*, also at Les Arcs, France.

The highest average speed in the Olympic

■ **Most overall titles**
Marc Girardelli (b. 18 Jul 1963), born in Italy, is now a naturalized citizen of Luxembourg but lives in Switzerland. He became the third skier in the history of the Alpine World Cup to win a record fourth overall title in 1991. He had previously won in 1985, 1986 and 1989.
(Photo: All-Sport/D. Cannon)

Highest altitude
Jean Afanassieff and Nicolas Jaeger skied from 8200 m *26 900 ft* to 6200 m *20 340 ft* on the 1978 French expedition on Mt Everest.

Steepest descent
The steepest descents in alpine skiing history have been by Sylvain Saudan. At the start of his descent from Mont Blanc on the north-east side down the Couloir Gervasutti from 4248 m *13 937 ft* on 17 Oct 1967 he skied to gradients of *c*. 60°.

Snow shoeing
The USSSA record for covering 1·6 km *1 mile* is 5 min 56·7 sec by Nick Akers of Edmonton, Alberta, Canada on 3 Feb 1991. The 100 m record is 15·06 sec by Scott Hannay of Westerlo, New York, USA on 25 Feb 1989.

Longest ski lift
The longest gondola ski lift is 6239 m *3·88 miles* long at Grindelwald-Männlichen, Switzerland (in two sections, but one gondola). The longest chair lift in the world was the Alpine Way to Kosciusko Chalet lift above Thredbo, near the Snowy Mountains, New South Wales, Australia. It took from 45 to 75 min to ascend the 5·6 km *3·5 miles*, according to the weather. It has now collapsed. The highest is at Chacaltaya, Bolivia, rising to 5029 m *16 500 ft*.

downhill race was 104·53 km/h *64·95 mph* by William D. Johnson (USA) (b. 30 Mar 1960) at Sarajevo, Yugoslavia on 16 Feb 1984. The fastest in a World Cup downhill is 107·82 km/h *67·00 mph* by Harti Weirather (Austria) (b. 25 Jan 1958) at Kitzbühel, Austria on 15 Jan 1982.

Highest speed — cross-country
Bill Koch (USA) (b. 13 Apr 1943) on 26 Mar 1981 skied ten times round a 5 km *3·11 mile* loop on Marlborough Pond, near Putney, Vermont, USA. He completed the 50 km in 1 hr 59 min 47 sec, an average speed of 25·045 km/h *15·57 mph*. A race includes uphill and downhill sections; the record time for a 50 km race in World Championships or Olympic Games is 2 hr 3 min 31·6 sec by Torgny Mogren (Sweden) in 1991, an average speed of 24·28 km/h *15·09 mph*.

Closest verdict The narrowest winning

Grass Skiing

Grass skis were first manufactured by Josef Kaiser (West Germany) in 1963. World Championships (now awarded for Super G, giant slalom, slalom and combined) were first held in 1979. The most titles won is ten by Ingrid Hirschhofer (Austria) 1979–89. The most by a man is seven by Erwin Gansner (Switzerland) 1981–7.

The speed record is 86·88 km/h *53·99 mph* by Erwin Gansner at Owen, Germany on 5 Sep 1982.

At the same venue Laurence Beck set a British record of 79·49 km/h *43·39 mph* on 8 Sep 1985.

24-hour skittle records

The highest score at West Country skittles by a team of eight is 99 051 by the 'Alkies' Skittles team at Courtlands Holiday Inn, Torquay, Devon on 4–5 Apr 1987; they reset the skittles after every ball. The highest long alley score is 78 223 by The Clarence House Eight at Portishead, Bristol, Avon on 17–18 Nov 1990. The highest hood skittle score is 124 932 pins by 12 players from the Semilong Working Men's Club, Northampton on 28–29 Apr 1990.

Table skittles

The highest score is 116 047 skittles by 12 players at the Castle Mona, Newcastle, Staffs on 15–16 Apr 1990.

margin in a championship ski race was one hundredth of a second by Thomas Wassberg (Sweden) over Juha Mieto (Finland) (b. 20 Nov 1949) in the Olympic 15-km cross-country race at Lake Placid, New York, USA on 17 Feb 1980. His winning time was 41 min 57·63 sec.

Longest run The longest all-downhill ski run in the world is the Weissfluhjoch-Küblis Parsenn course, near Davos, Switzerland, which measures 12·23 km *7·6 miles*. The run from the Aiguille du Midi top of the Chamonix lift (vertical lift 2759 m *9052 ft*) across the Vallée Blanche is 20·9 km *13 miles*.

Most competitors A total of 1700 downhill skiers competed at Åre, Jämtland, Sweden on 30 Apr 1984.

Longest races The world's greatest Nordic ski race is the Vasaloppet, which commemorates an event of 1521 when Gustav Vasa (1496–1560), later King Gustavus Eriksson, fled 85·8 km *53·3 miles* from Mora to Sälen, Sweden. He was overtaken by loyal, speedy scouts on skis, who persuaded him to return eastwards to Mora to lead a rebellion and become the king of Sweden. The re-enactment of this return journey is now an annual event at 89 km *55·3 miles*. There was a record 10 934 starters on 6 Mar 1977 and a record 10 633 finishers on 4 Mar 1979. The fastest time is 3 hr 48 min 55 sec, by Bengt Hassis (Sweden) on 2 Mar 1986.

The Finlandia Ski Race, 75 km *46·6 miles* from Hämeenlinna to Lahti, on 26 Feb 1984 had a record 13 226 starters and 12 909 finishers.

The longest downhill race is the *Inferno* in Switzerland, 15·8 km *9·8 miles* from the top of the Schilthorn to Lauterbrunnen. The record entry was 1401 in 1981 and the record time 15 min 26·44 sec by Ueli Grossniklaus (Switzerland) in 1987.

Long-distance (Nordic) In 24 hours Seppo-Juhani Savolainen covered 415·5 km *258·2 miles* at Saariselkä, Finland on 8–9 Apr 1988. The women's record is 330 km *205·05 miles* by Sisko Kainulaisen at Jyväskylä, Finland on 23–24 Mar 1985.

In 48 hours Bjørn Løkken (Norway) (b. 27 Nov 1937) covered 513·568 km *319 miles 205 yd* on 11–13 Mar 1982.

Freestyle The first World Championships were held at Tignes, France in 1986, titles being awarded in ballet, moguls, aerials and combined. A record two titles have been won by Lloyd Langlois (Canada), aerials, 1986 and 1989, Jan Buchner (USA), ballet, 1986 and 1989, and Edgar Grospiron (France), moguls, 1989 and 1991. The three seperate disciplines were included in the 1988 Olympics but only as demonstration events. Moguls will be contested with full status at the 1992 Olympics.

Ski-bob Origins The ski-bob was the invention of J. C. Stevenson of Hartford, Connecticut, USA in 1891, and patented (No. 47334) on 19 Apr 1892 as a 'bicycle with ski-runners'. The *Fédération Internationale de Skibob* was founded on 14 Jan 1961 in Innsbruck, Austria and the first World Championships were held at Bad Hofgastein, Austria in 1967.

The highest speed attained is 166 km/h *103·4 mph* by Erich Brenter (Austria) (b. 1940) at Cervinia, Italy in 1964.

World Championships The only ski-bobbers to retain a world championship are: men—Alois Fischbauer (Austria)

MOST WORLD CUP TITLES

ALPINE (instituted 1967)

MEN

OVERALL	4	Gustavo Thoeni (Italy)	1971–3, 1975
	4	Pirmin Zurbriggen (Switzerland)	1984, 1987–8, 1990
	4	Marc Girardelli (Luxembourg)	1985–6, 1989, 1991
DOWNHILL	5	Franz Klammer (Austria)	1975–8, 1983
SLALOM	8	Ingemar Stenmark (Sweden)	1975–81, 1983
GIANT SLALOM	7	Ingemar Stenmark	1975–6, 1978–81, 1984
SUPER GIANT SLALOM	4	Pirmin Zurbriggen (Switzerland)	1987–90

Two men have won four titles in one year: Jean-Claude Killy (France) (b. 30 Aug 1943) won all four possible disciplines (downhill, slalom, giant slalom and overall) in 1967; and Pirmin Zurbriggen (Switzerland) (b. 4 Feb 1963) won four of the five possible disciplines (downhill, giant slalom, Super giant slalom [added 1986] and overall) in 1987.

WOMEN

OVERALL	6	Annemarie Moser-Pröll (Austria)	1971–5, 1979
DOWNHILL	7	Annemarie Moser-Pröll	1971–5, 1978–9
SLALOM	4	Erika Hess (Switzerland)	1981–3, 1985
GIANT SLALOM	4	Vreni Schneider (Switzerland)	1986–7, 1989, 1991
SUPER GIANT SLALOM	3	Carole Merle (France)	1989–91

NORDIC (instituted 1981)

MEN

JUMPING	4	Matti Nykänen (Finland)	1983, 1985–6, 1988
CROSS-COUNTRY	5	Gunde Svan (Sweden)	1984–6, 1988–9

WOMEN

CROSS-COUNTRY	3	Marjo Matikainen (Finland)	1986–8

(b. 6 Oct 1951), 1973 and 1975, Robert Mühlberger (West Germany), 1979 and 1981; women—Gerhilde Schiffkorn (Austria) (b. 22 Mar 1950), 1967 and 1969, Gertrude Geberth (Austria) (b. 18 Oct 1951), 1971 and 1973.

Skipping

Ten-mile skip-run Vadivelu Karunakaren (India) skipped 10 miles *16 km* in 58 min at Madras, India, 1 Feb 1990.

Most turns *10 seconds* 128 by Albert Rayner (GB) (b. 19 Apr 1923), Stanford Sports, Birmingham, W Mids, 19 Nov 1982.

1 minute 425 by Robert Commers (USA) (b. 15 May 1950) at The Holiday Inn, Jamestown, New York, USA, 23 Feb 1990.

One hour 14 628 by Park Bong Tae (South Korea) at Pusan, South Korea, 2 Jul 1989.

On a single rope, team of 90 160 by students from the Nishigoshi Higashi Elementary School, Kumamoto, Japan, 27 Feb 1987.

On a tightrope 358 (consecutive) by Julian Albulet (USA) at Las Vegas, Nevada, USA, 2 Jul 1990.

Most consecutive multiple turns *Double* 10 709 by Frank Oliveri (USA) at Rochester, New York, USA, 7 May 1988.

Double (with cross) 2411 by Ken Solis (USA) at North Shore-Elite Fitness and Racquets Club, Glendale, Wisconsin, USA, 29 Mar 1988.

Treble 423 by Shozo Hamada (Japan) at Saitama, Japan, 1 Jun 1987.

Quadruple 51 by Katsumi Suzuki (Japan) at Saitama, Japan, 29 May 1975.

Quintuple 6 by Hideyuki Tateda (Japan) (b. 1968) at Aomori, Japan, 19 Jun 1982.

Most on a rope (minimum 12 turns obligatory) 220 by a team at the International Rope Skipping Competition, Greeley, Colorado, USA, 28 Jun 1990.

Snooker

Origins Research shows that snooker was originated by Colonel Sir Neville Francis Fitzgerald Chamberlain (1856–1944) as a hybrid of 'black pool', 'pyramids' and billiards, in Jubbulpore, India in 1875. It did not reach England until 1885, where the modern scoring system was adopted in 1891. Championships were not started until 1916. The World Professional Championship was instituted in 1927.

Most world titles The world professional title was won a record 15 times by Joe Davis, on the first 15 occasions it was contested, 1927–40 and 1946. The most wins in the Amateur Championships (instituted 1963) have been two by: Gary Owen (England) in 1963 and 1966; Ray Edmonds (England) 1972 and 1974; and Paul Mifsud (Malta) 1985–6.

Maureen Baynton (*née* Barrett) won a record eight Women's Amateur Championships between 1954 and 1968, as well as seven at billiards.

World Championships *Youngest* The youngest man to win a world title is Stephen O'Connor (Ireland) (b. 16 Oct 1972), who was 18 yr 40 days when he won the World Amateur Snooker Championship in Colombo, Sri Lanka on 25 Nov 1990. Stephen Hendry (Scotland) (b. 13 Jan 1969) became the youngest World Professional champion, at 21 yr 106 days on 29 Apr 1990. He had been the youngest winner of a major title, at 18 yr 285 days, when he won the Rothmans Grand Prix on 25 Oct 1987.

Stacey Hillyard (England) (b. 5 Sep 1969) won the Women's World Amateur Championship in October 1984 at the age of 15.

Highest breaks Over 200 players have achieved the 'maximum' break of 147. The first to do so was E. J. 'Murt' O'Donoghue (b. New Zealand 1901) at Griffiths, New South Wales, Australia on 26 Sep 1934. The first officially ratified 147 was by Joe Davis against Willie Smith at Leicester Square Hall, London on 22 Jan 1955. The first achieved in a major tournaments were by John Spencer (b. 18 Sep 1935) at Slough, Berks on 13 Jan 1979, but the table had oversized pockets, and by Steve Davis (b. 22 Aug 1957), who had a ratified break of 147 against John Spencer in the Lada Classic at Oldham, Greater Manchester on 11 Jan 1982. The youngest to score a competitive maximum was Ronnie O'Sullivan (b. 5 Dec 1975) at 15 yr 98 days during the English Amateur Championship (Southern Area) at Aldershot, Hants on 12 Mar 1991. Cliff Thorburn (Canada) (b. 16 Jan 1948) has scored two tournament 147 breaks on 23 Apr 1983 (still the only one in the World Professional Championship) and 8 Mar 1989. Steve Duggan (b. 10 Apr 1958) made a break of 148 in a witnessed practice frame in Doncaster, S Yorks on 27 Apr 1988. The break involved a free ball, which therefore created an 'extra' red, when all 15 reds were still on the table. In these very exceptional circumstances, the maximum break is 155. The only '16 red' clearance ever completed in a tournament was by Steve James (b. 2 May 1961) who made 135 against Alex Higgins (b. 18 Mar 1949) in the World Professional Championships at Sheffield, S Yorks on 14 Apr 1990.

The first non-professional to score a maximun break was Geet Sethi (India) in the Indian Amateur Championships on 21 Feb 1988.

Three consecutive century breaks were first compiled in a major tournament by Steve Davis: 108, 101 and 104 at Stoke-on-Trent, Staffs on 10 Sep 1985. Doug Mountjoy (b. 8 Jun 1942) equalled the feat: 131, 106 and 124 at Preston, Lancs on 27 Nov 1988. Jim Meadowcroft (b. 15 Dec 1946) made four consecutive frame clearances of 105, 115, 117 and 125 in witnessed practice at Connaught Leisure Centre, Worthing, W Sussex on 27 Jan 1982.

The first century break by a woman in competitive play was 114 by Stacey Hillyard in a league match at Bournemouth, Dorset on 15 Jan 1985. The highest break by a woman in competition is 116 by Allison Fisher in the British Open at Solihull, W Mids on 7 Oct 1989.

Softball

Origins Softball, a derivative of baseball, was invented by George Hancock at the Farragut Boat Club of Chicago, Illinois in 1887. Rules were first codified in Minneapolis, Minnesota, USA in 1895 as kitten ball. The name softball was introduced by Walter Hakanson at a meeting of the National Recreation Congress in 1926. The name was adopted throughout the USA in 1930. Rules were formalized in 1933 by the International Joint Rules Committee for Softball and adopted by the Amateur Softball Association of America. The International Softball Federation was formed in 1950 as governing body for both fast pitch and slow pitch. It was reorganized in 1965. Women's fast pitch softball has been added to the Olympic programme for 1996.

Most titles The USA has won the men's world championship (instituted 1966) five times, 1966, 1968, 1976 (shared) 1980 and 1988, and the women's title (instituted 1965) three times in 1974, 1978 and 1986. The

world's first slow-pitch championships for men's teams was held in Oklahoma City, USA in 1987, when the winners were the USA.

Speedway

Motorcycle racing on large dirt track surfaces has been traced back to 1902 in the United States. The first fully documented motorcycle track races were at the Portman Road Ground, Ipswich, Suffolk on 2 Jul 1904. Two heats and a final were contested, F. E. Barker winning in 5 min 54·2 sec for three miles. Modern speedway has developed from the 'short track' races held at the West Maitland Agricultural (New South Wales, Australia) Show on 22 Dec 1923, by Johnnie Hoskins (New Zealand) (1892–1987).

He brought the sport to Britain, where it evolved with small diameter track racing at Droylsden, Manchester on 25 Jun 1927 and a cinder track event at High Beech, Essex on 19 Feb 1928.

World Championships The World Speedway Championship was inaugurated at Wembley, London on 10 Sep 1936. The most wins have been six by Ivan Gerald Mauger (New Zealand) (b. 4 Oct 1939) in 1968–70, 1972, 1977 and 1979. Barry Briggs (New Zealand) (b. 30 Dec 1934) made a record 18 appearances in the finals (1954–70, 1972), won the world title in 1957–8, 1964 and 1966, and scored a record 201 points in world championship competition from 87 races.

Ivan Mauger also won four World Team Cups (three for GB), two World Pairs (including one unofficial) and three world long track titles. Ove Fundin (Sweden) (b. 23 May 1933) won 12 world titles: five individual, one Pairs, and six World Team Cup medals in 1956–70. In 1985 Erik Gundersen (Denmark) became the first man to hold world titles at individual, pairs, team and long-track events simultaneously.

The World Pairs Championships (instituted unofficially 1968, officially 1970) have been won a record seven times, by; England/Great Britain, 1972, 1976–8, 1980 and 1983–4; and Denmark, 1979, 1985–90. The most successful individuals in the World Pairs have been Erik Gundersen (b. 8 Oct 1959) and Hans Hollen Neilsen (b. 26 Dec 1959) with five wins for Denmark. They won as a pair, 1986–9, and Gundersen also won with Tommy Knudsen in 1985 and Nielsen with Jan O' Pedersen in 1990. Maximum points (then 30) were scored in the World Pairs Championship by: Jerzy Szczakiel (b. 28 Jan 1949) and Andrzej Wyglenda (Poland) at Rybnik, Poland in 1971; and Arthur Dennis Sigalos (b. 16 Aug 1959) and Robert Benjamin 'Bobby' Schwartz (USA) (b. 10 Aug 1956) at Liverpool, New South Wales, Australia on 11 Dec 1982.

The World Team Cup (instituted 1960) has been won a record nine times by England/Great Britain (Great Britain 1968, 1971–3; England 1974–5, 1977, 1980, 1989). Hans Nielsen (Denmark) has ridden in a record eight Team wins.

British Championships League racing was introduced to British speedway in 1929 and consisted of a Southern League and Northern Dirt Track League, the National League was formulated in 1932 and continued to 1964. The Wembley Lions who won in 1932, 1946–7, 1949–53, had a record eight victories. In 1965 it was

replaced by the British League which Belle Vue (who had six National League wins, 1933–6, 1939 and 1963) have won four times, including three times in succession (1970–72). Wimbledon was the only club to have competed every year since 1929 in Southern, National and British Leagues before their closure on 5 Jun 1991.

In league racing the highest score recorded was when Berwick beat Exeter 78–18 in the 16-heat formula for the National League on 27 May 1989. A maximum possible score was achieved by Bristol when they defeated Glasgow (White City) 70–14 on 7 Oct 1949 in the National League Division Two. The highest number of League points scored by an individual in a season was 563 by Hans Nielsen for Oxford in the British League in 1988. The League career record is 6471 points by Nigel Boocock (b. 17 Sep 1937), 1955–80.

Oxford set a record of 28 successive wins in the British League in 1986.

Belle Vue (Manchester) had a record nine victories (1933–7, 1946–7, 1949 and 1958) in the National Trophy Knock-out Competition (held 1931–64). This was replaced in 1965 by the Knock-Out Cup, which has been won eight times including joint holders in 1986 by Cradley Heath who were twice Provincial League winners, 1961 and 1963. The highest recorded score in this competition is 81–25, when Hull beat Sheffield in 1979.

The British League riders Championship was instituted in 1965 and is an annual event contested by the top scorers from each team. Ivan Mauger (New Zealand) holds the records for appearances, 15 and points scored, 146, 1965–79. The most wins is three by Hans Nielsen, 1986–7 and 1990. The National League Riders Championship was instituted in 1968. Stephen Lawson (b. 11 Dec 1957) has made a record nine appearances and John Jackson (b. 26 Jun 1952) has scored a record 67 points.

Squash Rackets

Although rackets (US spelling racquets) with a soft ball was played in 1817 at Harrow School, Harrow, London, there was no recognized champion of any country until John A. Miskey of Philadelphia, Pennsylvania, USA won the American Amateur Singles Championship in 1907.

World Championships Jahangir Khan (Pakistan) (b. 10 Dec 1963) won six World Open (instituted 1976) titles, 1981–85 and 1988, and the ISRF world individual title (formerly World Amateur, instituted 1967) in 1979, 1983 and 1985. Geoffrey B. Hunt (Australia) (b. 11 Mar 1947) won four World Open titles, 1976–7 and 1979–80 and three World Amateur, 1967, 1969 and 1971. The most women's World Open titles is three by Susan Devoy (New Zealand) (b. 4 Jan 1964), 1985, 1987 and 1990.

Pakistan (1977, 1981, 1983, 1985 and 1987) and Australia (1967, 1969, 1971, 1973 and 1989) have each won five men's world titles. England won the women's title in 1985, 1987, 1989 and 1990, following Great Britain's win in 1979.

Most titles *Open Championship* The most wins in the Open Championship held annually in Britain, is ten by Jahangir Khan, in successive years, 1982–91. Hashim Khan (Pakistan) (b. 1915) won seven times, 1950–55 and 1957, and also won the Vintage title six times in 1978–83.

Highest waves ridden
Waimea Bay, Hawaii reputedly provides the most consistently high waves, often reaching the ridable limit of 9–10 m *30–35 ft*. The highest wave ever ridden was the *tsunami* of 'perhaps 50 ft', which struck Minole, Hawaii on 3 Apr 1868, and was ridden to save his life by a Hawaiian named Holua.

The most British Open women's titles is 16 by Heather Pamela McKay (*née* Blundell) (Australia) (b. 31 Jul 1941) from 1961 to 1977. She also won the World Open title in 1976 and 1979.

Amateur Championship The most wins in the Amateur Championship is six by Abdelfattah Amr Bey (Egypt) (b. 14 Feb 1910), who won in 1931–3 and 1935–7. Norman Francis Borrett (b. 1 Oct 1917) of England won in 1946–50.

Unbeaten sequences Heather McKay was unbeaten from 1962 to 1980. Jahangir Khan was unbeaten from his loss to Geoff Hunt at the British Open on 10 Apr 1981 until Ross Norman (New Zealand) ended his sequence in the World Open final on 11 Nov 1986.

Longest and shortest championship matches The longest recorded competitive match was one of 2 hr 45 min when Jahangir Khan beat Gamal Awad (Egypt) (b. 8 Sep 1955) 9–10, 9–5, 9–7, 9–2, the first game lasting a record 1 hr 11 min, in the final of the Patrick International Festival at Chichester, W Sussex on 30 Mar 1983. Lucy Soutter (GB) beat Hugolein van Hoorn (Netherlands) in just 7½ min (9–0, 9–0, 9–0) in the British Under-21 Open Championship at Lamb's Squash Club, London on 17 Jan 1988.

Most international appearances The men's record is 122 by David Gotto (b. 25 Dec 1948) for Ireland. The women's record is 87 by Marjorie Croke (*née* Burke) (b. 31 May 1961) for Ireland, 1981–90.

Surfing

The traditional Polynesian sport of surfing in a canoe (*ehorooe*) was first recorded by Captain James Cook, (1728–79) on his first voyage at Tahiti in December 1771. Surfing on a board (*Amo Amo iluna ka lau oka nalu*) was first described as 'most perilous and extraordinary ... altogether astonishing and is scarcely to be credited' by Lt (later Capt.) James King, in March 1779 at Kealakekua Bay, Hawaii Island. A surfer was first depicted by this voyage's official artist John Webber. The sport was revived at Waikiki by 1900. Hollow boards were introduced in 1929 and the light plastic foam type in 1956.

Most titles World Amateur Championships were inaugurated in May 1964 at Sydney, Australia. The most titles is three by Michael Novakov (Australia) who won the Kneeboard event in 1982, 1984 and 1986. A World Professional series was started in 1975. The men's title has been won five times by Mark Richards (Australia), 1975 and 1979–82 and the women's title (instituted 1979) four times by Freida Zamba (USA), 1984–6, 1988.

Longest ride Sea wave About four to six times each year rideable surfing waves break in Matanchen Bay near San Blas, Nayarit, Mexico which makes rides of *c.* 1700 m *5700 ft* possible.

River bore The longest recorded rides on a river bore have been set on the Severn bore, England. The official British Surfing Association record for riding a surfboard in a standing position is 4 km *2·5 mile* by David Lawson from Lower Rea to Lower Parting on 27 Sep 1988. The longest ride on a surfboard standing or lying down is 4·73 km *2·94 miles* by Colin Kerr Wilson (b. 23 Jun 1954) on 23 May 1982.

The bore on the Ch'ient'ang'kian (see Chapter 1) was ridden for the first time by Stuart Matthews (GB) on 26 Sep 1988. The wave on this occasion was 3·6–4·5 m *12–15 ft* high and was ridden in the standing position for 600 m *656 yd*.

Swimming

In Japan, swimming in schools was ordered by Imperial edict of Emperor Go-Yozei (1586–1611) in 1603 but competition was known from 36 BC. Seawater bathing was fashionable at Scarborough, N Yorks as early as 1660. The earliest pool was Pearless Pool, north London, opened in 1743.

In Great Britain competitive swimming originated from at least 1791. Swimming races were particularly popular in the 1820s in Liverpool, where the first pool opened at St George's Pier Head, in 1828.

Largest pools The largest swimming pool in the world is the seawater Orthlieb Pool in Casablanca, Morocco. It is 480 m *1574 ft* long and 75 m *246 ft* wide, and has an area of 3·6 ha *8·9 acres*. The largest land-locked swimming pool with heated water was the Fleishhacker Pool on Sloat Boulevard, near Great Highway, San Francisco, California, USA. It measured 305 × 46 m *1000 × 150 ft* and up to 4·26 m *14 ft* deep and contained 28 390 hectolitres *7 500 000 gal* of heated water. It was opened on 2 May 1925 but has now been abandoned. The largest land-locked pool in current use is Willow Lake at Warren, Ohio, USA. It measures 183 m × 46 m *600 × 150 ft*. The greatest spectator accommodation is 13 614 at Osaka, Japan. The largest in use in the United Kingdom is the Royal Commonwealth Pool, Edinburgh, completed in 1970 with 2000 permanent seats, but the covered over and unused pool at Earls Court, London (opened 1937) could seat some 12 000 spectators.

Fastest swimmer In a 25-yd pool, Tom Jager (USA) (b. 6 Oct 1964) achieved an average speed of 8·64 km/h *5·37 mph* for 50 yards in 19·05 sec at Nashville, Tennessee, USA on 23 Mar 1990. The women's fastest is 7·21 km/h *4·48 mph* by Yang Wenyi (China) in her 50 m world record (see World Record table).

Most world records Men: 32, Arne Borg (Sweden) (1901–87), 1921–9. Women: 42, Ragnhild Hveger (Denmark) (b. 10 Dec 1920), 1936–42. For currently recognized events (only metric distances in 50 m pools) the most is 26 by Mark Andrew Spitz (USA) (b. 10 Feb 1950), 1967–72, and 23 by Kornelia Ender (GDR) (b. 25 Oct 1958), 1973–6.

The most world records set in a single pool is 86 in the North Sydney pool, Australia between 1955 and 1978. This total includes 48 imperial distance records which ceased to be recognized in 1969. The pool, which was built in 1936, was originally 55 yards long but was shortened to 50 metres in 1964.

Most world titles In the World Championships (instituted 1973) the most medals won is 13 by Michael Gross (West Germany) (b. 17 Jun 1964), five gold, five silver and three bronze, 1982–90. The most by a woman is ten by Kornelia Ender with eight gold and two silver in 1973 and 1975. The most gold medals is six (two individual and four relay) by James Paul Montgomery (USA) (b. 24 Jan 1955) in 1973 and 1975. The most medals at a single championship is seven by Matthew Nicholas Biondi (USA) (b. 8 Oct 1965), three gold, one silver, three bronze, in 1986.

OLYMPIC RECORDS

Most medals Men The greatest number of Olympic gold medals won is nine by Mark Spitz (USA): 100 m and 200 m freestyle 1972; 100 m and 200 m butterfly 1972; 4 × 100 m freestyle 1968 and 1972; 4 × 200 m freestyle 1968 and 1972; 4 × 100 m medley 1972. *All but one of these performances (the 4 × 200 m freestyle of 1968) were also new world records.* He also won a silver (100 m butterfly) and a bronze (100 m freestyle) in 1968 for a record 11 medals. His record seven medals at one Games in 1972 was equalled by Matt Biondi (USA) who won five gold, a silver and a bronze in 1988.

Women The record number of gold medals won by a woman is six by Kristin Otto (GDR) (b. 7 Feb 1965) at Seoul in 1988: 100 m freestyle, backstroke and butterfly, 50 m freestyle, 4 × 100 m freestyle and 4 × 100 m medley. Dawn Fraser (Australia) (b. 4 Sep 1937) is the only swimmer to win the same event, the 100 m freestyle, on three successive occasions (1956, 1960 and 1964).

The most medals won by a woman is eight by: Dawn Fraser, four golds: 100 m freestyle 1956, 1960 and 1964, 4 × 100 m freestyle 1956 and four silvers: 400 m freestyle 1956, 4 × 100 m freestyle 1960 and 1964, 4 × 100 m medley 1960, Kornelia Ender, four golds: 100 m and 200 m freestyle, 100 m butterfly and 4 × 100 m medley in 1976 and four silvers: 200 m individual medley 1972, 4 × 100 m medley 1972, 4 × 100 m freestyle 1972 and 1976 and Shirley Babashoff (USA) (b. 3 Jan 1957), who won two golds (4 × 100 m freestyle 1972 and 1976) and six silvers (100 m freestyle 1972, 200 m freestyle 1972 and 1976, 400 m and 800 m freestyle 1976, 4 × 100 m medley 1976).

Most individual gold medals The

SWIMMING—WORLD RECORDS (*set in 50 m pools*)

MEN

Event	Time	Name, country and date of birth	Place	Date
FREESTYLE				
50 metres	21·81	Tom Jager (USA) (b. 6 Oct 1964)	Nashville, Tennessee, USA	24 Mar 1990
100 metres	48·42	Matthew Nicholas Biondi (USA) (b. 8 Oct 1955)	Austin, Texas, USA	10 Aug 1988
200 metres	1:46·69	Giorgio Lamberti (Italy) (b. 28 Jan 1969)	Bonn, Germany	15 Aug 1989
400 metres	3:46·95	Uwe Dassler (GDR) (b. 11 Feb 1967)	Seoul, South Korea	23 Sep 1988
800 metres	7:50·64	Vladimir Salnikov (USSR) (b. 21 May 1960)	Moscow, USSR	4 Jul 1986
1500 metres	14:50·36	Jörg Hoffmann (Germany) (b. 29 Jan 1970)	Perth, Australia	13 Jan 1991
4 × 100 metres relay	3:16·53	United States	Seoul, South Korea	23 Sep 1988
		(Christopher Jacobs, Troy Dalbey, Tom Jager, Matthew Nicholas Biondi)		
4 × 200 metres relay	7:12·51	United States	Seoul, South Korea	21 Sep 1988
		(Troy Dalbey, Matthew Cetlinski, Douglas Gjertsen, Matthew Nicholas Biondi)		
BREASTSTROKE				
100 metres	1:01·45	Norbert Rozsa (Hungary)	Perth, Australia	7 Jan 1991
	1:01·45	Vasiliy Ivanov (USSR)	Moscow, USSR	11 Jun 1991
200 metres	2:11·23	Michael Barrowman (USA) (b. 4 Dec 1968)	Perth, Australia	11 Jan 1991
BUTTERFLY				
100 metres	52·84	Pedro Pablo Morales (USA) (b. 5 Dec 1964)	Orlando, Florida, USA	23 Jun 1986
200 metres	1:55·69	Melvin Stewart (USA) (b. 18 Nov 1968)	Perth, Australia	12 Jan 1991
BACKSTROKE				
100 metres	54·51	David Berkoff (USA) (b. 30 Nov 1966)	Seoul, South Korea	24 Sep 1988
200 metres	1:58·14	Igor Polyanskiy (USSR) (b. 20 Mar 1967)	Erfurt, Germany	3 Mar 1985
MEDLEY				
200 metres	1:59·36	Tamás Darnyi (Hungary) (b. 3 Jun 1967)	Perth, Australia	13 Jan 1991
400 metres	4:12·36	Tamás Darnyi (Hungary)	Perth, Australia	8 Jan 1991
4 × 100 metres relay	3:36·93	United States	Seoul, South Korea	25 Sep 1988
		(David Berkoff, Richard Schroeder, Matthew Nicholas Biondi, Christopher Jacobs)		

WOMEN

Event	Time	Name, country and date of birth	Place	Date
FREESTYLE				
50 metres	24·98	Yang Wenyi (China) (b. 11 Jan 1972)	Guangzhou, China	11 Apr 1988
100 metres	54·73	Kristin Otto (GDR) (b. 7 Feb 1965)	Madrid, Spain (relay first leg)	19 Aug 1986
200 metres	1:57·55	Heike Friedrich (GDR) (b. 18 Apr 1970)	East Berlin, Germany	18 Jun 1986
400 metres	4:03·85	Janet Evans (USA) (b. 28 Aug 1971)	Seoul, South Korea	22 Sep 1988
800 metres	8:16·22	Janet Evans (USA)	Tokyo, Japan	20 Aug 1989
1500 metres	15:52·10	Janet Evans (USA)	Orlando, Florida, USA	26 Mar 1988
4 × 100 metres relay	3:40·57	GDR	Madrid, Spain	19 Aug 1986
		(Kristin Otto, Manuela Stellmach, Sabina Schulze, Heike Friedrich)		
4 × 200 metres relay	7:55·47	GDR	Strasbourg, France	18 Aug 1987
		(Manuela Stellmach, Astrid Strauss, Anke Möhring, Heike Friedrich)		
BREASTSTROKE				
100 metres	1:07·91	Silke Hörner (GDR) (b. 12 Sep 1965)	Strasbourg, France	21 Aug 1987
200 metres	2:26·71	Silke Hörner (GDR)	Seoul, South Korea	21 Sep 1988
BUTTERFLY				
100 metres	57·93	Mary Terstegge Meagher (USA) (b. 27 Oct 1964)	Milwaukee, Wisconsin, USA	16 Aug 1981
200 metres	2:05·96	Mary Terstegge Meagher (USA)	Milwaukee, Wisconsin, USA	13 Aug 1981
BACKSTROKE				
100 metres	1:00·59	Ina Kleber (GDR) (b. 29 Sep 1964) (relay first leg)	Moscow, USSR	24 Aug 1984
200 metres	2:08·60	Betsy Mitchell (USA) (b. 15 Jan 1966)	Orlando, Florida, USA	27 Jun 1986
MEDLEY				
200 metres	2:11·73	Ute Geweniger (GDR) (b. 24 Feb 1964)	East Berlin, Germany	4 Jul 1981
400 metres	4:36·10	Petra Schneider (GDR) (b. 11 Jan 1963)	Guayaquil, Ecuador	1 Aug 1982
4 × 100 metres relay	4:03·69	GDR	Moscow, USSR	24 Aug 1984
		(Ina Kleber, Sylvia Gerasch, Ines Geissler, Birgit Meineke (now Heukrodt))		

record number of individual gold medals won is four by: Charles Meldrum Daniels (USA) (1884–1973) (100 m freestyle 1906 and 1908, 220 yd freestyle 1904, 440 yd freestyle 1904); Roland Matthes (GDR) (b. 17 Nov 1950) with 100 m and 200 m backstroke 1968 and 1972; Mark Spitz and Kristin Otto, and the divers Pat McCormick and Greg Louganis (see Diving).

Most medals *British* The record number of gold medals won by a British swimmer (excluding water polo, *q.v.*) is four by Henry Taylor (1885–1951) in the mile freestyle (1906), 400 m freestyle (1908), 1500 m freestyle (1908) and 4 × 200 m freestyle (1908).

Henry Taylor won a record eight medals in all with a silver (400 m freestyle 1906) and three bronzes (4 × 200 m freestyle 1906, 1912, 1920). The most medals by a British woman is four by Margaret Joyce Cooper (now Badcock) (b. 18 Apr 1909) with one silver (4 × 100 m freestyle 1928) and three bronze (100 m freestyle 1928, 100 m backstroke 1928, 4 × 100 m freestyle 1932).

Closest verdict The closest verdict in the Olympic Games was in Los Angeles, California on 29 Jul 1984, when Nancy Lynn Hogshead (b. 17 Apr 1962) and Carrie Lynne Steinseifer (b. 12 Feb 1968) (both USA) dead-heated for the women's 100 m freestyle gold medal in 55·92 sec. In the 1972 men's 400 m individual medley Gunnar Larsson (Sweden) (b. 12 May 1951) beat Aleksander Timothy McKee (USA) (b. 14 Mar 1953) by just 2/1000 th second, just 3 mm. Now timings are determined only to hundredths.

DIVING

Most Olympic medals The most medals won by a diver is five by: Klaus Dibiasi (b. Austria, 6 Oct 1947) (Italy)

High diving
The highest regularly performed head-first dives are those by professional divers at La Quebrada, Acapulco, Mexico, into water 3·65 m *12 ft* deep. The base rocks necessitate a leap of 8·22 m *27 ft* out.

SWIMMING

SHORT-COURSE SWIMMING WORLD BESTS (set in 25 m pools)

MEN

Event	Time	Name	Date	
FREESTYLE				
50 metres	21·76	Nils Rudolph (GDR) (b. 18 Aug 1965)	Bonn, Germany	11 Feb 1990
100 metres	48·2†	Michael Gross (West Germany) (b. 17 Jun 1964)	Offenbach, Germany	11 Feb 1988
	48·33	Tommy Werner (Sweden) (b. 31 Mar 1966)	Malmö, Sweden	19 Mar 1989
200 metres	1:43·64	Giorgio Lamberti (Italy) (b. 28 Jan 1969)	Bonn, Germany	11 Feb 1990
400 metres	3:40·81	Anders Holmertz (Sweden) (b. 1 Dec 1968)	Paris, France	4 Feb 1990
800 metres	7:38·75	Michael Gross (West Germany)	Bonn, Germany	8 Feb 1985
1500 metres	14:37·60	Vladimir Salnikov (USSR) (b. 21 May 1960)	Göteberg, Sweden	19 Dec 1982
4 × 50 metres relay	1:27·95	West Germany	Bonn, Germany	14 Feb 1988
4 × 100 metres relay	3:14·00	Sweden	Malmö, Sweden	19 Mar 1989
4 × 200 metres relay	7:05·17	West Germany	Bonn, Germany	9 Feb 1986
BACKSTROKE				
50 metres	25·06	Mark Tewksbury (Canada) (b. 2 Jul 1968)	Saskatoon, Canada	2 Mar 1990
100 metres	52·58	Mark Tewksbury (Canada)	Sheffield, S Yorks	30 Mar 1991
200 metres	1:56·60	Tamás Darnyi (Hungary) (b. 3 Jun 1967)	Bonn, Germany	8 Feb 1987
BREASTSTROKE				
50 metres	27·15	Dmitriy Volkov (USSR) (b. 3 Mar 1966)	Saint-Paul de la Réunion, France	30 Dec 1989
100 metres	59·30	Dmitriy Volkov (USSR)	Bonn, Germany	11 Feb 1990
200 metres	2:08·15	Nicholas Gillingham (GB) (b. 22 Jan 1967)	Leicester	27 Jan 1991
BUTTERFLY				
50 metres	24·05	Nils Rudolph (Germany)	Sheffield, S Yorks	30 Mar 1991
100 metres	52·07	Marcel Gery (Canada) (b. 15 Mar 1965)	Leicester	23 Feb 1990
200 metres	1:54·78	Michael Gross (West Germany)	Bonn, Germany	9 Feb 1985
MEDLEY				
100 metres	54·66	Josef Hladky (Germany)	Bonn, Germany	16 Mar 1991
200 metres	1:58·18	Pedro Pablo Morales (USA) (b. 5 Dec 1964)	Los Angeles, California, USA	26 Apr 1987
400 metres	4:09·64	Alex Baumann (Canada) (b. Prague 21 Apr 1964)	Halifax, Canada	7 Mar 1987
4 × 50 metres relay	1:38·72	USA	Bonn, Germany	14 Feb 1988
4 × 100 metres relay	3:36·66	University of Calgary (Canada)	Saskatoon, Canada	3 Mar 1990

WOMEN

Event	Time	Name	Date	
FREESTYLE				
50 metres	24·81	Livia Copariu (Romania) (b. 1973)	Sibiu, Romania	8 Apr 1989
100 metres	53·48	Livia Copariu (Romania)	Sibiu, Romania	7 Apr 1989
200 metres	1:56·35	Birgit Meineke (GDR) (b. 4 Jul 1964)	Indianapolis, Indiana, USA	7 Jan 1983
400 metres	4:02·05	Astrid Strauss (GDR) (b. 24 Dec 1968)	Bonn, Germany	8 Feb 1987
800 metres	8:15·34	Astrid Strauss (GDR)	Bonn, Germany	6 Feb 1987
1500 metres	15:43·31	Petra Schneider (GDR) (b. 11 Jan 1963)	Gainesville, Florida, USA	10 Jan 1982
4 × 50 metres relay	1:42·13	West Germany	Bonn, Germany	13 Feb 1988
4 × 100 metres relay	3:38·77	GDR	Monte Carlo, Monaco	12 Dec 1987
BACKSTROKE				
50 metres	28·91	Svenja Schlicht (West Germany) (b. 26 Jun 1966)	Bonn, Germany	8 Feb 1987
100 metres	59·89	Betsy Mitchell (USA) (b. 15 Jan 1966)	Los Angeles, California, USA	26 Apr 1987
200 metres	2:07·74	Cornelia Sirch (GDR) (b. 23 Oct 1966)	Indianapolis, Indiana, USA	9 Jan 1983
	2:07·74	Dagmar Hase (Germany)	Victoria, Canada	9 Apr 1991
BREASTSTROKE				
100 metres	1:07·05	Silke Hörner (GDR) (b. 12 Sep 1965)	Bonn, Germany	8 Feb 1986
200 metres	2:22·92	Susanne Börnike (GDR) (b. 13 Aug 1968)	Bonn, Germany	4 Feb 1989
BUTTERFLY				
50 metres	27·30	Qian Hong (China)	Perth, Australia	6 Jan 1991
100 metres *	58·91	Mary Terstegge Meagher (USA) (b. 27 Aug 1964)	Gainesville, Florida, USA	3 Jan 1981
200 metres	2:05·65	Mary Meagher (USA)	Gainesville, Florida, USA	2 Jan 1981
MEDLEY				
100 metres	1:02·75	Marion Zoller (Netherlands)	Sheffield, S Yorks	30 Mar 1991
200 metres	2:10·60	Petra Schneider (GDR)	Gainesville, Florida, USA	8 Jan 1982
400 metres	4:31·36	Noemi Lung (Romania) (b. 16 May 1968)	Paris, France	31 Jan 1987
4 × 50 metres relay	1:54·37	GDR	Bonn, Germany	14 Feb 1988
4 × 100 metres relay	4:02·85	GDR	Indianapolis, Indiana, USA	8 Jan 1983

slower than long-course bests. † hand timed for relay first leg.

High diving

The world record high dive is 53·9 m *176 ft 10 in*, by Olivier Favre (Switzerland) at Villers-le-Lac, France on 30 Aug 1987.

The women's record is 36·80 m *120 ft 9 in*, by Lucy Wardle (US) at Ocean Park, Hong Kong on 6 Apr 1985.

(three gold, two silver), 1964–76; and Gregory Efthimios Louganis (USA) (b. 29 Jan 1960) (four golds, one silver), 1976, 1984, 1988. Dibiasi is the only diver to win the same event (highboard) at three successive Games (1968, 1972 and 1976). Two divers have won the highboard and springboard doubles at two Games: Patricia Joan McCormick (*née* Keller) (USA) (b. 12 May 1930), 1952 and 1956 and Louganis, 1984 and 1988.

British The highest placing by a Briton has been the silver medal by Beatrice Eileen Armstrong (later Purdy) (1894–1981) in the 1920 highboard event. The best placings by male divers are the bronze medals by Harold Clarke (b. 1888) (plain high diving, 1924) and Brian Eric Phelps (b. 21 Apr 1944) (highboard, 1960).

Most world titles Greg Louganis (USA) won a record five world titles, highboard in 1978, and both highboard and springboard in 1982 and 1986, as well as four Olympic gold medals in 1984 and 1988. Three gold medals at one event have also been won by Philip George Boggs (USA) (1949–90), springboard 1973, 1975 and 1978.

Highest scores Greg Louganis achieved record scores at the 1984 Olympic Games in Los Angeles, California, USA with 754·41 points for the 11-dive springboard event and 710·91 for the highboard. At the world championships in Guayaquil, Ecuador in 1984 he was awarded a perfect score of 10·0 by all seven judges for his highboard inward 1 ½ somersault in the pike position.

The first diver to be awarded a score of 10·0 by all seven judges was Michael Holman Finneran (b. 21 Sep 1948) in the 1972 US Olympic Trials, in Chicago, Illinois, for a backward 1 ½ somersault, 2 ½ twist, from the 10 m board.

CHANNEL SWIMMING

The first to swim the English Channel from shore to shore (without a life jacket) was the Merchant Navy captain Matthew Webb (1848–83) who swam an estimated 61 km *38 miles* to make the 33 km *21 mile* crossing from Dover, England to Calais Sands, France, in 21 hr 45 min from 12:56 p.m. to 10:41 a.m., 24–25 Aug 1875. Paul Boyton (USA) had swum from Cap Gris-Nez to the South Foreland in his patent life-saving suit in 23 hr 30 min on 28–29 May 1875. There is good evidence that Jean-Marie Saletti, a French soldier, escaped from a British prison hulk off Dover by swimming to Boulogne in July or August 1815.

The first crossing from France to England was made by Enrico Tiraboschi, a wealthy Italian living in Argentina, in 16 hr 33 min on 12 Aug 1923, to win the *Daily Sketch* prize of £1000.

The first woman to succeed was Gertrude Caroline Ederle (USA) (b. 23 Oct 1906) who swam from Cap Gris-Nez, France to Deal, England on 6 Aug 1926, in the then overall record time of 14 hr 39 min.

The first woman to swim from England to France was Florence Chadwick (USA) (b. 1918) in 16 hr 19 min on 11 Sep 1951. The first Englishwoman to succeed was Mercedes Gleitze (later Carey) (1900–81) who swam from France to England in 15 hr 15 min on 7 Oct 1927. The first twins to complete the crossing were Carole and Sarah Hunt (b. 23 Aug 1962) who swam from England and landed together in France after 9 hr 29 min on 6 Aug 1988.

Fastest The official Channel Swimming Association (founded 1927) record is 7 hr 40 min by Penny Dean (b. 21 Mar 1955) of California, USA, from Shakespeare Beach, Dover to Cap Gris-Nez, France on 29 Jul 1978. The fastest France-England time is 8 hr 5 min by Richard Davey (b. 23 Jun 1965) in 1988.

The fastest crossing by a relay team is 6 hr 52 min (England to France) by the US National Swim Team on 1 Aug 1981. They went on to complete the fastest two-way relay in 14 hr 18 min.

Earliest and latest The earliest date in the year on which the Channel has been swum is 30 May by Kevin Murphy (GB) (b. 1949) in 1990 in a time of 13 hr 16 min and with the water at a temperature of 12°C *54°F*. The latest is 28 October by Michael Peter Read (GB) (b. 9 Jun 1941) in 1979.

Youngest and oldest The youngest conqueror is Thomas Gregory (GB) (b. 9 Oct 1976) who swam from Cap Gris-Nez to Shakespeare Point, Dover in 11 hr 54 min on 6 Sep 1988, when he was aged 11 yr 333 days. The youngest girl is Samantha Claire Druce (GB) (b. 21 Apr 1971) who was 12 yr 119 days on 18 Aug 1983 when she swam from Dover to Cap Gris-Nez in 15 hr 27 min. *The Channel Swimming Association has since introduced a rule stating that the minimum age for a Channel attempt is twelve.*

The oldest has been Bertram Clifford Batt (b. 22 Dec 1919), of Australia at 67 years

■ World best

241 days when he swam from Cap Gris-Nez to Dover in 18 hr 37 min from 19–20 Aug 1987. The oldest woman was Stella Ada Rosina Taylor (b. 20 Dec 1929) aged 45 years 250 days when she did the swim in 18 hr 15 min on 26 Aug 1975.

Double crossing The first double crossing was by Antonio Abertondo (Argentina) (b. 1919), in 43 hr 10 min on 20–22 Sep 1961. Kevin Murphy completed the first double crossing by a Briton in 35 hr 10 min on 6 Aug 1970. The first swimmer to achieve a crossing both ways was Edward Harry Temme (1904–78) on 5 Aug 1927 and 19 Aug 1934.

The fastest double crossing was in 16 hr 10 min by Philip Rush (New Zealand) (b. 6 Nov 1963) on 17 Aug 1987. In setting this record, he completed the fastest ever crossing by a man, 7 hr 55 min (England to France), and went on to complete the fastest ever triple crossing in 28 hr 21 min on 17–18 Aug 1987. The women's record is 18 hr 15 min by Irene van der Laan (Netherlands) (b. 27 Dec 1960) on 18 Aug 1983. The first British woman to achieve the double crossing was Alison Streeter (b. 29 Aug 1964) in 21 hr 16 min on 4 Aug 1983.

Triple crossing The first triple crossing was by Jon Erikson (USA) (b. 6 Sep 1954) in 38 hr 27 min on 11–12 Aug 1981. The first by a woman was by Alison Streeter in 34 hr 40 min on 2–3 Aug 1990. For the fastest, see Double crossing.

Most conquests The greatest number of Channel conquests is 31 by Michael Read (GB) from 24 Aug 1969 to 19 Aug 1984, including a record six in one year. The most by a woman is 19 (including five two-way)

■ **World record**

Matt Biondi and Troy Dalbey celebrate after the US team had set a world record time of 7 min 12·51 sec for the 4 × 200 metres freestyle at the Olympic Games at Seoul, South Korea on 21 Sep 1988. (Photo: All-Sport (USA))

■ **World best**

Nick Gillingham (GB) celebrates setting the then 200 metres breaststroke world record of 2 min 12·90 sec, to win the European title at Bonn, Germany on 18 Aug 1989. However, the record lasted a mere two days but he has the consolation of being the current holder of the indoor world best for this distance with 2 min 8·15 sec set at Leicester on 27 Jan 1991. (Photo: All-Sport/S. Bruty)

BRITISH NATIONAL RECORDS

MEN

Event	Time	Name and date of birth	Place	Date
FREESTYLE				
50 metres	23·13	Mark Andrew Foster (b.12 May 1970)	Crystal Palace, London	1 Aug 1987
100 metres	50·57	Andrew David Jameson (b. 19 Feb 1965)	Orlando, Florida, USA	25 Mar 1988
200 metres	1:50·54	Paul Tony Howe (b. 8 Jan 1968)	Rome, Italy	9 Aug 1990
400 metres	3:50·01	Kevin Thomas Boyd (b. 23 Jun 1966)	Seoul, South Korea	23 Sep 1988
800 metres	8:01·87	Kevin Thomas Boyd	Orlando, Florida, USA	26 Mar 1988
1500 metres	15:11·17	Ian Wilson (b. 19 Dec 1970)	Perth, Australia	13 Jan 1991
4 ×100 metres relay	3:21·71	GB (Andrew David Jameson, Mark Andrew Foster, Michael Wenham Fibbens, Roland Lee)	Seoul, South Korea	23 Sep 1988
4 ×200 metres relay	7:24·78	GB (Neil Cochran, Paul Robert Easter, Paul Tony Howe, Andrew Astbury)	Los Angeles, California, USA	30 Jul 1984
BREASTSTROKE				
100 metres	1:01·49	Adrian David Moorhouse (GB) (b. 24 May 1964)	Bonn, Germany	15 Aug 1989
	1:01·49	Adrian Moorhouse (GB)	Auckland, New Zealand	25 Jan 1990
	1:01·49	Adrian Moorhouse (GB)	Crystal Palace, London	26 Jul 1990
200 metres	2:12·90	Nicholas Gillingham (b. 22 Jan 1967)	Bonn, Germany	18 Aug 1989
BUTTERFLY				
100 metres	53·30	Andrew David Jameson	Seoul, South Korea	21 Sep 1988
200 metres	2:00·21	Philip Hubble (b. 19 Jul 1960)	Split, Yugoslavia	11 Sep 1981
BACKSTROKE				
100 metres	57·08	Martin Harris (b. 21 May 1969)	Perth, Australia	12 Jan 1991
200 metres	2:03·20	Gary Michael Binfield (b. 13 Mar 1966)	Auckland, New Zealand	27 Jan 1990
MEDLEY				
200 metres	2:03·20	Neil Cochran (b. 12 Apr 1965)	Orlando, Florida, USA	25 Mar 1988
400 metres	4:24·20	John Philip Davey (b. 29 Dec 1964)	Crystal Palace, London	31 Jul 1987
4 ×100 metres relay	3:42·01	GB (Neil Cochran, Adrian David Moorhouse, Andrew David Jameson, Roland Lee)	Strasbourg, France	23 Aug 1987

WOMEN

Event	Time	Name and date of birth	Place	Date
FREESTYLE				
50 metres	25·90	Alison Sheppard (b. 5 Nov 1972)	Cumbernauld, Strathclyde	3 Nov 1990
100 metres	56·60	June Alexandra Croft (b. 17 Jun 1963)	Amersfoort, Netherlands	31 Jan 1982
200 metres	1:59·74	June Croft	Brisbane, Australia	4 Oct 1982
400 metres	4:07·68	Sarah Hardcastle (b. 9 April 1969)	Edinburgh, Lothian	27 Jul 1986
800 metres	8:24·77	Sarah Hardcastle	Edinburgh, Lothian	29 Jul 1986
1500 metres	16:43·95	Sarah Hardcastle	Montreal, Canada	18 Apr 1985
4 ×100 metres relay	3:48·87	Great Britain (Karen Pickering, Sharron Davies, Caroline Woodcock, Joanne Coull)	Bonn, Germany	17 Aug 1989
4 ×200 metres relay	8:03·70	England (Annabelle Cripps, Sarah Hardcastle, Karen Marie Mellor, Zara Letitia Long)	Edinburgh, Lothian	25 Jul 1986
BREASTSTROKE				
100 metres	1:10·39	Susannah 'Suki' Brownsdon (b. 16 Oct 1965)	Strasbourg, France	21 Aug 1987
200 metres	2:31·57	Jean Cameron Hill (b. 15 Jul 1964)	Strasbourg, France	19 Aug 1987
BUTTERFLY				
100 metres	1:01·33	Madeleine Scarborough (b. 18 Aug 1964)	Auckland, New Zealand	28 Jan 1990
200 metres	2:11·82	Sharon Page (b. 1971)	Cumbernauld, Strathclyde	4 Aug 1984
BACKSTROKE				
100 metres	1:03·16	Sharon Page	Cumbernauld, Strathclyde	3 Nov 1990
200 metres	2:14·74	Joanne Deakins (b. 20 Nov 1972)	Auckland, New Zealand	30 Jan 1990
MEDLEY				
200 metres	2:17·21	Jean Cameron Hill	Edinburgh, Lothian	21 Jul 1986
400 metres	4:46·83	Sharron Davies (b. 1 Nov 1962)	Moscow, USSR	26 Jul 1980
4 ×100 metres relay	4:11·88	England (Joanne Deakins, Susannah 'Suki' Brownsdon, Madeleine Scarborough, Karen Pickering)	Auckland, New Zealand	29 Jan 1990

by Cynthia 'Cindy' M. Nicholas (Canada) (b. 20 Aug 1957) from 29 Jul 1975 to 14 Sep 1982.

LONG-DISTANCE SWIMMING —

Longest swims The greatest recorded distance ever swum is 2938 km *1826 miles* down the Mississippi River, USA between Ford Dam near Minneapolis, Minnesota and Carrollton Ave, New Orleans, Louisiana, by Fred P. Newton, (b. 1903) of Clinton, Oklahoma from 6 Jul to 29 Dec 1930. He was 742 hr in the water.

The greatest distance covered in a continuous swim is 481·5 km *299 miles* by Ricardo Hoffmann (b. 5 Oct 1941), from Corrientes to Santa Elena, Argentina in the River Paraná in 84 hr 37 min on 3–6 Mar 1981.

The longest ocean swim is one of 207·3 km *128·8 miles* by Walter Poenisch Sr (USA) (b. 1914) who started from Havana, Cuba, and arrived at Little Duck Key, Florida, USA (in a shark cage and wearing flippers) 34 hr 15 min later on 11–13 Jul 1978.

In 1966 Mihir Sen of Calcutta, India uniquely swam the Palk Strait from Sri Lanka to India (in 25 hr 36 min on 5–6 Apr); the Straits of Gibraltar (in 8 hr 1 min on 24 Aug); the length of the Dardanelles (in 13 hr 55 min on 12 Sep); the Bosphorus (in 4 hr on 21 Sep), and the length of the Panama Canal (in 34 hr 15 min on 29–31 Oct).

Irish Channel The swimming of the 37 km *23 mile* wide North Channel from Donaghadee, Northern Ireland to Portpatrick, Scotland was first accomplished by Tom Blower of Nottingham in 15 hr 26 min in 1947. A record time of 9 hr 53 min 42 sec was set by Alison Streeter on 22 Aug 1988. She was also the first person to complete the crossing from Scotland to Northern Ireland, in 10 hr 4 min on 25 Aug 1989. The first Irish-born swimmer to achieve the crossing was Ted Keenan on 11 Aug 1973 in 11–13°C *52–56°F* water in 18 hr 27 min. The

first Scottish-born was Margaret Kidd, 22, in 15 hr 25 min 3 sec on 23 Aug 1988.

Lake swims The fastest time for swimming the 36·5 km *22·7 mile* long Loch Ness is 9 hr 57 min by David Trevor Morgan (b. 25 Sep 1963) on 31 Jul 1983. The first successful swim was by Brenda Sherratt (b. 1948) of West Bollington, Cheshire on 26–27 Jul 1966. David Morgan achieved a double crossing of Loch Ness in 23 hr 4 min on 1 Aug 1983. In 1988 he also uniquely swam Loch Ness in 11 hr 9 min on 16 Jul, Loch Lomond 34·6 km *21·5 miles* in 11 hr 48 min on 18 Jul and the English Channel in 11 hr 35 min on 20–21 Jul. The fastest time for swimming Lake Windermere, 16·9 km *10·5 miles* is 3 hr 49 min 56 sec by Karen Toole, 17, of Darlington on 5 Sep 1981. The fastest time for the Lake Windermere International Championship, 26·5 km *16·5 miles,* is 5 hr 56 min 4 sec by Jay Wilkerson (USA) (b. 9 Sep 1968); women, 6 hr 3 min 54 sec by Martha Jahn (USA) (b. 1 Apr 1963), both on 11 Aug 1990.

24 hours Anders Forvass (Sweden) swam 101·9 km *63·3 miles* at the 25-metre Linköping public swimming pool, Sweden on 28–29 Oct 1989. In a 50 metre pool, Evan Barry (Australia) swam 96·7 km *60·08 miles,* at the Valley Pool, Brisbane, Australia on 19–20 Dec 1987.

The women's record is 82·1 km *51·01 miles* by Irene van der Laan (Netherlands) at Amersfoort, Netherlands on 20–21 Sep 1985.

Greatest lifetime distance Gustave Brickner (b. 10 Feb 1912) of Charleroi, Pennsylvania, USA in 59 years to November 1986 recorded 61 977 km *38 512 miles.*

Long-distance relays The New Zealand national relay team of 20 swimmers swam a record 182·807 km *113·59 miles* in Lower Hutt, New Zealand in 24 hours, passing 160 km *100 miles* in 20 hr 47 min 13 sec on 9–10 Dec 1983. The 24 hours club

record by a team of five is 154·93 km *96·27 miles* by the City of Newcastle ASC on 16–17 Dec 1986. A women's team from the club swam 143·11 km *88·93 miles* on the same occasion. The most participants in a one-day swim relay is 2135, each swimming a length, organized by Syracuse YMCA in Syracuse, New York, USA on 11 Apr 1986.

The longest duration swim relay was 233 hr 15 min for 903·7 km by a team of 15 from Maccabi Water Polo team at Sydney Football Stadium swimming pool, Sydney, Australia on 1–11 Dec 1988.

Underwater swimming Paul Cryne (GB) and Samir Sawan al Awami of Qatar swam 78·92 km *49·04 miles* in a 24 hr period from Doha, Qatar to Umm Said and back on 21–22 Feb 1985 using sub-aqua equipment. They were swimming underwater for 95·5 per cent of the time. A relay team of six swam 151·987 km *94·44 miles* in a swimming pool at Olomouc, Czechoslovakia on 17–18 Oct 1987.

Sponsored swimming The greatest amount of money collected in a charity swim was £108 040 in 'Splash '89' organized by the Royal Bank of Scotland Swimming Club and was held at the Royal Commonwealth Pool, Edinburgh, Lothian on 28–29 Jan 1989, 3012 swimmers took part. The record for an event staged at several pools was £548 006.14 by 'Penguin Swimathon '88', 5482 swimmers participated at 43 pools throughout London on 26–28 Feb 1988.

Table Tennis

Origins The earliest evidence relating to a game resembling table tennis has been found in the catalogues of London sports goods manufacturers in the 1880s. The old Ping Pong Association was formed in 1902 but the game proved only a temporary craze

until resuscitated in 1921. The International Table Tennis Federation was founded in 1926 and the English Table Tennis Association was formed on 24 Apr 1927. Table Tennis was included at the Olympic Games for the first time in 1988.

Most titles World G. Viktor Barna (1911–72) (b. Hungary, Gyözö Braun) won a record five singles, 1930, 1932–5 and eight men's doubles, 1929–35, 1939 in the World Championships (first held in 1926). Angelica Rozeanu (Romania) (b. 15 Oct 1921) won a record six women's singles, 1950–55, and Maria Mednyanszky (Hungary) (1901–79) won seven women's doubles, 1928, 1930–35.

With two more at mixed doubles, Viktor Barna won 15 world titles in all, while 18 have been won by Maria Mednyanszky.

With the staging of championships biennially the breaking of the above records would now be very difficult.

The most men's team titles (Swaythling Cup) is 12 by Hungary, 1927–31, 1933–5, 1938, 1949, 1952, 1979. The women's record (Marcel Corbillon Cup) is nine by China, 1965 and eight successive 1975–89 (biennially).

English Open (instituted 1921) Richard Bergmann (Austria, then GB) (1920–70) won a record six singles, 1939–40, 1948, 1950, 1952, 1954 and Viktor Barna won seven men's doubles titles, 1931, 1933–5, 1938–9, 1949. The women's singles record is six by Maria Alexandru (Romania) (b. 1941), 1963–4, 1970–72, 1974 and Diane Rowe (GB) (now Scholer) (b. 14 Apr 1933) won 12 women's doubles titles, 1950–56, 1960, 1962–5.

Viktor Barna won 20 titles in all and Diane Rowe 17. Her twin Rosalind (now Mrs Cornett) has won nine (two in singles).

English Closed The most titles won is 25 by Desmond Hugh Douglas (b. 20 Jul 1955), a record 11 men's singles, 1976,

Counter hitting
The record number of hits in 60 sec is 172 by Thomas Busin and Stefan Renold, both of Switzerland, on 4 Nov 1989. The women's record is 168 by the sisters Lisa (b. 9 Mar 1967) and Jackie (b. 9 Sep 1964) Bellinger at Crest Hotel, Luton, Beds on 14 Jul 1987. With a bat in each hand, Gary D. Fisher of Olympia, Washington, USA completed 5000 consecutive volleys over the net in 44 min 28 sec on 25 Jun 1979.

TENNIS

Table Tennis Internationals

The youngest ever international was Joy Foster, aged 8 when she represented Jamaica in the West Indies Championships at Port of Spain, Trinidad in Aug 1958.

The youngest ever to play for England was Nicola Deaton (b. 29 Oct 1976), aged 13 yr 336 days, against Sweden at Burton on Trent, Staffs on 30 Sep 1990.

Jill Parker played for England on a record 413 occasions, 1967–83.

Highest speed

No conclusive measurements have been published but in a lecture M. Sklorz (West Germany) stated that a smashed ball had been measured at speeds up to 170 km/h *105·6 mph*.

Lawn Tennis

Olympics

Tennis was re-introduced to the Olympic Games in 1988, having originally been included at the Games from 1896 to 1924. It was also a demonstration sport in 1968 and 1984.

A record four gold medals as well as a silver and a bronze, were won by Max Decugis (France) (1882–1978), 1900–20. A women's record five medals (one gold, two silver, two bronze) were won by Kitty McKane (later Mrs Godfree) (GB) (b. 7 May 1897) in 1920 and 1924.

1979–87 and 1990, 10 men's doubles and 4 mixed doubles. A record seven women's singles were won by Jill Patricia Hammersley (now Parker, *née* Shirley) (b. 6 Dec 1951) in 1973–6, 1978–9, 1981.

Taekwondo

Taekwondo is a martial art, with all activities based on defensive spirit, developed over 20 centuries in Korea. It was officially recognized as part of Korean tradition and culture on 11 Apr 1955. The first World Taekwondo Championships were organized by the Korean Taekwondo Association and were held at Seoul in 1973. The World Taekwondo Federation was then formed and has organized biennial championships.

Most titles The most world titles won is four by Chung Kook-hyun (South Korea), light-middleweight 1982–3, welterweight 1985, 1987. Taekwondo was included as a demonstration sport at the 1988 Olympic Games.

Tennis (Lawn)

Origins The modern game is generally agreed to have evolved as an outdoor form of the indoor game of tennis (see Real Tennis). 'Field tennis' is mentioned in an English magazine, *Sporting Magazine*, of 29 Sep 1793. The earliest club for such a game, variously called Pelota or Lawn Rackets, was the Leamington Club founded in 1872 by Major Harry Gem. The earliest attempt to commercialize the game was by Major Walter Clopton Wingfield (1833–1912) who patented a form called 'sphairistike' on 23 Feb 1874. It soon became called lawn tennis. Amateur players were permitted to play with and against professionals in 'open' tournaments in 1968.

Grand Slam The grand slam is to hold at the same time all four of the world's major championship singles: Wimbledon, US, Australian and French Open championships. The first man to have won all four was Frederick John Perry (GB) (b. 18 May 1909) when he won the French title in 1935. The first man to hold all four championships simultaneously was John Donald Budge (USA) (b. 13 Jun 1915) in 1938, and with Wimbledon and US in 1937, he won six successive grand slam tournaments. The first man to achieve the grand slam twice was Rodney George Laver (Australia) (b. 9 Aug 1938) as an amateur in 1962 and again in 1969 when the titles were open to professionals.

Four women have achieved the grand slam and the first three won six successive grand slam tournaments: Maureen Catherine Connolly (USA) (1934–69), in 1953; Margaret Jean Court (*née* Smith) (Australia) (b. 16 Jul 1942) in 1970; and Martina Navrátilová (USA) (b. 18 Oct 1956) in 1983–4. The fourth was Stefanie Maria 'Steffi' Graf (West Germany) (b. 14 Jun 1969) in 1988, when she also won the women's singles Olympic gold medal. Pamela Howard Shriver (USA) (b. 4 Jul 1962) with Navrátilová won a record eight successive grand slam tournament women's doubles titles and 109 successive matches in all events from April 1983 to July 1985.

The first doubles pair to win the grand slam were the Australians Frank Allan Sedgeman (b. 29 Oct 1927) and Kenneth Bruce McGregor (b. 2 Jun 1929) in 1951.

The most singles championships won in grand slam tournaments is 24 by Margaret Court (11 Australian, 5 USA, 5 French, 3 Wimbledon), 1960–73. She also won the US Amateur in 1969 and 1970 when this was held as well as the US Open. The men's record is 12 by Roy Stanley Emerson (Australia) (b. 3 Nov 1936) (6 Australian, 2 each French, USA, Wimbledon), 1961–7.

The most grand slam tournament wins by a doubles partnership is 20 by Althea Louise Brough (USA) (b. 11 Mar 1923) and Margaret Evelyn Du Pont (*née* Osborne) (USA) (b. 4 Mar 1918), (12 USA, 5 Wimbledon, 3 French), 1942–57; and by Martina Navrátilová and Pam Shriver, (7 Australian, 5 Wimbledon, 4 French, 4 USA), 1981–9.

WIMBLEDON CHAMPIONSHIPS

Most wins *Women* Billie-Jean King (USA) (*née* Moffit) (b. 22 Nov 1943) won a record 20 titles between 1961 and 1979, six singles, ten women's doubles and four mixed doubles. Elizabeth Montague Ryan (USA) (1892–1979) won a record 19 doubles (12 women's, 7 mixed) titles from 1914 to 1934.

Men The greatest number of titles by a man has been 13 by Hugh Laurence Doherty (GB) (1875–1919) with five singles titles (1902–6) and a record eight men's doubles (1897–1901, 1903–5) partnered by his brother Reginald Frank (1872–1910).

Singles Martina Navrátilová has won a record nine titles, 1978–9, 1982–7 and 1990. The most men's singles wins since the Challenge Round was abolished in 1922 is five consecutively, by Björn Borg (Sweden) in 1976–80. William Charles Renshaw (GB) (1861–1904) won seven singles in 1881–6 and 1889.

Mixed doubles The male record is four titles shared by: Elias Victor Seixas (USA) (b. 30 Aug 1923) in 1953–6; Kenneth Norman Fletcher (Australia) (b. 15 Jun 1940) in 1963, 1965–6, 1968; and Owen Keir Davidson (Australia) (b. 4 Oct 1943) in 1967, 1971, 1973–4. The female record is seven by Elizabeth Ryan (USA) from 1919 to 1932.

Most appearances Arthur William Charles 'Wentworth' Gore (1868–1928) (GB) made a record 36 appearances at Wimbledon between 1888 and 1927. In 1964, Jean Borotra (b. 13 Aug 1898) of France made his 35th appearance since 1922. In 1977 he appeared in the Veterans' Doubles aged 78.

Youngest champions The youngest champion was Charlotte 'Lottie' Dod (1871–1960), who was 15 yr 285 days when she won in 1887. The youngest male champion was Boris Becker (West Germany) (b. 22 Nov 1967) who won the men's singles title in 1985 at 17 yr 227 days. The youngest ever player at Wimbledon was reputedly Mita Klima (Austria) who was 13 yr in the 1907 singles competition. The youngest seed was Jennifer Capriati (USA) (b. 29 Mar 1976) at 14 yr 89 days for her first match on 26 Jun 1990. She won this match making her the youngest ever winner at Wimbledon.

Oldest champions The oldest champion was Margaret Evelyn du Pont (*née* Osborne) at 44 yr 125 days when she won the mixed doubles in 1962 with Neale Fraser (Australia). The oldest singles champion was Arthur Gore (GB) in 1909 at 41 yr 182 days.

Greatest crowd The record crowd for one day was 39 813 on 26 Jun 1986. The record for the whole championship was 403 706 in 1989.

UNITED STATES CHAMPIONSHIPS

Most wins Margaret Evelyn du Pont (*née* Osborne) won a record 25 titles between 1941 and 1960. She won a record 13 women's doubles (12 with Althea Louise Brough), nine mixed doubles and three singles. The men's record is 16 by William Tatem Tilden, including seven men's singles, 1920–25, 1929 – a record for singles shared with: Richard Dudley Sears (1861–1943), 1881–87; William A. Larned (1872–1926), 1901–2, 1907–11, and at women's singles by: Molla Mallory (*née* Bjurstedt) (1892–1959), 1915–16, 1918, 1920–22, 1926; and Helen Newington Moody (*née* Wills) (USA) (b. 6 Oct 1905), 1923–5, 1927–9, 1931.

Youngest and oldest The youngest champion was Vincent Richards (1903–59), who was 15 yr 139 days when he won the men's doubles with Bill Tilden in 1918. The youngest singles champion was Tracy Ann Austin (b. 12 Dec 1962) who was 16 yr 271 days when she won the women's singles in 1979. The youngest men's champion was Pete Sampras (b. 12 Aug 1971) who was 19 yr 28 days when he won in 1990. The oldest champion was Margaret du Pont who won the mixed doubles at 42 yr 166 days in 1960. The oldest singles champion was William Larned at 38 yr 242 days in 1911.

FRENCH CHAMPIONSHIPS

Most wins (from international status 1925) Margaret Court won a record 13 titles, five singles, four women's doubles and four mixed doubles, 1962–73. The men's record is nine by Henri Cochet (France) (1901–87), four singles, three men's doubles and two mixed doubles, 1926–30. The singles record is seven by Chris Evert, 1974–75, 1979–80, 1983, 1985–86. Björn Borg won a record six men's singles, 1974–75, 1978–81.

Youngest and oldest The youngest doubles champions were the 1981 mixed doubles winners, Andrea Jaeger (b. 4 Jun 1965) at 15 yr 339 days and Jimmy Arias (b. 16 Aug 1964) at 16 yr 296 days. The youngest singles winners have been: Monica Seles (Yugoslavia) (b. 2 Dec 1973) who won the 1990 women's title at 16 yr 169 days in 1990 and Michael Chang (USA) (b. 22 Feb 1972) the men's at 17 yr 109 days in 1989. The oldest champion was Elizabeth Ryan who won the 1934 women's doubles with Simone Mathieu (France) at 42 yr 88 days. The oldest singles champion was Andrés Gimeno (Spain) (b. 3 Aug 1937) in 1972 at 34 yr 301 days.

AUSTRALIAN CHAMPIONSHIPS

Most wins Margaret Jean Court (*née* Smith) (b. 16 Jul 1942) won the women's singles 11 times (1960–66, 1969–71 and 1973) as well as eight women's doubles and two mixed doubles, for a record total of 21 titles. A record six men's singles were won by Roy Stanley Emerson (Qld) (b. 3 Nov 1936), 1961 and 1963–7. Thelma Dorothy Long (*née* Coyne) (b. 30 May 1918) won a record 12 women's doubles and four mixed doubles for a record total of 16 doubles titles. Adrian Karl Quist (b. 4 Aug 1913) won ten consecutive men's doubles from 1936 to 1950 (the last eight with John Bromwich) and three men's singles.

Longest span, oldest and youngest Thelma Long won her first (1936) and last (1958) titles 22 years apart. Kenneth Robert Rosewall (b. 2 Nov 1934) won the singles in 1953 and in 1972 was, 19 years later, at 37 yr 62 days, the oldest singles winner. The oldest champion was (Sir) Norman Everard Brookes (1877–1968), who was 46 yr 2 months when he won the 1924 men's doubles. The youngest champions were Rodney W. Heath, aged 17, when he won the men's singles in 1905, and and Monica Seles, who won the women's singles at 17 yr 55 days in 1991.

GRAND PRIX MASTERS

The first Grand Prix Masters Championships were staged in Tokyo, Japan in 1970. They were held in New York, USA annually from 1977 to 1989, with qualification to this annual event by relative success in the preceding year's Grand Prix tournaments. The event was replaced from 1990 by thr ATP Tour Championship, held in Frankfurt, Germany. A record five titles have been won by Ivan Lendl, 1982–3, two in 1986 (January and December) and 1987. He appeared in nine successive finals, 1980–8. James Scott Connors (USA) (b. 2 Sep 1952) uniquely qualified for 14 consecutive years, 1972–85. He chose not to play in 1975, 1976 and 1985, and won in 1977. He qualified again in 1987 and 1988, but did not play in 1988.

A record seven doubles titles were won by John Patrick McEnroe (b. 16 Feb 1959) and Peter Fleming (b. 21 Jan 1955) (both USA), 1978–84.

INTERNATIONAL TEAM

Davis Cup (instituted 1900)
The most wins in the Davis Cup, the men's international team championship, has been 29 by the USA between 1900 and 1990. The most appearances for Cup winners is eight by Roy Emerson (Australia), 1959–62, 1964–7. Bill Tilden (USA) played in a record 28 matches in the final, winning a record 21, 17 out of 22 singles and 4 out of 6 doubles. He was in seven winning sides, 1920–26 and then four losing sides, 1927–30.

The British Isles/Great Britain have won nine times, in 1903–6, 1912, 1933–6.

Nicola Pietrangeli (Italy) (b. 11 Sep 1933) played a record 163 rubbers (66 ties), 1954 to 1972, winning 120. He played 109 singles (winning 78) and 54 doubles (winning 42).

The record number of rubbers by a British player is 65 (winning 43) by Michael J. Sangster (b. 9 Sep 1940), 1960–68; the most wins is 45 from 52 rubbers by Fred Perry, including 34 of 38 singles, 1931–6.

Wightman Cup (instituted 1923)
The annual women's match was won 51 times by the United States and 10 times by Great Britain. The contest was suspended from 1990 after a series of whitewashes by the US team. Virginia Wade (GB) (b. 10 Jul 1945) played in a record 21 ties and 56 rubbers, 1965–85, with a British record 19 wins. Christine Marie Evert (USA) (b. 21 Dec 1954) won all 26 of her singles matches, 1971 to 1985 and including doubles achieved a record 34 wins from 38 rubbers played. Jennifer Capriati became at 13 yr 168 days, the youngest ever Wightman Cup player when she beat Clare Wood (GB) 6–0, 6–0 at Williamsburg, Virginia, USA on 14 Sep 1989.

Federation Cup (instituted 1963)
The most wins in the Federation Cup, the women's international team championship, is 14 by the USA between 1963 and 1990. Virginia Wade (GB) played each year from 1967 to 1983, in a record 57 ties, playing 100 rubbers, including 56 singles (winning 36) and 44 doubles (winning 30).

Chris Evert won her first 29 singles matches, 1977–86. Her overall record, 1977–89 was 40 wins in 42 singles and 16 wins in 18 doubles matches.

Longest span as national champion
Keith Gledhill (b. 17 Feb 1911) won the US National Boys' Doubles Championship with Sidney Wood in August 1926. Sixty-one years later he won the US National 75 and over Men's Doubles Championship with Elbert Lewis at Goleta, California, USA in August 1987.

Dorothy May Bundy-Cheney (USA) (b. September 1916) won 180 US national titles at various age groups from 1941 to March 1988.

Most county titles
Philip Siviter (b. 16 Mar 1953) won 21 consecutive county men's singles titles, 1970–76 Worcestershire, 1977–90 Hereford & Worcester.

International contest Longest span
Jean Borotra (France) (b. 13 Aug 1898) played in every one of the twice yearly contests between the International Club of France and the I.C. of Great Britain from the first in 1929 to his 100th match at Wimbledon on 1–3 Nov 1985. On that occasion he played a mixed doubles against Kitty Godfree (GB). Both were former Wimbledon singles champions, and aged 87 and 88 respectively.

Highest earnings
Ivan Lendl (Czecho-slovakia) (b. 7 Mar 1960) won a men's season's record $2 344 367 in 1989 and has record career earnings of $17 238 027 to 24 May 1991. The season's record for a woman is $2 173 556 in 1984 (including a $1 million Grand Slam bonus) by Martina Navrátilová. Earnings from special restricted events and team tennis are not included. Navrátilová's lifetime earnings by 16 Jun 1991 reached $16 916 282.

The greatest first-place prizemoney ever won is $2 million by Pete Sampras when he won the Grand Slam Cup at Munich, Germany on 16 Dec 1990. In the final he beat Brad Gilbert (USA) (b. 9 Aug 1961) 6–3, 6–4, 6–2. Gilbert received $1 million, also well in excess of the previous record figure. The highest total prize money was $6 349 250 for the 1990 US Open Championships.

Greatest crowd
A record 30 472 people were at the Astrodome, Houston, Texas, USA on 20 Sep 1973, when Billie-Jean King (née Moffitt) (USA) (b. 22 Nov 1943) beat Robert Larimore Riggs (USA) (b. 25 Feb 1918). The record for an orthodox tennis match is 25 578 at Sydney, New South Wales, Australia on 27 Dec 1954 in the Davis Cup Challenge Round (first day) Australia v. USA.

Longest game
The longest known singles game was one of 37 deuces (80 points) between Anthony Fawcett (Rhodesia) and Keith Glass (GB) in the first round

of the Surrey Championships at Surbiton, Surrey on 26 May 1975. It lasted 31 min. Noëlle van Lottum and Sandra Begijn played a game lasting 52 min in the semi-finals of the Dutch Indoor Championships at Ede, Gelderland on 12 Feb 1984.

The longest tiebreak was 26–24 for the fourth and decisive set of a first round men's doubles at the Wimbledon Championships on 1 Jul 1985. Jan Gunnarsson (Sweden) and Michael Mortensen (Denmark) defeated John Frawley (Australia) and Victor Pecci (Paraguay) 6–3, 6–4, 3–6, 7–6.

The longest rally in tournament play was one of 643 times over the net between Vicky Nelson and Jean Hepner at Richmond, Virginia, USA in October 1984. The 6 hr 22 min match was won by Nelson 6–4, 7–6. It concluded with a 1 hr 47 min tiebreak, 13–11, for which one point took 29 minutes.

Will Duggan and Ron Kapp (both USA) performed a rally of 6202 strokes which took 3 hr 33 min at Santa Barbara Municipal Stadium, California, USA on 12 Mar 1988.

Tiddlywinks

World Championships Larry Kahn (USA) has won the singles title 12 times, and the pairs title a record five times between 1977 and 1991.

National Championships Alan Dean (b. 22 Jul 1949) won the singles title six times, 1971–3, 1976, 1978 and 1986, and the pairs title six times. Jonathan Mapley (b. 1947) won the pairs title seven times, 1972, 1975, 1977, 1980, 1983–4 and 1987.

Potting records The record for potting 24 winks from 18 in *45 cm* is 21·8 sec by Stephen Williams (Altrincham Grammar School) in May 1966. Allen R. Astles (University of Wales) potted 10 000 winks in 3 hr 51 min 46 sec at Aberystwyth, Dyfed in February 1966.

On 21 Oct 1989 several records were set by members of the Cambridge University Tiddlywinks Club at Queens' College, Cambridge and these included: 41 winks potted in relay in three minutes by Patrick Barrie, Nick Inglis, Geoff Myers and Andy Purvis, a long jump of 9·17 m *30 ft 1 in* by Andy Purvis and a high jump 3·49 m *11 ft 5 in* by Adrian Jones, David Smith and Ed Wynn.

Trampolining

Trampolines were used in show business at least as early as 'The Walloons' of the period 1910–12. The sport of trampolining (from the Spanish word *trampolin*, a springboard) dates from 1936, when the prototype 'T' model trampoline was developed by George Nissen (USA).

Most titles World Championships were instituted in 1964. A record five titles were won by Judy Wills (USA) (b. 1948) in the women's event, 1964–8. Five men have won two titles.

A record seven United Kingdom titles have been won by Wendy Wright (1969–70, 1972–5, 1977). The most by a man has been five by Stewart Matthews (b. 19 Feb 1962) (1976–80).

Youngest international British Andrea Holmes (b. 2 Jan 1970) competed for Britain at 12 yr 131 days in the World Championships at Montana, USA on 13 May 1982.

Somersaults Christopher Gibson performed 3025 consecutive somersaults at Shipley Park, Derbys on 17 Nov 1989.

The most complete somersaults in one minute is 75 by Richard Cobbing of Lightwater, Surrey, at BBC Television Centre, London for *Record Breakers* on 8 Nov 1989. The most baranis in a minute is 78 by Zoe Finn of Chatham, Kent at BBC Television Centre, London for *Blue Peter* on 25 Jan 1988.

Triathlon

The triathlon combines long-distance swimming, cycling and running. Distances for each of the phases can vary, but for the best established event, the Hawaii Ironman (instituted 1978), competitors first swim 3·8 km *2·4 miles*, then cycle 180 km *112 miles*, and finally run a full marathon of 42·195 km *26 miles 385 yards*. Record times for the Hawaii Ironman are: (men) 8 hr 9 min 16 sec Mark Allen (USA); (women) 9 hr 0 min 56 sec Paula Newby-Fraser (Zimbabwe) both on 15 Oct 1989. Dave Scott (USA) has won a record six races, 1980, 1982–4 and 1986–7. The fastest time recorded over the Ironman distances is 8 hr 1 min 32 sec by Dave Scott at Lake Biwa, Japan on 30 Jul 1989.

World Championships After earlier abortive efforts a world governing body *L'Union Internationale de Triathlon* (UIT) was founded at Avignon, France on 1 Apr 1989, staging the first official World Championships in August 1989.

A 'World Championship' race has been held annually in Nice, France from 1982; the distances 3200 m, 120 km and 32 km respectively, with the swim increased to 4000 m from 1988. Mark Allen has won eight times, 1982–6, 1989–91. Paula Newby-Fraser has a record three women's wins 1989–91. Record times — men, Mark Allen 5 hr 46 min 10 sec in 1986, and women, Erin Baker (New Zealand) 6 hr 27 min 6 sec in 1988.

Largest field The largest field in a triathlon race has been 3888 finishers in the Bud Lite US Triathlon race at Chicago in 1987. This series encompasses races over 1500 m, 40 km and 10 km for the three phases.

Tug of War

Origins Though ancient China and Egypt have been suggested as the originators of the sport, it is known that Neolithic flint miners in Norfolk practised 'rope-pulling'. The first rules were those framed by the New York AC in 1879. Tug of War was an Olympic sport from 1900 until 1920. In 1958 the Tug-of-War Association was formed to administer Britain's 600 clubs. World Championships have been held annually from 1975, with a women's event introduced in 1986.

Most titles The most successful team at the World Championships has been England, who have won 15 of the 25 titles in all categories, 1975–88. Sweden have won all four titles, 520 kg and 560 kg, at the two Womens World Championships held, 1986 and 1988.

The Wood Treatment team (formerly the Bosley Farmers) of Cheshire won 20 consecutive AAA Catchweight Championships 1959–78, two world titles (1975–6) and ten European titles at 720 kg. Hilary Brown (b. 13 Apr 1934) was in every team. Trevor Brian Thomas (b. 1943) of British Aircraft Corporation Club is the only holder of three winners' medals in the European Open club competitions and added a world gold medal in 1988.

Longest pulls *Duration* The longest recorded pull (prior to the introduction of AAA rules) is one of 2 hr 41 min when 'H' Company beat 'E' Company of the 2nd Battalion of the Sherwood Foresters (Derbyshire Regiment) at Jubbulpore, India on 12 Aug 1889. The longest recorded pull under AAA rules (in which lying on the ground or entrenching the feet is not permitted) is one of 24 min 45 sec for the first pull between the Republic of Ireland

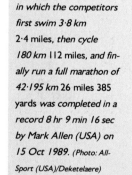

and England during the world championships (640 kg class) at Malmö, Sweden on 18 Sep 1988. The record time for 'The Pull' (instituted 1898), across the Black River, between freshman and sophomore teams at Hope College, Holland, Michigan, USA, is 3 hr 51 min on 23 Sep 1977, but the method of bracing the feet precludes this replacing the preceding records.

Distance The longest tug of war is the 2·6 km *1·616 miles* Supertug across the Little Traverse Bay, Lake Michigan, USA. It has been contested annually since 1980 between two teams of 20 from Bay View Inn and Harbor Inn.

Volleyball

The game was invented as *mintonette* in 1895 by William G. Morgan at the YMCA gymnasium at Holyoke, Massachusetts, USA. The International Volleyball Association was formed in Paris in April 1947.

The Amateur (now English) Volleyball Association of Great Britain was formed in May 1955.

Most world titles World Championships were instituted in 1949 for men and 1952 for women. The USSR has won six men's titles (1949, 1952, 1960, 1962, 1978 and 1982) and five women's (1952, 1956, 1960, 1970 and 1990)

Most Olympic titles The sport was introduced to the Olympic Games for both men and women in 1964. The USSR has won a record three men's (1964, 1968 and 1980) and four women's (1968, 1972, 1980 and 1988) titles. The only player to win four medals is Inna Valeryevna Ryskal (USSR) (b. 15 Jun 1944), who won women's silver medals in 1964 and 1976 and golds in 1968 and 1972. The record for men is held by Yuriy Mikhailovich Poyarkov (USSR) (b. 10 Feb 1937) who won gold medals in 1964 and 1968 and a bronze in 1972, and by Katsutoshi Nekoda (Japan) (b. 1 Feb 1944) who won gold in 1972, silver in 1968 and bronze in 1964.

Most internationals *British* Ucal Ashman (b. 10 Nov 1957) made a record 153 men's international appearances for England, 1976–86. The women's record is 171 by Ann Jarvis (b. 3 Jun 1955) for England, 1974–87.

Water Polo

Water polo was developed in England as 'water soccer' in 1869 and first included in the Olympic Games in Paris in 1900.

Most Olympic titles Hungary has won the Olympic tournament most often with six wins in 1932, 1936, 1952, 1956, 1964 and 1976. Great Britain won in 1900, 1908, 1912 and 1920.

Five players share the record of three gold medals; Britons George Wilkinson (1879 –1946) in 1900, 1908, 1912; Paulo 'Paul' Radmilovic (1886–1968), and Charles Sidney Smith (1879–1951) in 1908, 1912, 1920; and Hungarians Deszö Gyarmati (b. 23 Oct 1927) and György Kárpáti (b. 23 Jun 1935) in 1952, 1956, 1964. Paul Radmilovic also won a gold medal for the 4×200 m freestyle swimming in 1908.

World Championships First held at the World Swimming Championships in

1973. The most wins is two by the USSR, 1975 and 1982, and Yugoslavia, 1986 and 1991. A women's competition was introduced in 1986, when it was won by Australia. The Netherlands won the second women's world title in 1991.

Most goals The greatest number of goals scored by an individual in an international is 13 by Debbie Handley for Australia (16) *v.* Canada (10) at the World Championship in Guayaquil, Ecuador in 1982.

Most international appearances The greatest number of international appearances is 412 by Aleksey Stepanovich Barkalov (USSR) (b. 18 Feb 1946), 1965–80.

The British record is 126 by Martyn Thomas, of Cheltenham, Glos, 1964–78.

Water Skiing

The origins of water skiing derive from walking on planks and aquaplaning. A 19th-century treatise on sorcerers refers to Eliseo of Tarentum who, in the 14th century, 'walks and dances' on the water. The first report of aquaplaning was on America's Pacific Coast in the early 1900s. At Scarborough, Yorkshire on 15 Jul 1914, a single plank-gliding contest was won by H. Storry.

The present day sport of water skiing was pioneered by Ralph W. Samuelson (1904–77) on Lake Pepin, Minnesota, USA, on two curved pine boards in the summer of 1922, although claims have been made for the birth of the sport on Lake Annecy (Haute Savoie), France at about the same time. The first world organization, the *Union Internationale de Ski Nautique*, was formed in Geneva on 27 Jul 1946.

Most titles World Overall Championships (instituted 1949) have been won four times by Sammy Duvall (USA) in 1981, 1983, 1985 and 1987 and three times by two women, Willa McGuire (*née* Worthington) of the USA in 1949–50 and 1955 and Elizabeth 'Liz' Allan-Shetter (USA) in 1965, 1969 and 1975. Liz Allan-Shetter has won a record eight individual championship events and is the only person to win all four titles — slalom, jumping, tricks and overall

in one year, at Copenhagen, Denmark in 1969. The USA have won the team championship on 17 successive occasions, 1957–89.

The most British Overall titles (instituted 1953) won by a man is seven by Michael Hazelwood (b. 14 Apr 1958) in 1974, 1976–9, 1981, 1983; the most by a woman is nine by Karen Jane Morse (b. 14 Aug 1956) in 1971–6, 1978, 1981, 1984.

Highest speed The fastest water skiing speed recorded is 230·26 km/h *143·08 mph* by Christopher Michael Massey (Australia) on the Hawkesbury River, Windsor, New South Wales, Australia on 6 Mar 1983. His drag boat driver was Stanley Charles Sainty. Donna Patterson Brice (b. 1953) set a feminine record of 178·8 km/h *111·11 mph* at Long Beach, California, USA on 21 Aug 1977.

The fastest recorded speed by a British skier over a measured kilometre is 154·38 km/h *95·93 mph* (average) on Lake Windermere, Cumbria on 16 Oct 1989 by Darren Kirkland. The fastest speed recorded by a British woman is 141·050 km/h *87·647 mph* by Nikki Carpenter on Lake Windermere, Cumbria on 18 Oct 1988.

Longest run The greatest distance travelled is 2126·14 km *1321·16 miles* by Steve Fontaine (USA) on 24–26 Oct 1988 at Jupiter Hills, Florida, USA.

Cross-Channel Steve Butterworth (GB) skiied across the English Channel in a record time of 57 min 57 sec from New Romney to Boulogne on 19 Sep 1988. He also went on to complete a double crossing in 1 hr 55 min 8 sec.

Barefoot The first person to water ski barefoot is reported to be Dick Pope Jr at Lake Eloise, Florida, USA on 6 Mar 1947. The barefoot duration record is 2 hr 42 min 39 sec by Billy Nichols (USA) (b. 1964) on Lake Weir, Florida, USA on 19 Nov 1978. The backward barefoot record is 39 min by Paul McManus (Australia).

The British duration record is 67 min 5 sec by John Doherty on 1 Oct 1974.

The official barefoot speed record is 218·44 km/h *135·74 mph* by Scott Michael Pellaton (b. 8 Oct 1956) over a quarter-mile

■ **Longest pull**
The longest recorded pull under AAA rules (in which lying on the ground or entrenching the feet is not permitted) is one of 24 min 45 sec for the first pull between the Republic of Ireland and England during the world championships (640 kg class) at Malmö, Sweden on 18 Sep 1988. The Irish team are seen here taking the strain in the 1990 championships.
(Photo: All-Sport/B. Martin)

Most skiers towed by one boat
A record 100 water skiers were towed on double skis over a nautical mile by the cruiser *Reef Cat* at Cairns, Queensland, Australia on 18 Oct 1986. This feat, organized by the Cairns and District Powerboat and Ski Club, was then replicated by 100 skiers on single skis.

Most Olympic medals

Norbert Schemansky (USA) (b. 30 May 1924) won a record four Olympic medals: gold, middle-heavyweight 1952; silver, heavyweight 1948; bronze, heavyweight 1960 and 1964.

Most titles

The most world title wins, including Olympic Games, is eight by: John Henry Davis (USA) (1921–84) in 1938, 1946–52; Tommy Kono (USA) (b. 27 Jun 1930) in 1952–9; and by Vasiliy Alekseyev (USSR) (b. 7 Jan 1942), 1970–77.

— WOMEN'S WEIGHTLIFTING RECORDS —

Official World records can only be set at World Championships, which were instituted in 1987. The venues have been: 1987, Daytona Beach, Florida, USA; 1988, Jakarta, Indonesia; 1989, Manchester, Great Britain; 1990, Sarajevo, Yugoslavia. However, this list includes superior marks (*), where applicable, made in the Asian Games.

Bodyweight	Lift	Weight kg	lb	Name and country	
44 kg 97 lb	Snatch	72·5	159¾	Xing Fen (China)	1989
	Jerk	95	209¼	Xing Fen (China) *	1990
	Total	165	363¾	Xing Fen (China)	1989
48 kg 105¾ lb	Snatch	75	165¼	Huang Xiaoyu (China)	1987
	Jerk	97·5	215	Huang Xiaoyu (China)	1989
	Total	172·5	380¼	Huang Xiaoyu (China)	1989
52 kg 114½ lb	Snatch	80	176¼	Peng Liping (China)	1988
	Jerk	107·5	237	Peng Liping (China)	1989
	Total	185	407¾	Peng Liping (China)	1989
56 kg 123¼ lb	Snatch	85	187¼	Xing Liwei (China) *	1990
	Jerk	107·5	237	Wu Haiqing (China)	1990
	Total	190	418¾	Wu Haiqing (China)	1990
60 kg 132¼ lb	Snatch	92·5	203¾	Ma Na (China) *	1990
	Jerk	115	253½	Ma Na (China) *	1990
	Total	207·5	457¼	Ma Na (China) *	1990
67·5 kg 148¾ lb	Snatch	100	220¼	Guo Qiuxiang (China) *	1990
	Jerk	122·5	270	Guo Qiuxiang (China)	1989
	Total	220	485	Guo Qiuxiang (China)	1989
75 kg 165¼ lb	Snatch	102·5	226	Milena Trendafilova (Bulgaria)	1990
	Jerk	135	297½	Milena Trendafilova (Bulgaria)	1990
	Total	237·5	523½	Milena Trendafilova (Bulgaria)	1990
82·5 kg 181¾ lb	Snatch	102·5	226	Li Hongling (China)	1989
	Jerk	137·5	303	Li Hongling (China)	1989
	Total	240	529	Li Hongling (China)	1989
+87·5 kg 242½ lb	Snatch	112·5	248	Karyn Marshall (USA)	1990
	Jerk	142·5	314	Li Yajuan (China)	1990
	Total	245	540	Li Yajuan (China)	1990

— MEN'S WEIGHTLIFTING RECORDS —

Bodyweight class	Lift	kg	lb	Name and country	Place	Date	
52 kg 114½ lb FLYWEIGHT	Snatch	120	264½	Sevdalin Marinov (Bulgaria)	Seoul, South Korea	18 Sep	1988
	Jerk	155	341¾	Ivan Ivanov (Bulgaria)	Athens, Greece	16 Sep	1989
	Total	272·5	600¾	Ivan Ivanov (Bulgaria)	Athens, Greece	16 Sep	1989
56 kg 123¼ lb BANTAMWEIGHT	Snatch	134·5	296½	Liu Shoubin (China)	Kemerovo, USSR	1 Mar	1989
	Jerk	171	377	Neno Terziiski (Bulgaria)	Ostrava, Czechoslovakia	6 Sep	1987
	Total	300	661¼	Naim Suleimanov (Bulgaria)	Varna, Bulgaria	11 May	1984
60 kg 132¼ lb FEATHERWEIGHT	Snatch	152·5	336	Naim Suleymanoğlu (Turkey)*	Seoul, South Korea	20 Sep	1988
	Jerk	190	418¾	Naim Suleymanoğlu (Turkey)*	Seoul, South Korea	20 Sep	1988
	Total	342·5	755	Naim Suleymanoğlu (Turkey)*	Seoul, South Korea	20 Sep	1988
67·5 kg 148¾ lb † LIGHTWEIGHT	Snatch	160	352¾	Israil Militosyan (USSR)	Athens, Greece	18 Sep	1989
	Jerk	200·5	442	Mikhail Petrov (Bulgaria)	Ostrava, Czechoslovakia	8 Sep	1987
	Total	355	782½	Mikhail Petrov (Bulgaria)	Seoul, South Korea	5 Dec	1987
75 kg 165¼ lb MIDDLEWEIGHT	Snatch	170	374¾	Angel Guenchev (Bulgaria)	Miskolc, Hungary	11 Dec	1987
	Jerk	215·5	475	Aleksandr Varbanov (Bulgaria)	Seoul, South Korea	5 Dec	1987
	Total	382·5	843¼	Aleksandr Varbanov (Bulgaria)	Plovdiv, Bulgaria	20 Feb	1988
82·5 kg 181¾ lb LIGHT-HEAVYWEIGHT	Snatch	183	403¼	Asen Zlatev (Bulgaria)	Melbourne, Australia	7 Dec	1986
	Jerk	225	496	Asen Zlatev (Bulgaria)	Sofia, Bulgaria	12 Nov	1986
	Total	405	892¾	Yurik Vardanyan (USSR)	Varna, Bulgaria	14 Sep	1984
90 kg 198¼ lb MIDDLE-HEAVYWEIGHT	Snatch	195·5	431	Blagoi Blagoyev (Bulgaria)	Varna, Bulgaria	1 May	1983
	Jerk	235	518	Anatoliy Khrapatiy (USSR)	Cardiff, South Glamorgan	29 Apr	1988
	Total	422·5	931¼	Viktor Solodov (USSR)	Varna, Bulgaria	15 Sep	1984
100 kg 220¼ lb	Snatch	200·5	442	Nicu Vlad (Romania)	Sofia, Bulgaria	14 Nov	1986
	Jerk	242·5	534½	Aleksandr Popov (USSR)	Tallinn, USSR	5 Mar	1988
	Total	440	970	Yuriy Zakharevich (USSR)	Odessa, USSR	4 Mar	1983
110 kg 242½ lb HEAVYWEIGHT	Snatch	210	462¾	Yuriy Zakharevich (USSR)	Seoul, South Korea	27 Sep	1988
	Jerk	250·5	552¼	Yuriy Zakharevich (USSR)	Cardiff, South Glamorgan	30 Apr	1988
	Total	455	1003	Yuriy Zakharevich (USSR)	Seoul, South Korea	27 Sep	1988
Over 110 kg 242½ lb SUPER-HEAVYWEIGHT	Snatch	216	476	Antonio Krastev (Bulgaria)	Ostrava, Czechoslovakia	13 Sep	1987
	Jerk	266	586¼	Leonid Taranenko (USSR)	Canberra, Australia	26 Nov	1988
	Total	475	1047	Leonid Taranenko (USSR)	Canberra, Australia	26 Nov	1988

* Formerly Naim Suleimanov or Neum Shalamanov of Bulgaria

† Angel Guenchev (Bulgaria) achieved 160 kg snatch, 202·5 kg jerk for a 362·5 kg total at Seoul, South Korea on 21 Sep 1988 but was subsequently disqualified on a positive drugs test.

WATER SKIING RECORDS
WORLD

SLALOM

MEN: 3 buoys on a 10·25 m line, Andrew Mapple (GB) (b. 3 Nov 1958), at Boynton Beach, Florida, USA on 29 Mar 1989.
WOMEN: 1 buoy on a 10·75 m line, Susi Graham (Canada) and Deena Mapple (née Brush) (USA) at West Palm Beach, Florida, USA on 13 Oct 1990.

TRICKS

MEN: 11 030 points, Tony Baggiano (USA) at Destin, Florida, USA on 15 Sep 1990.
WOMEN: 8460 points, Tawn Larsen (USA) at Sparta, New Jersey, USA on 29 Aug 1988.

JUMPING

MEN: 62·4 m 205 ft, Sammy Duvall (USA) at Shreveport, Florida, USA on 24 Jul 1988.
WOMEN: 47·5 m 156 ft, Deena Mapple (USA) at Charlotte, North Carolina, USA on 9 Jul 1988.

BRITISH
SLALOM

MEN: (see World Listing)
WOMEN: 5 buoys at 12 m, Philippa Roberts, Grand Der, France, August 1986.

TRICKS

MEN: 8650 points, John Battleday (b. 1 Feb 1957) at Lyon, France on 5 Aug 1984.
WOMEN: 6820 points, Nicola Rasey (b. 6 Jun 1966) at Martigues, France on 27 Oct 1984.

JUMPING

MEN: 61·9 m 203 ft Michael Hazelwood at Birmingham, Alabama, USA on 30 Jun 1986.
WOMEN: 44·9 m 147 ft, Kathy Hulme (b. 11 Feb 1959) at Kirtons Farm, Reading, Berkshire on 1 Aug 1982.

course at Chandler, Arizona, California, USA in November 1989. The fastest by a woman is 118·56 km/h 73·67 mph by Karen Toms (Australia) on the Hawkesbury River, Windsor, New South Wales on 31 Mar 1984.

The British records are: (men) 114·86 km/h 71·37 mph by Richard Mainwaring (b. 4 Jun 1953) at Holme Pierrepont, Notts on 2 Dec 1978; (women) 80·25 km/h 49·86 mph by Michele Doherty (b. 28 May 1964) (also 71·54 km/h 44·45 mph backwards), both at Witney, Oxon on 18 Oct 1986.

The fastest official speed backwards barefoot is 100 km/h 62 mph by Robert Wing (Australia) (b. 13 Aug 1957) on 3 Apr 1982.

The barefoot jump record is: men 23·30 m 76 ft 5 in by Mike Seipel (USA) at Jacksonville, Florida, USA on 13 Oct 1990 and women 16·50 m 54 ft 1 in by Debbie Pugh (Australia) in 1990.

The British records are: men 19·10 m 62 ft 8 in by Christopher Harris in Germany in 1986 and women 12·3 m 40 ft 4 in by Beverley Collins at La Mede, France on 23 Jul 1989.

Weightlifting

Competitions for lifting weights of stone were held in the ancient Olympic Games. The first championships entitled 'world' were staged at the Café Monico, Piccadilly, London on 28 Mar 1891 and then in Vienna, Austria on 19–20 Jul 1898, subsequently recognized by the IWF. Prior to that time, weightlifting consisted of professional exhibitions in which some of the advertised poundages were open to doubt.

The *Fédération Internationalé Haltérophile et Culturiste*, now the International Weightlifting Federation (IWF), was established in 1905, and its first official championships were held in Tallinn, Estonia, USSR on 29–30 Apr 1922.

There are two standard lifts: the 'snatch' and the 'clean and jerk' (or 'jerk'). Totals of the two lifts determine competition results. The 'press', which was a standard lift, was abolished in 1972.

Youngest world record holder Naim Suleimanov (later Neum Shalamanov) (Bulgaria) (b. 23 Jan 1967) (now Naim Suleymanoğlü of Turkey) set 56-kg world records for clean and jerk (160 kg) and total (285 kg) at 16 yr 62 days at Allentown, New Jersey, USA on 26 Mar 1983.

Most successful British lifter The only British lifter to win an Olympic title has been Launceston Elliot (1874–1930), the open one-handed lift champion in 1896 at Athens. Louis George Martin (b. Jamaica, 11 Nov 1936) won four world and European mid-heavyweight titles in 1959, 1962–3, 1965. He won an Olympic silver medal in 1964 and a bronze in 1960 and three Commonwealth gold medals in 1962, 1966, 1970. His total of British titles was 12.

Heaviest lift to bodyweight The first man to clean and jerk more than three times his bodyweight was Stefan Topurov (Bulgaria) (b. 11 Aug 1964), who lifted 180 kg *396¾ lb* at Moscow, USSR on 24 Oct 1983. The first man to snatch two-and-a-half times his own bodyweight was Naim Suleymanoğlü (Turkey), who lifted 150 kg *330½ lb* at Cardiff, S Glam on 27 Apr 1988. The first woman to clean and jerk more than two times her own bodyweight was Cheng Jinling (China), who lifted 90 kg *198 lb* in the 44 kg class of the World Championships at Jakarta, Indonesia in December 1988.

Women's World Championships These are held annually, first at Daytona Beach, Florida in October 1987. Women's world records have been ratified for the best marks at these championships. The heaviest lift for any of the nine weight categories has been the 142·5 kg *314 lb* jerk by Li Yajuani (China) (b. 1971) for over 82·5 kg at Sarajevo in May in 1990.

POWERLIFTING

The sport of powerlifting was first contested at national level in Great Britain in 1958. The first US Championships were held in 1964. The International Powerlifting Federation was founded in 1972, a year after the first, unofficial world championships were held. Offical championships have been held annually for men from 1973 and for women from 1980. The three standard lifts are squat, bench press and dead lift, the totals from the three lifts determining results.

Most world titles *World* The winner of the most world titles is Hideaki Inaba (Japan) with 15, at 52 kg 1974–83, 1985–9. The most by a women is six by Beverley Francis (Australia) (b. 15 Feb 1955) at 75 kg 1980, 1982; 82·5kg 1981, 1983–5. The most by a British lifter is seven by Ron Collins: 75 kg 1972–4, 82 kg 1975–7 and 1979.

British Edward John Pengelly (b. 8 Dec 1949) has won a record 14 consecutive national titles, 60 kg 1976–9, 67½ kg 1980–89. He has also won four world titles, 60 kg 1976–7, 1979, 67½ kg 1985, and a record ten European titles, 60 kg 1978–9, 67½ kg 1981, 1983–9.

24-hour and 1-hour lifts A dead-lifting record of 2 503 760 kg *5 519 839 lb* in 24 hr was set by a team of ten from HM Prison Wandsworth, London on 26–27 May 1990. The 24 hr deadlift record by an individual is 371 094 kg *818 121 lb* by Anthony Wright at HM Prison Featherstone, Wolverhampton, W Mids on 31 Aug–1 Sep 1990.

A bench press record of 3 869 011 kg *8 529 699 lb* was set by a nine-man team from the Hogarth Barbell Club, Chiswick, London on 18–19 Jul 1987. An individual bench press record of 514 750 kg *1 134 828 lb* was set by John 'Jack' Atherton at HMP

Powerlifting feats Lamar Gant (USA) was the first man to deadlift five times his own bodyweight, lifting 299·5 kg *661 lb* when 59·5 kg *132 lb* in 1985.

The greatest power lift by a woman is a squat of 285 kg *628 lb* by Lorraine Constanzo (USA) at Dayton, Ohio, USA on 21 Nov 1987. Cammie Lynn Lusko (USA) (b. 5 Apr 1958) became the first woman to lift more than her bodyweight with one arm, with 59·5 kg *131 lb* at a bodyweight of 58·3 kg *128·5 lb*, at Milwaukee, Wisconsin, USA on 21 May 1983.

WORLD POWERLIFTING RECORDS (All weights in kilograms)

Class MEN	Squat		Bench Press		Deadlift		Total	
52 kg	245·5	Magnus Karlsson (Swe) 1990	146·5	Joe Cunha (USA) 1982	237·5	Hideaki Inaba (Jap) 1987	587·5	Hideaki Inaba 1987
56 kg	242·5	Hideaki Inaba 1988	160·5	Hiroyuki Isagawa (Jap) 1989	289·5	Lamar Gant (USA) 1982	625	Lamar Gant 1982
60 kg	295	Joe Bradley (USA) 1980	180	Joe Bradley 1980	310	Lamar Gant 1988	707·5	Joe Bradley 1982
67·5 kg	300	Jessie Jackson (USA) 1987	200	Kristoffer Hulecki (Swe) 1985	315	Daniel Austin (USA) 1989	762·5	Daniel Austin 1989
75 kg	328	Ausby Alexander (USA) 1989	217·5	James Rouse (USA) 1980	333	Jarmo Virtanen (Finland) 1988	850	Rick Gaugler (USA) 1982
82·5 kg	379·5	Mike Bridges (USA) 1982	240	Mike Bridges 1981	357·5	Veli Kumpuniemi (Fin) 1980	952·5	Mike Bridges 1982
90 kg	375	Fred Hatfield (USA) 1980	255	Mike MacDonald (USA) 1980	372·5	Walter Thomas (USA) 1982	937·5	Mike Bridges 1980
100 kg	422·5	Ed Coan (USA) 1989	261·5	Mike MacDonald 1977	378	Ed Coan 1989	1032·5	Ed Coan 1989
110 kg	393·5	Dan Wohleber (USA) 1981	270	Jeffrey Magruder (USA) 1982	395	John Kuc (USA) 1980	1000	John Kuc 1980
125 kg	413	Kirk Karwoski (USA) 1990	278·5	Tom Hardman (USA) 1982	387·5	Lars Norén (Swe) 1987	1005	Ernie Hackett (USA) 1982
125 + kg	445	Dwayne Fely (USA) 1982	300	Bill Kazmaier (USA) 1981	406	Lars Norén 1988	1100	Bill Kazmaier 1981
WOMEN								
44 kg	142·5	Delcy Palk (USA) 1988	75	Teri Hoyt (USA) 1982	165	Nancy Belliveau (USA) 1985	352·5	Marie-France Vassart (Bel) 1985
48 kg	150	Claudine Cognac (France) 1990	82·5	Michelle Evris (USA) 1981	182·5	Majik Jones (USA) 1984	390	Majik Jones 1984
52 kg	173·5	Sisi Dolman (Neth) 1989	95	Mary Ryan (USA) 1984	197·5	Diana Rowell (USA) 1984	427·5	Diana Rowell 1984
56 kg	191	Mary Jeffrey (USA) 1989	115	Mary Jeffrey (née Ryan) 1988	200·5	Joy Burt (Canada) 1989	485	Mary Jeffrey 1988
60 kg	200·5	Ruthi Shafer (USA) 1983	105·5	Judith Auerbach (USA) 1989	213	Ruthi Shafer 1983	502·5	Vicki Steenrod (USA) 1985
67·5 kg	230	Ruthi Shafer 1984	120	Vicki Steenrod 1989	244	Ruthi Shafer 1984	565	Ruthi Shafer 1984
75 kg	225	Sumita Laha (Ind) 1989	142·5	Liz Odendaal (Neth) 1989	230	Liz Odendaal 1989	577·5	Liz Odendaal 1989
82·5 kg	230	Juanita Trujillo (USA) 1986	150	Beverley Francis (Aus) 1981	230	Cathy Millen (NZ) 1990	577·5	Beverley Francis 1983
90 kg	252·5	Lorraine Constanzo (USA) 1988	130	Lorraine Constanzo 1988	227·5	Lorraine Constanzo 1988	607·5	Lorraine Constanzo 1988
90 +kg	262·5	Lorraine Constanzo 1987	137·5	Myrtle Augee (GB) 1989	237·5	Lorraine Constanzo 1987	622·5	Lorraine Constanzo 1987

BRITISH POWERLIFTING RECORDS (All weights in kilograms)

MEN	Squat		Bench Press		Deadlift		Total	
52 kg	217·5	Phil Stringer 1980	130	Phil Stringer 1981	225	John Maxwell 1988	530	Phil Stringer 1982
56 kg	235	Phil Stringer 1982	137·5	Phil Stringer 1983	229	Precious McKenzie 1973	567·5	Narendra Bhairo 1982
60 kg	247·5	Tony Galvez 1981	142·5	Clint Lewis 1985	275	Eddy Pengelly 1977	645	Eddy Pengelly 1979
67·5 kg	275	Eddy Pengelly 1981	165	Hassan Salih 1979	295	Eddy Pengelly 1982	710	Eddy Pengelly 1982
75 kg	302·5	John Howells 1979	185	Peter Fiore 1981	310	Robert Limerick 1984	760	Steve Alexander 1983
82·5 kg	337·5	Mike Duffy 1984	210	Mike Duffy 1981	355	Ron Collins 1980	855	Ron Collins 1980
90 kg	347·5	David Caldwell 1985	227·5	Jeff Chandler 1985	350·5	Ron Collins 1980	870	David Caldwell 1985
100 kg	380	Tony Stevens 1984	225	Tony Stevens 1985	362·5	Tony Stevens 1984	955	Tony Stevens 1984
110 kg	372·5	Tony Stevens 1984	250	John Neighbour 1990	380	Arthur White 1982	940	John Neighbour 1987
125 kg	390	John Neighbour 1990	250	John Neighbour 1990	372·5	David Carter 1989	957·5	Steven Zetolofsky 1984
125 +kg	380	Steven Zetolofsky 1979	258	Terry Purdoe 1971	377·5	Andy Kerr 1982	982·5	Andy Kerr 1983
WOMEN								
44 kg	127·5	Helen Wolsey 1990	68	Helen Wolsey 1991	152·5	Helen Wolsey 1990	345	Helen Wolsey 1990
48 kg	132·5	Helen Wolsey 1990	75	Suzanne Smith 1985	155	Helen Wolsey 1990	355	Helen Wolsey 1990
52 kg	143	Jenny Hunter 1988	82	Jenny Hunter 1988	173·5	Jenny Hunter 1988	395	Jenny Hunter 1988
56 kg	158	Jenny Hunter 1988	88	Jenny Hunter 1988	182·5	Jenny Hunter 1988	420	Jenny Hunter 1988
60 kg	163	Rita Bass 1988	90	Hayley Trafford 1989	185	Rita Bass 1990	422·5	Rita Bass 1989
67·5 kg	175	Debbie Thomas 1988	100	Angie Rajic 1991	197·5	Julie Orton 1989	435	Amanda Smith 1988
75 kg	202·5	Judith Oakes 1989	115	Judith Oakes 1989	215	Judith Oakes 1989	532·5	Judith Oakes 1989
82·5 kg	215	Judith Oakes 1988	122·5	Joanne Williams 1990	217·5	Judith Oakes 1989	542·5	Judith Oakes 1988
90 kg	200	Beverley Martin 1989	115	Joanne Williams 1989	215	Beverley Martin 1990	495	Beverley Martin 1989
90 +kg	220·5	Myrtle Augee 1991	137·5	Myrtle Augee 1989	230	Myrtle Augee 1989	587·5	Myrtle Augee 1989

Featherstone, W Mids on 27 May 1990. A squat record of 2 168 625 kg *4 780 994 lb* was set by a ten-man team from St Albans Weightlifting Club and Ware Boys Club, Herts on 20–21 Jul 1986. A record 133 380 arm-curling repetitions using three 22 kg *48½ lb* weightlifting bars and dumb-bells was achieved by a team of nine from Intrim Health and Fitness Club at Gosport, Hants on 4–5 Aug 1989.

Michael Williams achieved 1438 repetitions of his bodyweight (67 kg *147·7 lb*) in one hour by bench presses at Don Styler's Gymnasium, Gosport, Hants on 17 Apr 1989.

Strandpulling The International Steel Strandpullers' Association was founded by Gavin Pearson (Scotland) in 1940. The greatest ratified poundage to date is a super-heavyweight right-arm push of 815 lb *369·5 kg* by Malcolm Bartlett (b. 9 Jun 1955) of Oldham, Greater Manchester. The record for the back press anyhow is 645 lb *292·5 kg* by Barry Anderson, at Leeds, W Yorks on 14 Jun 1975. A record 22 British Open titles have been won by Ian Storton (b. 2 Feb 1951) of Morecambe, Lancs, 1974–88.

Wrestling

The earliest depictions of wrestling holds and falls on wall plaques and a statue indicate that organized wrestling dates from *c.* 2750–2600 BC. It was the most popular sport in the ancient Olympic Games and victors were recorded from 708 BC. The Greco-Roman style is of French origin and arose about 1860. The International Amateur Wrestling Federation (FILA) was founded in 1912.

Most titles *Olympic* Three Olympic titles have been won by: Carl Westergren (Sweden) (1895–1958) in 1920, 1924 and 1932; Ivar Johansson (Sweden) (1903–79) in 1932 (two) and 1936; and Aleksandr Vasilyevich Medved (USSR) (b. 16 Sep 1937) in 1964, 1968 and 1972. Four Olympic medals were won by: Eino Leino (Finland) (b. 7 Apr 1891) at freestyle 1920–32; and by Imre Polyák (Hungary) (b. 16 Apr 1932) at Greco-Roman in 1952–64.

World The freestyler Aleksandr Medved (USSR) won a record ten World Championships, 1962–4, 1966–72 at three weight categories. The only wrestler to win the same title in seven successive years has been Valeriy Grigoryevich Rezantsev (USSR) (b. 2 Feb 1947) in the Greco-Roman 90 kg class in 1970–76, including the Olympic Games of 1972 and 1976.

Most titles and longest span *British* The most British titles won in one weight class is 13 by welterweight Fitzlloyd Walker (b. 7 Mar 1957), 1979–91. The longest span for BAWA titles is 24 years by George Mackenzie (1890–1957) between 1909 and 1933. He represented Great Britain in five successive Olympiads, 1908 to 1928.

Most wins In international competition, Osamu Watanabe (b. 21 Oct 1940), of Japan, the 1964 Olympic freestyle 63 kg champion, was unbeaten and unscored-upon in 189 consecutive matches. Outside of FILA sanctioned competition, Wade Schalles (USA) won 821 bouts from 1964 to 1984, with 530 of these victories by pin.

SUMO WRESTLING

The sport's origins in Japan date from *c.*

23 BC. The heaviest ever *rikishi* is Samoan-American Salevaa Fuali Atisnoe of Hawaii, alias Konishiki, who in 1988 had a peak weight of 252 kg *556 lb*. He is also the first foreign *rikishi* to attain the second highest rank of *ozeki* or champion. Weight is amassed by over-alimentation with a high-protein stew called *chankonabe*.

The most successful wrestlers have been *yokozuna* Sadaji Akiyoshi (b. 1912), alias Futabayama, winner of 69 consecutive bouts in the 1930s, *yokozuna* Koki Naya (b. 1940), alias Taiho ('Great Bird'), who won the Emperor's Cup 32 times up to his retirement in 1971 and the *ozeki* Tameemon Torokichi, alias Raiden (1767–1825), who in 21 years (1789–1810) won 254 bouts and lost only ten for the highest ever winning percentage of 96·2. Taiho and Futabayama share the record of eight perfect tournaments without a single loss. The youngest of the 62 men to attain the rank of *yokozuna* (grand champion) was Toshimitsu Ogata (b. 16 May 1953), alias Kitanoumi, in July 1974 aged 21 years and two months. He set a record in 1978 winning 82 of the 90 bouts that top *rikishi* fight annually.

Yokozuna Mitsugu Akimoto (b. 1 Jun 1955), alias Chiyonofuji, set a record for domination of one of the six annual tournaments by winning the Kyushu Basho for eight successive years, 1981–88. He also holds the record for most career wins, 1045 and most *Makunouchi* (top division) wins, 807. He retired in May 1991 but remains in sumo as a training coach.

Hawaiian-born Jesse Kuhaulua (b. 16 Jun 1944), now a Japanese citizen named Daigoro Watanabe, alias Takamiyama and a stablemaster in the Japan Sumo Association with the sumo elder (*toshiyori*) name of Azumazeki Oyakata, was the first non-Japanese to win an official top-division tournament, in July 1972 and in 1981 he set a record of 1231 consecutive top-division bouts. He weighed in at 204 kg *450 lb* before his retirement in 1984.

Yukio Shoji (b. 14 Nov 1948), alias Aobajo, did not miss a single bout in his 22-year career, 1964–86, and contested a record 1631 consecutive bouts. Kenji Hatano (b. 4 Jan 1948), alias Oshio, contested a record 1891 non-consecutive bouts in his 26-year career, 1962–88, the longest in modern sumo history.

Katsumi Yamanaka (b. 16 Mar 1967), alias Akinoshima, set a *kinboshi* (gold star) record of 13 upsets of *yokozuna* by a *maegashira* (ordinary *Makunouchi* wrestler). Hawaiian-born Chad Rowan (b. 8 May 1969), alias Akebono, scored a record 18 consecutive *kachi-koshi* (majority of wins in a tournament) from his sumo entry in March 1988 to March 1991.

Yachting

Yachting in England dates from the £100 stake race between Charles II and his brother James, Duke of York, on the Thames on 1 Sep 1661 over 23 miles from Greenwich to Gravesend. The oldest club in the world is the Royal Cork Yacht Club which claims descent from the Cork Harbour Water Club, established in Ireland by 1720.

The oldest active club in Britain is the Starcross Yacht Club at Powderham Point, Devon. Its first regatta was held in 1772. The oldest existing club to have been truly formed as a yacht club is the Royal Yacht Squadron, Cowes, Isle of Wight, instituted

as 'The Yacht Club' at a meeting at the Thatched House Tavern, St James's Street, London on 1 Jun 1815.

Olympic titles The first sportsman ever to win individual gold medals in four successive Olympic Games was Paul B. Elvström (Denmark) (b. 25 Feb 1928) in the Firefly class in 1948 and the Finn class in 1952, 1956 and 1960. He also won eight other world titles in a total of six classes. The lowest number of penalty points by the winner of any class in an Olympic regatta is three points (five wins, one disqualified and one second in seven starts) by *Superdocious* of the Flying Dutchman class (Lt Rodney Stuart Pattisson, RN (b. 5 Aug 1943) and Iain Somerled Macdonald-Smith (b. 3 Jul 1945)) at Acapulco Bay, Mexico in October 1968.

British The only British yachtsman to win in two Olympic regattas is Rodney Pattisson in 1968 (see above) and again with *Superdoso* crewed by Christopher Davies (b. 29 Jun 1946) at Kiel, Germany in 1972. He gained a silver medal in 1976 with Julian Brooke Houghton (b. 16 Dec 1946).

Admiral's Cup and ocean racing The ocean racing series which has had the most participating nations (three boats allowed to each nation) is the Admiral's Cup organized by the Royal Ocean Racing Club. A record 19 nations competed in 1975, 1977 and 1979. Britain has a record nine wins.

Modern ocean racing (in moderate or small sailing yachts, rather than professionally manned sailing ships) began with a race from Brooklyn, New York, USA to Bermuda, 630 nautical miles *1166 km* organized by Thomas Fleming Day, editor of the magazine *The Rudder* in June 1906. The race is still held today in every even numbered year, though the course is now Newport, Rhode Island, USA to Bermuda.

The race still regularly run with the earliest foundation for any type of craft and either kind of water (fresh or salt) is the Chicago to Mackinac race on Lakes Michigan and Huron, first sailed in 1898. It was held again in 1904, then annually until the present day, except for 1917–20. The record for the course (333 nautical miles *616 km*) is 1 day 1 hr 50 min (average speed 12·89 knots *23·84 km/h*) by the sloop *Pied Piper*, owned by Dick Jennings (USA) in 1987.

The current record holder of the elapsed time records for both the premier American and British ocean races (the Newport, Rhode Island, to Bermuda race and the Fastnet race) is the sloop *Nirvana*, owned by Marvin Green (USA). The record for the Bermuda race, 635 nautical miles *1176 km*, is 2 days 14 hr 29 min in 1982 and for the Fastnet race, 605 nautical miles *1120 km*, is 2 days 12 hr 41 min in 1985, an average speed of 10·16 knots *18·81 km/h* and 9·97 knots *18·45 km* respectively.

Longest race The world's longest sailing race is the Vendée Globe Challenge, the first of which started from Les Sables d'Olonne, France on 26 Nov 1989. The distance circumnavigated was 22 500 nautical miles *41 652 km*. The race is for boats between 50–60 ft, sailed single-handed. The record time on the course is 109 days 8 hr 48 min 50 sec by Titouan Lamazou (France) (b. 1955) in the sloop *Ecureuil d'Aquitaine* which finished at Les Sables on 19 Mar 1990.

The oldest regular sailing race around the world is the quadrennial Whitbread Round the World race (instituted August 1973) organized by the Royal Naval Sailing Association. It starts in England and the course around the world and the number of legs with stops at specified ports are varied race to race. The distance for 1989–90 was 32 000 nautical miles *59 239 km* from Southampton and return, with stops and re-starts at Punta del Este, Uruguay; Fremantle, Australia; Auckland, New Zealand; Punta del Este, Uruguay and Fort Lauderdale, Florida, USA.

America's Cup The America's Cup was originally won as an outright prize by the schooner *America* on 22 Aug 1851 at Cowes and was later offered by the New York Yacht Club as a challenge trophy. On 8 Aug 1870 J. Ashbury's *Cambria* (GB) failed to capture the trophy from the *Magic*, owned by F. Osgood (USA). The Cup has been challenged 27 times, the United States were undefeated winning 77 races and only losing eight until 1983 when *Australia II*, skippered by John Bertrand and owned by a Perth syndicate headed by Alan Bond beat *Liberty* 4–3, the narrowest series victory, at Newport, Rhode Island, USA.

Dennis Walter Conner (USA) (b. 16 Sep 1942) has been helmsman of American boats four times in succession: in 1980, when he successfully defended; in 1983, when he steered the defender, but lost; in 1987 when he regained the trophy, and in 1988, when he again successfully defended. He was also starting helmsman in 1974 with Ted Hood as skipper. Charlie Barr (USA) (1864–1911) in 1899, 1901 and 1903 and Harold S. Vanderbilt (USA) (1884–1970) in 1930, 1934 and 1937, each steered the successful Cup defender three times in succession.

The largest yacht to have competed in the America's Cup was the 1903 defender, the gaff rigged cutter *Reliance* with an overall length of 43·89 m *144 ft*, a record sail area of 1501 m² *16 160 ft²* and a rig of 53·3 m *175 ft* high.

Regattas The most consistently sailed regatta is that at Cowes, where the first race for a gold cup took place on 10 Aug 1826. Since then there has been a regatta with one or more races in early August every year except for 1915–18 and 1940–45. The greatest number of boats to take part in Cowes 'Week' was in 1990 when there were 661 in 19 classes.

Yacht and dinghy classes The oldest racing class still sailing is the Water Wag class of Dublin, formed in 1887. The design of the boat was changed in 1900 to that which is still used today. The oldest classes in Britain, both established in 1898 and both still racing in the same design of boat are the Seabird Half Rater, centreboard sailing dinghy of Abersoch and other north-west ports, and the Yorkshire Onedesign keel boat which race from the Royal Yorkshire Yacht Club at Bridlington, Humberside.

The first international class for racing dinghies was the 14 foot International, whose principal trophy in Britain is the Prince of Wales Cup which has been contested annually since 1927 (except 1940–45). The most win is 12 by Stewart Harold Morris between 1932 and 1965.

Highest speeds The highest speed reached under sail on water by any craft over a 500-metre timed run is by a boardsailer Thierry Bielak (France) at 44·66 knots *82·71 km/h* at Saintes Maries de-la-Mer canal, Camargue, France on 18 Apr 1991. The women's record was set at the same venue by Brigitte Gimenez (France) (b. 6 Oct 1961) who achieved 39·45 knots *73·05 km/h* in December 1990.

The British records are (men) 41·22 knots *76·33 km/h* by Nick Luget and (women) 34·61 knots *64·09 km/h* by Samantha Harrison, both at Saintes Maries de-la-Mer on 22 Mar 1991.

Most competitors The most boats ever to start in a single race was 2072 in the Round Zeeland (Denmark) race on 21 Jun 1984, over a course of 235 nautical miles *435 km*. The greatest number to start in a race in Britain was 1781 keeled yachts and multihulls on 17 Jun 1989 from Cowes in the Annual Round-the-Island Race. The fastest time achieved in this annual event is 3 hr 55 min 28 sec by the trimaran *Paragon*, owned and sailed by Michael Whipp on 31 May 1986.

The largest trans-oceanic race was the ARC (Atlantic Rally for Cruisers), when 204 boats of the 209 starters from 24 nations completed the race from Las Palmas de Gran Canaria (Canary Islands) to Barbados in 1989.

Highest The greatest altitude at which sailing has taken place is 4910 m *16 109 ft* on Laguna Huallatani, Bolivia, in Mirror Dinghy 55448, variously by Peter Williams, Gordon Siddeley, Keith Robinson and Brian Barrett, on 19 Nov 1977.

BOARDSAILING

The High Court ruled on 7 Apr 1982 that Peter Chilvers (when aged 12) had devised a prototype of a boardsailer in 1958 in England. In 1968 Henry Hoyle Schweitzer and Jim Drake pioneered the sport, often termed windsurfing, in California, USA. World Championships were first held in 1973 and the sport was added to the Olympic Games in 1984 when the winner was Stephan van den Berg (Netherlands) (b. 20 Feb 1962), who also won five world titles 1979–83.

Highest altitude Richard Franklin of Liverpool boardsailed at a record height of 5190 m *17 027 ft* in an unnamed glacial meltwater near Cerro Wila Lloje, Bolivia in South America on 31 Jul 1988.

■ **Round the world**
(below) The yacht Maiden (skipper Tracy Edwards) at the end of the 1989/90 Whitbread Round the World race. Edwards was the first woman to skipper an all-female crew in the race, and it is the longest ocean race completed by an all-female crew.
(Photo: All-Sport/D. Smith)

STOP PRESS

THE NATURAL WORLD

Volcanoes — largest active (p. 18) There was a minor eruption of Mauna Loa shortly after the total eclipse of the sun, which was clearly visible from Hawaii, on 11 Jul 1991.

THE LIVING WORLD

Longest-eared rabbit (p. 32) 'Sweet Majestic Star', a black English lop rabbit owned by Therese and Cheryl Seward of Exeter, Devon, has ears measuring 724 mm *28½ in* long and 184 mm *7¼ in* wide.

Largest toad (p. 39) The largest toad ever recorded is a marine toad (*Bufo marinus*) named *Prinsen* ('The Prince'), owned by Håkan Forsberg of Åkers Styckebruk, Sweden. It weighed 2·65 kg *5 lb 13½ oz* and measured 38 cm *15 in* from snout to vent (53·9 cm *21 1/5 in* when extended) in March 1991.

Mantle of bees (p. 45) Jed Shaner was covered by a mantle of an estimated 343 000 bees weighing 36·3 kg *80 lb* at Staunton, Virginia, USA on 29 Jun 1991.

THE HUMAN BEING

Earliest hominoid (p. 60) A hominoid jaw-bone with three molars, discovered in the Otavi Hills, Namibia on 4 Jun 1991 by Mark Pickford of the College de France, has been dated to 10–15 million years old.

Oldest mother (p. 65) It was reported in the British Medical Journal (June 1991) that a mother gave birth at the age of 59 years.

Lightest baby (p. 65) A premature baby girl weighing 280 g *9·9 oz* was born at Loyola University Medical Center, Illinois, USA. The birth was reported 18 months later, on 29 May 1991.

Hiccoughing (p. 74) Charles Osborne died on 1 May 1991.

Balancing on one foot (p. 74) The longest recorded duration for balancing on one foot is 45 hr 25 min by Leslie Silva at Negombo, Sri Lanka from 6–8 Apr 1991.

THE HUMAN WORLD

Elections — largest (p. 85) For the Indian elections held on 20 May, 12 Jun and 15 Jun 1991, the electorate was around 520 million people, although details of votes cast are not yet available. As a result of the elections, P. V. Narasimha Rao of the Congress (I) Party became the country's new Prime Minister.

Patent case (p. 89) In the Polaroid Corporation/Kodak case, both companies filed appeals and eventually it was agreed that Kodak would pay $925 million.

Largest narcotics haul (p. 92) In Britain, cocaine with a value of £101 million was seized in 'Operation Klondyke', which resulted in three fishermen from the Scottish Highlands being jailed for between 15 and 25 years on 30 May 1991. The operation involved 18 months of surveillance and the cooperation of officers in Britain, Spain and Colombia.

Defence spending (p. 97) The UK defence budget for 1991/92 is £24·027 billion.

Longest march (p. 98) A team of nine representing II Squadron RAF Regiment from RAF Hullavington, Wilts, each man carrying a 18·14 kg *40 lb* pack, including a rifle, completed the London marathon in 4 hr 33 min 58 sec on 21 Apr 1991.

SCIENCE AND TECHNOLOGY

Oil spills (p. 111) The worst single assault ever made upon the eco-system was released on 19 Jan 1991 by the Iraqi President Saddam Hussein, who ordered the pumping of Gulf crude from the Sea Island terminal, Kuwait, and from seven large tankers. The best estimate of the outflow is between 700 000 and 1 050 000 tonnes *4–6 million barrels*. On 17 February Hussein ordered the dynamiting and firing of 510 wellheads in the Burgan and five other Kuwaiti oilfields, thus raising oil and soot clouds to 6700 m *22 000 ft*, and so polluting the crops of southern Iran and carrying as far east as India and now the fields of Pakistan.

Pendulum (p. 115) A reconstruction of Focault's pendulum has been installed at the Convention Centre in Portland, Oregon, USA. Weighing 408·24 kg *900 lb*, it swings from a cable 27·43 m *90 ft* long suspended 7 m *23 ft* above the heads of visitors.

Space flight (p. 120) Helen Sharman (b. 30 May 1963) became the first Briton in space when she flew aboard the Soviet vessel Soyuz TM12 on 18 May 1991.

Longest manned space flight (p. 120) The most experienced space traveller is the Soviet flight engineer Musa Manarov, who has clocked up 541 days 31 min 10 sec on two spaceflights in 1987–88 and 1990–1.

BUILDING AND STRUCTURES

Tallest structures (p. 122) On 10 Aug 1991 the Warszawa radio mast, the world's tallest structure, was reported to have fallen during renovation, causing £17 million damage.

Roller coasters (p. 128) The longest roller coaster in the world is *The Ultimate* at Lightwater Valley, Ripon, N Yorks. The run stretches for 2·29 km *1·42 miles*.

The tallest wooden coaster is *Mean Streak* at Cedar Point Amusement Park, Sandusky, Ohio, USA. It is 49·07 m *161 ft* tall at its highest point and has a top speed of 104 km/h *65 mph*.

Public house visiting (p. 129) Peter Hill, Joseph Hill, Rob Jones and John Drew, 'The Blackcountry Ale Tairsters' of Tipton, W Mids, have now visited 3800 different public houses.

Advertising signs (p. 133) The highest is the logo 'I' at the top of the 73-storey, 309·98 m *1017 ft* high First Interstate World Center building in Los Angeles, California, USA.

Snow and ice constructions (p. 139) A snow structure standing 22·17 m *74 ft* high and named *Yukichian*, ('the Snow Girl') was built by villagers of Sumon and Niigata, Japan on 3 Mar 1991.

TRANSPORT

Highest mileage (p. 151) The highest recorded mileage for a car is 2 065 563 km *1 283 517 miles* on 11 Jul 1991 for a 1963 Volkswagen 'Beetle' owned by Albert Klein of Pasadena, California, USA.

Driving around Ireland (p. 152) Larry Mooney (driver), Paul Gleeson and Alan Park (navigators), all of Northern Ireland, drove around the 32 counties of northern and southern Ireland in a time of 12 hr 19 min between 21–22 Jun 1991, covering a distance of 1008 km *626·4 miles* at an average speed of 81·84 km/h *50·85 mph*.

Longest fuel range (p. 152) The greatest distance driven on a single fuel fill in a standard vehicle (178·6 litres *39·3 gal* carried in factory optional twin fuel tanks) without refuelling is 2605 km *1618·7 miles* by a Tempo Trax diesel pick-up. Driven by Rajendra and Lal Singh of India in 49 hr 24 min 25 sec from 17–19 Jun 1991, the fuel average was 41·2 mpg *14·59 km/litre*.

Two-side-wheel driving (p. 152) Sven-Erik Söderman of Sweden drove a Daf 2800 7·5-ton truck on two wheels for a distance of 10·83 km *6·73 miles* at Mora Siljan airport, Delecarlia, Sweden on 19 May 1991.

Fastest caravan (p. 153) The speed record for a caravan is 204·02 km/h *126·76 mph*, driven by Charlie Kovacs at Mangalore Airfield, Seymour, Victoria, Australia on 18 Apr 1991.

Motorcycle duration (p. 155) The longest time a motor scooter has been kept in non-stop motion is 1001 hrs for a Kinetic Honda DX 100 cc ridden by Har Parkash Rishi, Amarjeet Singh and Navjot Chadha of India. The team covered a distance of 30 965 km *19 241 miles* at Traffic Park, Pune, Maharashtra, India between 22 April and 3 June 1990.

Biggest motorcyle pyramid (p. 155) The Corps of Signals Indian Army, Motorcycle Display Team, the 'Dare Devils', established a world record with a pyramid of 40 men on seven motorcycles. The pyramid, which was held together by muscle and determination only, with no straps, harnesses or any other aids, travelled a distance of 400 m *1312 ft* on 15 Feb 1991.

Rail travel — Four points of the compass (p. 159) Norma and Ronald Carter and their son Jonathan (14) of Whitkirk, Leeds, together with Bob Reid of Victoria, Australia, visited stations at the extreme points of the compass in Great Britain in a time of 42 hr 37 min from 11–13 Jul 1991.

Parachuting (p. 165) On 8 Jun 1991 Don Kellner of Pennsylvania, USA made his 15 000th parachute descent.

THE BUSINESS WORLD

Jumble sale (p. 168) The greatest amount of money raised at a one-day sale is $195 388·53 at the 59th one-day rummage sale organized by the Winnetka Congregational Church, Illinois, USA on 9 May 1991.

Richest men (p. 170) *Forbes* magazine estimated in its issue of 22 Jul 1991 that Taikichiro Mori, aged 87, of Japan was the world's richest man, with assets of $15 billion. A former economics professor, he now owns some 80 offices.

Coin balancing (p. 171) The tallest single column of coins ever stacked on the edge of a coin was made up of 253 Indian one rupee pieces on top of a vertical five rupee coin, by Dipak Syal of Yamuna Nagar, India on 3 May 1991.

Coin snatching (p. 171) The greatest number of 10p pieces clean-caught from being flipped from the back of a forearm into the same downward palm is 254, by Dean Gould of Felixstowe, Suffolk on 12 Jul 1991.

Dow Jones index (p. 173) The highest closing figure for the Dow Jones Industrial average was 3035·33 on 3 Jun 1991, a rise of 7·83 points on the day. The index closed above 3000 points for the first time on 17 Apr 1991, at 3004·46.

FT-SE 100 index (p. 173) The highest closing figure for the FT-SE 100 share index was 2601·7 on 2 Aug 1991, a gain of 10 points on the day. This was the first time it had closed above 2600 points. The highest ever trading level was 2612·4, achieved on 29 Jul 1991 — the first time through the 2600 mark.

Postage stamps (p. 175) The record price paid at auction in the UK for a single stamp is £203 500 (including buyer's premium), for a Bermuda 1854 Perot Postmaster's stamp (1d red on bluish wove paper) affixed to an entire letter. It was sold by Christie's Robson Lowe, London on 13 Jun 1991.

Sheep birthweights (p. 178) The lowest live birthweight recorded for a lamb is 900 g *1 lb 15¾ oz* for a female badger-faced Welsh mountain lamb named 'Lyle', born on 8 Jun 1991 at Thorpe Park, Chertsey, Surrey. Her larger male twin, 'Tate', weighed 1·31 kg *2 lb 14¹/₅ oz*.

Sheep shearing (p. 178) The British solo record for shearing lambs is 817, set by Philip Evans at Pant Farm, Merthyr Cynog, Powys on 20 Jul 1991.

THE ARTS AND ENTERTAINMENTS

Sand sculpture (p. 180) The longest sand sculpture ever made was the 26 375·9 m *86 535 ft* long sculpture named 'The GTE Directories Ultimate Sand Castle', built by more than 10 000 volunteers at Myrtle Beach, South Carolina, USA on 31 May 1991.

Largest guitar (p. 191) A guitar measuring 11·63 m *38 ft 2 in* tall, 4·87 m *16 ft* wide and weighing 446 kg *1865 lb* was made by students of Shakamak High School in Jasonville, Indiana, USA and unveiled on 17 May 1991.

Dancing dragon (p. 195) The longest dancing dragon, created for the 3rd International Abilympics in 1991, measured 921·41 m *3023 ft* from the end of its tongue to the tip of its tail and took four months to construct. A total of 1024 people brought the dragon to life, making it dance for 2 minutes at the Happy Valley racecourse, Hong Kong on 11 Aug 1991.

Stilt-walking (p. 199) The fastest stilt-walker on record is Roy Luiking, who covered 100 m *328 ft* on 30·48 cm *1 ft* high stilts in 13·14 sec at Didam, Netherlands on 2 Jun 1991.

HUMAN ACHIEVEMENTS

Party giving (p. 208) The world's biggest birthday party was attended by 75 000 people at Buffalo, New York, USA on 4 Jul 1991 as part of the 1991 Friendship Festival to celebrate the 215th birthday of the United States and Canada's 115th birthday.

Leap-frogging (p. 211) The greatest distance covered was 1603·2 km *996·2 miles* by 14 students from Stanford University, California, USA, who started leap-frogging on 16 May 1991 and stopped 244 hr 43 min later on 26 May.

Needle threading (p. 211) The record number of times that a strand of cotton has been threaded through a number 13 needle in 2 hr is 8927, set by Dipak Syal of Yamuna Nagar, India on 8 May 1991.

Cocktail (p. 213) The largest cocktail on record is one of 3000 litres *659·9 gal*, made by Ettore Diana at Lazise, Italy on 4 Oct 1989 and named 'Ciao'.

Popcorn (p. 214) The largest box of popcorn contained 154 m³ *5438·16 ft³* of popped corn. It measured 16·83 × 3·09 m *52 ft 7¼ in × 10 ft 1½ in* and was filled by Stanly County at Stanly Community College, Albemarle, North Carolina, USA from 6–8 Aug 1991. The average depth was 3·12 m *10 ft 2½ in*.

Stick of rock (p. 214) The largest stick of rock was one weighing 413·6 kg *911 lb 13 oz*. It was 5·03 m *16 ft 6 in* long and 43·2 cm *17 in* thick, and was made by the Coronation Rock Company of Blackpool, Lancs on 20 Jul 1991.

Yorkshire pudding (p. 214) The largest Yorkshire pudding was one measuring 9·18 × 4·58 m *30 ft 1¼ in × 15 ft 0¼ in* (42·04 m² *452·2 ft²*). It was made by staff from the catering department of Rotherham Council at Rotherham, S Yorks on 1 Aug 1991 to celebrate Yorkshire Day.

Greeting cards (p. 216) The Commerce Day Christmas card, made by students of University College, Dublin, Republic of Ireland and posted on 6 Dec 1990 to the city's Central Remedial Clinic for handicapped children, measured a world record 252 m² *2712·5 ft²* (30 × 8·4 m *98·4 × 27·5 ft*).

Cigarette lighters (p. 216) Frans Van der Heijden has collected 30 316 different lighters to date.

Jigsaw puzzles (p. 217) The world's largest jigsaw puzzle measures 1050 m² *11 302·2 ft²* and consists of 2250 pieces. Assembled on 19 Mar 1991, it was devised by J.N. Nichols (Vimto) plc of Manchester, and designed and built by students from Manchester Polytechnic.

SPORTS AND GAMES

American football (p. 222) The Birmingham Bulls won the Coca-Cola Bowl for a record-equalling second time on 4 Aug 1991. They had previously won in 1988.

Athletics (p. 227) World records: Men, 4 × 100m relay, USA (Mike Marsh, Leroy Burrell, Dennis Mitchell and Carl Lewis) 37·67 sec at Zürich, Switzerland on 7 Aug 1991. Pole vault, Sergey Bubka (USSR) 6·10 m *20 ft ¼ in* at Malmö, Sweden on 5 Aug 1991.

(p. 229) Donald James Thompson (b. 20 Jan 1933), aged 58 yr 89 days, became the oldest British full international when he took part in the 200 km walk at Bazencourt, France on 20–21 Apr 1991. In the same race Edmund Harold Shillabeer (b. 2 Aug 1939) became Britain's oldest international débutant at the age of 51 yr 260 days.

(p. 231) British records: Women, 400 m hurdles, Sally Gunnell 53·61 sec at Zürich on 7 Aug 1991. Triple Jump, Evette Finikin (b. 25 Sep 1963) 13·46 m *44 ft 2 in* at Birmingham, W Mids on 26 Jul 1991.

(p. 232) Walking (world): 50 km road walk, Sandra Brown (b. 1 Apr 1949) 4 hr 50 min 51 sec at Basildon, Essex on 13 Jul 1991.

Baseball (p. 235) Stolen bases, Rickey Henderson 973; Strikeouts, Nolan Ryan 5453, both to 11 Aug 1991.

Billiards (p. 239) Raymond Ceulemans won a 20th world three-cushion title in 1990.

Board games (p. 240) Stephen Twigge completed a game of solitaire in 10 seconds at Scissett Baths, W Yorks on 2 Aug 1991.

Cricket (p. 249) Ian Botham played his 98th Test in August 1991. He has scored 5154 runs (av. 34·36), taken 379 wickets (av. 28·23) and 115 catches in his Test career.

(p. 250) Recent research suggests that the youngest first class player was Esmail Ahmed Baporia (India) (b. 24 Apr 1939) who was aged 11 yr 261 days on his début for Gujarat v. Baroda at Ahmedabad, India on 10 Jan 1951.

Cycling (p. 253–4) Stephen Pulton cycled the Three Peaks route in a time of 41 hr 51 min on 1–2 Jul 1980.

Darts (p. 254) Highest 24-hour individual score, 518 060 by Davy Richardson-Page at Blucher Social Club, Newcastle on 6–7 Jul 1991.

Football (Association) (p. 260) The record transfer fee between two British clubs is £2·9 million (including VAT and other levies) paid by Liverpool to Derby County for Dean Saunders (b. 21 Jun 1964) on 14 Jul 1991. The highest fee for a British player is the £5·5 million paid by Bari of Italy to Aston Villa for David Platt (b. 10 Jun 1966) on 21 Jul 1991.

Golf (p. 264) Joseph Martin 'Jodie' Mudd (USA) (b. 23 Apr 1960) equalled the lowest score for any round of The Open, 63, in the final round at Royal Birkdale on 21 Jul 1991.

Gymnastics (p. 267) Press-ups (One-arm, 5 hours), 7683, John Decker at Congleton Cricket Club, Cheshire on 16 Jun 1991. Sit-ups (24 hours), 65 001, Marc Scriven at St John's Sports Centre, Worcester on 21–22 Jun 1991; Burpees (1 hour), 1619 by Paddy Doyle at Birmingham International Convention Centre on 21 Jun 1991.

Judo (p. 276) Naoya Ogawa (Japan) won a record-equalling fourth world title at Barcelona on 28 Jul 1991 winning the Open category. He had previously won the Open in 1987 and 1989 and Over 95 kg in 1989.

Motor racing (p. 279) After the Hungarian Grand Prix on 11 Aug 1991, Alain Prost had scored 686·5 points from 179 races, Ricardo Patrese had started 218 races and Ayrton Senna had achieved 57 pole positions from 120 races (31 wins).

Abseiling (p. 284) Recent research has shown that a team of eight men from the Code 4 Rescue unit abseiled 342 m *1122 ft* down the CN Tower, Toronto, Canada on 26 Jun 1985.

Netball (p. 284) Australia won a record sixth world title on 14 Jul 1991 at Sydney defeating New Zealand 53–52. During the 1991 World Championships, the Cook Islands defeated Vanuatu, 120–38 on 9 July to set a new highest team score.

Rugby union (p. 291, 292) David Campese has scored 40 tries in a record 57 international appearances for Australia and Michael Lynagh has scored a record 620 points in 46 matches, also for Australia.

Speedway (p. 297) Denmark won the World Pairs title for a record eighth time on 20 Jul 1991. Hans Nielsen was a member of the team for a record sixth time.

Swimming (p. 299) World record: Men, 200 m backstroke, Martin Lopez-Zubero (Spain) 1:57·50 at Fort Lauderdale, Florida, USA on 13 Aug 1991.

(p. 301) Suzy Moroney (Australia) completed the fastest double crossing of the English Channel by a female, 17 hr 14 min, on 23 Jul 1991.

(p. 302) British record: Men, 200 m freestyle, Paul Palmer 1:50·50 at Antwerp, Belgium on 1 Aug 1991.

(p. 303) The most participants in a one-day swim relay was 2145, each swimming a length, organized by Jeff D. VanBuren and David W. Thompson at Hamilton College at Clinton, New York, USA on 8 Apr 1989.

STOP PRESS

INDEX

INDEX

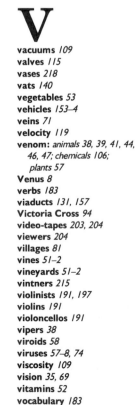

INDEX

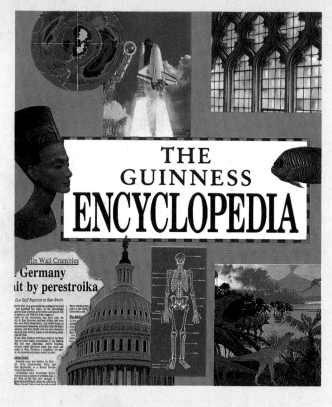
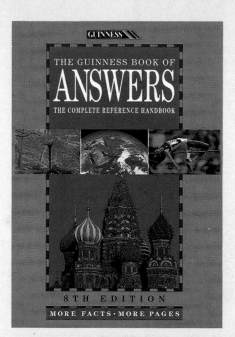